The Tangled Web

A Life of Sir Richard Burton

*Presented to the Central Library,
Bexleyheath, with the compliments
of the author.*

Jon R. Godsall

1 Nov 2008

As palace mirror'd in the stream,
   as vapour mingled in the skies,
So weaves the brain of mortal man
   the tangled web of Truth and Lies.

R.F. Burton, *The Kasidah*, Canto VI, stanza iv.

The Tangled Web

Matador
9 De Montfort Mews
Leicester LE1 7FW, UK
Tel: (+44) 116 255 9311 / 9312
Email: books@troubador.co.uk
Web: www.troubador.co.uk/matador

ISBN 978 1906510 428

Mixed Sources
Product group from well-managed
forests and other controlled sources
www.fsc.org Cert no. TF-COC-2082
© 1996 Forest Stewardship Council

Typeset in 12pt Garamond by Troubador Publishing Ltd, Leicester, UK
Printed in the UK by The Cromwell Press Ltd, Trowbridge, Wilts, UK

Matador is an imprint of Troubador Publishing Ltd

To Jenny

CONTENTS

LIST OF ILLUSTRATIONS

PICTURE CREDITS

The author wishes to thank the following copyright holders for allowing him to use their photographs, as follows. All other plates are in the author's own collection, or are out of copyright, or the copyright holder has not proved traceable.

4 (Dr Donald B. Baker); 5 (St Albans' Museums); 21 (The Director and the Board of Trustees, Royal Botanic Gardens, Kew); 34 (Malcolm Pinhorn); 6, 16, 17, 18, 20. 22, 23, 25, 26, 29, 35, 37 (Mary S. Lovell).

ACKNOWLEDGEMENTS

Throughout the many years it has taken me to complete this book I have incurred numerous debts, both in this country and abroad. I should, therefore, like to express my gratitude to the staff of the following institutions, who have been kind enough to spend time answering my letters, and providing me with copies of important documentary material. Some, by now, will have moved on to other appointments or retired. To others, my thanks will be, sadly, posthumous.

In the United Kingdom, I would particularly like to mention:

Mrs Christine Kelly, archivist of the Royal Geographical Society until her retirement at the end of June, 1992, to whom I owe an immense debt of gratitude. During a correspondence extending well over a decade, she showed unfailing kindness, patience, and courtesy, and was generous to a fault with her time in carrying out research on my behalf, and answering my many, and no doubt exasperating, questions.

Miss Elizabeth Talbot Rice, formerly Research and Information Officer at the National Army Museum gave me an enormous amount of help on a variety of military matters over a number of years. She was especially helpful in conducting research at the PRO on my behalf in connection with the military career of Burton's father, J. N. Burton, which initially proved elusive. More recently, I have received considerable help from Ms Kate Portelli of the Museum's Department of Archives, Photographs, Film and Sound.

I am particularly grateful to Dr C.J. Kitching, formerly Asst Keeper of the Search Dept, PRO, Chancery Lane, and to Gillian L. Beech, initially of the Search Dept at Kew, later of the Map Dept. Ms Beech provided me with invaluable help during the mid-1970s, in finding my way amongst the Foreign Office documents relating to Burton's consular career, until then ignored by his previous biographers.

I owe an especial debt to Andrew Griffin and Ian Baxter of the India Office Library and Records for their unstinting help over a long period in tracing extremely important manuscript material relating to Burton, and placing their expert knowledge of the institution's holdings at my disposal.

I would also like to express my thanks to Mrs Beverley Emery, assistant to the Hon Librarian, Miss B. J. Kirkpatrick at the Royal Anthropological Institute, London, who kindly accessed books and other material for me from Burton's personal library. Thanks are also due to Gemma Hunter, then Curator of the Burton Collection, Orleans Gallery, Richmond upon Thames, and her assistant, Ruth Briant, for allowing me to examine the fascinating Miscellaneous Items forming part of this collection, transferred from the Camberwell Library in 1969.

I must thank Dr Richard Pankhurst, former Librarian of the Royal Asiatic Society and, in particular his successor, M.J. Pollock. As a Fellow of the Society, I was able to make considerable use of the Oscar Eckenstein Collection, a superb archive of books, letters, and memorabilia, never before consulted by any of Burton's biographers. It proved particularly interesting for containing the correspondence carried on between Burton's bibliographer, N.M. Penzer and Eckenstein in 1920. This revealed that Penzer failed to acknowledge the very considerable debt he owed to Eckenstein in the compilation of his *Annotated Bibliography*, published in 1923.

I would also like to thank Mr Robert Jago, archivist, of the Wiltshire and Swindon Record Office, Trowbridge, for supplying me with copies of documents and help during my research of the Burton Papers in the very important Arundell Collection, which only became available to Burton scholars in 1991. Thanks also to his colleague Steve Hobbs, his successor in the post, who very generously placed the whole of the Collection, both written and photographic, at my disposal without cost or restriction.

Thanks are due to Dr Richard J. Olney, Director of Guides and Surveys at the Royal Commission on Historical Manuscripts, London, for extremely useful information and advice. I would also like to add a word of thanks to the Commission's former Secretary, G. R. C. Davis, who was of great help in resolving a matter of copyright involving the Scottish Record Office. Also to Dr S. G. Roberts, then Research Assistant at the Royal Commission, for drawing my attention to 'four letters (described as "racy") from Burton to Admiral Henry Murray, 1862-63,' reported as being in the possession of Mrs E. Murray, Edinburgh. In fact, I found that these letters had been deposited in the Record Office by her in 1970, and placed with the papers belonging to her husband's grandfather, the Hon Sir Charles A. Murray.

I will long remember the kindness of the late Sister Margaret Helen, Archivist of New Hall School, Boreham, near Chelmsford, Essex. Not only did she spend time copying by hand extremely interesting and amusing archival material relating to Isabel Burton's schooldays there, she also gave me an introduction to Lady Burton's great niece, Mrs Dorothy Flemming, as mentioned in my Introduction notes.

I have been particularly well served by a number of members of Oxford University. I must offer a special word of thanks to Mrs Clare Hopkins, Archivist, Trinity College, who supplied me with extremely important material from the archives of Burton's old college. I am also extremely grateful to the late A. F. L. Beeston, Laudian Professor of Arabic and Fellow of St John's, J. R. Madicott, Fellow and Librarian, Exeter College, Dr Robin Darwall-Smith, Archivist of University College and Magdalen College, Mrs Elizabeth Boardman, Archivist, Oriel College, R. G. M. Nisbet, Corpus Christi Professor of Latin, John G. Griffiths, Public Orator, and Ellis Evans, Professor of Celtic, Jesus College, J. L. I. Fennell, Professor of Russian and Fellow of New College.

Over many years, I have found the expert staff of the Bodleian Library, Oxford, unfailingly helpful in searching for information and prompt in answering questions. In particular, I would name, A. D. S. Roberts, Keeper of Oriental Books, R. Vyse, Dept of Western MSS, T. D. Rogers and S. R. Tomlinson. I am especially grateful to Doris Nicholson of the Oriental Collections, who unearthed for me some very interesting details about the distinguished Spanish Arabist, Don Pascual de Gayangos, responsible for showing Burton the correct way of writing the Arabic alphabet.

As always, the London Library has been invaluable in providing most of the books necessary for my research, and the staff extremely knowledgeable and co-operative.

Thanks are due to former Keepers of the National Library of Scotland, Dr James S. Ritchie, and the late Dr Thomas I. Rae, for providing me with letters from J. H. Speke to C. P. Rigby, and C. P. Rigby to James A. Grant. Also letters fom Speke to Blackwood in the Blackwood Papers, c.1860. I am particularly grateful to Iain F. Maciver, Head of Manuscripts Division not only for providing me with copies of letters in the Scott Papers, but very kindly answering questions on a number of other matters. I would also like to acknowledge the help of Dr Paul Barnaby, Project Officer, the Walter Scott Digital Archive, Special Collections Division, Edinburgh University Library.

I would also like to place on record my gratitude to the following:
H.W. Hodgson, Divisional Librarian, County Library, B.C. Jones, County Archivist and D. Bowcock, Assistant County Archivist, The Record Office, Carlisle; Miss S.J. MacPherson, Archivist-in-Charge,

Archives Dept, Record Office, County Hall, Kendal; A. M. Carr, Local Studies Librarian, Shrewsbury, Shropshire; C.L. Brodie, Archives Dept, Central Regional Council, Stirling, Scotland; T. Pickersgill, Asst Regimental Secretary,The Duke of Wellington's Regiment, Halifax, W. Yorks; I.P. Collis, County Archivist, Somerset Record Office, Taunton; R. Bryant, City Archivist and V. J. Kite, Area Librarian, Bath; C. Collier, Parish Clerk, Walcot Church House, Bath; E. Mitchell, Secretary to the Librarian, The Royal College of Surgeons of England, London; D.N. Cole, Librarian, Royal College of Physicians, London; C.P. Finlayson, Keeper of Manuscripts, Edinburgh University Library; Paul Rutledge, Norfolk Record Office, Norwich; P. Walne, County Archivist, Record Office, County Hall, Herts; M.V. Roberts, Keeper of Enquiry Services, Guildhall Library, London; E. McNeill, Librarian and Keeper of the Records, the Hon Society of the Middle Temple, London; W.W.S. Breem, Librarian, The Honourable Society of the Inner Temple, London; G. Holborn, Librarian, Lincoln's Inn Library, London; A.A. Dibben, County Records Officer, and C. R. Davey, County Archivist, County Record Office, Lewes, E. Sussex; D.R.C. West, OBE, The Hon Archivist, Malborough College, Wilts; C. Hall, The Parker Library, Corpus Christi College, Cambridge, Dr E.S. Leedham-Green, Deputy Keeper, University Archives, Cambridge; J. Wells, Asst Under-Librarian, Cambridge University Library; S. Green, Brighton Library, E. Sussex; A. James, Asst Librarian, Society of Antiquaries of London; S.K. Ashcroft for Mrs S. Head, Local Studies Librarian, Herts; Mrs A. Doughty and A. McCormack, for County Archivist, Surrey Record Office, Kingston upon Thames; R.A. Shaw, Local History Librarian, Battersea District Library, London; D. Jones, Chief Librarian and Curator, Richmond upon Thames; L. White, and his successor, J.P. Wells, as County Librarian, Oxford; N.J. Bond, Divisional Librarian, Central Berkshire; R.O. Hall, Bursar, Winchester College, Hants; P. Honan, Prof of English and American Literature, Leeds University; R.A. Bowden, Archivist, Marylebone Library, London; W. Serjeant, County Archivist, Suffolk Record Office, Bury St Edmunds; Rev W. J. Elliott, Rector, St Nicholas's Church, Elstree, Herts; R.A. Shaw, Local History Librarian, London Borough of Wandsworth; W.C. Brooks, local historian, Borehamwood, Herts; G. Cocks, Curator, City Museum, St Albans, Herts; M.Y. Williams, Borough Archivist, London Borough of Lambeth; Lt Col G. P. Wood, MC, Argyll and Sutherland Highlanders, Stirling; P. Scott, Chief Librarian, Upper Norwood Public Library, London; A.O. Meakin, Chief Librarian, Central Library, Croydon; H.P. White, Naval Historical Library, Ministry of Defence, London; K.C. Harrison, City Librarian, City of Westminster, London; C. Pettit, Asst Reference Librarian (Local Studies), County Library, Dorchester, Dorset; P.R. Gifford, Librarian, Local Studies, Colchester, Essex; D.H. Simpson, Librarian, the Royal Commonwealth Society, London; Prof C. Fyfe, Edinburgh University; Prof A. Rutherford, Aberdeen University; Staff at the Library and Records Dept, Foreign and Commonwealth Office, London; J.E. Treble, Ministry of Defence, London; D. Randall, Asst Archivist, Staffordshire Record Office, Stafford; R.J. Hampson, Area Librarian, Montgomery, Powys; Dr T.A. Heathcote, Curator, the Royal Military Academy Collection, Sandhurst; R.R. Aspinall, Librarian, Port of London Authority; M. Goulding, Trinity House Pilotage Service, London; N.E. Upham, Curator of Models, Dept of Ships, and G. Stow, National Maritime Museum, Greenwich; R.G. Roberts, Director of Libraries and Amenities, Central Library, Hull, Humberside; N.H. Robinson, Librarian, the Royal Society, London; J.R. Elliott, Area Librarian, West Devon, Plymouth; G. Langley, County Reference Librarian, Avon; M.E. Williams, City Archivist, and S. Lang, Asst Archivist, Record Office, Bristol; M. Barnes, City Librarian, Westminster, London; J. Cowlard, Library Information Officer, National Meteorological Library, Bracknell, Berkshire; A. Monk, Public Information Unit, Royal Greenwich Observatory, Herstmonceux Castle, E. Sussex; D. Claiden, P&O Information and Public Relations, and S. Rabson, Group Librarian, P&O, London; K.R. Cox, Chief Librarian, London Borough of Lewisham; Prof R.B. Sergeant, Director, and Dr R. Bidwell, Secretary, Middle East Centre, University of Cambridge; A. Spallone, Librarian, Institute of Italian Culture, London; B. Bright, Superintendent Registrar, Hull,

Humberside; P. Scott, Chief Librarian, Upper Norwood Sub-Library, London; Mgr Ralph Brown, Vicar General, Archbishop's House, Westminster; G.L.E. Lindow and his successor Capt D.S. Wyatt, OBE, as Secretary to The Athenaeum Club, London; R.H.N. Creswell, Regional Co-ordinator (Publicity), Grindlay's Bank, London; Librarian, Linnaean Society, London; I.J. Clarke, District Librarian, Daventry, Northants; P.I. King, Chief Archivist, Northamptonshire Record Office; L. de Sousa Rebelo, King's College, London; J.P. Fuller, Curator, Victoria and Albert Museum; R. Evison, Archive Asst, National Portrait Gallery, London; G.K. Senior, Director of Libraries, Museums, Arts Dept, St Helens, Lancs; M.J. Swarbrick, Chief Archivist, Victoria Library, London; F.D. Cole, Director of Libraries and Arts, London Borough of Camden; P. Lumsden, Librarian, Garrick Club; W.E. Usher, Librarian, Beefsteak Club, London; Lady Chapman, Archivist, Madame Tussaud's, London; R. Goodall, Professor of Fencing. British Academy of Fencing; J. Pienne, Secretary, Amateur Fencing Association, London; Chief Librarian,Whitehall Library, Ministry of Defence; G.M. Wilson, Keeper of Edged Weapons, and B. Clifford, Senior Curator (Library), Royal Armouries, HM Tower of London; D. G. Moir, Secretary, Scottish Geographical Society; D. Bromwich, Somerset Studies Librarian, Taunton; Col A.V. Tennuci, Curator and Secretary, RAMC Historical Museum, Aldershot; A.J. Duggan, Director, and E. J. Freeman, Librarian, the Wellcome Institute for the History and Understanding of Medicine, London; Dr Hugh Platt, Suffolk; B. Horder, Librarian, Royal College of Veterinary Surgeons, London; D.N. Clark-Lowes, Librarian, the Incorporated Society for Psychical Research, London; M.G. Grimwade, Secretary, Barnes and Mortlake Historical Society; J. Nielsen, Asst Librarian, Reader Services, Wellcome Library for the History and Understanding of Medicine; A.G. Lee, Librarian, St John's College, Cambridge; B. Burton, Librarian and P. Salinger, Librarian (Ancient Near East, Semitics & Judaica), School of Oriental and African Studies, University of London; D. Howell. Hon Secretary,The Royal Society of Marine Artists, London; J. Sayers, Company Secretary, Federation of British Artists, London; G. Muschenheim, Information Officer, Goethe-Institut, London; R.D. Harman, Superintendent of the Palace, Hampton Court, Surrey; D.M.M. Shorrocks, County Archivist, Somerset Record Office; H.T. Norris, Emeritus Professor of Arabic, SOAS, A. Gray, Archivist, Cornwall Record Office, Truro; Dr R. Gray, SOAS; K. Sweetmore, Archivist, British Records Association; David Knight, Archivist, Stonyhurst College, Lancs; Mrs Diana Harding, Archivist, Royal Yacht Squadron, Cowes; Anne Rainsbury, Curator, Chepstow Museum, Gwent; Doug Hindmarch, Local Studies Officer, Sheffield Library; Diane Clements, Director, and Mrs K.A. Jowett, Senior Assistant Librarian, The Library and Museum of Freemasonry, London; C. Martin McGibbon, Grand Secretary, and Robert L.D. Cooper, Curator, The Grand Lodge of Scotland of Antient, Free and Accepted Masons, Edinburgh.

Outside the United Kingdom, I need to thank Geraldine Willis, Librarian, Representative Church Body Library, Church of Ireland, Dublin. Also Dr G. Slevin, Chief Herald, Genealogical Office, Dublin Castle, Dr William O'Sullivan, Keeper of Manuscripts, University of Dublin, W. Spence, Dean of Tuam, Galway, who directed my attention to the existence of the letters of Archdeacon Edmund Burton in the PRO, Dublin, and to P. Connolly, Archivist, PRO, who gave me permission to quote from them.

I would also like to express my gratitude to the following French and Swiss librarians and archivists: J. d'Orleans, and his successor, C. Clepkens, Le Directeur des Services Generaux,Ville de Tours, B. de Fournoux, Le Directeur des archives d'Indre-et-Loire, Tours, R. Fillet, Le Conservateur en Chef, Bibliothèque Municipale, Ville de Tours, Andrée L'Heritier, Conservateur, Bibliothèque Nationale, Paris, P. Bougard, Le Directeur des Services d'Archives du Pas-de-Calais, the Librarian, Bibliothèque Municipale de Boulogne-sur-Mer, Jean-Loup Bourget, Cultural Attaché, French Embassy, London, Prof Marcel M. Chartier, Le Secrétaire Général, Société de Géographie, Paris. Also J. S. Mauerhofer, Swiss National Library, Information Centre Helvetica, Berne, and P. Gsteiger, Bernese State Archives.

Thanks are due to Richard Tötterman, formerly Finnish Ambassador in London, who kindly supplied me with information about his distinguished countryman, the 19th century Finnish explorer and orientalist, Dr G. A. Wallin. V. Ivanov, former Secretary of the Russian Embassy, London, was kind enough to make an unofficial translation of a letter addressed to me from A. Treshnikov, President of the Geographical Society of the USSR, and Corresponding Member of the USSR Academy of Science, Leningrad (now St Petersburg).

I recall with pleasure correspondence, and later, 'Burton talk' in this country, with Dr James A. Casada, Professor of History, Winthrop College, Rock Hill, South Carolina, USA, whose excellent up-date of Penzer's *An Annotated Bibliography* has considerably smoothed the way for later Burton scholars. I must also mention an interesting and fruitful correspondence with Burke Casari, a Burton collector of Lincoln, Nebraska, and Donald K. Pollock, an anthropologist, then of Rochester University, New York.

I would also like to acknowledge the help of the following: Sir Roger Fulford, Brigadier O.F.G. Hogg, Elizabeth, Lady Longford, Dorothy Middleton, Meriol Trevor, H.W. Drax, Winifred Cooper, Josephine Birchenough, the Rev David Standley, Sir Edward Playfair, John Bowden, Susan Bagshawe and Dr I. Fullagar. I would like to single out for special thanks, Keith McLuckie and Tony Waugh, whose computer skills have been indispensable in the production of this book. My thanks also to Barrie Maynard for placing his photographic expertise at my disposal.

One of the most fascinating aspects of my research has been locating present-day descendants of the Baker, Burton, Arundell and Stisted families.

Among members of the Baker family, I would like to mention: In the USA, Dr Marjory Foster, of Topeka, Kansas, great-great-granddaughter of Richard Baker, Burton's maternal grandfather. In this country, his great-grandson, Dr Donald Burton Baker, a former entomologist at the University Museum of Natural History, Oxford, with whom I corresponded on Baker family matters for almost five years before his unexpected death in 2004. I have also to thank his cousin, Richard Justin Baker, for supplying me with copies of miniatures of Richard Baker and Richard George, his son by a first marriage.

Of the Burton family: The late Lord Hunt of Llanfair Waterdine, KG, CBE, DSO, who, as Col John Hunt, led the first-ever successful assault on Everest in 1953. Lord Hunt, a former PRGS, was Burton's great-great-nephew, related through Burton's aunt, Catherine D'Aguilar (née Burton). I drew up a genealogy of the Burton family for Lord Hunt in 1993, which he asked the then Director and Secretary, Dr John Hemming, to place either in one of the eight original Burton volumes he was donating to the Society, or in the archives.

Of the Arundell family: Major-General P. F. Fagan, CB, MBE, whose mother, Isabel Mairi Arundell, was the second daughter of the 15th Lord Arundell of Wardour, and Lady Burton's great niece. General Fagan was born in Wardour Castle in 1935, and spent much of his childhood there, until the family was forced to leave following his uncle's death. Writing to me in 1994, General Fagan said that, 'Until perhaps 20 years ago, my mother owned the Burton belt – the belt he wore on his travels with numerous medals on it, from the Royal Geographical Society amongst others. Much to my chagrin, I discovered she had sold it at about that time, but have no record now of its whereabouts.'

Of the Stisted family: The late Brigadier J.N. Stisted, OBE, of the Royal Scots, great-great-nephew of Lt General Sir W.H. Stisted, KCB, Burton's brother-in-law. Brigadier Stisted kindly allowed me to make a copy of the family genealogy drawn up for him by the College of Arms. He also lent me a photograph of a painting of Lt General Stisted, commissioned during his tenure of office as Lt Governor of Ontario, which now forms part of the J. Ross Roberston Collection, Toronto Public Library, Public Archives of Canada.

On a more formal note, I would like to thank the owners and trustees of the following archives for permission to quote from manuscripts in their possession. In the United Kingdom: The Director and

Secretary of the Royal Geographical Society; The British Library; the Bodleian Library; the Master and Fellows of Trinity College, Cambridge; The Curator, Orleans House Gallery, Richmond-upon-Thames; the Trustees of the National Library of Scotland; The Director of the National Army Museum; Wiltshire and Swindon Record Office. In the Republic of Ireland: the PRO, Dublin. In the USA: the Huntington Library, San Marino, California.

I cannot bring this long list of acknowledgements to a close, without expressing my warmest and sincerest thanks to a valued friend, the acclaimed biographer, Mary S. Lovell. Despite her own pressing literary commitments, she has been unfailingly generous over a number of years with her time, offering much-needed advice and encouragement. If this were not enough, she placed her entire Burton archive at my disposal in 2003, inviting both my wife and myself to her delightful home in Gloucestershire to carry out the necessary research. When completing this proved difficult, she had no hesitation in suggesting that I take away her files for later photocopying at leisure.

An important part of Mary Lovell's archive consisted of Burton material once belonging to the superb collection of her close friend, the late Quentin Keynes, who died in February, 2003. Before his death, he gave her written carte blanche to use any of his materials in return for her transcribing them for him. I am extremely grateful to Mrs Lovell for permission to quote extracts from these, as well as numerous other letters from her private collection, in particular those from the Huntington Library. Although she gifted her entire Burton archive to the Orleans House Gallery, Richmond, in 2006, she asked, on my behalf, that previous written permissions should be honoured. I would like to thank the Gallery's Curator, Mark de Novellis, and Rachel Tranter, Head of Arts, Education and Children's Services, for their willingness to do so.

It is impossible to adequately acknowledge the debt I owe my wife, without whose long-time support this biography would never have been completed, much less come to print. It is, in a very real sense, as much hers as it is mine, and I am pleased to dedicate it to her. I need also to mention our three daughters, Deborah, Kathryn, and Rebecca, now grown up with their own families, who must have suffered from my obsession with Burton. Perhaps they will view this book as a slight recompense, and tangible evidence that Burton's ghost has finally been laid to rest.

MAP I

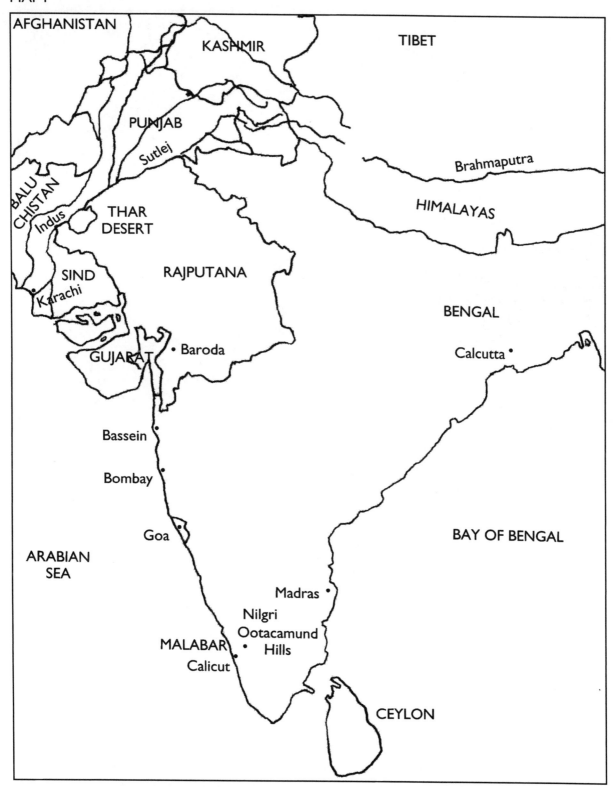

AFGHANISTAN

KASHMIR

TIBET

PUNJAB

Sutlej

Brahmaputra

BALU CHISTAN

Indus

THAR DESERT

HIMALAYAS

SIND

Karachi

RAJPUTANA

BENGAL

Calcutta

GUJARAT

Baroda

Bassein

Bombay

BAY OF BENGAL

Goa

ARABIAN SEA

Madras

Nilgri Ootacamund Hills

MALABAR

Calicut

CEYLON

Burton's service with the 18th BNI in western India, 1842-9

MAP 2

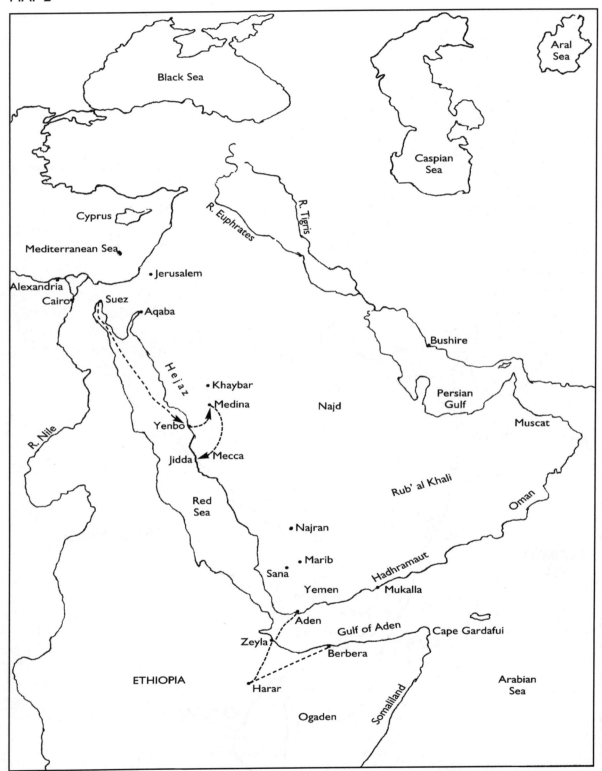

Burton's pilgrimage to Medina and Mecca, 1853, followed by the abortive Somali Expedition, 1854-5.

MAP 3

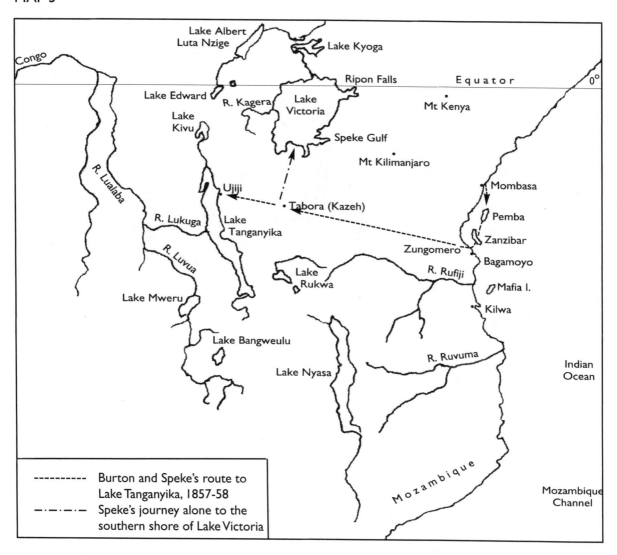

The East African Expedition set up to find the Great Inland Sea and, if possible,
locate the source of the Nile, 1857-58.

MAP 4

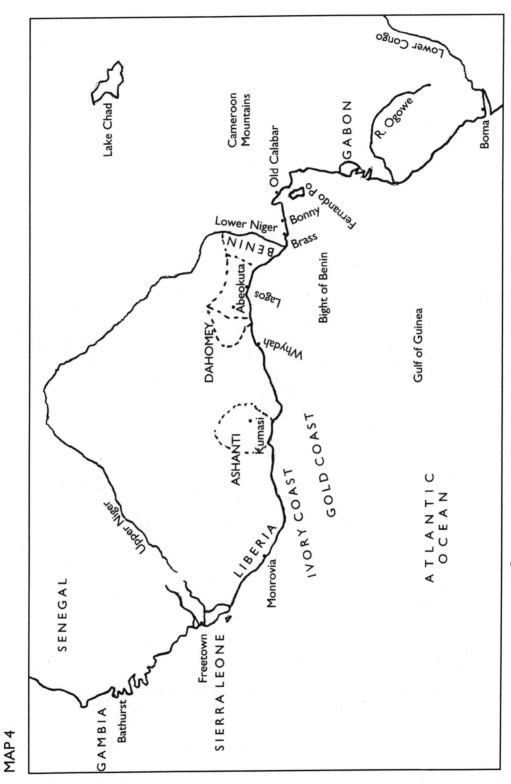

Burton appointed HBM's consul at Fernando Po, West Africa, 1861-4.

FOREWORD

Explorer, diplomat, anthropologist, orientalist, archaeologist, linguist, translator, swordsman and poet, Sir Richard Francis Burton (1821-90) stands on the brink of the Victorian era and the modern age. Mythologized and self-mythologized during his own lifetime, Burton was further eulogized after his death by various "Keepers of the Flame," starting with his widow, Isabel's, *Life*.

This has made Burton's appeal to writers, scholars, historians and the wider public all the more enduring. Successive biographers and curators have represented and reinterpreted him afresh for each generation. In recent years, Burton's life and reputation have been re-examined and re-assessed from a number of post-colonial, post-feminist and post-modern perspectives. Mary S. Lovell's biography, *A Rage to Live* and Orleans House Gallery exhibitions including *Lady Burton's Gift to the Nation* (1998) and *Burton: The Case for and Against* (2005) have been part of this ongoing process.

The presentation of Burton and the myths that have sprung up around him are central to Jon R. Godsall's work, and transformed what started off as a biography into a biographical study. Godsall examines the mythologizing process in this authoritative account. 'It became apparent early on in my research, that the truth had to be painstakingly searched for at almost every step along the way.' This meticulous quest for truth has unearthed a wealth of new material, never before studied or placed within the public domain. The book questions the various 'givens' that have passed down about Burton – the claims made by previous biographers of his pioneering position as explorer, scientist, and eminent literary figure. Godsall's aim, however, is not that of the iconoclast. He does not set out to destroy a reputation, but to present 'a truer picture – a more rigorous and balanced appraisal of the man and his exploits.' Challenging many previous assumptions, this book will undoubtedly make an invaluable contribution to Burton scholarship.

Mark De Novellis
Curator of Exhibitions and Collections
Orleans House Gallery, London.

The Richmond upon Thames Borough Art Collection, cared for by Orleans House Gallery in Twickenham, comprises over 2,400 works of art and objects and spans the mid-18th century to the present day. The collection offers a visual map of a changing borough and the people and places associated with its development, history, and heritage.

The collection also includes a number of items relating to Burton's life. Following his death in 1890, funds were so limited, that Lady Burton was forced to request donations in order to give him the resting place he had always wanted – above ground in an Arab tent. In return, she pledged a number of items to the nation. These found a permanent home at Orleans House Gallery and Richmond Local Studies Collection, when they were transferred from Camberwell Public Library in 1969.

It is these books, paintings, photographs, drawings, and personal effects that, more than any other items in the collection, generate the most interest and research requests from around the globe. Highlights include items presented to Burton on his travels, including spears and a necklace made from human bone, his sewing kit, fez, slippers, boots, swords, and casts made at his death of his hand and foot. Recently, the Burton Collection was greatly enhanced by the invaluable addition of the Lovell Archive, which comprises Mary S. Lovell's extensive research for her biography, *A Rage to Live*.

INTRODUCTION

(1)

'As the prime minister of an Eastern despot, he would have been splendid.'[1]

Writing in 1915, a quarter of a century after Burton's death, Frank Harris, journalist, man of letters, and 'social buccaneer,' according to his friend, Bernard Shaw, said that he had always thought Carlyle and Burton 'were the two greatest governors ever given to England. The one for England herself, and as an example to the world of the way to turn a feudal, chivalrous state into a great modern industrial state; the other, the best possible governor of Mahommedan peoples – two more prophets whom England did not stone, did not even take the trouble to listen to.'[2]

Although credited with shrewd political sense, Harris's opinion can only be regarded as crass in the extreme. Nevertheless, it has the merit of linking together two remarkable figures of the nineteenth century. While poles apart in most respects, they were curiously allied in certain matters of temperament and traits of character, and highly interesting as to the status of their respective marriages to exceptional women. Moreover, there can be little doubt that Carlyle, unquestionably the strongest moral force in the literature of the Victorian era, was influential in the formulation of the more extreme of Burton's political views.[3]

A perceptive critic reviewing one of Burton's early books on India, highlighted the fact that, for a young man he seemed to have adopted some very extreme opinions. Burton was warned that the fault from which he had most to fear was 'a disregard of those well-established rules of moderation which no one can transgress with impunity.'[4] Moderation, however, was no more part of Burton's makeup than it was of Carlyle's, who called himself a Bedouin, 'a freelance owing no allegiance save to his Maker and his own conscience.'[5] It is unsurprising, therefore, that Burton, who delighted as much as Carlyle in overturning the household gods of Victorian liberal bourgeois opinion and trampling them underfoot, should be drawn to the later and harsher pronouncements of Carlyle's political philosophy.

For Carlyle, history was essentially biography, and above all the biography of Great Men. Greatness lay in the exercise of the heroic virtues, which were capable of realisation in any sphere of human activity. As expressed in his printed series of lectures, *On Heroes, Hero-Worship, and the Heroic in History* (1841), the hero's shape was Protean: he could be divinity, prophet, poet, man of letters, king. Burton's heroes were extensions of himself: men not only of dynamic personality, but despotic, ruthless and self-willed, who had decisively changed the course of history.

In his essay on *Chartism* (1839), in which Carlyle first applied his ideas to contemporary politics, he called for the hand of the just, strong man as the way to solve society's ills. 'Napoleon was not president of a republic. Cromwell tried hard to rule that way, but found he could not. These, "the armed soldiers of democracy", had to chain democracy under their feet, and become Despots over it, before they could work out the earnest obscure purpose of democracy itself.'[6] There was a great deal of strength but precious little justice evident, however, in the regime of Dr José Gaspar Rodriguez de Francia, the Perpetual Dictator of Paraguay, whom Carlyle felt able to praise several years later for hanging and shooting his political opponents.[7] Coincidentally, Burton, too, was equally impressed by 'the wonderful energy and indomitable will,' of a later Paraguayan dictator, Marshal President Francisco Solano Lopez, who, during the War of the Triple Alliance, stood accused of torture, starving to death prisoners of war, and flogging to death men, women, and children, even ordering the beating of his own mother.[8] As a spirited advocate of rule by the mailed fist, at least for non-white races in the main, it was always a pleasure Burton found, 'after travelling through the semi-republican tribes of Africa, to arrive at the headquarters of a strong and sanguinary despotism.'[9] And he wanted his readers to believe that Eastern despotisms had 'arrived nearer the idea of equality and fraternity than any republic ever invented.'[10]

In his *Latter-Day Pamphlets*, Carlyle turned from recommending the strong leader to a wholesale and virulent denunciation of philanthropy, one of his *bêtes noires*. 'Most sick I am, O friends,' he wrote, 'of this sugary disastrous jargon of philanthropy, the reign of love, new era of brotherhood, and not Paradise to the well-deserving, but Paradise to All-and-Sundry.'[11] Philanthropy, which Burton scornfully described as having become a profession, is given short shrift in several of his books, where he is equally contemptuous of what he calls the 'weakly Humanitarianism of our modern day,' and its 'effeminate hysterical altruism.'[12]

There was, of course, a meeting of minds with regard to racial matters, both Carlyle and Burton being especially critical of the views and practices of "Exeter Hall," a convenient tag for the many missionary and philanthropic societies which used this venue in the Strand for their annual meetings. In Burton's opinion, 'ignorance, not knowledge, sentimentality, not sense, sway the mind on racial questions.'[13] His own views as to 'the Negro's Place in Nature,' were plain: 'a conviction of the innate and enduring inferiority of a race which has had so many opportunities of acquiring civilization, but which has ever deliberately rejected improvement,' and that the negro is 'best when "held to labour" by better and wiser men than himself.'[14] This is very similar in language and tone to Carlyle's own opinions in his "Occasional Discourse on the Nigger Question": 'decidedly you will have to be servants to those that are born *wiser* than you, that are born lords of you; servants to the Whites, if they *are* (as what mortal can doubt they are) born wiser than you. That you may depend on it, my obscure Black friends, is and was always the Law of the World, for you and for all men: to *be* servants, the more foolish of us to the more wise.'[15]

Marriage to two such opinionated, self-centred, and autocratic men was never going to be easy. In Jane Welsh Carlyle's case, she was finally broken on the wheels of her husband's selfishness and egotism. Isabel Burton, on the other hand, proved a survivor. Of immense loyalty, she was also infinitely resourceful. She began by being useful. She ended by being indispensable. Jane complained to Froude, that Carlyle had robbed her of the creed in which she had been brought up, but had failed to put anything in its place. Against all the odds, Isabel Burton's Catholicism remained intact throughout her marriage, providing a cushion and a rationale for her disappointments and sorrows.

Childlessness does not appear to have figured among them. During the Burtons' visit to India in 1876, a woman asked Isabel if they had any children, and received the startling response, "No, thank God; nothing to separate me from my Dick."[16] For Jane, who had longed for children and was denied them, it was not only an irreparable, but an unforgivable, loss. The weight of the available evidence points to Carlyle's being impotent. Unfortunately, in the case of the Burtons' marriage, there is no Froude or Geraldine Jewsbury to shed light on their sexual relationship. Was it, on its physical side, a sham, or had venereal disease made Burton sterile? These are important, even vital questions, to which, unfortunately, there can be no final, definitive answers.[17]

Towards the end of her life, Jane confessed to Froude that she had married for ambition: "Carlyle has exceeded all my wildest hopes ever imagined of him – and I am miserable."[18] Ambition was also an important factor in Isabel's assessment of marriage, which she divided into three classes – Love, Ambition, and Life. In marrying Burton, she was convinced that she had found a man in whom all three were united. 'Some understand Ambition as Title, Wealth, Estates;' she wrote in her journal, 'I understand it as Fame, Name, Power.[19] Burton achieved the first two of these, the third eluded him. 'Downing Street never trusted him with power,' remarked his friend, Ouida, the romantic novelist, 'and the distrust galled him bitterly.'[20]

Carlyle, memorably described by Ruskin as having been 'born in the clouds and struck by the lightning,' a *vates*, a seer, is largely neglected today. A similar fate was predicted for Burton. Reviewing Thomas Wright's *The Life of Sir Richard Burton* in March,1906, the *Times Literary Supplement* claimed that, apart from his translations, Burton was much more a personality and an actor than a thinker, a born explorer, or a man of action. It forecast that, unless his reputation as a linguist and more especially as an Arabic scholar and translator was promptly vindicated, it was inclined to think that in thirty or forty years' time, beyond a small circle of antiquaries and specialists, Burton's name would be almost wholly forgotten.[21]

Given the widespread and highly favourable Press coverage fifteen years later on the centenary of Burton's birth, this seemed a pretty fanciful suggestion. Ironically, it was *The Times* which led the way in fulsome praise, describing him as 'an Englishman who, physically, morally, and mentally was built on the heroic scale.' It pointed out that those of his contemporaries who had recorded their impressions of him, agreed that 'he was one of the greatest personalities of the age....traveller, scholar, linguist, swordsman, poet, and four times Consul, whose original and intrepid genius led him to explore almost every quarter of the globe except the Far East and Australasia, and in spirit the speech, thought, and habits of many and diverse races of mankind.'[22]

The paper also printed an extract from a letter from Dr F. Grenfell Baker, Burton's travelling medical attendant at the time of his death, in which he pleaded for the erection of some form of adequate monument, which would be 'appropriate to his wondrous career, and worthy of that Empire he did so much to enrich and to uphold, and in which he so thoroughly believed.' There was little likelihood, of course, of a statue of the translator of the unexpurgated version of *The Thousand and One Nights* adorning Trafalgar Square or the Embankment. Nevertheless, the widespread interest generated by all the publicity resulted in a more useful, if prosaic, proposal, for the establishment of an annual Memorial Lecture and the award of a bronze medal. 'It was agreed,' wrote *The Times* in its report, 'that as Sir Richard Burton was, above all things, a great pioneer, preference should be given in selecting the annual lecturers to pioneers in the countries and the subjects in those countries, in which Sir Richard Burton was especially interested.'[23] The scheme was supported by many of the great and the good. Queen Victoria's third, and favourite son, Prince Arthur, Duke of Connaught, agreed to act as patron, and the list of those co-opted on to the Committee to collect funds, read like a *Who's Who* of the British Establishment.[24]

The first Memorial Lecture, held under the auspices of the Royal Asiatic Society, was given four years later on 16 June 1925, by the Arabian explorer and orientalist, H.St John B. Philby.[25] He was an apt choice. Like Burton, he was a man with an enormous range of interests and a huge appetite for life, a brilliant linguist, arrogant, bloody-minded and intolerant of authority, a man ambitious for fame who pursued his own course, always convinced that he was right. He was also tough and resilient in the face of adversity. 'My planned career has all gone awry,' he would later write, in words that Burton could well have applied to himself, 'and been shattered into fragments. My nature perhaps could not fit into any plan or groove. But at each crash I have carved my way back into life......and made good despite the efforts of my enemies to stifle me.'[26]

By the 1930s, however, the *Times Literary Supplement*'s forecast was proved to have been prescient. 'No Englishman of the nineteenth century lived a more romantic life,' remarked Sir Arnold Talbot Wilson in the Fifth Burton Memorial Lecture in 1937, 'the lives of few aroused more acrid controversy. Yet he is little remembered today.'[27]

It was not until the post-war years, in particular the 1960s, that a general resurgence of interest in Burton began. Four biographies appeared in quick succession in the United States. In this country, a more relaxed and common-sense attitude towards the frank discussion of sex, saw the reprinting in 1963 of two famous manuals of erotic technique, hitherto generally unavailable: the 3rd century AD *Kama Sutra of Vatsyayana. The Hindu Art of Love*, jointly brought out in 1883 by Burton and his friend, F.F. Arbuthnot, under the imprint of the so-called Kama Shastra Society; and Burton's translation three years later of the 16th century, *The Perfumed Garden of the Cheikh Nefzaoui. A Manual of Arabian Erotology*. The reprinting of many of Burton's other works followed during that, and succeeding decades. Important critical assessments of Burton, particularly regarding his attitude towards the Arab world and British imperialism were made by such scholars as Thomas Assad in *Three Victorian Travellers*, Edward Said in his controversial *Orientalism*, and by Kathryn Tidrick in *Heart-Beguiling Araby*. More recently, the Syrian-born scholar, Rana Kabbani, has added her voice, citing Burton as the traveller who 'did most to asseverate the fiction of an erotic East.'

William Tinsley, who published a number of Burton's books, remarked as far back as 1900 on the strange fact that, during the author's lifetime, not one of them sold to anything like the same extent as those of Barth, Beke, Livingstone, Du Chaillu, Speke, Grant, Baker, Stanley, and several other well-known travellers. It was worth noting, however, he went on, that 'a complete set of Burton's books are at the present time, and, indeed, have been for some years, worth double the sum of all the complete sets of books by all the travellers I have mentioned.'[28] The possibility of obtaining a complete set these days is pretty remote, even if one could afford to do so, individual titles selling for hundreds, sometimes thousands of pounds. The same can be said of Burton's letters, manuscripts and drawings which have long been eagerly sought by collectors. A sale of his topographical pictures at Christie's in London, for example, on 16 July 1993, realised more than £52,000.

Even today, as during his lifetime, Burton is capable of generating controversy, and two important sales in recent times have caused a public outcry. The first was in 1986, when his personal library held by the Royal Anthropological Institute since 1955, was sold to the Christensen Fund of California for $500,000, and placed on indefinite loan in the Huntington Library. The second, involved a response of an altogether different kind. In the spring of 2001, it was reported that the Board of Deputies of British Jews, strapped for cash like the RAI, proposed selling Burton's notorious anti-Semitic MS, containing the medieval 'blood libel', the alleged ritual murder by Sephardim or Eastern Jews of Christian children at Passover.[29] Assigned, after a court-case, to the President of the Board in 1909, it was expected that the MS would fetch £150,000 - £200,000. Protests by many British Jews were ignored, and the sale went ahead at Christie's on 6 June 2001. Although it rocketed within seconds from an opening bid of £80,000 to £140,000, it failed to reach its reserve price and was withdrawn.

(2)

Keeper of the Flame

Like many other people at the time, both in this country and in the United States, I first became acquainted with Burton through the award-winning television series, *The Search for the Nile*, screened by the BBC in the autumn of 1971.[30] It left me with a determination to embark on my own search for Burton.

A biographer researching the life of someone long dead, is particularly fortunate if presented with the chance of meeting with a living link with that past which he or she is trying to recreate. This, however, was my remarkable good luck some five years or so into my research. Late in 1981, I was privileged to obtain an introduction to a remarkable old lady, Mrs Dorothy Flemming.[31] Then in her early nineties, she was old enough to have seen Queen Victoria drive through Hyde Park in an open carriage on her way to the palace after a visit to Windsor, 'an ageing lady in black,' as she later recalled for me, 'wearing a truly ugly mushroom hat.'[32] What made my acquaintance with her memorable, however, giving it an added *frisson*, was the fact that she was the only person still alive to have known Lady Burton. Not only that, as Lady Burton's great-niece, Dorothy, or 'Dortie' as she was known in the family, had been taken by her mother to spend the day with "Great-Aunt Puss" at Mortlake, a year or so before her death in 1896. Having set off in the family landau from their London home in Ovington Square, South Kensington,

"I vividly remember," she said, "arriving at a dingy little house, and standing at the front door to greet us was a mountain of a woman dressed in widow's weeds, who spoke with a deep contralto voice. She was devoted to my mother, and throughout, what was for me, an interminably long day, she never stopped talking; everything she said was punctuated by the words 'Dear Richard' or, every now and then, 'Agnes dear,' when addressing my mother. Of me she took not the slightest notice, and I sat silently by, as only a well-brought-up little Victorian girl should, afraid to move my little bare legs, closely watched by her horrid little pug dog, for if I did it would come up and sniff and growl. Perhaps because I had to sit for so long in a dark drawing-room with Richard's things slung all over the place, I can still remember a few of them. There was his top-hat in a glass case, his gold-knobbed walking stick. What I imagine would have been his consul's uniform and hat. Photo after photo of him, which remained in my mind for it was a most extraordinary face.

After lunch, we were taken to the mausoleum, which seemed to be just round the corner, and when I asked why it looked like a tent I was told not to chatter. My elders, both too stout to kneel, I was dumped down on the cold wet grass, while we said a De Profundis for his naughty old soul."[33]

The house, 2 (now 65) North Worple Way, one of a number of late-Victorian semi-detached suburban villas dotted about Mortlake, lay close to the Richmond branch of the London and South Western Railway.[34] Lady Burton had purchased it early in 1892, calling it "Our Cottage," in memoriam, as she explained to a visiting journalist, 'because for the last five years of Sir Richard's life, we never went to any nice place, without his saying to me, "I wonder if this would do for *our* cottage."'[35] Burton's name-plate, once affixed to his private door at the consulate in Trieste, was now attached to the door of Lady Burton's bedroom in the rear of the house. In the window stood a plain deal writing table and chair, one of many used by him for his literary work. It was seated here, with a clear view across the nearby cemetery of St Mary Magdalen Church where her husband lay interred in his marble tent, that Lady Burton, terminally ill with ovarian cancer, wrote the massive two-volume *Life* of her husband. 'The books and papers are tidied and classified,' she remarked, 'but my papers are not; but I was afraid to trust to sufficient life if I took six months to put them in order, so I have hurried on to give these pages to the world……..'[36]

So, what did the world think? The book was widely reviewed both here and abroad, and Lady Burton was able to write to a friend early in 1894, that she had had her head 'quite turned' by its success. Although *The Times of India* confessed to being disturbed by what it called 'the note of indiscriminate eulogy as well as by the wail of anguish' running through the book, it believed, nevertheless, that while detracting from its merit 'as a final summing up of the character of one of the most many-sided men of our time, they give it at the same time a charm all their own.'[37] This was not a view shared by the leading English literary journal, *The*

Athenaeum, which thought it 'adulatory to the point of absurdity, its complete lack of anything approaching to criticism, let alone fairly balanced judgement, depriving it of reality.'[38] *The Chicago Post,* on the other hand, found it 'very human and very illogical, but exceedingly naïve and the most unscholarly biography of a scholar ever written.'[39] This was a view endorsed in the weighty and lengthy judgement of *The Edinburgh Review.* For all its faults, it thought the book 'both interesting and amusing, and is one which will be read and ought to be read, for its matter, if not for its literary merit.'[40]

(3)

What is Truth; said jesting Pilate; And would not stay for an Answer.[41]

Unfortunately, the measures adopted by Lady Burton in the writing of her biography, were meant to ensure that the private sources for a large part of its matter would not be available to those wishing to follow in her footsteps. Having engaged in an orgy of burning in the weeks immediately following her husband's death, famously of the MS of a new and unfinished translation of *The Perfumed Garden,* she later destroyed all his private notebooks once her book was completed. All his early journals and those from 1862 to 1890 were among a long list of items to be burnt after her death, according to the private instructions she left for her younger sister and executor, Dilly.

The loss of this material is, of course, incalculable. Even so, it is far from being the only problem. Aside from any question of Lady Burton's mendacity, Burton's was a life, as Ouida remarked, 'which presented innumerable difficulties to the biographer. He was a man of great reserve, of the most varied experiences, of the most complicated character.' And she went on to comment on a very important fact which Burton's biographers have preferred to sweep under the carpet, that 'for the chief part of his experiences it was necessary to rely upon himself.'[42] This immediately poses the question as to how much credence can be placed in Burton as a witness?

Pejorative comments on the alleged propensities for lying of those whom Burton classed as semi-civilised or barbarian, run like a thread through many of his books. As for himself, he confessed that, 'like most boys of strong imagination and acute feeling,' he 'was a resolute and unblushing liar; I used to ridicule the idea of my honour being in any way attached to telling the truth.' Years later, on realising 'that a lie was contemptible, it ran into quite the other extreme, a disagreeable habit of scrupulously telling the truth whether it was timely or not.'[43]

In fact, we find his insisting, almost obsessively, on the need for truth, time and time again. 'All truth must be ultimately salutary, and all deception pernicious,' he wrote in his book on *Zanzibar,* quoting the *Edinburgh Review*'s editor, Francis Jeffrey, at the head of his chapter on 'The East African Expedition of 1857-1859.'[44] In a later chapter devoted to a memoir of his erstwhile companion, John Hanning Speke, he repeated the words he had used six years earlier in *The Nile Basin*: 'I claim only the right of telling the truth and the whole truth, and of speaking freely of another as I would be spoken of myself in my own biography.'[45] Similar sentiments were reportedly expressed by Burton during the early stages of writing his autobiography in 1876. 'Whilst dictating to me,' Lady Burton wrote, 'I sometimes remarked, "Oh, do you think it would be well to write this?" and the answer always was, "Yes! I do not see the use of writing a biography at all, unless it is the exact truth, a very photograph of the man or woman in question."'[46]

It all sounds highly laudable and convincing. So convincing, indeed, for Burton's biographers to have been persuaded on far too many occasions into accepting his claims at face value, ignoring the all-important caveat that, 'The biographer does not trust his witnesses living or dead.'[47] It became apparent early on in my research, that the truth had to be painstakingly searched for at almost every step along the way. In doing so, I uncovered a wealth of new material which had never before been used. I have already placed some of this information in the public domain.[48]

Pursuing this method gradually changed the nature of my book from a biography into a biographical enquiry, as it did for Richard Aldington writing about T.E. Lawrence in the 1950s. He, of course, set out to destroy a reputation. That is not the purpose of this book. Rather, it is to give a truer picture and, at the same time, a more rigorous and balanced appraisal of the man and his exploits. As well as sweeping away the many errors which continue to bedevil Burton biography, therefore, I have also taken a more critical look at the claims made for him as to his status in the various fields to which he made contributions. According to the late Fawn M. Brodie, Burton shines 'in three constellations of gifted men.' First, as an explorer, he occupies the front rank with Livingstone, Stanley, Baker and Speke. Second, he belonged to that group of British scientists, including Charles Darwin, Francis Galton, Thomas Lyell, and Thomas Huxley, 'who pushed back the frontiers of man's knowledge of man in an explosion of enthusiastic discovery.' Third, that 'he was a literary figure of great distinction.'[49]

The first of these claims is, I believe, debatable, the second patently absurd, and the third in need of qualification. According to *The Edinburgh Review*, Burton 'with all his ability, with all his linguistic facility and outstanding conquests...never attained the art of writing English.'[50] This is sheer travesty. Certainly, Burton was no poet, a fact which he was forced by the critics of the day to acknowledge publicly. A strong case can also be made out for believing that he has been vastly overrated as a translator. There is no doubt, however, that he was a natural writer, his prose style well described in his early days as an author as, 'free and flowing without special literary merits – the style of a man who knows books but likes life, motion, and talk better.'[51]

Although often regarded as an ephemeral type of literature, most of Burton's travel books are still well-worth reading. Apart from any question of his sardonic humour and pungent irony, they score over so many others of his contemporaries in the same field, in perfectly satisfying Dr Johnson's criteria for such literature, in their being 'good in proportion to what a man has previously in his mind; his knowing what to observe; his power of contrasting one mode of life with another. As the Spanish proverb says, "he who would bring home the wealth of the Indies, must carry the wealth of the Indies with him." So it is in travelling; a man must carry knowledge with him, if he would bring home knowledge.'[52]

It can be said with equal truth of Burton, as the great sixteenth century Portuguese poet, Luis de Camões, said of himself, that he had left his life scattered in pieces about the world. Although unable to claim to have followed everywhere in Burton's footsteps, I have covered a great deal of the same ground, albeit in a radically changed world. While Burton was prepared to undergo discomfort, at least in the wild, he never actively sought it. He would have delighted in the fast air-travel available today. He would, of course, have travelled first-class and, just as certainly, complained about the service.

CHAPTER ONE

WHITE SMOCK, BLACK CASSOCK AND RED COAT

'We are a servile, aristocracy-loving, lord-ridden people, who regard the land with as much reverence as we still do the peerage and the baronetage.'[1]

By late March, 1821, it was clear that Napoleon Bonaparte, the man who not only changed the history of France but also much of western Europe was dying. 'Death is nothing,' he had written with a young man's rhetorical flourish in 1804, 'but to live defeated is to die every day.' Now aged fifty-one, an exile for six years on the remote wind-swept island of St Helena in the South Atlantic, he was facing its stark reality. In April, weak and in great pain, he dictated his will, asking for his ashes to rest on the banks of the Seine, and blaming 'the English oligarchy and its hired assassins,' for his premature death. The end came on 5 May. Among the five British medical officers of the garrison present at the autopsy carried out that afternoon by the late emperor's personal physician, Francesco Antommarchi, was Richard Burton's uncle, Surgeon Francis Burton of the 66th Regiment.[2]

Coincidentally, his nephew was born in England that same month when Napoleon's life began ebbing away. Despite his father and uncle having fought against Bonaparte in the Napoleonic Wars, Burton grew up admiring the late French emperor. 'To me,' he wrote, 'Alexander is the first person of the triad which humanity has yet produced, the other two being Julius Caesar and Napoleon.' Having such a high regard for absolute rulers who put their stamp on history, Burton liked to believe that blood of the Sun King, Louis XIV, ran in his veins. "Why! I would rather be the bastard of a King, than the son of an honest man," he is reported to have said to Sir Bernard Burke, when discussing his supposed Bourbon blood during a visit to Dublin Castle in 1865.[3] Although followed by a gust of laughter, this was no doubt a true expression of his feelings. Nevertheless, despite being an aristocrat at heart and an autocrat by nature, Burton was born into the affluence and ease of the British upper middle-class.

The privileged life-style he was thus able to enjoy for the first twenty-odd years of his life, rested almost solely upon the wealth of one man, his maternal grandfather, Richard Baker. Apart from describing Baker as a 'sharp old man of business,' a talent conspicuously absent in his elder grandson, Burton displayed little knowledge of, or even interest in, his grandfather's life and affairs.

A miniature painted some time during the early years of the nineteenth century, when Baker was in his late thirties to early forties, shows a pleasant-featured man of slim build, with sandy hair parted in the middle, clean-shaven apart from a smudge of hair on the cheekbones.[4] The influence of Beau Brummel, the undisputed leader of fashion at the time, is apparent in the smartly tailored cut-away jacket, the stiff high-collared white shirt, white neck-cloth and white bow tie. Baker stares out from the portrait with a cool, confident gaze, as befits a prosperous fund-holder and rentier, his fingers in a variety of real estate pies scattered across Hampshire and the Home Counties, together with properties in the City.[5] Despite Pitt's introduction of income tax to help fund the war with Napoleon, 'a vile, Jacobin, jumped-up-jack-in-the-box, piece of impertinence,' spluttered one irate Georgian gentleman, the British upper classes had never had it so good.

During the late autumn of 1806, Baker and his family moved from the parish of St Andrew Undershaft in the heart of the City, to Nine Elms Lane in Battersea on the south side of the river. Although soon destined to be swallowed up in London's urban sprawl, Battersea was one of many villages still ringing the capital. Two-horsed coaches carried passengers along turnpike roads to and from London daily, allowing Baker to keep in regular contact with his attorney, business adviser and friend, Samuel Dendy, who had chambers in Chancery Lane. Reading for the Bar was still the fashionable thing to do, providing an entrée into good society. Doubtless having arranged with Dendy to provide at a later date some of the necessary legal training at his London office, Baker sent the son of his first marriage, Richard George, up to Trinity College, Oxford, the following year, at the same time entering his name at Lincoln's Inn.[6]

Three years later, the Bakers moved to Brighton, 'thought by the stockjobbers,' as that old curmudgeon William Cobbett later sourly observed, 'to afford a salubrious air.' The Sussex resort had long been patronised by the fashionable and wealthy, ever since Dr Richard Russell had popularised the sea-water cure. The arrival of the Prince of Wales in September 1783, gave it the royal seal of approval, bringing the *bon ton* flocking to the town in their droves. Among some of the more disreputable aristocratic friends of the Prince of Wales, whom he frequently entertained at Brighton, were members of the notorious Barrymore family, rarely out of the news for their outrageous, anti-social behaviour.

In 1813, perhaps being dunned by his creditors, Henry the 8th earl , sold off a small estate he owned in Hertfordshire. It was snapped up by Richard Baker. At the age of fifty-one, he had finally achieved his ambition, shared by most Georgian men of means, of owning a country seat.

Barham House, named from its close proximity to Barham Wood (later Borehamwood) was an elegant three-storied Georgian mansion, situated in what is now known as Allum Lane, about a mile from the hillside village of Elstree. The extensive grounds included well-timbered pleasure gardens, stocked with ornamental shrubs and flowers, a large walled kitchen and fruit garden containing a greenhouse and vinery, and three meadows of undulating pasture land, together with a picturesque lake.[7] It was here, according to Burton, that he was born on 19 March 1821.

It was untrue, and he knew it to be untrue when he began to dictate his autobiography to his wife during their voyage to India early in 1876. After all, he had entered his correct place of birth, Torquay, South Devon, in the Admissions Register of Trinity College, Oxford, as far back as 1840. So, why did he find it necessary to lie? The reason plainly lay in his, and especially his wife's, snobbish obsession with rank and status, of which being born at the 'right address' formed part. The young American novelist, Henry James, who settled in London in the winter of 1876, was not long in becoming aware that, 'The essential hierarchical plan of English society, is the great and ever-present fact.....There is hardly a detail of life that does in some degree not betray it.'[8]

Isabel Burton, highly conscious of being an Arundell of Wardour, one of the leading Old English Catholic families whose pedigree could be traced in the pages of *Burke's Peerage*, regarded such a hierarchy as being somehow pre-ordained. The purpose of the aristocracy, in her opinion, was 'to float upon the surface of the world.' She was, therefore, in favour of making the House of Lords more powerful than the

House of Commons, since 'God made them nobles, and gave them money and lands, power and influence, to govern, simply that they might benefit their own country.' After all, as she pointed out, 'God grades even in the Bible, some to rule, and others to serve.'[9] While Burton could express approval, therefore, for Brazil's lack of snobbery, 'where no man feels degraded by honest industry, however humble,' it was a far different matter when it came to admitting to any such links in his own ancestry. Consequently, he and his wife were keen to insist on the alleged Bourbon connection. They were equally insistent on there being an old abeyant baronetcy in the Burton family, Isabel even going so far as to tamper with a letter from Clarenceaux King of Arms, in order to lend credence to the claim.[˘]

This was all of a piece with the equally spurious claims made in Burton's brief notes on the 'family history.' His grandfather, he said, 'was the Rev Edward Burton, Rector of Tuam in Galway (who with his brother, eventually Bishop Burton of Killala, were the first of our branch to settle in Ireland).' These two Burtons of Barker Hill, he went on, traced their lineage from the Burtons of Longnor (sic), like Lord Conyngham and Sir Charles Burton of Pollacton, the two being collateral descendants of Francis Pierpoint Burton, first Marquis of Conygham. 'The notable man of the family was Sir Edward Burton, a desperate Yorkist, who was made a Knight Banneret by Edward IV, after the second battle of St Albans, and who added to his arms the Cross with four roses.'[11]

Most of this information can be dismissed out of hand either as historically inaccurate or wholly irrelevant. Edward Burton was not rector of Tuam, since the benefice was impropriate, but Vicar of Annaghdown. His brother Edmund Burton became Dean, not Bishop, of Killala. As for Sir Edward Burton, he was made a Knight Banneret after the battle of Towton, the biggest and bloodiest battle of the Wars of the Roses. The second battle of St Albans was a Lancastrian and not a Yorkist victory. The matter is academic, however, since there is nothing in the pages of *Burke's Landed Gentry* or *Irish Family Records*, which substantiates Burton's claims for the Burtons of Shap having any connection whatever with this old Shropshire family of landed gentry, or its younger Mainwaring-Burton line in Ireland.[12] So, who were Burton's real ancestors?[13]

The Shap Parish Registers from 1559-1830, are far from complete. 'It must have been a rare event,' as their editor has remarked, 'when anyone made his or her way over the bleak Shap fells to the parish church in winter.' The oldest of the volumes is a mere fragment, and there are only twenty Burtons listed in the Index to the published version.[14] The earliest entry records the marriage of Margaret Burton to Thomas Castley, 9 September 1582. The registers record another such marriage one hundred and fifty years later, when John Castley married Elizabeth Burton in June 1732.

Much of Westmorland was farmed by a class of yeomen, some owning the freehold of their land, others holding it by customary tenure of the lord of the manor. Their farms generally were small. They kept flocks of the tough Herdwick breed of sheep, which roamed the surrounding hills, able to survive what was often a harsh, uncompromising environment. Kendal was the centre of the booming woollen industry, to which trains of pack-horses brought in the wool from miles around, along rough, narrow tracks across the fells. It was to the ranks of these 'statesmen' as they were known in this northern county, that the Burtons belonged.[15]

The fragmentary nature of the records only makes it possible to trace a direct line back to Richard Burton's great-great-grandfather, Frank. In 1710, his eldest son, James, was born on the family farm at Hegdale, a tiny hamlet near Rossgill in the Lowther Valley. He was baptised on 8 May at the parish church of St Michael in Shap, the small grey town straggling along the ancient high road between England and Scotland.[16]

At the age of thirty, James married Sarah Holme by licence, his future brother-in-law, John Castley, acting as surety.[17] Sarah, then living at Scarside in the parish of Orton, was a daughter of the late Edmund Holme, who had farmed along the beautiful valley of the Lyvennet at Crosby Ravensworth, some few miles across the fells to the east of Shap. Edmund had been a prosperous yeoman farmer, and when he died in 1717 had left property amounting to £600. He bequeathed the farm and its chattels to his wife, Agnes, and left a legacy of £20 to each of his eight children.[18]

James brought his bride back to Rossgill, where three children were born during the next six years. In 1738, the family moved into what was, probably, a larger farmhouse at Barker Hill, close to the foaming waters of the Lowther River.[19] Between 1739-47, a period during which the Jacobite army of Bonnie Prince Charlie trudged south through Shap in snow and ice to put a Stuart back on the throne of England, six more children were born. The last, named Edward, after Sarah's younger brother, would become Richard Burton's grandfather.[20]

The town-bred Daniel Defoe, who toured large parts of Britain in the early years of the eighteenth century for his patron, Robert Harley, Earl of Oxford, described Westmorland as 'eminent only for being the wildest, most barren and frightful in England, even in Wales itself.'[20] This was an exaggeration. It was also far from being a cultural wilderness. For the bright, hardworking boy, even of poor parentage, an education held out the promise of horizons stretching far beyond those of the surrounding rain-soaked fells.

Although illiterate herself, Sarah's younger brother, Edward, had gone up to Queen's College, Oxford, in the year of her marriage.[22] He disappears from view until 1748, when the school records indicate that he was appointed headmaster of Sevenoaks School in Kent.[23] By then, the Burtons' eldest son, Edmund, was aged eleven, possibly educated up to that time at one of the local grammar schools. With a view to his eventually entering the Church, he was taken on the long arduous journey south to live with, and be educated by, his uncle.[24] Three years later, at the youthful age of fourteen, he was admitted to St John's College, Cambridge, as a sizar, in those days, the poorest, most despised class of undergraduates.[25]

In July 1763, a year after his being ordained priest, Edmund married Catherine Baxter of Atherstone in Warwickshire, a woman twelve years his senior.[26] It was a prudent marriage. Catherine's mother was the sister of John Ryder of Nuneaton, absentee Archbishop of Tuam, in the far west of Ireland. Three years later, through the patronage of the Archbishop, Edmund was appointed Vicar of Kiltullagh, a village some twenty miles east of the town of Galway.[27] Within only five years, after holding the office of Prebendary, first at Kilmeen, and then at Faldown, Edmund was appointed Arch-Deacon of Tuam.[28]

For almost ten years the Arch-Deacon and his wife enjoyed free quarters in the Archbishop's Palace, Edmund acting as agent for the revenues of the see, amounting to some £8,000-£9,000 derived from 86,000 acres of episcopal land. Fifteen of his letters survive from between 1763-83, all but two written to his brother-in-law and man of business, Robert Baxter, a lawyer of Furnivall's Inn, London.[29] In 1782 Catherine died, and Edmund was forced to leave the Palace.[30]

Although the letters are largely concerned with everyday mundane affairs, they give at least a flavour of Edmund's personality. By contrast, his much younger brother, Edward, is a shadowy, elusive figure. There are no means of knowing where he received his early education, and in what circumstances he joined his elder brother in Ireland. There is, certainly, no truth in Georgiana Stisted's assertion that 'on being presented with his Irish benefice [Edward] left the Lake Country with his brother Edmond [sic]....'[31] The records show that an Edward Burton entered Trinity College, Dublin, as a pensioner in 1767. After graduating BA in 1772, he became LLB four years later.[32] Whether he ever practised law before taking holy orders it is impossible to say. At some unknown date, perhaps through the influence of one of the members of the highly influential Kirwan family with whom the Burtons were very friendly, he was appointed Vicar of Annaghdown, a parish on the south-eastern shore of the island-studded waters of Lough Corrib.[33]

Georgiana is probably on firmer ground in asserting that, 'four sons and four daughters were the result of Edward's marriage to Maria Margaretta Campbell.'[34] Only one of the daughters, however, Catherine, a posthumous child born in 1795, the year after her father's death, can be independently identified and facts about her life traced in written records.[35] The two eldest sons, James Edward and John, tutored at home by their father, followed him to Trinity College, Dublin.[36]

At the time of the bloody events of the Great Irish Rebellion and the French invasion in 1798, the two younger sons, Joseph Netterville and Francis, were aged fifteen and eleven respectively.[37] On 22 August of that year, the French general, Jean-Joseph Humbert had landed in Killala Bay, county Mayo, with a force of 1,030 men and 70 officers, intended as the vanguard of a much larger army which never materialised. After a short, one-sided skirmish with the local yeomanry and militia, Humbert commandeered the residence of Bishop Joseph Stock, known locally as the castle.[38] The following morning he ordered a detachment of a hundred men to advance on Ballina. The carabineers and yeomanry proved to be no match for the battle-hardened French soldiers. After putting up a token resistance they fled, leaving one of their number behind to be taken prisoner.

By Saturday, 25 August, the French were ready to march on the walled town of Castlebar. Avoiding the obvious route via the coach-road to Foxford, Humbert struck off across country through the wildest and most rugged part of the barony of Tirawley. The sudden appearance of his forces from an unexpected quarter early on Monday morning, took the garrison by surprise. Amidst a heavy cannonade that was immediately loosed off, the French grenadiers charged. Without a shot being fired, the panic-stricken Irish militia turned tail and ran, tossing aside their weapons and equipment in their eagerness to escape. Looting and pillaging on the way, they only stopped on reaching Tuam, some twenty-seven miles from the scene of the action.

The British government's response to this ignominious rout, known waggishly thereafter as the Races of Castlebar, was unusually swift. Within hours of receiving the news, huge reinforcements of British militia were embarked for Ireland. On 29 August, two Highland regiments, together with the Louth Militia, joined General Lake at Tuam. By 2 September, when the Viceroy and commander-in-chief, Lord Cornwallis arrived, this normally quiet market town was swarming with almost 8,000 soldiers. The excitement generated by these colourful, if alarming, events, played out in the context of the Revolutionary War between Britain and France, must have had a profound and lasting effect on Joseph and his brother. Both would later join the British Army, one as an officer in the infantry, the other as an assistant surgeon.[39]

Burton described his father as being a lieutenant-colonel in the 36th Regiment, having enlisted at the age of seventeen, 'when he ought to have been at school.' Volunteers were called for in Ireland, and 'those who brought a certain number into the field received commissions gratis.' Sons of old Grandmamma Burton's tenants 'volunteercd by the dozen…and when the young master got his commission, they all, with the exception of one or two, levanted, bolted, and deserted.'[40]

The truth is, that Burton knew very little about his father's army career. Joseph Netterville Burton never served in the 36th Regiment,[41] and attained the rank of lieutenant-colonel only towards the latter part of his life. It is also highly unlikely that he received his commission in the manner indicated. The losses sustained by the army during the Napoleonic Wars made it easy for any young man who was literate, of good health and character, to obtain a commission.[42] It is clear from the Army List, that Joseph was commissioned into the 31st Regiment as a lieutenant on 4 November 1805, a fortnight after the battle of Trafalgar, and the death of Vice-Admiral Lord Nelson. He was aged twenty-two. The regiment, consisting of nearly a thousand men, marched to London from Steyning Barracks on the 2nd and 3rd of January 1806, having had the honour of being summoned to attend Nelson's funeral.[43] Three months later, Joseph embarked at Tilbury with his regiment, part of the reinforcements ordered out to defend the vital island of Sicily from Napoleon.[44]

CHAPTER TWO

A STROKE OF GOOD FORTUNE

According to Burton's misleading account, the only service his father saw was in Sicily, under Sir John Moore, where 'he fell in love with Italy.'[1] Moore, in fact, only took over the command from General Henry Fox for three months, and the 31st Regiment saw action in two campaigns. The first was in Egypt, where an under-strength brigade led by Brigadier-General the Hon Robert Meade, was ambushed and a quarter of its officers and men cut down by a murderous hail of fire in the narrow streets of Rosetta.[2] The second was seven years later at the storming of the Heights of Genoa, when the 31st Regiment formed part of an expedition ordered to operate in Italy under the command of Lord William Bentinck.[3] During the intervening years, it shuttled monotonously between Sicily and Malta.

Such enforced tedium could, and did, lead to quarrelling and even 'calling out.' Young hard-drinking Irish officers, in particular, were notorious for their bullying and duelling habits. "By Jasus, gentlemen," said one newly-joined ensign, addressing the assembled officers after mess, "I am conscious you must have the meanest opinion of my courage. Here have I been no less than six weeks with the regiment, and the divil of a duel have I fought yet. Now, Captain C. you are the senior captain, and if you please I will begin with you first: so name your time and place."[4]

If Burton is to be believed, his father shot and wounded a brother officer on two separate occasions, each time nursing him back to health. Such behaviour was regarded as seriously prejudicial to military discipline. An 1808 copy of the Articles of War, stated that any officer issuing a challenge was to be cashiered. The penalty even extended to any officer who knowingly allowed a duel to take place. These regulations were largely nullified, however, by the age-old custom of hushing up any non-fatal incidents taking place within the corps.[5]

On 31 March 1814, more than 40,000 men of the victorious Allied armies made a ceremonial entry into Paris, with bands playing and banners flying. Six days later, Napoleon abdicated. By 4 May, the former Emperor, the master of Europe, now a shabby and unprepossessing figure with lank hair and snuff-stained clothes, was in exile on the island of Elba, declaring that from now on he wanted to live like a justice of the peace.[6]

With no further prospect of military action in sight, Joseph, now promoted to captain, exchanged into the 2nd. Battalion.[7] In October, it was disbanded at Portsmouth.[8] It appears, however, that he did not return to this country. One of the regiment's monthly returns shows that he was given permission to live an unlimited time abroad.[9] Burton later recorded that, when his father decided to move from France to Italy in, or around, 1834, Grandmamma Baker insinuated, 'that in the olden day, there had been a Sicilian young woman who received the Englishman's pay, and so distributed it as to keep off claims.'[10] It is possible, therefore, that it was not only the Italian climate that Joseph fell in love with.

Burton, obviously, had no idea of his father's movements during these years. 'When peace was concluded,' he wrote vaguely, and, obviously, incorrectly, 'he came to England and visited Ireland. As that did not suit him, he returned to his regiment in England.'[11]

When, eventually, Joseph arrived back from Italy, and returned to the active list, it was not to his old regiment. Instead, from 20 May 1819, he became a captain in the 33rd Foot, more popularly known as the Duke of Wellington's Regiment.[12] For most of that year the regiment was garrisoned in the Channel Islands. In October, however, it was transferred to Portsmouth. Richard Baker owned property at Portsea on the outskirts of the city. It was, possibly, at a ball given by officers of the regiment, while Baker was on a visit there with his family, that Joseph first met his future wife, Martha, Richard and Sarah Baker's slim, rather plain and delicate, twenty-three year old second daughter.[13] 'To be fond of dancing was,' as the Bennet daughters were firmly convinced of Mr Bingley, in Jane Austen's Pride and Prejudice, 'a certain step towards falling in love.' After all, it was at a dance that the novelist herself had met with the love of her life, the young penniless law student, Tom Lefroy. Whatever the case, Joseph and Martha's courtship proved to be a pretty whirlwind affair.

The only documentary evidence which provides a clue as to the date of their marriage is an 1822 draft of Richard Baker's will. This shows that an indenture of settlement was drawn up between the various parties on, or around, 29 February 1820, and was contingent on the marriage being 'had and solemnised on or before the 25th of March next ensuing (being an event which happened)...' Burton claimed that the marriage 'was favoured by his mother-in-law and opposed by his father-in-law.' Sarah, like her daughter, was probably bowled over by the handsome, bronzed, dark-haired Anglo-Irishman, with piercing black eyes, a captivating brogue, and a nice line in blarney. Richard Baker, on the other hand, his feet planted very firmly on the ground, may well have considered that a daughter of his deserved better than a thirty-seven year old junior army officer, with scarcely two half-pennies to scratch together.

If such was the case, it is impossible to know how far Richard Baker took his opposition. Unlike her elder sister, Sarah, five years later, Martha was not married in her own parish.[14] Several factors suggest that the couple may have been married in Scotland, a month or so before Headquarters of Joseph's regiment arrived at Stirling Castle.[15] It was the 33rd's commanding officer, Lt Col (later Major-General) W.G.K. Elphinstone who, according to Burton, acted as best man.[16] If, indeed, Richard Baker boycotted the wedding, the bride was most likely given away by Joseph's brother, Francis, who, as it happened, was then at Edinburgh University, studying for his MD degree.[17] Last, but not least, Baker's wife, Sarah, was a Macgregor, possibly from this Central Region of Scotland.[18]

That summer, Queen Caroline, the estranged wife of George IV, went on trial, accused of an adulterous relationship with her Italian major-domo, Bartolomeo Pergami.[19] By the Bill of Pains and Penalties introduced by the Prime Minister, Lord Liverpool, it was enacted that she should be deprived of the title of Queen, and that the marriage between her and the King, should be 'for ever, wholly annulled, and made void.'

The grossly fat and flamboyant Queen was hugely popular throughout the country. In particular, she was the darling of the London mobs, who hurled insults at the King and booed his ministers, especially the Duke of Wellington, who had the windows of his carriage broken. 'Since I have been in the world,' remarked the diarist Fulke Greville, 'I never remember any question which so exclusively absorbed men's thoughts.'[20] For Burton's father, as his son later told the story, the trial which began in a suffocatingly hot House of Lords on 17 August 1820, had particularly unfortunate consequences.

According to this version of events, having been town-major during the Queen's stay at Genoa, Lt

Colonel J.N. Burton, as he is incorrectly described, was ordered by the War Office to appear as a witness against her.[21] However, Caroline having been on the best of terms with all the officers there, he acted like a gentleman, and flatly refused. He was punished, therefore, by being put on half-pay by the Duke of Wellington. This was particularly unfortunate since Lord William Bentinck, Governor-General of India, was about to take him on as his aide-de-camp. As a result, he lost all contact with the army, and afterwards lived entirely abroad. 'His decision was never criticised by the rest of the family,' wrote Burton, 'though I began life as an East India cadet, and my brother in a marching regiment, whilst our cousins were in the guards and rifles and other crack corps of the Army.'[22] This shows a sympathetic, if rueful, understanding of his father's position. It also points the praiseworthy moral of a man willing not only to jeopardise, but to throw away, his career for the sake of his principles. Unfortunately, it is a tissue of lies.

Queen Caroline was at Genoa from March to November 1815, a period indeed when the 1st Battalion of the 31st Regiment was stationed there from July of that year to February 1816. In keeping with Caroline's outlandish behaviour during the earlier stages of her European tour, the Genoese public and members of the British garrison, were treated to the novel spectacle of a stout middle-aged woman decked out incongruously in youthful pink and white frippery, being drawn through the streets in a gilt and mother-of-pearl phaeton. As has already been seen, however, Captain Joseph Burton, by that time having exchanged into the 2nd Battalion, which was then disbanded, had gone on half-pay voluntarily.

Nor was that all. Only naval officers were called as witnesses at the trial. The Duke of Wellington was Master-General of the Ordnance at this period, not Commander-in-Chief of the Army, a post held by the Duke of York.[23] He was, therefore, in no position to put any officer on half-pay. As for Lord Bentinck, he was not appointed Governor-General of India until seven years later. Furthermore, it is scarcely credible that he would have appointed an obscure deputy assistant quarter-master general as his ADC, assuming that he had heard of J.N. Burton in the first place.

Burton's father did not lose all contact with the army. It was only by keeping a weather-eye open as to what was going on, and exchanging into other regiments, at least on paper, that he eventually became a brevet-major in 1837, and a lieutenant-colonel fourteen years later.[24] As for Burton's cousins, only one, Francis Algernon Plunkett Burton, son of Admiral Ryder Burton, was in a crack regiment, the Coldstream Guards. The other, Dr John Edward Burton, was in the Royal African Colonial Corps, hardly in the same category by any stretch of the imagination.[25] Burton entered the Indian Army according to a later account, conveniently forgotten, because he wished to see more of the world, and have a greater chance of taking part in military action. As for his brother, Edward, he joined an ordinary infantry regiment, since that was all the family purse would stretch to.

Georgiana Stisted made no reference whatever to the Queen Caroline affair in her biography. Instead, she blamed asthma for Colonel Burton, as she called him, having to give up soldiering. 'Although a stalwart, broad-chested man,' she wrote, 'he was seized in the prime of life by bronchial asthma, a complaint which, appearing in one of its severest forms, utterly incapacitated him for active service.' In the hope of being fit enough at some future date to rejoin his regiment, he retained his commission, but 'went on half-pay, as it proved, for the remainder of his life.'[26]

J.N. Burton certainly went on half-pay again in 1820, although it had nothing whatever to do with the reasons advanced by Burton or his niece. A few months after arriving in Scotland, the 33rd Regiment was posted to Jamaica. Up Park Camp, located a few miles outside Kingston on the south-east coast, was a notoriously unhealthy place, a 'White Man's Grave.' Three officers and forty-nine non-commissioned officers of Joseph's regiment later died from malaria, shortly after their arrival. In fact it had such a reputation as a fever den, that certain Members of the House of Commons some years earlier, had advised the Government to send out coffins with the soldiers.[27] Unwilling to face such a prospect, and with a comfortable future as a gentleman of leisure now assured, Joseph exchanged into the 37th Regiment on 19 October 1820, and went on half-pay.

With Martha, now four months' pregnant, Joseph decided to winter in Torquay, south Devon. Set in the magnificent sweep of Torbay, and backed by wooded hills, it had grown from being a mere fishing village in the eighteenth century into a fashionable watering-place, due mainly to the use of Torbay by Earl St Vincent's Channel squadron during the late war. Its mild climate had also attracted those who, in normal circumstances, would have stayed in the south of France.[28]

Small properties for limited families could be leased for the season. There were even cottage-villas with gardens and shrubberies available on the hills for those wanting a detached residence. As one would expect of a thriving town, whose population had more than doubled in twenty years, there was no lack of amenities.[29] Besides enjoying a leisurely stroll along the sea-front, visitors could travel farther afield on horse or foot through the beautiful surrounding countryside. Local boats and trawlers from Brixham supplied the market with excellent fish, including lobster. The Baths at the end of the pier, opened to the public three year earlier, offered the choice of hot, tepid, shower, vapour, and cold sea baths. Cole's Library on the Strand could cater for the most genteel taste in literature, and every evening at seven, the Exeter Mail arrived outside the Post Office, bringing letters from as far afield as London.

Five months later, probably attended by her mother and sisters, Martha gave birth to a son. On 2 September, he was christened Richard Francis Burton, after his grandfather and uncle, in St Nicholas, the parish church of Elstree.[30] By this time, his parents had taken up residence in a wing of Barham House. Undoubtedly, Burton, who in 1886 was refused permission to borrow the Wortley-Montagu manuscripts from the Bodleian Library, Oxford, would have been astonished to know that the house where he had once lived as a child, had also been home to the manuscripts' owner during the late 1750s, Lady Wortley-Montagu's highly eccentric and wayward son, Edward. Admitting proudly never to have 'committed a *small* folly,' he had become a student of oriental languages from an early age, later regarded himself as a Muslim, and contemplated making a journey to Mecca. Unlike Burton, his ambition was never fulfilled.[31]

In a gloss which he wrote on Baker's will, Burton blamed his mother for depriving him of a fortune. Richard Baker, he claimed, had decided to make him his sole beneficiary, because he was born with red hair, an unusual thing in the Burton family. His mother, however, 'had a wild half-brother, Richard Baker, junior, a barrister-at-law, who refused a judgeship in Australia, and died a soap-boiler.' She was so fond of him, that she managed to persuade her father to delay the signing of the will, 'to the prejudice of her own babe.' Baker, however, eventually drove to see his lawyers, Messrs Dendy, intending to put his signature to the document. Just as he was alighting from his carriage, he collapsed and died of a heart-attack. The document being unsigned, the property was divided. 'It would now be worth half a million,' Burton wrote.[32] That he should be the sole heir to his grandfather's estate because he had red hair, seems a strange sort of fantasy. That he should accuse his mother of being responsible for betraying his interests, appears bizarre in the extreme. This is especially the case, since documentary evidence shows the claim to be to totally without foundation.

There are few hard facts that can be discovered about Martha's half-brother, Richard George Baker. After graduating from Trinity College, Oxford, in 1812,[33] he was first admitted to Lincoln's Inn, and then to the Inner Temple. He was called to the Bar in 1813, and seems to have spent much, if not all, of his working life as a special pleader on the Northern circuit.[34] As well as being, himself, a beneficiary under his father's will, he was also one of the three lawyers party to the indenture of settlement drawn up prior to the marriage of Burton's parents.

There may well be some truth in the claim of his being something of a madcap. His father first published his will on 5 September 1812, when the family was living at Brighton. During the next eleven years eight codicils were added. It is clear from the second of these, dated 14 January 1815, that Richard Baker disinherited his son. One of several stories later circulating in the Baker family about Richard George, is that he belonged to the fast living, high spending set of the Prince of Wales famously associated, of course, with Brighton. While this cannot be confirmed, records at the Jockey Club reveal that he owned a race-horse even while an undergraduate at Oxford.[35] The piling up of betting debts from which Richard Baker had to rescue him, may well have been the reason for his being cut out of his father's will. If, indeed, it was a warning shot intended to curb his son's extravagance, it appears to have worked, since he was reinstated two years later in a codicil of 28 February 1817.

Precisely how wealthy Richard Baker was, it is impossible to tell from the terms of his will alone.[36] Certainly well short of the amount claimed by Burton. Richard Baker, he said, 'tied up every farthing of his daughter's property, £30,000...', so that her husband could not touch it. Burton regarded this as a shrewd move, since his father, allegedly, had a taste for speculation, and the money would quickly have disappeared.

He was certainly correct about his mother's money being put in trust. Until the Married Women's Property Acts in the '70s and '80s, the Common Law denied women ownership of their own property. In the opinion of the eminent eighteenth century jurist, Sir William Blackstone, it was sufficient to say that 'in marriage husband and wife are one person, and that person is the husband.' It was usual, therefore, for daughters from even moderately wealthy families to have money put in trust for them. Although unable to touch the capital, they could at least draw on the interest for their own needs, giving them a measure of financial independence.

Burton wildly inflated, however, the amount of his grandfather's bequest. Richard Baker's will shows that he settled on each of his daughters, not £30,000, but the far more modest sum of £8,000.[37] Under the terms of the indenture drawn up before Martha and Joseph's wedding, Baker agreed to pay this amount to his executors 'at or before the expiration of one calendar month next after my decease with interest down to the time of paying the said sum of £8,000.' The money would be invested in public stocks or funds, or in Government or real security or securities, 'the same for the time being invested unto the said Martha, now the wife of the said Joseph Netterville Burton, for and during her life for her separate use independent of her husband.' At five per cent, this would bring in £400 a year.

Richard Baker's wife, Sarah, was left an annuity of £600. The rest of the property at her husband's death, would be divided equally between the three daughters and step-son. Baker also left an annual sum of £100 for the maintenance, education, and benefit of sons and daughters, until they reached the age of twenty-one, or married. This could be increased to £200 if the executors thought it necessary.

Burton's claim that his parents went abroad when he was a few months old and settled in Tours, is not borne out by the evidence. Fragmentary documents in the city's archives for the period 1816-24, which list the names of English residents, contain no mention of the Burtons.[38] It seems pretty certain, therefore, that Joseph and Martha lived at Barham House from 1821 up to, and probably a short time after, Richard Baker's death on 16 September 1824.[39] By then, Martha had given birth to two other children: Maria Catherine Eliza on 18 March 1823, and another son, Edward Joseph Netterville, born 3 July 1824, a happy event overshadowed by her father's death some two months later.[40] It is apparent from a legal document dated 15 May 1825, by which Joseph and Martha received a further £7,100 from the Baker estate, that they were then living in the village of Hadley, not far from Elstree, in the adjoining county of Middlesex.[41]

There is every likelihood that, by that date, for reasons of economy and the opportunity of enjoying a more agreeable climate, Joseph had made plans for their permanently settling in France. Two important family events, however, probably contrived to keep them in England for the remainder of that year. The first, was the marriage of Martha's elder sister, Sarah, to her husband's younger brother, Francis. Since their initial meeting at Joseph and Martha's wedding five years earlier, where their romance may have first blossomed, Francis's military duties had kept the couple apart for prolonged periods.[42] Shortly after returning to this country from St Helena in late July, the regiment was posted to Sunderland in the north of England, and then to Boyle in the north-west of Ireland. By exchanging into the 12th Lancers on 30 June 1825, Francis was able to return to England. Three months later, he and Sarah were married at Elstree parish church.[43] Fortunately, no one present could have foreseen how tragically short the marriage was destined to be.

Surprisingly, Martha's much loved half-brother, Richard George, now aged thirty-six, had also decided to settle down. Possibly in December of that same year, he married Louise Buckingham Rolfe, a young woman twenty years his junior.[44] It was probably not until early in the spring of 1826, therefore, that the Burtons left England to start a new life in France.[45]

CHAPTER THREE

A BLAZE OF LIGHT WITHOUT A FOCUS

Tours, in west-central France, contained one of many English colonies scattered across the Continent at this period. Despite the English enjoying a good relationship with the native population, there was little socialising between them. They had their own doctor, parson, and schoolmaster and, like all expatriates, were intensely patriotic and nationalistic.

The commune de Saint-Symphorien was, in the words of a contemporary guide-book, 'The Terrain Choisi' of the English. It enjoyed a reputation for being healthy, was conveniently situated near the town and, from its position high up on the right bank of the Loire, commanded a splendid view of the picturesque Touraine countryside.[1] Beauséjour, a spacious eighteenth-century château rented by Burton's parents, occupied a site half-way up these heights, off the present rue de Vilde. It had a large garden, its own vineyard, even its own chapel, and was only a few minutes' walk to the Pont Neuf which led across the river into Tours. Burton, in later years, remembered it with deep affection.[2] He, himself, was remembered as being somewhat surly in manner, extremely mischievous, and liable to outbursts of temper. These unfortunate traits were said to be compensated by his being very brave and affectionate.

At the age of six, in the process of kicking his way through a succession of nurses, and having learned the rudiments of the 3Rs, Burton was sent to one of the many primary schools in the town. Despite Beauséjour's close proximity to Tours, the extremely busy Pont Neuf proved to be almost impassable from the heat and dust in the summer, and clogged with mud in the winter. The château, therefore, was reluctantly given up, and the family moved across the river into a house in the rue de l'Archevêché. It was then regarded as the best thoroughfare in Tours, close to the Place and the Archbishop's palace.[3] The school, with its hacked and ink-spotted desks, was run by a lame Irishman by the name of Clough. Most were English pupils, with a sprinkling of French, forming what Burton called 'an ungodly article.' Shortly afterwards Clough disappeared, and was replaced by John Gilchrist, a Scottish pedagogue who took a sadistic pleasure in caning his pupils across the palm of the hand with a rattan.

The use of the guillotine for capital crimes was commonplace at this period. The newspapers were full of accounts of executions for poisoning, kidnapping, etc. Sites in Tours such as La Place du Champ de Mars, Place d'Aumont, and Place de l'Archevêché were often used, despite complaints by people in the neighbourhood of the noise and inconvenience they caused. On one occasion, by way of a school-treat, or perhaps a dire warning, Gilchrist took his pupils along to witness the execution of a woman who had poisoned her small family. Having been told to look away when the knife fell, it was inevitable that 'every small neck was craned and eyes strained to look, and the result was that the whole school played at guillotine for a week, happily without serious accidents.' Burton later decided that such an education was a mistake. 'To succeed in English life,' he said, 'boys must be brought up in a particular groove. First the preparatory school, then Eton and Oxford, with an occasional excursion to France, Italy and Germany, to learn languages, not of Stratford-atte-Bowe, and to find out that England is not the whole world.'[4]

As it was, he and his classmates became 'perfect devilets'. Fighting with sticks, stones, fists, and in season, snowballs, ranked as their major amusements. This was varied by truanting from school, in order to play at being Robinson Crusoes in the wood at the top of the Tranchée. The mature Burton criticised his parents for having little idea of bringing up their children. However, they appeared to be far from unique in this respect, since he described all Anglo-French boys generally, as being 'remarkable young ruffians who, at ten years of age, cocked their hats and loved the ladies.' By then, apparently, they had also graduated to breaking church windows, and using their fathers' guns for peppering the gravestones in the local cemetery.

These diverting bouts of juvenile delinquency came to an end for Burton in, or around, 1830. Shooting of a more fatal kind had broken out in Paris. Les Trois Glorieuses, as the general insurrection of July 27-29 became known among the French, toppled Charles X from his throne, and sent him scurrying to England. Joseph and Martha, after giving the matter much thought, and influenced perhaps by sundry cries of *"À bas les Anglais!"* decided to follow suit. Travelling involved a major upheaval. The shabby old carriages were wheeled out of the coach-house and refurbished. Every nook and cranny was stuffed with miscellaneous items of luggage. The rest was auctioned. Goodbyes were said, and the Burtons began the long exhausting journey to England.

Joseph Burton had, by now, planned his sons' future education. They were to go to Eton, and then on to Oxford or Cambridge. In the meantime, they would need to attend a preparatory school. After taking advice, the choice fell on one kept by the Rev Daniel Charles Delafosse at Richmond in Surrey. After several unsuccessful attempts at finding suitable accommodation, Joseph took a house in "Maids of Honour Row," adjoining the gatehouse of the old royal palace, one of a block of four built for the attendants of Princess Caroline of Wales, by George I.

The school, standing between the Green and the Old Town, had formerly been a large private residence. It had been opened in 1764 by the Rev Delafosse's grandfather, Charles, who had settled in Richmond five years earlier. Placing an advertisement in the London papers at the time, he described the school as 'roomy and elegant, the gardens extensive, the play-place, study, walled round, and in full view of the master's parlour; there is also a commodious place for exercise in rainy or cold weather.' The advertisement concluded that 'in short notwithstanding, Mr. Delafosse has such accommodation for his boarders as few, if any, private schools in the Kingdom can equal, yet his terms are extremely moderate, and every article relative to health, morals, and education, will assuredly be attended to.'[5]

Unsurprisingly, Burton's assessment of the school was far removed from that of its founder. Not without some exaggeration, he called it 'the kind of Dotheboys Hall, to which, in those days, gentlemen were contented to send their sons, paying a hundred a year, besides "perquisites" (plunder): on the Continent the same treatment could be had for £20.' House and school were near enough for Burton and Edward to have attended as day scholars. Instead they were sent as boarders, the parents no doubt convinced that an unbroken regime of discipline was needed to curb their sons' wildness.

The Rev Delafosse, master since 1811, appears in the reminiscences of one of his old pupils as 'a tyrant and a most unmerciful beater.' Two boys who ran away, were locked in a room for more than a day after being captured, fastened to a heavy weight, and flogged at intervals. The punishment only came to an end when the master's daughters interceded on their behalf.[6] If this had taken place before Burton entered the school, the Rev Delafosse must have considerably mellowed. Although quite unfitted, in Burton's estimation, to be a schoolmaster, Delafosse, bluff, portly, bewhiskered, and a great user of snuff, rarely used the rod, and was something of a favourite with the boys.[7]

The school hours were from seven till nine, ten to one, and three to five. In the best traditions of academic institutions, there was nothing good that could be said of the meals doled out by the headmaster's thin-lipped wife. Breakfast at 8 am was a wedge of bread with a thin veneer of butter, and washed down with watery milk from chipped mugs. Dinner, three hours later, was the usual 'stickjaw' pudding, sinewy meat, and spoiled vegetables. Although the boys were allowed tea from home, it was rarely seen. Maria remembered her brother at this time as 'a thin, dark little boy, with small features and large black eyes, [who] was extremely proud, sensitive, shy, nervous, and of a melancholy and nervous disposition.' His pride, apparently, led him into a continual series of fights, which took place in the schoolroom, the older boys acting as referees.[8]

Before the end of 1831, according to Burton's dating, there was an outbreak of measles in the school. Several boys died, and the remainder were temporarily dispersed. To avoid infecting their sister, Burton and his brother were taken to stay with their now widowed aunt Sarah at her house in Cumberland Street, London.[9] The rest of the female ménage consisted of Grandmamma Baker, aunt Georgiana, Burton's favourite, and Miss Margaret Morgan, the Baker sisters' former governess.

The two boys were overjoyed at this unexpected holiday. However, Richard fell ill a few days later. After being nursed by aunt Georgiana and Miss Morgan, he and his brother were taken to enjoy the fresh sea-breezes at Ramsgate. The two lost no opportunity of working on their aunt's fears at the danger they might face by returning to school. Joseph, who by now was 'thoroughly sick of "Maids of Honour Row," and "Richmond Green," 'and longed for a chance to return to shooting and boar-hunting in the French forests, decided that in future, his sons would be educated abroad.

The services of a Miss Ruxton, plump and red-faced, were secured as governess for Maria. It may well have been the Rev Delafosse, himself, who was, indirectly, responsible for obtaining the sons' tutor. One of his grandfather's pupils, Stephen Peter Rigaud, had gone on to study at Exeter College, Oxford. He was presently Radcliffe Observer and Savilian Professor of Astronomy. Possibly, through Rigaud's contacts at his college, Joseph Burton obtained the services of one of its undergraduates, Henry Ramus Dupré.

Burton who never had a good word to say for his young tutor, described him as 'an awkward-looking John Bull article, with a narrow forehead, eyes close together, and thick lips, which secured him a perpetual course of caricaturing.' Although there is a great deal of information, largely unedifying, about the father, there is little recorded about Henry himself.

He was born on 8 October 1810, the third son of the Rev Thomas Dupré, Headmaster of Berkhamsted School, Hertfordshire, and formerly a Fellow of Exeter College, Oxford. The school's historian has described Thomas Dupré's career there, until his long-overdue resignation in 1841, as 'a scandal from start to finish.'[10] Henry was sent from Berkhamsted to Winchester College in 1824, as a scholar, during the wardenship of the egregious Isaac Huntingford.[11] He left in 1828, and matriculated at Exeter College on December 11 of that year. There is no record, however, of his having taken a degree. The college registers show that he was in residence until December 1832, suggesting that Burton was at Delafosse's school for longer than is implied by his account.[12]

The Burtons probably left for the Continent early in 1833, the children whooping for joy as the white cliffs of Dover receded in the distance. In Burton's more mature view, they were too young at the time to realise the disadvantages under which they were being placed. As a result, 'we never thoroughly understood English society, nor did Society understand us.' Furthermore, he added wistfully, no doubt having his erstwhile companion, John Hanning Speke, in mind, 'it is a real advantage to belong to some parish. It is a great thing, when you have won a battle, or explored Central Africa, to be welcomed home by some little corner of the Great World, which takes a pride in your exploits, because they reflect honour upon itself. In the contrary condition you are a waif, a stray; you are a blaze of light without a focus.'[13]

Miss Ruxton and Henry Dupré, no doubt, with firm ideas on discipline, soon had a foretaste of life to come when their young charges gave them the slip while out walking in Paris. The children, familiar with the city, returned to the hotel well in advance of their unfortunate guardians, reporting that governess and tutor had been run over by an omnibus.

It was a peculiarity of the English colonists, apparently, not to return to the same place once they had left. Unsuccessful in finding a suitable country house near Orleans, they moved on to Blois. Here, as at Tours, they settled into a house on the high ground above the right bank of the River Loire. By this time, Miss Ruxton had decided that life with the Burton family was not for her and left. Dupré, obviously made of much sterner mettle, stayed for the next seven years until paid off in England.

A schoolroom was set up, and the boys' noses immediately set to the grindstone, studying Greek and Latin for six or seven hours a day. Masters to teach French, dancing, and fencing, were soon hired. The last, an old soldier, was the favourite, and the boys spent most of their leisure hours practising with the foil. Failing to use masks at first, Burton accidentally thrust his foil down Edward's throat, nearly destroying his uvula. Burton also tried his hand at falconry, an interest he would retain for many years. His earliest, fumbling efforts, however, failed. The bird died, and was mourned sufficiently for the experiment not to be repeated until many years later during his military service in Sind.[14]

By the end of the year, they were all thoroughly tired of Blois, especially his parents who, Burton said, 'were imperceptibly lapsing into invalids, like people who have no other business in life except to be sick.' Joseph now began to talk about settling permanently in Italy. Such a proposal upset Grandmamma Baker, who was worried about Martha's health, and would find it more difficult and expensive to visit her daughter and grandchildren in the future. Her angry, "You'll kill your wife, Sir, "and insinuations about Joseph's youthful indiscretions while serving in Sicily, largely fell on deaf ears. A severe winter in Blois made up Joseph's mind. Leaving in the early spring by coach and chaise, the family travelled to Marseilles, and embarked for Leghorn. Finding the place not their liking, they went on to Pisa. There, they took lodgings in a huge block of buildings opposite the bridge over the Arno.

The work of education continued. Two new masters were engaged, one to teach Italian, the other the violin. Burton, unlike Edward, had no talent for music. It was not long before lessons in this instrument were brought to an abrupt and untimely end, by his breaking the violin over the unfortunate master's head. Burton described Pisa as 'the dullest abode known to man.' The English and Italians ignored one another, there was no club, no dinner-parties or dancing as at Tours and Blois. Most of the colonists passed the time strolling about the Quai, or basking in the wintry sunshine. Siena, where they spent the summer of 1835, was equally uninspiring.

In September, the parents decided to stay at Rome during Holy Week of the following year. They broke the journey by stopping at Florence, and renting a house on the north side of the Arno, near the Boboli Gardens. This gave the Burton children an opportunity of seeing the city's magnificent art collections. At Rome, the family secured apartments in the Piazza di Spagna, the capital's English colony. They then got down to the serious business of sight-seeing with Mrs Starke's guide-book under their arms.

Having to cross the malarious Pontine Marshes, they left Rome in time to reach Naples before the beginning of the hot season. A satisfactory house was found upon the Chiaja. Having agreed to take it for the next season, the family crossed to Sorrento, where they were joined by aunt Georgiana and Margaret Morgan. The children thoroughly enjoyed themselves, bathing in the clear water, investigating old smugglers' caves, and making boat trips to Ischia, Procida, Capri, and Salerno. The two brothers also recklessly crept over the dangerous crumbling natural arch at Sorrento to prove to the Italians that it was possible.

Being a man of active mind with little to do, Joseph turned to chemical experiments as a way of filling his time. He bought Samuel Parkes's, *The Chemical Catechism*, one of several books on chemistry 'read with care' by the young Charles Darwin while at Shrewsbury public school.[15] Designed, according to the author, 'to render the promulgation of chemical science subservient to the cause of morality and religion,' it became an instant best-seller.[16] If Burton is to be believed, his father only succeeded in producing a certain substance which he called soap, and another, citric acid, spoiling thousands of lemons in the process.

Once settled at Naples, Joseph engaged the celebrated marine painter, Caraccioli, to teach his sons oil-painting, and the equally famous, Cavalli, as fencing-master.[17] For some unexplained reason, however, the house on the Chiaja was eventually given up, and the family moved to one inside the city. Here they experienced, at first hand, the consequences of a terrible cholera epidemic. Having already met with it in France, Siena, and Rome, it now only excited the brothers' curiosity. After persuading an Italian man-servant to procure the necessary garb, they did the rounds of the houses with the dead carts. Outside the city were huge stone-lined pits, where the black and rigid corpses of the victims were thrown 'like so much rubbish into the festering heap below, and the decay caused a lambent blue flame about the sides of the pit which lit up a mass of human corruption, worthy to be described by Dante.'

Behind the Chiaja was the red light district. Receiving promising hand signals from one of its inhabitants, Burton and his brother paid her a visit. Having plenty of pocket-money, they 'offered to stand treat, as the phrase is, for the whole neighbourhood.' The orgy, he said, was tremendous, and they were lucky to get home unhurt and unseen by the parents before morning. The resulting correspondence, 'consisting in equal parts of pure love on our side, and extreme debauchery on the syren's' was discovered, and brought about a tremendous scene. The boys climbed to the tops of the chimneys to escape their furious father and tutor. Only after extracting a promise to forgive their behaviour, did they come down.

After this affair, there was no question of remaining in the city. The family left in the spring of 1838 and, in due course, arrived at Pau, the capital of the Basses Pyrenees. Summer was spent in the cooler climate of Bagnieres de Bigorres, after which the family returned to Pau, and settled in at a house over the arcade in the Place Gramont. Here the boys were provided with a French teacher of mathematics, a radical socialist who hated rank and wealth. They also took lessons in boxing with the firm intention one day of thrashing their tutor. Whatever time they could spare, they spent in the local barracks, fencing with the soldiers and learning to smoke and consume large quantities of the strongest cognac.

This landed Burton into further trouble with his father. Crawling upstairs after a heavy drinking bout with a Jamaica Irishman, he met his mother on the stairs. On a plea of sickness, Martha helped him into bed. His pale face and glazed eyes worried her enough to fetch his father. It took Joseph only a moment to recognise the symptoms and, turning on his heel, exclaimed "The beast's in liquor." The mother immediately burst into tears, as much in the expectation of the blazing row that would inevitably follow, as for her son's drunkenness. The following day, having succeeded in cooling Joseph's anger, she gave her disgraced son a five-franc piece, making him promise to be better behaved in the future, and never to read Lord Chesterfield's *Letters to His Son*, of which she had a horror.[18]

Many years later, Burton drew on his memory of this domestic scene for his *Arabian Nights'* translation of the Tale of Al Nur al-Din and Miriam the Girdle-Girl:

'Now the merchant loved not wine-drinkers; and he said to Nur al-din, "Woe to thee, O my son!" – (the son strikes his father unconscious)...they sprinkled water on him till he recovered when he would have beaten his son, but the mother withheld him...'

In a footnote Burton remarked: 'How true to nature this scene is; the fond mother excusing her son, and the practical father putting the excuse aside. European paternity, however, would probably exclaim, "The beast's in liquor!"'.[19]

While at Pau, Burton picked up the Bearnais patois, a mixture of French, Spanish, and Provençale. It endeared him to the country people, who were delighted to be spoken to in their own language. He also found it not only helped in learning Provençale, but later assisted him in out of the way places, even as far away as Brazil.

With the coming of the warm four months, the Burtons decamped to the picturesque little village of Argeles not far from Lourdes. Here Burton and his brother fell in love with the pretty daughters of the Baron de Meydell. Following their return, the family took a house on the south side of the Arno, belonging to a widow by the name of Pini. The boys kept up their studies. Burton was particularly glad that he continued with drawing and painting, since he was able later to illustrate his own books. He never ceased to regret, however, lacking the musical talent to transcribe the music he listened to on his travels. With that ability he said, 'I might have collected some two thousand motives from Europe, Asia, and America, and have produced a musical note-book which would have been useful to a Bellini, Donizetti, or a Boito.'

There were other amorous affairs. Strange ladies put their heads out of windows in unaccustomed streets, surprising the father with their, "Oh! S'or Riccardo! Oh! S'or Edoardo." They fell in love with the daughters of the widow Pini, even so far as to make, and have accepted, proposals of marriage. An insuperable difficulty arose, however, about having the ceremonies performed. The brothers also became acquainted with a number of students from the medical school of the university, whose influence was far from good.

The winter at Pisa ended disastrously. In high spirits from consuming too much punch, Burton and his brother sallied forth into the streets after a midnight revel, determined on making mischief. After hustling some inoffensive passers-by, the watch was called, and the brothers took to their heels. Edward who had shorter legs was caught, and locked up for the night in the local guard-house. This was the last straw for Joseph. The family packed its belongings and, just before the onset of the hot weather, transferred itself to the cool, woodland surroundings of the Bagni di Lucca.

The family break-up, which had been looming for some time, occurred about the middle of summer. His sons' outrageous behaviour had permanently soured the father's temper, Burton said, 'He could no longer use the rod, but he could make himself very unpleasant with his tongue.'

Although aged nineteen, it is evident that leaving his mother placed Burton under considerable emotional strain, one that he never came to terms with. He noted later in India that, to the Hindu mother, her child was everything, even when he had grown up. Family ties were just as strong in Italy. 'Italians,' he wrote with bitter irony, 'marvelled at the Spartan nature of the British mother, who, after the habits of fifteen years, can so easily part with her children at the cost of a lachrymose last embrace, and watering her prandial beefsteak with tears.'

Leaving his wife and daughter behind at the Baths, Joseph, accompanied by Dupré, travelled with his sons to northern Switzerland. Here they split up, the father proceeding to England with Edward, and Dupré remaining behind at the medicinal spa of Bad Schinznach in the picturesque Canton of Aargau with the elder son. The baths with their noxious sulphur water had been chosen, said Burton, because he was suffering from exanthemata, brought on by checked perspiration. Exanthem is an eruptive skin disease, or an eruption associated with measles, smallpox, or scarletina. Later medical evidence suggests in my view that Burton, in fact, was suffering from something far more serious.

At the end of six weeks, he and his tutor returned to England. The rendezvous was a house in Hampstead, which had been taken by Grandmamma Baker and the two aunts, for the summer months.

There was then a second parting. The father, obviously considering that Edward's talent for music needed fostering, had arranged for him to be placed with 'the Rev William Havergal, rector of some country parish……[who] was in the musical line, and delighted in organ-playing.'[20] Burton was later banned from corresponding with his brother, having turned the Rev Havergal's name 'into a peculiar form of ridicule.'

In the meantime, he accompanied his father to Cambridge where his widowed aunt, Catherine, had settled while her son, John Burton d'Aguilar, completed his studies at St John's College. Through the kindness of James Scholefield, the Regius Professor of Greek at the university, Joseph was given some idea of his son's capabilities. His worst fears were soon confirmed. Scholefield examined Burton in Virgil and Homer, and found him 'lamentably deficient.' He had only a hazy idea of the Lord's Prayer, was unable to recite the whole of the Apostle's Creed, and had never heard of the Thirty-nine Articles to which every undergraduate had to subscribe at the matriculation ceremony. It was clear that a great deal of work needed to be done before the start of the Michaelmas term. Furthermore, arrangements needed to be made for the continued treatment of Burton's medical condition .

CHAPTER FOUR

A LITTLE LEARNING

Untruthful! My nephew Algernon?
Impossible! He is an Oxonian.
Oscar Wilde

In February 1837, the young Princess Victoria had hardly been able to contain her excitement at seeing her first train 'pass with surprising quickness, striking sparks as it flew along the railroad, enveloped in clouds of smoke & making a loud noise.' It was, she thought, 'a curious thing indeed!'[1] Too curious for Oxford University, Convocation of which in March of the following year, successfully petitioned Parliament against the Didcot Branch Railway being allowed access to the city.[2] As a consequence, the nearest railway station was at Steventon, some ten miles away to the south-west.[3]

It is highly likely, therefore, that Burton caught his first glimpse of Oxford's famous skyline from the London coach bringing him and his father in by the Henley road. From the top of Rose-hill, he would have had an unbroken view of the university's ancient grey buildings appearing to rise straight out of lush willow-dotted meadows, cornfields, market gardens and orchards, as yet unspoiled by that 'base and brickish skirt' of later years.

According to Burton's version of events, having arrived there during the Long Vacation, he was unable to take rooms at once in Trinity College, where his name had been entered. Arrangements, therefore, had been made for him to be lodged and coached by a certain Dr Greenhill, a general practitioner and physician at the Radcliffe Infirmary. The Greenhills were an old Hertfordshire family of landed gentry. In 1644, the then owner of the manor of Abbots Langley, Francis Combe died, leaving all his possessions to Sidney Sussex College, Cambridge, and Trinity College, Oxford. The two colleges then leased the estate to various members of the Greenhill family, who were related to Francis Combe, through his second wife, Anne.[4] It may well have been through Richard George Baker's contacts in the county or at Oxford, that Dr Greenhill's services were obtained.

Lately married to Dr Arnold's attractive niece, Laura Ward, the young doctor was a product, indeed an exemplar, of Arnold's system at Rugby, where religious and moral principles, combined with gentlemanly conduct, took precedence over intellectual ability.[5] A High Churchman, appointed churchwarden at St Mary's by John Henry (later Cardinal) Newman, and a member of Dr Pusey's theological society, his house was the meeting place of many of the leading figures in the Oxford Movement. Doubtless, Burton's father had high hopes that some of this plentiful supply of piety would rub off on his son.

Although earnest and high-minded, Greenhill was a man of considerable charm, good humour, and kindness.[6] Having spent a miserable first year at Trinity himself, he was in a position to understand and sympathise with his pupil's aversion to entering on university studies.[7] More crucially for Burton's future, he was also 'a man of much curious learning on ancient and medieval medicine,' an interest which eventually led Burton down the road of Oriental studies.'[8]

Greenhill, having taken his bride to Paris for their honeymoon, 'in order to show her the world,' as Burton wrote tongue-in-cheek, 'and to indulge himself in a little dissecting,' he was given temporary lodgings at the home of Dr Greenhill's friend, Dr James Adey Ogle.[9] A widower since 1835, Dr Ogle lived with his large family at 63-64 St Giles, an old rambling house opposite the entrance to St John's College.[10] Burton appears to have enjoyed his short stay there. However, as soon as Dr Greenhill and his new bride returned to their home, Burton was taken there by his father, and duly consigned to his new tutor.

Since Burton left matters deliberately vague, it is impossible to state with absolute precision the time-scale of the above events. Fortunately, the Greenhills' marriage certificate provides a useful marker. It shows that the couple were married by licence at the parish church of St Andrew, Rugby, on 21 September 1840. Burton, by his own admission, therefore, must have arrived at Oxford some time after that date, in other words, *very* late into the Long Vacation which extended from 11 July to 10 October. If the Greenhills did, indeed, travel to Paris as Burton claimed, they are unlikely to have returned from their honeymoon until some time during the first week in October, possibly later. This would have left little or no time for Burton to receive any coaching before the beginning of the new term.[11]

As soon as it began, he said, 'I transferred myself from Dr Greenhill to Trinity College.' His entry was prefaced, according to his own account, by his challenging to a duel, Continental style, a fellow-undergraduate who had the temerity to laugh at the 'splendid moustache,' which he had grown while abroad.[12] Only when the College authorities issued formal orders, he said, did he shave it off.[13] Having taken up residence in 'a pair of dog-holes, called rooms, overlooking the garden of the Master of Balliol,' Burton was advised by a kindly college porter, to 'sport his oak', to keep out older hands intent, on such occasions, on playing tricks upon 'fresh young gentlemen.'[14] Burton's response was to leave the door wide open, with a poker heating in the fire, ready to repel any intruders. 'This,' he explained, 'was part and parcel of that unhappy education abroad. In English public schools, boys learn first "to take," and then "to give." They begin by being tossed, and then by tossing others in the blanket.'[15]

All this, and much more besides, has been copied into every biography since. It belongs, nevertheless, to the realm of fiction. Documents in the college archives show, that Burton was not in residence at Trinity throughout the whole of the university year, 1840-41. Instead, he spent the whole of that time lodging with Dr Greenhill at 91 High Street.[16] This was highly unusual at this period, when there was generally sufficient room for all undergraduates at the various colleges.[17] Besides, the University's clerical hierarchy was convinced of the need to protect impressionable young men from the perils posed by landladies and female servants in lodging houses. It was not until after 1868 that students were given permission to live out of college in specially licensed premises.

So what had Burton to hide, that he found it necessary to lie so comprehensively? The reason, I believe, is that he had already lied about the true nature of his complaint, which had prompted his visit to the Hapsburg baths in the Aargau. In my view, he was suffering not from exanthemata, but a venereal disease, possibly syphilis.[18] This would also explain a fact which has never been questioned, as to why he was placed at Oxford in the care of a medical practitioner rather than an ordinary tutor. Since Dr Greenhill's credentials were impeccable both in a professional and private capacity, there would have been no problem in Burton's obtaining permission to live out. Furthermore, given doctor-patient confidentiality, there was no likelihood of the College authorities becoming aware of Burton's true condition.

His so-called 'splendid moustache', in fact, was only an incipient one, as Francis Hitchman's biography, based on Burton's own private papers, shows.[19] A very large number of those suffering from secondary syphilis, exhibit a skin rash at some stage of their illness. Syphilis, however, has been called 'the great mimic,' since it can be mistaken on superficial examination for a number of other complaints. This is particularly the case with the rash, which can closely resemble that associated with measles, small-pox, or a number of other skin diseases, including exanthemata. The earliest blemishes often appear on the edges of the ribs or the sides of the trunk. These later spread to the rest of the body. The face is largely unaffected by the disease, except around the mouth, where the rash may become pustular.[20] If such were the case, then Burton would have found it impossible to shave that area closely.

It was not until 19 November, almost six weeks into the Michaelmas term, that he presented himself for matriculation. Dressed in cap and gown, he was taken to Senate House to appear before the Vice-Chancellor, Philip Wynter, President of St John's College. After signing his name to the Thirty-nine Articles, and promising to observe the Statutes of the University, Burton entered the following details in the Admissions register: 'Ego Ricardus Francicus Burton, filius natu major Josephi Burton Armigeri de Tuam in Hibernia natus apud Torquay, in comitatu Devon. Annos circiter 19, admissus sum commensalis inferioris ordinis, die 19, Novembris 1840 sub tutamine magistrorum Short, Williams et Kensington.'[21] The ceremony concluded with the payment of, so-called, Caution money of £30, together with £5 for utensils.[22] As a fully fledged member of Oxford University, he was now entitled to attend lectures.

Of his three tutors, the Rev Thomas or "Tommy" Short, as he was better known, was far and away Burton's favourite, and the only one to feature in his autobiographical fragment.[23] He was a Fellow for sixty-three years (1816-79), and a Tutor for forty-one of them (1815-56). In 1828, he had failed by only one vote in being elected Headmaster of Rugby in place of Dr Arnold. 'He knew his books by heart,' said the Rev William Tuckwell, 'expounding them with fluency and humour; he ranked with the best Oxford whist players, and kept a spacious cellar of old port wine. But he was especially notable as a conversationalist which constituted a fine art in Oxford once.'[24]

Isaac Williams, on the other hand, curate to Newman at St Mary's, was a man of totally different character and temperament. A poet and theologian, there was in Williams, according to Roundell Palmer, later Lord Selborne, 'a deficiency of the strong and manly qualities requisite for a tutor, but he possessed many acquirements and an intense vein of morality.'[25] Among the leading members of the Oxford Movement, he later wrote critically of Short, that 'though very good-natured and kind, [he] seemed almost incapable of looking on college matters in a moral or religious light.'[26]

Burton was not long in discovering that the university was 'first and foremost,' as the fictional Tom Brown remarked in a letter to his friend Arthur at Rugby, 'an awfully idle place.'[27] The day began with compulsory chapel at 8 a.m. It was, however, a complete travesty, the service being raced through at considerable speed, many men using the time for cramming their lecture books.[28] Breakfast was succeeded by a couple of dry, uninspiring lectures, the subject of bitter complaint by generations of students. Samuel Johnson while at Pembroke College in the previous century, declared contemptuously 'that his Tutor's lecture on logic was not worth the twopenny fine imposed for missing it.'[29] Nothing had changed more than a century later. When A.P. Stanley came up to Oxford as Rugby's first open scholarship winner, he found that, of the three classical lectures he was required to attend, those on Livy and Pindar, were, in his words, 'absolutely useless.'[30] The rest of the day was the student's own, to do as he pleased. Apart from the so-called 'reading set,' hoping for high honours, to which Burton claimed, initially, to have belonged, most were pleased to do as little as possible.

The afternoons were given over to recreation. Unable to afford horses, Burton did what almost everyone else did, and that was to walk. A favourite destination was Bagley Wood, lying some five miles to the south of Oxford, near to the village of Kennington, a spot, as Matthew Arnold wrote,

> Where most the gipsies by the turf-edged way
> Pitch their smoked tents, and every bush you see
> With scarlet patches tagg'd and shreds of grey,
> Above the forest-ground called Thessaly.[31]

It was there, according to Burton, that his 'walks somehow or other always ended,….where a pretty gypsy girl (Selina) dressed in silks and satins, sat in state to receive the shillings and homage of the under-graduates.'

Comparatively few men boated at this period. Burton claimed to have worked hard, under a coach, at sculling and rowing, becoming an oar in the College's Torpid. William Gifford Palgrave who came up to Trinity from Charterhouse a couple of years later, was asked to join the College eight, not because of his skill in rowing, but, as he remarked: 'The fact is that there is great difficulty in filling up the crew and they are glad to get anyone of tolerable strength.'[32]

What Burton called 'the great solace' of his life, however, was fencing. When he first entered Oxford, its only *salle d'armes* was run by William Henry Angelo. He was the youngest son of the famous Harry Angelo, who had given fencing lessons to Byron, and whose premises at 13 Bond Street, London, had been patronised by the leading actors of the day. 'Old William,' however, as he was affectionately known, had none of his father's skill and flair, and eventually left to manage his brother's Academy in St James's.[33]

His place was taken by Archibald Maclaren, who quickly made his mark with a gymnastic and fencing salon in Alfred Street.[34] It was here that Burton struck up, what was to be, a life-long friendship with Alfred Bate Richards, a tall, muscular undergraduate in his final year at Exeter College.[35] He was a man, as Burton found, with whom it was 'unadvisable to box,' but was easily mastered with foil and broadsword.

In November 1841, Richards, who went on to follow a literary and journalistic career, brought out a thirty-six page pamphlet, somewhat luridly entitled *Oxford Unmasked*, which he published anonymously at his own expense. It was, he wrote, 'An Attempt to Describe Some of the Abuses in That University.' He dedicated it 'without permission' to Sir Robert Peel, then Prime Minister and sitting MP for the University. Rather rhetorical in style, but bubbling over with a young's man's burning indignation, it quickly went through five editions. It had 'always been a matter of wonder,' he remarked scathingly, 'why it should, in these days, be considered necessary, that the great founts of national education should be entirely at the distribution and under the control of one class of men: why the waters of learning, rendered turbid and polluted by interest and bigotry, should be thus ladled forth by priestly hands alone.' And what do they teach? 'Why, literally nothing, beyond something of what they miscall "*divinity*"…and at best a little of Aristotle's and Plato's philosophy, wretchedly garbled; logic by rote; and the INFALLIBILITY OF THE CHURCH! Such, truly, is the course of study at Oxford, prescribed by college tutors.'[36] It was strong stuff. Many of his criticisms were later voiced by Burton who, strangely, in view of their friendship, made no reference to the pamphlet which had created such a furore at the time.

Probably in an attempt to please his father, Burton, shortly after the Christmas break, competed for the Open scholarships offered by University College.[37] Trinity had thrown open its scholarships to the whole University as early as 1816, Balliol in 1828. It was not until 1837 that University College decided to found two new Scholarships of the annual value of £30, 'to be open without limitation, and tenable for four years.'[38] The first elections took place in late February or early March of the following year.[39]

Burton failed, 'beaten,' so he said, 'by a man who turned a chorus of Aeschylus into doggerel.' This is total nonsense. Scholarships were highly prized and very demanding, and competition for them was intense among the most able undergraduates and scholars from the leading public schools. When Benjamin Jowett came up to Balliol from St Paul's in 1835, to sit for the prestigious Open Scholarship, also worth £30, he was one of some thirty or more candidates.[40] University College was far from being in the same academic league as Balliol.[41] Nevertheless, there is no reason to believe that the examinations were any less difficult. Those elected in 1841 were an Oriel undergraduate, Henry Clarence Pigou, and Edward Hayes Plumptre, from University College, nephew of its Master, Frederick Charles Plumptre.[42]

Even had he been the 'reading man' he claimed to have been up till then, Burton's desultory studies in the more recent past with a poorly qualified tutor, and no yardstick by which to measure his attainments, would have placed him out of the running for competing with any chance of success in such an onerous examination. The chief reason, he alleged, for his failure, is that he upset his examiners by speaking what he termed 'real (Roman) Latin, and Greek Romaically by accent', the latter picked up from one of the Rhodo-Kanakis merchants at Marseilles.[43]

It is true that a wide divergence had taken place, as he pointed out, between the English pronunciation of Latin and the Italianate since the days of Chaucer. Latin in England, however, had always been pronounced with the contemporary English vowel sounds. As these gradually changed over time, especially as a result of the so-called 'Great Vowel Shift' in the fifteenth century, so the pronunciation of Latin followed.[44] It had nothing to do with furthering the break with Rome, as he suggested, during the reign of Elizabeth I. Besides, there was no such thing as 'real' Latin. Even the Classical Pronunciation eventually reconstructed by scholars, and reported on by the Philological Society at St John's College, Cambridge, in 1885, was only an approximation based on the best available evidence.[45]

Burton even claimed to have been laughed at during his first lecture at Trinity, for speaking after the Roman fashion. This, he said, was because he 'did not know the English pronunciation, only known in England.' This, again, is a patent fiction. Not only did he know it, but he had been using it for the last decade. His late tutor, Henry Dupré was a product, albeit a mediocre one, of Berkampstead and Winchester, then of Exeter College, which employed the English pronunciation, to say nothing of its use by his current mentor, Dr Greenhill.

We are told that Greenhill poured cold water on Burton's hopes of getting a first-class degree. In his turn, Burton quoted his own failure to secure a scholarship, as evidence that those with the ability to gain the highest honours, should not waste time learning foreign languages or pursuing a general education. Consequently, he washed his hands of the whole affair, turning instead to spending time at Oriel which, next to Christ Church, as Thomas Hughes observed, was the least addicted of any of the Oxford Colleges, 'to reading for the schools, or indeed to intellectual work of any kind.'[46] Unfortunately, there are no means of checking this aspect of Burton's account. It seems highly improbable, nevertheless, that such a decision could, or would, have been taken while lodging with Dr Greenhill, a man known for his conscientiousness and resolution.

What can be believed is, that at some time early in 1841, Greenhill introduced Burton to Arabic, a language he had begun studying in order to translate Rhazes's famous *Treatise on the Small-Pox and Measles*.[47] Burton was immediately drawn to this difficult language. Not only did it present a challenge, but it offered a novel and exotic experience to an appetite jaded after years feeding on the classics. He claimed to have made rapid progress in Erpenius's *Grammar*.[48] While it was Greenhill who was responsible for initiating Burton 'into the mysteries of Arabic,' it was left to a visitor, the distinguished Spanish scholar and orientalist, Don Pascual de Gayangos, to show him the correct way of writing the Arabic script, from right to left.[49]

Gayangos (1809-97) spent a large part of his life in England. He 'wrote the Castilian and the English,' as the historian, George Ticknor, remarked,' with equal purity and elegance,' and was a regular contributor to *The Athenaeum* in the late thirties and early forties. His speciality was Islamic history and geography, and in 1841 he was in London publishing his translation of Al Makkari on the Mohammedan rule in Spain for the "Oriental Fund Society."[50]

The remarkably comprehensive records of the Bodleian Library, reveal that Gayangos was in Oxford from Monday, 29 March to Thursday, 1 April 1841, engaged in research in the Duke Humfreys Library.[51] This means that he must have been helping Burton write the Arabic alphabet correctly, only some three to four weeks after he had, allegedly, competed for the University College scholarships. By which time, moreover, he was, in his own words, 'well on' in Erpenius's *Grammatica Arabica*.

Burton claimed to have become highly critical early on of the college teaching, for having no order and system. He regarded its philology as ridiculous, doing nothing to stimulate the reasoning powers. 'Learning foreign languages, as a child learns its own,' he very perceptively remarked, 'is mostly a work of pure memory, which requires, after childhood, every artificial assistance possible.'[52] With this in mind, he devised his own system of learning the basic essentials of a language in two months, something he was to apply with notable success later in India.[53]

At this period, he said, trying to learn Arabic at Oxford was not easy. The historian, Edward Gibbon, at Magdalen in the previous century, had encountered the same difficulty, his tutor, Dr Waldegrave, actively discouraging him from wishing to learn the language.[54] The great Orientalist, Sir William Jones, had come up to University College from Harrow in 1764, having already taught himself the Hebrew and Arabic scripts. Facing the same discouragement as Gibbon, Jones learnt Arabic from a Syrian, Mirza, whom he had met in London, and brought up to Oxford, spending part of each morning in re-translating the *Arabian Nights*.[55] Although there was a Regius Professor, Burton said, he was too busy doing other things. 'If an unhappy undergraduate went up to him, and wanted to learn, he was assured that it was the duty of a professor to teach a class, and not an individual.'[56]

This is incorrect. There was no Regius Professor of Arabic. There were, however, two professorships in the language. The principal one, the Laudian chair, had been endowed by William Laud, Chancellor of the University, and Archbishop of Canterbury, in 1634. During Burton's period at Oxford, the chair was occupied by Stephen Reay. The other chair, known as the Lord Almoner's Reader in Arabic, almost a sinecure appointment, was held by John Macbride, who combined it with acting as principal of Magdalen Hall.[57]

The 'Regius Professor' whom Burton obviously had in mind, was Edward Bouverie Pusey who, with Newman, was the leading Tractarian. Although Professor of Hebrew, he had also studied Arabic because of its linguistic affinities with that language.[58] Pusey was undoubtedly the best qualified Arabic scholar in the university at that time, and, with little bibliographical help, was responsible for producing the first comprehensive catalogue of Arabic manuscripts in the Bodleian Library. It is highly unlikely, therefore, that any 'unhappy undergraduate' would, or could, have approached Pusey, 'always a recluse,' as Tuckwell said, 'and after his wife's death in 1839, invisible except when preaching.'[59]

In view of the criticisms voiced by Gibbon, Jones, and Burton, it needs pointing out that it was not until 1883 that the University first conceded that Arabic and other oriental studies were proper subjects for undergraduates. Laud, himself, had never intended Arabic at Oxford to be anything other than, what we now call, a post-graduate study, and the original statutes of his chair prescribe that instruction should be given only in the vacations, thus ensuring that none of the younger members of the university was diverted from his proper term-time studies.[60]

Burton, who might be said to have enjoyed almost nothing during his short career at Oxford admitted, nevertheless, to being deeply impressed by the preaching of John Henry Newman, one of the great religious figures of the nineteenth century. Unlike Dr Pusey, whose University sermons at St Mary's Burton found recondite and badly delivered, there was 'a stamp and seal' upon Newman's delivery, 'a solemn music and sweetness, which made him singularly attractive.' These are fine words. Unfortunately, they are not Burton's own, but were plagiarised by him from a report in *The Times*, of an address given by the Rt Hon W.E. Gladstone at a conference on "Pew and Pulpit," delivered at the City Temple, Holborn Viaduct, on 22 March 1877. Not only did Burton quote the above words verbatim, he also copied the rest of Gladstone's observations on Newman's mode of preaching, merely changing a word here and there.[61]

Keeping up the pretence of living in college, Burton claimed to have met Newman and Dr Arnold at a dinner to which he had been invited by Dr Greenhill. Expecting much from two such eminent men, he was disappointed by their conversation, which 'was mostly confined to discussing the size of the Apostles in the Cathedral of St Peter's in Rome,' and that with little clear recollection.[62] The known facts, however, of which Burton was clearly unaware, show his anecdote to be completely untrue. Both Newman and Arnold, in the often acrimonious war of words generated by the Tractarian Movement, were adversaries, poles apart in their thinking. They had not met since 1828, when Arnold took his BD degree, and Newman disputed with him in the Divinity School. They were unexpectedly brought together in February 1842.

Arnold, appointed Regius Professor of Modern History, had delivered his inaugural lecture at the Sheldonian Theatre in December 1841; the rest in the Lent term following. As chance would have it, he was invited by the Provost, Dr Hawkins, to dine at his old college, Oriel. In the absence of the Dean, it fell to Newman, as Senior Fellow, to help entertain their guest. Potentially embarrassing, the meeting went off better than expected. It was to be their last. Four months later, Arnold was dead from a heart attack.[63]

During his first year, all of Burton's vacations were spent with his relations in London. In the Long Vacation of 1841, however, he and his brother Edward, accompanied by aunt Catherine and her two daughters, joined their sister and parents at Wiesbaden for a family reunion. Capital of the duchy of Nassau, in south-western Germany, it was a popular resort among the leisured classes in Victorian times, famous for its twenty-seven hot saline springs, its mild climate, and its park-like setting. Apart from the occasional dance at the Kursaal, and a flutter at the gaming tables in the casino, the brothers mainly amused themselves at the fencing-room. Here they discovered a new style of play with the schläger, a pointless rapier with razor-like edges, a weapon favoured by students for settling their affairs of honour.

While on a visit to the old university town of Heidelberg, Burton pleaded with his father to be allowed to leave Oxford and to enter the army, or, failing that, to emigrate to Canada or Australia.[64] Joseph Burton, however, was insistent that his elder son continue his university studies.

Returning to Oxford, and to residence in college for the first time,[65] Burton, if he is to be believed, cast about for some means of being sent down, short of expulsion, this implying 'ungentlemanly conduct.' It was not until the Lent term of 1842 that 'fortune put the clue' into his hands. A famous steeplechaser of the day, Oliver the Irishman, was due to race at Oxford. To avoid the possibility of 'disgraceful scenes' taking place, the University authorities imposed a ban on anyone's attending the meeting. To ensure its effectiveness, the whole of the undergraduate body was ordered to be present at the college lecture, specially timed to coincide with the race.

Burton, together with a number of other undergraduates from the various colleges, was determined to see Oliver ride, and ignored the ban. A 'tandem was ordered to wait behind Worcester College, and when they should have been attending a musty lecture in the tutor's room, they were flicking across the country at the rate of twelve miles an hour.' The following day, they were summoned to appear before the proctors to account for their actions. While his fellow culprits appeared suitably contrite, Burton argued the point forcefully, if not wisely. 'Consequently,' he wrote, 'when all were rusticated, I was singled out from the *Hoi polloi*, by an especial recommendation not to return to Oxford from a Rus.'[66]

Burton's account, like everything else in his Oxford chapter, has never been questioned. It has, nevertheless, a number of puzzling aspects. Not least is the name of the celebrated steeplechaser, whom Burton oddly refers to as 'Oliver the Irishman.' Tom Oliver, who, with Jem Mason, was the most successful steeple-chaser of his day, came in fact from Sussex. His real nickname was 'Black Tom,' a reference to his swarthy, gypsy-like complexion.[67] As for the alleged 'disgraceful scenes' taking place at such events, in the previous year, Dr Arnold, hardly one's idea of a permissive headmaster, allowed his pupils to attend a steeplechase meeting at Dunchurch, to watch Jem Mason ride his famous horse, Lottery.

Hunting and sporting men were always a small minority of the undergraduate body of the University. At Trinity, according to Blakiston, such men 'were rarely refused leave of absence from lecture.'[68] It seems a preposterous claim, in my view, that the undergraduates of one college, Trinity, let alone the whole of the University would be gated to avoid the possibility of trouble taking place at a race-course by a small number of undergraduates.

In his, so-called, 'Little Autobiography' written only eight years later, Burton treats his punishment as an ordinary rustication. 'The testy old lady, Alma Mater, was easily persuaded to consign, *for a time* [my italics], to "country nursing" the froward brat who showed not a whit of filial regard for her.'[69] I believe the whole story was concocted by Burton to conceal the real reason for his being sent down or even, perhaps, voluntarily quitting. Responsions, better known as "Little Go," a public examination sat by undergraduates in the second year was looming, with every possibility of his suffering humiliating failure.[70] He may well have got the idea of the steeplechase episode, from *The Adventures of Mr Verdant Green*, in which the hero travels in a tandem to the Chipping Norton Steeple-chase with his friends, Mr Bouncer, Mr Smalls, and Mr Fosbrooke. On the return journey, they are caught by the proctor, accompanied by marshal and bull-dogs, who suddenly appear from behind the toll-house at Peyman's Gate. The following day, Verdant hears his sentence, which is to 'translate all your lectures; have your name crossed on the buttery and kitchen books; and be confined to chapel, hall, and college.'[71]

Burton could not resist lying, however, even about his departure. In his 'Little Autobiography' he described leaving Oxford in a high dog-cart, his unidentified 'companion in misfortune too-tooing lustily through a "yard of tin", as the dons started up from their game of bowls to witness the departure of the forbidden vehicle.'[72] Writing a quarter of a century later, he identified his companion as Anderson of Oriel, who 'had proposed that we should leave in a splurge – "go up from the land with a soar." ' The dog-cart has now become a tandem, which 'unfortunately went over the bed of best flowers,' and it is Burton who is found 'artistically performing upon a yard of tin trumpet,' and 'waving adieu to my friends, and kissing my hand to the pretty shop-girls.'[73]

Unfortunately, for the credibility of Burton's story, the records at Oriel show that J.T. Anderson was in residence every term from Michaelmas 1840 to Michaelmas 1842. He then went out of residence for a term, for whatever reason. After a further period in college, Easter and Act Term 1843, the Tutorial Register contains the entry 'Sent away – went to New Inn Hall.' His name was removed from the Buttery Book at the beginning of the new quarter in September 1843.[74]

It is far more likely, therefore, that Burton's departure from Trinity on, or around, 11 March 1842, was a pretty low-key affair. The final entry for him in the College archive, records a payment of 2d for the porter.[75] His luggage was probably taken to The Mitre in the High Street, from where he caught a coach to London.

CHAPTER FIVE

A PASSAGE TO INDIA

Given the commitment in time and money which Joseph Burton had invested in his son's education, it was, perhaps, fortunate for Burton that news of his disgrace was conducted by correspondence. Since there were no trains on any part of the mail-route to Italy at this time, it might well have taken up to a month before a reply would have been received from Lucca or Pisa.[1] He remained significantly silent about his father's reaction. Burton's punishment, of course, did not necessarily mean the end of his university career. Although prohibited from returning to Trinity College, if that is the true story, there were Halls where an undergraduate, dismissed for whatever reason from his own college, could resume his studies where he had left off.[2]

By this time, however, Joseph must have had his fill of his elder son's antics. Asked what he intended to do with his life, Burton reiterated that he wished to enter the army, preferably the Indian service. This would give him the chance, as he thought, of seeing the world, and taking part in military action. Georgiana Stisted may well be correct in suggesting that there was no alternative. 'His father, much too irate to exert himself very actively in helping forward a youth, whom he looked upon as an undutiful scapegrace, considered John Company's service quite good enough for his elder son.'[3]

Recent events, certainly justified Burton in thinking that joining the Indian army augured well for seeing service in the field. For some time, the two great empires of Russia and Great Britain had faced each other, mutually hostile and suspicious, across the mountain fastnesses of Afghanistan. It was the British government's policy to ensure the integrity of this state as a buffer-zone against possible Russian expansion towards India.

Its ruler, Dost Mohammed, was regarded as having pro-Russian sympathies, thus posing a threat to British strategic interests. Against the advice of our agent in Kabul, Alexander Burnes, the governor-general, Lord Auckland, decided to replace him with the deposed Shah Shujah, who had been living for some time under the protection of the Indian government. The Army of the Indus, despatched for the purpose, encountered little resistance. Coincidentally, Burton's future brother-in-law, Lt (later Lt-Gen Sir) Henry William Stisted, of the Queen's (Second) Royal Regiment of Foot, took part in this successful operation. At the storming of Ghuznee, when a terrific explosion tore down the gate and its defences, Stisted received an arrow in the calf of his leg. He is reported to have shouted out, "Why damn me, they are shooting off their ramrods!" not realizing the nature of his wound. He is also said to have shaken his leg, and laughingly called out to the storming party as it passed him lying on the ground, "Who shot Cock Robin?"[4]

Dost Mohammed fled to Bokhara, and on 20 August 1839, the egregious Shah Shujah was back in possession of his kingdom. Sir William Hay Macnaghten, who had been mainly responsible for advising Lord Auckland to intervene in Afghan affairs, took his place as envoy and minister at the court. It was an ill-starred venture. On 2 November 1841, Burnes was hacked to death by a screaming mob at the Residency in Kabul. Only a month or so later, Macnaghten was also murdered, his decapitated head and limbs paraded in triumph around the streets, and his body suspended from a meat-hook in the bazaar.

On 6 January 1842, the Afghans dictated a humiliating treaty of evacuation to the gout-ridden and wholly ineffective British Commander-in-Chief, Major-General Elphinstone.[5] Its terms were never honoured. The British army and its camp followers numbering some 13,500, streamed out of Kabul in the middle of winter, the snow-covered passes ahead of them infested with hostile tribesmen. In the words of a later report, 'The Affghans appear to have wallowed in blood, and to have gratified their ferocity and bigotry to the utmost...'[6] Only one of the British personnel, Dr Brydon, survived, to reach Jellalabad and to enter legend a week later.

It was not until March that the full scale of the disaster became known to a shocked British public, accustomed to believing in the invincibility of British might. His aunts, said Burton, were 'patriotic enough to burst into tears when they heard of it.' *The Times*, in its leader column, was scathing in its comments: 'And so ends the first act of this most disastrous war. Few of our readers can remember so heavy, none, probably, so terrible, a reverse to English arms. And for all we have to thank ourselves.'[7] It was against the background of this catastrophe, the worst since the establishment of British power in India, that Burton sought to join the army of the Honourable East India Company.[8]

A commission in the British army was normally obtained through purchase, and was virtually the property of the officer holding it. This was not the case with a Company officer, who obtained a commission by receiving an appointment or nomination from a member of the Court of Directors. It was only later that Burton discovered that officers in the British army regarded themselves as a cut above those in the East India service, an attitude fostered by the various forms of discrimination practised against Company officers by the highest military authorities.[9]

Sensitive to earlier charges of jobbery, the Company operated strict rules, which prohibited members of the Company's committee of patronage from actually selling the appointments in their gift. Nominations, however, were sometimes given to relatives or friends of directors who, in their turn, might sell them. It was through a friend, according to Burton, that he received his nomination. 'My conviction is,' he wrote, 'that the commission cost £500.'

A Parliamentary committee set up as far back as 1809 to investigate allegations of abuses in Company patronage, discovered that a cadetship was worth £500, as against £3,000 for an Indian writership, and £10,000 for one in Canton.[10] These sums, however, represented an actuarial valuation, not their cost as such. Burton's service papers show that he was nominated by J. Loch, Esq, a member of the Court of Directors, and a former Chairman, at the recommendation of Joseph Maitland, of East India House.[11] Since this was the Company's administrative headquarters in London, there is no likelihood of any sum of money having changed hands as Burton suggested. In fact, he knew the contrary to be the case, since one of the questions in his Cadet's application form specifically asked: 'Do you believe that any person has received, or is to receive any pecuniary consideration, or anything convertible, in any mode, into a pecuniary benefit, on account of your nomination?' to which Burton answered: 'No.' A further statement to this effect was signed by Aunt Georgiana on The Parent's or Guardian's Certificate, dated 31 May 1842.[12]

There can be little doubt that Burton owed his commission to the influence of his future uncle, Robert Bagshaw, a leading Freemason with numerous friends and acquaintances in the East India trade.[13] Bagshaw would have been personally known to Joseph Maitland, who certified that he was 'was well acquainted with his [Burton's] family, character, and connexions....'[14]

The next thing was to obtain an outfit, which proved to be not only inordinately expensive, but 'absurdly profuse.' There were a number of military tailors in London to choose from for the dress and undress uniform, such as Jones in Charing Cross, Buckmaster in Old Bond Street, Dolan in St Martin's Lane, Moseley in Piccadilly. Costs of the same sort of items varied a great deal, and there was also a wide difference between the different regiments. The general average for fitting out an infantry officer was around £53. For an officer in the fashionable Hussars, it could be as much as £400. Horse appointments, obtainable from Messrs Laurie, Oxford Street or Gibson and Peat in Princes Street, Cavendish Square, could come to almost £40.

But this was only the beginning. The 'dozens and dozens of white jackets and trousers' mentioned by Burton, were, in fact, only a tiny part of what was considered to be the 'actual necessaries of a bachelor on the voyage to India by a sailing vessel.' In addition to numerous shirts, sheets, pillow cases, towels, silk pocket-handkerchiefs, loose cotton drawers 'for sleeping or bathing in,' and white kid gloves, to name but a few, the traveller was also advised to pack 3 lbs of Windsor soap, 6 lbs of short wax candles, and a bucket and rope, 'serviceable in drawing up salt water whenever wanted.'[15] Everything was securely packed in bullock-trunks, specially made and sold at the outfitters. Burton was probably not short of the mark in claiming that, 'The unfortunate cadets, or rather their parents, were in fact plundered by everything that touched them.'

All this time, apparently, he had been thoroughly enjoying himself, fencing at Angelo's Academy in St James's,[16] and boxing at the Horse-Shoe public-house in Tichbourne Street, Haymarket, run by Owen Swift, former light-weight champion of England.[17] As the time approached for his departure, he gave up these activities to concentrate on learning Hindustani with Duncan Forbes, professor of Oriental languages at King's College, London.[18]

Until partition, Hindustani was the *lingua franca* of modern India, spread throughout the sub-continent by the Mughals and merchants. It was given this name and popularised among Europeans by John Borthwick Gilchrist. Gilchrist, the first president of Fort William College in Calcutta, founded to train British civil servants, saw it as the means of having effective intercourse with the native population instead of Persian, the language of the court and government. The gruff, pipe-smoking Forbes, who spoke all his Oriental languages with a broad Scottish accent, had acted for a time as assistant to Gilchrist, after returning from the Calcutta Academy in 1826. He was impressed by Burton's efforts to teach himself Arabic. Although Forbes appears to have preferred telling anecdotes to teaching, Burton claimed to have laid a fair foundation in the language before leaving for India.[19]

He was duly sworn in at East India House in Leadenhall Street, 'a wonderful dull and smoky old place,' he called it, where the essayist Charles Lamb had 'served the Philistines' for thirty years or more.[20] Wanting the greatest freedom for himself, he said, and having an uncle, 'an old general of invalids,' and one of his D'Aguilar cousins married to a judge at Calcutta, he had elected to be sent to Bombay, rather than the Bengal Presidency.[21] Burton, however, had no uncle at Calcutta, at least not one in a position to subject him to the surveillance he said he wished to avoid. The 'old general of invalids' was, in fact, lieutenant-colonel George Thomas D'Aguilar, who had married Burton's aunt Catherine in 1814. He had died at Calcutta on 9 October 1839, and was buried in the South Park Cemetery.[22] Burton's other claim which, unfortunately, cannot be tested, may well be equally untrue.

The question of a passage to India now arose. Until the Charter of 1813, which broke the East India Company's monopoly on trade with the East, all journeys round the Cape were undertaken by East Indiamen. Most were privately owned, though built to the specification, and often to the design, of the Company which chartered them for so many voyages at an agreed rate per ton. Its civil and military personnel, too, travelled under a scale of fares graded according to rank laid down by the Court of

Directors. Senior passengers sat at the captain's table. Small fry, such as assistant surgeons and cadets, messed with the third officer.[23]

The advent in the 1830s of the steam-ship on the Overland Route through Egypt to India, an innovation strongly resisted for many years by the East India Company, provided a much quicker, and to many a more interesting, alternative.[24] In terms of cost there was little to choose between the two. The fare to Bombay aboard an East Indiaman for a single passenger in a side-cabin below was £120. Apart from incidental expenses incurred in travelling through Egypt, this was identical to that on the Overland Route. The Peninsular and Oriental Steam Navigation Company (P&O) charged around £60 for the voyage from Southampton to Alexandria. The passage money included an excellent table, wines, liqueurs, stewards' fees, and the carriage of 5 cwt of personal luggage. A further £60 was payable at Suez for the journey by Company steamer to Bombay via Aden.[25]

It is obvious that the Burtons' purse did not extend to either of these alternatives. With Robert Bagshaw's help, therefore, a passage was booked aboard the *John Knox*. A Liverpool-built barque of 540 tons burden, it was commanded by Richard B. Cleland, and was then loading in St Katherine's Dock, just down-river from the Tower of London. It was advertised by the shipping agent as, 'one of the fastest in the Bombay trade [and] produces a most favourable opportunity to shippers or passengers, having first rate accommodation and carries a surgeon.'[26] In fact, the average speed of these flat-bottomed, square-rigged vessels, which were slow to respond to the helm and unable to sail close to the wind, was only three or four knots per hour. For sailing characteristics and speed they did not compare with the 'aristocrats of the sea,' the larger East Indiamen built at Blackwall up to the middle of the century, nor the new generation of clipper ships built after 1850.[27]

A chill north-easterly wind, later veering to the south-east, was blowing across the river when the *John Knox* warped out of its basin on 17 June. Having cleared the Custom House, it made its way down the busy river with the ebbing tide, and dropped anchor an hour or so later in Greenwich Reach. The following day Burton, his head already shaved against the coming tropical heat, embarked with his luggage and with a battle-scarred bull-terrier bitch in tow.[28] There was a tearful farewell from the family entourage as the high-masted barque dropped slowly down-stream. Burton later admitted to feeling 'the scantiest regret,' except for his relatives, at leaving Europe. At Gravesend, where the sea-pilot came aboard to guide the ship through the hazardous sandbanks of the estuary, rain had fallen early from an overcast sky. As the day wore on, the barometer steadily fell, and late in the evening there was a loud rumbling of thunder from the SSW, and frequent squalls. By the following day, under a full spread of sail, the *John Knox* was off the Downs, where the journey to India really began.

Small merchant vessels chartered to the Company like the *John Knox*, flush-decked and with three masts, typically had only one deck-house on the after-deck, and the galley where the food was cooked. The rest of the accommodation for the crew and most of the passengers was below decks. There was a small scuttle entrance, no lighting or ventilation, no tables or seats, and sea-chests formed the only pieces of furniture. It was an uncomfortable, noisy, smelly, cheek by jowl existence. Burton, nevertheless as his wife later remarked, 'was always thoroughly happy aboard a ship, and was so sorry when the voyage was over. He never knew what sea-sickness was.' He found himself one of ten passengers. Two were young Ensigns, Isaac Boileau of the 22nd (Cheshire) Regiment, and Charles Thompson of the 18th Bombay Native Infantry.[29] The others were a Mr Richmond, who was going out to a commercial house in Bombay, his three servants, and 'three sturdy wives of sergeants,' as Burton described them, Mrs Louis, Mrs Foyer, and Mrs Delver.[30]

Boxing, practising gymnastics, playing a shrill-sounding flageolet for his own, if no one else's, entertainment, and teaching his brother officers the use of the sword, helped to break the monotony of the long voyage. Burton also devoured all the eastern books on board. It would be interesting to know how much his later attitude towards Indians and native culture was influenced, if at all, by James Mill's *A History of India* , one of a number of books stuffed in his trunk as a cadet's 'essential outfit.' Following its publication in 1817, it quickly established itself as a standard text-book for British administrators training for service in India. In the House of Commons in 1833, Macaulay, then Secretary of the India Board, described it with undeserved hyperbole as, 'on the whole the greatest historical work which has appeared in our language since that of Gibbon.' By 1840, however, it was being severely criticised by the Oriental scholar, Horace Hayman Wilson, Boden professor of Sanskrit at Oxford, and Examiner at Hailebury.[31] In the preface to his edition of the history, he warned that it was evil in its tendency and was 'calculated to destroy all sympathy between the ruler and the ruled.' He added further that, in his view, the influence of Mill's book was responsible 'for that harsh and illiberal spirit' which he saw among the newcomers to the Company's service.[32]

Burton devoted the chief part of his time, however, to the study of Hindustani. He was lucky in finding that Mr Richmond's three servants could speak the language. Burton got them to talk to him, and help him read stories from a text-book written by John Shakespeare, professor of Hindustani at the Addiscombe training-college.[33]

The ship ran steadily towards the Line, becalmed for a while in the doldrums, meeting-place of the north-east and south-east trade winds near the Equator. At the end of the south-east trades, it worked its way through the variables, and made the best of its way towards the Cape, finding plenty of strong wester-lies by sailing some way south. Rounding the Cape in winter presented the awesome spectacle of, 'Waves measuring miles in length' rolling up from the South Pole, 'in lines as regular as those of soldiers marching over a dead plain.' Instead of bearing up for the Mozambique Channel or Inner Passage, the *John Knox* headed north-east in a wide loop across the Indian Ocean between the Seychelles and the Maldives. On the morning of 28 October, after almost five months at sea, Burton caught his first glimpse of Bombay harbour, 'its scenery,' according to one observer, 'justly considered the most lovely in the world.'[34] Determinedly heterodox, Burton later professed disappointment, describing it as 'a great splay thing, too long for its height,' and without 'one of the perpendiculars that distinguish Parthenope.'

Further disappointment followed when the Government pilot came aboard. His replies shattered the excited cadets' hopes of military glory. Although the garrison at Ghuzni had surrendered, Sale's force at Jellalabad, and Nott's at Candahar, had held out successfully until help had arrived in the autumn. A relief force under General Pollock had forced the Khyber Pass, joined up with Sale and Nott, and then occupied Kabul. Shah Shujah had been murdered by his own subjects and, on 12 October, Pollock, after destroying the ancient and famous Four Bazaars had withdrawn from the Afghan capital. The tarnished reputation of the British army was seen, at least in part, to be vindicated.

CHAPTER SIX

JEWEL IN THE CROWN

Burton landed in a grubby shore-boat at the Apollo Bundah, in the sticky humid heat of the post-monsoon season. He was immediately surrounded by a noisy, seething mass of palanquin bearers and half-naked coolies clamouring for his custom. 'If the object of these attentions is a cadet,' said Mrs Postans, an experienced Anglo-Indian observer of the time, 'an individual readily to be distinguished by an experienced eye, some half-dozen dirty-looking Musselmen run along by the open door of the palankeen, crying out as they vehemently jostle each other, "I master's servant – I get master everything!", a promise she assured her readers, 'not to be believed.'[1]

It was the responsibility of the Superintending Officer to provide immediate quarters for the newly arrived cadet.[2] Bombay at this time was full of low-class taverns masquerading as hotels, most of them run by Parsees. Perhaps as a stop-gap due to lack of Army accommodation elsewhere, Burton ended up in the so-called British Hotel, situated in the narrowest, dirtiest street in the Fort.[3] Its rooms were merely spaces partitioned off with thin cloth walls, over which drunken fellow-guests were in the habit of peering at night. As for its food, its teas and curries, Burton said, were designed to haunt 'the censorium of memory for the rest of man's natural life.'

He managed to stand this for only a few days. Then, by spinning a yarn about his 'Irish relatives' to the good-natured assistant garrison surgeon, Dr James 'Paddy' Ryan,[4] was diagnosed as suffering from 'seasoning sickness,' and transferred to what, by courtesy, was called the Sanitarium.[5] This consisted of some half-dozen nondescript thatched bungalows, each standing in its own little bit of compound, which the tenants shared with bandicoot rats and lizards. Ostensibly ill, they spent a boisterous time, living mostly out of doors under mosquito nets, with a bottle of cognac for medicine stowed away under the bed. No furniture was provided, so Burton was forced to buy a bed, table, and chairs from a little Parsee broker popularly known as 'The General,' who could supply anything – at a price.

The Sanitarium looking out on to Back Bay was hardly well-sited. The foreshore was commonly used for interring the carcasses of dead cattle and other carrion. Furthermore, one of the wooden slaughterhouses built on stakes below the high-water mark, spilled blood and offal on to the mud, where it putrefied in the heat. There were also several cemeteries close by, and the Hindu smashan, or burning-ground.[6] There was little decency, Burton recalled, in the way it was conducted. The pyres of the 'fire-birth' were erected on the sand, heads and limbs were allowed to fall off, and when the wind was in the right quarter, the smell of roast Hindu was most unpleasant.[7]

Despite its lack of sanitation and cultural amenities, Bombay in those days was one of the most fascinating cosmopolitan cities in the East. Few places were more picturesque than the great Bhendi bazaar, at the centre of the Old Town in the fort, which saw:

> The beautiful Parsee women, with their gay green and orange-coloured sarees, chatting at the wells to the graceful, handsome sepoys, whose high caste compels them to draw water for themselves; the crowded ways, peopled with professors of almost every known creed and natives of almost every land; the open shops, filled with goods to suit all tastes, 'corn, and wine, and oil,' in their literal senses, with women's bracelets (a trade in itself), culinary utensils, and fair ivory work; the gorgeous temples, beneath whose porticoes young girls weave blossoms of fresh flowers;….. the streets devoted to the cunning work of gold and silver; the richly carved decorations: the variety of costumes that meet the eye, and the languages that fall upon the ear……[8]

It took some years of hard study before Burton was able to walk into such a bazaar, able to distinguish the various castes, knowing something about their manners and customs, religion and superstitions.

Captain Cleland had introduced Burton to his sister, married to an adjutant of the 25th Regiment of Sepoys. She, in her turn, had introduced him to Bombay society, which he soon found reason to dislike. More to his taste was his introduction to the night-time native life of the bazaar, 'a place of dissipation, to put it mildly,' he wrote, 'whose attractions consisted of dark young persons in gaudy dresses, mock jewels, and hair japanned with coconut oil.'[9]

He was not long in discovering that India, western India in particular, offered only two main pursuits for the Britisher: sport on the one hand, and studying the people and their languages on the other. It was the second which he seems to have already determined was to be his chosen field, and the one in which he was to excel. He resumed his study of Hindustani, recommended by 'the General' to a bearded, white-hatted old Parsee priest named Dosabhai Sohrabji, the best-known munshi, or language-master, in Bombay. In just a few weeks, Burton managed to get through the Akhlak-i-Hindi and the Tota-Kahani. The former, otherwise known as the 'Ethics of India,' was based on the Panca-Tantra, a highly popular Sanskrit collection of animal tales, intended to teach political wisdom or cunning. It was widely translated, circulating in Europe as The Fables of Bidpai, or Pilpay.[10] The Tota-Kahani, was the Hindustani version of 'Aesop's Fables. Impressed, the munshi in later times would always quote his pupil, 'as a man who could learn a language running.'

After six weeks or so, Burton received orders to join the 18th Bombay Native Infantry Regiment at Baroda, in Gujarat. He embarked at Bombay in a pattymar, a long, high-sterned native craft fitted with a large lateen sail.[11] On board were his high-spirited Kattywar horse, and a dozen servants headed by a handsome Goanese-Portuguese major-domo named Salavador Soares. Every evening during the leisurely voyage northwards, Burton made a point of going ashore to wander round such towns as Bassein, Broach, and Surat, associated with the earliest days of the British presence in India.

At the end of a fortnight, they reached Tankaria Bunder, a small landing-place in the Bay of Cambay. There, Burton hired carts, and the party began its slow four-day march to headquarters across the flat, brilliantly green Gujarat countryside. 'Wondrous peaceful and quiet lay those little Indian villages,' he recalled, ' outlaid by glorious banyan and pipal trees, topes or clumps of giant figs which rain a most grateful shade, and sometimes provided by the piety of some long-departed Chief with a tank of cut stone, a *baura* or draw-well of fine masonry and large dimensions.'

Burton, introduced to his fellow-officers, found their numbers very much depleted. Since 1824, regiments of the East India Company, organised on the same lines as the British army, had consisted of one battalion only. One 'wing' or half battalion of the 18th BNI was at Baroda. The other, containing a larger number of officers, had been stationed for some time at Mhow, on the borders of the Bengal Presidency.

Having taken up quarters in a bungalow, 'a thatched article not unlike a cowshed,' Burton immediately plunged into his language studies. Despite the difficulty and expense of obtaining good instructors, he spent almost all his leisure time – up to twelve hours a day – grappling with Hindustani,. He also found time to revise the little Arabic he had learnt at Oxford. 'Two *moonshees*,' he said, 'barely sufficed for me.' The intensity of his obsession, was undoubtedly motivated by a wish to expunge the memory of his recent failure and humiliation. Success was absolutely vital to his self-esteem. It was also just as important to prove to his parents, his father in particular, that he had the ability and the will to succeed in his chosen profession.

Few officers in those days with any ambition, stayed out of choice for any length of time with their own regiments. There were a number from the 18th BNI who were on detached service, holding well-paid Staff appointments in irregular corps, or in civil or political employment.[12] For the officer without benefit of interest, Burton said, two roads in India led to preferment. The quickest and most direct was 'getting a flesh wound, cutting down a few of the enemy, and doing something eccentric, so that your name may creep into a despatch.' The other, 'a more rugged and tortuous one,' was the study of languages, 'still you have only to plod steadily along its length, and sooner or later you must come to a "staff appointment."'[13] It was, in fact, a mixture of interest and languages which eventually brought him this prize.

Burton was able to spend such a great deal of time on linguistic matters, since the military duties at the Cantonment were neither lengthy nor onerous. The day began before dawn with a wash in cold water and a cup of tea. Work started as soon as it was light, lasting till shortly after sunrise. Burton had taught himself many of the drill movements from books, and was already proficient with the sword. He had little, therefore, to learn for the manoeuvres on the parade ground. Nevertheless, he gave a great deal of attention to military matters, he said, 'for the ominous words, "tail of the Afghan storm" were in many men's mouths.'

The morning parade was followed by a bath, then the officers gathered for a *chota-hazri*, or light breakfast of tea or coffee, biscuit, bread and butter, and fruit. Breakfast proper was at 9 o'clock. Most men then went off to amuse themselves in various ways, some at the billiard-room, others for a day's sport. The countryside around Baroda offered plenty of opportunities for hunting. Tigers roamed the dense jungle to the east of the city, and elephants could be borrowed from native friends for a day's shooting. Trained cheetahs were always available for smaller game. A large species of antelope called the nilghai, and the highly-prized black buck, browsed on the broad plains to the north. There were old grey boars in abundance. Nevertheless, the uneven terrain around Baroda made hunting them on horseback extremely dangerous. Burton bought an old grey Arab, which followed its quarry like a bloodhound. In the usual cruel fashion of the day, he trained by spearing pariah dogs, and his first success, he said, brought him a well-deserved accident. Unaware of the killing power of the sharp leaf-like blade, he made a powerful thrust at the animal. The point passed right through its body, and into the ground. He was instantly catapulted out of the saddle and thrown with some danger to his life, over the horse's head.

Luncheon, or 'tiffin', as it was better known, was at 2 pm. It consisted of various meat dishes and the usual curry, washed down with bottled beer. This was followed by two or three Manila cheroots, and a siesta. Considering this an unhealthy regime, Burton contented himself, instead, with a biscuit and a glass of port. Following a constitutional ride in the evening, the day ended with dinner in the Mess at 7 pm.

There was little or no young, unattached, white female society in a country station like Baroda.[14] In fact, the bibi, or white woman, was comparatively rare at this period in India. Consequently, Burton found that most of the older officers were more or less morganatically married to Indian women. It was a practice soon adopted by their juniors. These were normally temporary unions, agreed by both parties to end when the regiment left the station. It was a system with obvious advantages and disadvantages. 'It connected the white stranger with the country and its people, gave him an interest in their manners and customs, and taught him thoroughly well their language.'[15] On the other hand, the unfortunate half-caste children of these marriages were despised by the races of both parents. As more and more white women came out to India, the practice came under attack, especially by those of the Evangelical movement, and others mindful of Victorian proprieties. The greatest danger in British India, as Burton pertinently observed, 'is the ever-growing gulf that yawns between the governors and the governed; they lose touch with one another, and such racial estrangement leads directly to racial hostility.'[16]

Having passed his drill, he was given command of a company. Until 1862, there were ten companies in a battalion, half of them commanded by captains, the other half by lieutenants. There can be little doubt that Burton was now in his element. He encouraged his men in sword-exercise, getting the best players along to his quarters for long practice bouts each day. At the end of the month, he presented a prize, generally a gaudy turban to the most proficient. Although he did his best, he said, he was never able to teach them how to use the foil.

While contemptuous of Indian sword-play, Burton, nevertheless, was willing to learn the native style of wrestling. He was easily beaten at first by a number of sepoys in his Company. This led him to try their training methods, which consisted mainly in washing down balls of unrefined sugar, called Gur, with bowls of strongly spiced hot milk. The result, after a week, was a blinding attack of bile.

Being nervous about snakes, he claimed to have taken lessons from a snake-charmer and 'was soon able to handle them with coolness.' Some years later when repeating this account, he admitted to having given up the practice as too dangerous.[17] His description in *Goa and the Blue Mountains*, however, of an Indian's hand being as cold and clammy as a snake, qualities which are not characteristic of the reptile, suggest that Burton never lost his fear of handling snakes.

As a break from the monotony of the Cantonment, he occasionally rode over to the nearby city of Baroda. Standing on the banks of the Vishwamitra river, the capital of the powerful Gaekwar family was a mixture of low huts and tall houses, with a shabby palace and the usual bazaar. The Gaekwars had been forced to cede land to the Company for military help in the past, and to accept a British Resident in 1802. The city contained some 150,000 people, 'mostly hostile,' said Burton, 'who eyed us with hateful eyes, and who seemed to have taught even their animals to abhor us.' The Gaekwar would sometimes arrange a spectacle: a fight between two elephants with cut tusks, a caged tiger and a buffalo, or two wild stallions. Burton found this less interesting than the cock-fighting, which he later practised in Sind.

He was highly critical of the East India Company's role in affairs at Baroda. Instead of acting the part of masters, they seemed to rule on sufferance. He was also vehemently opposed to what he called 'the hateful doctrine' then gaining currency, that 'prestige is humbug.' His strongest comments were reserved for Richard Cobden, the leader, with John Bright, of the so-called Manchester or Free Trade School which opposed imperial expansion. Both Burton's uncle, Robert Bagshaw and his father, John, incidentally, were enthusiastic Free-traders. A firm believer, with certain reservations, in British imperialism, Burton was scornful of the view of this 'professional reformer,' as he termed Cobden, that the people of India would 'prefer to be ruled badly by its own colour, kith and kin, than subject itself to the humiliation of being better governed by a succession of transient intruders from the Antipodes.'[18]

The recent defeat of the British army in Afghanistan still rankled. No wonder, therefore, that the whole of the Cantonment went wild with excitement at the news of General Napier's victories in Sind at the battles of Meanee and Dabba in February and March, 1843.

By this time, Burton felt thoroughly confident of passing an Interpreter's examination in Hindustani. In early April, therefore, he obtained two months' leave of absence to visit Bombay. On this occasion he hired a tent, pitching it in the Strangers' Lines on the Esplanade.[19] Immediately, with the assistance of Dosabhai Sohrabji, he set about working at the fine detail of the language. On 5 May, he joined eleven other candidates for examination in the Town Hall.

THE TANGLED WEB

Interpreter examinations 'were not without a certain amount of difficulty,' he explained. They consisted of making a written translation, reading and translating *viva voce* from a native book, and holding a conversation with a moonshee, in this case, Mohammed Makba, a Concanee Muslim. The examining committee was headed by Major-General Vans-Kennedy, for eighteen years Judge-Advocate-General to the Bombay Army, and presently Oriental translator to the Bombay Government. He was a kindly, scholarly recluse whom an earlier Governor, Mountstuart Elphinstone, had once described as the most learned man of his acquaintance. He was 'a curious spectacle,' said Burton, 'suggesting only a skeleton dressed in a frock-coat or worn-out blue uniform.[20]

Burton passed his examination at the head of the list. It was the sweet taste of success he had needed. Intent now on tackling Gujarati, he laid in the requisite supply of books, and left Bombay for his regiment on 12 May.

The rainy season broke in June. Rain brought by the south-west monsoon fell in torrents, sometimes for a week on end, flooding the surrounding countryside. For three months the weather alternated between humid heat and damp, raw cold. The air was full of flying insects, 'which would have astonished Egypt,' Burton said, 'in the age of the plagues.' Every glass in the Mess needed to be covered, and it was hardly safe to open one's mouth. Except on rare occasions when the sun showed itself, shooting was almost impossible. What for most of his brother officers was a period of deadly ennui, was a heaven-sent opportunity for Burton. There were no parades, no duties. He was free to spend most of his time studying Gujarati, with a Nagar Brahman, a high-caste Hindu mendicant, named Him Chand.[21]

Wrongly assuming 'naga,' to be the Sanskrit word meaning serpent, a recent biographer devoted an entire chapter to Burton's supposedly becoming 'a fully practising snake priest,' handling snakes, 'particularly cobras under the tutelage of Him Chand.'[22] This, of course, flies in the face of Burton's own statement that he soon gave up handling such reptiles as too dangerous. More to the point, it is a complete misreading of 'naga' which, in this context, is derived from the Hindi word 'nanga,' cognate with the Sanskrit nagna, meaning 'naked.' It refers, in fact, to a naked mendicant belonging to any Hindu sect, particularly Dadupanthis, followers of the sixteenth century saint, Dadu, whose members were allowed to carry arms and serve as mercenaries. This accounts for Him Chand's presence in the British cantonment in Baroda.

As well as immersing himself in Gujarati, Burton managed to find time to take elementary lessons from the regimental pandit in Sanskrit, the classical literary language of the Hindus of India. Under his two teachers he 'became as well acquainted, as a stranger can, with the practice of Hinduism.'[23] Nevertheless, he supplemented this by consulting the publications of the Bombay Asiatic Society,[24] and reading up on Moor[25] and Ward. The latter, an anabaptist missionary, had published *A View of the History, Literature and Religion of the Hindoos* in 1811.[26] His work was heavily drawn on by John Mill in Book II of his *History of India*, who described Ward as 'the writer, who above all others, had furnished superabundant evidence of the immoral influence of the Hindu religion and the deep depravity it is calculated to produce.'[27] Eventually, if Burton is to be believed, his Hindu teacher officially allowed him to wear the Janeo, or Brahminical thread.[28]

On 10 August 1843, Burton's name appeared in Regimental Orders as Interpreter to his Corps. Only twelve days later, he obtained permission for a second visit to the Bombay Presidency. Intended to run from 10 September to 30 October, his leave was later extended to 19 November. He made the journey with a friend in the 4th NI brigaded with his own at Baroda, Lt (later General) Alexander Robert Manson, whom he met up with at Surat. After the rains, the route was knee-deep in mud, and with the ship sailing straight into the teeth of the south-west monsoon, progress at sea was slow. It was 26 September before they reached Bombay.

It was no weather for pitching a tent, and Burton was fortunate in finding lodgings in the Town Hall.

The examination before General Vans-Kennedy took place on 16 October. Once again Burton headed the list. On this occasion his sense of achievement would have been all the greater, since he beat Lt Christopher Palmer Rigby of the 16th Bombay NI, the most brilliant linguist in the Company's service. There seems little doubt that Burton knew the details of Rigby's career up to that date, and was intent not only on matching his achievements, but surpassing them. Rigby had come out to India as a sixteen year old cadet in 1836. Like Burton he saw that, without interest, his only means of advancement to a staff appointment lay in his own efforts. Between that date and October 1843, he had passed Interpreter examinations in four native languages: Hindustani, Maharatta, Persian, and Gujarati. The two latter were passed in the same year, despite a debilitating illness. During the next three years, he would add two more languages to their number, Canarese and Arabic.[29] He was undoubtedly a formidable rival. In later years, he would become an equally formidable enemy.

On 10 November, Burton received orders to rejoin his regiment, which had been posted to Sind. By 26 December, it was encamped on the Esplanade at Bombay, everyone cock-a-hoop at the prospect of seeing active service before long. On New Year's Day, 1844, the corps embarked on board the Company's steamship *Semiramis*, and set sail for Karachi.

CHAPTER SEVEN

THE UNHAPPY VALLEY

Crammed with six hundred sepoys and a number of European officers and their servants, there was little to do aboard the *Semiramis* other than to eat, smoke, and sweat under an awning 'about as efficacious to protect you from Phoebus's fury,' Burton observed, 'as a lady's park parasol against a gin-palace on fire.' Uncomfortable as the voyage was, it proved extremely important for Burton's future. One of his fellow-passengers was Captain Walter Scott, the only son of Thomas, the younger and favourite brother of the famous novelist, Sir Walter. Shortly after his son's birth in June 1807, Thomas Scott had misappropriated rents while acting as manager of the estates of Lord Abercorn. Having then absconded, Sir Walter, who had agreed to stand as guarantor for the regular payment of the rents, was left to settle the loss as best he could. Although nearly brought to the edge of ruin, he had come to the rescue of 'Poor Tom,' whom he described in his autobiography as 'a man of infinite humour and excellent parts.'[1]

Sir Walter had also taken a close interest in his young nephew's welfare. In 1821, having promised to 'do all that is in my power to stand in the place of a father to him,' he had managed to persuade his brother, then living in Canada, to allow "little Walter" to come and live with him in Scotland. Educated entirely at his uncle's expense at Edinburgh University and then at the military college at Addiscombe, Scott had gone out to India in June 1826 as a lieutenant in the Bombay Engineers. Over the years, he had gained extensive experience in a variety of civil engineering projects in the Poona Division, Ahmednuggur, southern Concan, the Deccan and the Southern Provinces. He had also qualified as an Interpreter in Hindustani to the Corps of Engineers. Praised by the Collector at Khandesh as a 'very able and intelligent officer,' for his work in overseeing the building of a road from Chandore to Sindwa, he had now been 'placed temporarily at the disposal of the Governor of Scinde for duty in that province, under General Orders, 24 November 1843.' On 14 January 1844, just over a week after landing in Sind, he was appointed 'to act as Field Engineer and to superintend the erection of public works at Kurrachee.'[2]

Burton immediately took to Scott, a handsome man of thirty-six, with pale blue eyes, regular features, yellow hair and a golden beard. He was, he said, 'a truly fine character….who never said a disagreeable word or did an ungraceful deed.' Having had the run during the summer months of Sir Walter's magnificent library at Abbotsford, the nephew had come to share his uncle's love for the feudal and chivalric past. Burton, too, like thousands of boys of his, and later generations, had thrilled at the exploits of Sir Walter's vividly drawn characters, the wide sweep of his canvas, teeming with exotic colours and richness. Many years later, after a visit with the poet Swinburne to the gorge at Malavaux and the ruins of the castle built by the Knights Templar, Burton told the poet that it was through reading about the Templars in Scott's

Ivanhoe, that he was first led to think about the East.[3] This chance meeting with Captain Scott was to influence Burton's life for the next five years. During that time, 'We never had a diverging thought, much less an unpleasant word;' Burton wrote, 'and when he died, at Berlin in 1875, I felt his loss as that of a near relation.'[4]

Four days out from Bombay, Burton caught his first glimpse of Sind, 'a glaring waste, with visible as well as palpable heat playing over its dirty yellow surface.' In an oblique reference to the happy valley of Dr Johnson's *Rasselas*, Burton would later describe the country as 'an unhappy valley, a compound of sand, stone, and silt.'

As in many other parts of India, the British had originally become involved in Sind through trade, the East India Company maintaining a trading factory in Lower Sind for short periods during the seventeenth and eighteenth centuries. From then on political considerations became paramount, the integrity of the country being regarded as vital to counter the perceived threats posed initially by France, and then by Russia, against our Indian Empire. First Lord Auckland, then Lord Ellenborough, his successor as Governor-General, rode rough-shod over the Talpur Mirs, the country's ruling dynasty. Any lingering remnants of their power were finally crushed by Sir Charles Napier in 1843, turning Sind into yet another province of empire.[5]

Sir Charles was fully aware before the event that, although Britain had no right to take over the country, it would do so, 'and a very advantageous, useful, humane piece of rascality it will be.'[6] A large body of opinion, both at home and in India, was far from supporting this view. Lieutenant-colonel James Outram, who had served as the British Political Agent in Sind, and then as Commissioner helping Sir Charles arrange a treaty, became one of his strongest and most trenchant critics.[7] The resulting long-running feud between the two men, 'divided Western Anglo-India,' as Burton said, ' into two opposing camps.' *The Times* was scathing in its attack on Lord Ellenborough, accusing him of having spent time planning the appropriation of Sind. It scornfully rejected any suggestion that a respect for the rights of other nations had played a part in the evacuation of Afghanistan, believing rather that 'the English statesman who carried into effect that withdrawal, while mouthing about his own generosity, was, in fact, and knew himself to be, only retreating pusillanimously before a formidable enemy, in order to gain an opportunity of plundering in security, a helpless, though perhaps shuffling, ally.'[8] Lord Mounstuart Elphinstone, the highly respected former Governor of Bombay, compared Lord Ellenborough's action to that of a bully, who, having been knocked down in the street, goes home to beat his wife in revenge.'[9]

Despite the dangerous wave-swept bar at its entrance, and the mud-choked channel leading up to the town, Karachi, the port of disembarkation, carried on a brisk trade with Persia, Arabia, and Western India.[10] Nevertheless, at closer view it was anything but imposing. The walled native town, dirty, smelly and noisy, consisted of wattle huts and tall mud houses topped with ventilators, clustering round the ruined walls of a native fort. Its dark, narrow, tortuous alleys ran with sewage and discarded detritus of all kinds. The only comparatively open space was the bazaar, 'a long line of miserable shops, covered with rude matting of date leaves.'

Of the 14,000 or so inhabitants, some 9,000 were Hindus. Many of them were very wealthy, influential merchants, who had agencies in all the neighbouring trading centres of any importance such as Muscat, Herat, Kabul, Kandahar and Multan. The rest were mostly Muslims, a great many of whom were fishermen and boatmen living outside the town walls. There were also the descendants of African slaves, to be seen everywhere 'with huge water-skins on their backs, or carrying burdens fit for buffaloes.' To the north and west, where there was a supply of suitable water, there were gardens, planted with vegetables and fruit trees. The rest was a salt or sandy desert. The large military cantonment, swarming with some 5,000 European and Native troops, spread over a slope a mile or so behind the town. For personal health reasons, Sir Charles

Napier had recently moved his administrative headquarters there, formerly located at Hyderabad some hundred miles to the north.

Appointed Governor of Sind by Lord Ellenborough at the end of March 1843, Napier had written in his journal a few days later: 'Omercote is ours!…This completes the conquest of Scinde; every place is in my possession, and, thank God! I have done with war! Now I shall work at Scinde as in Cephalonia to do good, to create, to improve, to end destruction and to raise up order.'[11] Contrary to the expectations of his opponents, Napier by, what Burton called, his 'enlightened despotism,' had pacified the province within a year. Under the Amirs, there had been widespread extortion of taxes from the villagers. Anyone foolish enough to refuse had a hot ramrod thrust up his anus as he hung from a beam by his thumbs. Napier divided the country into three large collectorates, manned by English officers with magistrates' powers. With the exception of the Beluchi feudal chieftains, he also banned the carrying of weapons, and established a well-armed, well-drilled police-force of some 2000 men.[12] Even so, Napier confessed to being unable to put a stop to one crime: wife-killing. 'They think that to kill a cat or dog is wrong, but I have hanged at least six for killing women: on the slightest quarrel she is chopped to pieces….. A chief came here yesterday to beg off another, a follower of his. "I'll hang him," said I. "What! hang him! He only killed his wife!" utter astonishment painted on his face.'[13]

Napier, of course, had his critics. Captain Keith Young, seconded from the Bengal Army in 1843 by Lord Ellenborough to become Napier's Judge Advocate-General, considered him a better military commander than civil governor. Young found that the Governor would not settle anything, and was unable to delegate. In particular, he was astonished to find that the province was still governed by military, and not civil, law.[14] Burton, for his part, was fully in favour of this, believing that a military government was 'the only form of legislature precisely adapted to these countries.' Despite Captain Young's initial reservations, he was eventually won over, impressed by Napier's 'earnest and untiring exertions on behalf of the people he governed; his strict justice; his amenity to all who approached him…..'[15]

Even so, the volatile temper and language of 'old Fagin' as the British soldiers had affectionately nicknamed their eagle-beaked commander was legendary, as was his eccentricity. A drawing of Sir Charles made by a member of his Staff on 24 May 1844 at the Durbar held for the Sindian chiefs to express their loyalty to Queen Victoria, shows the general dressed in a dirty old flannel jacket, trousers of white cloth, not over-clean, hunting cap, and no braces. Appended to the original drawing is a certificate signed by numerous members of the Sind Staff vouching for its being exact and not a caricature. Someone later added the remark, 'Correct, but the stockings are not shown down-at-heel as they ought to have been.'[16]

While having at heart the best interests of the ordinary people he governed, Napier, like so many of the English in India, was never able to converse in any of the country's languages. He had once made an attempt to learn Hindustani, but fell asleep after only a few minutes, his munshi being either too polite, or too afraid, to wake him. Burton, with his eye to the main chance, knowing Napier's need for officers able to speak the vernacular dialect, immediately found himself a teacher and a text-book. The conditions for study, however, were anything but favourable. They were billeted in tents, there were daily dust-storms, unending drills and brigade parades, and, as interpreter to his regiment, much of Burton's time was occupied in attending long-drawn-out courts-martial.

A month or two later, he was transferred with his corps to Gharra, some forty miles to the east of Karachi. As always for Burton, a change of scene came as a welcome relief. 'By far the most agreeable and wholesome part of regimental life in India,' he wrote, 'is the march; the hours are reasonable, the work not too severe, and the results, in appetite and sleep, admirable.' After spending a week or more preparing for the move, Burton set out in the cool of an early morning mounted on a dromedary. Its wooden saddle was covered with a thickly quilted gaudy-coloured silk cushion. Little bells dangled from the animal's necklace of blue beads, their tinklings believed to act as a talisman against the evil eye. Loaded up on four baggage camels were his tent and its furniture, table and chair, canteen and crockery, couch, carpet, and chest of drawers. There was the usual large retinue of servants in attendance, a head servant, a "boy," his assistant, two horse-keepers, one to look after Burton's shaggy Arab pony, a grass cutter, a pair of camel drivers, a washerwoman and several assorted female helpers. And, of course, there was "Pepper," Burton's snappy little terrier.

The journey along the road of the Five Torrents, which wound over low hills, dry river beds, bare rocks and sandy desert, was a leisurely affair, with stops at Jemadar-Ka-Landa, a typical Sind village, and Wuttajee. This, as he pungently put it, 'afforded the unusual convenience of a caravanserai; a deserted mosque having been desecrated into utility.'

His initial euphoria at the move was short-lived. Situated on a creek running up from Karachi to within twenty-four miles of Tattah, the ancient crumbling capital of Lower Sind, Gharra proved to be a windy, desolate, barren spot of rock and sand. Close by was the large native village, a dirty heap of mud and mat hovels, 'whose timorous inhabitants shunned us as walking pestilences.' In this part of Lars or Lower Sind, the summer temperature could soar to a mind-sapping 115 degrees Fahrenheit, ten more if one were under canvas. Knowing their field service was only temporary, their predecessors had not built barracks or bungalows. Lacking the wherewithal to build, Burton was forced to swelter through the whole of a hot season in a single-poled tent. He only managed to avoid suffocation by sitting under a table draped with a wet cloth.

This was all the incentive he needed to throw aside Sindi for Marathi, (Maharatee in his spelling), the Indo-Aryan language of western and central India. By way of repeated examinations, he hoped eventually to escape this new purgatory – permanently. Despite the fierce, enervating heat, with the expert assistance of the regimental *pundit* and an excellent dictionary, he was able to travel to the Bombay Presidency in September for examination. As usual, he led the list of half a dozen candidates.[17] Only two years after arriving in India, therefore, Burton had achieved the remarkable feat of qualifying as an interpreter in three vernacular languages.

Returning to Karachi, probably in late October, he promptly engaged the services of a Persian *munshi*, Mirza Mohammed Hosayn of Shiraz, and began an extensive course of reading in what he described as 'that most elegant of Oriental languages.' In Sind, where the language widely differed in pronunciation, idiom and vocabulary from the dialect of Shiraz and Isfahan, it was rarely used by the native population in conversation, being reserved for literature, official business, and letter-writing.

The following month, as a result of Captain Scott's patronage, Burton found himself gazetted as one of his four assistants in the Canal Department of the Sind Survey.[18] What Burton deliberately failed to disclose in his account was, that his services had been applied for by Scott three months earlier. His request, however, had been turned down. On 19 August 1844, Sir Charles's nephew and *aide-de-camp*, Captain William C.E. Napier, wrote to Scott informing him that:

> The General says he is sorry that he cannot appoint Burton *at present* to the Survey, because he is under a cloud, which has not yet been cleared up. He has been behaving rather bumptiously to his Commanding Officer, and the matter is not yet settled. Until it is, it is impossible for the General to give him an appointment. It is a pity, for he evidently could be very useful to you. Perhaps it may all come right in time.[19]

This would be Burton's first, but not his last, serious brush with his commanding officer, Major Henry Nicholas Corsellis. Humility was not part of Burton's makeup, and his recent examination successes may well have gone to his head, making him even more conceited than usual. Good linguists, as he was to say on more than one occasion, 'are often bad characters – mostly "too clever by half."'[20] Convinced that this brash young subaltern needed taking down a peg, Corsellis let him stew in his own juice for three months, literally as well as metaphorically. He then withdrew his objections to Burton's secondment to the Canal Department.

Sind had been irrigated by means of artificial canals from time immemorial. As far back as the eighth century, the Arab conquerors in assessing the land tax found it necessary to differentiate between land watered from the public canals and that watered privately by artificial means. It had been Lord Ellenborough's idea to have a survey undertaken of the country's ancient watercourses and canals. He, therefore, obtained the services of a brilliant engineer, Captain (later Sir) William Erskine Baker, then Superintendent of the Delhi Canal.[21] Baker, appointed the first Superintendent of canals and forests in Sind, was helped by several scientific officers, some of them seconded from the Survey of India.[22] In July 1844, after carrying out a number of surveys in the north of the province with his three assistants, Baker returned to Karachi. As well as submitting a number of important reports to Sir Charles, including a highly detailed Memorandum on the irrigation of Sind, Baker also tendered his resignation.[23] While Napier had been fully aware from the outset that Baker's appointment was only temporary, his departure, nevertheless, came as a severe blow. 'I have lost Baker:' he wrote in his journal, 'he is very clever and very active, it is a great loss for Scinde.'[24] Fortunately, he had, what he called 'a capital engineer' in Captain Scott, who had been Baker's contemporary at Addiscombe and passed out with him in the same year. He now took over the onerous job of trying to run the department adequately with a dearth of engineers.[25]

Conscious, perhaps, of lacking Captain Baker's background and expertise in irrigation, Scott had sent to Italy for a series of books upon the canalization of the Po valley. As Burton freely admitted, his familiarity with this area and, particularly, his ability to read and translate these valuable Italian works on hydrodynamics for Scott, was a significant, if not the only, factor in his being given this staff appointment. Although lacking in any scientific or technical training, Burton quickly picked up the use of compass, theodolite, and spirit-level. During this initial training period, he teamed up with a fellow officer in the department, Lt Thomas Colvin Blagrave, who no doubt acted as his mentor. Aged twenty-six, he was three years' Burton's senior, a seasoned young officer on the Survey, originally seconded, like Captain Baker, from the Bengal Presidency.[26]

The department's work that cold season, involved taking levels along canals, making rough maps of a number of the province's riverine forests, and plotting survey routes along the western border with Beluchistan. Blagrave and Burton were directed to carry out their survey at Fulayli, the main branch of the Indus in Wicholo or Central Sind, and its continuation, the Guni river. The party, comprising Government Khalassis or surveying assistants, Hindu rodmen and chainmen, and Afghan "horsekeepers," set out on 10 December. Six baggage camels carried all the necessary tents and equipment, and the ubiquitous "Pepper" was, as always, in attendance. During the hot season it was possible to roast a steak or cook an egg on the sand within minutes. Even now, in the so-called cold season, the sun was still fierce enough to blister and burn the skin. For maximum coolness and the better to blend in with their surroundings, the two officers had adopted native costume: a muslin turban, a muslin pirhan or shirt with loose hanging arms, a pair of voluminous blue silk shalwars or drawers drawn tight round the ankles, a long white cotton coat, and Oriental slippers known as papooshes.

About a week or so later they arrived in the district lying immediately around Hyderabad. Located on the most northerly hill of the Ganjo Takkar ridge, it had formerly been the capital of the country under the Talpur rulers, its huge imposing fort occupied by the reigning family. Since the removal of the seat of government to Karachi, it had undergone a steady decline. Arrangements had already been made with the military authorities there, for a camel courier to keep the party regularly supplied with papers, ham and beer during their three-months' stay. They would have to rely on buying any other necessities at the various villages as they moved around.

Towards the end of March the Indus would begin to rise, slowly at first, and then more rapidly. By the middle of May the Fulayli river encircled the city, and the whole of the surrounding countryside was covered with a patina of emerald green, the gardens famous for their fruits in full bloom. Everywhere would be heard 'the monotonous creaking of Persian wheels.... and the shouts of the peasants goading their cattle, or hooting away and slinging clay pellets at hungry flocks of impudent birds.' However, it was now the dead season, after the Kharif or autumn sowing, the trees withered and scraggy, the fields covered in a layer of white, shiny clay. The water-level now at its lowest, stagnant fetid pools lay at intervals along the winding reaches of the silted up river bed. 'Nothing but sunshine seems to flourish,' wrote Burton, 'nothing to abound but dust and glare.'

While quartered at Hyderabad, Sir Charles Napier had watched Sindhi and Cutchi labourers building a wall little more than twenty feet high. 'Four men loaded little baskets into which they put eight bricks,' he wrote incredulously, 'and drew up one basket, mind! One basket in 5 minutes by my watch.'[27] Burton expressed similar exasperation at, what he regarded as, the apathy and idleness of the Sindhi 'navvy'. Sind, he claimed was 'an Eastern Ireland on a large scale.....all would rather want with ease than be wealthy with toil.'

Despite these harsh strictures, he obviously enjoyed mixing with the Sindi people. While working at Hoosree, a large straggling village on the left bank of the Fulayli, some sixteen miles south-east of Hyderabad, the surveying party came across what passed for a Traveller's Bungalow. A two-roomed mud house with a verandah, it was so securely walled round that Burton felt like being incarcerated in an uncomfortably large grave. 'Some Englishmen,' he wrote, 'delight in isolating themselves from the sable and tawny members of their species. For my part, I infinitely prefer to be in a place where one can be giggled at by the young, and scowled at by old ladies, as they pass to and from the well; where one can throw sugar-plums to, and watch the passions thereby called into being from sweet, innocent, and artless childhood; where we can excite men by sketching them, and showing them the caricature.; startle the grey-beard by disputing his dogmas; and wrangle about theology with the angry beggars.'[28]

Burton was also interested in discovering that Fulalyi was one of several provinces inhabited by the Jats who, from their appearance and other peculiarities, he believed, were 'connected by consanguinity with that peculiar race the Gypsies.' Their dialect, Jatki, proved that they had originally come from the Punjab. Once numbered among the ruling classes during the time of the Kalhoras, they had lost this position when the Baluch people – referred to as Belochis by Burton – arrived in the country. A somewhat unattractive and dirty race, some earned a meagre living as farmers or shepherds, roaming with their flocks from one oasis to another. Most were breeders of camels, so much so that the words Jat and a sarwan, that is a camel man, had become synonymous. While there is no question of Burton's having a drop of Gypsy blood in his lineage, it was a group for whom he came to feel a close affinity, and in whom he retained a life-long interest.[29]

Despite claiming to have always acted upon the Latin maxim, *Omne solum forti patria*, 'For every region is a strong man's home,' Burton could not avoid being overcome by a wave of nostalgia for home and family on Christmas day. 'Of all the melancholy suicidal seasons,' he observed, 'none so bad as a birthday, an old festival, or any other time connected with the memory of the past, coming round upon the sojourner in a strange land.' Fortunately, he had plenty to divert his mind during these months. Nevertheless, it was not all work, and he seems to have had sufficient leisure to enjoy some field sports and cock-fighting.

During a visit to the village of Ibrahim Khan, a Talpur chief who had supported the British in the late war with Afghanistan, Burton was able to indulge his long-standing interest in falconry. The Falconers' Society of England, founded in 1770, which had helped keep the sport alive, had been wound up in 1838, following the death of its manager, Lord Berners. 'Judge, therefore, gentle reader,' Burton wrote in the preface to the short and highly entertaining monograph which he brought out on the subject some years later, 'how great was my joy when I found myself in a country where the noble sport flourishes in all its pristine glory. I shall never forget the profound satisfaction with which, after securing the services of an experienced Beloch, I succeeded in seeling a hawk for the first time.'[30]

A day spent shooting wild duck in the ponds and pools of the Haran Shikargah, near to Ibrahim Khan's village, also provided another welcome diversion. Shikargahs were the walled-in hunting preserves of the Talpur Mirs. Strictly protected by punitive game laws from interference and trespass by the common people, these dense tamarisk jungles and forests of mimosa which flourished alongside the Indus and its many branches, answered the dual purpose of preserving game and supplying the whole country with timber.[31] Though he made light of the incident later, this day's sport nearly cost Burton his life.

Towards evening, just as he, and his friend, Lt Blagrave, were about to leave, they lighted upon a little Jheel or lake, covered with thousands of duck. The opportunity was too good to miss. Responding to Blagrave's whispered suggestion that they approach the birds from opposite sides, Burton began to wade across a kind of ditch connecting two ponds. It proved to be deeper than he thought. In a short space of time he found himself up to the ears in mud and water. Wearing a pair of large jack-boots and wide Turkish trousers, with a shooting-jacket composed of oil cloth, hare pockets, and clutching a double-barrelled Westley and Richard rifle, it was well-nigh impossible to swim. Attempting to scramble up the soft slimy bank proved equally impracticable. Every submersion promised to be his last. Eventually realising his friend's predicament, Blagrave dashed to the rescue. With the help of the terrified beaters, who saw themselves being blamed for the accident, Burton was eventually hauled out by the collar largely none the worse for his ordeal.

Early in April, 1845, with the waters of the Indus rapidly rising, the survey came to an end. After making a brief call on his friends in the regiment now stationed at Hyderabad, Burton set off with Blagrave for the headquarters of the Survey in Karachi. All the rough sketches and topographical data amassed throughout the cold season now had to be accurately plotted on maps. This was work, of course, for a highly skilled engineer. Of his own contributions to the department, Burton said almost nothing. Lacking any technical expertise and with only a short rough and ready training so far, he appears to have spent many hours practising latitudes and longitudes. Determining geographical latitude involved his using a sextant to measure the angle of the noon Sun above the horizon. From this angle and the exact time as measured by a chronometer, latitude could then be calculated from published tables. Burton blamed his frequent peering through the sextant's telescope for short-sightedness later developing in his right eye.

As always, he pressed on with his linguistic studies, concentrating particularly on improving his fluency in the Persian language in order to pass his Interpreter's examination. To this end he spent a great deal of his leisure time in the company of Mirza Ali Akbar, who had served as Sir Charles Napier's munshi at the battles of Miani and Dubba. Lodging with him at his bungalow outside the camp, was another excellent Persian scholar, Mirza Daud.

Burton also claimed to have seen a great deal of Mirza Hosayn, better known as Abu'l-Hasan Khan, a younger brother of the Agha Khan Mahallati, the Persian nobleman who was the first holder of the title of *imam*, or spiritual leader of the Isma'ili sect of Shi'ite Muslims.[32] The dates in the historical records, however, show this to be one of Burton's tall stories, since he could not possibly have known Abu'l Hasan Khan at any time during 1845 or thereafter.

Having fled his country after a failed rebellion, the Agha Khan had thrown in his lot with the British. After assisting them during the Afghan War, and later in the conquest of Sind, he settled there with his followers and was pensioned by Sir Charles Napier. In April 1844, with the tacit approval, or even connivance, of the British, the Agha Khan sent his second brother, Muhammad Baqir Khan, to capture the fortress of Bampur (Banfahl). in Baluchistan. A short while afterwards, he despatched Sardar Abu'l Khan, who eventually took the stronghold as well as going on to enjoy other military successes in the region. Some time in June or July of 1846, however, the Sardar was defeated in battle by a Qajar army, the fortress was demolished, and he was taken as a prisoner to Tehran. Despite his hostile activities, Abul Hasan was pardoned, and allowed to settle at Shahr-i-Babak, where he lived to a ripe old age.[33]

Burton's recent work on the Survey had brought him, for the first time, into close contact with the ordinary Sindian people. As a result, he not only began to see the country and its inhabitants in a new light, but felt a strong urge to know a great deal more. Fortunately, his increased pay as a Staff Officer augmented by full *batta*, enabled him to collect together quite a large number of books, and to gather around him those whose wide experience of the province could help make them more meaningful.

By 1845, there was already a considerable literature of one sort or another on Sind – accounts of early British missions to the country, political, geographical and commercial reports submitted to Government, Parliamentary Papers and, of course, descriptions of the military campaigns leading up to the conquest of the country. Several of the earliest publications were to become classics of their kind, such as *Travels in Belochistan and Sinde* by Lieutenant Henry Pottinger (1816), *Narrative of a Visit to the Court of Scinde* by Dr James Burne (1831), and *Travels into Bokhara, Containing a Narrative of a Voyage on the Indus* by Lieutenant Alexander Burne (1835). The most recent addition to the list was Captain T. Postans' *Personal Observations on Sindh*, published in July 1843. Postans, formerly assistant to Sir Henry Pottinger, Political Agent in Sind and Baluchistan from 1836-40, had enjoyed, what he called, 'unusual advantages for collecting his materials.' His book, descriptive of conditions during the last years of Talpur rule, was undoubtedly, the most comprehensive and authoritative to date. Even so, Burton claimed that, 'After reading all the works published upon the subject, I felt convinced that none but Mr Crow and Captain James J. MacMurdo had dipped beneath the superficies of things.'

Lieutenant Alexander Burne had been sent, ostensibly, on a government mission in 1830 to Ranjit Singh in Lahore. Its real purpose, however, was to survey and chart the course of the Indus beyond Hyderabad. He decided 'to retain the character of a European, accommodating myself in dress, habits, and customs, to those with whom I should mingle.' Despite being a skilled linguist, fluent in Persian, Arabic and Hindustani, he had done this 'in an utter hopelessness of supporting the disguise of a native; and from having observed that no European traveller had ever sojourned in such countries without suspicion, and seldom without discovery.'[34]

So how did Burton set about systematically collecting material for an ethnological study, which a reviewer would later describe as 'perhaps the most complete account which has yet appeared of the Indus Valley.'?[35] 'The European official,' Burton claimed, 'seldom, if ever, sees anything in its real light, so dense is the veil with which the fearfulness, the duplicity, the prejudice, and the superstitions of the natives hang before his eyes.'[36] Burton was convinced, therefore, that it was only by passing himself off as an Oriental, that he would ever penetrate behind this veil and gain a true insight into native affairs. After experimenting with various disguises, he finally adopted the persona of a half-Arab, half-Iranian Shi'ite Muslim called Mirza Abdullah hailing from Bushire, the port at the end of an ancient trade route to Shiraz, Isfahan, and Tehran, near the head of the Persian Gulf. With shoulder-length hair, a long beard, and his face and hands, arms and feet stained with a thin coat of henna, his physical disguise was complete. As far as his pronunciation of the native dialect was concerned, he knew that it would not pass muster among the Sindian population. His strange accent, however, could be quite plausibly attributed to his mixed parentage. In the event of any problems arising, his munshi was usually at hand to give him support. The chance of being detected, therefore, was a very slim one.

Burton lists a wide range of activities in which he engaged in his role as a wealthy itinerant merchant selling fine linen, calicoes, and muslins. These included being admitted to harems, entering strangers' houses with scant ceremony, passing the evening in mosques listening to ragged students mumbling in Arabic from soiled and dog-eared pages of theology, debating the finer points of the Muslim faith with long-bearded mullahs, or mingling with the hemp-drinkers and opium-eaters in the estaminets. Most of these activities must have taken place at a much later date when Burton was stationed at Hyderabad, or on the move with the Survey. What is more likely at this early stage, is that he began in a small, unambitious way as a market trader, renting a shop now and again in Karachi, and stocking it with 'clammy dates, viscid molasses, tobacco, ginger, rancid oil, and strong-smelling sweetmeats.'

It is necessary at this point to digress for a moment, to consider two points at issue connected with Burton's adoption of this disguise. Both concern claims made by Lady Burton, first that Rudyard Kipling based his character of Strickland on Burton, and that her husband acted as an intelligence officer for Sir Charles Napier. Neither has any basis in fact.

Strickland, Kipling's 'unconvincing Sherlock Holmes of all disguises,' as Angus Wilson describes him, appears in several of the *Plain Tales From The Hills*, first published in 1888. He later popped up again several times in Kipling's masterpiece, *Kim*. Strickland ' held the extraordinary theory,' Kipling wrote, 'that a Policeman in India should try to know as much about the natives as the natives themselves.....and, following out his absurd theory, dabbled in unsavoury places no respectable man would think of exploring – all among the native riff-raff.' While other men went off to the hills for ten days, 'Strickland took leave for what he called *shikar*, put on the disguise that appealed at the time, stepped down into the brown crowd, and was swallowed up for a while.'[37] No one knows to what extent, if at all, Kipling based his fictional characters on real people. It is certainly the case that Burton's name does not figure, nor could it, among the two that have been suggested as models by those acquainted with the Punjab around 1870-1880.[38]

Hard on the heels of this spurious claim came another, made with the same object, that of inflating Burton's reputation and importance. In this particular case, it also gave Isabel the opportunity of riding her favourite hobby-horse, that of castigating 'dense and narrow-minded Governments,' for denying Burton the just rewards due to men who risked their lives. 'He was sent out amongst the wild tribes of the hills and plains,' she wrote, 'to collect information for Sir Charles. He did not go as a British officer or Commissioner, because he knew he would see nothing, but what the natives chose him to see.....Richard would be in a dozen different capacities on his travels, but when he returned, he was rich with news and information for Sir Charles, for he arrived at secrets quite out of the reach of the British Army.'[39]

There is, however, not a scintilla of evidence that Burton was ever called upon to carry out any such covert missions for Sir Charles, nor that any was remotely necessary. As we have already seen, Sind had been pacified within a year, and the defeated amirs sent into exile in far-off Bengal. The country was now ruled according to strict military law. Some 5,000 troops were stationed at various strategic points throughout the province and, with the exception of the chiefs, none of its inhabitants was allowed to carry weapons about his person. 'Large bodies of armed men,' as Burton himself pointed out, 'were thereby prevented from meeting to concert conspiracies...'[40] In a hastily sketched Memoir on Scinde written for the British Government in 1846, Sir Charles remarked that, since being governor, there had never been any doubt as to 'the public tranquillity.....And there never will be while I am here, because that tranquillity has been based, not on force of arms after the battles, but upon the justice and kindness of the government towards all ranks.'[41]

Needless to say, the hare started by Lady Burton is still running, and Burton's purported role as an intelligence officer has now become firmly enshrined in Burton lore. More recently it has received its ultimate embellishment in the fantasy world created by an American biographer. Here, Burton is no longer a mere intelligence officer for Sir Charles Napier. He has become a player in the Great Game, one of many clandestine agents working for British Intelligence dedicated to checking the inexorable advance of Tsarist Russia across Central Asia towards our Indian empire.[42] In this bizarre scenario, the Sind Survey is portrayed as a front for Burton's spying activities, a forerunner of the Survey of India's later use of so-called pundits. These native explorers trained in the use of ingenious surveying techniques, were then sent out, often disguised as Buddhist pilgrims, to map and report on the unknown and lawless regions of northern Afghanistan, Turkestan, and Tibet. All this makes for a ripping yarn, the very stuff of schoolboy fiction – which, of course, in this case it is.

It is now further necessary to examine the merits of Burton's own claim of being asked to carry out a covert mission of a rather different kind during this year for Sir Charles Napier.

Female prostitution was rife throughout British cities during the Victorian era. Around mid-century it was estimated that in London alone some 8,000 women were making a living selling sex. Something as visible could hardly be ignored, and was an issue that was widely debated in the leading journals of the day. Burton, therefore, was able to write freely in his ethnological study about the courtezans of Sind. What he could not do, was openly discuss male homosexuality.

It was not until forty years on that he was able to deal with the subject in detail in the Terminal Essay of his translation of the *Arabian Nights*. The term 'homosexuality' was not to enter the language until 1892, two years after Burton's death. Instead, he employs the word 'pederasty.' This is not an exact equivalent. Homosexuality means taking part in sexual activity with members of one's own sex without regard to the precise type of sexual practice engaged in. Pederasty, on the other hand, specifically means engaging in anal intercourse with a boy.

Burton would have us believe that he first encountered the practice quite by chance in 1845. According to his account, Sir Charles had been informed of there being three brothels in Karachi, 'in which not women but boys and eunuchs, the former demanding nearly a double price [7 annas to 4], lay for hire.' Apparently, this particular detail aroused Sir Charles's curiosity. In the event, the reason proved to be 'that the scrotum of the unmutilated boy could be used as a kind of bridle for directing the movement of the animal.' Being the only British officer who could speak Sindi, Burton was asked indirectly to make inquiries and to report back on the subject. He was only prepared to do so, however, on the express condition that his report would not be forwarded to the Bombay Government, 'from whom supporters of the Conqueror's policy could expect scant favour, justice, or mercy.'

Disguised as Mirza Abdulla, and accompanied by his munshi, Mirza Mohammed Husayn, Burton spent numerous evenings in Karachi visiting these brothels and compiling a detailed report. This was duly sent to Sir Charles. Unfortunately, when he later resigned from his post, Burton's dossier was left behind in Government House. It later found its way together with others to Bombay. The result was as expected. 'A friend in the Secretariat informed me that my summary dismissal from the Service had been formally proposed by one of Sir Charles Napier's successors, whose decease compels me *parcere sepulto*. But this excess of modesty was not allowed."[43]

Burton's biographers have been unanimous in their acceptance of his account. In their various ways, however, they have seemed determined to misrepresent, embellish and, in more recent times, completely alter what he wrote about the subject. Fawn Brodie's role in this has been crucial, since the gratuitous changes she made to the text have been copied either directly or with variations into most biographies since. Gone is the detail about Sir Charles's alleged interest in the reason for the price differential charged at the male bordellos, which supposedly prompted Burton's investigation. Gone, too, is the further detail of his being asked *indirectly* to make enquiries into the matter. Instead, in Brodie's version. 'Napier was disturbed by rumours that certain homosexual brothels in Karachi were corrupting his troops and asked Burton to investigate.'[44]

To compound matters, she goes on to claim that Napier, 'immediately destroyed the brothels, noting in his diary that he had improved public morality in the area "by putting down the infamous beasts, who dressed as women, plied their trade in the Meers' time openly," noting that among the chief clients had been the Ameers themselves, whose financial records revealed their deep involvement.'

In the first place this is a totally unwarranted assumption, since there is no documentary evidence as to when these brothels were closed, nor can she link such closure with Burton's alleged inquiry. Furthermore, Napier did not write this in his diary. It appears in a letter written *to* Sir Charles Napier in 1850 by Captain Rathborne, the former Collector at Hyderabad.[45] Rathborne was widely regarded as the author of the "letters of Omega," which first appeared in the Government-backed *Karrachee Advertiser* and gave, according to Burton, a description of 'the vices of the Sind Amirs in language the very reverse of ambiguous.'[46] Perhaps we should look no further than Rathborne's exposé of the male sex trade as the reason for Sir Charles Napier's action.

Fawn Brodie had searches undertaken for Burton's report at the India Office in London, as well as at Delhi and Lahore. All drew a blank. She came to the conclusion that this 'intelligence report', as she chose to call it, which, allegedly, had badly damaged Burton's Army career, had been destroyed as earlier suggested by Burton's bibliographer, Dr Norman Penzer.[47] What neither Mrs Brodie nor her successors seems prepared to contemplate is that Burton was lying, and that the document looked for by the archivists was never found, because it never existed.

There is not a shred of evidence that Burton's Army career in India was ever blighted. Quite the contrary. A typical military inspector's report on Burton, described him in glowing terms as an officer who, 'Evinces a zeal for the service and attention and zeal to his duties (as Lt) highly creditable.'[48]

So how much credence should we place in Burton's account? While the materials for arriving at a definitive answer are missing, almost certainly we should ask a number of questions before attempting to arrive at a conclusion. Houses of male prostitution, apparently, were common in Persia, the boys being 'prepared with extreme care by diets, baths, depilation, unguents, and a host of artists in cosmetics. Le Vice is looked upon at most as a peccadillo.'[49] It is clearly apparent from the space Burton devoted to the subject, and the obvious relish with which he related anecdotes about sodomy that he was fascinated by the practice.

Might it not be more likely, therefore, that a great deal of Burton's knowledge of pederasty in general, and what went on in the male brothels of Karachi in particular, derived from his close association with his Persian mentors, than through undertaking a supposed mission for Sir Charles Napier?

Then again, what should we make of Burton's alleged concern that his report should not fall into the hands of the Bombay Government? How, we may ask, would anyone in the Bombay Government possibly know, or even care, whether Burton was a supporter of Sir Charles's actions? He was, after all, a junior officer at the time, bound as was every other soldier to obey whatever orders he was given. Furthermore, in the Preface to *Sindh and the Races that Inhabit the Valley of the Indus*, which was published only six years after these alleged events took place, he wrote, 'The author has sedulously shunned all allusion to the "still vexed" questions concerning the conquest of Sindh, which for some years has been before the public. It was his intention to write a work interesting to the linguist and the ethnographer, not to enlist himself in the ranks of political partisanship.'[50]

In conclusion, we should also notice Burton's studied avoidance of identifying certain people. Who was it, for instance, that initially passed on the information to Sir Charles as to there being three male bordellos in Karachi? Who asked Burton to make enquiries and report back on his findings? Who was his friend in the Secretariat, and who, of Sir Charles's successors – located at Government House in Karachi it needs to be said, and not Bombay – proposed his summary dismissal from the Service? In the latter case, Burton refused to identify the person concerned, ostensibly on the ground of not wishing to speak ill of the dead. He had not shown the same compunction some years earlier, however, in describing the Governor-General of India, as 'the late Lord Dalhousie of pernicious memory.'[51] It should also be borne in mind that this was not the only occasion on which Burton used the device of the unattributable source.

Should we admire him, therefore, for exercising, what might appear on the face of it, admirable discretion, or should we suspect him of gross prevarication? His translation of the *Arabian Nights*, after all, was available in a limited edition to private subscribers only, and the man at the centre of the story, Sir Charles Napier, had been dead for over thirty years. His immediate successor as Civil Commissioner in Sind, Robert Keith Pringle (1802-97), was now an old man of eighty-three. Sir Henry Bartle Frere (1815-84), who had followed him in government had died the previous year. General Henry Dundas, third Viscount Melville (1801-76), who had taken over the military command of the Sind Division in 1847, had died nine years earlier. If, indeed, Burton was guilty of dissimulation, he had every reason to feel safe from contradiction.

Shortly after being appointed Governor of Sind in 1843, Sir Charles drew up ambitious plans for improving the facilities of the harbour at Karachi. These included widening the entrance, constructing docks, building a timber pier at Kiamari Point for native vessels and lighters, and creating a causeway between that point and the town. Conflicting pressures on time and resources, however, meant that only the last two were started during his administration.

That July, work on the causeway had struck a snag, when the barrier painstakingly erected to keep the Indus at bay had been badly undermined, leaving Scott, the superintending engineer, thoroughly dispirited. Sir Charles, for whom setbacks only served to rouse him to greater efforts, wrote to Scott in his typical breezy fashion, not only to bolster his confidence but to offer practical advice: 'I am sorry that the River has rolled over us this time, but we shall do the job yet. There is a thing called Experience without which, men *must* be exposed to mistakes; and so do not let this one act [?] dowse [?] your spirit.....let me hear daily in a few lines how matters go....I began the work without sanction and I expect to be blown up as well as the bund.[52]

By November, with work on the Mole proceeding smoothly, Scott decided to lead a surveying party on an extended tour to the north of the province. He chose Burton to accompany him, mainly, one must presume, in the role of interpreter. This journey has been portrayed by some as yet another intelligence mission.[53] It was nothing of the sort. Its purpose was primarily to allow Scott to obtain an overview of the work already carried out in the region on the canals and waterways by Captain Baker and his assistants. He also wanted to follow up on certain suggestions contained in their reports, one with regard to a projected road between Sukkur and Shikapur.

Two days after leaving Karachi, the group arrived at Kotree, the headquarters of the Indus flotilla. They were then ferried to the opposite bank, from where they rode into Hyderabad. After spending what Burton called 'a very jolly week' there, they recrossed the Indus and set off northwards by easy marches, averaging 12-15 miles a day. Initially following the right bank of the river, they then turned almost due west, travelling through wild desert country before arriving at one of the barren little range of hills extending from the Halah or Baluch Mountains.

Two miles beyond the well at Sibt, where the party stopped to replenish its water supply, was the so-called Mimosa Bank. A mere line of earth and stones thrown across the narrow neck of the valley, it served nevertheless to divert rainfall on to the plateau, instead of the precious water being allowed to drain away uselessly to the Indus. It was now so seriously damaged by the force of the spring rains, that Scott set up temporary camp there in order to carry out the necessary repairs. The extended halt, however, provided Burton with the welcome opportunity of studying a Baluchi family at close quarters. Although allowing himself to comment briefly on the origin, physical appearance, character and language of these nomadic herdsmen, the ethnology of Baluchistan as he later had to admit, 'has been too accurately described by modern travellers to require much further elucidation.' Nevertheless, there was one point in particular, which he thought merited attention. 'Pottinger and Postans,' he claimed, 'seem determined to derive this people from the Jews: the former depends upon the similarity of customs, forgetting how much the Koran owed to the Law and the Prophets: the latter relies upon the unsatisfactory testimony of dress.'[54] This is a complete misrepresentation of their position, all the more culpable since it is highly likely that their books formed part of a number Burton carried with him in his saddlebags on the journey.

Four stages on from Onurpoor, was the little village of Lukkee. Three miles distant, towering into the clear blue sky above the yellow, flat alluvial plain, could be seen the peaks and pinnacles of the majestic Lukkee Range. A morning's ride from the village, part of it through a defile so narrow that the camels were forced to march in Indian file dangerously close to the rushing waters of the Indus, brought them to Sehwan.

It was Christmas Day when they rode into the ancient city along its dirty, dusty streets. Located 146 miles from Karachi along the direct road, it had once been of some military and religious importance. It was now in rapid decline, a hot, squalid, dilapidated, stench-ridden place, 'remarkable,' Burton said, ' for the rascality of its inhabitants, the mausoleum of its patron-saint, Shah-Baz, and the abundance of its beggars, devotees, and courtezans.' They were instantly surrounded by a noisy, ragged crowd of pauper cripples, young and old of both sexes. Everyone seemed to be a mendicant, 'the very babies,' he remarked, 'look impatient to be begging.'

Alexander the Great had swept through this region with his army in the spring of 326 BC. While Captain Postans believed that the remains of the old fortification in Sehwan probably dated from this period, Burton dismissed the suggestion. He shared E.B. Eastwick's view, 'that the country of Sindh, though traversed by the classic waters of the Indus, and trodden by the armies of every invader of Hindustan, produces few monuments of antiquity useful to the historiographer, or interesting to the archaeologist.'[55] Both men, of course, had died well before the excavations undertaken in the 1920s by the archaeologists, Sir John Marshall and Sir Mortimer Wheeler, revealed the existence of what became known as the Indus Civilization, which had flourished in these parts roughly between c.2500-1700 BC.

A two days' march north-westward along the right bank of the Aral River, brought Scott's party to Lake Manchar. After the barren Lukkee Hills and the malodorous streets and alleyways of Sehwan, the lake offered a feast for the senses. Almost hiding part of its glittering surface from view, was a multitude of birds of bright variegated colours. At least a hundred swarthy-skinned Mohana or fishermen could be seen at work. During the searing heat of summer, however, its almost stagnant waters were a fertile breeding ground for swarms of insects and fever.

Covering the next hundred miles or so in a march of eight stages, Scott's men arrived at the large bustling town of Larkhana. Picturesquely situated on the banks of the large Ghar canal, it was the capital of one of the most fertile districts of Sind, yielding rich harvests of wheat, rice and gram, and fruits such as the mango, date and guava. A network of irrigation canals criss-crossed the plain, drawing life-giving water from the Indus and its effluent, the Narrah or Snake River, which ran into the northern end of Lake Manchar. The town itself was an important centre of commerce. Its position on the main road between Karachi and Shikarpur, meant that it was also a favourite stop-over for caravans and itinerant merchants. This was no doubt the reason, as Burton observed, for its being 'celebrated for anything but morality.'

There were two kinds of prostitutes in Sind. The Rangeli, as he explained, was a low courtezan of the Jatki race who eked out a bare living by peddling sex in villages close to the main roads, to support themselves and their men-folk. The more respectable class was the Kanyari. Like the Nautch girl of India, 'she generally unites the occupation of dancing with the more immoral part of her trade.[56]

The beauty of these dancing girls was legendary. The young Lt Henry Pottinger in the early part of the century recalled that, while at Tattah and Hyderabad, 'among the numerous sets of dancing girls, who came at different times to exhibit before us, I do not remember to have seen one who was not distinguished by loveliness of face, or the symmetry of her figure, and in most instances, both of these were strikingly combined.'[57]

No entertainment was complete without such an exhibition, the monotony of which, according to Captain Postans, was 'somewhat questionably broken by the ladies' imbibing, largely during the performance, of spirits to excite them to greater exertion.' He expressed astonishment at the amount they could drink of the extremely intoxicating liquor prepared from sugar or date, without suffering any apparent effect.[58]

While in political employment at Shikarpur several years earlier, E.B. Eastwick had received an invitation from Ibrahim Shah, the minister at Hyderabad, to a nautch in what was known as the Kazi's garden. Eastwick was not impressed, considering the Sindian dancing girls inferior to those he had seen in India. One of the troupe he singled out for mention, whose name was "Moonbeam" (Mahtab), he thought 'rather pretty; but on the whole there was no risk of being fascinated.'[59] Burton's lingering description of her face and figure after attending a nautch in Larkhana given by this now celebrated dancer and her sisters, clearly demonstrates that she fascinated him.[60]

Highly sought after performers such as Mahtab could expect to receive up to one hundred rupees for an evening's performance. Naturally, they charged correspondingly high sums for their sexual favours, some excessively so, in order to boost their charms. Burton reported having heard on one occasion, of a respectable merchant paying as much as two hundred rupees for a single visit. Whether he, himself, had a sexual liaison with the beautiful 'donna of Larkhana,' can only be a matter for conjecture. What does appear certain is that, some time later, he was able to persuade Nur Jan, the youngest and prettiest of Mahtab's sisters, to become his mistress. Although he made only two fleeting references to her in print, a stanza in an unpublished autobiographical poem shows the hold this lovely courtezan had on his affections:

> The Nubians & the Abyssinians
> Sent me at least a score of minions.
> Cashmere was not behind.
> But of them all the fair Nur Jan,
> The Venus of Belochistan,
> Was most to my mind.[61]

Only a few weeks after Scott and Burton's departure on their northern tour the First Sikh War had broken out. On 28 December, Sir Charles Napier dashed off a letter to his sister, Emily, Lady Bunbury, in Naples:

> I have only time to tear off this to you and George – I am crushed with interruptions and duties. The war is declared the Sikhs have passed the River – Sir Henry and Sir Hugh in full march to attack them....
> Henry (sic) Gough's letter to me is dated 14 instant that he would fight his Battle on the 18th December. He tells me that he has the largest force of Europeans ever assembled in India....My troops are all in march for the north and six regiments coming up from Bombay with 12 field pieces...I shall be able to enter the Sikh's (sic) territory with 10,000 and nearly 50 pieces of cannon.[62]

Although rumours of the war were rife everywhere, it was probably more than a fortnight later that Scott and Burton received official confirmation. In Burton's version of events, which will be examined later, Scott received a brief letter from Captain John Napier, Sir Charles's military secretary. Dated, Karachi, 3 January

1846, it read: 'The General says you may allow as many of your assistants as you can spare to join their regiments, if going on service, with the understanding that they must resign their appointments, and will not be reappointed, etc.'

The news made Burton desperate to go. Surveying work, however, still remained to be carried out, especially around Sukkur and Shikarpur, an important mercantile centre some twenty-four miles to the north-west. Once completed, Burton lost no time in applying himself to volunteering for the campaign. Having persuaded Scott, much against his will, to send in his resignation, Burton personally called upon General James Simpson, Napier's second-in-command. His application was refused. Happily for Burton, an order suddenly arrived from Bengal ordering all the assistants in the department to provide sureties. He immediately wrote an official letter stating that no one would stand bail for him. This letter did the trick, and he was ordered to join his corps.

By this time a large force had been assembled on the plain near Rohri, a town facing Sukkur on the opposite bank of the Indus. It presented a brilliant spectacle with 13,000 men in colourful uniforms, the camp glittering with white tents, and the river swarming with boats, pontoons and dhundis laden with supplies. The order to begin the march on the old walled city of Multan, the "Key of the Punjab," was given on 23 February. The long column wound its way for a fortnight in a thick cloud of dust and stifling heat. Despite these trying conditions, everyone was in the highest spirits. At Bahawalpur, however, news suddenly spread through the ranks, 'chilling as the damp of a Scindian dawn,' that the war was over.

This was indeed the case. The Sikhs, after crossing the Sutlej on 11 December 1845, had been defeated in four fiercely contested battles at Mudki, Firozpur, Ludhiana, and Sobraon. The last had been fought and won on 10 February, almost a fortnight before Napier's forces had set out, highlighting the slowness of contemporary communications in India. Burton's friend, Lt T. C. Blagrave, who had taken part in this bloody battle, wrote to him three days later, giving a long and graphic account: 'I wish you could only have seen it, it was a beautiful sight, and at first like a glorious Grand Review. We got the order at 11 on the 9th to be ready at 3 o'clock to move against them....[later]...the carnage in the river was awful, hundreds falling every minute or else rushing the ford...I wish you could have been on the engagement it was the finest and most exciting I have ever seen.[63]

This thought was no doubt uppermost in Burton's mind as he returned with the army to Rohri by 2 April. After halting there for a few days, it continued its slow march south, arriving back at the old regimental headquarters near Hyderabad, just over a fortnight later. A mixture of disappointment and physical weariness had contrived to sour everyone's temper. According to Burton, he had been making up doggerel rhymes on his fellow-officers' names in the Mess. Only too aware of his commanding officer's touchiness, he passed him over. At this, Lt Col Corsellis took offence, whereupon Burton wrote the following epitaph:

> Here lieth the body of Colonel Corsellis;
> The rest of the fellow, I fancy, in hell is.

A bitter quarrel ensued. 'I shall say no more upon the subject,' Burton added, 'it is perhaps the part of my life upon which my mind dwells with the least satisfaction.' Before examining the probable reason for this, it is necessary to retrace our steps a little way in order to consider a highly important piece of evidence, which shows that Burton was less than truthful in his account of rejoining his corps. Ironically, it appears in a letter written by Burton's father in response to one from Captain Scott of 19 April, containing some unwelcome news regarding his son.

It is clear from this letter that, by tendering his resignation to General Simpson, who was obviously unaware at the time of the true situation, Burton had deliberately flouted an order from Sir Charles Napier and, in consequence, had been removed from under Scott's command. What is also clear is that J.N. Burton whom, surprisingly, the letter reveals as a doting father, wished to shoulder the responsibility for the actions of his 'beloved son,' at the same time putting the very best gloss he could on them.

While greatly regretting what had happened, 'Richard,' he said, 'only acted up to the instructions I repeatedly gave him, namely "never to hold a situation which might possibly prevent his seeing service especially until he should have made a good name for himself in the field of battle."' For his own part, he was convinced that his son had never intended to disobey Sir Charles's order. Quite the reverse, since 'he imagined nothing could raise him so high in the estimation of the general *sans peure et sans lâche* as distinguishing himself in action which I am sure Richard intended to do if an opportunity offered.' Furthermore, and obviously intended by Joseph as a potent, if not clinching argument, 'Had the Army of Scinde seen service on the banks of the Sutlej so that the officers returned some with medals, some with promotion, might they not say to my son, "You remained behind surveying and pocketing rupees whilst we were risking our lives gaining laurels on the field of battle." How could he avoid these imputations but by acting as he did? Though his life is dearer to me than that of any other being in existence, I hope that he will always risk it by every means whenever his reputation as a soldier or his patriotism as an englishman (sic) may be in question.'

The disclosure in this letter of the real reason for Burton's loss of his staff appointment, points to his having tampered with the wording in John Napier's letter to Scott of 3 January, in order to account for his not returning to the Survey. He certainly did not give the full text, which may well have included Sir Charles Napier's order forbidding him from volunteering for active service in the Sikh campaign. We may regard as equally spurious, the alleged despatch which suddenly, and highly conveniently, arrived out of the blue from Bengal, instructing members of the Survey to provide sureties. It was standard practice for members of the Indian Civil Service to sign a good behaviour bond prior to taking up their appointments, with two sureties each in the sum of £500. While no money was deposited, any Civil Servant found guilty of financial impropriety resulted in the sureties being legally obliged to pay the Company £500 each. There are no records of military officers being obliged to sign such bonds.

Despite Burton's present predicament, Joseph, who had obviously been pulling strings behind the scenes on his son's behalf, had high hopes for his future. 'I am very anxious that Richard may pass his examination in the persian (sic) language in the course of this year, as it may possibly bring him into notice in Bombay, for I think it would be advisable for him to pay visits to persons of account to whom he has had letter of introduction. Sir Ths McMahon offered me a situation for Richard in the irregular cavalry, for which the latter ought to feel very grateful. I did not accept the general's kind offer lest Richard should be removed from his studies.'[64]

Now, not only had Burton been removed from his lucrative position on the Survey, which had helped to fund those studies, he was also in bad odour with Sir Charles Napier. Given that he had thousands of men under his command, how had Sir Charles found out that Burton was back with his corps? The obvious source of this information appears to be the 18th BNI's commanding officer, Lt Col Henry Corsellis. Was this the real reason for Burton's animosity towards him? If so, why did he later come to regret his action?

The little information about Corsellis that exists, shows that had recently suffered a double personal tragedy. His only son, aged eighteen, had died at Bombay in 1844, and that same year, his wife Sarah, had died on board the *Linton* on the way home to England. Corsellis, no doubt a broken man, survived his wife by less than four years.[65] In the light of these tragic circumstances, the 'Epitaph,' in itself a grim foreshadowing of the future, must have been deeply wounding. While Burton could regret his statement, he was, no doubt, too ashamed to give the reason.

He was further plagued by domestic troubles. One involved, what he termed 'complications' with Nur Jan, without disclosing, of course, who she was and the nature of their relationship. Casting about for an ADC the previous December before moving north with the army, General Sir James Simpson informed Sir Charles Napier that he had found someone to suit him, 'but he has that disgraceful incumbrance of a black woman and family…….Nearly every officer in the 18th is similarly circumstanced, and in this respect I never saw a corps so bedevilled. I hope to break some of these disgraceful liaisons when they move.'[66] If Burton was already enjoying one of these 'disgraceful liaisons,' it would have made life extremely difficult with Nur Jan now in the picture. Unfortunately, it is an episode in Burton's life, like so many others, which must remain forever shrouded in mystery. To cap his problems, he sustained a painful injury to his foot, when his mud bungalow collapsed after a torrential overnight downpour, almost trapping him and his old Afghan munshi inside. 'The things melt away after a night's rain,' he said, 'like ice in a London ball-room.'[67]

Despite his domestic difficulties, perhaps to escape them, Burton resumed his journeys disguised as Mirza Abdullah. His favourite resort for picking up useful information and stray gossip was the tall, crumbling mud house of an old Darby and Joan couple living on the banks of the Fulayli River about a mile from the Fort of Hyderabad. The once beautiful Khanum Jan who, many years earlier, had fled her home in Kandahar to elope with her now partially sighted husband, the tailor, Mohammed Bakhsh, had since become the local match-maker in affairs of the heart. On these occasions, Burton and his old Persian munshi, Mohammed Husayn, were turned out of the house to sit in the garden. It was a dolce vita existence, relaxing in the shade of a huge tamarind tree, the air sweetened by beds of fragrant basil. Close by could be seen the broad stretch of the Fulayli River, flowing swiftly between its wooded banks, colourful groups of people boarding or stepping off the ferry, while his companion, Mohammed Husayn quietly intoned the musical verse of 'mysterious, philosophical, transcendental Hafiz.'

This idyll was too good to last. The hot season of 1846 (April-September), turned out to be unusually sickly. The white regiments at Karachi, particularly the 78th Highlanders, were badly affected. Hyderabad, on the other hand, escaped relatively lightly. Even so, Burton was forced to go into sick quarters in early July, and left his regiment in early September with, what he described as 'a strong case.'

Burton's brief version of events, of course, leaves certain important facts unstated: first, as to what sickness affected the white regiments so badly, and especially what his 'strong case,' was meant to convey. What he deliberately fails to mention here, is that what he merely calls the 'unusually sickly season,' was one of the worst Asiatic cholera epidemics ever to sweep across India. It later arrived with equally devastating results in Europe and England. Sir Charles Napier wrote in his journal for 9 July 1846, 'I have lost my journal from 26th April and since then nothing but great suffering has been my fate. John's first illness; then his child's; and then the terrible cholera which swept off my soldiers; and, oh God! Its last blow struck down my beloved nephew after he and I had laid his child in its grave. I laid him by her side; he who from his infancy I had saved and cherished, and whom I so loved…'[68]

So, what was the reason this time for Burton's dissimulation? It has to be, that he deliberately avoided being specific, so that he could speak just as vaguely about his own illness. This points to its being the kind of complaint that he wished to keep concealed: in other words, his chronic genito-urethral complaint, possibly exacerbated now by gonorrhoea. His military records show that he was given extensions of leave on sick certificate from early September to the end of the year, and then again to 28 January 1847.[69]

It was probably during part of this latter period that Burton came under the care of John Frederick Steinhaueser, later to become his closest friend. Son of a prosperous London merchant living in Westbourne Terrace, Bayswater, Steinhaueser had qualified as a Member of the Royal College of Surgeons in May, 1838. It was not until July 1845, that he entered the Bombay Army as an assistant surgeon. On arrival there in December, he was placed at the disposal of the Superintending Surgeon in Scinde. After holding various temporary relief posts, he was sent, again in a temporary capacity, in October 1846, to Hyderabad, to relieve Assistant Surgeon Freeman from the medical charge of the 18th Bombay NI. This lasted until January 1847, when he moved to Karachi.[70]

Under the existing furlough regulations, it was necessary for Burton to appear before a medical board at Bombay, as well as possess a certificate signed by his corps' surgeon. The board's most distinguished member was Henry Carter, a well-known scientific figure in Bombay, later elected an FRS and winner of its prestigious Copley Medal. After service in Sind, he had been appointed Medical Officer of the brig *Palinurus*, during its survey of the south-east coast of Arabia. He was now the Presidency's Oculist and Assistant Civil Surgeon. He and Burton had become closely acquainted through the latter's visits to Bombay for examination, and his studies at the Royal Asiatic Society of which Carter was now the Hon Secretary.[71] This pretty well ensured that Burton's passing the Board was a mere formality, and his being allowed two years' sick leave to the Neilgherry Hills.

Sadly, his long-time friend and munshi, Mohammed Hosayn, had already returned to Persia. Burton, therefore, engaged the services of an Arab 'coach,' a young Abyssinian, Haji Jauhar, and his wife. Hiring a pattymar, the *Darya Prashad* ("Joy of the Ocean") and accompanied by his servants and horses, Burton set sail for Goa on 20 February 1847.

CHAPTER EIGHT

GOLDEN GOA

Almost three hundred years earlier, the young Portuguese poet, Luis Vaz de Camões (rendered as Camoens by Burton) had also set out for Goa, but in rather different circumstances. On 15 June 1552, the Feast of Corpus Christi, he had become involved in an argument between two of his friends and a minor Court official, Gonçalo Borges, near the Convent of S. Domingo in Lisbon. Something of a hot-head, Camões had drawn his sword on their behalf, wounding Borges in the neck during the ensuing melée. Although a super-ficial wound, the offence was regarded with the utmost gravity, given the importance of the religious occasion and the Court's presence in the city. Camões was thrown into prison, where he languished for over eight months. Possibly through the intercession of an influential friend, he was pardoned and released on the payment of a fine, having also expressed his willingness to serve the King in India. He felt none of Burton's elation, however, when the day came for leaving his native land. Setting sail from Lisbon aboard the *Saõ Benito*, on or around Palm Sunday, 23 March 1553, he went, as he later wrote, 'as one leaving this world for the next.'

Much of Camões' best lyrical poetry was written at Goa. It was here also, probably between 1555-8, that he completed the *Lusiads*, the great national epic structured around the first voyage of Vasco da Gama, on which he had been working for twenty years. Although he had signed on as a common soldier in the King's service for three years, seventeen were to elapse before he was able to return home to see his manuscript published in 1572.

Burton failed to disclose when he first became acquainted with Camões' work. 'Those who favour me by reading this version,' he wrote in the Preface to his translation of the *Lusiads* over thirty years later, 'are spared the long recital of why, how, and when Portugal's Maro [the Roman poet, Virgil] became to me the perfection of a traveller's study.'[1] It was, however, what he described as, ' the "Epic Life," of the poet, which first attracted him, 'one of the most romantic and adventurous of an age of adventure and romance.' With the passing of time, Burton identified more and more with Camões, seeing his own trials and disappoint-ments mirrored in those of the long-dead Portuguese poet. For years, as he later admitted, he carried about a pocket volume of the *Lusiads*, poring over its stanzas, and pencilling in his translation at the end of his journeys. It is highly probable, that the practice began on this voyage in February 1847 down the Arabian Sea.

The island of Goa was sighted in the early evening of the third day. Although largely rugged and hilly particularly towards its centre, along the coast there were plains fringed with coconut groves, rice fields, and orchards of mango and jack-trees. Two rivers separating the island from the mainland, the Mandovi and the

Zuari, flowed into the ocean each side of the cape, or Cabo, forming two large and deep anchorages. In the view of the seventeenth century traveller, Jean Baptiste Tavernier, Baron d'Aubonne, the harbour was one of the best in the world.[2]

Occupying a central position on the western coast of India, and favoured by many natural advantages, the island rapidly rose to prominence in ancient times. At the period of the Portuguese invasion, it was one of the principal emporiums of trade along this coast, attracting people of all races and creeds from various parts of Asia. It was also highly important in being the rendezvous for the Muslims of the peninsula at the time of the *haj* to Mecca, who embarked there for the port of Jedda on the Red Sea.

As part of his overall strategy for dealing a death-blow to Muslim trade in the East, it was seized by Affonso de Albuquerque in November, 1510. Its capture, however, was indelibly stained with the blood of innocent women and children who were mercilessly put to the sword. As Diu served as the Portuguese outpost controlling the passage into Indian waters in the north, so Goa became their central place of arms and commerce. Here, the pepper and ginger of the South India coast, and in particular, the more precious and highly lucrative spices, the cinnamon, mace and cloves from the farther East, gradually began to pile up on the island's quaysides.

In its heyday, under successive viceroys, it enjoyed unparalleled prosperity, becoming known as Goa Dourada or Golden Goa, a byword for fabulous wealth. 'Whoever hath seen Goa,' ran the Portuguese proverb, 'need not see Lisbon.' Yet all this magnificence was not to last. 'In less than a century and a half after da Gama landed on the shores of India,' as Burton remarked, 'the splendour of Goa had departed for ever.'

The view from the entrance of the harbour was picturesque and imposing. Crowning the headland to the left was the impressive fortress of Aguada, with a series of batteries commanding the sea-coast, built in 1612 to protect the northern shores of the Mandovi estuary from Dutch and Maratha raiders. In the centre was the Cabo, with a splendid palace, used as a summer residence by the Governors of Goa. To the right, towered the thick walls of the fortress of Mormugão. As the *Darya Prashad* nosed its way through the harbour up to the mouth of the Mandovi, two other fortresses came into view, Reis Magos and Gaspar Dias. Some five miles further up-river lay Panjim or Panaji, Goa's new capital since 1843, with the pretty little village of Ribander adjoining it.

Immediately after disembarking, Salvador was despatched to search for accommodation, eventually securing a house with six rooms, kitchen, stable and back court for a peppercorn rent of 14 shillings a month. Over the next two days, Burton toured the city and was granted an audience at the palace with the grandiloquently named, Governor-General of all the Indies, Dom Pestanha. Interesting as it might appear from the river, Panjim, as Burton found, lost much of its apparent appeal on closer inspection.

Fortunately, his prime interest lay elsewhere, in Old Goa, some six miles eastwards along the Mandovi river. Hiring a covered canoe, Burton stocked it with supplies sufficient for several days together with jars of fresh water, 'a necessary precaution,' he believed, ' against ague and malaria.' Without further ado, he set off up-stream accompanied by the trusty Salvador and their self-appointed guide, John Thomas, pledged 'to show de Goa to the Bombay gentlemans.' The sun was setting as they alighted at the landing place a little beyond the arsenal.

Its crumbling ruins etched later in a dramatic chiaroscuro as the moon rose slowly over the sea, brought to Burton's mind 'the Arab's eloquent description of the "City with Impenetrable Gates, still, without a voice, or a cheery inhabitant: the owl hooting in its quarters, and birds skimming in circles in its areas, and the raven croaking in its great thoroughfare streets as if bewailing those that had been in it."'[3] Was it here, one wonders, amongst this wreckage of empire, that Burton was first moved to translate a few stanzas of the *Lusiads*, 'the labour and solace,' as he would describe it, of so many of his later years?[4]

Foremost among the many churches visited the following day was the 16th century basilica of Bom Jesus, containing the magnificent tomb of St Francis Xavier.[5] Naturally, Burton was also interested in visiting the Nunnery of Santa Monaca, as he mistakenly called it, 'an order said to be strict in the extreme.' Just as naturally, his interest was more profane than sacred. According to the Dutch traveller and historian, Jan Huygen van Linschoten, who spent five years, from 1583-88, in the service of the Dominican Archbishop of Goa, Vincente de Fonseca: 'The towne hath in it all sortes of Cloysters and Churches as Lisbone [hath] onely it wanteth Nunnes, for the men cannot get the women to travel so farre, where they should be shut up, and forsake Venus, with whome (so that they may enjoy and fulfill their lustes) they had rather loose their lives, whereof they make small account.'

This deficiency was rectified in 1606, when a convent of Augustinian nuns was founded by the archbishop, Fr Aleixo de Menezez, and dedicated to St Monica, the mother of St Augustine of Hippo. The nuns were nearly all natives of India, and more or less coloured. It fell into such a state of disrepair, however, that in 1835, a fact of which Burton appears to have been unaware, the nuns were transferred to another building, C. da Graça.[6]

Despite his best efforts, all he and his servant saw was a variety of black handmaids and the portress. A deaf ear was turned to hints that an introduction to the prioress would be acceptable. They were also denied permission to visit the cloisters. An inveterate as well as an incomparable story-teller, Burton then launched into an ingenious and amusing tale of a romantic escapade to account for this refusal. It had, allegedly, taken place a decade or so earlier, and involved a young lieutenant, Salvador's earlier master, and a very pretty white girl, who taught Latin to the young novices. This officer is transparently Burton's narcissistic view of himself, 'a very clever gentleman, who knew everything. He could talk to each man of a multitude in his own language, and all of them would appear equally surprised and delighted with him. Besides, his faith was every man's faith.'[7]

The plot hinged on the young nun's being snatched from her room at the dead of night, the guards having previously been drugged with datura, a powerful narcotic, mixed in with their tobacco. It ended farcically. In his hurry, Lt – took a wrong turning. His accomplice, an Afghan servant named Khudadad, picked up what he believed to be the sleeping form of his master's beloved, only to discover to their horror a short while later, that he was carrying the far from beautiful form of the sub-prioress. Leaving her bound and gagged, they made good their escape.[8]

Such a brief summary does less than justice to this cloak and dagger story. Literally so, the young officer setting off at night in native dress, turban pulled down low over his blackened face, and armed with a sharp long-bladed knife. It is vintage Burton, the incredible told with a straight face, and told so convincingly that we are left wondering…..

On returning from Old Goa to Panjim, Burton next tried his luck at the Santa Casa de Misericordia, the Holy House of Mercy. Besides their spiritual duties, these charitable brotherhoods, modelled on those in Lisbon, were dedicated to providing help and comfort for those in need. This particular establishment contained some fifty young women. Most were orphans of all colours, class, and age, who remained there until they received offers of marriage. Burton pretended to want to interview the young ladies with a view to proposing marriage. His request was given short shrift, and he was told in no uncertain terms by the Mother Superior that ,'We are people under Government and do not keep a naughty house.'

This was followed by an equally abortive visit to Seroda some fifteen miles south of Panjim. Burton found the town dirty in the extreme, a chaotic mix of houses, pagodas, tombs, tanks with high parapets and huge flights of steps, peepul trees, and bazaars. The supposedly beautiful Hindu dancing girls whom they had been led to expect, turned out to be 'common-looking Maharatta women.' On his return, obviously having exhausted his interest in the area, Burton addressed a note to Senhor Gomez, the Governor-General's

Secretary for permission to leave Goa. Four days later he was off the port of Calicut on the Malabar coast.

It was here, after an epoch-making voyage round the Cape, that the ships of Vasco Da Gama's small fleet dropped anchor on 19 May 1498. Da Gama and his companions were given a friendly reception by the Zamorin raja of Calicut. Intrigues set in train by the foreign Arab merchants, however, who saw their long-standing monopoly of trade via the Red Sea threatened by this new sea-route, almost led to disaster. A treacherous massacre, fortunately, having been averted, Da Gama sailed three and half months later for home with rich cargoes, presents, and a letter from the Zamorin to the Portuguese King, Emmanuel, suggesting the establishment of mutually beneficial trading links. At Cannanore, farther up the coast, the raja is reputed to have pressed on the Portuguese more spices and merchandise than their vessels could hold, and signed a treaty of friendship with them written on gold leaf.

Faced with the choice of peaceful trade with a handful of ports along the Malabar coast or armed monopoly, Emmanuel chose the latter. On Da Gama's second expedition in 1502, bombardment of Calicut by the guns of his ships replaced the former hand of friendship. The capture and plundering of peaceful Arab merchant vessels off the port was followed by the most appalling cruelties, barbarous in the extreme, even by the standards of the day.[9]

Calicut, however, was no longer the noble and wealthy city described by Camoens. Instead, Burton found 'a huge mass of huts and hovels each built in its own yard of cocoas, vast and peculiar-looking mosques, a chapel or two, courts and cutcheries, a hospital, barracks, and a variety of bungalows.' There were few old monuments to be seen. The fort erected by the Portuguese had long since crumbled into dust. In fact, some maintained that the present city was not the one referred to in the *Lusiads*. For his part, Burton preferred to believe that it was here that 'Da Gama first cast anchor and stepped forth from his weather-beaten ship at the head of his mail-clad warriors upon the land of promise.'[10]

On the pretext of being discouraged from visiting the present Samiry Raja, who held aloof from meeting with Europeans, Burton decided to call upon the far less wealthy, if more sociable, cadet of the House of Yelliah. A ride of some three miles through high-banked lanes and over dykes built across the mud-filled paddy-fields, brought them to the village of Mangaon. The rajah, who received them with all the honours, turned out to be a little dark man, dressed in a splendid coat of cloth of gold, a strangely shaped hat of the same material, and red silk tights. The small room in which they met was packed with furniture, somewhat reminiscent of the *Old Curiosity Shop*, with cheap coloured prints, some obviously torn from magazines, on the walls. After some twenty minutes spent in conversation through an interpreter, they took their leave. There was a great deal of shrieking as they turned a corner and suddenly met in the gateway, young ladies belonging to the palace. 'They and their attendants,' wrote Burton innocently, 'appeared as much annoyed as we were gratified to catch a sight of Nair female beauty,' this being the real reason, of course, for his visit. The women were very young, pretty, with long black hair, and 'their toilette, in all save the ornamental parts of ring and necklace, were decidedly scanty.'[11]

It was the custom, as Burton was at pains to explain, for modest women of the Tiyar family to expose the whole of the person above the waist. Only prostitutes were compelled to have the bosom covered. Since this class of Hindu mainly provided European residents with nurses and other menial jobs, many of the Europeans had tried to put a stop to the custom. 'The proposal, however, has generally been met pretty much in the same spirit as would be displayed were the converse suggested to an Englishwoman.'[12]

Since leaving Bombay, Burton had shown himself in no hurry to get to Ootacamund. Still intent on seeing as much as possible of the country, he avoided the short cut up the Koondah Range. Instead, he chose the far longer route, skirting the sea-shore as far as Punani before turning inland to begin the long winding ascent up to the Neilgherry Hills. After passing through the magnificent, if unhealthy, Wulliyar jungle, they arrived by a rough road at Coimbatore, a straggling line of houses, bazaars, and white bungalows, each standing in its own wide bit of compound. A ride of twenty miles finally brought them to Matypolliam at the foot of the Neilgherry Hills. 'You would scarcely believe,' he remarked, 'that the inmates of that little bungalow which peeps over the brow of the mountain are enjoying an Alpine, almost a European climate, while we are still in the discomfort of the tropics.'[13]

John Sullivan, the outstanding figure in the history of Ooty as it was always called, had been the first to suggest to the Madras Government that it would make a superb hill-station for the British in southern India. The construction of a pass had begun in 1821, prisoners from Coimbatore jail being impressed to make the road. Advantage was initially taken of the indigenous tribesmen, the Todas, land being bought from them for the derisory sum of a rupee an acre. They soon learned, however, to strike a hard bargain. In 1828, the original plan was extended to make the hills into a sanatorium for military convalescents.[14]

It was probably not until some time in May, when Burton reported his arrival to Major McMurdo, the Military Commandant. Having had a good look around, Burton was pleased by the non-military appearance and sound of Ooty. By general consent, uniform was banished except for balls and parties. He found a friend, Lt Walter Neil Dyett, later to lose his right arm at Multan, who invited Burton to share his quarters. During the first couple of weeks Burton savoured the delight of roaming over the English-like countryside, 'Malvern at the fairest season,' was one earlier visitor's assessment of it. The novelty of the place, however, was not long in wearing off. Although there appears to have been a great many activities going on, as far as he was concerned, there was a dearth of amusements. 'Among the ladies we have elderlies who enjoy tea, and delight in scandal, grass widows...spinsters of every kind from the little girl in bib and tucker to the full-blown Anglo-Indian young lady who discourses on her papa, the Colonel, and disdains to look at anything below the rank of a field officer.'[15]

Burton gives the impression that he tried, but failed, to study while he was there. He paints a picture of borrowing 'some friend's Akhlak ei Hindi (The Ethics of India), rummaging through his trunk for a Shakespeare's grammar and buying a second-hand copy of Forbes's dictionary...but your mind refuses to rise again to its task. You find that Ootacamund is no place for study.' The truth is that, once settled in, he appears to have done little else. Despite his claim to the contrary, he did translate the Akhlak while he was there.[16] He also seems to have kept aloof from society, spending much of his time writing letters to the *Bombay Times*, studying Telegu and Toda, as well as Persian and Arabic.

None of this can have been easy since, towards the end of May, he suffered an attack of, what he called, rheumatic ophthalmia. He blamed this condition, no doubt a purulent conjunctivitis, on the sudden change from the dryness of Sind to the damp cold of the Neilgherries. It may well have resulted instead from a recent gonorrhoeal infection. It was to last for two years, and was not cured until he left India.

Despite this, Burton seems to have had little difficulty, for which he gave no explanation, in persuading his medical officer at Ooty that he was well enough to return to duty long before the expiration of his leave. While boredom no doubt played a part in his departure after only four months, it is likely that there were other, more pressing, reasons involved. Foremost amongst them must have been his desire to please his father by sitting his Persian examination that year, already postponed by his earlier illness. In the meanwhile, there had also been important changes in Sind. Sir Charles Napier had resigned in July, and Lt Colonel Henry Corsellis had left on sick leave to England. In the light of later events, it is highly probable that Burton received a letter, perhaps some time in July or August from Captain Scott, offering to reinstate him on the Survey team, should he be fit enough to return to the province.

On 1 September, 'glad as a partridge-shooter,' Burton rode down the Western Ghats, this time taking the short-cut down the Koondah Range. Twelve days later he was back at Calicut, where he stayed for a further fortnight. Aside from Mr Collector Connolly, who was brutally murdered by a band of fanatical Moplahs shortly after Burton's departure, there were scarcely twenty Europeans in the place. It was now the tail-end of the south-west monsoon, and Burton pitied the dreary lives these expatriates must lead during this season, with no other sounds in their ears than the roaring of the wind, the pelting of the rain, and the creaking of the palm trees.

It was in just such weather that he embarked for Bombay aboard the steamship, *Seaforth*, on 27 September, making brief visits en route to Mangalor and Goa. His arrival at Bombay three days later left him with a fortnight to work with a *munshi* in putting the finishing touch to his studies. On 15 October he sat his examination in Persian, topping the list of some thirty candidates. As well as being complimented by the examiners, he was later awarded an 'honorarium' of Rs 1000 (roughly equivalent to £3,800 in modern currency) by Government, 'similar to that bestowed on Lt Rigby.'[17] Only eight days later his name appeared in the Calcutta Gazette, as 'Appointed Assistant in the Scinde Survey,' clear proof that Scott must have applied for him at a much earlier date, knowing of Burton's return.

Perhaps too embarrassed by his early return to seek help from Henry Carter, Burton turned to a young Irish medic to prescribe for his condition. He strongly recommended applying citric ointment around the orbit of the eye. Persevering with this treatment, Burton said, led to his developing 'ugly symptoms of mercurialism,' which eventually drove him from India. Possibly leading a promiscuous sexual life-style, it is likely that the treatment was not confined to the orbit of the eye. Burton returned to Karachi in the s.s. *Dwarka*, coincidentally the small vessel in which he later sailed from Jedda to Suez following his pilgrimage to Mecca.

In the periods when not troubled by his ophthalmia, Burton resumed his study of Sindi under Munshi Nandu, and Arabic under Shaykh Hashim, a small half-Bedawin originally from Muscat, whom Burton had imported from Bombay. Under his tuition, Burton began 'the systematic study of practical Moslem divinity, learned about a quarter of the Koran by heart, and became proficient in prayer.'[18]

He claimed to have always wanted to visit Mecca during the pilgrimage season. 'Written descriptions by hearsay of its rites and ceremonies were common enough in all languages, European as well as native, but none satisfied me, because none seemed practically to know anything about the matter.'[19] This second claim, of course, is thoroughly dishonest, since it was written just under a quarter of a century after his so-called 'Pilgrimage', Burton's citing in his account those who had preceded him, and incorporating the detailed first-hand descriptions of J.L. Burckhardt and Ali Bey el Abassi in his text.[20] 'So to this preparation,' he went on, 'I devoted all my time and energy.' This, too, needs taking with a large pinch of salt. As an officer in the East India Company's Army, he could not possibly have foreseen any circumstances in the future which might enable him to carry out such a scheme. It was obviously inserted in the later autobiography to give the impression that his 'Pilgrimage' was the natural outcome of something for which he had been preparing for years.

He also made what he called a 'sympathetic study of Sufism.' Sufism or *Tasawwuf* as it is called in Arabic, is the inner, mystical dimension of Islam. Although there have been various suggestions as to the derivation of the word *Sufi*, the one most generally accepted is that it is from the Arabic word *suf*, meaning wool, and refers to the earlier ascetics' wearing of coarse woollen garments to symbolise their detachment from the material world.

The movement had originated in the 8th century as a reaction to certain features of orthodox Islam, in particular its sterile legalism, the worldliness of the Ummayyad and Abbasid caliphates, and the arid intellectualism of the theologians. Instead, Sufis encouraged a desire for inner, personal experience of the Divine, through meditation (*dhikr*: remembrance) and other practices. They rejected wealth and class distinctions, modelling themselves on the simpler lives led by Muhammad, the first caliphs, and the poor wandering dervishes or faqirs.

It is highly probable that Burton came to Sufism through his reading of the great 13th-15th century

Persian poets, such as Jalal ad-Din ar-Rumi, Sa'adi, Hafez, and 'Abd or-Rahman Jami. He described them as the 'high priests' of this religion of beauty, the rites of which were 'wine, music, and dancing spiritually considered, and its places of worship meadows and gardens, where the perfume of the rose and the song of the nightingale, by charming the heart, are supposed to improve the mind of the listener.'[21] No one, he believed, had done this better than Hafez, in whose lyrical poetry, 'we find learning and love of pleasure, wonderful powers of imagination, and a fulness of meaning, which none but Persians can appreciate.'[22]

It was not until the 12th and 13th centuries that Sufi orders or religious brotherhoods emerged. Each had its distinctive path towards experiencing the divine reality, the master who had already passed through its stages providing the necessary guidance for his followers. Burton was initiated into the Qadiriyya order, believed to be the oldest of the Sufi orders of Islam, under the high-sounding name of Bismillah-Shah, 'King in the name of Allah.' Eventually, after a probationary period, so he claimed, he was elevated to the rank of *murshid*, or Master in the mystic craft.[23] In Volume II, Appendix 1, of his *Personal Narrative of a Pilgrimage to El-Medinah and Meccah* (1855-56), Burton provided a translation of what he described as 'A Murshid's Diploma.' A modern Arabic scholar, however, has pointed out that it is nothing more than an *ijiza*, or licence, stating that Burton had been 'given instruction in the Saying of Unity with authority to recite it 165 times after each *farida* (obligatory ritual prayer) and on any other occasion according to his ability.'[24]

He varied this mystical study with that of Sikhism, the religion founded in the Punjab by the Indian prophet, Guru Nanak (1469-1539), in the late fifteenth century. Its doctrines and practices owed much to the Indian mystic and poet, Kabir (1440-1518), whose disciple Nanak was. In an attempt to build a bridge between Hindu and Muslim thought, Kabir took from each what he regarded as the best of its doctrines. This became the inspiration for Guru Nanak in establishing his new religion. As a student of both Hinduism and Islam, Burton, therefore, would have found much that was familiar to him.

While Guru Nanak accepted Hinduism's belief in the transmigration of souls, he rejected its caste system, believing in the essential equality of all men and women. He condemned idolatry and, what he regarded, as empty devotional acts. In the words of the religion's sacred text, the *Adi Granth* : 'I perform neither the Hindu worship nor the Muslim prayer; To the sole Formless Lord in my heart I bow. We are neither Hindus nor Muslims; Our body and life belong to the One Supreme Being who alone is both Ram and Allah for us.'[25]

Although holding a Staff appointment, and drawing the appropriate allowances, Burton, because of his eye condition, appears to have carried out little surveying. He, therefore, made up for it, he said, by writing long reports about the country and the people, which were sent to the Bombay Government, and duly printed in its Selections. The first of these, 'Notes relative to the Population of Sind; and the Customs, Language and Literature of the People,' was submitted to Government on 31 December, 1847.[26] This was followed just over two months later, on 2 March 1848 by, 'Brief Notes relative to the Division of Time, and Articles of Cultivation in Sind; to which are appended Remarks on the Modes of Intoxication in that Province.' This was written in collaboration with his friend, Surgeon John Ellerton Stocks of the Bombay Medical Establishment, Vaccinator in Sind.[27] There is no doubt that these appended remarks were written by Burton himself from personal experience.

One of the main reasons for, what he later called, 'the Scindian's degeneracy,' was the 'prevalence of drunkenness throughout the province. Wines and opium were only affordable by the upper echelons of society. The ordinary people had to 'content themselves with the many preparations of the deleterious bhang, in England called Indian hemp,' to which they became thoroughly addicted. They could be found regularly indulging their mind-blowing habit at establishments called daira, located on the outskirts of all large towns. Burton admitted to having often taken the drug himself, 'rather for curiosity to discover what its attractions might be, than for aught of pleasurable I ever experienced.' He recollected on one occasion 'being persuaded that my leg was revolving upon its knees as an axis, and could distinctly feel as well as hear it strike against and pass through the shoulder during each revolution.'[28]

In addition to these sociological studies, Burton later sent two linguistic papers to the Bombay branch of the Royal Asiatic Society. The first of these, 'Remarks on Dr Dorn's Chrestomathy of the Afghan Tongue,' was written with the assistance of an Afghan mullah, Akhund Burhan Al-Din'.[29] Boris Andreevich Dorn was the first Russian ever to study Afghan, and to introduce it into the syllabus of St Petersburg University. As well as compiling a grammar of Pushtu, he also wrote several works on the history and ethnography of the Afghans.[30] Burton's second paper was devoted to a 'Grammar of the Jataki or Belochki Dialect.'[31]

An account written by Walter Abraham, who had been Dr Stocks's botanical draughtsman at Karachi in 1847, paints a graphic picture of Burton's life at this period:

> When I knew him, [wrote Abraham] he was master of half a dozen languages, which he wrote and spoke so fluently that a stranger who did not see him and heard him speaking would fancy he heard a native. His domestic servants were – a Portuguese, with whom he spoke Portuguese and Goanese, an African, a Persian, and a Sindi or Belochee. These spoke their mother-tongue to Sir Richard as he was engaged in his studies with moonshees, who relieved each other every two hours, from ten to four daily...
>
> His habits at home were perfectly Persian or Arabic. His hair was dressed *a la Persian* – long and shaved from the forehead to the top of his head; his eyes by some means or other he employed, resembled Persian or Arabic; he used the Turkish bath and wore a cowl; and when he went out for a ride he used a wig and goggles...
>
> He was such a jovial companion, that his bungalow was the resort of the learned men of the place, such as Major (afterwards General) Scott, Lieutenant (and now General) Alfred de Lisle, Lieutenant Edward Dansey of Mooltan notoriety, Dr Stocks, and many others....[32]

An uneasy peace had followed the ending of the Sikh War in 1846. Defeat, and its aftermath, a punitive and humiliating treaty, had left a smouldering legacy of bitterness and hatred in the Sikh Army and among dissident landowners. It needed only the right moment to fan it into the flames of open insurrection. That moment came in April 1848. Two young British political officers, Peter Vans Agnew and Lieutenant William Anderson, sent from Lahore to Multan to arrange the setting up of a British administration, were murdered.[33] The late ruler, the Dewan Mul Raj, whose power and prestige had been systematically eroded by the British, was quickly elected war leader. Over the next few months, the rebellion spread like wild-fire throughout the Punjab.

A military response was not long delayed. Following two victories by a large force of levies under Major Herbert Edwardes, the Sikhs were pushed back into the ancient walled city of Multan. By mid-September, the repulse of one attack, and the defection of Shere Singh's forces convinced the British commander, Major-General Whish, that it would be better to abandon the siege until reinforcements were sent up the Indus from units of the Bombay Army stationed in Sind.

News of the murder of Vans Agnew and Anderson had reached Burton at Karachi by 2 May. It represented, in his view, one of the 'two most exciting items of intelligence' that spring, the other being the declaration of a republic in France. War was obviously inevitable, and with it the possibility of seeing active service at last, something denied him two years earlier. On 14 November, five days after Lord Gough's Army of the Punjab crossed the Sutlej, Burton wrote a letter of commiseration to his cousin Sarah, whose mother had died in September. It appeared that he had already heard the news from his father's last letter from Italy. However, 'he wishes me not to mention it to my mother,' adding that 'he has fear for her mind if it be abruptly alluded to...I will keep this letter open ten or twelve days longer, as that time will decide my fate. A furious affair has broken out in Mooltan and the Punjaub and I have applied to the General commanding to go up with him on his personal staff. A few days more will decide the business – and I am not a little anxious about it, for though suffering from my old complaint – ophthalmia – yet these opportunities are too far between to be lost.'

He returned to the letter on 25 November and, without comment, added a postcript, 'I am not going up to the siege of Multan, as the general with whom I had expected to be sent is recalled. Pray be kind enough to send on the enclosed to my father. I was afraid to direct it to him in Italy as it contains papers of some importance. You are welcome to the perusal, if you think it worth the trouble.'[34]

It was almost forty year later when Burton's expanded, and carefully misrepresented, version of what had happened at this time, appeared in print.[35] He had applied, he said, 'in almost suppliant terms,' for the post of Interpreter to the Bombay force. Scott, Steinhaeuser, Stocks, Dansey, and numerous other friends had already been ordered up. General Auchmuty's secretary, however, had written back informing him that the post had been filled. What made matters worse, was that the officer selected was only qualified in Hindustani, whereas Burton had passed examinations in six native languages, including Multani. The result was to bring on a severe bout of rheumatic ophthalmia, which could be cured only by a return to Europe. 'Sick, sorry, and almost in tears of rage, I bade adieu to my friends and comrades in Sind. At Bombay there was no difficulty in passing the Medical Board, and I embarked at Bombay for a passage round the Cape...' Burton concluded his account by claiming that his career in India 'had been in my eyes a failure, and by no fault of my own; the dwarfish demon called "Interest" had fought against me, and as usual had won the fight.'

Accepting Burton's version of events at face value, his earliest biographers were not slow in identifying the reason underlying this, apparent, miscarriage of justice. For Burton's niece, Georgiana Stisted, it lay in his failure to curry favour with those in authority and, what was worse, being openly critical of them.[36] It is, however, the claim first advanced by Thomas Wright, that Burton's report on the male bordellos of Karachi was produced against him, which has since gained general acceptance.[37] I have already given my reasons for questioning the existence of this document. What, therefore, did happen?

It will be remembered that Burton wrote to Sarah in mid-November 1848, precisely the time when the Bombay reinforcements should have arrived at Multan. That he was able to express the hope, or rather the expectation as he phrased it, of joining them at this date, lay in the fact that they were delayed in Sind, while the choice of an officer to command them was resolved.

The Bombay Government had chosen Major-General (later Sir) Samuel Auchmuty, a Peninsular War veteran then serving on the General Staff of the Bombay Army, in charge of the Sind Division. The Supreme Government in Calcutta, however, had already approved the appointment of Major-General Whish, who was junior to Auchmuty. There was no real dilemma, only poor communications. The choice of the paramount authority, naturally, took precedence. Auchmuty's command was cancelled – what Burton referred to as his recall – and he was superseded by a more junior officer, Brigadier Dundas. It was 10 December before the advance body of reinforcements from Sind arrived at Multan. With it were two of Burton's closest friends, Major Walter Scott, who had gone up as Dundas's chief of engineers, and John Frederick Steinhaeuser, seconded from the 26th Bombay Native Infantry to serve as medical officer with the force.

Burton's military records show that he became 'qualified to transact public business in the Sindi language on 7 September 1848, and in the Punjabee by 13 December.'[38] By that date, therefore, he had finally matched Lt C.P. Rigby's feat of passing examinations in six native languages. Burton now shared with Rigby the distinction of being the most brilliant linguist in the Indian Army. Was this not in itself, therefore, clear proof that Burton was, as he claimed, the victim of prejudice or misdirected patronage? The answer quite simply is, 'No.'

What Burton's biographers have failed to appreciate – and he, himself, of course, was not at pains to point it out – is the crucial fact that it was not simply a question of an officer trying to be useful and offering his services. The post of Interpreter was a Staff appointment and, as such, highly prized not only for the status it conferred, but also for the valuable financial reward it offered. Burton, as we know, had held such a post with his own regiment, on merit, in Gujerati and Maharatta. Thanks to the interest of Scott, he held yet another Staff appointment as an Assistant in the Sind Survey. On this ground alone it would have been grossly unfair for Burton to have displaced an officer already chosen, or in process of being considered.

Burton told the story with the express purpose of making it appear invidious on the part of the military authorities, in selecting an officer with only a tithe of his linguistic qualifications. Hindustani, however, was the military *lingua franca* of north-western India and, therefore, perfectly adequate for the purposes of the campaign. Had there been no other overriding reason, Burton's linguistic brilliance on this occasion would have been, in a sense, an irrelevance. What is, perhaps, the most remarkable aspect of the affair is that his remaining a 'carpet soldier' after all, a victim not of 'Interest' but of events, should have rankled for so long, and made him fabricate a quite baseless charge.

Naturally, we must be equally dismissive of his contention that emotional distress caused by his alleged victimization brought on a serious attack of ophthalmia. One recent biographer treats Burton's condition as if it were of psychosomatic origin, finding its cause in Burton's guilt over the Karachi report and his failure to secure the post of interpreter.[39] As will be seen later, his departure from India was solely for medical reasons.

Burton left Sind on 13 March 1849, the day after the Second Sikh War, of which he had so much wanted to be a part, came to an end. On 30 March, with all the pomp and ceremony of full Durbar, the Punjab was formally annexed to our Empire in India. Two days later, the brig *Eliza*, carrying Burton and his Afghan servant, Khudabaksh, warped out of Bombay harbour, and ran before the north-east monsoon towards the distant Cape.

CHAPTER NINE

HOME OF THE STRANGER

'Nowhere else than upon the sea,' wrote Joseph Conrad, 'do the weeks and months fall away quicker into the past. They seem to be left astern as the light air-bubbles in the swirls of the ship's wake.[1] There are no means of knowing whether this was true or not for Burton, broken in health and cooped up in the cramped quarters of the brig. Nevertheless, exchanging sea-air for the enervating climates of Karachi and Bombay can only have had an invigorating and inspiriting effect on him.

On Wednesday, 5 September, just over five months out of Bombay, the *Eliza* dropped anchor off Plymouth. The following Saturday, the Mercantile Register column of the weekly Plymouth, *Devonport and Stonehouse Herald*, carried this brief and misspelled entry: 'Off the Port – Eliza, Corry, sailed from Bombay for London, on the 1st April – general cargo. She landed here Hicks Esq Surgeon of the ship, R.F. Benton (sic) of the Bombay Army and a Native Servant.'[2]

Two years later, in the only published reference he ever made to his arrival in England, Burton contrasted his own reaction at seeing the glaring waste of the Sind coastline for the first time, with that of his servant, as the pilot boat ferried them ashore along the broad reaches of the Sound: "Allah, Allah!" exclaimed Khudabaksh, as he caught sight of the town, and the green hills, and the woody parks, and the pretty places round about the place with the breakwater; "what manner of men must you Feringhis be, that leave such a bihisht and travel to such accursed holes as ours, without manacles and the persuasions of the chob!"[3]

Appearances, nevertheless, were deceptive. In July 1848, *The Times* had carried a short report from Bucharest on the alarming spread of cholera in the city, which had brought government to a halt, and sent thousands fleeing in panic to the mountains. Within only three months, it was announcing its arrival in this country. By June 1849 it had reached epidemic proportions. Almost five hundred people had died since July in Plymouth. In London, the disease had already claimed more than nine thousand victims. More were being buried each week as *The Times's* leader-writer pointed out, than had been killed on the British side at Waterloo, and almost as many as had perished in the icy passes of Kabul during the infamous retreat from Afghanistan.[4]

Having taken a fast train to London, Burton was now comfortably installed with his aunt and uncle, Georgiana and Robert Bagshaw, in a household where cholera was never likely to be more than a talking point over the breakfast toast and marmalade.[5] 9 York Place, Portman Square, was one of a set of highly fashionable late-Georgian terraced houses in Upper Baker Street close to Regent's Park. A short distance down the New Road (now the Marylebone Road) was the parish church, where three years earlier the poet,

Robert Browning, had contracted a secret marriage with Elizabeth Barrett, before whisking her off to Italy a week later.[6] Adjoining the church was 1 Devonshire Terrace, a handsome house facing York Gate, where Charles Dickens was writing the latest number of *David Copperfield*.

Like that author's Mr Dombey, who had appeared before the public the previous year, Burton's uncle was a rich City merchant, the son of a Coventry banker, John Bagshaw. The father had founded the family firm of Bagshaw and Company at Calcutta in the early years of the century. With his lucrative business interests in the East India trade, he had combined the Chairmanship of the Calcutta and Diamond Harbour Docks and Railway Company. After nearly twenty years in India, he had returned to England loaded with the wealth of an old time nabob.[7] He lost no time entering Parliament as a Liberal free-trader, and becoming a director of several railway companies. Later, as well as renting a house in London close to his son, he built himself Cliff House, an Italianate mansion standing in spacious grounds outside Harwich in Essex, where he set about developing nearby Dovercourt as a new town.[8]

Robert Bagshaw had continued his father's links with the East, although he had been frustrated in his ambition of entering Parliament at the Yarmouth election in 1848.[9] Aunt Georgiana, who had given every indication of remaining a spinster, had married Robert on 25 July 1842, at St Mary's Church, Marylebone, only a month after Burton had left for India. She was now the proud mistress of a large establishment, boasting its liveried butler, footman, coachman and groom, in addition to numerous other servants.[10] Her marriage, and consequent departure from the house in Cumberland Street, had been only part of the gradual break-up of the old family group, which had been intact when Burton left for India seven years earlier. Grandmamma Baker had died in 1846, followed two years later after a lingering illness, by Aunt Sarah.[11] Soon, there was to be further change, Eliza looking forward to her own wedding in the following June, which would mean moving away from London. Only her sister Sarah and Margaret Morgan, the aunts' former governess and companion, would be left to inhabit the old house.

After spending an unknown period in London, Burton left to join his family at their winter quarters in Pisa.[12] It was a city of which he always spoke in derogatory terms. Yet, after a long absence, it must have seemed a sort of home-coming to re-enter once again one of the familiar old palazzi on the south side of the Lung Arno, to which his parents returned year after year like migratory birds.

There had been changes here, too. Burton's sister, Maria, had married Captain Henry Stisted of the Queen's Second Royal Regiment, on 30 October 1845, at Florence.[13] There were now two children, Georgiana aged four, and Maria, a few months old, for the grandparents to dote on.[14] Only Edward was missing from the family group. Having gone up to Trinity College, Cambridge, in 1843, his father had bought him a commission in the 37th, or Royal Hampshire, Regiment, two years later. In 1846, the regiment had sailed for Ceylon, where it remained for the next ten years.[15]

While Burton professed to dislike Pisa, he loved the Tuscan countryside, with its gently rolling landscape, its farms and villas, its vineyards and orchards, its dark cypresses and hill-top villages. And he always had a special place in his heart for Florence. However, after the heady but short-lived triumphs that year of the leaders of the Risorgimento, Mazzini and Garibaldi, the City of Flowers like the rest of Tuscany, was now under the heel of the Austrians. Brawls were continually breaking out between the people of Florence and the Austrian soldiers. Two soldiers had lately been killed in the suburb of St Nicholas, and several had been wounded. The inhabitants had even attempted to erect barricades, but had been 'prevented by the timely arrival of the police.'[16] Burton, in his only reference to this period in Italy, later recalled being, 'at Florence in 1850 when our fair country-women added not a little to its trouble by dividing into two factions, the Italian and the Austrian. Some wore national colours, others went so far as to refuse waltzes proposed to them by partizans of the hostile nation.'[17]

The family, minus Burton's father, returned to England that spring to attend Eliza Burton's wedding, and possibly, that of Robert Bagshaw's younger sister, Lucy. One of Georgiana's earliest memories was of crossing the snow-covered Alps in a travelling carriage. Inside the large lumbering vehicle were her mother and uncle, her sister and herself, an English maid, and 'a romantic but surly Asiatic, named Allahdad.' Burton was oftener outside the carriage than in it, 'as the noise made by his two small nieces rendered pedestrian exercise, even in the snow, an agreeable and almost necessary variety. Very good-humouredly, however, did he bear the uproar, now and then giving us bits of snow which we hoped might be sugar.'[18]

Lucy's wedding to the Rev Thomas Dealtry, only son of the Bishop of Madras, took place on Saturday, 1 June, at St Margaret's, Westminster.[19] Four days later, Eliza was married to John Edward Harryman Pryce at the parish church of St Andrew, Clifton, the fashionable suburb of Bristol. Pryce, belonging to an old Welsh family, was the youngest son of the late Richard Pryce of Gunley Hall, Chirbury, Montgomeryshire. He was also, lately, a captain in the Queen's 2nd Royal Regiment, a brother officer and a close friend of Maria's husband, Henry Stisted. Sadly, Eliza, aged only twenty-one, died at her home, Trelydan Hall, Montgomeryshire, on 8 April of the following year, shortly after giving birth to a son, Edward Stisted Mostyn Pryce.[20]

Burton stayed for a while with his sister at Dover. Once only a garrison town and a port of embarkation for the Continent, it had increased in size and gentility with the new passion for seaside holidays and sea-bathing. Doctors were even recommending the drinking of sea-water, mixed with port wine, milk or beef-tea, to make it more palatable. He also appears to have visited Royal Leamington Spa for its saline waters, and tried the fashionable water cure at Malvern, patronised by the likes of Carlyle, Dickens, Darwin and Tennyson.

Medical knowledge had scarcely advanced since the previous century and quackery still abounded. Advertisements appeared daily in *The Times*, claiming to cure everything under the sun. One, preposterously named preparation, Dr Sibly's Reanimating Solar Tincture, was 'strongly recommended to the public in all cases of debility, lassitude, consumption, nervous and rheumatic complaints and indigestion.' Burton, nevertheless, as Georgiana Stisted commented, 'While far from blind to the mistakes made by the faculty, and unpleasantly conscious of the real injury inflicted by the drastic drugs then in vogue...was never without some pet surgeon or physician.'

Prompted by the need for economy, Burton moved to Boulogne, probably some time in April 1851. Under the Company's regulations, 'Every officer on sick certificate for a period not exceeding 2 years, is granted his full regimental allowances.'[21] As from April of that year, these allowances would be severely curtailed, and Burton would need to rein in his expenses.[22] He first booked into one of the town's many cheap hotels. Some time later, according to Georgiana, almost our only source for this period, 'relatives received dismal letters complaining of dulness and low spirits.'[23] This resulted in his being temporarily joined by his sister and nieces, and later by his parents.

It appears to have been in Italy, if not on the voyage home, that Burton first began writing up accounts of his experiences in India. His output, as throughout his life, was astonishing. Despite ill-health, he had produced four books by 1851, totalling over fifteen hundred pages. Three published that year. The fourth, which was ready towards the latter part of 1851, came out in the early part of the following year.

The first to appear was *Goa and the Blue Mountains; or Six Months of Sick Leave*, published by Richard Bentley. Described by the author as owing 'Its Existence To Her Friendly Suggestions,' it was dedicated to Miss Elizabeth Stisted, 'In Token Of Gratitude And Affection.' One biographer has wrongly identified her with one of the handsome cousins with whom Burton is supposed to have fallen in love.[24] She was, in fact, his middle-aged sister-in-law, who had married William Henry Wood at Naples on 30 September 1830.[25] Unfortunately, the Stisted pedigree is silent on any other details, leaving it a mystery as to why Elizabeth was using her maiden name at this period.

Although a first book, *Goa and the Blue Mountains* is in no sense an apprentice work. Everything of the later Burton is here: his racy style, his breezy facetious type of humour mixed with the sardonic, his vivid pen-pictures of people and places, his powers as a raconteur, his dogmatism, and his perverse delight in taking an unorthodox and unpopular point of view in religion and politics.

The book was lucky enough to be reviewed in the *Athenaeum*, in which, unusually, books for review were given to experts in their field.[26] Conceding that the author was, 'beyond question a smart, active, intelligent and acute subaltern,' the reviewer then went on to describe the book as 'a curious piece of patchwork, made up of the most heterogeneous materials.' He suggested that, 'A judicious friend would very likely have burnt one-third of the manuscript, and ordered him to rewrite most of the rest.' The result would have been 'a volume descriptive of Goa and the Malabar coast of India so well written and full of information that it might have laid the foundation of distinguished fame.'[27]

Hard on its heels, appeared *Scinde, or the Unhappy Valley*, and *Sindh, and the Races that Inhabit the Valley of the Indus*. The first was dedicated to Lt Col Walter Scott, the second, 'With Much Respect,' to the Honourable the Court of Directors of the East India Company. In view of Burton's later malicious remarks about the East India Company Directors, it is interesting to note not only the different tone, but the diametrically opposed view expressed here: 'In conclusion it may be remarked that the following pages might have long remained in the obscurity of MS had not they been drawn from it by the liberal patronage which the Court of Directors of the Honourable East India Company have ever been ready to extend to their servants.'[28]

It should also be noted, that there is no mention in his service records of his having submitted to the Court of Directors in 1851, 'certain remarks upon the subject of Anglo-Indian misrule,' the publication allegedly being 'refused with many threats.'[29] It is yet another example of Burton's concocting a tale, when the parties concerned were in no position to answer back.

The reviewer of *Goa* had recognised that Burton was 'by no means an ordinary observer or an ordinary seeker of adventures.' He was equally complimentary of his *Scinde*. While regretting that some of its pages were 'still at variance with the rules of good taste,' he praised the author for the diligence of his inquiries into the language, literature and conditions of the native population. At the same time, he was critical of Burton's views on questions of Eastern policy, particularly with regard to the treatment of natives. 'For a young man, he seems to have adopted some very extreme opinions, and it is perhaps not too much to say that the faults from which he has most to fear, is a disregard of those well-established rules of moderation which no one can transgress with impunity.' It was a highly perceptive judgement, which Burton would have done well to ponder.

Instead, stung by the reviewer's criticism of his extreme opinions, Burton appended a lengthy Postscript to his next book, *Falconry in the Valley of the Indus*. 'The greatest difficulty a raw writer on Indian subjects has to contend with,' he claimed, 'is a proper comprehension of the *ignorance crasse* which besets the mind of the home-reader and his oracle the critic.'[30] He then launched into an autobiographical account of his life, showing how his service in India had led him to form his 'estimate of the native character.'

The reviewer was distinctly unimpressed by Burton's provocative comments. 'It would be well,' he remarked urbanely, 'if authors when they are consciously angry – with or without cause – would have a great distrust of themselves – and this would have the first beneficial effect of leading them to inquire whether they really have cause or not. Mr Burton, however, while he wants the wit to see the wisdom of this, wants also we fear the wit – our readers shall be the judges – to have turned that wisdom to good account had he perceived it. In addition to the other most unlucky feature of his rejoinder – for his own sake, it is to be regretted that he defends himself with more of the pugnacity than the polish of his profession.' The reviewer concluded his crushing reply with the words: 'If he ever learns to reason – as well as to write – he will know better – and we can afford to give him ample leisure for acquiring that accomplishment.'[31]

Probably advised by Maria, Burton swallowed his pride and wrote a letter the following week to *The Athenaeum*, 'with great courtesy and excellent temper,' as the reviewer described it, explaining the reason for his 'Postscript.' Had he persevered in that approach, instead of indulging in his usual abrasive style of self-justification and personal insult, he would have saved himself many an unnecessary and bitter quarrel.

There were other examples, of course, of Burton's totally lacking in tact and patience. 'If people bored him,' Georgiana said, 'he would take up a book, or even leave the room with scant ceremony.' As a result, certain members of the English community crossed the road when they saw him approaching. On the other hand, she asserted, he had made many warm friends.

As for his health, 'Liver trouble, chest affections, internal inflammation prostrated him for many a weary hour during the earlier part of his furlough.' Despite suffering extreme pain, he showed amazing fortitude, 'often actually misleading the bystanders with respect to the gravity of the case.' Although some of the symptoms listed by Georgiana, especially his suffering severely from inflammation of the bladder, come close to fitting Burton's case, his illness had nothing whatever to do with, what she described as, the 'climate and hardships of India.' The first documentary evidence, a medical certificate, showing Burton's real condition, is dated 22 October 1851. Signed by Frederick Le Mesurier, MD, late Medical Inspector, South Madras, it reads:

> I certify that I have known Lieut. R.F. Burton, 18th Regiment Bombay N.I. for nearly twelve months. I have carefully examined him as to the state of his health, and I find that he has suffered severely from ophthalmia, stricture of the urethra, and enlarged testicle, and that the diseases and their necessary treatment have induced a degree of constitutional irritation which at present renders him unfit for Regimental duty. I have no hesitation in recommending that six months extension of leave be granted to him as being necessary.

This recommendation was endorsed by P.B. Lucas, FRCS, 58 Rue de l'Écu, Boulogne, who stated that he had been attending Burton for the last six months.[32]

Urethritis is the usual manifestation of an acute gonorrhoeal infection. Without effective treatment, unknown in Burton's time, this could lead, as it appears to have done in his case, to chronic urethritis with stricture of the urethra. This is a narrowing of the duct for urine and sperm, between the bladder and the head of the penis. The infection tends to spread. In the male, it may include the rear portion of the urethra, the prostate, and the seminal vesicles.

What is known as the epididymis, is the elongated coiled duct which provides for storage, transit, and maturation of spermatozoa. It begins in the testis and ends in the urethra. Gonococcal infection of the epididymis usually affects one side only of the duct and, to the examiner's feel, when infected and swollen, might commonly be described as an enlarged testicle. Involvement of the epididymides frequently leads to sterility, and could well account for Burton's later childless marriage. Gonorrhoea may also involve the conjunctiva of the eye, as it appears to have done in his case. Given his extremely painful condition, the amount of literary work that he was able to achieve in a relatively short time, is nothing short of astonishing. One may agree with Georgiana that, 'Pain rather stimulated than depressed the action of his powerful brain.'

Apart from his writing, Burton appears to have fenced regularly at an establishment run by Mon H. Constantin, at 3 place du Mont-a-Cardon, one of two Salle d'Armes in Boulogne at this time.[33] He was also keenly interested in the use of the bayonet, to the extent of its being something of a hobby-horse. In *Goa and the Blue Mountains*, he criticised what he described as 'new-fangled fashions' compelling the officers to be scientific instead of practical men. 'We moderns seem determined to discourage personal prowess, gymnastics, and the perpetual practice of weapons in which our forefathers took such pride. How many good men and true have been lost in the late wars in consequence of our neglecting to instruct them in the bayonet exercise.'[34] In a later book, he returned to this theme, claiming that 'The British is, and for years has been, the only army in Europe that does not learn the use of this weapon.'[35]

While at Boulogne, he prepared a short monograph on the subject entitled *A Complete System of Bayonet Exercise*, now one of Burton's rarest books. Lady Burton declared, typically, that like all he did, it was undervalued at the time, 'but still it has long been the one used by the Horseguards.' Obviously ignorant as to the identity of Col Sykes, she said that he sent for Burton, and 'sharply rebuked him with printing a book that would do far more harm than good. It was thought that bayonet exercise would make the men unsteady in the ranks.'[36]

Burton's bibliographer, Norman Penzer, even went so far as to claim that it 'forms one of the most important books on the bayonet ever published, and to it can be traced the change in the systems of bayonet drill adopted in most European countries. I believe I am correct in saying that until about ten years ago it was impossible to find any work on the subject which was not based on Burton's work. Large numbers of it were purchased by foreign army authorities (particularly German).'[37]

In fact, his assertion is copied almost verbatim, and without acknowledgement, from a letter sent to him by a Burton collector, Oscar Eckenstein, in 1920. Interestingly, it runs completely counter to Penzer's original estimate of the *Bayonet Exercise*, as almost worthless.[38]

In the opinion of a leading expert on the subject of edged weapons, one should be sceptical of any statement suggesting that any one person 'invented' a bayonet exercise. 'As soon as bayonets were adopted,' he says, 'soldiers must have practised and exercised with them, although the early exercises were not written down. Burton was certainly not the first person to publish a bayonet exercise, or to describe how bayonets should be used in battle. Probably the earliest such exercise is that by A. Gordon, *A Treatise on the Science of Defence for the Sword, Bayonet and Pike in Close Action* (London, 1805).'[39]

Too coincidental to be accidental, in my view, is that Burton's book was published in the same year as one by Henry Angelo IVth, of the famous fencing dynasty, who became head of the Academy in St James's Street in 1852. It may well be that Burton, who probably fenced at the Academy when in London, got to hear that Henry Angelo was proposing to write a manual on the bayonet for the British Army. He, therefore, decided to write one himself hoping to have it accepted. Whatever Burton's knowledge of that weapon, he could not compete with Angelo, who was a professional fencing instructor. Although Burton sent in his monograph, it was Angelo's work which duly appeared in 1853, 'Authorised by the Adjutant-General's Office, Horse Guards.'[40]

If we are to believe Georgiana, Burton, a handsome and powerfully magnetic man, had a great many love affairs at this time. Well aware of her brother's eccentric views and roving temperament, Maria encouraged 'only the most promising.' It was a brief flirtation, however, at Boulogne, with a young convent-educated girl, Isabel Arundell, which led Burton a decade later, into a singular marriage.

The Arundells of Wardour were a very old Norman family, settled in the West country since around the middle of the thirteenth century. Their name derived from the French *hirondelle*, meaning swallow, six swallows forming part of the family's coat of arms. Despite the similarity in spelling, the Arundells had no connection whatever with the Howards, holders of the Dukedom of Norfolk and the Earldom of Arundel in Sussex.

Isabel's father, Henry Raymond Arundell, was born on 27 June 1799, at Bathford in Somerset. He grew up, however, at Ashcombe Hall in the parish of Berwick St John, situated among the rolling chalk downs and wooded valleys of south Wiltshire. The estate had been bought in 1763 by Henry, 8th Baron Arundell of Wardour. It then appears to have been taken on a long lease by Henry Raymond's paternal grandfather, James Everard, the third and youngest son of Henry, the 6th Baron.[41]

The estate lay only a few miles to the south-east of Wardour Castle. The original fourteenth century fortress had been almost totally destroyed during the Civil War. Although retaining the name, the new Wardour Castle was, in fact, an enormous Palladian mansion, built for Henry, 8th Lord Arundell, between 1770-76. The west wing, as well as containing suites for guests, housed a large ornate Roman Catholic chapel. It was probably here that Henry Raymond's family regularly worshipped. It is equally likely that it was from its attendant Jesuit priest that he received his early education.

At the age of fifteen, Henry, like his older cousin, James Everard, later the 10th Baron, was sent to Stonyhurst College, the palatial Jesuit foundation at Hurst Green, near Clitheroe in north-east Lancashire. Since the universities of Oxford and Cambridge were closed to Catholics, Stonyhurst offered an advanced academic course on completion of the normal school curriculum. Lay pupils, therefore, were able to spend a further two years studying philosophy, which formed the first part of the Jesuit seminary training. It appears that Henry took advantage of this opportunity for further study, not leaving Stonyhurst until 1 September 1818, when he was aged nineteen.

Among his contemporaries at the school were the two sons of Sir William Gerard, 11th Bt, John, his much younger brother, Robert Tolver, together with William, grandson of the 9th Bt.[42] The Gerards of Garswood Hall, Ashton-in-Makerfield, Newton-le-Willows, were a very wealthy local family, Lords of the Manor of Windle (now St Helens), and owning estates in Billinge, Ashton, Bryn, their old place of residence, and many other local areas. Among their many friends in the county were members of the Stanley family, Earls of Derby, seated at Knowsley Hall.

It was possibly as a result of an invitation to Garswood Hall, that Henry Arundell first became acquainted with John Gerard's younger sister, Eliza, later to become his second wife. In 1816, aged ten, she was sent to New Hall School at Boreham in Essex, leaving there six years later. Like Stonyhurst, the school had its roots on the continent, a young English girl of nineteen, Susan Hawley, founding the first monastery of English Canonesses of the Holy Sepulchre at Liège in 1642.[43]

In 1819, Mary Isabella, the second daughter of Sir Thomas Hugh Clifford Constable, of Burton Constable Hall in east Yorkshire, joined the school. Although some three or four years older than Eliza, and only to spend a year at New Hall, the two became close and long-standing friends. It may be supposed that it was through Henry Arundell's close ties with members of the Gerard family, that he was eventually introduced to Mary Isabella. A romance blossomed and they were married on 27 September 1827.

Death cast an ever-present shadow over the child-bed at this period. On 2 October 1828, three months after giving birth to a son, Mary Isabella died, probably from puerperal fever. After her death, the young widower, as Isabel Burton later wrote, 'only found consolation talking to my mother of his lost wife. From sympathy grew pity, from pity grew love.' In April 1830, only eighteen months after the death of his first wife, Henry married Eliza Gerard. Obviously regarding this as somewhat too short an interval, Isabel, in her account, doubled it to three years.

Accepting an invitation from Henry's cousin, James Everard, now 10th Lord Arundell, the couple lived for a time immediately following their marriage, in a wing of Wardour Castle.[44] Her parents then moved into a house in Montagu Place, Bryanston Square, London, following Lord Arundell's death. This could hardly be the case, since James Everard died at Rome in 1834. By then, Isabel, born on 20 March 1831 at 4 Great Cumberland Place, was already three years old.[45] She is similarly misleading in claiming that she was named Isabel after her father's first wife. As we have seen, her correct name was Mary Isabella, and it was this second name she was given at her christening. For whatever reason, it was a name Isabel disliked intensely. She never owned to it, and only used it when required to do so in official documents.

Primogeniture may well have been responsible for all the halls, villas and walled parks, rivalling 'the splendour of royal seats,' enthused over by the American, Ralph Waldo Emerson, during his visits to England in 1833 and 1847. It was a system of inheritance, however, which left the majority of the younger sons of the aristocracy and gentry in relatively poor circumstances, forced to find whatever means they could to support themselves and their families. This was the situation presently facing Henry Arundell, himself the descendant of younger sons.

Henry appears to have had no ambition to enter one of the great professions, now open to Catholics as a result of various government statutes.[46] Instead, in 1835, after the birth of his fourth child, Blanche, he went into business with his younger brother, Renfric, as a wine-merchant at 60 Mount Street on the Grosvenor Estate.[47] The occupation of vinter was a genteel enough one and could be, financially, very rewarding. It made John Ruskin's father extremely wealthy, able to send his son to Christ Church, Oxford, as a gentleman-commoner in 1836.

Unlike Renfric, Henry never seems to have come to terms with being forced to earn his living in trade, apparently regarding it as tantamount to being a blot on the Arundell escutcheon.[48] Isabel was guilty of the same kind of snobbery, anxious to give the impression that her father was a leisured man of means. In the more than two thousand pages of *The Life* and *The Romance*, there is not a single reference to the family business. It was left to her niece, Georgiana Stisted, to publicise the fact, with malice aforethought, in her so-called *True Life*.

Early on in 1841, the Arundells moved from London, taking a ten-year lease on Furze Hall at Ingatestone in the county of Essex. After Freyerning Hall, it was the oldest house of any size in the parish, quite the cream of the neighbourhood as one local remarked to a later tenant.[49] Isabel described it as, 'a white, straggling, old-fashioned, half cottage, half farm-house, built by bits, about a hundred yards from the road, from which it was completely hidden by trees.' Standing in extensive gardens, and situated in picturesque undulating countryside dotted with farms and covered with woodland, it provided an idyllic situation for the Arundells' growing family.

On 3 June of that year, after tearful farewells to her brothers and sisters, Isabel was driven the dozen or so miles to New Hall School, Boreham, 2 miles north-east of Chelmsford, to begin her schooling.[50] The annual cost of full board per pupil was £47.00, reduced to £40.00 if two or more children of a family attended at the same time. Of course, the expenses did not stop there, as entries in the account-books reveal: a pair of gloves, for example, costing 1/11d; 2 yards of black ribbon 1/4d; a beaver bonnet, 9/6d; 3 pairs of gloves, 5/9d; a pair of shoes, 6/6d.

While Henry Arundell initially settled the bills by means of bank notes and gold, he found it increasingly difficult to do so with the passing of time. Lacking the ready money, he came to a novel arrangement with the school, giving a whole new meaning to cash-flow problems and liquid assets. An entry in the account-book for 3 July 1842-31 March following, shows credit of £21 3s being allowed for wine, the balance of £11 11s 8d being paid in April by 6 gallons of brandy. Other entries for that and later years show credit allowed for further amounts of brandy and sherry. One bill for £19 17s 4d in 1845 was settled with a pipe of port, that is a cask, usually containing 105 gallons. Precisely how the community's sisters eventually disposed of this large quantity of alcohol can only be a matter for speculation.

According to Isabel, she left New Hall when she was sixteen. 'In one sense my leaving school so early,' she wrote, 'was a misfortune; I was just at an age when one begins to understand and love one's studies. I ought to have been kept at the convent, or sent to some foreign school; but both my mother and father wanted me at home with them.' In fact, Isabel left the school on 24 July 1846, when she had just turned fifteen, and the real reason for her departure was that her continued education with Blanche now at the school and a growing family, was proving too great a drain on the household's finances. Besides, a considerable sum of money now needed putting aside to meet the high cost of Isabel's eventual 'coming out.'

If Isabel is to be believed, her return home left her with a great deal of time on her hands, much of which she passed in the woods, reading and contemplating. Whether she enjoyed as much leisure as she claimed is a moot point. Eighteen year old, Theodore, was living at home, having completed his education at Stonyhurst.[51] Another girl, Emmeline Mary, had been born in 1843. Now, Isabel's mother was pregnant yet again with a fourth daughter, Elizabeth Mary Regis, born in 1847.

In March of that year, Disraeli's *Tancred; or the New Crusade*, was published, the last in the trilogy of his 'Young England' novels. Despite its attracting a great deal of hostile criticism, Disraeli told Benjamin Jowett many years later that, of all his novels, *Tancred* was his favourite. After reading it, the Society hostess, Lady Blessington, praised the author for having 'made me comprehend the East better than all the books I have ever read on it.' This was Isabel's experience. 'Disraeli's *Tancred* and similar occult books were my favourite, she wrote, 'but *Tancred*, with its glamour of the East, was the chief of them, and I used to think out after a fashion my future life, and try to solve great problems.'

Isabel was also attracted by 'gypsies, Bedawin Arabs, and everything Eastern and mystic, and especially about a wild and lawless life.' If any Romany gypsies happened to be camping in the vicinity, she would pass an hour or so around the camp-fire in their company. She was particularly drawn to Hagar Burton, 'a tall, slender, handsome, refined woman,' who called her Daisy. At their final meeting at Ingatestone, Hagar, obviously a skilled practitioner in the art of reading character and extracting relevant information, cast Isabel's horoscope. As translated from the Romany by her, the most important part of it for Isabel ran:

> You will cross the sea and be in the same town with your Destiny and know it not. Every obstacle will rise up against you, and such a combination of circumstances, that it will require all your courage, energy and intelligence to meet them.....but God will be with you, so you will always win...You will bear the name of our tribe, and be right proud of it....Your life is all wandering, change, and adventure. One soul in two bodies in life and death, never long apart...[52]

After moving back to London for her first season, probably some time late in 1849, she made her *début* the following year at a fancy ball at Almack's. Established by William Almack in 1765, these assembly rooms in King Street, St James, were at the centre of late eighteenth century social life for the rich, and remained so well into the next century. 'At the present time,' wrote Captain R.H. Gronow, 'one can hardly conceive the importance which was attached to Almack's, the seventh heaven of the fashionable world.'[53] It was also a matrimonial bazaar. While Isabel was happy enough to join in various activities with a number of eligible young men, marriage, however, was not an option. 'Mothers considered me crazy, and almost insolent,' she wrote, 'because I was not ready to snap at any good *parti*; and I have seen dukes' daughters gladly accept men that poor humble I would have turned up my nose at.'

On the other hand, the French literary and art critic, Hippolyte Taine, a keen observer of the mid-Victorian scene, observed that, 'A young English girl will not marry unless through inclination; she weaves a romance for herself, and this dream forms part of her pride, of her chastity...' This was certainly the case with Isabel. Her ideal, written down at the time in her diary, so she assured her readers, but bearing all the hallmarks of its being composed largely, if not wholly, *post factum*,

> 'had protected me and kept me from fulfilling the vocation of my sex – breeding fools and chronicling small

beer.[54] My ideal is about six feet in height; he has not an ounce of fat on him; he has broad and muscular shoulders, a powerful, deep chest; he is a Hercules of manly strength. He has black hair, a brown complexion, a clever forehead, sagacious eye-brows, large black, wondrous eyes – those strange eyes you dare not take yours off them. He is a soldier and a *man*; he is accustomed to command and to be obeyed......[55]

The season over, and strict economy called for, the Arundells gave up their London residence and sailed for Boulogne. After a slow climb up the steep Grand Rue, their carriage eventually rumbled through the Porte des Dunes, one of four towered gateways into the Haute Ville, and drew up outside 4 Rue des Basse Chambres. The street has since been renamed the Rue de Pressy, after an eighteenth-century Bishop of Boulogne. The narrow, cobbled thoroughfare, however, with its tall terraced houses with painted shutters, and attics lit by dormer windows reminiscent of large dog-kennels, remains essentially unchanged.'If this were but 300 miles farther off,' wrote Charles Dickens, who took a house at Boulogne during the summer of 1853, 'how the English would rave about it! I do assure you that there are picturesque people, and town, and country, about this place. that quite fill up the eye and fancy.'[56] For Isabel, initially, at least, Boulogne, especially after the glitter and excitement of the London season, was a sad let-down. Gradually, however, she and her younger sister, Blanche, became reconciled to what they called their European Botany Bay.

Much of their time was spent studying French, music and other accomplishments at the adjoining Sacré Coeur convent. By way of diversion, they were often allowed to walk along the tree-lined Ramparts to do their reading. This was varied by daily strolls at the fashionable hour with their mother down the Grande Rue, and along the Rue de l'Écu and the Quai, to the end of the Pier. The liveliest establishment in the town, a sort of Casino, and a hot-bed of mouth-watering gossip and flirtation, was strictly out of bounds. It was all very decorous, and thoroughly boring. Things were shortly to change. One day when Isabel and Blanche were walking on the Ramparts, 'the vision of my awakening brain came towards us.' Dressed in a black, short, shaggy coat, and shouldering a short cane, he was everything she had imagined, in height and appearance, including the 'large, black flashing eyes with long lashes, that pierced one through and through.' He gave her a short, penetrating stare, as if reading her thoughts. Isabel was magnetised. A little further on, she turned to her sister, and whispered, "That man will marry me."

Burton was there again the following day, this time following in their footsteps. Armed with a piece of chalk, he wrote on the wall , "May I speak with you?" Isabel, having glanced behind, took up the chalk which he had left on the wall, and wrote back, "No, mother will be angry." Unfortunately, 'mother found it, and was angry.' The result was that greater restraints were placed on their movements. To anyone familiar with the breadth and extent of the stone wall bordering the Ramparts of the Haute Ville, Isabel's account of Mrs Arundell's finding a chalked message somewhere along its considerable length, let alone recognising it as belonging to her eldest daughter, will sound pretty far-fetched. But this is to spoil a good story.

At their next meeting, again on the Ramparts, Burton was not only escorting but seriously flirting with the pretty daughter of a cousin of her father. Having been formally introduced, Isabel started at his name. 'Like a flash came back to me the prophecy of Hagar Burton......And again I thrilled through and through.' Too shy to do so herself, Isabel left it to her cousin to ask Burton to write something for her at the time. He did so, and thereafter she wore the piece of paper next to her heart. This same cousin also gave a tea party and dance at which Burton was present, 'like a star among rushlights!' She kept the sash where he had put his arm around her waist to waltz, and the gloves that his hand had held, and never wore them again.

Although not commented on by Isabel, her mother had given birth at Boulogne to, what proved to be, her last child. Weak, perhaps, after so many pregnancies, the baby, Raymond Ignatius, failed to thrive. He died on 27 March 1852, and his mother's spirit probably died with him. Meanwhile, political events in France had taken a turn for the worse. Three months earlier, on 2 December 1851, Napoleon's nephew,

Charles-Louis Napoleon Bonaparte, later Napoleon III, staged a *coup d'état*. On 4 December, his only opponents, the Republicans, were defeated in street fighting in Paris, as they were in other towns and in some regions. Thousands of arrests and deportations followed.

There was great popular excitement in Boulogne, where some eighteen hundred soldiers had been billeted. Foreign reaction to the *coup d'état* had, on the whole, been favourable. It was roundly condemned, however, in the independent press of Britain and Belgium. This resulted in some minor acts of hostility towards the English in Boulogne, as elsewhere. The Arundells had their windows broken on several occasions, and their pet dog was killed.

9 May 1852 was fixed for their return home, all agreeing 'that anything in London would be preferable to Boulogne.' Unwilling to add to her pain, Isabel decided against saying goodbye to Burton. It was the early hours of the morning when the steam-packet left for Folkestone. While Isabel's family went down to their berths, she remained on deck, intent on watching the town for as long as she could see its lights, 'for after all it contained all I wanted, and who [sic] I thought I should never see more.'

CHAPTER TEN

HEART-BEGUILING ARABY

On 24 May 1852, Sir Roderick Murchison in his Presidential Address to the Royal Geographical Society in London,[1] touched on a matter which was soon to have a profound effect on Burton's life and career: the breakdown in negotiations which had recently taken place between Dr Georg August Wallin of Finland, and the Imperial Geographical Society of St Petersburg, for a long-term exploration of the Arabian peninsula.

Dr Wallin, professor of Oriental Literature at Helsinki University, had already completed two important journeys in Arabia by the time Burton had returned to England in 1849.[2] The interest they had aroused among leading members of the RGS, resulted in personal discussions with the explorer in London and, later, by correspondence.[3] As a result, it became 'the anxious desire of the Council,' Sir Roderick explained, 'to enable this profound scholar to revisit Arabia for a series of years, and there to obtain a deeper insight into the real condition of very large interior tracts still entirely unknown to the civilized world.'

Finland at that time was a Russian grand-duchy.[4] Faced with the problem of financing such an ambitious programme, the London Society approached its younger counterpart in St Petersburg with plans for a joint venture. It was delighted with the response of its President, the Grand Duke Constantine.[5] For a while, everything appeared to be going smoothly. By the end of 1851, however, as a result of financial misunderstandings, negotiations between Dr Wallin and the Imperial Society were broken off, and the Finnish explorer, bitterly disappointed, returned to his own country.

Despite this set-back, Sir Roderick Murchison viewed the project as being only temporarily suspended. He continued to hope that it would be still be possible, with the help of the Government and the East India Company, which had shown an interest, to finance an expedition into the interior of Arabia. 'Dr Wallin was,' he claimed, 'a child of the desert, and perhaps the only European perfectly qualified by training and knowledge to dispel our ignorance of a land so interesting to the earliest history of mankind.'[6] It was an opinion he was shortly to revise.

By October, doubtless because Maria and the children had returned to England, and his mother to Lucca, Burton relinquished the apartment in the Rue des Pipots, and took a smaller set of rooms at 1, Rue d'Aumont, inside the Haute Ville. His health showed few signs of improvement. Although his ophthalmia appears to have cleared up, Dr Lucas's report, dated 18 October, testified to a return of the painful urethral stricture and swelling of Burton's left testicle. A further six months' extension of leave was recommended, 'for the perfect cure of both these affections,' as Dr Lucas optimistically put it.[7]

Shortly afterwards, Burton came to London. Besides being examined by the East India Company's own physician, who fully endorsed Dr Lucas's opinion,[8] Burton made a contact of far-reaching importance. This was with Major-General Monteith, a retired Company officer, and a founder member of the Royal Geographical Society.[9] Burton did not disclose when, or how, this meeting took place. It resulted, however, in Burton's offering his services to the Society, in place of Dr Wallin, to explore in Arabia. Wheels were now set in motion for him to meet some of its leading members.

Besides Sir Roderick Murchison, there was Capt W.H. Smyth, a former President of the Society, Dr Norton Shaw, and Col W.H. Sykes. Shaw, the dynamic Assistant Secretary, fluent in Swedish, having conducted the correspondence with Wallin, was familiar with every detail of the earlier plans.[10] Sykes, keenly interested in seeing an accurate map of Arabia drawn up, not only sat on the RGS Council, but was also a Director of the East India Company. It was probably Sykes who had been responsible for the EIC's interest in the scheme.[11]

Burton, of course, was already known to Sykes, personally, and through his books, as a highly intelligent officer, an acute observer, and a brilliant linguist. The 'Postcript' to Burton's most recent publication, *Falconry in the Valley of the Indus*, had fortuitously revealed another talent: the ability to disguise himself so effectively as an Oriental, that he had been able to move around easily and unsuspected in native Sindian circles. Here was a man, Sykes was convinced, and he must have had little difficulty in convincing the others, who could successfully pick up the mantle Dr Wallin had so recently, and unfortunately, laid down. Briefed, therefore, as to his future course of action, Burton returned to Boulogne.

Having, for whatever reason, given up his rooms in the Haute Ville, Burton temporarily booked into the Hotel de Paris, close to the harbour. There, he penned a brief statement of his intentions which the Committee on Expeditions could formally consider at its meeting later that month. 'I propose,' he wrote, 'to explore the country extending from Muskat to Aden, especially Shakr and Hadramaut. I wish particularly to trace the ancient cities of Himyar, and to travel as far inland as circumstances permit.' Enclosing a covering letter, and a long list of questions addressed to Dr Wallin, Burton despatched it to Dr Norton Shaw by the next packet-steamer.[12]

A day or two later, he found himself new lodgings at 2, Rue Neuve Chausée, located at a convenient distance from Dr Lucas's surgery. Possibly armed with a letter of introduction from Col Sykes, Burton called on Lt Col James Outram, then relaxing in Boulogne before returning to England to attend the Duke of Wellington's funeral. Outram, until recently British Resident at Baroda, had run foul of the Bombay Government for his outspoken criticism of the bribery and corruption endemic there. In spite of this display of official displeasure, Sykes must have felt that support from Outram, admired throughout India as a soldier and administrator, would carry weight in recommending Burton's plans to the Company.

Despite there being no urgency, Burton decided to waste no time in writing a formal letter to the Court, outlining his scheme and requesting permission to carry it out. Before considering what he wrote, it would be as well to recall his declared aims, set out very summarily at the beginning of his book. 'Through the medium of General Monteith,' he wrote, 'I offered my services to the Royal Geographical Society of London, for the purpose of removing that opprobrium to modern adventure, the huge white blot which in our maps still notes the eastern and central regions of Arabia.' This may now be compared with the main substance of his long letter, dated Friday, 6 November 1852:

My furlough expiring in April prox. I am desirous when permitted to return to India, of making myself in some way useful to the promotion of science. No traveller, I believe, has ever penetrated into the interior of that part of Arabia, which extends from Muskat to Aden, including the provinces of Shayr and Shakr, Hazramaut the Region of frankincense, and the Himyaritic land of ancient fame. The meagre details which I have gathered from various sources, leads me to suppose that the long belt of mountains which lines the coast is intersected by rich and fertile valleys which support large and powerful tribes.

Should the Honourable the Court of Directors think proper to grant me permission to explore that interesting region, I would use my best endeavours to make as accurate a survey of it as circumstances will permit.
I could also ascertain the nature and extent of its resources, and attempt to remove the obstructions which the
ignorance or the apathy of the natives may have opposed to the establishment of direct commercial relations
with the Western coast of our Indian Empire. Finally, I might investigate the Natural History of this
Unknown Region, define the limits of that vast tract described by "Great Sandy Desert" in our maps, compile
an extensive vocabulary of the Mahri or modern Himyaritic dialect, and I doubt not that ethnographical
details of an interesting description will result from my labours.

Burton then listed his qualifications for this scientific expedition: eight years devoted to the study of
Oriental manners, customs and literature;[13] almost four years' service with the Scinde Survey, and an ability
to sketch, model, and speak the Arabic language. He had besides, 'a superficial knowledge of medicine,' and
the necessary strength for travelling in wild country. Although anticipating some difficulty in carrying out
the project, he foresaw little danger since his plan was to disguise himself as a petty trader and physician.
'Moreover, I doubt not, ' he wrote, 'I should be mistaken for an Arab even in the midst of Mecca.'
Promising to avoid the politically unstable areas around Aden and Ras El-Khamal, Burton closed by
quoting Dr Carter's opinion that he should 'find few obstacles to success.'[14]

The letter outlines a bold and audacious plan. What is equally striking, is that it bears little or no resemblance to what appeared later in print. Not only did Burton suppress every single aspect of this projected
journey, with one exception, he subtly relocated the area to be explored: southern and south-eastern Arabia
in his letter, eastern and central Arabia in his book. There, briefly expanding on his professed aims, he
wrote, 'I had intended had the period of leave originally applied for been granted, to land at Muscat – a
favourable starting place – and there to apply myself, slowly and surely to the task of spanning the deserts.'
Only in this one respect may the letter and the book be said to share a common factor, though even here
there is equivocation. Spanning the deserts means quite plainly to cross them, and it has always been
assumed that Burton's intention was to pioneer a trail across the vast and trackless wastes of the Rub'a al-
Khali, the 'Empty Quarter.' In his letter, however, he merely states his wish to 'define the limits,' an aim far
more easily realized, one might suppose, by skirting its boundaries. Furthermore, as can be seen, Burton
made no official request for leave in this letter.

There can be little doubt that most, if not all, of Burton's aims were formulated for him by Dr Shaw
and Col Sykes, parties to the late negotiations with Dr Wallin. The Society's interest in South Arabia,
geographically a *terra incognita*, but with a rich and tumultuous history, was one of long-standing. It is
clearly apparent in a letter written to Wallin in November 1851 by Dr Shaw.[15] After taking care to assure
the rather prickly explorer that the Council had no wish to tie him down with regulations, feeling that such
'a learned and enterprising traveller' should be allowed to exercise his own judgement, Shaw continued
rather magisterially, 'It appears to me very desirable that the province of Hadramaut should form one of the
objects of your mission.'

Although much of the South Arabian coastline had been surveyed by officers of the Indian Navy,[16]
little was known about the interior. This was mainly due to the well-deserved reputation of its inhabitants
for religious fanaticism and xenophobia. The deepest penetration of Hadramaut had been made in 1843 by a
German explorer, Adolphe Baron von Wrede. However, at Seef, von Wrede had been dragged from his
camel, manhandled, and locked up as an English spy. He was lucky to escape with his life.[17]

Burton's supposed interest in the Himyaritic dialect and the region's ethnology, can also be traced to
Shaw's letter to Dr Wallin. After recommending the province of Hadramaut for exploration, he wrote, 'and

that next to the Geography of Arabia, its Ethnology and Philology ought to be carefully examined.' Unlike Burton, Wallin was an explorer who was also an academic, with a specialist knowledge in comparative linguistics. His friendship with Fulgence Fresnel, the French consul at Jeddah, who was among the first to devote serious study to the Himyaritic script, had whetted Wallin's desire to do the same.[18] He also wanted to travel into Mahra in the north-east of Hadramaut, to examine Fresnel's theory – which, in Burton's letter, appears an established fact – that the language spoken there was a dialect of ancient Himyaritic. In spite of the enormous range of Burton's interests, however, there is nothing which suggests that he had any more than a passing interest in the South Arabian script, or the pre-Islamic civilisation of the region.

On 15 November, after Burton's proposal was read and discussed by the RGS's Committee on Expeditions, which included Sir Roderick Murchison and Col W.H. Sykes, a recommendation was made to the Council that, 'the negotiations with Dr. Wallin for this purpose having failed on account of the demand of that learned traveller for the sum of £400 per annum during six years, the attention of the Hon the Court of Directors of the East India Company be invited to Lieut. Burton's proposition, with the hope that he may be permitted to carry out his proposal on his return to India, with full pay, and without loss of time during his absence.'[19]

This recommendation received the strong support of Sir Roderick Murchison. On 22 December, he followed it with a long letter to the Company, stating that 'it is the opinion of the Council of the Royal Geographical Society, that Lieutenant Burton who has expressed a desire to be employed in exploring the interior of the southern portion of Arabia, is singularly well-qualified to execute such a task...' After covering the same ground as Burton in his application, Murchison reminded the Directors of their former support for the scheme, pointing out in a postscript, that, 'The perfectly successful exploration of Northern Arabia by Professor Wallin during a series of years and his return to his native country in good health, are the best proofs that no unnecessary risks will be incurred by any traveller who is well-versed in the language and habits of the natives.'[20] Ironically, unknown to Murchison and the rest of the explorer's friends in London at the time, Wallin, shortly after returning to Finland from St Petersburg, had died from a heart attack on the eve of his forty-first birthday.

After being awarded his Brevet de Point in Boulogne on December 15, Burton returned to England to spend Christmas with his sister and relatives. Enjoying his newly-won status as Maître d'Armes, he must also have looked forward to an equally successful conclusion to his application to the East India Company Directors.

Business at East India House, suspended over the holiday period, resumed soon afterwards. According to Burton's published account, a deputation consisting of Sir Roderick Murchison, Col P. Yorke, and Dr Norton Shaw 'honoured me by warmly supporting in a personal interview with the chairman of the Honourable the Court of Directors to the East India Company, my application for three years' leave of absence on special duty from India to Muscat. But they were unable to prevail upon Sir James Hogg, who, remembering the fatalities which of late years have befallen sundry soldier-travellers, refused his sanction, alleging as a reason that the contemplated journey was of too dangerous a nature.'[21] This is not an accurate representation of events, nor one that is fair to the chairman of the Company.

In the first place, Sir Roderick and his colleagues met not only with Sir James, but also with the vice-chairman, Mr Russell Ellice. Furthermore, and of far greater significance, Sir James Hogg, whatever his personal feelings towards the proposed venture, could not have 'refused his sanction.' The Court of Directors was the executive body of the Company, possessing plenary powers and authority, subject only to the supervision and, if necessary, the directives of the Government Board of Control. Sir James Hogg did not even possess the right of veto over Committee or Court decisions, though, it may be safely assumed, his views and recommendations would be closely listened to.

What really happened was a far more involved process than Burton's simplistic, and deliberately misleading, account suggests. His letter and accompanying testimonials of 6 November, were first laid before the Revenue, Judicial, and Legislative Committee, by the Court of Directors for its consideration. A draft reply, ready by the end of December, was approved at a meeting of the Committee on 5 January 1853. The Court of Directors then gave its formal assent, and it was finally passed to the Board of Control for its official sanction.[22]

On 20 January, almost identically-worded letters were sent to Burton and Sir Roderick Murchison.[23] Permission was refused. In line with its normal policy, no explanation was given, no expression of regret offered. So, why was Burton's application turned down, backed as it was by such a prestigious body as the Royal Geographical Society, headed by Sir Roderick Murchison one of the most distinguished and influential men of his day?

The reason, or reasons, can only be conjectured. It may well be that the overriding consideration was the dangerous nature of the enterprise. Financial considerations may also have figured highly in its decision . Since the Company was being asked to dip its hand into its pocket for this venture, it was entitled to look for a worthwhile return on its investment. One may assume that it found Burton's commercial argument unconvincing.

To compensate for his disappointment, Burton claimed that he was allowed an additional year's furlough, 'in order to pursue my Arabic studies in lands where the language is best learned.'[24] The documentary evidence, however, throws a somewhat different light on this assertion. Probably through Col Sykes, Burton got wind of the Court's decision at some stage before it received final approval, allowing him sufficient time to formulate a contingency plan. Nothing, if not resourceful, he wrote the following masterly piece of improvisation to the Military Secretary at East India House, dated 19 January, the day *before* the letters of refusal were sent:

Sir,

With reference to the extension of leave granted to me by the Honourable Court of Directors, which will expire on the 28th of April, 1853, I have the honour to request the Court's permission to return to my duty in India. But having occupied myself with the study of Arabic, I feel desirous of mastering the Egyptian accent and literature of that peculiar idiom, for which purpose I have the honour to apply to the Court for leave to remain some little time in Egypt, being careful to reach India within the Parliamentary limits of an officer's continuous leave of absence from his duty.[25]

Burton also sent a note to Col Sykes telling him that he was sending the letter that day, and asking him to be kind enough to back it.[26] It is to be presumed that Sykes alone, among the EIC Directors, was aware that exploration in Arabia was the real purpose in mind. Or, as Burton expressed it somewhat egocentrically in his book, 'to prove by trial, that what might be perilous to other travellers is safe to me.' The crucial test was to be 'a visit to El Hejaz, at once the most dangerous point by which a European can enter Arabia.'

Since he was officially sick until the end of April, it now became imperative for him, just as officially, to be declared well. A Dr John Scott was found, living at 13 Shalton Street who, having 'carefully examined Lt. R.F. Burton,' discovered most fortunately, that he was 'in a fit condition of health for returning to his military duty in India.'[27] All that remained was to see if the Directors would be willing to grant yet another extension of leave.

In a terse statement received just over a fortnight later, Burton was granted a further six months, but warned that, if he failed to reach his Presidency on, or before, the end of March, 1854, he would be out of the service.[28] Burton immediately dashed off a note to Dr Norton Shaw telling him the good news. Although obliged to travel to Bristol that weekend, he would be back in town on Monday. 'Have spoken to Sykes and Sir Roderick about Committee,' he added. 'Abandon myself to you and Providence.'[29]

On 7 February, the Committee on Expeditions met, and invited Burton to draw up a proposal in writing in order to lay it before the Council. His principal object as expressed later in his book was, 'To cross the unknown Arabian Peninsula in a direct line from either El-Medinah to Muscat, or diagonally from Meccah to Makalla on the Indian Ocean.' It should come as no surprise at this stage, to find that this does not accord with the plan read and considered by the Council at the time. Quite plainly and straightforwardly it was, 'to join the Egyptian caravan from Cairo, and to penetrate via Medina and Mecca, through the province of Hadramaut to the southern coast of Arabia, upon receiving from the Council the sum of £200.'[30] In view of Burton's later prevarications, these, his real intentions, need to be kept firmly in mind.

A final meeting of the Committee, chaired by Sir Roderick Murchison, was held on 10 March 1853. Those present included Sir Woodbine Parish, Sir John Gardner Wilkinson, Col P. York, Lt Raper, RN, and Burton himself. The Minutes recording this meeting are worth quoting in full:

> Lieut. Burton's offer of 'proceeding via Egypt, join the Damascus Caravan, visit Medina and Mecca, and thence to pass through the Province of Hadramaut to the Southern Coast of Arabia on receiving from the Council the sum of £200,' having again been taken into consideration, it was:
>
> 1st. resolved that, in "in accordance with the Resolution of Council of the 14th of February, the sum of £100 be paid to Lieut. Burton, to enable him to complete his outfit and to reach Arabia."
>
> 2.   "That Lieut. Burton be further empowered to draw on the Society for another £100 and no more from any port in southern Arabia where he may have occasion for it."
>
> 3.   The above resolution having been read to Lieut. Burton was agreed by him, and Lieut. Burton explained to the Committee the methods he proposed to pursue in order to render his travels in Arabia successful."
>
> 4.   Lieut. Burton having next repeated that he intended to set out on his journey from England on the 4th of April this year, and that he would avail himself of every safe opportunity of communicating the results to the Society, the Committee adjourned.[31]

Once more, Burton was the heir of Dr. Wallin. As Sir Roderick Murchison had pointed out the previous year, the Society had no funds of its own to finance the Finnish explorer's expedition. It could only afford to contribute £200, half of which had been advanced by the Government, and the other half by the East India Company.[32] The Society, however, had offered to supplement this by supplying Wallin with a free passage, passports, and protection. In view of the time and expense involved, Wallin was inclined to regard this offer as almost derisory. Burton, on the other hand, with only ten months or so at his disposal, and a far less ambitious programme, was well-entitled to describe it as a liberal provision.[33]

Sir Woodbine Parish advised that an order should be made out on the Society's bankers. Sir Roderick even offered to give one on his own, Coutts & Co. Burton declined both suggestions. 'I, having more experience in Oriental travelling,' he wrote, 'begged only to be furnished with a diminutive piece of paper permitting me to draw upon the Society.'[34] This, provided later by Shaw, was made as small as possible in order to fit into a talisman case.

By choosing to travel to the Hadramaut via Mecca, Burton undoubtedly hoped to place his credentials as a devout Muslim beyond reproach. As a *bona fide* pilgrim, he would then be in a position of far greater safety among the fanatical inhabitants of the southern Arabian province. He also regarded the 'revered title' as probably being of great use to him when wandering among Muslim races elsewhere.[35]

The choice of entering the Hedjaz from Egypt was, seemingly, far from ideal. Fresnel had advised

Wallin to travel via Syria in order to lessen the danger of detection. The need for economy, however, forced him to disregard this advice. Burton, himself, was constrained by time, choosing, therefore, to travel from Egypt in order to join up later with the Damascus Caravan.

Less than a month remained before Burton's departure. In Georgiana Stisted's version of events – and it is the only one there is – he spent most of his time in London, with the occasional trip to Bath to see his parents and sister. At the end of his final and longest visit, having an aversion to goodbyes, he suddenly left one morning when the rest of the household was asleep. He left behind a farewell letter to his mother, and a small quantity of valuables to be divided between her and Maria.[36]

CHAPTER ELEVEN

THE MASK OF ISLAM

Disguised as a Persian, complete with flowing jubbah, shaven head, and a growth of beard and moustache,[1] Burton left Southampton aboard the P&O's newest and largest liner, *Bengal*, at mid-afternoon, Monday, 4 April 1853.[2] Apart from a brother officer, Captain Henry Grindlay of the 3rd European Light Cavalry, ostensibly travelling as his interpreter, and an important recent acquaintance, John Wingfield Larking, only the ship's captain and an attaché of the Turkish embassy in London returning to Constantinople, were aware of Burton's true identity.[3]

Destined eventually for the Calcutta-Suez run, the *Bengal* offered a standard of comfort and cuisine to its 135 first-class passengers, comparable to the best of the London hotels. It also appears to have offered unlimited amounts of wine, beer, and spirits. Although the drinking of alcohol was prohibited by the Qur'an, it was an offer, apparently, that Burton could not refuse.[4] 'If you see Larking,' he wrote to Norton Shaw from Cairo in November, 'pray give him my best salaams & tell him my throat is all safe still,' adding in a highly boyish vein, 'What fun we had on board the steamer.'[5]

Late in the afternoon of 17 April, the *Bengal* dropped anchor outside Alexandria harbour, and the passengers were ferried ashore.[6] Swarming around them was the usual flotilla of native craft crammed with Arabs shouting out offers of porterage, a noise Harriet Martineau, compared to that of a frog concert in a Carolina swamp.[7]

Carefully fostering the illusion of a True Believer, Burton gave audible and visible praise to Allah for seeing him safely to the end of the journey. Then, elbowing his way through the dense crowds to Larking's waiting carriage, he responded, native fashion, to a young beggar's call for bakshish with a curt "Mafish," roughly equivalent in Arabic to "I have left my purse at home." Within half an hour, he was enjoying the cool surroundings of *The Sycamores*, Larking's tree-shaded villa alongside the Mahmudiyah Canal, reclining Eastern fashion on a divan, drinking coffee, and sucking contentedly on a chibuk.

Burton had a powerful ally in Larking, though he took great care to conceal the status of his host, and the precise role he played. A member of a wealthy Kentish family, Larking had set up as a merchant in Alexandria during the early 1830s, in association with Samuel Briggs. Briggs, a well-known and highly respected merchant and banker, who later became Larking's brother-in-law, was a partner in the mercantile house of Briggs, Schutz, and Walmas and between 1803-10 acted as pro-Consul in Egypt and agent of the powerful Levant Company at Alexandria.[8] From 1838-41 Larking was HM consul at the port, succeeding Robert Thurburn, himself a partner in the house of Briggs and Co.[9] For fifty years or more, until his death in 1891, Larking occupied a unique position in the Levant, holding the post of agent in this country for the

Egyptian government. He was the first Englishman to acquire such a commanding influence in Egypt, and the favour he enjoyed during Mahomet Ali's reign (1805-48) was continued under succeeding Khedives. It was said, that there was no one of any note in Turkey, Syria or Egypt with whom he was not acquainted and by whom he was not respected.[10]

Once lodged in the seclusion of an out-house in Larking's garden, Burton lost no time in pursuing the daily routine he had followed aboard the *Bengal*, of forcing himself to think and act like a Muslim. Engaging the services of a shaykh, he renewed his studies of the Qur'an. He also set about mastering once again the complicated rituals of salah or prayer, the second pillar of the Islamic faith, regarded by its followers as the 'Key of Paradise.'

In his leisure time he visited the mosque, strolled around the city sightseeing, visited the coffee-houses and went shopping in the bazaars. He also grasped at the opportunity of watching a performance of Al-nahl, the Bee-Dance, which he characterised briefly as 'a pleasant spectacle.' It was, in fact, a highly erotic dance. Egypt had long been famous for its dancing-girls, particularly the Ghawazee, who combined lascivious dancing in public with prostitution. The government, however, had banned them as far back as June, 1834. The French novelist, Flaubert, writing from Cairo in 1850 complained to his friend, Louis Bouilhet, about the lack of good brothels. A connoisseur of prostitutes, Flaubert travelled up the Nile as far as Esna in Upper Egypt where they were in exile, to visit the voluptuous Syrian courtezan, Kuchuk Hanem. Salome-like, she danced the Bee for him, gradually shedding her clothing as she moved slowly and sensually, rolling her stomach and shaking her large, firm breasts, until she stood quite naked.[11]

Burton was equally uncommunicative in describing the hammam, or hot bath, one of the great indulgences of Egypt, according to the Arabic scholar, W.E. Lane. In a footnote, Burton referred to it as 'being a kind of religious establishment,' in the sense that no Muslim could pray in a state of uncleanliness. He went on to observe without further comment, that it 'has been too often noticed to bear another description.'[12]

It was not until over thirty years later in the Terminal Essay to his translation of the *Arabian Nights*, that he referred to the pathic boys who haunted the public baths as in the days of Catullus.[13] Flaubert was more explicit. In his letter to Bouilhet he said that sodomy was quite accepted there, that all the boys were bardashes, and it was at the baths that such acts took place.[14]

It was there, naturally, that Burton would have been most at risk had he not been circumcised. In the opinion of an earlier pilgrim to Mecca, 'Even to travellers in Mahometan countries, I look upon the safety of their journey as almost impossible, unless they have previously submitted to this rite.' Mr Bankes, the employer of another pilgrim, Giovanni Finati, who had a dread of circumcision, commented, 'Ali Bey is correct; the danger is doubled by non-compliance with the custom.'[15] Circumcision was also something that troubled Burckhardt. He wrote to a friend from Assiut on 6 July 1813: 'I have received a letter of Mr Fiott of Messina…in several of his letters he seriously advises me to undergo a certain operation…..To engage me still further he adds – in his last letter, the expression "I think it would do you no harm (meaning bodily harm)." ' It is not known whether he took the advice.[16]

In 1893, A.S. Bicknell, whose brother, Herman Bicknell, travelled successfully to Mecca in 1862, without any disguise, claimed to know positively that Burton was protected by the 'ceremony', as he put it.[17] This was quite possibly the case. Burton, himself, had written that, 'No evil results are expected from the circumcision of adults; it has often been tried in the cases of African slaves. The cure, however, is generally protracted for the period of at least six weeks.'[18]There is a further possibility, of course, that Burton was circumcised as a child. Although the practice was not generally adopted in Britain until the 1890s, and viewed by one writer 'primarily as an imperial phenomenon,' J.N. Burton, having taken part in military campaigns in hot countries, particularly Egypt, may well have been convinced of its hygienic benefits.[19] If, however, such an operation needed to be carried out before Burton left England it might, especially in view of his long-standing urinary complaint, have been painful as well as potentially dangerous. Herman Bicknell, in fact, himself an army surgeon, nearly lost his life through blood-poisoning following the operation.[20]

There is no mention in Burton's paper to the RGS of his practising as a doctor until after reaching Cairo. In his book, however, he makes much of being besieged at his door while at Alexandria by men, women, and children, eager for his pills and potions. These people as Burton knew from Lane's *Manners and Customs of the Modern Egyptians*, were highly superstitious, like the Muslims of Sind. Their own doctors were totally ignorant of the practices and skills of their own profession. The majority of the people relied for cures and protection against various evils on Providence or on charms, many based on the Qur'an.

This was just up Burton's street, having 'been a dabbler in medical and mystical study' since his youth. He was convinced that uncivilised peoples, as he called them, in warm latitudes, did not suffer from the wide variety of illnesses which beset 'more polished nations.' In fact, they could all be boiled down to one type – ague. It was a highly convenient, if misconceived, assumption.

Some five weeks later, Burton felt that he was ready to move on to Cairo. His intention was to travel in the character of a wandering darwaysh, a chartered vagabond of whom no questions would be asked. He, therefore, exchanged a new jubbah for his shaykh's tattered za-abut, a large-sleeved, home-spun robe, more appropriate for his new status. He also changed his name from Mirza to Shaykh, having, as he claimed, found out his mistake. This was a nonsense. According to Burton, the idea of assuming a Persian disguise before leaving London had been Captain Grindlay's. 'Little thought at the time the adviser or the advised,' wrote Burton in his book, 'how valuable was the suggestion.' It was, of course, nothing of the sort, as Burton observed in his paper to the RGS.[21]

The assumption of Persian nationality, in fact, was an albatross around Burton's neck, until he got better advice in Cairo and changed it. One did not need Burton's encyclopaedic knowledge of the Muslim faith, to know that the Persians as Shi'ites were heretics, detested, if not hated, by the Sunni majority. There is also every reason to believe that Burton was familiar with Dr Wallin's paper, in which he referred to the 'hated presence of the Persians,' on his journey to Mecca.[22]

The truth of the matter is that Burton knew of no other disguise at the time that he could adopt, with the same chance of success. In neither Arabic nor Persian on their own, was his pronunciation or the inflexion of his voice good enough to pass muster as a native of these countries. Furthermore, he was insufficiently versed in Sunni rituals to avoid detection. Although now calling himself, Shaykh Abdullah, he was still in essence Mirza Abdullah of Bushire, whose supposed half-Arab, half-Iranian ancestry could be used to account for any linguistic mistakes.

Burton also claimed to have forgotten to provide himself with a passport before leaving England. With the distinguished Egyptologist, Sir Gardner Wilkinson, and J.W. Larking on hand to give him advice, this is scarcely credible. Again, the truth seems to have been that Burton originally intended travelling to Alexandria in his own person, as did Dr Wallin. Once having adopted a disguise, he would rely on Larking to square matters with the local British consul in getting the appropriate tezkirah, or passport. In the event, he was persuaded by Grindlay that it would be amusing, as well as good practice in his future role, to pose as a Persian during the voyage to Alexandria.

Although Burton gives the impression of obtaining his tezkirah from the British consulate with some difficulty, 'involving,' as he put it, 'much unclean dressing, and an unlimited expenditure of broken English,' it was undoubtedly stage-managed, the consul, F.H. Gilbert, knowing perfectly well with whom he was dealing.[23] Burton's passport declared him to be an Indo-British subject named Abdullah, a doctor by profession, aged thirty.[24] It is possible that the second stage, obtaining the Zabit, or police magistrate's counter-signature, was genuine, giving Burton a chance to test his disguise and, as it turned out, his patience, in dealing with the tortuous ways of Turkish bureaucracy.

The reason he gave for taking so much trouble was that, 'to pass through the Muslim's holy land you must either be a born believer, or have become one.' He could not own to being a 'Burma' or renegade, 'to be pointed at, shunned and catechised, an object of suspicion to the many, and an object of contempt to all.' That would have obstructed the object of his wanderings. 'The convert is always watched with Argus eyes, and men do not willingly give information to a "new Muslim", especially a Frank; they suspect his conversion to be feigned or forced, look upon him as a spy, and let him see as little of life as possible.'[25] This repeated what Burton had written several years earlier, that 'Islam like many other faiths, professing to respect the convert, despises and distrusts him.'[26] Lady Burton's repetition of this view in her biography of her husband, was disputed by A.S. Bicknell, 'whose assertion,' he said, 'that apparent converts "do not get to see the inner secret places," 'betrays a curious ignorance of what that city contains, and what is required of pilgrims.'

As we shall see, difficulties with his passport recur several times later in Burton's narrative, all to do with his initial choice of destination, and a later wish to change it, as well as a change of identity. The issue, however, is clouded throughout, the necessary facts being deliberately omitted. It is not until one hundred and forty pages on, for example, that he informs readers that pilgrims arriving at Alexandria were divided into three groups by means of their passports, to travel the three main routes: Suez, Kusayr, and the Hajj route round the Gulf of Aqabah. Once the choice had been made, so Burton claimed, the Government turned a deaf ear to anyone wishing to change his mind. What he chose to conceal, was the route appearing on his passport. It was, of course, the third, which would show that he meant to travel to Mecca all along and not, as he later claimed, to Muscat. Despite his collecting information about El Hejaz during his stay at Alexandria, Burton seems to have been curiously unaware at the time of obtaining his passport, that the Hajj route did not touch El Medinah, which he wanted to visit.

In the meantime, he had provided himself with the small amount of necessaries required for the journey: a bag containing a miswak, a stick of softwood chewed at one end, which did duty as a toothbrush, soap and a comb, a change or two of clothing, and a zemzemiyah, or goatskin waterbag. His bedding and furniture comprised a coarse Persian rug, a cotton stuffed pillow, a blanket and a sheet. He had also bought a huge yellow cotton umbrella for shade. An important item was a large 'housewife', made for him by Elizabeth Stisted, a large roll of canvas, carefully soiled, with pockets containing needles and thread, cobbler's wax, buttons, etc.[27] 'The sight of a man darning his coat, or patching his slippers,' Burton said, 'teems with pleasing ideas of humility.' His equipment was completed by a large rosary, a dagger, a brass inkstand and penholder stuck in his belt, where he had secreted 25 gold sovereigns.[28]

His bed rolled up easily into a bundle, and his wardrobe was carried in a pair of native Khurjin or saddle-bags. Having mistakenly bought drugs in England, he had the unnecessary trouble of looking after them during the voyage. He found out later that he could have bought them cheaper in Alexandria or Cairo. To protect them, he purchased a strong wooden box capable of withstanding 'falling off a camel twice a day.'

Having made his farewells, Burton left *The Sycamores* towards the end of May in a mule-drawn trap to catch the shallow-draught steamer, popularly known among Europeans as the 'Little Asthmatic', that wheezed its way between Alexandria and Cairo. The mainstream of the Nile being at its lowest during April and May, the craft kept going aground. The journey, therefore, which should have taken thirty hours took three days and nights instead.

He had booked a deck passage, on the noisy crowded boat, where 'a roasting sun pierced the canvas awning like hot water through a gauze veil.' Beyond the banks of the canal, the people and the dry dusty landscape reminded Burton of Sind, and the canal with its high-sterned boats and lateen sails, could have been the Indus. As a darwaysh, he sat apart from the Infidel, smoking continuously, with occasional interruptions to say prayers and tell his beads. He quenched his thirst with muddy water scooped from the canal with a leather bucket, and munched bread and garlic, as he put it, 'with a desperate sanctimoniousness.'

He spent much of the voyage conversing in Hindustani and Persian with two passengers who had stumbled aboard at the last minute. One, Miyan Khudabaksh Namdar, was a plump, dusky Indian from Lahore, with 'an eternal smile and treacherous eyes.' After trading as a shawl merchant in London and Paris, he had settled in Cairo following a pilgrimage to Mecca. His companion, Haji Wali, was a merchant at Alexandria accompanying Khudabaksh to Cairo on law business. He would prove invaluable to Burton later.

On arriving at Bulaq, Khudabaksh insisted on Burton's staying with him as his guest, advancing 'cogent reasons for changing my mind.' This, undoubtedly, is Burton's oblique way of saying that the Indian had penetrated his disguise, and that he needed a longer apprenticeship. He remained at his host's house near the Ezbekiyah Gardens for almost a fortnight. At the end of that time, his patience was exhausted. His host had 'become a civilised man – talked European politics – learned to admire if not to understand liberty – liberal ideas!' anathema, of course, to Burton. It appears that he had also become a little too familiar for his liking, having the temerity to regard himself as being on an equal footing with an Englishman.

Burton learned some disturbing opinions from Khudabaksh: that the Frank everywhere in the East is considered a contemptible being, as well as dangerous. That only in and around the three Presidencies was the British Government popular. Elsewhere, the people would be glad to see a change. 'Where in the history of the world,' Burton commented, 'do we read that such foreign domination ever made itself popular?'[29] Such recognition, of course, in no way changed his imperialistic stance, or undermined his firm conviction that Britain had a right to govern India.

In due course, Burton moved into one of the many caravanserai dotted about the city. He was unsuccessful in obtaining lodgings in one of the best, the Wakalah Khan Khalil, adjoining the huge bustling market, with its maze of alleyways and shops. Instead, he had to put up with one further north, the Wakalah Siladar, in el Guwaniya, the Greek Quarter, swarming with drunken Christians.

Quite by chance, he would have us believe, he found Haji Wali, staying there.[30] He was a bluff, genial man in his mid-forties, of average height, with a large round head, closely shaven, set on a bull neck, a thin red beard, and handsome smiling features. Originally from Russia, he was a man of the world, who had learnt to shed his Muslim prejudices. "I believe in Allah and his Prophet, and in nothing else," was his creed. He immediately took it upon himself to act as Burton's guide, and helped to protect him from being cheated by tradesmen.

They quickly became friends, calling upon each other frequently, eating together, and passing the time in a mosque, or some other place of public recreation. They began to smoke hashish or Indian hemp, the most potent of the cannabis preparations, covertly at first, and then quite openly. Burton, it will be remembered, had taken the drug in India, allegedly curious to discover what its attractions were, rather than for the pleasure he ever experienced. He now called it a 'fascinating drug,' and forecast, totally inaccurately, that one day Egypt would supply the Western world with it, when its 'solid merits,' which he left unspecified, were eventually appreciated.

Haji Wali who, like Khudabaksh, had seen through Burton's disguise, now gave him two pieces of advice. Since Cairo was overrun with doctors, he suggested that Burton become a teacher of languages instead. This, Burton chose to ignore. He accepted, however, his companion's strong recommendation to put aside everything connected with Persia and the Persians. "If you persist in being an Ajami," he pointed out, "you will get yourself into trouble; in Egypt you will be cursed, in Arabia you will be beaten because you are a heretic; you will pay the treble of what other travellers pay, and if you fall sick, you may die by the roadside."[31]

After prolonged discussion, Burton decided to pass himself off as a Pathan, born in India of Afghan parents, who had settled in the country, been educated at Rangoon, and sent out into the world to wander as men of that race frequently are from early youth. To sustain the role required a knowledge of Persian, Hindustani, and Arabic, which he knew sufficiently well to pass muster. Any trifling mistake could be ascribed to his long residence in Rangoon. He assumed the bland, accommodating manners of an Indian physician, and the dress of a small effendi or gentleman. He still passed himself off, however, as a darwaysh. "Let it be known that you are under a vow to visit all the holy places of Islam," was Haji Wali's advice. "This will persuade any questioners that you are a man of rank under a cloud, and you will receive much more civility than perhaps you deserve," he said with a dry laugh.[32]

Shortly after settling into the wakalah, Burton set out to enhance his reputation as a doctor. He scored his first success with an Arab slave-dealer living in the opposite room, whose Abyssinian slaves constantly fell sick. Burton claimed to have cured one girl, though of what he does not say. Since she was worth £15, the slave-dealer was very grateful. As a consequence, Burton had to dose half a dozen others 'in order to cure them of the pernicious and price-lowering habit of snoring.'[33] An amazing elixir, indeed, given that modern medical science has failed to solve the problem. All that he required for his services was for the slave-dealer to show him round Cairo, and explain 'certain mysteries in his craft.'

According to Edward Lane, the earlier site of the market for black slaves in Cairo, the Wekalet el-Gellaba, or wekela of the slave merchants, had been a little to the south of the Khan el-Khalili. It had then been moved to Kair-Bey, its crowded and filthy state widely believed to be the cause of the spread of infectious diseases throughout the city.[34] Unaware of the identity of his questioner, the slave-dealer spoke freely on the subject of slave-hunting in the Somali country and Zanzibar, 'of all things most interesting to me.' In a letter to Dr Norton Shaw from Cairo in November, Burton wrote that he 'had found out a spy of old Mahomet Ali, who let me into all sorts of secrets about the country [Zanzibar], and wanted me to accompany him. I should have done so had I not been bound for Arabia.'[35]

As a gentleman, it was necessary for Burton to employ at least one servant. After hiring a Berberi, who had to be dismissed for stabbing a fellow-servant, Burton was forced to choose others, who turned out to be equally unsatisfactory. He ended up by employing an Indian boy, Shaykh Nur, who 'being completely dependent upon me…was therefore less likely to watch and especially to prate about my proceedings.'

Burton next set out to find a teacher, his pretext being that, as an Indian doctor, he wanted to read Arabic works on medicine, and to perfect himself in divinity and pronunciation. He chose to study the theology of the Shafe'i School. On the one hand, it was the least rigorous of the Four Orthodox. On the other, it most resembled the Shiah heresy, which his long association with Persians in India had made him familiar.[36] Such a choice convinced those around him that he was a rank heretic, 'for the Ajami taught by his religion to conceal offensive tenets in lands where the open expression would be dangerous, always represents himself to be a Shafe'i.'

He found a teacher in Shaykh Mohammed al Attar, or the druggist, with whom he studied several hours a day in the El Azhar Mosque.[37] A thin, watery-eyed old man of about fifty-eight, heavily wrinkled and bearded, he had once been prosperous as a khatib or preacher in one of Mahomet Ali's mosques, until his dismissal by the late Pasha. He now kept a shop in the Jamaliyah Quarter, 'a perfect gem of Nilotic queerness,' outside which Burton and Haji Wali often sat of an evening, smoking and drinking coffee.

Ramadan, the holy month of fasting and the fourth pillar of the Muslim faith, occurred in June that year. Like the Jewish Yom Kippur, it is a period of atonement. Being the height of summer, it was also 'a fearful infliction.' Throughout the month, from dawn to dusk, everyone was required to abstain from food, drink, and sexual intercourse. The chief effect on True Believers, Burton sardonically commented, was 'to darken their tempers into positive gloom…The Mosques were crowded with a sulky, grumbling population making themselves offensive to one another on earth, whilst working their way to heaven.'[38]

The end was marked by the firing of a gun at the Citadel, followed by the cry of the muezzin calling men to prayer. People immediately flocked on to the streets in good humour, many filling Ezbekiyah, with its picturesque gardens, and Greek or Turkish bands. Sometimes Burton and Haji Wali would walk to the Citadel on the Mokottam Hills and sit on the ramparts, enjoying a magnificent view over the moonlit city. At other times they escaped from Cairo's stifling atmosphere into the wilderness beyond the City of the Dead. 'Seated upon some mound of ruins we inhaled the fine air of the Desert, inspiriting as a cordial.'

Ramadan was succeeded by the Id al-Fitre, the festival of breaking fast, which occupied the first three days of Shawwal, the tenth month. It was a time for official receptions and private visits, the giving of presents, the wearing of new clothes, and the visiting of the graves of relatives. The favourite resort was the large cemetery outside the Bab el Nasr, which resembled a packed and noisy fair-ground.

This year's Id, however, according to Burton, was made gloomy, comparatively speaking, by the state of politics. The report of war with Russia, with France, with England, that was going to land three million men at Suez, and with Infideldom in general, ran through Egypt. The government armouries, arsenals and manufactories were crowded with kidnapped workmen, and those who intended going on pilgrimage, feared forcible detention. This, however, gives a diametrically opposite picture from that in a letter to Shaw only four months later, in which he speaks of Egypt being 'little agitated by war.'[39]

Among Burton's acquaintances was a precocious, street-wise, eighteen-year-old Meccan boy, Mohammed al Basyuni, from whom Burton bought the one-piece pilgrim cloth, called 'Al Ihram,' and the Kafan or shroud.[40] Even without the documentary evidence from the RGS this, in itself, is proof that Burton intended to go to Mecca. Mohammed was returning there after visiting Constantinople, and was eager to accompany Burton in the character of a 'companion.' He had travelled too much, however, to suit Burton, 'he had visited India, he had seen Englishmen, and he had lived with the Nawab Balu of Surat.'[41] He had been a regular visitor till Burton, allegedly, cured one of his friends of an ophthalmia, after which he left his address and disappeared.

During Ramadan, Burton had collected stores for his forthcoming journey: tea, coffee, sugar, biscuit, oil, vinegar, tobacco, lanterns, cooking pots, a small bell-shaped tent, and three water-skins for the desert. These provisions were distributed among a kaafas or hamper made of palm-sticks, and a huge sahharah or wooden box covered with leather. He now claimed the need to top up his money supply, having spent all his ready money at Cairo. Yet his expenses had been minimal. He had lived as the guest of Larking, and informed Norton Shaw after the pilgrimage, that he had 'lived almost for nothing' at Cairo. He also claimed to have had been advised by a native acquaintance to take at least £80, and 'considering the expense of outfit for the desert trek, the sum did not appear excessive.'[42] This, in my view, needs to be taken with a very large pinch of salt.

It will be remembered that Burton at his last interview in London, had asked to be furnished with a draft on a small piece of paper, 'I having more experience of Oriental travelling than Sir Woodbine Parrish and Sir Roderick Murchison.' Yet in his narrative, he described being unable to prevail on the native money-changers to accept it, because of its insignificant size and appearance! He was forced to seek help, therefore, from 'a compatriot at Cairo,' Sam Shepheard, the proprietor of the British Hotel. How much help, Burton did not say. A letter written after the 'pilgrimage' reveals the sum to have been £70.[43]

Burton was now faced with a passport problem, claiming that his Alexandrian passport required a double-visa, one at the police office, the other at the British Consulate. But, as we have seen, it already carried a double visa, giving him permission to travel anywhere in Egypt. It is only at this stage in his narrative, that he reveals to the reader the three routes to Mecca, and the Government's disinclination to change the route once chosen. Part of the difficulty facing him, aside from the assumption of a new identity, was his original choice of route, that is, via Akabah, which he now wanted to change to Suez.

If Burton had read Burckhardt's *Travels in Arabia* before leaving England, he would have discovered the following important information concerning the Cairo Caravan. Although written around 1816, it was in all essentials still unchanged: 'The Caravan assembles for several days at a place eastward of the Gardens near Cairo, about 1 hour distant called El Hassoua, and then proceeds to Birket el Hadj, four hours distant where they remain two days. From this place the caravan starts on the 27th of the month Showal; it travels only by night....The caravan does not visit Medina.'[44]

What Burton really needed was a new passport. This required the co-operation of the British Consul. Dr Alfred Septimus Walne, however, was a stickler for protocol, and refused to help.[45] Burton was now faced with a dilemma. Rather oddly, having advised Burton to make a complete break with anything Persian, Haji Wali is now supposed to have taken Burton to his own consulate, the Persian. The price asked for was exorbitant. Fortunately, the matter appeared to be resolved when Shaykh Mohammed suggested asking assistance from the Principal of the Afghan College at the El Azhar Mosque. At six pm the following day, Burton, passing himself off as Abdullah Khan, a title assumed in India and other countries by all Afghan and Pathans, rode to the Citadel with his new patron. A clerk filled in a printed paper in the Turkish language, certifying Burton on the priest's authority to be one Abdullah, the son of Yusf (Joseph), originally from Kabul. For the trifling sum of 5 piastres, his new identity was validated. Burton confessed to being overjoyed, while saying nothing at this point, however, about how he would obtain the necessary visa.

Precisely when he intended leaving the city, Burton fails to make clear. His departure, however, was allegedly precipitated following a drinking bout with a fierce-looking Yuzbashi, or Captain of Albanian Irregulars, Ali Agha, on leave from El Hejaz, whom he met in Haji Wali's room in the caravanserai. 'In Egypt,' Burton said, 'these men...were the terror of the population. In El Hejaz their recklessness awes even the Bedouins...'[46] The heavy drinking session of Araki, eventually ended with Ali Agha's rising, and demanding a troupe of dancing girls to give a performance. Told that the Pasha had forbidden such things, he moved towards the door vowing that he would make the Pasha himself dance for them.

He then staggered outside on to the gallery, Burton trying to restrain him, sending someone who was coming up the stairs flying back down, followed by a volley of oaths. Bursting open one of the doors, he entered a room where two old women were sleeping with their husbands, starting a noisy slanging match. Put to flight by their tongues, he reeled downstairs, where he fell on the sleeping night-porter, vowing to drink his blood. He was finally half-dragged, half-carried to his room shouting that he had raped all the women in Alexandria, Cairo, and Suez, 'an extensive field of operations,' Burton remarked drily, and put to bed.

This drunken fracas supposedly cost Burton his reputation, and Haji Wali advised him to leave quickly. Taking leave of his friends, he told them by way of precaution that his destination was Mecca via Jeddah, really intending, if possible, to reach El-Medinah by way of Yambu. 'Conceal,' says the Arab proverb, 'thy tenets, thy treasure, and thy travelling.'

Burton hired two dromedaries and their attendant Bedouins from a Badawi of Tur, on Mountain Sinai, who was making his way home. Although this was somewhat ostentatious for his rank, Burton wanted his servant mounted, in order to make a forced march, to find out to what extent, what he called, 'a four years' life of European effeminacy,' had sapped his powers of endurance. 'There were few better tests than an 84 miles' ride in midsummer on a bad wooden saddle, borne by a worse dromedary across the Suez Desert.' Burton despatched Shaykh Nur with the heavy luggage for Suez, two days before the end of the Id, that is, 1 July. The journey of a laden camel would take roughly two and a half days. After spending the remaining time with Haji Wali, Burton was advised to mount about mid-afternoon, in order to arrive at Suez by the evening of the following day. Having distributed presents, Burton took his leave, crossed his legs over the pommel, and passed through the Bab el Nasr on to the deserted Suez road.

He journeyed on under a searing sun without experiencing the slightest feeling of boredom. 'Around lie drifted sand-heaps upon which every puff of wind leaves its trace in solid waves, flayed rocks, the very skeletons of mountains, and hard unbroken plains over which he who rides is spurred by the idea that the bursting of a water-skin, or the pricking of a camel's hoofs, would be certain death or torture.'[47] Pitting his puny strength against the forces of Nature and emerging triumphant, Burton found immensely satisfying.

At sunset, he turned off the road, to be suddenly accosted by Mohammed al-Basyuni, the young Meccan who had wanted to accompany him from Cairo. He was now without money, and would accept no excuse. After stopping for a meal and a rest, they continued the journey, reaching the Central Station on the Transit route used by the vans at midnight, where they slept under its walls until dawn. In the afternoon, they turned off the road into a dry water-course not far from number 13 station, where they encountered a group of poor Maghrabi pilgrims. Burton gave them some water, a little bread and some money. They then demanded more with threatening looks, fingering their knives. Burton's pistols, however, kept them at bay. There was never any real danger, as he admitted, since 'The Suez road, by the wise regulation of Mohammed Ali has become as safe to European travellers as that between Hampstead and Highgate.'[48]

It was already night when he rode through the tumble-down gateway of Suez. He now spent some time in and out of the wakalahs in a fruitless search for Shaykh Nur. By chance, he heard that an Indian had taken lodgings in a hostelry called Jirjis Zahr, the 'George,' run by a Copt, a consular agent of Belgium.

Meanwhile, Mohammed had come across some friends from Medina, returning to the pilgrimage after a begging tour through Egypt and Turkey. One was an effeminate Daghistani from the East Caucasus, Omar Effendi, short, plump, soft-featured and beardless, looking fifteen, although almost twice that age, with a strong antipathy towards the opposite sex. Accompanying him was an African of highly volatile temper, born and bred a slave in his household, known as Sa'ad the Demon. The third was Shaykh Hamid Sammad, the 'Clarified Butter Seller,' a nickname derived from a celebrated saint and Sufi of the Qadariyyah Order, who was a perfect specimen of the town Arab, and a man of many skills. Sali Shakkar made up the fourth of the group, a mixture of Turk and Arab, around sixteen years old, greedy, selfish, and supercilious. They hospitably invited Burton to share their supper and their sleeping quarters. He declined their offer, feeling anything but sociable. Apart from worrying about his missing effects, every bone in his body ached, and he was badly sunburned. He managed to persuade the porter to find him an empty room, and fell into a troubled and uncomfortable sleep.

The following morning, having visited the Governor, Ja'afar Bey, Burton returned with an attendant to Shaykh Nur's room, intending to have it forced open. The measure proved unnecessary. Just as Burton entered the caravanserai, his servant appeared full of apologies, having spent the night carousing with Indian Lascars aboard one of the coal-hulks.

Mohammed's friends wasted no time in asking Burton for a loan, having barely two dollars of ready money between them. Their boxes, however, 'were full of valuables, arms, clothes, pipes, slippers, sweet-meats, etc., but nothing short of starvation would have induced them to pledge the smallest article.' Calculating that travelling in a group would help in shielding him from detection, he agreed, drawing up an agreement highly in his favour. He suddenly became a person of some importance. 'This elevation,' he said, 'led me into an imprudence which might have cost me dear; aroused the only doubt about me ever expressed during the summer's tour.' His friends, rummaging through his effects had taken little notice of his copper-cased watch, even his compass, having seen one at Constantinople. Sight of his sextant, however, at once aroused suspicion, especially on the part of Mohammed, who, when Burton had left the room, accused him of being an Infidel from India. This charge was rejected by Omar Effendi who had read the letter which Burton had written that morning to Haji Wali, and had at various times 'received categorical replies to certain questions in high theology.' He and the others, more concerned with holding on to their loans, rejected the accusation, and Mohammed was told to 'Fear Allah.' Nevertheless, in the interests of safety, Burton decided to leave the instrument behind.

However, in a lecture given thirteen years later to members of the Royal family in Brazil, Burton claimed to have first met his Muslim friends, not in Suez, but in Cairo, where he 'doctored them and lent them some trifling sums.' They had also helped him 'to collect proper stores for the journey.'[49] If this is the true version, as seems likely, it suggests that Burton deliberately tampered with the chronology in his book, in order to manufacture the above scene.

Dr Wallin's only instruments had been a watch, a compass, and thermometer. Even so, these led to suspicions as to his orthodoxy, even to his being a Frank. Following his first journey, he wrote, 'I am very vexed at not owning astronomical instruments; for I could have probably determined the position of the places I stayed at, if I had had the instruments and had known how to use them, which I suppose does not need much practice.'[50] He was well aware for the ambitious project he had in mind in 1851, that, if this were to be a scientific journey, 'travel as a dervish or a Bedouin' was not possible. Supplying surveying instruments for Dr Wallin had formed part of the RGS's provision for this expedition. This was not the case with Burton, and there is no record of his having indented for any.

The party agreed not to lose any time in securing places on board a craft bound for Yambu. Hearing that his Turkish passport was not in order for travelling from Suez, his friends advised Burton to have it signed by the Governor, while they busied themselves about the harbour. They warned him that if he displayed his Turkish tazkirah obtained from the Citadel, he would be ordered to wait for the Cairo Caravan.

A clerk quickly spotted the document's irregularity, and pointed out that nothing would persuade the Bey to allow Burton to continue his journey. This would mean his having to travel either via Kusayr, or riding down through Sinai to the harbour of Tur, on the slim chance of finding a vessel sailing to the Hejaz. His only hope at Suez was to seek help from the British Vice-Consul, George West.[51] Burton deliberately took Mohammed with him, concocting a fictitious tale for the benefit of his companions, that he had been a benefactor to the British nation in Afghanistan.

West, who had been warned to expect Burton, was extremely kind and helpful.[52] When objections were made to signing, what Burton now described as his Alexandrian tazkirah, West said that he would on his own authority, supply him with a new passport as a British subject from Suez to Arabia. As a result, the document was returned to him on the second day. In his paper for the RGS Burton wrote, 'I should have been detained at Suez had it not been for the stout aid of Her Britannic Majesty's Vice-Consul, Mr West, who persuaded the Bey to overlook the informality of my passport, and to allow me to embark on board a pilgrim ship.[53]

A deal was struck with the owner of the Silk al-Zahab 'The Golden Thread' or 'Wire' for places on the poop, the best part of the vessel at this time of the year. Members of the group would need to buy their own water, but the ship would supply them with fuel for cooking. On 6 July, amid great noise and confusion, they were poled to the little pier where the Bey personally examined all the passports. About 10 am, the sail was hoisted, and they ran down the channel to the roadstead, boarded from another ship as they went by about a score of Maghrabi, to where the pilgrim ship lay at anchor.

The vessel which was to take them down the Red Sea was a sambuk of about 50 tons, undecked except on the poop.[54] Although carrying two forward raking masts, there was only one sheet, a huge triangular sail. There were no means of reefing, no compass, no log, no sounding line or spare ropes, and no trace of a chart. The owner had promised to take 60 passengers, a sufficient number for a boat of this size, with huge piles of luggage scattered all over the vessel. Instead, there were 130, mostly Badawin from el Maghrib, described by Burton as 'perhaps the greatest ruffians in Islam.' Sa'ad the Demon, taken on as a member of the crew, lost no time in clearing the poop of intruders by the simple expedient of throwing them off, allowing Burton and his companions to settle down as comfortably as they could in a space no bigger than ten feet by eight. He, himself, found a spare bed-frame slung over the ship's side, and gave its owner a dollar for its use throughout the voyage.

Fighting was not long in breaking out below in the over-crowded vessel between a few old Turks from Anatolia and Caramania, and the wild Maghrabis from the deserts about Tripoli and Tunis. When this had subsided, the latter asked for their difficulties to be relieved by taking about half a dozen of them on the poop. This was resisted. Sa'ad flung his group a bundle of well-greased ashen staves, as the Maghrabis 'swarmed towards the poop like hornets, and encouraged each other with cries of "Allaho Akbar!"' Those on the poop, however, had the advantage of the high ground, and the Maghrabis' palm sticks and short daggers were no match for the quarter-staves. To these were added the contents of a large water-jar, which Burton claimed to have pushed down upon them, causing them to retreat in some confusion.[55]

That afternoon the sail was shaken out, the pilgrims meanwhile reciting the Fatihah, the short opening sura of the Qur'an, with upraised hands. Burton took a last, long look at the Union Jack flying over the British Consulate. The momentary regret, he felt, however, 'was stifled by the heart-bounding which prospects of an adventure excite, and by the real pleasure of leaving Egypt.'

CHAPTER TWELVE

THE HAJ

The 'Golden Wire' sailed slowly southwards along the Arabian coast. At sunset, the ship dropped anchor to avoid the notoriously dangerous reefs and shoals of the Red Sea, the passengers coming ashore for the night. For the two hours following sunrise the rays of the sun were endurable; after that, they became a fiery ordeal. The Turkish baby on board seemed to be dying, too weak even to cry. Burton remarked on the kindness his companions showed to the mother and her children, most taking it in turns to nurse the baby.

He, himself, kept to a strict regimen, having unlimited confidence in a moderate rice and water diet, both then and later, to protect him against the sun's blistering heat. He avoided regular washing, believing that warm water was debilitating, and cold water led to fever. Instead he relied on a little oil or melted butter, with an occasional bath of lukewarm water and henna paste, to cool his skin. The only remedy to combat thirst, in his opinion, was patience. After suffering for an hour or two, it became easy.[1]

An hour or so before sunset on 15 July, the ship glided into Marsa Mahar. While wading ashore over sharp rocks, Burton felt a sudden stabbing pain in one of his toes. On landing, he extracted what appeared to be a bit of thorn, and gave it no more thought. Probably the poisonous spine of a sea-urchin, common in these seas, it was to cause him a great deal of pain and inconvenience later.[2]

Twelve days after leaving Suez, the ship arrived at Yambu. Everyone thankfully disembarked, staggering ashore with cramped legs, some feeling feverish, others covered with boils, 'all with brains adust by reason of the sun.' His foot was now so painful, that he could hardly bear to put it on the ground. While his friends proceeded to the Custom House, Burton, leaning on Shaykh Nur's shoulder, limped up from the harbour to inspect the town.

Although an important port, and bearing the title 'Gate of the Holy City,' it was otherwise unremarkable. The houses in the wide streets were roughly built of crumbling limestone and coralline, with large crudely-fashioned mashrabiyah. Apart from the Custom House fronting the harbour, the only public buildings were some white-washed mosques, a wakalah or two, a saint's tomb, and a hammam, a mere date-leaf shed run by an old Turk and his surly Albanian assistant. There was the usual suk, and numerous filthy, fly-haunted cafés.

It was in one of these that his friends eventually found him resting his foot. Together they went off to the wakalah near the bazaar, where they managed to obtain an upper room facing the sea, and relatively free of flies. That afternoon, they sent for a Mukharrij, an Arab agent, to supply them with camels. A bargain was eventually struck, whereby they agreed to pay three dollars for each animal, half down, the other half on reaching their destination. Burton hired two, one to carry his luggage and his servant, the other for

Mohammed and himself. Since the Hazimi clan was 'out,' it was arranged that they should join a grain-caravan guarded by an escort of irregular cavalry, setting out during the evening of the following day.

They spent the forenoon laying in a stock of provisions, and making ready for the journey. To make it easier to take notes, Burton bought a shugduf or litter, his lameness providing a convenient excuse for riding in what was generally regarded as a somewhat effeminate means of travel.[3] He was careful, however, to ride a saddled camel when entering a populated area. Following advice, he dressed as an Arab to avoid paying the Jizyat, a capitation tax extorted by the settled tribes from strangers. He was also warned not to speak any language but Arabic when they were in the vicinity of a village.

Besides the appropriate arms, a sword, and a matchlock slung behind him, Burton also carried in a secret pocket, a small pistol with a spring dagger, which he was always careful to keep concealed. He also wore what appeared to be a 'Hamail,' the pilgrim's outward sign of his holy mission. This was a pocket Qur'an in a gold embroidered crimson velvet or red morocco case, hanging by red silk cords over the left shoulder. Instead, the case contained three compartments, one holding his watch and compass, another his ready money, whilst the third held a penknife, pencils, and slips of paper, small enough to conceal in the hollow of his hand. These were to be used for writing and drawing. Once his sketches were made, he cut up the paper into square pieces and, after numbering them, hid them in the canisters containing his medicines. He warned any traveller, however, against sketching in front of the Bedouins, who would certainly proceed to extreme measures, suspecting him to be a spy or a sorcerer.[4]

Burton avoided mentioning something equally ingenious which had been provided for him in London by the well-known bookseller, Bernard Quaritch. This was a copy of Freytag's *Arabic Dictionary*, specially bound to resemble a pair of Oriental manuscripts, so that Burton 'would have a key in linguistic difficulties, and a useful study, while apparently intent on his Moslem devotions.'[5]

In order to make a 'fair copy', he carried a long thin diary, specially made for him at Cairo, which fitted snugly into a breast-pocket without being seen. Although he began by writing his notes in Arabic, he switched to writing his journal in English once there appeared no risk involved. On more than one occasion as an experiment, he showed what he had written on a loose piece of paper to his companions, 'and astonished them with the strange characters derived from Solomon and Alexander, the Lord of the two Horns, which we Afghans still use.'[6]

To avoid suspicion when asking for information, he had an abstract of Arab genealogies, and always began his questioning with, for example, "You men of Harb, on what lineage do ye pride yourselves?" Although it was necessary to keep notes and sketches private, these people, Burton said, do not object to a learned man writing in a MS, as if commenting on it, and for other purposes he may retire into solitude and pray.

At 7 pm on 18 July, the little party of twelve camels tied head to tail, passed through the gates of Yambu, and took a due easterly course across the desert plain between the Radwah Hills and the sea-shore. After an eight-hour march, they rendezvoused with the grain califa, 200 hundred camels with their armed drivers, 'truculent looking as the contrabandists of the Pyrenees,' and seven Irregular Turkish horsemen for escort. For two days they travelled through a desolate, sun-scorched landscape. "What could have tied the leg of Allah's prophet to this bit of Jehannum?" Burton asked his companions. "Wallah!" one replied with grim humour, "because he could not afford a trip to Stamboul."[7] On 20 July they entered El Hamra, a long straggling village, which was the middle station between Yambu and El Medina. There, on the following day they were able to join up with another caravan from Mecca taking the same route.

At dawn four days later, voices dropped to a whisper as they entered the notorious gorge called Shuab el Haj, the Pilgrimage Pass. Suddenly firing broke out from the rocks above, and Badawin boys and men could be seen swarming up the heights from where they were able to fire with perfect impunity.

'Unfortunately,' said Burton, 'if one had been hit and killed, it might have caused an uprising over the country.' Their own party, therefore, made a great deal of noise and smoke to little effect. By the time they were through the gorge, twelve men, as well as camels and other baggage animals, had been killed.

Just after sunrise the following morning, Burton found his companions recklessly hurrying on their camels. "More robbers?" he inquired of a neighbour. "No, we are walking upon our eyes – in a minute we shall see El-Medina."[8] Crossing the dry El Akik fiumara, they presently arrived at a broad flight of steps cut into the black basalt rock. Upon reaching the top, and passing through a lane of lava with steep banks, they caught their first sight of the Holy City standing among its gardens and orchards in the plain below. Everyone stopped, and dismounting in time-honoured fashion, broke out into rapturous exclamations in praise of Allah and his Prophet, their features working with emotion and their eyes filled with tears. 'It was impossible,' Burton remarked, 'not to enter into the spirit of my companions, and truly I believe that for some minutes my enthusiasm rose as high as theirs.'[9] Remounting, he made a rough sketch of the town, and began questioning the camel-men about it and the surrounding countryside.

Although the sun was only beginning to rise through the mists from behind a low hill, crowds were already streaming out from the town to meet the caravan. His companions preferred to walk, eager to kiss, embrace, and shake hands with their relations and friends. 'Truly the Arabs show more heart on these occasions,' Burton observed, 'than any Oriental people I know.'[10]

After entering by the Ambari gateway, they proceeded to Shaykh Hamid's house, a modest-sized building occupying two sides of the large open space known as the Barr el Munakkah. The Shaykh had gone on earlier to prepare for his guests. He now appeared completely transformed, handsomely dressed, and almost formal in his behaviour. He led Burton up dark winding steps to the majlis or sitting-room on the first floor, where pipes stood already filled, diwans spread, and coffee boiling on a brazier in the passage.

It was not long before the room filled with visitors, who came and went until midday. The main topic of conversation was the Holy War. 'Abdel Mejid would dispose of the "Moskow" (the common name for the Russians in Egypt and El Hejaz); after which he would turn his victorious army against all the idolators of Feringistan, beginning with the English, French, and the Aroam or Greeks.'[11] By this date, 25 July, the Russians had crossed the Pruth and occupied the Turkish provinces as far as the Danube. The Turks, however, did not declare war until 4 October. Burton, when asked for his opinion, took care to agree with the popular view.

Excluding his prefatory remarks, it is at this stage in his narrative that Burton begins mentioning difficulties likely to interfere with his alleged aim of crossing the Arabian peninsula to Muscat. The Bedouins, he said, looking forward to the spoils of Europe, had decided there was to be an Arab contingent. Feuding had broken out, since everyone wanted to go, and there was inter-tribal fighting everywhere.

The adult visitors were succeeded by a headlong rush of badly-behaved children. This was sufficient for Burton to offend against Arab etiquette and inform his host that he was hungry, thirsty, and tired, and wanted to be left alone before the next day's visit to the haram. Profuse in his apologies, the Shaykh immediately attended to his request.

Having performed the necessary ablutions, they set out early the next morning for the Masjid El Nabawi, or the Prophet's Mosque. According to a saying attributed to Mohammed, 'One prayer in this my mosque is more productive than a thousand in other places, save only the Masjid El Haram.'[12] The Ziyarat, or Visitation, however, unlike the hajj, obligatory for every Muslim once in a lifetime, counted only as a meritorious action.

His foot being extremely painful, Burton rode through the muddy, freshly watered streets on a wretched lame, raw-backed, one-eared donkey, provided by Shaykh Hamid, an animal despised by the Bedouins. The Prophet's Mosque suddenly came into view, hemmed in by commonplace buildings, robbing it in Burton's opinion, of any beauty and dignity. Entering by a small flight of steps at the Bab al-Ramhah, the 'Gate of Pity,' he confessed to being astonished 'by the mean and tawdry appearance of a place so universally venerated in the Moslem world.' The longer he looked at it, 'the more it suggested the resemblance of a museum of second-rate art, a curiosity-shop, full of ornaments that are not accessories, and decorated with pauper splendour.'[13]

After prayers, it was time to distribute alms. The place swarmed with beggars. To avoid being distracted by them, Burton had earlier given two dollars in small change to Mohammed, with strict instructions to make the sum last throughout the visit to the mosque. Leaving him to cope as best he could, Burton turned his attention to the Rauzah. The most elaborate part of the mosque, it was gaudily decorated so as to resemble a garden. It was far from impressive during the day. Lit up at night, however, by oil lamps and huge wax candles, with its congregation of visitors handsomely attired, the eye became less critical.

After further prayer, they arrived at the Hujrah or 'Chamber' in the south-east of the building, separated on all sides from the walls of the mosque by a broad, railed passage. Inside were reputed to be three tombs facing southwards, enclosed either by blank stone walls or strong wooden boards. Praying as they went, Shaykh Hamid allowed Burton to draw near the little window, called the Prophet's, and look in. After straining his eyes for a while, he caught sight of a curtain or, rather, hangings, carrying three inscriptions in large gold letters announcing that behind them lay Allah's Prophet and the first two caliphs, Abubekr and Omar. Mohammed's tomb was distinguished from the others by a large pearl rosary and an ornament, the famous Kaukab el Durri, popularly regarded as a 'jewel of the jewels of Paradise.' To Burton's eyes , it resembled 'the round stoppers of glass, used for the humbler sorts of decanters,' adding, however, that he was not close enough to give a fair judgement.[14]

Not having seen the tomb himself, or met anyone who had, he was forced to describe it from books. This was not an easy matter, since the few that existed gave discrepant accounts. According to El Samanhudi, quoted by Burckhardt, the curtain covered a square building of black stones. The tombs were deep holes, and the coffin containing the body of the Prophet was cased with silver, having on the top a marble slab inscribed "Bismillah! Allahumma salli alayh!" (In the name of Allah! Allah have mercy upon him!) Even this distinguished scholar, however, contradicted himself. Consequently, said Burton, 'although every Moslem, learned and simple, firmly believes that Mohammed's remains are interred in the Hujrah at El Medinah, I cannot help suspecting that the place is doubtful as that of the Holy Sepulchre at Jerusalem.'[15]

He took care to make a ground plan of the Prophet's Mosque, since Burckhardt had been too ill to do so. Unfortunately, some of Burton's papers and sketches which he had placed for safety among his medicines, were damaged when one of the bottles broke. This meant, he said, that in certain minor details, his drawing was not absolutely trustworthy.

During his stay at Medina – he was there for just over five weeks – Burton not only visited the most important religious sites in the vicinity of the city, but collected an impressive amount of ethnographical data.

Most of the slaves, he discovered, were brought from Mecca by the Jallabs, or drivers. The majority of the best were exported to Egypt, Medina receiving the remainder. Some of these came from Abyssinia. The greater part, however, was driven from the Galla country, and shipped from ports along the Somali coast. A little black boy and girl cost around 1000 piastres each. Eunuchs were double that sum. Galla girls, a rarity in the Medina slave-market, were highly prized and commanded a high price, 'because their skins are always cool in the hottest weather.'[16]

There were no prostitutes' quarters as at Mecca, Cairo, or Jeddah. Scandals seldom occurred, and the women, he was informed, behaved with great decency. Burton glossed this in his text with an extremely long footnote in Latin on the supposed origins and results of male and female circumcision:

The practice among the Arabs of both sexes is a very ancient one……. It is now regarded as a matter of hygiene and health for men, and for young women, a remedy against lust…the Asiatic races considering that women are far more lustful than men. In Aristotle's view, the clitoris is excised because it is the seat and source of sexual pleasure. The philosopher, however, was unaware of the unnatural consequences of such mutilation. While it diminished the capacity of women for love and pleasure, it resulted in an increase in cruelty, debauchery, and insatiable desire.[17]

Towards the end of August, the Great Caravan arrived from Damascus, bringing a new curtain for the Prophet's Hujrah. When Burton looked out of his window that morning, the Barr el Munakkah had been transformed from a dusty waste, with a few Bedouins and hair tents, into a town of tents of every colour and shape. He painted a masterly picture of the vibrant, noisy scene, with: 'Huge white Syrian drome-daries…jingling large bells, and bearing shugdufs like miniature green tents, swaying and tossing upon their backs; gorgeous Takhtrawan, or litters borne between camels or mules with scarlet and brass trappings; Bedouins bestriding naked-backed Deluls (a she-dromedary) and clinging like apes to the hairy humps; Arnaut, Turkish, and Kurd irregular horsemen, fiercer in their mirth than Roman peasants in their rage……' Noise and confusion reigned everywhere.

A splendid comet blazing in the western sky had made the Medinites predict the usual disasters, believing 'that the dread star foreshadows all manner of calamities.'[18] Suddenly and coincidentally, the Hawazim and the Hawamid began fighting among themselves. 'This quarrel,' Burton claimed, 'put an end to any lingering possibility of my prosecuting my journey to Muscat, as originally intended.' In a footnote, he wrote, 'Anciently there was a caravan from Muscat to El Medinah. My friends could not tell me when the line had been given up, but all were agreed that for years they had not seen an Oman caravan, the pilgrims preferring to enter El Hejaz via Jeddah.'[19]

Whether there really was intertribal fighting at this time, is of no consequence, since we know that crossing the peninsula to Muscat was never part of Burton's original plan. As for the footnote, it reads very much like his adaptation of information written by Burckhardt in 1814: 'I have seen the route of an Indian pilgrim caravan, laid down in several maps as starting from Maskat and coming by Nejd to Mekka; but I could obtain no information respecting it…Those persons whom I questioned assured me that no such caravan had arrived within their memory.'[20]

Elaborating further on what is wholly a cock-and-bull story, Burton said that on the way from Yambu to El Medinah, he had secretly made friends with a man called Mujrim of the Beni Harbs, who understood that Burton had a particular reason for undertaking the perilous journey. Although unable to promise to act as a guide, he offered to make enquiries about the route, and to bring Burton the answer at noonday, a time when all the household was asleep. He had almost agreed to travel with him about the end of August, 'in which case I should have slipped out of Hamid's house,' said Burton, 'and started like a Bedouin towards the Indian Ocean.' The plan supposedly fell through. Mujrim put off the day till the end of September, and then when pressed, admitted that 'no traveller, nay, not a Bedouin, could leave the city in that direction, even as far as Khaybar.' As for Shaykh Hamid, he thought Burton mad for wishing to travel northwards when all the world was travelling south.

Despite being bitterly disappointed at first, he became resigned to the fact that under the most favourable circumstances, a Bedouin trip from El Medinah to Muscat, a distance of 1,500-1,600 miles, would have taken 10 months. As it was, he had to be in Bombay by the end of March or forfeit his commission. Furthermore, having entered Arabia by El Hejaz, he had been obliged to leave behind 'all my instruments,' except a watch and a pocket compass. This, of course, was a novel excuse, since he had previously mentioned having only the sextant, allegedly left behind at Suez.

The deliberately false impression that the Holy City was a substitute forced on Burton, is reinforced in his book, with its page captioned, 'What drove me to Mecca.' As for his intended journey to the Hadramaut, Burton is totally and quite cynically silent. Only in his paper to the RGS did he make a brief passing reference to the province, when referring to the Rub'a el Khali: 'At El Medina I heard a tradition that in days of yore a high road ran from the city, passing through this wild region to Hadramaut. It had, however, been deserted for ages, and my informants considered me demented when I talked of travelling by it.'[21]

The Damascus Caravan was due to start on 1 September. Burton, nevertheless, planned to stay at Medina until the last moment, intending to accompany the Kafilat el Tayyarah or the 'Flying Caravan', which normally left the following day. Suddenly, a rumour spread that there would be no Tayyarah, and that all pilgrims were advised to travel by the Damascus Caravan.

Early the next day, Shayk Hamid returned hurriedly from the bazaar confirming the truth of the rumour, and that they were to start the next morning down the Darb el Sharki. Although Hamid was horror-struck, Burton was overjoyed. Burckhardt had visited and described the Darb el Sultani, the 'High' or 'Royal' Road. No European had, as yet, travelled down by Harun el Rashid's and the Lady Zubaydah's celebrated route through the Nejd Desert. Hurried preparations were made for the journey. While Burton patched the water-skins, Shaykh Nur was despatched to lay in provisions for fourteen days. In his turn, Hamid arranged for the hiring of camel-men, returning in due course with a boy and a white bearded old Bedouin, by the name of Masud.

At 9 o'clock the following morning, Burton found himself standing opposite the Egyptian Gate surrounded by his friends who had accompanied him on foot to take leave with due honour. Then in company with some Turks and Meccans, he passed through the little gate near the castle, and headed for the north. After an hour they came to the Nejd Road, and a well-known place called Al Ghadir, where they turned to take farewell of the Holy City. 'All the pilgrims dismounted, and took a fond and yearning leave of the venerable minarets and the green dome, to them the most interesting spot on earth.'[22]

The caravan was striking in its varied and colourful appearance, contrasting strongly with the dark, barren landscape. There were at least seven hundred people on foot, others on horseback, in litters, or riding on splendid Syrian camels. The morning sun struck fire from the arms surrounding the striped Mahmal,[23] and lit up the scarlet and gilt litters of the grandees. The living, however, was simple on these marches. The pouches inside and outside the shugduf contained provisions and water, which they helped themselves to when inclined. At certain times during the day, vendors came around selling sherbet, lemonade, hot coffee, and water-pipes. During the night halt, provisions were cooked – rice, or kichri, a mixture of pulse and rice eaten with chutney and lime-pickle, varied occasionally with tough mutton and indigestible goat.

Burton immediately took to old Shaykh Masud. He, for his part, regarded his companion as worthy to hear about his battles, his genealogy, and his family affairs. The rest of the party could not contain their contempt when they heard Burton asking various questions about torrents, hills, and the directions of places. "Let the Father of Moustachios be," said the old man,; "he is friendly with the Bedouins, and knows better than you all."[24]

At El Suwayrkiyah, just under a hundred miles from Medina, they were now in territory belonging to the Sherif of Meccah. They made a halt there, and decided to have a small feast. The Samum as usual was blowing hard, affecting the travellers' tempers. A fight broke out between a Turk and an Arab, the Turk eventually dealing the Arab a heavy blow. That same night, so Burton heard, his assailant had ripped open the Turk's stomach with a dagger. The dying victim was wrapped in his shroud, and placed in a half-dug grave, the general practice with the poor and the solitary. 'It is impossible to contemplate such a fate without horror,' Burton wrote; 'the torturing thirst of a wound, the burning sun heating the brain to madness, and – worst of all, for they do not wait till death – the attacks of the jackal, the vulture, and the raven of the wild.'[25]

On 5 September, their route took them over a high table-land. 'That night as darkness fell, the black basaltic field was dotted with the huge and doubtful forms of spongy-footed camels with silent tread, looming like phantoms in the midnight air; the hot wind moaned, and whirled from the torches' sheets of flame and fiery smoke, while ever and anon a swift-travelling Takhtrawan, drawn by mules, and surrounded by runners bearing giant mashal (cressets) threw a passing glow of red light upon the dark road and the dusky multitude.'[26]

Two days later, they arrived at El Zaribah where the ceremony of El Ihram was performed, the assumption of the holy garb. A barber shaved their heads, cut their nails and trimmed their moustaches. The pilgrims then bathed and perfumed themselves, after which they donned two new cotton cloths, each six feet long by three and a half broad, with narrow red stripes and fringes. Their heads and feet remained bare. A leather purse was the only article which they were allowed to carry around their necks. This was followed by prayers, and 'a drowsy exhortation to be good and faithful pilgrims, to abstain from the enormously long list of things forbidden to the faithful at this season.'

Early that evening, the caravan approached a dry river-valley flanked on either side by steep buttresses of rock, through which they were to travel all that night Some way in they were ambushed by members of the Utabayah tribe. A shot rang out, and a high-trotting dromedary in front of Burton rolled over on its side, shot through the heart. Confusion immediately reigned, everyone trying to urge his animal forward out of danger. It was left to the Wahhabis to come to the rescue. Galloping up on camels, and taking up a position, one body began to fire upon the Utabayah robbers, whilst two or three hundred, dismounting, swarmed up the hill, putting the robbers to flight.

On Sunday, 11 September, Burton was roused from sleep by a general excitement, "Mecca! Mecca!" cried some voices; "The Sanctuary! O the Sanctuary!" exclaimed others, and all burst into loud "labbaykas", sometimes broken by sobs. Peering out from his litter, Burton could just see the dim outline of a large city by the light of the southern stars. Within the hour, they were entering Mecca by the Mabidah or northern suburb, the site of the Sherif's palace. At the Sulaymaniyah or Afghan quarter, his party turned off the main road into a bye-way and ascended the rocky heights of Jebel Hindi along dark deserted streets. Then they began a descent, until by 2 am they found themselves at the house of Mohammed. Leaving Burton in the street, he rushed upstairs to embrace his mother. He presently returned, his normally boisterous and jaunty demeanour now changed to one of grave and attentive courtesy. 'I had become his guest.' After a light meal, Burton lay down anxious to snatch an hour or two of sleep before having to perform their 'Tawaf el Kudum', or 'Circumambulation of Arrival', at the Haram or Great Mosque.

They rose at sunrise, and having bathed, proceeded in pilgrim dress to the Sanctuary. Entering by the Bab el Ziyadah, the main northern door, they descended two long flights of steps. After traversing the cloister, they caught sight of the Kaabah, the cube-shaped shrine located near the centre of the Great Mosque, considered by Muslims everywhere to be the most sacred spot on earth. Covering it was an enormous black cloth of brocade, the kiswah, embroidered in gold lettering with the legend, 'There is no God but Allah and Mohammed is his prophet,' and verses from the Qur'an.

There at last it lay [he wrote], the bourn of my long and weary pilgrimage, realising the plans and hopes of many and many a year.[27] The mirage of Fancy invested the huge catafalque and its gloomy pall with peculiar charms. I may truly say that, of all the worshippers who clung weeping to the curtain, or who pressed their beating hearts to the stone, none felt for the moment a deeper emotion than did the Hajj from the far north. It was as if the poetical legends of the Arabs spoke truth, and that the waving wings of angels, not the sweet breath of morning, were agitating and swelling the black covering of the shrine. But to confess humbling truth, theirs was the high feeling of religious enthusiasm, mine was the ecstasy of gratified pride.[28]

After performing the set number of prayers and prostrations, they drank a cup of holy water from the well Zem Zem. The flavour was salt-bitter, much like a tea-spoonful of Epsom salts in a large tumbler of tepid water.

At the south-east corner of the Kaabah near the door, was the famous Black Stone or Hajar, an irregular oval about seven inches in diameter worn smooth by the touch and kisses of millions of pilgrims. According to Muslim tradition, it had been given to Adam on his expulsion from Paradise in order to obtain forgiveness of his sins. Early on, they were prevented from touching the stone by the sheer number of pilgrims surrounding it. At the end of the Tawaf, or circumambulation, however, it was considered advisable to kiss it. For a time, Burton despaired of ever doing so because of the swarming crowds. Mohammed, however, was equal to the occasion. Assisted by some half-dozen stalwart Meccans, they forced a way through the crowd. After reaching the stone, they monopolised its use for fully ten minutes. Having kissed it and rubbed his hands and forehead upon it, Burton came away persuaded that it was a big aerolite. After performing various other rites, and thoroughly worn out, with scorched feet and burning head, he left the mosque.

Accompanied by Mohammed, and followed by Shaykh Nur with a lantern and prayer-rug, Burton returned to the mosque in the evening as a spectator. The oval pavement around the Kaabah, lit by moonlight, was crowded with men, women and children. He stayed in the Haram until 2 am, in the hope of seeing it empty. But the next day was to witness the departure for Arafat. Many, therefore, passed the night in the mosque. Shortly after his companions fell asleep, Burton approached the Kaabah intent on obtaining a bit of the torn, old Kiswah, but too many eyes were looking on. The opportunity, however, was favourable for a survey, and with a piece of tape, and the simple process of stepping and spanning, he managed to measure all the objects about which he was curious. Eventually arriving back at the house, he and his companions snatched a few hours' sleep on the Mastabah in the stifling heat.

On Monday, 12 September, dressed in their Ihram, they followed the road by which they had entered Mecca. Dead animals littered the ground. Arafat was about six hours' march, or 12 miles on the Taif road, due east of Mecca. They arrived there in a shorter time, but their weary camels during the last third of the way frequently threw themselves down on the ground. Between Muna and Arafat, Burton saw no less than five men collapse and die on the highway. They had deliberately dragged themselves out to die, where the spirit it was believed would depart to instant beatitude.

The following day began with military sounds. From noon onwards, the hum and murmur of the multitude increased, and people could be seen swarming in all directions. The pilgrims crowded up to the foot of the mountains. Then a solemn silence fell on the assembly, a sign that the preacher had begun the Sermon of the Standing (Khutbat el Wafkah), which lasted till near sunset.

At dawn on Wednesday, 14 September, a gun warned pilgrims to lose no time. They were now to mount for 'the throwing.' Carrying the seven pebbles brought from Muzdalifah, they found a huge crowd milling around in the narrow road opposite the Jamrat el Akabah, more popularly known as the Shaytan el Kabir – the Great Devil. This is a dwarf buttress made of rough masonry about eight feet high by two and a half feet broad, placed against a rough wall of stones at the Meccan entrance to Muna. Finding an opening in the crowd with difficulty, they approached within five cubits of the place, and holding each stone between the thumb and the forefinger of the right hand, threw it at the pillar, exclaiming, "In the name of Allah, and Allah is mighty! (I do this) in hatred of the Fiend and to his shame." They were now permitted to remove the Ihram, and to revert to Ihlal, the normal state of Islam.

Shortly after returning to Mecca, Mohammed hurried up in a state of excitement, exclaiming, "Rise, Effendi! bathe, dress, and follow me!" A crowd had gathered around the Kaabah, and Burton had no wish to stand bareheaded and barefooted in the midday September sun. At the cry of, "Open a path for the Haji who would enter the House," the onlookers made way. Two strong Meccans raised him in their arms, whilst a third drew him in from above. Having passed on Burton's personal details to the guardians of the shrine, Mohammed was then allowed to conduct him round the building and recite the prayers. 'I will not deny,' Burton said, 'that looking at the windowless walls, the officials at the door, and the crowd below…my feelings were those of the trapped-rat description.' This, however, did not prevent his carefully observing the scene during the long prayers, and making a rough plan with a pencil on his white Ihram.

Burton returned home exhausted, and washed with henna and warm water to ease the pain of his sunburned arms, shoulders, and chest. The house was empty, all the Turkish pilgrims being still at Muna and the Kabirah. The old lady fussed over Burton, who had won her heart by praising the graceless boy, Mohammed. Like all mothers, he observed, she dearly loved the scamp of the family. Having heard that Burton had not yet sacrificed a sheep at Muna, she advised his doing so without the slightest delay.

Clearly having no stomach to take part in this communal slaughter, Burton stood by watching this sacrificial rite. Many of the pilgrims dragged their unfortunate victims to a smooth rock near the Akabah, others stood in front of their tents. The animal's face was turned towards the Kaabah, and its throat slit, the pilgrim exclaiming at the same time, "Bismillah! Allahu Akbar!" The surface of the valley was not long in resembling the bloodiest slaughter-house.

On Friday, 16 September, the camels appeared at early dawn, and were loaded without delay. Burton, in particular, was anxious to escape the fetid air of Muna where they were encamped, and to return to Mecca for the sermon. The land stank. Five or six thousand animals had been butchered, and dismembered in this 'Devil's Punchbowl.' Flies swarmed everywhere.

Once back at Mecca they bathed and, as noonday approached, hurried to the Haram in order to hear the sermon. Burton was awestruck by the scene before him:

> The vast quadrangle was crowded with worshippers sitting in long rows, and everywhere facing the central black tower: the showy colours of their dresses were not to be surpassed by the garden of the most brilliant flowers, and such diversity of detail would probably not be seen massed together in any other building……
>
> Apparently in the midst and raised above the crowd by a tall, pointed pulpit whose gilt spire flamed in the sun, sat the preacher, an old man with snowy beard…As the majestic figure began to exert itself there was a deep silence…towards the end of the sermon, every third or fourth word was followed by the simultaneous rise and fall of thousands of voices.
>
> I have seen the religious ceremonies of many lands, but never – nowhere – aught so solemn, so impressive as this spectacle.[29]

His few remaining days at Mecca were spent performing the, so-called, Little Pilgrimage and visiting further holy sites. The latter section of his book, however, is marked by sheer fudge and lies. In one breath, Burton claimed to have insufficient money even to buy a sheep. In the next, to have enquired about the possibility of his proceeding eastward. "Wallah! Effendi," Umar is reported to have exclaimed, "thou art surely mad." Burton's travelling towards the Nafud Desert would, indeed, have been madness, given that his real destination as proposed in London lay to the south of the Arabian peninsula..

He reportedly learned from Umar, that the Bedouins of El Hejaz, were in a highly volatile state caused by reports of the Holy War, lack of money, and rumours of quarrels between the Sherif and the Pasha. Shaykh Masud is even supposed to have advised Burton to remain at Mecca for some months before proceeding to San'a.[30] This sudden, intriguing reference to the capital of the Yemen, provides the vital clue to what, I believe, Burton had originally planned as his route to the Hadramaut.

According to Burckhardt, two pilgrim caravans used to arrive at Mecca from Yemen in earlier times.

The one known as Hadj el Kebsy started from Sada and followed a path along the mountains to Ta'if. The other, composed of Yemenis, Persians and Indians "who had arrived in the harbour of the country, came along the coast." This caravan had been discontinued about 1803 and, when Burckhardt was writing, had not been re-established.[31] Even if it had, it would clearly not have suited Burton's purposes, since the journey from Mecca to San'a, done mostly on foot, had taken 43 days.[32]

Most pilgrims from Yemen, as from Oman,[33] now chose to travel by the easier and quicker sea-route. What seems likely, therefore, is that like Carsten Niebuhr and the other members of the Danish Expedition of 1762-3, Burton originally intended travelling down the Red Sea from Jedda, either to Luhayyah or Hudaydah.[34] In September, the prevailing winds south of 20 degrees were still mainly the favourable northerlies, shifting to variable.[35] The voyage, therefore, should not have taken much longer than a fortnight or so. From there he could have crossed the Tihamah, climbed to San'a in the Yemen Highlands, and then made his way into the Hadramaut by joining one of the merchant caravans.

The modern traveller, writer, and Arabist, Freya Stark, citing Hamdani and Yaqut, said there were two roads: one to the north, and still in existence, which was a short cut, and was 'used by caravans between Hadramaut and Yemen whenever there is a condition of comparative tranquillity along that wild border.' The other was the main road, also referred to by several Arab writers and was the 'route still the one most generally followed by caravans from San'a.' It was twelve stages there to the Wadi Hadramaut.[36] Depending on the frequency of caravans, the journey should not have taken Burton more than six weeks altogether from Mecca. This would have left him ample time for exploring – he had another six months at his disposal – before shipping from Makalla to Aden with the north-east monsoon, and then to Bombay by Company steamer.

As we have already seen, Burton was familiar with the fate of Adolphe von Wrede ten years earlier, and was only too aware of the dangers facing him in the Hadramaut. He later described the inhabitants as 'feared by the soft Indians and Africans for their hardness and determination,' quoting the common proverb that, 'If you meet a viper and a Hazrami, spare the viper.'[37] Many years later in his *Arabian Nights*, he observed that 'the hard nature of these people, the Swiss of Arabia, offers peculiar obstacles to exploration.'[38] These factors in themselves were enough to give Burton pause, if not wholly to deter him. There were others, however. As a later letter from Cairo reveals, he had no stomach for further Arabian exploration. Furthermore, he had accumulated a mass of notes and sketches of his itinerary, and was eager to return to Cairo where they could be transcribed for publication. Burton's excuse was that he saw that his 'star was not in the ascendant, and resolved to reserve myself for a more propitious conjuncture by returning to Egypt.' After resting for a while at Cairo, he then proposed starting a second time for the interior via Muwaylah.[39] This of course was entirely spurious. Even had it been honestly meant, it would have been entirely irrelevant to the purposes of the RGS, which had paid him £200 to explore in the Hadramaut, and not around the Gulf of Akabah.

Around 20-21 September, Burton hired two camels, sending on his heavy boxes with Shaykh, now Haji Nur, to Jeddah. Umar Effendi planned to wait at Mecca till his father had started in command of the drome-dary caravan, when he would secretly take an ass, and join Burton at the port. Bidding a long farewell to his friends, Burton rode out into the open plain, feeling 'a thrill of pleasure, such as only the captive delivered from his dungeon can experience.' Dr Wallin, too, had been eager to escape from the city for fear of detec-tion, contrasting strongly with Burckhardt, who felt 'terribly at ease in Mecca.'

Once again, Burton's description of events dating from his arrival in Jeddah to the end of his narrative, sounds wholly contrived. Allegedly, 'not having more than ten pence of borrowed coin,' and with the camel-men and donkey-boy clamouring for their money, he needed to cash the draft given to him by the RGS at the British Vice-Consulate. As will be seen later from a letter written from Suez, there is no mention of any such draft being drawn on. Burton's account as given in *The Life*, which contains variations from the text of his book, probably due to later tampering with the original manuscript, describes his being left cooling his heels outside the Vice-Consulate for a long time, and hearing someone say, "Let the dirty nigger wait." When, eventually, the Vice-Consul, Charles J.D. Cole, consented to see him, Burton presented him with a bit of paper as if it were a money order, on which were scrawled the words, "Don't recognise me; I am Dick Burton, but I am not safe yet. Give me some money (naming the sum), which will be returned from London, and don't take any notice of me." After this, Cole frequently invited him to the Consulate after dark.[40]

Burton now claimed to be still hesitating about his next voyage, not wishing to travel *down* the Red Sea alone in this season. One morning Umar Effendi appeared, weary, and fearful of pursuit. After giving him a pipe and hot tea, he was hidden in a dark hole and covered over with grass. His father appeared next morning, but left after a fruitless search. Returning from the Hammam that evening, Burton found the house in an uproar. The father had returned with a group of friends and relatives, and Umar Effendi was eventually discovered, and led away unresisting.

Deprived of a companion, Burton decided to return to Egypt as quickly as possible. Mohammed, having obtained all Burton's disposable articles, and hinted that after Burton's return to India, a present of 20 dollars would find him at Mecca, departed with an unaccountable coolness. Burton, we are led to believe, had taken him on board the *Dwarka*, when booking a passage to Suez. Mohammed's earlier suspicions were at last confirmed. "Now I understand," he said later to his fellow-servant, "your master is a Sahib from India, he hath laughed at our beards."

Burton spent his remaining days at the Vice-Consulate, glad of the company of a fellow-countryman, and the chance of talking 'shop' about the service. On 26 September, the *Dwarka* steamed out of Jeddah on its voyage up the Red Sea, anchoring a week later in Suez Harbour.[41]

CHAPTER THIRTEEN

THE FLESHPOTS OF EGYPT

Burton spent the next three months in Egypt . This is only apparent from a passing reference to this period in the first volume of his *Pilgrimage*.[1] No details were furnished either by Burton at the time, or later in his wife's biography. He would claim in his third volume, that he was detained in Egypt by illness, until it was necessary for him to return to India.[2] The implication, naturally, was that nothing happened there to merit attention.

In fact, the very reverse is true. This is clear from letters written to Dr Norton Shaw from Suez and Cairo.[3] Burton, undoubtedly, spent the first fortnight recuperating, sorting through his notes and sketches, and enjoying the 'open-hearted hospitality' of George West, at the British Consulate in Suez. It was not until early in the morning of 16 October, following the late-night arrival of the P&O liner, *Madras*, with passengers and mail from Calcutta, that Burton hurriedly set about writing two letters to Dr Shaw.

His devoted his 'official' letter to giving a brief outline of his late itinerary. As in the expanded account in his book, it contained no reference whatever to his real, and unaccomplished, mission to the Hadramaut. He promised that his detailed notes and sketches would be forwarded to the Society as soon as he had time to write them out. However, since the journey had slightly undermined his health, he was unable to give a definite date as to when he would be ready to make a second attempt. He concluded by informing Shaw that bills would shortly be presented to the Society for cash sums of £70 and £30, obtained respectively from Sam Shepheard of the British Hotel [Cairo], and Hugh Thurburn of Alexandria. There was no mention of any sum of money obtained on the RGS draft, allegedly presented to Charles Cole at Jeddah only a month earlier. How could there be? The amounts make it clear, that Burton had drawn on all the money allotted to him *before* leaving for Arabia.

The private letter, dashed off in pencil, expressed concern at the Society's possible displeasure at his not having written sooner. 'Couldn't,' he wrote, 'I was quite a nigger at Cairo and saw no English. Besides, having nothing whatever to say, I thought it best to say nothing.' This, of course, was totally disingenuous. Burton had ample opportunities through his contacts at Alexandria, Cairo, and Suez, to pass on information to the Society. As for having nothing whatever to say, he spent almost the whole of one volume describing his experiences at these places.

Conscious, obviously, that some incredulity might be expressed at his having drawn on the whole of the £200, especially since he had only completed the preliminaries of his mission, he asked Shaw not to be 'astonished at the Coin going sharp.' Although he had lived for nothing at Cairo, the Hejaz was extremely expensive. It is highly probable, in my view, that Burton deliberately exaggerated the costs, and that a substantial amount of the second £100 remained, which he later used to finance his hotel and other expenses at Cairo.

Asking, somewhat inconsequentially, if the Society wanted him to go from Akaba to the Dead Sea, he quickly passed on to what was, obviously, the *raison d'être* of the letter. He had heard that the Society was intending to send an expedition to Zanzibar. '"Dakilah," as the Arabs say, "I take refuge with you." 'I shall strain every nerve to command it, or rather get the command – and if you assist me, I'm a made man. I want Platte with me and a young fellow called Taylor to do the actual instrument work and self.[4] Only plenty of time! And a few muskets to carry things with a high hand.'

Burton's unidentified informant, however, was wrong. There is nothing in the Minute Books or the Presidential Address for that year, or the preceding one, which suggests that the RGS was contemplating an expedition to Zanzibar.[5] Promising Shaw to write by the next mail, Burton added a hasty postscript asking for his arrival in Egypt to be reported in some London paper to notify friends of his safe return.[6] Some hours later, he was aboard one of the Overland Transit vans on his way back to Cairo.[7]

The following day, Burton booked into Shepheard's Hotel overlooking the green expanse of the Ezbekiyah Square. Although the best hotel in Cairo, it was far from being the marble and plush palace torched by violent anti-British demonstrators in January 1952. In fact, Shepheard's in those days, as recalled by the American Consul-General, Edwin de Leon, 'presented more the aspect of a grim old barrack than that of a hostelry, with its stone walls four feet in thickness and paved likewise with stone, capable of standing a long siege if necessary.'[8] Nevertheless, it had long enjoyed the reputation of being the fashionable resort of the Egyptian tourist. 'Perhaps in no hotel in the world,' observed the correspondent of *The Illustrated London News*, 'do you find such an assembly of the people of rank and fashion from all countries as are found daily sitting down to the table d'hôte in the grand salon of this establishment.' Even so, by modern standards, the hotel's tariff was surprisingly reasonable. For 280 piastres per week (£2 6s 8d), guests received full board and lodging. By the end of his stay, therefore, exclusive of any other necessary expenses, Burton would have run up a bill of 3,360 piastres. This suggests, in my view, that he used the remainder of the RGS's £200 to wholly subsidise his prolonged stay in Egypt.

It was a month before he wrote again, a delay which he blamed on having been laid up with dysentery since his departure from Suez. 'I won't say it was aggravated by disgust at my failure in crossing the Peninsular (*sic*),' he said, 'but joking apart the "physic" of a successful man differs widely from that of the poor devil who has failed.' This sentiment is in marked contrast with that later expressed in the valedictory paragraph of his book, where, quoting Fahsien, he wrote that his heart was 'moved with emotions of gratitude that I have been permitted to effect the objects I had in view.'[9]

After living in primitive, unhygienic conditions for several months, it was entirely plausible, of course, that Burton should be suffering from a mild form of dysentery. In its more serious form, it could be fatal. Earlier explorers such as Frederick Hornemann, Ali Bey el Abassi, and Johann Ludwig Burckhardt, had died from the disease. Burton's previous and subsequent behaviour, however, as well as the contents of his letters, suggest that it was little more than a convenient excuse for staying in Egypt as long as it suited him to do so.

Much of his long letter consisted of haphazard jottings written in a racy style. He was living in the hotel, he said, with a young fellow called Sankey, a traveller in Barbary,[10] and someone whom he mistakenly referred to as Galeazzo Visconti, the Revolutionary.[11] Shepheard's, he assured Shaw, with mock gravity, was 'a precious scene of depravity, showing what Cairo can do at a pinch and beating the Arabian Nights all to chalks. That too when the Pacha has positively forbidden fornication.'[12]

Being the height of the season, the place was full of 'swell tourists. No end of gents who keep journals & will doubtless commemorate their Nile boats and Dragomans in mortal prose. We've an American missionary woman at the hotel who purposes authorship: 'tis to be hoped she won't write as she conversations's. As I am still dressed in nigger fashion & called the Haji, she thinks me a Jew. But at dinner I catch her gimlet eye & see the ear well open and consequently, Oh, Shaw! Wonderful are the tales of Yemen which are conveyed to her sensorium.' Their content may well be imagined from his later description of Yemen as being 'the most demoralised country, and San'a the most depraved city in Arabia.'[13]

Mixed up with these gossipy comments, however, were some important pieces of information. Two weeks earlier, Burton's friend of the Sind days, Dr John Ellerton Stocks, turned up at Shepheard's on his way back to England on sick-leave. In conversation with Stocks, who had volunteered for the original expedition, Burton now learned of the RGS's long-standing interest in exploring Somaliland. 'The Bombay Government, a short time before this,' he informed Shaw with sardonic humour, 'sanctioned an expedition to the Somali coast, or rather, country. But Carter (the Palinurus doctor) not relishing the chance of losing his cod – that misguided people are in the habit of cutting them off and hanging them as ornaments round their arms – refused to explore the interior.'

Burton later claimed to have 'conceived the idea of reviving the Somali Expedition,' *after* his return from the Hejaz to Bombay.[14] The letter clearly shows this to be untrue. He told Shaw that he would be ready to explore 'the Inferno' as he called it, the following summer, if he could obtain leave. Since it was reported that Sir James Hogg was to continue as Chairman of the East India Company, Burton would have to rely on the Bombay Government.[15] He was convinced that Lord Elphinstone would easily give his consent. If the Duke of Newcastle went out, that would suit him even better. He had been assured by Stocks, that he would not meet any opposition to the scheme at Bombay. On the other hand, he would not find anyone active in helping him either. As a result, Burton added pointedly, they would require some outside pressure. He forecast that he would probably have regained his health by the winter, since he already felt better and stronger. He had to be back in India by March, and would be ready to start for Somaliland immediately after the hot season. 'Want one summer for Amharic,' he added, 'and the vulgar tongue.'

The exploration of Zanzibar, nevertheless, continued uppermost in his mind. He repeated his wish to lead a scientific expedition there, confident of its success if he could obtain Government money for a small team to accompany him, one to survey, another for medicine and botany. He believed that, if given permission, Stocks, in spite of being on furlough, would be willing to join him. 'Above all things he's an excellent chap, but a mad bitch. Very mad.' Burton was convinced that there were good reasons for sending a mission to Zanzibar. It was one of the headquarters of slavery, the Americans were quietly but surely carrying off the commerce of the country, and it had huge, undeveloped resources.

Plainly doubtful of Shaw's response to this new-found enthusiasm for Zanzibar, especially since the Society had funded him handsomely for exploring in the Hadramaut, he wrote, 'You will ask why I now prefer Zanzibar to Arabia?' His answer, rather mystifyingly, was that he had now tried both sides of Arabia,[16] and could see no practical results. It was delightful travelling there, of course, he added hastily, careful not to give the impression that Arabia was a total dead letter, and nothing would give him greater pleasure than leave for three or four years to the eastern coast. However, 'nothing except more discovery of deserts, valleys, and tribes would come of it; no horses, no spices and scant credit as von Wrede's book – a ridiculous affair if report here speaks truly of how he collected it – will take the maidenhead of the subject.'

This is an extraordinary declaration, of course, for someone ostensibly dedicated to 'spanning the deserts' and 'removing the huge white blot' on the map of Arabia. It is also noteworthy in showing that he could not bring himself to mention the Hadramaut by name, instead referring to it obliquely as 'the subject.' Ironically, Baron von Wrede's book did not appear until 1870, nine years after his death.[17]

Cairo was a cosmopolitan gossip shop, and in the comparatively short time Burton had been there, he had become friendly not only with Linant de Bellefond, the brilliant French engineer, but with several other travellers: James Hamilton and Charles Didier, who had recently returned from North Africa, and were planning a trip to Arabia; and a young German, Heinrich Freiherr von Maltzan who was stimulated enough in his discussions with Burton at Shepheard's Hotel, into going in disguise to Mecca seven years later.[18] In particular, Burton became 'very thick,' with Arnaud d'Abbadie, the younger of two brothers of Irish-French extraction, who had spent ten years (1838-48) in a monumental survey of Ethiopian geography, geology, archaeology, and natural history.[19] Arnaud had recently returned for a short visit, and Burton obviously met him while he was recovering from a bout of illness before returning to France. It was possibly in conversation with Arnaud d'Abbadie that Burton had his imagination fired by accounts of the mysterious city of Harar, the ancient capital of the Muslim Adal state in the Chercher highlands of eastern Ethiopia.

It was the appearance in Cairo of another man, however, which would have the greatest impact on Burton. 'Krapf just arrived from Zanzibar,' he wrote flippantly, 'with discoveries about the sources of the White Nile, Kiliamanjaro & Mts of Moon which remind one of de Lunatico.' In spite of his facetiousness, his intentions were serious enough. 'I have not seen him,' he went on, 'but don't intend to miss the spectacle, especially to pump what really has been done and what remains to be done.'

The Rev Dr Johann Ludwig Krapf, after being expelled from Abyssinia with other Protestant missionaries in 1842, had established a mission station two years later at Rabbai Mpia just outside Mombasa on the East African coast. Popularly known as the Mombas Mission, its energetic members as Burton later described them, had 'the honour of having made the first systematic attempt to explore and open up the Zanzibar interior. It was their discoveries which excited a spirit of inquiry which led to the exploration of the Lake Regions.'[20] On 11 May 1848, during a journey into the Jagga Highlands, Krapf's missionary colleague, Johann Rebmann, had made the first European sighting of the snow-capped peak of Kilimanjaro. This was followed in the same year by Krapf, himself, who glimpsed the snow-covered summit of Mt Kenya, after leaving Kitui on 3 December.[21]

These discoveries were not long in sparking off renewed interest in the description of the Nile sources by the second century Alexandrian geographer, Ptolemy. The basis of his account was a story originally told by a Greek merchant, Diogenes, to the Syrian geographer, Marinus of Tyre, in the first century AD.[22] By that time, as is clear from the *Periplus of the Erythraean Sea*, Greek merchants from Alexandria were already sailing down the east coast of Africa as far as Rhapta, a port on the mainland, probably facing the island of Zanzibar. Ptolemy related how 'one Diogenes, returning from India, was caught, when off Cape Aromata (Guardafui), by a gale from the north, and was then driven with the land on his right hand, till in twenty-five days he came abreast of the lakes whence the Nile flows, and which are a little north of Rhapta.' With every appearance of scientific accuracy, he placed one on his map in latitude 6° S, longitude 57° E, the other in latitude 7° S, and longitude 65°. Flowing from the lakes were two rivers, which he showed as meeting at 2° north of the equator and in 60° longitude.[23] Rather strangely, in a quite separate chapter, he added a further detail: 'The shores of this gulf – the shallow seas as far as Prasum – are inhabited by cannibals, on the West of whom throughout, extend the Mountains of the Moon, from which the lakes of the Nile receive the snows.'[24]

It will be seen in a few months, to what extent Burton was affected by the missionaries' discoveries and Ptolemy's theories. In the meantime, he told Shaw that he was working at the sketches which he had made at Mecca and Medina. 'There are artists here who can assist me but none in India. So notes go on slowly especially as writing works one's brain and brain works one's belly.' He claimed that he was preparing a paper for the Society, which they would receive in the Spring. 'I only hope they understand the reason of my silence.'

The real reason for his silence, of course, is that he was doing everything for himself, and little or nothing for the Society. Plainly confident that he would eventually receive permission to explore in Somaliland, he was in a hurry to complete as much of his manuscript as he could before returning to India. It is clear from a reference in Burton's own book, that only a month after arriving in Cairo, he was well on the way towards finishing what would eventually be volume one of his *Pilgrimage*.[25]

Burton sent his final letter a month later. 'You'll be astonished,' he said, perhaps redundantly, 'when you see my direction. Still here.' He now claimed to be just recovering from his dysentery, and hoped before the end of the month to be quite well. He then intended, he said, 'to start off in Sinai direction and see what is to be done there.' He repeated the excuses of his former letter, that progress on his notes was slow, and he had sketches to complete and a variety of work in hand, which he did not specify. Since the journey would make a great gap in his writing time, he would be unable to send Shaw his first instalment until May.

He reported that Lord Elphinstone had passed through Cairo on his way to Bombay, and he had accompanied him to the Pyramids.[26] 'I flatter myself that leave will not be withheld,' he said, 'and if so I only want your help to get up something like an expedition to Zanzibar. If time be only allowed me I will pass over to the Atlantic.' If the Society wanted, he would apply for leave to Arabia, but Zanzibar appeared to be the field. He told Shaw that he would meet Krapf in England. 'He is, I hope, only my John the Baptist. I must be *au courant* of his discoveries.[27]

It only now remained for him to wind up his affairs in Cairo. He had no intention, of course, of making any journey to Sinai. Neither did he intend immediately returning to Bombay, which is the impression he gives in his book. What he now proposed was to leave Egypt within a few weeks and stop off at Aden. By doing so, he could, in a sense, combine business with pleasure. In the first instance, he would be able to discuss questions relating to Somaliland with the Political Agent, Captain S. B. Haines, and his assistant, Lieutenant C. J. Cruttenden.[28] In the second, he would be able to renew his friendship with John F. Steinhaeuser, who had been appointed Civil Surgeon at the colony earlier that year.[29]

Burton left Cairo on 16 January 1854, accompanied by Charles Didier and his English companion, the Abbé James Hamilton bound for Suez.[30] After a leisurely three-day caravan journey across the desert they parted, his companions proceeding down the Red Sea in a hired sambuk for Jedda, and Burton embarking on one of the EIC's steamers for Aden.

His only reference to this visit was made more than thirty years later in the *Arabian Nights*. Writing in the Foreword that the translation was 'a natural outcome' of his Pilgrimage to El-Medinah & Meccah, he went on: 'At Aden in the so-called winter of 1852 [*sic*],[31] I put up with my old and dear friend Steinhaeuser....and when talking over Arabia and the Arabs we at once came to the same conclusion that while the name of this wondrous treasury of Moslem folklore is familiar to almost every child, no general reader is aware of the valuables it contains, nor indeed will the door open to any but Arabists.' Before he left, they agreed to collaborate in producing 'a full, complete, unvarnished, uncastrated copy of the great original,' Steinhaeuser translating the prose, and Burton the metrical part.[32]

The impression is clearly given that Steinhaeuser was familiar with Arabic at this time. This is manifestly untrue. His army records show that he had qualified as an interpreter in Hindustani in 1851.[33] It was his only linguistic qualification, and remained so for the rest of his Army service. He was, therefore, in no position to understand any of the Arabic text of the *Arabian Nights*, other than what Burton told him. I believe that Burton's claim that the two were to collaborate in translation is a lie, but on this occasion done from a worthy motive. By linking their names together in this way, Burton sought to keep alive the memory of his closest friend, whose death in 1866 at the early age of fifty-one, touched him deeply.

Furthermore, Burton's real opinion at the time towards translating this work, was rather different from the impression given in 1885. 'The most familiar of books in England, next to the Bible,' he wrote, 'it is one of the least known, the reason being that about one-fifth is utterly unfit for translation, and the most sanguine Orientalist would not dare to render literally more than three-quarters of the remainder.'[34]

Aden had important commercial links not only with the Somali coast, but with the Horn of Africa in general. Frequently under attack from the Arabs in the hinterland, the colony's very existence depended on an unhindered flow of essential supplies coming across the Gulf. With growing French interest in the region, ports such as Berbera and Tajura, also had a strategic significance. Both Haines and Cruttenden, therefore, kept a keen eye on what was going on in Somaliland, and were able to furnish Burton with a great deal of useful advice and information.

He also familiarised himself with the town's Somali Quarter, giving him an opportunity of briefly studying the people and their language. Some eighteen hundred of them were living there in 1854, many without shelter or any visible means of support, who just squatted down wherever they could find a space.[35] Through Capt Haines, Burton was introduced to several Somali chiefs, who promised him safe conduct in travelling through their territories during his expedition. Having spent a highly profitable fortnight at Aden, Burton left for Bombay, arriving there on 21 February 1854.

CHAPTER FOURTEEN

PREPARING FOR THE INFERNO

Burton left no written record of this period either at Bombay or, later, at Aden. An outline of his stay, therefore, has to be pieced together from military records, supplemented by material from other sources. Only in one respect did he shed light on it, and that quite fortuitously, through the dedication of his book to 'The Honorable James Grant Lumsden…. within whose hospitable walls my project of African travel was matured….'

According to Thomas Wright, Burton met Lumsden on board ship, when he was returning to Bombay from Egypt in his Arab dress. Struck by Burton's appearance, Lumsden turned to a friend and remarked, "What a clever intellectual face that Arab has!" Overhearing the remark, Burton 'made some humorous comment in English, and thus commenced a pleasant friendship.'[1] Wright, however, was totally ignorant of the real facts concerning Burton's stay in, or departure from, Egypt, nor did he know anything about Lumsden's professional background. Although the anecdote has been repeated in every biography since, it represents, in my opinion, yet another example of Wright's use of fictitious embroidery.

The son of an Army officer, Lumsden was educated at Haileybury, and went out to India as a Writer in 1826. During the ensuing years, his obvious abilities brought him promotion to a number of important posts as Political Agent, Collector, Magistrate, and Judge. In 1848 he was appointed Secretary to Government in the Judicial, General, and Persian Department.[2] He and Burton may well have become personally acquainted the previous year, when Burton sat his Persian examination in Bombay. On 28 November 1853 Lumsden was appointed Provisional Member of Council, becoming a full member the following February.[3] Burton now had two of the most powerful men in the Presidency on his side.

Lumsden's house, where Burton spent the next four months, was situated some miles to the north of Bombay at Chinchpoogly, a quiet leafy suburb not far from the Governor's residence at Parel. Known as *Belair*, it was a large imposing stone building standing in its own grounds, surrounded by shrubbery and overshadowed by tall graceful coconut palms and tamarinds.[4] The narrow channel separating Bombay island from the mainland was close by, providing a welcome sea-breeze in the evenings during the sticky enervating heat of the hot season, which was now fast approaching. The two men appear to have got on famously. Burton's conversation, by turns intellectual and earthy, must have come as a revelation to someone like Lumsden, who had spent a rather dull, conventional existence in the Indian political service. It was possibly at *Belair* that Burton was introduced to a young man of twenty-one, a recent entrant into the Bombay Civil Service, Forster Fitzgerald Arbuthnot, on whom Burton must have had much the same effect.[5] The two became life-long friends, collaborating almost thirty years later through the so-called Kama

Shastra Society, in the translation and printing mainly of works of Eastern erotica, beginning with the famous *Kama Sutra*.

Probably at the Governor's request, Burton was given temporary employment in the Political Department. This effectively released him from military duties, allowing him to concentrate most of his energy on preparing for the forthcoming expedition. It also gave him the freedom to continue working on the manuscript of his book, and completing his papers for the RGS.[6] Besides working at *Belair*, Burton was no doubt able to enjoy the facilities of the libraries of Bombay's two learned societies, the Geographical, and the Royal Asiatic Society, whose Hon Secretary, as we have already seen, was Burton's friend, Henry Carter.[7]

It was Burton's practice never to travel in a region where he was unfamiliar with the language. He was, of course, fluent in Arabic, which was widely enough known throughout Somalia to enjoy the status almost of a second language. Nevertheless, he immediately embarked on a study of the indigenous tongue. Henry Salt had printed a vocabulary of the Somali language in an appendix to his book on Abyssinia.[8] Lt C.P. Rigby had more recently published specimens derived from a collection of words made by Capt T. Smee.[9] It was Rigby's 'An Outline of the Somauli Language, with Vocabulary,' however, which provided Burton with his most important learning aid.[10] Later, in his only criticism of, what he called, Rigby's 'excellent paper' with its 'modest title,' Burton questioned the author's assertion that the Somali language was totally dissimilar to Arabic in construction.[11]

Important as was Rigby's contribution, Burton's biggest debt was owed to three papers on the Somali country written by Lt C.J. Cruttenden. On the night of 1 August 1843, the steam frigate *Memnon* carrying the mails from Bombay to Suez was wrecked in a gale off Ras Assair on the north-east coast of Africa. In his capacity as Assistant Political Agent, Cruttenden was sent to oversee the salvage operation. He was there for six months and, during that time, made use of every opportunity for making 'frequent short excursions inland' to study the country and its people.[12]

His resulting report was followed five years later by two further papers on Somalia. The shorter of these is important for its description of the Wadi Nogal, which Burton would later ask Lt John Hanning Speke to explore. 'This "happy valley",' as Cruttenden described it, 'is spoken of in the most glowing terms by the natives, and apparently forms their great route for trade. The people of Ogahden, Murreyhan &c., bring all their gums, ivory and ghee along this valley as being the safest and least fatiguing route, and the people are described as a peaceful race, who subsist chiefly by the chace (*sic*), and by their sale of ostrich feathers, myrrh and ghee.' In Cruttenden's opinion, the valley offered a suitable and safe starting point for the traveller.[13]

A much longer article appeared later that year, based on visits to the Somali tribes inhabiting the African coast westward from Burnt island to Zayla, and on information obtained about the southern branches of the Darood living along the banks of the Webbe Shebeyli.[14] Among many other subjects, it dealt with Harar and the fair at Berbera, from which Burton quoted copiously. Cruttenden also commented on the feasibility of travelling in the region. 'From Gananeh to Berbera is 24 days for a Kafila, from the Webbe Shebeyli 19 days, and from Ogahden 9 days.' He considered the journey fully practicable for a European, if known to the Somali tribes on the coast.[15]

By late April, Burton was ready to submit his application to the Bombay Government.[16] Little of its detailed and wide-ranging contents, however, later appeared in the preface to Burton's book.

After recalling the Royal Geographical Society's earlier attempt to gain the East India Company's support for exploring Somalia,[17] Burton listed his own qualifications for conducting such an expedition, which he considered was 'still most desirable.' Not only had he studied all the relevant literature on the subject, he could also speak Arabic, and was now studying Somali, the vulgar tongue of conversation. His recent journey in the Hejaz would, he believed, 'plead in his favour as regards the temper, prudence, and *savoir faire* necessary for those who surmount the difficulties of pioneering a path for civilization through the semi-barbarous tribes of Africa.' Furthermore, he could cite several works published both in England and in India, as proof of his ability to prepare the results of exploration to meet the public eye. As for his general fitness, he had received a letter from Captain Haines containing, amongst other subjects, several allusions to it, but 'couched in terms too flattering to be quoted by myself.'

With regards to the scientific aims of the expedition, he felt it unnecessary to more than touch on the advantage of opening up to geographical research a region marked 'unexplored' in the best maps. Not only was it interesting in its situation, it was even more interesting in the huge variety of ethnographical and physiological questions which it posed. This applied equally to the studies of botany and natural history.

In the light of recent events, he considered the opening up of the region through the Haines (or Shebelle) and Ganana rivers, highly advisable from a political point of view. The Austrian Government, he claimed:

> having established a militant mission in forts and strong places armed with cannon, North and South of the Equator, proposes, in course of time, to use an army of natives trained like the "voyageurs" of Canada, to convey the rich and various productions of the interior down the navigable streams to the Eastern Ocean. No expense is spared to secure success for this novel enterprise, as those who have lately resided at Cairo will know. The missionaries are hot in their hopes that before a few years have elapsed they will have opened a line of connection with Zanzibar, where the produce of their industry can be shipped to Suez. Gt Britain has higher interests at stake than Austria, greater inducements and far more opportunities to establish a centre of traffic in these lands, and it is evident that an effort on its part to secure the command of the Eastern coast of Africa is now desirable.

Burton was no scientist, and his claims for the scientific benefits to be derived from the expedition were markedly extravagant. This was also the case with his political assessment, which was largely a travesty of events in Central Africa, following on the opening up of the White Nile route southwards to missionaries and traders by three Egyptian expeditions, 1839-42. As for his 'militant missions,' they belonged to the realm of fantasy. The missionaries failed to establish any friendly and meaningful rapport with the surrounding tribes, and their numbers were decimated by fever and disease. When the trader, J.A. Vayssière visited the station at Gondokoro in 1853, he found only three weak and dispirited priests, relying for their safety on four small-calibre cannon of the sort used for salutes and signalling.[18] In the year Burton was writing, the station was abandoned.[19]

Quoting from the reports of Lts Christopher[20] and Dansey,[21] Burton then went on to consider his proposed expedition in, what he called, 'its most important point of view, the commercial.' Referring to the great annual fair at Berbera, 'where the widely diverging radii of caravan roads from inner Africa meet,' he cited Dansey's suggestion of appointing a Government official to act as an adviser in controlling and preventing petty tribal feuds, which presently acted 'to frighten away the timid merchants (African and Foreign).' He forecast that, in less than a year, this would result in the growth of a large and permanent town.

Given the necessary permission, he intended to lose no time in leaving Bombay. While it would be impossible to travel in the Somali country during the rains, he could use the time profitably in preparing for the expedition at Aden. He had been advised by Capt Haines and Lt Cruttenden, 'two most competent counsellors,' to leave Aden for Berbera early in October. From there, if possible, 'he would push forward to Hurrur, the capital of the Somali country. My route would then be SW to Ganana, whence it is conceived I could make my way SE to Zanzibar.'

He had met Somali chiefs at Aden, who had offered him safe conduct through their territory. He felt able to trust them, because they had interests under British protection. From Zanzibar, his movements would be governed by circumstances. If his services were required in India, he would have to return there by a coasting voyage. If, on the other hand, he were allowed to penetrate westwards, he would seek the assistance of a Major Hamerton in securing the interests of His Highness the Imam of Muscat, and advance towards Central Africa.'[22] And now Burton came to what, undoubtedly for him, was the nub of the letter:

> It may be permitted me to observe that I cannot contemplate without enthusiasm, the possibility of bringing my compass to bear upon the Jebel Hamar, those "Mountains of the Moon," whose very existence have not, until lately, been proved by those geographers of 2000 years – a range white with eternal snows even in the blaze of the African summer, supposed to be the father of the mysterious Nile, briefly a tract invested with all the romance of wild fable and hoar antiquity, and to this day the [most] worthwhile subject to which human energy and enterprise could be devoted. For unnumbered centuries, explorers have attempted the unknown source of the "White River" by voyaging and travelling metaphorically and literally against the stream. I shall be the first to try by a more feasible line to begin with the head.

One need go no further than this eloquent passage for the key to understanding the nature of Burton's later attitude towards his erstwhile companion, Speke. It explains, too, his dogged refusal over many years, to accept that this, the greatest prize offered to the explorer, was irrevocably beyond his grasp. Burton, of course, was not entirely honest in claiming to be the first to try to trace the river's source by starting at the head. Based on his own investigations, the geographer, Dr Charles Beke, placed the sources of the Nile at a relatively short distance from the coast, within the dominions of the Imam of Muscat.[23] Convinced that the eastern seaboard offered the easiest route into central intertropical Africa, he collected a subscription and, in February 1849, sent out a young German professor, Dr Friedrich Bialloblotzky, to make the attempt. Following the murder of a French naval officer, M. Maizan, the coast was a veritable hornets' nest. Hamerton, therefore, supported by the missionary, Dr Krapf, refused the professor access to the African mainland.[24]

Obviously advised by Dr Carter, Burton said that as far as expenses were concerned, he wanted no more than had been sanctioned for the previous expedition. 'In an undertaking of such importance, pay is the least thing to be considered.' He was quite prepared to start 'alone and unattended.' In order to do justice to the subject, however, he would require a Medical Officer, whose duty would be to make a collection of fauna and flora. He, therefore, recommended the botanist, Dr Stocks, then on furlough in England, who had asked to be informed if permission to travel were given. He had also received an offer to accompany him from Lt Herne of the Bombay Fusiliers, 'an officer accustomed to daguerreotype, and to take astronomical observations, and was well-known for his ingenuity in mathematics.'[25]

In addition, he required a well-educated Indian youth, a Muslim if possible, to assist him in making a chart of the country day by day, and in laying down the longitudes, latitudes, and altitudes of their various stations. He, himself, would pursue philological enquiries, keep the Ephemeris, summarise the information collected by his colleagues, and prepare a work worthy of placing before the public. He could obtain the guides, guards and animals at Aden. He would need surveying instruments, and letters from Government or from the Political Department at Aden, addressed to certain chiefs. A list of their names had been forwarded to him by Lt Cruttenden. He would also need a few presents for them, mainly fine Abyssinian tobes, together with an ordinary fowling-piece for each one. Burton concluded by pointing out that, if his project were approved by the Right Hon the Governor in Council, 'the sooner he was allowed to get in touch with the literary societies of Europe, and to begin preparations for the journey, the more satisfactory would be its results.'

Just over a week later, he was informed by Government, that his letter had been 'perused with very great interest by the Rt Hon the Governor in Council,' and would be referred for the favourable consideration of the Hon the Court of Directors at the earliest opportunity. In the meantime he was asked to give a succinct account of the expenses involved.[26] The Hon Board met on 8 May. After acknowledging the long-held view of the RGS, one moreover supported by the Court of Directors, as to the importance of an expedition to Somalia, it went on to give Burton a remarkable character reference:

> The extraordinary facility in acquiring languages possessed by Lt Burton, of which six successful examinations constitute a very imperfect illustration, his power of adapting himself to various classes of men and circumstances, his keen relish for adventure combined with judgement and promptitude, as exhibited in his early visit to Mecca, his quick observation and facility of composition, have impressed Government with the conviction that Lt Burton has very rare qualifications for the important mission which he proposes to undertake, and that his researches will enable him to produce a work which will be recognised by scholars of all countries as a valuable contribution to scientific literature.

As Burton expected, the Board found the proposed expenses of 500 rupees per month 'reasonable and moderate.'[27] It also pointed to another advantage overlooked by him, namely, the possibility of introducing into India a regular supply of the hardy breed of horses and mules found in the Somali country.[28] As to the question of his further researches in Africa, it was felt that a decision on these could be deferred until the results of the expedition could be assessed. Furthermore, if Burton was granted permission to undertake the expedition, he should take steps to complete it within twelve months from the date of its commencement.

On 9 May, Burton was informed that his proposals would be referred to the Hon The Court of Directors by the following day's overland mail. In the meantime, he was permitted to proceed to Aden for a period of six months, in order to complete his study of the Somali language, and to obtain whatever preliminary information he could from the merchants living there.

Unknown to Burton, a month before he sent in his application, a Lt Henchy of the Madras Artillery had also applied to explore in Somalia. His application to the Chief Secretary to the Government, Fort St George, was forwarded to Bombay. On 28 April he was informed that, after the appointment of a permanent successor to Capt Haines, his request would be taken into consideration.[29]

Shortly after the Board's letter was sent to the Court of Directors in London, news of Burton's proposed expedition and his impending departure for Aden appeared in *The Bombay Times*. Henchy wrote to Burton, and received the following reply:

> I heard of your application to the Bombay Government, and would be delighted if you would apply to your Government to accompany me. We would not start before the beginning of October, but our time might be usefully spent at Aden making ready for the journey. I leave this for Aden on the 20th June with surveying instruments and everything required. It is expected that the Court will give leave, and now that Colonel Outram is to be at Aden, we shall receive every assistance from the local authorities. I am working at Somalee, the language with which you are conversant, and hope soon to master it. Will you kindly let me have a line saying what your plans are....[30]

This letter is particularly interesting for two reasons. On the one hand, it shows Burton's friendly and positive attitude towards Henchy, which is completely at odds with the later garbled and malicious version purveyed by Speke. On the other, it presents a totally different impression of Col Outram from that later conveyed by Burton. On 8 June, Henchy wrote to Fort St George, requesting leave for six months in order to join Burton at Aden. This letter was sent on to Bombay, stating that the Madras Government was prepared to grant Lt Henchy the necessary leave. So far, matters appeared to be progressing smoothly. As Burton had intimated, he and Lt Herne left for Aden on 20 June aboard the steam frigate *Auckland*.[31]

The British had seized Aden from the Sultan of Lahej in January 1839, thus becoming the first colonial possession of Queen Victoria's reign.[32] Apart from its important strategic position near the entrance of the Red Sea, and its value as a maritime coaling station, it had nothing whatever to recommend it. For the British soldier, it was about as popular a posting as Northern Ireland was during the 'Troubles', with every chance of being shot or stabbed, if foolhardy enough to venture beyond the massive fortifications into the interior. The town of grey stone houses and part of the military cantonment were in a 'Devil's Punchbowl,' hemmed in on three sides by dark brooding volcanic mountains. From May to September it was stifling hot, subject to the oppressive shamal, the sand-laden north wind blowing from the Arabian desert. Only among the hills at Steamer Point on the western side of the peninsula, the preserve mainly of senior officers, was it at all bearable for Europeans, with cool breezes coming off the sea.

Aden would not have been Burton's cup of tea even in better circumstances. He was averse to the gold-fish bowl atmosphere of small colonial circles. He also disliked the starch and march mentality of garrison life. He was contemptuous of the military caste-system, the dull routine and duller rules which insisted that waistcoats were to be worn no matter what the weather, and that visits were to be paid at mid-morning when the temperature stood at 120 degrees. In fact, 'where briefly, the march of mind is at a dead halt and the march of matter is in double quick time to the hospital or sick-quarters.'[33]

Col (later Lt General Sir) James Outram, the newly appointed Political Resident and Commandant, had been in Calcutta in December 1853, fully expecting to return to his post as Resident at Baroda. Lord Elphinstone, however, had written to the Governor-General, Lord Dalhousie, suggesting instead that Outram should be transferred to Aden. Outram later received a letter from the Governor-General stating that, 'The great importance of that position [Aden] in the event of a war being commenced in Europe, which may take any imaginable turn in the course of its progress, has caused me fully to enter into Lord Elphinstone's anxiety to see you there, and to share with him the anticipation of the confidence which your presence in such a position would give to all of us.'[34]

Accordingly, early in May 1854, the Bombay Government was informed that the services of Col Outram were placed at its disposal for employment in the joint military and political capacity.[35] On 26 June, the temporary commandant, Brigadier Clarke, handed over charge of the Residency to Outram, shortly before Burton and Herne's arrival.[36] With Lord Elphinstone's approval, Outram chose as his assistant, Lt R.L. Playfair, a fluent Arabic speaker, who had accompanied him a on a quasi-political mission to Syria, 1848-50.[37]

Outram, however, was far from well. According to Burton, he 'hardly left the house and looked like a weary old man with yellow skin and bloated nose like [a] nutmeg grater, hipped and disgusted.' Four years earlier, Outram had passed on his fears to a friend, Captain W.J. Eastwick, that his tobacco was being poisoned, the result of intrigues at the Gaekwar's court to get rid of him. This was pooh-poohed by Burton as apparently 'one of those obscure diseases of the brain which develop after long years in the tropics. When natives, Hindus or Hindis, do poison you, there is no mistake. They are not such bunglers in these matters as Europeans are...'[38]

At the end of June, Lt Henchy's letter, requesting permission to accompany Burton, was sent from Bombay to Outram, for any remarks he might care to make.[39] The following month, he recommended to Government that Henchy's application should be refused, 'for I find that while stationed at Aden, he incurred the hostility of the Somali tribes here, arising out of circumstances which I do not think it necessary to detail, but so serious a nature as to excite them to mob that officer on one occasion, when he was, I am informed, preserved with some difficulty from maltreatment at their hands.'[40]

His informant was, undoubtedly, Playfair. Not only was he a fellow-officer in Henchy's regiment, but he had been stationed at Aden as assistant executive engineer during the period in question (March to September 1853). Burton suppressed any allusion to Henchy in *First Footsteps*. Eighteen years later, he published a brief and opaque version of the matter, though without mentioning Henchy's name, and clearly displaying hostility towards Outram.[41]

The reason for Outram's reticence is apparent from Burton's later unpublished review of Goldsmid's biography. It appears that Henchy, referred to only as Lieutenant xxxx, had 'had certain affairs with Somali women [which] had made him an object of vengeance to the wild men and I strongly dissuaded him from taking the step.' Nevertheless, Colonel Outram 'who had a kind and feeling as well as a large heart,' was willing to allow Lt Henchy to join the expedition if Burton applied for him on his own responsibility. This, he refused to do.[42]

Earlier that year, a French steam frigate *La Caiman*, had been wrecked off Zayla. As in the case of an earlier incident involving the English brig *Mary Ann*, the survivors had been given assistance by the governor, El Hajj Sharmarkay. Despite the keen political rivalry existing between Britain and France, Sharmarkay was invited to Aden to receive presents from the British Government for his humane action. He arrived on 25 July, and Outram presented him with two double-barrelled Westley Richards fowling pieces.[43]

Sharmakay stayed for the next fortnight, and Burton took the opportunity of meeting this 'remarkable man.' He was a physically impressive figure, tall, one-eyed, and lean, aged about sixty, with a henna-stained tuft of hair on each side of his chin, his head and upper lip shaved Shafei style. Chiefly through British influence, he had risen from humble beginnings to be the chief of his tribe. Despite his age, he was full of energy, 'meditating nothing,' wrote Burton, 'but the conquest of Harar and Berbera, which would make him master of the sea-board, and extend his power as far as Abyssinia.'[44]

Burton now enlisted Sharmarkay's help for a daring venture which he had in mind – an unaccompanied journey to Harar, beginning in October. He asked him to select an *abban* or protector, and to provide camels and mules, paying him the money in advance. The city, of course, appeared on Burton's projected route to Zanzibar. 'The more adventurous Abyssinian travellers,' he wrote in his book, 'Salt and Stuart, Krapf and Isenberg, Barker and Rochet – not to mention divers Roman Catholic Missioners – attempted Harar, but attempted it in vain.[45] The bigoted ruler and barbarous people threatened death to the Infidel who ventured within their walls.' There was a tradition, according to Lt Cruttenden, that the prosperity of the city depended on excluding all travellers not of the Muslim faith, especially Christians.[46] Being a stronghold of slavery, the English in particular were, 'the most hated and dreaded…It was therefore a point of honor….to utilise my title of Haji by entering the city, visiting the ruler, and returning in safety, after breaking the guardian spell.'[47]

By undertaking this hazardous journey, Burton hoped to silence the expedition's many critics of whom, apparently, the Political Resident was one. Burton later publicly blamed Outram for forcing him to change his plans, alleging quite falsely, 'that the Political Resident refused to sanction the scheme proposed'[48] Whatever Outram's own private views about the Somali Expedition, there is not one iota of documentary evidence that he made any official objection to it. All the evidence, in fact, points to his having fully co-operated in the preparations then in progress.[49]

Shortly after mid-September, a tall, fair-haired young Company Officer, Lt John Hanning Speke, disembarked at Aden from the P&O liner from Calcutta, ahead of a mountain of luggage. Having shown a greater aptitude for bird-nesting than book-learning, he had been shipped out to India as a cadet in 1844 at the tender age of seventeen. Later that year he was gazetted as an ensign in the 46th Bengal Native Infantry. The idea of exploring in East Africa had occurred to him in 1849, so he said, after serving in the Sikh Wars with Sir Colin Campbell's so-called *Fighting Brigade*. His intention, later disputed by Burton, was 'to strike the Nile at its head, and then sail down the river to Egypt.' Speke's self-declared aim, however, was not geographical discovery, but to collect 'the fauna of those regions, to complete and fully develop a museum in my father's house, a nucleus of which I had already formed from the rich menageries of India, the Himalayan Mountains and Tibet.'[50] For the last five years, he had used his leaves to indulge his passion for hunting and collecting, neatly solving at the same time the problem of living economically in order to be able to finance his ambitious project. He had now served ten years in India, and was ready to carry it through during a three years' furlough.

Having been led to believe by Captain S.B. Haines, that he could penetrate Somalia, Speke was taken aback by getting a blunt refusal from the new Political Resident. Outram said that 'he would not only withhold his influence, but would prohibit my going there at all, as the countries opposite to Aden were so dangerous for any foreigners to travel in, that he considered it his duty as a Christian to prevent, as far as he was able, anybody from hazarding his life there.'[51] Speke was not one to give up easily. Outram eventually relented, easing his conscience should anything untoward happen, according to Speke, by suggesting that he should ask Burton if he were willing to attach him to the Somali Expedition. If so, the Resident would support Speke's application, and have his furlough cancelled. Burton consented, and Speke was immediately installed as a member of the expedition.

The documentary evidence reveals, however, that the process was not quite as immediate, smooth, and harmonious, as Speke later made out. Far from slipping 'into the role of a quietly adoring younger brother,' as described by one biographer,'[52] there was tension between the two men early on. Around 26 September, Burton received the sad and unexpected news that Dr Stocks had died in England.[53] Replying just under a week later to a question from Outram, Burton said that he expected to derive considerable benefit from Speke's co-operation. Provided that Speke was placed under his orders, he was agreeable to his accompanying the expedition. With the generous sum allowed for the expenses of the journey, he could well afford to include him in the party. However, he went on, he had informed Speke some days earlier that 'he was unable to apply for him at present,' since the death of Dr Stocks had, to a certain extent, altered his plans. He now intended applying for the services of Lt Stroyan of the Indian Navy, with the object of making his survey a geographical one. Meanwhile, with Col Outram's permission, he would direct Lt Speke to a safe place near Berbera. During his own absence in Harar, Speke could 'forward the views of Sir W.J. Hooker and other men of science,' by making botanical and other collections.[54]

This, for whatever reason, was not to Speke's liking. Two days later, an angry Burton was writing to the Political Resident, strongly protesting against Speke's declared wish to enter Somalia via Berbera, especially in view of his having officially applied to accompany the expedition. It rested with Government, Burton remarked tendentiously, 'to forbid its servants interfering with its political interests by incurring useless danger. Berbera would not be completely safe for at least twenty days. However, if Lt Speke so desired, he could land in the Warsungali country, and push inland towards the Wady Nogal at once, of course on his own responsibility.' In order to prevent any unpleasant discussion arising, he wondered whether it was in Col Outram's power to put Speke temporarily on duty without delay.[55]

Burton's potent argument about Government's interests and needless danger was, of course, tantamount to tossing Outram's own private views about the Somali Expedition back into his lap. The Political Resident could hardly ignore it. His directive to Speke that same day, however, suggests that it was done with less than good grace. As a result of Burton's protest, he said, he was 'reluctantly constrained' to forbid Speke's proposed visit to Berbera, 'at any other time, or under other circumstances than may be sanctioned by Lt. Burton under whose orders I have at your own request recommended to Government that you may be placed, and under whose command should you join the Expedition you must consider yourself while employed in East Africa.' In the meantime, pending the sanction of Government, he took upon himself the responsibility of putting Speke temporarily on duty.[56]

On 9 October, Burton received news from Bombay that the Court of Directors had agreed to his proposals. In its despatch, the Court stated that permission was given on the clear understanding that he was 'not to incur immoderate risk' in carrying out his researches. He was to 'carefully feel his way, and not to proceed unless he had reasonable grounds for believing that his own life and that of his associates will not be seriously endangered.' It believed that the Shoa Mission, under the late Major Harris, had committed a serious error in creating suspicion by a 'display of magnificence and extravagant expenditure.' This would be avoided by the manner in which the present exploration was to be carried out. 'It is to be considered not official, but undertaken by Lt Burton as a private traveller, the Government giving no more protection to him than they would to any individual totally unconnected with the Service.' The despatch concluded, by acknowledging the fact that Burton appeared 'eminently qualified to conduct such an expedition, which required not only peculiar attainments, but the combination of energy and perseverance with prudence and discretion.'[57] In the light of later events, some of these words would come to have a hollow ring.

The Court's instructions have been criticised as being 'not very sensible or honest' on the ground that 'the Company could not, in fact, avoid responsibility, if there were trouble.'[58] But the directives had no such implication. They were based on two important considerations. The first was humane. Two soldiers and a Portuguese attendant attached to the Shoa Mission, had been attacked at night and killed by Eesa tribesmen. The Court was, obviously, anxious to avoid any such loss of life. The second was diplomatic. The last thing the Company wanted to do, was to give the impression that the expedition formed part of a plan of intervention in Somalia by the British Government.

Burton acknowledged the Company's letter on 10 October. He pointed out, as he had done to Outram, that the death of Dr Stocks had led him, to a certain extent, to alter his original plan. 'I no longer indulge the hope,' he wrote, 'that the Expedition will distinguish itself by important botanical discovery, although having received from Sir W. Hooker ample instructions concerning collection, we may be able to forward many interesting specimens.' His primary aim now would be 'a geographical and commercial survey of Eastern Africa.'[59] Unless provided with the means of accurate observation, of course, there was little hope of doing justice to the work. The Expedition had an adequate supply of instruments and sufficient finances. All it required now was an able surveyor. He suggested Lt Stroyan, described by his fellow officers of the Indian Navy as being 'accustomed to hard travelling, in the habit of surveying, and exceedingly skilfull [sic] in the use of instruments.' In the event of his request being granted, he had left instructions for Lt Stroyan, since he expected 'to start almost immediately on a trial journey from Zayla inland.'[60]

Burton, of course, already had an 'able surveyor' in Herne, who had been specially detached from his regiment for that very reason. Speke, too, as he had stated in his letter of application to Government, had been told by Burton that he would 'gladly avail himself of my services as Assistant Surveyor.' Since Stroyan had expressed a wish to join the expedition while Burton was still at Bombay, this request could be regarded merely as a ploy to get this likeable young Scot taken on its strength. There was, possibly, another, and more, objective reason. Unlike Herne and Speke, Stroyan was a professionally trained and highly experienced marine surveyor and draughtsman, 'distinguished,' as Burton later wrote, 'by his surveys on the coast of Western India, in Sindh, and on the Panjab Rivers.'[61] Such recognised professionalism might be thought to lend greater authority to what Burton now intended. In the event, it was a fateful decision.

The directions left for Stroyan, formed part of a revised plan adopted, according to Speke, to give the expedition maximum protection. Burton intended to wait until the break-up of the Berbera Fair, and the departure of the caravans inland. The expedition would then follow the usual caravan route through the Ogaden to the Webbe Shebelle, carry on to Ganana, and then make its way, by whatever means, to the Zanzibar coast.[62]

Lt. Herne was instructed to establish a camp at Berbera at the opening of the fair season. When joined by Lt Stroyan, they were to study the country's productive resources, investigate the state of the slave trade, and collect carriage animals for the forthcoming journey. In the event of Burton's being detained by the Emir of Harar, they were 'to demand restitution before allowing the great caravan, which supplies the city with the luxuries of life, to leave the coast.'[63] Speke was to proceed to Bunder Guray, a small harbour on the Warsingali frontier. From there, he was to travel southwards as far as possible. After passing over the maritime hill-range, he was to turn westward, inspect the Wady Nogal, and, after buying horses and camels, make a direct march on Berbera to meet Herne and Stroyan not later than 15 January 1855. His duties were quite onerous, but this time, obviously, much to his liking. They included noting the watershed of the country, plotting his route, keeping detailed notes on everything he saw, collecting specimens of natural history in all its branches, and registering all meteorological phenomena. It was the Himalayas and Tibet all over again.

There was no public money for this undertaking at the time, said Speke, 'as the Indian Government had stipulated that the whole sum they would advance for this great expedition should not exceed £1,000, and, for security's sake, had decided on paying it by instalments at £250 at a time. I, therefore, desirous to render as much assistance as lay within my power to further the cause I had embarked on, volunteered to advance the necessary sum from my own private resources, trusting to Lt. Burton's promises in the future for being repaid.'[64]

Col Outram, consulted by Speke as to what clothes he should wear, was opposed to their going in disguise, considering that 'lowering ourselves in this manner would operate against me in the estimation of the natives.' Burton, however, was going in disguise to Harar, and 'thought it better we should appear as his disciples.' Lt. Herne had already bought his dress, and Speke, much against his will, was obliged to follow suit. 'It was anything but pleasant to the feel. I had a huge hot turban, a long close-fitting gown, baggy loose drawers, drawn in at the ankle, sandals on my naked feet, and a silk girdle decorated with pistols and dirk.'[65]

He had arrived at Aden with almost £400 worth of cheap articles of barter chosen for being 'as tempting and seductive as I could find, for the simple-minded negroes of Africa.' Burton later scoffed at these 'notions', describing them as 'all manner of cheap and useless chow-chow, guns and revolvers, swords and cutlery, and beads and cloth, which the "simple-minded Negro of Africa" would have rejected with disdain.'[66] For this immediate journey, Speke had spent £120 in buying miscellaneous articles at Aden to give away as presents to the native chiefs. In addition he carried with him a wide variety of arms and ammunition, large camel-boxes for storing specimens of natural history, one sextant and artificial horizon, a selection of thermometers, and a primitive camera obscura, which he had made at Aden under Herne's supervision. On 18 October, his preparations complete, Speke left by an Arab vessel for the African coast.

In a letter, written two days earlier to Col Outram, Burton enclosed receipts for an advance of salary he had received, requesting a similar advance for Lt Herne, and listing the weapons and ammunition which they were going to take with them. 'The Somalis who are to accompany us appear to attach the greatest importance to our being well-provided with firearms.' All were of the Habr Gerhajis tribe. Two were policemen, obtained for Burton by Col Outram.[67] One, Mohammed Mahmud, more generally known as El

Hammal, or the porter, bull-necked and with lamp-black skin, was appointed to manage affairs. The other was nicknamed Long Guled because of his lank, skeleton-like appearance. The third member of the party, Abdy Abokr, with his 'smattering of learning and prodigious rascality' was dubbed the Mulla "End of Time" – an allusion to the prophesied corruption of the Moslem priesthood in the last epoch of the world.'

Burton proposed travelling in his well-tried persona of a Muslim merchant, El Haj Abdulla, equipped with a small stock of cloth, tobacco, rice, dates, trinkets, and other articles. 'Usually of gentle birth, he is everywhere welcomed and respected, and he bears in his mind and his manner that, if Allah please, he may become prime minister a month after he has sold you a yard of cloth.'[68]

The time was fast approaching for his departure, as indeed it was for Col Outram. He had been in failing health in September and had informed Lord Elphinstone of his condition. By that time, however, when Outram had been at Aden for barely two months, his services had been requested by the Government of India, to act as Political Resident at Lucknow in succession to Col Sleeman, the highest political post in the Governor-General's gift.[69] His successor was Col (later General Sir) William Marcus Coghlan of the Bombay Artillery, an old friend and brother campaigner. Coghlan landed at Aden on 23 October, and immediately took charge of the Residency. Outram, waiting only for a steamer to take him to Calcutta, left four days later.[70]

On Sunday, 29 October, Burton himself embarked at the Mala Bunder aboard the half-decked foyst, *Sahalah*.[71] Following an old Arab custom, his friend Steinhaueser, threw the slipper of blessing at his back. In the still fierce heat of the late afternoon, the sails were hoisted, and the ship set off across the wide expanse of Back Bay headed for the Somali coast.

CHAPTER FIFTEEN

THE FORBIDDEN CITY

Burton and his companions caught sight of Zayla around noon two days later, its whitewashed houses and minarets visible through the shimmering heat above the dark line of its defensive wall flanked by round towers. First mentioned by the Arab historian and geographer, Al-Yaqubi (d.897),[1] it was one of numerous Muslim coastal trading stations which had sprung up to cater for the huge increase in the slave trade during the earliest period of Muslim expansion into north-east Africa, between the 10th and 12th centuries.[2] Slaves were still an important part of its trade, although far short of the huge numbers remarked on by Ludovico di Varthema, 'Gentleman of Rome,' who visited the town in 1503 AD.[3]

The haven, however, was still 'rude and despicable' as Varthema had described it three and a half centuries earlier. The *Sahalah* having dropped anchor among the twenty or so native vessels moored there, Burton dressed, clambered over the side into a small boat, and was pushed ashore by his companions. At the Bab el Sahil, the Seaward or Northern Gate, they were met by a guard. After donning clean tobes and arming themselves, he escorted them along the dusty roads of the old Arab town, until eventually they were ushered into the presence of the governor, El Hajj Sharmarkay.

Although the two men had already met at Aden, Burton's adoption of the persona of a Muslim merchant, required them to appear as strangers. After half an hour's audience in an austere, barn-like building with a damp earthen floor, the Hajj led the way to one of his large houses of white-washed coralline and mud. Burton found an upper room already prepared for them, the floor spread with mats and cushions, with a Kursi or cot, covered with fine Persian rugs and gaudy silks and satin pillows for his own use. That night, with the well-known sounds of El Islam in his ears, he fell asleep, 'feeling once more at home.'[4]

Much to his annoyance, however, the mules which he had ordered and paid for at Aden, had not been procured. Although the governor sent immediately to the neighbouring port of Tajurrah, Burton was delayed at Zayla for almost a month before they arrived. Fortunately, being a self-confessed 'amateur barbarian,' he slipped quickly and naturally into the free and easy ways of Somali society.

Most of his time was spent entertaining a twice-daily influx of visitors. 'It argues "peculiarity," I own,' he wrote, 'to enjoy such a life. In the first place there is no woman's society: El Islam seems purposely to have loosened the ties between the sexes in order to strengthen the bonds which connect man and man. Secondly, your house is by no means your castle…he who objects to having his head shaved in public, to seeing his friends combing their locks in his sitting-room, to having his property unceremoniously handled, or to being addressed familiarly by a perfect stranger, had better avoid Somaliland.'[5]

Nevertheless, he found time to add to the detailed ethnological notes he had already made at Aden. He described the Somalis as 'nothing but a slice of the great Galla nation Islamised and Semiticised by repeated immigrations from Arabia.'[6] Though Islam in Somalia was mainly of the strict Shafi'ite sect of the Sunni denomination, Burton claimed that the Somali pastoralists were 'Nominal Mahommedans, El Islam hangs so lightly upon them, that apparently they care little for making it binding upon others.' Without actually naming him, a modern scholar of the region has dismissed Burton's claim as 'very mistaken,' contending that, while in certain respects the circumstances of the settled cultivators of the south more closely resembled the general pattern of Islam, there was 'no distinction between the two communities in their observance of the five "pillars" of their faith.'[7]

While enjoying their company, Burton, nevertheless, found the Somalis fickle and hard to please, 'light-minded as the Abyssinians….soft, merry and affectionate souls, they pass without any apparent transition into a state of fury, when they are capable of terrible atrocities.'[8] It seemed to him, that they were happier at Aden than in their native country. 'There I have often seen a man clapping his hands and dancing, childlike, alone to relieve the exuberance of his spirits; here they become, as the Mongols and other pastoral people, a melancholy race, who will sit for hours upon a bank gazing at the moon, or crooning some old ditty under the trees.'[9]

As for the Somali women, they were, as he slyly put it, 'of the Venus Kallipyga order of beauty.' It was not until many years later, that he revealed that their protuberant buttocks had a sexual connotation. 'The prominence of the glutaei muscles is always insisted upon,' he wrote, 'because it is supposed to promise well in a bed-fellow. In Somaliland where the people are sub-steatopygous a rich man who can afford the luxury, will have the girls drawn up in line and choose her to wife who projects further behind.'[10]

In a possible veiled reference to his own personal sexual experiences there, he claimed that, 'As a general rule Somali women prefer *amourettes* with strangers, following the Arab proverb, "The newcomer filleth the eye."' In a further sweeping generalization, he called them prolific but bad mothers, neither loved nor respected by their children. A later authority on this region has disputed this claim, pointing out that 'Somali women are very fond of their children, and consequently infanticide is of the greatest rarity.'[11] Burton also insisted that they were 'of cold temperament, the result of artificial as well as natural causes.' He attributed this to the extreme form of female genital mutilation practised in Somalia, known as infibulation. This barbarous practice involved the excision of all the female external genitalia. What remained of the labia majora was then sewn together, leaving a small opening for the passage of urine and the menstrual flow.[12] If Burton is to be believed, the unnatural consequence was, that ,'While it diminished the capacity of women for love and pleasure, it resulted in an increase of cruelty, debauchery, and insatiable desire.'[13]

By the end of the month, Sharmarkay had supplied Burton with five camels, engaged an Abban or protector, two women cooks and a fourth servant. He did so under protest, however, warning Burton that the road swarmed with brigands, that the Eesa had lately murdered his son, that the small-pox was depopulating Harar, and that the emir or prince was certain destruction. 'One death to a man is a serious thing,' remarked Burton in his best sardonic manner, 'a dozen neutralize one another. I contented myself with determining the good Sharmarkay to be the true Oriental hyperbolist.'[14]

Two routes led from Zayla to Harar. The more direct consisted of eight long stages passing through the Eesa territory, and then two through the mountains of the Nola tribe of Gallas. Sharmarkay strongly objected to Burton's travelling by this route, stressing the danger posed by these militant tribes, who engaged in the horrific practice of male genital emasculation.[15] 'They seek the honour of murder, to use their own phrase, "as though it were a gain," and will spear a pregnant woman in hopes that the unborn child may be a male.' He suggested instead the more circuitous road, which passed south along the coast. A march of some 50 miles through the Eesa territory would bring them to the lands of the Gudabursi and

Girhi Somal. Here, carrying strong recommendations from Sharmarkay to certain principal families of these tribes, they would be, comparatively speaking, safe.

On 27 November 1854, El Haj Abdullah and his party, attended by the governor, his son Mohammed, and a detachment of Arab soldiers, passed through the Ashurbara or southern gate of Zayla. After a half mile march they exchanged affectionate farewells, shook hands, and parted.

Their little caravan was initially led by Raghe, a minor Eesa chief of the Mummasan clan. Sharmarkay had appointed him their *abban* or protector, his presence guaranteeing their safety in the case of any danger. Burton's three attendants rode alongside the camels, dressed in dazzling white tobes edged with bright red borders, their mops of frizzled hair glistening with grease. Burton followed, mounted on a splendid white mule, a double-barrelled gun lying across his lap, and his Colt's six-shooters stuffed into a roughly- made pair of holsters. They were not long into their journey before their two buxom cooks, Samewda Yusuf and Aybla Farih, were nicknamed Shehrazade and Deenarzade, a tribute to Burton's having kept his Somali audience enthralled with stories from the *Arabian Nights* while at Zayla. They, in their turn, were waited on by a one-eyed Zayla lad, Yusuf, nicknamed the "Kalendar." A Bedouin woman driving a donkey, brought up the rear.

They spent six monotonous days trekking over the hard, stoneless maritime plain of Zayla. Although it was December, Burton's arms were burned raw by the fiery sun which 'singed as through a magnifying-glass.' The meagre supply of water they managed to obtain from a few wells proved to be bitter and unpalatable. As they advanced south-westwards into the interior, the country gradually improved, and the air became distinctly cooler. By 3 December, they were at the southern frontier of the Eesa tribe, below the hills which formed the first step to the highlands of Ethiopia.

Wherever they halted, they were immediately surrounded by wandering groups of Bedouins. "Traitorous as an Easa," was a Zayla proverb, 'where the people tell you that these Bedouins with the left hand offer you a bowl of milk and stab with the right.' Burton, however, found them nothing but pleasant and amenable. 'They were importunate beggars, but a pinch of snuff or a handful of tobacco always made us friends: they begged me to settle among them, they offered me sundry wives....they declared that after a few days' residence, I should become one of themselves.'[16]

By 7 December, they had reached the summit of the maritime chain. For the next fortnight they slowly wended their way through the lands of the Gudabirsi, the undulating ground a mixture of thorn-clad hills and fertile valleys. Burton found some of the Bedouin girls 'not wanting in attractions.' One of the prettiest to whom he gave a bead necklace, 'repaid me by opining that I was painted white.'

On 23 December the caravan crossed the yellow, shrivelled up grasslands of the Marar Prairie. On their arrival at Wilensi, four days later, upon hearing that small-pox was still raging in Harar, Schehrazade and Deenarzade begged to be left behind. The Kalendar, therefore, was instructed to remain in charge of them. After a halt of two days the rest of the caravan set off for Sagarrah, escorted by an old Girhi Bedouin, known as Said Wal, or Mad Said.

Sharmarkay had given Burton a letter to the Gerad Adan, chief of the Girhi. However, the outbreak of a family feud between him and his brother-in-law, their Gudabirsi protector, made the latter cautious about committing himself. They were forced to cool their heels there until "Dahabo," one of the chief's six wives, and his eldest son Sherwa, came to their kraal to escort them onwards.

They spent six days as the guests of the Gerad Adan bin Kaushan, a tall, strong, wiry Bedouin with 'a tricky smile and an uncertain eye.' Now, with Harar so close at hand, Burton had to shame two of his Somali attendants into accompanying him, by threatening to travel alone. He left the End of Time behind in charge of the heavy luggage, and a letter to be forwarded to Lts Herne and Stroyan at Berbera, directing them what to do in case of accidents. An ass carried only what was absolutely necessary – a change of clothes, a book or two, a few biscuits, ammunition, and a little tobacco.

It will be recalled that Burton claimed that, because of their well-known opposition to the slave-trade, the English were the most hated and dreaded of all foreigners. Despite this, he intended as 'a point of honor,' to use his title of haji in order to enter Harar, and 'break the guardian spell.' He now did a complete *volte face*. His light skin having given rise to the suspicion in the villages through which they passed that he was a Turk, he decided to abandon his disguise. He then concocted an English letter purporting to be from the Political Agent at Aden to the Amir of Harar. He claimed, hardly convincingly, that two reasons influenced him in this decision. Firstly, in these lands, it was 'a point of honour not to conceal tribe or nation.' This immediately raises the question as to why he was not acquainted with the fact early on by Sharmarkay or others at Aden or Zayla. Secondly, and completely at odds with what he had claimed earlier of the English, he described the Ottoman as being 'more hated and feared than the Frank.' By the Ottoman or Turk, Burton, of course, had in mind the Egyptians, the late Muhammed Ali's imperial ambitions having directly threatened Abyssinia and the surrounding region. The people here had every reason to be suspicious and fearful. Within twenty years, a military force under Ra'uf Pasha, by then already in possession of Zayla and Berbera, crossed the desert and annexed Harar.

Burton caught his first glimpse of the 'forbidden city' early in the afternoon of 3 January 1855. A long sombre line on the crest of a hill some two miles distant, it contrasted strikingly with the usual whitewashed towns of the East. Initially, he experienced a deep sense of disappointment: 'nothing conspicuous appeared but two grey minarets of rude shape: many would have grudged exposing three lives to win so paltry a prize.' This was soon replaced by a feeling of euphoria, as he remembered that, 'of all that have attempted, none ever succeeded in entering that pile of stones.'[17]

After being kept waiting for an hour at the eastern gate, they were directed by a grim-faced guard to follow him. It happened to be a levée-day, and a number of Galla chieftains passing in and out of the palace prolonged their anxious wait. At last, after being ordered to take off his slippers and hand over his weapons, an order to which Burton objected, they were escorted to the palace-door.

A curtain was pulled aside, and he entered a large darkened room with a loud salaam. His greeting of "Peace be upon ye!" was courteously returned by a young man aged about twenty-four or twenty-five, plain and thin-bearded, with a sickly yellow complexion, wrinkled brows and protruding eyes. Obviously an invalid – Burton initially diagnosed consumption, then later chronic bronchitis – he sat reclined upon a raised cot, his elbow resting on a pillow, from which protruded the hilt of a Cutch sabre. He looked very much like an Indian Rajah, with a flowing robe of crimson cloth, edged with snowy white fur, and a narrow white turban twisted tightly round a tall conical cap of red velvet. As Burton walked towards the throne, four or five chamberlains seized his arms, according to custom, and hurried him on till he bent over the Emir Ahmed bin Abubekr's extended fingers, 'Which however I did not kiss, being naturally averse to performing that operation upon any but a woman's hand.'

The venerable grey-haired wazir or prime minister, Gerad Mohammed, then began enquiring as to his name, nation, and business at Harar. After handing over his letter, Burton explained in Arabic that they had travelled from Aden 'bearing the compliments of their Daulah or governor,' and that they had entered Harar 'to see the light of H.H's countenance.' An allusion to the friendship formerly existing between the English and the recently deceased chief Abubakr, brought a smile to the Amir's lips. The audience over, Burton was invited to become the prince's guest during the rest of his stay. That night, having retired to his quarters in the Emir's second palace, he was struck by the extreme novelty of their position. Here he was, 'under the roof of a bigoted prince whose least word was death; amongst a people who detest foreigners; the only European that had ever passed over their inhospitable threshold, and the fated instrument of their future downfall.'

Throughout the ensuing days, which passed monotonously enough, a closer inspection of Harar only served to reinforce Burton's initial impression of the city. It had seen better days. The streets and alleys were like mountain roads, and strewn with enormous rubbish heaps, inhabited by packs of mangy and one-eyed dogs. The houses, flat-roofed, with small holes for windows and coarsely-made wooden shutters, were built of sandstone and granite cemented with a reddish clay, giving them a dingy appearance. Most had large court-yards and separate apartments for women. There were hardly any public buildings: the bazaar was a long street; the jami or cathedral mosque a kind of barn decorated with two queer old minarets, and the palaces were single-storied houses with large courts, protected by doors of holcus stalks.

Although crammed with mosques and renowned for its sanctity, erudition, and fanaticism, trade was Harar's life-blood. Three caravans set out annually for Berbera, the largest leaving in March, consisting of at least 3,000 people and an equal number of camels. 'He who commands at Berbera, holds the beard of Harar in his hand,' was a well-known saying within the walls of the city. Its hand-woven tobes were famous throughout Eastern Africa. It also served as the main centre for the coffee, wars-dye, cotton, gums, tobacco, and the grain which flooded in from the whole of the surrounding Galla country.

While the men were particularly unprepossessing in appearance, Burton was struck by the pretty Abyssinian features of the women and surprised by their complete lack of self-consciousness. They went unveiled, and largely barefoot. Their hair, held in place by blue muslin or network, was tied in two large bunches below the ears. Their only ornaments were armlets of buffalo horn, coral necklaces, gilt hair pins and Birmingham rings. However, unlike the soft, low and plaintive voices of the Bedouin women which, to Burton, seemed 'rather like music than mere utterance,' the voices of the Harari women were harsh and unpleasant. Besides, 'they chewed tobacco with effrontery, drank beer, and demeaned themselves accordingly.'

As the epidemic of small-pox showed no signs of abating, Burton found a convenient excuse for hastening their departure. 'These African towns.' he wrote, 'are all prisons on a large scale. "You enter at your own bidding – you leave at another's" – is the native proverb, true and significant.' He regarded his dismissal at the end of ten days, as being due to a report by a young man of the Ayyal Gedid clan, 'that three brothers had landed in the Somali country, that two of them were anxiously awaiting at Berbera the return of the third and that though dressed as Moslems, they really were Englishmen in government employ.' The very real prospect of having his caravans cut off, should anything untoward happen, acted as a strong incentive, Burton believed, for the Emir's getting rid of his dangerous guest. Even so, he had no cause for complaint. He had been treated very hospitably by the Emir, who finally dismissed him with a present of a mule, and a letter addressed to the Political Resident in Arabia. Not long after, the Emir wrote to Aden asking to be sent an English doctor, proof, in Burton's opinion, that his modest attempt at establishing friendly relations between the prince and the British authorities had paid off.[18]

Well before dawn on Saturday, 13 January, the mules were saddled up and loaded with their few belongings. After snatching a hasty breakfast, Burton and his companions quickly mounted and spurred their animals through the dark deserted streets. 'Suddenly my weakness and sickness left me – so potent a drug is joy! – and, as we passed the gates loudly salaaming to the warders, who were crouching over a fire inside, a weight of care and anxiety fell from me like a cloak of lead.' It was that self-same feeling of elation, that rush of adrenalin he had experienced on leaving Mecca. Just as soon, it drained away leaving him 'musing upon how melancholy a thing is success. Whilst failure inspirits a man, attainment reads the sad prosy lesson that all our glories

"Are shadows, not substantial things."

Truly, said the sayer, "disappointment is the salt of life" – a salutary bitter which strengthens the mind for fresh exertion and gives a double value to the prize.'[19]

After a stop-over at Saggarah for the night, they rode on to Wilensi the next morning. Loud congratulations and shouts of joy greeted their arrival, and the evening ended in a feast. They stayed there for a week in order to lay in stock and build up sufficient strength for the long desert march ahead of them. Burton also worked from sunrise to sunset compiling a vocabulary of the Harari tongue, and mastering its syntax.[20]

On Sunday, 21 January, their messenger returned from the city bringing supplies for the road. By this time Burton's vocabulary was finished. He was already ten days behind schedule, and aware that his comrades at Berbera were certain to be worried for his safety. He started out with the intention of reaching the coast within a fortnight. Three days later, it was obvious from the slow pace of the caravan as they crossed the Marar Prairie, that this was a wildly over-optimistic assessment.

The timely appearance of a former abban, the 'valiant Beuh,' who reported that a guide was available in the area, gave Burton an idea. He suggested that Beuh should escort the women, camels, and baggage under the command of the Kalendar to Zayla. In the meanwhile, Burton and his companions carrying arms and provisions for only four days, would press on through the lands of the hostile Habr Awal.

Burton pocketed all his remaining provisions, five biscuits, a few limes, and several lumps of sugar, conscious that any delay or accident to their mules would starve them. One water-bottle had to do for the whole party. On 26 January, they made their way to a village belonging to the Ugaz or chief of the Gudabirsi tribe. An offer of five dollars persuaded one of their number, "Dubayr" – the Donkey, to act as their guide.

In his paper for the RGS, Burton declined to give a description of his return route to Berbera, dismissing it as 'a mere adventure of uncommon hardship.' The soaring temperatures of the desert, and, in particular, the lack of water also made it an extremely foolhardy one. 'The demon of Thirst rode like Care behind us. For 24 hours we did not taste water, the sun parched our brains, the mirage mocked us at every turn, and the effect was a species of monomania. As I jogged along with eyes closed against the fiery air, no image unconnected with the want of water suggested itself……I opened my eyes to a heat-reeking plain, and a sky of that eternal metallic blue so lovely to painter and poet, so blank and death-like to us…..'

On one occasion, after surviving without water for thirty-six hours, they were saved by a bird, the *katta*, or sand-grouse, which was seen flying towards the nearer hills. 'These birds must drink at least once a day,' Burton wrote, 'and generally towards evening, when they are safe to carry water in their bills to their young. I cried out, "See, the *katta!* the *katta!*" Suddenly the bird plunged down about a hundred yards away. Jumping from their saddles, they ran forward and found a little shaft of deliciously cool water into which men and beasts plunged their heads and drank their fill.

It was two o'clock in the morning of the fifth day – a remarkable feat – when they finally stumbled into Berbera. By then, the mules, pushed to the limit, bloodied by spear-pricks and cut to the bone by their saddles, were in a sorry state. Members of the party had fared little better. To his enormous relief, Burton discovered that his comrades were still waiting for him in a hut in the Ayyal Gedid quarter.

After visiting some interesting ruins on the outskirts, Burton was keen to leave.[21] 'The town had become intolerable, the heat under a mat house was extreme, and the wind and the dust were almost as bad as Aden, and the dirt perhaps even worse.' On 5 February, after directing Herne and Stroyan to march if possible, without incurring great risk, upon the "Elephant Valley," about 7 days' journey WSW of Berbera, Burton boarded a cranky old sailing vessel, the *El Kasab* or *The Reed*. Four days later, after a very rough passage, he was back in Aden.

He immediately set to work preparing for the next, and major, stage of the expedition. With his hands full, he was extremely grateful, therefore, for the offer by his friend, Lieutenant Dansey, himself a talented linguist, to write out and revise his notes on the Harari language.[22]

Burton also had another linguistic matter on his mind. On 18 February 1855 he wrote to the Political Resident, stating that, before leaving for Africa, about September or October, he had been examined by Lt Playfair in the Arabic language and his papers sent to Bombay. At the same time he had addressed an official letter to the Examination Committee there. Since returning from Africa, he had been unable to find any notice of his examination in General Orders, nor had he received any personal communication on the subject. Presumably on the grounds that no news is good news, he asked therefore, "to be considered a passed interpreter in the Arabic language," and to receive the appropriate munshi allowance. This, as he pointed out, had been granted to him for the Sindhi and Multani dialects in which he had passed examinations at Karachi.[23]

Burton made only two public references to his having passed in Arabic. In September 1886, he wrote to Lord Iddesleigh, Minister for Foreign Affairs, asking to be allowed to retire prematurely from the Consular Service on full pension. With it, he sent a ten-point statement of his "Services." Ninth in this list was his claim to have "learned twenty-nine languages, [and] passed official examinations in eight Eastern languages, notably Arabic, Persian, and Hindustani."[24] The first part of this claim is, of course, beyond proof. The second is patently untrue. Burton's qualifications as an interpreter in six not eight oriental languages are duly noted in his service record.[25] There is no mention of any pass in Arabic. This also applies to the *Bombay Gazette*, which records passes in other oriental languages, but none for Arabic for 1854-55.[26]

Burton only referred specifically to the 1854 examination in the last of the Supplemental volumes of the *Arabian Nights*, which appeared in 1888. Stung by criticism from, what he called, the "Lane-Poole clique," that he was ignorant of Arabic, Burton outlined his progress in the language, dating from his student days at Oxford. 'At Aden where I passed the official examination, Captain [sic] (now Sir R. Lambert) Playfair, and the Rev G. Percy Badger to whom my papers were submitted, were pleased to report favourably on my proficiency....in fact of this and sundry other subjects it may be said without immodesty that I have forgotten as much as many Arabists have learned.'[27]

The truth is that Burton failed his Arabic examination. As a result of his writing to Brigadier Coghlan, Burton was sent a copy of the Resolution of the Examination Committee of the previous year.[28] Unlike his own letter, however, it was not copied into the *Bombay Public Proceedings*, nor was any indication given as to its contents. This is especially unfortunate, since the document cannot now be traced. Fortunately, two letters written by the Arabic scholar, the Rev George Percy Badger, to Burton in 1872, help to shed light on the reasons for the Examination Committee's arriving at this astonishing decision.

Having heard that Burton was very vindictive, and not wishing to incur his animosity, Badger had refused repeated requests by Outram and Playfair to preside over the committee which examined him at Aden in 1854. Badger was subsequently told that the Bombay authorities refused to pass Burton on the ground that the Examination was informal, or contrary to rule, and that he should have been examined at Bombay. Furthermore, despite Playfair's qualification in Arabic having been accepted by the Madras College, the committee at Bombay was not prepared to accept his certification of Burton's undoubted capabilities.[29] 'However,' Badger wrote, 'I may now tell you what perhaps you never heard before. Playfair sent your papers to me, and after looking over them I sent them back to him with a note eulogising your attainments and, if I remember rightly, remarking upon the absurdity of the Bombay Committee being made the judge of your proficiency, inasmuch as I did not believe that any of them possessed a tithe of the knowledge of Arabic which you did.'[30] While it may not have any bearing on the matter, it is interesting to note that the President of the Bombay Examination Committee which failed Burton was none other than Captain C.P. Rigby.

Speke had forwarded his journal to Playfair on 20 December 1854. He, himself, however, did not arrive back at Aden until 17 February 1855.[31] He had failed to reach the Wady Nogal, mainly through the dishonesty of his *abban*, Sumunter. Speke's problems had been further compounded by the choice of Ahmed as interpreter, who belonged to the same tribe. Consequently, 'they invariably acted in concert against me like two brothers.' Burton was furious, and several days later wrote to the Political Resident, asking him to enquire into the case. 'If such conduct be allowed to pass unnoticed, or rather I should say if it be not visited with severe chastisement, I apprehend that it will be most problematical to the future proceedings of the Expedition.'[32] As a result of his intervention, Sumunter was speedily put on trial in the Aden Police Court, and found guilty.[33] His sentence was exemplary. Despite having a wife and family at Aden, as well as a thriving business as a merchant, he was sentenced to two months' imprisonment, fined two hundred rupees, and banished from the colony.

Brigadier Coghlan sent Burton's highly detailed and wide-ranging report to Government on 22 February 1855. Among other subjects it gave an overview of the conduct of the expedition; descriptions of Zayla, Harar, and Berbera and the operations of the slave-trade, together with his suggestions for ending it; proposed the establishment of a British Agency at Berbera, and summarised the political information collected during a three months' tour through the Western Somali country.[34]

Despite Speke's failure to reach the Wady Nogal Burton, nevertheless, praised his determination in collecting specimens of the fauna,[35] and for casting light on the arid and thinly populated territories of the Wassangeli and Dulbahanta tribes. He promised to lose no time in preparing Speke's notes for transmission to Government, keeping a copy for a general work on Eastern Africa. He also asked for permission to forward his own notes to the RGS of London and Paris, and to prepare his diary for publication at some future date. 'In these papers all political allusions will be carefully avoided, the form shall be purely geographical, and the latter which shall contain a grammatical outline and a vocabulary of the Harar dialect, is intended to be a mere narrative of adventure.'

Together with Speke, whom Burton now appeared to regard as the senior partner of the group, he proposed keeping to their original plan of entering Somalia via Berbera. Nothing worthwhile, however, could be achieved in a short time. He hoped, therefore, that the Bombay Government would obtain leave for them for a second year. This would enable them to successfully complete their exploration of the Eastern Horn of Africa. There was also the possibility that the expedition 'may extend to the Aethiopic Olympus (Kilimanjaro) and settle the question of its eternal snows.'

He concluded by asking for the Government's support for his application for promotion to the brevet rank of major. He believed that the higher his military rank the more political and scientific weight would be attached to his reports and publications by the learned societies of England and France. Furthermore, the Somalis, he claimed, 'were highly conscious of "status" and deferential to rank,......'[36]

Burton had arrived back at Aden to find a letter from England containing news of his mother's death from heart disease on 10 December 1854.[37] To what extent, if at all, he was emotionally affected by it, it is impossible to say. The paper's black-edging was the only outward sign of his bereavement when writing to Dr Norton Shaw on 25 February. Given his success in penetrating Harar, he was convinced that the Court of Directors would grant his application for a second year's leave, especially if backed by the RGS:

> My plans (public) are now to march southward to the Webbe Shebayli and Ganana.[38] Privately & entre nous I want to settle the question of Krapf and "eternal snows." There is little doubt of the White Nile being there-abouts. And you will hear with pleasure that there is an open route through Africa to the Atlantic. I heard of it at Harar & will give the whole account. ....Our difficulties will be principally amongst the penis cutting people. Altogether the prospects of the "Somali Expedition" are bright enough: there are difficulties however. This time we march as masters with 20 guns and horses etc., so that by day we need not fear a host.[39]

Burton now accepted Speke's suggestion, that he should go to Berbera to assist Herne in obtaining the requisite number of animals. He asked Speke to see what he could first do at Kurrum, and as soon as he had collected enough, to march with them along the sea-shore to Berbera. Speke was delighted. This time, with the help of Lt Dansey, he was supplied with an excellent guide and interpreter, Mahmoud, a Somali of the Mijjertheyn tribe. Better known at Aden as El Balyuz, or the Ambassador, a sobriquet he had acquired from having accompanied Lt Cruttenden on a number of occasions to the Somali country, he had the reputation of being one of the shrewdest and best informed of his countrymen.

Before leaving, Speke applied to the Government for some well-trained Somali policemen. Unfortunately, there were already too few for the colony's needs, and his request was turned down. He was, therefore, forced into engaging a motley crowd of raw recruits, Egyptians, Nubians, Arabs, and Seedis, to form an escort, arming them with his sabres and muskets. Sending seven of these men immediately to Berbera together with eight camels he had brought over from Bunder Goray, Speke embarked for Kurrum with the rest of his party on the evening of 21 March.

Four days later, Burton informed the Political Resident that he had completed his preparations, and was ready to start for Berbera within the week. Having heard that a ship-of-war was about to be despatched to Mussowah, he asked for, 'A passage for myself and a few personal servants and the presence of the vessel for a few days would naturally assist me in starting early from the coast.'[40] For whatever reason, his departure was delayed, and it was not until 5 April that he finally left Aden aboard HEI Company's schooner, *Mahi*.

Speke had arrived in Berbera two days earlier to find the place humming with activity. Four days later, there was great excitement as the huge Harar caravan could be seen streaming over the plain, its flanks guarded by groups of armed outriders. In all some three thousand people were making their way towards the town, as many head of cattle, and five hundred or more slaves chained together for sale in the market. Later that morning, the *Mahi* dropped anchor in the crowded harbour. Unfortunately, it was unable to stay as Burton had requested. Needed to relieve the *Elphinstone* blockading the seaboard, it left that same evening, firing a salute as a signal to the Somalis that the Expedition was travelling under the auspices of the British Government.

Burton claimed to have been reasonably satisfied with his reception at Berbera. Although the chiefs were displeased at the sentence handed out to Sumunter, they listened respectfully, nevertheless, to a letter from the Political Resident at Aden, asking them to treat members of the Expedition with consideration and hospitality. Even so, they must have experienced mounting anger as well as surprise on being told by Burton, 'that English gentlemen visiting their countries will not hereafter consider themselves obliged to travel like Arabs and Banyans under the charge of Abbans or Protectors.' This, of course, was diametrically opposed to what he had written in *The Pilgrimage*, that 'he clearly is in the wrong who refuses to conform to custom.' This high-handed decision to overturn at a stroke an ancient and lucrative practice, was later criticised by Speke and Playfair, who described it as 'the *termina causa* of all the mishaps which befell the expedition.'[41]

Chosen to be within range of the *Mahi's* heavy guns, their camp was situated on an isolated rocky ridge, about three-quarters of a mile from the town. The officers' tents were drawn up in one line, Lt Stroyan's on the extreme right about twelve paces from the "Rowtie" shared by Burton and Herne, with Speke some distance to the left. The baggage was placed between Speke's and Herne's tents. Fifty-six camels were tethered in front on a sandy bed below the ridge. Six or seven horses and mules stood in the rear. Each of the forty-two armed men was on the alert during the daytime. At night two sentries were posted. They were regularly relieved, and visited at times by El Balyuz, now the ras, or leader of the caravan, and by Burton or his companions. None of the many Englishmen who had visited Berbera during the space of thirty years had ever been attacked, and 'apparently there was as little to fear in it as within the fortifications of Aden.'[42]

On 9 April, a thunderstorm moving in from the southern hills behind their camp, signalled the onset of the Gugi, or south-west Somali monsoon. The eventual downpour precipitated the break-up of the Fair. Burton and his companions were now faced with a serious dilemma: whether to accompany the great Ogaden caravan then preparing to leave, or wait for a vessel expected daily from Aden, bringing them letters and instruments from England. They chose the latter alternative with disastrous consequences.

By the 15th, Berbera was a ghost town. Its only living creatures were a few diseased and dying cattle, and one little girl, showing the symptoms of small-pox, heartlessly abandoned by her parents with a few provisions 'to die like a dog on the inhospitable plain....'

Three days later, a small Arab buggalow on its way to Aynterad from Aden sailed into the deserted creek to see if anything remained of the fair. On board were about a dozen Somalis, including four women.[43] Frightened of travelling into the interior alone, they pleaded to be allowed to accompany the Expedition. Worried about the drain on their resources with so many extra mouths to feed, Burton reluctantly refused the men. The four women, however, after offering to do various menial jobs around the camp, were allowed to stay.

Shortly after sunset, as members of the expedition were relaxing in front of the tents, they were startled by the sound of gunfire coming from the rear. On investigation, three men were found walking quietly into the camp, leading ponies by the reins. Disobeying strict orders to shoot directly at any intruders failing to respond to their challenge, the guards were firing instead into the air immediately over their heads.

Initially, the men were suspected of being scouts acting as the forerunners of a Somali raid. Under interrogation, however, they claimed to have been sent by the elders of their tribe, the Habr Awal, worried that the ship might contain building material belonging to their old enemy, Sharmarkay. Rumours were rife that he was waiting for an opportunity to occupy Berbera by building forts, as he had done on previous occasions. This was entirely plausible, given that it was one of several Speke had heard circulating at Kurrum. Satisfied with their explanation, given under solemn oath, the men were treated hospitably, and allowed to leave at their leisure.

Between two and three in the morning of the 19th, Burton was woken by the Balyuz shouting that the enemy was upon them. 'Hearing a rush of men, like a stormy wind,' he sprang up, calling for his sabre. At the same time he despatched Herne to the rear and left of the camp, to try to ascertain the strength of the attacking force. Eventually finding himself alone, Herne returned hurriedly to the tent, reporting that their twelve armed servants had fled, and that the enemy amounted to about 150 men. Meanwhile, Burton had aroused the other two officers. Stroyan failed to make an appearance, and was not seen alive again. Speke, as soon as he was convinced that this was not a false alarm, quickly joined Burton and Herne in the rowtie.

While his companions blazed away with their revolvers, the darkness made it difficult to avoid the jabbing of spears and the long heavy daggers thrown at their legs through and under the opening of the tent. Furthermore, it soon became apparent that the Somalis were employing the familiar Arab stratagem of battering down the tent with war clubs and stones, thus trapping the occupants in its folds.

Giving the order to escape, Burton stepped outside with his sabre at the ready, closely followed by Herne and Speke. They were immediately faced with the daunting sight of about twenty Somalis kneeling and crouching near the tent entrance. Numerous other dusky figures could be seen and heard some way off. Momentarily hesitating, Speke was struck on the inside of his knee by a stone, causing his leg to buckle under him. As he limped back under the fly of the tent 'to take a better survey,' Burton called out, "Don't step back, or they will think we are retiring." Incensed by this implied rebuke, Speke strode forward, firing as he went. Pressing the muzzle of his Dean and Adams revolver against the chest of the largest man blocking his path, Speke pulled the trigger, only to find it had jammed. Just as he was about to club the man in the face with it, Speke, received a sharp blow across the chest, and collapsed to the ground, gasping for breath. In an instant, he was taken prisoner. His intended victim, after wrenching the pistol from Speke's grasp, then began fumbling between his thighs, making Speke's hairs stand on end. 'I feared that they belonged to a tribe called Eesa, who are notorious not only for their ferocity in fighting, but for the unmanly mutilations they delight in. The men were in reality feeling whether, after an Arab fashion, I was carrying a dagger between my legs, to rip up a foe after his victim was supposed to be powerless.' Having tied his hands behind his back, Speke's captors led him away to the rear, 'as he supposed to be slaughtered.'

Burton, meanwhile, after breaking through the enemy at the tent entrance, slashed his way through a dozen Somalis, war-clubs raining down blows on him as he did so. In trying his best to protect Burton, the Balyuz almost fell a victim to his sword. Mistaking him in the darkness for one of the enemy, Burton turned to cut him down. As the Balyuz cried out in alarm, Burton hesitated. In that split second, a Somali stepped forward and hurled his javelin. It sliced its way through Burton's left cheek, embedding itself in his jaw.

Following the Balyuz, who led him to a place where he believed his comrades had taken refuge, Burton sent a messenger to bring back the Aynterad vessel from the spit in the middle of the harbour. He spent the rest of the night searching for his comrades, forced to lie down at intervals from the excruciating pain of his wound and loss of blood. As dawn broke, he summoned up his little remaining strength and managed to stagger to the spit at the head of the creek, where he was carried into the buggalow. Once on board, he persuaded the crew to arm themselves and return to the scene of the disaster.

He was presently joined by Herne, who, apart from a few bruises, had survived completely unscathed. He had originally followed close on Burton's heels, using the butt-end of his empty revolver on the heads of the enemy. As he did so, he had come upon a dozen Somalis, who, though they loudly shouted out, "Kill the Franks who are killing the Somal," allowed him to pass unmolested. He had then looked for his friends in the empty huts of the town until dawn, when he was joined by the Balyuz who had been on a similar mission.

Speke, on the other hand, still missing at this point, had undergone a traumatic experience at the hands of some of his captors. Following a victory song, and slow solemn martial procession around the camp, the Somalis set about looting. 'A more complete and ferocious melée,' he wrote, 'I never witnessed.' Suddenly word went round that another tribe had heard of the attack, and was on its way to deprive them of their spoils. Instantly, the camp cleared, the oldest men leading the way. The most sadistic of Speke's jailers, however, did not join them. Instead, he stepped forward, as Speke described it, 'and coolly stabbed me with his spear.' In trying to defend himself, Speke suffered further severe wounds to his shoulder, hand, and left thigh. Warming to his work, the Somali dropped the rope holding his prisoner, stepped back a dozen paces, 'and rushing on me with savage fury, plunged his spear through the thick part of my right thigh into the ground, passing in between the thigh-bone and the large sinew beneath.'

'Smelling death,' in Burton's phrase, Speke suddenly leapt to his feet, giving his tormentor a hard back-hander in the face with his double-bound fists. Taking advantage of the man's momentary surprise, Speke ran helter-skelter towards the sea. Having successfully run the gauntlet of a hail of spears hurled in his direction, he finally sat down on the sand, faint from loss of blood. Giving himself a few minutes to recover and to unpick the knots binding his hands, he hobbled towards the town, eventually meeting up with the search party sent out to find him.

Returning later to the now deserted camp, Burton and his companions found that the Somalis had carried away all their cloth, tobacco, swords and other weapons. They had ignored the heavy sacks of grain, the books, broken boxes, damaged instruments, and various items for which they saw no use. These were later loaded onto the ship, and the heavier articles set on fire. Stroyan's badly mutilated body was found sprawled near his tent. A spear had pierced his heart, another his abdomen. There was a gaping wound across his forehead, and his body had been bludgeoned black and blue with war clubs. In addition, his 'thighs showed marks of violence,' Burton's euphemism for Stroyan's having been genitally mutilated after death.

'We were overwhelmed with grief:' Burton wrote, 'we had lived together like brothers.' They set sail that evening, hoping to inter their friend's remains at Aden. By the following morning, however, decomposition had set in so rapidly that they were forced to bury him at sea, his late close companion, Herne, reading the burial service.

In the absence of Dr Steinhaueser who was on sick leave, Burton and Speke were examined by the Acting Civil Surgeon, Dr Costelloe, on Sunday, 22 April 1855.[44] He stated in his report that the spear had entered the left side of Burton's face and had come out on the right, removing two molar teeth and dividing the roof of the palate.[45] He considered it a serious wound, 'and as he (Burton) had recently suffered from secondary syphilis (he) must immediately proceed to Europe as it would not be proper to allow him to remain in Aden during the approaching hot weather.'[46]

This latter diagnosis, I believe, should be treated with a high degree of scepticism. It appears to rely solely on Burton's own evidence, and not on any symptoms of secondary infection noted by Costelloe himself. The last thing Burton would have wanted, was to be sent for treatment at Bombay or elsewhere in India, and then ordered back to his regiment. In the light of how little time he later spent in England, I suspect a co-operative Irish medic.

As for Speke, Costelloe reported that he had received eleven wounds chiefly from spears, the most serious being one to the right thigh. Astonishingly, within three weeks, he was able to walk normally, 'a touching lesson,' as Burton remarked, 'how difficult it is to kill a man in sound health.'

Having appointed Herne to watch the proceedings of the official inquiry into the disaster, which opened on Tuesday, 24 April, Burton left for England the following day.

CHAPTER SIXTEEN

OH, WHAT A LOVELY WAR!

Fourteen months had elapsed since the declaration of war against Russia.[1] Then, in a mood of public euphoria, volunteers had flooded the Horse Guards in Whitehall. A week before the first troops left for Malta with bands playing and crowds cheering, *The Times* had declared that, though unable to match the great military nations on the Continent in the number of troops we could send, we would 'endeavour to compensate for this by perfect discipline, effective equipment, carefully selected officers, and above all, by the unflinching courage of our soldiers.'[2] Tragically, for too long, only the last of these criteria was met.

The national mood had radically altered since those early, heady days. Newspaper reports, none more so than in *The Times* itself, by its *Special Correspondent*, W.H. Russell, had graphically brought home to the public the scale of the administrative muddle, the incompetence of the Army's high command, and the sufferings of the British troops, especially in the terrible winter of 1854-55.[3] The Crimean campaign was, as Russell observed, 'soldiering with the gilding off.' Burton's twenty-eight year old cousin, Captain Francis Plunkett Burton had gone in a blaze of glory with the Coldstream Guards the previous year. After wintering on the heights above Sebastopol, he had returned to this country in May, his health permanently broken.[4]

Burton arrived back in London on Derby Day, an opportunity taken by the huge crowds gathered on Epsom Downs to forget the conflict in the Crimea for twenty-four hours. After seeking medical and dental help for his injuries, and visiting his father in Bath, he settled into the East India United Service Club, to prepare his Somali journal for publication. The first two volumes of the *Pilgrimage*, were almost ready for the press. The late arrival from India of his remaining manuscript, however, deferred publication of the volume on Mecca until early the following year.[5]

In Burton's absence, the work of editing the manuscript had been undertaken by a friend, Thomas Wolley.[6] As well as thanking the RGS for giving invaluable assistance, Wolley, in his Preface, acknowledged the 'kindness of an Eastern scholar of more than European reputation,' who had helped with revising the sheets before they were passed to the printer. The scholar, as Stanley Lane-Poole later revealed, was the distinguished Egyptologist, Sir John Gardner Wilkinson. According to Lane-Poole, Sir John removed a great deal of 'unpleasant garbage' in order to make the book publishable.[7] Undoubtedly of a sexual nature, much of it eventually found its way into Burton's notes to his translation of the *Arabian Nights*.

With a nod and a wink from Burton, Wolley ended his Preface, by hoping that the author's untiring energy and talent for observation and research would 'induce the Government of this country and India to provide him with men and means…to pursue his adventurous and useful career in other countries equally difficult of access, and, if possible, of still greater interest than the Eastern shore of the Red Sea.'[8]

Burton was unaware at this time of the highly critical attitude taken by the Aden and Bombay authorities towards his leadership of the Somali Expedition. This, too, was the position of the Royal Geographical Society. Lord Ellesmere, in his Presidential Address of 28 May, informed the Society that he had recently come across a paragraph in a German newspaper announcing Burton's safe return to Aden after an expedition to the Somali peninsula. This had been shortly confirmed by a letter from Burton to the Secretary, 'written in a spirit of dauntless joviality, which marks the character of the writer.'[9] This was far from being Burton's present feeling. A visit to his mother's grave in Walcot cemetery, and Stroyan's death for which he must have felt more responsibility that he cared to admit, had left him profoundly depressed. It was in this troubled state of mind that he looked to service in the Crimea as offering an opportunity for recovering his spirits. Only someone profoundly unaware of the true horrors of the Russian campaign could have thought so.

It was against the background of the public excitement in London over the long-awaited report of the Commons' Select Committee into the condition of the army before Sebastopol,[10] that Burton set about volunteering for war service. Four months earlier, General Sir James Simpson[11] had been sent to the Crimea by Lord Panmure, the new Secretary of State for War.[12] His brief was to report on the competence of the Staff officers, who were under strong criticism at home. Having served under him at Sakhar, Burton must have felt pretty confident that this would stand him in good stead for obtaining a position.

Shortly after reading his paper on Harar to the Royal Geographical Society,[13] he left London for France. After breaking his journey at Boulogne to spend several days with his sister and brother, now on a three-year furlough to Europe,[14] Burton caught a train for Paris. By Sunday, 17 June, he was aboard one of the packets of the Messageries Impériales, steaming out of Marseilles, bound for Constantinople. A week later, he was off Seraglio Point. Seven months earlier, Florence Nightingale had disembarked there in the pouring rain with her little group of nurses, to be rowed across the Bosphorus to the Dantean Hell of the Barrack Hospital at Scutari.[15]

Burton stayed only one night, booking into the Hotel d'Angleterre at Pera on the other side of the Golden Horn, run by Alexander Kinglake's former dragoman, 'the accomplished Mysseri.'[16] Criticism of the hotel and its owner in *The Times* provoked one reader into claiming that there was 'hardly a writer of modern Eastern travels, who has not found some words of grateful praise for Missiri and his hotel.'[17] Not surprisingly, Burton was one of the exceptions. He professed to find Misseri's wines atrocious, his cookery third-rate, and his prices first-rate. The following day, accompanied by Fred Wingfield, lately appointed assistant to William Filder, the much-maligned Commissary-General,[18] Burton set off up the Bosphorus for Balaclava.

It was only seven months since the port had been a scene of living nightmare, devastated first by a hurricane which totally destroyed the shipping in the harbour, and then by cholera. 'Words,' wrote W.H. Russell, 'could not describe its filth, its horrors.' As winter had given way to spring things had radically improved. A degree of cleanliness had been introduced among the sutlers and riff-raff of the town. A decent road had been built through Kadikeui to camp and the front. A month before Burton's arrival, the Sanitary Commission had supervised the clearing of the harbour of its devil's brew of sewage, bloated carcasses of horses, mules and sheep, swilling around with the putrefying mass of amputated arms and legs dumped there after the battle.

In May, the spirits of the soldiers had been raised by the spectacular success of the allied expeditionary force's attack on the Russian naval base at Kertch, commanding the entrance to the Sea of Azov. This had been followed a fortnight later by the equally successful assault by British and French troops on the Mamelon and the Quarries. The storming of the Redan, however, on 18 June, in concert with the French onslaught on the Malakoff, had been a disaster. The British Army was thrown into a mood of deep depression. 'You cannot conceive the miserable apathy, the ne'er-do-wellness of the Crimea,' Burton informed Dr Norton Shaw. 'Some curse seems hovering over our army. Our fellows are sensibly dispirited.' There were rumours that part of the army would fall back to Scutari, and after another attack on the Malakoff, 'the very spot which ought not to be attacked, would retire into winter quarters, breezy huts and battered tents.' However, it was almost impossible, he went on, 'to believe what is said by 10,000 gentlemen who have no earthly purpose in life but to seek solace in grumbling, fretting, and reporting.'[19]

Under the strain of this latest debacle, the health of the British commander, Lord Raglan, gave way, and he died in the evening of 28 June, the day Burton arrived in the Crimea. Whatever Lord Raglan's high personal qualities, Burton said, he was too old and infirm 'to come up to the idea of Sir Charles Napier's model officer, eternally on horseback, with a sword in his hand, eating, sleeping, and drinking in the saddle.'[20] The British Army badly needed someone of this stamp to raise its morale and give it an infusion of new life. Instead, it got Sir James Simpson, 'that worthy old gentle-woman,' as Lord Clarendon rather unkindly described him.[21]

During the week following his arrival, Burton passed the time visiting the front and camp with Wingfield and other friends. He then called on the new Commander-in-Chief at Headquarters, and found that his rush to the Crimea had been in vain. All appointments had been filled. The only alternatives to returning to England was either service with the Irregular Cavalry, the Bashi-Bazouks, or the Turkish Contingent. Burton claimed that his choice was readily made. 'There was indeed no comparison between serving under Major-General W.F. Beatson, an experienced light-cavalry man, who had seen rough work in the saddle from Spain to Eastern Hindustan; and under an individual, half-civilian, half-reformed Adjutant-General, whose speciality was, and ever had been foolscap – literally and metaphorically.'[22]

This offensive remark was Burton's way of publicly revenging himself on Sir Robert John Hussey Vivian who, in some undisclosed way, was involved in Burton's eventual resignation from the Bashi-Bazouks. Appointed Adjutant-General of the Madras Army in 1849, Vivian had returned to England in 1854, becoming a Director of the East India Company the following year. In May he had been appointed to command the Turkish Contingent in the Crimea. This body of troops appears to have been the brain-child of the British ambassador at the Porte, Lord Stratford de Redcliffe.[23] He had suggested taking twenty-five thousand of the best Turkish troops into British pay, commanded by British officers of field rank, leaving the Turkish officers of major and below unchanged. It was a plan which met with some success.

In spite of his later claim to the contrary, it is apparent from Burton's letter to Shaw,[24] that he shortly returned to Constantinople, and was given command of a company in this force. It seems that Burton was then informed by a friend that he was wanted by General Beatson. In his published account, however, Burton said he had written an official letter from the Crimea to the general, whom he had once met at Boulogne. He was therefore delighted when his name appeared in Orders. Lacking information, it is difficult to follow the exact chronology of Burton's movements at this time. One must assume from his letter to Shaw that, after resigning his appointment in the Turkish Contingent, Burton left immediately for the Dardanelles, where the Bashi-Bazouks had their Headquarters. Shortly afterwards, he returned to Constantinople, apparently on official business for General Beatson to the British ambassador, then at his summer residence on the Bosphorus. On 22 July, Burton wrote to Lord Stratford de Redcliffe from Pera, acknowledging the receipt of an enclosure addressed to General Beatson. He expressed deep regret that it had not reached him till the 20th. He now needed to visit Malta with as little delay as possible. It was probably late July, therefore, before Burton finally settled in with his new corps.

The war had turned the nearby village from a quiet backwater into a bustling little town. It had two Pashas, Civil and Military, and a large garrison of Turkish regular soldiers. General Beatson's house-cum-headquarters, where he lived with his wife and two daughters, was a low, rambling building close to the sea and near to a long line of old windmills. The regiments of the Bashi-Bazouks were camped out on the hills to the north of the town.

On 17 August, Burton was promoted to the local rank of Captain.[25] The following day he wrote to Shaw thanking him, the RGS, and various other friends, for their efforts on his behalf. He said that General Beatson had recommended him for a lieutenant-colonelcy, made him his Military Secretary, and had requested him temporarily as his Deputy Adjutant-General. He was cautious, however. 'Only entre-nous, my name has not yet been gazetted, and perhaps Col Grundy or some other stiff-necked individual might found an objection upon the score of certain assertions in El-Medinah.'[26] Ironically, just as he was about to enjoy this new-found success, relations between General Beatson and the British and Turkish authorities, never good, were becoming strained to the limit.

Beatson had first approached the British Government in 1854 with a plan of forming a corps of Bashi-Bazouks to give cavalry support to the allied armies. His offer had been accepted by the Foreign Office, and in May of that year he had reported to Lord Stratford de Redcliffe at Constantinople. Lord Raglan, however, said Burton, was averse to 'the idea of commanding men who kidnapped Bulgarians and roasted Russians.'[27] Furthermore, 'it was contrary to precedent: Irregulars were unknown at Waterloo, and the idea was offensive, because it was unknown to the good stock and pipe-clay school.'[28]

After a long delay, Beatson finally received the go-ahead from the British Government, and was promoted to the local rank of major-general. He left Constantinople in November of that year, and established his headquarters at the Dardanelles. Three months later he sent out British officers on a recruiting drive into Syria and different parts of Asia Minor, as well as into Bulgaria, Albania, Rumelia, and Macedonia, in European Turkey.

Things began rather inauspiciously. The first to arrive on 5 June 1855, were six hundred and fifty Albanians whose behaviour had scandalised people at Salonica, bringing a flood of protests to the British Embassy. Once at the Dardanelles, around one hundred and fifty of them mutinied and rode off. After attacking a police-station, where one of their number was held in custody, they went on an orgy of looting throughout the countryside. The remainder flatly refused to take part in any action against their comrades. Matters were only brought under control, when Turkish troops were sent from Constantinople, and a British man-of-war dropped anchor near the camp. The following month five hundred Syrians arrived from Beirut. On 21 July, fifty rode off to indulge in similar lawless behaviour.

Burton thought the original idea of raising this corps had been excellent. It had badly miscarried, in his judgement, largely through the fault of the War Office in not sending out enough officers. As a result, the men were left lying about on the hillsides with little to do. Captain Edward Money, appointed to one of the regiments about the same time as Burton, was shocked at how little seemed to be going on. Asked what he did with himself during the day, his commanding officer, a young man of twenty-eight, replied, "Eat a little, drink a little, smoke a little, and sleep a great deal."[29] There were no roll-calls or evening parades, no drilling or disciplining of the men. The same officer questioned about the lack of discipline told Money, "I don't think you can improve them; you must remember what they are, a wild harum-scarum set of devils; discipline them, and they'd be good for nothing." General Beatson, it appeared, contented himself with riding around the camp each morning and evening listening to their grievances. As soon as Burton was made Chief of Staff, he claimed to have persuaded General Beatson to change his policy with regard to drill and discipline. He also pointed out the wisdom of setting up a riding-school for a number of infantry officers who were unsteady in the saddle, and opening a salle d'armes to teach all the officers the best use of their swords.

Like his commander, Burton seemed to take a pretty lenient view of the Bashi-Bazouks' activities. The Arnauts or Albanians, he said, were in the habit of fighting when they were drunk, involving a peculiar style of duelling. Attended by their seconds and close friends, they stood facing each other at close quarters, each holding a cocked pistol in his right hand and a glass of raki in the left. The first to drain his glass was entitled to fire, 'and generally blazed away with fatal effect.'[30] Perhaps it was his own brand of lawlessness which gave Burton a peculiar empathy with these wild, fierce men, who had little regard for life. If they had been in Egypt, the Hejaz, or any other part of theTurkish world, he contended, they would have committed a dozen murders a day. As it was, 'Out of a few trifling set-tos among themselves, and an occasional bullying of the townspeople,' he told Shaw, 'the talkers of Constantinople have done wonders – they have ravished women, demolished towns, found out "outrages" and "abominable cruelties"; and ended by murdering General Beatson.' A report of this alleged incident appeared in *The Times* on 3 August, quoting from two despatches in the Paris newspapers, one from Constantinople of 26 July, the other from Vienna five days later. The truth, Burton insisted, was that 'Not an English lady of the half-dozen in the place has been obliged to leave it.'[31]

In fact, he thought the Bashi-Bazouks at the Dardanelles compared very favourably with the unruly French detachments at Gallipoli, and the rowdy inmates of the Nagara Hospital. However, although he regarded the mutinies as 'mere skylarking,' this was not a view shared by the Turkish authorities at the Dardanelles, or the British Ambassador. To him, they were a bunch of miscreants who, if they were paid by Russia, could not serve her cause better.[32]

General Beatson, very much in the Napier mould, blunt, combative, and outspoken, did not help matters. Even Burton, temperamentally similar in many ways, confessed to being astonished at the tactless manner and bellicose tone adopted by the general in many of his letters. Only after some persuasion did he allow Burton to tone them down. Even so, on one occasion, after completing his copy, Burton looked into the envelope and found that Beatson had added a postscript: 'This is official, but I would have your Lordship to know that I also wear a black coat.' Fortunately, the offending passage was quickly removed. Imagine the effect, Burton said, 'of a formal challenge to combat, "pistols for two and coffee for one," upon the rancorous old man of Constantinople, whose anger burnt like red-hot fire, and whose revenge was always at white heat.'[33]

Even so, Lord Stratford de Redcliffe was highly incensed against Beatson for a letter he had written to him, following a number of incidents at the Dardanelles. It appeared that the Bashi-Bazouks were in the habit of swaggering around the bazaar, taking what they wanted, and then refusing to pay. Shopkeepers foolish enough to protest, were subjected to abuse and violence. The Turkish Governor took up the matter with the Porte, and his complaints were forwarded to the British ambassador. Lord Stratford wrote to General Beatson, asking him to conduct an investigation into the allegations, and punish those responsible. Beatson's reply was typically dry and provocative. He said he would make full enquiries, and if any of his men were found guilty he would hang them. On the other hand, if he found no one guilty, he would hang the Turkish Governor.[34]

As a result of the desertions and depredations that had taken place, the ambassador ordered the setting up of a Court of Enquiry at the Dardanelles. It was a mixed commission composed of civil and military men, empowered not only to investigate but to sentence. Presided over by Brigadier-General J.G.S. Neill of the Turkish Contingent,[35] it consisted of three Turkish and two British consular officials. Of the latter, one was the vice-consul at the Dardanelles, Mr Calvert. The other, James Henry Skene, occupied a similar position at Constantinople. He was also General Vivian's private secretary, and sat as the personal representative of Lord Stratford de Redcliffe. The Commission was not far into its investigations, before General Beatson became involved in a bitter row with Brigadier-General Neill. It ended with Beatson's brusquely declining to have anything further to do with him. Skene was placed in an invidious position, the general telling him in forthright terms that, if he continued to associate with the brigadier, he would no longer be welcome as a guest in his house.

Ironically, in view of Beatson's hostile attitude to the Court of Enquiry, it had nothing but praise for the Bashi-Bazouks inside the camp. Its criticism was wholly reserved for their behaviour outside it. According to *The Times's* correspondent in Constantinople, General Beatson was supposed to have boasted of the obedience of his troops to himself and his officers. However, the correspondent went on, 'it would appear as if they imagined that docility on parade entitled them to enliven their hours of leisure by such objectionable pastimes as robbery, rape, and murder.'[36]

The results of the Enquiry containing, no doubt, an adverse report on General Beatson's uncooperative behaviour, were eventually sent to Lord Stratford de Redcliffe. He, in turn, passed them on to London. In late August, General Beatson received a despatch from the Secretary of State for War, Lord Panmure, ordering him on the ground of the undisciplined state of his troops, to place them under General Vivian. Beatson, however, was unwilling to serve under Vivian, described by Burton as a 'man redolent of pipe-clay and red-tape.' He immediately tendered his resignation which, initially, was not accepted.[37] It is against this background, that Burton's claim of having volunteered the use of the Bashi-Bazouks for the relief of Kars needs to be considered.

In the summer of 1854, a large Russian army commanded by General Muravief twice inflicted defeat on Turkish forces near this fortress town, in what was then known as Turkish Armenia. As a result, Colonel (later General Sir) Fenwick Williams, was sent there by Lord Raglan as Queen's Commissioner to liaise with the Turkish commander, Zarif Mustapha Pasha. Appalled by what he found, Williams decided to stay. He immediately set about organising the town's supplies and defences against the expected Russian siege, which began in June, 1855.

Eventually, the plight of the beleaguered garrison, diplomatically left to starve according to Burton, became a scandal. It was only at a late stage, having ignored up to eighty despatches from Col Williams asking for help, that Lord Stratford de Redcliffe, fearing official censure, wrote to General Vivian with a view to sending the Turkish Contingent on a secret mission to end the siege.[38] Vivian replied, however, that he was unable to procure the necessary transport. 'So I felt the game was in my hands,' Burton said, 'and proceeded in glorious elation of spirits to submit my project for the relief of Kars.' The resulting scene, he said, passed description. The ambassador 'shouted at me in a rage, "You are the most impudent man in the Bombay Army, Sir!" ending with, "Of course you'll dine with us today?"'[39] It was not until some months later that Burton discovered the reason. 'Kars was doomed to fall as a makeweight for the capture of half of Sebastopol, and a Captain of Bashi-Bazouks (myself) had madly attempted to arrest the course of haute politique.'[40]

This, Burton's version of events, first appeared in Hitchman's biography of Burton in 1887.[41] It was reviewed the following year in *The Athenaeum*, where this section was quoted.[42] In a letter to the journal, Stanley Lane-Poole who had lately published a biography of Lord Stratford de Redcliffe, challenged Burton's account, describing it as 'a strange inversion of facts.'[43] The originator of the plan to relieve Kars, he said, was not Burton, but the newly appointed Turkish Seraskier, or War Minster, Mohammed Rushdi. Dating to as far back as 27 June 1855, the proposal involved using the newly-formed Turkish Contingent under General Vivian, and part of Beatson's Horse, to make a diversion from Redoutkale and Kutais. Far from dragging his feet, as Burton had claimed, Lord Stratford de Redcliffe had given the plan his enthusiastic support, recommending it to the British Government in both his official and private letters. The Cabinet, however, was totally opposed to the transfer of the Turkish Contingent to Asia. Its own plan was that Kars should be relieved by way of Trebizond, and by Turkish troops alone. On 4 July, the Foreign Secretary, Lord Clarendon, wired the ambassador that the plan for reinforcing the army at Kars contained in his despatches of 30 June and 1 July was disapproved.

In a sneering, personalised, and totally irrelevant reply to Lane-Poole's criticism, Burton claimed to have 'told a true tale and no more.'[44] Lane-Poole retorted that it was 'a question between documents and Sir Richard Burton's word.'[45] The historical evidence shows that, in September when Burton was at Constantinople ostensibly proposing his scheme for relieving Kars with 2,640 Bashi-Bazouks, a Turkish army of 40,000 under Omar Pasha was already on its way for that purpose.[46] The most telling evidence, however, against Burton's ever having suggested such a scheme is to be found in his own letter of 18 August 1855, to Dr Norton Shaw. There, he wrote, '.....and as for affairs at Kars, they are too desperate to be retrieved by the efforts of 10,000 or 12,000 Turks. The whole country between Kars and Erzerum might rise in a moment against us, this would be followed by a Russian movement in Persia, and then the tide of war would set full Eastwards...'

By way of consolation the ambassador, so Burton claimed, made an indirect offer through Lord Napier and Ettrick, of commissioning him to pay an official visit to Schamyl, the legendary leader of the Muslim mountaineers of Dagestan and the Chechen region. The Persian ruler, Fath 'Ali Shah had lost the Caucasus to Russia by the treaties of Golestan in 1813, and Turkmanchay in 1828. Two years later, Schamyl had joined the Naqshbandiyah, a sect of Muslim Sufis engaged in a jihad against the Russians. In 1834, on being elected imam, he had proclaimed Dagestan an independent Muslim state. Since then, he had been a thorn in the side of tsarist Russia, sending out his well-organised and fanatical bands on wide-ranging and highly successful attacks on Russian positions in the Caucasus.

Burton said that he consulted with Charles Alison and Percy Smythe at the embassy.[47] They considered the scheme feasible, in spite of the dangers involved in a long ride through Russian territory. However, nothing came of it. Lord Stratford was unwilling, or unable, to give any promise of money, arms, or troops. Without such concrete proposals, Burton pointed out, Schamyl 'will infallibly set me down for a spy, and any chance of returning to Constantinople will be uncommonly small.'[48]

While it cannot be dismissed out of hand, little credence can be placed on the claim, attached as a rider to one which is certainly spurious. It is also highly unlikely in the context in which it would have had to be made. The priority of making such a proposal belonged to Laurence Oliphant, who had written a book describing his travels down the Volga and through the country of the Don Cossacks shortly before the outbreak of the Crimean War.[49] On the voyage from Yalta to Odessa, he had heard wonderful stories about Schamyl Bey from German passengers who had been in Circassia. He recognised that, if once the tribes could stop quarrelling among themselves, 'the organization of a combined force under the command of European officers who have long directed the operations of the Circassian army would prove most formidable to Russia.'[50] An independent Circassia presented a powerful barrier to tsarist aggression. The ability of Russian troops, however, 'to march with impunity across those mighty passes, and acquire new provinces to the south and eastward,' could eventually threaten our empire in India.[51] He became convinced, therefore, of the enormous strategic and political importance of making an alliance with the Muslim guerilla leader, to act in concert either with General Vivian's Turkish Contingent or Omar Pasha's troops. He had been disappointed of being sent on the mission himself in 1854. Attempts by two others having failed,[52] he managed to persuade the Foreign Secretary, Lord Clarendon, in August, 1855, to send him to Constantinople, armed with a letter for the ambassador.

It was on this voyage from Marseilles, that Oliphant had his first meeting with John Hanning Speke then on his way to join the Turkish Contingent. He wrote to his mother, 'Of course he is dying to go back and try again (that is, to discover the equatorial lakes of Africa & the source of the Nile), but is going to take a turn at Sebastopol first.'[53] At Constantinople, however, Lord Stratford de Redcliffe, given discretionary powers by the Foreign Office, exercised them against allowing the mission to proceed. Nothing had changed since John Longworth had been sent to Schamyl in April of that year. He had got no further than the Circassian coast before being sent back. It was obvious to the ambassador, that Schamyl was not interested in help from Christian sources, and that he was as intent on being independent of Turkey as he was of Russia.

Returning to the Dardanelles, Burton found his corps once more in trouble. On the morning of 26 September, the plain between the camp and the town was covered with Turkish regular troops: some five hundred infantry and two hundred and fifty cavalry. Eight field pieces were drawn up in position, and the warship *Oberon* was lying off in the Straits, commanding the approaches to the camp. The business community in the town had closed its shops, and the British consulate was deserted.

The reason for this extraordinary state of affairs, Burton inaccurately attributed to an exaggerated account of a trifling squabble between the French medical orderlies and the Bashi-Bazouks. Such an affray had taken place, but at an earlier date. It was hardly trifling, but it was not the cause of the present trouble. In view of the numerous disturbances involving the use of weapons by the Bashi-Bazouks, the Turkish Governor had asked General Beatson to order his men not to carry arms when coming into town. Beatson had declined to do so on the ground that it was against the traditions of the men he commanded.

Shortly afterwards, a serious incident occurred in which an Albanian officer attempted to rape the wife of one of his comrades, an officer in the Arab regiment. In the resulting clash between the two men, the husband received a deep sabre cut on the shoulder. The offender, managing to evade the police, regained the safety of the camp. A few days later he reappeared quite brazenly in the town. On being recognised by a soldier and told to accompany him to the Governor, the Albanian officer responded by shooting at the soldier, seriously wounding him in the thigh. It was only when his pistols misfired, that he was eventually overcome and thrown into jail.

The Civil Governor immediately summoned a Council, comprising the British and French consuls, and the Military Pasha. It was unanimously decided that, in future, any Bashi-Bazouks who entered the town carrying arms would, if necessary, be forcibly disarmed.[54] The Governor informed General Beatson that, unless he received a reply that day agreeing to his request for a ban on carrying weapons, he had no alternative but to adopt coercive measures. No such assurance was given, and a huge show of force was decided on. This led to a great furore in the camp, the native officers and men regarding it as an insult which should be met with force. Happily this was avoided. General Beatson issued the necessary order, the men submitted quietly, and the Turkish troops were withdrawn.

Nevertheless, this incident proved to be the final straw. Under order from General Vivian, Beatson was relieved of his command and directed to hand it over to Major-General M.W. Smith, who arrived at the Dardanelles on 29 September.[55] Beatson at the time was temporarily incapacitated, having been kicked on the head by his horse. According to Burton, he and a Major Berkley, having collected a delegation of as many officers as they could, went to General Smith to lay their case before him. They said that all the reports were false, and that they could demonstrate the disciplined state of the Bashi-Bazouks. They also suggested that Brigadier Brett might be directed to assume temporary command until fresh orders could be received from General Vivian. Brigadier-General Smith felt unable to comply with this request, 'so we both declared that we would send in our resignations. After an insult of the kind, we felt that we could no longer serve with self-respect.'[56]

This version differs in certain respects from General Beatson's own account. According to him, he sent for his officers who were acquainted with the Turkish language, and asked them what the effect would be of a sudden transfer of command. As a result, Beatson sent a letter to General Smith stating that he took upon himself the responsibility as senior officer, of transferring the command to Brigadier-General Brett while awaiting fresh instructions from General Vivian. He reported what he had done to Lord Panmure, and had a personal interview with General Smith who, he said, expressed no disapproval.[57]

Just over four years later, alleged events at this time became the subject of a libel action brought by

General Beatson against J.H. Skene, then HM's consul at Aleppo. The charges were, that when General Smith arrived at the Dardanelles, General Beatson assembled the commanding officers of the regiment, and actually tried to persuade them to make a mutiny in their regiments against General Smith, and against the authority of General Vivian. Two of these commanding officers, Lt Cols O'Reilly and Shirley, left the room saying they were soldiers and could not listen to language which they thought most improper and mutinous. Furthermore, that General Beatson had a sort of round-robin prepared by the chief interpreter. This was sent round to the different officers in the hope that they would sign it, refusing to serve under any other general but himself. Both of these mutinous orders were said to have originated with Captain Burton. He was also alleged to have kept the order from Lord Panmure, placing the Irregular Horse under General Vivian, locked up for three weeks, unknown to anyone but General Beatson. As a consequence, the order was not promulgated until after General Smith had arrived.

Although General Beatson lost the action on the ground that Skene's words were privileged, he effectually cleared his character of the charges against him. The jury, following Mr Baron Bramwell's lead criticised Skene, expressing 'their strong opinion upon the fact that when the defendant found out how unfounded the charges were, he had not retracted them.' Called as a witness at the trial, Burton, under cross-examination by Mr Bovill, was asked if he had been offered the option of a court-martial or resignation. 'It is long ago;' Burton replied, somewhat unconvincingly, given his total recall in other matters. 'I don't think it offered me the option of a court-martial. The letter making the offer is destroyed and I have no copy. I was offered the opportunity of resigning. I had applied to be permitted to resign previously.' Re-examined later, Burton said that his reason for resigning 'was because I did not consider myself well treated by General Vivian.'[58] None of these latter facts, of course, appeared in Burton's later account of his Crimean War experiences.

He left the Dardanelles with Beatson on 30 September. Having arrived at Buyukdere, a report was sent to General Vivian, who shortly afterwards came on board. According to Burton's rather unlikely account, Vivian listened favourably to Beatson's urgent request to be allowed to return at once to the Dardanelles. He then left at midday, stating that he would need to call on Lord Stratford de Redcliffe for instructions. A few hours later, General Beatson received a strongly-worded letter of rejection from the ambassador. There was nothing more to be done, and on 18 October both men left Therapia for England.

CHAPTER SEVENTEEN

THE LURE OF THE NILE

Although Burton returned to England under a cloud, his spirits must have been quickly raised by the critical acclaim he found accorded to his *Pilgrimage*. Judged by its real aims, as we have seen, his journey to Arabia was largely a failure. His book, however, by virtue of its subject, its narrative power, its vivid descriptive passages, and humour, became a popular as well as a critical success. It brought him the fame he craved, and gave him a position, according to one reviewer, 'equal to that most celebrated of Eastern travellers, Burckhardt.'[1]

The Athenaeum, which had crossed swords with Burton four years earlier, now had nothing but praise for the author and his work. 'Having done so much, Mr Burton has a claim to no ordinary attention when he writes…He has produced a book which unites characteristics hardly thought compatible – the solid old Oriental knowledge – the lively familiarity of a contemporary of *Eothen* – and a wild adventurousness like that of Mr Gordon Cumming.'[2] Equally flattering, *Blackwood's Magazine* suggested that, 'Perhaps there has never been a story of permanent disguise, so complete and successful.'[3]

Burton must have spent much of the next three months working at the manuscript of his journey to Harar, published the following spring under the title of *First Footsteps in East Africa*. It was a bulky volume, the printed text running to 458 pages, bristling with footnotes, and with four appendices.[4] The first of these was headed, the 'Diary and Observations Made by Lieutenant Speke, When Attempting to Reach the Wady Nogal.' It will be recalled that Burton had made a summary of Speke's journal at Aden in February, 1855, sending it along with his own report to the Bombay authorities before leaving for the African mainland. He had stated at the time that he would retain a copy for a general report on Eastern Africa. This being no longer feasible, Burton decided to include it with his own book.

Unfortunately, he could not refrain from appending a number of gratuitous comments, claiming that, despite Speke's misfortunes, his life had never been in real danger, and that some allowance needed to be made for the people of the country. Besides, he was known to be working for the Government, and 'savages cannot believe that a man wastes his rice and cloth to collect dead beasts and to ascertain the direction of streams.' He was also known to be a Christian, was ignorant of the Muslim faith, and being familiar with neither the Arabic nor the Somali tongue, was forced to communicate with the people through the medium of his dishonest interpreter and Abban.[5]

In October of that year, Laurence Oliphant in an otherwise highly complimentary review of Burton's book, criticised the résumé for lacking the interest of a personal narrative, and greatly regretting, 'that the experiences of one whose extensive wanderings had already so well-qualified him for the task, and who had shown himself so able an explorer, should not then have been chronicled at a greater length, and thrown into a form which would have rendered them more interesting to the general reader.'[6]

Burton later chose to regard these remarks as a deliberate provocation. 'This brand was not foolishly thrown:' he wrote, 'it kindled a fire which did not consume the less fiercely because it was smothered. Some two years afterwards, when in the heart of Africa, and half-delirious with fever, my companion let fall certain expressions which, to my infinite surprise, showed that he had been nursing three great grievances. The front of the offence was that his diary had been spoiled. Secondly he felt injured because he had derived no profit from a publication which had not proved paying to me. Thirdly, he was hurt because I had forwarded to the Calcutta Museum of Natural History, as expressly bound by my instructions, his collections, of which he might have kept duplicates.'[7]

Did Speke have any justification for accusing Burton of mis-using his diary, and his later claim that he had printed it 'to swell his own book.'?[8] In his letter to Government of 28 April 1854, Burton had stated that he would 'digest the mass of information collected by my coadjutors, and prepare a work worthy to meet the public eye.' Speke, who was not part of the expedition at that stage, was obviously unaware of this fact. At the same time, *First Footsteps, or An Exploration of Harar*, as it was subtitled, was clearly not a general report on Eastern Africa, for which Speke's abridged diary had ostensibly been retained. It might be thought, therefore, that he was justified in feeling aggrieved at his diary being consigned to the outer darkness, as he no doubt saw it, of an appendix.

But was he entitled to take this view? Burton described Speke's having, 'recorded his misadventures in a diary whose style to say nothing of sentiments and geographical assertions, rendered it in my opinion unfit for publication.' Was this mere spleen, or should he be believed? Later events connected with the ghost-writing of Speke's *Journal of the Discovery of the Source of the Nile* , of which Burton, like the rest of the reading public was completely unaware, suggest that he should.

Initially, Speke was installed at Strathtyrum, John Blackwood's country mansion situated about a mile from St Andrews, 'shut up in a room and told to write his book.' The experiment failed. Blackwood, who had guaranteed the explorer the £2,000 offered by John Murray, together with a similar arrangement regarding the contingent profits, was clearly worried. On 24 July 1863, he wrote despairingly to his nephew that he had 'been sweating over Speke's MS this morning, and what is to be done I know not...' As to his notes, 'They are written in such an abominable, childish, unintelligible way, it is impossible to say what anybody could make of them, and yet he is full of matter, and when he talks and explains, all is right.' Ironically, it was only with the assistance of another Burton, the historian, John Hill Burton, that 'the MS was finally got into shape and the book published the following December.'[9]

As well as giving unwitting offence to Speke, Burton reneged on his undertaking given to the Bombay Government that, in preparing his diary for publication, he would avoid all political allusions. Instead, he used part of his long Preface, dated 10 February 1856, to launch an eloquent and outspoken attack on the passive imperialism of the East India Company: its studied avoidance of any head-on clashes with the Yemeni Arabs, and its policy of containment rather than expansion. 'For half a generation,' he wrote, 'we have been masters of Aden, filling Southern Arabia with our calicos and rupees – what is the present state of affairs? We are dared by the Bedouins to come forth behind our stone walls and fight like men on the plain,....gross insults are the sole acknowledgement of our peaceful overtures...and our forbearance to attack is universally asserted and believed to arise from mere cowardice.'[10]

Broadening the argument of his thesis that, 'Peace is the dream of the wise, war is the history of man,'[11] Burton cited an earlier generation of Englishmen who, according to him, 'were celebrated for gaining ground in both hemispheres,' lands, he said scornfully, which 'were not won by a peace policy.' It was sheer folly for the philanthropist – always a term of abuse with Burton – and the political economist, to believe that, by giving up colonies, withdrawing behind compact frontiers, and by trying to maintain a balance of power, that Britain could still retain its leading position among the great nations of the world. 'Never!' he said resoundingly. 'The facts of history prove nothing more than this: a race either progresses or retrogrades, either increases or diminishes: the children of Time, like their sire, cannot stand still.'[12]

Such bellicose sentiments were hardly likely at any other time to endear Burton to his superiors either in London or India. They were especially inopportune at that particular juncture. The large file on the Somali Expedition had been sent by the Bombay Government in June 1855 to the Governor-General, then at his summer quarters in the Neilgherry Hills. Having read all the evidence, Lord Dalhousie endorsed the official criticism of Burton and his companions. Given the nature of the country and its people, he said bluntly, their 'negligence and disregard of all common prudence and ordinary precautions cannot be extenuated, far less excused.' Although authorising Brigadier Coghlan to carry out the measures he had suggested, he disagreed with the Resident's demanding such a large sum of money as 15,000Rs. In fact, he was opposed to levying a fine at all.[13] 'The reason of the objection,' Burton commented scathingly in a footnote, 'is not apparent. A savage people is imperfectly punished by a few deaths: the fine is the only true way to produce a lasting impression upon their heads and hearts. Moreover, it is the custom of India and the East generally, and is in reality the only safeguard of a traveller's property.' And Burton was in no doubt as to what punishment should be meted out to the offenders. They should be hanged on the spot where the murder had been committed, their bodies burned and the ashes thrown into the sea to avoid their becoming martyrs. 'This precaution should invariably be adopted,' he said, 'when Moslems assassinate Infidels.'[14]

As far as compensation for their losses was concerned, Dalhousie did not think that the officers had any just claim on the Government, 'having regard to the conduct of the expedition.' It was not until 13 June 1857, however, that they were officially informed of this fact. 'For this,' Burton wrote later, 'we had no redress. The Right Hon. the Governor-General of India, the late Lord Dalhousie of pernicious memory, thought more of using our injuries to cut off the slave-trade, than of doing us justice, although justice might easily have been done.'[15]

In August, 1855, the Court of Directors had written to the Bombay Government, informing them that, 'The disaster to the Somali Expedition renders it, in our opinion, inexpedient to entertain any application for its further prosecution.' If Burton was aware of this directive, he certainly gave no hint of it, nor of the damaging attacks that had been made on his reputation. In concluding his Preface, he expressed the hope that the project would be revived at an early date. 'Nothing is required but permission to renew the attempt – an indulgence which will not be refused by a Government raised by energy, enterprise, and perseverance from the ranks of merchant society to national wealth and imperial grandeur.'[16]

The reality was, that this particular door into Africa was now firmly closed. Recent events elsewhere in that continent, however, were about to open another.

In an article published as far back as 1835,[17] based on 'original and authentic sources,' the then highly respected "armchair geographer," W.D. Cooley, had given a description of a great inland sea. Known to the Arabs of Zanzibar by the general African name of Ziwa, that is *the lake*, it was called by those living on its shores Nassa, or N'yassa, which means *the sea*. Having been heard of by the Portuguese on the Zambezi, through their northern neighbours, the Maravis, it had been named by European geographers, lake Maravi. It was said that, four days beyond Keslingo, towards the WSW, the traveller reached a mountain named N'jese. From its summit, some fifty miles distant, could be seen the great inland sea, N'yassa, dotted with innumerable islands. According to the M'iao, even after 'paddling five or six hours a day, and resting every night on an island, it would take two moons to reach the farthest limit of the lake…Its breadth is three days' good paddling in a canoe.'[18]

During a six months' residence in Tanga in 1854 to study the Kisambara language, the German missionary Dr James Erhardt, heard from the ivory traders there, that the great stretch of water known as the Sea of Uniamisi 'was simply a continuation of the Lake Nyassa, the latter, according to them, striking out westward from its northerly direction, and then spreading itself out to an even greater expanse than hitherto, so as to approach the mountains which pass through the centre of the continent, and form a most impenetrable barrier and watershed....'

Erhardt was unwilling at first to give unqualified credence to their claims. However, he found it rather remarkable that others travelling into the interior from different starting points along a tract of coast extending from some six degrees of latitude, eventually arrived at a Baheri or inland sea. Collecting this data, Erhardt plotted it on a large map. In November of that year (1854), discussing the matter with his colleague, Johann Rebmann, 'at one and the same moment, the problem flashed on both of us as solved by the simple supposition that where geographical hypotheses had hitherto supposed an enormous mountain-land, we must now look for an enormous valley and an inland sea.'[19]

The following year, Erhardt sent a large and very detailed map to the missionary magazine, *Das Calwer Missionblatt* at Wittenberg. From there, Dr Heinrich Barth of the Missionary Society, who had recently returned from exploring in north and central Africa, sent a small facsimile drawn by Rebmann, together with three letters written by the missionary from Mombasa, to his friend, Dr Augustus Petermann in London.

Petermann, cartographer and founder/editor of the *Geographische Mitteilungen*, and a regular correspondent in geographical affairs for *The Athenaeum*, published an account in that journal on 29 September 1855.[20] The huge inner sea, said Petermann, was shown as occupying the vast space between the equator and 10° S. lat. and between 23° and nearly 30° E. long. Greenwich, having at its southern extremity Lake Nyassa attached to it like a tailpiece. This immense body of water, with an area twice as large as the Black Sea, was inscribed with the name 'Ukerewe or Inner Sea of Unamezi,' its narrow, elongated south-eastern end bearing that of 'Lake Niassa.' However unsatisfactory the internal evidence of the account, Petermann went on, 'it confirms and establishes one very important fact, namely, that there is only one large lake in Southern Africa. This was the opinion long since held by Mr. W.D. Cooley...whose views were opposed till now by the accounts of the missionaries in Eastern Africa, as they maintained that, in addition to Lake Nyassa, there existed another large lake in Moenemoezi.'

The Church Missionary Society had forwarded Erhardt's map to the RGS in August 1855. Its accompanying paper was read at a meeting on 26 November 1855.[21] Discussion continued at another meeting on 10 December, at which James M'Queen called into question the conclusions in Erhardt's paper. He contended that there were two lakes, not one single large one.[22] This was a view shared by Dr Charles Beke, who wrote a long letter to *The Athenaeum* in the following April from Mauritius. He had been told by the son of Mohammed bin Khamis, one of Cooley's principal authorities, who happened to be in Mauritius, that there were two lakes. One, the Nyassa, was much smaller and more southerly, and nearer to the coast, while the other, the Monowezi Lake, was considerably larger, more towards the north, and much further in the interior. The distinction between the two lakes, he had been told, was perfectly well-known to the Sawahilis of Zanzibar who traded with the interior. The roads to the lakes were also quite distinct and in different directions.[23]

Dr Petermann had concluded his *Athenaeum* article by calling for 'a determined and able man like Dr Barth to follow up discoveries and researches partially made.'[24] It is impossible to know precisely when Burton first became aware of the discussions going on about this alleged great inland sea. Although not yet a Fellow himself, it is reasonable to assume that his friendship with such leading lights of the RGS as Dr Norton Shaw, Col W.H. Sykes, and the Hon Henry A. Murray, resulted in his being fully informed of the situation shortly after his arrival in this country from the Dardanelles.

In response to the ongoing lively debate, the Society was not long in giving serious consideration to organising an expedition to test the truth of the missionaries' claims. In March, 1856, Shaw sent Erhardt a letter asking for detailed advice about mounting a limited expedition to East Africa. Burton later mistakenly claimed that Erhardt, himself, offered to explore there, a claim also echoed by Speke.[25] In his reply, Erhardt said that the island of Zanzibar was presently the key to that region, and that the intending traveller would organise his caravan to the interior from there. He recommended a weighty introduction to the Imam of Muscat. That done, however, 'the friendship of Arabs should no longer be cultivated as the Arab government and Arab slave dealers will only try to frustrate his ends.' This turned out to be untrue, as did Erhardt's claim that the English, French, and American consuls were not men from whom assistance could be expected.

Erhardt went on to advise about the language necessary, the Kisawahil, and the wages of the porters. As to the route, the easiest, shortest, and most frequently used way into the interior was from Kiloa. The party, he suggested, should start from there in July, August, or September, the most healthy season of the year. A long stay on the coast, he warned, was dangerous in every point of view.[26]

An Expedition Committee chaired by one of the Society's two Vice-Presidents, the veteran Arctic explorer, Sir George Back, met on 19 March. Having discussed a motion by Col Sykes 'regarding the project of an Expedition to explore a part of Africa between the coast of Zanzibar and the inland Sea of Uniamesi,' Erhardt's letter was read out, to which Francis Galton added some useful remarks of his own. The committee then concluded that it would advisable to defer any further discussion on the subject to a future meeting when they could have the assistance of Col Sykes and the Rev Erhardt.[27]

In the meantime, Dr Shaw wrote again to Erhardt for advice on the expenses that might be involved in mounting such an expedition. Erhardt replied that the chief expenses would consist of the wages of twenty porters at 6 dollars a head to accompany the traveller from Zanzibar or Kiroa to the Niasa and to stay with him till he returns, goods such as cloth, beads, night-caps, knives, needles, and gay-coloured prints. Other expenses would involve the hire of a boat to Kiroa [Kilwa], gunpowder, muskets, flints, food etc. The whole expedition, in his view, 'if nicely managed should certainly not exceed 300 dollars or £30 English.' With astonishing naiveté, Erhardt expressed the hope that 'these expenses will not frighten you out of such an undertaking as advocating an expedition to East Africa.'[28] Burton later referred to Erhardt's estimate of expenses, when he mistakenly referred to the missionary's proposal 'to land with an outfit of 300 dollars at Kilwa......' In a footnote he criticised it as 'highly injurious to future travellers...The consequence of his proposal was simply this: With £5000 instead of £1000...the East African Expedition could have explored the whole central area.'[29]

On 9 April, Burton wrote a formal letter of application to Dr Shaw:

I venture to request through you that the Roy. Geog. Soc. of Great Brit. will afford me their powerful aid in carrying out my original project of penetrating into Eastern Africa....Lately Colonel Sykes, Deputy Chairman of the Hon. EIC informed me that the plan might be revived by a recommendation from the R,Geog.Soc....I am prepared to start alone & if judged necessary – disguised as an Arab merchant. Should, however, the R. Geog. Soc. incline towards an expedition, with the idea that a virgin country of such extent as the line proposed could scarcely be investigated by a single traveller, I shall be happy to place before them a detailed scheme for operations in the interior combined with a survey of the coast.[30]

At a meeting of the Expedition Committee three days later, chaired by Col Sykes, the letters from Erhardt and Burton were read out. After considering the several maps and notes relating to the Eastern Coast, and the objects to be attained by an Expedition, the Committee:

Resolved, that, not less on the ground of geographical discovery, than for the probable commercial and, it may be, political advantages and the establishment of an amicable intercourse with the various tribes, it be recommended to the Council to invite the co-operation of Her Majesty's Government and that of the East India Company in an Expedition from Zanzibar, or its neighbourhood, to ascertain in the first instance, the limits of the Inland Sea or Lake known to exist, to record such geographical facts as may be desirable, to determine the exportable products of the country and the ethnography of the tribes. In addition to these advantages, the expedition may lead to the solution of that geographical problem, the determination of the head sources of the White Nile.

The Committee then directed Shaw to write to Burton to say that his claims would be duly considered.[31]

Fully confident of obtaining the RGS's full backing, Burton submitted his plans a week later:

> The RGS desire, I believe, to form an expedition principally for the 1) purpose of ascertaining the limits of the Ujiji Lake, 2) secondarily, to determine the exportable produce of the interior & the ethnography of the tribes...
>
> Proceeding to India, at the close of next Sept. I would there make preparations for the journey. An order from Govt. would enable me to collect from the vessels in Bo.[Bombay] Harbour a sufficient number (from 10-12) of the Swahili blacks [this is annotated at a later date in pencil, 'Not Swahilis – runaway slaves'] used in the steamers as coal trimmers & coal-hands....I have already had the honour to record my willingness to proceed alone to E. Africa. Yet it would scarcely be wise to stake success upon a single life when 2 or 3 travellers would at all times be safer & in case of accident more likely to preserve the results of their labours. I should therefore propose as my companion, Lt. Speke of the B.A. [Bengal Army]. If aided with a sergeant or non-commissioned officer for the purpose of assisting us in observations & surveys we should be enable to perform a more perfect work.
>
> The RGS would doubtless not be contented with a mere exploration of the Ujiji Lakes. It is generally believed that the sources of the White Nile are to be found among the mass of mountains lying between 1° S. & 1° N. lat., & 32° & 36° E. long. Moreover, the routes of Arab caravans who in 18 months have crossed Africa returning from Benguela to Mozambique, force upon us the feasibility of extensive exploration. These two are separate and distinct objects. They would, however, be greatly facilitated by a preparatory exped. to the U. Lakes as the information there procured by an intelligent eyewitness would serve for the better guidance of his successors....[32]

Burton's stated reason for choosing Speke to accompany him to the Lakes was, 'because he had suffered with me in purse and person at Berberah, and because he, like the rest of the party, could not obtain redress.'[33] This, however, was not the whole story. It is clear from his later posthumous portrait of Speke that Burton, despite his reservations about the man, was impressed by his erstwhile companion's qualities as an explorer. During his years spent trekking through some of the remotest parts of Little Tibet, Speke had not only indulged 'his passion for shooting, collecting and preserving,' he had taught himself geodesy in, what Burton described somewhat patronisingly, as 'a rude but highly efficient manner.' He had also become adept at constructing sketches and field-maps. Furthermore, long experience in 'tracing out the course of streams, crossing passes, and rounding heights, gave him,' Burton said, 'an uncommonly acute "eye for country" – by no means a usual accomplishment even with the professional surveyor.'[34] Plainly, he would be an asset on this expedition.

Speke, however, was in Turkey. Like Burton he had lost no time in volunteering for the Crimean campaign on returning to England. He, too, had seen no active service, spending most of his time stationed with the Turkish Contingent at Kertch. Now, with the ending of the war, and with no prospect in sight of returning to Africa, he had decided to try his hand at collecting the fauna in Circassia and other parts of Asia. He had bought guns and other necessary equipment, and a brother officer of the Bengal Army, Captain Edmund Smyth, had agreed to join him.

In late April, Smyth wrote to the RGS from Constantinople, asking it to use its influence in helping them to obtain passports in order to cross over into Russian territory.[35] Shaw replied that there was little chance of obtaining such passports, the time being hardly propitious for working in these regions. He pointed out to Speke that an expedition to explore Africa was once again being organized by Burton, and advised his joining it. By the same mail, a letter arrived from Burton with just such an invitation, and a promise that it would involve no expense since the Home and Indian Governments had each promised to contribute £1,000. This, Speke's account, gives the impression that there was certainty about these amounts at this stage. There was not. Without a second thought for his Caucasian expedition or, it appears, for Capt Smyth, Speke immediately sold his equipment, and took the first mail to England.

A third meeting of the Expedition Committee was held on 23 June, attended by Burton who explained his requirements.[36] He wished to be accompanied on the expedition, he said, by Lt Speke of the 46th Bengal Native Infantry, who had been with him in Abyssinia. He also wanted Dr Steinhaueser then stationed at Aden, and Corporal Church of the Royal Sappers and Miners, 'who had served so effectively on the African Expedition under Dr Vogel.'[37]

Burton also expressed the hope that the Hon the Court of Directors would place him on the same allowances as he had enjoyed on his former expedition. He also wanted a free passage to Bombay, where, he hoped, the necessary surveying instruments, guns and ammunition, would be supplied. From there, he wanted passage to Zanzibar in one of the Company's cruisers. Finally, he would require strong letters of support to Col Hamerton, the Hon Company's Agent there.

Two days later, the Committee met again to discuss receipt of a letter from the Foreign Secretary, Lord Clarendon, to the President, Admiral Beechey. The minutes of the meeting do not disclose its contents. It has to be assumed, therefore, that it contained the Government's pledge to pay £1,000 towards the cost of the expedition. Dr Norton Shaw was asked to send a copy to the East India Company, expressing hope for an early and favourable answer.

CHAPTER EIGHTEEN

BRIEF ENCOUNTER

Outside the pages of Isabel Burton's biography, we have only the briefest of glimpses of Burton's social and personal life at this period. He undoubtedly saw a great deal of his friend, A.B. Richards, who was a member of the Windham club, only two doors away from the EIUSC in St James's Square. Burton was also a regular guest at the convivial get-togethers held after each meeting of the RGS at Admiral Murray's bachelor quarters in Albany, Mayfair.[1] The tall, prematurely white-haired Murray, known to his friends as "The Skipper", was a highly popular host, who delighted in bringing together a wide diversity of men. Bishop Wilberforce, known to his detractors as 'Soapy Sam,' was occasionally a guest, though, as Galton remarked, Burton's 'usual conversation in those days was not exactly of a stamp suitable to episcopal society.'[2]

His reputation, of course, had already brought him to the notice of Richard Monckton Milnes, later Lord Houghton. One of the best-known and most influential men of the day, Disraeli had gently satirised him in *Tancred* as Vavasour:

Mr Vavasour was a social favourite, a poet and a real poet, and a troubadour, as well as a member of Parliament; travelled, sweet-tempered, and good-hearted, amusing and clever........ Vavasour liked to know everybody who was known, and to see everything which ought to be seen. He was also of opinion that everybody who was known ought to know him, and that the spectacle, however splendid or exciting, was not quite perfect without his presence.[3]

The campaigning Anglican clergyman and novelist, Charles Kingsley, recalled meeting Burton some time in July at Milnes's London residence at 16 Upper Brook Street. 'I was at Monckton Milnes's last night,' he wrote to his wife, Fanny, 'and went home with *Mecca* Burton and sat till 3 am with him. A splendid little fellow – just off to find the Mountains of the Moon.'[4]

Four years on from having last seen Burton in Boulogne, Isabel Arundell still remained completely obsessed by him. Strong willed and stubborn, she had dug in her heels over marriage to any other man. 'They say it is time I married,' she wrote in her diary,' (perhaps it is); but it is never time to marry a man one does not love, because such a deed can never be undone. Richard may be a delusion of my brain. But how dull is reality. With all to make me happy, I pine and hanker after him, my other half, to fill this void, for I feel as if I were not complete.'

Just like Florence Nightingale's *Cassandra*, a fictional character which she had created in 1852 to voice her own private feelings of utter despair, Isabel felt trapped in the vacuity and boredom of her upper-class existence. She envied Burton's 'wild, roving, vagabond life,' convinced that as she was 'young, strong, and hardy, with good nerves, and no fine notions, I should be just the girl for him;....I am sure I am not born for a jog-trot life; I am too restless and romantic...Now with a soldier of fortune, and a soldier at heart, one would go everywhere, and lead a life worth living. What others dare I can dare. And why should I not?'[5]

Appalled by accounts of the terrible suffering endured by British soldiers in the Crimea during the winter of 1854-55, Isabel had offered her services as a nurse to Florence Nightingale on three occasions. Each time she was turned down on the grounds of being too young and inexperienced. Always eminently practical when faced with adversity, Isabel turned her attention instead to giving much-needed help to the almost destitute wives and families of the soldiers. She formed a club of young upper-class women, complete with scarlet sash, flag, stamped paper, list and seal. Initially it was called the "Whistle Club," each of its members carrying a tiny silver whistle for protection. When this was no longer found necessary, the name was changed to the "Stella Club," 'in honour,' as she explained,' of the morning star – my star.'[6] The club was a runaway success, Isabel alone collecting a hundred guineas by shillings and sixpences in only ten days. She also found it a salutary experience. 'I know now the misery of London, and in making my rounds I could give details that would come up to some of the descriptions in *The Mysteries of Paris* or a shilling shocker.'

Following the signing of the treaty of Paris on 30 March 1856, which brought the Crimean War to an end, the London Season was soon in full swing again. Racing got under way at Ascot Heath. Although still called "Aristocratic Ascot" by members of the racing fraternity, its "glories" had all but disappeared with the opening of the Staines and Wokingham Railway. There were now appreciably fewer carriages, and the atmosphere had become more like Epsom.

Gold Cup day, Thursday, 12 June, was a red-letter day in the racing calendar, memorable for the attendance of Queen Victoria and the Prince Consort, together with the Royal suite, and a host of distinguished English and foreign guests. Undeterred by leaden skies and a piercingly cold wind, people in their droves trooped hopefully towards the course, while vehicles poured out of Windsor, clogging the roads and the drives through the park, and throwing up dense clouds of dust much to the consternation of the ladies in their best bonnets and heavily flounced dresses.

Like many others, the Arundells were probably at Ascot, less for a flutter than for a chance of getting a grandstand view of the Royal entourage descending the hill along the 'new mile' – eleven carriages-and-four, five of them drawn by beautiful grey ponies, with attendants and outriders dressed in scarlet livery.

Perhaps as big a highlight for Isabel that day, was her chance meeting at the racecourse with the gypsy, Hagar Burton, whom she had not seen since her younger days at Furze Hall. Breaking away from the milling crowds, she shook Isabel's hand. "Are you Daisy Burton yet?" she asked. "Would to God that I were!" Isabel replied fervently 'The other's face lit up. "Patience; it is just coming." The gypsy barely had time to wave her hand before being unceremoniously pushed away from the carriage. 'I never saw her again,' wrote Isabel, 'but I was engaged to Richard two months later.'[7]

Since early in 1854, the Arundells had been living at 32 Oxford Square, part of an area sometimes known as Tyburnia, bounded by Sussex Gardens, and the Bayswater and Edgware roads.[8] So far, it had been a very hot August, and Isabel, together with her younger sister Blanche and a friend, were walking in the Botanical Gardens in nearby Regent's Park.[9]

In all probability, this unidentified 'friend,' was John Hugh Wadham Smyth Pigott, whom Blanche was to marry a year later. Although almost sixteen years Blanche's senior, he must have seemed the ideal suitor in the eyes of Mrs Arundell. Catholic of course, he was a friend of the Prince of Wales, and an enormously wealthy landowner. A long-standing member of the exclusive Royal Yacht Squadron, and a keen if not fanatical sailor, he and Blanche had met at Cowes, where he owned two yachts.[10] With the ending of Cowes

Week, August 5 –11, the couple had returned to London. Clearly, Isabel's role that day in the Botanical Gardens, was to act as chaperone for her young unmarried sister.

Some way into their leisurely stroll around the Inner Circle, Isabel suddenly caught sight of Burton 'walking with the gorgeous creature of Boulogne – then married.'[11] Whether this was Destiny at work as Isabel liked to claim, or whether Louisa, perhaps, had dropped a broad hint that she would be in the Gardens with Burton that particular day and at that particular time, must remain a matter for conjecture. They immediately stopped, exchanged greetings, and asked each other numerous questions about the four intervening years. Before she left, Burton pointedly asked if she came there often. "Oh yes," she replied, just as pointedly, "we always come and read and study here from eleven to one, because it is so much nicer than staying in the hot rooms at this season." Murmuring agreement, he caught sight of the book she was carrying and asked what she was studying. Isabel showed him her well-thumbed copy of Disraeli's *Tancred*.

Naturally, it was a book with which Burton was thoroughly familiar. It served to establish an immediate rapport between them, Burton going on to elaborate for her the book's leading ideas and its overriding philosophy expressed by the great Jewish banker, Sidonia: 'All is race – there is no other truth.' As Isabel left after about an hour , she overheard him say to his companion, "Do you know that your cousin has grown charming?" I could not have believed that the little schoolgirl of Boulogne would have become such a sweet girl,' and she heard Louisa say "Ugh!" in a tone of mock disgust.

The following day when Isabel and Blanche arrived, he was there again, alone this time, composing 'some poetry to show Monckton Milnes on some pet subject.' Burton rose at their approach, and stepping forward called out laughingly, "You won't chalk up, 'Mother will be angry,' as you did when you were a little girl?" They walked together around the Gardens, chatting again over old times and about people and things in general. About the third day, 'his manner gradually altered towards me; we had begun to know each other, and what might have been an ideal love before was now a reality.' By this time, too, Blanche unaccountably disappears from Isabel's narrative.

Possibly that self-same day, having heard through the grapevine that he had received permission from the East India Company to join the expedition, Burton dashed off a short note to Dr Norton Shaw, who was then away from London:

> My Dear Shaw,
>
> All right. Yesterday I heard privately that it is settled. So after a little run through Baden Baden I return to get all ready. Pray see Church when you come back and request him to join the party. If he cannot be with us, I leave you to find a good honest John Bull who does not fear niggers.
>
> PS I've ordered a metallic boat from America, revolvers and other useful articles.[12]

The letter gives the clear impression that his departure for Germany was pretty imminent. According to Isabel, however, she and Burton had one brief fortnight of uninterrupted happiness, at the end of which he stole his arm around her waist, laid his cheek against hers, and asked her, "Could you do anything so sickly as to give up civilization? And if I can get the Consulate at Damascus, will you marry me and go and live there?"[13] He asked her not to give him an immediate answer, since it would mean such a huge sacrifice, and involve leading a life like that of Lady Hester Stanhope. Isabel, overcome with emotion, was silent for so long, that Burton apologised for asking for so much. Finding her voice at last, Isabel said, "I do not want to think it over – I have been thinking it over for six years, ever since I first saw you at Boulogne. I have prayed for you every morning and night. I have followed all your career intimately. I have read every word you ever wrote, and I would rather have a crust of bread with you than be queen of all the world, and so I say now, Yes, *yes*, YES!" Burton, naturally, was well aware of the difficulties of their position. "Your people will not give you to me," he said. "I know that," Isabel replied spiritedly, "but I belong to myself – I give myself away."

Nevertheless, they thought it inadvisable to announce their engagement to Isabel's mother, 'for it would have brought a hornets' nest about our heads, and not furthered our cause – and besides, we were afraid of my being sent away, or of being otherwise watched and hindered; so we agreed to keep it a secret until he came back.'[14]

In the light of later events, we might well consider that Isabel was responsible for heavily over-egging the pudding as far as their relationship was concerned. It raises the intriguing question, of course, as to why Burton, allegedly deeply in love at this stage, could so easily tear himself away from Isabel merely to enjoy the expensive pleasures of Baden-Baden in the Black Forest. Little wonder that she omitted any mention of this trip from her narrative.

We have further to question that entering the consular service, let alone the absurd suggestion of his attempting to obtain the plum posting of the Consulate at Damascus, was ever in Burton's mind at this period. Instead, it reads like a fictional projection into the past by Isabel, of what actually happened many years later. He had returned from the Dardanelles 'determined,' in his own words, which Isabel suppressed in her own biography, 'to follow none but the career of an explorer and a pathfinder.' Only by remaining in the service of the HEIC, would he have any chance of fulfilling this goal. The humdrum existence of a consul only became an unwelcome, if necessary, option some years later.

In the event, Burton did more than merely take the waters at Baden-Baden. On 7 September he was writing to Shaw from Hamburg. Without disclosing the reason for his being there, he stated that he would be in England on or about the 20th of that month. 'Enclosed is the rough copy of the E.A. Exped. Plan. Col. Sykes did not give in hand his other plan, he showed it to me & placed it in a drawer on the right side of his desk. Pray have the letters ready for my return. Hamerton is they say coming home in which case an official addressed to HBM's Consul Zanzibar would be best......'

While Burton had heard, unofficially, of the East India Company's decision, it was not until 30 August that the Deputy Secretary of the EIC wrote an official reply to the Royal Geographical Society.[15] The Court of Directors, Shaw was informed, was willing to co-operate with HM's Government 'in giving effect to a measure which they believe will contribute to the general advancement of science, and the development of Eastern Commerce.' They were, therefore, prepared 'in compliance with the request of the Council of the Royal Geographical Society, to authorise the employment of Captain Burton of the Bombay Army on this special service for two years, without prejudice to his position as a regimental officer, on full pay, and Regimental allowances.' They were also prepared 'to issue such instructions to the authorities in India as may be calculated to facilitate its operations, with especial reference to the exercise of their influence with the Imaum of Muscat, from whose territory it is proposed that the expedition should start.'

Speke's position, on the other hand, looked anything but promising. In June, he had discovered to his consternation that the Government in India intent on increasing its Indo-European forces, had sent an urgent request to Leadenhall Street that officers should not have their leave extended, or be placed on duty out of India. The India House authorities, therefore, although privately sympathetic to Speke's case, felt it necessary to withhold their permission. 'I was now between two fires. I had sacrificed my Caucasian expedition, and could not speak with the authorities in India.[16]

Things looked so desperate that an approach to the highest authority in India was contemplated, but as Burton wrote to Shaw in June, 'I've been speaking to some knowing coves who all advise no reference to the

Governor-General. It will delay us for months, if not knock the thing on the head.'[17] It was finally decided that Speke would travel with Burton to Bombay, trusting to luck that the Government there would be prepared to give him provisional permission.[18]

This was not the only problem. Having now learned that the EIC was not prepared to match the Government's grant of £1,000, Speke claimed that he objected to go, 'as I did not wish, for one reason, to put myself under any money obligations to Captain Burton; and for another, I thought I had paid enough for a public cause in the Somali country, without having gained any advantage to myself.' While this sounds perfectly reasonable on the face of it, it should be taken, I believe, with a large pinch of salt. There was no likelihood of his voluntarily passing up this heaven-sent opportunity of returning to Africa. More credible, if somewhat exaggerated perhaps, is his claim that Burton, knowing 'nothing of astronomical surveying, of physical geography, or of collecting specimens,' was keen to see him go.[19]

Burton received his official appointment from the RGS Council to take charge of the expedition on 1 October 1856, together with lengthy instructions for its conduct drawn up by Francis Galton.[20] An important part of these read:

> The great object of the expedition is to penetrate inland from Kilwa, or some other place on the East Coast of Africa, and make the best of your way to the reputed Lake of Nyassa.....
>
> Having obtained all the information you require in this quarter, you are to proceed northward towards the range of mountains marked upon our maps as containing the probable source of the 'Bahr el Abiad,' which it will be your next great object to discover.
>
> From the limited sum of money appropriated to the purpose of this expedition, it will be necessary to practise the most rigid economy. The Council have directed £250 to be placed at your disposal at Bombay for the purpose of providing the necessaries for the expedition; and on your arrival at Zanzibar you will be provided with £250 more for any additions to your outfit that may be required. You will also be authorised to draw upon Colonel Hamerton to the amount of £250...the remaining sum of £250 being reserved for your return home, or in case of extreme emergency.
>
> It is to be most distinctly understood that the Royal Geographical Society will not consider itself responsible for any sums otherwise procured or drawn without its express authority, and that the parties drawing such bills will be themselves liable for these............
>
> Wishing you success in this gallant enterprise, and that you may return in health to this country, covered with honour....'[21]

This might be all very well for Burton. For Isabel, however, 'The idea of waiting for willing parents and a grateful country appeared so distant that I should scarcely be worth the having by the time all the obstacles were removed.' She also had to be prepared for his sudden departure on his receiving certain information.'[22]

On the morning of 3 October, Isabel went to meet him as usual, and they agreed to see each other the following day. Burton, she claimed, had traced a little sketch map for her of what he expected to find in the Lake Regions. It is printed in the *Life*, and is completely spurious, containing features such as lakes Tanganyika, Victoria Nyanza and Albert, the existence of which, let alone their positions, was not suspected at this period. In showing the Rusizi river flowing northwards from Lake Tanganyika into Lake Albert, not discovered until March 1864, and thence into the White Nile, it obviously belongs to a much later period, when Burton was bent on trying to convince British geographers that Tanganyika was the Nile's real source.

Besides giving him Hagar Burton's horoscope, she placed round his neck a medal of the Blessed Virgin on a steel chain. Known to Catholics as 'the miraculous medal,' it dated from 1830, when St Catherine Laboure, of the Daughters of Charity, reputedly experienced two visions of the Virgin Mary in Paris. After the second vision, a voice was heard to say, "Have a medal struck after this model. Those who wear it will receive great graces." Originally called "the medal of the Immaculate Conception," it quickly became known as the Miraculous Medal, after so many remarkable graces and favours were supposedly granted through it.

Some years later, Burton would contemptuously dismiss this kind of medal and the Cross, together with numerous other talismans belonging to pagan Africa and the world religions, as 'the tomfooleries of faith.[23] According to Isabel, however, he promised to wear it throughout the journey, and show it to her on his return. She had offered it to him on a gold chain, which he refused, saying " they will cut my throat for it out there." He also gave Isabel a short six-stanza poem. It was not, however, a tender love lyric addressed to her personally, of the kind he had tossed off by the score in India, but to the goddess 'Fame', whose image he wore, 'Within a heart well fit to be thy shrine.' If Thomas Wright is to be believed, he also gave a copy to Louisa Segrave.

To what extent we can believe any of Isabel's melodramatic account of her reaction to Burton's departure, given her love of the occult, can only be a matter for speculation. That afternoon, Burton is said to have made a courtesy call at Oxford Square. The conversation was friendly but formal, Isabel believing that she would be seeing him the following day. The family was attending a play that evening, and Isabel begged Burton to come. He said he would try, but that if he was unable, she was to appreciate that he had some important business to transact.

Topping the bill that week at the Royal Princess's Theatre in Oxford Street, was Sheridan's tragedy, *Pizarro*, with the famous actor-manager, Charles Kean in the part of Rolla, and his wife, Ellen Keane (née Tree), as Elvira.[24] The Arundells had seats in one of the theatre's four tiers of boxes. At 10.30 pm Isabel thought she saw Burton on the other side of the house, looking into their box. She smiled and beckoned to him to come down. He then disappeared. A few minutes passed without his making an appearance. 'Something cold struck my heart; I felt that I should not see him again, and I moved to the back of the box, the tears streaming down my face….happily for me Cora was bewailing her husband's loss on the stage, and as I am invariably soft at tragedy, my distress caused no sensation.'

Isabel passed a restless night, unable to sleep. Dozing off at last, she dreamt that she could feel Burton's arms around her. "I am going now, my poor girl," he said. "My time is up and I have gone; but I will come again – I shall be back in less than three years. I am your Destiny."'

Pointing to the clock, which stood at two, he held up a letter at the same time fixing her with his piercing stare. Placing it on the table, he said, "That is for your sister – not for you." He went to the door, and after giving her another of those long peculiar looks, disappeared from sight. This is the *Romance* version of what is alleged to have happened. In the *Life* account, however, not only is the wording slightly different, but Isabel describes it in paranormal terms, experienced not as a dream but while awake, with Burton's appearance being preceded by a warm current of air drifting towards her bed.

She immediately roused one of her brothers, in whom she confided. "Richard is gone to Africa," she sobbed, "and I shall not see him for three years." He dismissed it as a nightmare, blaming it on the lobster she had had for supper. She spent that night sitting in her brother's armchair. At eight o'clock the next morning, a letter arrived for her sister Blanche, enclosing one for Isabel. Richard had found it too painful to part from her, and thought they would suffer less that way. He requested Blanche to break the news gently to her sister, and to give her the letter, which assured her that they would be reunited in 1859. He had received some secret information, which had prompted him to leave England immediately in case of being detained as a witness at some trial. He had left his lodgings in London at 10.30 the preceding evening, when she thought she had seen him at the theatre, and sailed at two o'clock from Southampton, when she saw him in her room.[25]

This might seem a text-book example of synchronicity, a term coined many years later by the Swiss psychologist, C.G. Jung, to describe events which coincide in time and appear to be meaningfully related, while having no discoverable causal connection. Unfortunately, the facts do not support Isabel's claim either as to times or place of departure. A.B. Richards dined with Burton on the day he left, before seeing him off at the railway station.[26] Under the terms of his instructions from the RGS, Burton was ordered to travel by the Overland Route to Bombay. Given the need for his precipitate departure from England, this meant his taking a reasonably early train from London Bridge in order to be certain of catching the Royal Mail steamer which left Dover for the Belgian port of Ostend every night, except Sunday, at 11.15 pm. From there, he and Speke, planned to cross Europe to Berlin, from where they would take a train south to the Austrian port of Trieste on the Adriatic. Here, they would be able to board a ship to Alexandria.

After Burton had gone, Isabel claimed to have received a letter from Bruges dated 9 October. This, too, is wholly unbelievable. The city is only some fourteen miles from Ostend, where Burton and Speke would have docked early in the morning of 4 October. Given Burton's need to put as much space as possible between him and the EIC authorities in London, it is hardly likely that he would have stayed any longer than was necessary to connect with a train for the next stage of the journey.

In fact, Isabel admitted to not having had another letter from Burton by 18 January 1857, confiding to her diary that she ' must meet this uncertainty with confidence, and not let my love be dependent on any action of his, because he is a strange man and not as other men. ....I must trust and pray to God; I must keep my faith in Him, and live a quiet life, employ myself only in endeavouring to make myself worthy, and surely this conduct will bring its reward.'

Meanwhile, Burton and Speke had arrived in Cairo on 4 November, where they booked into Shepheard's Hotel. 'Captain Burton has just come,' wrote its owner rather tetchily to his wife the following day, 'to bother me about his expedition to the interior of Africa.' Before leaving for Suez, Burton and Speke also took the opportunity of meeting the Count d'Escayrac de Lauture, to inspect the expedition of which he was the leader, then being fitted out by HH Abbas Pasha.'

A report on this expedition had appeared in *The Athenaeum's* 'Our Weekly Gossip' column on 30 August:

> The mystery of the Nile is about to be attacked on every side...Captain Burton is preparing a new expedition...The Pasha of Egypt has ordered a new expedition under M. le Comte d'Escaryac de Lauture, an experienced African traveller and the author of a recent book on Sudan and of other treatises on African geography...Count de Lauture has just left London, having been in communication with the Secretary of the Royal Geographical Society on the subject of the Expedition, which is intended to start for Cairo early in October....Count de Lauture and Captain Burton will advance in friendly rivalry from opposite quarters towards the sources of the Nile, and perhaps meet on a common ground to solve the most attractive of geographical problems. Could not Dr Vogel be instructed to co-operate with this investigation? The way from Lake Chad to the upper waters of the Nile is not impracticable to a traveller as skilled as Vogel...The convergence of these three expeditions on a single point would most likely clear the mystery, and if it cleared it at all, would do so in a pleasant manner....[27]

A further account had appeared in *The Times* on 27 September, written by Mr Anthony W. Twyford, its British member. '.....nothing,' he wrote, 'has been neglected that could by any possibility interest the scientific world....The expenses of this expedition will be considerable, as the Viceroy has provided it with everything that can forward its success...Thus the problem of the sources of the Nile is near its solution.....'[28]

Twyford's assessment proved to be premature. Although Burton later commented that, 'the contrast between an Egyptian expedition and an English exploration impressed us unpleasantly,' it proved a complete failure. In fact, a non-starter, the expedition being abandoned at the end of January, 1857, at the fourth cataract.[29]

This was not the only unpleasant experience. The news which had sent Burton hot-foot from England, had now arrived in Cairo – a letter, dated 24 October, from the Court of Directors, ordering his immediate return to London at the request of the Secretary of State for War, to appear as a witness at the court-martial then pending on Col A. Shirley. He was ordered to proceed 'by the steamer direct from Alexandria to Southampton,' and not through France.[30] A letter of the same date was also sent to Dr Norton Shaw, brusquely informing him that Burton's 'services will not be available for the Expedition in Africa, until his attendance in this country is dispensed with.'[31]

Burton deliberately avoided replying to this letter until he arrived at Aden. Writing from there on 14 November, he stated that the steamer by which he had been meant to return had left Alexandria on 6 November around 10 am. He received, and acknowledged, the Company's official letter from the British Consulate on the same day around noon. It was, therefore, impossible for him to carry out the order within the limits specified.[32] No mention, he went on, had been made about his returning by the next steamer, 'probably because the Court-Martial pending upon Col. A. Shirley will before that time have come to a close...I need scarcely say, that should I, on arrival at Bombay, find an order to that effect, it shall be instantly and implicitly obeyed.'

Burton knew full well, of course, that he had nothing to fear on that score. By the time his letter reached London from Aden, and before any reply could be received at Bombay, he and Speke would be at Zanzibar, well beyond the clutches of the EIC. 'As a servant of the East India Company,' he went on, 'in whose interests I have conscientiously and energetically exerted myself for the space of 14 years, I cannot but request the Court of Directors to use their powerful influence in my behalf. Private interests cannot be weighed against public duty.'[33] Obviously not satisfied that this alone would be enough, Burton wrote to Shaw on the same date, asking him to use his interest 'to the effect that, as an officer virtually in your service, I may be permitted to carry out the views of your Society. I start this evening for Bombay.'[34]

It was while at Aden, that Burton and Speke learned that the blockade of the Somali coast imposed on 4 September 1855, had been raised without compensation for the losses sustained on their previous expedition. 'This step appears, politically speaking, a mistake,' Burton wrote scathingly.... 'If it be determined for social reasons at Aden that the blockade should cease and mutton become cheap, a certain percentage could be paid upon the exports of Berberah till such time as our losses, which, including those of Government, amount to £1380, are made good.'[35]

The two men arrived in Bombay on 23 November, where affairs began to look a great deal rosier. 'Lord Elphinstone,' said Speke, 'saw at a glance of how much importance to the improvement of the commercial objects of his Presidency this exploring expedition was likely to be. The Secretary to Government, Mr Anderson, who was equally of this view, treated the matter as a great national object and, at the request of Captain Burton, drew up an official application to incorporate me in the expedition and sent it to the Government at Calcutta, with the recommendation of his Lordship; whilst I, in anticipation of the sanction of the Governor-General, Lord Canning, was permitted to accompany Captain Burton to Zanzibar...'[36] The services of Dr Steinhaeuser, who was keen to join them, were also applied for from the Medical Board.

During the week's stay, Speke saw to the completion of their outfit in scientific instruments. For observations, however, both men would have to rely on their own efforts, since neither sergeants nor native students was available at the Bombay Observatory. They were able, however, to engage two Goanese cook "boys", Valentine Rodriguez and Gaetano Andrade as servants. By the time for departure, Burton had spent

£70 in preliminary expenses out of the £250 which he was permitted to draw.

Their preparations completed, the two explorers left for Zanzibar on 2 December aboard the eighteen gun, 387 tons sloop-of-war, *Elphinstone*. They were seen on board by Grant Lumsden who, with the Governor of Bombay, had been most helpful in their behalf. Shaking their hands, he 'bade us go in and win – deserve success if we could not command it.' Later, looking back through his journal of those times, Burton found it radiating boundless enthusiasm:'Of the gladdest moments in human life, methinks, is the departure upon a distant journey into unknown lands. Shaking off with one mighty effort the fetters of Habit, the leaden weight of Routine, the cloak of many Cares, and the slavery of Home, man feels once more happy….Somewhat boisterous,' he remarked, 'but true.'

The voyage occupied eighteen and a half days. Even so, it was not long enough for all the tasks that needed doing. Burton read up on everything that had been written about Zanzibar, and both he and Speke 'rubbed up our acquaintance with the sextant and the altitude and azimuth; and we registered barometer and thermometer, so as to have a base for observations ashore.' Burton, nevertheless, managed to find the time to write a very long memorandum addressed to the RGS, which was later to land him in hot water. 'I have little to report that may be interesting to geographers; but perhaps some account of political affairs in the Red Sea may be deemed worthy to be transmitted to the Court of Directors or to the Foreign Office.[37] He wrote nothing, apparently, to Isabel.

After sixteen days at sea they glimpsed Pemba. The wind dropped with the setting of the sun, and they were forced to anchor that night under Tumbatu Island, south-west of Point Nunguwi. It was the early hours of the next morning when they caught sight of the island of Zanzibar, coming in with the pilot, the air cool and heavy with the fragrance of cloves. As the ship carefully manoeuvred its way through the razor-sharp coral reef, they could see the Arab town facing north. In the centre, commanding the anchorage was a square-curtained fort. To its right and left were the Imam's palace, the various Consulates, the large flat-roofed buildings of the leading residents, dazzling white, and behind, barely concealed, the dingy-matted hovels of the inner-town. 'Zanzibar city to become picturesque or pleasing,' wrote Burton , who would later write about it extensively, 'must be viewed, like Stanbul, from afar.'

Strangely, the guard-ship, an old 50-gun frigate belonging to HH the Sayyid was not displaying colours as was customary when a foreign ship entered port. Flags were also absent from all the masts. Dropping anchor in Front Bay, and flying the Sayyid's blood-red ensign at the main-mast, and the Union-Jack at the fore, the gunners of the *Elphinstone* fired off a 21-gun salute. Bunting immediately flew up ashore, while the *Victoria*, a gun-ship of the Muscat navy roared back a 22-gun response. Unknowingly, they had arrived on the last day of Muslim mourning for Sayyid Said, 'our native friend and ally, who had for so many years been calling for volunteers and explorers, and from whom the East African expedition had been taught to expect every manner of aid except the pecuniary.'[38]

Anxious to know how matters now stood, Burton and Speke lost no time in scrambling down the side of the ship, to be rowed ashore to the British Consulate.

CHAPTER NINETEEN

A COASTAL EXCURSION

Lt Col Atkins Hamerton, who greeted them warmly was a tall, broad-shouldered Irishman who had been appointed HEIC's Agent and HM's Consul on the island in 1841, two years after the British had signed a commercial treaty with Sayyid Said.[1] It was not long before the blunt and forceful Hamerton had raised British prestige which had sunk to a low ebb. Contemptuous of Arabs, whom he regarded as 'a miserable class,' he also began to exercise a high-handed authority over the Sultan. 'The British consul,' claimed Richard Waters, his, not disinterested, American counterpart, 'is not a favourite of the Sultan, but he is so much afraid of the injury he may do him, that he is more subservient to him than he would otherwise be.'[2] Following complaints to the British Government by Sayyid Said in 1845, the Foreign Secretary, Lord Aberdeen, ordered Hamerton's recall. The Bombay Government, however, accepted the consul's explanation that he was the victim of local intrigues for having exposed the corrupt practices of Said's officials. Always jealous of interference by the home government in matters which it regarded as being solely within its own jurisdiction, it refused to co-operate in finding a replacement. Aberdeen's Government fell, and the matter was not pursued by Palmerston.

Despite this temporary clouding of his reputation, visitors to the island over the years, English and foreign alike, came away impressed by Hamerton's genuine friendliness and hospitality. None more so than Captain Guillain in 1846,who was then exploring along the east coast of Africa. Despite Anglo-French rivalry, he described Hamerton's greeting him with the greatest cordiality and kindness. He was, said Guillain, borrowing the English idiom, 'a good fellow,' and highly sociable. He also recognised that, behind the charming and affable exterior, lay a shrewd mind with a profound knowledge of political affairs.[3]

Although only fifty-two, what Burton described as 'ennui and sickness', had turned Hamerton's hair and beard prematurely white, and his face a deathly pale. If Burton knew of the consul's history of drunkenness, he kept it to himself. It had not only earned the disapproval of the missionary, Dr Ludwig Krapf, but had been commented on by many French visitors. Hamerton was now suffering from a very serious liver complaint, the result of excessive and chronic alcohol consumption. He had over the years, literally, been drinking himself to death.

While his recent illness had left him physically weak and listless, Speke reported finding Hamerton 'vivacious in temperament, and full of amusing anecdotes which kept the whole town alive.' Not only did he put his house at the disposal of the explorers, seeing to the landing of all their kit and putting it safely in store at the Consulate, but he made them feel at home. 'His generosity,' said Speke, 'was boundless, and his influence so great, that he virtually commanded all societies here.'[4] Furthermore, Hamerton proved Dr

recent misfortunes, their health had distinctly improved. For his part, his mission accomplished, Burton felt a burden of care lifted from his shoulders.

The rainy season broke on 14 May, bringing fine cool mornings, clear warm sun, and deliciously cold nights. However, not having received a single word from the agents contracted to forward their supplies, they were now facing grave difficulties. They had to engage porters for the hammocks, feed seventy-five mouths, pay several Sultans, and incur the heavy expenses of a two hundred and sixty miles' journey back to Unyanyembe. Burton had no alternative, therefore, to supplementing what they had, with what he called, his own little patrimony. 'One thousand pounds,' he wrote, 'does not go far when it has to be divided amongst a couple of hundred greedy savages in two and a half years.'[6]

For some days past there had been rumours of a large caravan of Wanyamwezi porters, commanded by an Arab merchant, approaching Kawele. Suddenly on 22 May, a crackle of muskets announced the arrival of strangers. By noon the Tembe was surrounded by boxes, bales, slaves, and parcels of papers and letters from Europe.

This good luck averted a looming crisis. Nevertheless, while these supplies were adequate for taking them to Unyanyembe, they were insufficient for exploring the southern end of lake Tanganyika, far less for returning to Zanzibar via the Nyassa and Kilwa lakes as Burton had hoped to do. It is noticeable that he says nothing about returning either then, or at a later stage, to explore the Northern lake.

Speke gave a different version of events in his book. He claimed that the Sheikh on an earlier occasion had volunteered, if they wished to carry out a survey of the lake, to return to Kazeh, and fetch some more African money, to meet the necessary expenses, 'I wished to finish off the navigation of the lake,' said Speke; 'but Captain Burton declared he would not, as he had had enough of canoe travelling, and thought our being short of cloth, and out of leave, would be sufficient excuse for him.'[7] Some years later, Speke was more graphic and overtly malicious in his account of his companion's response, alleging that:'Burton who had had enough of Africa said, "I will be damned if I go any more on the Lake, I always like leaving the work half done that I might have something left to return to." I then at once proposed that we should return to Kazeh and visit the Nyanza, to which he objected saying that it had better be left for another time, when I said no we have not completed our work on this Lake and geographers will expect it from us.......'[8]

On 18 June they arrived at Yombo, where they met some of their goods coming up from the coast sent by the French Consul, and a second packet of letters. One from Burton's sister, Maria, contained news of the death of their father, who had passed away on 6 September 1857, after a six weeks' illness. 'Such tidings,' he wrote, 'are severely felt by the wanderer, who, living long behind the world, is unable to mark its gradual changes...and who expects again to meet each old familiar face ready to smile upon his return, as it was to weep at his departure.'[9] Kazeh was reached towards the end of June, where they were warmly greeted by the hospitable Snay bin Amir, who had made special preparations to receive his guests. Burton now had the satisfaction of finding that his last order on Zanzibar for four hundred dollars worth of cloth and beads had arrived.

All succumbed to fever during the first week following their return. Burton once more suffered from swelling and numbness of the extremities, while Speke was afflicted with deafness and poor vision, which prevented his observing correctly. On 24 June, Burton forwarded his field book to the RGS, together with a map of the large northern lake drawn up by Speke from information mostly supplied by their Arab inform- ants, principally Snay bin Amir. He also enclosed a long and important letter. It now only remained, Burton said, to ascertain whether the Arabs had not exaggerated the lake's dimensions. He later claimed to have despatched Speke on his short expedition to Nyanza. This is untrue. In this letter, Burton wrote, 'Captain Speke has *volunteered* [my italics] when he and the rest of the main party are recovered from their present state of universal sickness to visit the Ukerewe Lake of which the Arabs give grand accounts. It lies nearly due north of Unyanyembe at a distance of from 12 to 15 marches. Thus we shall be able to bring home authentic details of the four great waters which drain Eastern and Central Africa: the Nyassa, the Chaga, the Ujiji Lake and the Ukerewe.'[10]

Burton later charged Speke with misrepresenting the state of his health in the second of his articles in *Blackwood's*, where he wrote, 'My companion was, most unfortunately, quite done up, but very graciously consented to wait with the Arabs to recruit his health.'[11] Burton denied this, claiming that he had other and more important work to do, going on to quote what Speke had written to the RGS on 2 July from Kazeh, 'To diminish the disappointment caused by the short-coming of our cloth, in not seeing the whole of the Sea of Ujiji, I have proposed to take a flying trip to the unknown lake, while Captain Burton prepares for our return homewards.'[12] This in no way alters the fact that Burton in his current state of health, could not possibly have gone on this trip. As Speke pointed out in his letter, 'this business must be done speedily else the ponds and puddles drying up will render our progress seawards difficult.' It will be remembered that Burton, following his severe bout of malaria at Sorora in the previous January, admitted that it prevented his walking any distance for nearly a year. This was further substantiated in his present letter of 24 June 1858, where he informed Shaw of being 'unable to walk or ride except in a hammock carried by Unyamwezi porters.'

Burton expressed his regret, that the Expedition had not been better financed. 'With £5000 we might, I believe, without difficulty, have spanned Africa from East to West.' This led him to bring up again the vexed question of paying the Expedition's personnel. He recalled Speke's letter of 20 November 1857, in which he had urged the necessity of rewarding their guide and attendants. Unfortunately, the promises made by the late Lt Col Hamerton could not be honoured:

> These are sums which we could not afford, nor can we on our return pay the high salaries promised in our presence to these men. By Said bin Salim, the guide, $1000 would be expected, by each Beloch, 13 in number, $100, and by each slave, in all, about $15.60. We have already expended at least £500 out of our own private resources. Expecting that a six months' march would take us to the Lake of Ujiji and back, ignoring also the Ukerewe Lake, we thought to come within the limits of the major sum allotted to us. But our exploration, delayed by sickness, accidents & the non-arrival of supplies, cannot be concluded under 18 months. I venture to urge this subject most forcibly upon the Expeditionary Committee of the Royal Geographical Society as, unless Lt. Col. Hamerton's promises be fulfilled by his successor, we shall be placed in a most disagreeable position at Zanzibar.

These were prescient words as far as he, himself, was concerned. Owing to the time taken for Speke's November 1857 letter to reach England, it was not until a week after Burton's latest letter was written, that the RGS acted on the earlier request. On 30 June 1858, the President, Sir Roderick Murchison, wrote to the Foreign Secretary:

> So long as Col. Hamerton lived, there could be no doubt of his continuing to give energetic support to these explorers; but since his death, fears have been entertained that his successor might not equally aid them, particularly in furnishing them with money and rewarding their guides. I hope therefore that your Lordship may deem it right to instruct the consular authorities at Zanzibar to support both by money and influence an expedition in which your Predecessor in office took the liveliest interest, and which has succeeded, almost beyond out hopes, in penetrating so far into the interior of Africa.[13]

In concluding his letter, Burton disclosed that he had received, what he described as, 'an official expression of disapprobation from the Rt Hon the Governor in Council, Bombay, "for want of discretion and due respect for the authorities to whom I am subordinate," in consequence of some remarks addressed to you upon the subject of political matters in the Red Sea.' As he further reiterated, the document had been forwarded, not for publication, but for the information of the Foreign Office or the Court of Directors of the East India Company. Burton stated that he had expressed his regret for having offended the Government to which he was much indebted, adding that 'at the same time I am at a loss to understand how I have offended.'[14] Burton, undoubtedly, received the letter of censure with the second packet of letters at Yombo on 18 June, informing the RGS of the fact a week later while at Kazeh. In his journal, printed in *The Life,* however, he manufactured a rather different story.

First, he deliberately moved the time forward to 6 December, when they had reached their old ground in the Ugogi Dhun. Here, they met another Caravan, 'which presently drew forth a packet of letters and papers.' This post, he said, 'brought me rather an amusing official wigging.' He dated this 1 July 1857. However, in Appendix F of *The Life,* where it is reprinted, it is dated 23 July. Because of the slowness of the postal service in Africa, he claimed to have received with the same post, a newspaper with an account of the massacre of nearly all the Christians at Jeddah, on the Red Sea. This, he said, took place on 30 June 1858, exactly eleven months after he had warned the Government. The truth is, that the letter from the Bombay Government arrived at Yombo twelve days *before* the massacre took place, making it impossible for Burton to have known about the event until much later.

Preparations were now put in hand for Speke to visit the Northern Lake. He had discovered during their first stop at Kazeh, that Snay had travelled up the lake's western flank to Kibuga, the capital of the kingdom of Uganda. Furthermore, he employed men who had lived and traded in Usoga. Snay advised anyone wishing to see the northern boundary of the lake to go to Kibuga armed with suitable presents, and make friends with the reigning monarch. Then, with his assistance either buy or construct boats on the shore of the lake, which was about five marches east of his capital.

Other Arab and Waswahili merchants corroborated Snay's statement, including a Hindu merchant called Musa. Speke said he singled out this man for mention, not only because of the straightforward way he had of telling his story, but also because they could converse with one another directly, thus avoiding any chance of errors. Although his informant had recently visited Kibuga and had lived with the reigning monarch, Sultan Mtesa, he had only a hazy idea of the physical features of the country beyond the point which he had reached. Nevertheless, he was able to produce a negro slave who had been to Usoga and had seen, what he called, the river Kivira. He described it as being much broader, deeper, and with a more powerful current than either the Katonga or Kitangule rivers. After issuing from the lake, it flowed in a north-westerly direction through stony hilly country. Speke later became convinced that this river was the Nile itself, although doubting it at the time until he made Snay change his original statement about the direction of its flow.

On 2 July, Speke informed Shaw that he was, 'off to the Ukerewe Lake to see if the accounts of it are true; by what we have heard I should expect to see something like a Lake, a piece of water almost boundless, for in such a strain report goes. Altho' the distance to it from this is far short of Ujiji, strange to say few Arabs have ever visited it, & of those at present here, none.' Burton, having been practically bed-ridden for the last eleven months and forced to travel most of the time in a hammock, was staying behind to get things ready for the return journey.

As for himself, blindness remained his greatest problem, sometimes affecting one eye then the other, sometimes both. It not only stopped his reading and writing but, more importantly for his peace of mind, he had been unable to take Lunars and fix the Longitude. Clearly frustrated, he blamed his more recent failure 'simply from want of an assistant to take the time, for Burton has always been ill; he won't sit out in the dew

& has a decided objection to the Sun, moreover when there happens to be a good opportunity for taking a Lunar his eyes become bad & so I always get disappointed.'

To make matters worse, he continued gloomily, it was 'a shocking country for sport.' All he had managed to shoot were a few antelopes and guinea-fowl, besides hippopotamus near the coast. Furthermore, there was 'literally nothing to write about in this uninteresting country, nothing could surpass these tracks, jungles, plains etc for dull sameness, the people are the same everywhere, in fact the whole country is one vast senseless mass of sameness.'[15]

Although eager to put Kazeh far behind him, it was not until a week later that Speke was able to leave with a small, strongly armed party, carrying enough kit for six weeks. After a sixteen days' trek, he caught his first glimpse of the northern lake on 3 August. Looking down at its pale blue waters sparkling in the early morning sun, 'I no longer felt any doubt,' he wrote, 'that the lake at my feet gave birth to that interesting river, the source of which has been the subject of so much speculation, and the object of so many explorers. The Arabs' tale was proved to the letter. This is a far more extensive lake than the Tanganyika; "so broad you could not see across it, and so long that nobody knew its length."' He now had the pleasure 'of perceiving that a map he had constructed on Arab testimony, and sent home to the Royal Geographical Society before leaving Unyanyembe, was so substantially correct that in its general outlines, I had nothing whatever to alter.'[16]

On 25 August, just as Burton was preparing to organise a little expedition to K'hokoro and the southern provinces, Speke reappeared. They had scarcely breakfasted, according to Burton, when his companion 'announced to me the startling fact that "he had discovered the sources of the White Nile."'

In his *Blackwood's* article, Speke said nothing about Burton's reaction to his claim, merely writing: 'Captain Burton greeted me on arrival at the old house, where I had the satisfaction of finding him greatly restored to health, and having everything about him in a high state of preservation for the journey homewards.'[17] He was more explicit later in his book, stating that,

> Captain Burton greeted me on arrival at the old house, and said he had been very anxious for some time past about our safety, as numerous reports had been set afloat with regard to the civil wars we had to circumvent, which had impressed the Arabs as well as himself with alarming fears. I laughed over the matter, but expressed my regret that he did not accompany me, as I felt quite certain in my mind I had discovered the source of the Nile. This he naturally objected to, even after hearing all my reasons for saying so, and therefore the subject was dropped. Nevertheless, the Captain accepted all my geography leading from Kaze to the Nile, and wrote it down in his book – contracting only my distances, which he thought exaggerated, and of course taking care to sever my lake from the Nile by his Mountains of the Moon.[18]

Speke made no reference to any tension in their relationship resulting from his announcement, which must have come as a bombshell to Burton. According to him, 'Jack changed his manners to me from this date. His difference of opinion was allowed to alter companionship. After a few days, it became evident to me that not a word could be uttered upon the subject of the lake, the Nile, and his *trouvaille* generally without offence. By a tacit agreement it was, therefore, avoided....'[19]

It was eventually settled in a meeting of all the Arabs, that the Caravan would return to the coast by the normal route. The explorers' two years' leave of absence was drawing to a close. Even if they had had sufficient outfit, they were not prepared to risk the consequences of taking an extra twelve months. However, they did not give up hopes, according to Burton, of making their return useful to geography by tracing the course of the Rufiji River, and of visiting the coast between the Usagara Mountains and Kilwa, an unknown line not likely to attract future travellers.

The caravan set off for the coast on 26 September 1858, Burton still needing to be carried in a hammock. Just over a week later, they reached Hanga. Here, Speke was taken dangerously ill with kichyomachyoma, more popularly known as 'little irons.' Shortly after arriving, in addition to deafness, he began to suffer from an inflamed eye and a swollen face. Worst of all was a mysterious pain, which moved around his body. He woke around dawn a week later, having suffered a horrible nightmare, in which a pack of tigers, leopards and other animals, harnessed with iron hooks, were dragging him along the ground with the speed of a whirlwind. The next spasm was less severe, but his mind began to wander. A third attack exhibited all the symptoms of hydrophobia, his limbs racked with cramps, his features drawn, and his eyes glazed. He began to bark with a peculiar chopping motion of the mouth and tongue, his lips protruding, the effect of difficulty in breathing. It so altered his appearance that he became unrecognizable, terrifying onlookers. As soon as he was able to speak, he called for pen and paper, and scribbled an incoherent letter of farewell to his family. This marked the crisis. For some weeks afterwards, he had to sleep in a half sitting-up position, propped up with pillows. The pains continued, but gradually lessened. When they ceased entirely, he mumured weakly to Burton, "Dick, the knives are sheathed."[20]

Burton described these illnesses as 'the effects of fever, and a mysterious manifestation of miasma in certain latitudes.' The dramatic symptomatology, however, appears to fit with the clinical syndrome of trichinosis. The early explorers lived largely on the flesh of wild animals, many of whom in that part of the world carry larvae of a small roundworm, *Trichinella spiralis*. When an infected piece of meat is eaten, the embryos contained in it are set free, developing into full-grown trichinellae, and from each pair of these 1000 or more new embryos can arise in a few weeks. They bore their way into the wall of the bowel, and from there wander all over the body, finally lodging themselves between the fibres of the voluntary muscles.[21]

During his delirium, all of Speke's long-pent-up grievances against Burton spilled out like a lava flow: the unauthorised use of his diary for which he had received no payment; the sending of his collection to the Calcutta Museum of Natural History; and Burton's imagined rebuke during the thick of the fight at Berbera. There were many more besides, things which Burton had unconsciously done, to which Speke took exception. The latest, was his not immediately accepting that Speke had discovered the sources of the Nile. Burton claimed that from his recovery he noticed 'that Speke's alacrity had vanished, that he was never contented by my arrangements, that he left all the management to me, and then complained that he had never been consulted. He quarrelled with their followers, and got himself insulted, and that having been unaccustomed to sickness, he neither could endure it himself, nor feel for it in others. He took pleasure in saying unkind, unpleasant things, and said he could not take an interest in any exploration if he did not command it.'[22]

Burton had a hammock rigged up for Speke. Luckily, an unloaded Caravan was passing down to the coast, and they managed to hire thirteen porters who agreed to carry them to Rubuga. Although Speke's sufferings continued, by the time they reached K'kok'ho in Ugogi, he was able to sleep, and his appetite had returned. He was now strong enough to be able to carry a heavy rifle, and go out hunting. Here, Burton, still far from well, shakily penned a letter to the Bombay Government, stating that unavoidable delays had made it impossible for them to return with the period prescribed, and asking for an extension of leave for 6 months from 2nd Dec 1858 to the 2nd July 1859.[23] On Christmas Day, 1858, they worked their way along the Kikoboga River, which they had to ford four times. They celebrated Christmas on chicken instead of roast beef, and a concoction of ground nuts sweetened with cane sugar took the place of plum pudding.

A week earlier, Norton Shaw had replied to a worried Mrs Speke, asking for information about her son's whereabouts. Shaw stated that nothing official or private had been received from her son or Captain Burton for a long time. Nevertheless, he pointed out that in that month's issue of the *Church Missionary*

Intelligencer, mention was made of their having arrived at the Great Lake, and that they were returning home. He also stated, that Lord Malmesbury had written to say that instructions were to be sent to the new Agent at Zanzibar, to afford them every possible assistance, and that 'Burton, as well as your son, is aware that the Mission can draw £250 now in case of need.'[24]

On 2 February 1859, Burton and Speke doffed their caps and gave three cheers as they caught their first glimpse of the Indian Ocean. The following day they passed through the poles decorated with skulls at the entrance to the maritime village of Konduchi. After protracted celebrations, a boat transferred most of their weeping followers to their homes. Despite their exploration having taken far longer than anticipated, and having arrived at the coast destitute, according to Burton,[25] he sent a note from Konduchi to the Consul at Zanzibar, requesting a coasting vessel in order to explore the Delta and the unknown course of the Rufiji River. On 9 February, the battela and stores required for this trip arrived, and the next day they set out for Kilwa, 'the Quiloa of De Gama, of Camoens, and of the Portuguese annalists.'

The expedition was a failure. Nearly all the boat crew died from cholera. They were unable to visit the course of the great Rufiji River, which was in flood. No man would take service on the infected vessel and, according to Burton, 'The Hindu Banyans who directed the copal trade of the river regions aroused against them the chiefs of the interior.'[26] This was a charge later rebutted by the Consul, C.P. Rigby, as having not the slightest foundation in fact. He stated that a young German explorer, Dr Albrecht Roscher, had taken passage with Burton and, after one day, left on foot accompanied by only one African boy, without saying where he was going. It later emerged that Dr Roscher travelled on foot to the Rufiji River, exploring its course for a considerable distance. On returning to Zanzibar, he spoke highly of the great hospitality and kindness he everywhere received from the Banyan settlers.[27] Burton, according to Rigby's information, went to the mouth of the Rufiji, and 'did not land there, or make any endeavour to do so, but sent for some of the principal Banians to come on board, and having as was his custom made notes from what they told him, sailed away.'[28] Whatever the truth of the matter, Burton and Speke sailed back from Kilwa, landing at Zanzibar on 4 March.

Utterly depressed, not even caring to talk, Burton spent much of the time at the Consulate reading French novels. Most, if not all, of his depression must have been rooted in the conviction, in spite of his later denial, that Speke was correct in claiming to have found the source of the Nile, thus robbing him of what he had prized most. Early that month, in a despatch to the Bombay Government reporting the explorers' safe arrival on the island, Rigby was writing that, 'Captain Speke is confidently of opinion that the northern end of this great lake (Nyanza) will prove to be the source of the White Nile.'[29]

Exactly what Burton's relations with the new Consul, C.P. Rigby were at the time, can only be implied from later remarks by both men. Rigby had been appointed Agent for the East India Company, with the local rank of Lieutenant-Colonel, on 10 March 1858, and HM's Consul there on 9 December.[30] He did not arrive at Zanzibar however, until 27 July 1858, having sustained severe injuries in an accident at Bombay, which confined him to bed for two months. Whatever else might have soured the relationship between the two men, Rigby, in the prevailing political climate, was deeply incensed by Burton's socialising with the French Consul, Ladislas Cochet, who had been so helpful to the two explorers following Hamerton's death.'Contrast Rigby's scruples as a host,' wrote his daughter in her memoir, 'with Burton's absence of proper feeling as a guest, when he foregathered on friendly terms with a man not on visiting terms with the said, viz. M. Cochet.'[31]

In the highly volatile period following Hamerton's death, Majid, deprived of the support of his oldest and closest ally, faced a real threat to his position from rival factions, particularly the al Harthi. While awaiting the arrival of Hamerton's successor, Majid turned to Ladislas Cochet of France, for support. The young Frenchman, who had only taken up his consular duties in February 1856, gave a sympathetic hearing to Majid, although powerless to provide practical assistance. With Rigby's arrival, Majid lost no time in trying to rebuild the British alliance. At the same time, he saw a way of bolstering his position, by highlighting attempts by French plantation owners from Reunion to obtain workers for their island. His stratagem was successful, convincing Rigby that French politics threatened Zanzibar's independence, as well as the British-led anti-slavery crusade.

The pace of events accelerated by February, 1859, when Majid's eldest brother, Thuwayni, despatched a large expedition from Muscat to invade the island. Forewarned, the British intercepted Thuwayni's ships, which turned back when faced with a threat of force.[32]

Whatever the main reason for Rigby's antipathy towards Burton, he and Speke, on the other hand, seem to have hit it off from the very start. Perhaps a week or so after the explorers' arrival at the Consulate, Rigby was writing to one of his correspondents, praising his new-found friend to the skies, 'Speke is a right, jolly, resolute fellow, Burton is not fit to hold a candle to him, and has done nothing in comparison with what Speke has, but Speke is a modest, unassuming man, not very ready with his pen, Burton will blow his trumpet and get the credit of the discoveries. Speke works, Burton lies on his back all day and picks other people's brains.'[33]

While welcoming Sayyid Majid's invitation to remain until the expected hostilities were over, Burton no longer felt at ease in the Consulate. 'I felt myself too conversant with local politics and too well aware of what was going on to be a pleasant companion to its new tenant.' Despite the resounding success of their mission, he now claimed to be, 'unwilling to leave the field of my labours while so much remained to be done.' With the gradual return of his health, he was prepared to wait at Zanzibar, 'till the answer to an application for leave of absence, and a request for additional funds could be received from the Government of Bombay and the Royal Geographical Society.'[34] It is a highly unlikely version of events, unsubstantiated by any documentary evidence. However, 'the evident anxiety of my host to disembarrass himself of his guest, and the nervous impatience of my companion – who could not endure the thought of losing an hour – compelled me, sorely, against my wish, to abandon my intentions.'[35]

As for the difficulties envisaged in rewarding members of the expedition, Burton seems to have hit on an effective way of dealing with them. When Said bin Salim, the Ras Kafilah, called twice or more at the Consulate, Burton simply refused to see him. He later claimed that, at the time, Rigby agreed with him that the Arab had been more than amply rewarded by the sum advanced to him by Lt Col Hamerton. As for the Jemadar and the Beloch who attended Burton to the doorway of the prince's durbar, 'I would not introduce them to their master or to the Consul, as such an introduction would have argued myself satisfied with their conduct; nor would I recommend them for promotion or reward.' However, writing later to the Expeditionary Committee of the RGS from Aden, Burton stated without comment that Sayyid Said had generously rewarded their Beloch escort, 'the money placed at out disposal rendering such an expense unavoidable.'[36] Ladha Dama made a half-hearted claim on behalf of the sons of Ramji, but withdrew it when Burton, allegedly, presented him with the facts of the case. 'As regards the propriety of these severe but equitable measures,' Burton wrote, 'my companion was, I believe, at the time of the same opinion as myself.'

As soon as the alarm over the threatened invasion had died down, Burton and Speke left Zanzibar on 22 March 1859, aboard a clipper-built barque, the *Dragon* of Salem, bound for Aden with the south-west monsoon. Just over a fortnight into the voyage, unknown to Burton, Speke wrote a letter to Rigby expressing his grave concern at what he regarded as the great wrong done to Ramji. 'I think now that you are fully aware of the whole matter you are in duty bound to see justice done to this unfortunate man.'[37] In suggesting such a course of action, Speke, unwittingly, was setting in motion a train of events that would ultimately have extremely serious consequences for Burton, besides resulting in the irreparable breakdown of their already strained relationship.

After a voyage of twenty-five days, the ship arrived off Aden on 16 April. The explorers spent the next few days as guests of Dr Steinhaeuser, 'who,' according to Burton, 'repeatedly informed me that all was not right.'[38] On Monday, 19 April, he wrote a letter to Norton Shaw. Its importance cannot be overestimated, nor the difficulty Burton must have found in writing it, since it provides clear, unambiguous proof, despite his later denials, that he did, indeed, believe Speke's claims were well-founded.

> A fresh attack of fever & general debility [he wrote] will delay me for a short time in the return to England, where both Captain Speke and I are about to proceed on medical certificate given by the Civil Surgeon of Aden. Captain Speke, however, will lay before you his maps & observations & two papers, one a diary of his passage on the Tanganyika lake between Ujiji & Kasengi, and the other his exploration of the Nyanza Ukerewe or Northern Lake. To this I would respectfully direct the serious attention of the Committee as there are good reasons for believing it to be the Source or the Principal feeder of the White Nile.

That same day, HMS *Furious*, carrying Lord Elgin and his private secretary, Laurence Oliphant, on their return journey from a diplomatic mission to China, dropped anchor in Back Bay. The vessel was due to leave immediately after coaling, and both explorers were offered a passage up the Red Sea to Suez. Speke accepted, Burton declined, citing continuing illness. One senses, however, that now, having openly handed the palm to Speke, the real reason lay in his reluctance to return to London.

CHAPTER TWENTY-TWO

AT DAGGERS DRAWN

Burton was to publish varying accounts about what Speke is supposed to have done after they parted company at Aden. The earliest occurred in his *Lake Regions*. Here, Burton straightforwardly and angrily wrote, 'that, after preceding me from England, with the spontaneous offer on his part of not appearing before the Society that originated the expedition until my return, he lost no time in taking measures to secure for himself the right of working the field which I had opened.'[1]

In *The Nile Basin*, published shortly after Speke's death in 1864, Burton provided additional, more specific, and slightly altered detail. He now wrote that his erstwhile companion, the day after his return to England (May 9 1859)[2] 'was induced to call at the rooms of the RGS, and to set on foot a new exploration. Having understood that he was to await my arrival in London before appearing in public, I was too late with my own project. This was to enter Eastern Africa via the Somali country, or by landing at the Arab town Mombas, whence the southeastern watershed of the Nilotic Basin might be easily determined. My offer was not preferred by the Council of the RGS.'[3] This is a thoroughly misleading version of events.

Burton made further changes in the chapter he devoted to Speke in his *Zanzibar*, which appeared eight years later. Here, he stated that Speke 'voluntarily promised, when reaching England, to visit his family in the country, and to await my arrival, that we might appear together before the RGS. But on board the *Furious* he was exposed to the worst influences, and he was persuaded to act in a manner which his own moral sense must have afterwards strongly condemned, if indeed it ever pardoned.'[4]

It was not until 1891, following critical comments by James Grant on Burton's obituary in *The Times*,[5] that Isabel identified Laurence Oliphant as having been the person responsible for Speke's eventual under-hand behaviour. She alleged that Oliphant, who had died three years earlier, and was therefore unable to speak in his defence, 'got hold of and poisoned Speke's mind against Richard. He said that Burton was a jealous man, and being Chief of the expedition, he would take all the glory of Nyanza; that if he were in Speke's place he would go up to the Royal Geographical Society at once, and get the command of a second expedition; that he would back him, and get others to. Speke resisted at first, but his vanity prevailed, and carried him along until one thing after another was piled up against the unconscious absentee.'[6]

There are no good reasons for believing this to be the case. We already know that Speke's burning resentment against Burton dated from their period together in Somalia. It is also clear from what he later wrote about the state of his mind when forced to leave Lake Nyanza, that he did not need the prompting of an Iago-like figure to act as he did. 'My reluctance to return may be easier imagined than described. I felt as much tantalised as the unhappy Tantalus must have been when unsuccessful in his bobbings for cherries in the cherry-orchard, and as much grieved as any mother would be at losing her first-born, and *resolved and planned forthwith to do everything that lay in my power to visit the lake again.*'[7]

His brief account of how he achieved this, first appeared in *Blackwood's Magazine* in May, 1860. He added a little more detail in his *Journal of the Discovery of the Source of the Nile*, published three years later:

> My third expedition to Africa [he wrote], which was avowedly for the purpose of establishing the truth of my assertion that the Victoria N'yanza which I discovered on the 30th July, 1858, would eventually prove to be the source of the Nile, may be said to have commenced on the 9th May, 1859, the first day after my return to England, when at the invitation of Sir Roderick Murchison, I called at his house to show him my map for the information of the Royal Geographical Society. Sir Roderick, I need only say, at once accepted my views; and knowing my ardent desire to prove to the world by actual inspection of the exit, that the Victoria N'yanza was the source of the Nile, seized the enlightened view that such a discovery should not be lost to the glory of England and the Society of which he was President; and said to me, "Speke, we must send you there again." I was then officially directed, much against my own inclination, to lecture at the Royal Geographical Society on the geography of Africa which I had, as the sole surveyor of the Second Expedition laid down on our maps.[8]

So how does his explanation square with the facts? According to Oliphant's most recent biographer, Speke, together with the members of Lord Elgin's mission landed 'to a heroes' welcome' at Plymouth on Saturday, 7 May. There is not the slightest evidence for this. On the contrary, their arrival was not reported in either of the two local papers or *The Times*.[9] If Speke travelled to his home at Jordans, as Burton later suggested was his intention, it must have been the briefest of visits. By the following day he was in London, booked into Hatchett's Hotel, Piccadilly. That same morning, he received a note from Norton Shaw, welcoming him back to London, and inviting him to the usual monthly meeting of the RGS at Whitehall Place the following day.

Speke replied that he would answer him verbally if they could get together prior to any such meeting, to talk over old times and sundry matters. 'My particular business in Africa was Geography,' he went on, 'as I may have told you before. I believe most firmly that the Nyanza is *one source* [my italics] of the Nile, if not the principal one.'[10] This is particularly interesting, as being the only occasion when Speke ever admitted the possibility of there being other sources.

At the time, Clements (later Sir Clements) Markham, a future President of the RGS, was a young married man working for the India Office, and living in Eccleston Square just off Belgrave Road. He later claimed to have been actively involved in the affair, 'When Speke came home from Burton's expedition before his chief,' he wrote, 'Dr. Norton Shaw brought him straight to my house, as he wanted advice. We talked the whole matter over for some time, and the next day I went with him to Sir Roderick...(who) at once took him up, but I rather misdoubted his want of loyalty to Burton.'[11]

It appears on this evidence, that Speke contrived to have himself 'invited' to Murchison's house in nearby Belgrave Square. This was obviously done not only with the intention of convincing Murchison that the northern lake was the probable source of the Nile – Burton at the time, as we have seen, supported this view – but in order to gain the President's personal backing for Speke's leading another expedition to the Lake Regions. In this, he was brilliantly successful, as events proved.

The Monday evening's lecture, 'Observations on the Geography of Central Africa' was given by James M'Queen. Speke would have preferred Cooley, some of whose papers showing 'great foresight and ability' had impressed him. Murchison, who was in the chair, then introduced Speke to the meeting, pointing out that he had only returned in the last two days from the very area covered by M'Queen's paper and was, therefore, able to supply some useful information.

After outlining the recent course of events there, Speke proceeded to give his reasons for believing the Nyanza Lake to be the great reservoir of the Nile, and for the river's regular swelling at Cairo on 18 June. This was due, in his opinion, to immense volumes of water pouring down in a north-easterly direction from the mountains at the northern end of Lake Tanganyika, supplemented by the rivers draining the western slopes of Mount Kenia. 'It would be highly erroneous,' he said, 'to suppose that the Nile would have any great fluctuations from any other source than periodical rains. Were the Nile supplied by snow, as some theorists think, its perennial volume would ever be the same.'

M'Queen, later one of Burton's closest and most effective allies, was having none of it. The question of the sources of the Nile, he said, had cost him a great deal of trouble and research. He was confident, therefore, that there was no material error either in longitude or latitude in the position he had ascribed to them, namely, a little to the eastwards of the meridian of 35°, and a little northward of the equator. He claimed that his paper and its associated map, would clearly show, not only that the Bahr-el-Abiad had no connection with Kiliamanjaro, but that it had no connection whatever with any lake or river to the south of the equator. As for the swelling of the river Nile, this 'proceeded from the tropical rains of the northern torrid zone, as had been stated emphatically to Julius Caesar by the Egyptian priest, Amorcis, 2000 years ago.'

Stepping into the fray with commendable diplomacy, Colonel Sykes suggested that the difficulties raised by M'Queen were quite reconcilable with the facts stated by Speke, 'for every great river had more than one source.' The only question needing to be answered was, which of those branches should be considered the chief source of the river.[12]

Burton arrived at Southampton aboard the P&O liner *Pera*, on the afternoon of Friday, 20 May.[13] He later complained bitterly that when he eventually reached London he 'found that everything had been done for, or rather against me. My companion stood forth in his true colours, an angry rival.'[14] A rival Speke certainly was, but not, at least then, an angry one. Writing to Shaw two days before Burton's arrival, about the possibility of his preparing a geographical paper for the 13th Proceedings, Speke said he would be happy to write one. 'At the same time,' he observed, 'I think it would be unfair to Captain Burton, Commandant of the Expedition, if I touched on anything not entirely relating to that branch. Especially as I know that Burton has been very industrious in observing and obtaining great masses of matter appertaining to the manners, customs & productive resources of the country traversed by the Expedition.'[15]

During that year's period of Lent, Isabel is said to have gone into a Retreat in the Convent at Norwich, where she 'strove to banish worldly thoughts,' committing her religious reflections to *Lamed*, one of her books of private devotion.[16] However, there was no Convent at Norwich at this date. It was not until October 1864, in fact, that six sisters of Notre Dame came to Norwich at the request of the Rev Canon Dalton, Rector of St John's – the first nuns to be seen since the Reformation.[17] Isabel is then said to have come out on Easter Day, and after visiting some friends for a few weeks, returned to London. 'Here she was greeted with the news that Speke had come home alone. The air was full of Speke, and the rumour reached her ears that Burton was staying on in Zanzibar in the hope of being allowed to return to Africa.' She was seized with a sense of despair. Just as she was thinking of returning to the Convent and becoming a Sister of Charity, she received six paltry lines of verse from Burton, couched in Catholic imagery. 'I knew then,' she said, 'it was all right.'

On 22 May, according to Isabel, she called at the address of a friend who happened to be out. Informed that she would be in for tea, she decided to wait for her return. Some five minutes later the door-bell rang, and she could hear another visitor being ushered in. The door was suddenly opened, and turning round expecting to see her friend, she saw Burton instead. 'For an instant we both stood dazed, and I cannot attempt to describe the joy that followed. He had landed the day before, and came to London, and now he had come to call on this friend to know where I was living, where to find me.'[18] This is pretty hard to swallow. Not only was Isabel listed in Burton's personal address book, by her own account she had also been deluging him with fortnightly journals, together with scraps from newspapers and accounts of books, addressed from Oxford Square for the last two years or more.

If any of the above scenario is not sheer fantasy, the meeting may well have been secretly arranged through an intermediary, to avoid Burton's having to call at Oxford Square, where with Mrs Arundell, at least, he was almost *persona non grata*. The couple then left the house, the friend apparently forgotten. Burton hailed a cab, and they went for a long drive, he with his arm around her waist, and she leaning her head on his shoulder. The first thing they did, according to Isabel, was to draw each other's pictures from their pockets, something not mentioned before, 'which, as we had not expected to meet, showed how carefully they had been kept.' It was a Burton 'sadly altered,' however, from when they had last met. His 'youth, health, spirits, and beauty were all gone for the time.' Nevertheless, 'Never did I feel the strength of my love as then.'

The following day, Burton and Speke attended the Anniversary Meeting of the RGS, the Council room densely packed with members of the Council and their friends, a great number of scientific men, and several ladies. In a short ceremony, the Founder's Gold Medal was awarded to Burton for having 'explored a vast region of Eastern and Central Africa never before traversed by any geographer; and for the discovery of the great internal lake of Tanganyika.'[19]

Murchison then went on to recount briefly, Burton's exploits up to, and including, the most recent with Speke. It soon became apparent, however, where his main interest lay. 'A marked feature of the expedition,' he said, 'is the journey of Captain Speke from Unyanyembe to the vast inland fresh-water lake called Nyanza.' After presenting Burton with the medal, rejoicing 'that the Council of this Society had it in their power to recompense your highly distinguished service,' Murchison spoke of taking 'this opportunity of expressing to you my hearty approbation of the very important part which your colleague Captain Speke has played in the course of the African expedition headed by yourself.' Later, in his Address to the Society, when he would further remark of Burton's meritorious services, he would 'dwell upon the subject of the vast interior lake of Nyanza, made by your associate when you were prostrated by illness – a discovery which in itself is worthy of the highest honour this Society can bestow.'

Burton's reply matched the occasion. He thanked Murchison for this honour, for his kind and flattering comments, and the Society for its generous support over the years. He then turned to his companion: 'To Captain Speke,' he said, 'are due those geographical results to which you have alluded in such flattering terms. Whilst I undertook the history and the ethnography, the languages and the peculiarities of the people, to Captain Speke fell the arduous task of delineating an exact topography, and of laying down our positions by astronomical observations – a labour to which at times even the undaunted Livingstone found himself unequal.' Burton concluded by expressing the desire that 'we may have a further opportunity of prosecuting our labours in this good cause.'[20]

True to his promise, Murchison devoted a large part of his Address to the Nile question, concentrating upon Speke's discovery of the northern lake. He spoke of his 'thriving upon hard field work,' leaving his 'invalid companion' to reach the great lake Nyanaza.[21] He hoped 'that when reinvigorated by a year's rest, the undaunted Speke may receive every encouragement to proceed from Zanzibar to his old station, and then carry out to demonstration the view which he now maintains, that the Lake Nyanza is the main source of the Nile.' Burton's feelings while the praises of Speke were being sung, and the Tanganyika discovery relegated to almost a geographical footnote, can only be imagined.

That evening, both men attended the Anniversary Dinner held at the Freemasons' Hall, Great Queen Street. Among, what *The Times* called, 'a glittering assembly of noblemen and gentlemen' were the Duke of Wellington, the Marquess of Salisbury, W.E. Gladstone, Viscount Strangford, the Minister of Denmark, and the Society's President elect, the Earl of Ripon. Laurence Oliphant was also there, in the absence of Lord Elgin, responding to a toast to 'The Opening of China and Japan'.[22]

In spite of Burton's complaint that when he reached London, 'everything had been done for, or rather against me,' an *ad hoc* Expedition sub-Committee met on 21 June, to consider proposals put forward earlier by both Burton and Speke for continuing their explorations in East Africa. The sub-Committee consisted of John Crawfurd, the distinguished orientalist and ethnologist, Francis Galton and Laurence Oliphant, who had recently been elected to the Council of the RGS. Both Burton and Speke attended the meeting. The sub-Committee reported that they had 'no hesitation in believing that great advantages to geographical science, and incidentally to commerce and civilization, must be expected from continuing these explorations of the Eastern side of the African continent which have been already so happily commenced by the two enter-prizing travellers.'

Only just over a week earlier at the RGS meeting at Burlington House, Galton had drawn attention to the closeness of the parallel between Burton and Speke's explorations, and those undertaken thirty-seven years earlier in the north of the same continent by Captains Denham and Clapperton. He suggested that Burton and Speke 'should henceforth take rank as the Denham and Clapperton of East Africa.' Galton spoke truer than, perhaps, he realized at the time. In 1822 Major Dixon Denham had led a government-sponsored expedition from Tripoli across the Sahara to Bornu in the Lake Chad Basin. There was mutual dislike from the start between Denham and Clapperton, men of completely different temperaments, and their relationship throughout was tense and acrimonious. Afterwards, Denham's official account of the expedition was written in such a biased way, as to leave the impression that the credit for its success was his alone.

No doubt having been informed by Oliphant of the tension existing between Burton and Speke, the committee diplomatically declared that they were 'of opinion that considering the vastness of the field of enquiry and the respective special qualifications of Captain Burton and Speke, the preferable course to pursue would be that they should proceed on their explorations by two distinct and independent routes.'

Burton's proposal of exploring the Eastern Horn of Africa 'on a line between the sea-board about Berbera and Gananah on the Jubba River, and from there westwards towards the Nyanza lake and the supposed sources of the Nile,' was essentially, of course, his old Somali plan taken off the shelf and dusted down. Even so, apart from its commercial potential, the committee regarded it as possessing great geograph-ical interest, especially since it offered the possibility of determining 'the existence of the reputed snowy mountains from which the headwaters of the Nile are supposed to flow, and the elevation and limits of the great central plateau.'[23]

Despite the sub-Committee's ringing endorsement of Burton's plan, we are justified, I believe, in questioning not only the seriousness with which it was put forward, but also its feasibility. Still suffering from ill-health Burton, unlike Speke, was unable to put a date on his departure. It will also be remembered that, following the disaster suffered by the Somali Expedition at Berbera, the East India Company had dismissed out of hand any plans for resurrecting it. There is no evidence that its attitude had changed in the meanwhile. Furthermore, the plan had no hope of succeeding without the help of the Aden authorities. Burton's criticism of them in his *First Footsteps*, was hardly likely to favour his cause. He would soon make it impossible by comments he would make in his next book. In fact, Burton's proposal resembles nothing so much as the last despairing throw of the dice by a gambler, who knows that his luck has run out.

Burton spent the earlier part of August in Dover with his sister. Maria's husband, Henry, now a lieutenant-colonel and a CB, who had been mentioned in despatches for gallantry during the relief of Cawnpore, had returned home, and the family spent several months together. 'We did our best to cheer him up,' wrote Burton's niece, Georgiana, 'for all that summer he seemed ailing and despondent.'[24] During these months, he was heavily involved in writing an account of the expedition for the RGS.[25] 'I had thought of running on to Vichy,' he wrote to Galton, 'but not being able to afford the time have taken to drenches of the water which appears to have worked muchly.'[26]

Some time later in the month, he broke off work to spend a week at Fryston Hall, Monckton Milnes's country mansion near Ferrybridge in the West Riding of Yorkshire. Thackeray, who clearly revelled in its atmosphere, described it as combining 'the graces of the château and the tavern.'[27] The hypochondriac Tennyson, more aware of its draughts, dubbed it 'Freezetown.'

For the visitor, the most striking feature, was the huge number of books to be seen crowding every room and passage in the house. Apart from their encyclopaedic range, many of them contained odd and fascinating tidbits: a bit of the skin of a famous criminal in a volume devoted to criminal trials; in another, a lock of Keats's hair. Of immense interest to Burton, would have been Milnes's large, and growing, collection of erotic and pornographic literature. In fact, his host laughingly described the house as Aphrodisiopolis. Only that year, a large quarto edition of 'Aretin d'Augustin Carrache ou Recueil de Postures Erotique... avec texte explicatif des sujets,' bought for him in Paris, had been sent through Customs with its pages gummed together.

While Burton suffered from periodic bouts of deep depression, Speke, on the other hand, was in buoyant mood. Early in September, he promised to send Rigby copies of two *Proceedings of the RGS* to show him 'what interest my discoveries have created in this land. Since I came home I have had no rest, being giddily hauled about from right to left and back again..... I feel that I shall never be robbed of the discovery of the Nile though some men may possibly step in and spoil my work by connecting the Nyanza with the Nile. I shall come down the Nile, if I ever get there, with swelling dignity, as our Vice-Consul Mr Petherick of Khartoum has offered to assist me to his utmost,'[28]

Citing ill-health, Burton declined an invitation to join Speke in delivering a paper to Section E at the meeting of the British Association in Aberdeen. Instead, he spent the time from early September to around the middle of October taking the waters at Beulah Spa, located near his sister's house in Upper Norwood. The spa, with its 25 acres of enclosed woodland, laid out as a pleasure garden by the noted architect, Decimus Burton, had been one of London's foremost pleasure resorts following its opening by the Countess of Essex in 1831. The arrival of the Crystal Palace in 1854, however, brought about its decline and eventual closure.[29]

Burton's presence at the spa, presented Speke with a further opportunity for venting his spleen on his erstwhile companion. Writing to his soul-mate Rigby, Speke thanked him for his 'very long and highly amusing letter. It has gone the rounds of the family circle,' he said, 'and been much chuckled over, especially that part description of the great Burton and his big boots. The boots were worn day and night until he arrived at Aden when shame alone induced his dropping them, and then he took to wearing quiet slippers an article much better adapted to the miserable condition of his weak legs and rotten feet...... B. is now engaged in washing his liver out at the hydropathic institute at Norwood. I hope those cleansing waters may wash him clean.'[30]

Towards the end of the month, Speke informed Shaw of having just received a letter from Burton. He professed to be much amused at hearing that Burton differed from him in his accounts of Africa, in particular that part relating to the north end of Nyanza. 'I thought he would,' Speke went on, 'for he used to snub me so unpleasantly when talking about anything, that I often kept my council. (sic) B. is one of those men who never <u>can</u> be wrong, and will never acknowledge an error so that when only two are talking together, talking becomes more of [a] bore than a pleasure.'[31]

The first part of Speke's diaries had already appeared in *Blackwood's* in September, entitled 'Journal of a Cruise on the Tanganyika Lake, Central Africa.' The second part came out the following month, 'Captain

J.H. Speke's Discovery of the Victoria Nyanza, The Supposed Source of the Nile.' Burton later wrote that these two papers 'opened a broad breach between my late companion and myself. They contained futilities which all readers could detect. A horse-shoe, or Chancellor's wig, some six thousand feet high and 180 miles in depth, was prolonged beyond the equator and gravely named "Mountains of the Moon." The Nyanza water, driven some 120 miles further north than when originally laid down from Arab information stultified one of the most important parts of our labours. Nor did I see why my companion should proceed to apply without consultation such names as "Speke Channel" and "Burton Point" to features which we had explored together.'[32]

Following his return, Isabel claimed to have met Burton, 'constantly,' though the facts suggest otherwise, and that he called upon her parents. 'I now put our marriage *seriously* before them,' she wrote, 'but without success as regards my mother.' At some unspecified date in October, Isabel further claimed to have sent a long letter to her mother in which she poured out her feelings for Burton. It was ostensibly written in response to her mother's "inviting my confidence", while she was "absent on some visits." Isabel described her at this time as being 'still a worldly woman of strong brain, of hasty temper, bigoted, and a Spartan with the elder half of her brood. We trembled before her, but we adored her, and we never got over her death in 1872.'

In this letter, Isabel went over where and why she fell in love with Burton, ranging over his accomplishments, and describing his character as being 'loveable in every way.' Without 'a particle of pettiness or snobbery in him,' he was 'the only being who awes me into respect, and to whose command I bow my head. And let me tell you another thing,' Isabel said, showing great perception, 'you and my father are immensely proud of your families....but from the present to the future, I believe that our proudest record will be our alliance with Richard Burton.'

He was, indeed, 'proud, fiery, satirical, ambitious.' But then, she worshipped ambition. 'Fancy achieving a good which affects millions, making your name a national one? It is infamous that most in the world live and die, and are never missed, and like us women, leave nothing but a tombstone. By ambition I mean men who have the will and power to change the face of things. I wish I were a man. If I were I would be Richard Burton; but being only a woman, I would be Richard Burton's wife.'

As to his lack of religion, 'At present he is following no form; at least none that he owns to. He says there is nothing between Agnosticism and Catholicity. He wishes to be married in the Catholic Church, says that I must practise my religion, and that our children must be Catholics, and will give such a promise in writing.' The only response to this letter, Isabel said, was an awful long and solemn sermon, telling me 'that Richard was not a Christian, and had no money.' Isabel said that she was not defending her letter to her mother. 'I only plead that I was fighting for my whole future, and my natural destiny.'[33]

These are only brief extracts from a document, eloquent in many respects, running to almost three thousand words. Did Isabel really write it at the time, or was it something that she later concocted? The question needs to be asked since, aside from the inherent crassness of the statement that there was 'nothing between Agnosticism and Catholicity,' Burton could not have used the former term in 1859. The word 'agnostic' was not coined by Professor Thomas Huxley until a decade later.[34] This important fact which has been overlooked by all of Burton's previous biographers serves, I believe, to cast grave doubts on the letter's authenticity.[35]

Whatever breach may have been opened up by the publication of Speke's diaries during September and October, was further widened by unexpected and unwelcome events a month later. On 8 November, Burton received a letter from the India Office, enclosing one from Rigby to the Government of Bombay on the non-payment of certain of the men hired by Burton to accompany the Expedition into Equatorial Africa. He was asked to comment on the statements contained in the letter, Sir Charles Wood being particularly anxious in knowing, 'why you took no steps to bring the services of the men who accompanied you, and your obligations to them, to the notice of the Bombay Government.'[36]

Apart from his two letters to Rigby in April, Speke had brought the matter up again in September, hoping that Rigby had persuaded Ramji to complain, and would 'assist him in getting his rightful dues; if he is not paid by any other means I must do so on return to Zanzibar.' He again made a much longer reference to the non-payment question when writing to Rigby in October.[37] By then, unknown to Speke, Rigby had written two letters, one official, the other private, to the Bombay Government on the subject.

He confessed to having felt extremely reluctant to interfere with anything connected with the non-payment of the men in question. Since, however, Said bin Salim and Ramji, had appealed to him, and Captain Speke had written him two private letters strongly insisting on the justice of their claims, he considered it his duty to bring the matter to the notice of Government, 'for I feel that if these men remain, after all they have endured in the service of British officers, our name for good faith in these countries will suffer, and that any future traveller, wishing to explore the interesting countries of the interior, will find no persons willing to accompany them from Zanzibar, or the opposite mainland.'[38]

Having given added weight to his case by wrapping it in the British flag, the terms of the resolution by the Board in Bombay on 19 August were entirely expected. Rigby was authorised to settle all outstanding claims in full, including repayment to the Sultan. He was also informed that he had 'acted with perfect propriety in bringing the subject to the notice of Government.'[39]

Burton had submitted his accounts early in June to the Council of the RGS, which then referred them to the Expedition Committee. On 13 October, he had written to Shaw, giving a short account of the pay of their escort. The Ras Kafilha, Said bin Salim, he said, did not deserve the additional reward promised in the case of good conduct. In the case of the Beloch escort, although he had written home for their reward, they had forfeited it as a result of their desertion and other acts of misconduct. As for Ramji, he had charged the extravagant sum of $300 at the outset for 10 slaves, which would have purchased the whole gang in the bazaar. Now, just under a month later, Burton was suddenly faced with having to justify his actions to East India House and the Secretary for India.

After dealing with Rigby's letter point by point, Burton professed his 'extreme surprise that Captain Speke should have written two private letters, forcibly pointing out the claims of these men to Captain Rigby, without having communicated the circumstances in any way to me, the chief of the Expedition. I have been in continuous correspondence with that officer since my departure from Zanzibar, and until this moment I have been impressed with the conviction that Captain Speke's opinion as to the claims of the guide and escort above alluded to was identical with my own.'[40] Obviously in a furious mood, Burton shortly afterwards wrote to Shaw that he did not wish 'to have any further private or direct communication with Speke. At the same time I am anxious that no mention of his name by me should be made without his being cognisant of it.'[41]

Just under a fortnight later, Speke informed Rigby that, 'Having read the letters which had passed between him and the Government at the Geographical Rooms, he saw in all Burton's answers, 'the same avoidance of the naked truth, it is that sort of thing that has always made me feel incensed against him, and although I felt obliged to travel with him, I entertained a loathing for him. I know that I ought to have hauled him up long before I did but felt compunction about doing it as he is my senior.'[42] Shortly afterwards, Speke, himself, sent a detailed statement of his views on the contents of Rigby's letter for Sir Charles Wood.

Captain Burton in concluding his letter, Speke said, expressed surprise at finding that he, Speke, still differed in opinion with him, yet at the same time writing friendly notes. 'I can only say,' Speke said with breath-taking hypocrisy,' that I never allow enmity to be rankling in my breast, yet am ever ready to refer anything discordant with my views, especially if that be on the question of equity.' He claimed that it was 'the greatest pain' to his feelings, that he had been compelled to give his views in the present letter, although they only contained what he had always said and expressed to Captain Burton in person.[43]

The following day, an Expedition Committee, chaired by Col Everest, met at the RGS, and resolved, 'That the Committee having examined the accounts of the East African Expedition as sent in by Captain Burton showing an outlay of £2,496 10s 5¼d, consider that this Expedition which obtained for its leader one of the Gold Medals of the Society and achieved results of such high importance, would have warranted the Expenditure of even a larger sum.'[44] Undoubtedly pleased and relieved at this decision, Burton wrote an official letter to Shaw on 20 December, requesting 'the kindly interest of the Council in obtaining for me from HM's Secretary of State for Foreign Affairs the balance of money expended by me amounting to £1,494 0s 5½d.'

As a result of the Expedition Committee's deliberations in the New Year, Shaw was directed to inform Burton that 'in the opinion of the Committee, the Society has no claims on the Foreign Office for any sum beyond the £1,000 already advanced towards defraying the expenses of the East Africa Expedition, but that the Committee will be gratified to learn that Capt. Burton has been reimbursed the extra sum laid out by him.'[45]

Its optimism, however, appeared sadly misplaced when, on 14 January, Burton was sent an official letter on the non-payment issue from East India House, sternly censuring his actions. He was further informed that his letter, and that of Captain Speke, would be forwarded to the Government of Bombay, 'with whom it will rest to determine whether you should be held pecuniarily responsible for the amount which has been paid in liquidation of the claims against you.'[46]

In a characteristically robust and combative reply, Burton asserted, 'that the character of the British Government has not, and cannot in my humble opinion have suffered in any way by withholding a purely conditional reward when forfeited by gross neglect and misconduct; and I venture to suggest that by encouraging such abuses serious obstacles will be thrown in the way of future exploration, and that the liberality of the British Government will be more esteemed by the native than its character for sound sense.'[47]

Having been the guest of Monckton Milnes at Fryston in August, it appears that during the following winter, he and Burton spent many bachelor evenings together in London. Although Isabel remained totally silent on the matter, it is clear from correspondence in the archives of the RGS and the Houghton Papers that Burton, after spending Christmas in England with his sister, left soon afterwards for the Continent. In a letter to Milnes from Boulogne of 22 January, he said that he was writing to him 'in the "home of the stranger," not however so much for the usual reasons as from the conviction that here I can work....There is a fatal necessity for... writing something more popular than a geographical report, & upon this I am now engaged.'

Since last meeting him, he had seen Hankey. The "sisters" are a humbug – Swiss women, and thorough mountaineers, a breed as unfit for debauchery as exists in this world. I told Hankey so and he remarked philosophically enough that they were sufficiently good for the public of pouillards. He showed me also a little poem entitled the Betuliad. I liked most every part of it except the name. You are writing for a very very small section who combine the enjoyment of verse with the practice of flagellation....Why not call it the Birchiad? If you want it corrected here I can do so. Hankey and I looked over the copy... at Paris and corrected the several errors.'[48]

Hankey, who had probably been introduced to Burton in London some time in the previous year, was Milnes's chief adviser and agent, responsible for stocking his erotic collection at Fryston. His favourite courier was a Mr Harris, manager of the Covent Garden Opera House, who travelled frequently to France on musical matters. Harris, who suffered from curvature of the spine, became adept in smuggling through Customs, not only quarto books but statuettes in the bend of his back.[49]

The son of a general, and a former Guards' officer, Hankey lived with his mistress at 2 Rue Lafitte, an apartment in a fashionable part of Paris looking out over the boulevard towards the Café Anglais and the Opéra Comique. In conversation with the Goncourt brothers, however, he professed to finding London more fun than Paris, since there was a house there kept by a Mrs Jenkins where he could whip girls and stick pins in them. H.S. Ashbee, the scholar and bibliographer, who met Hankey many years later, referred to him as 'a remarkable man, quite a study, he appears to me like a second de Sade without the intellect. He has given himself up body and soul to the erotic mania, thinks of nothing else, lives for nothing else.'[50]

After leaving Hankey, Burton had returned to Boulogne, and settled down to write. However, he was 'interrupted by Beatson's confounded suit. One could not refuse to assist him as he really has been ill-treated after a fashion; so I showed up in the witness-box. My evidence has not been printed quite correctly, n'importe.. There is little hope of my escaping from this place before the ninth of February.'[51]

Following their return to England, a disagreement over money matters had helped to fuel the increasingly acrimonious dispute between Burton and Speke.[52] Having spent more than £1,400 of his own money, Burton was asking Speke for £600. Speke pointed out at the beginning of February that, as the Indian Government had decided to grant his full pay and allowances from 2 December 1856 to 14 May 1859, he would be prepared to pay 'half of the excess of expenditure which accrued to the Expedition.' It was conditional, however, on Burton's formally requesting a refund from the Government on their behalf.

Burton's response was immediate. The debt, he declared, was one which Speke had contracted unconditionally in Africa. After refusing point blank to accept Speke's terms, which he considered insolent, he went on, 'Had I known you then as well as I do now, I should have required receipts for what was left a debt of honour. I must be content to pay the penalty of ignorance.'[53]

Writing to Milnes from Boulogne on 10 February, Burton thanked him for 'the extracts, secondly for the paternal admonition, "be very careful how you use this," – to which I reply pace tua, that I invented capping it. Fred Hankey wrote to me today, "I have just written de nouveau /sic/ to the person who is to get the Bituliad printed at Bruxelles (sic etiam) saying I must have rendezvous immediately to settle the whole matter without loss of time."

I am rather tempted to stay through the carnival....These small Saturnalia bring with them pleasant memories...

Besides which this is a good place to work in. I am staying at the Chateau d'Outreau with an old friend...Harrow boy, Captain of the Greys, first class at Oxford, Holy Orders and Divinity, great in metaphysics, tall in mathematics, and a very stiff drinker.'[54]

Just under a week later, Burton wrote to Shaw that he was 'bothered – that old woman at the head of the India House has been writing rot to me, & has received in consequence in reply a severe blowing up. You shall see the papers when I return.

Tonight DV I shall be in Paris for the end of the Carnival, after that to London about the last of next week.'[55]

Once back in this country, Burton wrote an official letter to the RGS, enclosing the decision arrived at by the Secretary of State for India in Council. 'In doing so I take the opportunity of again distinctly denying the stigma cast upon me by the Secretary of State for India in Council, namely that the "character of the British Government has suffered" by the non-payment of a claim which it appears to me has been left entirely in the hands of Captains Rigby and Speke.

I have furthermore to inform you that in early May Messrs. Longman propose to print a work upon the subject of the Lake Regions of Central Africa...'[56]

Just under a week later, Burton wrote to Shaw, asking him to inform the Committee of the RGS that, on or around the 16th of that month [it was actually on the 12th], he had officially applied to the Under-Secretary of State for India for '"refundment of the sums disbursed by me in forwarding the objects of the East African Expedition," and appending the favourable opinion expressed by the Council.'[57] Burton's letter had been received at the India Office on 17 March, and a frosty minute drafted in the Political Department in reply. 'In estimating the excess of expenditure over receipt, Captain Burton ought to have taken into account the amount of the Indian pay & allowances received by himself and Captain Speke – these being the contribution of the Indian Exchequer towards the expenses of the Expedition. Nothing else was promised to them by this Government..'[58]

On 10 April, the day on which Burton penned the Preface to his *Lake Regions*, Shaw received an undated note from him. 'My dear Shaw, I return from Paris on Thursday and leave for America on Saturday.' Burton did not disclose the reason for his being in France again, which could have been connected with Milnes or Hankey. On the other hand, it may possibly have been related to the award to him and Speke of La Grande Medaille d'Or de la Société de Géographie, Paris – its highest award, 'pour la découverte la plus importante en géographie.'[59]

Burton's activities in this country and in France since returning from Africa could have left him little time for seeing Isabel. Yet nothing in his behaviour suggests that he was one jot affected by their being apart. Naturally, there is no hint of this in her highly suspect version of events shortly to take place, tricked out with the usual premonition of something dire about to happen.

According to Isabel, she was out walking with two friends one day in April, when 'a tightening of the heart came over me that I had known before.' Returning home, she said to her sister, "I am not going to see Richard for some time." She said, "Why, you will see him tomorrow." "No I shall not," Isabel replied; "I don't know what is the matter." A tap came at the door, and a note with the well-known writing was put into my hand. I knew my fate, and with deep-drawn breath I opened it. He had left – could not bear the pain of saying goodbye; would be absent for nine months on a journey to see Salt Lake City. He would then come back, and see whether I had made up my mind to choose between him, and my mother, to marry him if I would; and if I had not the courage to risk it, he would go back to India, and from thence to other explorations. I was to take nine months to think about it.'

CHAPTER TWENTY-THREE

SAINTS AND SINNERS

Burton probably left Euston Station for Liverpool on Friday, 20 April, where he booked into the Adelphi Hotel. The distinguished American author, Nathaniel Hawthorne, who was the United States' Consul at Liverpool from 1853-57, described England's great commercial city as, 'Sitting, as it were, in the gateway between the Old World and the New, where the steamers and packets landed the greater part of our wandering countrymen, and received them again when their wanderings were done.'[1] Amongst those of his compatriots who passed through this gateway during the late 1830s and early 1840s, were members of a new and highly controversial religious movement, the Church of Jesus-Christ of Latter-day Saints, founded at Fayette, Seneca County, in up-state New York in April 1830.[2]

Almost a year earlier, the movement's founder and Prophet, Joseph Smith, claimed to have received divine instructions to appoint twelve disciples, 'to go into the world to preach my gospel unto every creature.'[3] It was not until 1 June 1837, the same month in which Princess Victoria acceded to the throne, that one of the apostles, Heber C. Kimball, was directed to go to England 'to open the door of salvation to that nation.' Later, another apostle, Orson Hyde, together with Willard Richards and Joseph Fielding, a British emigrant who had recently settled in Canada, were chosen to join him. Shortly after the missionaries landed at Liverpool on 20 July, Fielding travelled to nearby Preston to see his brother, a minister at Vauxhall Chapel, and it was there that Mormonism was first preached in Britain.[4] After a year spent in preaching, distributing tracts, and working with the poor and unemployed in various parts of the country, the missionaries returned to the States in July 1838.

A second mission arrived at Liverpool two years later. It included Brigham Young, the movement's future charismatic leader and first President of the Church, of whom it was predicted at his ordination in 1835 that he would travel abroad, 'behold heavenly messengers going forth,' and 'do wonders in the name of Jesus' by the power invested in him by the priesthood. Young later recalled that, despite having 'landed......as strangers in a strange land, and penniless,' they had made many friends, established churches in practically every important town and city in Great Britain, baptized between seven and eight thousand, seen to the printing of 5,000 Books of Mormon, 3,000 Hymn Books, 2,500 volumes of the missionary journal, *The Millenial Star*, and 50,000 tracts.[5] They had also organized the emigration of 1,000 converts to Zion, and set up a permanent shipping agency. It was an impressive record in such a short space of time.

'Emigration in Mormondom, like El Hajj in El Islam,' as Burton pointed out, 'is the fulfilment of a divine command.'[6] Besides this religious imperative, however, there were pressing economic reasons for a rapid increase in population, following the Saints' epic trek from Nauvoo, western Illinois, to the barren wastes of the Salt Lake Valley throughout the spring and harsh prairie winter of 1846.[7] Emigration, there-fore, organized through, what was called, the Perpetual Emigrating Company, was at the forefront of the Church's policy in the 1850s.[8] By adopting such means it hoped, eventually, to transport some 30,000 British converts over the vast distance between this country and the Far West of the United States.[9]

The Times attributed the Mormons' undoubted success in this field to the fact that, 'Their arguments were addressed to a mass that was already on the move both in mind and body. The time of distress which just preceded the great emigrant movement was exactly the time at which the highly coloured pictures of peace, comfort and prosperity in a new land, drawn by a Mormon missionary, could tell most powerfully upon our own people, crushed by low wages and tempted to look upon their own country as a scene of immoveable hardship, inequality and oppression.'[10]

Burton gave no indication as to when he first became acquainted with Mormonism. Given his keen interest in the world religions and sexual mores, it is probable that his attention was drawn at a fairly early stage to this new sect, whose 'combination of Judaism, Mohamedanism, socialism, despotism, and the grossest superstition, with much practical good sense,' made it, in the words of one commentator, 'the most singular phenomenon of modern times.'[11] By 'Mohamedanism' was meant, of course, the Mormon Church's adoption of plural marriage, or polygamy as it was better known. It formed part of a 'revelation' from Joseph Smith announced at Nauvoo, 12 July 1843. Claims that the Mormons were practising polygamy, however, were always strenuously denied by the Church Elders. It was only publicly announced at Utah in 1852, and to the British Mission in the *Millenial Star*, 1 January 1853.

There was a considerable body of literature on the subject of Mormonism by the 1850s, most of it hostile. Lacking first-hand knowledge at this period, Burton could hardly fail to be influenced by such views. In his posthumously published essay, 'El Islam, or the Rank of Mohammedanism Among the Religions of the World,' he refers to 'the shallow imposture Mormonism.'[12] This is most likely his adapta-tion of the phrase, 'this miserable imposture,' used by J.W. Conybeare in his long and highly critical article on the Mormons published in *The Edinburgh Review* in April 1854.[13]

Despite the different impression given by Burton's journal entries, there is every reason to believe that his decision to visit the States and the Mormon community in Utah, was strongly influenced by discussions with his friend, the Hon Henry A. Murray. Murray's grandfather, John, 4th earl of Dunmore (1732-1809) had served as the last British governor of Virginia. Henry was also related by marriage to the family of the American soldier, Brigadier-General James S. Wadsworth, later killed while serving with the Federal Army in the Civil War. Murray had twice visited the States, first in 1826, and then again in the early 1850s. Following this last visit, he had written a book describing his extensive travels. 'While in these parts [St Louis, Missouri],' he wrote, 'I made some enquiries as to that mysterious body of religious lunatics – the followers of a Western Mahomet, by name Joe Smith – who rejoice in the name of Mormons; but since my return to England, I have found such a concise and valuable account of them in that valuable work by Mr Horace Mann, entitled Religious Worship in England, that I have determined to turn wholesale plagiarist, as Mr Mann's work being purely statistical, may possibly have never met the reader's eye.' Murray's Chapter X, headed 'Latter-Day Saints and River Scenes,' carries such debunking captions as: 'Joe and the Angel; Joe Turned Author; Joe and the Professor; Joe and his Priesthood; Joe's Business,' etc.[14] If Burton set out for the States with a similar prejudiced view of the Mormons, he would later go on to write one of the most unbiased accounts of this religious community which had appeared until then.

Burton left Liverpool aboard the 1,800 ton Cunard liner *SS Canada* on Saturday, 21 April, bound for

Halifax and Boston with Her Majesty's mails. The following day, while the ship lay at anchor off Cork harbour unloading and taking on mail, Burton scribbled a short note to Norton Shaw, asking him to direct five of his private copies of *The Lake Regions* without delay to Dr Hooker of Kew Gardens, Drs Gray and Günsner of the British Museum, Adam White, Esq., and Sir Roderick Murchison. He had called upon the latter, who was not in town, and 'enclosed a PPC card (sic) 'to Miladi.' 'This change,' he went on, 'is very jolly. Stiggins is drinking fresh and we look forward to great fun.[15]

Stiggins's name had cropped up in one of Speke's letters of the previous month to Blackwood, in which he asked the publisher if he had 'seen a profligate individual called "Styggins?" I gave him a ticket to go and look you up. He is a very nice fellow but louche.'[16] His name also figured in another of Speke's letters written later that year to C.P. Rigby.[17] So, who was this somewhat oddly-named companion of Burton on his trip to America?

It was not until 1872, when recalling his friend, Steinhaueser, who had died six years earlier, that Burton revealed that they had 'wandered together over the United States......'[18] Rather than joining Burton 'somewhere in America,' as suggested by Fawn Brodie the two men probably met up in Boulogne some time in March before travelling together to England.

In 1956, a package arrived at the British Museum's Department of Manuscripts, containing fragments of a manuscript journal and diary written by Burton during his voyage to America.[19] The fragments, brief extracts from which were first printed by Mrs Brodie, consist of eighteen unlined pages, four single, the remainder verso and recto. Of these, the right-hand side carries the text, while the left is mainly used for miscellaneous items – nautical, meteorological and on-board observations, insertions etc. sometimes written horizontally, sometimes diagonally.[20]

The journal contains two conflicting accounts of Burton's decision to travel to America. On the first single page, headed Chapt.1 he writes:

Wearying of the wide and trodden paths through slow-progressing Europe, "of the mingled gorgeousness of foreign travels and the East," and of the monotonous savagery which characterises Africa, I resolved to recruit my health and spirits by a turn between the Atlantic and the Pacific, and to enrich my mental picture-gallery with a few rapid sketches of the mighty Western world.

"Seek thy fellow-traveller before thy trip," says the seventh Arab law. Happily for me, an old friend returned from Europe, after depositing the remnants of his....[indecipherable] as the wise do, in the Holy Land. A thoroughly civilised man, he suited my purposes...........

A different version, however, appears a little later:

"I'll tell you what it is, h'm?" exclaimed Stiggins with a look of afflatus of inspiration and an outward jerking of the fingers of both hands – a gesture indicative of considerable excitement – "I'll go to America!"

"Yes, I'll go to America. I'll radically change my meat and drink. I'll go in for the food of the country, world-famous canvas backs and other provocations of thirst. I'll drink mint juleps, brandy smashes, whisky-skies, gin-sling, cock-tail sherry-cobblers, rum-salads, streaks of lightning, morning glory.

"It'll be a most interesting experiment..... Will you come with me and eat and drink through America, h'm?"

I could not say no after drinking with him on and off for 15 years..........

So I replied in the affirmative...........

We resolved to leave without delay, and to hurry on the necessary preparations. £300 each was considered sufficient – if we take more said my friend we shall only throw it away...[21]

Steinhaueser's habit of heavy drinking, plus his recent visit to the Holy Land, provide the clues, I believe, as to the origin of his humorous nickname, which has puzzled biographers since. Stiggins is the prim-faced, red-nosed religious humbug in Charles Dickens's *The Pickwick Papers*, pastor of the local chapel near to The Marquis of Granby public-house in Dorking run by Mrs Weller. Her constant companion, much to the disgust of Sam Weller's father, Stiggins, in addition to consuming large helpings of buttered toast, had a distinct partiality for helping himself to her hot pineapple rum-and-water dashed with a slice of lemon.[22]

While Fawn Brodie failed to make the connection between Steinhaueser and Stiggins, she made an even more important error with regard to what she described as 'the intimate journal fragments, written in a script so illegible it was almost a code.' It was her failure, excusable it has to be said, to make adequate sense of Burton's writing, which led her badly astray in commenting on his supposed 'responsiveness to strangers and his frequent fluctuation from interest and quick affection to momentary hatred.'[23] The diary, in fact, is headed 'Leaves from Miss A-B-'s Diary,' and represent the daily jottings of an attractive and flirtatious young woman, travelling to America with her aunt.

Why Burton should choose to adopt a female *persona* poses an intriguing question, especially since he was not a writer of fiction. It has been suggested that it is a 'spoof' diary, probably written to amuse Steinhaueser or even Isabel on his return.'[24] Even after allowing for changing tastes in humour, however, it is difficult to imagine anyone being even faintly amused by such embarrassingly banal entries as:

23 April 1860

Saw the sailor heaving a log – always thought that a log meant a piece of timber, and now find that it is the Captain's diary. Mean to keep *my log* out of the way.
Heavy rain, the sky was quite covered. We were told that the Captain had taken the sun yesterday – when will he give it up again?

or

25 April 1860

Hurricane from N to S. The stewardess calls it a squall. I suppose because it makes the poor dear children cry.

The 'spoof' diary, theory, of course, fails to account for Isabel Burton's wishing to burn it. There is an alternative interpretation, that the diary represents Burton's indulging in a cross-dressing fantasy, acting out the role of a woman. Part of the entry for 1 May reads, 'Put on my scarlet jacket and black merino skirt. …..The gentlemen proposed a May Ball. I put on my new poplin…My hair was a chignon and I wore the sweetest little circle of a pin in my back hair.' Burton would later quote Goethe's saying 'that the highest type of man must always contain something of the feminine.'[25] He even went so far as to claim in his *Arabian Nights*, that 'Amongst men the mixture of the feminine with the masculine temperaments leads to sodomy.'[26] Was there more of the feminine in Burton's makeup than met the eye? On this reading, far from handing around his diary for the amusement of his friends, he would have taken great care, like his female *alter ego*, to keep '*his* log out of the way.'

Following the ship's arrival at Halifax, Nova Scotia, on 2 May, Burton continues the narrative in his own person, bolstering it in typical fashion with an array of facts about the city's history, population, climate, economy, and its status as a military and naval base. After spending some three hours sightseeing in and about the steep streets of the town, the men returned to the ship, 'unanimous as to one point, viz that hanging was a favour compared to Halifax.'

While Burton later wrote of, 'Having wandered through every State of the Anglo-American Republic,' he left no account of his and Steinhaeuser's itinerary after landing at Boston on 4 May.[27] We can, however, catch brief glimpses from scattered references in some of Burton's books and surviving memorabilia.[28] No doubt carrying letters of introduction from Henry Murray, it is likely that the two men continued northwards through New England before travelling via Lower Canada to the Great Lakes.[29] They then, probably, continued down the eastern seaboard as far as south-eastern Virginia, making whistle-stops at the major cities on the way.

After sightseeing in New York, the men stopped off at Philadelphia, where the gorilla trophies of the young African explorer, M. Du Chaillu, were on display at the Academy of Natural Sciences.[30] Keen to enjoy what he called, 'a little Indian fighting,' Burton also made a point while at Washington DC of calling on the Hon John B. Floyd, Secretary of War. Burton was not only very courteously received, but provided with introductory letters addressed to the officers commanding various departments in the West. Having visited the home and burial place of George Washington at Mount Vernon, on the Potomac River, the couple continued on to Richmond and then Williamsburg, the historic former state capital. Burton later looked back nostalgically on his stay in Virginia, 'that old Dominion of Queen Elizabeth where still linger traces of the glorious cavalier and the noble feudal spirit, which (alas!), have almost disappeared from the mother country....'[31] After a leisurely journey through the states of the deep South, it was probably around late July when the two men arrived at the great bustling cotton port of New Orleans, Louisiana.

Probably spending no more than a day or so there, Burton booked a passage aboard a Mississippi steamboat bound for St Louis, Missouri, some 1,218 miles up-river.[32] Whether Steinhaueser accompanied him on this stage of the journey or left Orleans for Europe, can only be a matter for speculation. This was still the golden age of river traffic. For cabin passengers, at least, the high-decked steamboats billowing black smoke from their towering twin stacks were a comfortable, even luxurious, form of travel. It could also be hazardous. In February of the previous year, one of the boilers of the Mississippi steamer, *Princess*, blew up, killing almost 200 people.[33] Henry Murray narrowly escaped with his life, when the vessel in which he was travelling down-river from St Louis to New Orleans, was rammed by another steamer in the darkness of the early morning and wrecked. Fifteen passengers and eighty head of cattle were drowned. Murray lost all his papers, his letters of credit, and his journal. In fact, 'I had also lost everything else except what I had on – rifles, gun, clothes – all were gone.'[34]

It was perhaps a week later when Burton's steamboat tied up alongside the crowded levee at St Louis. Disembarking, he booked into Planter's House Hotel, Fourth, between Pine and Chestnut Street. Dickens, who stayed there in 1842, described it as 'built like an English hospital, with long passages and bare walls, and skylights above the room doors for the free circulation of air.' Nevertheless, he praised it as being 'an excellent house,' the proprietors having 'most bountiful notions of providing the creature comforts.'

One of Burton's fellow guests with whom he struck up an acquaintance was Lt James Jackson Dana of the US Artillery, who was to be his future travelling companion. Dana, his young wife, Thesta, and their two-year-old daughter, May, were on their way to Camp Floyd, in Utah Territory, some forty or so miles beyond Salt Lake City. Needing precise information about the route, Lt Dana left with his family for St Joseph by railroad on Thursday, 2 August. Burton followed two days later, having used the time profitably to buy a ticket for the Central Overland, California and Pike's Peak Express stagecoach, to stock up with a few provisions and medicines, and to kit himself out for the long journey ahead.

St Joseph was a large waterside town on the west of the State of Missouri, some 500 miles up river from St Louis. During the major gold rush years of 1849-52, it had boomed as a steamboat base and supply depot for wagon trains westward. In the opinion of one gold seeker, Eleazar Ingalls, it was 'the greatest place for gambling and all over rascality that I was ever in.' Little seems to have had changed over the years, one visitor in June 1859 describing it as 'the muddiest, nastiest border ruffian town on the earth.'

Promptly at 8 a.m. on Tuesday, 7 August 1860, a Concord coach drawn by a team of four mules pulled up outside the Patee Hotel, where Burton and his fellow passengers were staying. These coaches built by the Abbot-Downing Company of Concord, New Hampshire, had revolutionised western travel. First used by the Butterfield Overland Express on the south-west route from St Louis or Memphis through Ft Smith, El Paso, and Ft Yuma, to San Francisco, they were far better suited for travelling across plains and deserts than any earlier vehicle.

The passengers' luggage was immediately slung on board with scant ceremony. The official limit was 25 pounds per person, any excess being charged at $1 per pound. Everyone, naturally, tried to stow away as much as possible, Company officials turning a blind eye to non-payment for bedding, stores, weapons, and openly encouraging the addition of numerous whiskey-kegs and cigar-boxes. An hour late in starting, they eventually rattled through the dusty streets of St Jo, and boarded the steam ferry, which carried them across to the left bank of the Missouri River. Once, in so-called, "Bleeding Kansas," they joined the great emigrant route from Missouri to California and Oregon. Ahead lay a journey of 1,136 miles, to be covered in forty-five stages over a period of just under three weeks.

Much of the land between the Missouri and Fort Kearney was gently rolling prairie. 'Nothing, I may remark, is more monotonous,' wrote Burton, 'except perhaps the African and Indian jungles, than these prairie tracks. You saw, as it were, the ends of the earth, and looked around in vain for some object upon which the eye might rest...' These vast, featureless plains had the same effect on Robert Louis Stevenson travelling aboard an emigrant train from New York to San Francisco in 1879. 'What livelihood can repay a human creature for a life spent in this huge sameness?,' he mused.... 'A sky full of stars is the most varied spectacle that he can hope.'[35]

Despite the often long stretches of driving in cold cramped conditions, the snatched few hours of sleep before an early start, mosquitoes and the rough and dusty roads, Burton appears to have thoroughly enjoyed himself. 'I could not but meditate,' he wrote, 'upon the difference between travel in the pure prairie air, despite an occasional "chill" and the perspiring miseries of an East Indian dawk, or of a trudge in the miasmatic and pestilential regions of Central Africa.'[36]

Although describing one day as being much like another, he still contrived to fill his journal with a mass of data, which later went to swell a book of more than 700 pages. Nothing escaped his attention, nor his criticism, particularly the squalor he encountered at some of the way stations. At Cold Springs, Burton got his first taste of 'the *rale* "Far West,"' myriads of flies disputing 'with us a dinner consisting of dough-nuts green and poisonous with saleratus, suspicious eggs in a massive greasy fritter, and rusty bacon, intolerably fat.'

There was, however, far more which Burton found novel and interesting. The long winding trains of wagons, for instance, 'those ships of the great American Sahara,' which, in the early morning light looked like 'lines of white cranes trooping slowly over the prairie.....' He was amused enough to write a long character sketch of the "ripper" or driver who 'can do nothing without whiskey, which he loves to call tarantula-juice, strychnine, red-eye, corn-juice, Jersey-lightning, leg-stretcher, tangle-leg, and many other hard and grotesque names.'

At Guittard's he caught his first glimpse of the arrival of a Pony Express rider. The brain-child of William H. Russell of the firm of Russell, Majors and Waddell, the service, which instantly caught the public imagination, had begun on 3 April of that year, delivering mail from St Joseph, Missouri, to Sacramento, California, in under ten days. Charging high rates, however, of from two to ten dollars an ounce, and lacking a government subsidy it only managed to survive until October of the following year, when the electric telegraph made it irrelevant.[37]

Naturally, with his acute ear for languages, Burton, like Dickens, was fascinated with American words and speech idioms, introducing a number of them into his account. In fact, among the books he had brought from England was John Russell Bartlett's *A Dictionary of Americanisms*, published in London the previous year, and praised by Burton as 'a glossary which the author's art has made amusing as a novel.' A "drink," as he pointed out, was any river: the "Big Drink" was the Mississippi. A creek, pronounced 'crik,' was not an arm of the sea, but a small stream of sweet water. Miss was still used for Mrs by western men and negroes. Referring to a Miss Moore, who kept a spotless way station, Mrs Dana explained to a puzzled Burton that every western wife, even if still in her teens, was called 'ole woman.' She also pointed out to him, 'one sign of demoralization on the part of Miss Moore. It was so microscopic that only a woman's acute eye could detect it. Miss Moore was teaching her children to say "Yes surr!" to every driver.'

Any hopes that Burton had of taking part in some Indian fighting, were rudely dashed when they arrived at Fort Kearney. Captain Sturgis, of the 1st U.S. Cavalry, had recently attacked a large body of Comanches, Kiowas, and Cheyenne near the Republican Fork of Kansas River, a little to the south of the fort. It was clear, that there would be no more fighting for some time to come. Burton was fortunate, nevertheless, in arriving just in time to witness the wholesale exodus of an Indian village to new grazing grounds. The weapons carried by the braves: small tomahawks or iron hatchets, leather targes, and bows and arrows protected from damp in deerskins and quivers decorated with beads and fringes, reminded him of their use among the Bedouins of El Hejaz. He also noticed that they treated their lean and ungroomed horses as cruelly as the Somal.

While the old women of the tribe 'were fearful to look upon,' his roving eye was caught by a pretty young Indian girl with large languishing eyes, glittering white teeth, and sleek, long black hair. 'Her figure had none of the fragility which distinguishes the higher races,' he remarked approvingly, 'who are apparently too delicate for human nature's daily food – porcelain, in fact, where pottery is wanted.' Obviously propositioned by the driver, she responded 'with a soft clear laugh – the principal charm of the Indian as of the smooth-throated African woman – at the same time showing him the palm of her right hand as though it had been a looking-glass. The gesture would have had a peculiar significance in Sindh; here, however, I afterwards learned, it simply conveys a refusal…'[38]

Clearly fascinated by a subject which he had merely touched on in his *Pilgrimage*, Burton later devoted a whole chapter to a wide-ranging and sympathetic ethnological essay on the Sioux or Dakota. Once the dread of all the neighbouring tribes, comparable to the great Anizeh race amongst the Bedouins of Arabia, the Sioux now faced extinction as a result of current Government policy. He described their language, like that of the Pawnee, as being easily learnt, government officials picking it up in the same way as the Anglo-Indian did Hindustani. A remarkable characteristic of the Prairie Indian, he noted, was his habit of also communicating, like the deaf and dumb, in sign language, something which he profusely illustrated in his book.[39] In fact, Burton later declared his intention, which was never fulfilled, of producing 'a system which may prove generally useful, especially to those beginning a foreign tongue.'[40]

Headed for Platte Bridge around the middle of August, Burton got his first glimpse of a slow-moving train of Mormon wagons making its way to Salt Lake City. '"British-English," Burton remarked, 'was written in capital letters upon the white eyelashes and tow-coloured curls of the children.' One young woman attempted to conceal a pretty face under a severe expression. 'I thought that perhaps she might be a Sultana,' he wrote sardonically, 'reserved for the establishment of some very magnificent Mormon bashaw; but the driver, when appealed to, responded with contempt, "Guess old Briggy wont stampede many o' that 'ere lot!"'

Four days later, striking away from the valley of the Sweetwater, and after winding up and down rugged hills and along broken hollows, they arrived at South Pass. The great watershed between the Atlantic and the Pacific, it was also the key to westward migration. Over 7,000 feet above sea-level, this gap in the Rockies was no narrow ravine hemmed in by sheer walls of rock, but 'an almost level table-land, of twenty miles from north to south, and four or five across: a field of battle large enough for all the armies of the world.'[41] Now in the high country, that evening they caught sight of the impressive peaks of the Wind River Mountains in the distance.

By 25 August they were through Echo Canyon, and labouring over the Wasatch, the last and highest mountain chain between Fort Bridger and the Great Salt Lake Valley. Emerging from Emigration Canyon around 6 pm that day, Salt Lake Valley presently came into view. Mormon advance scouts, Orson Pratt and Erastes Snow, had first entered the valley on 21 July 1847. They were followed three days later by Wilford Woodruffe's carriage, in which Brigham Young lay ill with Rocky Mountain fever. Raising himself with difficulty from the floor, Young looked out on what was to be their new home. 'The spirit of light,' he later wrote in his journal, 'rested on and hovered over the valley, and I felt there that the Saints would find protection and safety.'[42] Now, at this self-same spot, Burton wrote:

> the pilgrim emigrants, like the Hajis of Mecca and Jerusalem, give vent to the emotions long pent up within their bosoms by sobs and tears, laughter and congratulations, psalms and hysterics. It is no wonder that the children dance, that strong men cheer and shout, and that nervous women, broken with fatigue and hope deferred, scream and faint; that the ignorant should fondly believe that the "Spirit of God pervades the very atmosphere," and that Zion on the tops of the mountains is nearer heaven than other parts of the earth. In good sooth, though uninfluenced by religious fervour – beyond the natural satisfaction of seeing a bran new Holy City – even I could not, after nineteen days in a mail-wagon, gaze upon the scene without emotion.[43]

Announcing Burton's arrival, the *Deseret News* described him as 'a traveler of distinction, generally known as the Hajee [*sic*] Burton, pilgrim to Mecca, explorer of Hurrur, and discoverer of the central African lakes.' While encountering kindness and hospitality from the many ordinary people that he met, there is no doubt that, as a distinguished foreign visitor, Burton was given special treatment by the Church Elders. Throughout the whole of his stay, he was allowed unlimited access to people of every class, from the Head of the Church down to the most lowly agricultural labourer. Furthermore, as a foreigner, he was free to ask questions on subjects which would have been taboo, had he been an American, especially an official. Nevertheless, there was 'in Mormondom,' as he admitted, 'as in all other exclusive faiths, whether Jewish, Hindu or other, an inner life into which I cannot flatter myself or deceive the reader with the idea of my having penetrated. At the same time it is only fair to state that no Gentile, even the unprejudiced, who are *rarae aves*, however long he may live or intimately he may be connected with Mormons, can expect to see anything but the superficies.'[44]

A couple of days after his arrival, Burton was shown around the city by Colonel Stambaugh of the Militia, the Surveyor-General of Utah. He was duly impressed by its size, the spaciousness of its streets, the quality of its shops, and the perfect safety at night enjoyed by its 9,000 to 12,000 inhabitants. The Mormon prophecy had been fulfilled, he wrote. In only twelve years, the once howling wilderness, the miserable preserve of half-naked Digger Indians, had 'blossomed like the rose.'

Despite appearing rather grave and humourless the Mormons, Burton found, were highly sociable. He had arrived at the wrong time of the year for the 'gay season.' He found, however, that they delighted in sleighing and private theatricals and, when money became available, intended building a theatre to vie with any back in the old country. This was no idle promise, the scheme coming to fruition during the following two years. Based on Drury Lane Theatre, London, and with its impressive central chandelier made by Brigham Young himself, it had a seating capacity for 3,000 people, and cost the community close on $100,000.[45]

The Sunday following his arrival, Burton was invited to dine with the Governor, the Hon Alfred Cumming and his charming wife, Elizabeth. In June 1857, on trumped-up charges, which were never investigated, that, 'The community and in part, the civil government of Utah Territory are in a state of substantial rebellion against the laws and authority of the United States,' the Secretary of War, John B. Floyd, ordered federal troops to move against the Territory. Cumming, a native of Augusta, Georgia, who, among other posts, had served as Superintendent of Indian Affairs on the Upper Missouri, was appointed by President Buchanan to succeed Brigham Young as Governor.

Receiving no official notification of these plans, Young chose to regard the troops as a hostile mob. He immediately declared martial law and activated the territorial militia, the Nauvoo Legion, promising that ,'If the army advanced into the territory, the Mormons would make a Moscow of every settlement, and a Potters field of every cañon.' Fortunately, wiser counsels prevailed, and a compromise settlement was eventually brokered with the President's approval. Even so, as a matter of diplomacy, Cumming avoided socialising with his predecessor, except on public occasions.

After dining with the Governor, several visitors later dropped by at Salt Lake House, the hotel where Burton was staying. Amongst them were Mr and Mrs Stenhouse. A Scotsman by birth and a journalist by profession, Elder Stenhouse was Burton's almost daily companion throughout his stay at Salt Lake City, and provided him with a great deal of information. Burton was struck by the strength of the man's faith, his utter conviction, 'that Mormonism is and must be true to the exclusion of all other systems.' He saw it as 'an instance of how the brain of man can, by mere force of habit and application, imbue itself with any idea.' Burton found his wife, Fanny, a charming, cultivated woman, able to speak excellent French.

On this particular occasion, the conversation turned to a discussion of plural marriage, 'and for the first time,' Burton wrote, 'I heard that phase of the family tie sensibly, nay learnedly, advocated on religious grounds by fair lips.' All this was a matter of some considerable irony given Mrs Stenhouse's real views at the time of which Burton was unaware, and the fact that, a little under a decade later, both she and her husband were to be numbered among the most famous, or notorious, of Mormon apostates.

Born at St Helier, Jersey, in 1829, Fanny Stenhouse had followed her parents into the Mormon Church, after attending a meeting in Southampton, addressed by a young missionary, Elder T.B.H. Stenhouse. After a short courtship, they were married on 6 February 1850. It was not until three years later, however, that she became aware of the 'revelation' of "Celestial Marriage," announced in the *Millenial Star*. 'I felt bitterly,' she later wrote, 'that this new doctrine was a degradation to woman, and I wondered why God should see fit to humiliate my sex in this way.'[46] Despite hating polygamy, she was in no position at this stage of her life, to question the divinity of its origin.

Her husband's subsequent embracing of the Godbeite heresy and his excommunication from the Church on 26 October 1869, at last gave Fanny the opportunity she needed to break from the Mormon faith. In 1872, having moved to New York with her husband, she was persuaded to bring out a pamphlet, *Polygamy in Utah*. Its success resulted in its being expanded two years later into the highly popular exposé, *Tell it All*. First issued in Hertford and Cincinnati, with a short introductory preface by Mrs Harriet Beecher Stowe, it went into several American editions before being published in England in 1880, as *An Englishwoman in Utah: The Story of a Life's Experience in Mormonism*.[47]

Having followed strict etiquette by first meeting with Governor Cumming, Burton was granted an interview on 30 August with the man he had really come to meet, President Brigham Young. After shaking hands 'with complete simplicity of manner,' Young invited Burton to be seated on a sofa at one side of his private office, and presented him to the five members of his inner circle of advisers.

Born in Vermont in 1801, but looking far younger than his fifty-nine years, Burton described the Prophet as, 'a well-preserved man,' with scarcely a grey hair in head. He was dressed much like a Quaker in grey homespun, its plainness set off with a decorative cravat and waistcoat. Simple and courteous in manner, he 'showed no signs of dogmatism, bigotry, or fanaticism.' He was known to eat simply and frugally. His favourite food was baked potatoes with a little butter-milk, washed down with water. Although portrayed by his enemies as 'hypocrite, swindler, forger, murderer,' no one looked it less. He was, in Burton's view, 'the St Paul of the New Dispensation: true and sincere, he gave point and energy, and consistency to the somewhat disjointed, turbulent, and unforeseeing fanaticism of Mr Joseph Smith; and if he has not been able to create, he has shown himself great in controlling circumstances.'[48]

At the end of an hour, the conversation beginning to flag, Burton rose, shook hands with all concerned and took his leave. He left with the impression, 'that the Prophet is no common man, and that he has none of the weakness and vanity which characterise the common uncommon man.'[49] This was a view shared by his French predecessor at Salt Lake City, Jules Remy, who thought that 'every impartial mind, knowing how difficult it is for any one of us to determine what is truth, will class him in the rank of great men, in the rank of those extraordinary men who appear at distant intervals, now to confer upon nations a benefit, now to serve as a scourge....'[50]

The conversation had ranged over a number of topics during Burton's hour-long interview with Brigham Young. Not wishing to give offence, however, he had deliberately avoided broaching the subject of the Prophet's own marital arrangements. The movement's founder, Joseph Smith, had reportedly said of Brigham Young, that "he could eat more eggs, and beget more children, than any man in the state of Illinois." According to Jules Remy, Young had a seraglio of seventeen women of various ages, one of them whom he had seen by chance in his garden, being strikingly beautiful. The number of his children, however, was unknown. In the preceding spring he had nine born to him in one week.[51] The subject, of course, was a gift to professional wits and raconteurs. Following his visit to Salt Lake City in 1864, the humorist, Artemus Ward, remarked in a lecture, that he 'undertook to count the long-stockings on the clothes line in [Brigham Young's] back yard one day; and I used up the multiplication table in less than half an hour.' The present scholarly estimate is that, ultimately, Young had twenty-seven wives, although he was eventually 'sealed' to around fifty more women, and had fifty-six children.

Burton admitted to approaching the subject of plurality with despair, 'so conflicting are opinions concerning it, and so difficult is it to naturalise in Europe the customs of Asia, Africa, and America, or to reconcile the habits of the 19th century A.D. with those of 1900 B.C.' He pointed to the widespread notion, particularly prevalent in England even among the educated, that the Mormons were Communists; that wives were held in common, and that a woman could have as many husbands as the husbands have wives. Nothing, in fact, was further from the truth. Their two mortal sins were adultery and the shedding of innocent blood.

As was usual among polygamists, the first wife was *the* wife, and assumed her husband's name and title. Her 'plurality partners' were called sisters. The first wife was married for time, the others were sealed for eternity. The practice was a direct result of the Mormons' literal interpretation of Scripture, coupled with a belief that a woman was unable to enter the heavenly kingdom without a husband to introduce her. There were also socio-economic factors involved: a need to increase the population, and the fact that servants were both rare and costly. It was cheaper, therefore, and more comfortable, Burton remarked, to marry them. In fact, many female converts, he claimed, were attracted to Mormonism by the prospect of becoming wives.

The result was that, what he called, 'the choice egotism of the heart called Love, subsides into a calm and unimpassioned domestic attachment: romance and reverence are transferred, with the true Mormon concentration, from Love and Liberty to Religion and the Church.'[52]

Much of this, undoubtedly, would have been wormwood and gall to Fanny Stenhouse and those of her persuasion, who had experienced the faith from within. She did not feel an inferior being, 'designed by the Lord for the especial glory and exaltation of man,' nor did she 'feel herself honoured if he would only make her the mother of his children – a creature who if very obedient and faithful throughout all the trials and tribulations of life, might some day be rewarded by becoming one of her husband's queens, but should even then shine only by virtue of the reflected light derived from the glory of her spouse and lord.'[53] In polygamy, as far as she was concerned, love died a natural death; it did not subside into a tender attachment. Nor was it anything but galling to a woman's pride to have it said that she had been cast aside for another.

It is only fair to point out, that many of these supposedly down-trodden women held a diametrically opposite view. In 1870, some three thousand Mormon women crowded into the Salt Lake Tabernacle, to protest against those not of their faith daring to criticize polygamy. One of the speakers was Emmeline Wells (1828-1921), a leading figure in Mormon politics and a powerful and tireless advocate of women's rights. "The world says polygamy makes women inferior to men – we think differently," she told the cheering crowds. "Polygamy gives women more time for thought, for mental culture, more freedom of action, a broader field of labor....[and] leads women more directly to God, the fountain of all truth...."[54]

Burton passed the following Sunday reading the Books of Mormon and of Moroni the Prophet. He struggled to get through more than a few chapters at a time, finding it 'monotonous as a sage-prairie.'[55] This was also the experience of an earlier English visitor, William Chandless, who found it 'hopelessly dull.' Mark Twain, naturally, gave it a humorous twist, describing it as 'chloroform in print.' In his view, 'If Joseph Smith composed this book, the act was a miracle – keeping awake while he did it was, at any rate.'[56]

One of Burton's favourite places of resort was the Historian and Recorder's Office, which contained a small collection of volumes, papers, both official and private, designs and other important documents, many of them written in the Deseret alphabet. Staying for around an hour, he made voluminous notes on the main factors which had affected Mormonism within recent times, besides asking questions about the country and its economy. 'At the office,' he wrote, 'the undying hatred of all things Gentile-federal has reached its climax; every slight offered to the faith by anti-Mormons is there laid up in lavender, every grievance is carefully recorded.'

During his third week, Burton went on a number of excursions. He also paid a visit to Camp Floyd, where he found a great deal of anti-Mormon feeling. "They hate us, and we hate them!" exclaimed one of the officers, expressing the general opinion. Any objections Burton put forward were immediately countered by the claim that, 'whenever a stranger enters Gt. S.L. City, one or two plausible Mormons are told off to amuse and hoodwink him.' There were a number of reasons for the Army's rancorous feelings towards them. One stemmed from the murder on 26 October 1853 of Captain T.W. Gunnison of the corps of Topographical Engineers, and eight of his party, near Nicollet on the Sevier River. Anti-Mormons claimed that the deed was carried out with the connivance of 'White Indians,' to prevent the exploration of a route to California, and the disclosures which were likely to follow. In fact, their accusations were wholly unfounded. As Jules Remy pointed out, the Pahvant Indians were solely responsible for the savage attack, carried out in reprisal for the killing of one of their tribe, and the wounding of two others, by some emigrants on their way to California.[57]

This was far from being the case, however, with the infamous Mountain Meadows Massacre, which took place four years later. Accepting that it was 'unfortunately too true,' Remy on this occasion asked, 'but is it not rather giving too great a fling to hatred to attribute without proof this horrible crime to the Mormons disguised as Indians?[58] Burton, as well as printing a somewhat erroneous account of the massacre from the anti-Mormon point of view, also included the Mormon denial 'that the massacre was committed by their number,' with their questioning 'the Gentiles why, if such be the case, the murderers are not brought to justice?'[59] As emerged later, the reason was simple: a deliberate cover-up by the Elders of the Church, and wholesale deception.

On 7 September 1857, 120 men, women and children of the Fancher wagon-train passing through southern Utah on its way to California, were cold-bloodedly murdered by Paiute Indians and Mormons at a remote grassy area called Mountain Meadows. "Thanks be to the Lord God of Israel," one of the Mormons, John D. Lee, is reported to have said, "who has this day delivered our enemies into our hands." It is not known how much Brigham Young was initially told of this infamous incident. While it was privately discussed, all open reference to it was suppressed. "The more you stir a manure pile," he is later said to have told a friend, "the worse it stinks." Publicly everything was blamed on the Indians. It was not until 1870 that Brigham Young, under pressure, excommunicated Lee, though secretly protecting him. When he was later arrested, orders were given that no Mormon should testify against him at his trial. At his second trial, Young ordered Mormons to cooperate. Lee, an unfortunate scapegoat, was found guilty, and on 23 March 1877 was executed by firing squad at the site of the massacre.[60]

Burton's sick-leave was due to expire on 16 October. It was vital, therefore for him to obtain a further six months' extension. During his visit to Camp Floyd, he had obviously brought up the matter with a Dr Porter, to whom he was introduced. Unfortunately, the doctor proved 'uncommonly and unnecessarily shy upon the subject of a "sick certificate."' This posed a tricky problem. Burton's claim in one part of his narrative that Salt Lake City was 'well provided with disciples of Aesculapius,' is not borne out by what he wrote later, nor by other visitors. William Chandless was told by one of his special acquaintances, a Mormon doctor on the plains, that the Mormons did not encourage doctors at all, considering '"administering" (i.e. anointing with oil, &c.) more efficacious.'[61]

Fortunately for Burton, the physician in question, W.F. Anderson MD, proved more amenable than his army counterpart in issuing him with a certificate. Even so, it was not strictly in accordance with the rules, requiring two signatures and the counter-signature of HBM's consul as proof that the signatures were genuine. 'But the signer was the only M.D. in the place,' he remarked, 'H.B.M.'s nearest consul was distant about 600 miles, and to suggest that a gentleman may be quietly forging or falsifying his signature is to incur an unjustifiable personal risk in the Far West.'

Around the middle of September, Burton began making plans for departure. He had already written letters to a number of his friends, including one to Norton Shaw, 'who read out the missive *magno cum risu audientium*.'

Salt Lake City, Deserat (sic), Utah Territory, Sept.7

My Dear Shaw,

You'll see my whereabouts by the envelope; I reached this place about a week ago and am living in the odour of sanctity, – a pretty strong one it is too, – apostles, prophets, et hoc genus. In about another week I expect to start for Carson Valley and San Francisco. The road is full of Indians and other scoundrels, but I've had my hair cropped so short that my scalp is not worth having. I hope to be in San Francisco in October and in England somewhere in November. Can you put my whereabouts in some paper or other, and thus save me the bother of writing to all my friends? Mind, I'm travelling for my health, which has suffered in Africa, enjoying the pure air of the prairies, and expecting to return in a state of renovation and perfectly ready to leave a card on Muata Yanoo, or any other tyrant of that kind.[62]

Burton's companions for part of the return journey, were to be an old acquaintance, Judge Flenniken, his son Thomas, and the Territorial Marshal, Mr Grice. For the sum of $150 each, Mr Kennedy, an Irishman, who was just about to drive thirty-three horses and mules to San Francisco had agreed to convey them, to provide an ambulance and three wagons. He had also promised to collect an adequately armed party. The marshal undertook to arrange their provisions for the journey. After spending his last night as the guest of the Stenhouses, Burton set out south the following day, 20 September, for Camp Floyd.

During his five days there as the guest of Captain Heth, besides enjoying an excursion to Timpanogos Canyon, Burton managed to meet up with an old Mormon, O. Porter Rockwell. Looking much like a jovial, devil-may-care English ruffian, Rockwell pulled out a dollar, and sent to the neighbouring distillery for a bottle of Valley Tan. It was 'smuggled in under a cloth,' Burton said, 'as though we had been respectables in a Moslem country, and we were asked to join him in a "squar' drink,"' that is, neat. A lot more squar drinks followed. Hearing that Burton was preparing for California, he advised against his taking the direct route, describing it 'as fit for travelling as hell for a powder magazine.'

Leaving Camp Floyd on 26 September, Burton and his companions spent their first night at a farmhouse, the guests of Mr Smith, marshal Grice's predecessor in office. Before settling down to sleep, they were entertained by a number of "shooting stories": that in and about Carson, Nevada Territory, a dead man for breakfast was the rule; that apart from accidents, there were no less than fifty murders per year. 'In a peculiar fit of liveliness an intoxicated gentleman will discharge his revolver in a ball-room, and when a "shyooting" begins in the thin walled frame houses, those not concerned avoid bullets and splinters by jumping into their beds.'

After a day spent resting and stocking up on certain necessities at Carson City, Burton introduced himself to Captain Dall, superintendent of the Ophir mines at Virginia City. Located astride the Comstock Lode, the biggest deposit of silver ore discovered in the history of mining, Virginia City had grown from a tiny scattering of houses to a city in less than two years, complete with gaslight, stock exchanges, theatres, churches, and forty-two saloons. Under Captain Dall's guidance, Burton spent the next two days inspecting the aptly-named Ophir Mine, the Comstock's richest. Lying along a claim nearly a quarter of a mile in length, it was priced by land speculators at an incredible $4,000 per foot.

With good horses, it was possible to travel by stage-coach from Carson City to San Francisco in two days. Mr Kennedy, however, wanted to see Burton safely to the end. The judge, in his turn, had entrusted him with looking after his son, Thomas, as far as Sacramento. Burton decided, therefore, to cross the Sierra Nevada Mountains by easy stages. Two days after reaching Diamond Springs and visiting the gold-diggings at Placerville, he left by coach for Folsom, from where he travelled by railroad to Sacramento. After cashing a bank draft and settling some outstanding debts with Mr Kennedy, he said his farewells and boarded the steamer *Queen City*. An eight- hour trip down the Sacramento River brought him finally to the 'El Dorado of the West.'

Burton spent ten pleasant days at San Francisco. Although plenty of tourist attractions remained to be seen, by this time he had had his fill of travelling. Besides, there was a presidential election in progress, and he wanted to see with his own eyes, 'the working of a system which has been facetiously called "universal suffering and vote by bullet."'[63] Despite numerous invitations, he politely but firmly declined 'to lecture upon the subject of Meccah and Medinah, Central Africa, Indian cotton, American politics, or everything in general.'

Leaving San Francisco on the 15th November, Burton arrived at a miserably wet, dull, and dirty Panama a month later. A visit to the acting Consul, however, resulted in his being introduced to the Military Governor, and to 'a charming country-woman, whose fascinating society made me regret that my stay could not be protracted.' Three days later, he was en route by train across the isthmus to Aspinwall (present-day

Colon). An adverse wind delayed the ship taking to him St Thomas, the vessel reaching the Danish settlement only just in time to connect with the *Seine* from New York. Fortunately, the voyage to England proved uneventful until the ship came within sight of Land's End, where it encountered a gale, followed later by a pea soup fog. As result, it was forced to cruise about for three days in the Solent and Southampton Water before being able to dock.

CHAPTER TWENTY-FOUR

MARRIAGE

So far, it had been one of the coldest winters on record. The Serpentine in Hyde Park, thickly coated with ice, became one great fair, covered with tents. At night the lake was lit up with blazing fires cooking chestnuts, the flaming torches of large numbers of skaters, and exploding fireworks. Despite heavy snowfalls in many eastern counties, rail services had not been affected.

Trailing a mountain of luggage, and chaperoned by her brother, Rodolphe, Isabel took the train from King's Cross some time in December, to spend part of the festive season with her relations, Sir Clifford and Lady Constable. Burton Constable, their seat in east Yorkshire, was one of the most splendid of the baronial halls of England. Like most of the great country houses, it was also a place of unbounded hospitality, especially at Christmas.[1]

During one of the evenings' celebrations, according to Isabel, a large number of guests were amusing themselves by singing around the piano, when someone propped up the music with *The Times* which had just arrived. In yet another example of that alleged serendipity so beloved by Isabel, the first announcement that caught her eye was that, "Captain Burton had just arrived from America." Notice of his ship's imminent arrival had actually appeared in the newspaper on Friday, 28 December.[2] However, as we have seen, it was three days' late in docking.[3] The announcement which Isabel read, therefore, did not appear until Tuesday, 1 January 1861:

> The Royal Mail Company steamship, *Seine*, Captain Richard Revett, arrived at Southampton yesterday.....
> The *Seine* brought 79 passengers among whom were Commander H.J. Evans, RN, from Jamaica; Captain R.S. (sic) Burton from California....

Her, ostensibly, fortuitous glimpse of this announcement, however, is unlikely to have happened in the way she described. News of daily shipping movements appeared on the paper's inside pages, in this particular case, page 7, column 5. It could only have been read, therefore, by someone who was *deliberately* turning to this page, and searching for this particular item.[4]

She found it difficult to carry on normally. Once given the opportunity, she retired to her room, where she spent the night packing, and racking her brain to think of a convincing excuse to account for her leaving. There were some twenty-five friends and relatives, including her brother, in the house, and she had masses of luggage. The surrounding countryside was blanketed in snow, and it was nine miles to Hull station.

However, in spite of learning of Burton's arrival only early in the evening, twelve hours later, we are led to believe, she had eventually hit on the idea of arranging for a telegram to be sent, ordering her back to London, 'under the impression that it was of the most vital importance.'

Burton's biographers, though puzzled, have swallowed Isabel's story, one writing that no one will ever know exactly how she achieved it.[5] The simple fact is, that she did not, since there were no telegraphic facilities at Hull until around a decade later.[6] The truth possibly is, that in the absence of any letters from him, Isabel had been instructed by Burton before his departure for America, to look out for news of his arrival in England in *The Times*. They would then meet at a prearranged rendezvous. When, eventually, she did come across the announcement, she left in a rush without worrying too much about whether her excuses were convincing or not. It was only very much later, when writing about this period of her life, that she felt the need to give her actions a fictional gloss.

She said nothing about her departure from Burton Constable, her parents' reaction to her precipitate return home, nothing about where, when, and how she and Burton met in London that same day. There was, obviously, much more to what happened, than Isabel was prepared to disclose. 'What a triumph it is to a woman's heart,' she enthused later, 'when she has patiently and courageously worked and prayed, and suffered, and the moment is realized that was the goal of her ambition.' It is far from certain, however, that it was the goal of Burton's ambition. Nothing that we know of his character and behaviour up till then, suggests that he was suffering from love, that 'choice egotism of the heart', as he had lately defined it in the manuscript of his journey to the States. In Isabel's rather stagey version, however, Burton is supposed to have said:

> I have waited for five years. The first three were inevitable on account of my journey to Africa, but the last two were not. Our lives are being spoiled by the unjust prejudices of your mother, and it is for you to consider whether you have not already done your duty in sacrificing two of the best years of your life out of respect for her. If *once* you *really* let me go, mind, I shall never come back, because I shall know that you have not got the strength of character which *my* wife must have. Now you must make up your mind to choose between your mother and me. If you choose me, we marry and I stay; if not, I go back to India and on other Explorations, and I return no more. Is your answer ready? I said, "Quite. I marry you this day three weeks, let who will say nay."[7]

Whatever the truth, what had hardly been a whirlwind romance, suddenly became a whirlwind marriage. Isabel wanted to be married on Wednesday, 23 January, because it was the Espousals of Our Lady and St Joseph. Burton is said to have objected to this day, and to the Friday, because they 'were our unlucky days.' The marriage, therefore, was fixed for Tuesday, 22 January. Isabel went straight to her parents, and told them what had happened. Her father, all too familiar with his wife's views and temper, and married long enough to have mastered the fine art of marital diplomacy, said, "I consent with all my heart, if your mother consents." Predictably, Mrs Arundell said, "Never!" Equally intransigent, Isabel replied that she intended marrying Burton whether her mother liked it or not. No doubt taken aback by this new feisty Isabel, Mrs Arundell offered her the compromise of marriage with her father and brothers only being present. Isabel rejected it out of hand as being a slight not only on Burton's family but herself.

Without further ado, she called on Cardinal Wiseman at his London home at 8 York Place, Portman Square.[8] Wiseman, long on familiar terms with the Arundell family, having ascertained that Isabel's mind was absolutely made up, told her to leave the matter in his hands, and invited Burton to call on him. There is every reason to believe that the two men got on like a house on fire. There had never been anything of the ascetic about Wiseman, who had a 'lobster salad, as well as a spiritual side,' according to F.W. Faber.[9] Not only was he highly sociable and a man of the world, he was also an Oriental scholar, who had been appointed to the chair of Oriental languages in Rome University at the early age of twenty-five. Like Burton, he was a brilliant linguist, reputed to be able to speak at least half a dozen languages, among them Arabic and Persian, and had been a member of the Royal Asiatic Society since its foundation.[10]

Wiseman asked Burton to give him three promises in writing, which he did: that Isabel would be allowed the free practice of her religion; that any children of the marriage would be brought up as Catholics; and that the ceremony would be conducted in a Catholic Church. Wiseman then sent for Isabel. She claimed that he promised her his protection, the procuring of a special dispensation from Rome, and that he would perform the wedding ceremony himself.

Isabel was probably being deliberately misleading, in claiming the need for a special dispensation from Rome. Under Catholic law, mixed religion known rather quaintly as an 'impedient impediment' required dispensation. However, the Bishops of England and Wales at that time had powers under what were called the 'quinnennial faculties' to dispense from this without intervention from Rome.[11] As to Wiseman's performing the ceremony, he was not then in the best of health. The once slightly built scholar had become a mountain of a man, his 'Immense,' as he was once reputedly called by one of his Irish parishioners, racked with heart problems and diabetes. He had returned from Rome in the summer of 1860 after another illness and operation *en route* in Paris. He now lived mainly in the country at Etloe House, Leyton, where he had spent his convalescence in the autumn of that year.

Wiseman then saw Mr Arundell, who explained how bitter his wife was about the affair, that she was threatened with paralysis, and had to be given every consideration. It was agreed, therefore, amongst the family, that, to avoid a quarrel, the wedding should be kept a secret. None of the family would be present, and Isabel would be attended only by friends.

She spent the remaining weeks preparing for her marriage making, unlike most brides-to-be, 'a very religious preparation, receiving the Sacraments. Gowns, presents, and wedding pageants had no part in it, no place.' In her devotional book, she wrote that, 'The Principal and leading features of my future life are going to be, "Marriage with Richard. My parents' blessing and pardon. A man-child. An appointment earned by literature and publishing. A little society. Doing a great deal of good. Much travelling."' She was aware of having 'undertaken a very peculiar man; I have asked a difficult mission of God, and that is to give me that man's body and soul. It is a grand mission; and after ten years and a half of prayer God has given it to me.'[12]

Isabel then set out seventeen rules for her guidance as a wife, among which were: 'Let you husband find in you a companion, friend, and adviser, and confidante; attend much to his creature comforts; allow smoking or anything else, for if you do not, *somebody else will*; improve and educate yourself in every way, that you may enter into his pursuits, and keep pace with the times, that he may not weary of you; be prepared at every moment to follow him at an hour's notice and to rough it like a man; keep up the honeymoon romance...do not make prudish bothers which only disgust, and are not true modesty; perpetually work up his interests with the world; hide his faults from every one and back him up through every difficulty and trouble, but with his peculiar temperament advocate peace whenever it is consistent with his honour before the world.'[13]

Peace, however, was presently not on the cards. If Burton was unaware of the turmoil he had created by his critical remarks on Speke and others in the *Lake Regions*, he had some inkling when he was shown a highly critical letter by Shaw, which Rigby had addressed to the RGS on 10 October 1860. Burton's reply was bitter and scornful, claiming that Rigby's 'virulent attack' had been motivated, not by a sense of public duty, but out of personal spite.[14]

There had been other angry reactions to remarks in the book, of which Burton was unaware. Stung by criticisms of the conduct of the Somali Expedition in Captain R.L. Playfair's *A History of Arabia Felix or*

Yemen,[15] Burton had launched a bitter attack on the Aden Residency, making three specific charges against it: that the Political authorities, by their coldness and active jealousy, were responsible for the tragic disaster at Berbera; that Playfair had officially published a deliberately false account of it, and that the consequent inquiry was held in his, Burton's, absence, and without his knowledge, and its findings secretly forwarded to Government.[16]

These allegations drew an immediate response from Playfair.[17] 'The unscrupulous statements of this officer,' he wrote scathingly in a long letter to the Bombay Government, 'may usually be disregarded, but where a distinct charge is made against a public office, it is necessary to expose its falsity.' He went on to rebut each charge in detail. He pointed out that Burton had been given unstinted help both by Sir James Outram and his successor, Brigadier Coghlan. Furthermore, that the evidence of Burton's own servants, without regard to others, backed up his, Playfair's, contention, that insufficient precautions were taken against possible surprise attack,[18] and that Burton's claim that an enquiry was instituted in his absence, was completely untrue. The expedition, as Playfair observed, 'returned from Berbera on Sunday, 22 April, the investigation commenced on the 24th in open court in presence of Lt Herne, especially appointed by Captain Burton to watch the proceedings. He, then left on the 25th by the steamer *Ganges*, and the Court's findings were forwarded to the Bombay Government 'in the regular course with Brigadier Coghlan's letter No.63, dated 7th May....'

Since he had based his case on official documents, Playfair asked to be allowed to publish his letter in the columns of *The Athenaeum.* Permission was refused, the Hon the Governor in Council considering it inexpedient, 'to permit Captain Burton's statement in his recent work to draw the Government or any Government officer into a controversy in a public print.' It was thought sufficient to assure Captain Playfair, 'that Government considers his vindication of the proceedings of the authorities at Aden to be complete.'[19]

Speke, whose character and achievements had also been denigrated in Burton's book, wrote to John Blackwood from Bagamoyo on 1 October 1860. He had 'heard today from Rigby.....that Burton had published some bitter things concerning myself in allusion to the lake expedition, and I must now say that if he has been impinging my honor in any way, I shall be very sorry that I have glossed over many of his trans-actions in the late papers which I sent to you for publication....If the spirit of Burton's victims could only raise their voices in England now and tell their tale without a fault,' he wrote with unwonted eloquence, 'what strange rebukes would appear against the would be injured man who injures without scruple yet feels more sensitively than most other men.'[20]

Isabel left Oxford Square by cab at nine o'clock on the morning of her wedding, ostensibly to visit a friend in the country. Instead, she drove to 26 Osnaburgh Street, Regent's Park, the home of Dr Bird and his sister, Alice.[21] The Birds, knowing the strength of Mrs Arundell's opposition to the marriage, had consented to Isabel's being married from their house, to 'throw the mantle of respectability' over it, and prevent gossip about its being a runaway match. Here, Isabel changed into a fawn-coloured dress, a black lace cloak, and a white bonnet, and together they drove to the Royal Bavarian Chapel in Warwick Street.[22] Burton was already waiting at the door, dressed against the bitter cold in a rough shooting jacket, with a cigar in his mouth, 'bravado,' according to his niece, 'to hide his deadly nervousness on taking such a step.'[23] He had, apparently, informed his sister of his impending marriage only days before the ceremony.

As Burton went in, Isabel was delighted to see that 'he took holy water and made a very large sign of the Cross.' The wedding ceremony was conducted after all, not by Cardinal Wiseman, who was ill, but by the Rector, the Rev Dr Edward Hearne, with Thomas Smith, the Registrar, in attendance. By Lord Hardwicke's Marriage Act of 1753, no one could be legally married except by a Church of England minister. The Marriage Act of 1836, however, permitted religious ceremonies in Catholic or Protestant dissenting places of worship, which would be legally binding provided the Civil Registrar was present.

The ceremony over, the couple returned with the Birds to their house for a simple lunch. They then 'went to Richard's bachelor lodgings,' consisting of a bedroom, a dressing-room, and a sitting-room, 'and we had very few pounds to bless ourselves with, but we were as happy as it is given to any mortals out of heaven to be.' Burton, of course, had no 'bachelor lodgings' other than those in the East India United Service Club in St James's Square, which was given as his place of residence on the marriage certificate. He had, therefore, taken rooms for them in Bury Street, a short distance from the square along King Street. Given that she was mistress for the first time in her life of her own establishment, in which she professed to have enjoyed so much happiness, it is odd that she felt the need to suppress its location. Not only did she avoid mentioning it in her biography, she also gave instructions to her publishers, Chapman and Hall, to ensure that the name of the street was made illegible in the reproduction of the letter which Burton wrote to her father the following day:

'My dear Father,

I have committed a highway robbery by marrying your daughter Isabel at Warwick St. Church and before the Registrar – the details she is writing to her mother.

It only remains to me to say that I have no liaisons of any sort, that the marriage is properly legal and "respectable." I want no money with Isabel: I can work, and it will be my care that time shall bring you nothing to regret.[24]

If Georgiana Stisted is to be believed, Burton's marriage 'upon which much misplaced sentiment has been lavished, surprised both friends and relatives; those who knew him best were perfectly aware that it surprised him most of all. He was past forty, for some years he had had no serious *affaire de coeur*, and he invariably declared in his private circle, in answer to occasional enquiries, that he intended to remain a bachelor – principally from inclination, and partly because his limited means and roving habits were unsuited for matrimony.'[25]

The implication is that Burton, somehow, was steam-rollered into marriage. He, himself, is supposed to have suggested as much. "I am surprised," said his cousin, Dr Edward J. Burton, speaking to him a few days later, "to find that you are married." "I am myself even more surprised than you," was the reply. "Isabel is a strong woman. She was determined to have her way, and she got it."[26]

If this is correctly reported, it is probably nothing more that Burton's drollery. Nothing that we know about him suggests that he could be forced into doing something to which he was opposed – especially something so permanent as marriage. He appears to have thought little, if at all, of Isabel, during his years of exploration and travel. The history of their 'romance' given only from her perspective, in which fact and fantasy are interwoven, poses an insoluble problem. This is further compounded by a lack of knowledge about Burton's own sexuality. Did he marry for love? Given his own pronounced egocentricity, could he even feel such an outgoing passion, or was it for him, a marriage of convenience, the time at last being right when an alliance with Isabel, and through her the Arundell family, with friends in high places, could prove useful in forging a new career?

In spite of what Burton is alleged to have said to Isabel, he was well aware that he had slammed the door on future explorations as a result of his recent conduct and criticism of the East India authorities. What was now staring him in the face were years of peace-time soldiering in India, and a painfully slow climb up the promotional ladder. As Dr Johnson said of hanging, such a sombre prospect must have concentrated Burton's mind wonderfully.

While living at Bury Street, Isabel was visited by her brothers who kept her informed of affairs at home. Some weeks later, according to Isabel, two of her aunts, Mrs Strickland-Standish, and Monica, Lady Gerard, got to hear that she had been seen going into bachelor quarters in London, and lost no time in passing on the news to Mrs Arundell. She in turned contacted her husband who was visiting in the country. He, allegedly telegraphed back, 'She is married to Dick Burton, and thank God for it.' At the same time he forwarded Burton's letter which, obviously, had been deliberately written in the first place to cover for his having known all along about the marriage.[27] In an accompanying note, he asked his wife to send one of their sons to fetch the couple, and to receive them properly.

This, we are led to believe, Mrs Arundell did. 'My mother behaved like a true lady and a true Christian,' Isabel wrote. 'She kissed us both and blessed us...and then mother embarrassed us very much by asking our pardon for flying in the face of God, and opposing what she now knew to be His will.' Burton, supposedly, was very touched. 'It was not long before she approved of the marriage more than anybody, and as she grew to know him, she loved him as much as her own sons...'[28] This, of course, was emphatically denied by Georgiana Stisted who claimed that, almost the last time she saw Mrs Arundell, 'she exclaimed in answer to some remark from her daughter, "Dick is no relation of mine."'

In her earlier *Reminiscences*, Georgiana reported that both Isabel and Burton 'stayed with us at Dovercourt in Essex almost immediately after their marriage, spending the rest of the winter and spring between that place and London.'[29] In her biography of Burton published five years later, however, she told a different story. She now claimed that shortly after his marriage, Burton 'fell ill with severe bronchitis, and leaving his wife to break the news to her people, and see how they were disposed to receive him, he went to Dovercourt, the home of a wealthy aunt for rest and careful nursing.'[30] In deciding which version is nearer the truth, we have to remember that both women had an axe to grind. Nevertheless, as we shall see later, other independent evidence shows that Burton was at Dovercourt throughout March and April, something which Isabel deliberately concealed. It also sounds more in character. It is not necessary, however, to accept Georgiana's reason for his being there. What is more likely, is that Burton found the Bagshaw's spacious house in Orwell Terrace, Dovercourt, looking out to the North Sea, a far quieter and more congenial place to work at his book, than the small flat in Bury Street.

The financial situation of the couple at this period has been variously discussed by their biographers. Of the earliest, W.H. Wilkins stated that, Burton 'had a small patrimony, and his pay; in all about £350 a year.'[31] According to Georgiana Stisted, 'When his wife's debts and his own were paid, Burton only had four thousand pounds remaining from his little patrimony, a sum which prudently invested in a joint annuity, brought in about £200. Besides 'this majestic income', there was his half-pay.[32] Thomas Wright, on the other hand, never averse to inventing when facts were unavailable, claimed that 'Burton was not without means, for on the death of his father he inherited some £16,000, but he threw his money about with the recklessness of an Aladdin.'[33] In our own time, some biographers have chosen one or other of these sources to draw on. Others have used a pick-and-mix technique to arrive at their figures.

The plain fact is that we don't know how much money they had. What can be stated with certainty, however, is that Thomas Wright's figure is ludicrous, even from the evidence of his own book. While writing on one page that Burton inherited £16,000, he quotes a letter on another from Burton to his cousin St George Burton, in which he writes, 'Had the old man left me his money or any chance of it, I should have applied for permission to take up the old family baronetcy.'[34] As J.N. Burton's will shows, he did not leave a penny to either of his sons, nor were their names even mentioned in the document. Instead, his personal estate amounting to between £1,000 and £1,500 was to be put in trust for his two grand-daughters, Georgiana and Maria Stisted.[35]

If the couple had any money worries they were quickly dispelled, when, 'Through the kindness of Lord

John Russell,' Isabel wrote, 'Richard obtained the Consulship of Fernando Po, in the Bight of Biafra, with a coast line of six or seven hundred miles for his jurisdiction, a deadly climate, and £700 a year. He was too glad to get his foot on the first rung of the ladder, so though it was called the "Foreign Office Grave", he cheerfully accepted it.'[36]

Throughout the nineteenth century, consular appointments were wholly in the private patronage of the Secretary of State for Foreign Affairs. Selection took place from a list of candidates in his possession. However, the only way of getting your name on the list, was either through being personally acquainted with the minister, or being recommended by some influential aristocrat or politician. As for Burton's getting his foot on the first rung of the ladder, there was no ladder in the Consular service, which lacked any system of promotion or rewards.

W.H. Wilkins wrote very sensibly that he could not 'take the view that Burton was ill-treated in not getting a better position; on the contrary, taking all the circumstances into consideration he was fortunate in obtaining this one...There is little doubt that even Fernando Po was given him through the influence of his wife.'[37] This was the view expressed some years earlier by the author of an article in *Vanity Fair*, who stated that it was actually Isabel herself who was directly responsible for Burton's getting the post.[38] In view of her later untiring efforts on his behalf, this is perfectly credible.

Writing to Milnes about his appointment from Dovercourt on 20 March 1861, Burton described Fernando Po as 'a kind of Juan Fernandez affair off the Bight of Benin, touching which the British sailor sings:

> Beware and take care of the Bight of Benin,
> There's one comes out for forty goes in.[39]

Needless to say I have gratefully accepted it. The dog that refuses the Governmental crumb shall never be allowed by a retributive destiny to pound with his teeth the Governmental loaf.' He went on to say that he wished to be retained upon the cadre of his Corps:

This is the case with Capt. Rigby, H.M.'s Consul at Zanzibar. And was the case with Mr. Cole at Jeddah – to quote no other names. They may quote against me the obsolete rule that the meridians of the Cape and Egypt are the furthest western points (from India) where no Indian officer can accept detached employment and yet remain in his regiment – but the objection would be ridiculous in this our day. Only, you see, there is nothing obsolete in official matters.

The book progresses apace – a month will see it among the Almanacs of Pat.Row. Every day brings with it a sense of relief, and a little load of matter lifted off the brain. I shall remember your advice, all the evidence shall issue from Mormon mouths, and be received with philosophical calmness and stoical serenity.[40]

Later in the month, Burton received official notification of his consular appointment from the Foreign Office. He was informed that he was restricted from trading, that his salary would commence ten days prior to his leaving for Fernando Po, and that he was granted a sum of £165 towards the expenses of his outfit and passage.[41]

He was also told to lose no time in taking up his appointment. This was thought to be particularly necessary, since his predecessor, T.J. Hutchinson, had been relieved of his post following serious allegations by a Mr Cheetham, a supercargo in the Old Kalabar River.[42] Earl Russell had appointed two naval officers to inquire into these charges on the spot. Meanwhile, Hutchinson had left his post on the urgent plea of sickness. Russell was anxious 'that a new Consul should be sent as soon as possible to Lagos and Fernando

Po as we now have no Consuls in the Bights.'[43] This was easier said than done, as a letter of 18 August 1860 from the FO to the Admiralty made clear. 'It is extremely difficult to find a fit person to be Consul at Fernando Po. The same difficulty occurred on Mr. Beecroft's death.[44] The best person would probably be some lieutenant in the navy who has been employed on the African coast.'[45]

Despite his instructions, Burton was in no hurry to leave. His book was still unfinished and Isabel, who had been living with her parents all this time, obviously wanted him to stay as long as possible.[46] This was particularly the case, since he had decided that Fernando Po was too dangerous for her to accompany him. 'Under normal circumstances,' as he remarked some years later, 'Equatorial Africa is certain death to the Englander. I am surprised at the combined folly and brutality of civilized husbands who, anxious to be widowers, poison, cut the throats, or smash the skulls of their better halves. The things can be as neatly and quietly, safely and respectably, effected by a few months of African air at Zanzibar or Fernando Po....'[47]

Burton had been a member of the East India United Service Club in St James's Square, almost from its inception. Now, some time around April-May, he was elected to the prestigious *Athenaeum Club*, the resort of almost everyone of note in the literary, scientific, and artistic world.[48] Surprisingly, in view of Burton's bitter attack on Speke, he was proposed by Speke's patron, Sir Roderick Murchison, and seconded by Richard Monckton Milnes.[49] If Burton was to lose connection with the Indian Army by his acceptance of the consulship of Fernando Po, he would need a club when in London. This, of course, is precisely what happened. The reasons, however, put forward successively by Francis Hitchman, Isabel, and W.H. Wilkins, for his being struck off the Indian Army List, are totally false. Even so, they have never been questioned by later biographers.

Allegedly basing her account entirely on Burton's own notes, Isabel set out his case at length in *The Life*, blaming his supersession on the 'mingled malice and meanness of his enemies.' Despite its being the common practice in times of peace, 'for Indian officers to be allowed to take up appointments and still remain on the cadre, temporarily or otherwise,' his acceptance of this miserable post was made the excuse for striking his name off the Indian Army list. 'He received no notice whatever, and he only realised, on seeing his successor gazetted, that his military career was actually ended, and his past life become like a blank sheet of paper.......they swept out his whole nineteen years' service as if they had never been, without a vestige of pay or pension. '

She then printed an undated letter, ostensibly written by Burton at the time, the contents of which directly contradicted her claim only a few lines earlier, that he had received no notice whatever, and would name no names.'[50]

So, what actually occurred? On 4 March 1861, Major Stock, the Acting Adjutant-General of the Bombay Army, wrote a letter to the Secretary to Government, Military Department:

Sir,

I am desired by the Commander-in-Chief to request you will bring under the notice of His Excellency the Honorable the Governor in Council the names of the undermentioned officers of the Bombay Army whose prolonged absence from their duty in England renders it extremely improbable that they can ever be expected to render efficient service, and his Excellency begs that under these circumstances a report may be made to the Right Honble. The Secretary of State for India, with a view to their being removed from the Army or subjected to a medical examination before they are permitted to return to India.

Burton was one of three officers named. The reply to the Inspection Report Question: "Has any officer been absent from duty for an unusual length of time?" ran as follows for Burton:

Lieut. Burton has performed but little duty in the Regiment and scarcely any in the Country. He has been on sick leave to England 3 or 4 times and once to the Neilgherries for protracted periods.

It will appear that out of a period of 18 years and 128 days Service, this officer has only performed 9 years & 18 days duty in India. Much of his time has been occupied in Foreign travel, and in making pilgrimmages (sic), the result of which has been to him the loss of health and the loss of his service to the Government of India. It seems, therefore, to the Commander-in-Chief hardly just to the army, that an officer who employs himself in this manner should be kept on its effective strength.[51]

Copies of the reports on the three officers concerned, were sent with a covering letter from the Military Department, Bombay, on 20 March 1861, to the Secretary of State in London. His reply to the Governor in November of that year, was as follows.

Sir,

With reference to para.4 of your despatch No.33 dated 20th March last in which you drew attention to the long periods which Captain R.F. Burton has been absent from his duty in India, I have to inform you that in July last that officer was desired to wait on the Examining Physician, who reported that he would probably be fit to return to India at the expiration of his leave of absence, *Captain Burton was accordingly informed that if he failed to arrive in India by the expiration of this leave, his name would be struck off the list of the Army* [my italics]. This officer having accepted the appointment of Consul at Fernando Po and proceeded to that place cannot arrive at Bombay before the date of the expiration of his leave of absence. His name must therefore be struck off the list of the Army from that date.[52]

Accordingly, Burton's name was removed from the Army List on 27 October 1861.

This was still several months in the future. On 5 June, Burton breakfasted at 16 Upper Brook Street, Milnes's town house, where he had his first meeting with the up-and-coming young poet, Algernon Swinburne. The two seem to have immediately taken to each other, though it would have been difficult to find men so physically dissimilar – Burton, tall, dark, and powerfully built, Swinburne, a tiny figure, with sloping shoulders, rigid back, and a large head crowned with a mass of violent red hair, set on a slender neck. 'Burton, who was by sixteen years Swinburne's senior,' Edmund Gosse wrote, 'was a personage of virile adventure, the hero of mysterious exploits in Asia and Africa; he was al-Haj Abdulla, the enchanted pilgrim who had penetrated to the holy city of Mecca. He represented in action everything of which Swinburne only dreamed.'[53]

According to Isabel, she and Burton had a 'glorious season.' Monckton Milnes settled the question of their position 'by asking his friend, the prime minister, Lord Palmerston, to give a party, and to let me be the bride of the evening.' Palmerston had sold his house in Carlton Gardens in 1855, and bought Cambridge House overlooking Green Park. The Saturday evening parties held there were glittering events, invitations to them being eagerly sought after. As the guests arrived, they were received by the Palmerstons at the top of the great flight of steps, Lady Palmerston looking regal in her diamonds and wearing the latest fashion in crinolines. It was more likely to have been one of these to which Isabel was invited, rather than one laid on especially in her honour. When she arrived, 'Lord Palmerston gave me his arm, and he introduced Richard and me to all the people we had not previously known, and my relatives clustered around us as well.'[54]

It was Queen Victoria's strict rule, not to receive anyone at Court who had made a runaway marriage. Isabel's initial concern, however, that her marriage with Burton might be regarded with disapproval proved groundless, and she was allowed to put her name down for a Drawing Room. Soon after 2 o'clock on 19 June 1861, Queen Victoria and Albert, accompanied by the Princess Alice, arrived at St James's from

Buckingham Palace attended by the Ladies and Gentlemen in Waiting. The Royal Body-Guard of the Honourable Corps of Gentlemen at Arms was on duty in the State Saloons. The Queen, in mourning for her mother, the Duchess of Kent, who had died three months earlier, was wearing a black paramatta train with a deep trimming of black crape, her head-dress formed of a black crape veil, covering a jet black tiara. After the introduction of the Foreign Ambassadors and Ministers the presentations took place in the Throne Room. Altogether, there were 211 ladies who had the honour to be presented to the Queen. Among the first group, consisting of recent brides, was 'Mrs Burton on her marriage, by Lady John Russell.'[55]

The happiness of the event was clouded soon afterwards, when Burton and Isabel lost practically all their possessions in a fire at Grindlay's Warehouse, except for the few boxes they had with them. 'The worst was that all his books, and his own poetry, which was beautiful,' wrote Isabel, especially one called "The Curse of Vishnu," and priceless Persian and Arabic manuscripts, that he had picked up in various out-of-the-way places, and a room full of costumes of every nation were burnt. He smiled, and said in a philosophical way, "Well, it is a great bore, but I dare say that the world will be none the worse for some of those manuscripts having been burnt." (a prophetic speech, as I now think of it). When he went down to ask for some compensation, he found that Grindlay was insured, but he was not – not, he said, that any money could repay him for the loss of the things.'[56]

Early in July, Burton read a paper to the Ethnological Society on M. du Chaillu's explorations in Equatorial Africa. Paul Belloni du Chaillu, born in France in 1835, had spent many of his early years in the Gabon, where his father acted as agent for Messrs Oppenheim. In 1832, aged only seventeen, he travelled to the USA with his natural history collection. As a result of a series of articles which appeared in the *New York Tribune*, he was sent on a mission to western Africa by the Academy of Natural Sciences.

The explorations which he carried out between 1855 to 1859, resulted in further valuable zoological collections, as well as extending geographical knowledge of a little-known country. A popular account of his travels had recently been published in London.[57] It was enthusiastically received by the general public, particularly for its accounts of the, then, little-known gorilla. In fact, it proved so popular, that a second edition was called for in June, 1861, and a third in July. It was, however, severely criticised by a number of distinguished zoologists and geographers. The former questioned many of his statements as to the natural history of the country explored. They also refused to accept his claims as to the habits and ferocity of 'that remarkable ape, the fierce and untameable gorilla,' as he called it,….'whose unconquerable ferocity has made it the terror of the bravest native hunters – an animal, too, of which hitherto naturalists and the civilised world knows so little, that the name even was not found in most natural histories.'[58]

Du Chaillu had arrived in England early in 1861. In his Preface to the First Edition, he acknowledged the warm welcome he had received from various learned societies, particularly the RGS, which allowed its rooms to be used for his collection. Du Chaillu, however, was to have an unfortunate experience at the Ethnological Society's meeting, which he attended to hear Burton read his paper. Angered by, what he regarded as the insulting and provocative remarks made about him by one of its members, T.A. Malone, the volatile little Frenchman suddenly leapt to his feet, and physically attacked him. In mitigation of du Chaillu's conduct, Burton wrote to *The Times*, which had reported the assault, that Malone, 'adopted a tone and style of address which would have caused the coolest temper to boil over. My wonder is that M. du Chaillu restrained himself so long.'[59] Naturally, this timely and welcome expression of support, bought Burton from then on the friendship of du Chaillu.

The Foreign Office was rather less friendly. A week after this incident, Burton received a terse letter from Earl Russell, instructing him 'to make arrangements for proceeding to your post at once (this being circled in the draft) at Fernando Po.'[60] This was replied to by Burton the following day from the EIUSC, in another of his cleverly worded letters to buy time:

The next steamer for Fernando Po leaves, I believe, on the 24th prox. If Lord John Russell thinks my presence at my post is immediately necessary, I shall at once take passage.

But the 24th July will carry me into the heart of the unhealthy season – a bad beginning in tropical climates. If, therefore, I can be spared from my post I shall take passage for the 24th August and arrive in September when the rains – the only tolerable time in West Africa – are about to set in.[61]

I should mention that Sir Ronald Martin forwarded about 3 months ago a "sick certificate" to the Foreign Office advising me to remain in Europe till September next.

I hope that this will not be interpreted that any personal risk would deter me from setting out at once. If any mission to, or attack upon, Dahome be contemplated, I would willingly serve on it.[62]

On 18 July, after been kept waiting for almost fourteen months, Burton was finally informed that his request for reimbursement of the money he had paid out of his own pocket for the East African Expedition had been turned down. 'I can but conclude,' he wrote in reply,' that the representations, or rather misrepresentations of those whose interest it has been to prolong my absence from Zanzibar, have led to a conclusion by which I feel deeply aggrieved – namely the non-recognition of my services by the Secretary of State for India in Council. And I venture to express a hope that when the Civil proceedings which are now being instituted by me against Captain (local Lieut. Colonel) Rigby, British Consul at Zanzibar, come on for trial, this correspondence may be adduced to show how successfully this officer has exerted his malice against me.'[63]

Writing from the Adelphi Hotel, Liverpool, the day before his departure, Burton informed Monckton Milnes, that the proofs of the "Saints" 'had been corrected and my wife will take them up to Town the day after tomorrow. She will tell Longmans that you have been good enough to offer your assistance touching debated passages. Cut out as much as you please – amputation I feel is wanting.......My wife is fretting herself into a fever which, as you may imagine, adds greatly to the pleasure of departure.....

I left Cameron drunk, and Albany half sober. To keep up my spirits, I toyed with the last stanza now added to the other....

> On the twenty-fourth of May,
> 'Tis Her Majesty's birthday,
> And she gave us all a drawing-room accordion
> Then just at 2 o'clock
> Sir F-S- showed his –
> To the ladies on the other side of Jordan.'[64]

Burton would not allow Isabel to accompany him until he had seen what Fernando Po was like. 'I was to go out, not now, but later,' she claimed, 'and then, perhaps, not to land, and to return and ply up and down between Teneriffe and London, and I, knowing he had Africa at his back, was in constant agitation for fear of his doing more of these Explorations into unknown lands. There were about eighteen men (West African merchants), and everybody took him away from me, and he had made me promise that if I was allowed on board and see him off, that I would not cry and unman him.'

There was a high wind blowing at the docks, and it was pouring with rain. One man stuck to them like a leech the whole time, preventing them from exchanging a word. 'How I hated him!' Isabel went down below, unpacked Burton's things, settled his cabin, and saw to the arrangements of his luggage. 'My whole life and soul was in that goodbye, and I found myself on board that tug, which flew faster and faster from the steamer. I saw a white handkerchief go up to his face. I then drove to the spot where I could see the steamer till she became a dot.'[65]

CHAPTER TWENTY-FIVE

WEST AFRICAN ODYSSEY
Part 1

Nostalgia, Burton maintained, was 'a disease as yet imperfectly recognised. The only remedy – preventive there was none – is constant occupation of mind if not of body.' It was a recommendation he was to follow to the letter. Throughout the next four years, his pen was never idle. As well as writing lengthy despatches to the Foreign Office, he published five books, as well as a stream of articles on his African travels, which appeared in such outlets as the *Proceedings* and the *Journal* of the RGS, the *Anthropological Review*, the *Transactions of the Ethnological Society*, and *Fraser's Magazine*. And, of course, letters to *The Times* and *The Athenaeum*.

The first of his books, *Wanderings in West Africa*, was later worked up from the journal Burton kept aboard the ASS *Blackland* on his outward-bound voyage. Dedicated to 'The True Friends of Africa – Not to the "Philanthropist or to Exeter Hall,"' it is conspicuous, even by the standards of the time, for its cultural arrogance and the virulence of its attack, some of it highly personalised, on the Africans of the Guinea coast, especially the liberated slaves, as well as on missionaries and the philanthropic movement. Knowing that it would go down like a lead balloon at the FO, Burton hid his identity under the *nom de plume* of 'A FRGS.'

Passing off deep-seated personal prejudice as ethnology, he poured contempt on, what he called, the futility of the negro's claim to equality and brotherhood. 'From humbly aspiring to be owned as a man,' he wrote, 'our black friend now boldly advances his claims to égalité and fraternité, as if there could be brotherhood between the crown and the clown!'[1] In terms reminiscent of the next century's apartheid era in South Africa, he considered it a political as well as a social mistake to allow these men to dine in the main cabin. 'The white man's position, 'he declared, 'is rendered far more precarious on the coast than it might be, if the black man were always kept in his proper place.'[2]

He was, of course, fiercely critical of Sierra Leone, first colonised from Britain in 1787 by settlers of African origin, and then by liberated slaves from all over West Africa. Describing what was the main centre of Christian missionary activity on the coast as 'this unfortunate, mistaken colony,' he lambasted, what he claimed was, the negro's habit of using the law against the white man. 'The British Constitution,' he asserted, ' determines that a man must be tried by his peers......No one raises the constitutional question, are these half-reclaimed barbarians my peers?'[3] Africa's salvation, he contended, lay not with Christianity, but with Islam, which had 'taught the African to make his first step in moral progress, which costs so much to barbarous nature; and it thus prepares him for a steady onward career, as far as his faculties can endure improvement.'

Early on the morning of 27 September, a day short of five weeks after leaving Liverpool, Burton caught his first glimpse of Fernando Po. The largest island in the Gulf of Guinea, it had been discovered around 1472 by the Portuguese navigator, Fernão do Po. Impressed by its beauty, he called it Ilha Formosa, or Beautiful Island, though it was not long in becoming better known by the name of the discoverer himself.[4] High volcanic mountains rose steeply from the narrow coastal plain, most covered to their summits in dense forests, and sprinkled with craters and crater lakes. Highest of all, was Clarence Peak or Pico de Santa Isabel, soaring to well over 9,000 feet above the north central landscape.

The Portuguese had been forced to cede the island to Spain in 1778. However, its first attempts at colonisation failed. With Spanish consent, the British took over temporary administration of the island in 1827, finding it extremely useful as a naval base for its armed cruisers engaged in suppressing the slave-trade in the Bight of Biafra. In 1843, Spain reasserted its formal rights over the island, appointing the British-born resident, John Beecroft, as 'Governor.'[5] In fact, it was not until fifteen years later, that a Spanish governor was sent out.

'I had eyes for little else that morning,' Burton wrote. Facing him from the anchorage in Clarence Cove, was a steep cliff almost a hundred feet high, ascended by two diverging winding paths. Along the top he could see a scattering of about a dozen whitewashed and thatched bungalows, framed against a background of tall palms. 'Arriving in these outer places,' he wrote, 'is the very abomination of desolation. I drop for a time my pen, in the distinct memory of our having felt uncommonly suicidal through that first night at Fernando Po...'[6]

Port Clarence, or Sta Isabel, as it was known to the Spaniards, offered nothing by way of consolation.[7] Mary Kingsley who landed there thirty years later, found it the very dullest town she knew on the coast. An air of dereliction hung over its shabby weed-grown streets and its cemetery, where Richard Lander, the Niger's explorer lay in an unmarked grave.[8] Even sailors from the monotonous south coast, as Burton observed, 'felt the ennui of Fernando Po to be deadly – gravelike.'[9]

It is clear that he was determined from the outset, to spend as little time there as possible. 'People die off on this coast like madmen,' he informed Monckton Milnes a few months later, 'you would stare at the statistics. I have no such present purpose, and therefore keep moving, six weeks settled would kill me.'[10]Hardly had he arrived, therefore, than he set off on the small Intercolonial steamer for a 'flying survey' of the remaining Oil Rivers in the delta. By 2 October he was back on the island, stranded, as he put it, with 'nothing to do, and no prospect of doing anything.'

The situation was not improved by the extremely dilapidated state of the Consulate. Writing to the Foreign Office six days later,[11] Burton complained that no repairs had been carried out in the four years since it had been built. It was now scarcely habitable. The thatched roof leaked, flooding the floor after heavy rain. The fences, undermined by white ants, were lying flat on the ground. The outhouses were in ruins, and the foundations of the building, planted on underground posts, were so rotten 'that every violent tornado threatens to blow it over the cliff.'[12] Enclosing an estimate for repairs, totalling £344 17s 4d, 'drawn out with due economy', as he took care to point out, Burton asked to be allowed to proceed with the work before the onset of the next rainy season.[13] With it, he sent another despatch, asking to be supplied with a number of surveying instruments.[14]

James Murray, the Assistant Under-Secretary in overall charge of the Consular Service, scribbled perplexed minutes to both requests: 'Is there any precedent for this at Fernando Po?' Edmund Hammond, the Permanent Under-Secretary, thought not, turning down the request for instruments with a frosty, 'No,' believing 'it would be objectionable and undesirable to supply our consuls with such instruments. With the exception of the chronometer, the other things can count but little.'[15] The Foreign Office proved equally uncooperative over paying for repairs to the Consulate. Despite a protracted correspondence, Burton was eventually forced to pay £250 for the repairs out of his own pocket. The matter was settled some years later in a way neither party could have foreseen at the time.

One of the reasons Burton gave to the FO for the building's needing renovation, was that British cruisers frequently touched at Fernando Po, and that the officers derived considerable benefit from change of air and scene on shore. There was no place where they could lodge, except at the Consulate.[16] It was one of these cruisers that now provided Burton with a means of escape. The day after writing his despatch, he accepted the offer of a passage to Lagos from the Commodore and Senior Officer of the West African squadron. It was the nearest point, he later claimed, where he could obtain various necessities such as a cook-boy, kitchen utensils, and a carpenter.[17] This, of course, was a complete smokescreen. The real reason was his hope of joining a diplomatic mission to Abeokuta, then being arranged.

Leaving Edward Laughlan, secretary of the Glasgow firm of Taylor and Laughland, to keep an eye on things, Burton boarded HMS *Arrogant* on Thursday, 10 October. Four days later he arrived off Lagos, where he immediately transferred to HMS *Prometheus*, commanded by Commander Norman Bedingfield. Burton's explanation to the FO the following month, was that he had travelled there for the purpose of finding a gun-boat to enable him to make an official visit to the Oil Rivers. As to his becoming attached to a treaty mission which was none of his business, well – 'Commander Bedingfield, the Senior Naval Officer of the Bights Division, was proposing to visit Abeokuta, and I availed myself of his kind offer to accompany him...'[18]

This expression of gratitude to Bedingfield was not, however, matched in Burton's book where he spoke of him in sarcastic and pejorative terms.[19] Bedingfield, of course, could be arrogant and conde-scending. He had had a short and stormy association with Livingstone as his second-in-command on the Zambezi Expedition, three years earlier.[20] Nevertheless, Burton's later public comments were both tasteless and unnecessary.

He spent the first week or so at Lagos, recently annexed by the British, suffering from an attack of 'seasoning fever.' Once recovered, he passed the time at the Consulate with Mr M'Coskry, then Acting-Governor, preparing for the journey, and enjoying Muslim society. By this time, Burton had found himself a servant in the person of Selim Agha, a Nubian with lamp-black skin and Semitic features. After spending more than twelve years in Europe, chiefly at a Scottish school in Aberdeenshire, he had returned to Africa only four years earlier with the Niger Expedition. He would prove his worth in gold, becoming Burton's right-hand man.[21]

On 29 October, the party left for Abeokuta in two of the *Prometheus's* gigs. Although not mentioned by Burton in his book, he helped Bedingfield conduct a sketch survey of the Ogun or Abeokuta River, which was published the following year by the Admiralty.[22] The ascent of the river was completed by 1 November. Abeokuta ('refuge among the rocks') sited on its east bank, had been founded some thirty or so years earlier by Sodeke, a hunter and leader of the Egba refugees from the Ibadan area. As well as attracting others later, fleeing from the collapsing Oyo Empire, and from the civil war among the Yorubas, it was also settled during the 1840s by Anglican and Baptist missionaries .

While Burton's visit allowed him full scope to air his prejudices about Exeter Hall philanthropy and the negro he, nevertheless, made a number of interesting comparative ethnological observations. Missing nothing, he gave a detailed description of the clothing, head-dress, hairstyle, tattoos and ornamentation of the people, remarking that 'in this country every tribe, sub-tribe, and even family has its blazon, whose infinite diversifications may be compared with the lines and ordinaries of European heraldry – a volume would not suffice to explain all the marks in detail.'

He dismissed as nonsense much that been talked about the Dahoman Amazons, hundreds of whom had been killed in the battle of Abeokuta in 1851. In fact, they were simply the slaves of the palace organised as royal property, and armed by the late King Gezo, who feared treason from the men. He discerned a striking similarity in the conditions imposed on 'those poor deluded African women who are admitted to the priest-hood, and many of those nuns who in Catholic Europe are forced to take the veil.' Unable to resist a dig at Mrs Arundell, he described the former as being only 'instruments in the hands of fraud and oppression, while the others are too often the victims of domestic tyranny and ambition.'[23]

Little was known about Yoruban mythology. 'Like all these religions, if they could be called such, there is a vagueness and a variety of explanation which, despite the advantage of alphabets and of a far superior organization, appears strikingly the worship of ancient Greece and Rome, and of modern India.'[24] Witchcraft was common. Nevertheless, in his opinion, it had its good side. 'Where the dark places of the earth are full of cruelty, its vague terrors form a salutary check upon the violence of husbands and masters, rulers and criminals. It is the power, and the only power of the weak.'[25] Of course, where there was witch-craft, there were talismans. 'Here the Grigri, as it is barbarously called, is the prophylactic of the Jews, the amulet of Christian Abyssinia and Syria, the Cross and the Miraculous Medal of Southern Europe…A folio volume,' he said, 'with a side-long glance at Isabel, 'might be filled with these fooleries of faith.' He regarded them 'as the vestiges of that fetishism which is the first dawn of religion in the breast of the savage, and which cannot fail to crop out even from the enlightened surface of monotheism….In the present state of human affairs, faith appears a necessary evil, an inseparable weakness.'[26]

A new treaty having being signed on 7 November 1861, the party left Abeokuta the following day. That night they broke their journey at the village of Baragu. Sleeping-quarters once arranged, rum and gin were passed around, and 'the merriment waxed fast and furious….. Our hosts were perfectly civil and obliging,' Burton wrote slyly, 'and so were our hostesses – rather too much so I could prove, if privileged to whisper into the reader's ear. But what would Mrs Grundy say?'[27] What Isabel later thought and said, can only be imagined. Leaving early the next morning, they arrived back at Lagos after twelve days' absence. After spending a further eleven days at the Consulate, Burton left aboard HMS *Bloodhound* on 2 November for an official visit to the Oil Rivers.

Just over three weeks later, the shallow-draught paddle-steamer entered the Nun, or Niger River, where it spent a day lying off the new missionary station, recently founded by the Rev Samuel Crowther.[28] Besides being important to trade, the Niger, in Burton's opinion, was 'destined to become the highway of African exploration, and the means, if there be any, of diffusing light throughout the interior of the "Dark Continent."'[29]

Sailing eastwards along the coast HMS *Bloodhound* arrived at the Brass River, once one of the great slaving stations. 'Did you ever hear of the Brass River?' Burton asked Milnes in a long letter of 1 December. 'I am almost ashamed to write to you from the place.' He had volunteered by this mail, he said, to visit Idahumu (Dahomey), and 'to bring the king to a sense of his duty.' As for Du Chaillu, 'the nearer one approaches the Gaboon, the more contradictory become reports. I know far less about the matter than I did when in England, and this will last till a three months' leisure enables me to visit the place personally. Therefore, reserve judgement. As yet I see no reason to disbelieve him.'[30]

On 5 December, the gun-boat anchored down-stream in the Bonny River. 'Obani', or Grand Bonny, as it was better known, was not only the most important trading station in the Bights of Benin and Biafra, but in West Africa as a whole. Yet, despite Europeans having traded there for two hundred years, Burton remarked, 'the native is still but little less barbarous than in any part of the African interior known to us…..Cannibalism was undoubted, iguana worship endured, and the Juju-house presented the disgusting spectacle of victims' skulls alternating with goats in long line to form an altar, while their privities putrefied in the sun suspended to a scaffold hard by.'[31]

Three days later, after calling on the native chief, 'King Pepple,' Burton set off with members of the

Bonny Court of Equity to New Calabar River, for a visit to its friendly old chief, Amakree. Courts of Equity were associations of the leading black and white traders in certain of the Oil Rivers. The post of chairman was held by one of the supercargoes in monthly rotation. Disputes were heard before the court, which could impose fines on defaulters. The trade of anyone foolish enough to refuse to submit to its jurisdiction was boycotted. 'King Amakree,' as Burton's immediate predecessor had pointed out,' is the most independent king to be met with anywhere on the coast; and I believe he owes this reputation to the fact of his not taking goods on trust from any supercargo, nor allowing his people to do it, consequently maintaining his high position.'[32]

After almost three weeks spent touring the Oil Rivers, HMS *Bloodhound* steamed into Ambas, or Victoria Bay on 10 December, dropping anchor off the mouth of Morton Cove close to the Victoria Missionary Station.

As luck would have it, Burton had arrived at a favourable moment for carrying out his 'long-cherished project' of exploring the Cameroons Mountain. A somewhat absurd claim, given that before March of that year, he had no idea that he would ever land up in West Africa. Gustav Mann, a twenty-five-year-old Hanoverian botanist, working for the British Government, had climbed a few hundred feet of the mountain the previous year.[33] Pressure of time, however, had compelled him to give up, and he had returned to Fernando Po. He was now back in Victoria, preparing to make a second attempt on what, at well over 13,000 feet, was the highest peak in sub-Saharan West and Central Africa. As Burton needed to visit the Cameroons River, Mann, so Burton claimed, 'agreed to break ground as soon as possible, to botanize on the way, and to await my arrival before attempting the peak.' He later publicly accused the young botanist of bad faith. 'I must, however, do him the justice to say that he set off without delay and did his best to be number one; he failed, however, and failed signally, as the sequel will show.'

Burton left for the Cameroons River on the following day, which he described to the Foreign Office as 'perhaps the most troublesome spot on the coast.'[34] The trade was in a thoroughly disorderly state because Cameroons like Old Calabar was a "Trust" river, and the European traders could not, or would not, form a Court of Equity like that of the Bonny River. There were four chiefs, all of whom were currently engaged in blood feuds. Several such affairs, he said, still awaited his arbitration. He had summoned the three principal chiefs, and persuaded them with great difficulty to sign an additional article to a treaty concluded with them by his predecessor, Mr Hutchinson, in July 1859.[35] It was only when a gun-boat was permanently stationed in the Bight of Biafra, he contended, that the agreement would be kept.

The presence of missionaries was a further source of trouble. 'These employes are almost invariably of mechanic origin, come out to the country at an early age, settle for life in comfort, if not in affluence, going home to marry, and bringing out their families. They learn the native dialects, so they are consulted by the people when legal defence against the violence and arrogance of the European is required. On the other hand, the missionary who boasts that he "has the standpoint of Archimedes" must in duty oppose the custom of the people by sacrifices, their wars, their polygamy, and their systems of slavery.' Even so, 'he will strain every part beyond the limits of the most elastic conscience to protect, to shelter, and to secure the escape of a fugitive servile.'[36]

On 13 December, the tour came to an abrupt end, when thirteen out of fifty-five white members of the crew of the *Bloodhound*, besides the commander and chief engineer, went down with fever. The medical officer protested against an intended visit to Old Calabar, the Kom Toro and the Rio del Re, the last two of which Burton had been anxious to open. The ship left the Cameroons River, therefore, Burton promising to return soon in order to settle the blood money due upon the most recent murders. Late that same night he was back in Fernando Po. 'As usual there is nothing to do here,' he later wrote, 'the whole work of the Consul lies in the "Oil Rivers."'

Burton stayed only four days, just long enough to collect an outfit necessary for a month in the jungle. The Rev Alfred Saker, who had always wanted to explore the mountain, had already volunteered to accompany him. Burton now gained another companion in M. Atilano Calvo Ituburu, Assessor or Assistant Judge and Secretary to Government at Fernando Po.

On returning to the Mission Station, Burton discovered that Mann had set out in advance to wait for them at Mapanya, the highest village on that part of the mountain. When Burton and his small party reached it the following day, the young botanist immediately informed them that he had just returned from the summit. Faces fell at this announcement. However, it soon became apparent that the time he had spent in walking made it impossible for him to have reached that spot. Mann, in his own account of the climb, makes no mention of having made any such claim.[37]

Rather pompously, Burton later wrote of the climb that, 'It was hardly, however, the mere ambition of leaving my mark, to *faire époque*, on Western Africa, that impelled me to the task. The desire of adventure was subsidiary to higher views.' One of these was to demonstrate that the Cameroons Mountains was ideally suited not only for a sanitorium but also for a convict station.[38] He claimed to have found an ideal spot for the former situated at 7,000 feet. 'Of the 60,000 runaway negroes in Canada,' he said, 'give me but 300, and I will make a path practicable for mules at the end of the dry season. Pestilent Lagos will acquire a "sick-bay", and where can a Lebanon be found equal to the majestic Cameroons?' He believed that the rains were not heavy, 'and I doubt not, indeed, that they are lighter than those of the Himalayas and the Neilgherry Hills.'[39] Burton was woefully wrong. The seaward facing side of the mountain has a mean annual rainfall of 400 inches (10,000mm), and is one of the wettest places in the world.

The Rev Saker left on Christmas Day, promising to return early the following month. Mann, who had begun so strongly, had been confined for some time to his hammock with sickness. The judge and Burton, therefore, decided on a reconnaissance of the great mountain on 27 December. After an early start, they stood around midday on the rim of a crater, where they rested for a quarter of an hour. They broke the silence with a cheer, 'the first Europeans, certainly – probably the first men whoever stood within gunshot of the giant sugarloaf whose now extinguished fires caught the old Carthaginians' gaze.' An hour later, they began walking round the cone. Here, however, the judge stopped, looking at the sheer rock-face ahead. Judging it beyond his powers, he advised Burton to reserve it for another day.[40] 'Subsequents almost make me regret that I had been most obstinate, ' wrote Burton, 'but on second thoughts – no! to be the first is everything; to be second is nothing.'

He began the final ascent with a single Kruboy. As they neared the summit, the porter 'sank down with thirst-glazed lips and he was allowed to remain behind.' What is far more likely is, that he was ordered to stay where he was, so that Burton could claim the glory for reaching the summit alone. By way of recording his claim, he built a little cairn of stones, placing under it a page torn from *Punch*.

Although Mann showed no trace of animosity towards Burton in his paper for the *Linnean Society*, he complained privately to friends in England. Sir Joseph Dalton Hooker later told Darwin that Burton:

> has in a public despatch filched away all poor Mann's credit for the ascent of the Cameroons, calls it his expedition, planned and carried out by him, and calls Mann his volunteer associate.[41] I never read anything so gross in all my life. Poor Mann had set his heart on the thing for 2 years, had failed the first time and was actually leaving Fernando Po for the ascent when Burton arrived at Fernando Po as Consul, did leave, and had ascended the mountain several weeks before Burton, following him, was at its foot, having prepared the way and provided guides and everything. I am quite disgusted, but hardly know how to act. I dislike and despise the Geogr. Soc. way of going on so much, that I do not like to bring the matter forward there, and as to having a quarrel with Burton, we all know what it is to touch pitch.[42]

Mann's complaints appear not to have reached Isabel's ears until late in 1862. Writing to Norton Shaw, she asked him to send her a private note about Mann. 'The Laughlands called on me yesterday,' she wrote, 'W.A. merchants, and in conversation mentioned Mr Mann "as such a nice person and great friends with our Consul.." Is it your opinion Mann is deceiving him, pretending to be friends with him and writing privately against him? It's very dangerous to say anything to Richard he is so hot-tempered, and makes himself so disagreeable to anyone if he takes a dislike, that I would not without serious cause say a word.'[43]

Having foolishly set out in a pair of loose waterproof boots, which chafed his feet raw, Burton was unable to walk for a month. Around the middle of January, while still incapacitated at Spring Camp near the summit, he wrote a detailed report for the Foreign Office on his recent visit to the Oil Rivers.[44] He also enclosed a letter requesting leave of absence. 'The Governors of Sierra Leone and of Cape Coast Castle and the Consul at Lagos,' he claimed, 'are allowed for the benefit of their health, three months annual leave to Madeira. I venture to hope that your Lordship will be pleased to extend this privilege to me.........Hoping that your Lordship will be pleased to consider how much more work a beneficial change of climate for three months in the year – I have already undergone two attacks of fever and ague – would enable me to do during the other nine.'[45] This was tersely minuted by James Murray at the FO on 20 May, 'No such permission has ever been given to the Consul at Lagos as Captain Burton states.' He was informed accordingly.[46]

On Monday, 27 January 1862, the Rev Saker having returned from Victoria, the Union Jack was hoisted, and the last bottle of champagne drunk. To commemorate their visit, they left a slip of sheet-lead on which their names had been roughly scratched, and two sixpences in an empty bottle. What Burton called his Christmas holidays were now over. A visit planned to last a fortnight had turned into six weeks. On Friday, 31 January 1862, he left Spring Camp, arriving back at Victoria on 2 February. Two days later he was back at Fernando Po, too late to meet Winwood Reade, who was later to become a close friend and supporter. In his book, published a year or so later, Reade recalled visiting the Consulate, being 'disappointed of an interview with Richard Burton who was up the Cameroons...During the few days I spent at Fernando Po I was located at his house, and had at my disposal a library of which the profound and varied nature was an index to that great mind.'[47]

Since his leaving England, various commissions from Burton had come to Isabel by every mail. The most daunting, as far as she was concerned, involved her travelling to Paris to present the Emperor and Empress with the relics of Napoleon Bonaparte, which had come into the possession of the Burton family. These comprised a lock of his hair, preserved for forty years in a glass watch-case, which Burton had had set in a handsome ring, and a sketch of the plaster-cast taken after Napoleon's death. Isabel was also instructed to take a richly bound set of Burton's books, and ask for an audience.

Having spent Christmas, 1861, with her family, she arrived alone in Paris at the end of December, and took rooms at 10 rue Pauquet de Villejust, in the Quartier Chaillot, on the left bank of the Seine. She duly left her presents and a letter at the Tuileries Palace, and waited for the royal summons.[48] Meanwhile, she settled down to write a letter on behalf of her husband. As is clear, Burton had no compunction either at this stage in his marriage, or later, in allowing his wife to fight his battles for him. It has to be said, of course, that Isabel was a willing and energetic combatant, who left no stone unturned in pushing his interests.[49]

At the end of December, she wrote to Norton Shaw, informing him that 'Dick' had asked her to apply to Sir Charles Wood for a pension, and to retire from the Indian Army as major. Since she was writing to Sir Charles by the same mail, she asked Shaw if he could persuade Sir Roderick Murchison and Lord Ashburton to back his application. 'After all, you know,' she said, 'it is Richard's devotion to the RG Society that has lost him India.' On a separate sheet of note-paper, she wrote a brief and enigmatic note, obviously with reference to Burton: 'I have had sets of these sent me anonymously, but I found out and got the abusive one suppressed. It emanates as well as the other from a large body of people.'[50]

She was still in Paris on 11 January, when she wrote again to Shaw. She had just received a letter from Dick, informing her that he was well, that he had had a stormy passage on the journey out, and that Fernando Po was a stinking hole at present, but that he hoped to make something better of it soon. He had told her that there would soon be stirring work on the rivers, and that his work was not to be done without a gunboat at his orders, and there was a nice little craft in the Bonny River that would just suit him.

Isabel said she was going out soon, and that Burton was repairing the Consulate. There was no furniture, only the bare walls. However, there was lots of good to be done there to the place, which he was setting about at once, and 'I believe I am to find my share among the female population. Everyone knows that Fernando Po is the forlorn hope of the Foreign Office. Yet perhaps it is the place of all others where he will find the most to do.'

Later that day, she wrote again to Shaw, having received another letter from 'Dear Richard'. He was sending a long report to the RGS. Isabel asked Shaw if he would send a line to her mother at 13 Oxford Terrace. 'When might you read it at Burlington House as some of my family would like to attend?'[51] This suggests that Mrs Arundell was now, perhaps, not only reconciled to her son-in-law, but quietly proud of his achievements.

Nothing, if not persistent, Isabel once again returned to the subject of pension and promotion for Burton. As to the abusive memorandum, she wished to avoid anything that would be bad taste such as publishing it. Paris was very gay. 'But I am here on his affairs and refuse all invitations as I do not care to go out without him.'[52]

Nothing came of Isabel's visit to Paris. There was no summons to the Tuileries Palace, and the presents, though declined, were not returned. She returned home feeling snubbed and embarrassed by the affair, the needless loss of the heirlooms creating ill-feeling in the Burton family. She blamed herself at the time, attributing the failure of her mission to 'want of experience and protection.' A.B. Richards described the offer of the gifts as simply 'an act of civility.' This is to strain credulity too far. A certain *quid pro quo* must have been envisaged. This something was, perhaps a letter of recommendation from Napoleon III, which would help smooth Burton's path when given the opportunity of visiting the French colony of Gabon in search of the gorilla.

His chance came in March. In his book, recounting his experiences in Gabon, which was not published until 1876, Burton started *in medias res*. He, thus, avoided the necessity for explaining why he was able to travel so far outside his Consular jurisdiction, and on matters totally unconnected with his official duties. His excuse at the time, concocted for the Foreign Office, was that he had left for the Gaboon River to meet the British merchants there, in order to inquire into a fancied grievance concerning British vessels not being allowed to carry their own colours beyond the island of Coniquet at the head of the Gaboon River.[53]

Burton left Fernando Po on 15 March 1862 aboard HMS *Griffon*, which was taking the mails south. Two days later, the ship was off Le Plateau (Libreville), capital of the French colony. Dressed in his consular uniform, he went ashore to meet Baron Didelot, Commandant Supérieur des Établissements de la Côte d'Or et du Gabon, and M.H.S.L. L'Aulnois, Lt. De Vaisseau et Commandant Particulier du Comptoir de Gabon. His next step was to request the pleasure of a visit from Messrs Hogg and Kirkwood, who were in charge of the English factories at Glass Town and Olomi. Burton's trip to 'Gorilla-Land' was, of course, limited by the cruise upon which the *Griffon* had been ordered. However, this was soon overcome. Mr Hogg borrowed a rather dilapidated old boat from the Rev William Walker of the Gaboon Mission. After manning it with three of his own Krumen, and collecting the necessary stores and supplies, Burton was able to set out on 19 March – his 41st birthday.

Two hours later he landed at Denistown, where he met the local chieftain, Roi Denis, and read out his introductory letter from Baron Didelot. After listening to Burton's offers of dollars, liquor and cloth, Roi

Denis said that all his hunters were in the plantations. However, for an increased consideration, he would allow his own son, Ogodembe, alias Paul, to accompany him. This was agreed, and Burton left for Mbata, known as La Plantation by the French. Presently, Forteune, the chief huntsman appointed by Roi Denis to take charge of Burton appeared. He was a man of note in his tribe, boasting that he had slain with his own hand, upwards of a hundred gorillas and anthropoid apes. 'I regret to say,' commented Burton with mock-gravity, 'that this young nobleman ended his leave-taking by introducing a pretty young woman with a pert expression as his sister, informing me that she was also my wife pro.temp.' He was sufficiently taken with this young woman, to include a sketch of her in his book, and in a letter to Monckton Milnes.

Burton spent his first bush evening drinking palm-wine and rum. 'One must begin by humouring Africans,' he said patronisingly, 'under pain of being considered a churl.' This , of course, had hardly been a leading characteristic of Burton's explorations in East Africa. "Young Prince," under the influence of drink, 'hospitably offered me his daughter-in-law, Azizeh, Forteune's second wife. Forteune then hinted that perhaps I might prefer his daughter.' Undoubtedly for Isabel's benefit, Burton claimed that both offers were declined.

He had come to Mbata to shoot a specimen of the gorilla and, if possible, to catch a youngster. The presence of numerous villages and constant firing, however, had driven away all the wild animals from the nearby river regions. Furthermore, he was constrained by time from wandering beyond the coast. Seemingly, with no prospect of bagging a gorilla there, Burton set out for Nche Mpolo, the headquarters of the "Young Prince." This proved to be a further waste of time and effort.

In conversation with Mr Walker at Glass Town, Burton was told, what by now he already knew, that he had taken the wrong line, and that he should have run two or three days up the Rimbwe, the first large influent on the southern bank of the Gaboon. Burton, therefore, decided to ascend the 'Old' Mpongwe or Gaboon River, to visit 'the Fan of whose cannibalism such curious tales had been told.' From Paul du Chaillu's illustrations, 'I fully expected to see a large-limbed and ferocious-looking race, with huge mousta-chios and plaited beards.' Instead, he found 'A finely made, light-coloured people of regular features and decidedly mild aspect.'[54] Furthermore, the result of his own enquiries into cannibalism amongst the Fans, significantly differed from that of M. du Chaillu. Perhaps in an attempt to avoid offending the young Frenchman, he added the caveat that 'Mayyan is held by a comparatively civilised race, who have probably learned to conceal a custom so distasteful to all their neighbours white and black; in the remoter districts cannibalism may yet assume far more hideous proportions.'[55]

Even so, Burton's investigation was disappointing in its lack of the sensational. His host, Mr Tippet, who had lived three years with these people knew only three cases of cannibalism. The Rev Walker agreed with other authorities, that it was a rare incident even in the wildest parts. Burton believed that it was a quasi-religious rite practised upon enemies slain in battle, an equivalent to human sacrifice.

A short and abortive expedition up the Londo River, in a last attempt at shooting or capturing a gorilla, persuaded Burton to abandon his quest. On 22 April, he boarded HMS *Griffon* which had just returned from the south coast, and at noon, three days later, he was back at Fernando Po. There, he found two despatches from London waiting for him. One was on the subject of the Consulate repairs. The other directed him to investigate King Pepple's demand for £400 from the African Steamship Company, in respect of the company's hulk *William Money* in the Bonny River.[56]

Burton, however, was compelled to delay his enquiries, 'by an unwillingness to expose the crew of a British ship-of-war to the fearful sickness of the Bonny River.' The first case of yellow fever had broken out there on 14 March 1862, and extended far into the following year, the later ravages, according to Burton, being concealed in case seamen might be deterred from sailing there. One ship, the *Osprey*, lost all her European crew, comprising 17 men, the master alone surviving.[57] Conditions were even worse at New

Calabar, where 6 supercargoes and 169 out of 278 whites died. Only a short while after Burton had left for the Gaboon River, the disease had spread to Fernando Po, carrying off 78 out of 250 Europeans.

The day after his return, Burton wrote to Monckton Milnes, thanking him for a copy of his highly favourable article on *The City of the Saints*, which had appeared in the *Edinburgh Review* earlier that year.[58] He informed MiInes, that du Chaillu had written to propose a trading and hunting partnership. It was an offer, however, which he did not intend to take up. He had now seen the very narrow field of du Chaillu's exploits. The Fans were no more cannibals than the people of Bonny, and they buried their dead very decently. 'Substantially his account is founded on fact, but fiction improves all things.' This was essentially the verdict of Winwood Reade who had preceded Burton to the Gabon. He described du Chaillu's book as a medley of fact and fiction, remarking that he 'has written much of the gorilla that is true, but which is not new; and a little that is new, but which is very far from being true.' Reade criticised du Chaillu for having 'been induced to sacrifice truth to effect, and the esteem of scientific men for a short-lived popularity.'[59]

Following HMS *Griffon's* return to Fernando Po, Burton was informed that an Englishman had been assaulted by a native in the Old Calabar River, one that Burton had not yet 'officially' visited. The gunboat was again put at his disposal, and on 1 May, only five days after returning from the Gabon, Burton left again for the delta.[60] The Old Calabar River turned out to be chartless, buoyless, and without pilots, and the *Griffon* was nearly wrecked off 'Tom Shott's Points' by a shipmaster who volunteered to pilot them. Eventually, it anchored safely off Duketown on Sunday, 4 May.

A meeting of the white traders was called for the next morning to consider the re-establishment of a Court of Equity based on the articles of the old treaties concluded by the late Governor Beecroft and Mr Consul Hutchinson, in 1856. This was duly agreed. 'In the present state of the river,' Burton wrote in his long report to the Foreign Office, 'some such measure was called for, where affairs have literally been managed by the revolver for the last six months.' However, persuading King Archebong and his chiefs to append their signatures to the articles of the new Court of Equity, proved to be anything but an easy matter.

The *Griffon's* captain, Cdr Perry, had been advised by the Commodore to leave the river, if possible, after the fifth day. Burton had already spent four, and a month seemed in prospect. At the request of the supercargoes, therefore, he wrote to King Archebong that he was expected to sign the articles before noon of the next day, under penalty of Burton's taking extreme measures. After clearing out his house and preparing to slip away into the bush, King Archebong thought better of the affair. He and his chiefs came on board before noon of the following day, and signed without further trouble. Their example was followed by Tom Eyo, John Eyo, and the chiefs of Creek Town. Burton was now free to attend to the charge of assault, which had brought him there in the first place.

This cleared up, he then proceeded with Cdr Perry and the supercargoes of Old Calabar, to inspect several markets in the Cross River. Passing by Creek Town, Burton called upon the friendly old chief Tom Eyo, and with the approval of all the missionaries and supercargoes, placed a footman's gold-lace hat on his head, which converted 'Father Tom', said Burton, into "King Eyo Honesty IV."

Burton informed the FO that, as soon as the season opened, he intended to travel once more to Ibu and the upper markets, which he had briefly visited on 9 May, and personally superintend the opening of the Cross and Calabar Rivers. 'The tribes of "middlemen" who now infested the coast from Benin to Cameroons, ' he said, 'could no longer be permitted to bar the great highways which Nature has run into the African interior.' On Wednesday, 14 May, Burton left for the Cameroons River in order to investigate the alleged killing of natives by British traders. As a result of the latest incident, Burton raised the question with the FO of British consuls on the African coast being invested with magisterial powers in order to deal at once with similar cases. The FO replied that, before HM's Government could issue such an order in

Council, it was necessary for there to be some treaty or agreement with the chiefs of the country, consenting to such power being exercised within their jurisdiction.

With this in view, a despatch had been sent to Mr Consul Hutchinson on 25 May (year not filled in), enclosing a draft treaty which he was instructed to propose to the various chiefs within his consular jurisdiction for their acceptance. However, the only chiefs who, at the time, consented entering into such an agreement, were Eyo Honesty and King Archebong, the chiefs of Duke and Creek Town in Old Calabar. Burton was told that, if he thought that the chiefs in the principal trading rivers were now willing for HM's consul to have the power of dealing with offences committed by British subjects within their territories, he had permission to propose their entering into the necessary agreement with HM's Government for that purpose.[61]

Burton had been absent from Fernando Po for just under three weeks, and was now to spend the longest time on the island since his arrival. Shortly after his return, he sent a long despatch to the FO detailing his trip to the Old Calabar River, and another on the state of the Consulate.[62] He also found one waiting for him from the FO, commenting on his earlier report on his visit to the Cameroons Mountains. 'I doubt not your report is full of interest,' Murray observed, 'but in consequence of the illegible character in which it is written, I am unable to make myself acquainted with its contents.' Burton was asked in future, therefore, to write in a larger and more distinct hand.[63] Murray went on, however, to praise Burton for his zeal and spirit of adventure which had prompted him to this undertaking. It seemed calculated, in his opinion, not only to advance geographical science, but also to prove of political importance in suggesting a location where the health of Europeans might be recruited after the deleterious effects of the climate on the coast. Copies of the report would be circulated to the Admiralty, War Department, and Geographical Society. In view of the expedition's results, Burton was also granted the expenses he had asked for, although it was 'contrary to the strict rule of the office' not to allow these when prior permission had not been given.

The following month, Burton received further critical comments on the illegibility of his handwriting, and directed to send duplicates of certain despatches[64] By the same mail, he also received permission, when a man-of-war was not available, to use the African mail-packets to visit the rivers within his consular jurisdiction 'when such visits are indispensably necessary…but you must in each case apply for permission to charge the expenses, explaining the grounds for taking the voyage.'[65]

With unlimited leisure at his disposal, Burton occupied part of it in editing Captain Randolph B. Marcy's *The Prairie Traveller*. He also wrote to his close friend, the Hon Henry Murray. Addressing him as 'Venerable Villain and Helmsman,' his letter, as the three others to Murray which are extant, is racy, full of light-hearted banter and malicious comment. 'You are thank goodness and despite gout as virulent and abusive as ever…Do reform your manners, cease to harp upon car.cop [carnal copulation] and set not to us youths an example of long and prosperous iniquity…The fact is you are breaking down with regular habits. You want a little gipsying and sleeping in the bush. You require a spell of temperance, sobriety, and chastity.'

Tongue-in-cheek, he suggested that Murray try the clairvoyante he had had suggested to him as a cure, though, he went on, 'I don't believe in any of its systems…My wife sent me a flannel shirt which I was to rub and return to her. I rubbed it on an old goat in the yard. By return of post came a cwt [hundredweight] of medicine, and directions about restoring my poor chest. Now that's too bad. The old goat now coughs, and I'll swear by the gods that his lungs are as good as mine.'

The rest of the letter is sprinkled with malicious references to various people. Petherick he described as a 'model ass', and 'as for that treble donkey Speke, I hope by this time that he is decently devoured by jackals.' Referring to Rigby as one who 'never could keep his hands from picking and stealing and his temper from evil-speaking, lying and calumny,' he promised to 'settle affairs with him some day.' As for

Thomas Hughes, author of *Tom Brown's Schooldays*, he was 'an earnest jackass, a kind of Tom Brown without the hair.'[66]

Having been marooned on Fernando Po for an unprecedented ten weeks, Burton had arranged to travel to Prince's Island off the coast of Gabon, aboard HMS *Bloodhound* , ostensibly for the benefit of his health. On 21 July, however, he hurriedly changed his plans following a visit to the Consulate by a Dr Henry, a merchant in the Benin River. According to Burton's anonymous account published the following year in *Fraser's Magazine*, Dr Henry's factory, during his absence from the river, had been attacked by 200 armed slaves led by a chieftain named Akabwa. Mrs Henry, threatened with rape and death, was forced to take refuge in a neighbouring factory. As a result of her ordeal, 'she fell ill with fever' and died of nervous depression on 11 June. Her husband, 'eager to punish his wife's murderers', visited Fernando Po in person, 'and on application easily persuaded HM's Consul so far to fall foul of "etiquette" as to undertake in a place beyond his jurisdiction the task of redress for, if not of active punishment.'[67]

Later, Burton concocted a different story to justify his actions to the Foreign Office. After describing the attack on the factory, he was at pains to point out that Mrs Henry was an Englishwoman, and that Dr Henry 'was unable to return and look after his property without my aid.' Moreover, 'he and Captain White only 10 days before his making the application to me, had saved Messrs Horsfall's establishment at the risk of their lives.' Therefore, 'The case being urgent, I resolved to attend to it though out of my jurisdiction, thinking that business of a higher importance had prevented his Excellency the Governor of Lagos visiting the Benin River.'[68]

Burton immediately wrote an urgent requisition to the *Bloodhound's* captain, Lt Cdr Stokes, 'whose feelings on the subject were equally excited.' The cruiser left on the night of 31 July, steaming the 270 miles through a succession of squalls, and dropping anchor off the Benin River three days later. On 5 August, Burton summoned the supercargoes and agents, together with Idgare, alias Governor Jerry, and his chiefs. The latter, 'after the usual prevarications, refused to come on board the *Bloodhound*.' All the white men in the River unanimously signed a request that trade should be stopped, as the only means of apprehending Akabwa.[69] The following day, Burton wrote to the FO and the Governor of Lagos, reporting the thoroughly disorganized state of the river.

On 7 August, a boat was despatched to catch the mail at Lagos, a hundred miles away. In the meantime, Burton and Lt Cdr Stokes decided to utilise the time before its return, in visiting the celebrated city of Wari. Unknown to them at the time, the boat was capsized and Mr Rigg, a West Indian, who was in charge of it was drowned. The crew was seized by the people of the Coast, belonging to the same tribe as the offenders, and held in captivity until a ransom was paid.

Wari was reached after nineteen hours of rowing, a short survey of the route being made on the way.[70] They found the place fallen into ruins since the death of King Elusa in 1848. A wooden cross in the jungle was the only trace of the once-celebrated Portuguese mission. 'Singularly wild and strange this emblem arose from a thicket of grass surrounded by dense jungle...hard by stood the usual ju-ju house...suggesting signs of the difficulties with which the Cross has to contend with in these lands where Nature runs riot...it has fought a good fight, but hitherto with signal failure.'[71] They interviewed Elusa's eldest sons, Chamwana and Ayaowu, whom the traders in the river had represented as capable of taking their father's place, and re-establishing a strong government. When, however, the affair of Akabwa was brought up, they pleaded their inability to deal with one so powerful.

After a late dinner Burton and his party retired to rest. 'The people of Wari and Benin,' he said, 'are touchy about and jealous of their wives....On the other hand, they are no less free with the other members of the family, sisters and daughters, and they appear to take offence if these ornaments of the house are not duly admired. We were often signalled by the men of the village, who nodded significantly to dark apartments: it is unnecessary to say that the offers were politely declined.'[72]

No message having been returned from Lagos, Burton decided in conjunction with Lt Cdr Stokes, Dr Henry and Captain White, to visit the city of Great Benin, whose king in past times had been the most powerful sovereign of Yoruba. On 17 August, after rowing for seventeen hours, they reached Gwato, the burial place of the great Egyptologist, Giovanni Belzoni. 'Many of the oldsters remembered the traveller,' Burton said, 'and talked admiringly of his huge black beard, his gigantic strength and his mighty stature – 6ft 6ins.' However, before he could set out for Timbuktu, he had contracted dysentery from drinking bad water, and died on 3 December 1823. He had been buried at the foot of a very large tree, but no one now knew where his grave was. Burton, therefore, had to be content with making a sketch of the tree, and sending home a handful of wild flowers.[73]

In the early part of the century, Gwato had contained many European factories. Now there was not one. The group passed the night there, and set out the next day, walking for nine hours and then sleeping in the bush. On 19 August, after a march of two hours over the worst of paths, they entered the city. When the usual preliminary visit had been paid to the 'Captain of War,' the dignitary next in rank to the king, they were led to their quarters. 'One of the first objects that met our sight was a negro freshly crucified after the African fashion, sitting on a stool with extended arms, lashed to a framework of poles. I fear it was in honour of our arrival.'[74] Benin, Burton said, had the smell of blood, and stank of death. 'Without any prepossessions for Exeter Hall policy, and far from owning that evangelization has succeeded, or ever will succeed in this part of Africa, I could not but compare the difference between Abeokuta, where there are missionary establishments, and Benin, which for years has remained a fallow field.'[75]

Near the outer gate of the palace was 'the form of a fine woman, seated and lashed hand and foot to a scaffolding of rough branches which raised her ten or twelve yards from the ground. The birds had been busy with her eyes, part of her bosom had been eaten away, and the skin was beginning to whiten..' In Africa, Burton wrote, 'the divinity that doth hedge a king, is a demon in a chamber of horrors.'[76]

On 21 August, having had two audiences with the king, they left Benin City, and reached the river the next day, where they heard of the loss of the despatch boat. Without special orders it was impossible for the *Bloodhound* to remain any longer. Moreover, it became evident as Burton later informed the FO that, without adopting the strongest measures, the outrage would remain unpunished. 'The Beninese have learned to despise Europeans.....Of course, out of my jurisdiction, I could not undertake any forcible measures.'[77] The *Bloodhound* steamed for Lagos on 27 August. The following day Burton landed, and reported the whole transaction to His Excellency, the Governor. However, 'a sharp attack of fever prevented my writing these details to your Lordship.'[78]

Waiting for him on his return to Fernando Po on 4 September, was a despatch from the FO, granting him two months' leave of absence. The draft carried a memo: 'I presume this means on full salary?'[79] According to *The Romance's* flawed version of events, this leave owed much to Isabel's worrying about a rumour that Burton was keeping a seraglio in Fernando Po. 'One day in October, when she could bear the loneliness and separation from her husband no longer, she went down to the Foreign Office, and cried her heart out to Sir Henry (then Mr.) Layard.'[80] Touched by her plight, Layard went upstairs, presently returning to say that 'he had got four months' leave for Burton, and had ordered the dispatch to be sent off that afternoon.' Isabel was so overcome, that she 'had to go and sit out in the Green Park till the excitement wore off; it was more to me than if he had given me a large fortune.'[81]

Isabel may well have gone to the Foreign Office, and acted as described. Her visit, however, could not have taken place in October, since the FO despatch is dated 22 July 1862. As to the sending of despatches, this of course was governed by the sailing times of the African Steamship Company. Furthermore, as can be seen, the length of leave awarded to Burton was only half that stated by Wilkins. It was copied by him from

The Life, where it was manufactured to give credence to what eventually happened.[82]

A week after Burton's return, he left in HMS *Bloodhound* for a visit to Batonga, one of the small centres of trade to the south under his Consular jurisdiction. After visiting the supercargoes, and hearing their grievances, Burton and Lt Cdr Stokes set off early on 15 September to climb the so-called Elephant Mountain. Soon afterwards, Lt Cdr Stokes suffered an attack of ague and fever. Even worse was to follow. On returning to the ship, they found that the commander's steward, whom they had left slightly unwell, had died of yellow fever, and was awaiting burial. Without waiting for an investigation to be carried out, Burton helped Stokes on board and at noon, on the 18th September, HMS *Bloodhound* stood out to sea in heavy weather.[83]

Three days after arriving back at the island, Burton forwarded to the Foreign Office an extract of orders recently issued by the Officer Commanding the West African Squadron to his naval commanders, on the proper use of gun-boats. 'You are to consider that it is only when British life and property are in jeopardy…..that you would be justified in despatching a vessel of war up the rivers and creeks. It is with reference to this state of affairs, and this only, that you will be guided in complying with or rejecting the requisitions of consuls for passage to these localities.' Although referring to consuls in general, Commodore Edmonstone's order, as Burton well knew, was aimed directly at him. 'I respectfully submit to your Lordship,' he wrote in his accompanying despatch, 'that under such circumstances, it is difficult for me to superintend, and much more difficult to advance trade in the rivers under my jurisdiction, and it requires little foresight to perceive that if the Bight of Biafra be left without a cruizer permanently stationed there, the export slave-trade will soon revive.'[84]

Before making his way to Madeira, Burton paid a previously postponed visit to the Bonny River to investigate a complaint made by the African Steamship Company against King Pepple, described by Burton as 'about the damndest scoundrel unhung.' The Foreign Office had sent him a reminder in July, asking him to report as well on two further matters there.[85]

One of these was, that Burton should discuss the subject of human sacrifice with King Pepple, at the same time informing him that HM's Government had no intention of giving political support. However, as Burton later pointed out, King Pepple had been absent from Bonny Town during this visit. Furthermore, the steamer stayed for too short a time for him to hold 'palavers' with the chiefs. More importantly, he was not on board an English cruiser. 'As was truly said by my predecessor, "A Consul's moral force without a ship-of-war is a moral farce." Nothing would be easier than to compel the Bonny people to forego the open display of cannibalism and human sacrifice, but it might be necessary to use strong measures. On the other hand, as the case of Abeokuta proved, it would be impossible to prevent such sacrifice. Such prevention sounds to an African as absurd as the "abolition of Christianity" to a European.'[86]

After an official tour round the 'Oil Rivers', Burton left his Consular jurisdiction on 7 November. According to the rest of his despatch, it was at Cape Palmas that news of yellow-fever having broken out at Santa Cruz and Teneriffe was received. On reaching the latter place, the Spanish passengers on board were unable to disembark. A written request was made to Captain Lowry of their ship, the SS *Athenian*, that he would place them in quarantine, and refrain from taking in coals and Colonials. The Captain, at some loss, according to Burton, agreed to do so.

On Thursday, 4 December, the ship reached Madeira, and the yellow fever flag could be seen flying to port and starboard. The passengers were entirely free from fever, and two, Burton being one of them, wished to disembark.[87] The following day, Captain Erskine, HM's Consul came alongside, and advised Captain Lowry to address him officially, requesting him to obtain permission from the authorities to land the passengers, and to inform them that if refused, he would have to take them to England under protest. In such circumstances, the authorities would be held responsible for losses and damage for the passage money, and the maintenance of the passengers, and for the Company's claim for detention. This was done, but to no effect. The Consul asked Burton if he would land in quarantine, to which he agreed. Even this, however, was not permitted.

On 2 December, Dr Norton Shaw had received a letter from Isabel. Her present orders, she said, were 'to start on the 8th, to go north to an uncle's (Sir R. Gerard who lives near Liverpool, handy for sailing), so I have to collect my traps, to order suitable trunks. Send all your news for Richard.'[88]

Isabel's preparations proved unnecessary, the SS *Athenian* docking at Liverpool on 12 December with Burton aboard.

CHAPTER TWENTY-SIX

WEST AFRICAN ODYSSEY
Part II

The Burtons spent a couple of days at Garswood, then left for London, taking rooms at 16 Edgware Road. Shortly after calling at the FO to report his arrival in this country, Burton wrote to Monckton Milnes with mock indignation of their having, 'The impudence to congratulate me upon a return to England – I pointed at the window which showed one of your abominable fogs.' Murray, he said, had gone north, and had written him a note 'enlarging upon the vigour of my <u>penis</u>. Sad the demoralization of the age – when even grey hairs talk about the human cock.'[1]

On 17 and 18 December, Burton wrote two long despatches to the FO, using the opportunity, not unexpectedly, to ask for an extension of his leave until January.[2] Four days later, he was writing to *The Times*, expressing astonishment at finding 'in your columns my name cited by a private correspondent, and passages from one of my private letters, quoted to the detriment of M. Paul du Chaillu.' These, no doubt, were the views he had expressed to Milnes in his letter from Fernando Po of 26 April, who had then been indiscreet enough to pass them on to a third party.

Burton's letter, therefore, was a damage limitation exercise, which found him leaning over backwards to praise du Chaillu:

> M. du Chaillu, and I differ upon many points. He may be wrong, or vice-versa; but that is still a question. I will briefly state that, after a residence of about three weeks in the Gaboon country, during which I walked to Cape Lopez and explored the south-eastern fork of the river beyond any former traveller, my opinion of M. du Chaillu's book is higher than it was before visiting the land of the great gorilla..... No one save the jealous European, doubts his having shot the great anthropoid (mind, I modestly disbelieve in the danger), and surely it is something for the French sportsman to have succeeded when three Englishmen – Mr. Levinson, Mr. Winwood Reade, and myself have failed.[3]

A day or so later, Burton and Isabel left London, now basking in an almost summer heat, to spend Christmas with the Arundell family at Wardour Castle.

Isabel had signally failed in her efforts to gain pension and promotion to major for Burton. He himself now brought up the subject with the FO in January. His object, he said, was not to return to India 'unless there be, as I expect, another and a Muslim crisis, when men who have studied the country and the people, would be required.' However, he would feel deeply grateful if the Foreign Secretary would enable him 'to obtain a local or honorary rank of lieutenant-colonel in HM's service, placed in a Spanish colony with a military governor, and thrown amongst British naval officers some of whom rank with me and are much my junior in years.' The only advantage he could expect from such promotion, 'would be the proving to those whom it might concern, that 'though "struck off", I am still honoured with the approbation of those under whom I serve.'[4] It was always a forlorn hope, as Burton must have known. Lord Russell's reply was brief and to the point, stating that he saw 'no sufficient reason for complying with your request.'[5]

On the same day as Burton sent this despatch he, together with ten others, attended the first meeting of the Anthropological Society of London. The Society's founder was Dr James Hunt, who had recently resigned as joint secretary of the Ethnological Society of London.[6] In setting up this new organization, he had taken as his model the Société d'Anthropologie, which had recently been established in Paris. Hunt, who had inherited a practice in stammering from his father, had published several books on human speech, one of which dealt in part with 'the great question of races and languages.'[7] He defined anthropology as 'the science of the whole nature of man.' Unlike the ethnology of the recent past, dominated by biblical dogma and the speculations of the polygenists and monogenists, 'anthropology would treat of man's relations to animals, his connection with the physical universe, the laws regulating his physical nature, his physiological characteristics – in short, everything pertaining to his nature.'[8]

Hunt's racial views were strongly influenced by Dr Robert Knox, who has been described as 'one of the key figures in the general western movement towards a dogmatic, pseudo-scientific racism: "Race is everything: literature, science, art – in a word, civilization depends on it.'[9] The first issue of the new Society's publication, the *Anthropological Review*, appeared on 1 May, carrying an article by Burton, 'A Day Among the Fans.'[10] It also included a notice and an anonymous review, possibly by Burton himself, of Marcy's *The Prairie Traveller*.[11]

In order to have sufficient time to consult with some of the Liverpool oil-traders, Burton, together with Isabel and her mother, left London for Garswood a week or so before his ship was due to sail. Isabel gives the impression that she pleaded at the last moment to be allowed to go with her husband. 'I told him I could not possibly go on as I was living; it was too miserable, one's husband in a place where one was not allowed to go, and I living with my mother like a girl – I was neither wife, nor maid, nor widow; so he took me with him...'[12] But Burton had already informed Henry Murray around Christmas that Isabel was going with him as far as Teneriffe, 'Thus far and no farther.'

They left aboard the ASS *Athenian* on Monday, 24 January 1863, in the worst storm within living memory. Every berth was full, so much so, that the captain chivalrously gave up own his cabin to both of them, so that Richard and she 'might not be separated an hour sooner than necessity compelled us to be.' That night the ship was pounded by mountainous seas, which swept over the deck, washing the quarter-master overboard and flooding the saloon and berths with water. Most of the women were screaming, and to add to the panic the lights went out. It was not until they had been a week at sea, that the weather really improved. Early on the morning of 2 February, they caught sight of Madeira, its dark mountain masses streaked with snow, sharply defined against a cloudless blue sky.

After being ferried ashore through the surf, they booked into Hollway's, a small but select boarding-house in the great square of Funchal. Here they found Lady Marianne Alford with her son, the first Lord Brownlow, Dr Frank, and a large party whose society, according to Isabel, they enjoyed immensely.[13] Burton informed Milnes that if the place had any fault, it was a little too pious. 'My wife,' he wrote, ' is too frantic with running about the churches and chapels and convents, and other places of idolatrous abominations to do anything else.'[14]

In was not until a week after settling in, that Burton got round to answering the FO's despatch of December, asking for his observations on the restrictions placed on consular use of the West African

Squadron's gunboats. Naturally, he rebutted all the charges. He admitted having been shown the order restricting his being supplied with a cruiser, unless British life and property were in actual jeopardy. However, 'in the case of HMS *Griffon*, Commander Perry, RN,' Burton claimed, to have been 'wholly unaware, and doubtless that able and energetic officer was equally so, that by remaining a few days at Fernando Po to recruit after a long visit to the "Oil Rivers" – not as Commodore Edmonstone states "that HM Consul might be enabled to explore its peak" – I was causing any inconvenience to the public service.' Burton also rejected criticism that he and Lt Cdr Stokes had shown a lack of prudence, resulting in the death of the captain's steward from yellow fever at Batonga.

While accepting that Commodore Edmonstone was justified in saying that "the rivers on the coast have been visited more frequently of late than in former years," Burton was convinced that 'they require still more visiting.' How little credence can be placed in these words, however, is well illustrated in the evidence he gave on this subject only two years later to the Parliamentary Select Committee appointed to report on establishments in West Africa. Asked by Lord Alfred Churchill as to how the trade was conducted there, Burton replied that it differed in each river. Churchill then went on, "There is no active supervision besides the casual visits of the Consul?" Burton replied, "Exactly so. I found the less the Consul went there the better."[15]

Commodore Edmonstone had also criticised Burton for over-stating the danger of slave-running. 'That officer,' Burton said, 'seems to forget the two cases of the *Constancia* captured in 1860 by Captain Ruby in the Cameroons River. Where we have commerce and sundry mission stations in the Benin River and in other places, the peculiar facility with which a cargo might be run was, when I visited them, a familiar topic of conversation, and I deemed it my duty to report the facts. Of this Commodore Edmonstone is probably quite unaware.'[16]

After a month spent making numerous excursions, the Burtons left for Teneriffe. Although Burton, himself, wanted to pass a few days at Santa Cruz, he fell in with Isabel's suggestion that it would be better to look for somewhere away from the yellow fever epidemic for now, and leave this until later.[17] After spending an uncomfortable night in filthy, flea-ridden accommodation at San Christoval de la Laguna, they moved on to Orotava, on the northern side of the island. Despite the discomforts, Isabel regarded it as the happiest moment of her life, having 'been through two mortally dull years (without travel) in commonplace, matter-of-fact Old England.'[18]

There were no hotels in the place, but they were able to hire a long dusty loft in a private house on the Square. Once the ballroom or reception room of a dead Marchesa, it was now merely used for storing lumber. With the help of a peasant servant, Isabel set about making the place spick and span. Three carved wooden doors opened on to a verandah balcony, which provided a splendid panoramic view of the surrounding countryside. On a clear day, they could see the snow-capped summit of Pico de Teide, which they later climbed. Here, said Isabel, 'we intended to pass a happy month – to read, to write, study, chat, walk, make excursions, and enjoy ourselves.'[19]

And it appears that they did. Burton dedicated his latest book, *Abeokuta and the Camaroons Mountains*, to her, writing: 'To My Best Friend My Wife These Pages Are Lovingly Inscribed,' and adding lines in Latin from a poem 'To His Mistress,' attributed to the Roman elegiac poet, Tibullus:

> O, I could live with thee in the wild wood
> Where human foot hath never worn a way;
> With thee, my city, and my solitude
>   Light of my night, sweet rest from cares by day.[20]

Isabel admitted to being very proud of this 'lovely inscription and motto,' writing in her own copy of the book, 'Thank you sweet love!'[21]

Isabel also wrote her first book about their experiences on Madeira and Teneriffe. Burton, however, 'would not let me print it, because he did not think it up to the mark. He thought I must study and copy many more years before I tried authorship.'[22]

What really happened according to the publisher, William Tinsley, is that she 'wrote, and we put into type, a book about *"The Great Teneriffe"*, and a set of proofs, making between three and four hundred pages in book form, were given to Burton as a surprise. But Mrs. Burton was the most surprised, for he ordered every particle of the book to be destroyed, and paid the costs, which were over a hundred pounds, out of his own pocket. I do not think he cared a dump about the expense, but his estimation of the book was not complimentary to the author.'[23] It was four years before Isabel's account appeared, not, however, in book-form, but as a four-part article in a magazine.[24]

They delayed leaving for Santa Cruz until the last moment. Then, after three or four days' sightseeing in the capital, a gun signalled the imminent departure of the steamer returning to England. 'How gladly I would have gone with him ;' Isabel said, 'even to the eleventh hour I had hoped that he would relent and let me go. But the climate was death to a white woman, and he was inexorable.'[25] However, in *The Life*, she gives the impression that she continued the journey with him to West Africa, 'but I was not allowed to *sleep* at Fernando Po....So I turned back again with a heavy heart, and had a passage back.....*via* Teneriffe and Madeira.' She added, 'I again passed a long and dreary time, during which he kept me either with my parents well at work,' which was undoubtedly true, but not her claim 'or at sea coming out and going back, with visits to Madeira and Teneriffe.'[26]

Burton should have been back at his Consulate by 27 April. Instead, he waited around at Lagos, where he had arrived six day earlier, in order to ask the new Commodore of the West African Squadron for a cruiser to visit the Oil Rivers.[27] Had Burton returned to Fernando Po, he would have found an important despatch waiting for him, which would, probably, have made this request unnecessary. Dated 27 January 1863, it ran: 'I have under my consideration your despatch of the 5th inst. pointing out the urgent necessity of your being provided with a crew to man the boat which was lately supplied to you by the Admiralty, to enable you sufficiently to carry out your Consular duties in the rivers of the Bight of Biafra. I have to state to you in reply that I am willing to grant you an allowance of £95 a year for this purpose. You will charge that sum in your annual account with the Lords Commissioners of the Admiralty.'[28] Why the Admiralty should suddenly allow Burton a boat, while it was still awaiting his response to Commodore Edmonstone's criticism, is unclear. Equally strange, is the fact that there is no evidence that Burton, who had campaigned for some time for this facility, ever bothered to make use of it.

Commodore Wilmot having arrived at Lagos a few days later, the two men travelled together to Epe, which had lately been burnt down under orders from the Governor of Lagos, Henry Stanhope Freeman.[29] 'What wonderful fellows these negroes are!' Burton remarked. 'If it had been in Arabia there would have been a blood feud for 200 years. Here in Africa, we were received with the greatest civility, and even gratitude, for having killed their people and burnt their village a month ago!'[30] Burton informed Wylde that, because of the demands of the Ashanti War, the Commodore had been unable to supply him with a cruiser. Wilmot and the Acting Governor were intending to visit Abeokuta the following day. However, 'I shall not accompany them, and can hardly expect that he will set matters right after the confusion and disagreement of the last year.' In the meantime, until a cruiser could be spared, 'I will run up to Dahome and make my bow to the King.'

Brief details of this visit are to be found in two private letters.[31] One is to Monckton Milnes, to whom Burton had written from Lagos on 7 May, and the other to an unknown recipient, possibly Norton Shaw, given in extract among the FO 84/1203 despatches. Both, bearing the same date, 31 May 1863, are addressed from Kauna or Kanna, the capital of Dahome, and are almost identical in wording and contents. It appears from his statement at a meeting of the British Association at Bath in September of the following year, that he was at Dahome from 18 May to 17 June.

He left Whydah for Kanna on 24 May, and had an easy journey to the capital. 'I have been here 3 days,' he remarked to Milnes in his usual sardonic style, 'and am grievously disappointed. Not a man killed, not a fellow tortured. The canoes floating in blood is a myth of myths. Poor Hankey must still wait for his peau de jeunesse…' As for the King, described by the newspapers as a "monster", he was 'a jolly looking party, about 45, with a pleasant face, a frank smile, and a shake of the fist like a British shopkeeper.' He had been well-received by the King, who had made him a captain in his Fanti Corps of Amazons. There had been a great deal of bosh spoken and written about these individuals, Burton said. 'I was looking forward with prodigious curiosity to the 5000 adult African virgins, never having met with a single specimen.' Most of them he had discovered were women taken in adultery, and given to the King for soldiering instead of being killed. 'They were mostly elderly, and all of them were hideous, the officers being decidedly chosen for the bigness of their bottoms.'

The King had presented him with a large cloth and small boy. In his turn, Burton had given the King a few presents – cloth, several boxes of liquors, malt whisky being his favourite, 'and (keep this quiet) three very dégagé coloured prints of white women in a state of Eve-ical toilette. This charmed him, and he inquired whether such articles are to be procured alive. I told (heaven forgive me) a fearful fib, and said that in my country, the women are of a farouche chastity.'

The King had given him a grand review the previous day, and then set off for a slave-hunt, which was to last a month or so. Burton, therefore, decided to leave Whydah that afternoon. After seeing something of the coast, Grand-Popo colonised by the French, and, probably, Porto Novo, he intended returning to Lagos. Yellow fever in the Bight of Biafra, however, ruled out any possibility of visiting the Oil Rivers even, in the unlikely event, of there being a cruiser available. Already 33 out of 200 had died at Bonny in 20 days. 'So, most probably,' he told Milnes, tongue-in-cheek, 'I shall go up the Niger and attempt Timbuctu in a canoe. Really, it will be a curious spectacle for the immortal gods to look down upon a chap starting in a hollowed log of wood for some thousand miles up a river with an infinitesimal chance of success! I ask myself "Why?" and the only echo is, "Damned fool. Enfer, needs must when the Devil drives."'

Burton returned to Fernando Po some time in late June. By then, he had been absent from the Consulate for eight months. Once again he was marooned on the island, made worse by the rains which had set in earlier than usual. 'The earth was all water, the vegetation all slime, the air half steam,' the right conditions he believed, for the reappearance of the yellow fever which had wiped out one-third of the white colony during the previous year. He was thoroughly depressed, and pondering how to escape, when HMS *Torch* steamed into Clarence Cove on 24 July and Cdr Smith offered Burton a passage down South, which he gratefully accepted. That at least is Burton's published version.[32] It appears from a despatch to the FO written four months later, however, that he had actually applied for the passage.[33] His excuse was, that he was compelled to leave by a severe attack of neuralgia! The climate, too, had 'become most dangerous,' and Mr Edward Laughlan had consented to act for him, 'till my return with restored health.'[34]

Before setting out, however, Burton waited for the arrival of the mail from London. A FO despatch with enclosures now raised his spirits even higher. These consisted of copies of two despatches from Commodore Wilmot, reporting the details of his visit to the King of Dahome in the previous December and January. It appeared from these, that Wilmot had not only been unsuccessful in persuading the King to give up the slave trade, but also in getting him to make any promise that he would bring a halt to his barbarous massacres or "Customs." The Government, nevertheless, thought it advisable to maintain friendly relations with the King, in the hope of eventually persuading him 'to give up his human sacrifices, and to turn his energies to the development of the resources of his country.'

Commdore Wilmot had led the King to expect that either he or some other officer would return to Abome at the end of six months. Unfortunately, his duties as the Senior Officer of the African Station, made it impossible for him to be absent from his command. 'Under these circumstances, HM's Government having every confidence in your judgement, discretion, and knowledge of the African character, have determined to entrust to you the duty of making known their views to the King and chiefs at Dahome.' Burton was told to be ready to leave for Abome, as soon as possible after the arrival of the packet from the Foreign Office with the African mails on 24 July. This would contain further detailed instructions for his guidance, together with presents for the King. In the meantime, Burton might consider it advisable to announce through the authorities at Whydah, that he would be shortly proceeding on this mission. The Foreign Secretary had already issued instructions to the Admiralty for Burton's being conveyed to and from Whydah in a man-of-war, and that the journey to Abome should not be undertaken until the close of the rainy season. His instructions would be forwarded to Lagos, and he was advised to be there to await the arrival of the next mail.[35]

Considering Burton's intentions, this was highly unlikely. Nevertheless, with an excuse for all seasons, this presented few problems. On 29 July, Burton left Fernando Po in the worm-eaten *Torch*. A week later, the vessel was off the red hills of Loanga. At the invitation of Cdr Hoskins, Burton transferred to *HMSS Zebra*, and began the 240 miles' journey south. He arrived at S. Paulo de Loanda, the capital of Angola, on 14 August. It was the first Portuguese colony he had seen in West Africa and, for the first time, something like a city. Years later, he recalled 'one charming face, but ten years in Africa cannot pass without the saddest changes.'[36]

At Loanda, he acknowledged the Foreign Secretary's last despatch, pointing out that, on account of the swamps, it would not be advisable to leave Whydah before December or January next. In giving his excuse for leaving Fernando Po, he made no mention, of course, of his future plans. After a short but very pleasant visit, Burton left on 22 August, this time aboard HMS *Griffon*, headed for the mouth of the Congo, 180 miles distant. It was not until November that he informed the FO of having landed at Banana Point on 30 August, 'accompanied by Cdr Perry of HMS *Griffon*, to whom I had officially represented the value of naval escort, at least as far as Boma.' The reason he gave for having travelled so far, was that, 'As my improvement in health was slow, I resolved to proceed towards the highlands of the Congo, which tradition represents to be a sanitarium.'[37]

His immediate concern, he said, was to collect news at the factories. Mr Elkman, of the Dutch factory, advised him to lose no time in setting out up-river before the impending rains. 'I wanted, however, a slight penetration for travel and determined to see something of the adjoining villages, especially the site of the historic Padrão.'[38] On 2 September, Burton and his party left Porto de Lenha for the Portuguese factory at Boma, where they presented their letters of introduction to Sr. Antonio Vicente Pereira.

This part of the river belonged to Nessalla, the 'Rei dos Reis,' or King of Kings. Without his permission, they would be unable to obtain an interpreter, canoe, or crew. They, therefore, visited him at Banza Chisalla, Burton taking a fine spangled cloak, a piece of chintz, and a case of ship's rum. After a great deal of wrangling, it was arranged that the king should forward them in a couple of his own canoes to Banza Nokki, supposedly the end of the river navigation. Burton was duly established with his books and instruments at Nkaye, using the delay in studying the country and the people, and making an extensive botanical collection.[39]

He was delighted with the country, a counterpart, he called it, of the Usambara Hills in Eastern Africa, and prophesied (wrongly) that, 'When the Lower Congo shall become the emporium of lawful trade, the white face will find a sanitarium in these portals of the Sierra del Crystal…and the region will become one of the "Paradises of Africa."'

At dawn on 16 September, the party began a short march from Banza Nkulu to the Yellala rapids. Before setting out, Burton had been warned that a shipful of goods would not take him past Nkulu. This was soon confirmed. In the evening, there was a palaver at which he publicly vented his exasperation. Eventually, ruffled feathers were smoothed all round, and the suggestion made that they return to Boma at once, organise a party, and march upon Congo Grande (S. Salvador). If determined upon being 'converted into black man,' Burton might join some trading party there into the interior.

Back at Boma by 19 September, Burton's preparations were, allegedly, brought to an abrupt conclusion five days later, by the arrival of a letter from the Commodore of the Station. This informed him that he had been appointed HM's Commissioner of Dahomey, and that unless he set sail immediately in HMS *Griffon*, no other opportunity would be found for some time. This, as Burton related it in his book was, of course, deliberately inaccurate, as the quoted despatches show. Not only did he already know of his appointment, but he had also made a prior arrangement with Cdr Perry to rendezvous at a given date. Leaving Boma on the evening of 25 September, he reached Banana Point two days later. The following day he boarded HMS *Griffon* for the first stage of his journey back to Fernando Po, arriving there on 24 October.

During his absence, three despatches had arrived from the FO relating to his mission to Dahome. The first listed the presents forwarded for presentation to the King. These comprised a forty-foot circular crimson silk damask tent with poles (contained in two boxes), a coat of mail and gauntlets, a richly embossed pipe with amber mouthpiece in a Morocco case, 2 richly embossed silver belts, and 2 silver and partly gilt waiters in oak cases.[40] The other two despatches set out Burton's detailed instructions.

It was appreciated that great difficulty would be experienced in trying to persuade the King to put an end to the human sacrifices, which prevailed more or less openly along the greater part of the western coast of Africa. Burton, nevertheless, was to use his best efforts in trying to mitigate the horrors of these "Customs."

HM's Government had complied with the King's wishes as far as was possible, with the exception of a carriage and horses. It would be a difficult matter to get English horses out to the coast, even supposing they arrived at their destination. It would also be very doubtful from the nature of the country and climate of their surviving long after their arrival. Obviously wishing to keep a card up its sleeve as a further inducement to the King to comply with its wishes, the FO instructed Burton to say that, if future relations were of such a nature as to warrant such proceedings, HM's Government would not hesitate to comply with the King's wishes in this respect.[41]

Burton was told that he should, if possible, stipulate with the King before proceeding to Abome, that there should be no human sacrifice during the time of his stay at the capital. The last packet from the West Coast had brought reports of the King's death from the effects of a wound received in one of his slave-hunting expeditions. Burton was told that, if these reports were true, he should know something about the character of the King's successor before proceeding to the Dahomean capital. However, whether to do this or not was left to his discretion.[42]

Burton acknowledged these despatches on 27 October. With respect to the list of presents, he said, although those named were sufficient for the King, he would also need to lay in at Whydah a certain amount of cloth and rum as "dash" to the ministers and Amazons. While he would make every effort to carry out the Foreign Secretary's wishes as to there being no human sacrifices during his stay at the capital, he thought that there was little likelihood of success. He believed that it would only be after many interviews, that he might be able to persuade the King to substitute animal for human victims.[43]

Before leaving for his mission, however, Burton unwittingly became embroiled in an affair which was to hang like an albatross around his neck for the next four years.[44] Early in May of that year, a brig called the *Harriet*, lately owned by a deceased liberated African and British subject, William Johnson, was escorted from Prince's Island to Fernando Po by a British man-of-war. While lying at anchor in Clarence Bay, it was declared unseaworthy and incapable of proceeding to its home port in Sierra Leone. During that month, Burton was away enjoying himself at Lagos, Epe, Dahomey, Grand Popo, etc. He then returned to his Consulate towards the end of June. Pleading neuralgia and the necessity for a change of air, he left for the Congo on 29 July.

Having been informed of the poor state of the ship, the executors of Johnson's estate, Messrs Pratt, Taylor, Jarrett, solicitors, sent Burton a letter of attorney on 13 August 1863, authorising him to sell the brig, and to forward the net proceeds after payment of all charges and expenses attending the sale. He was also asked to ship the *Harriet's* cargo of palm-oil to England, all the books connected with the vessel, and one puncheon of black soap. It was only in November, however, that Burton, having been back on the island for a month from his unofficial visit to the Congo, carried out these instructions. After public notice had been given of the intended sale, the brig was auctioned at the Consulate on 21 November, Selim Agha acting as auctioneer, and announcing the terms of sale in English and Portuguese.

According to Isabel, who later took up the case on Burton's behalf, 'When this brig was for sale, Mr Edward Laughland (sic) said he would buy it in behalf of his employers, and give Captain Burton his note of hand for the money, £280. Captain Burton was at this juncture ordered to Dahome, gave his receipt for the amount which he had never seen or trucked, and left Edward Laughland to act for him with full instructions to forward the money to the owners at Sierra Leone.'[45] The money never reached them. It later emerged, that Edward Laughlan had been provisioning the crew to such an extent from May onwards, that the executors, instead of being beneficiaries, were now debtors to the house that Laughlan was acting for. Of course, if Burton had been on the island carrying out his consular duties, the problem should never have arisen. Since it had, it was up to him to have taken the appropriate action. Despite Isabel's claim, Burton did not leave for Dahomey until eight days after the auction. Instead, he seems to have abrogated all his responsibilities and left everything in Laughlan's hands.[46]

Burton embarked aboard HMSS *Antelope* on 29 November to a salute of seventeen guns. Four days later the vessel was off Lagos. Burton went ashore and hastily collected the presents for the King sent by the Foreign Office. Mr John Cruickshank, the Assistant Surgeon, who had been detailed for duty in Dahome, helped by laying in a few stores. The following day, they left Lagos and on 5 December were anchored off Whydah, just too late for Burton to have a discussion with Commodore Wilmot. Having waited around for Burton for a fortnight, he had been forced to steam northwards. They landed in a surf-boat to singing and shouting, and were met on the beach by the Rev Peter Bernasko, native teacher and Principal of the Wesleyan Mission. They were then escorted into the town with shouting, firing, singing and dancing.

It was almost mid-December when the party set out for Kana. On arrival, they were visited by the King's chief physician and archi-magus, Buko-No Uro, looking, Burton said archly, 'somewhat leaner than before, probably the result of his latest nuptials with one of the King's stalwart daughters.'[47] Although, ostensibly, he had come pay his respects, his real motive, according to Burton, was to find out what presents he had brought, and especially to know whether various items specified to Commodore Wilmot, chiefly a carriage and pair, were on their way. As a token of friendship, he announced that their reception would take place that day, and that they would proceed to Agbome the following day. When the review was over, the Yevogan, or "White man's chief," again came up, shook hands with them, and preceded by the most numerous of the companies, set out in the direction of the palace, leaving Burton's party to follow.

They finished the journey in hammocks, making three official tours of the Addogwin market-place, each time stopping to salute the palace gate. They retired about 100 yards, and facing eastwards sat down till summoned to 'the presence.' The heat was excessive, and the dancers' dust had stained them red. After half an hour, they were motioned to rise and advance by the To-no-nun, or chief eunuch, chief of the body attendants upon the sovereign. They entered through the royal gate, first removing their swords and closing their umbrellas. After walking hurriedly across half of the palace yard, they halted at a circle of loose white sand, where the ministers prostrated themselves. Burton and his companions raised their hats and caps, and bowed several times to the King who was sitting under a covering of thatch.

They were then made to advance very slowly towards the King, the native officials bending almost double. Like his father, the King dressed simply, which set off his manly and stalwart form. After the usual quadruple bowings and hand-wavings the King arose, tucked in his toga, descended from the estade, donned his slippers, and advancing, shook hands with Burton. A group of the royal wives, sat in a semi-circle behind the King. 'If perspiration appears upon the royal brow,' Burton wrote, ' it is instantly removed with the softest cloth by the gentlest hands. If the King sneezes, all present touch the ground with their foreheads.' This intense personal veneration reminded Burton of the accounts of Mohammed the apostle and his followers left by contemporary writers. 'But without analysing too far,' he said, 'I suspect that in Dahome it is rather the principle than the person that is respected, the despotism more than the despot, the turban rather than the wearer.'

After the toasts, salutes were fired. When this was over, they were informed that another deputation was to be received. They, therefore, moved aside, and sat under a gorgeous tent canopy. Here, Burton produced his journals and sketch-books. The King, he said, was always pleased to see this. More than once afterwards, he told him 'that no white man had ever before taken so much trouble, and that everything should be shown to me. The Pagan African is in this point, a great contrast to his more civilised Moslem brother, and to the wilder tribes of Asia, who fear the pen as they do the fiend.'

The King was detained at Kana by various cases affecting human life. No less than 150 Amazons were found to be pregnant, 'so difficult is chastity in the Tropics.' They confessed and were brought to trial with their paramours. Eight men were condemned to death, and would probably be executed at the Customs. The majority were imprisoned or banished to inland villages. Some were pardoned. Female criminals were executed by officers of their own sex within the palace walls, not in the presence of men. 'Dahome is, therefore, in one point,' Burton observed, 'more civilised than Great Britain, where they still, wondrous to relate, "hang away", even women, and in public.' On Sunday, 20 December, the party left for their lodging, a large barn with a thatched roof resting on posts, and a verandah. It was to be their home for nearly two months. In front was a small dark room, oppressively hot, and without a breath of wind. Burton, immediately and unceremoniously, knocked a window through the back wall of clay, and provided it with a shutter made out of a claret case, turning it into what he regarded as a reasonable study.

The next day King Gelele made a ceremonious entry into his capital. Covered by four white umbrellas, he was carried by twelve women in a hammock of yellow silk, and three parasols, yellow, purple, and blue-red were waved and twisted over him, to act as fans. The following day might have been one of rest, but the King could not curb his impatience to see the presents sent by the British Government. At 10.15 the party set out for the Komasi palace, and placed their chairs opposite the Agwaji Gate. After waiting around for half an hour, they received a summons to enter.

When the presents were examined, the tent was found to be too small. Although it was probably more impressive than anything belonging to the King, the only part of it he admired, said Burton, was the ginger-bread lion on the pole-top. The pipe was never used. The belts caused great disappointment, the officials declaring that bracelets had been mentioned to Commodore Wilmot. 'Africans are offended,' declared Burton, 'if their wishes are not exactly consulted, and they mulishly look upon any such small oversight as an intended slight.'[48] The silver waiters were very much admired. The coat of mail was found to be too heavy, the gauntlet was too small. As to the carriage and horses, 'I vainly for the dozenth time, explained the difficulty of sending them. It was disposed of at once with cavalier coolness…If the horses died upon the beach at Whydah, no matter.'[49]

Early on 28 December, a discharge of musketry near the palace and the arrival of a royal message, announced the beginning of the King's Annual Customs, and that the party's presence at the palace was expected. They delayed as long as was decent, and shortly after noon, mounted their hammocks, and proceeded to the Komasi house. The word 'custom,' Burton explained, was used to signify the charges paid to the King at a certain season of the year. The Grand Customs were performed only after the death of a king. They exceeded the annual rites in splendour and bloodshed. The Annual Customs formed, in fact, a continuation of the Grand customs, periodically supplying the departed monarch with fresh attendants in the shadowy world. They were called by the people Khwe-Ta-Nun, the Yearly Head-thing. The number of victims, however, had been exaggerated. 'For instance,' he wrote, 'the Europe-wide report that the King floated a canoe and paddles himself in a tank full of human blood.' This arose from the custom of collecting the gore of their victims in one or two pits about two feet deep and four feet in diameter. He had estimated a total of, at most, 80 during the period of his mission, and of these none, except the criminal element, was Dahoman.

A victim shed stood in the Uhun-jiro market-place outside the Ako-Chyo Gate. Inside were twenty victims. All were seated on cage stools and were bound to posts which passed between their legs. The confinement, in Burton's opinion, was not cruel. Each victim had an attendant squatting behind him to keep off the flies; all were fed four times a day, and were untied at night for sleep. 'A European under the circumstances,' he said, 'would have attempted escape, and in all probability would have succeeded; these men will allow themselves to be led to slaughter like lambs.' He also counted nine victims on the ground floor and ten above, lashed to nearly every second post of the front opposite the palace. They resembled in every way those of the market shed, and looked wholly unconcerned, whilst their appearance did not attract the least attention. 'Yet I felt haunted by the presence of these morituri, with whose fate the dance, the song, the dole, and the noisy merriment of the thoughtless mob afforded the saddest contrast.'

After a ceremonial display and speeches, Burton again sent a message officially objecting to be present at any human sacrifice, and declaring that if any death took place before him, he would at once return to Whydah. Men-huwu, or human sacrifice, in Dahome, had been thoroughly misunderstood by the press and public at home, Burton claimed. 'The Dahoman sovereign must enter deadland with royal state, accompanied by a ghostly court of leopard wives, head wives, birthday wives, Afa wives, eunuch-singers and drummers etc.' The same process extended through the Continent to the south-eastern country of the Cazembe. Every year, also, tradition dictated that prisoners of war and all criminals should be sent to increase the King's retinue. 'England,' he contended, 'was hardly in a position to criticise, when in the year of grace 1864 we hung four murderers upon the same gibbet before 10,000 gaping souls at Liverpool.'

As to the so-called Amazons, he traced their origins to the masculine physique of the women, enabling them to compete with men in enduring hardships, and privations. He had noted this physical equality of the sexes in the Grand Bonny and the Oil Rivers. One of his predecessors in Dahomey, Commander Forbes, had described the effects of enforced celibacy on the Amazons, as making them 'forget the other desires of our fallen nature.' Burton disagreed, being convinced that 'all the passions are sisters. I believe that bloodshed causes these women to remember, not to forget love…Seeing the host of women who find a morbid pleasure in attending the maimed and dying, I must think that it is a tribute paid to sexuality by those who object to the ordinary means.'[50]

At 11 am on the fifth and last day of the King's So-Sin Custom, Burton and his party proceeded to the Komasi House, where the ceremony called by strangers , 'The Procession of the King's Wealth,' was to take place. The approach to the Palace was not pleasant. The market-shed was empty, its nine occupants having been executed. Four corpses were sitting in pairs upon the Gold-Coast stools, supported by a double-storied scaffold. A short distance away on a similar structure were two victims. Between these was a gallows of thin posts with a single victim hanging by his heels, head downwards. Finally, close to the path, was a fork-shaped yoke for two, dangling side by side. They then passed to the south-eastern gate of the Komasi House. In front of sundry little black dolls, stuck in the ground on both sides of the entrance, lay a dozen heads, their necks cleanly severed, their faces looking downwards. Within the palace entrance were two more.

In an extract from a letter to an unknown recipient, merely dated 'December,' filed with the FO despatch, Burton said that the King would be going to war in February, 'making a point that I should stay until all is done.' He then intended to apply for the King's permission to visit the Waki Mountains, which could be seen to the north of Agbome. His study of the language was advancing well, despite daily audiences from midday to six in a sun that would cook a steak. 'I make myself at home, smoke when the King lights his pipe, and punish his liquor, and this, combined with visiting and writing down all I see, passes the time.'[51] As always, Burton made excellent use of this time. He wrote in the Preface to his book, that its pages were the result of a three months' personal study of Dahome, his work extending over the day, and often half through the night. The amount of detail he accumulated was enormous, and his analyses of custom and belief proved to be remarkably authoritative. The American anthropologist, Melville J. Herskovits, who studied Dahomean society in the 1930s, made numerous references to Burton's book, describing it as 'the most valuable of all the long series of works on Dahomey which preceded him.'[52]

It was not customary to address royalty, Burton said, even if one were familiar with the language. The king's words were spoken to the interpreter, who passed them on to the visitor, and the answer returned by the same route. Burton had, possibly, made tentative beginnings in the Ffon language at Whydah, having had the loan of vocabularies and other papers from Abbé François Berghero of the French Catholic Mission.[53] Burton described the language as 'one of the poorest, the meagrest, and the most incult of the great and rich Yoruban family.' It was harsh and explosive, and as one of Burton's Krumen justly observed, "Dis country wouf, he break man tooth."'.'[54]

Burton, naturally, studied the sexual practices of the Dahoman. The phallic symbol was to be seen everywhere. 'The Dahoman Priapus was a clay figure of any size between a giant and a pigmy, crouched upon the ground as if contemplating its own attributes.'[55] The prostitutes, licensed by royal authority and subject to an annual tax, were confined to a particular district. They were supplied from the palace, and 'the peculiar male and female system which pervades the court rendering eunuchesses necessary as well as eunuchs, demands Heterae for the women as well as for the male fighters. I was hardly prepared for this amount of cynicism amongst mere barbarians; although in that wonderful book, the Arabian Nights, which has been degraded by Europe into mere fairy tales, the lover is always jealous, not of his own, but of the opposite sex.'[56]

Furthermore, it was the usual practice in many regions of the world where male circumcision took place, for the woman to be 'subjected either, as in Egypt, to mutilation of the clitoris, performed in early infancy, when that part is prominent, or as in the Somal and the Upper Nilotic tribes described by M. Werne, to mutilation combined with excision of the nymphae and fibulation, the wounded surfaces being roughly stitched together.'[57] In Dahomey, the very reverse took place. Here, the lips of the female genitalia, 'locally called Tu must, from the earliest years, be manipulated by professional old women, as is the bosom among the embryo prostitutes of China. If this is neglected, lady friends will deride and denigrate the mother, declaring that she has neglected her daughter's education, and the juniors will laugh at the daughter as a coward, who would not prepare herself for marriage.'[58]

After spending nearly six weeks in Agbome, the Government's message had still not been delivered in person to the King. Fast losing patience, Burton informed him, therefore, that until some respect was paid to his instructions, he would not appear again at the palace. On 8 February, he received an official letter from Commodore Wilmot stating that a cruiser was waiting to take him to the Oil Rivers. This news rendered strong measures necessary. On the morning of the following day, the party's boxes and bags were produced, and ostentatiously packed in the compound. At the same time, Messrs Bernasko and Dawson went to the palace with a message that, unless faith was kept with the Consul, he would be setting out the next day. This produced almost immediate results. Around mid-afternoon on 13 February, the Bako-no's messenger hurried them in full dress to the palace. Even so, they were kept waiting in the hot sun for several hours.

After the necessary formalities, Gelele rose and shook hands with them. Returning to his seat, he expressed surprise at having heard of Burton's complaining about him, in spite of their having been the best of friends. Burton replied that, while he had no personal grievance against the King, it had been totally unacceptable behaviour to delay the delivery of so important a message for two months. The King replied that he had been busy, and anyway knew its contents.

Burton, in no mood to mince his words, delivered his message. The king, 'who had never heard so much truth before in all his life,' although plainly annoyed, kept his temper under control. He justified the slave trade as an ancestral custom established by white men, to whom he would sell all they wanted. That the customs of his kingdom compelled him to make war, and that unless he sold his captives he would have to kill them, which England, perhaps, would like even less. As to human sacrifice, Gelele declared that he executed only criminals and prisoners-of-war, who, if they could, would do the same to him.

For his own part, Burton confessed to being unimpressed by the King's answers. Whatever his personal courtesies, they compared badly with his determination to ignore, even in the smallest detail, the wishes of Her Majesty's Government. At the end of this rather tense audience, the King suggested to Burton that if his mind was 'no longer stirred', they might drink together. He then arose to conduct them outside the palace. He shook hands cordially, told Burton that he was 'a good man,' but, rolling his head, 'too angry,' and bade them farewell.

After spending a few days at Whydah, chiefly in the company of the priests of the French Mission, Burton boarded HMS *Jaseur* for a tour round the Oil Rivers. He left no specific account of his tour, but it is possible to trace some of his movements from the detailed report he sent to the FO on his return to Fernando Po. It appears to have passed without incident, except at Bonny, where he had a serious brush with King Pepple.

On Burton's arrival in the Bonny River on 23 March, he called a meeting of the Court of Equity. King Pepple having refused to be present on board HMS *Jaseur*, Burton had him forcibly removed from his canoe, and compelled him to attend. It appeared from one of the King's notes, that he considered his visit to England had cancelled all previous treaties and obligations with the British Government. Burton, therefore, decided on strong measures. He fined King Pepple 240 puncheons of tradable palm-oil, which were to be deposited at the end of six months in the hands of the then Chairman of the Court of Equity. The King was also banned from living at Bonny Town.[59]

That same day, Burton wrote a 'Private and Confidential' letter to the FO on his mission to Dahome. He blamed the delay in delivering his "message", partly on the "Grand Custom" and the King's preparations for war. However, in his opinion, it was chiefly due to the King's disappointment at the presents sent by HM's Government, instead of those mentioned by Commodore Wilmot. Burton also suggested that the King had, perhaps, seen too many Government servants and white men – 'three several visits having been paid to him during the year' – not to have his African suspicions aroused. Nevertheless, he regarded his mission as having been successful to the extent that, 'for the first time such displays as parading the victims and slaughtering them within hearing, if not within sight of an English officer, were omitted.'

Burton then went on to make some highly critical remarks about the Wesleyan missionaries who had been attached to the mission. 'I would by no means accuse Mr. Bernasko of evil designs,' he wrote, 'but he lacks, African-like, moral courage to tell the truth.'[60] As for his friend, Mr Dawson, there was nothing good he could say in his favour. 'He is known to have administered an abortion to his sister-in-law…is the "own correspondent" of a Methodistical paper called "The West African Times" and, hitherto, he has strongly advocated sending to Agbome, Mr. T.B. Freeman of Accra, also a person of colour.' He had 'no personal feelings against Mr. Dawson,' Burton claimed, 'but I think it proper that your Lordship should know of his peculiarities.'

Stating, somewhat unconvincingly, that he did not wish in any way to disparage the previous Mission, he claimed that, 'Everything was reported notably in too favourable a light. Commodore Wilmot's despatches were compiled from the notes of Dr. Haran, HMS Brisk, and there are evident marks of the Hibernian hand. The excellent officer who conducted the last Mission also deemed it, he tells us, wise to conform in every point to the whims and humours of the people. These semi-barbarous and ignorant chiefs, of course, expect every visitor to do the same, and thus all road to progress is stopped.'[61]

Burton's malicious remarks about the Rev Bernasko were, in a sense, repaid by the latter, who wrote afterwards, 'The manner and customs of the Dahomans, or Africans generally, are not as the civilised Europeans; therefore, one who has an interest in their civilization ought not to go amongst them with a hot passion and a harsh temper. I say that Africa is still ignorant. The Commissioner, in fact, Rev. Sir, did not go to Dahomey with any patient heart. In a thoroughly bad mood,' observed Bernasko, 'Burton at his leave-taking put on a long face to the presence of the King , which no European has ever done so.' It appears that Gelele called the African pastor back later, and complained, 'that if the Queen send such Commissioners to him [it] will spoil everything and break the friendship between England and Dahomey.'[62]

With his letter outlining his mission to Dahomey, Burton enclosed one requesting leave. Claiming that his health had suffered from the last rainy season, he requested permission to absent himself from the island during the three wet months when the climate was thoroughly malarious, and when business was at its dullest. If this request was granted, he would leave Mr Wilson in charge of the Consulate, 'a gentleman in whom all confidence may be reposed.'[63]

The following day Burton wrote to Monckton Milnes, now Lord Houghton, thanking him for his suggestions about Dahome. 'But if I am delicate how disburden myself of really interesting knowledge.' He was sending three specimens of his difficulty, in the hope that Houghton could 'hint how to express these things. If not, I shall go at the subject like a bull (in dog-Latin and little Greek).' As to du Chaillu, 'I begin to fear he is on the humbug once more, & this time he will fail. For the rest of his days he shall sit in the shadow of the gorilla.' He told Houghton that he had 'applied for leave, and am bolting to Spain for the purpose of weeping over the downfall of El Islam in the halls of the Alhambra. I am so dead sick of Fetishism, and so anxious for a little of the "Higher Law."' 'Poor old Hankey,' he concluded his letter. 'I did so much to get him a human hide at Agbome and I failed.'[64]

Burton was back at Fernando Po on 3 April. Having completed a report for the FO on the trade, politics, and personalities of the Oil Rivers, he set about the task of arranging and editing his Dahomey journals for publication. 'After two years of constant quarrelling,' he wrote in his Preface, 'the beautiful island and I are now "fast friends."' In this new, apparent mood of serenity, he devoted the first chapter to its praise, 'I Fall in Love With Fernando Po.' He was now living 800 feet up in a house, 'Buena Vista,' built by an official of the woods and forests, who was then absent on private affairs in Spain.

Although somewhat primitive, life, nevertheless, was pleasant. He wrote in the garden at sunrise and sunset, read hard during the day and, after dark, settled down comfortably to a pipe and a new book of travels. Whether he was as celibate as he claimed, is an open question. His "niggers" as he described them, were, 'as Krumen should be, employed all day long in clearing, cutting, and planting – it is quite the counterpart of a landowner's existence in the Southern States.' They called themselves 'his children,' that is to say, his slaves. In fact, Burton remarked, 'no white man who has lived long in the outer tropics can prevent the feeling that he is pro tempore, the lord, the master, and the proprietor of the black humanity placed under him….. if a little "moral influence" were not applied to their lives, they would be dozing or quarrelling all day in their quarters, and twanging a native guitar half the night.'[65]

This view, along with many others, highly depreciatory of the negro and the philanthropist, Burton included in Chap XIX of the second volume of his book on Dahomey. The material, largely written at Agbome, was given the same title, 'On The Negro's Place in Nature,' as that used by his friend, James Hunt, for a lecture given before the Anthropological Society of London in November 1863.[66] It was prefaced with an extract from the rabidly anti-negro article in the 1797 edition of the *Encyclopaedia Britannica*,[67] and a letter in which Burton praised Hunt's 'courageous paper', which he had read with 'pleasure and profit.'

Like other students of anthropology, he said, he was grateful to him, for having shown 'the great gulf, moral and physical, separating the black from the white races of men, and for having placed in so striking a light the physiological cause of the difference – namely, the arrested physical development of the negro.'[68] The hollowness of Burton's position, and his unprincipled willingness to adopt a diametrically opposite view when it suited him , is nowhere better illustrated than in his comments only a year later in his *Wit and Wisdom From West Africa*. Here, he wrote that his specimens might 'go a long way towards refuting the old-fashioned doctrine of an essential inequality of the Negroes with the rest of mankind, which now and then shows itself, not only in America, but also in Europe..'[69]

Shortly after completing his Preface, a despatch arrived from the FO, designed to spoil Burton's idyllic mood at 'Buena Vista.' An application had been received from the Admiralty, the despatch ran, respecting the cost of his entertainment on board Her Majesty's ships "Griffon" and "Zebra" in the previous August and September. Burton was asked, therefore, 'to explain in detail the circumstances under which you considered yourself justified in asking for these passages in HM's ships.' He was told that, in future, he was to pay the cost of all passages himself, and then to ask whether he would be reimbursed, after Lord Russell had had the chance to consider whether the passage was, or was not, in the interests of the public service. The draft of this despatch was minuted by James Murray: '…Meanwhile he must not leave his post without permission. His frequent absences have already been much complained of.'[70] Burton, however, did precisely that on Saturday, 7 May.

He later turned up at Teneriffe, from where he wrote to the FO just under a month later. He said that the two tours round the Oil Rivers and two visits to Dahomey during the last year, 'have rendered a complete change of climate necessary for the recovery of my health. The more so as the West African coast is at this moment very unhealthy, and the worst season of the year is coming on.' He asked for permission, therefore, to be absent from the Consulate until the end of the rains some time in September.[71]

On 11 June, Burton wrote again to the FO that he had heard from private sources, that Lord Russell had granted him four months' leave, and ordered his return to England. In the circumstances, he hoped that his Lordship would allow him to defer his return to England till August 1864, 'the state of my health requiring some repose.'[72] What Isabel thought of Burton's spending two months at Teneriffe among, what he had described as the enchanting dark-haired, dark-eyed women of the island, we shall never know.[73] Of course, she omitted any mention of his visit there in her biography.

Just under three weeks later, the FO informed Burton that Lord Russell had not ordered him to return to England, but simply granted him four months' leave of absence 'in order to enable you, if you thought proper, to come to England on your private affairs.' He was told that this leave would expire on 7 September, when he was to return to his post at Fernando Po.[74] The last communication Burton received at Teneriffe, was a demand from the FO for him 'to pay to the credit of "Naval Funds", in the hands of Her Majesty's Paymaster-General, the sum of £6 6s due by him to the officer commanding HMS "Torch".' On 12 August Burton arrived back in Liverpool where, in Isabel's description, 'we had a second joyous meeting …. – this time to part no more as previously.'[75]

CHAPTER TWENTY-SEVEN

DEATH IN THE AFTERNOON

Once back in London, Burton wasted no time getting in touch with his friends, Lord Houghton and Admiral Murray. As we have already seen, he was particularly anxious to have Milnes's advice on the best way of presenting the 'anthropological' information for his book, almost ready for the press. 'Caro Milnes, ' he wrote from his London address on the day of his arrival, 'I called at 16 and heard that you are expected. Henry Murray is still in town, we feed together this day. I want much to consult you about Dahomey, having proposed to raise a she-corps in England, all about 40 and past bearing...'[1]

Later that month, Burton and Isabel visited Milnes at Fryston. Among the guests was Arminius Vambery, a lame, tetchy, little Hungarian Jew, who had become the "lion" of the 1864 season for his journey across Central Asia disguised as a dervish.[2] As a surprise, Milnes had him hide behind one of the doors, and as Burton and Isabel entered the drawing-room, recite the first Sura of the Qu'ran with perfect intonation. Burton was taken aback but, according to Vambery, immediately recognised his identity, even though the two had not met before.[3] Isabel recalled Vambery entertaining the company with Hungarian tales, and 'Richard, cross-legged on a cushion, reciting and reading "Omar el Khayyam," alternately in Persian and English, and chanting the call to prayer, "Allahhu Akbar."'[4]

During late August and into early September, Burton was involved in a spate of correspondence with the FO. In one of these despatches he asked for permission to draw upon the Lords Commissioners of HM's Treasury for the sum of £43, the amount of expenses incurred on his visit to the Congo.[5] The following day, he was writing yet again, this time being forced to employ all his ingenuity in trying to justify his using the naval vessels, *Griffon* and *Zebra*, for this unofficial visit. Russell was not convinced. His answer was briefly minuted at the FO, 'This is entirely a private affair. In accordance with our usual custom [it] must be paid by Captain Burton himself.'[6]

In the same TNA file of despatches, there is a copy of Burton's detailed Report on his ascent of the Congo, headed 'Printed for the use of the Foreign Office, Sept. 6 1864. Confidential.' Included with it is a very interesting memorandum on Burton's request for reimbursement, written by W.H. Wylde, not unsympathetic, but clear-sighted about Burton's excuses:

> In submitting the accompanying application for Lord Russell's decision, it is only right to state that this expedition of Captain Burton's up the Congo was undertaken without permission, and that the river is several hundred miles beyond his Consular jurisdiction. The excuse given for undertaking this expedition was the impaired state of his health, and the tradition that the highlands of the Upper Congo were represented to be a sanitarium.

I believe, however, that as long as there is a river unexplored, a mountain unascended, within Captain Burton's reach, his health will always be impaired, until he has accomplished both the one and the other, though it may be to the detriment of his Consular duties. Captain Burton's report, which is an interesting one, is annexed. The expenses incurred (£43) are not great, and Lord Russell may, perhaps, consider the information acquired of sufficient public interest to warrant the reimbursement of Captain Burton of the amount of expenses incurred.

I think, however, that Captain Burton ought to be warned that if he undertakes expeditions without the previous sanction of the Secretary of State, he will have to defray the expenses out of his own pocket.

Wylde's advice, however, was ignored. Another Minute from Murray, while ordering copies of Burton's Report to be sent to the Board of Trade, the Admiralty, and the RGS, at the same time denied his expenses on the grounds that his journey was not on the public service, and had been undertaken without Lord Russell's authority.[7]

While Burton had been in West Africa, Speke's East African Expedition had scored a spectacular success. On 6 July 1862, Speke had written to Sir Roderick Murchison from Bandowarogo at the Kibuga or palace of Mtesa in Uganda: 'As you proved yourself a good father to me by getting up this expedition, so I hope now you will consider me a worthy son for without doubt I am on the northern slopes of Africa, and the Victoria Nyanza is the true and indisputable source of the Nile.'[8]

This was followed by a long silence. It was not until late April of the following year, that *The Times* published a letter from Sir Roderick, informing them that he had just heard from Mr Layard, Under-Secretary for Foreign Affairs, that a telegram had just reached the Foreign Office, announcing the safe arrival of Capts Speke and Grant at Khartoum on the White Nile.[9] In a further letter to the newspaper in May, Murchison quoted, without date, what Speke had written to him about the sources of the Nile:

I said I would do it, and I have done it. The Victoria Nyanza is the great reservoir of the sacred Bahr el Abiad (White Nile)...I think I may safely says (he adds) that I never felt so rejoiced as I did when Petherick delivered to me your letter, notifying that the Royal Geographical Society had adjudicated to me their Founder's Medal (for the discovery of the Lake Victoria Nyanza)...

'The discovery of Speke and Grant,' Sir Roderick went on, 'by which the southernmost limit of the basin of the Nile is determined to be four degrees south of the equator, is the most remarkable geographical feat of our age, and is, indeed, an achievement of which all our countrymen may well be proud.'[10]

After being fêted in Egypt by the Khedive, Speke and Grant arrived back at Southampton aboard the P&O liner, *Pera*, on 17 June, to be met by Col Rigby and a civic deputation. Five days later a special meeting of the RGS was convened at Burlington House, which was packed to overflowing, 'a great number of ladies being present,' as *The Illustrated London News* reported. Sir Roderick Murchison was in the chair, and Speke and Grant had great difficulty in making their way to the platform. Immediately they were recognised, 'they were greeted with hearty and reiterated cheers.'[11] The following night, Speke lectured on his discovery at the Royal Institution before a glittering assembly, which included HRH the Prince of Wales, the Comte de Paris and several members of the late Royal family of France, as well as Sir Roderick Murchison and a numerous suite.[12]

As soon as he could break free from these official engagements, Speke travelled to Edinburgh to consult with Blackwood's which had contracted to publish his manuscript. The members of the firm, however, were not long in realizing what a mammoth task faced them. As we have already seen, the problem was only solved by enlisting the help of the Scottish historian, John Hill Burton, who, after a great deal of time and trouble, succeeded in making the manuscript publishable.[13]

It was not until Friday, 6 November, therefore, that the people of Taunton were able to welcome Speke on his return to his home county of Somerset. On his arrival at the station, he was loudly cheered by thousands of people. A grand procession was formed, which then proceeded to the Shire Hall, where an address was presented by the civic authorities on behalf of the inhabitants. At a meeting of the Bailiffs of the previous day, there was a suggestion of a public dinner being 'one of the best ways for bringing public feeling into a focus.' It was thought that a bust, to be placed in the Hall, would form a fitting memorial. There was also the hope expressed, that 'our most gracious Queen would confer some signal mark of her royal approval, and that Parliament would acknowledge his services in some substantial way.'[14]

Speke's *Journal of the Discovery of the Source of the Nile*, was published on 16 December. In its review, *The Athenaeum* praised it as a great story plainly told. 'Like the labours of Livingstone in another department of African travel, it is a triumph of English pluck, sagacity and skill, in one of the grandest and most important labours undertaken by civilized men.' Nevertheless, the book was criticised for lacking in generosity. 'Captain Speke has done so fine a thing that he would have lost nothing in renown, and would have gained much in sympathy by a free and full acknowledgement of what had been done by others in preparing the way for his own successful feat.' In particular, the journal drew attention to Speke's comments which had upset the Egyptian Government, and his 'contemptuous and insulting' remarks about Mr Petherick. 'All this,' it said, 'is very sad to read.'[15]

Three days later, Speke was honoured with a banquet in the Grand Jury Room at the Shire Hall, Taunton, decked from floor to ceiling with every conceivable decoration. Replying to the toast to Speke and Grant, Mr Danby Seymour, MP and Member of the RGS Council, reminded the guests that 'Captain Speke was not one who went out to explore the regions of Africa for any purpose of his own; but he was an officer in Her Majesty's service, sent out by the Geographical Society, in conjunction with the Foreign Office of this country, for the great purpose, namely, that of exploring those regions in which he had a reasonable supposition that the source of the Nile would be found.' Now looking at the book of Captain Speke, which he had examined attentively, they would there see the extraordinary discoveries which Captain Speke had made, and 'I own I had no idea of the extent of these discoveries till I had read the work.'[16]

Nor, it must be added, had any other members of the RGS, and it is hard to avoid the suspicion that Seymour's remark was a double-edged compliment. It will be remembered that Burton, as leader of the second East African Expedition, had written an enormously long report in 1859, which had filled the Society's journal. Only then did he go ahead with publishing a more popular version. This was not the case with Speke who, by the date of the appearance of his *Journal*, had written nothing for the Society. According to his biographer, it was not until July 1864 that 'Speke interrupted other work to fulfil his obligations to the Royal Geographical Society by submitting a report for its journal.'[17]

This is not strictly accurate. The Society, in fact, received Speke's manuscript on 22 March, just before he travelled to Paris. A proof of his paper was not returned to him until 16 April by a clerk, H.W. Farley, who expressed regret that it was held up owing to the death of Mr Greenfield.[18] He informed Speke that Mr Markham wanted it returned at the earliest possible date, 'as the Journal is only delayed on its account.'[19] However, what Speke had sent was a skimpy paper, entitled 'The Upper Basin of the Nile, from Inspection and Information.' So skimpy as to be insulting, considering that his published *Journal* ran to 658 pages with a large fold-up map. The Council must have felt snubbed, and it must have come as something of a slap in the face for Sir Roderick Murchison who had been Speke's warmest supporter from the very beginning.

A special Council Meeting was convened, therefore, on 13 May with Sir Roderick in the chair. As a result, the Hon Sec, Mr W. Spottiswode, wrote to Speke the following day, stating that he was 'directed by the President and Council of the Royal Geographical Society to express their regret that owing to the very brief and imperfect character of the notes which you have furnished them, and to the absence as yet of any map (or means to construct one), they feel compelled to publish the present volume of their Journal without any account of the important mission entrusted to yourself and Captain Grant.' This was not all. They went on to draw Speke's 'serious attention' to the terms under which he had been sent, ending by asking him to return the journals and other MSS relating to the expedition 'which the Council permitted you to take away last autumn for the purpose of your book, as well as for the preparation of an official account of the expedition.'[20]

The Minutes show, however, some dithering followed the despatch of this letter. A Special Committee meeting held on 1 June, decided on publishing Speke's paper, but that it should be preceded by a Memorandum. This decision was reversed on 13 June, the Committee deciding that the Journal should be issued at once without Speke's paper. On 27 June, the meeting reverted to its original decision. It was, therefore, published in a very late 1863 Journal, with the prefatory Memorandum registering the Council's obvious displeasure, a public rebuke unique in the Journal's history:

> In publishing the following observations with the accompanying Map and Tables, relating to the part of Africa traversed by Captains Speke and Grant, the Council regret that so very important a subject should be illustrated in their Journal, only by this short memoir, which Captain Speke has entitled the 'Upper Basin of the Nile.' As the author has not transmitted, for publication in the Transactions of the Royal Geographical Society, any other materials or diary of his travels, the reader must look for further information in the published work of Captain Speke, respecting the important expedition with which he was entrusted, and in which he has been supported throughout by the President and Council of the Society, as testified indeed by Captain Speke himself in the concluding paragraph of his memoir.[21]

Speke was currently engaged in correcting the proofs of a second book, based on his earlier Blackwood articles describing his experiences in Somaliland.[22] With these memories stirring inside him, he wrote to John Blackwood from North Wales in July, 'How I wish I had got that blackguard Burton's nose now between my finger and thumb – I shall never travel with a male companion again in a wild country, and certainly shall never think again of writing a personal narrative since it only leads to getting abused when describing disagreeable truths....'[23] He had further angry words to say about Burton when writing to Blackwood from the Grand Hotel, Paris, just under a week before Burton arrived back in this country:

> Don't be afraid on my account of what I have written for it only exists between B the B and myself, whether we fight it out with the quill or the fist. I won't let him come to England quietly as we stand at present. He was cut by his Regiment for not accepting a challenge, and now my Regt. expects me to tackle him some way or other, to say nothing of my own feelings of honor. I think I have been very mild considering the amount of injustice he has done me...I can prove what I have said whilst he being the aggressor has brought it all on himself....[24]

The chance to fight it out came in September, not with quill or fist, but in public debate at the meeting of the British Association for the Advancement of Science, to be held at the Royal Mineral Water Hospital, Bath, between the 14th and the 23rd of the month. According to Isabel, 'Laurence Oliphant conveyed to Richard that Speke had said that "if Burton appeared on the platform at Bath.....he would kick him." I remember Richard's answer – "Well, *that* settles it! By God, he *shall* kick me;" and so to Bath we went.'[25] There can be little doubt, however, that Burton had already planned to attend the meeting, to offer a paper on the Nile Sources critical of Speke's claims, hence his request to the FO for an extension of leave until the end of the month. Speke, as it happened, was then staying at nearby Neston Park, the Wiltshire estate of his uncle, John Fuller, and was invited to take part in the discussion.

The business of the Association began on 14 September, the day after the Burtons booked into the Royal Hotel. The General Committee held its first meeting in the Guildhall, High Street, at 1 o'clock, for the election of sectional officers and various other matters. It was 'rendered unusually amusing' according to the local newspaper report, 'by the predicament into which Mr. Carter Blake' – a friend of Burton and Hunt – 'plunged it on behalf of the Anthropological Society, by submitting the motion entered for proposal at the final meeting at Newcastle for establishing a special sub-section for anthropology.' The proposal, however, was heavily defeated, the almost unanimous view being that 'every possible facility already existed for the reading of any papers relating either to the distribution of the various races, or to the anatomical and natural history of Man.'[26]

Section E, Geography and Ethnology, was presided over by Sir Roderick Murchison, with David Livingstone as one of five Vice-Presidents. A great many others, among them Burton, Speke, Galton, Sykes, and Vambery, formed the Committee. That evening, in the packed theatre, brightly lit by gas chandeliers, Burton sat on the stage with some of the Association's most distinguished members, to listen to the Inaugural Speech given by the new President, Sir Charles Lyell, the country's leading geologist.

The date for the discussion about the Nile Sources, and the claims of Lake Tanganyika and a north-eastern water, then unnamed, versus the Victoria Nyanza, was fixed for 16 September. On the day previous, Burton recalled passing his former companion as he sat on the president's right hand. He 'could not but remark the immense change of feature, of expression, and of general appearance which his severe labours, complicated perhaps by deafness and dimness of sight, had wrought in him.' They looked at each other without showing any signs of recognition. 'Some one beckoned to him from the bottom of the hall. At 1.30 pm he arose, and ejaculating, "I can't stand this any longer," he left the room. Three hours afterwards he was a corpse.'[27]

According to Francis Galton, it was customary each morning, a little before the President and Committee of the several sections took their seats, to meet in a separate room to discuss matters requiring immediate settlement, and to select papers which were to be read the following day. On this occasion, this business had been completed, and Sir James Alexander was urging that the Council of the Association should be requested by the Committee to bring Captain Speke's services to the notice of Government, and to ask for their appropriate recognition.[28] Just at this point, a messenger brought a letter to the President, Sir Roderick Murchison. He motioned to the Secretary, who was seated at his left hand, to read it. In the meantime, Sir Roderick continued to attend to Sir James. It was evident from the expression of the Secretary's face, that the letter contained serious news. While Sir James continued speaking, the letter was circulated and read by each in turn, including Burton, who, according to Galton, sat opposite to him. It was to say that Speke had accidentally shot himself dead, by drawing a gun after him while getting over a hedge.[29]

Section E resumed its sitting, whereupon a formal motion of offering condolences was passed unanimously.[30] Burton then read a paper on 'The Ethnology of Dahome,'[31] after which the President said that Captain Burton wished to express his feelings with regard to the untimely death of the explorer, Captain Speke. As he could not trust himself to address the meeting, he had recorded his sentiments in a note, which the Secretary would read: "I cannot touch upon African matters without a few words of deeply felt allusion to my old colleague, Captain Speke. The differences of opinion that are known to have existed between us while he was alive, make it more incumbent on me to publicly express my sincere feelings of admiration for his character and enterprise, and a deep sense of his loss now that he is so suddenly removed from among his geographical associates."[32]

The meeting then continued with John Petherick reading a paper containing the latest news from Africa of the explorations of Samuel Baker.[33] A discussion followed, in which Burton and Drs Bryne and Kirk took part, regarding the light which recent discoveries had thrown on the sources of the Nile. With the aid of a map, Burton stated his opinion that Lake Victoria was not the most southerly head of the Nile, but that this title belonged to Lake Tanganyika, which he believed was the western lake of Ptolemy.[34] It still remained, however, to be decided whether a river flowed out of the northern end of this lake into the Lake Luta N'Zige, and thence into the Nile. Dr Kirk, the companion of Livingstone, supported Burton's views insofar as he believed the drainage of Lake Tanganyika was not to the south into Lake Nyassa. He expressed deep regret, however, that Burton had not collected specimens of fish from the lake, since the examination of their species would have gone far to settling the question.[35]

That same afternoon, an inquest into the circumstances of Speke's death, was being held at Monk's Park, Corsham, the residence of his brother, William. The first witness to give evidence was George Fuller, who said the deceased had fired off both barrels before the accident occurred. Around 4 o'clock he, Fuller, had got over a low part of a loose stone wall, some two feet high. When he was about sixty yards from that place, he heard the report of a gun, and looking round thinking to see some birds, saw Speke standing on the same part of the wall without his gun. Shortly afterwards, he saw Speke fall into the field. He went immediately to his assistance, and found him bleeding from a wound in the chest, which he tried to staunch. Speke remained conscious for a short while and spoke to him. Fuller said that he stayed for about five minutes, and then left him in charge of his game-keeper, Daniel Davis, while he went for assistance. One barrel, the right, was then at half-cock, the left-hand barrel was discharged. In his evidence, Davis said that Speke died about a quarter of an hour after the gun was discharged. He described the weapon as a Lanchester breech-loader without a safety-guard. It was his opinion that the gun was quite safe, 'and in the same state as gentlemen's usually are.'

The surgeon, Mr Snow of Box, found Speke dead when he arrived. He observed a wound on the left hand side, 'such as would be made by a cartridge if the muzzle of the gun was close to the body. It led in a direction upwards and towards the spine, passing through the lungs and dividing all the large blood vessels near the heart.' The coroner pointed out to the members of the jury what verdict he thought they should return. They unanimously recorded a verdict that, 'The deceased died from the accidental discharge of his own gun, after living a quarter of an hour.'[36]

Burton shortly afterwards wrote to Frank Wilson at Fernando Po, 'Nothing will be known of Speke's death. I saw him at 1.30 p.m., and 4 p.m. he was dead. The charitable say that he shot himself, the uncharitable that I shot him.'[37] Writing some years later, Burton remarked that, 'The calamity had been the more unexpected as he was ever remarkable for the caution with which he handled his weapon.' Burton went on to point out that he always made a point of ascertaining a fellow-traveller's habits in that matter, and he observed that 'even when our canoe was shaken and upthrown by the hippopotamus he never allowed his gun to look at him or at others.'[38]

The Times's obituary described Speke's death as having produced a sensation akin to that of a national misfortune. It described him as a gallant soldier, and 'a sagacious and enterprising traveller, who by sheer pluck and endurance solved the problem which has vexed the curiosity of mankind since the dawn of history….' This unfortunate accident, it said, would put an end to the controversy which was to have amused the Geographical at Bath. Captain Speke and Captain Burton could no longer be pitted against each other in a gladiatorial exhibition:

It must be very hard for Captain Burton, [it went on] who had won so many prizes, to reflect that he was once slumbering under the shadow of the very highest prize of all, while another and a less experienced hand reached over him and plucked the fruit...In fact poor Burton was ill and Speke was well; Speke was shooting Egyptian geese and catching perch in the lake while Burton lay in his hammock. Moreover Speke had the happy sagacity to guess the vast importance of the discovery on which he had lighted. Burton was very near gaining the blue riband of the Geographers, but he did not gain it. In all future time Captain Speke, whose loss we deplore, must be remembered as the discoverer of the source of the Nile.[39]

This drew a sharp response from Burton two days later, claiming that 'the popular version of the discovery of Lake Nyanza, and of the "settlement of the Nile sources" was in advance of fact.' After going over the old ground, he said that in his latest expedition, Speke had succeeded in striking the NE shoulder of a water which many geographers regarded as the broadening of the Kitangula River, not his original Nyanza. Most foreign geographers, Burton claimed, considered the Asua affluent coming from the SE to be the true Nile. However, Drs Livingstone and Kirk, after visiting the Nyassa lake, and finding no affluent from the Tanganyika, 'compel us to believe,' Burton said, repeating what he had outlined at the British Association discussion on 16 September, 'that the latter drains into the "Luta Nzigi", and is thus the western lake reservoir of Ptolemy – Nyanza being the eastern.' Since he was about to publish a pamphlet upon this subject, he would say no more at present. 'You will, however, perceive that...the discovery of the Nile sources can hardly be a thing settled for all future time.'[40]

There had been suggestions that Speke should be buried in Westminster Abbey. Whether such a proposal was ever seriously considered is not known. In the event, Speke was buried in the family vault at St Andrew's Church, Dowlish Wake, on Friday, 23 September 1864, where his brother was the incumbent. Among the two thousand mourners present were Grant, Murchison, and Livingstone.

Four days later, a letter appeared in *The Times* from Sir Roderick Murchison, stating that he and his friends had decided 'to bring about the erection of a suitable monument to commemorate the exploits of a man who....(setting aside all disputes respecting the source of the Nile) unquestionably determined the existence and position of the great water-basin whence the Nile flows.' Ensuing events were to show only too clearly the transience of Speke's fame. In February 1866, Rigby, then recently returned from India, wrote to Grant that he had 'received the Delhi Gazette with the notice about Speke's Memorial, very few fresh subscriptions had come in. I sent copies of the Circular to the Governor of Bombay & all the Bombay Editors, & to the President of the Bombay Geographical Society, which is taking it up & asked for subscriptions limited to 15 Rs each.'[41]

In his Anniversary Address for that year, Sir Roderick Murchison announced that the Society had received royal permission for a memorial to be erected in one of the walks in Kensington Gardens. However, he avoided mentioning the poor response to the Memorial Fund. Writing to Grant again in June, Rigby said that 'poor Speke's monument....is nearly ready to put up but money is wanting.' He had sent a copy of the printed notice to a great many people both in this country and India, 'but it does not appear to have been productive of a single guinea. General George Lawrence told me he would subscribe himself and write to his brother the Governor-General to interest him. I sent him some copies, but he neither subscribed nor took any notice of it. I sent a copy to Sir Bartle Frere & wrote him a private letter with it, he has not subscribed, nor have I heard of a single subscription received through the Bombay Geographical Society.'[42] The monument of red polished granite carrying the simple, unprovocative inscription, 'In Memory of Speke, Victoria Nyanza, and the Nile 1864,' was eventually erected. There is nothing in the Minutes of the Council of the RGS, however, regarding the arrangements for its erection, which seem to have been carried out solely by Sir Roderick Murchsion. If there was an unveiling ceremony, it was not reported in *The Times* or even in the RGS Journal. Except by his family and a few close friends, Speke appears to have been quickly forgotten.[43]

After the break-up of the British Association meeting, the Burtons went for a short stay with Thomas Wright, the antiquary, at his home in Shropshire.[44] On Burton's return to London he found that he was still being dunned for money by the FO. It had written to him in October stating that it had been applied to by the Lords Commissioners of the Admiralty for the repayment of the cost of stores supplied to him in September 1862 from HMS *Brisk*, amounting to the sum of £42 13s 4d. Burton was instructed to pay that sum into the credit of "Naval Funds" in the hands of HM's Registrar-General, and to inform Murray of having done so.[45] This was followed three days later by another request for money. He was informed that, since it was clear to Lord Russell from Burton's explanation in his letter of 3 September, that his voyage on board the *Griffon* and the *Zebra* were undertaken on his own account, he was directed to pay the cost of his entertainment on board these vessels, a sum amounting to £47 2s 0d.[46] In all, therefore, Burton owed the Admiralty almost £90.

Although Isabel had accompanied Burton to Bath and Shropshire, she had been frantically busy behind the scenes, trying to prevent his return to Fernando Po. While Burton, himself, may have had certain reservations about directly canvassing the FO for another post, Isabel, with her own future happiness at stake, had no such inhibitions. It appears that she directly petitioned the Foreign Secretary, detailing Burton's services (as she saw them), complaining of the miserable Fernando Po posting, and pleading for one where she could join her husband. It is impossible to say whether Russell was amused or exasperated by Isabel's pleas. However, he replied courteously enough to her letter, writing from his wife's home in Scotland. Although Russell was generally regarded as something of a cold fish, his letter betrays a nice sense of humorous irony:

Dear Mrs Burton,

I know the climate in which your husband is working so zealously and well is an unhealthy one, but it is not true to say that he is the smallest of consuls in the worst part of the world. Many have inferior salaries, and some are in more unhealthy places.

However, if I find a vacancy of a post with an equal salary and a better position, I will not forget his services. I do not imagine he would wish for a less active post.

He has performed his mission to Dahome very creditably, to my entire satisfaction.[47]

Isabel's pleas paid off. In May of that year, the post of Consul at Santos, Brazil, had become vacant through the death of Captain Sir Henry Vere Huntley, RN.[48] Since then, affairs had been run by the Vice-Consul, John Hayden, manager of Maria & Co's bank. Burton received official notification of his new appointment to the Santos posting, just over three weeks after the receipt of Lord Russell's letter. The salary of £500 was identical with that at Fernando Po, though his office expenses were £50 less, and he was only allowed £85 for outfit[49] The date of his appointment is deliberately misrepresented in *The Life* as having taken place in May of the following year. This was done, as we shall see, in order to lend credibility to Isabel's returning from Portugal ostensibly to 'wind up affairs.' Ironically, through the interest of Sir Roderick Murchison, the Consulate of Fernando Po was offered to Speke's erstwhile companion, James Grant.[50] He declined and returned to his army career in India. David Livingstone then used his influence to obtain the post for his younger brother, Charles.[51]

Burton left London some time after the middle of November, to stay with a Mrs Anna Maria Burton at Churchill House, near Daventry in Northamptonshire. It was here that he wrote the 'Advertisement' to *The Nile Basin*, which was published at the end of November, or the early part of December. It consisted of two parts: Part 1 was an expanded version of the *Memoir* on the Nile sources read before the RGS on 14

November, introduced by an 'Advertisement' and Prefatory Remarks. Part II, and much the larger section, was devoted to a reprint of James M'Queen's 'valuable and original letters,' as Burton chose to call them on 'Captain Speke's Discovery of the Source of the Nile.'[52] These had first appeared in *The Morning Advertizer*, shortly after the publication of Speke's *Journal*.

The writer of a brilliantly witty and amusing article, thought to be Viscount Strangford, which had appeared in *The Saturday Review* several months earlier, observed that, 'Outraged self-love, like faith, will not only move mountains, but will visibly create or destroy them; especially the Mountains of the Moon, Kilimandjaro, and Kenia, and the horseshoe around the head of Lake Tanganyika with which Captain Speke has lately been playing fast and loose....'[53] In similar fashion, Burton, while claiming that he had 'no wish to depreciate the services to geography of Speke and Grant,' proceeded to make the most, of what he now called, 'the supposed Nyanza,' and the 'so-called lake,' disappear under his hand. He was prepared, he said, to accept only two parts of Speke's map: first, the southern part seen by him, 'when he was *despatched* [my italics] from Kazeh, whilst I prepared for the toilsome march upon Kilwa, and secondly, the north-eastern water which he touched in January-July 1862.'

Speke was extremely vulnerable on a number of other fronts, and Burton spared no pains in attacking what he called the 'extreme looseness of Speke's geography.' One such glaring example was his having given Victoria Nyanza four outlets. 'It is strange,' as Sir Harry Johnston later observed, 'that so great a geographer should have had such elementary notions about hydrography....much as the Portuguese in earlier days provided lakes in the centre of Africa, which fed impartially the Congo, the Nile and the Zambezi.'[54]

Burton's aim, of course, was to discredit Speke's geographical claims in order to assert the primacy of his own: that Lake Tanganyika was Ptolemy's western lake reservoir, draining into the White Nile via the Ruzizi River and the Luta Nzige. M'Queen's strategy, on the other hand, was to blow Speke's claims sky-high by belittling the man. Character assassination was the name of the game. Initially attacking Speke's 'spiteful and ungenerous' treatment of John Petherick, M'Queen moved on to portraying Speke as a heartless, lip-smacking lecher, measuring one of Rumanika's fat wives, so that he could 'obtain a good view of her naked; amusing himself 'in drinking pombe...and in splashing in the Nyanza in company with the king's naked queen, when not engaging in witnessing the execution of some of them.' M'Queen also found time to make sport with Speke's errors and inconsistencies, such as making the Nile run upwards instead of downwards on two occasions, remarking on the absurdity of his giving African places English names, and his inclusion of a 'wonderful Hindoo map of the Nile,' which M'Queen had heard on good authority was a forgery.

It was as Alan Moorhead said, 'all very Victorian, very malicious, very hypocritical...' It was also completely tasteless and insensitive given that Speke had died only some two months or so earlier. The most devastating response to the book's publication, appeared in *Blackwood's* in January of the following year, undoubtedly from the fluent pen of Laurence Oliphant. Had Burton

confined himself to attacking the living, it would not have been thought worth while to give publicity to his sentiments, but the decencies of society may not be outraged with impunity beyond a certain point, and we can only put Captain Burton in his true light before the public by showing that his real object in publishing the work before us and calling it the "Nile Basin" is to discredit, not the discoveries of an explorer, but the memory of a deceased fellow traveller. Would it not have been the instinct of a generous mind to have allowed the very controversy to slumber, rather than excite it by allusions in it to the disparagement of one who was no longer alive to defend himself? If the contents of the Nile Basin, which has yet to be discovered, are half as offensive as the contents of that basin which Captain Burton has presented to us, we do not envy the discoverer.[55]

Burton returned to London in late November or early December, to find a despatch from the FO waiting for him. Enclosed with it was a letter from the Sierra Leone lawyers, Pratt, Taylor, and Jarrett, executors of the Johnson estate, complaining that they had not received the money due from the sale of the *Harriet*, 'in spite of repeated requests.' Burton was ordered by Earl Russell to immediately contact them with an explanation.[56] It was not until 10 December, however, that he sent a reply. He informed Earl Russell that in August 1863 he had gone to the Congo River. After his return he had sold the brig on 21 November, and on the 29th of that month had proceeded to Dahomey. None of the correspondence alluded to (12 Nov 1863 and 12 May 1864) had been forwarded to him. In May 1864 he had left the West Coast of Africa, and since then had had no correspondence with Sierra Leone.[57] Burton was sadly mistaken, however, in thinking that this explanation would prove to be a satisfactory resolution of the matter.

None of this, of course, was reported by Isabel, who wrote that, in spite of Speke's death, they had a delightful winter, moving around from one country house to another. In early January, they spent just under a week with the Stanleys at Alderley Park in Cheshire, their visit recorded in the journals of Lord Amberley, Earl Russell's eldest son, and his wife, Kate Stanley.[58] Amberley described Burton as 'a very dark man, with a fierce scowling eye & a repulsive hard face; but exceedingly clever and amusing in conversation.' Isabel was 'a pleasant and lively woman, talks much and fast, seems excitable & is a Roman Catholic into the bargain.'

That afternoon, while several of them were sitting in the library after lunch, Isabel began telling them about her many mesmeric experiences. Writing afterwards in *The Life*, she described Burton as a great mesmeriser, preferring women, especially those of the blue-eyed, yellow-haired type. He had begun with her as soon as they were married. She had disliked it at first, and used to resist, but after a while she consented. He used to mesmerise her readily, but he never allowed anyone else to do it, nor did she. Once mesmerised, he had only to say "Talk", and she used to tell everything she knew. Laughingly, he used to tell everybody, "It is the only way to get a woman to tell you the truth." Often, she had told him things she would have preferred keeping to herself.[59]

After dinner on this particular occasion, Burton succeeded in mesmerising Kate's elder sister, Blanche. Isabel who had not been present in the room at the time got to hear of it, and there was an awful row between Burton and his wife after everyone else had gone to bed. She was concerned that 'he would now be doing it with women who were not so nice.' Angrily dismissing this as folly he, nevertheless, had threatened 'that if any man mesmerised her he would kill the man and her too, a threat I dare say he is quite capable of executing.'[60] Such behaviour suggests that, for both of them, mesmerism had powerful sexual connotations. For her, perhaps, it provided a release of pent-up desires; for him a form of prurient voyeurism.

The Burtons left on Monday, 9 January 1865, spending the next two months touring Ireland. They returned to England probably in late February or early March. During Burton's absence, Earl Russell had received another letter from the executors of the Johnson estate in Sierra Leone, dated 24 January 1865, restating the fact that they had not received the £280 owing from the sale of the *Harriet*, that they were being annoyed by the creditors of the estate, and asking the Foreign Secretary once more to intervene with Burton on their behalf. This Russell did in a letter sent in February, requesting him to take immediate steps to pay the amount in question to Johnson's executors.[61] The letter must have come as a nasty shock to Burton, who thought he had satisfactorily disposed of the matter. It was over a fortnight before he replied to the Foreign Office stating that the proceeds of the sale were never made over to him personally. In all probability, he went on vaguely, they had been made over to Mr Edward Laughlan who had acted for him during his absence in Dahome 'The sad effects of the local climate,' Burton suggested, 'may have prevented his accounting for the sum received.' Having heard that Mr Edward Laughlan was still an invalid, he had written to Mr John Laughland of Glasgow for information on the subject.[62]

Laughland enclosed with his reply, an account which showed a balance, after extracting the proceeds of the vessel, in his favour of £29 9s 6d, which did not include what was owed to Burton in Consul's fee, auction charges, and commission. In other words, it was the executors who owed Laughland and Burton money, and not the other way round. Armed with this information, a no doubt relieved Burton wrote to James Murray two days later.[63]

Around about this time, according to Isabel, while they were on a rail journey, Burton took a book out of his pocket, as if just bought at a stall, and handed it to her to read. She was delighted with it, she said, and kept reading him passages from it with peals of laughter. We are led to believe that it was only some time later, seeing the amused expression on his face, that it occurred to her that Burton himself was the author.[64]

The book was called *Lithophonema* or 'Stone Talk', a long satirical poem extending to 3,675 lines written in a loose octosyllabic couplet form.[65] Burton concealed his identity under the pseudonym of Frank Baker, derived from his own second name, and his mother's family name. He dedicated it to James Hain Friswell, 'My Old Friend, The Author of "The Gentle Life,"' who appears to have seen it through the press. The poem may be regarded as an up-dated version, in a typical Burton manner, of the medieval dream vision. For Piers Plowman falling asleep one May morning beside a brook on the Malvern Hills, and dreaming a marvellous dream, read Dr Polyglott (Burton) coming to on a London pavement around three o'clock in the morning, after a heavy drinking session with his friend, Charley Wode, a certain No-shire squire (Milnes). Instead of Holy Church appearing as it does to Piers, Dr Polyglott hears a voice coming from one of the paving-stones where he is lying, and Fleet Street suddenly comes alight, and alive with human heads. One head, in particular, speaks to him, one with a Hindu face, Ram Mohun Roy. This, of course, was the name of the great religious, social, and educational pioneer in the Hindu community during the nineteenth century. Here, as the other persona of the poem, he acts as a critic of Dr Polyglott's views, and the vehicle of its satire.

The poem embodies, among other things, Burton's highly critical views on British policy and society between the Reform Bill of 1832 and the 1860s. Many of them can be found in his other books, others are new. The Stone, for example, incensed at Polyglott's criticism of the Romans, compares them favourably with men like Clive, Hastings, Dalhousie, and Napier, whom he classes as bandits, and the policy of pagan Rome with imperial Britain and her 'philanthropic aims.' He accuses Britain of plundering, not like warriors, but like highwaymen. The Stone also lashes out at modern patriotism, at Popery, and Christianity's so-called brotherly love. A nation of shopkeepers, he asserts, can never hope to be truly philanthropical –'Did China sink beneath the seas/ What would result? Demand for teas!'

It is on the treatment dealt the starving pauper mother, however, that Burton's lines are at their most powerful. Having died in a reformatory for prostitutes or in jail, her body finally ends up on the dissecting bench:

> The scalpel's work when past and done,
> They shovel pieces, not of one,
> But half-a-dozen subjects dead –
> One arm, three legs, and dubious head –
> That, ere the mass begins to fester,
> The priest may pray for 'this our sister.'

Isabel, alarmed, showed the poem to Monckton Milnes, who thought it would do Burton a great deal of harm with the 'powers that were.' He advised her, therefore, to buy up all the copies which she did. It would appear that the precaution was totally unnecessary. Burton took as the poem's motto, the famous words in St Augustine's story of his conversion, "Tolle, Lege," (Take up and read). It was advice that the reading public largely ignored. The publisher's statement shows that only 200 copies were printed, 128 were sent to the press, author etc., 65 copies were left on the publisher's hands, and only 7 were sold at 3s 7d, knocked down from the original price of 5s. Of the £50 paid out by Burton, he got back £6 14s 1d.

Early in April, the Anthropological Society of London celebrated the election of five hundred fellows into the Society, by giving Burton, its senior vice-president a public dinner. Replying to Lord Stanley's toast, Burton recalled with pride how he had taken the chair two years earlier when the Society was founded, and its members numbered only eleven. As a writer and traveller during the last fifteen years, 'he had found it impossible to publish those physiological observations, always interesting to our common humanity, and at times so valuable. The Memoirs of the Anthropological Society act the Good Samaritan to facts which the publisher and the drawing-room table proudly pass by. Secondly, there was no arena for the public discussion of opinions now deemed paradoxical, and known to be unpopular. The rooms of the Anthropological Society now offer a refuge to destitute truth.'[66]

Later that month, Burton was called to give evidence before the Parliamentary Select Committee on British Establishments in West Africa. It appears that Livingstone afterwards, 'felt that Burton's evidence had done a lot of damage and had set back for years any hopes of a more positive British policy towards colonization.' Burton, supposedly, had derided the economic potential of West Africa, and had claimed that the missionaries there were doing more harm than good. Livingstone was angry enough to write a sympathetic letter to Dr Tidman with condolences for the 'lies' and 'aspersions of that beastly fellow Burton against the missionaries of the West Coast.' 'Burton,' Livingstone had gone on, 'seems to be a moral idiot. His conduct in Africa was so bad that it cannot be spoken of without disgust – systematically wicked, impure, and untruthful.'[67]

Far from deriding the economic potential of West Africa, Burton told the Chairman, the Rt Hon (later Sir) Charles Adderley, that he had the highest beliefs in the mercantile prospects of the Niger. 'We might easily supply the whole basin of the Niger and the eastern Niger at least at a third of the price at which they are supplied at present by the caravan trade of the north.' He was, however, against the British taking any territory in the Bight of Biafra, and as little as possible in the Bight of Benin. Apart from Lagos, where the Consul could do all the work necessary with the help of a cruiser, he believed that all the Government establishments, both civil and military, could be dispensed with on that coast.

Burton was predictable in his remarks on the native population of Sierra Leone. Asked by Lord Stanley if he considered that the Sierra Leone people had a bad reputation, Burton replied that the civilised Christian convert there was dreaded on the Coast. 'He has been trained up in police courts, can examine a witness as well as any lawyer in England, his great missionary interest can raise a cry at once.' Sir Francis Baring nicely showed up Burton's prejudice when he asked if, with regard to the comforts of life, carriages, horses, and so on, the black merchant did not live very much on the same footing as the European? "Externally, quite so," Burton replied; "internally not so much. He delights in carriages and horses, and a broad cloth coat with a large velvet collar, but in the house all this is removed, and he places a rag round his waist."

Sir Francis. "He takes off his coat?"

Burton. "Yes, and with his coat he takes off his manners."

Sir Francis. "Europeans take off their coats in India?"

Burton. "Yes, no doubt."[68]

It is obvious that James Murray contacted Burton again on 17 April over John Laughland's letter and accounts. Just over a fortnight later, Burton wrote to Earl Russell, enclosing Laughland's reply to Murray's communication, and trusting that his Lordship would find it satisfactory. It is only at this stage in her biography – without, of course, breathing a word of the *Harriet* affair – that Isabel claimed to have represented to Lord Russell how miserable their lives were, being always separated by the climate of Fernando Po, 'and he very kindly transferred us to Santos, in the Brazils, where I could go.' The appointment, it will be remembered, had really been made six months earlier. However, Isabel's fiction, the reason for which will appear shortly, lent credence to her story that she and Burton would go out to Portugal for a trip. At the end of it, he would go on to Rio de Janeiro, she would return to London 'to wind up affairs, and then join him at Santos.'

The Burtons left Southampton on Tuesday, 9 May.[69] They arrived four days later at Lisbon, after experiencing very bad weather. The *Braganza Hotel* where they took up residence, was crowded with a diplomatic mission from London, there to give the Garter to the King of Portugal. The Burtons were initially put up in the garret. After two days, they were given a very pleasant suite of rooms overlooking the Tagus and a large part of Lisbon. Even so, their spacious, whitewashed bedroom, was overrun with cockroaches, some as much as three inches long. Isabel at first used to stand on a chair and scream, annoying Burton a great deal. 'A nice sort of traveller and companion you are going to make,' she reported his saying. The result was, that a piqued Isabel got down, fetched a basin of water and a slipper, and, fighting her revulsion, in two hours knocked ninety-seven of them into it. It cured her, she said. Even so, they changed rooms a short while afterwards.

Cockroaches were to be the least of their worries. It is clear from a letter written by Burton to the FO from the hotel three days after their arrival, that he had been informed on the Saturday before their departure, without being given any official explanation, that the issue of his salary was to be discontinued. His passage was paid, increasing his difficulties. He was later given to understand that the stoppage was on account of the brig *Harriet*, concerning which, he said, a long explanation had been forwarded on 26 April, by Mr John Laughland.[70] On the day before his departure, Burton had written to the FO, recalling John Laughland's statement which showed that the £280 had been used by Mr Edward Laughlan, Acting Consul during Burton's absence in Dahomey, to settle an account due to the firms of Messrs Taylor & Laughland, of which he was the chief agent at Fernando Po. The money, Burton said, had never passed through his hands, therefore, he could not be held responsible for it.[71]

This was not the view of the FO, a Memo of the same date also showing the extent of its displeasure with his conduct. Captain Burton, it said, seemed determined to avoid settling the case in the only way in which he could properly close it. After briefly recalling the facts, it cuttingly accused Burton, 'whose receipt must be held to be of more value than his statements that he never received the money,' of trying to throw the blame on his own Acting Consul. Burton, however, was solely responsible. They must necessarily insist upon his doing what he had been told long ago, to settle the question himself personally with the executors, by retaining out of Burton's salary the amount which he had acknowledged to have received as Consul.[72]

Faced with this serious situation, Burton asked Earl Russell for an extension of leave in order to get into contact with John Laughland and others from Lisbon, rather than from Santos, where no reply to a letter could reach him in less than two months and a half. The FO despatch a week later was brusque and unsympathetic. He was instructed to proceed to his post and settle the matter there with the executors.[73]

The affair must have cast a long shadow over the holiday. They stayed for a month, not two as Isabel claimed. Burton then left for Rio on 13 June, leaving Isabel to pick up the pieces in England[74] Once there, she lost no time in contacting John Laughland, with the result that the two went together for a meeting with James Murray at the FO. Everything appeared to be satisfactorily explained at this interview, and Burton was allowed to draw the March and June quarters of his pay.[75]

In the meantime, Isabel attended what she called 'some very interesting experiments at Mr William Crookes, both chemically and spiritualistically.' The Burtons had probably been introduced to Crookes by Dr Bird's sister, Alice, a mutual friend. Crookes, a chemist and physicist, was famous for having discovered the element, thallium, four years earlier, and later for his cathode-ray studies, which were fundamental in the development of atomic physics. He had also developed a scientific interest in spiritualism, eventually becoming convinced of the reality of psychical phenomena. Later, this led to his being duped by D.D. Home and Florence Cook.[76]

Although Crookes had inherited a large fortune from his father, he had visions of making a far larger one by the process known as gold amalgamation. In February 1865, therefore, he lodged his first patent application. It was turned down, however, since his sodium-amalgam process had been patented a year earlier by a German-American scientist, Professor Henry Wurtz. To cater for the different varieties of ores, Crookes specified three separate amalgams. The only hope in South America seemed to be based upon prospects in Brazil. Burton, it appears, as soon as he became aware of Crookes's scheme, offered to take charge of his interests there. Later, on Burton's advice, Crookes took out another patent, specifying the use of a small admixture of silver instead of zinc in the amalgam.[77] Nothing, however, ever came of the scheme.

During the middle of August, Isabel wrote to Lord Houghton informing him of her departure date, and stating that she continued to get 'cheery notes at intervals from dear Richard.' He was amusing himself on the Coast and intended joining her in Rio on 9th October. She then went on to ask Lord Houghton, if he could, 'without any trouble or unpleasantness to himself,' write to the Duc D'Aumale to ask 'if he would give us a good word with the Comte and Comtess D'Eu at Rio. I suppose one doesn't ask for a letter of introduction but whatever is <u>right</u> for the Royal family. We shall be present in the usual way & Richard must come under their notice in his official capacity, but one is always better received if one knows somebody at <u>home</u> who is interested about one, & if you could do this it would be very kind, as it is the only good society on the Coast (the entourage of the Emperor). I should not like Richard to begin with any other.' Isabel said she was travelling about saying goodbyes, and was returning to London on the 23rd. '27 Upper Montagu Street will find me if you shd be so kind as to write…..'[78]

By the end of August, having spent two and a half months in England, not the month as she claimed, Isabel had settled their affairs to her satisfaction. With just over a week to go before leaving for South America, she spent most of it in retreat at the Convent of the Assumption, Kensington Square. 'I am to bear *all* joyfully, as an atonement to save Richard,' she wrote in her devotional book. 'How thoughtful for me has been God's dispensation!…How I have bowed down before my husband's intellect! If I lost Richard life would be worthless. Yet he and I and life are perishable, and will soon be over; but God and my soul and eternity are everlasting. I pray to be better moulded to the will of God, and for Love of Him to become indifferent to what may befall me.'[79] On 8 September she left London, and the following day sailed from Southampton.

CHAPTER TWENTY-EIGHT

EXILED IN BRAZIL

The Royal Mail Company's steamship arrived at Recife (Pernambuco) on 27 September. To her consternation, Isabel discovered that all the letters she had written to Burton since they had parted at Lisbon were piled up in the post-office. Four days later, after beating down the coast in heavy weather, the ship docked at Rio, and the couple had a happy reunion. They booked into the Estrangeiros Hotel, enjoyed a great deal of hospitality, both naval and diplomatic, and went on a number of excursions and picnics. Isabel also suffered her first bout of fever.

Santos, 120 miles south of Rio, was ordinarily reached by a rather uncomfortable local steamer. However, as soon as Isabel was fit enough to be moved, they were given a lift aboard a naval man-of-war. According to her, they reached Santos on 9 October.[1] However, the dating on a brief letter from Burton to Milnes indicates that they were still at Rio on 23 October.[2]

Today the world's leading coffee port, Santos was then little better than a mangrove swamp, much like the West Coast of Africa Burton had recently left. Lying only a few feet above sea-level on the inner side of the flat Ilha de São Vicente, heavy seas sometimes washed into the gardens, scattering whalebones about in all directions, and ruining the flowers. Burton, having inspected the place before Isabel's arrival, had concluded that São Paulo healthily situated on top of the Serra, and some thirty miles inland, needed a consul as much as Santos on the fever-ridden coast. Very conveniently, Charles A. Glennie, the vice-consul, whose sights were set on being consul one day, was so attached to Santos where he had lived for the past forty years, that, according to Isabel, 'the only hardship he would have known would have been to live out of it.' Burton, therefore, at least in theory, would only need to commute between the two places as occasion required.

São Paulo was a pretty, white, straggling town on a hill, three thousand feet above sea-level, with a view of mountains in the distance. Although uncomfortably hot between nine and four in the summer, it was reasonably cool at other times. Unlike Santos, there were no cockroaches, fleas, bugs, or sandflies. There were, however, mosquitoes and jiggers. The latter, Isabel discovered through painful personal experience, were little tick-like insects, that burrowed into your foot under the toe-nail and laid a large sac of eggs. In extreme circumstances, failure to remove them in time could result in the amputation of toes and feet.

While Burton returned to Santos to set up his Consulate, Isabel stayed behind to look for a house. Initially, she took a furnished apartment in the town, feeling that if Burton had to be away often –which was more than a distinct probability – she would not feel particularly safe 'amongst lawless people and beasts', with only her Irish maid to keep her company. Almost a fortnight later, she left to rejoin Burton. 'I do hate

Santos,' she wrote to her family in December. 'The climate is beastly, the people fluffy. The stinks, the vermin, the food, the niggers are all of a piece.' Besides, with the steaming heat rising from the mangrove swamps, they were plagued with sand-flies and mosquitoes. The only tolerable place was the Barra, which boasted a magnificent sandy beach speckled with rose-coloured shells, fronting a wide bay and surrounded by picturesque mountain scenery. After spending a fortnight or so there, Isabel became feverish. She, therefore, left for São Paulo, while Burton set off south to Iguape, on some unexplained business, possibly to investigate the lead mines there.

Shortly after her return, Isabel engaged a black servant called Chico. A recently emancipated slave, he was thirty-five years old, a dwarf about four feet tall, perfectly proportioned, and as black as coal. He was also very intelligent, and a jack of all trades. From then on, he became Isabel's right-hand man, and stayed with them the whole time they were in Brazil.

It appears from one of Isabel's letters, that Burton left around 18 December for another visit to the mines, leaving her to celebrate her first Christmas in a strange country, alone. It was not until a month later that he returned to Santos, 'so I conclude he will be up here in a few days. It is our fifth wedding day on the 22nd....' By the time he reappeared, Isabel had rented another property, an old convent, No 72 Rua do Carmo. Opening on to the street, it ran a long way back, providing an unbroken view of the countryside. She immediately set about cleaning, painting, whitewashing, and wall-papering, engaging slaves and paying them as if they were free men. All were Catholics, so Isabel made a small chapel for them, which she painted herself. The slaves in Brazil were allowed to believe, she said, that they had no souls, and nothing to look forward to. She, however, taught them the dubiously comforting doctrine, that, not only did they have souls, but that 'although they were condemned by class and colour and custom to be slaves upon earth, just as it was in the Bible, that once dead, they and we would stand equal before God.'[3] The priest used to come to the little Oratory, where Isabel had the bishop's permission to have mass and sacraments, and they all received communion together. The house had two other interesting features. One was Burton's study, a very long room with a terrace at the end, and equipped with a telescope and other items necessary for astronomy. Occupying the centre of the house was a large, all-purpose room opening on the stairs. Directly below, was a room Isabel kept as a hospice for the needy and homeless after dark, where they were fed and housed, before being turned out in the early morning.

Since the *Harriet* affair was totally suppressed by Isabel and W.H. Wilkins in their biographies, there is no mention of the acute financial embarrassment that the Burtons must have suffered as the result of the FO's action over his pay. On 6 May 1866, while he was away on a nineteen days' visit to the interior, Isabel wrote a long letter to the Foreign Secretary, pointing out that Burton's pay had been stopped since 30 June of the previous year, and for the second time. He, himself, refused any further explanations believing it to be useless. She, therefore, was taking the liberty of doing so for him.

Despite her visit to the FO with John Laughland, Burton's pay was again stopped, 'we think perhaps on account of a scurrilous pamphlet which a black lawyer named Rainy has written as if he were employed by the owners, and which is only a return for all that Capt. Burton has written in dispraise of the Sierra Leone negro, and is untrue as the explanation I now send is true…'[4]

Rainy, in fact, was employed by the owners, the executors having invested him in August 1865 with the power of attorney to sue Burton for the £280. His sixty-six page pamphlet, *The Censor Censured*, privately printed in London, appeared some time towards the end of that year. Written with eloquence and forensic skill, it was dedicated 'To the African People.'[5]

Referring to Burton's *Wanderings in West Africa*, he said that he had not come across any books of travel, 'since the extravagant stories told by Munchausen,' to equal it. He characterised Burton's judgements on Sierra Leone as 'a vile national slander,' conclusions arrived at after a three days' visit. After setting out the whole of the correspondence which had taken place regarding the sale of the *Harriet*, interspersed with his comments, Rainy spoke of challenging 'the whole record of official or commercial life for such a lamentable instance of culpability or neglect.'[6] He said that he would not pain Burton, by dwelling upon the transparent hollowness of his defence, ie his absence from Fernando Po:

> An official absent from his post, and none of the communications addressed to him forwarded? This is rather a sorry look out for Her Majesty's Government in the event of a delicate or important matter arising. But giving Captain Burton full credit for the clumsy manner which he, by his own confession discharges his official duties – May I ask: was he absent when he pocketed the proceeds of the sale and signed the receipt? He most assuredly was not then absent in the flesh, although to the protracted dismay of Johnson's executors, he was absent in mind as far as the transmission of the proceeds of the sale of the "Harriet" was concerned. The only plausible presumption is, that Captain Burton has a soul which rises superior to vulgar accounts....[7]

Although Burton was innocent of the charge of pocketing any money, this unwonted publicity was damaging to his reputation at home. Rigby referred to the pamphlet in a letter to Grant, giving a somewhat garbled version of what had happened. 'The agents are going to sue Burton in a Civil Court,' he said, '& he will have to come home.'[8] In another letter a few months later, he told Grant that Rainy had sent a copy of his pamphlet to the Royal Geographical Society, and that he, himself, had written to Rainy to try to obtain a copy, but without success.[9]

On 28 May, Lord Clarendon wrote to Burton, enclosing a copy of the letter from the executors asking for Government assistance in recovering the money. 'I am advised by the Law Officer of the Crown that the assistance requested should be rendered, and that you should be made properly responsible for acts done in your name and on your behalf.' An inquiry was to be made on the spot. In the meanwhile, Burton's pay was suspended.[10]

At the beginning of June, Isabel travelled to Rio with Burton, who had been invited to give an account of his travels before Pedro II and his Empress.[11] Later that month they were presented at the court which had transferred to summer quarters at Petropolis, some 2,667 feet above sea level. Burton was dressed in his consular uniform, and Isabel in 'grand toilet.' Pedro II, whose reign lasted almost half a century, was the most enlightened statesman, simple, modest, and caring little for the trappings of royalty, who was never happier than when conversing with scholars. On their second visit, the Emperor kept Burton talking two and a half hours on various affairs, and asking his opinion on the resources of the country. Only the previous month, Burton had written to H.E. Edward Thornton, the British Envoy and Minister Plenipotentiary at Rio pointing out that, 'At present the province of São Paulo has not been able to show a pound of coal. If allowed to travel I do not despair of discovering an article which will materially develop the physical and moral capabilities of this vast empire.'[12]

Later that month, Burton and Isabel went down to Rio with the intention of taking out a patent, presumably for Crooke's gold amalgamation process. Whilst there, Isabel became covered with boils, unable to sit or stand, walk or lie down without pain, irritated and depressed beyond words. Matters were made worse by one of her best friends, Mrs Elliot, wife of the Admiral, having to leave for England because of her husband's promotion. There was one apparent gleam of light, however, Burton being informed that he had obtained his concession to the lead mines of Iporanga in São Paulo. Isabel doesn't go into details about this, and the facts only emerged later through official correspondence. They were cock-a-hoop about it, and Burton, leaving Isabel to receive the papers, set off for an unstated destination in search of a sea-serpent reputed to be one hundred and sixty feet long! 'But I do not tell this,' Isabel informed her family, 'as it might get him into a row with the F.O.' No sooner had Burton gone, however, than Isabel received a letter informing her that the Council of State had raised an objection to the concessions documents being printed. The result was that she was forced to remain in the hotel in Rio on her own, and at great expense, in order to fight the case as best she could.

Isabel left Rio on 11 August, with regret for some things, especially those friends she had made there, who wanted her to stay for a ball on the 14th. However, she knew that Burton's travels would be finished that day, 'and he would feel dull and lonely at home alone.' They met sooner than expected. The next day, at 4 o'clock in the morning, 'Poor Richard came off from the coast in a canoe in a gale wind,' and the captain obliged Isabel by laying to and bringing him in. Burton's canoe had been upset, and he had spent two days in the water, fortunately shallow.

For a while, after Rio society, Isabel found what she called the 'farmhouse life' of São Paulo, with no one to speak to, very dull. However, it did not take her long to become reconciled to it once again. She need not have worried about Burton's feeling dull and lonely at home. On 22 August, he left to stay with priests of the Capuchin Order at their *chacara*, or country-house, just outside the town. They were the best educated men in the province, from whom Burton felt he could always learn something. Obviously keenly aware of his shortcomings in science and mathematics, he took up the study of astronomy with Fray João, and metaphysics, physics, and algebra, with Père Germain. It 'feels odd going to school near 50,' he wrote to one correspondent, 'but n'importe.'

Shortly after his arrival in Brazil, Burton had also begun the study of the Tupy-Guarani languages.[13] After Arawakan, they were the second largest group of the South American Indian languages, used by the first European traders and missionaries as contact languages in their dealings with the Indians. He also had at least a couple of literary works in hand. One was Camoen's *The Lusiads*, begun years earlier in Goa, and *Vikram and the Vampire; or Tales of Indian Devilry*, his adaptation of eleven stories taken from the Baital Pachisi.[14]

Writing to her parents on 15 September, probably in response to their comments on her suffering from boils, Isabel said that she did not think that the climate disagreed with her. It was more money affairs and local miseries. She would not feel justified in coming home except for serious illness. She had 'just domesticated and tamed Richard a little; and it would not do to give him an excuse for becoming a wandering vagabond again.' What he needed was a comfortable and respectable home, and a tight hand upon his purse-strings. She also felt that she had a mission, which amply filled her time.

They led a very regular life. They were up at 5 am, and out for a walk. She then went to Mass and the market. Afterwards, Burton gave her a lesson in fencing and Indian clubs. Having bathed in cold water, they dressed and breakfasted at 11 am. Isabel then carried out her domestic work, followed by singing practice and studying Portuguese. After helping Burton with his literature, they dined at six, and retired to bed at nine or ten.[15] It is clear that Isabel also took a good deal of Burton's consular work off his shoulders, later describing herself lightheartedly in a letter to Lord Houghton, as 'the vice-consul.' She presently had to copy several reports for the Foreign Office: one of thirty-two pages on cotton, another of one hundred and twenty-five pages on geographical matters, and a third of eighty pages, on general trade. Since it was for Lord Stanley, she said, she did it cheerfully.[16]

Stanley, who had replaced Earl Clarendon as Foreign Secretary in Derby's third cabinet, was notably sympathetic, partisan even, towards Burton's position in the *Harriet* affair.[17] In a Memo, Lord Stanley said that he had read Burton's explanation carefully. While recognising that he was legally responsible for Laughlan's acts, he could see force in Burton's plea, since he was absent on duty, that 'summum jus' become 'summa juria.'[18] As to his being evasive in giving accounts, Lord Stanley thought Burton's defence 'reasonable and probable.' The alleged extravagance of expenditure could only be investigated on the spot. He saw no reason why Burton's letter should not be forwarded. Since Burton spoke of his reputation for integrity,

Lord Stanley thought it should be explained that there was no charge against him in that respect. He did not believe it wise to stop the whole salary of a consul kept at his post, and who might not have private means. 'Are we not in such a case responsible morally for his getting into debt, which he must do?'[19]

Having obtained permission from Edward Thornton to visit Sarocaba and the iron mines of the province of São Paulo,[20] Burton left on 10 December with two companions, three horse-boys, and a long string of mules, and was away twenty-six days. According to Isabel, she accompanied him part of the way. 'We parted,' she wrote, 'on a little mountain with a church at the top – a most romantic spot.'[21] She returned alone with one mounted slave. Since Isabel wrote to her parents from Rio on 8 December, having suffered, what she described as a mild attack of cholera, it might be thought that she would not have been in any position to make the return journey in time to have travelled with Burton. Nor could she possibly have spent Christmas with him in spite of claiming to have done so in *The Life*. She actually spent it in Rio with friends, having come there to sell one of Burton's books, and continue work on a gold concession.[22]

It appears that Burton eventually obtained the concession for the lead mines of Iporanga. However, as reported by Isabel, Sir Edward Thornton, was very angry with him, taking it in the sense of Consuls trading and reported him home. 'Fortunately,' she said, 'we had the large mind of Lord Stanley (Lord Derby) at the head of the Foreign Office, and he, knowing how caged and misplaced Richard was at such a Consulate, thought that he might be allowed that little bit of amusement, and sent back a despatch that he did not think that being interested in mineral production could be exactly classed under the head of trading.'[23] This was a complete travesty of the facts as the relevant despatch from Thornton shows:

> Lord Stanley's attention has been called to a mining concession lately granted by the Brazilian Government to you, in conjunction with Señor Augusto Teixera Coicubra. His Lordship has consequently instructed me to inform you that in seeking this concession at the hands of the Brazilian Government you must have overlooked the fact that you are by your instructions prohibited from trading; and it is evident that a concession for working mines which is clearly a trading proceeding would be incompatible with your official functions.
>
> Lord Stanley adds that the seeking for such a concession for yourself was inconsistent with para.VII of the General Instructions in which it is laid down that a Consul cannot ask or accept favour for himself from the Governor of the country in which he resides, and that if you asked the same concession and favour of your partner you have also disregarded the rule laid down in the same instructions that a Consul should not recommend his private friends abroad or at home "for employment of trust or profit" under that Government.[24]

So, despite the time and expense involved, Burton's hopes of making himself rich on that score came to nothing.

There is every reason to believe that he kept up a regular correspondence with Swinburne, although only one letter survives from this period. The poet had written to Lord Houghton shortly after Burton left for Brazil in 1865. 'As my tempter and favourite audience has gone to Santos, I may hope to be a good boy again, after such a "jolly swishing" as Rodin alone can and dare administer. The Captain was too many for me, & I may have shaken the thyrsus in your face. But after this half, I mean to be no end good.[25]

Literary success, at least among the younger generation, had come to Swinburne in that year, first with *Atalanta in Calydon,* followed by the first series of *Poems and Ballads* in the late autumn of 1866. These won him immediate celebrity and notoriety. John Morley described Swinburne as having 'revealed to the world a mind all aflame with the feverish carnality of a schoolboy over the dirtiest passages in Lempriere. It is not every poet who asks us to go hear him tuning his lyre in a stye.'[26] Picking up on this metaphor, *Punch* described Swinburne as 'Mr Swineborn.' Despite these puritanical comments, however, 'the real marvel of *Poems and Ballads*,' as Sir Arthur Quiller-Couch has said, 'lay of course in its poetry, ...here was a man who, five hundred years after Chaucer.....had suddenly discovered a new door and thrust it open upon what seemed endless vistas of beauty.'[27]

Writing to Burton on 11 January 1867, Swinburne said that he was currently working on 'a sort of etude a la Balzac plus the poetry [Lesbia Brandon], which he considered would 'be more offensive and objectionable to Britannia than anything I have yet done.'[28]

Charles A.P.V. Robinson, Commander and Senior Officer, Bights Division, had arrived at Fernando Po on 1 Nov 1866, and immediately commenced enquires into the *Harriet* affair. Now, having received Commander Robinson's report, James Murray saw a means of bringing the long-running contentious issue to a satisfactory conclusion. In a Memo of 22 January 1867, he said that he found Burton to be a creditor to the Foreign Office for certain repairs to the Consulate at Fernando Po. Settlement was only delayed because they were waiting for the account and vouchers which Burton had been required to send. The money payable to him would be enough, if not more, to pay off the claim on the *Harriet*, 'and the settlement is therefore considered rendered easy.'

This was a solution, of course, plucked out of the air, since there is no documentary evidence that the FO ever had any intention of paying Burton for the repairs he carried out on the Consulate. Murray, therefore, proposed writing to Burton, stating that the result of the investigation proved that he was liable to the executors for the sum of £280, for which he had given a receipt, less charges incidental in the ship. However, as the charges made in his behalf by Mr Laughlan had been proved to be excessive, he had to leave it to the executors as to whether they wished to make reasonable allowance for this, and Burton would pay the balance rather than the whole.[29] Letters containing the FO's decision were sent to all parties concerned on 31 January 1867. Burton was also told that the suspension of his salary pending the inquiry was now rescinded, and that his pay would be issued in the usual manner. Consul Livingstone was informed that, as a result of the enquiry, it would no longer be possible for Edward Laughlan to perform any consular duties at Fernando Po in the future.

That same month, in an undated despatch to Edward Thornton, Burton asked for permission to visit the valley of the Iguape River, 'where according to native rumour there is some prospect of slave importation being attempted.' Burton said that he should be able to collect materials for a report to the Minister between the middle of February and the last week of March.[30] Permission was given. Burton, however, returned in March, 'knocked up by six weeks in the wild,' according to Isabel, 'and he broke out with fever. I felt affected and the whole house squeamish.' Isabel's remedy was to rush Burton off to the Barra, where they stayed in 'what they dare to call the hotel..... It is as hot as the lower regions; and if one could take off one's flesh and sit in one's bones, one would be too glad.[31]

On 5 April, H.W. Bates, the Asst Secretary of the RGS,[32] wrote Burton a letter, which must have sent his spirits soaring:

> Before this reaches you, you will have seen in the papers the accounts of the reported death of Dr.Livingstone. We have received no further news since the letter published in The Times of March 26th. According to Dr. Kirk who has very carefully examined (cross-examined) the 9 Johanna men who escaped, Livingstone before he was cut down, had solved the problem of the northern termination of Lake Nyassa. After reading Kirk's carefully written letter in which he sets out this conclusion, I must say I thoroughly agree with him. Lake Nyassa ends in a marshy creek (or Lake Nyassa's end) without current about 10° 30′ S. lat.
>
> Now one of my chief objects in writing to you, is to tell you what is being done in consequence of this.

Mr. Findlay believes it will strengthen the hypothesis of Tanganyika being the head of the Nile, and you will be after all the discoverer. I am spurring Findlay to write a short paper on the subject for our Society: he has made some discovery about levels – of Albert Nyanza and the water visited by Laçerda. If he make a readable paper we will have it read at an evening meeting. He has borrowed of me your MS translation of Laçerda's journey to Cazembe, which was deposited in my hands by the brother of Winwood Reade, & which I know you would wish to be lent to Mr.Findlay for such a purpose.[33]

Burton had been almost two years in the country without an official holiday. Early in May, he wrote to Thornton asking for an extended leave to visit the gold and diamond mines of Central Minas Geraes, via Petropolis, Barbacena, and the prairies and highlands of Brazil. It is highly unlikely that he told the Minister that he also intended canoeing down the 1,500 miles of Brazil's great São Francisco River from Sabara to the sea. This time, Isabel and Chico would travel with him. Back came a highly amenable reply from Thornton, that he would have much pleasure in granting the leave asked for. On Burton's arrival in Petropolis, he would be glad to hear what persons would be most useful for him to have letters of introduction to, and would do his best to obtain them.[34]

Obviously in revenge for Thornton's reporting him to the FO, neither of these facts is acknowledged in Burton's book describing his travels, where the minister's name is suppressed. Instead, Lord Stanley receives the credit for Burton's leave – no mention that it was requested, only that it 'was graciously allowed' – and the impression given that the various introductions he received were the result of his own efforts. Responsibility for the Santos Consulate having been handed over to Charles Glennie, the three left for Rio on 21 May. They were there for almost three weeks. On 5 June, obviously still smarting at his treatment over the *Harriet* affair, Burton wrote a long, bitter, self-justificatory and libellous letter to Lord Stanley.

As the case then stood, he said, he wished to make 'a respectful but most energetic protest against the great wrong which has been done to me, and to request that justice might be done to my former representative, Mr. Edward Laughlan as well as to myself.' Burton claimed that, 'Some excitement was caused in a clique best characterised as the negro-worshipper by my book called "Wanderings in West Africa," by sundry of my lectures before certain societies, and by my relations of travel in Abeokuta and Dahome. As might be expected, the negro-worshippers did not attempt to defend his black idol; in the old noble way he proceeded to retaliate by slander and defamation.'

The consequence of a FO letter of 31 January 1867 to the solicitors, was a leader in *The African Times* of 'unusual and transparent virulence,' suggesting that Burton was unfit for employment under HM's Government, and should be removed from his post. 'All this fury,' he said, 'because I do not hold the black to be equal to the white man, and because I would prefer seeing the missionary at home in Spitalfields than abroad in West Africa!' He had served his country in four parts of the world for more than a quarter of a century. His conduct had met with as much approval as could reasonably be expected 'by a man who had, perhaps, been sometimes indiscreet in speaking what he believed to be the truth.' He now earnestly asked for justice: first, that all the papers connected with the case might be submitted for revision to the Law Adviser of the Crown; second, that the sum placed in his name by Messrs Hampton and Burgin might be forwarded to him in full; and finally, that either his despatch might be published, or some other means as public as the aggravated insult to his character might be adopted for his protection.[35]

A FO memorandum appended to this letter was brief and to the point: 'I do not see anything in this letter calculated to show that the course adopted was wrong or illegal; but there can be no objection to comply with his request to refer it to the Law Adviser.' This was done, and the final despatch, which brought the curtain down on the *Harriet* affair, was sent to Burton on 23 July 1867. It stated that Lord Stanley had submitted Burton's representation and the whole of the previous correspondence to the proper

Law Officer of the Crown. He had advised that there were not sufficient grounds for altering the decision of HM's Government as already communicated to Burton. Lord Stanley added, however, that it was open to Burton or to his agent in this country to recover at law from Messrs Hampton and Burgin, any just claims that he might have against them for the expenses incurred in maintaining the crew of the *Harriet* before she was sold. But he should remember, 'that they will set against any such claim the loss of interest between 1863 and 1867 on the proceeds of the sale of the vessel and the expenses to which their clients have been put in establishing their case.'[36]

After enjoying what Burton drily called, 'the excitements of the Rio season,' he and Isabel left the Brazilian capital on 12 June. They sailed across the Bay from the Prainha in a small paddle-steamer, which eventually brought them to a rickety little plank jetty at the northern end called the Mana landing-place. From there, a little railroad ran eleven miles through a mangrove and papyrus flat to the foot of the Estrella range of mountains. Here, they changed the train for a carriage drawn by four mules, and began a steep winding ascent up the mountains covered with tropical forest. Within two hours they were at Petropolis, and booked in at the Hotel Inglez. Some days later they set off at daybreak for Juiz de Forez in a large char-a-banc, the heavier luggage having been sent ahead by public coach. It was sunset when they drove up to a chalet and were guests in an empty house. That evening, they were serenaded in the moonlight by a band of villagers. The most agreeable part of the following day was spent in the gardens of the château of Commendador Procopio Ferrreira Lage, an enormously wealthy Brazilian planter.

From there, they travelled on to Barbacena, which proved to be a dead-alive kind of place. The streets were deserted and there was not even a market. At nearly four thousand feet, it was bitterly cold except in the sun. Many of the houses were shut up, the young men having left to fight in the war with Paraguay. On Wednesday, 19 June, they left the last remnant of civilization behind, taking to the saddle to cross the campos or Brazilian prairies, avoiding the most populous part of Minas, lying almost due north between Barbacena and Diamantia. Besides themselves, their party consisted of a Mr E, Mr James Fitzpatrick, in charge of the three baggage mules, Chico, two slaves on foot as guides, and two spare animals as remounts. Dr Renault, the French Vice-Consul, had supplied Burton with letters, 'recommendations' in this country often proving more valuable than banknotes.

It was early July when they finally they arrived at the village outside the Morro Velho colony. As the bells rang nine, they alighted at the entrance of the Casa Granda, and were welcomed by Mr Gordon, the Superintendent of the São João d'El Rei Mining Company, and his wife. Morro Velho was a bustling, lively place in an extensive, elevated valley, surrounded by mountains and divided into districts or settlements. Mr Gordon was like a local king there and all over the province.

On Wednesday, 10 July, they left Morro Velho for a short trip, Gordon wishing Burton to inspect a seam of ore of disputed substance – that, at least, is Isabel's story. At the end of eleven days, they returned and found the church bells ringing, and pretty girls with sprays of flowers in their hair on their way to Mass. Forbidden by Burton to attend, Isabel paid two old women to hear Mass for her, much to the amusement of the party.

Among other things, Burton and Isabel were determined to go down the mine reputed to be the largest, deepest, and richest gold mine in Brazil. It was considered something of an event for a woman to do so, especially since Mrs Gordon, who had lived at Morro Velho nine and a half years, had never done so. She now decided to accompany Isabel, the two women dressing themselves in brown Holland trousers, blouse, belt, and stiff leather hats, with a candle stuck on their heads with a dab of clay. There were two means of descent, either by ladder or by bucket. The ladders, nearly a thousand yards long, were preferred by the miners, since their safety depended only on themselves. The alternative was to descend in a big iron bucket weighing nearly a ton, called a 'kibble', normally used for carrying ore. It was attached to a carriage running on a shaft of iron-shod wood, descending at an angle of 46°.

So powerful was the pressure in places, the biggest trunks of the Brazilian forest giants had been split or crushed. The vertical height, 1,134 feet and the 108 feet breadth were unparalleled in mining, suggesting to Burton a cavern, a huge Palace of Darkness. 'Through this Dantesque Inferno, gnomes and kobolds glided above in ghostly fashion, half-naked figures muffled by the mist. Here, dark bodies gleaming with beaded heat-drops, hung by chains in what seemed frightful positions; there they swung like Leotard from place to place; here they swarmed up loose ropes like the Troglodytes; there they moved over scaffolds which even to look up at, would make a nervous temperament dizzy.'[37]

In the evening, Burton gave a lecture on his travels, and the miners and their officers put on a short concert for them. Burton had been preparing – Isabel, in her account writes 'we' – to canoe from Sabara down the Rio das Velhas and the Rio São Francisco to the sea, visiting among many other places, the diamond mines at Diamantina on the way. The expedition, she said, was to be Richard, herself (if permitted), and Mr. E -. 'I was entreating to go, and my fate was hanging in the balance, when the question was settled for me by an accident.' Coming down from the platform after singing at a concert, she fell awkwardly and sprained her ankle severely. 'This was a dreadful bore for Richard,' she said, 'who could not take me, and did not like to leave me…..' Burton, of course, had never intended taking her, writing to a correspondent from Rio in June, that, 'My wife accompanies me part of the trip.'[38] 'My old longing for the pleasures of life in the back woods,' he later wrote – for solitude – was strong upon me as in Bube land. I sighed unaimiably to be again out of reach of my kind so to speak – once more to meet Nature face to face. This food of the soul….is like absence, which, says the Proverb, extinguishes the little "passions" and inflames the great.'[39] Burton, 'good-naturedly' postponed his journey for ten days. Isabel was confined to bed for five days, and then allowed to move around on crutches, litter and sofa, which lasted for a further twenty days.

On 6 August, they set off from Morro Velho over the picturesque mountainous road to Sabara, Isabel carried in a covered litter with a mule at front and back. The next morning, accompanied by all the Sabara VIPs, they walked to the Porto da Ponte Grande, where the ajojo or raft lay. An old Noah's Ark, as Burton described it, consisted of two canoes lashed together, boarded over, and covered with an awning like a tent. For the rest, there was a little brick stove, benches, and a writing-table. It was crewed by two blacks in the stern, and two in the bow to paddle and pole, and one to cook for Burton and attend on him. Isabel and he went aboard, and a young woman of the party broke a bottle of caxassi over the craft's bows, exclaiming, "Brig *Eliza*". Two pairs of slippers were thrown at Burton's head, and, amid many shouted 'vivas' from the assembled crowd, the party embarked for a trial trip. Towards sunset they arrived at Roca Grande. There, Isabel took leave of Burton just as the sun was setting behind the mountains. She was not to expect him until she saw him. It might be two months, four, or six. Not quite what Edward Thornton had in mind, of course, when he granted the leave. From the bank, Isabel watched with dim eyes until the *Eliza* disappeared round a bend in the river. Burton, himself, confessed to having felt an unusual loneliness as the kind faces faded in the distance.

Isabel stayed with the Gordons until she was fit enough to ride all day without injuring herself. She left on Sunday, 25 August, taking with her seven animals, two slaves, and a muleteer borrowed from Mr Gordon. She appears to have taken a week to reach Petropolis, arriving there around 2 September. Early the following morning, she started out for Rio. On board the little steamer that crossed the bay, she was so ashamed of her appearance that she hid in the ladies' cabin. Her boots were in shreds, her only dress was torn in about forty places, her hat was in ribbons, and her face was swollen and burned the colour of mahogany.

Isabel spent the next few days resting her sprained ankle, and reading and answering her mail from

View from Barker Hill, near Shap, Westmorland (now part of Cumbria), of the site of James Burton's farm, demolished some time between 1858-98.

Richard Baker (c.1762-1824), Burton's maternal grandfather, described by his elder grandson as 'a sharp old man of business.'

Sarah Baker (c.1772-1846), Burton's maternal grandmother.

Richard George Baker (c.1788-1864), barrister of the Inner Temple, and Richard Baker's son by his first marriage.

Barham House, Elstree, Hertfordshire, where Burton spent the first five years of his life.

Richard Burton, c.1848, wearing the native dress he adopted while working in the field for the Sind Survey.

A portrait of Burton and his sister, Maria, painted in Boulogne by Claude Jacquand, c.1851.

The author (left), speaking with John L. Bird, present owner of Furze Hall, near Ingatestone, Essex, where Isabel Arundell spent part of her childhood and youth.

4 Rue des Basses Chambres (extreme left), the Haute Ville, Boulogne-sur-Mer, where the Arundell family moved for economy in c. 1850.

Painting of an Arab Shaykh in his Travelling Dress, by the Victorian artist/traveller, Thomas Seddon.

Sketch of Al Madinah by a Native Artist.

The Pilgrim's Costume.

Lt Gen Sir James Outram (1803-63), Political Resident and
Commandant at Aden in 1854 during the planning of the
Somali Expedition.

A view from the Coffee Stream of Harar, the "Forbidden City."

HH Ahmed Bin Abibakr, Amir of Harar.

An engraving from Burton's sketch of Zanzibar.

Studio portrait of Burton sitting in his tent on the East African Expedition.

John Hanning Speke (1827- 64), Burton's companion and second in command on the Somali and East African expeditions and, later, his bitter enemy.

The Royal Bavarian Chapel, Warwick Street, London, where Richard Burton and Isabel Arundell were married on 22 January 1861.

The consulate building at Fernando Po, which Burton described to the FO as being planted on posts which were so rotten, 'that every violent tornado threatens to blow it over the cliff'.

Gustav Mann (1836-1916), German botanist, born in Hanover. He was initially a gardener at the Royal Botanic Gardens, Kew, before becoming a plant collector, the first on Mt Cameroon.

The Arundell family on a visit to Wardour Castle, Wiltshire, in December 1862. Annotated by Isabel, the group consists of 'Back row l to r: Rudolph, Emmeline, Richard, Papa, Puss. Front: Blanche, Mama, Uncle Renfric. Jack.'

Sir Roderick Murchison with members of Section E, Geography and Ethnology, at the meeting of the British Association for the Advancement of Science in Bath in 1864.

The memorial to Speke, marking the spot where he died on 15 Sept 1864.

Isabel with members of the naval and diplomatic service at the Brazilian capital, Rio de Janeiro.

Edward Henry Stanley (1826-93), 15th earl of Derby, foreign secretary, 1868 and 1874-8, a 'fellow anthropologist' and sympathetic friend of Burton.

The Rt Hon Sir Henry Elliot, GCB, second son of Gilbert, second Earl of Minto. He served as British ambassador at the Porte from 1867-77.

A photograph of Isabel aged 38, taken in 1869 before setting off to join her husband in Damascus.

S. Jackson Eldridge, HBM's Consul-General of Syria, maliciously described by Isabel Burton as 'fearfully jealous of his superior subordinate.'

'The Moon,' Isabel Burton's Syrian maid.

Forster Fitzgerald Arbuthnot (1833-1901), close
friend and founder member with Burton of the
so-called Kama Shastra Society of Benares.

John Payne (1842-1916), poet and translator of the
Arabian Nights, who gave Burton invaluable
assistance with his more famous literal,
unexpurgated version.

Dr Frederick Grenfell Baker (1853-1930), born at
Lahore, son of an Indian Army officer. After being
in private practice from 1884-87, he acted as
Burton's travelling physician until his death in 1890.

Leonard Smithers (1861-1907), solicitor and
publisher of pornographic works, who collaborated
with Burton in translating the *Priapeia* and the
Carmina of Catullus. He later acted as literary
adviser to Isabel Burton.

Isabel Burton, c.1892, wearing the Mary Stuart
head-dress which she had adopted for Lady
Murray's fancy-dress ball at Cannes in 1887.

'Our Cottage' in Mortlake, where Isabel Burton wrote the two-volume *Life* of her husband.

Neglected for many years, and broken into by vandals in the 1970s, the Burton mausoleum has since been renovated. It is now listed by the Department of the Environment as a building of historical and architectural importance.

Mrs Dorothy ("Dortie") Flemming (1889-1989), Lady Burton's great niece,
at the door of her house in Whitby in 1982, aged 93.

home. She then travelled down to Santos. At the end of October, she returned to Rio, hoping for news of Burton of whom she had heard nothing for over two months. The English steamer from Bahia came in on 1 November, but Burton was not on it. Isabel, naturally, was worried in case Burton had been taken ill, made a prisoner, or had his money stolen, since he was in the habit of carrying large sums hanging out of his pocket. Unless he arrived within two or three weeks, she even thought of making the long journey to the Paulo Affonso Falls and up-river in search of him. Wilfrid Scawen Blunt recalled meeting with Isabel at Rio on his way to the British Legation at Buenos Aires. He hadn't seen her since the late fifties or early sixties, when he met her at the house of her aunt, Monica, Lady Gerard. He remembered her then as a quiet, fair-haired, rather pretty girl of the convent type. 'She had developed,' he said, 'into a sociable and very talkative woman, clever, but at the same time foolish, overflowing with stories of which her husband was always the hero. Her devotion to him was very real, and she was entirely under his domination, an hypnotic domination Burton used to boast of....'[40]

It was probably not until around mid-January, 1868, by which time Isabel was beside herself with worry, that Burton turned up unexpectedly – on the one steamer she failed to meet – and was quite angry that she had not come on board to meet him! Shortly after returning, he looked unwell, but went on persisting that there was nothing wrong with him. He even had plans for further travels, starting in July, 'going off for an exploration amongst the [Tupi] Indians,' as Isabel explained in a letter to Lord Houghton, 'where I shall be de trop, and as it will occupy 8 months, I am going part of the way with him, then ride down to the coast and embark for England, remain six months, see all my friends, civilise myself a little, buy some clothes and be back again before his return.'[41]

This was not to be. Around the middle of April, Burton felt so feverish that he was forced to go to bed. He became very ill with a pain in his side, and went through fearful agonies unable to move hand or foot, to speak, swallow, or breathe, without a paroxysm of pain that made him scream for a quarter of an hour. Isabel thought he was dying. A doctor came up from Rio on the eighth day of his illness, and took up quarters in the house. On hearing Isabel's account, and after examining Burton, he said he did not know if he could save him, but would do his best. His diagnosis was pneumonia and hepatitis.[42] In her account to her mother, when Isabel thought Burton was dying, she said to him, "The doctor has tried all his remedies; now let me try one of mine." She sprinkled some holy water on his head, knelt down and prayed, and put on the blessed scapulars. He had not been able to raise his head for days to have the pillow turned, but he raised it of his own accord, sufficiently to let the string pass under his head, and had no pain. According to Isabel, it was a 'silent consent.' The result was that Burton lay quite still for about an hour, and then said in a whisper. "Zoo, I think I'm a little better." From then on, he made a slow and painful recovery.[43]

At the end of seven weeks, Isabel took him down to the Barra to convalesce, where he sat on the sands letting the sea roll over him. Possibly as the result of the depression than can follow hepatitis, Burton told Isabel on their return to São Paulo, that he could stand Brazil no longer. He blamed it for giving him his illness, it was far away from the world, and career-wise, it was a dead end. This came as a severe blow to Isabel, since up to then it was the only home that she had really shared with him. However, Burton's wish was her command. From Santos, on 15 June, Burton wrote to George Buckley Matthew, who had taken over from Edward Thornton, expressing his hope for sick leave 'to change air further south.'[44]

Isabel who hadn't been out of the house while looking after Burton, and was thoroughly exhausted and in poor health herself, wrote home from along the coast the following day, 'In this country, if you are well, all right; but the moment you are ailing, lie down and die, for it is no use trying to live. I kept Richard alive by never taking my eyes off him for eight weeks, and perpetually standing at his bedside with one thing and another. But who in a general way will get any one to do that for them?' She also expressed in her letter a deep love for 'the virgin forests of South America in which I am now sitting alone, far from any human creature, with gaudy butterflies and birds fluttering around me, big vegetation, and a shark playing in the boiling green sea, which washes up to my feet, and the bold mountain background on a very blue sky, the thick foliage covered with wild flowers and creepers such as no hothouse in England could grow....'[45]

The house and its contents were sold, and Burton and Isabel left São Paulo for the last time on 31 July.[46] He was to start with her for Rio, then turn south on a leisurely trip via Rosario, Rio Grande do Sul, Buenos Airies, Montevideo, the Plata River, and Paraguay, to see the war.[47] He would then travel to the Pacific coast, returning by way of the Straits of Magellan, Buenos Aires and Rio to England. Isabel, as she said, was to have all her work cut out for her, returning to London to see if she could persuade the Foreign Office to give him another post. In addition she was to try and work the Iporanga Mines from there, 'whole mountains of lead and quicksilver, also gold and copper (twenty-eight square miles).' She was also 'to bring out his "Highlands of Brazil," the "Journey of Lacerda," and a second edition of "Mecca", "Uruguay," Iracema," and "Manuel de Moraes." '[48] After a fortnight spent enjoying the hospitalities of Rio de Janeiro, Isabel saw Burton aboard the small Intercolonial steamer, *Arno*, on 6 August 1868. He left that day, she three days later.

Shortly after arriving at Buenos Airies, Burton ran into an old acquaintance, a Mr Gould., whom he had not seen for over a decade. Gould, obviously a person of some influence, had just returned from a visit to the camp of Marshal-President Lopez.[49] Very helpfully, he gave Burton an introductory letter to the officer commanding HMS *Linnet*, which was overseeing British interests in Paraguayan waters. He also introduced him to the Brazilian Envoy Extraordinary, M. de Amaral.

Burton was also presented to one of the most prominent people in South America, President D. Bartholome Mitre, since 1862 actual President and Commander-in-Chief. A statistician, geographer, linguist, and orator, he also impressed Burton with his knowledge of books. He had heard something of Burton's travels, and received him like an old acquaintance. Burton's admiration of Mitre, however, did not blind him to the fact 'that his later career bears upon it the stain of a profound political immorality...whose result is the present disastrous and by no means honourable war.'[50]

From Buenos Aires, Burton went up the Parana River to Rosario, missing seeing Consul Hutchinson, his predecessor at Fernando Po, who was on sick leave in England. On his return, he spent a week with a couple of acquaintances at the river port of Corrientes, the site three years earlier of the decisive defeat of a Paraguayan invasion force. Its streets after dark were anything but safe as he discovered, and carrying a revolver was a necessity. 'If an unknown asks you at night for a light, you stick your cigar in the barrel and politely offer it to him without offence being given or taken.'[51]

By 22 August, Burton was at the key river-fortress of Humaita, entering upon what he called the proper scenes of the Paraguayan War. He carried from Corrientes an introductory letter to Commodore Francisco Cordeiro de Torres Alvim, Captain of the Fleet. Two days later, the Commodore arrived in a little steam-launch and offered Lt Cdr Bush and Burton a passage up-stream as far as Timbo, where the mass of the armoured fleet lay at anchor. From the deck of the vessel, the left bank could be seen riddled by shot from Parrott guns, with the rotting corpses of Paraguayans and members of the Argentine Voluntary Legion lying scattered under the trees where they had fallen. Higher up-river, steamers were busily embarking the wounded for the several hospitals down-stream.

Early in the afternoon of 1 September, the Brazilian squadron moved up to the mouth of the Tebicuary, whose lines had lately been abandoned by Marshal President Lopez. Burton's visit was now ended. On the evening of 3 September, he bade a regretful farewell to his hosts, and transferred to the Clyde steamer, *Vale of Doon*. Early the next morning, they ran up the Tebicuary. Nothing remained after his short visit but to return to Buenos Aires, and await the course of events. A month later, Burton went up the Uruguay River on a short visit to General Justo José de Urquiza, 'a man whose history is that of the Argentine

Confederation.' Aware of Burton's intention of crossing the Pampas, then in a somewhat troubled state, the General presented Burton with his photograph and a letter of safe conduct addressed in peremptory terms to the "Indian" chiefs and to their Gaucho companions. Thus armed, Burton said, he felt more secure than if protected by the flags of England and France. Detestable weather, which left the roads knee-deep in mud, prevented Burton's visiting Uruguayana and the upper Uruguay. He was, therefore, forced one again to return to Buenos Aires.

According to Wilfrid Blunt, the announcement of Burton's arrival had been widely trailed beforehand in the local newspapers. It was said that he had plans for exploring Patagonia and the western Pampas, and of climbing the highest peaks in the Andes, including the hitherto unclimbed summit of Aconcagua. It soon became apparent, however, that Burton was in no fit state to carry them out. Although he carried on talking for a while about this project to all those prepared to listen, the subject was gradually dropped, and ended up by becoming something of a joke among his friends.

Blunt considered that Burton at the time was at the rock-bottom of his whole career, and barely respectable in his behaviour. The boredom of his consular life at Santos had temporarily turned him into an alcoholic, and he rarely went to bed sober. He regularly dressed in 'a rusty black coat with crumpled black silk stock, a costume which his muscular frame and immense chest made singularly and incongruously hideous, above it a countenance the most sinister I have seen, dark, cruel, treacherous, with eyes like a wild beast's.'

Blunt recalled first meeting Burton at a dinner-party. With him was a man who claimed to be Sir Roger Tichborne, ostensibly in Buenos Aires to collect evidence for the lawsuit he was about to bring, to establish his identity and legal right to the baronetcy and the family estates. According to Blunt, the two, 'a strangely disreputable couple,' spent a great deal of time together,' and he, himself, saw a good deal of both. Burton's visit to the Pampas, however, 'ended tamely enough in his crossing it with the Claimant, the two inside the ordinary diligence, to Mendoza and thence on mules to the Pacific.'[52] This is completely at variance with Burton's own contemporary account and the evidence he gave at the Tichborne trial two years later.

Accompanied by William C. Maxwell, a fellow-passenger with whom Burton had struck up a friendship on his voyage south from Rio, he 'wandered about quaint Cordoba.....one of the oldest of the scattered cities with which the Spaniards had built up a kind of skeleton civilization.' Then, together with Major Ignacio Rickard, RA, they inspected the Sierra San Luiz, and visited the scene of the terrible earthquake at Mendoza.[53] After crossing the Andes by the Uspallata Pass, they rested at Santiago de Chile before embarking at Valparaiso for Peru.

CHAPTER TWENTY-NINE

AN AUSPICIOUS HOMECOMING

The Royal Mail Company's steamship, *La Plata*, carrying Isabel back to England docked at Southampton early on Tuesday, 1 September 1868. She was met by her mother and her two sisters, Emmeline and Elizabeth, both now in their twenties, wilting under what they described as the "tropical weather." The happiness of the family reunion, however, was overshadowed for her by the shock of learning that her step-brother, Theodore, had died only nine days earlier.[1]

Fortunately for Isabel, her numerous business and literary commitments left her with little or no time to dwell on Theo's death. Burton, obviously keen to circumvent the FO's ban on his trading, had asked her to find some way, if possible, of working the Iporanga mines from London, probably under her name. This proved impossible. Isabel also failed to find a market for the Brazilian translations, *The Uruguay*, and *Iracema* and *Manuel de Moraes*.[2] She was luckier in persuading Burton's usual publisher, William Tinsley, to accept the manuscript of *The Highlands of the Brazil*, although she had to contribute £250 [worth more than £10,000 in today's money] towards the cost of publication.

A fortnight elapsed before she found time to get in touch with Lord Houghton, taking refuge in a white lie that she had landed from Brazil only a few days earlier. Writing from her mother's house on black-edged paper, she asked Lord Houghton to send her Richard's copy of *Mecca*, which she believed Winwood Reade had given him. 'He wants me to have it brought out as a railway book. I think the subject is worn out, but must obey orders.' Since she was presently editing his book on Brazil, or rather going to, together with five other smaller items, she would be forced to stay in London for some time.[3]

Regretfully declining an invitation from Lord Houghton late in the following month to visit Fryston, Isabel said she was so occupied with publishers and keeping an eye out for FO jobs for Richard, that she dare not leave town. She had, however, allowed herself a short break at Wardour, from where she had returned only the previous night.[4]

It was getting on towards the middle of November when Isabel felt able to accept Lord Houghton's offer, having cleared a visit to Fryston for a few days with William Tinsley, on the promise of 'taking plenty of proofs with me.' Lord Stanley would be addressing his constituents at King's Lynn, 'so that will be no hindrance, besides I have bothered him pretty well and if Richard does not get well served, it won't be the fault of his hard-working wife. It will be a shame if he goes out and gives me nothing. Every relation I have, and they are legion, the entire old Roman Catholic clan, are red hot conservatives, so that when *your* side comes in, I can expect no quarter and can't ask it.'

In the meantime, she continued, the family was in shock over yet another unexpected bereavement. A favourite aunt, Lady Lawson, formerly Mimosa Gerard, had recently come up to London for an operation. Everything appeared to have gone successfully. The following day, however, she had a sudden relapse and died within a few minutes. All the members of the family were going down to Brough in east Yorkshire for the funeral on 12 November. This, Isabel thought, would 'be the proper day for me to come to you , because it wd seem unfeeling not to stay with them as long as they are here.' She was already in deep mourning for her step-brother, 'and I shall not be, therefore, able to dress very <u>extensively</u> but I dare say Lady Houghton won't care about that.'[5]

Burton had dedicated his latest book, without permission, to Lord Stanley, describing him as 'a brother anthropologist.' Now Isabel, also apparently without permission from her husband, and certainly without the prior knowledge of the publisher, inserted a Preface of her own:

> Before the reader dives into the interior of Brazil with my husband as a medium, let me address two words to him.
>
> I have returned home, on six months' leave of absence, after three years in Brazil. One of the many commissions I am to execute for Captain Burton is to see the following pages through the press.
>
> It has been my privilege during these three years, to have been his almost constant companion; and I consider that to travel, write, read, and study under such a master is no small boon to any one desirous of seeing and learning. Although he frequently informs me, in a certain oriental way, that "the Moslem can permit no equality with women," yet he has chosen me, his pupil, for this distinction, in preference to a more competent stranger.
>
> As long as there is anything difficult to do, a risk to be incurred, or any chance of improving the mind and of educating oneself, I am a very faithful disciple; but I now begin to feel that, while he and his readers are old friends, I am humbly standing unknown in the shadow of his glory. It is therefore time for me respectfully but firmly to assert that, although I proudly accept of the trust confided in me, and pledge myself not to avail myself of my discretionary powers to alter one word of the original text, I protest vehemently against his religious and moral sentiments, which belie a good and chivalrous life. I point the finger of indignation particularly at what misrepresents our Holy Roman Catholic Church, and at what upholds that unnatural and repulsive law, Polygamy, which the Author is careful not to practise himself, but from a high moral pedestal he preaches to the ignorant as a means of population in young countries.[6]

Her motive in writing it, as she later explained to William Tinsley, was that 'my few words soften off what offends different classes of people [about] Captain Burton and explains him to the public. A man's own wife may do this....'[7] Tinsley was far from convinced by her argument at the time. He feared that its inclusion would undermine the author's authority and, therefore, the sales of the book which, he felt, had limited appeal anyway, and jeopardise, if not scupper, their joint investment. Isabel, stubborn to the last, was determined that it should stay.

Dec 4th 1868

Dear Mr Tinsley,

....It would be more profitable to smash up the book than <u>not</u> to let the preface stand as it is. The Queen <u>hates</u> polygamy, and <u>I am acting under orders</u>. The British public hates polygamy. Captain Burton has chaffed the public long enough. I now intend to make it my business that it shall understand him.

The Brazilian Govt. is Catholic. The Empress Ultra-Papist. Do you think that the Emperor wd order 3 or

4,000 copies to be distributed in his Empire if Capt. Burton's animus were not somewhat annulled...? The men in your office who set you against my preface are underhand enemies to my husband...Believe me if I could publish anything like a difference between us all London would buy it up – so it won't damage you!

~~We cannot well risk an appointment of £950 a year for the sake of one £250.~~ Please ~~be quiet~~ about this and let it be.[8]

Isabel had her way and, of course, was proved right. The Press lapped up her feisty Preface, enjoying the spectacle of what appeared to be a purely spontaneous and defiant reaction to some of her husband's extreme opinions. However, as is clear from a letter she later wrote to Lord Houghton, Burton knew in advance what she was going to put in.[9] Far from registering any objection, he was clearly all for it. In fact, there is more than a hint of its being stage-managed, both being keenly aware that such controversy was more likely to stimulate rather than depress sales.

The book fared less well at the hands of the critics. *The Athenaeum* found it hard work, promising much, but delivering little. 'Captain Burton tells us in two or three places that this book contains his material for a future book. Properly digested, worked over, above all weeded, they will be valuable to both writer and reader. As they now stand, we cannot think they will benefit the first, and we are sure that they will not tempt the second.'[10]

By February 1868, Disraeli had, at last, succeeded in climbing 'to the top of the greasy pole,' as he put it, taking over as prime minister from Lord Derby who retired from politics. It was generally regarded, however, as a 'caretaker' premiership. The Reform Act of 1867 having almost doubled the electorate, everyone eagerly looked forward to see what effects this would have on the electoral fortunes of both parties. At the general election held on Wednesday, 2 December 1868, the Liberals swept to victory with a majority of 112 seats. Disraeli resigned without waiting to meet Parliament, and Queen Victoria called on Gladstone to form a new government.

The following day, in what must have been almost the last act of Stanley before leaving office, he sent a despatch to Burton informing him 'that the Queen has been graciously pleased to appoint you to be Her Majesty's Consul at Damascus in the place of Mr. Rogers, who has been appointed Her Majesty's Consul at Cairo.....'[11] Just over a month later, after getting wind that efforts were on foot to have his appointment cancelled, Isabel wrote to Burton on 7 January 1869:

My Darling,

If you get this, come home by the shortest route. Telegraph from Lisbon and Southampton, and I will meet you at latter and have all snug.

Strictly private. The new Government have tried to upset some of the appointments made by the last. There is no little jealousy about yours. Others wanted it even at £700 a year and were refused. Lord Stanley thinks so, and so do I, that you may as well be on the ground as soon as possible.[12]

In spite of sending copies to Rio, Buenos Airies, and Valparaiso, none reached him. It was not until 30 March, the day of his return to Buenos Airies via the Magellan Strait, that Burton wrote to James Hammond acknowledging Lord Stanley's despatches of 3rd and 7th December. He said that he would return to England on his way to his post by the next Royal Mail steam-packet leaving on 26 April. In the meantime, he intended utilising the delay, 'by proceeding to Paraguay to finish a report upon the present exceptional and sanguinary war which I have already commenced on a former journey.'[13]

After visiting Asuncion, the strategic Paraguayan city captured in 1868, and occupied and administered by Brazil until 1876, Burton made his way by rail to the Allied front at Luque. Here he met the Commander-in-Chief of the Allied Army, Marshal Guilherme Xavier de Souza. By 21 April, Burton was back in Buenos Airies, spending the remaining days among friends, before embarking for Rio.

Just under a week before Burton set sail for England, Sir Henry Elliot, Ambassador to the Porte, wrote to the new Foreign Secretary, Lord Clarendon, expressing, what he said, was the view taken at Damascus of Burton's appointment. He pointed out that Damascus was probably the most fanatical city in the Empire, and the presence there of a person who had penetrated to the Prophet's Shrine, was regarded as certain to cause demonstrations against him, that might result in unfortunate consequences. 'By the Mussulman population, Captain Burton is regarded either as having insulted their children by taking part as an unbeliever in their most sacred rites, or else having, at the time, been a Mahomedan, and having become a renegade. Under either supposition, he would be regarded with aversion by most, and with hatred by very many of the population.' It was his duty, Elliot said, to draw Lord Clarendon's attention to a consideration, as he diplomatically phrased it, 'which was probably lost sight of when Captain Burton was selected for the post.'[14]

Sir Henry made his own personal view of the appointment clear in a private letter to Earl Granville, Lord Clarendon's successor, two years later:

I was astounded when I heard that [Lord Stanley] had named Burton, whose character was so well known in the East as to make it a certainty that trouble would come from it....The fact of the matter is that Eastern travellers are for the most part exactly the people least fitted to fill the responsible position of Consuls in Turkey. They have got accustomed to overbearing exercise of authority and to a neglect of anything like sense in dealing with the people about them. Which may be necessary in the wilds, but which cannot be tolerated at or near the seat of administration.[15]

Burton arrived at Southampton on 1 June 1869, looking in much the same disreputable state as Isabel had, when she arrived at Rio from the mines. Once back in London, they booked into Howlett's Hotel, a small family hotel in Manchester Street. Burton then set about making himself look presentable for a party and reception that had been laid on for him.

The following morning he called at the FO to report his arrival in person and pay his respects to Lord Stanley and his successor, Lord Clarendon. He followed this by going the rounds of publishers, cartographers, and commissions. That night he and Isabel went to an Admiralty party, and from there to one at the Foreign Office; the next night to the Royal Literary Fund, where he made a speech. He dined with Sir Roderick Murchison, and attended a meeting at the RGS, 'found it slow, and was not satisfied with his reception.' He also went to a Levee at St James's Palace.

In the meantime he had asked for, and been granted, six weeks' leave of absence by Lord Clarendon, before proceeding to Damascus. Writing to the FO, Burton said that he had been advised after his last attack of hepatitis in Brazil, to take a course of Vichy waters before taking up residence for some years in a hot climate. He asked for permission, therefore, to proceed to Beirut via Vichy.[16]

In his reply, sanctioning this request, Murray said that he took this opportunity of repeating what Lord Clarendon had told Burton verbally, that very serious objections to his appointment had reached the Foreign Secretary from official quarters. That, although Lord Clarendon had allowed the appointment to go forward on receiving Burton's assurances that the objections raised were unfounded, 'his Lordship has warned you that if the feeling stated to exist against you on the part of the authorities and the people at that place should prevent the proper performance by you of your official duties, it would be his Lordship's duty immediately to recall you.'[17] A copy of this letter was despatched to Sir Henry Elliot three days later. Burton responded by renewing in writing what he had said to Lord Clarendon: that neither the authorities nor the people of Damascus would show him any but the most friendly feelings, as had happened in Egypt and Zanzibar. However, as designing persons might have attempted to complicate the situation, he undertook 'to act with unusual prudence, and, under all circumstances, to hold myself only answerable for all the consequences.'[18]

Shortly after returning to England, Isabel had announced her intention to Lord Houghton of attempting to have Burton created a KCB, suggesting that he might care to back her up. The honours awarded to Grant and Baker while he, himself, had been passed over, clearly remained a festering sore with Burton. He was unaware that Grant was far from happy at the treatment he, and Speke in particular, had received. While expressing his gratitude to Sir Roderick Murchison for commending him to Lord Clarendon for a CB, Grant thought it 'a shame to Government, that the family of Speke's should be so wholly ignored.' Had his 'name been coupled as it always has been, with that of my companion in the Gazette, I should have been proud to wear the honor but, to see his name forgotten and to read my name following Bakers (sic) – is as you must allow somewhat humiliating after our memorable expedition.'[19]

Murchison was clearly upset and alarmed on later learning from Grant's sister, Mrs Mackenzie, that her brother regarded the award of a CB an insult, and was considering rejecting it. 'This honour,' he wrote, ' has been coveted and prized by very distinguished Colonels in the Indian Army who have long served the Crown and to repudiate it would be astounding.' It is obvious that Murchison was also hurt at Grant's forgetfulness of the efforts he had made at the time to obtain honours for the two men. Finding it impossible to obtain a baronetcy for the Speke family, he had tried to obtain CBs for both explorers, with a knighthood for Speke as leader of the expedition. Despite having raised the matter with the prime minister, Lord Palmerston, this, too, was refused, 'and I retired quite disgusted. Of course after such snubbing I resolved never more to seek for any honour for a traveller however distinguished.'[20]

Even had she known about Murchison's resolution, it is doubtful if Isabel would have taken any notice. Having canvassed the support of some thirty of Burton's most influential friends, she circulated a long letter through Murchison, making, what were plainly, exaggerated, inaccurate, and irrelevant claims to bolster his case. 'It would be a great help to Captain Burton,' she said, 'to leave England with the prestige of having received some mark of approval from his country for his past services, and as Sir Samuel Baker is already knighted and made a CB for his one expedition, Captain Burton would like to have something higher for his many services, and in the shape of a military distinction for his past unacknowledged military services, that is, a KCB.'[21] Lord Clarendon was unimpressed. He told Isabel quite bluntly that if he had one to give away, there were many people he would prefer to give it to than Burton.

Although deliberately ignored by Isabel in her biography, nothing is more certain than that Burton, having been back in this country for some three weeks or more, had lost no time in resuming his association with Swinburne. The poet had spent the early months of that year at Holmwood, his parents' home near Henley-on-Thames, working on a textual study of the poems of Shelley. At the end of April, after paying a short visit to Benjamin Jowett at Balliol College, Oxford, Swinburne returned to his lodgings at 22a Dorset Street, where he remained throughout June writing a review of Victor Hugo's recently published romance, *L'homme qui rit*, for *The Fortnightly Review*.[22]

Despite his promise to Lord Houghton four years earlier to 'be no end good,' the poet had become a chronic alcoholic, subject to fainting fits undoubtedly brought on through his intemperance. On one occasion, Edmund Gosse recalled standing outside 16 Cheyne Walk, D.G. Rossetti's house in Chelsea, when a hansom cab drew up. Out stepped the fastidiously dressed figure of the critic and essayist, Walter Pater, followed by Swinburne, who tumbled out into the road on his hands and knees, his top hat rolling into the gutter. His public behaviour was often no less outrageous. Several such drunken incidents occurred at the Arts Club in Hanover Square where he was a member, leading to his eventual forced resignation.

Despite the best efforts of Dr George Bird, who was his close and admiring friend as well as physician, Swinburne seemed intent on drinking himself into an early grave. As Admiral Swinburne once remarked wearily to Dr Bird's sister, Alice, "Miss Bird, God has endowed my son with genius, but He has not vouchsafed to grant him self-control."[23] Swinburne had already spent two periods during 1867 and 1868, convalescing in Etretat on the Normandy coast with his Welsh friend and confidant, George Powell. Possibly with Dr Bird's blessing, Burton now offered Swinburne the opportunity of accompanying him to Vichy for the water cure. The poet leapt at the invitation.

By early July Burton had had his fill of the London season, vowing in a letter to his Brazilian friend, Albert Tootal, never to return again except during autumn or winter. 'It has been a life of bed at 8 am, no breakfast, lunch at 2 pm, dine at 8.30 and then soiree. Not so tiring when one is broken to it, but deadly monotonous.'[24] A week later, he informed the Foreign Secretary that he was leaving England en route for Damascus. That day, he and Isabel took the ferry to France, spending a nostalgic few days visiting their old haunts at Boulogne and, inevitably, finding the town greatly changed, and not for the better.

Shortly after Isabel's return to England to 'pay, pack, and follow,' Burton was joined by Swinburne. The reason why Burton wanted his wife out of the way is not far to seek. There is a strong probability that it was on the journey to Vichy, that Burton stopped off at Paris in order to introduce the young poet to Hankey. A week or so later, an ecstatic Swinburne wrote to Powell that, after leaving Vichy, he hoped to meet Paul de Saint-Victor, Théophile Gautier, and perhaps Flaubert at the rooms of a friend in Paris. 'He is *the* Sadisque collector of European fame. His erotic collection of books, engravings, etc, is unrivalled upon earth – unequalled, I should imagine, in heaven.'[25]

Burton and Swinburne arrived at Vichy on 24 July. During the ensuing weeks, they toured the beautiful Auvergne countryside together. They also made a foursome in the evenings with the artist, Frederick (later Lord) Leighton, already known to Swinburne, and the former operatic singer, Mrs Adelaide Sartoris (née Kemble), now grown grotesquely fat. Here, in the words of Edmund Gosse, 'This quartette of brilliant compatriots met daily, and entertained one another to the top of their bent. Many years later when the other three were dead, Swinburne celebrated this enchanting month at Vichy in a poem called "Reminiscences," which for some reason or other, he would never include in any one of his volumes.'[26]

Shortly after Burton set off for Vichy, Isabel confessed to feeling unhappy, and wishing to join him. She may well have felt uneasy, of course, over Burton's friendship with Swinburne. There can be little doubt that she felt extremely annoyed at being excluded, especially when she discovered that their Brazilian friend, Mr J.J. Aubertin, was also joining him there. Without further ado, she packed her bags and set off for Vichy with him.

The day after Isabel's arrival on 9 August, Swinburne wrote to his sister, Alice, 'I feel now as if I knew for the first time what it is to have an elder brother. He is the most cordial, sympathetic friend to me it is possible to have, & it is a treat to have him to myself instead of having as in London to share him with all the world….. I rather begrudge Mrs. Burton's arrival here on Monday, though we are excellent friends, & I dare say I shall see none the less of him.'[27] Writing to his mother, Lady Jane, three days later, Swinburne was even more fulsome in his praise of Burton:

'but if you had seen <u>him</u>, when the heat & the climb and the <u>bothers</u> of travelling were too much for me in the <u>very</u> hot weather – nursing, helping, waiting on me – and going out to get me books to read in bed – & always thoughtful, kind, ready, & so bright and fresh that nothing but a lizard (I suppose that it is the most insensible thing going) – could have resisted his influence – I feel sure you <u>would</u> like him (you remember you said you didn't) and then, love him as I do – & I tell you this, he is so good, so true, kind, noble & brave, that I never expect to see his like again.'[28]

The water cure over, Swinburne, now much improved in health, accompanied the Burtons to Lyons, where he left for Paris. They carried on to Turin, sight-seeing on the way. From there they drove to Brindisi, where Isabel saw Burton off to Damascus. A few hours later she made her way back to England.

During the next few weeks, Isabel worked flat out in order to be able to join him the quicker. Despite Stratford, in Essex, being a major industrial settlement at the time, it lacked an adequate and continuous piped water supply. It relied heavily, therefore, on pumps drawing up water from at least six wells. One of Isabel's first commissions was to visit this area to watch their operation, since Burton was anxious to be able to produce water, if possible, whenever they stopped in the desert.[29] Not knowing exactly what Damascus was like, she invested in a pony-carriage, and her uncle, Sir Robert Gerard, gave her a very old family chariot. As well as taking lessons in removing and re-assembling wheels and axles, she learned to do the same with her owns guns and pistols. She also spent time stocking up on household items for their future home.

Amazingly, in the midst of all these preparations, Isabel found time to write to the newspapers. She wrote to *The Daily Telegraph* on 23 October as to the possible whereabouts of Dr Livingstone, stating that she had written to her husband to supply the public with a complete account of the scene, which might suggest the best means of rescuing him. She also wrote to *The Times* on 12 November complaining of Sir Roderick Murchison's omission at the latest RGS meeting, of her husband's name in connection with the sources of the Nile. In similar vein, she wrote to *The Athenaeum* just over a week later to claim Burton's 'proper place among the five explorers of the lakes, *second* to Livingstone as explorer....and *first* as lake discoverer.'[30]

After a tearful family farewell, Isabel left for Dover in a howling gale on 16 December, accompanied by her brother, Rodolphe, and her two sisters. It proved too dangerous to embark, and Isabel was forced to spend the night in a small uncomfortable inn nearby. She left for Calais the following morning. The sea was still '"mountains high"....but what cared I?' she later wrote, 'I had shaken the dust off my feet of what Mrs. Grundy is pleased to call respectability – the harness of European society. My destination was Damascus, the dream of my chidlhood and girlhood. I am to live among Bedouin Arab chiefs; I shall smell the desert air; I shall have tents, horses, weapons, and be free, like Lady Hester Stanhope...I will follow in the steps of Tancred.'[31]

The unforeseen delay, however, resulted in Isabel's missing her scheduled connection to Marseilles. She also lost two of her many trunks, both of which turned up intact some months later, one containing nearly all her money, some £300 in gold sovereigns, and the other all the little luxuries she had collected for the journey. Since the P&O *Tanjore* was due to sail on 19 December, there was no time to eat or sleep in Paris, but to press on by an excruciatingly slow train. At Marseilles, Isabel wrote letters home, and was on board the *Tanjore* by 8 am on the 19th. Five days later the ship was off Alexandria, and Isabel came ashore on Eastern ground for the first time on Christmas Day. The P&O agent was helpfulness himself, taking charge of everything and attending to all her wants. A passage was secured aboard a Russian steamer, the *Ceres*, which was sailing within twenty-four hours, and Isabel spent a great deal of money sending a telegram to Beirut which arrived after her. 'It was a strange Christmas night,' she said, 'spent alone in a small Alexandrian hotel, passed in writing letters home, and thinking of the merry family parties and festivities – and of my mother.'

The deck of the *Ceres* was extremely dirty, crowded with passengers from every part of the East, mostly pilgrims for the Haj. Even so, Isabel found it 'the most interesting part of the ship, to one who had always been dreaming of the East.' The vessel anchored very early off Beirut on the morning of the 29th. Burton was not there to meet her, however, Isabel feeling very indignant, much as he had at Rio the previous year.

Around 9 am, the Vice-Consul, Mr Jago, came aboard, kindly offering her every assistance, and taking her ashore with her luggage to the Bellvue Hotel facing the sea.[32] She then accompanied him to call on Consul-General Eldridge, who, despite his wife being ill, invited her to lunch, and showed her how to smoke her first nargileh.[33] Isabel again sent a telegram to Burton, which also arrived after her.

The diligence to Damascus having already gone, Isabel spent the evening writing home letters and forwarding small mementoes from the bazaars. The following morning she was kindly provided with what, she called, 'a shabby little omnibus,' drawn by three broken-down horses, with one of Eldridge's splendidly dressed kawasses as guard during the journey. Squeezed into it and on it, besides herself, was her English maid, a large pet St Bernard dog, two brindle bull-terriers and two of the Yarborough breed, together with a mountain of luggage.

The seventy odd mile journey to Damascus was accomplished in two days with an overnight stop at Shtorra. It was sunset of a dreary winter's evening when she entered the town, confessing that her first impression of it was anything but favourable. The weather was bitterly cold, wild dogs roamed the slushy narrow streets littered with refuse, and, after fifteen days and nights non-stop travelling from London she was thoroughly exhausted. She went straight to an inn, known by courtesy as Demitri's Hotel. Burton arrived an hour later, greeting her, she said, in 'that matter-of-fact way, with which he was wont to repress his emotions. I could *feel* that he was both surprised and overjoyed.' The contrast with his attentive, thoughtful, and kind behaviour towards Swinburne at Vichy is illuminating, and speaks volumes for the nature of the Burtons' relationship. He had been there for three months, she said, the climate and loneliness having had a bad effect upon him both mentally and physically.[34] A more likely explanation, not mentioned by Isabel, is the fact of his having climbed to the summit of Mount Hermon with Captain Warren, RE, on 29 October, and having gone on an expedition in the eastern Hauran with a French entomologist, in December.[35]

After a hot meal, they warmed themselves over a large brass dish filled with glowing charcoal embers, and then settled down comfortably with a cigarette and drink to plan for their future.

CHAPTER THIRTY

THE PEARL OF THE EAST

Burton's predecessor, Edward Rogers, had lived in a large house in Damascus itself.[1] The Burtons, however, felt hemmed in there, with the windows of the houses barred and latticed, and the thirteen gates of the city locked at sunset. They, therefore, set about looking for more congenial living quarters. After a long search, they rented a bare-walled, whitewashed cottage high up in the large northern suburb of Salahiyyeh, linked to Damascus by numerous country houses. It was only a short ride to the city in one direction along a road paved and bordered with trees, and to the desert in another.

Salahiyyah, 'Of the Saints,' had received its name in the 5th century (AH), when it was settled by Turcomans, to which a colony of Kurds was later added. In early times the place had been noted for its school and mosques, most now in a ruinous condition. The finest mosque was that erected over the tomb of Muhi ed-Din ibn el-Arabi, the celebrated 12th-13th century Muslim mystic philosopher, who had settled in Damascus in 1223.

The Burtons' house, with projecting latticed windows, overhung the road. There were gardens front and back, a mosque on one side, and a hammam on the other. Across the road among apricot orchards, Isabel had her stables. Just beyond the village, with its domes and minarets, and numerous trees, there was a patch of desert sand, and a high sand-coloured mountain, called Jabal Qasioun, the Camomile Mountain. This barren hill was held sacred by the Muslims, who believed that Adam had once lived there, that it was there that Abraham had learned the unity of God, and that it had once been visited by Mohammed while still a camel-driver. According to this hoary old legend, he remarked that man could only enter one paradise, and he preferred to go to the one above. He, therefore, sat down and, after feasting his eyes on the city below, went away without entering its gates.

Burton and Isabel interrupted their moving in to watch the colourful spectacle of the departure of the Damascus Caravan around the middle of January. As an important place of rendezvous, the annual Haj pilgrimage brought in a great deal of revenue to the city. The great caravan reached it around the middle of the month of Ramadan, and from then until its departure on the 15th of the following month, the streets and bazaars were packed with noisy jostling crowds eager alike to buy and sell.

The Burtons joined the Haj on the third day, riding sixty miles along the Darb el Sultani to Mazarib before bidding a formal farewell to the chief authorities in the caravan. Burton 'was looked upon by all as a friend to the Moslem,' so Isabel claimed, 'and consequently the Sultan, and no opposition would have been shown to him had he also made a pilgrimage to the jealously guarded Haramayn, or the Holy Cities of the Moslems…'[2]

As the envoy of a great Power, Burton was provided with a number of dragomans, or gentleman secretaries, together with kawasses, who looked like cavalry soldiers. To prevent her being molested on the streets, Isabel was attended by a dragoman interpreter and four kawasses with highly decorated swords and uniforms.

Even so, she and Burton used to live a great deal with the native population, and as natives, in order to gain an insight into their lives. They wore European dress in Damascus and Beirut, and Eastern dress up-country or in the desert, eating the local dishes. If Isabel went to a harem, she often dressed like a Muslim woman with her face covered, and sat in the bazaar, and let her Arab maid do all the talking.[3] They attended all sorts of ceremonies, circumcisions, weddings, funerals, or dervishes' dances. Burton frequented the cafés and the mosques, the evening story-tellers' haunts, Isabel the charm shops, where the fortune-tellers hung out, administering love philtres. They mixed with all classes, religions, races, and tongues, Burton's knowledge of Arabic and Persian, enabling him to enjoy intimate relations with the Arab tribes and all the chief authorities.

Among their close friends was Abd al Qadir, the exiled Algerian leader, a Sufi of the Qadiriyya order, dark, handsome and with dignified bearing.[4] Another, was the Hon Jane Digby, who had married Lord Ellenborough at the age of seventeen, and whose divorce four years later became a cause célèbre. Thereafter, her ubiquitous life was strewn with a succession of discarded lovers, husbands, and children. She had finally made her home at Damascus, marrying a Bedawin Shaykh, Mijwal el Mezrab. They lived half the year in a beautiful house in Damascus, and the other half in his Bedawi tents. Charming and intelligent though he was, Isabel found it incomprehensible that Jane 'could have given up all that she had in England to live with that dirty little black – or nearly so – husband.' Burton, apparently, thought her the cleverest woman he had ever met, 'for whom life's poetry never sank to prose.' Not only was she perfectly fluent in nine languages, she could also read and write in them. She also painted, sculpted, and was musical.

According to Isabel, she was unmistakably an English lady, 'well born and bred, and she was delighted to greet in me one of her own order.' They became great friends and, in Isabel's version of events, Jane 'dictated to me the whole of her biography, and most romantic and interesting it is.' This was to become a matter of public contention some years later. 'I took a great interest in the poor thing,' Isabel said condescendingly,…. 'she appeared to be quite foolishly in love with him…though the object of her devotion astonished me…Poor thing! She was far more sinned against than sinning….'[5]

As soon as Isabel was thoroughly settled in, she began to hold weekly receptions.[6] Visitors dropped in throughout the day, the dragomans interpreting for her, and the kawasses resplendent in scarlet and gold, keeping guard by turns. Her visitors sat around on divans, smoking and chatting, the servants constantly engaged in bringing up relays of nargilehs, chibouques, cigarettes, sweet-meats, sherbets, Turkish coffee and tea. If there were Muslim women present, she had two reception-rooms, shuttling from one to another, since the women refused to unveil before strange men.

The most distinguished of her visitors was the Wali, or Governor-General of Syria. He arrived in state one day, dressed in full uniform and with a large entourage. He was extremely polite and friendly, reminding Isabel of 'an old tom-cat: he was dressed in furs, was indolent and fat, and walked on his toes and purred.'[7] Her first impression was that he was a kind-hearted old creature, although not very intelligent and easily led. She was not long in discovering, however, that the cat had claws, Rashid becoming jealous, so she claimed, of Burton's influence.

It is Puss's claws, however, which are in evidence here. Although Burton's biographers have been content to take her malicious, unflattering portrait of Mehmed Rashid Pasha at face value, it is way off the mark in almost every respect. Far from being the effete, indolent old man of Isabel's caricature, Rashid was a highly intelligent, resourceful, and able governor. Nor is there any truth in Burton's later assertion that the

Wali 'learned the usual hatred of Europeans' in Paris.[8] He was, in fact, thoroughly westernised in his dress and tastes, a man of culture with a broad interest in the arts.

Born in 1824, he was three years younger than Burton. The son of an officer of Macedonian origin in the service of Muhammad Ali Pasha, the ruler of Egypt, he was sent in the late 1840s to Paris to complete his education. On returning to Constantinople in 1850, now fluent in both French and Arabic, he was offered an appointment in the tercüme odasi, the translation bureau. Part of the department which later evolved into the foreign ministry, it became the proving ground for some of the most distinguished Ottoman officials in the nineteenth century.

Rashid's abilities were quickly recognised, leading to a number of rapid promotions both in Constantinople and the provinces. At the age of forty, having gained the eye of the Grand Vizier, Fuad Pasha, he was raised to the rank of vizier, and appointed Wali, or Governor-General of Izmir in western Turkey. Two years later, in 1866, after the fall of Fuad Pasha, he was made Wali of Syria.[9]

Under the Grand Viziership of Mehmed Amin Ali Pasha, Rashid's brief was to implement the westernising reforms of the Tanzimat movement.[10] It was also to crush the unruly elements in the province, such as the Druze and the Bedouin, who threatened the stability and integrity of the Ottoman social order. It was a brief which he carried out harshly and effectively.[11] Like Sir Charles Napier in Sind, he was a hard-riding official throughout his period of office, who led from the front. Both believed in hitting the enemy hard, and then offering the velvet glove of friendship.

Burton's jurisdiction extended from Baghdad on the east to Nablus on the south, and as far north as the Aleppo district. He was responsible for the post for Baghdad through the Desert, as well as the safety of commerce, and protection of travellers, and the few English residents, missions, schools, and protected subjects.

Even so, his duties hardly appeared onerous. After rising at dawn he went down to the Consulate at midday, remaining there till four or five. Nevertheless, Isabel insisted, it was also necessary for him 'to scour mountain and desert, to ride hard, and to know everything that is going on in the country, and personally,' she was at pains to stress, 'not through dragomans only.'[12] A good excuse, if any were needed, for Burton's being absent on 'expeditions, often for days, sometimes on business and sometimes to visit the Druze chiefs,' during the first three months of their life at Damascus. It was a practice, of course, that Burton was to continue, and one that would lead, inevitably, to conflict with the Governor-General.

Ever since arriving in Damascus, Burton had set his sights on visiting the ancient ruined city of Palmyra, the biblical 'Tadmor in the wilderness' (Judges 9:18), supposedly built by Solomon to secure the route for the caravans that imported the treasures of India, Persia, and Mesopotamia. Famed also for Zenobia, the warrior queen who had ruled the city in its days of splendour, and had been led through Rome bound in fetters of gold, after its conquest. Writing close to the time, Isabel used the pretext of Burton's having 'semi-official business' at Karyatayn to veil his real intentions. She was careful to point out that it was within his jurisdiction, and that she 'resolved to accompany him, in the hopes of pushing on to Palmyra.'[13]

Isabel's heroine, Lady Hester Stanhope, had been the first European woman to visit it in 1813.[14] Several Englishmen had also been there, but always accompanied by large numbers of the tribe El Mezrab. Burton wanted to end what amounted to a system of blackmail, by demonstrating that the 150 miles' journey through the desert could be done without such a costly escort. This reason could not be openly stated, of course, while Jane Digby was still alive. Isabel, therefore, in her *The Inner Life of Syria* published seven years later, concocted the excuse that, 'The tribe of Mezrab which usually escorts travellers, had been much worsted in some desert fights with the Wuld Ali, and was at the moment too weakened to be able to guarantee our safety.'[15]

A number of people had originally expressed an interest in joining the expedition. In the event, this dwindled to two: Vicomte de Perrochel, a French traveller and author, and M. Ionine, the Russian Consul for Damascus. They set out on 5 April. Apart from inclement weather, they encountered no difficulties on the journey, arriving at Palmyra on the eighth day. Isabel thought it the most imposing sight that she had ever seen, 'so gigantic, so extensive, so desolate was this splendid city of the dead rising out of, and half buried in a sea of sand. One felt as if one were wandering in some forgotten world.'[16] Burton came across some caves, and the party spent several days excavating, discovering human artefacts and bones. They also found some Greek statues, one life-size of Zenobia. They left Palmyra ten days later on Easter Monday, returning by the most direct route, Burton intent on getting back to Damascus by Friday, when the Baghdad and English mails came in.

The following month, Burton informed his Brazilian friend, Albert Tootal, that he had his translation of Hans Stade in hand, and expected to finish the notes and preface in a few days more.[17] It would then go to England in August with his wife. He intended to begin the Lowlands of Brazil in a few days, 'a kind of make weight for the highlands.' Given all the later recriminations surrounding his recall, he went on to make the startling admission of having a presentiment that his 'stay in Damascus won't be long *and am quite prepared for a move.* [my italics] If here till next autumn I shall dress as a Bedouin, get camels and ride off into the Nejd – part not yet visited by any European. But that must be when the Conservatives come in.' In the meantime, he was writing from morning till night, completing arrears of work, 'after which I will cut the damned hole.'[18]

His writing plans, however, were shortly interrupted by an outbreak of cholera followed by an epidemic of scarlet fever. Doing everything she could to help, Isabel herself succumbed to illness. Burton, therefore, took her to Beirut to recover and convalesce. While going on several local excursions together, Beirut was far too confining for Burton. Leaving Isabel to her own devices, he travelled south as far as Tyre, Sidon, Carmel, and Juneh. 'I was too weak to go with him,' Isabel explained, 'which I regretted very much, as I would have given a great deal to have visited the grave of Lady Hester Stanhope.'[19]

Although their house occupied the highest ground in Salihiyyah, the summer heat became stifling. On 25 June, eleven days after returning from Beirut, they moved to summer quarters at Bludan, a Greek Orthodox village about twenty-seven miles across country from Damascus, 5,000 feet up in the mountains. The large stone house belonged to a distinguished former Consul, Sir Richard Wood. A wild waste of garden full of fruit trees extended on every side of the property, with a stream with two small waterfalls rushing through the grounds. Their days there were 'a perfection of living.' The mails came once a fortnight, and Burton was obliged to ride into Damascus every few days to see that all was going on well.

A few weeks later they received a visit from two young men, Edward Henry Palmer, and Charles Tyrwhitt Drake, who camped out in the garden.[20] Palmer, a Fellow of St John's College, Cambridge, was highly gifted in so many ways, and a brilliant linguist. After failing in his application for the post of oriental secretary to the British legation in Persia, he had been selected in 1869 to accompany Captain (later Sir) Charles Wilson RE, and others, on their survey of Sinai, under the auspices of the Palestine Exploration Fund.[21] His main duty was to collect the correct names of places from the Bedouins, and thus establish the correct nomenclature of the Sinai peninsula. That summer he returned to England only to leave it again on 16 December for another expedition.

This time he was accompanied by the twenty-three year old Drake, already a seasoned traveller in the East and fluent in Arabic. The two men travelled alone on foot, walking the six hundred miles from Sinai to Jerusalem, identifying sites and searching for inscriptions. During this pioneering venture, they explored for the first time, the so-called, Desert of the Wanderings (Tih), and many unknown parts of Edom and Moab.[22]

Burton's presence being required in Ba'albek in July, according to Isabel, straining our credulity beyond its limits, 'I gladly embraced the opportunity of visiting the far-famed ruins.' So, too, did Palmer and Drake, who, despite their recent strenuous exertions, left with the Burtons only two days after arriving. Shortly after camping under the famous 'Cedars of Lebanon,' Palmer and Drake left for Beirut via Tripoli. The Burtons, therefore, set off back to Bludan, stopping off at Diman, the summer residence of the Patriarch of Antioch and of all the East. 'His Beatitude gave me a number of pious things,' wrote Isabel, 'among others a bit of the true Cross, which I still wear.'[23]

Two days later they arrived at Zahleh, 'a strange out of the world town,' where Miss Ellen Wilson, Superintendent of a Protestant missionary school in the district, offered them hospitality. One of the pupils at Miss Wilson's establishment was an intelligent young girl named Khamoor, 'The Moon.' A native of the Lebanon, and of poor Greek Orthodox parents, she was aged about seventeen, very pretty with her hair dressed in two long jet-black plaits. Miss Wilson said that the girl needed a change of air, and a month at Bludan would do her good. By this time, Isabel and the girl had taken a liking to each other, and were both glad of the offer. The only condition was that she was never to be taken to a Catholic Church.

Unfortunately, Miss Wilson had failed to tell Isabel that all her girls had recently suffered from fever, until she herself was struck down, followed in turn by Burton and then Isabel. While he managed to shake off his illness, Isabel failed to rally. At sunset on 11 August, she was lifted out of bed, put into a litter and carried back home. Once there, Isabel thought she was cured. However, a constant succession of fainting fits and an aversion to food lasted for three weeks, leaving her very weak and low spirited. 'I do yearn to get home again,' she wrote plaintively to her sister, Dilly. 'The sight of you all will do me good. I want a little nourishment & a little petting & a little quiet, but I have one more expedition to make – first to the stronghold of the Druses & to the wild Arabs of the Ba'kaa or I should not be satisfied with my work.'[24]

Three days earlier, a mounted messenger arrived in the late evening with letters from Nasif Meshaka, Chief Dragoman of the British Consulate and Mr Wright, the chief missionary at Damascus. According to Meshaka, the Christians of Damascus were in a state of great alarm, two young Jews having been caught scrawling signs of crosses in the streets and the lavatory of a mosque at Suk el Jedid, as had happened before the massacre of 1860. Wright corroborated the fear, though he saw no good reason for it. It appeared, however, said Isabel, 'that one of those eruptions of ill-feeling which are periodical and epidemic in Damascus, resulting from so many religions, tongues, and races, was about to simmer into full boil.'[25]

By an unfortunate combination of circumstances, all the chief authorities as well as the consuls were absent from the city. There would be nobody, therefore, to take responsibility. In ten minutes, Burton and Isabel had made their plans, saddled the horses, and cleaned their weapons. Burton refused to take Isabel, 'because he intended to protect Damascus, and he wanted me to protect Bludan and Zebedani.' That night, she accompanied Burton down the mountainside, he taking half the men, and leaving the other half behind. When they arrived in the plain, 'We shook hands like two brothers and parted. Tears, or any display of affection, would have cost us our reputation.'

Although the local authorities expressed extreme surprise on hearing the news, Burton was insistent that, unless certain measures were immediately taken, he would have to telegraph Constantinople.[26] He asked for a guard of soldiers to be posted in every street, and for each to be patrolled during the night. He, himself would go the rounds with Holo Pasha, Acting Governor of the City. The soldiers in the barracks were to be warned that at the first sign of mutiny, they would be sent to the Danube. An order was to be issued that no Jew or Christian was to leave the house until all was quiet. These measures continued in force for three days. Not a drop of blood was shed, said Isabel, and the Christians who had fled to the mountains returned to the city. 'There is no doubt,' she remarked conclusively, 'that my husband saved Damascus from a very unpleasant episode.'

Although life returned to its normal routine there was, according to Isabel, a great deal of ill-feeling simmering between the Muslims and Christians all this summer. Even before this last incident – or, rather, non-incident – Isabel had been personally involved in one which was potentially explosive. As she told it, she used to ride down to the adjoining village of Zebedani to hear Mass, attended by only one servant. Loved by the people her main problem was to pass through the crowds that came to kiss her hand, or her habit.

On this particular occasion, she was riding alone through the village, everyone as usual standing up and saluting her. Suddenly a young Muslim of about twenty-two, Hasan, thrust himself in front of her horse, shouting out, "What fellows you fellahin are to salute this Christian woman! I will show you how to treat her." His reply to Isabel's, "What is the meaning of this?" was to threaten to pull her off her horse and duck her. "I am a Beg, you are a Beg. Salute me." Isabel's response was immediate. Leaping from her horse, she seized the young man by the throat, and set about thrashing him with the butt-end of her whip until he shouted for mercy. Her servant, whom she described as being a little way in the rear, thinking that she was being attacked, raced to the rescue. Six men flung themselves upon Hasan, and in the ensuing struggle her servant's gun went off, fortunately hitting no one.

Isabel returned home, and waited to see if an apology would be offered, but none came. The Christians told her that if she allowed this incident to pass in silence, they would be unable to stay in the village. She, therefore, reported the matter to the Wali. At this particular time, Isabel said, he was not ill-disposed towards Burton, and behaved like a gentleman. He apologised to Isabel, and threatened to send soldiers to burn and sack the home of Hasan and his family. She interceded, however, and they escaped with a light sentence of a few weeks in prison. She also reported the incident to Consul-General Eldridge, who had already heard a garbled version of what had happened.

Early in October, half the servants, together with the English maid, the pet animals, baggage and furniture, were sent under escort direct to winter quarters in Damascus. Having already visited Ba'albak and the northern Libanus, the Burtons returned by a roundabout route via the southern part of the mountain, home of the Druzes. After a courtesy visit to the Sitt Jumblatt, head of the great Druze house, and his Excellence Franco Pasha, Governor of the Libanus, they climbed part of the way up Mount Hermon.[27] Here, Burton removed a stone covered with a Greek inscription discovered earlier by Captain Warren, later shipping it off to England. The excursion ended with a gallop to the Waters of Merom, a call upon the only Bedawi 'Emir' in that region, and an inspection of the hospitable Druze villages clinging to the southern and eastern sides of Mount Hermon. 'The winter was now setting in apace,' said Burton, 'suggesting repose, or at least short excursions to those who can rest only by change of exertion.'[28]

The Burtons were to experience some troublesome and unpleasant times during the next few months. There were people at Damascus, Isabel complained, who were always trying to damage them with the Government at home, and sending lying reports to the Foreign Office. Burton had first fallen out with a freelance missionary, Mr Mentor Mott, living at Beirut, who had come to Damascus earlier that year and attempted to proselytise. Convinced that his activities would endanger the lives of the Christian community, Burton cautioned him, at the same time reporting him to the Consul-General. The result was that he made an enemy of the missionary.[29]

Burton also quarrelled with the Jewish money-lenders, whose nefarious practices he described in a despatch to Sir Henry Elliot in November.[30] Damascus, he said, contained a total of forty-eight adult males protected by HM's Consulate.[31] The most important were David Harari, Tshek Toby, and Yaakub Stambouly. They were Jews, who had been admitted to, or whose fathers, acquired, a foreign nationality, given with the benevolent object of saving them from Muslim cruelty and oppression in days gone by. These protégés had extended what was granted for the preservation of their lives, liberties, and property, to transactions which rested entirely for success on British protection.

He instanced the case of Mr Yaakub Stambouly who, since the death of his father in 1861, had been allowing bills signed by the ignorant peasantry of the province, to accumulate at simple and compound interest. This had resulted in the liabilities of the villagers becoming greater than the value of the whole village. Some villages had been partly depopulated by his exactions. For about a year, a Special Commission had been sitting on the case. Its intricacies complicated by his unwillingness to settle anything, had wearied out all its members. He corrupted, or attempted to corrupt all those with whom he had dealings. With his Excellency's permission, Burton concluded, he would inform them that British protection extended to preserving their persons and property from all injustices and violence. It would not assist them to recover debts from the Ottoman Government, or from the villagers of the Province, and that it would not abet them in impressing or in detaining the latter.[32]

Apart from the usury issue, there was also the matter of Burton's having temporarily taken away protection from the Jewish masters of the boys caught drawing crosses. Some Jewish moneylenders, seeing a chance to get rid of Burton, according to Isabel, reported to Sir Moses Montefiore and Sir Francis Goldsmid in England that he had tortured the boys.[33] Goldsmid immediately wrote to the Foreign Office, 'I hear that the lady to whom Captain Burton is married is believed to be a bigoted Roman Catholic, and to be likely to influence him against Jews.'

Isabel was not in a position to make a public rebuttal of Goldsmid's aspersions. However, as soon as she heard of it, she wrote a spirited reply to the Foreign Secretary. She accused Goldsmid of accepting the tissue of untruths made by the chief moneylenders, because they were his co-religionists. As for the charge of being bigoted, if three Catholics were guilty of having done one-half of what these three Jews had done, she would never rest until she had brought them to justice. She only laid claim to one prejudice, and that was against hypocrisy:

> My husband would be quite unfitted for public life if he were to allow me to influence him in the manner
> described, and I should be unworthy to be any good man's wife if I were to attempt it. My religion is God's
> poor. There is no religious war between us and the Jews, but there was a refusal to use the name of England to
> aid three rich and influential Jews in acts of injustice to, and persecution of, the poor; to imprison and let them
> die in gaol in order to extort what they have not the power to give, and to prevent foreign and fraudulent
> money transactions being carried out in the name of Her Majesty's Government...[34]

The Burtons spent Christmas Day at Beirut at the invitation of the Consul-General. Also staying there was Charles M. Kennedy from the Foreign Office. The Burtons thought it only right to invite him to Damascus, an invitation he accepted a few weeks later. Since this was to be an official visit, they went out of their way to make an impression. Apparently, he found everything in order at the Consulate, going on to pay official calls with Burton. During the next few days, Isabel not only showed him most of the sights of Damascus, but held a large *soirée* one evening in his honour.

What is missing from her account, however, is the reason for Kennedy's visit, which neither she nor Wilkins disclosed. It was, in fact, part of a rationalization and cost-cutting exercise by the Foreign Office, and Kennedy who was Senior Clerk in the Commercial Department, was there to vet the consular arrangements for Syria.[35] The salary of the Consulate at Damascus had been raised at the time of Burton's appointment. Writing to Earl Granville the following January, Sir Henry Elliot said that he had long questioned the necessity for keeping it up at its present scale. He was only waiting for Kennedy's report, before submitting the question of its reduction to the Foreign Secretary.[36]

Kennedy would state, in fact, that Beirut and Damascus were so near, and communications between the places so easy that, in the abstract, it seemed better to station resident Vice-Consuls at theses places. Both would be under the superintendence of the Consul-General who should reside at, or visit each place, according to the requirements of the public service. If the Consulate at Damascus were to be placed on a revised footing as a Vice-Consulate, the salary would fall by £200 with a further drop of £100 in office expenses.[37] Such a reduction in salary and status would, of necessity, lead to Burton's having to seek another Consulate elsewhere.

Such was also in the mind of Rashid Pasha, though for different reasons. This is clear from a long and highly critical letter calculated to do Burton maximum damage with the Government, which he wrote to the Ottoman Grand Vizier, Aali Pasha, on 11 January 1871. 'The Sublime Porte,' he remarked, in the manner of Antony's oration over the dead Caesar, 'does not wish to elaborate on the personal conduct of this official, on his long and frequent absences to the point where the relations of the Imperial Authorities with him, and his own affairs, suffer. Furthermore, it won't pursue the matter of the excursions he makes everywhere accompanied by his wife, both of them exposed to all kinds of danger, as in the hunting of wild beasts to which they give themselves over, where accidents of any sort are likely to occur.'

He accused Burton of having 'a very special aversion for the Muslim nation,' always portraying the Muslims over-excited, and the Christians as terrified. He then turned to the matter of Isabel's horse-whipping the young Muslim. In his version of events, she had struck him because he had not risen as she rode past. Nor had her servant's gun gone off accidentally in a struggle, but had actually been fired at the young man for being insolent. An enquiry had been opened immediately, a fact, if fact it was, not mentioned by Isabel. Burton, whose part in it she had also failed to disclose, was accused of not having pursued the matter regularly and legally. Instead, he had misrepresented the affair, returning to his familiar theme of claiming that Christians were threatened, that security in the area no longer existed, and that they were on the brink of the events of 1860.[38]

'Such is the Consul which the British Government has sent to Damascus, and with whom the Imperial authorities have made, and are continuing to make up to the present time, fruitless efforts to maintain cordial relations.' In exposing the attitude and behaviour of Mr Burton, the Ministry of Foreign Affairs hoped that the British Embassy would not hesitate to consider the measures which he had fully deserved by his behaviour.[39]

An extract from this Confidential Memorandum was sent by Sir Henry Elliot to Lord Granville four days later. In his covering letter, Elliot remarked on the difficulty of obtaining accurate information as to what was being done by Government agents at such a distant place as Damascus. He was, therefore, loath to accept the criticism passed by hostile, and perhaps interested parties, or by Turkish officials, who may have had differences with them. Nevertheless, his Lordship had been aware for some time of his (Elliot's) belief that Burton's proceedings were such as to give grounds for anxiety. Even so, it would have been impossible for him to cite any one act to justify Burton's removal from his Consulate. As for the horse-whipping incident, he had 'vaguely and unofficially' heard of it. An unwillingness, however, to have the name of a lady brought forward in such an affair prevented his investigating it further.[40]

Ostensibly to conduct an important enquiry into the affairs of a British-protected subject, Burton set out the following month in the company of M. Zelmina Fuchs for Hums and Hama on the northern border of the consular district of Damascus. The real reason for his visit, however, was to inspect the inscriptions at Hama at the request of Mr (later Sir) Walter Besant, Secretary of the Palestine Exploration Fund.[41] The stones had been noticed as early as 1812 by J.L. Burckhardt, who stated that, 'in the corner of a house in the Bazar was a stone with a number of small figures and signs, which appeared to be a kind of hieroglyphic writing, though it did not resemble that of Egypt.'[42] They had remained in obscurity until 1870, when Mr Augustus Johnson, US Consul-General at Beirut and the Rev S. Jessup of the Syrian Mission, saw them while wandering through the Bazaar of the old town.

Burton examined, and later sent home, facsimiles of the four unique basaltic stones, whose character raised in cameo, apparently represented, he said, a system of local hieroglyphics peculiar to that part of Syria. They formed, in his opinion, the connecting link between picture-writing and the true alphabet. A few years later, scholars such as Wright, Ward, and Sayce, suggested 'Hittite' as a better word to describe the inscriptions.[43]

Burton and his companion returned to Damascus via the northern Jebel el Hulah, using the opportunity to examine the magnificent Crusaders' castle, Crac des Chevaliers, and the plain of the Eleutherus river. The hardships of the march were considerable. Most of the country was flooded, and the rushing torrents and deep ditches caused long detours. Heavy rains had begun shortly after they left Hama, accompanied by strong winds, which ended in snow and sleet. Soon afterwards, a Jewish servant of M. Zelmina Fuchs fell sick and died. Burton himself suffered from frost-bite. Back in Damascus by 10 March, Burton bought the originals of the copies of the inscriptions held by Dr Bliss, intending to send them home to the Secretary of the Anthropological Institute. However, he learned that Tyrwhitt Drake had already set out for the East in order to investigate the stones for the Palestine Exploration Fund Society.

A short while later, Burton telegraphed the Foreign Secretary for sick-leave, which was granted. It is doubtful whether his health really required such leave. It seems instead to have been a pretext for allowing the Burtons to pass Holy Week in Jerusalem, and for him to visit the Hauran later. However, it could not be taken until the end of March according to Isabel, since his presence was required in Damascus.[44] The truth of the matter is that this fitted in better with their travel arrangements. The fact that there was nothing radically wrong with Burton's health, seems to be borne out from a visit the Burtons received on 17 March from Lord Stafford and Swinburne's cousin, Algernon (Bertie) Mitford, later the first Lord Redesdale.

Redesdale thoroughly enjoyed his stay in Damascus in Burton's company, whose abilities as a guide, he regarded as unrivalled. 'We used to wander through the city penetrating into all sorts of nooks and hidden places unexplored by tourists; sometimes he would take me to visit some Turkish or Arab friend of his, giving me a glimpse of that Oriental life to which only men such as himself, versed in all the mysteries of faith and manners, have access….the light that he could throw upon matters which are riddles to most men, even to old residents among Moslem peoples, was a revelation.' One morning according to Redesdale, Burton came to him with a roll of manuscripts under his arm. '"There," he said, "you shall have the first sight of this." It was the first two or three chapters of his translation of the "Arabian Nights." He assured me that he had shown the translation to nobody.'[45]

Redesdale was highly critical of Isabel's manner towards the Muslims among whom she lived, 'and whom it was her husband's business to conciliate.' He recalled one occasion when they came across a Muslim who was prostrate before the tomb of a holy saint. 'She did not actually strike him with her riding-whip, but she made as though she was going to do, and insisted on the poor man making room for her to go up to the tomb.' Redesdale left the mosque in disgust. 'If actuated by no higher motive,' he remarked, 'she should have reflected upon the harm which such conduct needs work upon her husband, to whom, to do her justice, she was entirely and most touchingly devoted. It is only fair to Burton's memory to show how heavily he was handicapped.'[46]

Things had been so well organized, that when it came to the time of departure for the Holy Land, Tyrwhitt Drake had arrived in Damascus. It was decided that Isabel would travel by sea, and meet Burton at Jerusalem, while he rode overland with Drake. Perhaps because the latter was being paid by the Palestine Exploration Fund to go to Hama and not anywhere else, Burton omitted Drake's name from his account of this trip.[47]

Isabel, after travelling to Beirut, was delayed by rough seas. She then embarked on the smallest, dirtiest, and smelliest steamer she had ever boarded. She spent twenty-four hours in Jaffa before going on to Ramleh, where she put up at the Franciscan monastery. After a seven and a half hours' journey, she at last 'reached the crest of the hill, and beheld Jerusalem beneath me. I reined in my horse, and with my face towards the Sepulchre gazed down upon the city of my longing eyes with silent emotion and prayer.' She booked into the Damascus Hotel, a quiet hostel free of tourists or trippers, 'for I had come on a devout pilgrimage.' Burton and Drake arrived in the evening. After exhausting every place and object of religious interest during Holy Week, they left Jerusalem on 24 April, arriving at Nazareth some ten days later.

Here, they found a group of travellers whom they had met earlier, and who gave them shelter until their own tents were pitched. The camps were on a small plain just outside the town, the Burtons' sited near a Greek Orthodox Church, and hidden from the others by a small rise. In *The Life*, Isabel devotes only a small amount of space to the incident that followed, which was to have serious repercussions for Burton.[48] According to the much fuller version in her private notes,[49] a Copt entered her tent the next morning, 'either for stealing or some other purpose.' She was still in bed, half awake, and heard the servants telling him to go. He refused and was very insolent. He then started throwing stones. Isabel, now thoroughly roused, called to her servants to leave him alone, but by this time they were angry, and had started beating him. A little affair of this sort, she claimed, would be hardly noticed in the usual way. Unluckily, the Greeks whom it didn't concern, were coming out of the church, and joined in on the Copt's side.

There were only six servants, and around one hundred and fifty Greeks. By this time, Burton and Drake hearing the noise, ran out of their tents half-dressed, and did everything to try and calm the situation. The response was a hail of stones.[50] A rich and respectable Greek called out, "Kill them all; I'll pay the blood money." Seeing that he could not appease the Greeks, and several of the servants already being badly injured, Burton fired a shot into the air. Isabel in the meantime dashed round to the other camps and called all the English and Americans with their guns. Their arrival scattered the Greeks just in time, according to Isabel, or none of them would have been left alive. The whole affair was over in less than ten minutes.

Later that the day, Burton reported the incident to a Turkish official and asked for redress. However, he had only twelve policemen, and was unable to do anything. Burton and the others, therefore, had to wait at Nazareth for five days, until the soldiers he had requested from St Jean d'Acre arrived. The Greeks were initially very insolent. However, on discovering that Burton was intent on having the offenders punished, they came in a body to beg pardon. The Bishop also sent word that he deeply regretted the part he had taken. According to Isabel, however, 'they were manufacturing the most untruthful and scandalous report of the affair, which they sent to Damascus and Beyrout, St. Jean d'Acre and Constantinople.'

In *The Inner Life of Syria* published five years later, Isabel claimed that the only mistake Burton made was 'thinking that the post being very unsafe, it would be better to defer sending his report of the affair to Constantinople and London, until he reached Damascus when he would explain the affair personally to the Wali. Meanwhile, the scandalous reports had already been sent,' she went on, 'and he appeared to be silent.'[51] The truth of the matter is that Burton, naïvely, thought that he could contain the affair, and prevent its ripples spreading wider.

Having arrived back in Damascus on 19 May, he immediately explained what had happened to the Wali, 'who condoled him in the kindest terms.'[52] He also wrote to a number of other officials, 'most of whom telegraphed and sent letters of satisfaction and regret.' According to Isabel, Sir Henry Elliot telegraphed to know what it all meant, 'and a full report was sent to Constantinople and London.' By reference to the date of departure from Nazareth, 10 May, however, given by Isabel,[53] and the Foreign Office Blue Book, this claim is shown to be false. Burton sent a despatch to Sir Henry Elliot on 20 May, describing violations carried out by Muslims of the Protestant cemetery in Damascus. He was completely silent on the Nazareth affair. The Ambassador, however, had become aware of it that same day, after receiving a letter giving the Greek version of the affray.[54]

Whatever the effect this latest embarrassment might have on Burton's superiors in Constantinople and London was, in a sense, irrelevant. Burton's future, unknown to him, had already been decided. A month earlier, Sir Henry Elliot, asked by the Foreign Secretary for his opinion regarding the complaint by the Porte of Burton's proceedings at Damascus, replied as follows:

> Your Lordship is aware that for some time past, I have not been satisfied with the manner in which her Majesty's Consulate at Damascus has been conducted, Captain Burton not having succeeded in giving greater satisfaction to the British subjects – whether Christian missionaries or protected Jews – than to the Ottoman authorities, and I cannot withhold the opinion that he is not well-suited to the post which he occupies.
>
> The complaint made by the Porte of his habit of spreading alarming news of impending massacres agrees with information which reached me through other independent channels, but neither that, nor the alleged frequency of his absence from his post, would of themselves suffice to warrant the recall of a British Consul. I consider, however, that his presence tends to unsettle the public mind at Damascus, and to keep alive a sentiment of insecurity, which may at any time become a source of danger, and that it would be very desirable that he should be removed whenever an opportunity for it might offer.
>
> As your Lordship has already decided to reduce the scale of the Consulate at Damascus, it might for the present be sufficient, in reply to the representation of the Porte, to inform them that a change would shortly be made.[55]

On 25 May, Lord Granville informed Sir Henry Elliot of his intention of transferring Burton from his post at Damascus to some other Consulate, and sanctioning the Ambassador's passing on his decision to the Porte.[56]

If Isabel is to be believed, Burton 'thought that everybody was satisfied and contented,' and that the "village row", as she termed it, was ended. In this cloud-cuckoo land, if such was the case, he set out to use up the remainder of his 'sick-leave.' According to Isabel, the Druzes having paid him several friendly visits, and frequently begged him to call upon them in the Hauran, he was keen to keep up neighbourly relations. 'He also wished to copy Greek inscriptions,' she added, 'and explore volcanoes which the road would show.'[57] This, of course, was the real purpose of his proposed expedition, a fact which Burton himself made clear in his *Unexplored Syria*. For upwards of a year and a half, he had been tantalised by the sight of the forbidden Tulul el Safa, the Tells or hillocks of the Safa region. He had also heard reports of a cistern, tank, or cave, called the Umm Niran, the Mother of Fires. The difficulty and danger of visiting these places, he claimed, arose simply from the relations at the time between the Governor-General and the hill-tribes of Bedawins who, mixed up with the Druzes, infested the area.

A few days after Burton and Drake's departure on Wednesday, 24 May, Isabel claimed that the Wali wrote her an extraordinary letter. In it, he accused Burton of having made a political meeting with the Druze chiefs in the Hauran, and of having done great harm to the Turkish Government. Knowing that Burton had done nothing of the kind, she wrote to the Wali telling him that he had been deceived, and asked him to wait until Burton's return. He pretended to be satisfied, 'but a Turkish plot had been laid on foot of which I knew nothing. A disturbance had been purposely created between the Bedawin and the Druzes which enabled the Turkish Government to attack the Druzes in the Hauran. The Wali allowed Burton to go in order to accuse him of meddling in Turkish affairs, and agitated for his recall.'

An extant copy of Rashid Pasha's letter shows Isabel to be lying. It was not written to her but to Burton, and is dated 6 June, the day before his return not a few days after his departure. Naturally, it was also responded to by him and not Isabel. Icily polite, Rashid pointed out to Burton that, when he first arrived in Syria, 'plunder, theft, and depredations were the order of the day. The perpetrators were the

Bedouins and the Druse.' Since then, all his efforts had been directed to giving the country the peace and security it was lacking, convincing the Druse of the friendly intentions of the Imperial Government, making them realise the need to pay taxes, and by offering guarantees to the Bedouins in order to ensure the non-violation of promises.

The policy had succeeded by preventing the Druse from having any contact with foreign agents, especially the English Consulate, the Druse 'imagining in their simplicity that England afforded them a very special protection.' He had explained all this to Burton's predecessor, Mr Rogers, who immediately stopped all contacts with the Druse, with beneficial results. 'Therefore, I will not pretend,' Rashid went on, 'that I was not exceedingly vexed to find that you had undertaken a journey in the Djebel, and that you had announced yourself to the sheikhs in an official letter.' He had also received a report that Burton had 'visited the Druse to reconcile them. If this is true it is a very serious matter and the feelings of the Vilayet on the matter should have been sounded out.'[58]

Responding to the letter two days later, Burton professed to be surprised at its contents. 'Nobody knows better than I of the peaceful conditions which the wise measures of the Imperial Government have established in the Hauran.' At the same time, he was unaware then as now, 'that a simple journey with the object of making a return visit to copy some inscriptions and to pass through an inhabited country (the Diret el Tulul) could have disturbed this security.' The only reason for his sending an official letter to the Sheiks was to gather them together without loss of time. As for the Druse, he did not think they were in need of being reconciled, 'and certainly I would never have contemplated such a serious step without the instructions of my Government.'[59]

Burton, however, was in as much trouble with the British Ambassador as he was with Turkish Governor-General. Three days earlier, Sir Henry Elliot had informed Lord Granville that, although he had despatches and letters from Burton up to 20 May, they did not contain a single allusion to the affray at Nazareth. He had, therefore, telegraphed him to report immediately by telegraph and post.[60] A flurry of letters from Burton to the Ambassador followed.

With the first, Burton sent enclosures which, he said, provided the best explanation of what had happened.[61] He followed this up two days later with an attack on, what he claimed were, the corrupt practices of the Governor-General in Northern Syria, and a justification for his visit to the Druzes of the Hauran. His was the only Consulate at Damascus, Burton claimed, which maintained a shadow of independence. He hoped, therefore, that the Ambassador would understand the reason, in case mischievous reports were circulated about it.[62]

On 11 June, Burton wrote yet again to Sir Henry Elliot, explaining the delay in reporting the Nazareth affair on the grounds of wishing to lay the case before the Ambassador complete in all its details.[63] His explanation of course, completely begged the question as to why he had not even mentioned the affray in his despatch to Constantinople of 20 May. A week later, after responding paragraph by paragraph to a further letter on the affray from Sir Henry Elliot, Burton went on to remark that:

> During the four years which I passed in the Brazils, the Argentine Republic, Chile, Peru and Paraguay, often travelling through the wildest parts of somewhat lawless regions, I cannot call to mind having had a single dispute. In Syria, however, party feeling carries everything before it. .....
>
> .... during my twenty months' residence at Damascus, I have laboured incessantly to promote justice and conciliation, with a due regard for our national dignity..... Those only wish me ill who are jealous of me, or are restrained, by my knowledge of the country and Eastern character, and by my insight into their plans, from carrying out the objects of their ambition, and from the unjust and corrupt measures which are now, especially under the present Administration, the curse of the country.[64]

Four days earlier, the Assistant Under-Secretary for Foreign Affairs, Odo Russell, had sent a letter to Burton enclosing a copy of Rashid Pasha's telegram to Aali Pasha, which had been passed on to Lord Granville by the Turkish Ambassador in London. Russell said that serious complaints regarding Burton's general proceedings had been made by the Porte to HM's Government. As from the receipt of this letter, therefore, Lord Granville, wished Burton to remain at the Consulate in Damascus until further notice.[65]

Another letter of the same date from the Ambassador to the Foreign Secretary, went on to give an extremely fair and considered assessment of the role which Burton had played as Consul. Without going into specific details, the general drift of the complaints made against him, was his determination to meddle in the internal administration of the district. The Governor had written to the Porte, that if Her Majesty's Consul were to assume the virtual position of Governor, it would be impossible for him to continue to direct the Government of the Province. Copy of a letter already forwarded to Lord Granville concerning the affair at Nazareth, while eloquently advocating Burton's proceedings, unconsciously but conclusively confirmed the Governor's complaint.[66]

After asserting that the Wali hated the Consuls of the Great Powers, the letter went on to say that his Excellency "still more hates Captain Burton, for he is virtually Governor here, and there is not much use for a Governor, and he dare not do anything wrong for fear of him, for he can neither bully nor bribe him." If, as he could hardly doubt, the Ambassador went on, this correctly described the position assumed by Captain Burton, it certainly appeared to show that he had misunderstood the duties and the mode of conduct to be followed by Her Majesty's Consular Agents, 'who by co-operation or by friendly remonstrances with the provincial authorities, as the case might seem to require, might contribute powerfully to the well-doing of a district, but who, by raising themselves up as rivals or antagonistic powers, cannot fail to produce a state of things which may lead to disastrous results.'

It was reasonable to assume that many abuses existed in the administration of the province. Captain Burton, however, in his desire to remedy them, had been insufficiently careful to avoid giving just cause for offence on the part of those who were responsible for its tranquillity.

Prior to Burton's appointment, he could 'not recollect either the local authorities or Her Majesty's Consul-General at Beirut, having been the least concerned about the state of the district. Since then, there had been growing unease that the British Consul's well-known opposition to the local authorities might be regarded by the restless population as an incitement to resist them.'[67]

In the meantime, Burton had become embroiled in a highly sensitive religious issue which led to a further clash with Rashid Pasha. This involved the case of a Muslim convert to Christianity. The man in question, Hadj Hassan el Arbagie, had reportedly been brought from Beirut to Damascus under police escort on the orders of the Governor-General. Burton informed Elliot that he immediately wrote to his Excellency that such an action was an infraction of the Treaty of 1856, which secured life and liberty to the so-called "renegades." In his reply, the Wali denied Burton's right to interfere in a matter concerning the subject of His Imperial Majesty, the Sultan. At the same time he forwarded a despatch which he had addressed to the Doyen of the Consular Corps, Beirut, complaining of the conduct of Protestant missionaries proselytising in secret.

Although the prisoner was later freed, it was rumoured that a group of young Muslims at Beirut intended to murder him after his return home.[68] Writing to the Ambassador two days later, Burton accused the Governor-General of having attempted to bribe Hassan in order to persuade him to apostatise. The convert refused, and was threatened with being sent to Constantinople with his hands "in wood." Burton hoped that such a step would not be permitted. 'It would deal a fatal blow in Syria to religious toleration. It would publicly prove our weakness by suggesting that, although supported by a Treaty which guaranteed life and liberty to all converts, we could not defend a convert from banishment.'

Shortly after taking charge of the Consulate, he went on, certain Muslims belonging to the Shazli order of Dervishes had converted to Catholicism.[69] Experiencing strong disapproval from the local authorities, they took refuge in the Spanish Casa Santa. However, as Catholic questions were then mainly the prerogative of France, he had not thought it proper to act in the matter. 'In conclusion, without wishing in any way to impede freedom of action in cases of conversion, I venture to suggest that missionaries, especially Protestant missionaries in Syria, be invited carefully and conscientiously to consider whether they are justified in exposing a Muslim convert to the imminent risk of losing his life, and by irritating a fanatical people to risk causing for themselves and their co-religionists such outbreaks of fury as characterised the last decade at Aleppo, Jeddah and Damascus.'[70]

Isabel devoted a very large section of Chapter XXI in *The Life*, to the Shazlis, printing a document entitled "The Christian Revival in Syria," which, she claimed, was written by Burton. According to her, 'When I brought out my "Inner Life of Syria," Richard brought me the following document, blushing like a schoolboy, and asked me to insert it in my own name – if I would mind, as I could not be godmother to the Shazlis, being godmother to *it*.'[71] The idea of Burton's 'blushing like a schoolboy' beggars belief, as does his authorship of the document as it stands. There is no reason to doubt that he was sufficiently interested enough in the Shazli conversions, to conduct his own investigations into this bizarre phenomenon, and to write about it. He had been familiar with this Sufi order for years, having referred to the Shaykh Shadhili, the Muslim holy man, who, reputedly, had introduced coffee-drinking into Arabia, in his *First Footsteps in East Africa*.[72] It is a measure of Isabel's disingenuousness, that we are asked to believe, for example, that Burton could write in the following vein: 'The conversion of the Mohammedans has begun at last, without England's sending out, as is her custom, shiploads of Bibles, or spending one fraction upon it; and in this great work, so glorious to Christianity, England, if old traditions are about to be verified, is to have a large share.'[73] Clearly, what she did, was to use Burton's straightforward report, which also contained observations he had made to Government, and embroider it with her own Catholic sentiments.

Obviously intent on portraying Burton's later recall as a form of martyrdom, Isabel then went on to claim that he suggested offering his protection from Muslim harassment to the 'at least twenty-five thousand secret Christians longing for baptism.' Having bought a tract of land for them and built a village, they could settle there unmolested. If he then requested the Patriarch Valerga of Jerusalem to come and baptise them, "would *you* be afraid," Burton is reportedly to have said to her, "to stand godmother for them with *me* on guard." Her immediate response was that she "would only be too proud to do it."

Having informed Lord Granville, the affair, she maintained, 'was hopelessly mismanaged, and his recall followed within the month; ......It broke his career, it shattered his life, it embittered him on religion.....I may be wrong, but I have always imagined that he thought Christ would stand by him, and see him through his troubles, but he did not like to speak of it.'[74]

Burton's real view of the situation, as distinct from Isabel's fantasy, is clear from a despatch which he sent to Sir Henry Elliot on 15 July. This 'revival,' clearly more a matter of self-interest than of faith, he attributed to the maladministration of Syria during the last five years, especially the last two under Rashid Pasha. As a result, he said, 'the Moslem is the only subject of the Porte who has no defender unless his purse be well-lined.' The so-called "Greek" Christians were backed, especially at the present time, by Russian influence and gold. The Latins received support from the ecclesiastics and from the Catholic Consulate. The Protestants and the Druzes looked to England for that help and support which her policy had wisely extended to them. 'But the Moslem Rayyah could not look to any of these sources for aid....he has at length learned to envy the privileges enjoyed by the various Christian sects, such as immunity from conscription and facilities of obtaining the justice which he cannot expect. El Islam will not help him – Christianity will.'[75]

The heat for some time had been almost unbearable in Damascus. 'We felt like the curled up leaves of a book,' Isabel said. 'Everyone who could fled.' She refused to go to summer quarters, however, because Burton could not do so. At last fever set in, and it became a necessity. Burton sent her away to Bludan, and the next day she resumed her old life of the previous summer. 'After a few weeks, 'Richard came up and joined me at Bludan with Charles Tyrwhitt Drake.'

What Isabel neglected to mention is that, in spite of Lord Granville's ban on Burton's leaving the Consulate at Damascus, she had sent a telegram to Sir Henry Elliot on 10 July, asking him to, 'Kindly telegraph permission to Captain Burton to go to summer quarters four hours' ride from Damascus. All the Consuls gone long ago; the whole household ill from excessive heat.' Isabel had counted on the Ambassador's not knowing of the Foreign Secretary's instructions to Burton. And she was right. It was not until ten days later, however, that Sir Henry telegraphed back that, 'there is nothing in the regulations of the service to prevent a Consul from going a few hours' distance from his usual residence without special leave.[76] The Ambassador later informed Lord Granville that, although he had been unaware of the Foreign Secretary's prohibition, he had not replied immediately to Mrs Burton's request, since 'I was convinced that there was something which had been kept back from me, and I felt, moreover, some hesitation in returning any answer to a request which, if made at all, should have come direct from the Consul.'[77]

While Burton had been at Damascus, he had twice inspected the most interesting features of the Jebel el Sharki, the Eastern Mountain. Taking advantage of Tyrwhitt Drake's visit, Burton resolved to connect the two excursions by a march from Jebel el Shakif to the northern end. The excursion lasted eight days, between 31 July and 7 August. During it, they saw in a range supposed to be impracticable, four temples, of which three were probably unvisited. They had prepared for entering on a map of Syria and Palestine, the name of five great mountain blocks, and traced out the principal gorges. Finally, they had determined the disputed altitude of the anti-Libanus.[78]

Unknown to Burton, this was to be his last excursion in Syria. On 22 July, Lord Granville sent a despatch, expressing regret at having

to inform you that the complaints which I have received from the Turkish Government in regard to your recent conduct and proceedings render it impossible that I should allow you to continue to perform any Consular functions in Syria, and I have, accordingly, to desire that you will, on receipt of this despatch, hand over the archives of Her Majesty's Consul at Damascus to the person whom Mr. Consul-General Eldridge will appoint to carry on the duties of the Consulate until further orders. You will, therefore, make your preparations for returning to this country with as little delay as possible.[79]

Two days later, Odo Russell sent Eldridge a copy of this despatch, with instructions to appoint someone until further arrangements had been made.

Unaware at this date of his recall, Burton sent two despatches both dated 9 August to Sir Henry Elliot. In the first, he complained of his rude treatment by Rashid Pasha in connection with his 'having protested, in the name of the British-protected Jews of Tiberias, against the illegal sale of ground containing a synagogue and a cemetery which they had proved to have been their property for centuries.' In the second, he drew attention to the unsatisfactory nature of the inquiry into the Nazareth affray, quoting from a letter written to him a week earlier by the Rev John Zeller, which stated that, "The investigation against the people who made the attack upon your party was suddenly broken off, and all the prisoners were set at liberty. The whole trial was, from the beginning, a wretched farce." His Excellency Rashid Pasha, Burton commented, 'has applied with instance for his recall, and it was evident that the sooner he was removed from Syria the better. At present he is one of the perils of the Empire.'[80]

It was Burton, however, who was the first to go. On 16 August, Isabel wrote, 'a bombshell fell in the midst of our happy life.' The horses were saddled at the door, and they were about to go for a ride, when a ragged messenger arrived with a note. It was from the Vice-Consul of Beirut, informing him that by order of the Consul-General he had arrived the previous day, and taken charge of the Damascus Consulate. Burton and Drake were in the saddle in five minutes, and galloped into the town without drawing rein. Some time later, a mounted messenger returned with a note from Burton: 'Don't be frightened – I am recalled. Pay, pack, and follow at convenience.'[81] Acknowledging Lord Granville's despatch the following day, Burton stated that he had handed over the archives of the Consulate to Mr Acting Consul Jago, and had made preparations for leaving Damascus the following morning.[82] In his journal for 18 August, Burton wrote:

Left Damascus for ever; started at three am in the dark, with a big lantern; all my men crying; alone in *coupé* of diligence, thanks to the pigs. Excitement of seeing all for the last time. All seemed sorry; a few groans. The sight of Bludan mountains in the distance at sunrise, where I have left my wife. *Ever again?* Felt soft. Dismissal ignominious, at the age of fifty, without a month's notice, or wages, or character.'[83]

Isabel went about as usual trying to be philosophical. In bed, so we are led to believe, she had one of her dreams. She thought some one pulled her, and said in a loud whisper, "Your husband wants you – get up and go to him!" After it happened three successive times, she jumped up, saddled her horse and rode five hours across country, over rocks and across swamps making for the diligence half-way house. She reached Beirut twenty-four hours before the steamer sailed. 'When Captain Burton had once received his recall,' she said, 'he never looked behind him, nor packed up anything, but went straight away.' She met him walking alone in the town, and looking so sad and so serious. Not even a Kawass was sent to attend on him, to see him out with a show of honour or respect. 'But I was there (thank God!) in my place, and he was so surprised and glad when he saw me! We had twenty-four hours to take counsel and comfort together.'

They received numerous expressions of regret and sympathy, except from the Consul-General, who cut them. At 4 o'clock on 20 August, Isabel went on board with Burton and saw the steamer off for England. As she stepped ashore, Burton's faithful servant, Habib, who had followed him, and arrived just ten minutes too late, flung himself down on the quayside in a passionate flood of tears. Exhausted, and with her clothes dry and stiff, Isabel took the night diligence back to Damascus. After spending a day with Miss Wilson, she returned to Bludan escorted by Tyrwhitt Drake, a Kawass, and servants.

The news of Burton's recall spread like wildfire. People from the surrounding villages poured in, and Muslims flung themselves on the ground shedding bitter tears and tearing their beards. "What have we done for your Diwan (Government) has done this things to us. Send some of us to go over to your land, and kneel at the feet of the Queen and pray that he may be sent back to us again."

Isabel broke up the establishment, packed Burton's books and sent them to England, and settled all affairs. This was made slow and difficult, she said, as the Government had temporarily left them without a farthing. It also showed the extent of their extravagance, apparently lacking any savings to draw on in such an emergency. At last she made her predicament known to her uncle, Sir Robert Gerard, who telegraphed to the Imperial Ottoman Bank, "to let his niece have any money she wanted."

On Monday, 11 September, she and Drake breakfasted with Jane Digby, spending the rest of the day with her. 'How I regret their departure,' Jane wrote in her diary, 'and how I shall miss her lively friendly society.' Afraid that a demonstration might result from the large number of people who wanted to accompany her along the road, Isabel planned to slip away quietly the following night. She and Jane spent the final day together at Salahiyyah. 'My last day,' Jane wrote sadly, 'and at night we parted, probably to meet no more in this world! Notwithstanding her hopes of his return here as Consul-General.'[84]

For some days Isabel had been sickening with fever, determined, nevertheless, not to be ill at Damascus and detained. But having braved what she regarded as 'the fatal 13th,' she set out on it, and 'was not destined to reach Beyrout.' When she arrived at that part of the Lebanon looking down upon the sea, near Khan el Kharayyah, she became delirious and was unable to carry on.

Fortunately, the village of her Syrian girl was located only half an hour from the road. Isabel was carried to her father's house, and lay there for ten days very ill, nursed by Khamoor and her English maid. When she had recovered sufficiently, Isabel wrote a long letter to Lord Derby, who had been responsible for appointing Burton to Damascus stating, what she described as, the true facts of the case, and exposing the falsehoods which had led to Burton's recall. As soon as she was well enough to move, she travelled to Beirut where she embarked aboard the Russian ship *Ceres* which had brought her to the Lebanon almost two years earlier.

Alexandria proved a culture shock to Isabel. 'Demi-semi Europeanised, Christianised, civilised natives are not pleasant,' she observed tartly. 'The Europeans put them on an equality and are too lazy to put them in their places.'[85] The Kawass of the Consulate, she observed in shocked surprise, 'answered me familiarly and sitting. Ours were obliged to stand and salute if any English person passed in the street, and if a Consul or his wife visited Damascus, one was on duty as long as they stayed, and one was on guard at the hotel or at our house for every English person of distinction. That is the difference between Nature and Civilization, between Moslem and Christian, and also of a Military or a Civilian master....'[86]

On 30 September Isabel took passage on the P&O *Candia*. A fortnight later the ship docked early at Southampton, and by early afternoon Isabel was on her way to join Burton and her family.

CHAPTER THIRTY-ONE

RECALLED

After landing in England on 18 September, Burton had made a brief visit to his in-laws at 14 Montagu Place, before booking in at Howlett's Hotel a couple of days later. From there he wrote to Lord Houghton informing him of his recall. 'I mention this to you as you are one of my oldest and best friends, but pray don't think that I have any grievance or that you are going to be bored by it. When shall I see you? I have dropped as it were from the clouds & found all London abroad.'[1] Almost a week later, in response to various queries by Lord Houghton, Burton said that his story was 'too long to tell you in a note. When my wife arrives (5th or 6th prox.) I shall do it all up in the form of a print, so that you can scan your eyes over it at once......On the 28th next I must run down for a few days with my sister, returning on the 2nd...Have you had any news of Hankey?'[2]

When Burton met Maria, the shock of his sudden recall, according to Georgiana, clearly showed in his attitude and behaviour. 'Never had we known him so wretched, so unnerved; his hands shook, his temper was strangely irritable, all that appreciation of fun and humour which rendered him such a cheery companion to old and young alike, had vanished.'[3] Unable to sleep, he sat up into the small hours of the morning smoking and talking with his brother-in-law.

The difference between their two careers must have struck Burton forcibly, and painfully, at this time. After distinguished military service in India, Henry Stisted at fifty-four, was now a major-general. He had recently served as lieutenant-governor of Ontario, and in May 1871, had been nominated a KCB. Burton, by contrast was a 'captain' only by courtesy, and was in bad odour with the Foreign Office. Georgiana, unfairly, laid the blame for the blighting of his career on what she called 'Isabel's 'imprudence and passion for proselytising.'

After spending only two days at Norwood, Burton returned to London where he found a despatch from Edmund Hammond notifying him of the recall of the Governor-General, Mohammed Rashid Pasha. We have already noticed Isabel's earlier malicious caricature of Rashid Pasha. Her account of his recall and subsequent events is equally malicious and untruthful. Writing to Lady Houghton in November, she claimed that, after the death of the Grand Vizier, Aali Pasha, 'it was then discovered that Rashid Pasha was an infamous man and he was dismissed with disgrace never to be reemployed and not even allowed to remain till the new Wali arrived.'[4] Similar sentiments with additional details were expressed later in *The Life*, where Burton's recall was described as being due to, 'A Pasha so corrupt that his own Government was obliged to recall him a month later, threaten him with chains, and throw him into a fortress, and his brains were blown out a short while after by a man he had oppressed.'[5] All these claims are utterly spurious.

Rashid Pasha had written a long private letter to Aali Pasha, at the end of July. He began by referring to his official letter of complaint written that day on Burton's conduct and the articles he published in *The Levant Herald*. In it, he had pointed out that, 'if Mr Burton is not replaced as soon as possible, and if the "Levant Herald" does not stop inserting correspondence of the same kind, it will become extremely difficult for me to govern the country with the authority and the consideration due to the person of the representative of the Imperial Government.' He asked permission, therefore, to bring a law-suit for libel against the Editor-in-Chief of the paper, the only person he could cite, since 'Mr Burton persists in hiding under the transparent but prudent veil of anonymity.'[6]

He then went on to ask to be allowed to return to Constantinople, on the grounds, 'that the difficult expeditions, the [onerous?] journeys I have made in the last five years in a burning desert and in a murderous climate have finished by ruining my health.' Nevertheless, his carrying on despite this, and the demands that this Vilyat made on him, 'one of the most difficult to govern,' only proved the extent of his devotion. He asked, therefore, to be granted any place, however modest, at the capital.[7]

Aali Pasha, who by now combined the offices of grand vizier, foreign minister, and minister of the interior, had fallen ill during the previous month. On 6 September he died leaving, what amounted to, a political vacuum, with no obvious candidate to succeed him. Despite the ensuing administrative problems caused by rival cliques, Rashid was recalled in the normal way, leaving Syria for the last time on 3 October 1871.

News of his recall caused a sensation. According to the Acting-Consul, Thomas Jago, petitions were going the round of the city and the province for signature, pleading with the Porte to rescind the order for his recall. Telegrams, too, in the same vein, had been despatched to Constantinople by the Spiritual Chiefs of the Christian and Jewish communities. Naturally, not all regretted his going. 'The feeling, however, among the people generally, was one of satisfaction. Apart from the innate love of change, sorely tried by the unusual duration of his tenure of office, the exigencies of the tax-gatherer and usurer, the misery of the past winter, and the stagnation of trade, had not tended to increase the popularity of the Executive among the poor; while the increase in peculation and corruption in all branches of the Administration, which followed his return from Constantinople, has neutralised the great esteem in which he was held up to that time.'[8]

Nevertheless, Rashid was too talented and experienced an official to be out of office for long. Within a short time of his return to Constantinople, he was appointed Wali of Herzogovina, Yenipazar and Bosnia, a post he held until early in 1873. He was then recalled and made Minister of Public Works, followed later that year by his appointment as Foreign Minister in the government, first of Shirvanizade Mehmed Rushdi Pasha, and then of Muterjim Mehmed Rushdi Pasha. He was engaged in writing a constitution for the Ottoman Empire, when he was cut down by an assassin's bullet on Thursday, 15 June 1876. In what was an act of personal and political revenge, a Circassian army officer, Hasan, apparently high on hemp, tricked his way into a meeting of government ministers at the house of the President of the Council of State. Firing two shots in quick succession, he first killed Huseyn Avni Pasha, the Minister of War, his real target, and then Rashid Pasha, who happened to be in the wrong place at the wrong time. Continuing unchecked on his deadly rampage, Hasan killed a further five people besides wounding eight others, before he was run through by a soldier and arrested.[9]

Although Burton exulted in the news of the former Governor-General's death, he was widely mourned, many telegrams of condolence being sent to the government and to his family in Constantinople. The verdict of historians is that he governed Syria as well as any Ottoman official in the latter half of the nineteenth century, leaving behind a substantial and enduring legacy for his successors.[10]

While Rashid Pasha was the main target for the Burtons' virulent abuse and misrepresentation, Consul-General Eldridge, 'fearfully jealous of his superior subordinate,' as Isabel would have us believe, came in for his share. Writing in libellous terms to Lady Houghton shortly after Burton's recall, Isabel described Eldridge as 'a very bad man,' whose wife was 'a paid spy for Igroalieff at Constantinople.' One of his three dragomen was 'a thief kicked out of the Imperial Ottoman Bank for stealing,' another, 'a gentleman who is light-fingered in the post office, and the third, 'a member of the most disreputable family of intriguers in the Levant.' As if this weren't enough, 'To these gentlemen Mr Eldridge entrusts the management of British interests in Syria, whilst he eats and drinks, draws his pay, plays with his barometers, neglects his work, [!] and employs his leisure hours in ruining hardworking and honest men like Richard.'[11] There is, of course, not the slightest evidence to suggest that Eldridge was anything other than a perfectly competent and hard-working official carrying out his wide-ranging responsibilities to the complete satisfaction of the Foreign Office.[12]

On reaching London, Isabel claimed that she found Burton had made no defence, treating the whole thing *de haut en bas*. This was hardly correct. As we have already seen, he intended writing up the whole thing on Isabel's return, and would have prepared detailed notes for this purpose. It was only two days after her arrival, that a very long letter written from her parents' house, was ready for despatch to Lord Granville. 'It becomes now my duty,' Burton wrote, 'in a matter not only so serious of itself but also important as regards the public interests, to lay the whole case before your Lordship from the time of my appointment to that of my recall.'[13]

It is instructive to place beside Burton's very long self-assessment of events, the observations which Sir Henry Elliot had been asked by Lord Granville to make on the misunderstanding between Burton and the Governor-General. What these highlighted in particular were Burton's utter lack of prudence and discretion, and his adoption of an attitude of rivalry towards the Turkish authorities who were responsible for the administration of the country. Elliot quoted from a recent despatch written by Burton, in which he observed that, 'In the days of Mr Richard Wood and Colonel Rose, when the English Government had some influence in Syria, the Governor-General and the Mushir used to rise from their seats when a Consular Dragoman entered the room, and ordered for him pipes and coffee. Those days are now gone.' Burton, however, had fallen 'into the error of endeavouring to recover for himself and his dragoman, a position neither aimed at by his colleagues nor compatible with the altered state of affairs, and he naturally encountered the strenuous opposition of the Governor-General.'[14]

The Ambassador claimed to have tried as far as possible to gather from independent sources, the opinions which had been formed in Syria with regard to Burton. He could not 'be blind to the unanimity,' he said, 'with which he is blamed even by those who consider him to have been actuated by a generous wish to support those whom he looked upon as oppressed; but he may be held to be disqualified for the post of HM's Consul at Damascus, without its being necessary to assume him to entertain all the hostile designs attributed to him by the Governor-General.'[15]

The impression given in *The Life* and *The Romance* is that Isabel fought a long drawn-out rearguard action against the FO to clear Burton's name. 'I applied myself for three months,' she wrote, 'in putting the case clearly before the Foreign Office in his name.'[16] There was no mention, however, of his 16 October letter. It was, in fact, only nine days later that Lord Granville replied: 'I do not think it necessary to follow you through recapitulation,' he wrote, 'or to enter into any review of your conduct in the post which you last held. I am willing to give you credit for having endeavoured, to the best of your ability and judgement, to carry on the duties which were entrusted to you. But, having come to the conclusion, on a review of the Consular establishment in Syria, that it was no longer necessary to maintain a full Consul at Damascus, at a cost to the public of £1000 a year, your withdrawal from that residence necessarily followed on the appointment of an officer of lower rank and at a lower rate of salary, to perform the Consular duties in that place.'[17]

It was, as intended, a perfect face-saving solution for Burton, who grasped it with both hands. 'It is gratifying to me,' he replied, 'to find that the cause of my recall from Damascus was not on account of any erroneous impression that ill-feeling existed against me on the part of the authorities or the people of Syria. This circumstance will render it unnecessary to trouble your Lordship with many other testimonials lately forwarded to me from the British-protected Jews of Tiberias and Safed, from the Druses, from the villages about Damascus, and from other section of the community.' With regard to his own future employment, 'it only remains for me to place myself at your Lordship's commands, in the assured hope that such employment would be of a nature to mark that I have not forfeited the approbation of HM's Government.'[18]

Isabel's version of the end of the affair is, that Richard got 'the *nearest thing* to an apology that one would expect out of a Government official, and an offer of several small posts which he indignantly refused.' The first of these claims is an obvious nonsense. As for the second, Isabel said that she found an entry in his journal which, significantly, she left undated, that he was offered Para, but would not take it. –"Too small a berth for me after Damascus."[19] In fact, this post, and this only,was offered to Burton towards the end of September *before* Isabel arrived back in England. The excuse he gave to the FO in declining it, was that his wife's health would be unable to stand up to the climate. 'But Richard is offered Para, £750 a year and yellow fever,' Isabel wrote scathingly to Lady Houghton in November. 'Perhaps tomorrow he may be offered the Fiji Islands. May Allah burn their houses etc etc.'[20]

Sir Roderick Murchison had suffered a stroke in November 1870, which left him paralysed down his left side. Despite this impairment, he prepared his last Anniversary Address to the Geographical Society in the spring of 1871, dictating it to his nephew. Burton noticed in his journal that his name had been left out once again. 'He was anxious,' according to Burton, 'to pay due honour to our modern travellers, to Livingstone and Gordon, Speke and Grant. He has done me the honour of not honouring me.' Later on, he wrote, 'Received a card from him to go and see him.'[21] In the middle of October, however, Murchison caught a cold during the course of his usual drive. An attack of bronchitis followed, and he died peacefully on the 22nd. He was buried five days later in Brompton Cemetery. The Queen and the Prince of Wales sent their carriages to join the procession, and the Prime Minister, Gladstone, walked behind the bier.[22]

Never one to let sleeping dogs lie, the following day Burton wrote to *The Times* on the subject of its obituary notice:

> Our lamented President, the late Sir Roderick Murchison, *forgot*, in his anniversary speech, to couple with the names of Speke, Grant and Baker, that of a man who led the first expedition into the Lake Regions, which are now known to send forth the Nile. You have done the same in the excellent notice above alluded to. The public has given more than their due to my humble labours in the cause of geography. I regret, however, to see no mention of my friends Winwood Reade and Paul du Chaillu, who have both worked hard in the same cause, who, by their adventurous journeys into the African interior have opened up new lands and who, being young men with long, and I hope, happy careers before them, will not benefit by sitting in the cold shade.[23]

The civil trial of Arthur Orton, the Tichborne Claimant, had begun in the Court of Common Pleas on 11 May 1871. It not only aroused enormous public interest, it also inflamed widespread latent anti-Catholic feeling, particularly anti-Jesuit, the Claimant's supporters portraying him as the victim of a priestly plot. It was of particular concern to the Arundell family, since there was a close connection by marriage with the Tichbornes.[24] Having met the Claimant in South America in 1868, when he had gone out to meet the Chile Commission, Burton was called upon to give evidence on Wednesday, 13 December, as to what had passed between them.

Examined by Mr Serjeant Ballantine, Burton said that, "On the 4th November I was at Beunos Airies preparing to cross the Pampas. I met the plaintiff at a place called Villa Nueva, now called Villa Maria....The plaintiff was then returning to Buenos Ayres. We heard from him that he had been at Cordova. We passed one evening together."

Asked by the Attorney-General, "Was this the first time you had ever seen the plaintiff?" Burton replied, "This was the first time I saw him."

Recalled after lunch at the request of the Attorney General, Burton was allowed to refresh his memory by reading from his journal: 'Went to the Hotel Oriental, kept by a most extortionate Pole. (Laughter.) There met Sir Roger Tichborne returning from Cordova, after remaining a week or so at Buenos Ayres. Sorry he could not join us [ie Maxwell and Major Richard]. He had letters urging him to return to England.'[25]

It will be remembered that, according to Wilfrid Scawen Blunt, Burton and the Claimant spent a great deal of time together at Buenos Aires. If Blunt is not guilty of invention, therefore, it makes Burton guilty of perjury, although it is not immediately apparent why he should wish to conceal a more intimate connection with the Claimant.

She and Burton, according to Isabel, had 'ten months of great poverty' – of the genteel sort, of course – 'and neglect (but great kindness from Society),' during which they were, supposedly reduced to their last £15. As Georgiana Stisted was careful to point out, 'Neither, it may be remembered, was remarkable for economy; but Isabel who held the purse-strings, used to get quite indignant when reminded of the duty of providing against rainy days…..However, she was not allowed to want. Each side of the family possessed its wealthy member, and the individuals in question, being as generous as they were rich, came to the assistance of our imprudent pair.'[26]

They spent a month at Garswood, Sir Robert paying their fares there and back, 'without knowing that we wanted anything,' so Isabel would have us believe. He also gave her £25, 'and from that time one little help or another came to keep us alive, without our asking for anything.'

Burton wrote to Milnes at the beginning of January 1872. 'We ran up north on Dec. 27, and on Thursday next go to Knowsley for a short visit, shortened by Lady May (or Mary)….[illegible] marriage in London.[27] ……Don't trouble yourself about writing, but perhaps some one about you will let me have a line. B[uckley] Matthew expected to see his daughter Mrs Earl (of L'pool). He wants me to do a "good action" to write about the Paraguayan War in The Times. But just at present I cannot afford good actions, and to tell you the truth my humour does not lie in that direction pour le moment. I think you will sympathise with me. Isabel passes on her best love to you and yours.'[28]

On 23 January Burton left to join his sister at Edinburgh, and Isabel returned to London. Three days later he informed W.H. Bates of having 'written to my wife to send a copy of Zanzibar to RGS for Kirk at Zanzibar, and another for Wakefield at Mombasah and only hope they may arrive in time…My mother-in-law is very ill, so I may be obliged to return as now to London. If not, I shall stay here till the end of February.'[29]

Burton's long-lost manuscript of his Zanzibar having gathered dust since turning up unexpectedly in February 1865, had lately been published. The long interval of a decade, he remarked, 'has given me time to work out the subject, and better still to write with calmness and temper upon a theme of the most temper-trying nature – chap.XII, vol.II will explain what I meant.'[30] This chapter is wholly devoted to an account of Speke, Burton's final attempt to exorcise the ghost of his late companion. 'I fully recognise the difficulty of writing a chapter with such a heading.' he wrote. 'Whatever is spoken will be deemed by some better unspoken; while others would wish me to say much that has been, they believe, unsaid. Those who know me, however, will hardly judge me capable of setting down ought unfairly, or of yielding after such length of years, to feelings of indignation, however justified they might have been considered in the past.'[31]

These were provocative words to C.P. Rigby, who wrote an angry assessment of it to Grant. 'I have waded through the tedious pages of the 2nd volume of this work with great difficulty, and the only result is increased disgust and contempt at the pitiful lying author who can thus revile the memory of his companion poor Speke.' He described Chapter 12 as being 'the raison d'être of the entire book, to give this false foul libeller the opportunity of spitting his venom at the memory of poor Speke,' and that 'a lapse of 10 years have (sic) only increased the venom there engendered in the breast of this unworthy concocter of books.'[32]

The press response, nevertheless, was generally very favourable, although the critic of *The Examiner* feared, 'that these two rambling, egotistical, and excessively bulky volumes will prove tiresome reading even to the most arduous student of African travel.'[33] *The Athenaeum*, however, was highly complimentary, 'welcoming with pleasure this new work from the prolific pen of the accomplished traveller in all four quarters of the globe.' The reviewer was particularly interested in the question raised in the book, as to whether the Victoria Nyanza of Speke was one single expanse of water or consisted of several lakes. 'The evidence that it is a single lake is certainly very imperfect.' He pointed to Burton's contention in *The Nile Basin* in 1864 having recently received material support from information collected by the Rev T. Wakefield, Church Missionary at Mombas, and published in the 40th volume of the RGS journal (1870). 'After all,' he observed, 'nothing is more likely than for Captain Speke to have been mistaken on the subject.'[34]

While in Edinburgh, Burton had been approached by a Mr Alfred Lock, an entrepreneur who had just obtained a concession from the Danish Government for working the sulphur beds at Myvatn in the northern part of Iceland. Anxious to know of its financial potential, he wanted a survey carried out, and was willing to pay for all the necessary expenses, together with a lump sum of £2,000 if the property realised expectations. Naturally, Burton jumped at the chance and, as Granton was to be his starting point, he spent part of the time in making preparations.

On 26 April, Frederick Leighton began to paint the portrait of Burton, which would later hang in the National Portrait Gallery, London. At this first sitting, according to Isabel, Burton was most anxious that Leighton should paint his necktie and pin, and kept saying to him every now and then, "Don't make me ugly; don't, there's a good fellow;" and Leighton kept chaffing him about his vanity, and appealing to Isabel to know if he was not making him pretty enough.[35] Not reported by Isabel was Burton's attempt 'to put Leighton on his mettle,' by continually looking up from his position in which he had been placed, and by violent contortions of the face jeopardized the idea Leighton had formulated.'[36]

The following month Burton was called to give evidence before a Select Committee on Diplomatic and Consular Services. He made them all laugh when he complained that the salary of Santos had been totally inadequate to his position, and that he had been obliged to use his own little capital to supplement his income. Asked 'how his predecessor (a baronet) had managed,' Burton replied, "By living in one room over a shop, and washing his own stockings."'[37] Part of Burton's evidence throws light on how much he needed to use his own money – and how much he was able to draw on – in order to live up to his standards. Burton said that a shilling in England had the purchasing power of 27 pence in Brazil, and of a dollar (4s 4d) at Fernando Po; in any case, his salary at Fernando Po was £750 and he spent £3,000 of his own; at Santos it was £700 and he could not live under £1,200, and at Damascus salary and office allowance amounted between them to £1,000 per annum, and he never spent less than £1,500.[38]

Shortly after mid-May, Burton left London en route for Iceland. By now, according to Georgiana, he was quite himself again, and apparently enjoying life. In spite of Edinburgh's abysmal climate, he liked the town, the bracing air 'correcting a tendency to liver troubles.' He was also flattered by the kindness and hospitality extended to him on all sides. Sir Henry Stisted's Regiment, the 93rd Highlanders,[39] stationed at the Castle, entertained in genuine Highland fashion, and at their house in Queen Street Burton 'met most of the leading Scotch families, who happened to be lingering in the northern capital.'[40]

He sailed from Granton en route to Iceland on 4 June. The following day, Mrs Arundell died, and was buried at Mortlake eight days later. Shortly afterwards, Lord Granville wrote to Isabel, to ask if she thought Burton would accept Trieste, Charles Lever having died. He advised her to urge him to take it, because they were not likely to have anything better for some time.[41]

Writing to her niece from Wardour Castle early the following month, Isabel confessed to not having 'cried nor slept since mother died (a month tomorrow). I go up again on Monday for final pack-up – to my convent ten days…then back in town in hopes of Nana [Burton] in August, about the 7th. Then we shall go to Spain, and to Trieste, our new appointment, if he [Burton] will take it as all our friends and relations wish, if only as a stop-gap for the present.'[42]

Although Isabel had immediately written off to Burton in Iceland, she was not able to send his acceptance until 15 July. 'We knew, of course,' she said, 'that after a post of £1000 a year, with work that was really diplomatic, and with a promise ahead of Marocco (sic), Teheran, and Constantinople before him, that a commercial town on £600 a year, and £100 office allowance, meant that his career was practically broken.'[43] This, of course, was absurd. It merely meant that, the Foreign Office having had its fingers burnt once, would not appoint Burton to any Muslim country in the future. This should to have been crystal clear to Burton. However, according to Isabel, 'he said he would stick on as long as there was ever a hope of getting Marocco.'

Burton embarked for his return on 1 September, arriving back in Edinburgh four days later. After staying with his sister for just over a week, he left for London. Although the speculation proved unsuccessful, the work had given Burton a fresh interest. The bracing summer benefited his health, and by his return, Georgiana said, he looked at least fifteen years younger. This was also clear from a letter to Lord Houghton, in which Burton spoke of Iceland having done him a power of good. 'You know I suppose,' he went on, 'that the boy Bunny (Arbuthnot) is now at Brighton (Union Club will find him). I hope to see him up here within a few days.' Burton added that he had interviewed Stanley the day before. 'I like him and think him the right sort. The RGS has as usual put its foot into the wrong hole, but what can you expect of a body which has as one of its heads Mr. Galton. The [fellow?]s Grundy, knows Grundy, and owes all his strength to Grundy…'[44]

The context of these disparaging remarks about Galton, was Henry Morton Stanley's 'discovery' at Ujiji of Livingstone for the *New York Herald* on 10 November 1871, which had caused deep resentment and jealousy at the RGS. Persuaded that Livingstone was badly in need of medicine and supplies the Council of the RGS under its new President, Sir Henry C. Rawlinson, decided in late 1871 to sponsor a relief expedition. The RGS, itself, set the ball rolling by contributing £500, and by the end of January 1872 more than £4,000 had been raised by public subscription. Writing to W.H. Bates, earlier that month, Burton expressed his approval of the Society's choice of Lt L.S. Dawson, to lead the expedition. 'I would not go for three reasons,' he went on. '1st rather infra dig. to discover a miss. 2nd Had the FO asked me I should of course have gone, but I won't let them get rid of me quietly. 3rd I look forward to W. Africa, the Congo & Gaboon for my next venture. East Africa is waxing trite and stale. My best wishes to Lt Dawson. He had better collect all the books on the subject.'[45] However, by the time the expedition arrived in Zanzibar, Stanley was already there, his mission completed several months earlier. Lt Dawson, turned out to be wholly inept as a leader, and the expedition a costly and embarrassing failure for the RGS.

'My success,' Stanley wrote on 29 July 1872 to the Rev Horace Waller, a leading member of the RGS, 'seems to have aroused considerable bitterness in the minds of those from whom I naturally expected a different reception.'[46] Furthermore, Stanley's attacks on Dr John Kirk, accusing him of being a traitor to Livingstone, incurred hostility towards him, not only from the geographers but from the press. Some of the tension was taken out of the atmosphere when the RGS suggested that Stanley, who had arrived in England at the beginning of August, should address a meeting of the Geographical Section of the British Association, presided over by Galton, to be held in Brighton in September. Failing at the third attempt to get going with his prepared speech about his geographical surveys with Livingstone on Lake Tanganyika, Stanley discarded it, and spoke off the cuff about his experiences in Africa. This failed to impress the professional geographers of the Association, prompting Galton to remark condescendingly at the end of the speech, that they had not come to hear sensational stories, but to discuss serious facts. Later, in an after-dinner speech given at a civic luncheon, Galton compounded the offence by tactlessly asking Stanley if he were a Welshman or not.[47]

At the end of August, despite this unfortunate reception, Stanley was honoured by Queen Victoria, who sent him a gold and lapis lazuli snuff-box decorated with jewels and inscribed with her initials. This was followed by a letter from Sir Henry Rawlinson, who had been entrusted with the duty of taking Stanley to meet the Queen at Dunrobin Castle, home of the Duke of Sutherland. Victoria took an instant dislike to the African explorer, finding him "a determined ugly little Man – with a strong American twang." She later wrote to King Leopold II, 'warning him against Stanley's harshness to the natives: far from opposing slavery, he kept female slaves for himself.'[48] A week later, much against the grain, Clements Markham, the Secretary of the RGS invited Stanley to dinner. Among the other guests was Burton and a young naval officer, Verney Lovett Cameron. Many years later, he recalled meeting Burton at this dinner, 'just before I started on my journey across Africa, and I well remember how kind and patient he was in answering my many enquiries, many of which must have seemed trivial and uninteresting to him.'[49]

It is ironic in view of Burton's obvious high regard for Stanley, that he would be responsible for the demolition of Burton's theories about the source of the Nile, proving Speke right, and Burton and his supporters wrong about the Victoria Nyanza. Already, during his stay with Livingstone, Stanley had discovered that the Rusizi River flowed *into* and *not out of* Lake Tanganyika. Cameron, too, in his cruise round the lake would later discover its outlet, missed by Burton and Speke, leading to the Lukuga River, and thence to the Lualaba, one of the Congo's main headstreams.

Burton had admitted in his recent letter to Lord Houghton that Trieste was 'a fall after Dam.[ascus].But affairs in Syria are getting into a grand mess.' He went on to claim to having taken, 'Trieste now, not to sacrifice the results of 30 years' public service. Otherwise I can get $30,000 by 100 lectures in the U. States. That would enable me to explore the Congo and the Mwataya Nvo.[50] My wife who has just lost a favourite brother, H. Arundell, RN on the West Coast would of course be against my going, but would yield in time.'[51]

Money matters were uppermost in Burton's mind when he wrote to Lord Granville early in October, pointing out that he had ceased to receive salary as HM's Consul at Damascus on 26 December 1871, and that he had been permitted to draw salary as HM's Consul at Trieste from 6 August 1872. During the interval he had received nothing. 'I venture to hope,' he wrote, 'that you will think it proper to move the Lords of the Treasury in my behalf to grant me this compensation.'

His request resulted in a very long Memo reviewing the whole of the case leading to his recall, and making certain unsympathetic observations.

Captain Burton, after making himself responsible for the consequences of going to Damascus, could hardly claim for these consequences. Late in March of the present year he wrote to ask for £550 on account of the expense entailed upon him by his sudden removal, as well as compensation for the abolition of office...In his present letter he does not repeat the first part of his claim which is probably greatly in excess of the expense he was really put to.

In case Lord Granville should consider that Captain Burton has any claim for his temporary loss of employment....the Treasury might be applied to for a gratuity during the time he was employed. The accompanying draft of Mr. Hammond, dated May 1872, which was drafted before Captain Burton received his present appointment, but which never went off, will show what it was once intended to say to the Treasury about his compensation.

> VB (?) Oc.3/72.

Does Lord Granville consider Captain Burton's claim for compensation a valid one? I do not think it is. Captain Burton remained unemployed for 8 months only, viz. Dec. 26th 1871 to August 8 1872, during which time he was offered another post by Lord Granville which he did not wish to accept, and he is now appointed to the valuable port of Trieste.

> E[dmund Hammond?] Oc. 3, 1872.

Granville commented: 'I think you are right.'[52]

Shortly afterwards, Dr Bird carried out an operation on Burton's back, to remove a tumour, resulting from a blow from a single-stick some years earlier. Burton 'sat astride on a chair, smoking a cigar and talking all the time, and in the afternoon he insisted on going down to Brighton.' Isabel was not allowed to accompany him, the purpose of Burton's visit, undoubtedly, being to meet his friend 'Bunny' to discuss publication of their joint translation of the *Ananga Ranga*.

In his Preface, Burton described this erotic treatise, originally in Sanskrit, as having 'been translated into every language of the East which boasts a literature, however humble. In Sanskrit and Prakrit (Marathi, Gujarati, Bengali, etc) it is called "Ananga Ranga," stage or form of the Bodiless One, Kama Deva (Kamadeva) the Hindu Cupid who was reduced to ashes by the fiery eye of Shiva and presently restored to life.' In Arabic, Hindustani and the Muslim dialects it was known as Lizzat-al-Nisa, or the Pleasure of Women.[53] Generally, throughout India, it was referred to as 'the Kama Shastra, the Scriptures of Kama or Lila Shastra, the Scripture of Play or Amorous Sport.'[54] Burton praised the author for 'the delicacy with which he has handled an exceedingly delicate theme.' It proved too delicate for the English printer who, the following year, 'on reading the proofs, became alarmed at the nature of the book, and refused to print off the edition.'

Following a large family get-together at Wardour Castle, Burton left Southampton for Trieste on 24 October. Isabel, after laying in the usual stock of everything needed by a Consul, followed by land on 18 November. Having arrived in Venice and booked into the Europa Hotel, she first sent a telegram and letter to Burton in Trieste, a mere six hours away, to announce her arrival. The following day, she hired a gondola in order to visit the old haunts she had not seen for fourteen years. Towards late afternoon, she thought it would only be courteous to call on the British Consul, Sir William Perry. After some misunderstanding on her part, Sir William took her in his gondola to the P&O ship *Morocco* sailing for Trieste, and there in the saloon seated at a table writing was Burton. "Hallo," he said, "what the devil are *you* doing here?" Isabel replied with the same question, while Sir William looked on intensely amused. According to Isabel, she had thought when Burton left her on 24 October, that he had headed straight for Trieste. He had also assumed that she, too, would do the same. So they had gone on writing and telegraphing to each other at Trieste, neither of them receiving any news.[55]

Later, in a despatch to the Foreign Office, Burton accounted for his eventual delay in arriving at Trieste, as being 'caused by the necessity of resting at Gibraltar.' He had been ordered to travel by sea, he said. 'Not wishing to press for further leave, I left London a fortnight sooner than my medical adviser wished, as the effects of an operation which I had undergone were still very painful. The SS "Morocco" in which I resumed my journey at Gibraltar should have reached Trieste on the 27th November, but was delayed by the quarantine…..'[56] The vessel, according to Isabel, was detained at Trieste for cargo, enabling them to spend several days in Venice sightseeing.

The explanations of both should, I believe, be taken with a large pinch of salt. Writing to a correspondent on 1 November, Isabel said that Burton had left for Trieste on the 24th, and that she had received a telegram from Gibraltar the previous day, 'sent at 3.15 and arrived here at 4.33 saying he had got there safe *but awful gales*. He was advised to go by sea as rest for his shoulder, which is still open, and I should think such a voyage *must* have been rather irritating and almost impossible for the surgeon to dress it as the wound is still kept open by being stuffed with cotton with a probe.'[57]

Far from resting at Gibraltar as he wished the FO to believe, Burton 'rushed up to Ronda in S. Spain,' as he later informed Albert Tootal. 'Very good run and was pelted with stones by boys to the tune of "He! Garibaldi."'[58] Built in an almost impregnable position on high rocky outcrops either side of the almost 300 ft deep Tajo gorge spanned by an eighteenth century arched bridge, Ronda was one of the most spectacularly located cities in Spain. Its Plaza de Toros was famous, of course, for being the spiritual home of bullfighting. However, Burton's prime reason for visiting the city, probably lay in his wishing to examine the remains of its Moorish conquerors, who had occupied Ronda from the 8th to the 15th century. It had finally fallen to the Catholic monarchs Ferdinand and Isabella on 20 May 1485.

On 6 December, probably having spent over a week at Venice, the Burtons crossed over to Trieste. On arrival they were met by Mr Brock, the Vice-Consul, and Mr O'Callaghan, the Consular Chaplain. It was remarked, wrote Isabel, '"that Captain and Mrs Burton (the new Consul) took up their quarters at the Hotel de la Ville, *he* walking along with his game-cock in his hand, and she with a bull-terrier," and it was thought that we must be very funny. We dined at *table d'hôte*, and we did not like the place at all.'[59]

CHAPTER THIRTY-TWO

TRIESTE – THE FIRST PHASE

Tucked away in the north-east corner of the Adriatic, Trieste was essentially a creation of the Austro-Hungarian Empire. In 1382, anxious to escape domination by Venice, the city placed itself under the protection of the Habsburg Duke Leopold III of Austria. It turned out to be a wise move in the long run, even though protection turned into annexation. Bent on expanding their colonial empire into a maritime one, the Habsburgs spent a fortune on developing Trieste into an important European port.

In the eighteenth century in the area around the Canal Grande, a splendid development of quayside promenades, squares embellished with fountains and statuary, imposing neo-classical houses and regular, spacious streets, grew up. It was named Borgo Teresiano after the Austrian Empress Maria Theresa, the driving force behind the project. The city's status as an imperial free port later acted as a magnet to shipping and insurance companies, shipbuilders and financiers, whose great palazzos trumpeted their civic influence as well as their enormous wealth. Even greater prosperity followed with the opening of the Suez Canal in 1869, allowing trade with India and the Far East.

Offering Charles Lever the appointment as British Consul there in 1867, the Foreign Secretary, Lord Derby, is reported to have said, "Here is six hundred a year for doing nothing, and you are just the man to do it." Even this failed, however, in reconciling Lever to the climate and society of Trieste, which he thought a vile place, 'half Holywell and half Wapping, where, whatever is not skipper is Jew.'[1] This was a deliberate travesty, of course, since Trieste was a cosmopolitan city composed of Austrians, Italians, Slavs, Greeks and Jews. Yet it contained a truth. Under Maria Theresa, the Jews had been offered generous inducements to settle in the city. They now formed its financial backbone, dominating the banking and insurance businesses, and forming the city's social and intellectual elite.

In fact, it was the leading Jewish family of Baron Morpurgo, synonymous for wealth and largesse, who were foremost in extending hospitality to the Burtons. After calling on them at the plush Hotel de la Ville, where they spent the first six months, the Morpurgos opened their house to them. This introduced them 'to all that was the best of Trieste,' as Isabel put it, 'and everybody called.' This must have initially posed an annoying problem for her, since she had made Burton responsible for looking after two boxes containing all her best clothes and part of her jewellery. 'He contrived to lose them on the road (value about £130) so when I arrived I had nothing to wear.' They had no redress, and when the boxes eventually arrived they had been ransacked.

Burton immediately cast about for a country retreat where he and Isabel could go when they wanted a change or felt out of sorts. Only an hour from Trieste, and some twelve hundred feet up on the Karso, the barren limestone plateau riddled with caverns and underground rivers, was the Slav village of Opicina. Close to the tall obelisk erected in 1830 to mark the completion of the Vienna to Trieste highway, was Daneu's, a rambling old country inn. From its terrace there was a panoramic view of Trieste and the country surrounding the Adriatic; at the rear, shrubberies and fields, and a view of the Karso backed by mountains. The air was fresh and invigorating. The Burtons took partly furnished rooms there, adding their own furniture as time went by. It soon became their favourite weekend retreat. They more or less waited on themselves, and always kept some literary work available there to carry on with.

The least domesticated of men, hotel living suited Burton down to the ground. It saved 'the bore (not to speak of the expense) of house-keeping,' as he explained to Lord Houghton, 'it allows one no end of time, it is in fact freedom. Servants here are a horror, either dolts or knaves, women whores & drunkards, often both.' He and Isabel kept fit with an hour's fencing and drill each day. The rest of their time was fully occupied in study and literary work of one sort or another. Burton was currently learning Russian and Slavonic, writing his Icelandic book and undertaking a fresh course of chemistry and botany. Isabel was learning German, Italian, and Arabic, writing her Syrian book, and keeping up her singing.

Although apparently pretty much contented with his lot at this time, Burton was clearly frustrated at no longer having any diplomatic responsibilities. He thought he now saw his chance in military events unfolding in Asia. Ever since the humiliating and costly retreat from Kabul in the 1840s, and the Indian Mutiny in 1857, successive British governments had regarded Afghanistan as a vital buffer state. The Russians' inexorable advance southward towards this country, therefore, posed an ever-present strategic problem. By 1865, Tashkent had been formally annexed, and Samarkand became part of the Russian Empire three years later. That same year, Bukhara virtually lost its independence as a result of the terms of a peace treaty forced on it. The Russians now controlled a vast swathe of territory extending as far as the northern bank of the Amu Darya, or Oxus, river. 'Why does not the FO make me Resident at Cabul,' Burton asked Lord Houghton, ' and find out all about what Russia is doing there? Especially on the northern frontier and in Badakhshan. I can ride…speak Pushtu (Afghan), Persian, Hindostani & so forth.'[2]

Just under a week later, he wrote in similar vein to a high-ranking military acquaintance of his, Lt General William Wylde, an eighty-five year old Peninsular War veteran. 'Trieste is very nice for a comfort loving old Gen'l but – what am I doing in this galley? Do put in a word for me and send me rejoicing Eastward Ho!….My wife asks to be kindly remembered to you and is quite ready to follow where her devoted husband leads.'[3] If any recommendations were made to Government on Burton's behalf, they fell on deaf ears.

It appears that the Burtons had already made plans shortly after arriving in Trieste, for visiting Rome during Holy Week, followed by a trip to Vienna. Unfortunately, Burton's letter requesting such leave is not extant among the Foreign Office files.[4] It is impossible to state with any certainty, therefore, as to what subterfuge he adopted. One must suppose it was the old chestnut on grounds of health, the recent operation on his back providing a plausible excuse, with the need to escape the debilitating effects of the Bora for a short while, and enjoy a warmer climate further south thrown in for good measure. Leaving Vice-Consul Brock in charge of the Consulate for the first, but far from the last, time, the couple set off down the Adriatic on 1 April for the Italian port of Ancona. From there, they travelled to Loreto, a small town a few miles to the south.

Since at least from the fifteenth century, the Santa Casa di Loreto, the 'Holy House' of Loreto, had been numbered among the most famous Catholic shrines in Italy. Its most conspicuous building was the basilica housing, what was believed by the Faithful to be, the very cottage at Nazareth in which the Holy Family had lived. Threatened with destruction by the Turks in 1291, angels apparently had conveyed the house from Palestine to a hill at Tersato in Illyria. Three years later, it was transported in similar fashion to a laurel grove in the vicinity of Recanati, from where it was finally moved by these same divine messengers in 1295 to its present site. Naturally, it was associated with appearances of the Virgin and miraculous cures. After spending what Isabel described as 'a delightful day in the Holy House,' she and Burton took the train to Rome, arriving there on the night of 3 April.

The following day they called on Lady Paget, wife of the British Ambassador, with whom Isabel remained friends for the rest of her life. Lady Paget later wrote of Burton that, 'Anybody might have taken him for an Arab, an illusion which was strengthened by his staining his underlids with kohl....His wife, an Arundell of Wardour, still bore great traces of beauty, though she, too, shared the Eastern predilection for pigments. She was genial, intelligent, and courageous in no ordinary way. Her defence of the poor dumb animals drew me strongly towards her.'[5] Isabel also saw a great deal of Cardinal Howard, a distant connection, who had been one of her 'favourite dancing partners when *he* was in the Life Guards and *I* was a girl.'[6] Burton, of course, enjoyed going over the old places he'd known in his boyhood, and showing them to Isabel. He also spent time writing long articles, which later appeared in *Macmillan's Magazine*.[7] Sadly, Isabel was doomed to disappointment in her dearest hope that the Pope would 'say something to make an impression on Richard.' Most annoyingly, his Holiness Pope Pius IX was taken ill the day before she arrived, and only recovered the day after she left.

After visiting the Catacombs and the Baths of Caracalla on a wet and miserable day, Isabel herself was taken ill, with what she described as, Roman fever.[8] It was only with some difficulty that she mustered enough strength to travel on to Florence, where she was forced to spend a week in bed. Even so, she and Burton managed to see a great deal of the novelist, Ouida, famous for her extravagant melodramatic romances of fashionable life. In 1867, she had begun her custom of staying at the new and luxurious Langham Hotel, when in London. Here, she gave men-only parties, Isabel being the only exception. William Allingham, the Anglo-Irish poet, who met her at one of these dinners, described her as 'dressed in green silk with a clever sinister face, her hair down, small hands and feet, and a voice like a carving-knife.'[9]

From Florence, the couple went on to Pistojia and Bologna, where Burton spent some time exploring the Etruscan remains. Unable to shake off the effects of the fever, Isabel was laid up once more at Venice. It was not until 25 April that they eventually arrived back at Trieste in a night of terrible gales. Excusing his late return in a despatch to the FO, Burton said that he 'had made all arrangements for returning within the fortnight when my wife fell seriously ill, and being unable to leave her I was delayed nearly a week at Florence and returned to my post only on this day.'[10]

Staying at Trieste only long enough to draw breath, change baggage, which was already packed, and without the knowledge of the Foreign Office, the Burtons sped off to Vienna, 'as Richard was engaged as a reporter to a newspaper for the Great Exhibition there.' Burton wrote two accounts for *The Athenaeum* describing the buildings in detail, and giving his impressions of the Exhibition, which in early May was still not completed. At 9 a.m. on 1 May, four days after their arrival, he and Isabel set out in a light drizzling rain, to see the opening ceremony. He described the vast 4,000 acres Prater Park in the north-east section of the city, as now bearing 'a city of its own, a solid and substantial settlement of zinc and stone. It would contain the citizens of Reykjavik in a corner; it would lodge easily and comfortably all the inhabitants of Iceland in a wing, and it would give standing room to the whole population of Syria and Palestine.'

Punctually at 11 a.m. the Imperial and Royal party appeared, and took its place upon the estrade. Following music by Johann Strauss, and a speech by the Archduke Protector, the Emperor, Francis Joseph I, 'declared officially the world's exhibition of the year of grace 1873 open to the world.' With the departure from the estrade of the Imperial party, 'All who had legs pressed forwards to secure places where the Imperial party could just be seen; a simum of dust filled the Rotunda, which became Araby the Blest in a storm, and the boarded ground resounded, as under a charge of cavalry.'[11]

They were delighted with everything except the high prices being charged for food and beverages at the hotels, where, according to Isabel, 'all portions were most homoeopathic.' She related an amusing anecdote in which a waiter brought Burton a doll's size cup of coffee. "What is that?" asked Richard, looking at it curiously, with his head on one side. "Coffee for one," sir." "Oh! Is it indeed?" inspecting it still more curiously. "H'm! bring me coffee for ten!" "Yes, sir," said the waiter, looking as if he thought it a capital joke, and presently returned with a common-sized cup of coffee.'[12]

Isabel, naturally, was in her element, plunged into three weeks of incessant Society and gaiety, which began at twelve and lasted until three or four in the morning. She was very much dazzled by the Viennese court. 'It is not to be wondered at that the Austrians are so loyal and wrapped up in their Imperial family,' she enthused. 'Everything they do is so gracious, and the Emperor enters so keenly into all the events that occur to his people.......not much danger of a republic *there*.'[13] Isabel, as an Arundell of Wardour and, therefore, an Austrian countess, was able to attend.[14] There was a difficulty, however, about Burton. Consuls, considered a species of lower life, were not admitted. Isabel was having none of it and insisted on having the matter brought to the attention of the Emperor. He immediately solved it by allowing Burton to come as an army officer. To cap it all, Isabel was sent for by the Crown Prince 'with a few others out of about 40 English ladies,' and the Prince of Wales spoke to her for about for half an hour.

Some of the shine was taken off the visit, however, when they came to pay the bill. In his second piece for *The Athenaeum*, Burton wrote that, 'For rooms you will pay six to eight florins each, and you will dine at E. Sacher's, or any other restaurant for five florins.'[15] It turned out that the quite expensive rooms at the Hotel zum Römischen Kaiser, which the Embassy had taken for them ostensibly at fifteen florins a day, were being charged at ten florins more, facing them with an unexpectedly large bill of £163.[16] 'We did not think it was good taste to make a fuss about it,' said Isabel, 'so we paid it.'

It is clear, however, that they allowed money to run through their fingers like water during their three weeks' stay without much thought of the consequences. Faced now with the need to practise the strictest economy for some while, they moved out of the hotel into a flat at the top of a tall building just opposite the Südbahn railway station. They began with six rooms which, over the years increased to no less than twenty-seven. A staff-reporter on *The World* who visited the Burtons some years later described each of the then ten rooms, as being completely lined with rough deal shelves, containing, perhaps, eight thousand or more volumes in every Western language, as well as in Arabic, Persian, and Hindustani. Every odd corner was piled with weapons, guns, pistols, boar-spears, swords of every kind and make, foils and masks, chronometers, barometers, and all kinds of scientific instruments. One cupboard was crammed with medicines necessary for Oriental expeditions, or for Isabel's Trieste poor. The bedrooms and dressing-rooms were furnished in Spartan simplicity with little iron bedsteads covered with bearskins. On the reading-tables besides the beds were copies of the Bible, Shakespeare, and Euclid, which accompanied them on all their journeys. Perhaps the most remarkable objects were the rough deal tables, which occupied most of the floor space. There must have been about eleven of them, each covered with writing material. 'Dick likes a separate table for every book,' Isabel explained, 'and when he is tired of one he goes to another.'

Three little rooms made up their 'den' where they lived, worked, and entertained their friends. 'If I had a campagna and garden and servants,' Burton remarked, 'I should feel tied, weighted down, in fact. With a flat, two or three maidservants, one has only to lock the door and go. It feels like "light marching order" as if we were always ready for an expedition.' Here Isabel received something like seventy very intimate friends every Friday, 'an exercise of hospitality,' Burton remarked, 'to which I have no objection, save one, and that is met by the height we live at. There is in the town a lot of old women of both sexes, who sit for hours talking about the weather and the cancans of the place, and this contingent cannot face the stairs.'[17]

In his interview for *The World*, Burton said revealingly, that he and Isabel were 'like an elder and younger brother living en garçon,' that is, a bachelor existence. After working all day, they wanted relaxation. For that purpose they had formed a little 'Mess' with fifteen friends at the table d'hôte of the Hotel de la Ville, where they got a good dinner and a pint of the country wine made on the hillside for a florin and a half. By this plan, 'we escape the boredom of housekeeping, and are relieved from the curse of domesticity, which we both hate.' At dinner they heard the news, if any, took their coffee, cigarettes and kirsch outside the hotel, then went homewards to read themselves to sleep.

As a change from the pressures of work at Trieste, they occasionally ran over to Venice and hired a gondola. Miramar, the glistening white sea-palace of the tragic Emperor Maximilian of Mexico built on a promontory jutting into the Bay of Grignano offered a further delightful opportunity for relaxation. Thrown open to the public, its grounds were 'most romantic and fanciful, full of covered terraces, shady walks, secluded places for reading, the ruins of a very old chapel, Italian gardens, and so on.' Isabel also pursued her interest in spiritualism. The house of the French Consul-General and his wife, Monsieur and Madame Léon Favre, was a rendezvous for frequent séances. It is likely that the recent deaths of her mother and younger brother, prompted Isabel, even more than usual, to try to make contact with the spirit world. Burton, presumably attended some of these meetings, sending in a short 'Testimony' on spiritualism to the movement's journal.[18]

After long delay, Burton's translation and annotation of *The Lands of Cazembe* was finally published early that summer by the RGS.[19] Two appendices, rejected by the Society on the grounds of their being controversial, were privately printed by Burton at Trieste on 17 July, 'especially for the use of my friends.' One was his 'Notes on "How I found Livingstone in Central Africa: travels, adventures and discoveries," by Henry M. Stanley,' the other 'Being a rejoinder to the "Memoir on the lake regions of East Africa reviewed, in reply to Captain Burton's letter in the 'Athenaeum', No.1899." By W.D. Cooley.'

A number of Burton's 'copious annotations' in *The Lands of Cazembe* were directed against his *bête noir*, Cooley. The latter, however, was given an opportunity of replying in January of the following year by *The Academy*, a journal founded five years earlier, 'designed to be the exponent and supreme organ of British scholarship, research and intellectual attainment.'[20] Undoubtedly, Cooley was chosen to review the book because of his deserved reputation for having an encyclopaedic knowledge of the early Portuguese travellers.[21] The editor may also have wished to fuel controversy, as well as to provide financial help to the now impoverished old man.

Age had dulled none of Cooley's critical faculties nor tempered any of his animosity towards the RGS and all its works. He was dismissive of the translations, which he described as having been 'offered to London publishers 30 years ago, and rejected by them, because found to be meagre and devoid of interest.' He, himself, in 1852 had given 'a summary but sufficient account of them' in a volume 'entitled *Inner Africa Laid Open*, a fact which Captain Burton cannot be ignorant.....While introducing the admirable Lacerda to the public, he himself makes the chief figure. He, therefore, annotates the volume copiously, his notes forming at least one-third of the volume, and most of them attacking me, chiefly by misrepresentation.'[22]

Writing to Albert Tootal in March, Burton said that he had he had 'not published anything of late but have been very hard at work writing violent leaders in various papers against Radicals. The change of government quite sets me free. I am in no hurry to leave Trieste as the little peninsular [sic] (Istria) abounds in interest. You will have seen the last meeting of the Anthrop, where my paper on the castillieri came on.[23] They are said to be the oldest remains in Europe. I shall start for Damatio in the spring and do Montenegro thoroughly. Then ready for anything or anywhere – but the Eastern Question may come up at any moment and then will be my time of triumph.'[24] Events, however, were not to turn out as Burton planned.

Early in May, probably in an attempt to recoup their recent heavy expenses, Burton brought up the matter of compensation again with the FO for the losses he claimed to have sustained in his recall from

Damascus. He was informed just under a fortnight later, however, that the Foreign Secretary 'cannot at this distance of time reopen the case.'[25] Attached to the draft reply was a minute. 'Consul's Department. Consul Burton at Trieste is ill. Lord Derby wishes him telegraphed to as follows: "Hearing you are seriously ill, Lord Derby grants you leave of absence without waiting for formal application." I have sent this off officially by post in the same sense.'

In Isabel's version in *The Life* as to the onset of Burton's illness, she said that he and others made an expedition up the Schneeburg Mountain, which was always covered with snow. She was careful not to explain why Burton was absent from his consulate at this period, obviously without official leave, climbing, what is the highest peak in lower Austria.[26] He used to amuse himself, she went on, by buying any amount of clothes and greatcoats, yet he always went out lightly clad to harden himself. So he set off on the expedition dressed in a thin coat and wearing thin shoes. Three days after arriving home on 14 May, he was taken very ill quite suddenly. Inflammation settled in the groin, a tumour formed, and he suffered tortures.

This is Isabel's rather inadequate cover story for Burton's real condition. It is clear from a doctor's report of the following year, that this was directly associated with the stricture of the urethra and swollen testicle, which had plagued him for years. By this date his condition had reached a crisis, and a major operation was essential. Isabel's use of the word 'tumour' may, of course, be her euphemism for the swollen left testicle. It might also relate to swollen inguinal lymph glands. It is quite possible that Burton had two STDs, that is gonorrhoea and syphilis, the inguinal lymph glands becoming enlarged in both diseases.

Isabel immediately sent for the best physician and the best surgeon in Trieste, who warned her that it would be a long illness. She, therefore, telegraphed home for a water-bed, a large supply of port, various remedies, soups, and so on, and put the beds on big iron rollers to make it easier to change him from one to another. 'He had 2 bad operations performed,' she explained to Lord Houghton,' – the last with chloroform. It took 2 bottles of chloroform and 40 minutes to get him under. The physician held one pulse, I the other and the surgeon chloroformed and cut – a hole a finger deep and 3 inches wide, but happily he was quite unconscious. (I thought I should have died).'[27] She sat beside him on a couch for seventy-eight days and nights, catching at brief opportunities to sleep when he slept. 'He was in such pain,' she told Houghton, 'weak as a child and unable to turn in bed without assistance.' She was afraid that 'his life would ebb away, but I kept up his strength with good port wine, egg-flips with brandy, cream and fresh eggs, Brand's essences, and something every hour.'[28]

At the very height of their troubles, they received the devastating news that their best friend, Charley Drake, had died in Jerusalem of typhoid fever.[29] He had joined them at Trieste the previous year for the benefit of his health, shortly after their return from Vienna. They had spent a delightful month showing him all the places of interest in Istria, Fiume and Pola, and the environs of Trieste, before crossing to Venice on 4 July to see him off. Burton, unfortunately, got hold of the letter before Isabel did. After reading it, he fell back in a faint, reopening the wound. 'He loved Drake,' she said, 'like a brother, and few know what a tender heart Richard has.' Isabel convinced herself that, although Drake talked quite as agnostically as Burton did, he was a good Protestant at heart and died a holy death.

Despite making satisfactory progress, Burton became convinced that he would never leave his room, and began to imagine that he was unable to swallow. Isabel, therefore, suggested taking him away, and the doctors reluctantly agreed, if it were possible. It was now the end of July, so Isabel went up to Opicina, and took a ground-floor suite of rooms at the inn. She ordered a carriage equipped with a bed, and an invalid chair for carrying up and down stairs. The next day men arrived with the chair, and Burton was lifted gently into it, and given a glass of port wine. After successfully negotiating the one hundred and twenty steps to the ground floor, he was placed equally gently into the carriage. The driver was ordered to walk the horses, and with Isabel holding Burton's hand, they set off for Opicina. After about a quarter of an hour, he said he was all right, and that they could go faster. After reaching the inn, Burton confessed to feeling as if he had made a journey into Central Africa, 'but I shall get well now.'

And so it proved. In a couple of days he was breakfasting and sitting out in the garden. After twelve days Isabel took him to Padua in order to consult with a celebrated old doctor, Pinalli. He gave Burton a thorough examination, ordered him to go to Battaglia for five days with the assurance that nature and bicarbonate of soda would do the rest. Although she glossed over her own condition in *The Life*, Isabel admitted to Lord Houghton at the time that she was 'quite broken down by fatigue and anxiety, and have gastric flu which affects my head and sight.' She, herself, was ordered by the doctor to go to Recoaro for a month to take the waters and have a complete rest. The two places were only five hours apart, as she told Houghton, 'so I can easily get back to him if he misses me.' Although her nerves were 'quite grim pro. tem', she had the great consolation that 'the doctors say that my tone and aura have kept the life in him and that without me, they would not have succeeded.'

After following the medical advice, both felt fit enough to go on a number of excursions. Back in Trieste by 21 September, they once more picked up the threads of their life in the Karso, driving or walking great distances over the country, searching for inscriptions and castellieri.

By the following month, Burton had made plans for sending Isabel to England to consult with Mr Lock about the sulphur mines in Iceland, and to find publishers for several of his books. She was to go on ahead armed with several pages of instructions, and he would join her later. 'I had only been two years in Trieste,' she said, 'and it made me exceedingly miserable; but whenever he put his foot down, I had to do it, whether I would or no.'[30]

The trip, however, gave Isabel the opportunity of parting with her Syrian maid, who had been so petted and spoiled over the years, that she would do only what she liked. It was pretty well impossible to marry her in Europe. Isabel, therefore, wrote to her father telling him that she proposed sending her home under the charge of the captain and stewardess of the first ship direct to Beirut. He should meet her there, and should try to marry her among her own people, if possible. Fortunately, Khamoor was very much taken with the idea of returning home to show off all her finery and with the substantial sum of money Isabel had put aside for a dowry. To her great relief, Isabel later heard that she had married one of her own people, and settled down in the Buka'a.

Having seen Khamoor aboard on 4 December, Isabel, herself, left four days later, making the journey almost non-stop to England, where she arrived on 12 December. With characteristic energy and single-mindedness, she immediately set about her assignments, sometimes working for thirteen hours a day and forgetting to eat. As well as searching for publishers for Burton, she needed one for herself, having completed the manuscript of *The Inner Life of Syria* on 20 November.

Despite her best efforts, Isabel was only successful in placing one of Burton's books, his *Ultima Thule; or; A Summer in Iceland*.[31] Nevertheless, it brought in much needed cash, Isabel accepting the publisher's latest offer, 'to purchase the absolute copyright of the work….at the price of one hundred and fifty guineas to be paid on publication and the proof sheets to be revised by the author.'[32] In current money, this would be worth close on £7,000.

While his book on Iceland had proved reasonably rewarding, this was far from being the case with regard to Burton's business relationship with Alfred G. Lock. Just under a week later, Isabel received a letter from Lock, anxious to clear up the serious misunderstanding which had arisen between them, and for his solicitors to settle terms with the Burtons' legal representative as quickly as possible. He pointed out that his arrangement to pay Burton £2,500 for reporting on the Nyvatn mines was, 'that the money should ostensibly be paid for the actual discovery of the mines further inland which he came upon in his journey to the desert.' This was done in the belief that, 'were it known that Capt. Burton received money for his report, his character would be considerably damaged, and the report would be looked upon as that of an interested party.'

He was now convinced not only that the Icelanders would never lease these new mines to him, but that being so far inland transport costs would swallow up all the profits. Furthermore, after spending a great deal of time, trouble, and money, he had discovered to his great surprise, 'that the <u>mercantile</u> world never heard of Capt. Burton, and will not place an atom of confidence in his report on <u>mining matters</u>.' Nevertheless, far from wishing to back out of the arrangement, or having 'some design for entrapping Lord Arundel (sic),' as she appeared to believe, he was strongly committed to seeing it through. This meant convincing capitalists, however, that Capt. Burton's testimony could be relied on, by demonstrating that some of his friends were subscribers.[33]

It was a case that would drag on for some time, without resulting in any satisfactory conclusion for the Burtons. Isabel was equally unsuccessful in her further attempt at obtaining a KCB for Burton, whom she described in a letter to Lord Houghton the following month as, 'pining at being passed over.' Her printed 'little resumé of his unrewarded services,' circulated as usual to a great many influential friends resulted at least in the Council of the RGS bringing, what it described as Burton's 'exceptional merits' to the attention of the Foreign Secretary. Recalling that it had bestowed its Founder's Medal on Burton in 1859 it, neverthe-less, regarded this, 'an inadequate reward for his long and successful career as a geographer and explorer.' The Council, therefore, ventured, 'to recommend Capt Burton to your Lordship for some further mark of the Royal favour wherever a fitting occasion arises.' No such 'fitting occasion,' however, ever arose under Disraeli's leadership.[34]

Earlier that month, Burton had written a racy letter addressed to 'Caro Houghton', and headed Trieste (+ Bora = purgatory):

> As the Yank said before the big fight with the B'ar, "God A'mighty it's not often I bother youse," but as now I have something worth telling you. Boy Bunny has been behaving like a trump and giving up his mind (as I, his Pa, have ever advised) to the study pure and simply (sic) of Hindu erotic literature.
>
> In p.46 of Koka Pandit translated I regret to say into our cleanly English tongue by two ruffians who sign themselves FFA and BRF you will find an allusion to the "holy sage Vatsyayana Muni."[35] He is the father of Ars Amoris in Sanskrit, lived about AD 100 and wrote a book in nine chapters which treats de omni re scribili et femina (?) He also quotes from no less than 9 other authors whose works have wholly perished. One of his chapters treats of courtezans, another of marrying one's own wife, and a 3rd of marrying other men's wives. It is <u>the</u> standard book. Bunny has ordered the MS from Benares, where the "holy sage" lived, and will begin to translate it at once.[36] <u>If it is thoroughly moral</u>, I hope to add some notes. And why, when old age creeps on, should one not devote oneself to popularising the precepts of the wise?
>
> We may meet in April or May next, for their soup, canned meats and vinegarish wine have emptied my veins. You might, if you have become Conservative, suggest to Mr. Diz. that Trieste is not half large enough to hold me, but I should be contented with Central Asia or even with northern Africa.'[37]

On 12 May, a week after Isabel attended the Drawing-room, 'Richard arrived himself, and we did a great deal of visiting and a great deal of Society in the evening.' However, she avoided saying anything about how Burton managed to get to England as planned. On 15 April, he sent a letter to the Foreign Secretary, 'My Lord, Finding myself unable to recover strength and energy at Trieste after my illness last summer, I have the honour to request that your Lordship will kindly allow me a month of sick leave in England, beginning with early May. It will be difficult for me to travel very fast. I enclose attested copy of the opinion given by my medical adviser.' Unsurprisingly, Dr Carlo Liebmann of Trieste, was able to endorse all of Burton's remarks in his accompanying medical certificate, recommending him to a 'temporary stay in his native country as the best means of ensuring complete recovery.'[38] After receiving the necessary permission on 26 April, Burton left the following day.[39] He reached England after, what he described to Albert Tootal as, 'a charming dawdle of a journey, 17 days from Trieste through Upper Italy, Switzerland, the Rhine etc. I expected to be disappointed with the latter after the great rivers of Africa, N. America and Brazil especially as I had not seen it for 20 years. Quite the reverse. I found it more picturesque and beautiful than ever.'[40]

That same month, Isabel's *The Inner Life of Syria* appeared to highly favourable notices in the Press.[41] *The Athenaeum* described the book as 'two rambling but amusing volumes, the title of which is incomplete, because instead of being called 'The Inner Life,' the book ought to be styled the "Inner and Outer Life of Syria, Palestine, and of the Heavens and Underground thereof." ...Of course, Mrs Burton's observations must sometimes be taken with reserve, even the vision in the cave in the Holy Land in which she expounds the Captain's merits to Queen Victoria.'[42]

Headed 'A Dream,' this is the most astonishing part of Isabel's book, comprising the whole of chapter XXVII. Whilst the wise might laugh at them, there were dreams, she gravely assured her readers, 'which enlighten one on sciences, religious and profane, on virtues and vices, on the government of nations, and on individuals; which show the disposition, sentiments, and secret designs of the people about us, and which require to be treated with infinite discretion.....one can learn higher things without miracles.'[43]

Having dreamt that she had died, instead of being sent to Purgatory, she was ordered by a Superior Angel Guardian to carry out certain difficult tasks, one of which included the not inconsiderable feat of reforming the world and redressing its wrongs. Readers were then treated to a long recital of Isabel's reactionary views on science, religion and politics, mixed in with unctuous flattery of Queen Victoria and the Royal family. After listening with remarkable patience to a detailed account of Burton's career, the Queen is described as being sufficiently moved to grant what, in Isabel's view, was Burton's 'just and right position according to his works and merits : Envoy Extraordinary and Minister Plenipotentiary to some Eastern Court, and KCB; likewise to be restored to honorary rank in the Army, which would be equivalent to that which he would have held, had his career not been ungenerously cut short.'

After travelling with her Guardian Angel to the Vatican, and settling the Papal States, the Pope sent Burton his blessing as one of God's elect. Among other things he said to her, "My daughter, why do you affect yourself at seeing your noble husband passed over in regard to worldly honours? Look at your husband and then look at the people who do get these honours and places, and cease to repine. It is not the will of God, for your husband is far greater than any of these....Take this as a sign. In the very place where Jesus said, 'No man is a prophet in his own country,' the people shall treat your husband as they treated Jesus..."[44]

Absurd in so many ways, this alleged dream, nevertheless, provides a valuable insight into the bizarre workings of Isabel's mind. It is also illuminating of Burton's too, since he could have censored or even forbidden Isabel's fatuous and tasteless eulogising, but chose not to.

On a rather more profane level, Burton took it into his head to make his fortune by producing, what was to be marketed, as 'Captain Burton's Tonic Bitters.' It was to be put in an attractive bottle, and to carry his picture. The label, designed by Burton, rather wordily informed the public that, 'This admirable Tonic and Digestive' had been 'compounded by a Swedish physician in 1565. He had been hospitably received in a Franciscan Convent and before his death he gave it as a token of gratitude to the Prior.' Having been 'extensively used by the monks as a restorative and stimulant during the last three centuries,' the prescription had been copied out for Burton by his Franciscan friend, Padre Fran Ayler. One tablespoonful was to be taken in a glass of water or sherry, or diluted cognac. Unfortunately for Burton's money-making plans, none of the public appears to have come forward to sample even that amount.

On 10 June, they were invited to meet Gladstone at Lord Houghton's. Very late in the evening, Mrs Gladstone reportedly said to Isabel, "I don't know what it is, but I can't get Mr. Gladstone away this evening." And Isabel replied, "I think I know what it is; he has got hold of my husband, Richard Burton, and they are both so interested one with the other, and have so many points of interest to talk over, that I venture to hope that you will not take him away." Gladstone's last entry in his diary for that day, however, reads, 'Dined at Ld. Houghton's.' He makes no mention of any conversation with Burton.[45] There were also numerous lectures and dinners, and some expeditions on the Thames. At Oxford, Burton met friends and acquaintances such as Benjamin Jowett, now Master of Balliol College, his old tutor, Thomas Short, still in harness at eighty-six, and his former fencing instructor, Archibald Maclaren. He revisited his old college, Trinity, and others such as Magdalen and Oriel. Isabel noted in their journals for 1875 that they often break-fasted and lunched twice in order to fulfil invitations.

On 14 June, his month up, Burton asked the Foreign Office for an extension of leave until the end of September, approximately, 'for the purpose of taking the waters of Vichy and establishing my health. I need hardly inform you that the climate of Trieste is very unhealthy during the present year, and without any epidemic we expect a mortality of 50 per thousand, that of London being 22.'[46] There was nothing wrong with Burton's health, of course, as the number of his activities suggests. What is also certain, is that he always intended to get leave to England, and then to ask for an extension. It was to become the classic pattern of his numerous requests for leave. A brief minute appended by Lord Derby to the draft despatch reads: 'Grant extension.' The following day, Burton wrote again to the FO requesting that:

> should no other officer have been chosen, to place my name on your list as a candidate for the Consulate-General, Tiflis, which I hear is to be established as soon as the Russian Government shall permit.[47] I have lately been studying the Slavonic dialect of Slav; it is cognate with Russian and a few months will make me perfect in the latter tongue which I formerly spoke. Your Lordship well knows that I am acquainted with Turkish and Persian. A military man wanted, my 19 years' service may be in my favour. I beg also to forward the enclosed, and to request that if your Lord thinks it a fair petition, that it may be presented and supported.

As the FO minute on this shows, the 'enclosed' was the printed statement of his services in support of being made a KCB, currently being circulated by Isabel. Another minute read: 'To bear in mind both requests, but question of name rests with the Russian Minister, and many considerations affecting application to Tiflis, which may interfere with his wishes.'[48]

The same day, Burton wrote to Lord Houghton on the same subject, stating that, having written and rewritten about the whole country around Trieste, he was sick of it. 'I want to be up and doing: Central Asia or Central Africa or something of the kind. I have applied for Tiflis. One of the clerks says, "Between us they are going to appoint a military man who knows something of the language." I replied, "I am a military man who knows something of the language....!" Diable! My broadsword exercises (quite new and my own invention) have been submitted to the Duke with his approval.[49] I have offered my Cavalry pistol gratis to the War Office.[50] I have – never mind. Do lend me a hand of help and send an elderly gentleman to Trieste.'[51]

With the granting of an extension of his sick leave ostensibly to visit Vichy, Burton, without the knowledge of the FO, left England on a business trip connected with the sulphur mines in Iceland. Isabel's only comment was: 'One morning we had breakfast with Sir Fredrick Leighton, and we had our last Sunday's Divan. We went to the Prince of Wales's Chiswick Party, and the same night Richard started off for another trip to Iceland.'[52] Isabel, when she has nothing to hide, is normally prodigal with dates. However, they are non-existent for this particular period. So when did Burton set off for Iceland?

The Prince and Princess of Wales's Garden Party, a huge gathering of the great and the good, at which Queen Victoria was present, was held at Chiswick House on Monday, 5 July.[53] According to Isabel, 'Richard was not gone more than six weeks, and then he returned with an attack of lumbago, followed by gout.' This time span is incorrect, and it was not a case of Burton's flitting off alone, as is shown by two short reports in *The Academy* on, what the journal described as, 'The Iceland Sulphur and Eruption Expedition.'

The first ran: 'Captain Burton left London on Monday evening to inspect the eruption and the sulphur mines of North-east Iceland. He heads a party of savans, who have hired the steamer *Fifeshire* for that purpose. Mrs Burton remains in London till he returns.'[54] As the second report indicates, the party of ten 'sailed from Leith on July 6, arrived at Husavik on the 11th, will stay fourteen days in Iceland, start to return on the 24th, and will be in London on the 30 inst.'[55] As soon as Burton was better, Isabel said, he left for the Continent. 'He went by ship to Rouen. He wished to go to Tours to revisit the old home of his childhood, and from thence to Vichy to do some good to the gout, and from there to make a pilgrimage, all by himself, to Paray le Monial, from whence he brought me beads and medals, and arrived in London on October 6th.'[56]

This is the first date provided by Isabel. Fortunately, FO documents reveal the background to this part of Burton's leave. On 22 August, Burton wrote to Lord Derby, stating that, 'on Wednesday approximately, the 25th August, I propose to leave London for Vichy with the intention of taking the waters till nearly the end of September.'[57] A month later, Burton wrote again to the FO from Hotel d'Espagne, Paris, enclosing 'copy of a medical certificate given to me by Dr. L.A. Ritterbandt, MD, who advises me to avoid passing the approaching winter in the rigorous climate of Trieste. Your Lordship doubtless knows that the mortality of that city ranges between 40 and 50 per thousand, and the average for London is 22 per annum. I would, therefore, request an extension of sick leave "from the end of September till the end of March 1876."'

The certificate, dated Vichy, 21 September 1875, reads: 'I have known Captain Burton for the last 16 years when I began to treat him after his return from Africa. He is now suffering from stricture of the urethra and functional derangement of the liver. The former is the result of a….[word indecipherable] which attacked him in 1874; and the latter has been influenced by the unwholesome climate of Trieste. There is no objection to his returning to his consulship at the latter place at the end of its vigorous winter, but I have strongly advised him to pass the cold season in a milder climate such as Egypt or, if he prefers it, in the Tropics.'[58] Since Burton was paying the medical piper, it is difficult to know if there is a word of truth in this. His 'stricture of the urethra' dated back, of course, to his days in India, and not to 1874; nor did his alleged 'functional derangement of the liver' have anything to do with the climate of Trieste. In fact, this 'diagnosis', is couched in the exact words used by the EIC doctors in England in the early 1850s, suggesting that the patient was dictating what the doctor wrote. As for the advice to winter, possibly in the Tropics, Burton had already planned where he and Isabel were going.

This request for yet another, and prolonged, extension of leave, gave the FO some food for thought. The draft of the despatch, annotated in pencil reads: 'How much leave has he had? Went on leave April 26th.' This is followed in ink: 'I am not aware that the Service will suffer by the prolonged absence of Captain Burton from his post, and I propose to grant him leave until the 31st December, and, in the first instance when, if the state of his health requires it, we can extend it to the 31st March. Mr. W[ylde].' 'I agree. Sept. 28th. Derby.'

The Burtons left for Trieste on 4 December, 'a never-to-be-forgotten-day – so dark, foggy, deep snow, and a red lurid light. All the gas and candles had to be lit at nine o'clock in the morning. London was like a Dante's snow hell; the squares were like a Christmas tree.'[59] A large family party accompanied them to the Pavilion at Folkestone to see them off. The Dover train was stuck in a snow-drift from six to twelve at night.

The boat was unable to cross, and the night train failed to arrive. It was blowing a gale at sea. By the 7th, weather conditions had sufficiently improved for them to be taken to the station in two sledges. After landing at Boulogne, they lingered to see old faces and old places: Constantin, Burton's old fencing-master, Caroline, the Queen of the Poissardes, who welcomed them with open arms, and, of course, the Ramparts. From there, they went on to Paris.

Burton now sent a further letter to the Foreign Office expressing the 'hope that your Lordship will prolong the 3 months' absence on sick leave recommended by Dr. Ritterbandt.' This resulted in a splutter of comments from unidentifiable officials at the FO: 'He asked for an extension last September till the end of April next.' [This was incorrect] and was granted leave till Dec. 31st. and told he might apply again if his health required it. I grant 3 months from the end of December, and say that Lord Derby hopes that at the expiration of this further leave, he will be able to return to his further duties.' In pencil: 'When did he leave his post?' 'April 27.' In ink again: 'Captain Burton will have completed 7 months' absence from his post on the 27th inst. [In fact, it would be 8 months] Is his leave to be extended and, if so, for how long? I doubt the state of his health requiring the extension asked for.' In another hand, someone else writes: 'He was very ill before he left Trieste, but since he came home he has been on an exploring expedition to Iceland. I heard the other day that he had gone, or was going, upon some other journey.' 'Ask for another medical certificate.' In a final note, initialled D[erby], the matter was firmly resolved: 'Give him the leave for the time originally asked for: till the end of April.'[60]

Staying long enough in Paris to receive this reply, the Burtons left on 16 December, stopping off at Turin and Milan to visit friends. They arrived at Trieste on Christmas Eve. Having accepted an invitation for Christmas lunch, they allowed all the servants to go out and see their friends. It turned out that Burton felt unwell on Christmas Day, and went to bed. There was nothing in the house except bread and olives, and Isabel ate her Christmas dinner by his bed.

Having concealed all of Burton's requests for leave, so she said nothing about their present plans for visiting India. It appears from W.H. Wilkins's version of events in *The Romance*, that Isabel had long wished 'to go there with her husband, and get him to show her all the familiar spots which he had described to her as having visited or lived at during his nineteen years' service in India.' Burton, naturally, was much taken with the idea. Getting got hold of a map, they drew a line down the centre from Kashmir to Cape Comorin, and, given the time at their disposal, worked out how much they could manage to see on the western side, leaving the eastern side for a future occasion.[61]

They spent eight days packing and finalising arrangements for their tour. A host of friends turned up for a farewell midday dinner, and then accompanied the couple to the dockside. Waiting for them was the Government boat provided by Burton's best friend, the local Minister of Finance and the Captain of the Port, which then ferried them out to the Austrian-Lloyd's *Calypso*. Late in the afternoon on the last day of the old year the ship weighed anchor, and they steamed down the Adriatic with a fresh breeze.

CHAPTER THIRTY-THREE

REMEMBRANCE OF THINGS PAST

The run from Trieste to Port Said took just under a week. After strolling for a while around the grubby, ramshackle Arab town, the Burtons dined at the Consulate. Here they were introduced to Ferdinand de Lesseps, the builder of the Suez Canal, besides meeting up with a number of old friends, among them the Rt Hon Stephen Cave, MP, and his wife. Coincidentally, Burton had written to Cave the previous month from Paris, on the possibility, suggested by the 'eminent "Ingenieur chemist, F. Maxwell Lyte,"' of forming a company of mixed nationality to exploit Egyptian deposits of rock salt. 'I need not point out to you the vast export trade which thus could be opened through the canal between Egypt and the Far East.'[1] Whether Burton had any hopes of profiting from this possible venture is unclear.

The next morning they began to steam slowly through the Canal. Far away to the east they could just glimpse the desert – 'the wild, waterless Wilderness of Sur, with its waves and pyramids of sand catching the morning rays of the sun.' Occasionally a group of Bedouin passed by with their camels and goats, reminding Isabel of 'those dear, dead days at Damascus.' On the thirteenth day, the *Calypso* dropped anchor at Jedda. Mr Gustavus Wylde, the Vice-Consul, son of Burton's boss at the FO, Henry Wylde, sent a boat and a kawwas to bring them off, insisting on their remaining at the Consulate for the eight days they were to spend there.

The ship finally left for Bombay crammed to the gunwales with some eight hundred Muslim pilgrims, high seas and driving monsoon rain eventually adding to their misery. Isabel crawled about the rolling and pitching ship with difficulty, administering what little food and help she could. One of the pilgrims died on the second day out, and was buried at sea. Even so, there was no mourning or wailing among his companions, firm in their belief that he had gone straight to heaven. It had a depressing effect on Isabel, however, who witnessed twenty-three funerals during the next twelve days.

Once ashore at Aden, Burton lost no time enquiring after the members of the party who had accompanied him to Harar. He discovered that Mohammed el Hammel had died only the previous year. Long Guled and the two women, Shehrazade and Deedarzade were still alive; the former in camp, the latter in Somaliland. Abdo (the End of Time) had died a natural death; the one-eyed Yusuf had been murdered by the Isa tribe; the boy, Hasan Hammas, was now a sergeant in the water-police.

Arriving at Bombay on 2 February, they booked into the plush Watson's Esplanade Hotel in the Kala Ghoda District, its cast-iron pillars and tiers of wrought-iron galleries, making it look, as one traveller remarked, 'something like a huge birdcage....risen like an exhalation from the earth.'[2] Being new to India, Isabel was enthralled by the novelty of its sights and sounds. Burton took her to see all the scenes he had once known, remarking how curious it was that, 'although I hated them when I was obliged to live here, now that I am not obliged I can look back upon these scenes with a certain amount of affection and interest, although I would not live here again for anything. The old recollections make me sad and melancholy.'³

They were fortunate during their stay there, in being taken under the wing of Burton's close friend, Arbuthnot. As 'Collector' or chief administrative official responsible for collecting the revenue, he was a very important local figure. Knowing everyone of note, he introduced the Burtons to Bombay Society besides spending a great deal of time taking them on excursions in his carriage or in his boat. After visiting the magnificent 7ᵗʰ century AD Caves of Elephanta in Bombay harbour, filled with exquisite stone sculptures of Hindu gods and goddesses, they drove out to Bandora, some twelve miles from the city, where Arbuthnot owned a palatial bungalow and stables, a quiet rural spot enjoying refreshing sea breezes. Towards sunset they were joined by the Duke of Sutherland (the former Lord Stafford, who had visited the Burtons at Damascus) and other friends. It was the eve of Muharram, the first month of the Muslim year, and young boys dressed like tigers came and performed some native dancing, mimicking fighting and clawing one another.

Besides sightseeing, there was also so much hospitality to enjoy, that they dined out every night. While Isabel found everything enchanting, Burton gives the impression in his book, *Sind Revisited*, of being thoroughly bored with this ceaseless social round. 'You went to a ball, and found it dull; to a concert – duller; to the barn theatre – dullest.' On 16 February, as obviously planned well beforehand, Burton wrote to the Earl of Derby, stating that as his health had 'somewhat improved by the climate of western India,' he had 'the honour to request that my sick leave may be prolonged during the ensuing quarter, beginning with April 1, 1876.'⁴ His request was interestingly minuted at the FO: 'As to granting this, Captain Burton has been absent from his post since April, and it can hardly be said if he is well enough to travel to India, that he is not well enough to perform his duties of his post.' Another remarked: 'I heard the other day that he intended visiting Zanzibar on his way home from India.' Lord Derby, as usual, ignored the pejorative remarks of his officials, and granted Burton's request without comment.⁵

News of the Burtons' arrival in Bombay had been reported in *The Times of India*. As a result, he received several letters during February and March from Bapojee Hurree, whom Burton had employed as far back as 1854 to copy parts of his *Pilgrimage* manuscript, while he was staying with the Hon J.G. Lumsden at Belair. Impressed with the man's work, Burton had presented him a number of Mahratta and English books, which he still had in his possession. Anxious to retrieve the former, he asked Bapoojee Hurree, presently living and working as a clerk in the Booldana district in Hyderabad, to bring them to Bombay, promising him in exchange a copy of his *Pilgrimage*. At Bapojee Hurree's request, he also wrote him a glowing reference.⁶ Burton was also contacted by his former Portuguese servant, Valentino A. Rodriguez, who had accompanied him on the East African Expedition. Now in service with the Collector at Ahmedabad in Gujarat state, Valentino expected to be free during April, '& will go to Bombay when if I am fortunate I would get an opportunity of seeing your honour again.'⁷

Shortly after receiving this letter, the Burtons left Bombay to visit the Karla Caves, built by Buddhist monks in the 3ʳᵈ-2ⁿᵈ century BC, and one of the finest examples of ancient rock-cut caves to be found in India. From there they travelled to Poona through the Indrauni valley, scene of the Peshwa intrigues against the British, and their great battles with the Maharattas. The journey that gave them the greatest pleasure, however, was to the princely state of Hyderabad in the Deccan, which was new to Burton as well.

Situated on the Deccan Plateau some 1,800 feet above sea-level, Hyderabad was by far the largest and the most important native city in India, ruled over by a strong ally of the British, the Nizam.⁸ The Burtons were invited to be guests of Major Nevill, the English officer commanding the Nizam's troops. His wife, coincidentally, was the eldest daughter of the late Charles Lever, Burton's immediate predecessor at the Trieste Consulate. That night, despite travelling for most of the day, they attended a dinner-party and ball at

Government House.

The Nizam's affairs were jointly managed by three immensely wealthy and powerful men: Sir Salar Jung acted as Regent and Prime Minister.[9] The Amir el-Kebir was co-Regent and Minister of Justice; the Wikar Shums ool Umara was his brother. After a tour of the city, described by one Muslim chronicler as 'a resort of heavenly peace and worldly comfort,' the Burtons made their way to the magnificent palace of Sir Salar Jung, After enjoying a splendid breakfast of European and Eastern dishes, they were shown his collection of weapons. There was every sort of gun, sword and dagger on display, with jewelled inlaid hilts, sometimes with dangling pearls and emeralds attached to them. Burton was in his element. They were then taken to see the stables, a place described by Isabel as resembling Burlington Arcade, open at both ends, with loose boxes where the shops would be. They contained about a hundred horses, all thoroughbred Arabs and Persians, each with its own groom.[10] That night the Burtons were invited to the Residency for a dinner-party given by Sir Richard and Lady Meade for Sir Salar Jung and his Ministers.

The next few days were a non-stop round of festivities: breakfasts, dinner-parties at the Residency and elsewhere, followed by numerous excursions. Invited to visit the palace of the Wikar Shums ool Umara, they were received with military honours by a guard of soldiers, and then ushered in to a band playing "God Save the Queen." The hall was swarming with retainers and servants, who pressed them to eat as they served the dishes, whispering into their ears, "Take mutton cutlet; 'im very good." As before, they inspected the weaponry, much of it inlaid with gold or set with jewels. The next day there was a display of gymnastics and arms. Their host also put on some cock-fighting which, naturally, interested Burton, but Isabel walked away.

The following day they drove to the country residence of the Amir el Kebir, a beautiful palace set in gardens filled with a variety of birds and flowers. They inspected the town riding on elephants, and afterwards returned to breakfast with the Amir. The highlight, however, was a trip to the massive granite fortress and ruined city of Golconda, some five miles west of Hyderabad. From 1518-1687 it had been capital of the Shi'ah kingdom, one of five Muslim sultanates in the Deccan. In 1687 the ruling dynasty of Qutb Shahis was overthrown by the Mughal emperor Aurangzebe, and Golconda became part of the Mughal Empire for the next three hundred or so years. There was a beautiful garden of palm trees, and a labyrinth of arches, and the Burtons wandered about this romantic spot lit by a crescent moon, while fireflies glistened around the white-domed tombs of the Qutb Shahi sultans. They discussed the famous and controversial Koh-i-noor, or 'Mountain of Light' diamond, associated in some sources with Golconda, Isabel later sending an account of its history to the *Morning Post* 'for which I was considerably chaffed by the Press.'

On their last night, Sir Salar Jung put on a magnificent *fête*, the company consisting of the Nizam's Court and Ministers, and about thirty-six selected Europeans. The festivities began with a *Nach*, followed by a splendid dinner of about fifty-six covers served in the principal *salamlik* by retainers in picturesque costumes. After a brief visit the following morning to the nearby city of Secunderabad, founded as a British cantonment in the eighteenth century, the Burtons returned to Bombay.

It was possibly at the end of the first week in March, that they made their trip to Sind. Leaving on a Friday by a steamer belonging to the British Steam Navigation Company, they arrived at Karachi early the following Monday morning. The town, Burton discovered, had become, externally at least, extremely respectable and dull. There was 'a general Bombay look about the place, the result of deep eaves supported by corbelled posts; of a grand Hindu establishment or two; of the new market-place, and of large school and native police-stations.'[11] Karachi was still the seat of the local government and the headquarters of the European regiment. The Sepoy, however, had disappeared from Sind, whilst India, Burton claimed, had reduced her Sepoy army to a mere absurdity.

The result, in his estimation, was the ruin of the Indian army. 'And did not Voltaire think and declare,' he went on, using the subject to air his imagined grievances and bolster his own ego at the same time, that, of all the ways of Providence, nothing is so inscrutable as the littleness of the minds that control the destinies of great nations. Some have distinctions, you know, forced upon them; others win it by means which honest men despise. They never report the truth, unless pleasant to the ear….. "These superficial specimens of humanity, who know which side their bread is buttered, owe their rise, their stars and their ribbons, their KCBs and pensions, not to the sterling merits of courage and ability, of talents and manliness, but to the oily tongue that knows so well to work the oracle, and to a readiness of changing tactics as the chameleon changes colour." In short, these gentlemen have mastered the "gospel of getting on"; the species "neglected Englishman" has not.[12]

For the remainder of the month, Burton took Isabel over the scenes of his former life there, 'saluting them, letting the changes sink into his mind,' she said, 'and taking an everlasting farewell of them.' They visited the old alligator tanks, where the young subalterns used to go and worry the creatures with their bull terriers; the spot where he had a brief flirtation with the beautiful Persian girl, Baroda where he was quartered for so long, and Gharra where he had lived so miserably. He was able to trace the foundations of the lines of his old regiment, where he said, "None of us died, because we were young and strong; but we led the life of salamanders." Then they went on to Nagar, and to Thatha and Kalyan Kot and the Mekli Hills, to Sundan, Jarak, and the Phuleli River where he had spent many a pleasant hour lounging on its banks with his munshi. They resumed their drive along the Tahir-Bazar Road: 'I am now bound for my old home. Novelties meet my eyes at every turn.' They turned left, and after a few yards, about a mile and a half from the Hyderabad Fort, entered old Mohammed Khan's Tanda, or walled village.

> What a change within! Some twenty-five natives, mostly negresses, haunt the houses which lodged our corps. The mess-house, to which so many recollections attach, still stands, thanks to its foundation of baked brick; but the front is converted into an open stable for human beings…Yonder is the house which nearly fell down, nearly crushing its inmate and his Munshi; the fireplaces are still half-filled up, and the floor is grown with Yawasi, or camel-thorn. How small and mean are the dimensions which loom so large in the pictures stored within the brain…How strange are the tricks of Memory, which, often hazy as a dream about the most important events of a man's life, religiously preserves the merest trifles! And how very unpleasant to meet one's Self, one's "Dead Self", thirty years younger!
>
> Adieu old home! I shall not perhaps see you again, but it is not in my power ever to forget you.[13]

By the beginning of April, Burton having seen everything in southern and northern Sind he wished to see, they returned down the Indus to Kotri. The following morning they took the down-train to Karachi, and from there, the steamer back to Bombay.

Just over a week later, they set out for Mahabaleshwar, the summer capital of the Bombay Presidency, almost 5,000 ft up in the Sahyadri Hills of the Western Ghats. The morning after their arrival, they rose very early and drove in a *tonga*, a sort of tea-cart, with small *tatoo* ponies, to Elphinstone Point to enjoy the view and to see the temples. Although a most delightful excursion, it was quite spoiled for Isabel by the brutal way in which the driver beat the ponies with his thick cowhide whip. They made several pleasant trips during their stay, and people were very hospitable. However, there was too much Society to suit their tastes. 'Tall carriages instead of basket chairs, and sables capped with black chimney-pots, look queer in the wild woods,' Isabel remarked.[14]

Only two days after returning to Bombay, they embarked aboard the British Indian Steamship Company's *Rajpootna*, for 'distant and deserted Goa,' £10 for a thirty-six hours' passage. Anchored off Panjim (New Goa), a large boat arrived to take them and their baggage ashore to prevent the ship's going aground on a suspected sandbank. This meant an eight mile row, a mile and a half of it across open sea, five miles of bay, and one and a half along the winding river to the little stone pier landing.

Goa, as they found, offered nothing but the barest necessities. There was no inn and no tent. They had either to sleep in their filthy open boat, or take their own tents and everything with them. However, the agent of one of the steamers, Mr Major and his wife, seeing their predicament, offered them a small room in their house with their only spare single bed. Fortunately, Isabel had bought a large straw Pondicherry reclining chair and a rug from the captain of the steamer. She and Burton, therefore, took it in turns to occupy the chair and the bed.

The climate was the worst Isabel had ever experienced. There was not a breath of air at night, and the thirst was agonising; even the water was hot. To make matters worse, the place was utterly dead. They were only able to hire a small down-at-heel *gari*, an open cart, with just enough room for two. The wheels wobbled, the spring on one side was broken, the lamps dangled, there was a deal box for their driver, a small boy, and the harness consisted of old rusty chains tied together with bits of string. The pony was broken down with mange, starvation and sores, Isabel, naturally insisting on seeing to him herself, and caring for him properly.

Burton wanted to revisit former scenes, and Isabel was assigned to study the Portuguese manuscripts of Old Goa. They used to leave their cart there, and have the pony taken out and fed, watered and rested, whilst they toured round the ruins of churches and monasteries. When they were thirsty, little boys for a piece of silver, would shin up the trees like monkeys, pick off coconuts, and chop off a section at the top. The milk was delightfully refreshing and as cold as ice. As a diversion from their other activities, they made two interesting expeditions by boat: one to Mr Major's coffee plantation, the other to Seroda, each occupying two or three days.

At last the time came round for them to leave Goa. The steamers were due once a fortnight, but this one was long overdue. Eventually they were informed by telegram that the steamer would pass Goa at midnight. After starting down-river in the evening, they were delayed by a violent thunderstorm and poor visibility at the mouth of the bay, which almost resulted in their losing their passage back to Europe.

They had mixed feelings about leaving India. On the one hand, they were glad to escape the intolerable heat and the approaching monsoon season. On the other, they were sorry to leave, given their ever-increasing interest in the country, and the growing number of friends. They stayed at Bombay no longer than was absolutely necessary, and then embarked for, what turned out to be, an uncomfortable return journey to Trieste in the Austrian-Lloyd's *Minerva*.

Shortly after disembarking at Suez, the Burtons were surrounded by a small group of friends of his Mecca days. They later took their *kayf* with the Arabs at "Moses' Well," some three miles into the Arabian Desert, who gave them delicious coffee and *narghilehs*. After stopping for over a fortnight at Cairo – a rather important period as will be seen later – the Burtons embarked for Trieste. As their ship approached, 'The beautiful little City, nestled in its corner in the mountains at the very top of the Adriatic, seemed to us the greenest and the most beautiful spot we had ever beheld, after hot India and barren Egypt and Arabia.'[15]

CHAPTER THIRTY-FOUR

THE GOLD MINES OF MIDIAN

After, what Burton called, 'the horrors of the Red Sea,' Trieste was delightfully cool, cold even, snow still lying on the slopes of the surrounding mountains. The political temperature in the nearby Balkan states, however, had risen alarmingly.

By July of the previous year, a series of natural disasters combined with chronic Turkish maladministration and religious persecution, had provoked serious insurrections in Bosnia and Herzegovina mainly by Christian peasants against their Muslim overlords. By May 1876, Serbs and Bulgars had joined the revolt. Turkey responded to attacks by Bulgarian comitadjis, or armed guerillas, by sending in the Bashi Bazouks to terrorise the civilian population. Throughout May and June they perpetrated appalling massacres of men, women, and children, accompanied by rape, torture and pillage.[1]

Under the so-called Berlin Memorandum of 13 May, the Eastern Powers, Austria-Hungary, Germany and Russia, called on Turkey to conclude an armistice with the rebels for two months, while carrying out prompt measures for reform as outlined in an earlier note by the Austro-Hungarian foreign minister, Count Andrassy. The price of refusal would be a concerted intervention to enforce a reasonable minimum. Suspicious of Russia's intentions, Disraeli foolishly rejected the Berlin proposals and, a fortnight later, ordered the British fleet to Besika Bay.

'This is an exciting moment,' Burton remarked in a letter to Grattan Geary, editor of *The Times of India*, written only two days after arriving back. 'Such a move, may very probably bring the Russians south of the Danube, in which case Turkey in Europe bursts up. We should be ashamed to support a power whose only policy is sheer rank murder.'[2] Early in July, Serbia and Montenegro declared war on the Ottoman Empire.

Such was the degree of Burton's absorption in the so-called Eastern Question, that three months later he declared his willingness to Geary to write an occasional letter for his paper. As a servant of Government, of course, the publication of views critical of its foreign policy, was wholly out of order. To avoid serious repercussions from the Foreign Office, therefore, Burton insisted that anything that appeared would have to be under an alias.[3] The letter also revealed that, by then, Burton was already writing for the radical liberal newspaper, *The Daily News*, under the pseudonym, "Conscience," 'but don't publish the fact.' As an ultra-Conservative in his politics, this was just the sort of paper whose views one would expect Burton to regard with anathema.[4] However, as he explained to Geary, 'I find myself herding with a strange lot, Shaftesbury, Bright and A. Herbert, but men who prefer patria to party must expect strange company.'

Amidst this period of crisis in Turkey's internal and external affairs, came news of the death, first of the sultan, Abdulaziz, on 4 June, followed eleven days later by the murders of Huseyn Avni, President of the Council of State and Rashid Pasha, the country's foreign minister. 'Serve the scoundrel right,' Burton remarked vindictively of Rashid in a letter to his cousin, Dr Edward Burton. 'He prevented my going to Constantinople and to Sana'a in Arabia.[5] I knew the murderous rascal too well to trust him.'

While Burton might exult in the death of the man whom he described as his 'arch-enemy,' he had cause to mourn other deaths that year. After a long wasting illness, his brother-in-law, Lt General Sir Henry Stisted had died from tuberculosis in the previous December. 'Maria writes to me about poor Stisted's death,' he informed his cousin. 'What an end to a successful life. I never yet saw a man so determined to kill himself. A great loss for Maria and the chicks.'[6]

Three months later on 19 March, Burton's old friend and mentor of his Sind days, General Walter Scott, died at Halbendorf in Saxony. Exactly a quarter of a century earlier, Burton had dedicated his *Scinde; or the Unhappy Valley* to Scott. It was with a heavy heart, that he now inscribed his *Sind Revisited*, which appeared the following year, to Scott's memory.

Only just under a week before Burton arrived back in Trieste, an even older friend, A.B. Richards, passed away at his home in Brunswick Square, London. His death, which surely must have come as a happy release after suffering excruciating pain for almost a year from cancer of the rectum, was certified by his friend and personal physician, Dr George Bird. Richards's death certificate, also reveals, what was obviously a closely guarded family secret, that he had a natural daughter, Edmée, who was present at her father's death. One senses that, like the poet Wordsworth's liaison in 1791 with the young Frenchwoman, Annette Vallon, by whom he had a daughter, Caroline, there is a fascinating story to be told here, if only the facts were available.

Fortunately, these sad events were partly counterbalanced that year by good news about another of his friends, the young naval officer, Verney Lovett Cameron. In 1872, the RGS, acutely embarrassed by the Lt Dawson débacle and privately miffed at H.M. Stanley's highly publicised success, appointed Cameron to lead, what was called, 'The Livingstone East Coast Search Expedition.' Together with three companions, including Livingstone's nephew, Robert Moffat, landed at Bagamoyo from Zanzibar on 2 February 1873. Eight months later, after learning of Livingstone's death earlier in the year, Cameron decided to press on to Ujiji in order to recover the missionary-explorer's papers and personal effects. By now he was alone, Moffat having died from fever early on in the expedition, and the other two men having decided to return to the coast. After circumnavigating Lake Tanganyika, Cameron made the bold, if unauthorised, decision to continue his journey across Africa. On the morning of 7 November 1875, more dead than alive from the effects of scurvy, he staggered into Katombela, a fishing village near Benguella on the Atlantic seaboard of Portuguese Angola.

As the first European to make an east-west crossing of the continent, he received a tumultuous welcome on his return home on 2 April 1876. He was praised by the world's press, fêted wherever he went, and showered with honours. The RGS, despite its strong reservations about the inordinate cost of the expedition, awarded him its Founder's Medal, he was made a CB, an honorary DCL was conferred on him by Oxford University, and he was promoted to the rank of Commander in the Navy.

In the first of two letters to Burton in late July, Cameron expressed how indebted he had been to Burton's *Lake Regions* while he was in Africa. He also thanked him 'most heartily for the kind way you fought my battles while I was away.' He was devoting all his energies to getting his book out in November 'in time for the Xmas publishing season when I will send you a copy.'[7] He had been 'trying to get a charter for a company but Government is averse to granting one. Several capitalists have been nibbling and I am still in communication with some. Money will be forthcoming I fancy as soon as there is a glut of unemployed capital in the country, but people are timid.'[8]

Cameron had written to the Council of the RGS just over a fortnight after arriving on the west coast, describing the African interior as 'mostly a magnificent and *healthy* country of unspeakable richness.' He also mentioned in his letter his intention of trying to form 'a great company....with a capital of £1,000,000 to £2,000,000 which would have Africa open in about three years if properly worked.'[9] Despite his initial optimism, his scheme never came to fruition. 'What I had on my return in 1876 to say about Africa in a commercial point of view,' he wrote many years later in the second edition of his book when the "scramble for Africa," was well under way, 'though amply borne out by recent occurrences, seemed in a great measure to fall flat on the ears of merchants and politicians.'[10]

The information contained in Cameron's second letter about Lake Tanganyika must have been extremely disillusioning to Burton, since it seriously undermined his theories about the lake and the Nile sources. In it, Cameron confirmed that, 'Many of the Arabs have now been to the North end and they all assured me that the water came in there.' Furthermore, 'Everything seemed to gravitate towards Lukuga and there is a gap in the mountains there. I have a small sketch of the entrance. After leaving the Lake I could see the valley of the Lukuga and that it distinctly was the drain of the lake. I hope this will tell you what you want to know.' It did anything but, of course. Cameron had discovered ninety-six rivers flowing into Lake Tanganyika but only one issuing out of it, the Lukuga. This eventually drained westwards into the much larger Lualaba river, which he believed, correctly as it turned out, to be the main headstream of the mighty Congo river. The discovery, of course, dealt a fatal blow to the belief cherished by Livingstone up to the day of his death, that the Lualaba fed the Nile.

Having translated the Brazilian epic poem, *O Uruguai*, Burton now tried his hand on the finest of the Italian Renaissance epics, Ludovico Ariosto's *Orlando furioso*. The poem, containing 40 cantos, and written in ottava rima, was a sequel to Matteo Boiardo's *Orlando innamorato*, which combined for the first time elements of both Arthurian and Carolingian traditions of Romance.[11] Burton, probably with too many irons in the fire, completed only four cantos, which met the same fate after his death as a number of his other unpublished works.[12] Although it is impossible to know what English versions of Ariosto Burton drew on, his mode of translating, in this particular case, can still be seen in the Italian edition of Ariosto which he used. As the librarian, Herbert Jones observed, 'there never was such a man for using books as mere tools........He would use the scissors on a fine edition as one cut out of a newspaper paragraph. He scrawled across title-pages, mutilated everything.' Instead of obtaining a cheap copy, or translating on a clean manuscript, Burton used a rare Milan edition of the *Orlando furioso*, illustrated by Gustave Doré. 'His stanzas are scrawled across the printed text,' Jones went on, 'across the very tissue paper even which shields the full-page illustrations.'[13]

Reviewing General Gordon's *Journals* in 1885, Burton stated that, shortly after being appointed to the Sudan in 1874, Gordon had consulted him about an Eastern harbour of export. He had suggested one north of the equator, which should separate Egypt from Zanzibar. His advice, however, was disregarded, and poor Admiral (then Capt. H.F. McKillop) brought upon himself much trouble. In 1876, Burton went on, Gordon offered him command of the Eastern Sudan with £1500 per annum, 'but as I asked for £2000 he was nettled, and wrote that he hardly expected so much devotion to £ s d. My answer was that every farthing (and something more) would be spent in the country, but the amount to spend would represent the measure of my power and influence. This satisfied him, and yet I could not accept the offer. We were at once too like and too unlike to act together without jarring.'[14]

Burton's memory, however, was at fault in several respects. Gordon first consulted him for advice about the area and the tribes around the Nile Basin in July 1875.[15] Furthermore, it was not until 21 June 1877, when Gordon, without any prior consultation, informed Burton that he had written to the Khedive 'to ask him to give you Darfur as Governor-General, with £1,600 a year, and a couple of secretaries at £300 a year each......I know that you have much important work at the Consulate, with the ship captains, etc., and of course it would not be easy to replace you; but it is not every day you use your knowledge of Asiatics or of Arabia. Now is the time to make your indelible mark in the world and in these countries. You will be remembered in the literary world, but I would sooner be remembered in Egypt as having made Darfur.'[16] Burton wrote back: 'My dear Gordon, You and I are too much alike. I could not serve under you, nor you under me. I do not look upon the Soudan as a lasting thing. I have nothing to depend upon but my salary; and I have a wife, and you do not.'[17] At this stage, of course, Burton, without mentioning them to Gordon, had other, and more lucrative plans, involving the Khedive of Egypt.

In *The Gold Mines of Midian*, Burton recalled how, in 1853, after he and Haji Wali had become close friends at the Wakalah Siladar, the latter had strolled one day into his room with a great air of mystery. Having shown him a small quantity of sand containing minute specks of gold, he had suggested they travel together as pauper pilgrims to the spot where it had been found. Instead, Burton asked the English Consul, Dr Walne, to notify H.H. Abbas Pasha of the discovery, with a view to working the diggings. His request had been ignored. As a result, Haji Wali had used the sand to powder a letter, and Burton had set out for Arabia. 'For nearly a quarter of a century my secret was kept to myself.' It was not until H.H. Ismail Pasha became Viceroy of Egypt, that the long-wished-for opportunity presented itself. Burton's old friend, Hugh Thurburn, after making enquiries at the Khan Khalil and other bazaars in Cairo, eventually traced Haji Wali, and informed Burton that a very old man of that name was living in New Bubastis.

With England now taking the leading role in the reform and development of Egypt, Burton thought this an opportune moment to act. Following his return from India, therefore, he passed through Zagazig, where, after a short conversation with Mr J.C.J. Clarke, Telegraphic Engineer and Directeur des Télégraphes, he 'placed him upon the scent which he cleverly and patiently followed. A long correspondence ensued.' The Haji, Burton claimed, despite his advanced age and alleged infirmities, appeared more anxious about the affair than might have been expected. He promised Mr Clarke that he would fetch a plan of the place from Alexandria. After five months of prevarication it emerged that no plan existed, but that a letter written in Turkish contained certain jottings as to the route.

In the meantime, His Highness, the Viceroy of Egypt, having heard from a mutual friend – undoubtedly the Marquis Alphonse Victor de Compiègne, whom Burton had seen much of in Cairo following his return from India – that he had obtained information as to the site of a gold-field many years earlier, 'honoured me with an invitation to report this matter in person.' To describe Haji Wali's meagre sprinklings of gold dust as evidence of a gold-mine was, of course, ludicrous. Anything, however, was grist to Burton's mill if it involved escaping from Trieste, and offered the chance of exploration. In February 1877, therefore, Burton applied to the Foreign Office for a month's leave, concealing, of course, the real reason for it. His request was obligingly backed by his physician, Dr Carlo Liebmann, who advised his leaving Trieste for a month, in consideration of what Burton called 'a ferocious winter, all Bora and Sirocco.'[18] With Lord Derby still at the FO, the result was a foregone conclusion. Burton now had the necessary leave for Egypt but not, it appears, the wherewithal to get there. After the expensive trip to India, the Burtons were strapped for cash. Dependable Uncle Gerard, however, no doubt spun a tale by Isabel, of the inevitable riches that would result from Burton's trip, came up again with the money.[19]

It had not been a happy year so far, for Isabel. Two of her 'dear old uncles......who were like fathers to me,' as she later informed Lord Houghton, had died within months of each other, one in December of the previous year, the other, Renfric, her father's business partner, on 21 February. Even more distressing, her sole remaining brother, Rodolphe, had contracted black small-pox in a cab, and died, aged only forty, on 23 January.[20] 'I was so grieved,' she said, 'that I shut myself up all December, January, February and March.'[21] Early in February, she entered a convent at Gorizia for a fortnight, followed by a pilgrimage to Monte

Santo. Burton, in the meantime, took advantage of Isabel's absence to make an unauthorised trip to Zagreb, the capital of Croatia, and several other places in the region.[22]

On 3 March, he left Trieste for Egypt, using the voyage to complete a draft review of Cameron's *Across Africa* for *The Times of India*.[23] Five days later he arrived at Alexandria, from where he travelled by train to Cairo. There he discovered that the Marquis de Compiègne had died following a duel just over a week earlier.[24] However, a Mr Frederick Smart announced Burton's arrival to the Khedive, and he was invited to the Abadin Palace the following day. 'The Land of Midian,' Burton observed, sounding as if he were making an effort to validate what followed, 'is Egyptian, in a region inhabited by Egyptian tribes, and held by Egyptian garrisons. I was at the right spot at the right moment, so I made no mystery of my long-guarded secret,[25] but placed all the particulars then known to me at the disposal of the Khedive, leaving him to recognize my services as he might think fit.' Burton described his reception by Ismail Pasha as 'peculiarly gracious.' His first audience, he remarked, 'taught me that this prince is a master of detail, whilst in promoting the prosperity of the country he has been taught by experience to exercise the utmost vigilance and discretion.'[26]

This was both sycophantic and absurd. Ismail, described by *Punch* as 'that coolest and craftiest of artful dodgers,'[27] was spendthrift in the extreme. He had inherited a precarious economy and a crushing burden of debt. Yet in the management of his finances, he was extravagant and unwise, laying himself open to unscrupulous exploitation. Burton's *bête noir*, Dr Walne, had remarked as far back as 1855 that, the then Khedive, Said Pasha, was 'rash and flighty and conceited, and is spoilt by the flattery of the foreigners who surround him; they tell him and he believes them that he is a universal genius. He undoes everything, does very little, and, I fear, is preparing us for some great catastrophe.'[28] According to Lord Cromer, who arrived in Egypt as one of the Commissioners of the Debt three years after Burton, 'Ismail Pasha added, on an average, about £7,000,000 a year for thirteen years to the debt of Egypt. For all practical purposes it may be said that the whole of the borrowed money, except £16,000,000 spent on the Suez Canal, was squandered.'[29] Burton, obsessed by the idea of making a fortune, allowed himself to be blinded as to the real state of affairs in Egypt. Large sums of money were already owed to contractors and others for goods supplied to the Egyptian Government. Its own employees were many months in arrears of pay. Nevertheless, whilst this went on, taxes were being collected with merciless severity for nine months, in some places, for a year, in advance, to service the debt.

Apparently, the Khedive at first appeared satisfied with the explanation that gold had been picked up by a pilgrim near the second or third caravan stations on the way from El Muwaylah to El Akabah. Burton confessed that, as he himself at that time, 'had never heard of the Mining-cities, my hopes of finding an Ophir, a California, were comparatively humble, I expected only a few "placers" which might, however, as gold formations are rarely sporadic and isolated, lead to an auriferous region.'[30]Although Burton does not say as much, it is clear that Ismail Pasha, even in his parlous financial state, was deeply sceptical of Burton's being able to fill the Egyptian treasury with much-needed gold. On 25 March, however, just as Burton was preparing to return to Trieste, Ismail decided to give the venture a try, and formally invited him to lead an expedition to where the metallic sand had been found.

A Government vessel was commandeered, and Burton left for Zagazig, where Haji Wali and Mr Clarke were waiting for him. Although Burton had not seen Haji Wali since 1854, he immediately recognised him. They embraced like long-lost brothers, and, after a few words of conversation, Burton found that his former companion remembered every detail. He immediately agreed to accompany Burton on condition of all his expenses being paid, and of a leaving a few *bent* (Napoleons) to support his family during his absence. Burton then left for Suez. Early the following morning, Friday, 30 March, M. George Mace, C.E. handed him a letter signed by H.H. Prince Husayn Kamil, Minister of Finance, detailing all the arrangements that had been made. Having been introduced to three Egyptian officers who were to join him, Burton formally took command.

They then called upon the Muhafiz (Governor) of Suez, H.E. Sa'id Bey, to meet the Captain commanding the corvette, and to finalise the time and way of embarkation. A French engineer, M. Marie volunteered to become caterer, and Mr Clark, then on 'sick leave,' to act as Burton's secretary. For the next twenty-four hours, work went on non-stop collecting the provisions and the furniture; camel-saddles, water-bags, large and small, kitchen implements, eating gear, and the thousand and one necessities for a three weeks' cruise and desert trip. 'Our mission, of course,' Burton said, 'was kept a profound secret.'

Haji Wali now began to give endless trouble, complaining of pains in his head, in his side, in his knees, and so forth. A doctor was sent for with the request that he supply Haji Wali with the most awful-tasting gout-mixture. As it turned out, two bottles of ale a day proved even more effective. 'Yet it was a serious step to take, as it were, a man of 82 by the neck, as he said, and to carry him off to Arabia.'[31] Burton confessed to feeling relieved of considerable responsibility, when he returned Haji Wali to his family in better condition than when he left it.

They embarked at 6 p.m. on Saturday, 31 March, the general belief at Suez being that they were going in search of petroleum, salt, sulphur, and ruins. At the New Port, they were received on board H.H.'s steam corvette, *Sinnar*, and at 10 p.m. steamed out of dock. By the morning of the second day, they lay at anchor in the open and dangerous roadstead of El Muwaylah. Two officials, military and civil, came aboard, and after reading the letter conveying the vice-regal orders, promised to supply them with 50 camels within three days.

Early on 3 April, Burton and M. Marie set out in a sambuk, accompanied by Lts Hassan and Abd el Kerim. The escort, ten soldiers, with the Chawush Ali and Marius, the chef, followed in another boat. After landing early the following day, they spent the next five days in and about the Wady Aynunah, waiting for the camels and inspecting the ruins. On 7 April, the caravan, preceded by the Sayyid el-Rahim straggled in. Two days later, they set out in a northerly direction towards the Zahd or Aynunah Mountains. The eastern frontier was still unexplored, and they heard of ruins far in the interior. The business of the next winter would be to trace the gold deposits to their sources in the north and east.

On 10 April, they set off in the direction of the White Mountain, then skirted the seaward base of the Jebel el-Zahd. After following two dried up river-beds, they came upon a scattering of tombs. About half-way along the second, the Wady Aynunah, Mr Clarke caught sight of a "written stone," a block of red porphyry, the same material inscribed with the Himyaritic inscriptions which had been copied by Seetzen in Yemen. It was carried off and deposited later with H.H. the Viceroy, after it had been photographed and copies sent to a number of eminent Oriental scholars. During the afternoon, they ascended the White Mountain. Burton was descending, when M. Marie shouted out that he had made a discovery. Projecting from a mass of quartz was a vein, which they immediately named Le Grand Filon. It later proved to be a highly composite formation containing some ten metals. After Burton's return to Cairo, he proposed to the Viceroy an immediate start with a party of engineers and a load of gun-cotton and dynamite, to blow up the vein in quantities weighing several tons, to transport them back to Cairo and exhibit to the world a specimen of the Midianite metal. However, on 25 April, the Russo-Turkish war broke out, resulting in heavy demands on men and money from Egypt. 'I felt that my proper place was at my post,' Burton said, expressing a highly unusual sentiment for him. Besides, the hot weather was rapidly approaching. The project, therefore, was to remain in abeyance until November, when it was thought that the campaign would cease to engross public attention.

Burton was convinced that gold-washing had never been forgotten at El-Muwaylah. He believed that it had been carried out in secret, bringing large fortunes to men who, ostensibly, dealt in charcoal. He could cite no evidence, however, in support of this belief. Some of the old people at Suez declared that the works were abandoned years ago because the material extracted failed to cover expenses. 'Exactly what would be bruited abroad of a rich placer,' Burton said, determined to see mystery where there was only common-sense economics. At El-Muwaylah, they embarked on board the *Sinnar*, sailing south that same day to inspect a 'mountain of sulphur,' and a turquoise mine of which they had been informed by the Bedawin. 18 April was their last day in Arabia. Besides specially chosen specimens intended for the Khedive, they carried away for analysis eight boxes full of metalliferous quartz, greenstone, porphyry, basalt, syenite and chloritic slate; fourteen water-bags of granite and other gravels; and twelve bags of sand for laboratory work.

As far as Burton was concerned, the high point of his visit to old Midian was the brief stay at Makna, and the glimpse of the Dahi, or true Desert, which it offered: 'What a contrast with the horrors of the civilised city…How easy to understand the full force of the Bedawi expression, "Praise be to Allah that once more we see the Nafud!"'[32]

The return voyage to Suez was spent in writing up reports, pounding the specimens, and treating the powder with mercury. On Saturday, 21 April, exactly three weeks after their departure, they took leave of all their friends of the SS *Sinnar*. A telegram was immediately despatched to the Viceroy announcing complete success, and applying for a special train. Nothing now remained but to pay the wages and the bakhshish of the two Europeans, Marius Isnard, the cook, and the kitchen help, Antonia. Not mentioned, of course, in Burton's book, was the despatch which he wrote that same day to the Foreign Office. It was, as with so many of them, economical with the truth:

My Lord,

I have the honour to report that about the end of March when I was preparing to return to Trieste, the Viceroy of Egypt favoured me with a special invitation to board the frigate 'Sinnar' with a guard of 3 officers and 20 men, to visit a neighbouring part of the Arabian coast, where I had ascertained the existence of gold about 25 years ago.

We left Suez on Saturday, March 31st, and returned here today, having discovered during our 16 days of travel the ruins of 6 large mining cities, and fine specimens of gold, silver, and other metals. The Land of Midian is, in fact, another California.

I venture to hope that under the peculiar circumstances of the case, your Lordship will be pleased to excuse the irregularity in not applying for leave, and to extend my leave of absence on urgent private affairs till the end of May.

This was minuted at the FO: 'He had a month's leave and left his post in March. I suppose he can have it extended, but he gives no reason for it. His account of gold-finding is too vague.'[33] Written sanction for Burton's extension of leave was given on 7 May, carrying an amusing note in the draft copy: 'This despatch had better go to the Vice-Consul at Trieste to be forwarded, as he is more likely to know where Burton is than we are.'[34]

The train to Cairo was frustratingly slow. Because war was expected, troops were getting ready for embarkation, and there was a general confusion and excitement. Mr Smart, unable to delay any longer had left for Alexandria, en route for Naples. Burton, however, had an audience with H.H. Prince Husayn Kamil Pasha, the young Minister of Finance, who questioned him about the trip. Next morning the Khedive, after receiving Burton's hearty acknowledgement of the princely way in which he had ordered the excursion, thanked him for his assurance that the Nile Valley had ever been the land of his predilection.[35] Ismail closely inspected the charts, maps, and plans of his staff officers, and, according to Burton, at once understood the advantage of working the ancient mines of Midian with modern appliances. Ismail also showed a great deal of interest in the measures which Burton briefly outlined. 'The first step would be to regiment the convicts who now do little beyond dying at the local Botany Bay, Fayzoghlu. These men could be divided into companies, officered from the Engineer branch of the service, and form a body like that which in the more economical and less sentimental days of English colonial history, distinguished themselves on the Gold Coast and in West Africa.'[36]

So, what were the "urgent private affairs" requiring an extension of Burton's leave? It turned out that Cairo, 'the literary place of the Arabs, *par excellence*, appeared to be the best place for investigating the origin of that mysterious alphabet known in Syria as El Mushajjar, the tree-shaped, the branchy, in fact the "palm-runes" of Icelandic Edda.'[37] Burton, in fact, had used the period before leaving for Midian to work on the Ogham inscriptions, and had already sent an article on the subject to *The Athenaeum*.[38] Despite the novelty of the subject, however, Burton said he would have to defer publication, 'as his researches were not then in a fit state to appear before the world.'

After paying his last respects to the Khedive, Burton left Cairo on 27 April. On 2 May, the Institut Egyptien at Alexandria conferred honorary membership on him, after which he delivered a short lecture. He embarked on board the Austrian Lloyd's SS *Aurora* on 6 May, and was back at Trieste six days later, 'restored to marvellous good health and spirits.'

CHAPTER THIRTY-FIVE

MIDIAN REVISITED

Burton remarked how, throughout the summer of 1877, he was haunted by, what he described as, memories of mysterious Midian. 'The Golden Region,' he said, 'appeared to me in the glory of primeval prosperity described by the Egyptian hieroglyphics; as rich in agriculture and in fertility, according to the old Hellenic travellers, as in the Centres of Civilization, and in the precious metals catalogued by the Sacred books of the Hebrews.'[1] Throughout that time he engaged in a long correspondence with many learned friends, besides making a painstaking study of the most up-to-date geographers, particularly German, in order to familiarise himself with all that was known of mining in Arabia generally, and in Midian in particular.

Around the middle of September, the Khedive offered Burton 'in an autograph letter full of the kindest expressions, the governorship of Dar-For.'[2] Burton declined the honour, as he phrased it, till he had completed his work in Midian, something he was invited to do during the ensuing winter. Generally, the official public, as Burton admitted, aware that he had brought back stones, not masses of gold and silver, were highly critical of the prospective waste of money from the public purse. The Khedive, however, 'who had mastered, with his usual accuracy of perception and judgement, the subject of Midian and her mines, was staunch in his resolve, and when one of the foreign financiers warned him that there were no public funds for such purpose, his Highness declared, *on dit*, that the costs of the Expedition should be defrayed at his own expense.'[3] This, as Burton would find, literally, to his cost, was a grand if empty gesture.

Although Burton had found no evidence of gold so far in his explorations in Midian, it is clear from a light-hearted letter written by Isabel in September to a stockbroker and businessman friend, Luke Ionides, that some sort of secret financial deal for exploiting any finds was being hatched. 'Richard wrote you a letter which you have never answered. You must please be a better boy and answer quickly, as Richard goes on 19 October. I am to follow in January. Meantime you and I are to transact all the business together, and if you don't answer "by express train and telegraph" you know what a fiend I shall become.' She added in a PS. 'My husband says there is nothing new to say only that in February he means to raise the funds in the manner proposed. If he is in Egypt he will communicate with you direct. If in Arabia through me and you must tell me what words to use in telegraphing. Also tell me this, we see quite well what immense advantages will accrue to you, but we don't see exactly what will accrue to us and I want to know.'[4]

This, however, was not the only financial scheme which Burton had under way at this period for making his fortune. According to N.M. Penzer, Burton, following his return to London after experiencing the hardships and privations of his pilgrimage to Medina and Mecca, 'tried to form a company for enabling the pilgrims to reach the Holy City with greater ease and comfort.'[5] The company was to trade under the name of The Hadjilik or Pilgrimage to Mecca Syndicate Ltd, with a capital of £10,000 in 100 shares of £100 each. Penzer's own copy of the original prospectus carried no date. He mistakenly believed, therefore, that this business venture belonged to the 1850s. In fact it is to be dated almost a quarter of a century later to the period of the Russo-Turkish war, more specifically September 1877. Furthermore, it was not prompted by any philanthropic motive as implied by Penzer.

The aim of the Syndicate was to organise a steamer service for pilgrims operating out of the major ports along the Mediterranean, Red Sea, Persian Gulf and Indian Ocean. Based on a figure of some 170,000 pilgrims using this means of travel for that year, at an average of £7 per head, this would result in a gross profit for the Syndicate of £1,900,000. It was believed that the net profit on this would be at the rate of £2 per head, not counting the additional profit to be made from freight and the sale of provisions. Given the present state of affairs, there was little doubt of its earning a dividend of at least 50 percent per annum for members. Since the war had taken a heavy toll of the steamer fleet of the Levant, pilgrims would be forced for many years to come into taking advantage of the service provided by the Syndicate.[6]

There are no clues as to the number or identity of the persons composing it, nor whether anyone ever applied for share certificates. Perhaps it sounded too good to be true to prospective investors, who may well have doubted that the steam power of the Levant would be out of action for so long as claimed. Whatever the case, it appears to have to come to nothing, and nothing further has come to light about it.

Isabel's letter to Luke Ionides gives the impression of Burton's arrangements for leaving England as being cut and dried. In fact, it was not until three days later that he wrote to the Foreign Office asking for three months' leave dating from 19 October. He said, somewhat in advance of fact, that H.H. the Viceroy of Egypt, had invited him again to visit the mines of Midian, in order to carry out an exploration which, it was believed, would promote the power and prosperity of the country. Since the funded debt of Egypt in 1876, including the Daira loans, amounted to £68,110,000, and there was a floating debt of about £26,000,000, making a grand total of over £90,000,000, Midian would have to be far richer in gold than the California Burton claimed it to be.[7]

'I will not conceal from your Lordship,' Burton went on, 'that his Highness will be gratified by my being permitted to accept his invitation for a short period, that the exploration, if successful, will be of the greatest personal advantage to me, and that absence from Trieste at a season when the cold winds set in will be very beneficial to my health, which has lately suffered from lumbago and neuralgia attacks.' As usual, he proposed leaving Mr Brock in charge of the Consulate, 'whose long and able services are a warrant that the duties of the office will be satisfactorily performed.'[8] Lord Derby, also as usual, agreed without question to Burton's request, and he set off for Cairo on 19 October.

On his arrival, Burton found to his consternation that an association for exploiting the discoveries of the first expedition had been formed in London by the Messiers Vignolles. Their representative, Gen Nuthall, formerly of the Madras Army, had twice visited the Egyptian capital during August and October, seeking a concession of the mines, and offering conditions which, according to Burton, were perfectly unacceptable. Somewhat forgetful of Haji Wali's role in the affair, Burton wrote complainingly that he 'was to share in the common fate of originators, discoverers, and inventors: the find was mine, the profits were to go elsewhere.'[9] Unfortunately, Gen Nuthall failed to see matters in that light. However, after a few friendly meetings he left Egypt believing in the possibility of their working together when the exploration was completed. Ismail, who had recently given Burton a verbal promise of either the concession, or four percent on gross produce, acted, so Burton said, *en prince*, 'simply remarking that the affair was in my hands, and that he would not interfere with me.' Of course, as Burton well knew from his experience in South America with the same Foreign Secretary, an attempt to obtain a mining concession broke the rule forbidding a Consul to trade.

In the meantime, the Viceroy had decided that the Expedition should not only carry out the work of discovery by tracing the precious metals to their source, but that specimens were to be brought back, large enough for assay and analyses, quantitative and qualitative, in London and Paris. Consequently, miners and mining apparatus were needed, with all the materials for quarrying and blasting. The Expedition was held up, however, for want of money. Not feeling in the best of health, Burton decided to make a flying trip to Karslbad, a spa highly popular with wealthy Europeans on the Tepla river in western Bohemia.[10] On 2 December, the Minister of Finance distributed one month's pay among the officials in arrears of salary ranging from seven to fifteen months, with a vague promise that all arrears would presently be made good. That same day, the Khedive issued 2,000 napoleons to the Expedition, in addition to the 620 already spent on instruments and provisions.[11]

Arrangements for a special train having been completed, the Expedition finally got under way on Thursday, 6 December. By this time, three precious weeks of fine autumnal weather had been lost. After stopping briefly at Zagazig to pick up Haji Wali, 'whom age had made only a little fatter and greedier,' the train carried on to Suez. On 10 December, they sailed from Suez Quay in the *Tayr el-Bar* ('Bird of the Sea') and boarded a gunboat. There was further delay when the engine broke down forcing it to return. It was not until Wednesday, 19 December, therefore, that Burton and his party landed at El-Muwaylah. Two days before disembarkation, Burton wrote again to the FO: 'I have the honour to report that finding a change of climate from Egypt advisable, I accepted a gracious invitation from His Highness the Khedive, to revisit the Land of Midian, where the splendid air has done me much good. Under these circumstances, I venture to hope that your Lordship will be pleased to extend my leave of absence for 3 months from the 19th January, 1878.' This was granted without demur by the Foreign Office.[12]

The usual palaver took place, starting pleasantly and ending disagreeably. Reports had circulated that Burton possessed some £22,000, mostly to be spent at Muwaylah. 'The unsettled Arabs plunder and slay,' he commented sourly; 'the settled Arabs slander and cheat.'[13] A whole day was spent in inspecting the soldiers and mules, in despatching a dromedary-post with news of their safe arrival (and Burton's request for extra leave), and arbitrating between the claims of the rival Bedawin. On 21 December, they left camp bound for the White Mountain and Aynunah. Christmas proved a failure. Not only had the Dragoman killed their last turkey, he had also forgotten to bring the plum-pudding from El-Muwaylah. Although there was champagne, it was hardly suited for washing down tough mutton. New Year's Day was celebrated with whisky-punch, the evening ending with music and dancing.

It was now the height of the cotton season and Old Haji Wali extremely worried that the Fellahs of Zagazig in his absence would neglect to pay their various debts, began to malinger. He lost no time in leaving the Expedition and returning to Egypt. According to Burton, they later had the malicious satisfaction of hearing that he was forced to spend a long quarantine at Tor.

The old man had given Burton a hand-sketch of the most primitive kind. Fortunately, they had no difficulty in identifying Haji Wali's tree, a solitary mimosa growing out from the sands of the Shigdawayn gorge to the right of the caravan track. As soon as the washing-trough was brought up from Sharma, they began operations by digging a trench at least 12 feet deep close to the tree. There was not a trace of the precious metal. This immediately made them suspect that Haji Wali might have bought a pinch of gold from the Bedawin, and mixed it with a handful of surface material. Had the assayer at Alexandria played him a trick? Or had an exceptionally heavy downpour washed down auriferous 'tailings'? Burton, clutching at straws, preferred to believe the latter to be the case.

Everyone in camp spoke openly of Tibr (gold) stored in quills, carried behind the ear, and sold at Suez – not at Cairo for fear of the consequences. Not even the poorest of the Arabs, however, could be persuaded by promises or bribes to break the taboo of silence. Burton admitted that the whole story might have been a hoax. On the other hand, he believed there was also a cogent reason for their reticence; 'the open mouth would not long have led to a sound throat.'

They wasted a whole fortnight at Maghair Shu'ayb, Burton bitterly regretting that the time had not been given to South Midian. After a week of washing for metals here it was time to move farther afield. Their week spent at Makna from January 25 – 2 February justified the pleasant impression left on Burton by the first visit. On 26 January, a caravan of four camels for the two quarrymen and the guide set off southwards, carrying sacks, tools, and other necessaries. They returned on the morning of the third day, bringing back rich specimens which prompted Burton to have the place surveyed. The second search party, however, proved a failure.

They now cruised from Makna to El-Akabah. With the ship's ancient boiler honeycombed with holes, Burton decided it would be safer to steam by day and anchor by night in some small bay. By the time of their arrival on 7 February, a group of camels had gathered on the shore, while inland were some 3,000 north-west African pilgrims, the Hajji el-Magharibah. An equally large number had already preceded them to Suez. Letters from there informed Burton's party that cholera had broken out at Mecca and Jedda, killing ninety-eight a day in both places. The area once cleared of pilgrims, the ship's gun was fired, and after a similar response, they received the visit of the port officials.

Accompanying them was Mohammed ibn Jad el—'Alawi, who styled himself Shaykh of El-'Akabah. Under his guidance they rowed to the site of Elath. Disembarking at the northern palm-clump, Burton inspected El-Dar, the old halting-place of the pilgrim-caravan before New 'Akabah was founded. After making arrangements for a dromedary-post to Suez, he wrote officially to Prince Husayn Pasha, requesting that his Highness would exchange the *Mukhbir* for a more seaworthy steamer. Furthermore, the delay at Maghair Shu'ayb had exhausted their resources, and the Expedition needed another month's additional rations for men and mules. The application was speedily granted, and 'my wife,' Burton wrote, 'who had reached Cairo, saw that the execution of the order was not put off till the end of March.'

Following Burton's departure from Trieste, Isabel had spent most of her time at Opicina, correcting the proofs of *The Gold Mines of Midian*. Early in November she wrote to Luke Ionides as to the procedure to be followed once gold was found. 'You will of course be the first to know, and before the Khedive knows. Richard thinks that let us say Egyptian [funds] are 33 or 34 – the discovery will raise them to 40 or even 50. Now if it is really what he expects it must be done on a large scale. Richard does not mean to risk a single shilling. Your business is to keep the secret of the funds, and to watch and catch the moment we will give you notice of, and the instant there is a rise to make use of it and to give him a share of what you and Fitz make by his means….. There would be lots ready to do it…but we want to put the profit in the hands of friends and relatives.[14]

Arrangements had been made on this second expedition, for Isabel to make her way to Cairo and Suez as soon as she had finished the proof-reading. On landing at Alexandria, she found letters and instructions, which left her puzzled, since she was not to attempt to join 'unless I could do it in proper order.' It remained for her to discover what 'proper order' meant. After visiting Cairo, she made her way to Zagazig, where she visited Mrs Clarke and the Levick family, who were very kind to her.

She was eventually informed that a ship was to be sent out, and that she was to have the offer of going by it. She was told privately, however, that the Khedive and the Governor, Said Bey, were hoping that she would refuse. There was a complete lack of privacy aboard the *Sinnar*, and she would be turning some of the crew out of their quarters. She declined, therefore, to everyone's relief, taking small rooms at the Suez hotel instead where she spent most of her time catching up on her correspondence.

There was a Franciscan Convent of Italian monks near the inn where she passed an hour or so every day. Consul West and his wife were also most hospitable, lending her a huge white donkey which nobody could break. Isabel, however, managed to take long desert rides on it, though she admitted that the animal nearly dislocated all her bones. General Charles Gordon arrived when she was there, and stayed a week, 'which I enjoyed very much, for of course I used to see him every day. He was certainly very eccentric, but very charming. I say eccentric, until you got to know and understand him.'[15] She was then obliged to travel to Cairo for four days to superintend the sending of the supplies Burton needed.

With their arrival, Burton decided to press on to El-Muwaylah, finishing, by the way, their work on quartz-prospecting on the 'Akabah Gulf. Unforeseen circumstances had already prevented them on two occasions from visiting the mysterious Hisma. They now decided to devote their energies to its exploration. Unfortunately, it was rumoured that the Ma'azah had decided to supply them with transport, and had sent messages in all directions to collect the animals. In Burton's view, this appeared very much like a gathering of war-men, and rendered a distant march to the east highly inadvisable. This was additionally disappointing, since he had heard that the Hisma was a region full of archaeological interest.

They now left the region explored by Europeans, their line to the south and south-east covering new ground. They would be entering South Midian, which extended to El Hejaz. As the march might last longer than expected, Burton ordered fresh supplies from El-Muwaylah to meet them in the interior via Ziba. At Shuwak, they allowed the camels a day of rest, whilst they planned and sketched, dug into, and described, the ruins.

During their day's halt at Ziba, Burton inquired about the Jebel el-Fayruz. The chief trader pleaded ignorance. The others denied knowing anything about turquoises; there were no such stones; the mines were exhausted. Burton, however, said that he knew this coast was visited for turquoises by Europeans; and that the gem had been, and still was sold at Suez and Cairo. The few free days before the arrival of the *Sinnar* for the return to El-Muwaylah, gave Burton an opportunity for studying the Alpine ranges of maritime Midian. He was particularly keen to collect specimens of botany and natural history from an altitude hitherto unreached by any other traveller in Western Arabia. Furthermore, there was geography as well as mineralogy to be carried out.

At El-Muwaylah, the two Shaykhs were paid off, and dismissed with due ceremony. Provisions were brought from the fort to the cove, useless implements were placed in store, and mules embarked. Last, but not least, their tender Mukkbir was to be despatched with mail for Suez. The whole Expedition, apart from the sick who were left at the fort, was now bound southwards. After 12 hours' steaming, they ran carefully into Sharm Dumaygah. Burton having 'resolved to pass a day at these old quarters of a certain Haji Abdullah.'[16] From there, the corvette sailed on southwards to El Wijh.

On the day of their arrival, Burton sent a hurried letter of invitation to Mohammed 'Afnan, Shaykh of the Baliyy, inviting him to visit the Expedition, and to bring with him 70 camels and dromedaries. His tents being pitched at a distance of 3 days' long march in the interior, Burton determined not to waste a precious week at the end of the cold season, and the party was once more divided. Anton, the Greek, was left as storekeeper, with orders to pitch a camp, to collect as many provisions as possible, and to prepare for this last journey into the interior. One group was directed to march along the shore southwards. After inspecting a third Jebel el-Kebrit, they would bring back notices of the Wady Hamz. Meanwhile, Burton and his party would proceed in the *Sinnar* to El-Haura, a roundabout cruise of 100 miles to the south.

Having returned to El-Wijh, their last march was to be the Bada plain where Burton planned to collect specimens of a traditional coal-mine, which Ismail considered of the highest importance. The first question to Burton on his return was whether the fuel had been found, 'and a shade of disappointment appeared when the answer distinctly declared it a myth.' Although he was not yet despairing of finding coal in Arabia, 'we can hardly expect volcanic rock to yield it.'

An order was given for the return march on 5 April. Five days later, after riding 17 miles, they found themselves once more at the sea-board. Their kind host, Captain Hasan Bey, came to meet them in his gig to return them to the *Sinnar*, its quarter-deck dressed with flags as if for a ball. The next day saw them at El-Wijh.. There, Burton dispensed pay and bakhshish to the companions of his Desert march, and shipped the men and mules with the material collected during the southern journey. The ship set off for Suez on the morning of 12 April, anchoring for the night in one of the bays of Jebel N'uman. The next day placed them at the Sharm Yaharr, where Burton took final leave of his companions.

On 20 April, while Isabel was at church during the 'Office' for Holy Saturday, a messenger from the Governor put a slip of paper in her hand. 'The *Sinnar* is in sight, the *Emetic* will await you later on to meet the ship.'[17] She found Burton looking ill and tired. Some delay was again necessary in order to telegraph his arrival, to apply for a special train, and to sort and pack their 25 tons of specimens. At Zagazig, a splendid dinner had been prepared for Burton and his wife by Monsieur Camille Vetter, a French cotton-merchant from Ettlingen. An Englishman who happened to be at Suez wrote to the *Home News*, 1 June 1878, 'I had occasion to be at Suez on the return of Haj Abdullah (Dick Burton) from Midian last month, and I noted the sensation his arrival created. His name is as well known amongst the natives in Egypt as if he had passed all his days amongst them.'[18]

Burton was back at Cairo on 22 April. It was not until just over a week later, however, that the 'Viceroy graciously sent his Junior Master of Ceremonies' to welcome him back, and he was at once honoured with audiences at the Khedival Palace, 'Abidin, and by Prince Husayn Kamil Pasha at Gizeh. The Khedive expressed satisfaction at Burton's recent work, and ordered several measures to be carried out. One was an exhibition of mineralogy and archaeology, maps, plans and sketches at the Hippodrome, which he himself opened. They created much interest, Burton said, but the discovery of a mining-country, some three hundred miles long, once immensely wealthy, and ready to become wealthy once more, was not likely to be accepted by every one. Jealous and obstructive officials, as he described them, 'did not think much of it.' Rivals opposed it with even less ceremony. Burton agreed that there was much to criticise in the collection which, according to him, had been put together with extreme carelessness by M. Marie. Furthermore, the latter when publicly asked by the Khedive, whether he was sure that such and such specimens contained gold, replied evasively that, 'Midian is a fine mining country.' This was commented on sneeringly by Burton: 'But we must not be hard upon M. Marie. He is an engineer, utterly ignorant of mineralogy and of assaying; he was told off to do the duty, and he did it as well as he could – in other words, very badly.'[19]

Numerous concessions had been applied for, some even from as far away as Australia. The Viceroy, however, had decided that careful analysis of the specimens should be made at his private expense. In London, M. Ferdinand de Lesseps volunteered to send specimens of the rock to the Parisian Academie des Sciences. According to Burton, Ismail spontaneously renewed his verbal promise, 'that I should be honoured with a concession, or that a royalty of five percent on the general produce of the mine should be the reward of the discovery.' Meanwhile he was kept hard at work drawing up a concise general description of the province, reporting upon the political and other measures which could benefit Midian, and lastly, suggesting the means best calculated in his opinion for successfully working the mines. During this time, Burton wrote a despatch to the FO – or, rather, it was written for him by Isabel as the hand-writing shows – stating that he was 'preparing a report on the state of that country and its wonderful mineral wealth, which I shall forward to your Lordship through Mr. Vivian, Consul-General and Political Agent at Cairo.'[20]

The Khedive, ignoring a call from the Commissioners of the Debt for a full-scale inquiry into Egypt's financial situation, had set up a partial inquiry of his own on 27 January 1878. Faced with finding a qualified person to conduct it, Ismail picked on General Gordon, and brought him back from the Sudan in March, which was when Isabel had met him. His reputation for integrity, the weight his name carried with the British public, were sufficient in Ismail's eyes to give credence to the Commission's findings. According to the Earl of Cromer, 'inexperience in financial questions would, it was thought, lead him to accept the accuracy of any facts and figures which were laid before him by the Egyptian Government.' Negotiations with Gordon, however, were not long in breaking down, and he returned to the Sudan. 'It was apparent to every one concerned, including Gordon himself,' said Cromer, 'that he was not fitted to conduct any financial inquiry. He wrote at the time that he felt sure that he "was only to be a figurehead."'[21]

During Burton's last audience with the Khedive, Ismail 'ably and lucidly resumed the history of the past measures, and the steps which he proposed for the future.' This was to be the setting up of a Compagnie de Recherche with the object of undertaking a serious exploitation. Burton was then courteously dismissed, and requested to take charge of the specimens and personally superintend the work of assaying. He and Isabel left Cairo on 10 May, in company with their friend, Mr Garswood, C.E. On 12 May, they boarded the SS Austro-Hungarian *Austria*, arriving back at Trieste five days later.

It was almost a month later, after hearing that the specimens had arrived at the London Docks, that Burton wrote a long letter to the Foreign Office requesting leave:

My Lord,

On the 9th ult. when the Viceroy of Egypt gave me his last audience, his Highness expressed a desire that I should take back to England a sufficient quantity of metalliferous rocks brought back by the last expedition to Midian, superintend personally the analysis and forward to his Highness the official report. My reply was that I could not do so without the permission of H.M.'s Government, and that before proceeding northwards it would be necessary for me to visit the Consulate of Trieste.

As reported to your Lordship, I arrived at this Consular post on the 17th May..........

I venture to hope that H.M.'s Government will be pleased to approve of my proceedings in having opened up a country which, once rich in mineral wealth, promises even greater profit in the future when the appliances of modern science shall take the place of the rude working of the engines. It is unnecessary for me to enlarge upon the advantages which an enriched Egypt will offer to England and to Anglo-Egyptian creditors, or upon the gain resulting to English companies who will undertake, under the concessionists, the working of the mines. It is evident that so large a region, and so wealthy in mineralogical produce, can be opened up with a general advantage to all those whom it concerns.

The work of the analysis is delicate, and in these days when the starting of companies is a special profession, it requires special supervision. I shall be sorry to trust the 25 tons of specimens, collected with so much labour and expense by the last expedition, in any hands but my own. I therefore hope that your Lordship will take into consideration the special circumstances of the case, and will be pleased to allow me 2 months leave on urgent private affairs, between the end of June and the end of August.[22]

Leave was granted, and Burton decided to make the voyage by "long sea." He and Isabel left on the evening of 6 July, reaching Liverpool just under three weeks later.

CHAPTER THIRTY-SIX

FOOLS' GOLD

The Burtons spent only a fortnight or so in England. The day before leaving for the British Association for the Advancement of Science meeting in Dublin, Burton sent the inevitable letter to the Foreign Office asking for an extension of leave. 'My Lord,' he wrote, 'I regret to say that the state of my health and the necessity of taking the best advice in London compels me to apply to your Lordship for a prolongation of leave. I venture to hope that you will be pleased to allow me 3 additional months after the end of the present month when my leave expires.'[1] The following day the couple left by the night mail for Dublin. Bram Stoker, who was waiting at Westland Row station early next morning to meet the actor, Henry Irving, noticed two other people in the compartment. 'I could not but be struck by the strangers,' he wrote of his first meeting with the Burtons. 'The lady was a big, handsome, blonde woman, clever looking and capable. But the man riveted my attention. He was dark and forceful, and masterful and ruthless. I have never seen so iron a countenance.'[2]

The Burtons stayed at Malahide Castle with Lord Talbot and his family, and had a delightful time, according to Isabel, meeting old friends, and making many charming acquaintances. Burton's lecture to Section E, Geographical, on the Land of Midian, was delivered on 19 August.[3] The first of his three lectures to the Anthropological, also on Midian, took place the next day.

Burton, in fact, milked the subject of Midian for all it was worth, contributing numerous papers to learned journals into 1880. On 23 August, he lectured on the Ogham Runes and El Mushajjar, at Sir Samuel Ferguson's, Isabel having to copy 'yards of trees'.[4] He eventually followed it up by writing an account of it for the Royal Society of Literature, and then had it made up into a pamphlet.[5]

Once back in London, Isabel immediately set about correcting the proofs of her book, *A.E.I.*, due out in November. Burton's *The Gold Mines of Midian* had already appeared to mixed reviews. *The Athenaeum* found that there was 'a freshness about his narrative which must engross the attention of all who turn to the pages of his latest contribution to geographical literature.'[6] *Vanity Fair*, however, was sarcastically uncomplimentary. 'Mr. Burton professes to have discovered a "new Ophir" and "unworked California," and to have opened inexhaustible sources of wealth to the Eastern world. To a benefactor of mankind, the venial sin of a dull book will be easily forgiven. At the same time it is difficult to explain why an author of his power and reputation should have published such a book.'[7] *The Globe* also felt 'obliged to confess to a sense of weariness during its perusal,' nor was it convinced that 'the facts collected by the author, or even the fresh discoveries just reported, are sufficiently strong evidence to justify the classification of Midian with Australia or California as a great gold-bearing land.'[8]

Such scepticism had not stopped Isabel from building castles in the air. 'I don't think, when we are millionaires, as we are going to be you know in 2 years,' she assured Lord Houghton,' that I shall ever court the fashionable world. We shall lead the same life with a steam-yacht & a pied à terre in London. I mean to do heaps of good (our wants are simple), but we shall collect around us an entourage which will be a perfection – old friends & everybody will be somebody worth knowing.....It is a pleasant dream to look forward to. Dick has worked 36 years & I have helped him now nearly 18 years. It is time we should have something for it, & I think these Midian mines are going to prove our reward.'[9]

Managing to snatch a free fortnight in October, they first ran up to Lancashire to stay with 'Uncle Gerard,' and to Knowsley, where Lady Derby had a large house-party. They then went on to see 'more cousins' of Isabel's at Carlton Towers, Yorkshire, and from there to Lord Houghton at Fryston. Shortly after returning to London on 19 October, they paid a visit to Lord and Lady Salisbury at Hatfield, 'where we had the pleasure of being again in the same house with Lord Beaconsfield.'[10] W.H. Wilkins remarked that, though Disraeli had much in common with the Burtons, in particular his love of the East and mysticism, he never did anything for them. He suggested that Burton's strong anti-Semitic views had something to do with this neglect. Whether this was the case or not, Isabel made overtures once again to have Burton made a KCB, with similar depressing results.

Barely a month after his visit to the Foreign Secretary at Hatfield House, Burton wrote yet another letter to Lord Salisbury requesting a further extension of leave: 'My Lord, I have the honour to request that you will be pleased to prolong my leave of absence during the quarter ending February 1879. Dr. Garrod who is still treating me, considers that a longer rest in England is advisable. Moreover, the death of Mr. Bagshaw, late M.P. for Harwich, affects me as regards property, and leaving for the Continent at once would injure my interests.'[11] Despite Dr Garrod's advice, we may well suspect that Burton was fit enough to return to his, hardly onerous, duties at Trieste. It is true, of course, that both he and Isabel had arrived in England in a poor state of health. Since returning from Ireland, however, as Isabel explained to Albert Tootal, they had 'put themselves under the doctor, refused all invitations, and nursed themselves well and got on with their work.'[12] As for his uncle's death affecting Burton as regards property, this was a bare-faced lie. Bagshaw had died, aged 74, on 14 August, while the Burtons were in Ireland, leaving assets totalling just under £45,000. However, in his closely-written, twelve-page will, there is not a single reference to Burton.[13]

A few months earlier, *The Daily News* in its review of *The Gold Mines of Midian*, had pointedly observed that Burton appeared 'to find the consular service in general and the consulate at Trieste in particular, as a Frenchman said of journalism, a capital career *pour en sortir*.[14] This was a matter again exercising officials in the Foreign Office, as the following memos appended to Burton's despatch show: 'Since the spring of 1875, Captain Burton has been at his post only 16 months.' This was responded to by the Foreign Secretary: 'Grant this extension, but add that Lord Salisbury trusts that he will be able to return to the port at the end of the time. As a matter of discipline he might certainly be told this, that if he does not revisit his port soon, the audit office will make remarks about his salary, but I have never known Captain Burton's long absences from any of his consulates to be productive of inconvenience to the public service.'[15]

On 12 November, Maria Stisted, the younger of Burton's two nieces, had died at Dovercourt of tuberculosis, aged only twenty-nine. Isabel, in *The Life*, is totally silent about Maria's death, as she was about Sir Henry's three years earlier. Yet she wrote a deeply sincere and touching letter of condolence from Brighton to Georgiana at the time. 'Please know and feel,' she wrote in conclusion, 'that though the world looks dark, you have always a staunch friend in me. Dick feels Minnie's death fearfully. He telegraphed to me and writes every day about it.'[16] When Burton's latest book on Midian appeared, he dedicated it to the memory of his 'Much Loved Niece.'

Despite this recent bereavement, Burton went ahead with a lecture to the British National Association of Spiritualists at Great Russell Street on 2 December. The subject allotted to him was 'Spiritualism' (or rather Magnetism, Occultism, and similar matters) 'in Eastern Lands.' Burton's introductory remarks are interesting for being a clear testament of his scientific, rationalist, and sceptical outlook.

He described himself as an agnostic and a materialist. 'We avoid asserting that spirits do not exist...we students are addicted to "suspension of judgement" – a mental operation apparently distasteful to the multitude.' Personally, he ignored the existence of soul and spirit, 'feeling no want of a self within a self, an I within an I.' One of the best features of the time, in his opinion, was the gospel of what was derisively called 'Doubt and Denial.' It showed mankind's determination 'no longer to be fooled with the fallacies of many faiths; his longing to supplant the fatuous fires of belief by the pure daylight of present reason, and his resolve to shed the lively ray of science upon the dark deceits and delusions, the frauds, the follies, and the failures of the past.'

Lord Beaconsfield, he observed, is "all on the side of the Angels."[17] I cannot but hold to the apes. And if he be a fallen angel I, at least, am a Simiad that has done something to develop itself.' This, of course, echoed Thomas Huxley's devastating reply to Bishop Samuel Wilberforce at the 1860 meeting of the British Association at Oxford: 'If then... the question is put to me, would I rather have a miserable ape for my grandfather or a man highly endowed by nature and possessed of great means of influence, and yet who employs these faculties and that influence for the mere purpose of introducing ridicule into a grave scientific discussion – I unhesitatingly affirm my preference for the ape.'[18]

At the conclusion of Burton's speech, Isabel, who had been taking notes stood up and asked to be allowed to make a remark. She regretted, she said, that she could not join in the general applause which greeted his lecture, which appeared to her to cater for all parties. 'I need not tell you,' she added, 'that he little thought tonight to find his wife amongst his opponents.'[19]

Burton, allowed by the Chairman to reply, said that Mrs Burton had accused him of 'trimming.' He said he thought they would agree that it was the first time he had ever trimmed, and he could certainly promise never to do it again. '*A man's wife knows, perhaps, too much about him.* I think it scarcely fair to have his character drawn by his wife. I do not think gentlemen would go to their wives, or that wives would go to their husbands in order to know exactly what they are.'[20]

Throughout this time, from the latter part of 1878 and extending into early 1879, the minerals from Midian were being assayed. M. Ferdinand de Lesseps took charge of some cases of specimens for analysis, but 'the poorest stuff,' Burton claimed, 'had been supplied to him by M. Marie, and the results of which I never heard, were probably nil.'[21] Dr John Percy, the distinguished lecturer in Metallurgy at the Royal School of Mines, concluded his report on the specimens given to him, that three from the same locality contained gold. The amount, however, was small, although he considered its presence not altogether unsatisfactory, 'and certainly to justify further exploration.' He thought it likely that what Burton had brought home had been rejected by the ancients as unworkable. Further exploration might, in his opinion, lead to the discovery of workable stuff. It would, however, require a great deal of time.[22]

Burton, naturally, described Dr Percy's as a very able report. 'We cannot but form a different and far higher idea of its (Midian's) mineral capabilities,' he said, 'than those who determine them by the simple inspection of a few specimens. The learned Dr. Percy at once hits the mark when he surmises that worthless samples were brought home, and this would necessarily occur when no metallurgist, no practical prospector, was present with the Expedition....all the specimens were collected *à ciel ouvert*, and wholly without judgement.'[23] According to Isabel, Burton 'determined on the following expedition to choose and send his own specimens and prove a very different tale.' But since Burton was neither a trained metallurgist nor a practical prospector in any real sense, it is difficult to see how those results, by his own reasoning, could fail to be any different.

But what 'following expedition' did Isabel supposedly have in mind? On 20 January 1879, she hastily scrawled a draft letter to the Khedive undoubtedly at Burton's dictation, proposing terms which, 'in his humble opinion,' would 'be most advantageous to the Khedive as well as to Egypt and satisfactory to those capitalists who would be asked to undertake the workings of the Mines of Midian.'

Burton then went on to rule out the need for any further expedition as suggested by the Khedive at their last interview, 'the expenses to be defrayed by working the gold and silver works which it was believed lie near the seaboard.' He pointed out that the results of his explorations did not justify [it], and there was 'nothing to induce people to subscribe money for such a purpose particularly in the existing depression in all financial circles.'

Instead, he asked for a concession for all minerals, including precious stones (with the exception of pearls), its limits to run from Fort El Molilah in the north to Wadi Hamz in the south, and extending eastwards to the volcanic region known as Harrah. The concession would be made out in his name and that of Mr Frederick Stuart. In return, they would offer twelve percent of net profits, bearing in mind the cost and special difficulties attending the venture. He thought this fair and equable. He was able to start the following month, and asked his Highness 'to kindly give the matter consideration and honour him with a reply accordingly.'

Appended to this draft letter was an itemised account of the amount spent by Burton up to that date. This comprised four passages to and from Cairo, including freight of baggage and dragoman; Foreign Office deductions from his Consular salary resulting from his absence; the hotel bill for his stay at Cairo; sundry purchases for the expeditions plus the cost of analysis in England as ordered by the Khedive. The whole came to the not inconsiderable sum of £525 5s 5d, equivalent to almost £23,000 in contemporary money.[24]

A week later, Burton sent a letter to the Foreign Secretary asking for yet more leave:

My Lord,

I have the honour to forward a paper lately published which will explain the object of my addressing your Lordship. I have been delayed by the printers. The future of an ancient mining country measuring some 300 miles long is of vital importance to Egypt, especially in her present financial situation, and not of unimportance to England. But in these days, the beginning of mining operations is a work of delicacy and difficulty. Nothing is easier than to ruin the first diggings; any carelessness, rashness, or over-expenditure, will give the finest mine a bad name in the market, from which it will not recover. This will notably be the case in the gold mines of Midian, when to normal difficulties must be added that of dealing with the Bedawin.

I need hardly enumerate my qualifications for the task; they are probably known to your Lordship. Midian is a peculiar country, and I am the only man with sufficient knowledge to conduct the work. But for efficient superintendence of the mines till such time as they can manage themselves, some leave of absence from my post will be necessary, nor have I any wish either to take foreign service or to give up the Consulship at Trieste.

It is now proposed by those who are ready to form a syndicate, that I shall proceed to Egypt in March, and remain there and in Midian until the hot season sets in, that is about June. As regards the winter of 1879-80, I will apply to your Lordship in case my services are, as I expect they will be, required by the mines, during the cold or working season.

This request resulted in two long and caustic memos from unidentifiable FO officials. The first ran: 'I do not see why the Midian gold-digging business should be made an excuse for Captain Burton's perpetual absence from his post. The public would have a good ground if he is to be allowed to have half the pay of his post, and to be always working for his own advantage and self-glorification. It would possibly be only fair that Captain Burton should cease to draw Consular salary when employed in Midian, if it is true as he says with characteristic modesty, that he is the only man who can do what is required there. There are, at all events, many men more fitted than he is to be Consul at Trieste.'

The second memo carried on the same theme: 'The reason why Captain Burton has always had such so much leave, is that successive Secretaries of State have always granted him as much as he has asked for; but I have never known the reasons for this unvarying compliance. I can suggest the following reasons for again granting his application: 1) That he is of no particular use at Trieste; 2) That the Vice-Consul Mr. Brock always does the work very well during his absence; and also, I believe, when he is at Trieste; 3) That the discovery of mines would be of great value to Egypt at the present moment, and that Captain Burton's services would, doubtless, be especially useful for that purpose; 4) That Captain and Mrs. Burton are known to a great many people, and have the ear of the Press and the Public, and they would make a tremendous outcry if the request were to be refused.' Written in red ink underneath, is Lord Salisbury's laconic comment: 'For all which excellent reasons grant the request.'[25]

Following his meeting in Dublin, Bram Stoker met up again with Burton several times throughout January and February. At a supper held in Irving's rooms in Grafton Street on the night of 8 February, he described how 'The subdued light and the quietude gave me a better opportunity of studying Burton's face; in addition to the fact that this time I sat opposite to him and not beside him. The predominant characteristics were the darkness of the face – the desert burning; the strong mouth and nose, and jaw and forehead – the latter somewhat bold – and the strong, deep, resonant voice. My first impression of the man as of steel was consolidated and enhanced.'

Bram Stoker was also a guest at a party held on 21 February at Bailey's Hotel, South Kensington, by William Mullan, to celebrate the publication of Isabel's book, *A.E.I.* 'We were each of us presented with a copy laid before us on the table.'[26] Press reaction was generally highly favourable. *The Saturday Review* remarked that the book had all the special characteristics of the author. 'There is the same sense that the writer has discovered the keystone of European, Asiatic and African policy; there is the same burning desire to put everybody and everything right, from Lord Beaconsfield to the directors of Austrian Lloyd's; there is, finally, the same genuine belief that she and her husband are the object of the whole world's suspicion, envy, or admiration. Fortunately, there is also the same animation and instinct for seizing on the picturesque point in a landscape or an incident.'[27] *The Athenaeum* praised the book, remarking that nothing was beneath the author's notice, and nothing beyond it. One of her great charms, it said, 'is her outspoken and evident sincerity. The ink flows faster from her pen than it would in the case of most writers of the sterner sex, who are weighed down by a sense of responsibility.'[28]

The same issue of the journal gave an equally friendly reception to Burton's *The Land of Midian (Revisited)*. It thought that anyone would have to be sceptical, indeed, who still doubted the existence of valuable mineral treasures in the Land of Midian. Whatever the outcome of Burton's "prospecting", it went on, 'there can be no doubt that he has materially added to our geographical knowledge. The region had been surveyed, something of its geology and natural history studied, and several cities mentioned by Ptolemy identified, and the ruins of a classical temple discovered in the Wadi Hanz.' This, in fact, would be the most important and enduring aspect of Burton's exploration of the area. Among the numerous papers he communicated to learned journals was an extensive and detailed report to the Royal Geographical Society on the 'Itineraries of the Second Khedival Expedition; Memoir explaining the New Map of Midian made by the Egyptian Staff-Officers', together with a folding map.[29] As David Hogarth observed, 'When a party as well equipped as Burton's, led by so learned and capable an observer, has quartered a narrow district, with full leisure and opportunity for survey, that district may be held explored.'[30]

The Burtons split up in April. Isabel was to go straight back to Trieste, he intended making a little tour through Hamburg, Berlin, Leipzig, to see the publisher Tauchnitz, and Dresden. During her stay in Paris, Isabel slipped down waxed stairs at her hotel, suffering serious injuries to her leg and back. Instead of following medical advice and staying there for six weeks, she had herself bound up and carried to the Gare de Lyon on the fourth day. Arriving at Turin twenty-four hours later, she had to be conveyed to the hotel, feeling too unwell to carry on. However, next day she insisted on going on to Mestre. There she suffered badly from the heat and the pain in her leg, while waiting four hours for a train. When it did arrive, it was a slow train, without any coupe-lits. Burton met her, and she was carried home and put to bed, which she was unable to leave for a long time.

Despite undergoing a prolonged course of shampooing and soap baths, Isabel never regained her full health. 'Strong health and nerves I had hitherto looked upon as a sort of right of nature,' she wrote, 'and supposed everybody had them, and had never felt grateful for them as a blessing; but I began to learn what suffering was from this date.'[31] Burton took her up to Opicina for a large part of the summer, and parties of friends were invited up to dinner. As soon as she was well enough, she and Burton travelled extensively. They first stopped off at Graz in south-eastern Austria, no doubt for Burton to visit the seventeenth century Armoury, with its unique historical collection of armour and weapons. Whilst there, they also saw a great deal of Brugsch Bey, director of the school of Egyptology at Cairo.[32] They then carried on to Baden, where Isabel spent three weeks bathing, and drinking the waters, varied with excursions to Vienna, 'to hunt up swords in the Museum for Richard's "Sword" book.'

On 22 September, Lady Salisbury sent a letter of sympathy to Isabel. 'It was indeed most trying,' she wrote, 'to have that accident in Paris just as you were recovering from your illness in London. I suppose you are now thinking of the preparations for your Egyptian trip,' Lady Salisbury went on, 'unless the new Khedive has stopped it, which he is not likely to have done, as its success would redound so much to his own advantage.'[33] It will be remembered that Burton had informed the FO in his letter of 27 January, that an unspecified group who were about to form a syndicate wanted him to go to Egypt in March. So, what had prevented his going? Lady Salisbury's letter points to very important changes which had taken place since then.

Through the months of April and May, it became more and more apparent that no satisfactory solution of Egypt's difficulties was possible, so long as Ismail Pasha remained Khedive. Acting under Lord Salisbury's instructions, Sir Frank Lascelles informed Ismail on 19 June that the French and English Governments were 'agreed to advise your Highness officially to abdicate and to leave Egypt.' If he acted on this advice, they would see that he was given a suitable Civil List pension, and that the order of succession remained intact. Ismail asked for time to consider the matter. While doing so, he sent special agents to the Sultan, and money was spent on bribes. By then, the European powers were agreed that the Khedive should go. The Sultan, however, wanted the deposition to come from him, and to appoint Prince Halim.

On 25 June there was, said the Earl of Cromer, 'a last flicker of resistance' from Ismail. Nevertheless, it was purely token, Ismail having already stowed many of his valuables aboard his yacht. Diplomatic pressure at Constantinople had also been successful in ensuring that Prince Tewfik and not Prince Halim would succeed Ismail as Khedive. On 26 June, the Sultan pointedly sent a telegram to Cairo addressed 'to the ex-Khedive Ismail Pasha.' Four days later, Ismail left Cairo for Alexandria. At his request there was no official ceremony. 'A large crowd, however, assembled to witness his departure. The ladies of the harem, dressed in black, were present in carriages outside the station and were loud in their lamentations.'[34] At Alexandria he embarked on board his yacht, the *Mahroussa*, said his farewells to those who had come to see him off, and sailed away to a very comfortable retirement in Naples, where the King of Naples had placed a residence at his disposal.[35]

In July, Gordon decided to resign his governor-generalship. Writing from the Red Sea, en route to Massawah on a mission to the Negus of Abyssinia, he told Burton that he liked the new Khedive immensely; 'but I warn you that all Midian guiles will be wasted on him, and Mrs. Burton ought to have taken the £3,000 I offered her at Suez, and which she scoffed at, saying, "You would want that for gloves." ..... No, the days of Arabian Nights are over, and stern economy now rules. Tewfik seeks "honour, not honours."'[36]

However, on 15 October, Burton asked for, and was granted, three months' leave of absence, starting the following month.[37] Isabel was very unhappy at his decision to go once again to Egypt to try his luck with the mines. Still, 'as there were such great hopes depending on it, and there was not enough money for both of us, he had to go and I had to stay.' This claim is contradicted in a letter which a worried Isabel wrote to Lord Houghton at the end of December: 'Swinburne writes me quite alarmed at your report of Dick's health. Telegraph to me & tell me what you know, & I shall start by next steamer. He sailed on 5th for Egypt in glorious health. I had a letter on 12th, one on 16th, a telegram on 24th all jolly & S's letter has given me quite a shock. I have telegraphed to Cairo at once, and am preparing to start by steamer the day after tomorrow according to answer. I was to have joined in February.......'[38] It proved a false alarm, Burton being in perfectly good health. He got no further than Egypt, however, where, according to Isabel, he 'ate his heart out in impotent rage and disgust at his bad luck.'

Gordon's mission to the Negus of Abyssinia had also proved abortive. He had been arrested and then thrown out. After a forced march over the Abyssinian Mountains in the depths of winter, he arrived in Cairo on 2 January 1880, and he and Burton met for the first time. Burton wrote later that he was astonished to find how unlike Gordon was to all his photographs. 'No photograph had represented those calm benevolent blue eyes and that modest reserved and even shy expression, blent with simple dignity, which, where he was intimate, changed to the sympathetic frankness of a child's face.'[39]

Having enjoyed three months of Egyptian sunshine, if nothing else, Burton wrote again to the FO on 9 February 1880, asking to be allowed 2 months' prolongation of leave on urgent private affairs from 5 March till 5 May. 'I have met,' he said without elaborating, 'with unexpected delays on the part of the Egyptian Ministry.'[40] Whether on prompting from Burton, or of her own accord, which is the more likely, Isabel wrote to Gordon, who was now back in England, for his help: 'You write to an orb which is setting, ' he replied, 'or rather, is set. I have no power to aid your husband in any way...In fact, my dear Mrs. Burton, I have done for myself with this Govt. & you may count me a feather, for I am worth no more. Will you send this to your husband? He is a first-rate fellow, & I wish I had seen him long ago (scratch this out, for he will fear I am going to borrow money).....'[41]

Isabel who had not completely recovered from her fall nine months previously, now fell ill again. The doctors advised her to see a bone-setter in London. She immediately sent a telegram to Burton who told her to go. She was nearly three months under Dr Maclagan. She also went as advised to Hutton, the bone-setter, who found something wrong with her ankle, back, and arm, as a consequence of her fall. His treatment to her back, fortunately, kept pain at bay for a long time. Returning to London after paying a brief visit to the King of the Belgians, Gordon called several times on Isabel, who was laid up at her lodgings in Upper Montagu Street. 'I remember on April 15, 1880, he asked me if I knew the origin of the Union Jack, and he sat down on my hearthrug before the fire, cross-legged, with a bit of paper and a pair of scissors, and he made me 3 or 4 Union Jacks, of which I pasted one in my journal of that day, and I never saw him again.'[42]

Nothing having come of Isabel's direct attempts to get a KCB for Burton, it appears that she now tried to obtain promotion of some sort for him by the back door. Precisely what is not clear, since her letter is not extant. It will be remembered that, while at Damascus, Isabel had been accused by Sir Francis Goldsmid of being likely to influence Burton against the Jews. She replied that her husband would be quite unfitted for public life if he were to allow her to influence him in such a manner. On this occasion, however, she saw nothing incongruous in writing to Lady Salisbury to do exactly that. Given the FO's low opinion of Burton as Consul, of course, there was never a chance, but had there been, it was now too late. Beaconsfield's Conservative Government had fallen, to be replaced by a Liberal administration under Gladstone on 23 April; 'a public misfortune,' in the words of Queen Victoria. It did, however, provide Lady Salisbury with a perfect excuse, couched in suitably diplomatic language: 'My Dear Mrs. Burton, – I received your note yesterday, and I fear it is too late to do anything, as the lists went in yesterday, and Lord Beaconsfield is with the Queen today. So we must bear our misfortunes as best we can, and hope for better days. I cannot help feeling that this change is too violent to last long. But who can say? It is altogether so astonishing. As regards Captain Burton, I hope you will not lose anything. So valuable a public servant will, I hope, be sure of recognition whatever Government is in office.'[43]

Unfortunately, on or around 2 May, Burton received recognition of a rather more unwelcome sort. Returning to his hotel after dining out late in Alexandria, he was set upon by a gang and left unconscious and bleeding. It emerged from Isabel's brief account of this affair, that Burton carried around with him a divining rod for gold! This was stolen, as was the signet ring off his finger. According to Isabel, 'he kept it a profound secret in order that it should be no hindrance to his going back to work in the mines of Midian.'

It had not needed a prolonged stay in Egypt, of course, for Burton to discover that the gold mines of Midian were a complete dead letter. According to Isabel, the new Khedive, Tewfik, did not consider himself bound by anything his father had done. The plain fact is that, whatever his personal inclinations, he had no alternative but to accept tight Franco-British control over the nation's finances. As a result, Burton lost all the money which he had advanced and partly borrowed for paying expenses, which they were convinced would eventually be refunded. This amounted to over £500, as we have already seen. Isabel, herself, admitted to losing £728. The reason for Burton's failure to realize his dream of riches was quite clear to Isabel. 'In all the expeditions that my husband has undertaken to different mines,' she wrote, 'the minerals are *there*, but there has been too much dishonesty by those employed to carry it out, for my husband ever to have had his proper share, as Explorer, Discoverer, and Reporter, or Leader of these Expeditions. Every man has been feathering his own nest, even in a small way, regardless of the public good, and where any other nation has been mixed up, it has cheated in favour of its own country.'[44] It was a sort of cold comfort.

CHAPTER THIRTY-SEVEN

CAMOENS AND KASIDAH

During the latter part of his stay in Cairo, Burton had addressed two letters to the new Foreign Secretary, Lord Granville, on the resurgence of slave trafficking in Egypt. In the second of these, he claimed that the importation of slaves 'has now assumed an importance which threatens to become scandalous.'[1]

Once back in Trieste, Burton drew the Foreign Secretary's attention to a further branch of the trade, which he had failed to mention in his previous two letters. This involved Abyssinians, including the Galla tribes, which would need controlling through the Red Sea.[2]

Isabel, who inserted this correspondence in *The Life*, then went on to print, what she described as, a private letter which Burton wrote to Lord Granville, requesting a temporary appointment in that area as Slave Commissioner. He asked for 'a salary of from £1,600 to £2,000 a year (£1,600 would do if allowed to keep Trieste on half-pay, £350 per annum), the use of a gun-boat, and a roving-commission, independent of the Consul-General of Egypt, but to act in concert with a Consul (such as young Wylde) appointed to the Soudan.' Since it was to be only temporary, he asked 'to be allowed to keep Trieste to fall back on when my work is done, and as a home for my wife when she cannot be with me.' He was prepared to 'guarantee that placed in such a position, in two years' time, the Red Sea *shall be as clear of slaves as if slavery had never existed.*'[3]

The letter carries no address or date, nor does Isabel print Lord Granville's response to Burton's request. Since there is no trace of the document in the FO files, doubt has to be cast on its ever being sent. Furthermore, although printed in the context of letters written in 1880, it cannot belong to that date. It must post-date 1883, the year in which Sir Evelyn Baring returned to Egypt as British Agent and Consul-General, invested with plenipotentiary powers.

Besides writing letters on slavery to the FO while in Cairo, Burton also completed his translation of *Os Lusiadas*, which had occupied him, on and off, for over thirty years. Describing it in the Preface as the most pleasing literary labour of his life, one of his chief aims, he declared, had been 'to produce a translation which shall associate my name, not unpleasantly, with that of "my master, Camoens."'[4]

In her capacity as 'editor', Isabel thought it necessary to say a few words in a Preface of her own. She felt uniquely qualified for that role, having 'shared his travels in Portugal, his four years up-country in Brazil; learnt the language with him.' Unsurprisingly, she thought Burton's translation stood apart from the rest. She was afraid, nevertheless, that it was 'too aesthetic for the British Public, and will not meet with its due meed of appreciation as the common translations have done.'[5]

Although dated Trieste, 19 July, Isabel's Preface must have been written at the baths at Monfalcone at the head of the Adriatic. This is clear from a letter she sent to Georgiana Stisted some time after her return to Trieste. 'My dearest Georgie,' she wrote. 'On leaving you I came on to Trieste, arriving 29th May, and found Dick just attacked by a virulent gout. We went up to the mountains directly without waiting even to unpack my things or rest, and as thirty-one days did not relieve him, I took him to Monfalcone for mud baths, where we passed three weeks, and that did good. We then returned home to change our baggage and start for Ober Ammergau.'[6] Both visits were unofficial, of course. While Isabel could justifiably describe Monfalcone as being in Burton's consular district, Ober Ammergau was well beyond these limits.

Four hours after leaving Murnau, they took up quarters in a pretty cottage with two whitewashed little rooms, no sheets, one spoon, one glass, no table, and a pint of water in a pie-dish. Since the landlady only provided accommodation, they had to dine out at a small eating-house in the village. Following Mass and Communion, the play began at eight the following morning and lasted eight hours (eighteen acts) with an hour and a half interval for food and rest. They then sat down and minutely described Ober-Ammergau, the Play, and their impressions. Isabel told Georgiana that she thought it 'glorious, so impressive, simple, natural. Dick rather criticises it.'[7]

Burton described his object in attending this "great religious drama in the beautiful highlands of Bavaria" as being 'artistic and critical, with an Orientalistic and anthropological side; the wish to compare, haply to trace, some affinity between the survival of the Christian "mystery," and the living scenes of El-Islam and Meccah.'[8]

He admitted, however, to finding it impossible to draw such a parallel. 'The former is performed by a company of hereditary and professional players; the latter by a moving multitude of devotees.[9] Oberammagau runs through the holy history of the Judaeo-Christian world. Meccah touches only upon the legend of Adam and Eve at Arafat, the tradition of Abraham and Ishmael at Mun and the Ka'abah, and finally absorbs itself in the life and career of Mohammed.' City and village shared only one thing in common; 'both throve upon the contributions of the pious.'[10]

It is clear from the dating of his remarks 'To the Reader' prefacing his long poem, *The Kasidah*, that Burton was in Vienna, again unofficially, some time in November. It appears that two issues of the first edition, published by Bernard Quaritch, appeared that year. In all, only about two hundred were printed, and fewer than one hundred sold.[11] As in the case of his *Stone Talk*, Burton concealed his identity. The full title ran, 'The Kasidah (couplets) of Haji Abdu El-Yezdi, A Lay of the Higher Law, Translated by his Friend and Pupil, F.B.' [Frank Baker] Burton claimed in his Notes that Haji Abdu was, or so it was believed, a native of Darabghird in the Yezd Province. However, he always preferred to style himself El-Hichmakani, a facetious surname meaning 'Of No-Hall, Nowhere.' Besides a knack of language learning, he had a well-stored memory. Briefly, 'he had every talent save that of using his talents.'

Kasidah literally means a 'purpose poem', and was a genre whose form was invented by pre-Islamic Arabs. It could vary from as few as twenty to more than one hundred verses, and normally contained an account of the poet's journey. It became in the Muslim world the characteristic form for panegyric. It could also serve for religious purposes as well. Burton, in the *persona* of the Haji, uses it for his own reflections 'upon the endless variety of systems, maintained with equal confidence and sufficiency, by men of equal ability and honesty.' His aim was to discover a system which would reconcile their differences.[12]

Isabel, who printed the poem in its entirety in *The Life*,[13] claimed that Burton wrote it on his return from Mecca, when he could secure any privacy. She described it in terms of absurd hyperbole as 'the most exquisite gem of Oriental poetry that I have ever heard or imagined, nor do I believe it has its equal, either from the pen of Hafiz, Saadi, Shakespeare, Milton, Swinburne, or any other.' It reminded her of the Rubaiyat of Omar Khayyam, 'Yet the "Kasidah" was written in 1853 – the Rubaiyat he did not know until eight years later.'

Certainly the introductory *mis-en-scène*, is the Haji taking leave of the Caravan setting out for Mecca. There is no internal evidence, however, which indicates precisely when the poem was written. There are a couple of references in the Notes to Omar Khayyam, and the citing of two stanzas from Fitzgerald's 'translation' of that poet. If the Notes are contemporaneous with the poem, this would make it post 1859. Fitzgerald's version did not attract attention until 1860, when it was 'discovered' by D.G. Rossetti, and then by Swinburne. More significantly, the line in Canto II, stanza 7, 'Ah me! my race of threescore years is short.....', which was almost exactly Burton's age in the latter part of 1880, suggests that the poem was written late in life, and represents the summation of his mature views.

The Scotsman was not taken in by the claim that that the poem was by Haji Abdu El-Yezdi. In its review of 8 February 1881, it said that, 'we more than suspect that this learned Oriental is a Mrs. Harris – "there is no sich a person."' Fawn Brodie quite missed the point of the reviewer's remarks about Mrs Harris, who is the often referred to, but non-existent, friend of Mrs Gamp in Dickens's *Martin Chuzzlewit*.[14] As a result she reached the odd, if amusing, conclusion that, 'Burton must have been outraged to see his poem dismissed as the work of an obscure woman, and this may have crystallized his determination to keep his authorship secret.'[15]

The reviewer described the poem as supremely agnostic, and said that there was 'considerable ability shown in touching on the various points of science and religion "which make for" scepticism, and it treats modern theories in the attitude of doubt, in imitation of the fine scepticism, which speaks in the verses of Omar Khayyam.' *The Edinburgh Review*, however, in its review of Lady Burton's *The Life* in 1893, was scathing in its comments on *The Kasidah*. It said that, 'we are obliged to say that it does not appeal to us for anything but dulness, stupidity, obscurity, and not unfrequently, blasphemy...That a really able man should write such rubbish is not the least strange thing in the story of his life. That any one, even his wife, should be able to read it, and should dare to commend it, is perhaps still more strange.'[16]

It is clear from a letter Isabel wrote to a close friend around the middle of January 1881, that she and Richard were thoroughly enjoying their life back at Trieste. She was feeling a lot better, and could now walk a little. They spent their weekends together at Opicina, saving up all the week's correspondence and newspapers to read and doing their translations. They had even set up a shooting range and brought up foils. 'The Triestines think us mad as hatters to come up here, on account of the weather, which is "seasonable" – *bora*, snow, and frozen fingers.....In fact I have a winter I love, a quiet Darby and Joan by our own fireside, which I so seldom get.'[17]

Three months later she was mourning the death of Disraeli, who had exerted such a strong influence on her earlier life as the author of *Tancred*, and later as Conservative statesman. For Burton, it provided an opportunity for expressing veiled anti-Semitic sentiments in reflecting on Disraeli's career as politician and littérateur. It appears, however, to have been a year or more before he committed his thoughts to paper in, what is now, a very rare pamphlet, *Lord Beaconsfield. A Sketch*.[18] 'It was judged advisable,' he wrote, 'to withhold a realistic study of the departed statesman till time had dulled the blow, till the Dailies and the other teachers had issued those *documents à servir* which lurk in the biographical pigeon-hole, writ large and wanting only a last sentence and a date.'[19]

The English middle-classes, Burton claimed, never understood Disraeli. Conversely, Disraeli to his dying day, could never read his English public. Part of his inability, in Burton's opinion, arose from the condition of his education, but essentially it was racial. 'The truth is that Disraeli was in nature as in name a very Hebrew of the Hebrews. He underwent the Jewish within the normal week and the Christian rite in his early teens. But even the waters of baptism cannot wash away blood.'[20] The Jew, Burton contended, owed his phenomenal position to a peculiar racial vitality. 'He is born under exceptional conditions, and his career is not subject to the rule of the ordinary. He is the only cosmopolite....'[21]

As for the literary Disraeli, he and the poet Byron, in Burton's view, shared one thing in common. 'Both had that exceeding sensitiveness, that womanly (not effeminate) softness of heart which find safety only in self-concealment from the coarse, hard and cruel world that girds it.' While this was also Burton's view of himself, he could not forgive Disraeli's failure to reward his services. 'His Hebrew blood made him love those who loved his people, and hate with the fiery racial hate, all who did not....the best title to promotion in any of the services under his premiership was emphatically not merit. A few drops of the precious Ichor that filtered down from the veins of Abraham, Isaac and Jacob would have outweighed the gifts of an admirable Crichton.'[22]

That year the Burtons decided to take, what Isabel called, their gout baths, at Duino, and not Monfalcone. Duino was a village picturesquely situated on an eminence overhanging the Adriatic, two hours' drive from Trieste, up in the Karso. Towering over it was the 15th century castle and fortress of the Hohenlohes where, in the early years of the next century, the great Austro-German poet, Rainer Maria Rilke, began writing his Duino Elegies.[23] The tiny rural inn where the Burtons took up lodgings was only a stone's throw from the castle. They remained there for some six weeks, probably during the last two weeks of May and most of June, taking the baths and spending much of the time in the company of the invalid Princess, her two sons and three daughters. This was, of course, without the knowledge or permission of the Foreign Office.

Besides passing many a pleasant hour on the rocks with the Princesses, fishing for crabs, swimming, boating and telling ghost stories, Isabel appears to have derived equal enjoyment from hitting back at the critics of Burton's translation of The Lusiads. 'I wrote the "Reviewers"' at Duino June last,' she later told her friend, Miss Bishop, 'and I enjoyed doing it immensely. I put all the reviews in a row on a big table, and lashed myself into a spiteful humour one by one, so that my usually suave pen was dipped with gall and caustic.'[24]

Isabel was referring to 'The Reviewer Reviewed,' added by her, as 'A Postscript,' obviously with Burton's approval and active involvement, to Volume 2 of his Camoens, His Life and his Lusiads, 1881.'[25]

Describing Burton's translation as being 'the only scholarlike and complete 'Lusiads', she then proceeded to pour scorn on a number of papers and journals which had dared to express adverse opinions. For example, The Scotsman (21 Feb 1881) had said that, 'Captain Burton is no poet, and his translation is nearly the most unendurable we ever saw.' The Manchester Examiner (Jan 17 1881) had complained that 'Captain Burton does not write in the English of today, nor apparently the English which was either written or spoken at any given period of history...' 'Was I right or wrong,' she exclaimed, 'when I said that Burton's Lusiads was too aesthetic for the British public? In sixty years time it will be appreciated.'[26]

After returning to Trieste to take part in all the celebrations marking the arrival of the British Squadron, the Burtons left for Veldes on 8 August. 'Now Richard was absent without leave from the F.O.,' said Isabel, as if it were a unique occasion, 'but of course he never left without the Consulate being in the charge of a Vice-Consul, and all money affairs settled.'[27] As a result of Burton's unauthorised absence, they were extremely worried in case of meeting any one they knew. Their worst fears were realized. As they sat in the restaurant, in strode the Ambassador's own Chaplain at Vienna. Burton immediately bolted up to the bedroom. Isabel, however, thought it wiser to brazen it out. She, therefore, went up to the Chaplain and explained what they were doing. 'He burst out laughing,' according to Isabel, and supposedly said, "My dear child, I am just doing exactly the same thing myself."' As a result, Burton came down again, and the three spent a convivial evening together. The Burtons then went on to Tarvis, St Michele, and from there to Salzburg where, it appears, Burton was attending a scientific Congress, probably as a correspondent. Later, at Ischl, they parted company, Isabel ordered to go back to Marienbad for treatment, while Burton carried on to Vienna.

On 7 September, Isabel was so ill that she was in a quandary as to how she could get to Vienna. However, she had herself put into a *coupé*, with room to lie down, and remained there throughout the more than eleven hours' journey. On her arrival, she discovered that Burton had arranged a dinner-party to meet her, so she had to dress and receive. Two days later they returned to Trieste, changed baggage and immediately set off for Venice to attend the great Geographical Congress which opened on 15 September.[28]

After an absence of more than six weeks, the Burtons, accompanied by V.L.Cameron, who had been staying with them, returned to Trieste. Like Burton, Cameron was one of those who believed that Britain had a 'right' to exploit the natural resources of Africa. During his journey across the continent, as we have already seen, he had reported to the RGS on the evidence he had found of mineral wealth: coal, gold, copper, iron and silver. As ever, it was gold that haunted the imagination of Burton, despite his recent failure in Midian; wealth that would break the shackles binding him to the Foreign Office.

Although gold had been brought back to England from the Gold Coast since 1551, nothing had been done to develop the industry. James Irvine, a Liverpool entrepreneur, had been the first to notice the native gold-washings in the spring of 1858, sufficient grains of gold being obtained for them to live upon all through the rainy season. It was a French trader, M.J. Bonat, however, who was the first to form a company in 1880, the shares held mostly in Paris. Unfortunately, a shortage of capital forced Bonat to close down. He published a statement of his discoveries, and Irvine sent out Mr R.B.N. Walker whose bona fides Burton had vouched for, to investigate. The result was the formation of the Guinea Gold Coast Mining Co, with Burton's name on the Board of Directors. This fact was not disclosed either by Burton in the book of his journey, or in *The Life*.

James Irvine now wrote to Burton, asking him to go out to the Gold Coast on behalf of the Company. According to Isabel, 'he was to have all his expenses paid, a large sum for his report, and shares in the mines.'[29] Cameron, invited by Burton to accompany him, returned to England to make final preparations. Burton wrote, in his own inimitable style, to the Foreign Office to ask for the necessary leave:

> My last winter in Trieste was found very trying after so many years in the Tropics. The opening of the present cold season has already proved more trying still. Your Lordship would confer upon me a great favour by allowing me to pass the quarter between Nov. 15th and Feb. 16th on the West African coast, where I shall find a genial and congenial climate, and also I can do good work by throwing additional light on the rich gold diggings so strongly recommended by "Wanderings in West Africa" as far back as 1863. Six English establishments have already been established, and I know nothing so likely as the mining industry to benefit the negro, even in domestic slavery, more terrible perhaps than the export.[30]

The request was granted in a despatch of 17 October.

Two years earlier, an anonymous writer had published specimens of a new translation of the *One Thousand and One Nights* in the *New Quarterly Magazine*, Jan-April 1879. The cudgels on behalf of Edward Lane's translation, described by this writer as unreadable, were immediately taken up in *The Academy* by Lane's nephew, Reginald Stuart Poole. 'Style,' he wrote, 'is of course, a matter of taste. Lane's is founded on an attempt to retain the Oriental colour.' However, he went on, 'The question of English style, might for the present be dropped, as, if a translator could not translate, it little matters in what form his results appear. But it may be questioned whether an Arab edifice should be decorated with old English wall-papers.'[31]

The anonymous writer was John Payne, whose translation of the French poet, François Villon, in 1878, had received wide critical praise. Notice of his translation of *The Nights* being ready for publication now appeared in *The Athenaeum* on 5 November 1881. Burton wrote to the journal three weeks later, stating that many years earlier, in collaboration with his old and lamented friend, Dr F. Steinhaeuser of the Bombay Army, he had begun to translate the whole of the '1001 Nights.'

> The book, mutilated in Europe to a collection of fairy tales, and miscalled the Arabian Nights, is unique as a study of anthropology. I determined to render every word with the literalism of Urquhart's Rabelais, and to save the publisher the trouble by printing my translation at Brussels. But *non omnia possumus*. Although a host of friends has been eager to subscribe, my work is still unfinished; nor could it be finished without a year's hard labour. I rejoice, therefore, to see that Mr. John Payne, under the Villon Society, has addressed himself to a realistic translation, without "abridgements or suppressions." I have only to wish him success, and to express a hope that he is resolved *verbum reddere verbo*, without deference to any prejudice which would prevent his being perfectly truthful to the original. I want to see that the book has fair play, and if it is not treated as it deserves, I shall still have to print my own version. "Villon", however, makes me hope for the best.[32]

The Burtons left Trieste on 18 November for Venice. It was so raw, damp, and cold that everybody was ill. They took rooms at the Britannia Hotel until the time came to leave, and then had a good passage to Fiume, where they stayed with old friends for almost a week. On the 25th they had just finished writing up Burton's biography begun five years earlier on the voyage to India, when the call came for him to leave. 'I watched till the ship was out of sight,' Isabel wrote, 'and felt very lonely.'

CHAPTER THIRTY-EIGHT

TO THE GOLD COAST FOR GOLD

Burton spent a pleasant week at Lisbon, meeting up with old friends, besides passing many hours in the Camonian room in the Bibliotheca Nacional. According to Thomas Wright, Payne, supposing that Burton had made considerable progress with his translation of the *Arabian Nights*, had written to him on 28 November suggesting collaboration. Payne's letter reached Burton before he left Lisbon. He wrote back: 'In April, at the latest, I hope to have the pleasure of shaking hands with you in London, and then we will talk over the 1000 *Nights and a Night*. At present it is useless to say anything more than this – I shall be most happy to collaborate with you.......I am an intense admirer of your Villon.'[1]

Burton was a fortnight at Madeira, enjoying its quasi-tropical climate, and nostalgically recalling his last visit there with Isabel in 1863. Cameron, who had been unavoidably delayed in England, joined him on 8 January.[2] Despite failing at Sierra Leone to hire Krumen for the Gold Coast, Burton discovered 'none of that extreme bumptiousness and pugnacious impudence,' which he claimed to have been aware of twenty years earlier. 'Most Englishmen,' he said, 'know negroes of pure blood as well as "coloured persons," who, at Oxford and elsewhere, have shown themselves fully equal in intellect and capacity to the white races of Europe and America. These men afford incontestable proof that the negro can be civilized, and a high responsibility rests upon them as the representatives of possible progress.'[3] This was a world away, of course, from the sentiments he had expressed twenty years earlier in *Wanderings in West Africa*.

Burton and Cameron arrived at the gold port of Axim on 25 January 1882. Struck by its lack of sanitation, Burton suggested that the convicts in the castle prison should be taken away from 'shot drill' and other absurdities, and made to clean up the place. Labour, of course, would have to be light. 'Unfortunately, humanitarianism does not allow the lash without reference to headquarters.'[4] Even so, life at Axim was pleasant enough. Sunday, said Burton, was known as 24 hours of general idleness and revelry. 'Your African Christian,' he observed sarcastically, 'is meticulous upon the subject of the "Sabbath"; he will do as little as possible for 6 days, and scrupulously repose upon the seventh. Whether he keeps it "holy" is quite another matter, into which I do not care to enquire.'[5]

The first mining business they had to transact was with Kwamina Blay of Attabo, Ahin or King of Amrehia, Western Appolonia. Carried in a large red-lined log basket by four servants, he arrived in state on 28 January, dressed in sky-blue silk, with a waist-cloth of marigold yellow, and wearing a tall cocked hat with a huge red and white plume together with a dwarf pigtail. Burton was particularly interested in the swords carried by members of the king's suite, the blades of which called afoa, he discovered, were licked when swearing. Cameron sketched them for Burton's *Book of the Sword* then in preparation, Ahin Blay later sending him a specimen of a weapon with two divergent blades which was used to cut off noses and ears.

Before embarking on the interview, comprising numerous compliments, the handing over of presents and liquoring up, Burton persuaded the Ahin and his elders to sign the document, enabling him to take possession of the Izrah mine. The papers were duly attested by witnesses, the visit ending with a royal progress to the fort, where the District Commissioner did whatever else was necessary.

In similar strain to his assessment of Midian, but with considerably more justification, Burton described the whole land as being impregnated with the precious metal. 'I find it richer in sedimentary gold than California was in 1859 (sic).' Both he and Cameron came to the conclusion that the Izrah Concession would pay well. But instead of the routine shafting and tunnelling, it needed to be treated by hydraulicking, and washing away the thirty feet of auriferous soil which covered the reef.

On 8 February they left Arabokasu intending to march upon the Inyoko Concession. As Burton was still weak from over-exposure to the sun, and could do little work for a week, Cameron and James Irvine's agent, Mr Grant, canoed the three hundred or so yards of the Papa lagoon. They then struck north, and after walking for three-quarters of an hour they reached the Inyoko Concession. Cameron found the shaft still open, and observed that the valley contained many holes and washing pits. One was pointed out to him as having yielded 20 ounces of dust in one day. 'These reports,' Burton said, 'recall the glories of California and Australia in the olden time.'[6]

Early in the forenoon of the following day, Burton and Cameron were carried in hammocks to Kikam village. King Blay, too lame to leave his house, had sent his interpreter to show them the Yirima or 'Choke-full' reef. However, according to Burton, 'the man, doubtless influenced by some intrigue gave us wrong information.' They breakfasted in the house, but all the doors were bolted and locked, and his people (the Safahin Etié's) were hardly willing to serve them drinking water. Unwilling to stay any longer in this uninviting and uninteresting post, they ordered their hammocks and, setting out at noon, reached Axim by the early evening.

They had no other reason to complain of their week's trip, except its inordinate expense. 'Apparently one must be the owner of a rich gold-mine to live in and travel on the Gold Coast. We had already in a fortnight got through £50 of silver sent from England, and this too, without including the expenses of bed and board.'[7]

On 15 February, they proceeded down the coast to inspect the mining lands of Prince's River, east of Axim. They travelled by surf-boat, determined to shoot the banks going, and to collect botanical specimens. On the return journey, in company with the chief, Mra Kwami, Burton, seemingly for the first time in his exploring life, was forcibly struck by the oddity of travelling through someone else's land.

> Fancy a band of negro explorers marching uninvited through the Squire's manor, strewing his lawn and tennis-ground with all manner of rubbish, housing their belongings in his dining and drawing-room and best bedrooms which are at once vacated by his wife and family;…..Fancy then inquiring curiously about his superstitions, and sitting in his pew, asking for bits of his East window, and criticising his "fetish" in general, ending with patting him on the back and calling him a "jolly old cock." Finally, fancy the Squire greatly enjoying such treatment, and feeling bitterly hurt unless handled after this fashion.[8]

Payne had informed Burton early in the year that, as his first volume was in type, it apparently should go to press at once, but that he would be pleased to submit subsequent volumes to him. Terms were also suggested. Burton replied from Axim, in a letter which reached Payne on 20 March. '……Of course you must go to press at once. I deeply regret it, but on arriving in England my time will be so completely taken up by the Gold Coast that I shall not have a moment's leisure. It would be a useless expense to keep up the type. Your terms about the royalty are more than liberal. I cannot accept them, however, except for value received, and it remains to be seen what time is at my disposal.'[9]

After a long palaver with the three claimants of the Akankon mining-ground, Burton and Cameron left Axim once more on 24 February, for the head of the Ancobra River.[10] Next morning, they embarked aboard a run-down steam-launch with the chief Apo of Asanta, owner of the Ingotro concession. This proved to be the largest they had yet seen, although dense forest had prevented its wealth from being explored.

Early in March, having neglected simple precautions, Burton and Cameron 'went down' on the same day. Cameron was prostrated by a bilious attack, Burton by ague and fever. Despite these attacks, they went by launch to Tumento, where Cameron grew rapidly worse. He suffered from excruciating pains in the legs, and confessed that even during his crossing of Africa, he could remember nothing as severe. In Burton's case, his attacks had changed from tertian to quotidian, every new paroxysm leaving him in a state of utter helplessness.

Convinced that matters might easily get worse, Burton proposed leaving. Furthermore, they were running short of ready money, and tornadoes were occurring daily. They decided, therefore, to run down the coast in order to regain health and strength for a new departure. Part of their original plan had been to combine their visit to the Gold Coast with an exploration of the so-called Kong Mountains. They had found so much to do upon the Ancobra River, however, that they had no time for exploration. 'Geography,' said Burton, 'is good, but Gold is better.'[11]

His search, nevertheless, for the precious metal was now over. As had happened with his companion, Speke, a quarter of a century earlier, the younger and more resilient Cameron partially recovered health within a week. He, therefore, decided to go north again on his own to inspect the working mines about Takwa for a second time and to finish his map. While Burton spoke of not wishing to spoil Cameron's work by being an encumbrance. one suspects that, by this time, he had had his fill of concessions, and wanted, as well as needed, a rest, and a change of surroundings. He proposed running down south and revisiting his old quarters at Fernando Po and the Oil Rivers, hardly the ideal places to convalesce from malaria.

In the meantime, he had plenty to occupy himself, writing up his notes, and meeting all the managers of the working mines who passed through Axim. When at last he was ready to embark aboard the SS Loanda, his health gave way, and he found that his convalescence would be a long-drawn-out affair. Where better to spend it than Madeira? A ship bound there was lying in port, and on the evening of 28 March it set off northwards, Burton regaining health and strength with every breath. He landed at Madeira on 13 April, enjoying a month's rest before boarding Cameron's steamer bound for England.[12]

During Burton's absence, Isabel had fretted herself into feeling quite ill. She worked at her usual occupations for the poor, and preventing cruelty to animals, studying and writing, and carrying out all the numerous directions contained in his letters. However, her doctor, Prof Liebman, had now discovered that she had, what she described as, 'the germs of an internal complaint.' She had noticed throughout that year that she had been getting weaker and weaker in the fencing-school, sometimes even fainting. She, therefore, stopped going.

Immediately she received news of the date of Burton's arrival, she left Trieste, spending a few days at Venice before travelling on to London via Paris and Boulogne. Shortly after her arrival, she consulted an eminent surgeon about her illness. He advised an operation, which he claimed would be a trifling matter. Understandably, Isabel had an ingrained fear of the surgeon's knife and anaesthetics. Her greatest concern, nevertheless, was the fact that an operation would incapacitate her for a considerable length of time. This meant that she would be unable to care for Burton on his return. She was also afraid that knowing about her illness would worry him. So for his sake, she refused the operation and kept her illness a secret from her husband.

On 15 May she travelled to Liverpool, staying at Garswood with her uncle until Burton and Cameron arrived five days later. That night, James Irvine and the rest of the directors gave a dinner to welcome them back. Since it was also meant to serve as publicity for their business scheme, Irvine had corresponded with Burton in Madeira as to whether the event would be better held in London. Irvine favoured the capital, convinced that the Press would take more notice of it there. A suggestion had also been made to invite Lord Derby to preside over the dinner, his acceptance being thought more likely if the event were held in London. Burton had disagreed on several grounds, and his view prevailed.[13]

On 22 May, he and Isabel returned to London, where he was due to lecture at the Society of Arts on 'Gold on the Gold Coast.' No sooner had they arrived, however, than he was taken quite ill, and had to retire to bed. It was not until just over a week later he had recovered sufficiently to deliver his lecture. That same day he also wrote to the Foreign Secretary, reporting his arrival in England, and requesting 'that your Lordship will be pleased to allow me two months additional leave in order to prepare for return to Trieste.'

This novel and highly imaginative excuse was greeted with a flurry of memos by officials at the FO. 'The Consular Regulations as to leave,' one wrote resignedly, 'have never, so far as I recollect, been applicable to Capt. Burton's requests for leave so I suppose this must be granted. It is well, however, to note that he has started a new reg. on wh. to hang his applications, ie "time to prepare for his return to Trieste." This was responded to by William Grant, the Chief Clerk, who thought that Burton was 'abusing the liberty wh. has been so often granted him. "Two months to prepare for returning to Trieste,"after being absent for about 6 months is rather strong.' One month was suggested and eventually endorsed by the Foreign Secretary.[14]

Isabel for reasons of her own, was not entirely satisfied with this arrangement. She, therefore, employed her considerable female wiles a few days later in an attempt to wring a further concession from the Foreign Secretary. This would mean allowing Burton to stay until the 15th rather than the 8th of July, ostensibly in order to take her to Marienbad:

> I have got the commencement of an internal malady, [she wrote] brought on by drinking bad water, and the doctors say I can get rid of it by going to Marienbad, and I have to choose between that & being separated again from my husband whom I have not seen for so long...At the same time that I make my private wishes known to you, be assured, that sooner the service should in any way suffer, or Lord Granville be displeased after all his kindness, & further I hold greatly to his retaining Trieste, to which place I am devoted – I will cheerfully go to Marienbad alone, in spite of my nervousness at the idea....[15]

It was just the sort of appeal to which the gentlemanly Lord Granville could hardly be immune. The extra week was granted.

As a result of the favourable reports brought back by Burton and Cameron, a public company was formed with a capital of £30,000. Both Burton and Cameron were now given places on the Boards of two new companies: the African Gold Coast Syndicate, and West African Gold Fields Ltd. Needless to say these infringed consular regulations, and Burton kept quiet about them.

He was a month later than he had anticipated in calling on Payne. During this meeting, according to Thomas Wright, Burton told Payne that he had no manuscript of any kind for the *Thousand and One Nights* beyond 'a sheet or two of notes.' From what Burton supposedly said later, it seemed that these represented a mere syllabus of the contents of the Boulac edition of *The Nights* – the only one of the four printed texts, viz., Calcutta, Macnaghten, Boulac, and Breslau used and combined by Payne, with which Burton was then familiar. Wright's evidence, of course, has to be recognised from the outset as of dubious validity, since he was intent on proving that Burton plagiarised almost the whole of Payne's translation.[16]

That Burton had only notes at this stage is contrary, of course, to what Lord Redesdale, not the most trustworthy source, and later, Bram Stoker, had reported of their meetings with Burton. Since the latter did not see the actual manuscript, if there really was one, it is impossible to know how much or how little Burton had done by 1879. Nor can a letter, headed 'Trieste, April 19, 1881,' written to Gerald Massey in which Burton speaks of 'working as hard as ever at a Gold Book and a Sword book, at the Arabian Nights and at the Lyrics of Camoens....' be used as confirmation of his currently being engaged in translation of *The Nights*. The references in this letter to his 'having rushed off in despair on July 15,' to the throwing of an Orsini bomb, and to his book on the Gold Coast, clearly indicate that the letter belongs to the latter part of 1882.[17]

In spite of Burton's advice to Payne to go ahead and publish his first volume, he held it up until Burton's return to England. Three other volumes were ready for printing, and the remainder merely wanted fair copying. Burton, as he had forecast, was caught up with the Gold Coast affair, and the possibility of collaboration fell through. Payne's first volume duly appeared, and as a result it was arranged that Burton should read Payne's subsequent proofs. He declined, however, to accept any payment unless his help proved necessary. In the meantime, the literalism of the translation had created an extraordinary stir. On 3 June, Burton wrote to Payne, 'Please send me a lot of advertisements. I can place a multitude of copies. Mrs. Grundy is beginning to roar; already I hear the voice of her. And I know her to be an arrant w- and tell her so, and don't care a – for her.'[18]

Payne's translation, in fact, had been condemned even before it appeared. William Wright, Sir Thomas Adams's Professor of Arabic at Cambridge, had declared in the previous December, that, 'If the work be ever published, I hope the attention of the proper authorities may be called to it with a view to its suppression. If Mr. Payne be, as I am glad to hear, a good Arabic and Persian scholar, both Orientalists and the general literary public have need of his talents and labour in other fields. There are plenty of works in both languages in the departments of poetry, history, biography, maths, and philosophy which require to be edited and translated before we can arrive at a right appreciation of Arabic and Persian scholarship in its palmy days.'[19]

On 14 July, announcing his intended departure for Trieste the following day, Burton asked Lord Granville's permission 'to proceed via Marienbad by easy stages, as the state of my wife's health forbids her travelling alone or by long stages.'[20] This provoked an explosive comment a fortnight later in one of the FO memos. 'The impudence of these Burtons exceeds belief. I don't believe Mrs B. is the least ill.' Since the Burtons 'have started,' wrote another, '& give no address at any of the easy stages to Marienbad it is useless to ansr. this letter.'[21]

Whatever the truth about Isabel's state of health, Burton left for Paris ahead of her on 15 July in order to join Cameron.[22] Isabel followed with her niece, Blanche Pigott, a week later. 'There is always something amusing to people who have seen everything themselves,' said Isabel, 'in taking a fresh young girl about.' Blanche was just out of her convent, and 'Richard and I, having no children, thought it rather fun having a daughter.'[23] It was the last day of July when they eventually arrived at Trieste, the journey having 'occupied fifteen instead of three days,' Burton blandly informed the FO, 'as African ailments found me out in Paris and at Turin.'[24]

The following day saw the opening of the Grand International Exhibition by his Imperial Excellency, Archduke Karl Ludwig. The city was illuminated at night almost as brilliantly as Venice had been for the Congress. Unfortunately, the gala occasion was ruined by Italian extremists. On the afternoon of the second day, as Burton reported to the FO, an Orsini shell was thrown at a procession passing down the High Street with a band.[25] This resulted in at least one death, several wounded, some badly, one being Burton's friend, Dr Dorn, editor of the *Triester Zeitung*. The motive, Burton said, was evidently to injure the Exhibition, the date of its opening giving it a kind of political significance. The city was in a state of turmoil, and a demonstration was held in front of the Italian Consulate-General. Disorders, he said, were expected.'[26]

Remarking on this serious state of affairs two days later in a letter to Payne, Burton said he expected more to come and dare not leave his post. While his wife, therefore, was to go to Marienbad, he had to content himself with the baths at Montfalcone, only an hour away by rail.'[27] Writing again to Payne on 14 August, Burton alluded to a proposed special quarto edition of Payne's *Nights*. The scheme, however, fell through. 'I am delighted with the idea,' he said, 'for though not a bibliophile in practice (£ s. d. preventing) I am entirely in theory.' There was also an amusing reference to a clergyman, says Wright, who after giving his name for a copy withdrew it. 'If the Rev. A. miss this opportunity,' said Burton gravely, 'he can only blame himself. It is very sad but not to be helped…' Later in the letter, also tongue in cheek, Burton claimed that, 'The fair sex appears wild to get at the Nights. I have received notes from two upon the nice subject, with no end of complaints about stern *parients*, brothers and brothers-in-law.'

Meanwhile, Isabel and Blanche were thoroughly enjoying themselves going for walks and drives, reading, studying German, with the odd excursion thrown in. Among the reading matter provided for its English clientele at Hotel Klinger in Marienbad was *Vanity Fair*. That month, three articles appeared it in between August 12-26, on the Consular Service. The third, rather pointedly entitled 'Amateur Consuls,' was wholly devoted to Burton. 'Without for a moment wishing to imply that any duties attaching to Capt. Burton's official capacity are neglected,' the very well-informed writer began urbanely, 'it is evident from his frequent prolonged absences from his various posts, that those duties, whatever may be their nature, can very frequently be performed by a deputy. From Santos, for instance, he obtained 6 months leave to explore the San Francisco; from Damascus he was absent for a similar period in the land of Bashan. From Trieste he went for a whole winter again to the same historic locality; not to mention his lengthened absences in Iceland, and recently on the Gold Coast. He may, therefore, fairly be taken as a type of the Amateur Consul – that is to say of the distinguished public worker who is rewarded by a Consulate, with no very onerous duties attached to it.'[28]

An obviously worried and annoyed Isabel, lost no time in writing a very slanted letter to the editor. Disregarding that part of the article which mentioned Burton's failing his Arabic examination, she complained that it was 'likely to make the public think that Captain Burton is living on the fat of the land. I do not want any one to put the "evil eye" upon the poor hard-earned little £600 a year – *well* earned by forty years' hard toil.' It was true, she went on glibly, and completely falsely, 'that Government had sometimes, but not often, spared him for a few months at a time to do larger works, which have been for more general public benefit and wider extended good; but all the journeys quoted in *Vanity* have been undertaken *between* his various posts, when he has been out of employment, or during the usually *allowed* leave that *other* men spend in Pall Mall.' Isabel then went on to claim that the magazine was mistaken on another point, using a morally questionable argument to bolster her case. 'The higher the post and the more important the duties,' she wrote, 'the greater is the ambition to discharge them nobly. How much more keenly would one feel as an Eastern diplomat, for instance, than settling a dispute between the cook and the mate of a merchant vessel, or signing passports? Your "Series" writer must have dipped his pen in vinegar and gall when he wrote about the "much-prized posts."'[29]

Certainly Burton might be excused thinking that someone had put the "evil eye" on his business schemes. Although he had tried to keep his directorships a secret, it was only a matter of time before news reached the Foreign Office. On 31 August, he had the highly uncongenial task of informing James Irivine that Lord Granville had requested his resignation from the post of Director of the West African Gold Fields

Co. In his reply, deeply regretting this decision, Irvine pointed out that, 'this carried with it the resignation of all the other things, all the same you have undoubtedly no choice in the matter, though it is not so long ago since I saw Lord Granville's name not only as a Director, but actually as Managing Director of a large colliery, or something of that kind.' In fact, Irvine was well short of the mark. The enormously wealthy Earl was not only the owner of Shelton collieries in the Potteries, he was also the principal owner of the huge Etruria Iron Works. There was a paradox here.

Irvine thought it would be sufficient for Burton to withdraw quietly, without making his resignation public. 'We must grin and bear it,' he suggested, 'until we are in such a position that we can take a different stand.'[30] This was difficult advice to follow in the circumstances. As had previously happened with his equally ill-starred ventures in Iceland and Midian, Burton would be left considerably out of pocket. 'I was always sorry,' Isabel said plaintively, 'when he got on the mine track, because he always ended in one way.'[31]

Early in September, Burton wrote to the FO of having read in the papers that there was the possibility of trouble in Muslim India. It was only reasonable, therefore, he claimed, to expect that there might be religious excitement in Egypt. 'For some years,' he said, 'I have enlarged upon the fact that eastern sub-tropical Africa could supply a large number of fighting-men who would not sympathise with the Egyptians – or Indian Mahommedans......'

If the Government thought proper, he went on, 'I could proceed to Zanzibar whose language is familiar to me, and organise a first levy of one thousand men. Commander Cameron, R.N., C.B., etc., who is also a good Kisawahili scholar would willingly accompany me.'[32] Even had the FO been interested in his scheme, there was never any need for these levies, and Burton's hopes of being able to leave Trieste for East Africa were disappointed.

Burton was now keeping up a regular and frequent correspondence with John Payne. That same month, he asked for a loan of Payne's copy of the Macnaghten, or Calcutta edition, enquiring at the same time of his first volume. 'What news of Vol.1? I am very anxious to see it, and so are many female correspondents. I look forward with great pleasure to the work.'[33] Writing again after hearing that an attack was to be made on Payne's volume in the press, Burton said, 'Perhaps it is best to let Mr R.S. Poole sing his song (intolerant little cad!)....Your book has no end of enemies, and I can stir up a small wasp's (sic) nest without once appearing in the matter. The best answer will be showing up a few of Lane's mistakes, but this must be done with the greatest care, so that no hole can be picked in the critique.'[34]

Early in October, Burton expressed his delight at hearing that a new edition of Lane was to be published, since it would draw attention to the subject. 'I must see what can be done with reviewers. *Saturday* and I are at drawn daggers, and — — is such a stiff young she-prig that I hardly know what is to be done about him. However, I shall begin work at once by writing and collecting the vulnerable points of the clique. — — - is a very much hated man and there will be no difficulty.'[35]

Of the 'opposing clique', as he called it, Burton wrote on 8 October, 'In my own case I should encourage a row with this *bête noir*; but I can readily understand your reason for wanting to keep him or it quiet.' Burton went on, 'I shall write today to Cotton saying what your suggested, and also to Tedder (Librarian Athenaeum Club) to know how RSP is best hit. Tedder hates him – so do most people. Meanwhile you must (either yourself or by proxy) get a list of Lane's *laches*. I regret to say my copy of his *Modern Egyptians* has been lost or stolen, and with it are gone the lists of his errata I had drawn up many years ago. Of course I don't know Arabic, but who does? One may know a part of it, a corner of the field, but all! Bah! Many thanks for your notes on the three sonnets (Camoens). Most hearty thanks for the trouble you have taken. The remarks are those of a scholar and translator.'[36]

Burton read the first proofs of Volume 2 that month, and returned them to Payne on 21 October. 'It will only be prudent to prepare for an attack,' he said. 'I am perfectly ready to justify a complete translation of the book. And if I am obliged to say what I think about Lane's Edition there will be hard hitting. Of course I wish to leave his bones in peace, but R.S. Poole may make that impossible. Curious to see three editions of the 1,001 *Nights* advertised at the same time, not to speak of the bastard.[37] I return you nine sheets [of proofs] by parcel post registered. You have done your work very well, and my part is confined to a very small amount of scribble which you will rub out at discretion.'[38] Later, Burton said that Payne required no assistance of any kind. He, therefore, refused any payment for reading the proofs.

Having failed only the previous month to persuade the FO to send him to Zanzibar, Burton was suddenly asked, out of the blue, to proceed on an important Government mission. At 4.40 p.m. on 27 October, he received an official telegram which ran: 'H.M.'s Government wish to avail themselves of your knowledge of Bedouins and the Sinai country, to assist in the search for Professor Palmer. There is a chance of his being still alive, though bodies of his companions, Charrington and Gill, have been found. Proceed at once to Ghazzeh; place yourself in communication with Consul Moore, who has gone from Jerusalem to institute enquiry.' A delighted Burton immediately wired back: 'Telegram received. Ready to start by first steamer. Will draw £100. Want gunboat from Alexandria to Ghazzeh or Sinai. Letter follows.'[39]

CHAPTER THIRTY-NINE

FIND PALMER!

European domination in Egypt was immediately reasserted following the abdication of Ismail. The financial and political measures subsequently carried out, however, did nothing to win over the forces of resistance that had grown up under the Khedive. A nationalist group had already come into being within the Assembly, prominent among whom was Sharif Pasha, prime minister from April to August 1879. In the army, a group of disaffected officers led by Arabi Pasha was deeply resentful of European control of their country. By 1881 these two groups had merged to form the National Party, al-Hizb al-Watani.

It was an uneasy alliance, and open tension appeared with a petition drawn up in January 1881 by Arabi and his colleagues against the war minister, Rifq Pasha, a Circassian. They were arrested and court-martialled, but released by mutineers. Tewfiq capitulated, dismissed Rifq, and appointed Barudi Pasha, one of Arabi's friends. The Arabists, nevertheless, still felt themselves under threat. A military demonstration in Cairo in Sept 1881 forced Tewfiq to appoint a new ministry under Sharif and to convoke the Assembly.

Meanwhile, the European powers were becoming alarmed at this turn of events. An Anglo-French note sent in January 1882 with the intention of bolstering the Khedive's position had precisely the opposite effect. Sharif resigned, and Barudi became prime minister with Arabi as his war minister. Rioting broke out on 11 June after British and French naval forces had been sent to Alexandria. Several hundred were killed or wounded, among the latter being the British Consul, Sir Charles Cookson. These riots forced Gladstone to concentrate on the Egyptian crisis. Although against military intervention, on 15 June the British cabinet was forced to consider this possibility.

Just over a week later, a conference of European powers was held in Constantinople to consider what could be done to persuade Turkey to intervene in Egypt.[1] The next day, Britain's hand was forced further by the exclusion of their Controllers-General from a sitting of the Nationalist Ministry in Cairo. At the same time, Arabi announced that any military intervention would be resisted by force.

Although the British cabinet was still reluctant to use troops, military planning went ahead. On 3 July, Sir Garnet Wolseley produced an outline plan for the employment of two infantry divisions and cavalry brigade for the seizure of the Canal, followed in due course by an advance on Cairo. The next day, secret orders were issued to the commanders of the chosen units. The Government still hoped that, if it came to intervention, this might be limited to the protection of the Canal. Nevertheless, as a precautionary measure, two battalions and a company of engineers were ordered from Malta to Cyprus under Major-General Alison, ready to act in conjunction with the Royal Navy.

So far as the origin and purpose of the mission are known, Palmer was sent by Gladstone's

Government to attempt to win over the Arab tribes and prevent their supporting the Egyptian rebels. He was also to use his influence backed by Egyptian gold, to safeguard the Suez Canal from Arab attack, and provide for its repair after possible damage at the hands of partisans of Arabi. On his arrival in Alexandria on 5 July 1882, Palmer received instructions from the naval commander, Admiral Sir Beauchamp Seymour, to proceed to Jaffa. From there, he was to enter the desert and make his way to Suez, interviewing the principal shaykhs along the route.

Meanwhile, rebel construction of seaward fortifications at Alexandria continued apace, causing concern to Admiral Seymour, while the presence of threatening Arab bands along the Canal, gave rise to fears for its safety. On 10 July, Seymour issued an ultimatum on his own authority that, unless the forts were surrendered to him within twenty-four hours, he would open fire. That evening French warships sailed away for Port Said, refusing to participate in the affair. After a heavy naval bombardment, the batteries were silenced by late afternoon. The following day, Arabi evacuated his troops and withdrew inland, leaving Alexandria in flames, while mobs roamed the streets looting and wreaking vengeance on any Europeans they could find. It was not until 14 July that Seymour landed seamen and marines to fight the fires and restore order.

On 11 July, Palmer had vanished, but 'Abdallah Effendi was riding his camel through the desert in great state, armed and dressed in the richest Syrian style,' giving handsome presents to his old acquaintances among the Tiyaj, and securing their support for the Khedive's cause against the rebel subjects of Egypt. The attitude of the Shaykhs appeared all that could be desired, Palmer reporting in optimistic terms that he had 'got hold of some of the very men whom Arabi Pasha had been trying to get on his own side, and when they are wanted I can have every Bedawi at my call from Suez to Gaza. I am certain of my success.'[2]

After three weeks' disappearance in the desert, Palmer joined the fleet at Suez on 1 August. The next day he was in the first boat that landed for the occupation of the port. He was now appointed interpreter-in-chief to HM's forces in Egypt, and placed on the staff of Admiral Sir W. Hewett, commander of naval operations in the Red Sea. Palmer, himself, was convinced that with £20,000 to £30,000 to buy their allegiance, he could raise a force of 50,000 Bedouin to guard or unblock the Suez Canal. On 6 August, a sum of £20,000 was placed at his disposal by the admiral, but Lord Northbrooke, the first Lord of the Admiralty, telegraphed his instructions that while Palmer was to keep the Bedouin 'available for patrol or transport duty,' he was only to spend 'a reasonable amount' until General Sir Garnet Wolseley arrived and could be consulted.

Palmer had been busily engaged for several days in arranging for a supply of camels for the army, but on 8 August he set out towards Nakhl to meet an assembly of leading shaykhs whom he had convened to arrange the final terms of their alliance. In accordance with Lord Northbrook's instructions, he took with him only £3,000 in English gold for the purpose, to begin with. He was ordered to take a naval officer as a guarantee of his official status, and chose Flag-Lt Harold Charrington. Captain William John Gill, RE, the well-known traveller also accompanied him, with the intention of cutting the telegraph wire which crossed the desert, and connected Cairo with Constantinople.[3] There were also two servants, besides camel drivers, and a certain Meter Abu-Sofia who, posing as a prominent shaykh, was engaged to act as guide and protector. It was the last time that Palmer and his companions were seen alive. The popular account at the time was that they were ambushed by Bedawi, and offered the choice of either being shot or jumping over a precipice. It was said that Charrington and Gill elected to be shot, and Palmer, covering his eyes, jumped over the precipice.

There is nothing in either Burton's or Isabel's account to suggest that he encountered any problems in going on this mission. However, as the FO despatches show, it was touch and go at first as to whether he would receive permission, and then, having arrived, whether he would be allowed to stay. In the event, he contrived to be away from Trieste for six weeks.

The day after receiving the telegram, Burton wrote to Lord Granville, returning thanks for the confidence shown in him by HM's Government. The telegram directing him to proceed to Ghazzah [Gaza] he said, had arrived late the previous evening, and was answered early that morning. Unfortunately, as he pointed out, HMSS, *Iris*, and the Austro-Hungarian weekly steamer sailed on Friday. There was, therefore, no possibility of his leaving Trieste till 3 November by Austrian-Lloyds. He had telegraphed his intention of drawing £100 sterling, and a voucher would be kept showing how that sum was spent.

If his friend, Professor Palmer was still alive, detained, as he hoped, by the Bedawin, it would be highly advisable that he should proceed from Alexandria to Ghazzah, or to Tor harbour in the so-called Sinaitic peninsula, on board one of HM's gun-boats. The appearance of a ship-of-war in those waters always exerted an influence which extended far and wide. He would confer with HM's Consul at Alexandria, and might possibly need to consult with HM's Consul-General at Cairo. Ghazza and Sinai were both distant places inhabited by wholly unconnected tribes of the Bedawin. Burton assured Lord Granville, that not a moment would be wasted. If there was any decisive intelligence concerning Professor Palmer to hand, he hoped that it would be telegraphed to him without delay.[4]

This carried the following memo: 'The Admiralty will want Consul Moore to start at once with Hopkin Effendi. Captain Burton not being able to start until November 3rd, it hardly seems worth his while going at all. Shall we telegraph to stop him or ask Admiralty?'

Although I have not seen a copy of the telegram in question, Burton's reply implies that the original request was countermanded. He telegraphed back: 'My passage being paid and preparations complete, may I run to Alexandria and Cairo to make sure, and come back quickly? Steamer sails early tomorrow.'[5] The memo responding to this ran: 'May go to Egypt as his passage is paid. Copy to Admiralty. What answer?' Permission was telegraphed that day.

Burton left Trieste by the first steamer, 3 November, and landed, late in the evening at Alexandria, five days later. The next morning Burton called at HM's Consulate and the office of the *Egyptian Gazette*. Here he was shown a different version of the affair, which had appeared in the local journal El-Ahram (*Les Pyramides*). This reported that the party was attacked by the Bedawin in Wady Sadr where all were killed, and that the guide Abu Safih (properly Matr Nasser) ran away with the bag containing the money. This probable version of what had taken place, afterwards confirmed by Colonel Warren, ignored, according to Burton, all details concerning the unlikely offer of different deaths, and Prof Palmer's throwing himself from the cliff. Burton telegraphed Lord Granville on the morning of 9 November, stating that he was not satisfied with reports of the deaths, and requesting permission to visit Suez. A letter would follow.[6] This carried the memo, 'There does not seem to be any advantage to his going to Suez, especially with what the Admiralty say with regard to possible friction between him and Colonel Warren. The Admiralty say that Lord Granville proposes to instruct him to return to his post. Wait until receipt of promised letter.'

Having learned what little he could from Captain Fitzroy, the senior naval officer, Burton proceeded to Cairo two days later. Here he called upon Lord Dufferin, Ambassador at the Porte, who had lately arrived in Egypt as British Commissioner to report on a scheme of reorganization, and the Consul-General, Sir Edward Malet. From there, Burton took a train to Suez.

From Zagazig to Suez was one of the most dangerous bits of railway travelled over by Europeans. A rickety stretch of twenty-six miles eventually brought him to Ismailiyeh, from where Wolseley's forces had marched on Cairo, and won a victory over Arabi at Tel-el-Kebir two months earlier.[7] From Ismailiyeh, Burton entered the wilderness, Arabia Deserta. 'The features are familiar,' he remarked, 'but they are ever fresh and they never pall.'

At the Suez Hotel on 14 November, he met up with Mr Consul West, Col (later Sir Charles) Warren, Lieutenants Haynes and Burton, and Captain Stephenson of H.M.S. *Carysfort*. As a result, Burton decided to return to Cairo to meet Moore from Ghazzah. 'Mr. Consul Moore is expected at Cairo on the 18th inst.,' he informed Lord Granville, 'and from him I expect to hear the latest intelligence concerning the assassins.'8 Burton left two days later than intended, supplied by Col Warren with a list of twenty-one names of the Bedawin, Terabin, Huwaytat, and their sub-tribes, the Dabbur, allegedly involved in the murders. These men were reported to have fled north towards Ghazzah, and to have taken refuge in Ottoman dominions, 'a fact suggesting that enquiry best be made in that direction.'

Burton left the train at Zagazig, passing the night in discussions with Mr Charles Clarke who had accompanied him to Midian. He had also been of great service to the British Army under Wolseley. Clarke, in fact, had been invited to join the Palmer mission. However, although on friendly terms with the powerful Bedawin chief, Sulayman Pasha El-Abazeh, he had foreseen disaster and declined. He promised Burton privately to collect information from the people, a potentially dangerous undertaking since he was stationed with a wife and young family on the edge of the desert.

Meeting up with Consul Moore at Cairo, Burton found that he was also convinced that much could be done at Ghazzah. After calling again upon Lord Dufferin and Sir Edward Malet, who both thought his presence there might prove advantageous, Burton left Cairo four days later. After consulting with Captain Fitzroy and Vice-Consul Jago at Alexandria, Burton telegraphed the FO for a gunboat to take him to Ghazzah, Jaffa, and back.

The vessel, HMS *Condor*, reached Minat (Ghazzah's harbour) on the afternoon of 27 November, somewhat too late to land. Next morning they took off a missionary, the Rev Schapira. He informed Burton that around 10 November, a fellah of Ghazzah named Mohammed al Khaysh, had reported to certain Christians, that a white man had been seen wandering in the east of the so-called Sinaitic Desert. The wanderer had met up with a tribe near El Akabar, and had approached the natives saying in true Arab fashion, "I am under your protection." When Col Warren was searching the wilderness, this fugitive was passed on to another tribe. He might have been the Syrian Christian from Beirut, Burton thought, engaged by Professor Palmer as an interpreter, or the Jewish servant whose relatives lived at Jaffa.

The following evening the *Condor* anchored off Jaffa, and M. Schapira and Burton agreed on their plan of operations. Next morning Commander Jeffreys landed Burton with the necessary ceremony, and, accompanied by the missionary, called upon the Consular Agent and the Turkish Governor. While in their presence, Burton received a telegram from the Foreign Secretary ordering him to return immediately to Trieste.

Writing to Lord Granville on 11 December, the day following his return, Burton admitted that his mission had clearly been hopeless:

> With all respect for the learning and knowledge of my friend, Professor Palmer, I cannot conceal from myself the marvellous imprudence of his proceedings. It has been suggested that his long and toilsome desert drive from Ghazzah to Suez in the mid-summer heats after many quiet years of English life may have somewhat affected his brain. He probably relied upon the short experience of a winter's march thirteen years earlier, and trusted to the honour of notorious thieves. He had been warned that, if taken prisoner, his life would be forfeited. Locally it was well known that he was proceeding in time of war under cover of buying camels, to raise the Bedawin of the Tih against the Egyptian rebels. He carried a large sum in gold.

Burton was confident that all the culprits would eventually be arrested, but the task was by no means so easy or so simple as had been reported. They would take refuge in Turkish territory, and the local Syrian authorities would do their best to avoid making enemies.

He expressed regret at not having volunteered at first to lead the expedition. Unfortunately, he had heard of the reported catastrophe only after Col Warren had been appointed to do the work. 'That officer,' he wrote, 'has shown great energy and tact in all his expeditions, but my proceedings would have been wholly different.'[9]

It is clear from a letter Burton wrote to Ouida some time in January that he was incensed at being peremptorily summoned home from Jaffa. 'This is simply making a fool of me. They wanted my name while the House of C. was sitting and then – nada [Spanish = nothing]. However I hope soon to throw up their rotten Consulate & start in life free. I've sent an article to Cornhill – if they dare print so much truth. We are not governing enough – England's normal fault in her Conquests. But Lord Dufferin is a first-rate man and if the ministers obey him all will be well.'[10]

Burton had written to Payne about the so-called Kama Shastra Society on 5 August 1882, three months before setting out for Egypt. 'I hope,' he wrote, ' you will not forget my friend, F.F. Arbuthnot, and benefit him by your advice about publishing when he applies to you for it. He has undertaken a peculiar branch of literature - the Hindu Erotic, which promises well.' Burton followed this up on 23 December, informing Payne of Arbuthnot's intention of paying him a visit. 'He has founded a society consisting of himself and myself,' ending his letter after sketching the idea, 'I hope that you will enjoy it.' Three weeks later, on 15 January 1883, he asked Payne if Arbuthnot had sent him his Vatsyayana [ie *Kama Sutra*]. 'He and I have started a Hindu Kama Shastra (*Ars Amoris* Society). It will make the Brit(ish) Pub(lic) stare. Please encourage him.'

When returning portions of Payne's proofs of the *Nights* in May, he wrote: 'You are "drawing it very mild." Has there been any unpleasantness about plain-speaking? Poor Abu Hassan is (as it were) castrated. I should say, "Be bold" (*Audace*, etc.) only you know better than I how far you can go and cannot go. I should simply translate every word.'[11] Later that month, he touched on the taboo subject of pederasty. 'Unfortunately,' Burton wrote, 'it is these offences against nature (which come so naturally to Greece and Persia, and which belong strictly to their fervid age) that give the book so much of its ethnological value.' He then referred to a paper which he had written showing the geographical limit of these offences, and drew a trumpet shape – 'a broad band across Europe and Asia, widening out into China and embracing all (aboriginal) America.'

'Curious is it not? Beyond the limits the practice is purely sporadic, within them endemic. I shall publish it some day and surprise the world. I don't live in England and I don't care a damn for public opinion. I would rather tread on Mrs. Grundy's pet corn than not. She may howl on her * * * * * * to her heart's content.'[12]

Quite out of the blue, it appears, Burton took a great dislike to their flat in Trieste where they had been living for over ten years. However, it appeared providential to Isabel later. The drainage became incurably bad, and after Burton fell really ill and his heart weak, it would have been impossible for him to climb the stairs. They ransacked the whole of Trieste, but found only one house suitable, the Palazzo Gossleth, and that was occupied. Providentially, it became vacant in June, and they moved in the following month.

Built by an English merchant at Largo del Promotorie, it had twenty rooms and an entrance large enough to drive a carriage through. Its numerous windows provided a marvellous panoramic view of the city and the Adriatic beyond. There was also a very large garden and campagna (orchard), overlooking the gulf in which the Austrian fleet always anchored.

Detesting little rooms, Burton insisted on having the biggest one in the house – so large that he could divide it into four parts, using one for sleeping, another for dressing, a third for writing, and the fourth for breakfasting. No matter that it faced directly north, received the full blast of the Bora, and never saw the sun. Despite being thoroughly heated in winter with a large stove, the badly-fitting sash-windows let in draughts, and everything inside got damp. To keep himself warm, Burton wore a fur-lined coat all day, and slept at night between buffalo-skins. He also provided himself with a little den, where he could turn the key on all intruders, when he was extra busy. It was only after they had been there for four years, that Isabel succeeded in persuading him to change to the best room in the house, which faced to the south and west.

They swam and bathed throughout that summer, discovering for the first time found that this exercise did not agree with them, and that their long swimming days were over. Instead of rising at 3 or 4 a.m. as they had done throughout their twenty-years of married life, they now got up at the comparatively late hour, for them of 6 or 6.30 a.m. They read and wrote a great deal in the garden, often spending much of the day there.

On 24 August, Burton wrote to Payne, 'Please keep up in Vol. V this literality in which you began. My test is that every Arab word should have its equivalent English....Pity we can't manage to end every volume with a tidbit! Would it be dishonest to transfer a tale from one night or nights to another or others? I fancy not, as this is done in various editions.'[13] Burton returned to the subject of literalism again on 1 October. 'What I mean by literalism is literally translating each noun (in the long lists which so often occur) in its turn, so that the student can use the translation. I hold the *Nights* the best class books, and when a man knows it he can get on with Arabs everywhere.'[14]

The following day, much to the regret of both, Blanche, 'our whilom daughter,' having been with them for eighteen months, had to return home. Isabel counted herself fortunate in having Ellen Bishop staying with her, 'not only a devoted friend, but so knowing about sickness.' After seeing their niece off, Burton walked home, and when Miss Bishop and Isabel had completed various commissions, they arrived at the palazzone to find Burton suffering his first serious attack of gout. In the absence of an informed clinical diagnosis it is impossible, of course, to know whether Burton was really suffering from this 'patrician malady,' or the slow debilitating effects of tertiary syphilis involving his heart and joints. 'A change now came over our circumstances for the worse,' Isabel said, 'and here we begin the last seven years of his life, three and a half years of long gout sickness, on and off, without any suspicion of danger, though much suffering, and three and a half years after that, when every moment was fear. He now began to notice in his journals when he heard the first nightingale, when the first cuckoo note in spring, and for some time past he had noticed the first swallow, and the first flight of swallows, and then their departure, with increasing sadness.' On 6 December, Burton wrote in his journal in red ink: 'Today, eleven years ago I came here; what a shame!!!'[15]

CHAPTER FORTY

THE ARABIAN NIGHTS' ENTERTAINMENT

Throughout the early part of 1884, Burton was extremely unwell, his condition not helped by his insistence on returning to the big room. During all of these attacks, Isabel never left his side, day or night. She admitted to disobeying the doctor's dietary orders occasionally, such as giving Burton large glasses of brandy-grog every night, 'or he would have been a dead man long ago.'

On 19 January, Burton, after asking for the remaining volumes of Payne's *Nights*, wrote, 'A friend here is reading them solemnly and with huge delight: he would be much disappointed to break off perforce halfway. When do you think the 9 vols. will be finished? Marvellous weather here. I am suffering from only one thing, a want to be in Upper Egypt. And, of course, they won't employ me. I have the reputation of "independent," a manner of "Oh!, no, we never mention it, sir," in the official catalogue, and the one unpardonable Chinese Gordon has been sacked for being "eccentric", which Society abominates. England is now ruled by irresponsible clerks, mostly snobs. My misfortunes in life began with not being a Frenchman. I hope to be in London next Spring, and to have a talk with you about my translation of the 1001.'[1]

The friend in question who was thoroughly enjoying reading Payne's translation of the *Nights*, was George L. Faber, HBM's Consul at Fiume, who recalled many years later dropping in unexpectedly on the Burtons on this, the Feast Day of St Joseph. He 'found Dick in bed, still under the effects of a bad attack of gout......I was told that he was not to talk much, but he said he would be glad if I would talk to him..' Faber spent the whole day at Burton's bedside, during the course of which he perked up considerably. Despite his condition, Burton's sardonic humour had obviously not deserted him. 'He said that St Joseph had nearly done for him,' Isabel claiming on the other hand, 'that had it not been for St Joseph he would have died.' Continuing in this bantering vein, he said that, 'they (meaning his wife), taking advantage of his weak state, had tried to smuggle the *padre* into his room that morning but that he had been one too many for them this time, and had kicked him (the *padre*) out.'[2]

On 4 February, however, Burton temporarily lost the use of his legs. After this he greatly improved until 14 March. He had been moved on to a divan in the drawing-room, upon which they had made a bed, for change of air. He was so well that Isabel thought she might take a walk in the garden. Hardly had she begun, when a servant rushed after her with the news that Burton was faint. He was so bad that she sent for two doctors. They gave him twenty-five drops of digitalis three times at intervals of fifty minutes, and for two days and nights she never left his side. Instead of a threatening thrombosis, however, it turned out to be flatulence around the heart, which could have been dispersed by drinking boiling-water. After two days, he was so well that he could be wheeled around the house in a chair. After two more bad attacks, all was well.

He rallied, and began to walk.

In late March he was allowed to go out for a drive, and from then on to sit in the garden. Isabel had a machine constructed to carry him up and down stairs, and a wheel-chair in the garden, so that he could drive about and get out and walk a few steps, leaning on her arm and using a stick. They had a present from home of good claret and port. He was very fond of port, the very last thing, of course, he should have been drinking. The doctor made his last regular visit on 8 April.

After long delay, Burton's *The Book of the Sword*, finally appeared in the early part of spring.[3] He confessed that the long period involved in researching the subject, had convinced him that to treat it comprehensively was impossible within reasonable limits. He had decided, therefore, to publish it in three parts. Part 1, contained in this volume, 'treats of the birth, parentage, and early career of the Sword.' Part II 'treats of the Sword fully grown.' Part III 'continues the memoirs of the Sword, which, after long declining, revives once more in our day.'[4]

However, reviewing the book in *The Academy*, Andrew Lang suggested that, 'Captain Burton is to be congratulated rather on the amount than on the arrangement of his material. The history of the sword might make a big book in any man's hands; in Captain Burton's there seems to be no reason why it should ever end at all.' He was particularly critical of the amount of, what he saw as, irrelevant matter. 'The historian who sticks to his subject will find Captain Burton's book a mine of information, but too full, we do not say of dross, but of alien metals, precious in their place, but out of place here.'[5]

On 15 April Burton wrote to Payne, 'I am just beginning to write a little and to hobble about (with a stick). A hard time since January 30! Let me congratulate you on being at Vol.ix. Your translation is excellent, and I am glad to see in *Academy* that you are working at Persian Tales. Which are they? In my youth I read many of them. Now that your 1001 are so nearly finished I am working at my translation.'[6]

According to Isabel, Burton had begun work on *The Nights* on 1 April. On the day he had written to Payne, she had hired an amanuensis, since attending Burton night and day, and dealing with all his correspondence and business, left her no time for copying. So at what stage was Burton's work? It will be remembered that, in his letter published in *The Athenaeum* in November 1881, he had stated that, many years ago, in collaboration with his old and lamented friend, Dr Steinhaeuser, he had begun to translate the whole of the 1001 Nights. 'Although a host of friends has been eager to subscribe,' he said, ' my work is still unfinished, nor could it be finished without a year's hard labour.'

In 'The Translator's Foreword' to volume 1 of *The Nights*, Burton further elaborated on the 'collaboration.' He claimed that Steinhaeuser was to have been responsible for the prose, and he the metrical part. We have already seen, of course, that Steinhaeuser was neither an Arabist nor a writer. Burton had also radically changed his mind from his belief in 1856 that 'about one-fifth is utterly unfit for translation, and the most sanguine Orientalist would not dare to render literally more than three-quarters of the remainder.'[7] While Burton was in Brazil, Steinhaeuser had died, and his valuable MSS left at Aden had been dispersed, so that 'very little of his labour came into my hands.' The pressure of other matters, however, meant that it progressed slowly. 'At length in the spring of 1879, the tedious process of copying began, and the work commenced to take finished form.'[8]

Thomas Wright disputed both Lady Burton's account of the inception and progress of the work, and Burton's own story in the Translator's Foreword. He declared that Burton told Payne in 1881 that, 'beyond notes and a syllabus of titles nothing had been done; and in 1883 wrote in a letter, 'I find my translation is a mere summary.'[9] This referred to the Bulak edition, the only one, according to Wright, that Burton was then familiar with.[10]

Aside from Wright's allegation, Burton's claim that his work began 'to take finished form in 1879,' is completely at variance with what he himself wrote later. 'During the autumn of '82, after my return from the Gold Coast...my task began in all possible earnest with ordering the old scraps of translation, and collating a vast heterogeneous collection of notes. I was fortunate to discover at unlettered Trieste, an excellent copyist, and willing to decipher a crabbed hand, and deft at reproducing facetious and drolatic words without thoroughly comprehending their significance. At first my exertions were fitful and the scene was mostly a sick-bed to which I was bound between October '83 and June '84.'[11]

In line with his object of reproducing *The Nights*, 'not virginibus puerisque, but in as perfect a picture as my powers permit,' he had carefully searched for the English equivalent of every Arabic word, no matter how low or "shocking" it might appear to polite ears. The general tone of *The Nights*, Burton insisted, was exceptionally high and pure. 'Here we having nothing of that immodest modern modesty which sees covert implication where nothing is implied, and "improper" allusion when propriety is not outraged; nor do we meet with the nineteenth century refinement, innocence of the word, not of the thought, morality of the tongue, not of the heart, and the sincere homage paid to virtue in the guise of perfect hypocrisy.'[12]

Unlike Payne's translation, explanatory notes were an essential part of his, believing as he did that the *Nights* could not be properly understood in the West without commentary. 'The accidents of my life, it may be said without presumption, my long dealings with Arabs and other Mohammedans, and my familiarity not only with their idiom but with their turn of thought, and with that racial individuality which baffles description, have given me certain advantages over the average student however deeply he may have studied.'[13] Nor was this all. These volumes, afforded him a long-sought opportunity 'of noting practices and customs which interest all mankind, and which "Society" will not hear mentioned.' He was confident that they would 'form a repertory of Eastern knowledge in its esoteric phase. The student who adds the notes of Lane to mine will know as much of the Moslem East and more than many Europeans who have spent half their lives in Orient lands.'[14]

Burton freely admitted to making 'ample use' of the work of some of his predecessors for his own translation. In particular, he cited the work of Scott, Lane, and Payne, 'the whole being blended by a *callida junctura* into a homogeneous mass.' Dr Jonathan Scott, HEIC's Persian Secretary for a time to Warren Hastings, the Governor-General of Bengal, had produced a translation of *The Nights* in 6 small 8vo volumes in 1811, based on the MS of Edward Wortley Montagu.[15] He had been followed by the Arabic scholar, Edward William Lane, whose version of *The Nights* Burton strongly criticised.[16] 'He chose the abbreviating Bulak edition,' he wrote, 'and, of its two hundred tales, he has omitted about half and by far the more characteristic.' Furthermore, Burton described them as 'rendered unreadable as Sale's Koran by their anglicised Latin, their sesquipedalian un-English words, and the stiff and stilted style of half a century ago when our prose was, perhaps, the worst in Europe.'[17] Burton reserved his praise for Payne's version, 'the first and most complete translation of the great compendium, "comprising about four times as much matter as that of Galland, and three times as much as other translators..."' He described it as 'the most readable....It succeeds admirably in the most difficult passages, and he often hits upon choice and special terms and the exact vernacular equivalent of the foreign word, so happily and picturesquely that all future translators must perforce use the same expression under pain of falling short.'[18]

According to Wright, Burton's obligations to Scott and Lane were infinitesimal. Instead, he claimed, 'practically the whole of Burton is founded on the whole of Payne.'[19] Wright alleged that Burton took from Payne at least three-quarters of the entire work, transferring many hundreds of sentences and clauses bodily. 'Sometimes we come upon a whole page with only a word or two altered. In short, amazing to say, the public have given Burton credit for a gift which he did not possess – that of being a great translator.'[20]

On 3 May, Burton wrote to the FO, requesting two months' leave of absence beginning between the middle and the end of May, 'in fact as soon as I am fit to travel.' His accompanying medical certificate, dated two days earlier, read: 'I, Dr. Arthur Castiglioni declare that I have been treating Captain Burton ever since

31st January for an attack of fever and catarrh, complicated with rheumatic gout. His health has greatly improved under my care, but I do not wish to see him exposed to the great heat of Trieste until he is strong enough to bear it. I have, therefore, advised him professionally, to try a change to the highlands of Syria for about two months, after which I hope to see him completely re-established.'21 This sounds very much like Burton's suggestion, rather than Dr Castiglioni's. In the event, Burton's health proved not to be up to travelling so far. He was not well enough to leave Trieste until 4 June. This was followed by a very trying journey to Graz, half-way to Vienna. On alighting from the train, he felt dizzy and could barely stand. The Hotel Daniele was just across the road, and leaning on Isabel he managed to get there. They stayed the whole of the next day in order for Burton to rest, and then went on to the Erherzog Karl Hotel in Vienna.

Two days later Burton began to feel much better, greatly enjoying meeting up again with Sir Augustus and Lady Paget. The Burtons left Vienna on Tuesday, 10 June, by an early train, and Burton was well enough to undergo the nine hours' journey to Marienbad. They booked into Klinger's Hotel, and here he rapidly progressed under care. On 20 June, Burton wrote to Payne, 'I should much like to know what you are doing with the three supplemental volumes, and I hope that each will refer readers to the sources when you borrow it. This will be a great aid to students. The more I examine your translation the better I like it. Mine will never be so popular because I stick so much to the text. No arrangements yet made about it, and MS will not be all ready till the end of January.'22

From Marienbad they visited Konigswort, where they enjoyed strolling about in the forests, making occasional expeditions, reading together, and occasionally having a professor read to them in German. On return, after the cure, they went back for a few days to Vienna before going on to Roitsch-Sauebrunn in Steiemark. By then, Burton had asked the FO for, and been granted, a month's extension of leave.23

It was from here that Burton wrote to Payne on 12 August. After enquiring about "the three supererogatory vols." he went on, 'We left Marienbad last of last month, and came to this place (a very pretty little spa utterly clear of Britishers), where we shall stay till the end of the month and then again for Trieste where we shall make plans for the winter. Will you kindly let me have the remaining volumes, and when you have a spare quarter of an hour I want a little assistance from you. When you sent me your Breslau you pencilled in each volume the places from which you had taken matter for translation (How wretchedly that Breslau is edited!) I want these notes scribbled out by way of saving time. Of course I shall have to read over the whole series: but meanwhile will content myself with your references.'24

Burton and Isabel stayed at Sauerbrunn until 3 September and then returned to Trieste. Here, Burton wrote again to Payne, 'On return here I found Vol.ix with your dedication which delighted me hugely. I did not notice your fine work in reviewing the Clouston treatise. I had not your express permission. Living so far from the world I am obliged to be very careful in these matters: one never knows what harm one may be doing unawares. Of course I shall speak of your translation in my preface, as it deserves to be spoken of.'25

After seeing a great many visitors and friends, the Burtons went up to Opicina, and immediately applied themselves to the task of advertising *The Nights*, the first two volumes being almost ready for print. They were now faced with the serious problem as to how many copies should be printed. The numbers advised by different people varied from 150 to 3,000. After giving it a great deal of thought, Burton chose 1,000 as a just middle. They then drew up a long list of friends, acquaintances, and strangers, likely to patronise the work, and Burton wrote three advertisements, lithographed and printed at Trieste. Some 24,000 to 30,000 were posted at a cost of £126.

These circulars produced about 800 favourable replies, the number later rising to 1,500 and then to 2,000.26 According to Thomas Wright these figures were only reached through the help of John Payne. Initially, only 300 favourable replies were received. A disappointed Isabel then wrote to Payne for advice.

As a result, he sent her the names of those who had subscribed to his own book, together with a list of other likely persons.[27]

At the beginning of October, Burton wrote to Payne thanking him for a complete, specially bound edition of his *Nights*: 'I am delighted with it, especially with the dedication...To my horror Quaritch sent me a loose vol. of his last catalogue with a notice beginning, "The only absolutely true translation of the [*Arabian Nights*], &c." My wife telegraphed to him and followed with a letter ordering it not to be printed. All in vain. I notice this only to let you know that the impertinence is wholly against my will. Life in Trieste is not propitious to work as in the Baths; yet I get on tolerably...'[28]

That month, Burton's version of *The Lyrics* of Camoens appeared with a long dedication written at Desterro, Trieste on 25 September, to: 'The Prince of the Lyric Poets of His Day, Algernon Charles Swinburne. ' It began, 'My Dear Swinburne, Accept the unequal exchange, my brass for your gold.' As Burton wrote at the end of 'The Translator's Foreword, 'It may conciliate some enmities and captivate, perhaps, some good-will, when I abjure all pretensions to rank as a Poet. No one more fully appreciates the difference between "making" and "translating"; between the Poétes (Creator) and the copier who aspires only to second prizes...'

Swinburne replied to Burton's compliment on 27 November, carefully avoiding any comment about the poetic quality of his translation:

> My Dear Burton, Your dedication makes me very proud and the kindness of its terms gives me a still heartier pleasure than that of mere pride in your friendship......
>
> The learning and research of your work are in many points beyond all praise of mine, but not more notable than the strength and skill that wield them. I am hungrily anticipating the Arabian Nights. Of course it is understood that Watts and I subscribe for a copy apiece. .... You both know how we look forward to our next meeting with you, when you *shall* not run away so soon as you did last time.[29]

Apart from Oswald Crawfurd's friendly review in *The Academy*, the general voice of criticism was unfavourable. *The Mail and Express*, New York wrote: 'Captain Burton who will persist in translating, has followed up his version of *The Lusiads* of Camoens, with a version of his Sonnets, Odes, and Sextines. We have not seen enough of Captain Burton's English in this instance to form any clear idea of it, and we do not care to see much of it, if it resembles the English into which he projected *The Lusiads*.'[30]

Unfortunately, this was the case. 'Alas!, wrote the reviewer in *The Athenaeum*, 'even the most kindly disposed judge must see one serious flaw, fatal to the success which so vast an expenditure of time and trouble deserved. Camoens is not "Englished in the volumes before us, he is "Burtoned", and that is a different matter. Captain Burton has constructed a dialect of his own, which is neither the English of the present day nor yet the English of Shakespeare, or of Spenser, or of Chaucer, and it is in this new language that his very able version is composed....And if his far-fetched words are likely to prove a stumbling-block to the ordinary reader, the strange way in which they are mixed must disturb the philologist.'[31]

Burton was ill throughout January and February of 1885, and Isabel pleaded with him to throw up the Service, and to live where it best suited him, even though they would have been very poor. "One winter may be an accident," she said, " but two winters is a caution; and you must never winter here again." Although agreeing with her in this respect, Burton was adamant about not throwing up the Service until he either obtained Morocco, or was allowed to retire on full pension. Although it was six years to Burton's retirement, that is what Isabel now determined to press for on returning to England.

The following month Burton wrote to the FO requesting two months leave of absence on urgent private affairs, beginning in early May. His object, he said, 'was to place myself under a London physician on account of rheumatism for which this part of Europe is notorious.'[32] Leave was granted, and the Burtons left for London on 19 May. They travelled together as far as Venice, before splitting up after a couple of days. Burton, who had been ordered to travel by sea for the benefit of his health set off for Liverpool, while Isabel returned to England by land, sightseeing in several European cities on the way.

CHAPTER FORTY-ONE

THE THOUSAND AND ONE NIGHTS
AND A KNIGHT

Burton's presence in England had, of course, the dual purpose of allowing him to consult a London physician and bring out *The Nights*. After putting himself under Dr Foakes for gout, both he and Isabel set about preparing to issue the book. Isabel, who had always taken a forceful, no-nonsense attitude to negotiating with publishers in the past, now took over the running of the business side of the enterprise.

Although the Burtons were now their own publishers, they needed to find a suitable printer willing to carry out the necessary work. This, as Burton well knew from attempting to issue the *Kama Shastra* in 1873, could be fraught with difficulties. He was not alone in encountering such problems relating to the sexual content of a book. Two years later, J. A. Symonds, met with strong disapproval from the compositor responsible for setting the type of the second volume of his *Studies of the Greek Poets*.

The following month Isabel contacted Mr Notcutt, business manager of Waterlow & Sons Ltd. 'Having made my husband two prom.,' she wrote, 'one not to read the MSS of his work and the 2nd not to let it out of my hands, I should like to be able to keep the one as well as the other. I shall call here on Monday after ten and a room should be placed at my disposal with the MSS for as long as you like. Let me know if this will do and satisfy the Directors.'[1]

As a result of her visit, a specimen contract was drawn up, part of which the Burtons found completely unacceptable. 'We are rather surprised at your last clause…..,' Isabel remarked severely, 'it is one which a man ought not to sign to save his life. It binds him and his body and soul and all the property he has or ever might have at the caprice or religious calls of every boy on your premises whose sister or aunt might be made a confidant of and thinks it her <u>duty</u> to make it known.' She then went on to 'honourably pledge ourselves never to divulge your name (Waterlow and Sons) either in private nor otherwise,' offering the further assurance that, 'if anything occurred we should have Messrs G. Lewis as our lawyer who would pull us through it for us and you.' As to any money owed to the firm, the sum required would be available for every volume as wanted, 'but we shall not leave £8,000 or £10,000 quiet till April without touching it. Yrs will be guaranteed not to be touched by the clause inserted.'[2]

Writing soon afterwards to the well-known novelist and anti-feminist journalist, Eliza Lynn Linton, Isabel effusively thanked her for her 'good work in procuring for Dick and me (who are sort of "Babes in the Woods" in business point of view) the friendly and strong protecting wing of the famous George Lewis. I shall D.V. go and cower under it tomorrow after five and feel safe from the den of thieves, the "Trade" as they call themselves – more villainous than dealing in horse flesh – also from that hideous humbug the

Society for the Suppression of Vice…'[3]

An amicable arrangement was eventually reached, and Burton was able to go ahead with publicising the book.

On 2 July, he sent out a prospectus announcing that he had 'much pleasure in informing the Subscribers…that he has placed the MSS in the hands of a high class firm of printers, who are now busily engaged in preparing the first volume. This will be ready towards the end of August, and it is anticipated that the subsequent volumes will be issued to the Subscribers at the rate of one volume per month.' Now numbering 2,000, they were invited to send in their subscriptions to Messrs Coutts' Bank, where a separate account had been opened for the purpose. Cheques were to be made payable to Mrs Isabel Burton. Obviously intended to whet a speculative appetite, the circular carried a P.S. – *Subscribers may be pleased to learn that Mr. PAYNE'S volumes issued at nine guineas, now fetch from fourteen to twenty-one.*

The following day Burton asked the Foreign Office to be allowed 3 months leave on urgent private affairs dating from July19, when his present leave expired. 'My health has suffered severely from the climate of Trieste during the last two years. I find it necessary to place myself under the charge of a London physician, who hopes in time to effect a cure.'[4] Surprisingly, this was minuted sympathetically: 'The climate of Trieste never agreed with Burton, and it first made inroads on his health soon after his appointment in 1872.' The request was granted by Lord Salisbury, who had formed a minority government a month earlier, taking over the foreign office as well as the premiership.

With the aim of persuading the FO to allow Burton to take early retirement from the Consular Service, Isabel wrote to her friend, Mrs Friswell:

> I send you <u>privately</u> copies of two papers, which will coach you up in the case of our hope that Dick may be pensioned & retire. Do you think you could forward them to your friend Mr Walter Herries Pollock, with a word from yourself, asking him to give us a lift in the "Saturday Review?" "Punch," "Truth," "Vy Fair," "The World," have done so, saying it is an exceptional case that all sides may agree upon as right. I <u>do</u> grieve at putting an extra strand of work upon you, but you can do me a great service, & how I wish I could ever do one for you.[5]

On 21 July, a family party was held to celebrate Mr Arundell's eighty-sixth birthday. It was to prove to be the last happy family meeting, since shortly afterwards he suffered a second stroke, from which he was not expected to recover. Only two days earlier, the Burtons had lunched with Lord Houghton who was also in poor health. Shortly after leaving for Vichy, he died on 11 August. Burton, in the meantime, paid several visits to Oxford, primarily to visit his old friend, Archibald Sayce, Fellow of Queen's College. It was from here on 1 August, that Burton dedicated the second volume of his *Nights* to John Payne. He returned, however, in time for Lord Houghton's funeral service at St Margaret's, Westminster Abbey, on 18 August.[6]

The first volume of the *Nights* appeared on 12 September 1885, handsomely bound in black cloth, with a broad gold diagonal band on both covers and back, enclosing lettering in black relief. There were Arabic designs in gold on both sides of the cover, the lettering on the back also being in gold. The volume was accompanied by a circular requesting that the book should not be exposed for sale in public places or permitted to fall into the hands of any save curious students of Moslem manners.[7]

Despite Burton's worries, the book on the whole received an excellent press. 'The publication of the first volume of Captain Burton's translation of the *Alf Layla*,' commented the Whitehall Review, 'enriches the world of Oriental investigation with a monument of labour and scholarship and of research.'[8] The *Nottingham Journal* was equally flattering. 'From an Oriental point of view, the work is masterly to a degree. The quatrains and couplets, reading like verses from Elizabethan mantels, and forming a perfect rosary of Eastern love, the constant succession of brilliant pictures, and the pleasures of meeting again our dear old friend Shahrazad, all these combine to give a unique charm and interest to this "perfect expositor" of the Medieval Moslem mind.'9

Naturally, there was an outcry in some quarters against the translation, prompting J.A. Symonds, to write to *The Academy* on 27 September, to protest against the hypocrisy which condemned the text. 'The real question is whether a word-for-word version of the *Arabian Nights* executed with peculiar literary vigour, exact scholarship and rare insight into Oriental modes of thought and feeling, can under any shadow of pretence be classed with "the garbage of the brothels."10 When English versions of Theocritus and Ovid, of Plato's Phaedrus and the Ecclesiazusae, now within the reach of every schoolboy, have been suppressed, then and not till then can a "plain and literal" rendering of the *Arabian Nights* be denied with any colour of consistency to adult readers.'11

The strongest and, in parts, most cogent criticism came from *The Edinburgh Review*. The reviewer, probably Reginald Lane-Poole, described Burton's translation as much less accurate than Payne's. In addition to this defect, 'His English is an unreadable compound of archaeology and "slang," abounding in Americanisms, and full of reaching after obsolete or foreign words and phrases, which may be interesting to the editor of the Philological Society's new English Dictionary, but are extremely annoying to any reader with a feeling for style.' It placed Burton's version, according to the reviewer, 'quite out of the category of English books.'

As for Burton's notes, 'Probably no European even if he had lived half a century in "Orient lands" has ever gathered together such an appalling collection of degrading customs and statistics of vice.' He described them as a 'disgrace and shame to printed literature.' In his view, the different versions 'had each its proper destination – Galland for the nursery, Lane for the Library, Payne for the study, and Burton for the sewers.'

The critic had earlier claimed that it was 'a well-known fact that the discussion and reading of depraved literature lead infallibly to the depravation of the reader's mind.' In his opinion, 'The less such things were thought and read about, the less they would be enacted in real life.'12

Burton's lengthy response was typically robust. It was also self-serving to some extent in its arguments. Nevertheless, it exhibited, what we would now regard as, an admirable common-sense attitude towards sex, and a surprising depth of psychological insight into the subject. He strongly denied 'that the childish indecencies and the unnatural vices of the original' could 'deprave any mind save that which is perfectly prepared to be depraved....The man must be prurient and lecherous as a dog-faced baboon in rut to have aught of passion excited by either.'13 Taking the high moral ground, he claimed that it was journals like the *Pall Mall Gazette*, one of his most vociferous critics, with its 'persistently sexual subjects and themes lubric,' which were responsible for 'more active and permanent damage to public morals than books and papers which were frankly gross and indecent.'14

He expressed regret for displaying 'the gross and bestial vices of the original in the rare places where obscenity becomes rampant.' However, he held it his duty 'to translate the text word for word, instead of garbling it and mangling it by perversion and castration.' If faced with prosecution as suggested by some sections of the Press, he was fully determined to appear in Court with his 'version of *The Nights* in one hand and bearing in the other the Bible (especially the Old Testament, a free translation from an ancient Oriental work) and Shakespeare, with Petronius Arbiter and Rabelais by way of support and reserve.'15

Broadening his argument, Burton criticised English society for being perfectly content to 'bring up both sexes and keep all ages in profound ignorance of sexual and intersexual relations, and the consequences of that imbecility were peculiarly cruel and afflicting.....Let us see what the modern English woman and her Anglo-American Sister have become under the working of a mock-modesty which, too often, acts cloak to real *dévorgondage* ; and how Respectability unmakes what Nature made. She has feet but no "toes"; ankles but no "calves"; knees but no "thighs"; a stomach but no "belly" nor "bowels"; a heart but no "bladder nor "groin"; a liver and no "kidneys"; hips and no "haunches"; a bust and nor "backside" nor "buttocks" : in fact she is a *monstrum*, a figure fit only to frighten the crows.'[16]

On 2 October, Burton asked the FO for yet another extension of leave. 'The enclosed certificate is given to me by the physician Dr. Castiglioni who attended me through the successive winters of Trieste, and who strongly enjoined me not to risk a third. I also feel that another attack like the last two will probably prove fatal. With your Lordship's permission, I propose to pass the coming cold season at Tangier on the seaboard of the southern Mediterranean, returning to my post at Trieste about the middle of March, when the climate although rigorous is not dangerous.'

Burton's request was interestingly minuted by an FO official, who had obviously been combing through the records: 'Captain Burton has had leave during the last five years including 1885 as follows:-

1880   (Jan. 1st – May 10th) ; (Aug. 15th – Sept. 1st).......4 months 27 dys.

1881   (Oct. 17th – July 31st)........9 mths 15 dys.
1882

1884   (June 4th – Sept. 3rd)......3 mths.

1885   (May 19th – Oct. 19th).....5 mths.

        Total = 1 yr 10 mths 14dys

Apparently unimpressed, Lord Salisbury wrote underneath: 'He is an old man, in his 65th year, I believe, and has been a good deal knocked about in his time. I, therefore, recommend granting this leave.'[17]

Later that month, hearing that Sir John Drummond-Hay was about to retire from Morocco, Burton applied for the post. Drummond-Hay had spent over forty years there, rising in 1872 to become minister plenipotentiary, and wielding enormous influence. It was the one thing Burton had stayed on for in the service, Isabel said, in the hopes of getting. His application was backed up by about fifty of the best names in England, and it seemed as if it was as good as promised to him. But was it? Would any Foreign Secretary, even one as sympathetic as Lord Salibury, choose Burton for such a post given his past record?

Burton left for Tangier towards the end of November, booking into the Continental Hotel close to the sea. On 15 January 1886, he wrote to Payne, describing Tangier as 'beastly but not bad for work...It is a place of absolute rascality, and large fortunes are made by selling European protections – a regular Augean stable.'[18] Nevertheless, his visit there provided him with personal insight into, what he believed, was the original manner of transmitting the tales of the *Nights*. 'I cannot take up the *Nights*, in their present condi-tion,' he wrote in his Terminal Essay, 'without feeling that the work has been written down from the Rawi or Nakkal, the conteur or professional story-teller...Moreover the *Nights* reads in many places like a hand-book or guide for the professional who would learn them by heart; here and there introducing his "gag" and "patter." To this "business" possibly we may attribute much of the ribaldry which starts up in unexpected places: it was meant simply to provoke a laugh.'[19]

Isabel was to have joined Burton as soon as she had completed her business in England. However, she received a telegram from him stating that there were outbreaks of cholera, and that she would not be allowed to land at Gibraltar. Anxious to be with Burton for their silver wedding anniversary, she immedi-ately telegraphed Sir John Adye, then commanding at Gibraltar, and asked if he would allow a Government boat to take her off the P&O, and put her straight on the Morocco boat. She received a favourable reply. At Gibraltar, Burton came off in a boat and Captain Baker kindly came for her with a Government launch, into which Burton changed. She found him not looking at all well and extremely low-spirited, 'but he got better and better, as he always did as soon as he was with me.'

On 5 February 1886 a telegram arrived addressed to 'Sir Richard Burton.' Reportedly, he tossed it over to her, and said: "Some fellow is playing me a practical joke, or else it is not for me. I shall not open it, so you may as well ring the bell and give it back again." "Oh no!" I said; "I *shall* open it if you don't." It was from Lord Salisbury, stating that the Queen, at his recommendation, had made Burton a KCMG in reward for his services. According to Isabel, Burton looked very serious and uncomfortable, and said, ' "Oh! I shall not accept it." I said, "You had better accept it, Jemmy, because it is a certain sign that they are going to give you the place." (Tangier, Marocco)'[20] Ironically, in view of Isabel's misplaced optimism, the motto of the KCMG order is "Auspicium melioris aevi," 'A pledge of better times.'[21]

After spending a pleasant week on the Rock, they began their journey back to Trieste in bad weather. Unfortunately, Isabel suffered a bad fall during the voyage, when the ladder between the upper and lower decks was washed away by heavy seas. Although making light of her injuries, it was evident by the time they reached Naples that she had hurt herself badly. Typically, Burton's response to his wife's welfare, was to insist that she continue her journey by land alone, whilst he, 'who thoroughly enjoyed the sea, rejoined the ship.'

Isabel travelled on to Rome by rail, then on to Florence and Bologna, touring the medieval parts of the cities. She arrived at Trieste on 20 March, to find three telegrams waiting for her. "Father very ill can you come?" "Father died today," "Father buried today at Mortlake." It was a severe blow, she said, and she felt it very much, because it was unexpected.[22]

Writing to Ouida early in April, Burton said that, 'On 23 ult I returned from a winter in Marocco [sic] and it kept me out of bed which is saying a great deal. Isabel joined me at Tangier and hated it – her fondest affection is all lavished upon this elongated sewer, Trieste.

Here we remain till the end of May when I must be again in London and look after the four remaining volumes of the Arabian Nights. You know I suppose that they have K.C.M.G'd me and I'm ungrateful enough to comment, "Half gives who late gives." '[23]

Burton's letter requesting leave is missing from the General Correspondence file at TNA. It can be safely assumed, nevertheless, that it was on the ground of that catch-all phrase, 'urgent private affairs.' However, since Burton had received his knighthood, Lord Salisbury's Conservative Government had fallen, and Gladstone had become Prime Minister for the third time. The 5th Earl of Rosebery was now, very briefly, Secretary of State for Foreign Affairs. His chilly response must have given Burton food for thought. 'I am directed by the Earl of Rosebery,' ran the reply, 'to state that his Lordship accedes to your application for leave of absence from the 1st of June to the 1st of August, but I am to observe that this is an exceptional favour as you only returned to your post at the end of March after an absence of 10 months, and as you have during the last 8 years been absent on leave for 3 years and 9 months, I am to state that such frequent and prolonged absences are contrary to the public service.'[24]

The Burtons left Trieste on 4 June, travelling via Innsbruck, Zurich, Basle, and Boulogne to England. After staying a few days at Folkestone with Lady Stisted and Georgiana, they took a train for London.

CHAPTER FORTY-TWO

A WALK THROUGH A PERFUMED GARDEN

On 27 June, the family assembled at 14 Montagu Place, where they dined and drank a silent toast to the memory of Henry Raymond Arundell, on what would have been his eighty-seventh birthday. 'It was a very melancholy time, for me,' Isabel wrote, '....dividing the property, packing up, and breaking up the old home, which had been our refuge on all the holidays of our married life.'[1] Naturally, Isabel said nothing about the value of her father's property. Henry Raymond Arundell's very long will, proved and registered nine days earlier, shows that the gross value of his personal estate amounted to just over £44,855. The furniture, plate, linen, pictures, prints, jewels and all household and personal effects of all kinds, except those belonging to his stock-in-trade as wine-dealer, were to be divided equally between the four married daughters: Isabel, Blanche, Elizabeth Mary Regis, and Emmeline Mary, the only surviving children of the family. Each was left a fourth part of their father's residuary estate in trust for their own use. This would give each daughter £10,714. In Isabel's case, however, her bequest was reduced by £1,800 because of loans outstanding.[2]

Just under three weeks before leaving Trieste for England, Burton had received a letter from the London booksellers, Robson and Kerslake, who were involved in clandestine publications. 'A book has recently appeared in Paris,' it ran, 'which we think will probably interest you – Le Jardin Parfumé – and thinking so, we have ventured to send a copy by book-post today, and beg your acceptance of it.'[3]

A manuscript copy of this 'Manual of Arabian Erotology' by Abu 'Abdullah Muhammad ibn Umar (al) Nafzawi, dated by modern scholarship to around 1410,[4] had been discovered some time before 1850 by an unknown French staff officer stationed in Algeria. He translated it into his own language, but it was almost twenty-five years before it was printed. Four French Army officers began secretly lithographing it on machines belonging to the French Government, but were discovered by their commanding officer when only thirty-five copies had been run off.[5] The work first appeared in 1876.

An excellent forgery of this so-called 'autograph edition,' which misdated the Arabic manuscript to the sixteenth century, was printed at Paris in 1885. Early the following year, the well-known French publisher, Isidore Liseux, published a corrected and revised text in a de-luxe edition limited to 220 copies.

On 29 June, Burton received a further letter on the subject, this time from another London bookseller, Edward Avery.[6]

Dear Sir,

I have laid your letter before the parties who reprinted one of your works and in consideration of your interest in the translation, they have requested me to make the following offer of 4 copies of AR [Ananga Ranga] and 6 copies of the Perfumed Garden, the latter when ready for delivery. (NB Messrs. Robson & Kerslake translate the French into English) which will be in about four weeks. At the same time, I am requested to point out to you that the work would not have been reprinted had your publishers been satisfied to supply the work at the original cost of 30 shillings, which allowed a reasonable profit on the sale. A similar offer is made to XYZ at the same time. I am also requested to state that should you be inclined to return the compliment, 2 copies of your translation of the Arabian Nights would be thankfully accepted.

Prospectus of Perfumed Garden by post.

Avery, an acquaintance of Swinburne and, later of Leonard Smithers, specialised in the sale of what Chief Inspector Drew of the Metropolitan Police would later describe in his court evidence as 'elaborately bound books…the grossest and most obscene pictures and photographs that one could well imagine, as well as a number of beautifully carved ivory models showing persons in the act of coition.' After successfully avoiding the attention of the law for twenty-five years, his luck ran out in 1900 when he was tricked into selling one of his more explicit items to a plain-clothes policeman. He was brought to trial and sentenced to four months' imprisonment after pleading guilty.[7]

Avery's claim that he had laid Burton's letter 'before the parties who reprinted one of your works,' was in fact a smoke-screen to cover his own personal involvement in this piracy. This is evident from a pencilled note on the inside of the front cover of one of the British Library's copies of The Kama Sutra, which reads: 'Published by Edward Avery of Gt College St – 145 Camden Town in March 1886.'

There are no means of knowing whether Burton responded to Avery's letter. What is clear, is that he temporarily laid aside his 'Terminal Essay' in order to translate the Liseux edition into English. On completion, it was issued by the Kama Shastra Society in seven or ten parts, in paper covers of varying tints of grey and fawn like the first edition of The Kama Sutra. Later in the year, the Society printed a second edition, now, however, bound in full vellum, with lettering and border in gold. It appears that Avery was also responsible for the piracy of this work. Referring in his Terminal Essay to the Kama Shastra editions, Burton went on to write bitterly: 'A rival version will be brought out by a bookseller whose Committee, as he calls it, appears to be the model of literary pirates, robbing the author as boldly and as openly as if they picked his pocket.'[8]

The contents of The Perfumed Garden are similar to those of The Kama Sutra and Ananga Ranga. What 'makes this treatise unique as a book of its kind,' wrote Burton, 'is the seriousness with which the most lascivious and obscene matters are presented. It is evident that the author is convinced of the importance of his subject, and that the desire to be of use to his fellow-men is the sole motive of his efforts.'[9]

Burton, nevertheless, expressed regret, 'that this work, so complete in many respects, is defective insofar as it makes no mention of a custom too common with the Arabs not to deserve particular attention. I speak of the taste so universal with the old Greeks and Romans, namely the preference they give to a boy before a woman, or even to treat the latter as a boy.'[10] In August 1884, the French writer, Guy de Maupassant, had written to a French publisher suggesting a reprint of the lithographic edition which had lately come to his notice. In his letter, Maupassant said that the translator 'has not dared to translate a chapter concerning a vice very common in this country – that of Pederasty.' What the officer, in fact, had omitted was not an entire chapter, but the long final section of the 21st or closing chapter.[11]

While there was nothing about pederasty in the Liseux edition which he was translating, Burton wrote about it at length in the final section of his Terminal Essay. He justified this on the grounds of being unwilling to ignore any subject which was interesting to the Orientalist and the Anthropologist. 'And they, methinks, do abundant harm who, for shame or disgust, would suppress the very mention of such matters.'

Since carrying out his report on the male brothels in Karachi in 1845, enquiries in many countries had led him to the conclusion that there existed, what he termed, a "Sotadic Zone".[12] Within this zone, according to Burton, the Vice was 'popular and endemic, held at worst to be a mere peccadillo, whilst the races to the North and South of the limits as defined, practised it only sporadically amid the opprobrium of their fellows who, as a rule, were physically incapable of performing the operation, and looked upon it with the liveliest disgust.'[13]

He accounted for the practice by supposing that within the Sotadic Zone, there was 'a blending of the masculine and feminine temperaments, a crasis which elsewhere occurs only sporadically.' However, in Volume 2 of the *Nights*, Burton was less tentative, claiming that, 'Amongst men the mixture of the feminine with the masculine temperaments leads to sodomy.'[14] Conversely, this blend in women led to lesbianism and tribadism.

Havelock Ellis (1859-1939) the leading English authority of his time on human sexual behaviour was critical of Burton's view. 'The theory of the Sotadic Zone,' he wrote, 'fails to account for the custom among the Normans, Celts, Scythians, Bulgars and Tartars, and, moreover, in various of these regions different views have prevailed at different periods. Burton was wholly unacquainted with the psychological investigations into sexual inversion which had, indeed, scarcely begun in his day.'[15]

Aware that his translation of *The Perfumed Garden* would shortly be pirated, Burton was now faced with the unwelcome prospect that the same might happen to his *Arabian Nights*. Such productions, printed and not published left their authors completely at the mercy of the unscrupulous. 'England and Anglo-America, be it observed,' he said, 'are the only self-styled civilized countries in the world where an author's brain-work is not held to be private property: his book is no book unless published and entered after a cost of seven presentation copies at "Stationers" Hall…'[16]

The book, therefore, was handed to a friend, the Irish novelist and journalist, Justin Huntley McCarthy, MP, who 'undertook the task of converting the grand old barbarian into a family man to be received by the "best circles."' His proofs, duly expurgated, were passed on to Isabel, 'who I may say,' Burton went on, 'had never read the original, and she struck out all that appeared to her over-free….' There were six volumes in all, the first two appeared later that year, the last in 1888.[17]

Attractively bound in white cloth, the front cover was decorated with two golden motifs, one Arabic, the other Christian: a crescent moon in the top left-hand corner balanced by the three lilies of St Joseph in the bottom right. Inside, was a portrait of Lady Burton, facing the title page printed rather floridly in brown and green inks. The book was dedicated 'To the Women of England…Believing That The Majority Can Appreciate Fine Language, Exquisite Poetry and Romantic Eastern Life, Just As Well As The Thousand Students And Scholars Who Secured The Original Thousand Copies.'

What she wanted to do, Isabel explained in her Preface, was 'to give to the English public for family reading the real thing, not the drawing-room tales which have been put before them as "Arabian Nights," for the past one hundred and eighty years, since the days of Professor Galland….

I can only add that the object of my colleague (Mr. Justin Huntly McCarthy, M.P.) has been to make as few omissions as possible, and that I guarantee that no mother shall regret her girl's reading the Arabian Nights. You will be deprived of nothing of the original save 215 out of 3,215 pages.'[18]

Few mothers were put to the test, since the edition was a complete failure. 'The public,' as Burton remarked with apparent satisfaction, 'would have none of it: even innocent girlhood tossed aside the chaste volumes in utter contempt, and would not condescend to aught save the thing, the whole thing, and nothing but the thing, unexpurgated and uncastrated. The result was an unexpected and unpleasant study of modern taste in highly respectable England.'[19] Of the thousand copies which were printed, only 457 were sold in the course of two years.

After Burton's death, Isabel wrote to the Writers' Club in 1895, revealing that her 'so-called edition was really my husband's and abridged by him. Mr Justin Huntly McCarthy Junior has the credit of it, and his name is on the fly-leaf, but on receiving it from him, we found his erasures were chiefly on Christianity, and that he had left in many stories that were not fit for general use, my husband did it himself, and then passed it on to me to read.'[20] It is clear, nevertheless, from a comparison of the two editions, that Isabel's explanation should be taken with a pinch of salt, and that she played a far more active role in the expurgation of the original than either she or her husband was prepared to admit.[21]

On 2 July, Burton was stunned to learn that Lord Rosebery had given Morocco to Mr (afterwards Sir) William Kirby-Green. According to Isabel, Burton, on hearing the news, said in his usual generous way: "Next to getting it one-self, the best thing is to know that a friend and a good man has got it." But when he came home and told Isabel, he said, "There is no rise for me now, and I don't want anything; but I have worked forty-four years for nothing. I am breaking up and want to go free."[22]

On the last day of that month, Burton wrote to the Foreign Secretary, asking for further leave: 'My Lord, I have the honour to forward a sick certificate from Dr. Baines, a medical man with acquaintance with my case. A return to Trieste during this most unwholesome season will hardly be advisable, and although I have no apprehension of cholera when in robust health, I should hesitate to expose myself to a particularly virulent form under other conditions.' Dr Baines, in certifying Burton, said that he found he was 'still weak and debilitated from rheumatism and fever contracted at Trieste. 'It would be most injurious, he said, to Burton's health to return. 'He still requires two or three months in a mild climate to regain his health and strength.'

This was sarcastically minuted at the Foreign Office: 'Lengthened practice makes it very easy to suggest that Burton's leave application should be sanctioned.' This was followed by a single terse instruction. 'Grant.' However, further sarcasm followed: '....I do not see how we can send Burton back to face "a peculiarly virulent form of cholera." If anything were to happen to him, he has assured me that the "whole civilised world would cry out upon us." Are we prepared for such a visitation?' Another minute read: 'It must be granted, and I think it right to call to Lord Iddesleigh's attention, the amount of leave Sir Richard Burton has had, and also on one occasion at least when he got sick leave he went to the West Coast of Africa in the employment of a mining company.'[23]

Following a visit to Scotland in August, Burton, with Isabel's energetic assistance, intensified his efforts to secure early retirement from the Consular Service. The first letter, addressed to the Rt Hon Lord Iddesleigh, was written by Burton in purple ink in a very scrawly hand on 8 September:

> I have the honour after serious consideration to submit the following request to you. After living for fourteen years in an unwholesome port, I find that the climate of Trieste as a constant residence undermines my health and incapacitates me for work. I have not had the promotion which would encourage me to hope for more, nor do I see the prospect of any post which I would accept with pleasure and satisfaction.
>
> I have, therefore, come to the determination after 44 years in the public service, 19 years in the army and twenty-five in the Consular Service, to be allowed five years' peace as compensation, and to retire now at the age of 65 on full pension.
>
> My services require no details in my address to your Lordship, but I would venture to note in the following pages a few of the facts which would seem to suggest my claims to some consideration on the part of H.M.'s Government, and which I venture to say will obtain the approval of the public at large.

This was followed by a ten-point statement of his "Services", beginning with his years in the Bombay Army, and ending with his having published over forty-six works, several of which had become standard.

Number 9 claimed that he had 'learned twenty-nine languages, passed official examinations in eight Eastern languages, notably Arabic, Persian, and Hindustani.' It is, of course, impossible to verify the accuracy of this former figure. Certainly, he was deliberately inaccurate with regard to the latter. As we have already seen, the correct number was six, and Arabic was not one of them.[24]

Burton's unheard of request caused a flutter of consternation at the FO, followed by a rash of memos. One ran: 'Check as to whether any precedent exists for granting appeal and as to statements of service.' This was followed by a response in another hand: 'I can't recall to mind any precedent for which Sir Richard Burton asks for. If the Consular Department has not the means of checking his statement of services, I would send him a blue form to fill in.' This is followed by a sarcastic question: 'Are periods of leave deducted, because if so, Sir Richard Burton's service would be diminished by about a half?' (VS) This was responded to: 'There is a column in the Supn. form for entering the period of leave absence, but it has not been the practice to give particulars on the ground that Clerks and others under this office only have rare leave. This can, however, be stated in the case of Sir Richard Burton.' The final instruction was, 'I would only deduct the extra leave.'[25]

Burton followed up his first letter by another, almost a week later. 'My Lord, I have the honour to report that I have written the following letter to Lord Salisbury in answer to the one I received from Mr. Daly.' This ran: 'I have received Mr. Daly's letter, and have the honour to reply that I should like to retain my post as Consul of Trieste till some arrangements can be made to enable me to live upon a sufficient pension. Perhaps if there is a deficiency from the Treasury to make up the Consular pension, his Lordship might recommend my services to the Civil List on the ground of literary and linguistic labours.

I trust that your Lordship will support me in this, I hope, not unreasonable request.'

This was minuted: 'No objection to his remaining.' In the Foreign Office file at this point, there are copies of Burton's "Services", and letters sent to Sir Thomas Villiers Lister and Admiral Mayne. As to the former, this carried the memo: 'This letter is almost identical with that of the 8th in which he asks to remain on, and has been told he may do so.' At the bottom of the letter to Mayne is written: 'If my military services could be taken into consideration, I might perhaps on three counts, military, consular, literary and linguistic, receive one sufficient pension. My wife and I have worked hard for the Conservative cause, and her relatives, notably Gerards and Arundells are devoted and hard-working Conservatives.'[26]

On 18 September, before relinquishing the keys of Montagu Place, the Burtons wandered all over the now empty house before taking a sad leave. That same evening, Henry Irving gave them a supper at the Continental at which Bram Stoker was present. On this occasion, he recalled, the conversation was chiefly on plays. 'Burton had a most vivid way of putting things – especially of the East. He had both a fine imaginative power and a memory richly stored not only from study but from personal experience. As he talked, fancy seemed to run riot in its alluring power; and the whole world of thought seemed to flame with gorgeous colour.'[27]

Burton completed his Terminal Essay at the Athenaeum Club at the end of September. 'Here end, to my sorrow,' he wrote in his L'Envoi, 'the labours of a quarter of a century.' However, they were not yet at an end. There were still six volumes of the *Supplemental Nights* to complete, two to be supplied from the Wortley Montagu Manuscript in the Bodleian Library, Oxford. Burton was then commuting between London and Oxford, copying as best he could from the manuscript.

The Arabic document consisted of seven volumes, written in 1764-5. There was also an additional volume containing a list of contents written in both English and Arabic, and an autograph note added by Dr Jonathan Scott when he sold the manuscript to the Bodleian Library for £50 in 1802.[28] Scott stated on the title-page that the manuscript had been 'brought from the East by Ed Wortley Montague (sic) Esqr', and that it had been 'bought at the sale of his manuscripts by the Rev Professor White of Oxford and disposed by him to Jonathan Scott from whom they were purchased by the Curators of the Bodleian Library.' At the time of the sale, he described the manuscript as 'the most perfect copy of the Arabian Nights, which has yet been imported into England (perhaps into Europe).' He later changed his tune, however, complaining of his disappointment on discovering 'upon perusal that the greater part of them were unfit to appear in an English dress. Very many of the tales were both immoral and indecent in the construction and of others the incidents are too meagre and puerile to interest a European reader of any taste,.......'[29]

On 13 September Burton had sent a letter through Dr R. Rost, Chief Librarian, India Office, to the Curators at the Bodleian stating that: 'Our friend, Dr. Steingass, has kindly consented to collaborate with me in retranslating from the Wortley Montagu MS of the Bodleian Library, Oxford, the tales originally in vol.vi of Dr. Jonathan Scott's A.N.' Burton then went on to ask, in view of Dr Steingass and himself having engagements in London, if the curators would allow the MS to be transferred, volume by volume to the India Office, and remain under the custody of its Chief Librarian. 'I may note that the Tales...contain nothing indelicate or immoral....Moreover, the MS, as far as I can learn, is never used at Oxford. I am the more anxious about the matter as the November fogs will drive me from England, and I want to finish an extract before winter sets in....'[30]

It appears from the Bodleian Library records, that the Librarian, E.B. Nicholson, prepared a note for the Curators' meeting on 23 September 1886, giving details of Burton's application for the loan of MSS. Bodl. Or. 550-556 to the India Office Library. He made no attempt to oppose the loan, and added a note saying that, according to Burton, the MSS contain "nothing indecent or immoral, in fact the whole MS is exceptionally pure."[31] In the correspondence on the subject, printed in *The Academy*, Burton stated that his official letter was forwarded at once by Dr Rost, 'but this was the only expeditious step. On Saturday, Sept. 25, the curators could form no quorum, the same thing took place on Saturday, October 9, and there was a prospect that the same would take place on Saturday, Oct. 23.[32] I am acquainted with many of the public libraries of Europe, but I know of none that would throw such obstacles in the way of students.'

The records show that, at the Curators' meeting of 30 October, the Librarian recorded that he was unable to recommend loans of three manuscripts under consideration on the grounds of rarity. No such reservation was made in relation to Burton's application, but, nevertheless, it was turned down. Unfortunately, there is no evidence in the Library records to show who may have objected to the loan, and on what grounds.[33]

Henry William Chandler, the Waynflete professor of moral and metaphysical philosophy at Oxford, had been appointed a curator of the Bodleian Library two years earlier. Although strongly opposed to the Library's practice of lending its rare books and manuscripts, he sympathised with Burton's predicament, reportedly saying to Isabel: "Who could have foreseen, when opposing all loans and laying down laws to limit the facilities of students, that directly afterwards Richard Burton would turn up and want an Arabic manuscript, a manuscript, moreover, which no man in the University can read, although it boasts of two Arabic professors.'[34]

It was impossible to find a copyist in Oxford, and those who offered themselves in London, Burton found unsatisfactory. At last, Isabel hit on the bright idea of photographing the pages required. She passed on her ideas to Professor Chandler, who thought it a most valuable suggestion for the University. He not only carried it out, but insisted on bearing all the expenses himself.[35] By this time, however, Burton was laid up with a bad attack of gout.

Recalling this period many years later, the Rev Archibald Sayce, then a fellow of Queen's College, said that he invited Burton to stay with him in the College, 'but he preferred putting up at the Mitre – "College," he said, was "a hotel of the ninth century" – and dining with me twice a week.'

One Sunday, Burton told him that he had gone to London the previous day to see his doctor, as he had experienced some twinges of gout. When the dessert was placed on the table, therefore, and Burton was about to help himself to a glass of College port, 'I put my hand on his arm and said, "Take claret instead; remember the gout!" "Oh," he replied, "the doctors now tell you that port is the best thing for the gout!" and before the evening was over he had drunk three glasses of it.'[36]

On 19 October, Isabel had a cab at the door ready to take her to Liverpool Street station for a visit to her convent in Essex.. Before she could step into it, she received a telegram saying, "Gout in both feet; come directly." Cancelling the cab, Isabel immediately started for Oxford. The following day, Sayce, while at breakfast, received a note from Isabel: "Do come and see us; Dick is down with the gout." He walked up the High Street to the Mitre 'and found Burton groaning in bed and Lady Burton packing up his clothes and preparing to carry him off to town.'[37] Everything was prearranged by telegraph, and Dr Foakes was to meet them at their lodging.

The physician's drugs, nevertheless, failed to provide relief. After six weeks in bed, Burton sent Isabel to fetch Dr Jonas Henrik Kellgren, a practitioner of Swedish medical gymnastic and manipulative treatment. It was nothing if not heroic. The ultra-sensitive gouty limb, 'is shampooed and twisted, and pumped up and down till the patient is in absolute agony, and as soon as he is able to stand upon it, he is driven round the room like a wild beast.'[38] Surprisingly, the treatment brought temporary relief. After a week, Burton was able to crawl downstairs, limp into a cab, and visit Kellgren's establishment in Eaton Square.

Such was the improvement that the Burtons decided to pass Christmas at Garswood, which Isabel regarded as a second home. Lord Gerard had been a kind and generous friend to both of them, and a second father to Isabel. They were saddened, therefore, at finding him seriously ill. With a great deal of difficulty, he was persuaded to go up to town and take the best medical advice. Two days later he was found dead in bed. While in the area, they took the opportunity of attending a large house party at Knowsley. After returning to London, they were invited to Hatfield for the Christmas celebrations.

On 5 January, the Burtons left London for Folkestone, staying at the Pavilion Hotel, where Burton could see his relations, who held several large receptions for them. A week later, they were shocked to receive a telegram announcing the death of the Foreign Secretary, Lord Iddesleigh. The following day, they crossed to Boulogne in fog and rain, from where they travelled on to Paris.

CHAPTER FORTY-THREE

SHOCKS AT THE FRENCH RIVIERA

As usual, when in Paris, the Burtons booked into the highly fashionable Hotel Meurice, the "Hotel of Kings," in the rue de Rivoli, overlooking the Tuileries Gardens.[1] The timing could not have been more propitious. At his first meeting with M. Hermann Zotenberg, the learned and genial Keeper of Eastern Manuscripts at the Bibliothèque Nationale in the rue de Richlieu, Burton was cock-a-hoop to discover that Zotenberg had recently bought a MS copy of *The Nights* for the National Library containing the Arabic originals of Zayn al-Asnam and Alaeddin, previously thought to be lost.

Losing no time in reporting this "find" to *The Academy* in London, Burton said that Zotenberg had 'most courteously offered to lend me his transcription of "Aladdin," and I am delighted with the opportunity of going back to the fountain-head instead of translating from the Hindustani translation.'[2]

Unfortunately, the artificial heating of the reading-room at the Bibliothèque Nationale proved too much for Burton's heavy cold, and he was obliged to suspend his work. On 20 January, he was feeling unwell, when Dr George Bird opportunely appeared. He suggested that they should go south without further delay. Fortunately for Burton, the Arabic scholar, Professor M. Houdas, kindly agreed to copy out the history of Zayn al-Asnam from the Sabbagh MS and send it on to him. Thus assured, the Burtons left the next day for Cannes.

After the chill air and grey skies of Paris, Cannes' warm sunshine and colourful scenery came as a revelation. It had first been popularised by the English aristocrat and Whig politician, Lord Henry Peter Brougham, who had a sumptuous villa built there in 1839. It wasn't long before he was joined by many other members of the British upper-crust, who followed his example. By 1870, the artist and poet, Edward Lear, who travelled widely for the benefit of his health, was complaining that Cannes was growing 'at the rate of 10 new hotels and 200 houses yearly.'

Burton described its Society as 'the gayest of the gay, ranging from Crown Princes of the oldest, to American millionaires of the newest.' Prominent among this assortment of the idle rich was the playboy Prince of Wales, now a fat, balding, middle-aged roué. The Burtons attended Lady Murray's fancy-dress ball given in his honour, where Burton, for the last time, appeared as a Bedawin Arab, and Isabel as Mary Stuart. Despite a packed social calendar of breakfasts, lunches, five o'clock teas, dinners, balls, and suppers, Burton appears to have found sufficient time to embark on his translation of Zayn al-Asnam. He was also able to inform the French publisher, Isidore Liseux, whom he had asked to obtain an Arabic copy of the *Jardin Parfumé* for him, that he had just bought a fine copy for 50 francs, and would 'not want any other or bother my friends any more in the matter.'

Early in the morning of Ash-Wednesday, a movement of the earth's crust deep below the Ligurian Sea sent powerful shock waves along the entire length of the Riviera, causing extensive damage and loss of life. This was followed by a series of after-shocks which continued throughout the morning. Neighbouring towns, especially Nice, Mentone, and Diana Marino, were particularly affected. In the hills behind San Remo, the church in the village of Baiardo collapsed on the congregation killing around two hundred people.

Cannes escaped relatively unscathed. The first tremor lasted for about a minute, rocking the Burtons' hotel but leaving it undamaged. Although guests were rushing out into the garden in a panic, Burton refused to budge. It was only after a third severe shock that he relented. The priests, he noted with obvious delight, 'had flocked to one church, and there were seventeen hundred scared people, who had neglected their religion, fighting to get into the confessionals.'

The following day, Isabel became worried about Burton, watching him dip his pen anywhere but in the ink. When he tried to say something, he was unable to find the words. When he walked, he knocked up against the furniture. He refused to take any medicine, because they were due to leave the next day for Nice to inspect the ruins, then on to Mentone from where they intended to make their way back to Trieste. Nevertheless, Isabel insisted on his seeing their old friend, Dr Frank, whom they had called on when they had first arrived in Cannes. He examined Burton, found him perfectly sound, and thought Isabel was worrying unduly. The same symptoms, nevertheless, recurred during the next two days. On the 26th, despite having packed up, Isabel refused to move. While admitting that the 'earthquake must have shaken me more than I was aware of,' Burton forbade her sending for Dr Frank, insisting that it would pass. Isabel, who thought otherwise, sent for the doctor.

Convinced that she was worrying unnecessarily, he was in no hurry to arrive. He stayed for half an hour, assuring them that everything was all right. Just as he was feeling Burton's pulse once more, prior to leaving, Burton suddenly suffered a severe attack of epileptiform convulsions, which lasted for about half an hour. Dr Frank assured Isabel that Burton did not suffer, but appeared doubtful as to whether he would recover.

Horrified that he might not have been 'properly baptised,' meaning of course the Catholic sacrament, she got some water, knelt down, and saying some prayers, baptised him. Shortly afterwards he recovered consciousness, completely unaware of what had happened.

For a time, he was confined to bed and sofa with a diet of broth and bromide, milk and soda-water, and was carefully nursed. It soon became clear, however, that it would be impossible for Burton to move without a travelling doctor in attendance. Although strenuously resisting the idea for several days, he was eventually won round. Isabel telegraphed to England, and a physician, Dr Ralph Leslie of Toronto, on the look-out for a temporary travelling appointment, was sent to them. After leaving Cannes on 9 March, they booked into the Hotel Victoria in Monte Carlo, Burton feeling well enough to make excursions to Mentone and Nice to inspect the ruins.

Several days later they decided to press on to Genoa, Burton having to be carefully and slowly transported the whole way. They then travelled on to Venice, where he immediately felt a great deal better, able to take trips in gondolas and short walks in the Piazzetta. Shortly after arriving back at Trieste, Burton informed the FO that, because of ill-health, he was unable to take over his duties as Consul. Dr Leslie signed a medical certificate to that effect the following day. This resulted in the usual exchange of memos at the FO as to whether Burton was or was not on leave, and whether he should continue on half-salary. One ran:

'Para. 22 of the General Consular Instructions requires that a Consul shall "report the date on which he resumes his duties." It seems to me that Sir Richard Burton should be kept on half-salary until he so reports.'

This was responded to sardonically in another hand, 'That is certainly the interpretation of the Regulations, but an application of it to Burton will beget another circular to the Crowned Heads of Europe and the Nobility of Great Britain, Scotland and Ireland, full of allusion to unrequited services and the base ingratitude of a heartless country.

'Still, it is just that he should not receive full salary…… Inform him that Mr. Cautley will continue to be Acting-Consul, and will be paid by the usual deductions from Sir Richard Burton's salary.'

A narrow piece of green paper in the Correspondence File contains Lord Salisbury's courteous but slightly exasperated directive: 'Might we not leave it alone? Burton is going to do the right thing. Perhaps an account of the two despatches will suffice. Simply acknowledge the receipt of the two despatches.'[3]

On 10 April, Isabel wrote to Alice Bird with a tale of woe: ' He [Burton] has been making daily progress to health. He is now out walking with his doctor. We had a consultation a few days ago. He will always require *great care and watching* all his life – diet and internal health; must not climb, as his heart is weak, nor take Turkish baths, nor overwork; and he may live so fifteen years, but he may die any moment of heart disease. And I need not say that I shall never have a really, happy, peaceful moment again. In the midst of this my uncle who was like a father to me, was found dead in bed. Then I have had a bad lip and money losses, and altogether a bad time of it.'[4]

From the 19th to the 22nd of June a grand gala was held to celebrate Queen Victoria's Golden Jubilee. An address was drawn up and sent to the Queen. The first day was devoted to a service in the Protestant church, which Burton and Isabel attended officially. On the second , there was a banquet and ball at the Jager. Burton was brought down by the doctor, and took the chair at the dinner, from which he made a loyal toast. It was the only occasion on which he ever consented to wear his KCMG order.

That July, it was abnormally hot even by Trieste standards. On 14 July Burton sent a request to the FO for 2 months' leave during the hot season, leaving the following day for summer quarters at Rohitsch-Sauerbrunn.[5] The great heat, however, tired Burton, and he suffered a fortnight of bad health. The English Squadron arrived at Trieste with the Duke and Duchess of Edinburgh, and other members of the Royal family on 9 September. The Burtons wanted to return to Trieste, but were forbidden by Dr Leslie. He said he could not guarantee Burton's life for half a day if he had to put on uniform, go on board, and be present at official receptions. Both , therefore, wrote their explanations and excuses to the Royal secretaries and, through them, offered their house to their Imperial Highness, if the need arose. They left Sauerbrunn on 18 September, breaking their journey with a three days' visit to Abbazia, near Fiume, in order to choose their rooms for the winter.

Back in Trieste, Dr Leslie received an offer of a yachting tour to India and China with some very wealthy man, which he was keen to accept. Burton was strongly opposed to having a replacement. Isabel, however, was now thoroughly broken down in health herself, and finding it more and more difficult to cope. Apologising to one of her regular correspondents, J.J. Fahie, for her delay in replying, she said that she had to 'do all my work, and mostly all Richard's too, and often keep up when I should like to go to bed, so that having to despatch about 20 letters a day, my own often have to wait, or it would be the last straw. Nevertheless, 'Richard is very good to me and gives me wonderful energy so I am never depressing but hope as ever.'[6]

Hearing that Dr Grenfell Baker, who had been one of the doctors attending Burton at Cannes was looking for a travelling appointment, Isabel persuaded Burton to let her write with an offer. She did so, and Baker relieved Dr Leslie on 15 October 1887.[7] According to Wright, Dr Baker accepted only on the condition that Burton followed his medical orders. This, it appears, was necessary, since Burton now regarded the time spent over his meals as time wasted, ravening his food like an animal in order to return to his work.[8]

Despite her declared optimism about their affairs, Isabel admitted in her recent letter to Fahie, that they were dreading a forthcoming biography of Burton 'as the editor is not competent. I did contribute a great deal in fact, his early life to about 29 years of age, but the editor has picked and chosen, and not put it as I meant.'

The 'editor' in question, a term as we shall see that Isabel specifically forbade him to use, was James Francis Hitchman, a forty-eight-year-old well-respected journalist and author. It might appear that he had all the right credentials to commend him to Lady Burton as a suitable biographer for her husband. Besides being editor of the Conservative-supporting *Manchester Courier*, and writing for the reviews and magazines, he was the author of biographies of Pope Pius the Ninth (1878) and Isabel's favourite politician, Lord Beaconsfield (1879). Hitchman was also an active member of the Primrose League, an organization founded four years earlier to promote the cause of Disraeli's brand of Conservatism among the wider electorate.

In the Preface to his book, Hitchman informed his readers that he had planned 'for many years to tell the adventurous and romantic life of Richard Burton and the idea had been encouraged by Lady Burton from the outset.' Besides providing material from her 'husband's voluminous collection of letters, diaries and notes.' she had also contributed 'an immense amount of information' on matters of which she had particular personal knowledge. Furthermore, he had also been able to add many things 'through her kindness,' which had, he hoped, 'turned what once threatened to be a mere compilation into a genuine contribution to contemporary history.' Admitting that his 'own part in these volumes has thus become a comparatively humble one,' he hoped to be 'allowed to claim the credit, as Carlyle did on a somewhat similar occasion, of having turned out "an honest piece of journey-work."'9

Privately, however, all was far from well. According to Isabel's highly partial and vindictive account of events written early the following year to Leonard Smithers, she said she had seen Hitchman only four times in her life. He had called on her one day, 'and tricked my heart with tales of poverty, sickness and large family, and asked me if I could prevail upon my husband to let him write his biography because he could sell it for £150. Upon my account my husband trusted him and said he might.'

During a period of great trouble and sickness, she had received 800 pages of proof-sheets, consisting of 'patches of my husband's own books, strung together with little links of Mr Hitchman's in shockingly bad English, and abusing everyone who has ever offended him in all his life, quite irrespective of the subject, as if he had only undertaken it to air his grievances.' They had 'tried to correct his proofs and cut out the abuse of people and things but when we wanted to make it ship shape and to leave out also some of our own (because we were too ill and troubled to read them in MSS) he began to quarrel, and say "*The book was his and not ours*' and he was not going to allow this or that.' Isabel further claimed that Hitchman had wished to insert 'edited by Mr H,' because he had 'got to be afraid of some of the things he had said against people.' She had learned of this just in time, and had sent 'a friend to the publisher who at once cancelled the word Editor which would have been an untruth.'10

Some time in late October, obviously worried as to how the book would be received by the public and its possible detrimental effect on Burton's standing with government, Isabel sent copies of Hitchman's proof-sheets to her friend, Oliver Notcutt, of Messrs Waterlow for his comments. They offered cold comfort. While he was unable to gauge the book's effect on their interests with government, he thought that the 'author had made a fatal mistake, and that is to constantly and persistently abuse the officials of the Foreign Office. Sir Richard fearlessly spoke his mind, and lost favour accordingly, but that is no reason why his biographer should have done so too. It would not have mattered (and no language could then have been too strong) had Sir Richard required nothing more from government. But it is to my mind sheer folly to hit a man one moment and to ask a favour of him the next.'11 There, for the moment at least, the matter rested.

On 22 November, Burton sent a letter to the FO requesting six months' sick-leave. By the time permission was granted, the Burtons had already left for Abbazia, looking forward to wintering in the mild climate of the Austrian Riviera. On 7 December, however, an unseasonal snow began falling which lasted for two months. Fortunately, besides going on a number of pleasant excursions, they had plenty to occupy their time, Burton needing to complete the last two volumes of his *Supplemental Nights*, and Isabel her *Household Edition*.

She was shortly to have her peace of mind unpleasantly disturbed. Just under a fortnight after their settling in, she was sent a cutting from the gossip-column of the Plymouth newspaper, *The Western Daily Mercury*. Under the caption, 'London Letter, From Our Own Correspondent,' the writer reported having 'just heard a funny story about the Sir Richard Burton biography, which is being prepared for the press by Mr. Hitchman, the editor of the *Manchester Courier*.' According to his informant, Hitchman 'strongly objects to the insertion of certain passages which suggest the pervading spirit of the latest English version of the "Arabian Nights' Entertainment," in the work which he has taken upon himself the task of editing. Lady Burton persists in the biography, the whole biography and nothing but the biography.' This had resulted in Mr Hitchman and Lady Burton daily fighting "terrific battles by telegraph." As to whether they were to 'be treated to the unexpurgated edition of what promises to be a book of interest and something more, only the future can discover.'[12]

Thoroughly incensed, Isabel immediately dashed off a letter to the Editor, strongly denying that there was any truth in these claims. 'I have proved to the world during 27 years of literature,' she said, 'that I never print what cannot be put into a girl's hands.' If she had made a mistake, it was to 'remark that "I thought a boy's ways, even if they were tiresome and not at all goody-goody, would be more interesting to readers after that boy became a great and clever man, than dry details of books already known to the public."' Hitchman had not agreed with her, and she had said no more. 'This paragraph,' she went on, 'has evidently been written to sell the book, but that a lady's name should be so <u>unwarrantably</u> and <u>impertinently</u> misused in consequence of doing a good-natured thing, ought to put a cachet on the shady quality of your informant.' In spite of revising her original draft, however, in which she intemperately described Hitchman as 'a stranger who ought to have been born with a red danger signal on his forehead,' Burton would not allow her to send it.[13]

That same day she wrote a letter to their solicitor, Mr Russell: 'Just look what a dreadful mess I have got into with this dreadful cad Hitchman who whined to me about his sickness and poverty till I gave him my notes & 25 guineas which I could not afford. He wouldn't dare do this to a man nor yet a woman of his own class. But because I am a lady he knows he has me at his mercy.

Can you show Marston. Can you threaten Hitchman that if there is a word more of the kind in the newspapers that you will go as far as you can against him for libel or anything to stop his foul temper and diabolical motives.'[14]

Surprisingly, Burton's appears to have been the restraining hand in this affair. Having had the satisfaction of venting her anger against Hitchman, he sensibly advised Isabel that this letter like the other drafts be quietly filed away.

Three months earlier, *The Saturday Review* had dismissed as 'a most poor, meagre and paltry production,' the *Short Sketch of the Career of Richard F. Burton*, an updated reprint of which had appeared the previous year.[15] The reviewer, possibly Mrs Lynn Linton, was nevertheless highly complimentary, even effusive, in her remarks about Burton himself. Recalling Lord Derby's remark of twenty years earlier that Burton's career was enough to make the reputation of six men, she claimed that it was now enough for sixteen. All the more reason to ask, therefore, why successive governments for so long had 'neglected to acknowledge Burton's achievements by the smallest distinction,' and why he had been 'kept for sixteen long years in the place where he could be of no use whatever....'[16]

The editor of *The Saturday Review*, however, chose a critic of a wholly different stamp to review

Hitchman's biography of Burton. In a malicious, perceptive, and hard-hitting critique, pointedly entitled, 'A Roving Consul,' he remarked on Hitchman's showing 'an anxious willingness to efface himself,' to the extent that, 'even when he appears to speak in his own person his utterances sound as if they written down by dictation.' This in essence, of course, is what had happened, Hitchman having transferred Burton's own material bodily into his own book, merely altering the personal pronoun. The book's purpose, according to the reviewer, was 'to show that Sir Richard Burton's "career has been blighted" ; that his contemporaries have not understood or appreciated him; that he is the victim of misrepresentation and prejudices; that he has lived six lives while other men were living one; that he has been "scandalously neglected" and treated with cruel injustice by each successive government; that his only rewards have been a Consulate in one of the least healthy towns of the Adriatic, a Knighthood and a retiring pension of £300 a year, and that posterity it may be hoped, will place him on the pedestal he ought to occupy.'

What followed was a highly effective piece of character assassination, the reviewer concerned to highlight Burton's flaws for public inspection: his 'overweening self-confidence' unleavened with any touch of generosity; his unwillingness to 'listen with patience to any view of the matter in the slightest degree divergent from his own.' The reviewer was particularly critical of the remarks made about Speke, 'not only in terms of disparagement but of bitter acrimony which, whatever, may be the rights and wrongs of the quarrel between them, must be shocking to all persons of fair mind and decent taste when spoken in cold blood of a dead colleague.' In fact, 'Any one who, unfortunately differs from Sir Richard in opinion, any one who is thought to have overlooked his merits is held up to scorn in these volumes.'

There was perhaps, an even more painful sting in the tail. 'By the way, we wonder what Consul or other servant of the Foreign Office, ever had such long and frequent leaves of absence, and spent so little time at his post (drawing salary all the time, it may be presumed) as Sir Richard Burton.' The reviewer concluded by hoping, 'that the want of generosity to which we have already alluded in Sir Richard Burton's estimate of almost every one but himself, may have been brought into stronger relief by Mr. Hitchman than the subject of this most unfortunate biography could have wished.'[17]

In her letter to Smithers written three weeks after the appearance of this devastating review, Isabel said she felt 'quite sure that Mr Walter Pollack, the Editor of the "Saturday" would not have allowed his paper (to use a proverb) to "kick the dying lion" if he knew a little behind the scenes.' She believed her 'only and best course is to remain perfectly silent and quiet, and let it blow over with dignity. Several of the greatest people in England have (like yourself) written expressing their disgust and indignation, amongst them are those who can put him in the position he has so well earned.' She intended, after a while, to 'publish the one he dictated to me and add what I know of him during 27 years of matrimony and 5 of engagement and that will be the *real* one.'[18]

On 5 March they said goodbye to their friends, and at four o'clock drove to Mattuglie to take the train to Trieste. A fortnight later, much to his relief, Burton completed the last volume of the *Supplemental Nights*.

In consideration of the state of his health, Burton, according to Isabel, is supposed to have written in his journal, that the FO, although unwilling to release him, was kind enough to let him judge when he could, or could not, stay at Trieste; in fact, an informal sick certificate. As the summer was premature, and he could not stay, he thought he might as well go back to England to see his *Supplemental Nights* brought out. This is sheer fiction as the following despatch from Burton shows: 'My Lord, With reference to your Lordship's despatch No.16 of Dec. 7, 1887, granting me 6 months' leave of absence from my post on the grounds of ill-health, I have the honour to request that your Lordship will be pleased to grant me a further leave of absence on the same grounds. I am still unable to attend the active duties of H.M.'s Consulate, which is still in charge of Mr. Philip Cautley, and I am advised by my medical attendant, whose certificate is enclosed, to remove to another climate within a fortnight.'

This carried the following memoranda: 'During the three years ended March 31st, 1888, Sir Richard Burton has had leave of absence as follows:

	yrs	mths	dys
May 20, 1885 – March 23 1886		10	5
June 6, 1886 – March 31 1888	1	9	25
Total =	2	8	

For 9 months 18 days out of the above period, Sir Richard Burton was at Trieste on leave of absence, Mr. Cautley performing the duties of the Consulate.'

'Grant extension. It is to be feared he will do no more work.'

Below, another official added in blue pencil the unsympathetic comment: 'Under such circumstances most Consuls retire.'[19]

Burton's request was granted on 18 May, by which time he had already set out for Switzerland, 'being advised by my medical friend,' as he informed the FO, 'to leave Trieste without delay.' The Burtons travelled first to Venice, then on to Milan where, according to "Richard's Journal" they 'called on the 20th, on the Emperor and Empress of Brazil (who had been most truly kind to us during our four years' stay; the Emperor was then thought to be dying, so we did not see them, nor did we ever see them again)...' However, this incident could not have taken place, since Pedro II was still Emperor, and living in Brazil. He, and the rest of the Royal family, were not banished to Europe as a result of a military coup until November 1889.[20]

After a leisurely progress through Switzerland, the Burtons left for Paris on 15 July, where they dined with Professor Zotenberg.[21] Three days later they crossed to Folkestone.

CHAPTER FORTY-FOUR

A LAST VISIT TO ENGLAND

After a brief overnight stop at Folkestone for Burton to see his sister and niece, the couple travelled on to London the following day where they booked into the St James's Hotel, Piccadilly. It had been two years since they had been in London and, naturally, there were a great number of friends to be seen, as well as business to transact.

Burton was delighted to be able to return to the comfort and quiet of his old club, the Athenaeum, in Pall Mall. Arriving by cab about half-past eleven or twelve, he would lunch there, followed by a siesta. From then until six when he was picked up either by Isabel or Dr Baker, he would pass the time reading or writing and chatting to fellow members. It was the first time he had enjoyed freedom from round-the-clock surveillance in three and a half years, and came as an immense relief to him. Dr Baker now took the opportunity of having a holiday, his place temporarily filled by Dr Leslie, who had returned to London.

Among Burton's regular correspondents was Leonard Charles Smithers who, in the next decade, became the publisher of that famous group of avant-garde artists and writers, the so-called Decadents, Beardsley, Wilde, and Dowson. It was during the summer of 1897 that Oscar Wilde, writing to his one of his friends, famously described Smithers as a man who 'loves first editions, especially of women: little girls are his passion. He is the most learned erotomaniac in Europe. He is also a delightful companion, and a dear fellow, very kind to me.'[1]

Smithers had first come to Burton's notice in February 1885, when, as a young man of only twenty-three, he wrote asking for his name to be put down as a subscriber for Burton's *Nights*. Born in the steelmaking town of Sheffield in south Yorkshire on 19 December 1861, he had studied law at Wesley College and was presently working for a local firm of solicitors, Meredith Roberts and Mills.[2]

Like some other lawyers of Burton's acquaintance such as John Payne, Theodore Watts and Edward Heron-Allen, Smithers' real interests lay elsewhere. In his case, it was the printing and publication of books, mainly of erotica. Some time after qualifying in 1884, he had struck up a friendship with Harry Sidney Nichols a young printer who also dealt in rare books. Nichols had moved to Sheffield from Leeds, where he had opened up, what he rather grandiosely termed, "Nichols' Great Emporium and Literary Lounge." Finding they shared the same tastes, the two men formed a loose partnership, and began the covert production and distribution of pornographic literature. By 1888, the London end of the marketing of these books was being handled by the bookseller, Edward Avery.

Since first making contact with Burton, Smithers had contrived to cement their relationship by sending gifts of books and, more recently in July, certain unspecified sketches which Burton in his letter of thanks, described as being 'most useful to me.' Towards the end of that month, Burton's curiosity was whetted by Smithers bringing up the subject of his translating a well-known Latin work, the scurrilous nature of which was such that it could not be included in a popular edition of the classics. 'Do you speak of a new translation of the Priapeia?' Burton asked. 'If so I should like to see it.'

The *Priapeia*, as later described by Smithers was, 'a collection of short poems in the shape of jocose Epigrams affixed to the statue of the god Priapus. These were often rude carvings from a tree trunk, human-shaped with a huge phallus…and they were placed in the gardens of the wealthy Romans, for the two-fold purpose of promoting fertility and of preventing depredations on the produce.'[3] The translation would eventually become the first publication of the, so-called, Erotika Biblion Society of Athens, a fictional imprint directly modelled on Burton and Arbuthnot's Kama Shastra Society of Benares. Smithers also closely followed Burton in annotating the Latin text 'from an erotic (and especially a paederastic) point of view,' and in providing it with a scholarly apparatus comprising an Introduction, Notes Explanatory and Illustrative and Excursus.

The Burtons spent the early part of August at Ramsgate, taking rooms at the Granville and making daily excursions to other seaside resorts along the Kent coast. After a week, according to Isabel, 'the air proved too strong for him,' and they returned to London, this time to the plush Langham Hotel in Portland Place. Despite its being the holiday season with many people out of town, old friends and relatives came and lunched and dined with them every day, which cheered up Burton immensely.

Dr Baker having returned from holiday, Burton made a brief visit to Oxford, where he needed to carry out some additional research at the Bodleian Library. From there they went to the Queen's Hotel, in Upper Norwood, to be near Burton's sister and niece for a fortnight, and enjoy the Crystal Palace.[4] Extreme restlessness had now become a leading symptom of Burton's complaint. It appeared to Isabel as if they were always on the move, Burton draining an area of its interest long before others had got as far as deciding whether they liked the place or not. When he arrived at this stage he would anxiously say: "Do you think I shall live to get out of this, and to see another place?" She used to reply, "Of course you will. Let us go today, if you feel like that." This was sufficient to quieten him for a while, and he would say: "Oh, no; say next Monday or Tuesday."[5]

They left London around the middle of October, spending ten days at the Pavilion in Folkestone in order for Burton to be near his sister and niece. 'They had tried hard to persuade him to spend the winter with them instead of going to Cannes, the year of the Riviera earthquake. Gypsy-like he abhorred the idea of tying himself down for any length of time. So long as it was possible even to be carried in and out of trains and steamers, travel he would.'[6] On 26 October, a gusty morning lit up occasionally by pale gleams of sunshine, the Burtons crossed to Boulogne. It was the last time that brother and sister would see each other.

The Burtons stayed for three days at Boulogne, before going on to Paris. Thankfully leaving behind the rain and fog of Paris on 2 November, they travelled to Geneva by the train de luxe, taking a suite at the Hotel Nationale. 'Today has been glorious,' Burton wrote in a postcard to his friend, W.F. Kirby, two days later, '– all sun and blue with Mont Blanc as clear as crystal.'

Here, Burton sent a letter to the FO requesting further leave until the end of March: 'My medical adviser, as the enclosed medical certificate shows, is of the opinion that I cannot without danger, endure the cold damp of Trieste during the ensuing winter, and is favourable to my trying the dry air of the sanitary stations about the Lake of Geneva, where I shall await your Lordship's reply.' Despite the despatch carrying a short memorandum: 'Is it to be granted? He has only acted 4 months since May 20, 1885,'[7] permission was given without further comment.

Towards the end of November, Burton gave his last public lecture to the Geneva Geographical Society. The President, M. Henri Saussure, after introducing Burton and giving a short summary of his travels, called upon him to speak. At first, Burton, who spoke chiefly on Mecca and Harar, was very nervous and tired, but gained in strength as he got into his stride. At the end he was asked to sit down, and questions were invited from the audience.[8]

Burton had written to Leonard Smithers back in September, thanking him for putting his name down as a subscriber for the *Priapeia*. 'Where do you think I can get a copy of the *Tableaux* [*Vivants*]?'[9] Expressing curiosity about the Erotika Biblion Society, he asked if Smithers had 'finally established it with list of members...subscribers, etc. Or is it like the Kama Shastra awaiting development?....to be flushed out with members. Something of the kind is necessary to abate a growing...bawdy publisher [Edward Avery] who asks guineas for books worth only shillings and who drums the market only for his own benefit. Avery is a most perfidious rogue; he pirated my friend Arbuthnot's book....What is the address of Mr Nichols? I presume the London agent is Robson and Kerslake of Coventry St....Nichols will be a useful man in the matter of the Scented Garden which progresses well – especially if he has a list of 250 subscribers to the Erotika Biblion Society. Beware of Robson and Kerslake, they are "in the trade".......perhaps it would be wise to repudiate them.'[10]

Undoubtedly in awe of Burton's reputation as a translator and linguist, it must have been with some trepidation that Smithers eventually sent his manuscript to Burton for his critical appraisal. Writing from Vevey on the east shore of Lake Geneva on 2 December, Burton observed that the translation of the *Priapeia* 'is (or rather should be) a scholarly publication.' He had 'only one objection to the workmanship. The sting of an epigram should be in its tail,' going on to provide Smithers with a number of Latin examples.[11]

Restrained as these comments were, they appear to have had a dispiriting effect on Smithers. Just over three weeks later, therefore, Burton was hastening to bolster the young man's confidence. 'Do not mistake me about *Priapeia*,' he wrote reassuringly. 'I like the first sheet very much and find it a scholarly preface.'[12]

On 22 January 1889, the Burtons moved to the Hotel des Alpes at Montreux. Friends marked their twenty-eighth wedding anniversary with presents, flowers and short speeches, Isabel becoming quite emotional. As for Burton, he disappeared, and locked himself in their room. After exhausting their interest in Montreux, the couple moved on to Lausanne.

At the beginning of March, they returned to Lucerne, and nine days later went down to Venice, arriving back at Trieste on 12 March. Here Isabel was weak for a long time, following a bout of influenza which had begun in Switzerland. Faced with an uncertain future, she decided to collect as many souvenirs as possible of the home she had taken to her heart. She therefore hired a talented young painter, Albert Letchford, with whom they were already acquainted, to paint the four views from their windows, and nine of their favourite interiors, including Burton studying in his bedroom. After completing this assignment, Letchford went on to paint Burton for the Stanley Exhibition, and one life-size fencing picture, which Isabel later exhibited at the Grosvenor Gallery.[13]

Around the middle of May, Burton informed W.F. Kirby that they would not be in England that year. 'I cannot remove myself so far from my books, and beside, I want a summer in Austria, probably at Closen or some place north of Vienna. We had a long ten months' holiday and must make up for time lost. *The Scented Garden* is very hard work, and I have to pay big sums to copyists and so forth. Yet it will, I think, repay the reader. What a national disgrace is this revival of Puritanism with its rampant cant and ignoble hypocrisy! I would most willingly fight about it, but I don't see my way.'[14]

Burton had written to Smithers earlier that month, stating that he did not think that the Post Office was directing its attention to Trieste, and that if he wanted 'any book sent home to England safely you could transact it to me and I would forward it at once. Collection seems confined to Holland and France. I have my own dodge for sending home parcels. About a week ago I applied to Mr Ashbee [to his private address] and he has not yet answered….Does the surveillance over Mr Nichols affect you?' In a further letter to Smithers just over three weeks later, Burton expressed the hope that his friends would keep him 'au courant of the Vizetelly business. It appears to me that the national purity is going too far and that a reaction will presently set in'[15] Given the current moral climate in England, this was a pretty forlorn hope.

As a result of an action brought by the National Vigilance Association during the previous year, the London publisher, Henry Vizetelly, had been charged with obscene libels for publishing translations of Emile Zola's *La Terre*, *Pot Bouille* and *Nana*. 'Zolaism,' as the *Methodist Times* described it, was a disease 'a study of the putrid…..No one can read Zola without moral contamination.'[16] Vizetelly appeared at the Old Bailey in October 1888, prosecuted by the Solicitor General, his junior being the future prime minister, H.H. Asquith. Seeing how the land lay when the jury objected to passages from *La Terre* being read out in open court, Vizetelly changed his plea to guilty. After promising to withdraw the books from circulation, he was bound over for twelve months and fined £100.[17]

Unfortunately, he made the mistake of allowing earlier published translations of Zola, which had not been the subject of the first trial, to continue in circulation. The National Vigilance Association again took action and, in May 1889, Vizetelly, now an old man of seventy, found himself once more in the dock at the Central Criminal Court. This time unable to pay the fine, he was given a three months' prison sentence.

Burton thanked Smithers early in June for keeping him 'informed concerning Vigilant Society,' agreeing with the other's view that 'these idiots are driving the trade underground to the detriment of everyone.' Despite these problems, however, there was to be 'no falling by the wayside…let's play hell and raise Cain.'[18] Even at this late stage, however, Smithers still needed reassurance as to the quality of his translation. 'You are unreasonably despondent about your volume,' Burton wrote. 'It is by no means a "poor amateurish piece of work"…..The commentary is excellent and I congratulate you upon it throughout.'[19]

With his *Priapeia* now almost ready for the printer, Smithers had suggested that they collaborate on a new and more elaborate edition, Burton providing a metrical version of Smither's prose translation of the Latin text. There would be fuller and more extensive notes on various sexual practices supplemented with erotic illustrations. While Burton approved of the suggestion, he pointed out that it would probably be another year before he was free from engagements. For whatever reason, he shortly afterwards changed his mind, and threw himself wholeheartedly into this new project.

The following month, only a short while after having resumed his Consular duties, Burton requested, and was granted further sick leave. On 1 July, he and Isabel returned to Adelsburg. However, they both fell sick there, and a week later moved on to Graz. After numerous excursions, they went to Murzuschlag, the station at the bottom of the Semmering, the most easterly and lowest of the great Alpine passes in east central Austria.

The heat, together with reports of cholera, had driven everyone out of the town to the mountains, and it was impossible to get a bed either for love or money. Ever resourceful, Isabel immediately took a carriage and drove up to the Lambach Hotel, situated on an eminence overlooking the town. All the rooms were occupied except one. After seeing Burton and Dr Baker settled in there, she and her maid, Lisa, went down into a sort of outhouse, where they had a little room leading out of the carriage stable, with pigs on one side and a wash-house on the other.

Early in August, they travelled to Maria-Zell, the Lourdes of Austria, nearly 3,000 feet up in the north Styrian Alps. They stayed there for a fortnight, then heard there was room on the Semmering. An annexe of the Sudbahn Hotel, it turned out to be a delightful place with glorious views of the soaring mountains covered with pine forests, exhilarating air, good food, and above all, quiet. Their idyll was shattered, however, when they got, what Isabel described as, 'a startling letter from the Foreign Office to Richard, wanting to know why he had had so much leave, although they had told him to take it.'[20]

The letter, dated 10 August, and, for good reason, not printed by Isabel, ran as follows: 'Sir, The Comptroller and Auditor-General notice that you have been absent from your post for a period of some two years and three months since June 1886, have remonstrated at so long and unprecedented an absence, and requested an explanation of the circumstances. I am, therefore, directed by the Marquis of Salisbury to request that you will, if possible, furnish such explanation as may enable his Lordship to reply.'

After providing a summary of Burton's requests for leave over this period, a perplexed official wrote: 'What answer should we return to the Audit office? One of the Examiners was here the other day, and he made the remark that Sir Richard Burton was an author, and that Sir Richard's prolonged leave was probably owing to that fact.'

This was commented on drily: 'I cannot suggest any answer except perhaps that absence from his post was a constitutional defect.'[21]

Burton replied at length on 19 August, enclosing a medical certificate from Dr Baker. One of the memoranda appended to Burton's letter reads: 'Sir Richard Burton's explanation must go to the Audit Office for what it is worth. I read between the lines that he is very angry. Another: 'Does Lord Salisbury want anything said to endorse Sir Richard Burton's explanations of his absence from his post, and sending it to the Audit Office?'

This was replied to very sympathetically and perceptively by the Prime Minister: 'There is no doubt that his health prevents constant attendance now. He is an officer whom one would wish to treat with all possible consideration, though his qualities have never been those which are best fitted for a commercial consulate. As the prime minister of an Eastern despot he would have been splendid.' Some time later, Lord Salisbury added below in red ink: 'Send the medical certificate to the Audit Officer, and inform him that in the course of Sir Richard Burton's services as an explorer and scientific traveller, special indulgences have been shown him in respect of illnesses contracted by him in that capacity. Salisbury. Sept. 4.'[22]

It was a neat solution, and the final Olympian word on the matter. A note later in the file stated, 'that the Chief Clerk thinks that the matter need not be pursued…'

Worried by the FO letter, Burton decided to cut their holiday short. Writing to Smithers the day after arriving at Vienna, Burton thanked him 'for the last sheets of Priapeia…it is delicate and artistic, we must avoid anything "bawdy." The volume must be large and handsome.' He asked Smithers to write him a 'line to Trieste, where we shall be about mid-September.[23] An attack of gout, however, resulted in Burton's returning to Trieste earlier than intended.

Just over a week after arriving back, Burton wrote to Smithers enclosing a specimen of the wording of the title-page of the *Priapeia*, which he wished to see in print. He was adamant that they should 'not hurry this affair, but allow Mr Nichols plenty of time to kick off. When this is done I must find a new lot of subscribers. It is not my…[intention?] just at present (with Garden, Penteramone etc in view) to be prominent in the matter, but when the time comes I can work with Quaritch, Rob[son] and Ker[slake]. Arbuthnot and [whole] of them. Let us say 500 copies at £3 3 0 – 320 pp, an outlay of £150 – £200 which we must share.'[24]

Smithers disagreed, however, with Burton's plan of allowing sufficient time to sell the 1st edition. 'I am rather afraid,' he wrote in his long reply, 'of Combrugghe (an Amsterdam publisher) & Avery reprinting the work if it takes well. A second edition *de luxe* would knock this on the head, and the two editions could sell well concurrently if the first has 4 months start – which it must have, as the second could not be prepared in less time.' These things considered, he thought it 'might be as well to get the subscription list filled as early as possible.' Expressing his satisfaction with Burton's proposal of dividing the expense and the profits equally, Smithers thought that the outlay would not be much in excess of £100, believing that he could get the volume printed at 3 shillings a page.[25]

On 6 November, Burton informed W.F. Kirby that they were starting on their winter's trip in nine days' time. 'From here to Brindisi, await the P. and O., then to Malta (ten days), Tunis (month) Tripoli and Algiers, where I hope to see the very last of *The Scented Garden*.'[26]

Crowds of friends came to see them off with bouquets of flowers. After landing the next day at Brindisi, strong gales forced them to stay there for several days waiting for the steamer taking them on to Malta. They finally left in the P&O *Rosetta* on 24 November, arriving the next day at Valetta, where they booked into the Royal Hotel. After being delayed again by storms, they finally left on 19 December. They had a nineteen hours' run to Tunis. They enjoyed this most of all, as it was decidedly the most Oriental, though it was neither so grand, nor so wild as Damascus. Burton had a slight attack of gout, but as soon as this passed, they saw everything that was to be seen.

The immediate problem now was how to get from Tunis to Algiers. Isabel, therefore, wrote to Sir Lambert Playfair, now Consul-General for the territory of Algeria and the northern coast of Africa: 'Dear Sir Lambert Playfair,' she wrote, 'First I owe you a thousand apologies for not addressing you properly, but I am sure you will excuse me because the F.O. List I have with me is so old. Seriously you will I fear think me very tiresome for asking advice & not taking it, but the fact is we are a pair of middle aged cripples & from what I hear the ferry is so far from the town that if I once got there, I should never come down to the town & never see anything so that I want you to transfer me to the Continental which they say is near the Orient & under a Swiss proprietor. I look forward to making your acquaintance and my husband also. We leave here on Tuesday 14th <u>DV</u> & we shall come along very slowly as he cannot travel much during the day. I fancy we shall get to Algiers about the 24th. I am sending all our heavy luggage by grand vitesse train straight (ship seemed so uncertain).'[27]

In the event, the Burtons ended up staying at the Hotel St George. Isabel described Algiers as an ideal place to look at. At first Burton was delighted with it, and thought he might end his days there. By the end of three weeks he had a complete change of mind. He wrote to Payne on 28 January, mainly about his failure to find manuscripts of *The Scented Garden* at Tunis. 'Today,' he went on, 'I am to see M. Macarthy, of the Algiers Bibliothèque Musée; but I am by no means sanguine. This place is a Paris after Tunis and Constantine, but like all France (and Frenchmen) in modern days as dirty as ditchwater.'[28]

On 16 February, they started for what Isabel called one of the great humbugs of the world, the baths at Hammam R'irha. They stayed there a week, during which it did nothing but pour with rain. Burton, however, was able to do a great deal of work on Catullus. In an undated letter from there, Burton advised Smithers to, 'Put off Rob[son] and Ker[slake]….the rascals want to reprint… If I were you I should certainly consider Catullus. Why draft roughly, we have plenty of time, especially as this interruption has occurred…..You must do your best to see if your house is watched. That can easily be done. You are the best judge about the probability of a search warrant; you should be perfectly prepared. The detective's blind is easily seen through. I suspect Vigilance Society…who clearly has scent of the book some time ago….As I told you, it is impossible for me to appear clearly as long as I hold Consulate.

Don't forget to consult me about anything. I am again working on Catullus. Pity we can't bring him out before Priapeia, no one could have said a word.'[29]

They were back in Trieste in time for Burton's sixty-ninth birthday. A week later, he wrote a follow-up letter to Mr A.G. Ellis of the British Museum whom he had contacted while in Algiers: 'It is very kind and friendly of you to write about *The Scented Garden* MSS….I know the two Paris MSS (one with its blundering name): they are the merest abridgements, both compressing Chapter 21 of 500 pages (Arabic) into a few lines. I must now write to Gotha and Copenhagen in order to find out if the copies there be full. Can you tell me what number of pages they contain?…'[30]

The Annual Report of the National Vigilance Association for 1890 described how, during that year, it had had several cases which it had brought under Lord Campbell's Obscene Publications Act. One of these which resulted in a successful prosecution, was against the exhibitors of Jules Garnier's illustrations of the works of Rabelais. It is against this background that the flurry of letters which passed between Burton and Smithers in the coming months should be understood.

Responding immediately and 'in haste' on 10 May to a letter from Smithers of a few days earlier, Burton wrote, 1. 'It will never do to withdraw the book after 41 names have applied for copies. 2 I cannot take too active a part while my direction is "Consulate Trieste", my service ends on March 19/91 after which I am free. 3. I propose my agent Mr O. Notcutt to forward the letters to you and have written to him...of course someone has played spy, but how can that affect you?' adding in a PS 'The first thing I would advise is to clear your house of copies, correspondence etc.'[31] The following day Burton warned Smithers that he 'must be fully prepared for search warrant, and we must avoid any questions being asked in the H[ouse] of C[ommons], now or at some future time.'[32]

Four days later he wrote: 'The thing is a misfortune and nobody's fault. But there is one precaution absolutely necessary. All the copies at the printer should be packed up and stored. We must then have patience and delay till times are quiet.

Of course no one can complain of translations from the classics, but the notes and discurses will bring me under the act.....'[33]

With Burton's retirement now less than a year away, Isabel was, if anything, even more paranoid about possible police action than she had been during the printing of the *Nights*. With this foremost in mind, she was in no mood to mince her words in writing a long letter the following day to Smithers without Burton's knowledge. She was particularly incensed that Smithers was concealing his identity, but that her 'husband was doing a most quixotic thing to him most dangerous' by allowing himself to be openly identified. 'Meanwhile you seem to be his evil genius. He puts his name forward and you are thoroughly screened and protected, and if there is a row, the pension which is to keep him for the remainder of his days, after an honourable career of 49 years, will most likely be withheld or reduced to a minimum.'

Nevertheless, she was at a loss to account for Burton's actions. 'What madness possesses him I cannot think – to risk a whole future for a miserable £500 possible gain. If not, the reason to do a service by lending his name to a man he never saw seems to me equally ridiculous.' Smithers was not to mention her letter to Burton. He could, however, show it to Arbuthnot, who was presently staying with them, and would be visiting Sheffield at her request in June on his return to England. 'You must not mind my writing so plainly,' she wrote in conclusion, 'there is too much at stake – at any rate when we make acquaintance you will forgive and say I was right.'[34]

The venture, having 'come to grief' as Burton phrased it in a letter to Smithers three days later, it was imperative that they get rid of it as fast as they could. He advised his seeing Quar[itch] and the others in order to find out what they were prepared to pay for the entire 500 copies. 'We can then commence Catullus and be more careful about wording the prospectus. Here is the problem. No one will pay the three guineas unless the book is appetising enough.' He thought it best not to be too optimistic regarding the search warrant or concealing the printer. 'Those Purity fellows are great at bribing and never know when an underling might sell you.' He had shown the book to Arbuthnot, who had been there for several days, and talked over various matters with him. 'He can after a fashion assist you with Quar. Rob. and Ker.'[35]

Smithers, taken aback and hurt by Isabel's blunt letter, obviously adopted a very contrite tone in his reply. 'I am very glad indeed of your letter.' she wrote. 'And I think very highly of you for it.' Nevertheless, she thought him 'quite mistaken in thinking that Sir Richard would not be prosecuted equally as well as you. We had the greatest risks and difficulties all through the 16 volumes of the Nights and it was only *Benares* saved us.' Although Sir Richard had 'warm friends and popular honour everywhere,' he also had 'a few bitter enemies he had quizzed and criticised in early days; and those are near the throne and always setting the Queen against him.' She had spent all her life, she continued, 'trying to control these untoward circumstances and restraining him to suit his interests......I dare not tell my husband I wrote to you – he would be very angry with me. He thinks as highly of you as you do of him.' She, therefore, asked Smithers not to write to her again, fearful that a letter might fall into Burton's hands, 'and would have done so if I had been out....'[36]

Writing to Smithers the following day, Burton thought it would be valuable to know how the *Priapeia* stood in regard to the common law. It was 'a canto of verses by Catullus etc. Catullus is openly published and never prosecuted. A private volume cannot "injure the minds of the people" nor in our case is it issued or published.' He thought Quaritch should be their last resort. 'It appears to me that your idea of sending circulars to safe names is very good and Mr N can give them.' Having left the letter open until the end of the month, Burton added, 'Bye the bye, when the detective showed warrant from Scot yard could you gather if he had been directed to look after a swindler hunting for subscriptions, or was he sent about Pr. in particular?'[37]

Not having heard from Smithers for some time, Burton wrote the following month noting that, 'no news is always good news.' Arbuthnot, he said, had written to him a few days earlier giving an account of his visit [to Sheffield] and voicing strong objections to Burton's resuming anything until he got his pension. In reply, Burton had asked Arbuthnot if he would object to their sending out no more than 20 copies 'to properly safe men so as to [discourage?] pirates.' He now went on to ask Smithers as to how much it would cost 'to cover up pages' where his name appeared. 'I should be most unwilling to do this but it might be necessary. Meanwhile I am most anxious to finish off Pr. and to take wholly to Catullus...'

Without Burton's knowledge, Isabel again intervened in the matter, slipping in a short note with his letter telling Smithers not to 'consent to <u>any</u> [copies] being sent out till next year. Arbuthnot says decidedly not....If the £50 is wanting I suppose £25 will be Richard's share. Write this to him. He will tell me what to do.'[38]

Writing to Smithers three days later thanking him for a letter dated much earlier in the month, Burton confessed to feeling very disappointed at receiving no sheets of *Priapeia* to correct or finish off. 'Also no account of Arbuthnot's visit to you and what is being said and done. On the other hand you have got rid of our trouble, but the enemy does not sleep.'

With regard to Catullus, he said, they had 'only two charges upon the public (1st) a more literal translation than anyone has yet dared to make and (2nd) notes which could not be published.' If these were brief, they had no right to charge £3 3s. 'I should be much inclined to £2. 2s. 0d and make it selling advertisement for Pr. at £3. 3. 0d. What do you say to this?' He thought they had made 'two distinct mistakes in the letter. (1) The prospectus is far too promising, and (2) the choice of direction in the last was a sad affair although not to be prevented. My friends will lose confidence in me if their letters be opened by the P.O. and returned.'

Intending to spend the summer in Switzerland, Burton had sent in a request for leave to the FO earlier that month. He informed Smithers, that if it was necessary to contact him on any important matters, it would be better to write direct to him, 'and not through the other person.' He had already begun copying Catullus, and would keep at it until Smithers sent him his prose. 'But I must not hurry myself, and do my work thoroughly.'[39]

On 1 July, he and Isabel left Trieste for what was to be their last ever trip together.

CHAPTER FORTY-FIVE

BURTON TAKES HIS FINAL LEAVE

They went first to Gorizia, and the next morning on to Tarvisio. Although set among breathtaking mountain scenery, neither of them was well enough to enjoy it. Isabel, in fact, had suffered from poor health since returning from their holiday in Austria, going down with peritonitis some three weeks after their return. After stopping for a day or two, they travelled on to Villach, and then to Lienz, the principal town and market centre of the East Tyrol district. From Innsbruck they made a four hours' run over the Arlberg Pass to Feldkirch, in order to visit Bertie Pigott, Isabel's sixteen year old nephew, who was studying at the large seventeenth century Jesuit college, highly popular at this period with the English Catholic upper classes.[1] After two days they left and arrived at Zurich in time for the great Schiefs-Statte fête, or the Rifle Association.

Isabel claimed that, during this Swiss trip, she did all she could to persuade Burton to leave the Service, and to stay in England till he was thoroughly rested and well. They would then return and pick up their things, or have them sent on. Burton, however, would not hear of it. This can be taken with a large pinch of salt. It was the more practically-minded Isabel who was all for Burton's staying in the service until he reached pensionable age. Writing to Smithers only two months earlier of the supposed fix she was in, she claimed that, 'Sir Richard wanted to throw up the Consulate last week and sell up my charming house here, because he could not keep his engagements with you otherwise. You cannot wonder if I felt and spoke strong language.'[2]

At Burton's request, primarily acting on advice from Arbuthnot, but also under pressure from Isabel, Smithers had been forced to make changes to the wording of the Introduction to the *Priapeia*, which had already gone to the printers. In his original version, he had clearly identified Burton as being responsible for the metrical translation. In its altered form, it was now pointed out that Burton's name had been 'inadvertently connected with the present work, 'and that it was 'only fair to state that under the circumstances he distinctly disclaims having taken any part in the issue.'[3] Burton appears to have been satisfied with the changes, agreeing with Smithers that, 'The disclaimer is, as you say strong, but everyone will see my hand in the book not to speak of the first prospectus which we sent out. In those to follow you should send just one, not mentioning the names of Outidanos and Neaniskos. Arbuthnot will do his best and so will Dr Lylie to whom I requested a copy being sent. I don't want to write in any of the copies until I return home pensioned.'[4]

Isabel, for her part, as she wrote to Lady White-Cooper, was looking forward to wintering with Burton in 'Greece and Constantinople, & in March his official term is up. I have my charming house till August,

[then] I have to wind up our affairs & get him home. ....I do not relish concentrating myself into a vulgar little flat with small means. On the other hand, <u>he</u> yearns for it, and I shall be proud and happy to have brought him home alive & safe after so many perils & trials for 30 years & latterly such broken health – that everything else must fade before it.'[5] This was hardly Burton's own view of his retirement. A couple of weeks before he died, he wrote to the book-seller, Bernard Quaritch: 'Nothing tries me so much as quiet domestic life. I don't know about "settling" in London, what we want is a pied-à-terre for books, etc, and facilities for running away at any given moment.'[6]

After leaving Zurich, they went up to Davos Platz, lying some five thousand feet above sea-level among the mountains of the Grisons, in the hope of meeting J. A. Symonds. The writer had arrived there as an invalid in August 1877, merely intending to enjoy a short break before continuing his journey to Egypt. Instead, it became his home for the remainder of his life, Symonds looking back on the years spent there as 'the healthiest, and the most active' of what he described as his 'chequered and perturbed existence.'[7] Unfortunately for the Burtons, Symonds had recently gone away, returning only the evening of their departure.

They had a delightful drive from Davos to Maloja in the Upper Engadine, one of the most beautiful valleys in Switzerland, with its dark forests, snow-capped peaks, and shimmering lakes. Among their fellow guests at the Hotel Kursaal, a luxurious palace at the head of the picturesque Sila Lake, was the recently married explorer, H.M. Stanley, and his wife, who were on a Continental tour.[8] Writing to *The Morning Post* in August, Isabel said that she and Burton 'had often seen Mr. Stanley in a casual way, but we had never lived in the same house, we had never got to know him.' Now, he and Burton were 'always together, exchanging their mutual experiences and ideas,' and admiration of each other's careers had 'developed into a sincere liking and friendship – on both sides – that I trust will last our lives.'[9]

One day, Mrs Stanley, described by Isabel, as 'a sweet, sympathetic, womanly woman with the highest and most refined intelligence,' played an amusing trick on Burton. She got a piece of paper, and turning part of it down, she asked him for his autograph. He readily complied, writing it in English and Arabic. She then turned up the back of the paper on which she had previously written: "I promise to put aside all other literature, and as soon as I return to Trieste, to write my own autobiography." They all signed underneath, and later Isabel had it framed. In his own autobiography, Stanley described Burton as appearing much broken in health. 'I proposed he should write his own reminiscences. He said he could not do so, because he should have to write of so many people. "Be charitable to them, and write only of their best qualities," I said. "I don't care a fig for charity; if I write at all, I must write truthfully, all I know," he replied.' Stanley believed that Burton might have been, 'One of the real great ones of England,' had he not been 'cursed with cynicism.'[10]

Snow fell so heavily during the last two or three days of August that the Burtons were eager to return to Italy. They said goodbye to friends on 1 September, and left in the early afternoon. Six days later, before leaving Venice for Trieste, they took a short trip on the Gran Canale in a gondola. 'How sorrowful it would have been,' wrote Isabel, 'could we have but foreseen that it was the last journey we should ever take together in this life! If we could but look forward, we should not be able to bear it.'[11]

They had left Maloja, fully intending to pass the following summer there, as Burton informed Smithers the day after their return to Trieste. 'I returned home yesterday night and found your letters of Aug 27 and 30. We can now correspond regularly till mid-November. I have read reprint of the Corrections sheet and deeply regret the necessity for the change. But you will see that to oppose the generous voice of friends and well-wishers would be impossible.' He thought the index was very good and not too detailed. 'As regards Catullus....we must avoid all trite notes and dwell at full length upon the notes which hurt our raison d'être in view of the loss of pederasty.'[12]

It is clear from the Translators' advertisement, that copies of *Priapeia* were ready for delivery some time during August 1890, although it would be more than a month before Burton received his own copy. 'I return Arbuthnot's,' he wrote in late September, 'who is as usual very nice and join him in congratulating you on the end of labour 1. My copy is not yet come, can there be any foul play in the matter? I delayed writing to you until your well-deserved holiday came to a close. We must begin Catullus in real earnest about beginning of October.'

In a somewhat amusing re-run of Isabel's earlier secret dealings with Smithers, Burton went on: 'As soon as you are comf [?] please write personally to my wife and repay advances with many thanks, saying nothing more or less private than about the baby. I do not wish her to know that we make coin by it. I wholly ignore Catullus. Let her have accounting as regularly as you please when there is anything to account for. Also direct letters to me, not to Lady B. because accidental opening of the same.' He said that he was 'working too hard at Scented Garden for other disport,' and was keeping 'Ausonius for the winter which will easily see him finished.'[13]

During these last few weeks, Burton repeatedly said to Isabel, "When the swallows form a dado round the house, when they are crowding on the window, in thousands, preparatory to flight, call me;" and he would watch them long and sadly.[14] Isabel had already begun to dismantle the house and to put away things to make it easier for packing on return, since they intended starting for Greece and Constantinople on 15 November.[15] The leave was to last until March 1891, when they would return to Trieste and stay until July. Those three months and a half were to be used to pack up, make their preparations, wind up all their affairs, and send their heavy baggage to England. After bidding farewell to Trieste, they were to pass July and August in Switzerland, and arrive in London in September.

Three days before he died, Burton told Isabel that a bird had been tapping at the window all morning, adding, "This is a bad omen you know." On Sunday, 19 October, Isabel attended Communion and Mass at 8 o'clock, and then returned and kissed Burton at his writing. 'He was engaged in the last part of *The Scented Garden*,' she said, 'which had occupied him seriously only six actual months.' She claimed, he said to her: "Tomorrow I shall have finished this, and I promise you that I will never write another book on this subject. I will take to our biography." She replied: "What a happiness that will be!" He took his usual walk of nearly two hours in the morning, breakfasting well. Friends came to tea, and he had another walk in the garden. During this, the last walk he ever took, he saw a little robin drowning in a tank in the garden. After asking Dr Baker to rescue it, he warmed it with his own hands, then put it in inside his fur coat, making a fuss of it until it was quite restored. He then saw that it was put in a cage to be looked after until it was well enough to fly away again.

That afternoon, he and Isabel sat together writing numerous letters which, when finished, she put on the hall table to be posted on the Monday morning. The only marked difference on this particular Sunday was, that whereas Burton was normally extremely punctual, at half-past seven he seemed to dawdle about his room, putting things away. He dined well, but sparingly, and was in good spirits. About half-past nine he got up and went to his bedroom, accompanied by Dr Baker, and they assisted him at his toilette. She then said the night prayers to him, and while she was doing so, a dog began to howl, which upset Isabel badly. Burton then asked for a novel, and Isabel gave him Robert Buchanan's *Martyrdom of Madeline*.[16]

Around midnight, he began to experience a gouty pain in his foot. Consulting their journals, she found that he had had 'real gout' three months previously, and said: "You know the doctor considers it a safety-valve that you should have healthy gout in your feet every three months for your head, and your general health." This appeared to satisfy Burton, and though he moaned and was restless, he tried to sleep. Isabel sat by him magnetising the foot locally, as she had the habit of doing to soothe the pain.[17] This gave him so much relief that he dozed a little.

At four o'clock the pain intensified, and Isabel suggested sending for Dr Baker. Burton was against disturbing him. Isabel, however, was having none of it, and the doctor was there in a few moments. After checking on Burton's heart and pulse, which appeared normal, and giving him some medicine, Dr Baker went back to bed. About half-past four, Burton complained of a feeling of suffocation. Isabel flew back to the doctor, who came and found Burton in a life-threatening condition. Isabel immediately summoned all the servants, sent in all directions for a priest, while she and Liza under Dr Baker's supervision, tried every remedy and restorative, to no avail. What later haunted her memory, is that for a minute or two Burton kept on crying: "Oh, Puss, chloroform – ether – or I am a dead man!" But she had to answer: "My darling, the doctor says it will kill you; he is doing all he knows." She was supporting him in her arms, when he became heavier and heavier as his life drained away, so that it became necessary to lay him on the bed. Dr Baker applied an electric battery to the heart, and kept it there until seven o'clock.[18] Kneeling down at Burton's side, Isabel held his hand, praying 'my heart out to God to keep his soul there (though he might be dead in appearance) till the priest arrived.'

Eventually, their parish priest, Pietro Martelani, hurried in. Motioning Isabel aside, he explained that he could not give Extreme Unction because Burton had not declared himself a Catholic. She begged him not to lose a moment in giving the Sacrament, 'for the soul was passing away, and that I had the means of satisfying him.' Isabel said that he looked at all three of them, and asked if Burton was dead. They all said, no. The priest immediately administered Extreme Unction, and said the prayers for the dying and the departing. 'By the clasp of the hand and a little trickle of blood running under the finger,' Isabel said, 'I judged that there was a little life until seven, and then I knew that…I was alone and desolate for ever.'[19]

Six years later, Georgiana Stisted described her aunt lying 'weeping and wailing on the floor, until at last, to terminate a disagreeable scene,' the priest consented to perform the last rites. 'Rome,' she said scathingly, 'took formal possession of Richard Burton's corpse, and pretended, moreover, with insufferable insolence, to take under her protection his soul.'[20] She stated that later, both Dr Baker and Lady Burton's maid, an eye-witness, agreed in declaring that Sir Richard had died before the priest's arrival. 'Be it understood we did not blame Dr. Baker. He was employed professionally by Lady Burton, and had no authority to resist an outrage which, moreover, was utterly unexpected.'[21]

As a result of Georgiana's hostile comments, Lady Burton's friend, the Baroness Paul de Ralli, wrote to Cardinal Vaughan early in the following year, enclosing the priest's version of what had happened that day.[22] Msgr Martelani testified that, on 20 October 1890 at six o'clock in the morning, he was called upon to assist at the last moments of Sir Richard Burton, British Consul. Aware of his having been brought up in the Evangelical religion, he had first called on Dr Giovanni Sust, the Provost of the Cathedral, for advice on what to do in the matter. He was told to go, and act as circumstances might dictate. When he entered the sick-room, it appeared that he was looking at a corpse. On asking if Burton was alive or dead, Lady Burton replied that he was still living, and the doctor nodded his head to confirm what she said.

The doctor was seated on the bed holding Sir Richard Burton's hand to feel the beat of the pulse, and from time to time administering either some form of restorative or giving an injection; the priest was unable to remember precisely which. 'These are things which one would certainly not do to a corpse, but only to a person still living; or if these acts were performed with the knowledge that the person in question was already dead, they could not be done without laying oneself open to an accusation of deception, all the more reprehensible if put in operation at such a solemn moment. In such a case, all the responsibility would fall upon the doctor in charge, who with a single word, or even a sign given secretly to the priest, would have been able to prevent the administration of the Holy Sacrament of Extreme Unction.' This, of course, was naïve in the extreme. Not only was Dr Baker an employee of Lady Burton and, therefore, placed in an extremely awkward, if not impossible, position, he was also acutely aware of the importance she attached to

Burton's dying in her Faith.

As to religion, the priest went on, Lady Burton had told him that her husband had received Extreme Unction some years earlier, 'being, if I mistake not, at Cannes, and that on this occasion he had abjured the heresy and professed himself as belonging to the Catholic Church.' This, of course, is completely at odds with what Isabel had said of that occasion, when she claimed to have baptised Burton while he lay seriously ill and unconscious.[23]

Given Lady Burton's declaration, Msgr Martelani decided to administer the last rites. Since it appeared that there was little time to lose, he wished to administer the Extreme Unction by means of one single anointing on the forehead, as was done in urgent cases, 'but Lady Burton said that death was not so imminent; therefore, she begged me to carry out fully the prescribed ceremony of Extreme Unction.'[24] That there was no need for hurry, of course, is completely contrary to what Isabel said in *The Life*, as we have seen.

Catherine de Ralli claimed that, as an intimate friend of the Burtons, everything said about their life at Trieste in the 'true' life had been written from dictation, and, furthermore, that she could name the authoress's informant, which made the book worthless for those who knew the source from which she had gained her information – the same source which had made Lady Burton's life hideous from the day of her husband's death to the time she had left this place.'[25]

W.H. Wilkins claimed that Georgiana's picture of Isabel's 'weeping and wailing on the floor' was a gross travesty of her grief, describing it as 'the outcome of a malevolent imagination from which nothing is sacred, not even a widow's tears.' He asserted – on the basis of no independent evidence – that Lady Burton, 'bore herself through the most awful trial of her life with quietude, fortitude, and resignation.' If the second charge were true, that Burton was never a Catholic at all, Wilkins continued, it followed that he was "kidnapped" by wife and the priest on his death-bed. Wilkins said that he did not claim that Burton was a Catholic, or that he was not. 'But what I do assert with all emphasis is that *he gave his wife reason to believe that he had become a Catholic*; and in this matter she acted in all good faith, in accordance with the highest dictates of her conscience and her duty.'[26]

Of course, she did nothing of the sort. Before Burton can be proved to be a Catholic, he must be proved to be a Christian, and all the evidence is against it. As Edwin de Leon commented: 'Richard Burton was self-reliant, self-sustained, seeking no support from heaven or earth, substituting self-will for faith and strenuous effort for Divine Assistance.'[27] Burton himself wrote in Canto IV of *The Kasidah*: 'Man worships self: his God is Man,' a theme he repeated later in his *Nights*: 'The more I study religions the more I am convinced that man never worshipped anything but himself.' Of the Faith in which he was now to be buried, he had written clearly, caustically, and without ambiguity:

> Vainly the heart on Providence calls,
>   such aid to seek were hardly wise
> For man must own the pitiless Law
>   that sways the globe and sevenfold skies.
>
> "Be ye Good Boys, go seek for Heav'en,
>   come pay the priest that holds the keys;"
> So spake, and speaks, and aye shall speak
>   the last to enter Heaven, – he.[28]

Isabel later observed to Major St George Burton that, 'To a Protestant, Dick's reception in the Holy Church must seem meaningless and void. He was dead before extreme unction was administered; and my sole idea was to satisfy myself that he and I would be buried according to the Catholic rites and lie together above ground in the Catholic cemetery. He was not strictly received, for he was dead, and the formula *Si es capax,* etc, saved the priest's face and satisfied the church.'[29]

The ensuing religious ceremonies, elaborate and prolonged, were all that Isabel could have hoped for. Albert Letchford who had been working in the house for nearly a year, painted a life-size picture of Burton after death. He also made a bust and took plaster-casts of one of Burton's hands and feet.[30] The bust was later bought by Arbuthnot, but broke in the casting.

Isabel was privately informed that, as a special dispensation, the Austrian Government was willing to allow Burton to be buried in England. This meant Burton's body having to be embalmed.[31] Terrified herself, of being buried alive, she requested that the left ulnar vein should be opened, and a strong charge of electricity should be applied for two hours. She kissed him, and then the embalmers came, and she was forced to leave the room. Afterwards, Burton was laid out in full uniform, the room dressed like a *chapelle ardente* [a chapel of rest] surrounded with candles and covered with wreaths sent by friends.

The Trieste authorities arranged a splendid military funeral, an honour never before accorded to a foreigner. Burton's coffin was draped with the Union Jack, on which lay his sword; his insignia and medals were displayed on a cushion, and a second hearse was smothered in garlands and flowers. The Consular Corps for the first time suspended their rule, and dressed in full uniform acted as pall-bearers. At their own request, a company representing the crew of a large English ship, which had just arrived in port, formed part of the *cortége*. Isabel came next, but was too overcome with grief to be fully aware of her surroundings. It seemed that everyone in Trieste who could drive or walk, turned out. Every flag in the town and harbour flew at half-mast.

After the funeral oration, and the singing of the children of the orphanage of the "Dies irae, dies illa," the coffin was placed in a small chapel in the burial ground, where Isabel remained behind the rest. Two days later, the superintendent of the cemetery had his own bedroom draped, adorned and consecrated as a *chapelle ardente*, and the coffin was moved there. It was kept decorated with lights and flowers, and Isabel was free to go and pray by Burton, and was allowed to keep him there while she was preparing to leave Trieste.

Some time, shortly after the funeral, Isabel wrote to Burton's sister: 'Our affairs are so numerous and we belonged to so many things that I have not strength enough to get them carried out before eight weeks, and I *could not* bear to arrive in Xmas holidays, but immediately after they are over, early January, I shall arrive, if I live, and pass through Folkestone on my way to Mortlake with the dear remains to make a tomb there for us two; and you must let me know whether you wish to see me or not.[32]

'I wish to go into a convent for a spiritual retreat for fifteen days, and after that I should like to live very quietly in a retired way in London till God shows me what I am to do or, *as I hope, will take me also*; and this my belief that I shall go in a few months is my only consolation.....I have not forgotten you, and what it means to you who loved each other so much. I shall save many little treasures for you. His and your father's watch, etc. There are hundreds of telegrams and letters and cards by every post from all parts of the world and the newspapers are full. The whole civilized world ringing with his praises, and appreciative of his merits – every one deeming it an honour to have known him.....Best love to dearest Georgy. I will write to her. Your affectionate and desolate Isabel.'[33]

Hints that all was not well in the Burton household during this period appear in *The Life*, where she wrote: 'The Master being dead – if I had been a sensible woman – I should have cleared my house out directly after the funeral; but I was too absorbed with the horrors of my now desolate position, and I had neither sense nor heart to make any changes. From this arose complications, misunderstandings, and heart-burnings enough to make life still more unbearable.'[34] Writing to one of her close friends much closer to these events, she sketched a rather more graphic, even melodramatic, account claiming that, 'During that time I swam in a sea of small horrors – wickedness, treachery, threats......'[35]

Some light is shed on the events there in two typed documents written by Isabel. The first is an undated carbon-copy, possibly written around July-September 1891, largely about the problems she encountered in the purchase of certain paintings of Burton by Albert Letchford. The other, her sworn deposition on the burning of the manuscript of *The Scented Garden*, dated 6 August 1893.[36] Both suffer from a major defect in giving only her side of the story, and that only partially.

Burton's funeral took place on, or around, 23 October 1890. Two days later, 'fearing that my mind or body may be affected by grief,' Isabel handed over power of attorney to Dr Baker and Albert Letchford, 'authorising them to take charge of me & our effects, & my dear husband's body, & convey us to England, & to carry out all the written instructions I have confided to Dr. Baker in a book, a portfolio, & 6 blue copy books marked 1.2.3., A.B.C.'[37] She also handed Dr Baker a cheque for £500, supplied by her trustees in London from her capital, in case there was any need to draw on it.

She then shut herself entirely alone in Burton's rooms for sixteen days, sorting and classifying his manuscripts, packing and arranging his books, and carrying out, what she claimed, were all his last wishes and written instructions. 'What a terrible time it was I passed in the midst of these relics, shutting myself away in solitude, and rejecting all offers of assistance, as I could not bear any one to witness what I had to go through, and also there were many private papers which I knew nobody ought to see but myself, and much that he particularly desired me to burn if anything happened to him.'[38]

'Much' was an understatement. According to Norman Penzer, 'In spite of many vigorous appeals from Miss Letchford (now Madame Nicastro), many poems, essays, and unfinished MSS. were committed to the fire.' She burned all his diaries and notebooks, and into the flames went the manuscript of *The Scented Garden*.' Her reasons for this action will be dealt with in the next chapter. 'Lady Burton,' he went on, 'seemed to lose all sense of reason in the presence of her confessor – a common and uneducated man – and at his slightest suggestion valuable papers were burned.' Daisy Letchford, it appears, wrote Penzer, 'many long and intensely interesting letters, describing her surreptitious reading of many of the MSS before they were burned, and the gems she found among them.'[39] Precisely how this was achieved, if we are to believe Isabel's version of events, is unclear.

According to her undated document, Isabel noticed a marked change in attitude towards her by Dr Baker, Albert Letchford and his sister, after 10 November 1890. Although failing to draw attention to it, this date is significant, of course, in marking the end of Isabel's burning spree. From then on, 'I found the young people gradually change their manner towards me, and grow colder and colder.' She also offers no reason for this, clearly unable to bring herself to admit, that they were utterly appalled and alienated by her whole-sale burning of Burton's works. In particular, no doubt, the burning of his MS of *The Scented Garden*, on which he had spent so much time and effort, particularly during the latter days of his life. Isabel complained of feeling more like a visitor in her own house than its mistress, spending a great deal of time alone, the young people's conversation generally petering out when she entered the room. She claimed that, 'Many things were said to her that would have terrified the brain of a weaker woman, and which always wounded my heart, because I could see no reason for it.' She expressed similar sentiments in a letter to Dr Baker early in the following year, where she spoke of the 'eleven weeks during which you were <u>anything</u> but kind – the why is only known to God and yourself....'[40] This can only be regarded as naïve and obtuse in the extreme.

By the time she came to write her deposition on *The Scented Garden* in 1893, she had the knives out for Dr Baker, now cast in the role of ring-leader of a conspiracy. '3 weeks after my husband's death,' she wrote opaquely, 'some incidents occurred of a nature which wounded the vanity of Dr Baker...and from having been treated with the greatest consideration and kindness as resident physician to Sir Richard Burton, he became my most bitter enemy.' No mention here, of her acknowledgement in the letter already quoted, of his '3 years care and attention to my beloved husband; your kindness and consideration for me at his death bed and for three weeks afterwards,' and later when she left Trieste for England. She now alleged that Dr Baker persuaded not only Albert Letchford to follow his lead, but the painter's sister, Daisy, their uncle, Peter Jones, Ursula, one of her housemaids, 'whom they sent to spy on all my actions,' and her husband's copyist, Mrs Maylor. The latter who is described in effect as a double agent, 'reporting back to both sides,' is supposed to have informed Isabel that 'they had begun to conspire against me the night after my husband died, even before he was buried.'

The impression is given that they lost no time in deliberately and calculatedly taking advantage of Isabel's vulnerable situation. No sooner had she appointed Dr Baker and Albert Letchford her guardians with full powers of attorney, 'than everything was resorted to, of treachery to frighten me to death. Dr Baker used to come into my room, and make frightful quarrels with me, they had visions of my husband walking about (without his hat) in the streets and under the house and I cannot tell what besides.'

Nor was this all. 'When they had got all the little I had to give, or remembrances of my husband and presents and what I had agreed to pay Mr Letchford for my pictures, he suddenly asked for £40 and Miss Letchford proposed that he should go to England with us, so that I should have to pay for Dr Baker, Mr Letchford, Miss Letchford, myself and a maid during the journey, stopping at Hotels, and at the Langham where I was going,' apart from Dr Baker who would be returning to his mother's house. Isabel 'gently remarked' that she could not afford the additional expense.

The arrival of her forty-eight-year-old cousin, Canon G.W. Waterton, who stayed a month, provided some welcome respite. Rector of the Church of Our Lady and St Joseph in Carlisle since 1879, Waterton had enjoyed a distinguished career at Ushaw College, the Catholic seminary not far from Durham. He took great pride in being a lineal descendant of the martyred 15th-16th century humanist and statesman, Sir Thomas More. He was also no less proud of being a nephew of the famous traveller, naturalist and eccentric, Charles Waterton.[41] Having obtained special dispensation from Rome, he said Mass in Isabel's chapel, gave her Communion every morning, and helped her with the books and manuscripts. Eventually, these, together with Isabel's numerous personal effects, were packed in two hundred and four cases.

Around the end of the first week in January 1891, Dr Baker and Albert Letchford moved out of the palazzo to stay with Mrs Letchford, Isabel wishing to clear the house of its beds, lamps and furniture. Daisy Letchford, however, stayed with her as a companion. On 20 January, Isabel had to go to the Sant' Anna cemetery to see Burton's remains prepared and loaded on board the Cunard liner *Palmyra*.[42] Feeling nervous and unwell, Isabel experienced difficulty in dressing herself and arranging her hair. Having parted at an earlier stage with her personal maid Eliza, for unspecified reasons, she called on Daisy Letchford to help, only to discover that she had left at daylight, without a word of warning and without saying goodbye. Isabel fainted, 'but on coming to I reasoned with myself, took courage in both hands and went through my dreadful day alone.'

Four days later, Albert Letchford called at the palazzo, claiming that Isabel had said defamatory things about his sister. He threatened to call her before a tribunal, thus effectively stopping her from making her journey back to England. He also claimed that Austrian law would be very severe and any damages punitive. 'I was quite alone in the house with only 3 maid-servants,' Isabel wrote, 'and having a weak heart and besides being very ill and broken I was very frightened of him and did as he bid me.' She, therefore, sat down and wrote a short note to Letchford's dictation, addressed to Mrs Letchford, solemnly swearing that she had 'never said anything detrimental to Miss L's character which of course would only have been downright scandal on my part.' She added that, 'Miss Letchford 'came to me as a friend in time of need and I deeply regret she does not accompany me to England as a friend as I hoped she would.'[43]

Shortly after he had left, Baron and Baroness Sartoris arrived on a visit. Isabel told them what had happened, and they agreed to stay with her. Presently, Letchford returned stating that the family was not satisfied, and that she needed to write more. With friends in the house, Isabel now 'took courage and refused.'

The following day, Isabel went round to Dr Baker's hotel to ask for the return of her two documents together with the £500 cheque. Later that morning he wrote a note apologising for missing her, 'but I was in bed and the people here are so slow.' Requesting an acknowledgement for sending the items, he reminded her that he had 'offered to return them some time back.' He was pleased to hear that she would be ready by Tuesday. He would 'be here till the messenger returns if you want anything & I shall go and pay farewell visits.'[44]

That same evening, while Isabel was dining with twenty friends in a last get-together, a letter arrived requiring an immediate reply.[45] It was from Albert Letchford, who, having heard from Dr Baker of Lady Burton's request for the return of her documents demanded that: unless full payment was made before 12 noon the following day for the painting of "Burton after death," and the portrait painted for the Stanley Exhibition, legal steps would be taken to recover the balance of £63. Should she be unable to pay, he wanted the picture of "Burton after death" returned, together with the balance of £13 due.

Isabel responded by appealing for "protection" from Governor Cav. Rinaldini and the chief of police, Cav. Pichler. She also called in an artist, Signor Lonza to give his opinion as to the price demanded. He valued "the dead picture" as a work of art at 150 florins, describing 200 florins for such a work as excessive. She, therefore, put the whole affair into the hands of her friend and lawyer, Dr Ettore Richetti. He advised her 'to concede something to buy my pictures in peace.' She eventually paid Letchford '£34 sterling more than I owe,' for the two pictures, as she explained in a letter to Prince Hohenlohe, but was perfectly willing '(because it is fair) to pay 500 florins more, for the full length fencing picture, the plaster hand after death, and a little unfinished sketch, the work to him of a few hours.'[46] Isabel blamed the affair on 'the mischief-making and misrepresentations of Miss Letchford his sister, who was my companion for 11 weeks, and whom God mercifully preserved me from bringing to England amongst my friends and relations.'

Before leaving the palazzo for the last time, she walked round all the now empty echoing rooms, memories flooding back of the once happy times spent there, mixed in with the sad events that had recently taken place. She then strolled round every part of the garden, standing for a while under the linden tree where she and Burton had so often sat, breaking off a little branch as a memento before leaving, which she later framed. She was met by a huge crowd of well-wishers at the station carrying flowers, finding it 'an awful trial,' as she confessed, 'not to make an exhibition of herself.' It came as a kind of relief when the train finally steamed out. For the next hour, however, as it wound along the picturesque route close to the sea, she never took her eyes off Trieste, the home where she had been so happy for eighteen years, and which she would never see again.

CHAPTER FORTY-SIX

SUMMONED BY BELLS

Death had not only robbed Isabel of her husband, but of the long-awaited FO pension which, meagre as it was, would have provided basic financial security for their life together in England.[1] She now faced an uncertain future alone. The chief source of her bravery, as she had informed Leonard Smithers in the immediate aftermath of Burton's death, was that she believed herself to be dying. In the event, she would exhibit amazing resilience as well as business acumen in the five or more years left to her.

Although portraying herself on more than one occasion as very poor, this gave a less than candid picture of her real financial situation. True, the amount of salary due to Burton at his death was a mere £31 15s 11d, and he left only £188 15s 1d in his will.[2] On the other hand, Isabel was not without means. Besides the £204 joint annuity taken out on his and her life, she had the money left in trust for her by her father as well a regular income from investments in Indian and British railway stock.[3]

Unknown to her, plans were already afoot to help secure her financial future, albeit in somewhat more modest terms than she had recently enjoyed. Immediately on hearing of Burton's death, Lord Salisbury had wired Trieste, expressing his 'great regret' at Lady Burton's loss. This, however, was not to be his final word on the matter. He let it be known via the FO grapevine to the PRGS, Sir E. Mounstuart Grant Duff, that the Government would be willing to grant a Civil List pension to Lady Burton, if a good enough case could be made out for her husband's services to science, and if the RGS Council was prepared to back it.[4]

As a result of a report drawn up by Francis Galton, a memorial in favour of the petition signed by the Presidents of the RGS, the Royal Asiatic Society, the Anthropological Institute, and the British Association for the Advancement of Science, was sent to W.H. Smith, First Lord of the Treasury, in early January 1891. Just over a fortnight later, the parties were informed 'that the Queen had been pleased graciously to approve of his recommendation that a Civil List pension of £150 be granted to Lady Burton, widow of the late Sir Richard Burton KCMG,' and that the necessary directions had been given.[5] Isabel was in Venice when the letter from the RGS caught up with her, writing back to the Secretary that she had 'received the good news all today because the snow at Trieste blocks us out from the world days together and as I left the day before yesterday en route for England the letters had to follow me. I cannot tell what a surprise and gratification it has been for me for it also honours my husband's memory besides relieving me of certain natural anxieties.'[6] She arrived in England on 7 February, first meeting with Burton's sister and niece, before joining her three sisters waiting for her at the Langham.

A fortnight earlier, a letter had appeared in *The Times*, announcing the setting up of a fund to provide a 'suitable memorial' in Mortlake Cemetery for Burton. After listing the names and contributions of some of the wealthy donors who had already subscribed, such as the Countess of Derby and Alderman Sir Polydore de Keyser, it went on : 'Should any balance exist after erecting the memorial, it will be devoted to bringing over to this country from Trieste, Sir Richard Burton's library and effects, and thus relieving Lady Burton of what would necessarily be a considerable expense to her.'[7]

The memorial in question was to be a mausoleum of Isabel's design, embodying in her words, 'the beautiful idea found in the tombs of Lydia and Lycia, and which is enshrined in the Taj Mahal at Agra.' It would at once serve to give concrete expression to 'the poetry contained in my husband's "Kasidah" with the religion he wished to die in.' Hating darkness all his life, to the extent that he would never have the blinds down, Burton would lie above ground in an Arab tent sculptured in dark Forest of Dean granite and white Carrara marble. Adorned with both Christian crucifix and Islamic nine-pointed star, it would be unique and 'by far the most beautiful, most romantic, most undeathlike resting place in the wide world.' To Isabel's great consternation, however, she found that the severe winter weather had brought work on the project to a standstill. It would be Easter, at the earliest, before the funeral could take place. Having discussed these new arrangements with Canon John Wenham, Isabel travelled up to Liverpool on 12 February with her sister, Dilly, to collect Burton's body when the *Palmyra* docked the following day.

Isabel had last written to Leonard Smithers in late December, asking him 'to settle up (as you proposed to do) to Xmas or rather say to the 31st January, and then start again because I am in want of ready money and my expenses are enormous until I am settled in England; the transport of the body and the funeral etc.'[8] She now returned to the same subject with even greater urgency: 'May I beg you now to settle with me at once, up to the 1st of July – according to the details of your letter to Dr Baker, which I have and I want money badly and shall be glad of your cheque. Later on I shall see you and talk of the future.'[9]

It was a cold damp evening, lit only by flaring torchlight, when Burton's coffin was temporarily placed in the crypt of St Mary Magdalen Church. After offering up prayers, Isabel and her sister returned to the Langham. Here she finally collapsed under the strain, passing much of the time from then until the end of April between bed and armchair. 'I cannot describe the horror of the seventy-six days,' she wrote, 'enhanced by the fog, which, after sunlight and air, was like being buried alive.'[10]

In the meantime, Smithers, although still weak after being seriously ill for a month with bronchitis and inflammation of the lungs, had recovered sufficiently by late February to send Isabel a profit and loss account connected with the sale of *Priapeia* and subscriptions for the *Catullus*. Expenses connected with the former were roughly £220, 'the large agency fees under the special circumstances having greatly swelled the cost, while the frequent changes of agency have embarrassed the book's sale.' He expressed confidence, however, in this item being much smaller in the future. So far he had received about £190 in cash. He was, therefore, able to enclose a cheque for £25, hoping to follow this with another for the same amount in the very near future. So far, the number of copies sold added up to about £240. He, therefore, suggested calling on Isabel in order to explain his accounts and his suggestions as to the disposal of the edition. What he had in mind as far as the *Catullus* was concerned, was to issue a public and a private edition. In his view, 'the press notices of the public edition will fetch subscribers not only to the private edition but also the earlier work.' Meanwhile, she was due £35, which he promised to remit immediately he received the subscription. 'As soon as I can get to work,' he ended optimistically, 'the sales will go steadily.'[11]

There was certainly no cause for optimism regarding the subscriptions for Burton's tomb. Instead of the £959 needed to cover spiralling costs, only twenty-four friends so far had subscribed a total of £139 15s. Such was Isabel's alarm at the financial embarrassment facing her, that she wrote to the editor of *The Times* what was, in all essentials, a begging letter. Claiming to have been 'left in comparative poverty,' by the death of her husband, 'but by no fault of his,' she thought 'that there would be no shame in appealing to the British nation to help me raise a small but characteristic monument to a man they so honoured, and who had devoted his life to the nation's interest in so many ways as Sir Richard Burton.'

The sum she had initially asked for was smaller, since she had no idea at the time how enormous the expenses would prove to be. Of her husband's library and effects, she had brought over 50 packages at her own expense, but 175 remained behind, which were beyond her means.[12]

Isabel returned to the subject at the end of the month, thanking certain people for their contributions, correcting an error, and stating that the total now stood at £490 7s. 6d. This still left her needing £459 12s 6d more. 'It is only a question of whether it comes out of my poor little patrimony,' she went on plaintively, 'or whether the nation makes me a present of it. I shall be a prouder and happier woman if it does.'[13]

Burton had supposedly not wished Isabel to know that he and Smithers were 'making coin' from *Priapeia*. However, she now appeared not only to be perfectly at ease, but positively eager, at receiving money from its sale. While thanking Smithers for his recent cheques, she was quick to point out that he had sold about 80 copies for £240. 'The edition was 500 copies which would have been about £1,500 and give us £740 or thereabouts….as you have [collected] £240 I am now entitled to £120 already…and I [hope] you will be able to let me have the remainder soon. You can see by the paper how much I want money just now to bridge over this awful time till about July. I shall be so glad to see you whenever you like. Do you think there is a chance of there being a good sale? What hinders it? I had no trouble with the A. Nights and this though smaller ought to have a good sale.'[14]

Work on Burton's mausoleum had fallen so far behind schedule, that his funeral was now fixed for Monday, 15 June, at eleven o'clock. The final arrangements, in fact, were only completed two hours before the ceremony began. Invitations had been sent to eight hundred and fifty-two people, and there was an open invitation to anyone who wanted to come. Four hundred succumbed to influenza, so Isabel claimed, but eight hundred appear to have turned up. Naturally, none of Burton's family attended. "Poor deluded woman!" wrote Georgiana scathingly of her aunt. "After all it was but a barren triumph. No wreath from Royalty, silent or outspoken disapprobation from right-minded people. In spite of numerous and pressing invitations, only one member of her husband's family, a distant cousin, accepted: his sister, niece, his favourite relatives, refused to countenance a Lie.'[15] The same note was struck by Francis Galton, who overcame his scruples and attended. He said he did not see more than three geographers there, one being Lord Northbrook, a former President of the Society. The place was swarming with Isabel's Catholic friends, so that, 'From pure isolation, we kept together the whole time. There were none of Burton's old associates. It was a ceremony quite alien to anything that I could conceive him to care for.'[16]

Three days before the funeral, Isabel had written a very long letter to *The Morning Post*. It was not, however, published until Friday, 19 June. Captioned 'Sir Richard Burton's Manuscripts,' it appeared at first glance merely to list Burton's unpublished material for the sake of those people who had expressed great interest as to what he might have left behind. What she described as his *magum opus*, *The Scented Garden*, had been completed apart from half a page. His *Penteramone* was ready for the press. 'Disjointed, and not quite complete,' was *Catullus*, 'a scrap of *Ausonius*, various small fragments, and poetry.' In addition, there was part of the next section on *The Sword*, one almost completed book on the gipsies, together with several unpublished MSS of earlier travels. Everything would eventually see the light of day. The problem was that she lacked the necessary money to print them on her own account. She intended, therefore, to 'do it by private subscription, and make one thing pay for another.'

It was only after a lengthy description of her role in the publication of the *Arabian Nights*, that she came to the *raison d'être* of her own letter. 'I have now a terrible confession to make to the world,' she wrote melodramatically, 'one which I know will close a great many houses against me, and deprive me of many friends whom I value.' Even then, she kept her readers on tenterhooks before finally divulging what she had done. After locking herself in Burton's rooms following his death, sorting and examining the manuscripts, she had come across this particular one, *The Scented Garden*, treating, so she claimed 'of a certain passion.' Not that one should suppose for a moment, she hastened to add, 'that Richard Burton ever wrote a thing from the impure point of view. He dissected a passion from every point of view, as a doctor may dissect a body....'

While her mind was in turmoil over the next few days as to what she should do, she also claimed to have received an offer of 6,000 guineas for the manuscript from a man she was not willing to identify. She turned it down, on the grounds that, 'Out of 1,500 men, 15 will probably read it in the spirit of science in which it was written, the other 1,485 will read it for filth's sake, and pass it to their friends, and the harm done may be incalculable.' It was dark when she sat on the floor before the fire still considering what to do. Was she prepared, she asked herself, to 'let that soul, which is part of your soul, be left out in cold and darkness till the end of time, till all those sins which may have been committed on account of reading those writings have been expiated, or passed away perhaps for ever?' The answer, despite every other consideration, was a definite, no. Having fetched the MSS, two large volumes, she laid them on the ground before her, then, 'Sorrowfully, reverently, and in fear and trembling, I burnt sheet after sheet until the whole of the volumes were consumed.' By this act, she believed, if her 'husband's soul were weighted down, the cords were cut and it was left free to soar to its native Heaven.'

Isabel ended her letter on a mawkish note. 'Goodbye, kind and beautiful world,' she wrote.' I am not going morbidly to shut myself up, but still we shall not meet.' The goodbye, in fact, turned out to be only a brief farewell, and the world proved anything but kind. Isabel's public confession rained down coals of fire on her head from Press and individuals alike. After returning from a short break in the country with one of her sisters, she was forced into writing once again publicly about *The Scented Garden* to *The Echo* and, later, to *The New Review*, doing a complete *volte face* as to the status of the book in the Burton canon. Prefacing these letters in *The Life*, she said that she had 'made the greatest mistake in the world; I did not know my public, I did not know England. I was under some delusion which I have often bewailed, that I was responsible to, or owed some explanation to, the would-be buyers of the book, nor can I *now* think how I could have imagined that it was, or described it as, my husband's *magnum opus*.'

She now insisted that the only value in the book, consisted in Burton's annotations, and there was no poetry. However, there are just over 400 lines of verse in *The Scented Garden*. No one, even skimming through, could fail to notice it. This fact, coupled with her completely false description of its treating of 'a certain passion,' strongly suggests that Isabel may not have read the manuscript at all. What is more likely, perhaps, is that she read only the earlier part. In her description, 'The first two chapters were a raw translation of part of the works of "Numa Numantius," without any annotations at all, or comments of any kind on Richard's part, and twenty chapters translation of Shaykh El Nafzawi from Arabic. In fact it was *all translation*, excepting the annotations on the Arabic work.'[17]

That Burton would have included extracts from the works of "Numa Numantius" without introduction or comment of any kind beggars belief. This reference, however, to the pen-name of Karl Heinrich Ulrichs (1825-95), pioneer of the modern gay movement is extremely interesting and important, and may well hold the key to the burning of *The Scented Garden*. After graduating in law and theology from Göttingen University in 1846, Ulrichs went on to study history at Berlin University. From 1849-57 he acted as legal adviser for the district court of Hildesheim in Hanover, but was dismissed two years later when his homosexuality became obvious. Shortly afterwards, writing initially under the pseudonym of "Numa Numantius", and then openly under his own name, he began a public crusade for the repeal of the repressive anti-homosexual laws in Germany, as well as advocating equality before the law for sexual minorities, suffering abuse and victimization for his efforts.

Whether Burton translated, or had translated for him, a number of Ulrich's pamphlets, is a moot point.

In Isabel's Deposition on the burning of *The Scented Garden*, in which she expressed concern at a rogue copy being passed off as Burton's own, she wrote: 'If any part of this "Scented Garden" contains two chapters of "Memnon" (works of Numa Numantius) it will be translated by Dr Baker to whom I gave as a keepsake, the German pamphlet, which he wanted, and who was very anxious that it should come to light. I was most anxious that it should not, for I have a letter written to my husband on October 11th 1890, by the talented and charming John Addington Symonds, in which he says, "I am quite astounded at your having Memnon translated, there is so much clotted nonsense in the book mixed up with curious suggestions that it hardly seems worth the trouble." He says further on in the letter which is a long one – "the best source of information regarding the author, would probably be the archives of the police in Berlin."'[18]

It is impossible for the homosexual Symonds to have written in these terms either of *Memnon* or its author, and points to Isabel's having tampered with the letter. Symonds stated in his *Memoirs,* that he 'had not read the extraordinary writings of Ulrichs' until some time after May 1889. Two years later, however, he included a long chapter on Ulrich's theory in his privately printed essay, *A Problem in Modern Ethics.*[19] Such was his interest, that he visited Ulrichs at Aquila in Italy, where he had been living since 1883, in order to discuss the subject with him. Symonds later wrote to his friend Edward Carpenter, that Ulrichs 'must be regarded as the real originator of a scientific handling of the phenomenon……There is a singular charm about the old man, great sweetness, the remains of refined beauty.'[20]

Deeply regrettable as it was, to say the least, from Isabel's point of view, Burton's historical survey of pederasty in his Terminal Essay, could be justified, however tenuously, on 'anthropological' grounds. In her eyes, the inclusion of Ulrich's *Memnon* at the head of *The Scented Garden* must have appeared to lack any justification whatsoever. Not only did it treat homosexual love as natural, it was also deeply personal. It gave an account of the "story of his heart," his romantic attitude from an early age towards members of his own sex, and celebrating such love in verse, as that to his friend, Eberhard, commemorating their first meeting 'at evening's hour' in woodland and exchanging kisses.

Isabel could only have been appalled, and determined, as she had said in her Deposition, that it should never see the light of day. At the same time, she could hardly detach it from the main body of the work, since the many would-be subscribers of the book would not be prepared to buy it in an emasculated form. It was either all or nothing. Concerned for her husband's posthumous reputation and everlasting soul, she chose the latter option, and consigned the entire manuscript to the flames.

The relationship between Isabel and Leonard Smithers, thrown together by circumstance might, eventually, be expected to wither and die. Instead, it flourished, motivated by mutual self-interest. Isabel found that she needed Smithers's publishing and legal expertise in order to forward her ambitious plans for publishing a new edition of Burton's works. Smithers, with a keen eye to being a beneficiary of these plans, particularly with regard to the *Arabian Nights,* sought to cultivate this friendship. It proved to be a financially rewarding, if sometimes uneasy, alliance.

A month after the funeral, Smithers informed Isabel, that he expected to be in London on business towards the end of July. He had been 'steadily working at Catullus,' which he was confident would prove a great success, and had found 'the amount of gross lines in the work very small indeed.' When they next met, he wanted to discuss the plans and prospects of the book with her. However, he had done nothing about *Priapeia* since last seeing her.[21]

In the meantime, Isabel had written to Smithers, requesting the immediate return of her husband's list of subscribers lent to him by Mr Notcutt for the *Arabian Nights.* Since she intended to gradually publish all of Burton's works, she asked him for the name and address of a cheap publisher in Sheffield. 'I would like [to] try him – and perhaps might run up to Sheffield to make arrangements and let you help me.'[22]

Smithers, naturally, was only too willing to lend her a hand. He explained that, acting as drama critic for a number of years for a local newspaper, he had always been able to get his printing done cheaply in the jobbing office. Although the manager responsible was now leaving, he [Smithers] was making arrangements to buy the press, type, etc himself, while retaining the services of the same compositor. He would, therefore, be able to get his work done even more cheaply than before. Once everything was shipshape, he not only expected to be able to offer considerable help with any publication she cared to issue, but would be able to get it printed and published and obtain the paper for it far more cheaply than she could. Furthermore, he was currently negotiating for a 'good rare and second-hand book shop in London, which if arranged this autumn as I expect it will be, will enable me to push the sale more rapidly of anything you may wish me to bring out.'[23]

This was an attractive proposition that offered everything that Isabel could have hoped for, and she was quick to respond. 'If you set up with the type and compositor as you say, I have no doubt I can put money in your way besides getting my work done more cheaply by you than anyone.' Nevertheless, past difficulties with printers had made her somewhat 'cautious and doubtful,' and she warned Smithers that she would be annoyed if anything went wrong. If she came to Sheffield, she would book into a hotel, despite his offer of accommodation at his own house, staying '2 or 3 days to understand and make all arrangements and in that case would wish it kept secret.'[24]

Although Smithers must have been pleased with Isabel's reply, he was obviously annoyed at her suggestion that anything might go wrong. He reminded her that he was 'not personally to blame for the awkwardness which arose over the Priapeia. Indeed, it was through my carefulness that the matter dropped and that no publicity was made.' He pointed out that the latest cheque he had sent to her for £25 represented almost half of the net profits so far made, except for a few pounds, which he had still to account for. He had preferred waiting until he 'could get safe opportunities for pushing the sale rather than – firstly run the risk of exposure or secondly deteriorate the value of the book by selling copies at low price. The book is bound to sell and sell at full price. It is only a question of time and patience.' Having almost completed negotiations for the London bookshop, he would shortly be in a position to push the sale of any of her books. Since he intended carrying on this business in addition to his legal work, it would put him 'in communication with a lot of fresh people – both trade and private customers – as half of my time will be spent in London.'[25]

Towards the end of July, Isabel went into 'severe retreat' at her old convent, New Hall, in Essex, which she regarded as a second home, and where she found 'a mental and physical tonic.' Although writing to Smithers on 8 August, the day after her return, it was almost a week before she received an acknowledgement. Then it was to inform her that his little daughter was lying close to death with 'consumption of the bowels.'[26] In a characteristic letter, embodying the consolations of her religion, Isabel offered well-meant words of comfort. 'How strange that one must condole and congratulate you in a breath. It is hard to part with a little one but if she has been baptised do not grieve, she is spared this very dreadful world to her guardian angel in heaven. See how gently God deals – He gives you a son to replace the one he takes. You must always see the Silver Lining behind the cloud. Do tell your wife that it is there.'[27]

While deeply affected by the loss of his daughter, Smithers's legal and business activities must have left him little time to grieve. Despite his advice cautioning patience, Isabel seemed intent on getting quicker, if substantially lower, returns, by selling off the remaining copies of the Priapeia. 'The largest buyer of remainders is Mr Glaisher of 265 High Holborn,' Smithers wrote at the end of August. 'But I think your Ladyship is wrong if you take less than £600 for the 385 copies, being the standard translation it is only a matter of time selling the whole edition....at £3 3 0.'[28]

This time, Isabel appears to have taken Smithers's comments to heart, and the remaindering plan was not brought up again. By now she had moved out of temporary lodgings at 5 Baker Street into No 67, where major changes and refurbishment had been carried out for her over the past few months. A visitor described the drawing-room as redolent of Eastern magnificence and colour. The floor was strewn with Persian rugs, a

Moroccan chandelier of eleven lamps hung from the ceiling, Oriental divans were scattered about and the pottery was real Istrian, Egyptian and Majolica ware. At the top of the house, Isabel had had built out a large room to store her husband's manuscripts, which she knew, as she used to say, as a shepherd knows his sheep. They lined three sides of the room, and filled many packing-cases on the floor. Not a day passed without her poring over them for hours.

She had scarcely settled into the house, when her younger sister, Blanche, died of cancer, and Isabel had to travel to Weston-super-Mare for the funeral.[29] Fortunately for her, in her grief-stricken state, Smithers took over the tricky and time-consuming task of handling the business of copyright ownership in Burton's books and arranging contracts. Fully aware of the potential value of her husband's *Nights*, she instructed Smithers to omit this from his brief, intending to sell it separately. While suggesting to Isabel that it might be offered to some big firm in the course of twelve months or so, later events make it clear that Smithers had every intention, if possible, of gaining the right to publish it himself little changed from Burton's original text. By the middle of November, Smithers was able to report back in which of Burton's books Isabel had absolute rights. He advised that it would 'be as well to commence negotiations as your ladyship pleases for the ten works I have enumerated as being your own property as these....are in considerable demand and ought to sell readily.'[30]

In truth, literary endeavours were never far from her mind. 'I dream always of my books and the pile of work,' she wrote to her friend, Ellen Bishop, just after Christmas. 'I am worrying on as well as I can with my miscellaneous writing. Fogs have kept us in black darkness and pea-soup thickness for 5 days without a lift....I passed Xmas night in the Convent of the Holy Souls. I went in my cab – the streets were one sheet of ice – and two flambeaux on each side...We had communion and 3 masses at midnight...I passed the night with our Lord and my darling, who had many masses for him in London and all over England that night....I am better and have stronger nerves, and am perhaps more peaceful.'[31] A bad bout of influenza in early January, however, almost brought her to death's door.

By now, the controversy over Isabel's burning of *The Scented Garden* had long since died down. It was suddenly reignited in March shortly after she returned to Baker Street, when the anti-feminist writer, Eliza Lynn Linton, whom she had regarded as a friend, launched a blistering attack on her in a magazine article. 'He was no sooner dead than his widow surrounded him with the emblems and rites of her own faith – which was not his. She did not shrink from inflicting this dishonour on the memory of a man who had systematically preached a doctrine so adverse to her own. She cared nothing for the integrity of the man she thus stultified – nothing for the grandeur of the intellect she thus belittled.'[32] Perhaps even more devastating from its compressed, alliterative use of language and powerful anti-Catholic sentiments, was Swinburne's *Elegy*, published a short while later:

> Priests and the soulless serfs of
> priests may swarm
> With vulturous acclamation, loud in
> lies,
> About his dust while yet his dust
> is warm
> Who mocked as sunlight mocks
> their base blind eyes.[33]

Even by late March, Isabel was still convalescing from her almost fatal attack of flu earlier in the year, her work and correspondence badly in arrears, as she explained in a letter to her friend, John J. Fahie. It is no wonder then, that she was in no fit mental or physical state at that time to respond to these attacks on her.[34] 'My life is now most retired,' she told Fahie – 'prayer and writing, writing and prayer. I pay no calls, I accept no invitations. I am preparing for my <u>great</u> journey, but hope to leave the reminiscences behind me.'[35]

A few months later, Isabel wrote to Leonard Smithers, thanking him for the letters he had sent her, which 'fully answer the purpose and I shall have I fancy enough for biography but will write to you if I have not. In these affairs I cannot afford to be particular what words I <u>see</u> nor do they do me any harm. I think Richard wished his men friends should think I did not know what he was engaged upon, and had he lived, one would have carried that idea out.'

After briefly touching on possible sales of the *Catullus,* she unexpectedly turned to the subject of Burton's obsessive interest in homosexuality, posing a question that, at once highlighted her deep-seated concern over the issue, and the strange nature of their marital relationship. 'I wish you could assure me on one point. Why did he wish the subject of unnatural crime to be largely aired and expounded? He had such an unbounded contempt for the vice and its votaries. I never asked him this question unfortunately, and though it may be a safe dissection for a live man to undertake, I think it is such a dangerous one for a dead man's memory, who, if his motives be <u>once misunderstood</u> cannot defend himself.......I do not know if you understand me. Perhaps few would or old women – but not women of the Lynn Linton school.'[36] Unfortunately, Smithers's response is no longer extant.

It is evident from a typed undated sheet of Memoranda belonging to this period that, by now, Isabel had clearly mapped out her publishing plans for the future.[37] Besides the question of her copyrights and the separate issue of the *AN*, this included selling her biography of Burton for £1,500. She also had several unpublished manuscripts of his to bring out separately. After a while, she wrote, 'when the Biography begins to pall, I propose that the buyer, or myself, should bring out a popular edition. I will then collect his pamphlets, correspondence with the Press, any interesting letters, and the pith of his Labours for England in two volumes called Labour and Wisdom of Sir Richard Burton. If I live long enough, I will write my own Autobiography and leave it to be published after my death.'[38] Given the nature of her illness and the almost daily pain she endured, it is amazing that she achieved most of these objectives.

Personal ill-health and the death of several members of her family had combined to prevent Isabel from fulfilling the promise she had made the previous year to readers of *The Morning Post* of beginning her biography of Burton that autumn. Despite her recent assurance to J.J. Fahie of engaging in nothing but prayer and writing, she seems to have been persuaded to take a short break that summer at the seaside resort of Ventnor in the Isle of Wight, as well as making several other visits. Her writing plans were then further delayed by spending some time at Ascot with her sister, Emmeline, whose husband, Richard van Zeller, died in early September. It was probably not until around the middle of that month, therefore, that she was able to settle down at Mortlake to concentrate on writing the biography.

By then Isabel had already begun negotiations with the large publishing firm of Chapman and Hall. After a personal visit some time in October by George Etheridge, the junior partner in the firm, a meeting with Edward Chapman was suggested for early on in the New Year 'either here or at your house in Baker Street with a view to entertaining the Biography & your edition of "The Arabian Nights."'[39]

Far from occupying her 'two or three years,' her bulky manuscript was completed in just eight months. Under an agreement signed with the publishers on 3 March 1893, Isabel was given an immediate cash-payment of £1,500 for an edition of 2,500 copies. Two months later she was granted a royalty of five shillings for every copy sold of the American edition.[40] During the next few months, while busy coping with the numerous problems connected with its publication, she was also negotiating through Smithers for the bringing out of the *Memorial Edition* of her husband's works.

Smithers, as we have seen, had his sights set all along on obtaining the publishing rights from Isabel in order to bring out a new edition of the *Arabian Nights* as close to the original as possible. Burton had made £10,000 clear profit from the enterprise, and Smithers was convinced that it was still a rift of gold waiting for further exploitation. At the same time, it has to be recognised that his motives were not entirely mercenary. Having always had a high regard for Burton, Smithers was keen to have his own name associated with that of the late great man. However, he was faced with one major problem, that of being able to raise enough capital to buy the copyright. He badly needed an investor willing and able to finance the project. He found him in Charles Edward Jeffcock, later described by Isabel, perhaps not quite accurately, as 'a gentleman who only wanted to dabble in books for amusement.'

A Sheffield man like Smithers, the thirty-six year old Jeffcock was immensely wealthy. A graduate of Jesus College, Cambridge, and a rugby blue, he was not only managing director of the Sheffield Coal Company, but held directorships in two other local collieries, besides being on the board of the Knottingly Brewery Company and the Rhodesian Town Purposes Company in South Africa. He had also married money. His wife, Caroline Bradley Frith, had inherited £200,000 from her father as well as being left a sizeable amount by her late brother.[41]

Jeffcock immediately eased the way for the speedy publication of the *Memorial Edition*, by buying up the copyrights in all of Burton's major books. Three, each with a preface contributed by Isabel, appeared that year, a fourth, and the last as it turned out, during the following year.[42] She was also able to dispose of the manuscript of Burton's translation of Basile's *Il Pentamerone*, though she was far from pleased at the result. 'I have had a great vexation in one sense,' she later wrote to her friend, Lady Walburga Paget – 'the Pentamerone came out, the publisher had contracted with me that I was to erase all the vulgar words; he broke his contract, and took no notice of the erasures, but published it all quite raw, and of course omitted my preface.'[43] It was a foretaste, had she but known it at the time, of what was to come.

In the meantime, it was Smithers's turn to feel extremely discomfited. Early in May, while negotiations were going on to buy the copyright of *The Nights*, he received a letter from Isabel informing him that she had had a better offer. Absolutely mortified, Smithers wrote back immediately expressing disbelief that she could do such a thing in view of their long relationship. He promised to be able to match any other offer, but she needed to be open in her dealings and not go behind his back when they had a verbal contract. He pointed out that he had always dealt fairly with her since Sir Richard's death, even giving up the *Priapeia* at her request, which had left him considerably out of pocket. He now felt that she was being disloyal, especially since he had already committed money to the project in partnership with Mr Jeffcock.[44]

It may well be that Isabel's 'better offer' from Chapman & Hall was no more than a bargaining ploy. In the event, a hastily arranged personal visit seems to have smoothed over matters, leading to Smithers's suggesting a proposition he might make to Jeffcock for the purchase of *The Nights*. These terms formed the basis of a contract that was later drawn up and signed by Isabel and Jeffcock on 24 May 1893. Under it, Isabel agreed to sell the whole of her husband's and hers *AN*, 'on condition of every immodest or coarse word being suppressed <u>now and for ever</u>, and that Mr Jeffcock, Mr Gregg (sic), Mr Smithers, and Mr Nichols, or all concerned agree to oppose any attempt at a "Black Book" on the part of others, and to abstain from making one themselves.' Smithers was to edit it, and the text was to be subject to her supervision. Her stereos were to be used for the 10 volumes, and the 6 Supplementals and the Terminal Essay were to 'be pruned by Smithers so as to admit of copyrighting the whole.' The edition would consist of 12 volumes, each selling at six shillings, and four shillings to the trade. Under this arrangement, she would receive £2,000 either down, or at 5 per cent, with a Royalty of £1,000 to be paid down as ready cash. In the space of a couple of months, therefore, from the sale of her biography and *The Nights* alone, Isabel had made £4,500, or getting on for a quarter of a million pounds in modern money.

Smithers would not be the only one to be upset along the way by Isabel's rather cavalier approach to conducting her business affairs. The following month George Etheridge wrote to her at Boscombe, near Bournemouth, where she was holidaying, regretting the fact that she had not let him see the slip of paper which she had sent out with the prospectus of her biography. In it, she had asked her friends to order the book direct from the publishers, and not from the booksellers. Naturally, the trade was up in arms about it, forcing Edward Chapman to circularise a note to the booksellers stating that her action had 'been done without our or Mr Etheridge's sanction.'[45]

After some delay, the biography was published on 12 July, and proved an immediate popular, if not a critical, success. Isabel later wrote to her friend, Madame Gutmansthal de Benvenuti. 'I have had my head quite turned by the great success of my book. First came about 100 half-nasty or wholly nasty critiques, then the book made its way. I have had three leading articles, over a thousand charming reviews, and have been inundated with the loveliest letters and invitations.[46]

Despite her undoubted feelings of euphoria over the reception of her book, Isabel continued to live in 'mortal dread' of there being an active conspiracy by Peter Jones and the Letchfords, to bring out a counterfeit *Scented Garden*, aided and abetted by Rose Maylor, who had typed Burton's erotic work, and could imitate his style. She had Smithers diplomatically investigate the matter, who reported back to her in late August, that his present impression was 'that...the Scented Garden plan does not exist, or at any rate has not got beyond the stage of idle talk.'[47] Far from being reassured, Isabel followed up her Deposition on the Burning of the Scented Garden of 6 August, with another such typed document written the following month. In it, she threatened legal action against anyone passing off such a forgery as Burton's original work.[48]

Now flush with money, Isabel embellished the mausoleum, putting up in honour of Burton's poem *The Kasidah*, festoons of camel bells from the desert in the roof, so that when the door was opened or closed, or at the elevation of the Mass, the 'tinkling of the camel bell,' would sound just as it did in the desert. On 22 January 1894, the date of their thirty-third wedding anniversary, Isabel passed the day in the mausoleum listening to the bells ringing for the first time.[49]

Having struck a bargain with Smithers to receive all the remaining copies of *Priapeia*, a draft agreement was at last drawn up for the printing of one thousand copies of the *Carmina* of Catullus, selling for 3 guineas. Double this price was asked for a large-paper edition, limited to fifty copies. As joint owners of the copyright, Smithers had originally contracted with Burton for both men to share equally in the expenses and the profits. He was now prepared 'to bear the entire expense of the issue,' in exchange for Lady Burton's assurance of revising and correcting her husband's translation, and making it 'complete and accurate as possible.' She, however, reserved the right 'to modify any words in the said verse translation which would injure the memory of her late husband.'[50]

Isabel's excuse for having procrastinated so long over its production, was because Burton's notes, 'which are mostly like pencilled cobwebs, strewn all over the Latin edition were headed, "Never show half-finished work to women or fools."'[51] The type-written copy which she eventually sent Smithers to edit was, as he complained in his Introduction, 'literally swarming with copyist's errors.' Nor was this all. The text contained a number of gaps, Isabel claiming that Burton intended to wait until he received Smithers's prose, before filling in the words now left in stars, to avoid their using the same expressions.

Smithers, now more sure of his ground, was not prepared to let this claim go unchallenged. 'Lady Burton,' he wrote, tactfully, but in essence denying her explanation, 'has without any reason consistently refused me even a glance at his MS, and in our previous work from the Latin, I did not find Sir Richard trouble himself in the least concerning our using like expressions.' Furthermore, Smithers had earlier taken care to point out to the book's private subscribers, that Burton had 'laid great stress on the necessity of thoroughly annotating each translation from an erotic (and especially a paederastic) point of view, but subsequent circumstances caused me to abandon that intention.'[52]

While Isabel could rest satisfied with having carried the day with the Catullus, it was Smithers who was to enjoy the sweet fruits of victory with regard to the *Arabian Nights*. That spring, as she later recounted to members of the Writers' Club, 'there began to be talk of not doing it upon the plan agreed, but of making what the Publishers called a nice Standard Library Edition.' Despite heated arguments throughout the summer and meetings with lawyers, nothing was resolved. During the editing and printing stage, C.E. Jeffcock, as was probably always his intention, gradually began selling his rights to Smithers and Nichols. Isabel, in the meantime, paid an unnamed journalist nine guineas to expurgate Burton's sixteen volumes containing all his latest corrections, emendations and fresh annotations, and sent the result to the publishers. They were pointedly ignored, Nichols declaring in no uncertain terms to her solicitor that he was 'not going to have the thing….petticoated.' Her efforts to seek legal redress came to nothing, the eminent barrister, Sir Frederick Pollock, declaring that she had no case. Exploiting a legal loophole, the publishers were able to argue that they had 'agreed to let you correct the proofs, but we did not contract to observe your corrections.'

Incensed, Isabel accused Smithers of taking advantage of her 'not being a lawyer but a lady,' and believing, therefore, that the contract she had signed, 'meant what it said.' Soon after its publication in November, however, she appears to have accepted the assurance of the publishers that this edition 'would do honour to my husband and myself, would be a thing to be proud of, would be entered at Stationer's Hall, would not require to be locked up, would in no way be hurtful to youth, and would be the Standard Library Edition of all ages….'[53]

Early the following year, Isabel succumbed to the prevailing epidemic of influenza. Though she rallied later after a month, she never recovered. She was no longer able to walk up and down stairs without assistance, or even across the room. She remained in Baker Street for the first six months of the year, and then she recovered sufficiently to be removed to Eastbourne for a change.

It was during the last years of her life when her health was failing, according to W.H. Wilkins, that Lady Burton was induced against her better judgement to have some dealings with certain so-called "spiritualists", who approached her under the plea of "communicating" with her husband. A somewhat different version, was afterwards given by the person at the centre of the public controversy which later blew up, Ada Goodrich Freer, otherwise known as "Miss X." Miss Freer was then a leading member of the Society for Psychical Research, and assistant editor of W.T. Stead's occult quarterly, *Borderland*, launched in 1893. She was charming, intelligent, and, as it turned out later, not a little unscrupulous.[54] She claimed that Lady Burton sent her a note in the spring of that year, saying that she would like to make her acquaintance. However, various difficulties made it impossible for them to meet until July. They were then a party of ten at Lady Burton's house in Baker Street, 'and I did not exchange a dozen sentences with my hostess….'[55]

They did not meet again until the spring of 1895. According to Ada Freer, on Friday, 26 July, she was staying at the country house of a Mr and Mrs D.A. A short time before, she had shared with Mr D. in the investigation of a haunted house. While there, they had made use of a Ouija board, upon which they had received some messages which had seemed interesting. With the idea of carrying this experiment further, they used the board that Friday evening. It immediately began to work, and some garbled messages appeared to be coming from Burton. These included a prophecy that Isabel had only eight more months to live, and a complaint about his tie-pin: 'You should not have given away my pin. You would not have lost it. I don't want a grocer's boy wearing my things.' More messages, supposedly, were picked up the following day..

A copy of the notes that were taken on these two occasions was forwarded to Lady Burton. She replied in cordial terms, sending her comments on these alleged messages. These are the papers containing, what Wilkins termed, ridiculous "revelations", which Lady Burton later signed. He said nothing, however, about what subsequently happened.

On Monday, 5 August, Miss Freer went down to Mortlake, where she found Lady Burton and Mr D. Before her arrival, Mr D. and Lady Burton had drawn up a list of questions, though they were not shown to her till the evening after dinner. In her account in *Borderland*, Miss Freer said that, after lunch, about 3 o'clock, they 'adjourned to a quiet place out of doors selected by Lady Burton.' However, in 1897, she revealed that this 'quiet place' was none other than the Burton mausoleum.

It was a cold drizzling afternoon, and they sat inside, with the door open to let in a better supply of light, and to let out the fumes of a small oil-stove. She and Mr M.D. sat at a small table on which rested the Ouija board. A portrait of Burton fetched from under the altar lay beside it. Isabel sat by the door, her note-book and the contents of a small hand-bag spread out on Burton's coffin. Isabel had an agenda paper of eight questions which she had prepared.

In response to later criticism in various journals, including a piece by W.H. Wilkins in the *Westminster Gazette*, Miss Freer said that Lady Burton desired that *Borderland* rather than the Society for Psychical Research 'with the critical methods of which she was not wholly in sympathy,' should be the vehicle for a public statement of what had happened. On 15 August, Lady Burton had sent her some special directions as to "disguising facts." The "séance" was to be called a "sitting," ...and the Mausoleum was to be called "a tent." Lady Burton had reminded her that there were two tents, one in the burial ground, the other in the garden, and it was not necessary to particularise. 'As her only reason for secrecy was the fear that the Mausoleum would be closed to her, it was not necessary to observe this injunction in writing *after* Lady Burton's death.'[56]

On 26 August, Ada Freer wrote to her friend, Lord Bute: 'Lady Burton is deeply impressed by the characteristic language and the curious details, and has already altered her will on the strength of certain statements of which I hardly understand the import. As one issue is that she has left me Sir Richard's valuable Arabian and Egyptian occult instruments, I can't complain.'[57] This is a tissue of lies. There is no mention of Ada Freer in Lady Burton's will, nor is there any indication that the will was altered.

Having removed to Eastbourne, Isabel took a cottage, Holywell Lodge, Meads, where she remained from September to 21 March of the following year. By this time it was clear that she was failing fast. When free from pain, she remained bright and cheerful, enjoying a joke as much as ever. In a letter written at this time to Georgiana she gave an amusing account of her establishment at Eastbourne: 'It consists,' she wrote, 'of my secretary [Miss Plowman] and nurse, and we have our meals together, and drive out together whenever I am able. Then my servants are a maid, house-parlour maid, a housemaid, and a cook (my Baker Street lot). The cottage [at Mortlake] is in charge of a policeman, and Baker Street a caretaker. My friend left three servants in the house, so we are ten altogether, and I have already sent one of mine back, as they have too much to eat, too little to do, and get quarrelsome and disagreeable.' She concluded: 'As to myself, I am so thin and weak that I cannot help thinking there must be atrophy, and in my own case my own idea is that I may be able to last till March.'[58]

Despite her frail condition, it appears that she kept in touch with Ada Freer, expressing the hope that they might meet for further sittings. If Miss Freer is to be believed, she did not desire them. 'Personally I definitely dislike and disapprove of any attempt to induce phenomena and the very word séance is associated in my mind with fraud, vulgarity and irreverence......'[59]

According to Wilkins's suspect statement, Isabel, after thinking the matter over, the absurdity of the thing struck her. 'She came to the conclusion that there was nothing in it at all, and that, as compared with the occultism of the East, this was mere *kindergarten*. She was very ill at the time, and unable to write herself, but she mentioned the matter to her sister at Eastbourne, and said: "The first thing I do when I get back to London will be to recall those silly papers."' Death, however, prevented this being done. Wilkins said that 'Mrs Fitzgerald at once communicated Lady Burton's dying wishes to the person in whose charge the papers were, and requested that they should not be published. But with a disregard alike for the wishes of the dead and the feelings of the living, the person rushed some of these absurd "communications" into print within a few weeks of Lady Burton's death, and despite all remonstrance was later proceeding to publish others, when stopped by a threat of legal proceedings from the executors.'[60]

As a rider to this affair, one may recall what Burton had said as far back as 1869: 'As regards the spirit theory I may again remark that, if after this life my psyche or pneuma, or whatever it may be, is to find itself at the mercy of every booby who pays half a crown to his or her medium, evidently the future state of this person will be much worse than the present.'[61]

Early in the New Year, 1896, Isabel rapidly became worse. She wrote to Madame Gutmansthal-Benvenuti: 'I never forget you, and I wish our thoughts were telephones. I am very bad, and my one prayer is to be able to get home to London. The doctor is going to remove me on the first possible day. I work every moment I am free from pain. You will be glad to hear that I have had permission from Rome for Mass and Communion in the house, which is a great blessing. I have no strength to dictate more.'[62]

On 20 March she was moved on a bed into an invalid carriage, and travelled back to London accompanied by her sister, the doctor, and a priest. On arriving at Victoria station, she said she felt so much better that she would walk along the platform to the cab. Mrs Fitzgerald alighted first, but on turning around, she found that Isabel had fainted.

Towards the morning she seemed better. She kept on saying: "Thank God I am home again!" During the night, however, she grew worse. The next morning, Passion Sunday, 22 March, after being given the Last Sacraments, she whispered: "Thank God," breathed a sigh, and died. Just under a week later, she was laid to rest beside her husband, the camel bells ringing out for the last time.

Isabel Burton had spent a large part of her life tirelessly attempting to bolster and defend his reputation. Undoubtedly, there will continue to be many and conflicting opinions about Burton. Nevertheless, now more than a century after his death, his position in the pantheon of great figures of the Victorian age seems assured. Deeply flawed certainly, yet a man who lived life to the full and one, as an obituarist wrote at the time of his death, 'who ever dared to be true to himself.'

In putting the final touches to this portrait of Burton, therefore, it seems fitting that he should speak for himself as to what he wished to represent as having been the guiding philosophy of his life:

> Do what thy manhood bids thee do,
>   from none but self expect applause;
> He noblest lives and noblest dies
>   who makes and keeps his self-made laws.
>
> All other Life is living Death,
>   a world where none but Phantoms dwell,
> A breath, a wind, a sound, a voice,
>   a tinkling of the camel-bell.

APPENDIX

BURTON AND FREEMASONRY

It might be said that Burton spent a large part of his adult life in quest of intellectual and spiritual enlightenment. The beginnings of his search for what can be termed as esoteric knowledge, can be traced back to his undergraduate days at Oxford. In his so-called *Little Autobiography* he recalled that, after 'throwing up the classics,' he turned instead to reading such books as 'Erpenius, Zadkiel, Falconry, Cornelius Agrippa, and the Art of Pluck.'

Zadkiel was the pseudonym of Richard James Morrison (1795-1874), a former naval lieutenant during the Napoleonic wars, who became interested in astrology and produced, what proved to be, a highly successful and lucrative almanac. Heinrich Cornelius Agrippa von Nettesheim (1486-1535) was the medieval German scholar, whose famous treatise, *De Occulta Philosophia*, was published in 1531. Divided into three books, it dealt with different forms of magic together with cabbalistic analyses of the Hebrew alphabet and Pythagorean numerology. His influence was later recognised by a perceptive reviewer of *Sindh and the Races*, who remarked that Burton's account of the Sindians' 'belief in and practice of the occult sciences, demonology, magic and alchemy, would have gladdened the heart of Cornelius Agrippa.' In 1865, Burton, himself, used the Ouroboros on the front cover of his *Stone Talk*. This depicted a snake devouring its own tail, and was a Gnostic and alchemical symbol expressing the cycle of life and nature, and the unity of all things.

Besides dabbling in the works of the above authors, Burton also struck up a friendship with John Varley (1778-1842), the well-known water-colour artist and astrologer, who had been a close friend of the poet, painter and mystic, William Blake.

While Burton's biographers have focused attention on his later studies of Indian religions and Islamic mysticism, they have completely ignored his earlier induction into Freemasonry. Burton's first brief allusion to the Craft occurs in his *Scinde; or the Unhappy Valley*. 'That strange-looking building without windows,' he points out to his fictitious British visitor, Mr Bull, on their tour around the environs of Karachi, 'is the Freemasons' Lodge, the *Jadoo Ghur*, or "Magic House," as the natives call it, considering the respectable order a band of sorcerers who meet in their philadelphion to worship the Shaitan and to concert diabolical plans and projects against Allah's chosen people, themselves.' Kipling uses the same native term for the big blue and white Masonic Lodge at Lahore in his novel *Kim*, where the boy's late father, Kimball O'Hara, a young colour-sergeant in the Mavericks, ostensibly an Irish regiment, had been a member.

Sharing certain similarities in its organization, as well as in its spirit of brotherhood and *esprit de corps*, Freemasonry has long appealed to members of the military, numbering among its ranks such distinguished soldiers as Wellington, Sir John Moore, Lord Kitchener, Viscount Wolseley, Earl Roberts and Earl Haig.

Sir Charles Napier was no exception. He was a keen and long-standing Freemason, who had been initiated, passed and raised to the degree of Master Mason on 16 June 1807, while serving as a major with the 50th Regiment in Guernsey. Replying to a toast given to him by the Masonic fraternity at Simla in 1850, at which many of the leading officers of the Indian army were present, he spoke of the great debt he owed to Freemasonry. Of how, once a prisoner 'without hope of being exchanged and expecting to be sent to Verdun,' a French officer, a brother mason, had managed to send a letter to England to inform Napier's family of his safety.

Five years earlier, after making a grant of land to the Masonic Lodge Hope, No. 350, at the western end of the cantonment at Karachi, Sir Charles had been invited to lay the foundation stone of a permanent structure. Despite lacking premises of its own, the Lodge appears to have existed unofficially since 1842. On 7 September 1847, perhaps to coincide with the opening of its new building, it was granted a charter by the Grand Lodge of Scotland.

It was not until almost forty years later in his Notes written for Francis Hitchman, that Burton revealed that he had become a Freemason while serving in India, and then only in the briefest and most disparaging terms. 'The Lodge "Hope" kindly made me "an entered apprentice," he wrote, 'but I had read Carlisle [sic] "The Atheistical Publisher," and the whole affair appeared to me a gigantic humbug, dating from the days of the Crusades, and as Cardinal Newman expressed it, "meaning a goose club." But I think better of it now, as it still serves political purposes in the East, and gives us a point against our French rivals and enemies.'

Although Burton gives the impression of the Lodge having made a spontaneous gesture on its part in making him a member, the truth is that he would have had to apply for membership. All candidates for initiation needed to be 'regularly proposed and seconded; be approved by the Brethren in open Lodge assembled, which is done by ballot, and must sign the usual declaration.'

There can be little doubt that Captain Walter Scott was responsible for proposing Burton. Scott came from a family of freemasons. His uncle, the novelist, Sir Walter, had been initiated, passed and raised on the same day in Lodge Canongate from Leith in 1801. In this he was only following in the footsteps of his father and maternal grandfather. Furthermore, two of Sir Walter's brothers, his son, son-in-law and grandson, were all members of the Craft. Captain Walter Scott, himself, had been initiated into Lodge Canongate Kilwinning No. 2 (Edinburgh) on 6 April 1836.

It was probably from Scott that Burton derived the fanciful notion that Freemasonry was connected with the Crusades, a theory used to explain its growth in Scotland. It was claimed by its adherents, without a shred of reliable evidence, that the Freemasons were descended from the Knights Templar, the religious military order of knighthood instituted by the Pope in 1118 to defend the Kingdom of Jerusalem and the surrounding area from Muslim attack.

It is not easily apparent why Burton chose to denigrate Freemasonry by quoting Cardinal Newman's rather weak jibe about its meaning a "goose club." This was an allusion to the founding of Grand Lodge in 1717, by the amalgamation of four London lodges which met at the Goose and Gridiron alehouse in St Paul's Churchyard, London. It may, of course, have been intended as a sop to the religious sensibilities of his wife. Freemasonry was anathema to the Roman Catholic Church, which had issued numerous encyclicals against it since 1738. On 20 April 1884, Leo XIII promulgated his famous encyclical, *Humanum Genus*, which was entirely devoted to an attack on the 'Sect of Freemasons,' describing it as 'the common enemy.'

We can only speculate as to Burton's reasons for 'humbly soliciting to be admitted to the mysteries and privileges of Ancient Freemasonry.' Was it prompted by self-interest, by the belief that it might help advance his military career? His reference to Richard Carlile suggests that it was motivated, in part at least, by the desire of testing the validity of his criticism of the order. Carlile (1790-1843), the radical journalist and freethinker who suffered relentless persecution by the authorities throughout his lifetime, wrote a number of publications attacking Freemasonry. The main thrust of his attack was on the organization's secrecy and its links with high-ranking members of society including the Royal Family.

His *Manual of Freemasonry* became a best-seller, a revised and enlarged third edition in one volume appearing in 1845, the year, possibly, when Burton became a Freemason. 'I am of opinion,' Carlile wrote at the head of his Introduction, 'that nothing useful to be known should be made a secret.' Paradoxically, while denying that the Freemasons had any secret, he asserted that 'there is a secret connected with their association and they have not known it.' In Carlile's view, 'The esoterical principle of Freemasonry, as of Christianity and Judaism is SUN WORSHIP AND SCIENCE, AS THE BASIS OF HUMAN CULTURE AND DISCIPLINE, the common Paganism of the human race.'

Burton's name does not appear on the roll of members of the Lodge Hope following the grant of a charter in 1847. Freemasonry, in fact, would prove to be merely one staging post along the long road of his unremitting search for enlightenment, for a coherent belief system which he could wholeheartedly embrace. Despite his best efforts, he remained sceptical to the last. 'We may believe what we are taught,' was the bleak message of *The Kasidah*, written almost four decades later, 'we can know nothing.'

NOTES

The following abbreviations have been used in the notes:

Manuscript Collections

BOD: Bodleian Library, Oxford.
BL: The British Library, formerly the British Museum Library.
EMC: Edwards Metcalf Collection (Private), Huntington Library, San Marino, California.
FO: Foreign Office Records (Consular Dept), Kew.
HL: Huntington Library, San Marino, California.
NAM: National Army Museum, London.
NAS: National Archives of Scotland, Edinburgh.
NLS: National Library of Scotland, Edinburgh.
OHG: Orleans House Gallery, Riverside, Twickenham, Richmond upon Thames.
OIOC: Oriental and India Office Collections, British Library. Formerly India Office Records (IOR).
QK: Quentin Keynes Collection (Private).
RAI: Royal Anthropological Society, London.
RAS: Royal Asiatic Society, London.
RGS: Royal Geographical Society, London.
SOAS: School of Oriental and African Studies, University of London.
TCC: Houghton Collection, Trinity College, Cambridge.
TNA: The National Archives, Kew, formerly the Public Record Office.
WSRO: Wiltshire and Swindon Record Office, Trowbridge.

NB: On the eve of publication, it came to the attention of the author that, since carrying out his research many years ago, the RGS had not only changed its reference numbering system for much of the material in its Archives, but in certain cases items had been transferred into different collections. The references cited in the Notes, therefore, are the old reference numbers, and future researchers will need to convert these to the new.

Notes to Introduction

1   Part of a minute on Burton, written by the British prime minister and foreign secretary, Lord Salisbury, to his Foreign Office officials in the Consular Dept, in TNA, FO 7/1153, August 1889.

2   F. Harris, *Contemporary Portraits*, First Series (London, 1915), p.178.

3   George Eliot wrote in *The Leader*, 27 October 1855: 'There is hardly a superior or active mind of this generation that has not been modified by Carlyle's writings; there has hardly been an English book written for the last ten or twelve years that would not have been different if Carlyle had not lived.' Quoted in I.M. Campbell, *Thomas Carlyle* (London, 1974), p.193.

4   Scinde; or the Unhappy Valley, *The Athenaeum*, No.1252, 25 Oct 1851, p.1,111.

5   J.A. Froude, *Thomas Carlyle. A History of the First Forty Years of his Life, 1795-1835* (London, 1882), ii, p.402.

6   'Chartism,' *Critical And Miscellaneous Essays. Collected And Republished By Thomas Carlyle.* (London, 1872), Vol.VI, p.146.

7   'Dr. Francia,' *Critical And Miscellaneous Essays*, (London, 1865), Vol.IV, pp.249-294.

8   R.F. Burton, *Letters from the Battlefields of Paraguay* (London, 1870), p.x.

9   *The Lands of Cazembe, Lacerda's Journey to Cazembe in 1798*. Translated and Annotated by Captain R.F. Burton, FRGS.......(RGS, John Murray, London, 1873), p.96n.

10   R.F. Burton, *The Book of the Thousand Nights and a Night* (London, 1885), Vol.10, p.59.

11   T.Carlyle, *Latter-Day Pamphlets*, No.II, March 1850, 'Model Prisons,' p.22.

12   R.F. Burton, *Camoens. His Life and His Lusiads. A Commentary* (London, 1881), i, p.56.

13   R.F.Burton, *A Mission to Gelele, King of Dahomey* (London, 1864), ii, p.183.

14   *Ibid.*, pp.179 & 204.

15   'Occasional Discourse on the Nigger Question,' *Critical And Miscellaneous Essays* (London, n.d.), Vol.VI. p.205. This essay also contains a strong and sustained attack on philanthropy and Exeter Hall.

16   WSRO. *The Times of India*, 26 August 1893.

17   In Camoens. *His Life and His Lusiads. A Commentary*, which contains a good deal of veiled self-portraiture, Burton writes, p.45: 'Nature (so-called) is peculiar, even enigmatical, in her action: she apparently prompts her choicest favourites to endow the world with as many copies of themselves as possible. And she succeeds in foiling their best endeavours. Again, Alexander, Caesar, and Buonaparte.' Is it also a side-long glance by Burton at his own failure to father children?

18   J.A. Froude, *Thomas Carlyle*, 1795-1835, i, p.291.

19   W.H. Wilkins (ed.), *The Romance of Isabel, Lady Burton* (London, 1896), i, p.161. Hereafter cited as The Romance.

20   'Richard Burton.' By Ouida [Madame Ramée], *The Fortnightly Review*, Vol.LXXXIX, New Series (Jan.-June, 1906), p.1044.

21   *Times Literary Supplement*, Friday, 9 March 1906, p.83. There is an interesting article by Jonathan Bishop, obviously based on one of the claims made in this review: 'The identities of Richard Burton: the explorer as actor,' in Victorian Studies, 1, No.1 (Sept. 1957), pp.119-35.

22   'An Explorer's Centenary. Richard Burton, 1821-90,' *The Times*, 19 March 1921, p.11.

23'   'Sir Richard Burton's Centenary. Memorial to a Great Pioneer,' *The Times,* 4 July 1921, p.20. Responsibility for the Memorial Lecture was handed over to the Royal Asiatic Society, which decided to hold it triennially, and substituted a silver medal for that of a bronze.

24   Among the large list was Baron Desborough, better known as "Willy" Grenfell, fencer, mountaineer, swimmer and big-game hunter, a known and admired "fixer," Lord Reay, Lord Meston, soldiers and oriental scholars such as Percy Molesworth Sykes and Sir Richard Carnac Temple, Sir Francis Younghusband, soldier, diplomat, explorer and geographer, then serving as PRGS, Sir George Frederick Kenyon, Keeper of Antiquities at the British Museum, Lord Lugard, a major figure in Britain's colonial history, the novelist, Sir Henry Rider Haggard and Rudyard Kipling, novelist, short-story writer and poet, chiefly remembered for his celebration of British imperialism.

25 'The subject of his lecture was 'The recent history of the Hedjaz: causes of King Hussein's failure,' *Journal of the Royal Asiatic Society* (1925), pp.597-603. It was delivered in the Lecture Theatre of the Royal United Service Institution, Whitehall. Other medallists have included Bertram Thomas (1931), Freya Stark (1934), Lt General Sir John Glubb (1940), and W.P. Thesiger (1966). The Memorial Lecture is still held, roughly triennially, though dragging out a somewhat pallid existence since the British retreat from Empire.

26 E. Monroe, *Philby of Arabia* (London, 1973), p.10.

27 *Journal of the Royal Asiatic Society* (1937), pp.569-73. According to his entry in the *DNB*, Wilson, soldier, explorer, civil administrator, author and politician was 'a convinced believer in the British Empire as a power to preserve peace and civilise backward races.' Aged 55 at the outbreak of World War II, he wangled a commission in the RAF, and served as an air-gunner on heavy bombers. He was killed on 31 May 1940, when his aircraft was shot down and crashed behind enemy lines.

28 W. Tinsley, *Random Recollections of an Old Publisher* (London, 1900), i, p.146.

29 Ironically, in 1985, scholars who expressed interest in reading the MS were denied access to it. Among these was Dr Colin Holmes, who wanted to consult it for his work on British anti-Semitism. Karen Gold, reporting on the MS in the *Times Higher Educational Supplement*, 4 January 1985, p.1, quoted the Board's secretary-general, Hayim Pinner, as saying that 'the restricted part of the book, which dealt with the "medieval blood-libel" on the Jews could not serve any useful purpose for anyone.'

30 A six-part dramatisation, scripted by Michael Hastings and Derek Marlowe, and narrated by the actor, James Mason, which won two Emmy awards in the USA. The role of Burton was taken by Kenneth Haigh, and Speke by John Quentin. A lecture, in response to the series, 'The Search for the Niles Sources,' setting out the historical facts, was given at the Royal Geographical Society by Dorothy Middleton on 7 February 1972. It was followed by a symposium, in which contributions were made by makers of the programme and academics, critical of its numerous inaccuracies.

31 I obtained the introduction through the kindness of Sister Margaret Helen, archivist of New Hall School, Boreham, Chelmsford, Essex, where Lady Burton had been a pupil from 1841-46. Mrs Flemming, née Smyth-Pigott, who was the grand-daughter of Lady Burton's younger sister, Blanche, attended the school from 1905-7, and kept in touch with it throughout her long life. Dorothy was born on 2 July 1889 at Brockley Court, part of the huge estate in Somerset owned by her grandfather. She died on 25 November 1989, four months after reaching her 100th birthday.

32 This, and her account of watching Queen Victoria's funeral from a window in the Edgware Road, are related in her fascinating, privately printed memoirs, *Four Score Years and Ten. A Miscellany of Memories.* I am bequeathing a copy of the original, unabridged typescript which is in my possession, together with Dorothy Flemming's letters to me, to the British Library.

33 This verbatim description forms part of a letter written to the author in December 1981. Mrs Flemming repeated the story, when I called on her in the spring of the following year at her home in Whitby, north Yorkshire.

34 The description of "Our Cottage" given by W.H. Wilkins in *The Romance*, ii, p.752, bears little relation to the house as it presently stands, and clearly indicates that Wilkins had never visited the place himself. On the basis of his account, doubts have been expressed that the present structure is the one referred to. However, the building is clearly shown on the Ordnance Survey map, 60 ins = I mile, 1894/5, resurveyed 1893, the period when Lady Burton was living there.

35 WSRO. Quoted in an article in *The Vegetarian*, 27 January 1894.

36 I. Burton, *The Life of Sir Richard F. Burton* (London, 1893), ii, p.434. Hereafter cited as *The Life*.

37 WSRO. *The Times of India*, 26 August 1893.

38 *The Athenaeum*, No.3431, 29 July 1893, p.149.

39 WSRO. *The Chicago Post*, Illinois, 20 August 1893.

40 'The Life of Captain Sir Richard F. Burton. By His Wife.' *The Edinburgh Review* 178, 1893, July – Oct. Art.VII, p.439. The review extends over 29 pages, pp.439-68.

41 Francis Bacon, 'Of Truth,' *Essays*, The World's Classics (OUP), p.5. It is clear that Burton, who was well-read in English literature, was familiar with this essay, briefly quoting from it, although not citing its source, in *The Lake*

Regions of Central Africa (London, 1860), ii, p.328: 'In this stage of society truth is no virtue. The "mixture of a lie" may add to pleasure amongst Europeans, in Africa it enters where neither pleasure nor profit can arise from the deception.' Bacon's original reads, pp.5-6: 'A mixture of a Lie doth ever adde Pleasure.'

42   *The Fortnightly Review*, Vol.LXXXIX, p.1039.

43   *The Life*, i, p.21. This was glossed by Lady Burton in a footnote: 'From that he became a man wholly truthful, wholly incorruptible, who never lost his "dignity," a man whose honour and integrity from the cradle to the grave was unimpeachable.'

44   R. Burton, *Zanzibar; City, Island and Coast* (London, 1872), ii, p.283.

45   *Ibid.*, p.372.

46   *The Life*, p.ix.

47   P.M. Kendall, *The Art of Biography* (London, 1965), p.22.

48   Jon R. Godsall, 'Fact and Fiction in Richard Burton's Personal Narrative of a Pilgrimage to El-Medinah and Meccah (1855-56),' *Journal of the Royal Asiatic Society*, Third Series, Vol.3, Part 3, November 1993, pp.331-51; 'Richard Burton's Somali Expedition, 1854-55: Its Wider Historical Context and Planning,' *Journal of the Royal Asiatic Society*, Vol.11, Part 2, July 2001, pp.135-73.

49   Fawn M. Brodie, *The Devil Drives* (London, 1984), p.16.

50   *The Edinburgh Review* 178, 1893, July-Oct, Art. VII, p.464.

51   R.F. Burton, *First Footsteps in East Africa* (London, 1856), reviewed in *The Athenaeum*, 19 July 1856, No. 1499, p.892.

52   J. Boswell, *The Life of Samuel Johnson* (Oxford, 1904), ii, p.216.

Notes to Chapter 1

1   'Richard Cobden to Mr Bright on Parliamentary Reform (Nov 4 1849),' in J. Morley, *The Life of Richard Cobden* (London, 1881), ii, p.54.

2   The other surgeons were: Mitchell, Livingstone, Arnott and Shortt. The five medical officers then signed the post-mortem report, which concluded that Bonaparte had died of a cancerous ulcer or carcinoma in his stomach. Apparently, without seeking any official permission, Francis Burton took a cast of Napoleon's head shortly after his death, and cut off a lock of his hair, which became a family heirloom. An account of what followed can be read in *The Life*, i, pp.5-11, 'Facts Connected With The Last Hours Of Napoleon.'

3   *Ibid*, i, p.397. As Ulster King of Arms, Sir Bernard Burke was the chief genealogical and heraldic authority in Ireland, an appointment dating back to the reign of King Edward VI. His apartments and the Office of Arms (now the Genealogical Office and Heraldic Museum) were housed in the Bedford Tower, Dublin Castle.

4   Black and white reproductions of painted miniatures of Richard Baker and his wife, Sarah, appear in Thomas Wright, *The Life of Sir Richard Burton* (London, 1906), i, pp. 43 & 45. They were then in the possession of Baker's great-grand-daughter, Nella Agg, of Hewlett's, Cheltenham. Unfortunately, they appear to be no longer extant. My description of Baker is based on a copy of the original owned by a present-day member of the family, Richard Justin Baker.

5   This information is derived from a draft copy of Richard Baker's will drawn up at Brighthelmstone [Brighton], on 5 September 1812. Brighthelmstone was later struck through, and Barham House substituted.

6   His entry in J. Foster, *Alumni Oxonienses, 1715-1886*, Vol.1, reads: 'Baker, Richard George, son of Richard of St Andrews, London, gent. Trinity College, matriculated 14 July 1807, aged 18; BA 1812, of Lincoln's Inn 1807.'

7   The ground plan in the 1931 sale catalogue, when the house was known as "Hillside," is slightly different from that shown in the plan taken from sale particulars of the Boreham House estate in 1883. It is impossible, of course, to know exactly how it looked during Richard Baker's tenancy, 1813-24. The house was bought by a local estate agent, demolished, and the grounds divided into building lots. The coach-house was retained, and later turned into flats. A piece of timber from the property, carrying the date 1681, is on permanent display in the County Record Office.

8   H. James, 'London at Midsummer,' *English Hours* (London, 1905), quoted in F. Bédarida, *A Social History of*

England, 1851-1900 (London, 1991), p.40.

9   I. Burton, *The Inner Life of Syria, Palestine and the Holy Land* (London, 1875), ii, pp.123-4.

10 The letter is in Isabel Burton's copy of *Notes on the Burton Genealogy*, formerly at the Royal Anthropological Institute, London, now at the Huntington Library, San Marino, California. Her published version is in *The Life*, i, p.14.

11 *The Life*, p.2.

12 The lineage of the Burtons of Longner Hall is set out in J.B. Burke, *Landed Gentry*, 18th edn, Vol.III, 1972. That of the junior branch of this family, Mainwaring-Burton, is in J.B. Burke, *Irish Family Records*, 1976.

13 Isabel Burton wrote to her cousin and his wife, Lord and Lady Arundell (John and Lucy) on 27 August 1876, thanking them for their 'kind and charming gift of the Life of Catherine Burton.' She said that she was expecting Dick back that night from a short trip, and would give it to him 'because he is intensely interested in all that concerns his own family name and in finding out things about his ancestors…..' (QK Coll). This has not been the case with any of Burton's previous biographers, who have merely copied his claims or completely ignored the subject.

14 M.E. Noble (ed. & copyist), *The Registers of the Parish of Shap in the County of Westmoreland. From 1559-1830* (Kendal, 1912).

15 There is a letter in the QK Coll from Burton to Isabel, written from Edinburgh, 24 Jan 1872, instructing her to 'rescind' all his references to Shap. This suggests that he may have discovered information about his ancestry which he preferred to conceal.

16 Baptismal record, Shap Parish Registers. His burial entry is dated 22 July 1778, where he is described as a husbandman. This term was usually applied to a tenant farmer as distinct from a yeoman who was, properly, a freeholder cultivating his own land.

17 Notice of this marriage appears in the index of Carlisle marriage bonds, Record Office, Carlisle, dated 14 October 1731.
    The baptism of Sarah Holme is entered in the parish registers, Crosby Ravensworth, for 19 Nov 1704. There are numerous Holmes listed in the Shap parish registers, the name being variously spelled with or without the letters 'e' and 's'. These registers show that Sarah Burton, widow of James Burton of Barker Hill, died on 7 May 1780, aged 76. Her will dated 6 Dec 1778, and signed with a cross, is in the Cumbria County Record Office, Carlisle. Agnes, her second daughter, acted as executrix.

18 Edmund Holme's will, also in the Carlisle Record Office, is dated 19 Sept 1717. According to the Bank of England's 'Equivalent Contemporary Values of the Pound,' £600 at this date roughly represented the equivalent as at June 2000, of £46,662.

19 Barker Hill, which is mentioned frequently in parish registers between 1582 and 1692, is said to be named from some earlier member of the family of George or Joseph Barker. See A.H. Smith, *The Place Names of Westmoreland* (Cambridge, 1967), English Place Names Society series, Part II, Vol.XLIII.
    The Barker Hill farm on the 1st edition Ordnance Survey map, 1858-59, published in 1861-2, is of cruciform shape with an L-shaped outbuilding. It also shown in this way on the revised edition, 1897. In the 2nd Edition, 1898, the farm has disappeared, leaving only the outbuilding, which survives to the present day.

20 The children of James and Sarah Burton born at Rossgill were: Elizabeth, 7 Dec 1732; Agnes, 4 April 1734; Edmund 4 April 1737. The remainder, born at Barker Hill, consisted of: Isabel, 26 April 1739; James, 14 May 1741; John, 2 Sept. 1743; Joseph and Mary, 15 May 1745 (twins, who probably died shortly after birth); Edward, 10 March 1747. The dates are probably for baptism, not birth.

21 D. Defoe, *A Tour Through England and Wales,* Everyman Library (London, 1959), ii, pp.269-70.

22 There is an entry for him in J. Foster, *Alumni Oxonienses,*1715-1886, Vol.II (London, 1888), p.680: 'Edward Holme, s. Edmund of Crosby Ravenside, Westmoreland, pleb. Queen's Coll., matric. 14 March 1731-32, aged 21; BA 1737, MA 1741.'

23 Now a well-known public school, Sevenoaks is one of only eight such founded before 1432. Edward Holme took over the headmastership from the Rev John Simpson, who, during his long stewardship (1716-48), had allowed the school roll to decline to only four pupils by 1748. Edward stayed for ten years. Unfortunately, I have failed to

discover any further facts about his later life and career.

St John's College, Cambridge, was chosen for Edmund since, for most of the 18th century, until overtaken by Trinity, it was the biggest and most richly endowed of the Cambridge colleges. See D.A. Winstanley, *Unreformed Cambridge* (Cambridge, 1935). William Pitt came up to Pembroke Hall in 1773 aged only 14, as did the Duke of Bedford to Trinity in 1779. The English Utilitarian philosopher, Jeremy Bentham, was only twelve when he entered Queen's College, Oxford, in 1760.

24   There is an entry in Isabel Burton's *Notes on the Burton Genealogy* (WSRO), which reads: 'The first of the Irish branch of our family, Edmund and Edward Burton, were the sons of a clergyman who lived at Barker Hill, Westmorland. They were educated by a wealthy uncle at St John's College, Cambridge, and both went into the Church. When the uncle died, it was found that he had left all his money to hospitals and charities, and the nephews being offered preferment in Ireland, settled in Galway.' While these details are largely incorrect, it is obvious that some knowledge of Edmund Holme and St John's College, Cambridge, existed in the family.

25   There is an entry for him in J. & J.A. Venn, *Alumni Cantabrigienses*, Part 1 to 1751, Vol.1 (Cambridge, 1922), p.265, and R.F. Scott (ed.) *Admissions to the College of St John the Evangelist*, part III, (Cambridge, 1903), p.136: July 1751-July 1752, Admissiones a Julii 2do 1751 (1) Burton, Edmund, son of James Burton, farmer (firmarii), Westmoreland; bred at Sevenoak, Kent (Mr Holme); admitted sizar, tutor and surety Mr Powell, 25 September, aet. past 14.' Edmund's younger brother, John, came up to St John's as a sizar sixteen years later. His entry is in J.A. Venn, *Alumni Cantabrigienses*, Part II, 1752-1900, Vol.1 (Cambridge, 1940), p. 468 and reads: 'Burton, John. Adm. Sizar at St John's, July 6, 1767; a clerk in Holy Orders. S. of James, farmer of Westmoreland. B. Sept. 22, 1742, at Shap. School, Bampton, Westmoreland (Rev William Collinson). Matric. Michs. 1767.' On the hardships faced by sizars, see D.A. Winstanley, *Unreformed Cambridge*, p.194ff. For a more personal view, the experience of Patrick Brontë, who came up to St John's College as a sizar in October 1802, can be read in J. Barker, *The Brontës* (London, 1994), pp.1-13.

26   According to a note on his entry in R.F. Scott, *Admissions to the College of St John the Evangelist*, p.609, 'Edmund was ordained Deacon 23 September 1759 by the Bishop of Peterborough and licensed to the curacy of Rushden, Northants, he was ordained Priest 6 June 1762 by the Bishop of Lincoln and licensed to the curacy of Puddington [*sic*], Beds.' This should read 'Toddington'. Edmund's curacy of Rushden, near Higham Ferrers, is not recorded in the entry for him in J. & J.A. Venn, *Alumni Cantabrigienses*, p.265.

27   This was an age of widespread ecclesiastical abuse and nepotism. The Archbishop made his eldest son prebendary of Tuam, then Dean of Lismore, as well as rector of Templemichael, co. Longford. The husband of his daughter Elizabeth, was appointed Archdeacon of Ardagh, a see which the Archbishop held *in commendam* with Tuam.

28   Pronounced 'Toom', the town was the seat of Turlough O'Conor, the famous twelfth century High King of Ireland. In that century it was chosen as the metropolitan see of Connacht, and by the time of the Anglo-Norman invasion, was well on the way to becoming the capital of the province. Before the Reformation it contained no less than three churches and two monasteries.

29   The letters, Ref M 3249, are housed in the Public Record Office of Ireland, Four Courts, Dublin. With them is a thirty-one page manuscript headed, 'Archdeacon Burton,' by Stanley Lane-Poole, MA, Litt.D, Dunganstown, County Wicklow. There are also some letters dated 1915 from Lane-Poole to an unnamed correspondent commenting on the Burton letters, and complaining of the difficulty he was having in getting the article published. In fact, it was never published, at least in the extended form of the original MS. A much abridged version entitled, 'Sir Richard Burton's Archdeacon,' eventually appeared in *Notes and Queries*, 11th Series, 5 June 1915, pp.425-6. Lane-Poole was wrong in his basic premise that Archdeacon Edmund Burton was Richard Burton's grandfather; probably deliberately so, given that no documentary material exists for the life of the Rev Edward Burton. The article contains other errors too. Nevertheless, it provides some very interesting and useful background information.

30   Her tombstone in the grass very near the east end of the old cathedral of St Mary's, reads: 'Under this stone lies Catherine Burton who died the 13th May 1782 aged 57 years. With tender gratitude for 18 years of uninterrupted happiness, her husband Archdeacon Burton erected this in memory of her virtues and his affliction.' It was a childless marriage. However, at some unknown date, Edmund remarried, his second wife, Martha Judge, bearing him

several children, one of whom, James Ryder Burton born in 1795, entered the Navy on 12 May 1806 as a Volunteer, at the early age of eleven. It was he who first made the spurious claim in print that his father was, 'Bishop of Killala, a collateral descendant of Fras. Pierpoint Burton, Lord Conyngham....' See W.R. O'Byrne, *A Naval Biographical Dictionary* (London, 1849), allegedly 'Compiled from Authentic and Family Documents.' Archdeacon Edmund Burton, who followed Walter Blake Kirwan as Dean of Killala in 1806, died on 22 March 1817, aged eighty. There is an abstract of his will, MS 512, 0/5, dated 16 February 1799, proved 1817, in the Genealogical Office (Office of Arms), Dublin Castle. Apart from the bequest to his wife, he left two guineas each to his Westmorland brother and sister, James and Agnes Burton.

31 G. Stisted, *The True Life of Capt. Sir Richard F. Burton* (London, 1896), p.1. Hereafter cited as *The True Life*.

32 G. D. Burtchaell and T.U. Sadleir (eds.), *Alumni Dublinenses* (Dublin, 1935), new edition with supplement. A pensioner is the equivalent of a commoner at Oxford. His schoolmaster is named as Mr Langhorne, but there is no additional information as to his earlier or later career.

33 The Kirwans were a very old established family in Ireland, a number of whom have entries in the *DNB*. Stanley Lane-Poole in his MS article, '*Archdeacon Burton*,' wrote, pp.10-11: 'Galway was well stocked with sportsmen & abounded in good houses. The famous "Tribes" were not extinct. There were Kirwans, Bodkins, Blakes, Lynches, Dalys, Brownes, Martins, Burkes, within riding distance; the O'Flaherty himself, no longer the terror of the country, was to be found on the estate of "Lemonfield" – surely a name breathing conviviality & punch – on the shores of Loch Corrib; whilst close to Tuam a Kirwan seat was known as "Friendly Quarters", redolent of the traditional hospitality of the Irish landlords.........' Edmund Burton appointed two members of the Kirwan family as guardians of his children. They were also made executors of his will, together with his wife. A similar close friendship is likely to have existed between the Kirwans and Edward Burton's family.

34 This matches the number listed in *Notes on the Burton Genealogy*, WSRO, p.1, and the copy in the RAI, p.2.

35 Her name appears on the card index of officers of the Bengal Army in the NAM, having married Lt (later Lt Col) George Thomas D'Aguilar (1783-1839) of the Bengal Establishment at Calcutta on 30 Aug 1814. Her son, the Rev John Burton D'Aguilar, graduated from St John's College, Cambridge in 1840, served as chaplain in the service of the HEIC in India, and then became Vicar of Ashwick, Somerset, dying in 1904. She died on 14 Nov 1887, aged 92, leaving almost £10,000 in her will. She is briefly mentioned in *The Life*, i, pp.68 & 84.

36 James entered the Church, becoming Prebendary of Donoughmore (Ross) from 1812-50, curate at Ballycotton, 1836, Vicar of Dysert Enos and Kilteale from 1841-50. He was married twice. His first wife was Margaret Boyce. After her death, he married Elizabeth Meredith in 1824. He died Nov or Dec 1850, aged 75. Richard Burton's cousin, Dr Edward John Burton, M.D. (1814-97), was the son of the Rev J.E. Burton's first marriage. See T. Wright, *The Life of Sir Richard Burton* (London, 1906), i, p.238, for Dr Burton's unfounded claim that he was born in the house of his father's brother, the [alleged] Bishop of Killala.

37 The Nettervilles were a very old Anglo-Norman family which had been settled in Ireland since the reign of Henry II in the 12th century. In the reign of James I, Nicholas Netterville was raised to the peerage of Ireland on 3 April 1622, as Viscount Netterville. The title became extinct on 7 April 1882, following the death of Arthur, 8th Viscount. See Sir Bernard Burke, *Dormant and Extinct Peerages*, 1883, p.392. The entry in *Burke's Irish Family Records*, 1976, for the Mainwaring-Burton line, a junior branch of the Burtons of Longner, which linked with the Conyngham family in the 18th century, shows that Katherine Burton, eldest daughter of Samuel Burton of Burton Hall, County Galway, married on 28 February 1731, the 5th Viscount Netterville. Elizabeth Kirwan, the third daughter of Joseph Kirwan of Hillsbrook, County Galway, married James, the 7th Viscount Netterville of County Meath on 7 April 1834. Friendship with both these Galway families, might well have been the reason for Edward's conferring the Netterville name on his third son, Joseph.

38 Dr Joseph Stock (1740-1813) was Bishop of Killala, during the period when Edmund Burton was Dean. Born and bred in Ireland, Stock had enjoyed a distinguished academic career at Trinity College, Dublin, where he became a Fellow. In 1793 he was collated prebendary of Lismore, resigning two years later to become headmaster of Portera Royal School, Enniskillen. In January 1798 as the result of family influence – his wife was the sister-in-law of Archbishop Newcome – he succeeded Joseph Porter as Bishop of Killala.

39 If we are to believe Burton, 'He had an especial ambition to enter the Church, but circumstances compelled him to

become a military surgeon in the 66th Regiment.' *The Life*. i, p.4.

40   *Ibid.*, p.49. In Lt Gen Sir W. Napier, *The Life and Opinions of General Sir Charles James Napier, G.C.B*, 4 vols (London, 1857), i, p.51, the author writes how 'Col. Napier (Charles's father) at the latter end of 1794 was appointed to the Londonderry regiment of which Lord Conyngham was colonel. He had only to discipline it….but had nothing to do with the mode of recruitment which he abhorred; for the men had been raised by the usual infamous mode of the times, that is to say false promises, the officers obtaining rank according to the number of recruits they brought.' Burton was familiar with this biography of his old commanding officer in Sind, and, knowing nothing about the real facts of his father's entry into the army, may well have adapted this passage to suit his own purpose. On the other hand, one in five of new officers in the regular army came from the Militia, having obtained their commissions by persuading forty of their men to transfer with them. M. Glover, *Wellington's Army* (Newton Abbot, 1977), p.40. Could this system have been the germ of Burton's story? Joseph Burton's age when he entered the British Army, suggests that he might have spent some time previously in the Militia, as in the case of his brother, Francis.

41   This incorrect detail has been copied into every biography of Burton from 1887 up to the present day. It was Joseph's brother, Francis, who served in the 36th regiment, from 10 March 1808 until 9 Sept 1813, joining it as an assistant surgeon from the 5th Garrison Battalion, North Devon Militia. Drew, *Medical Officers in the British Army*, Vol.1 (1660-98), entry no. 2712, p.180. Coincidentally, Roderick Impey Murchison, then a youth of fifteen, entered this regiment as an ensign in 1807, in later years becoming a distinguished President of the Royal Geographical Society.

42   See M. Glover, *Wellington's Army*, p.36.

43   *The Times*, Wednesday, 8 January 1806.

44   For the regiment's official history see Col H.W. Pearse, DSO, *History of the 31st Huntingdonshire Regt. And 70th Foot Surrey Regt, Subsequently 1st and 2nd Battalions of the East Surrey Regiment*, Vol.1, 1702-1914 (London, 1916). Joseph Burton's name appears in the list of 21 lieutenants who served in the Revolutionary War, p.89. A force of 6,000 men was already concentrated in Sicily in February 1806. A reinforcement of four battalions, one of which was the 31st, left England in April under the command of Brigadier-General, the Hon Robert Meade, the senior lieutenant-colonel of the regiment. *Ibid.*, p.91.

Notes to Chapter 2

1   *The Life*, i, p.3. Moore had served in Ireland during the Great Rebellion. He remained there on the staff of Sir Ralph Abercromby until June 1799. By 1806, knighted and gazetted lieutenant-general, Moore wrote to a friend in March of that year, that he was 'tired of the trifling details of a home command,' and had turned his thoughts 'to India as the greatest and most important command that could fall to a British officer.' However, the government was not keen on his travelling so far from this country. The following month he was offered, and accepted, the post of second-in-command to General Henry Fox in the Mediterranean. C. Oman, *Sir John Moore* (London, 1953), p.362. In 1809, he was mortally wounded at the battle of Corunna, his death mourned in one of the most famous funeral elegies in the English language, 'Burial of Sir John Moore at Corunna,' written by the young Irish poet and clergyman, Charles Wolfe (1791-1823).

2   The entry for Captain J.N. Burton in Hart's Army List for 1856, the only time in which he appears, shows that he served in Egypt in 1807, and at the Heights of Genoa. The British government, following a failed attack on Turkey, which was sympathetic to the French cause, decided to seize Alexandria in order to forestall a second French landing in Egypt. Early in 1807, a force of 6,000 men was despatched under the command of Major-General Mackenzie-Frazer with Major-General Wauchope as his second-in-command. Three British infantry regiments were included in the expedition, the senior being the 1st Battalion of the 31st Regiment. The first detachment of the expedition arrived at Alexandria on 16 March, and the town surrendered four days later. A scarcity of supplies there, led to Gen Mackenzie-Frazer's being advised by the British Consul, to occupy Rosetta. A weak brigade

under Brigadier the Hon Robert Meade of the 31st was ordered to march on the town, where a failure to take necessary military precautions led to a bloody ambush. Major-General Wauchope was killed, and Brigadier-General Meade seriously wounded.

3   Lord William Henry Cavendish Bentinck (1774-1839), second son of the 3rd duke of Portland, commissioned as an ensign into the Coldstream Guards at the age of seventeen. Appointed governor of Madras in 1803, he was recalled in 1806 following a serious mutiny among native troops, for which he was held ultimately responsible. After being placed in charge of a brigade at Corunna in Spain, he was appointed commander of the British troops in Sicily. His liberal proclamations at Genoa proved embarrassing to the British government, and he was recalled in 1815.

4   Memoirs of Captain George Ellers, 12th Foot, quoted in C.W.C. Oman, *Welllington's Army, 1809-1814* (London, 1912), p.43.

5   See W. Douglas, *Duelling Days in the Army* (London, 1887), pp.vii-viii. However, if one of the protagonists died as a result, the survivor could be tried for murder. E. Samuel, *An Historical Account of the British Army and of the Law Military* (London, 1816), cites a Major Campbell of the 21st Regiment who, in 1807, was convicted and hanged for the murder of a brother officer whom he had shot in a duel.

6   Under the terms of the Treaty of Fontainebleau, Napoleon was granted 'full sovereignty and property' over the island of Elba, with an annual income of two million francs, protection by a guard of 400 volunteers, and allowed to retain his title of Emperor.

7   TNA, WO 25/64, folio 33, monthly returns of the 31st Regiment, show that Joseph was promoted captain on 21 April 1814. The return of 25 April show him as employed as deputy assistant quartermaster-general. ('A quartermaster-general is a staff officer who is chief of the department exercising control over all matters relating to the quartering, encamping, marching and equipment of troops.' *OED*, 2nd edn XII, p.997). The return of 25 July shows him promoted to captain in the 2nd Battalion, and struck off the strength of the 1st Battalion.

8   The 2nd Battalion was disbanded at Portsmouth on 14 October 1814, and the officers and men fit for service were transferred to the 1st Battalion, which they joined at Messina on 6 May 1815. See Col H.W. Pearse, DSO, *History of the 31st Huntingdonshire Regt*, p.95.

9   TNA, WO 25-3232

10   *The Life*, i, p.35.

11   *Ibid.*, p.3.

12   Annual Army List. The regiment had Yorkshire associations, Sowerby, near Halifax, being regarded as its original recruiting-ground. In 1782 it was known as the First Yorkshire West Riding Regiment, the nickname of 'Havercake Lads' dating from around the same time. Its later title of the Duke of Wellington's (West Riding) Regiment derived from Wellington's taking over the Colonelcy of the regiment in 1806, succeeding Lord Cornwallis who died in India, two months after his re-appointment as governor-general. See A. Lee, *History of the 33rd Foot* (Norwich, 1922), p.9.

13   The plainness of Martha Baker is Burton's assessment of his mother's looks, *The Life*, i, p.3. Georgiana Stisted, more romantically inclined, described Martha as having 'luxuriant brown hair, large grey eyes, tall, graceful figure, and tiny hands and feet,' and 'if not so regular in feature, quite as attractive as her husband.' *The True Life*, pp.4-5.

14   There is no reference whatever to Martha and J.N. Burton in the comprehensive index of marriages performed in Hertfordshire prior to 1837.

15   If the marriage did, indeed, take place in Scotland, there are two problems associated with tracing it, which I have failed to overcome: (i) registration was not compulsory before 1 January 1855; (ii) there are no means of knowing whether the ceremony was performed in Stirling or Edinburgh, nor in what parish.

16   *The Life*, i, p.94. William George Keith Elphinstone, Major-General, 1782-1842. He purchased the Colonelcy of the 33rd Regiment on 30 September 1811, and emerged from the battle of Waterloo with great credit. He continued to command the regiment during the occupation of French territory from 1815-18, and in England until 12 April 1821. He then exchanged into the 16th Light Dragoons, and went on half-pay a year later.

17   Francis Burton was a student in the Faculty of Medicine for one session, 1819-20, during which he attended classes

in the Institutes of Medicine, Materia Medica, Clinical Medicine, Chemistry and Botany. At the end of the session, he submitted an eighteen-page thesis printed, as required by the rules, in Latin, entitled 'De agitatione nervosa vulneribus sclopetariis quandoque inflicta.' He graduated MD on 1 August 1820. In 1820-21, he went on to pass the MRCS examination.

18   Rob Roy Macgregor the red-haired, bearded freebooter, was a folk-hero of the Central Region, whose blood Burton also liked to think ran in his veins. Sir Walter Scott's historical romance *Rob Roy*, first appeared in 1817-18, and in February 1819 was dramatised in a theatre in Edinburgh.

19   See R.Fulford, *The Trial of Queen Caroline* (London, 1967).

20   Cited in C. Hibbert, *George IV, Regent and King, 1811-30* (London, 1973), p.157. Charles Cavendish Fulke Greville (1794-1865), was friendly with most of the leading statesmen of his time. He kept a political diary, *The Greville Memoirs: (i) A Journal of the Reigns of King George IV and King William IV* (3 vols, 1874), (ii) *A Journal of the Reign of Queen Victoria (to 1860)* (5 vols, 1880).

21   A town major was an officer on the staff of a Governor of a district, or on that of an officer commanding a district or encampment. He issued orders to the troops, and read out standing orders to incoming troops as they arrived. He commanded according to the rank he held in the Army, but if his only commission was that of Town-major or Fort-major, he took rank as the most junior captain. The modern equivalent is garrison adjutant or in certain cases CSO II. There is nothing in his Army records, which substantiates the claim in *Notes on the Burton Genealogy*, p.1, that he owed this appointment to his having 'greatly distinguished himself at the taking of Genoa.' The term is incorrectly printed as 'town-mayor' in *The Life*, i, p.17.

22   *Ibid.*, p.17.

23   The Duke of Wellington was made Master-General of the Ordnance on 1 January1819 (Patent 59, George III, 5th Part, No.13, p.95), and held that post until 10 May 1827, when he was succeeded by Henry, 1st Marquess of Anglesey (Patent 8, George IV, Part 5, No.20, p.199). Wellington's part in the Queen Caroline affair was to negotiate a compromise settlement with the Attorney-General, Henry Brougham. Under its terms, she would receive £50,000, live abroad, and allow her name to be omitted from the Liturgy.

24   The monthly and annual Army Lists provide a sketch of J.N. Burton's career: In the annual Army Lists from 19 Oct 1820, he is a captain on the half-pay list of the 37th Foot up to, and including, the 1854 List. The 1856-57 List has two entries for him, one under lieutenant-colonel, giving his seniority date as 11 Nov 1851; the other under 'Resignations and Retirements' giving his rank as lieutenant-colonel.

In the monthly Army Lists, p.188, he is shown as follows: Captain Joseph N. Burton 35 Foot to be major in the Army 10 January 1837. Brevet Major Joseph N. Burton 34 Foot to be lieutenant-colonel in the Army, 11 November 1851.

25   Francis Algernon Plunkett Burton (1826-65), Ensign and Lieutenant on 8 May 1846; lieutenant and captain on 27 June 1851; retired as captain and lieutenant-colonel on 25 May 1865. These double ranks are peculiar to the Guards regiments.

Edward John Burton, Entered Army as Assistant Surgeon in the Royal African Corps (afds 3 West Indian Regt) 11 May 1838. He retired on half-pay as Staff Surgeon Major, and was gazetted hon Deputy Inspector General of Hospitals, on 20 Dec 1864. Declined this honorary rank, which was cancelled 1 Sept 1865. MD, Edinburgh, 1836. There is a full entry for him in *Register of Officers in the Army Medical Service*, No.4513, p.303.

26   *The True Life*, p.4.

27   A. Lee, *History of the 33rd Foot*, pp.260-61.

28   See O. Blewitt, *The Panorama of Torquay*, 2nd edn (London &Torquay, 1832).

29   According to O. Blewitt, p.51, the population of the parish of Tormohun (including Torquay and Tor) was 838 in 1801, 1,350 in 1811, and 1,925 in 1821.

30   St. Nicholas Parish Church, Elstree, the Rev David Felix officiating. Baptismal entry No.149 for 1821, bishop's transcripts of the register entries: (parents) Joseph Netterville Burton and Martha Burton, (abode) Boreham Wood, Elstree, (father's quality, trade or profession), Esquire or Captain in His Majesty's Service.

31   See J. Curling, *Edward Wortley Montagu (1713-1776), The Man in the Iron Wig* (London, 1954). The Arabic MSS, in seven volumes, written in 1764-5, contain a complete collection of the *Arabian Nights' Entertainments*. They

once belonged to Edward Wortley Montagu's library, and are briefly noted in W.D. Macray, *Annals of the Bodleian Library*, 2nd edn (Oxford, 1890), p.281.

32   *The Life*, i, p.16. 'He was born to be rich,' wrote Lady Burton, 'and he liked to be thought rich.' *Ibid.*, ii, p.267. It is obvious here, that Burton wanted it to be thought that he would have been wealthy but for the intervention of his mother.

33   J. Foster, *Alumni Oxonienses, 1715-1886* (London, 1888), Vol.1: 'Baker, Richard George, son of Richard of St. Andrews, London, gent. Trinity College, matriculated 14 July 1807 aged 18; BA 1812, of Lincoln's Inn 1807.'

34   Lincoln's Inn Admissions, 3 August 1807: 'Richard George Baker of Trinity College, gent., aged 19, eldest son of Richard Baker of Battersea, Surrey, Esq.' He is first mentioned in the Law List for 1820, where he is said to have been living at 1 New Court, Temple, and to be in the Northern Circuit. By 1823 he is listed as Manchester special pleader, Chester assizes and Lancashire sessions. His entry continues with minor variations to 1841, when the fact of his being called to the Bar at the Inner Temple on 26 November 1813 is also noted. This latter fact is all that is recorded until his last entry in 1880. However, as his death certificate shows, he had died long before this date, on 25 January 1864.
Special Pleaders were members of an Inn of Court, who devoted themselves to the drawing of pleadings (ie technical documents drawn up by counsel on either side in civil cases, with the purpose of clarifying the precise issues at stake), and to attending at judges' chambers. Jowitt's Dictionary, 1977 edn. Special pleaders no longer exist: Bar Council Annual Statement, 1948.

35   *General Stud Book*, Vol.1, listed in second half of 1810 under the names of Richard Baker, Arthur Orton and Charles Beckwith. The latter may well have been a relation, since 'Beckwith' was Martha Baker's middle name, possibly derived from the maiden name of her father's first wife. Dr Donald B. Baker informed me that some present-day members of the family interested in racing, tried to re-register Richard George's racing colours, only to find that they had been adopted by the late Queen Mother.

36   At the foot of the last page of Baker's will, there is an entry dated 10 Nov 1824, which reads: 'Robert Colmer and Samuel Dendy Esquires, two of the executors in this will named were duly sworn as well to the truth and due performance of the said will as of the eight codicils annexed thereto, as usual, also that the deceaseds goods and chattels and credits do not amount to the sum of eighty thousand pounds.'

37   Jane Austen in *Emma*, describes her heroine as being 'the heiress of £30,000.' It seems to have been the sort of princely sum associated with great heiresses. According to the Bank of England's table of equivalent contemporary values of the pound, it represents £1,193,700 in present-day money, as of June 2000.

38   Série M, personelle et administration générale, sous-série 4M police et sûreté générale. In this series, under '4M 105 Renseignements confidentiels (1823-24) – de nombreaux Anglais sont signalés, le nom de Burton n'est pas mentionné.' Also '4M 425 – police générale. Anglais résidant à Tours, passeports (1816-1823). Etat des Anglais à Tours (1822) (dans cette liste, le nom de Burton ne figure pas), and 'sous-série 6F: recherches des archivistes, travaux, correspondance, enquêtes, 6F 351. Anglais en Touraine, XIXème – Xième siècle (le nom de Burton n'est pas mentionné).' Information from J. d'Orléans, Le directeur des archives d'Indre-et-Loire.

39   Richard Baker of Barham House, Elstree, b. [1762], died Elstree 16 Sept 1824 aged 62 years. Buried Elstree Parish Church on 25 Sept 1824. Register VII, p.14, entry 106. A tablet recording his death, formerly inside the church, is now attached to the east wall of the tower.

40   The births of both children are recorded in the Elstree parish registers, though Captain Joseph Netterville Burton is wrongly described as "an officer in His Majesty's Navy." The parents' address is given in 1823 as Barham Wood, and in 1824 just as Elstree.

41   WSRO. Copy. Additional Settlement Upon Trust for Joseph Netterville Burton Esq & Martha his Wife.

42   Francis Burton's military career is briefly sketched in R. Drew, *Medical Officers in the British Army, 1660-1960*, Vol.1: 1660-1898 (London, 1960), p.180, entry 2712.

43   The bishop's transcripts of register entries, record the marriage of Francis Burton, Esq of the parish of St Michael, Coventry, bachelor, and Sarah Baker of Elstree, spinster, by licence, 27 September 1825.

44   Before Lord Hardwicke's Marriage Act of 1753, there was no lower legal age of marriage, except during the 1650s when it was sixteen for men and fourteen for women. In 1753, it was set at fourteen for men and twelve for women.

This ruling remained in force until the Age of Marriage Act in 1929, which raised it to sixteen for both. Louise, better known as Lucy, was the daughter of a merchant, John Samuel Rolfe. Mary Ann, the first of their seven children, was born on 26 September 1826. The remainder of Richard George's life is shrouded in obscurity. He apparently died intestate at his home in Hammersmith on 25 January 1864, which suggests that he continued to live beyond his means. His widow remarried on 23 August 1866, and by 1881 was a widow again. She died, aged 80, on 10 May 1889.

45   According to *Notes on the Burton Genealogy* (formerly at RAI), p.7, Burton is said to have gone to France in 1825. However, another source, *A Sketch of the Career of Richard F Burton*, By Alfred Bates Richards, Andrew Wilson, St. Clair Baddeley (London, 1886), p.2, states that Burton's 'education as a traveller and linguist commenced in his *fifth year*, when he was taken to the Continent.' [my italics]. For the reasons given, I believe 1826 to be the more likely date.

Notes to Chapter 3

1   'Its proximity to the town, its position from which the eye may wander over an immense extent of the richest fields and meadows, the beautiful hills on the left bank of the Cher, forming a background of nearly thirty miles in length from east to west, the meanderings of the Loire and Cher through a highly picturesque country, the noble Chateaux in the distance, the bird's eye view of the bridge and town, all these united have gained such a preference for this commune that a choice of residences cannot always be had.' *The Handbook for English Visitors in Tours and Touraine* (Tours & London, 1847), pp.111-12. Houses for large or small families could be had, either furnished or unfurnished, although there were few of the latter kind. Rents ranged from £30 to £120 a year for a furnished house out of town.

2   The château has an entry in J.-X, Carré de Busserole, *Dictionnaire géographique, historique et biographie d'Indre-et-Loire et de l'ancienne province de Touraine* (Mémoires de la société archaeologique de Touraine), tome 1 (Tours, 1878), p.19. It is also mentioned in R. Ranjard, *la Touraine archéologique, guide de touriste en Indre-et-Loire* (Tours, 1930). Burton visited Beauséjour in 1875, before starting his autobiography early in the following year on the journey to India. See *The Life*, i, p.18. The mansion has since been demolished. It is commemorated in the Allée de Beauséjour, a small lane leading off the steep rue de Vilde. Today, it still appears a relatively high income area, containing large houses screened with high walls and trees. The *commune* of St Symphorien was absorbed into the city of Tours in 1964.

3   La rue de l'Archevêché has now become la rue Emile Zola, and still contains buildings dating back to the period when the Burtons lived there. It leads directly into the square of the Archbishop's Palace, which today is known as Place François Sicard, and contains a public garden. The old Archbishop's Palace in Burton's time had already been converted into a museum, known as le Musée des Beaux-Arts. The population at this period in Tours-Nord numbered 1,122, and in the city itself, 21, 928. *Annuaires d'Indre-et-Loire*, 1829.

4   *The Life*, p.21.

5   A. Barkas, *An Interesting Corner of Richmond Green* (1914), p.3. The only extant drawing of the building is a faded copy of a water-colour, dated 1820, in an extra-illustrated edition of Manning and Bray's *History of Surrey* in the British Library. Its hand-written caption reads: 'Rev. Charles Delafosse's School now the site of the Gas Office.'

6   A.H. Hassall, *The Narrative of a Busy Life* (1893), an unpublished manuscript from Richmond Notes, Vol.19, p.1027ff.

7   The Rev Daniel Charles Delafosse left the school in 1838, and became vicar of Wandsworth. In 1844 he was instituted Rector of Sheen, where he died in 1859. The school remained empty for a year after Delafosse's departure. Then, under the name of 'The Royal Naval Female School' it became an institution used for the maintenance and education of the daughters of naval and marine officers. When the Naval School moved to St Margaret's by the riverside in 1856, the premises were taken over for use as a Cavalry College. Soon afterwards, however, a disastrous fire broke out, which destroyed almost the entire building. A Barkas, *An Interesting Corner of Richmond Green*, pp.5-6.

8   'Very few were the schoolboys we met with in after life,' wrote Burton. 'The only schoolboy who did anything worthy, was Bobby Delafosse (who was appointed to the 26th Regiment, N.I.) who showed immense pluck, and died fighting bravely in the Indian Mutiny. I met him in Bombay shortly before I went off to the North-West Provinces, but my remembrances of the school were so painful, that I could not bear to recognise him.' *The Life*, i, pp.30-31. Burton was mistaken in believing that Robert M.D. Delafosse, or "Bobby", the headmaster's third son, died in the Indian Mutiny. He was killed in action in 1844, aged only twenty-three. It was another, much younger, member of the Delafosse family, Lieutenant (later General) Henry George Delafosse (1835-1905), who took part in the Indian Mutiny, and survived. There are numerous references to him in A. Ward, *Our Bones Are Scattered* (London, 1996).

9   According to his entry in R. Drew, *Medical Officers in the British Army*, Francis Burton died in London on 24 Oct 1828. The cause of his death is not given, though he may well have suffered long-term damage to his health, through having taken part in the disastrous Walcheren expedition of 1809 in which no fewer than 23,000 men died of disease in four months. Bishop's transcripts record his burial at Elstree on 1 Nov 1828. J. E. Cussan, *History of Hertfordshire, Cashio Hundred* (1881), p.79, transcribes a tablet in the church erected to his memory, which shows that he was interred in the vault of his father-in-law, Richard Baker.

10   B.H. Garnons Williams, *A History of Berkhamsted School, 1541-1972* (Berkhamsted, 1980), p.122. Thomas Dupré had eleven children. Although Garnons Williams describes Henry Ramus as the third son (p.127), according to J.R. Maddicott, Librarian of Exeter College, Oxford, he was the fourth. He was named after an old school and college friend of his father, the Rev William Henry Ramus.

11   Warden of Winchester College from 1789-1832, 'one who was a lickspittle to the great and a bully to the young, a pedant, a liar and a cheat.' J. D'E Firth, *Winchester College, 1394* (Winchester, 1949), p.92.

12   It also suggests that the date, 1830, given by Burton for the family's departure from France, is to be preferred to that of 1832 as given in *Notes on the Burton Genealogy* (RAI), p.7.

13   *The Life*, i, p.32.

14   See R.F. Burton, *Falconry in the Valley of the Indus* (London, 1852).

15   See G. de Beer (ed.), *Charles Darwin, Thomas Henry Huxley, Autobiographies* (Oxford, 1974), p.24.

16   S. Parkes, *The Chemical Catechism*, 12 edn (London, 1826), Preface to the Eighth Edition, p.2. Originally written 'to make his only child proficient in his favourite pursuit,' the first edition of 1,500 copies – the smallest he ever printed – was published on 12 May 1806, and sold so rapidly as to make a second necessary on 26 Oct 1807. Eleven editions were called for in eighteen years. The work was translated into a number of European languages, the Spanish government ordering it to be used in its schools.

17   David Howell, Hon Secretary, The Royal Society of Marine Artists, was unable to find any information about Caraccioli. Similarly, Mrs Bridget Clifford, Senior Curator (Library) at the Royal Armouries, HM Tower of London, drew a blank with regard to Cavalli. 'There is no entry for him in Thimm's *A Complete Bibliography of Fencing and Duelling* (John Lane, 1986),' and colleagues of Mrs Clifford in Leeds, 'scoured the indices of our fencing books in vain.'

18   Philip Dormer Stanhope, 4th Earl of Chesterfield (1694-1773), diplomat and wit, now best remembered as the author of *Letters to his Son* and those to *his Godson*, and for his unfortunate relationship with Dr Samuel Johnson, which resulted in Johnson's famous letter addressed to him on 7 February 1775, attacking patrons. When Chesterfield's *Letters* to his natural son, Philip Stanhope, were published, Johnson remarked quite unjustifiably that 'they teach the morals of a whore, and the manners of a dancing master.' J. Boswell, *The Life of Samuel Johnson, LL.D.*, 2 vols (London, 1904), i, p.177. Dickens further damaged Chesterfield's reputation by caricaturing him in *Barnaby Rudge* as Sir John Chester, describing him as 'an elegant and polite, but heartless and unprincipled gentleman.'

19   R.F. Burton, *A Plain and Literal Translation of the Arabian Nights' Entertainments, Now Entituled The Book of the Thousand Nights and a Night* (Kamashastra Society, 1885), Vol.8, p.287.

20   The only person fitting Burton's description is the Rev William Henry Havergal (1793-1870). His *DNB* entry describes him as a writer of sacred music who, from the age of fourteen, often played the organ in his parish church. He matriculated at St Edmund's Hall in 1812, graduated BA in 1816, and proceeded MA three years later.

On 13 November 1829, he was presented with the rectory of Astley, Worcestershire. He was only partially sighted at this period.

Notes to Chapter 4

1   Queen Victoria's Journal, Royal Archives, 8 February, quoted in E. Longford, *Victoria R.I.* (London, 2000), p.58.
2   Convocation argued 'that the existing means of communication with London were fully adequate, that greater facilities for that communication would be injurious to the discipline of the University, and that the works adjoining the river would cause floods by impeding the water-course.' See G.V. Cox, *Recollections of Oxford* (London, 1868), p.284.
3   Not at Abingdon as stated by Burton in *The Life*, i, p.77. The 'Great Western' was opened as far as Steventon (near Didcot) on 1 June 1840, 'to and from which place Oxford passengers were conveyed in coaches and omnibuses.' G.V. Cox, *Recollections*, p.297.
4   For an account of the Casio Hundred, see William Paget (ed.), *The Victoria History of the Counties of England. Hertfordshire* (London, 1908), ii, pp.323-4.
5   William Alexander Greenhill (1814-94), youngest son of George Greenhill, treasurer of the Stationers' Company. He entered Rugby in 1828, the year of Dr Thomas Arnold's appointment to the Headmastership. Four years later he went up to Trinity College, Oxford, on an exhibition, having failed to obtain a scholarship. Intent on a career in medicine, he studied at the Radcliffe Infirmary and in Paris (1836-7), graduating MB in 1839, and MD in 1841. He was appointed to the Radcliffe Infirmary in 1839, a post which he held until 1851, when he left Oxford and settled in Hastings. He was a prolific writer in the fields of medicine and religion, and contributed numerous articles to the *DNB*. On Gladstone's recommendation, he was granted a civil list pension of £60 in 1881.
6   See Oxford University College Histories: H.E.D. Blakiston, *Trinity* (London, 1898), p.221, where Greenhill is described as a man 'of great and unostentatious generosity to poor students.' It appears that he put £20 into an envelope, and sent it anonymously to the poverty-stricken young Benjamin Jowett then in his first year at Balliol, telling him to use it to pay for extra tuition, so that he could compete more successfully for the Hertford Latin Scholarship. Greenhill later revealed his identity, becoming Jowett's first correspondent. See G. Faber, *Jowett. A Portrait with Background* (London, 1957), p.127. Faber erred, however, in describing Greenhill as 'Among the young Balliol graduates.'
7   Five letters written to him by Thomas Arnold were printed in A.P. Stanley, *Life and Correspondence of Dr Arnold*, Teachers' Edition (London, 1901): LV, 25 Feb. 1833, pp.300-1; LXXXV, 29 Oct. 1834, pp.339-40; XCVII, 30 March 1835, pp.356-7; CXXVIII, 9 May 1836, pp.405-6; CXLI, 31 Oct. 1836, pp.422-24. Sir Benjamin Ward Richardson in his Memoir on Greenhill, *The Asclepiad*, Vol.XI, Second Series (London, 1895), wrote, p.166: 'From what he told me personally, I do not consider that he formed any great attraction to Oxford, as a school, nor to his classical studies there.'
8   See H.E.D. Blakiston, *Trinity*, p.221.
9   James Adey Ogle (1792-1857). The son of a doctor, Ogle, after two years at Eton (1808-10), entered as a Commoner at Trinity College, where he obtained a scholarship the following year. In 1813, he took first class honours in mathematics, going on to study medicine on the Continent, and in Edinburgh. On graduating MD in 1820, he was appointed mathematical tutor at Trinity College. He later held several medical professorships.
10 The house was demolished in the 1920s for the building of the Dominican priory, Blackfriars (Doran Webb, 1921-9). Two of Dr Ogle's daughters married men well-known in Oxford. One married Manuel Johnson (1805-59) who, in 1839, succeeded Professor Rigaud, as head of the Radcliffe Observatory. In 1856, her twin-sister, Amelia, married James Bowling Mozley, an active member of the Oxford Movement, who later became Regius Professor of Divinity.
11 According to Sir B.W. Richardson, *The Asclepiad*, pp.170-71, Greenhill 'was not greatly impressed by the Parisian schools of his day…France, in fact, did not seem to agree with him…..'
12 While staying at Hurstmonceaux in 1840, A.P. Stanley received an invitation from Archibald Tait of Balliol to join

him at Bonn. 'Of the students themselves and their life, he is a minute observer. One of his walking companions he described as "certainly as pleasing, handsome, and gentlemanlike, with the exception of moustachios, as you would wish to see." The duels, of which there had been 300 that term, strike him as "more childish than anything else."' See R.E. Prothero, *The Life and Correspondence of Arthur Penrhyn* Stanley, *D.D.* (London, 1893), i, p.222.

13   *The Life*, p.70. There was, in fact, nothing in the Laudian Statutes prohibiting a member of a college from wearing a moustache or beard. On the other hand, the pressure to conform to the current fashion of mutton-chop whiskers alone, would have been strong. See N. Bentley, *The Victorian Scene. A Picture Book of the Period, 1837-1901* (London, 1968), p.121.

14   See C. Bede, *The Adventures of Mr. Verdant Green. An Oxford Freshman* (London, n.d.), p.28: 'Mr. Filcher [Verdant's scout, or personal servant] then went on to point out the properties and capabilities of the rooms, and also their mechanical contrivances. "This is the hoak, this 'ere outer door is, sir, which the gentlemen sports, that is to say, shuts, sir, when they're a'readin.' This well-known book, published in three parts between 1853-56, went through numerous editions. It was written and illustrated by Edward Bradley, whom Burton met at Marienbad in June 1884, and gives a highly amusing, yet accurate, account, of undergraduate life at Oxford during the 1840s.

15   *The Life*, p.71.

16   John Ruskin came up to Christ Church, Oxford in 1836, his mother taking rooms at 90 High Street to be near to her son. There is a fine sketch of St Mary's and All Soul's College done by Ruskin, probably in 1838, a view Burton would have been familiar with from the front windows of the adjoining property.

17   See D. Balsdon, *Oxford Then and Now* (London, 1970), p.28. There were about 120 undergraduates at Exeter College when William Morris came up to the university in 1853. As a result of the overcrowding, he and Burne-Jones had to go into lodgings for their first two terms. However, 'No undergraduate was then allowed to spend the night out of college in any circumstances.' The problem was solved by requiring them to 'sleep in the third room of sets belonging to seniors....' See J.W. Mackail, *The Life of William Morris* (London, 1899), i, p.32. According to *The Oxford University Calendar*, 1840, there were 77 Commoners and 10 Gentlemen-Commoners in residence at Trinity.

18   Richard Ellmann, *Oscar Wilde* (London, 1988), p.88, believed that Wilde contracted syphilis at Oxford, 'reportedly from a woman prostitute.'

19   F. Hitchman, *Richard F. Burton, K.C.M.G.: His Early, Private and Public Life* (London, 1887), i, p.83.

20   See J.B. Wyngaarden, MD & L.H. Smith, Jr, MD (eds.), *Cecil Textbook of Medicine*, 16th edn (Philadelphia, 1982), ii, p.1576.

21   Trinity College Archive, Admissions Register C, p.8. This standardised form of words, repeated with appropriate changes by each candidate, translates as follows: 'I, Richard Francis Burton, son of major Joseph Burton, gentleman, of Tuam in Ireland, was born in Torquay, in the county of Devon. On this day, 19 November 1840, aged about 19, I have been admitted as a Commoner of the Lower Order, under the tutelage of fellows, Short, Williams and Kensington.'

22   Trinity College Archive, Accounts, III/C/2. Caution money was a refundable sum, deposited as a security for good conduct. Accounts III/G/1840-41. Buttery Book; First Quarter ending 17 Dec 1840.

23   See *The Life*, i, pp.78 & 90; ii, p.167. The only facts concerning Arthur Kensington are those shown in his entry in J. Foster, *Alumni Oxonienses*, 1715-1886 (London, 1891), Vol.II, p.787; o.s. John Pooley, of Surrey, arm. Oriel College, matric. 14 June 1832, aged 17; scholar Trinity College, 1833, B.A. 1836, M.A. 1739; maths lecturer, fellow 1838-42, tutor and dean 1839; of Lincoln's Inn, 1837, died 27 Sept. 1876. After relinquishing his fellowship, he appears to have left Oxford. There is no record, however, of his having gone on to pursue a career in law or the Church.

24   W. Tuckwell, *Reminiscences of Oxford* 2nd edn (London, 1907), pp.229. Towards the end of his long life, Short became blind, dying in 1879 at Solihull, near Birmingham. According to *The Life*, ii, p.167: 'On the 31st May I find in Richard's journal, "Poor Tommy Short dead, ninety years old;" ....After Richard's death I found one of the Rev. Thomas Short's cards kept amongst his treasures.'

25   Quoted in his entry in the *DNB*.

26   See Sir George Prevost (ed.), *The Autobiography of Isaac Williams, B.D.* 3rd edn (London, 1893), p.80. In 1841-42,

his close connection with the Tractarians resulted in his becoming embroiled in controversy during his contest with James Garbett for the Poetry Professorship. Although the stronger candidate, Williams withdrew, married shortly afterwards, and left Oxford.

27   T.Hughes, *Tom Brown at Oxford* (London, 1861), new edn, 1886, p.6.

28   Junior students were called upon to act as 'prickbills,' a duty which involved standing at the entrance to the chapel, and marking off the names of those attending. In Academical Abuses Disclosed, 1832, the writer remarked that, 'After the doors are closed the reader commences the Church of England service, which, stopping only for want of breath, and being ably seconded by the responder (the rest being totally indifferent) he generally succeeds in running through in fifteen minutes and some odd seconds. Such is the mockery of religion which he is compelled to attend twice a day.' See V.H.H. Green, *A History of Oxford* (London, 1974), p.168. A similar picture is drawn in T. Hughes, *Tom Brown at Oxford*, p.8, and C. Bede, *The Adventures of Verdant Green*, pp.45-6.

29   C.E. Mallett, *A History of the University of Oxford* (London, 1927, reprinted 1968), iii, p.130.

30   R.E. Protheroe, *The Life and Correspondence of Arthur Penrhyn Stanley, D.D.* (London, 1893), i, p.127.

31   The Scholar-Gipsy, from *Poems by Matthew Arnold* (1853). G.V. Cox, *Recollections of Oxford*, pp.352-3, noted that in 1850, 'The "Cowley Enclosure", coolly and cruelly "cut off forty-seven pathways," within two miles of Oxford....substituting for them eight new ones...dull, and dusty, and formal by the new roadside..... This enclosure, accompanied by that of Bullingdon Common with its nice turf for a canter, only required (what soon followed) the enclosure of Bagley Wood, to cut off not only fresh air from Oxford students in general, but from its future students in Scientia Naturali in particular, the only remaining localities for botanical and physiological pursuits.'

32   M.Allen, *Palgrave of Arabia* (London, 1972), p.94. 'The "Torpid boats" were originally the second boats of a college, which until 1837 rowed with the "Eights." In 1838, the Torpids were made a class by themselves, and raced in the days between the Eight-Oared Races. In 1852 they were moved to the Lent Term, and reorganized on their present basis.' W.E. Sherwood, quoted in the *OED*. T. Hughes, p.xxvii, described the torpids as being 'filled with the refuse of the rowing men – generally awkward or very young oarsmen.'

33   See J.D. Aylward, *The House of Angelo – A Dynasty of Swordsmen* (London, 1953), pp.157, 165, and 190.

34   There is an amusing description of Maclaren's fencing-school and gymnasium in C. Bede, *The Adventures of Verdant Green*, pp.258-9. Originally housed in two rooms, Maclaren, between 1858-59, had a large, special purpose gymnasium built on the corner of Bear Lane and Alfred Street. There are references to MacLaren in F. MacCarthy, *William Morris. A Life for Our Time* (London, 1994), pp.73 & 77.

35   Alfred Bate Richards (1820-76), eldest son of John Richards, MP for Knaresborough, West Riding of Yorkshire, from 1832-7. Richards was educated at Edinburgh high school and Westminster. He matriculated at Exeter College, Oxford on 19 Oct 1837, and entered his name as a law student at Lincoln's Inn on 18 May 1839. He graduated BA in 1841, and was called to the Bar at Lincoln's Inn on 20 Nov 1845. In 1870, he was appointed editor of *The Morning Advertizer* in succession to James Grant, a post which he held until his death on 12 June 1876. His compilation, *A Short Sketch of the Career of Captain Richard F. Burton* .....By an Old Oxonian, was published by Edward Mullan in 1880. His middle name 'Bate' is consistently misspelled by biographers, taking their lead from the mistake in printing Richards's name in the reissue of *A Short Sketch* in 1886. Lady Burton in *The Life*, correctly spells his name in Vol 1 on pp.5 and 15, and then incorrectly in Vol 1, pp.73 & 91; and again in Vol 2, pp.4, 10, and 49. In Vol.1, p.151, she refers to him as Alfred Richard Bates!

36   *Oxford Unmasked*, By A Graduate, pp.13 & 18. The dedication of my own copy of this rare pamphlet from the Bodleian Library, Oxford, Gough Add. Oxon 8 215.3, is dated August, 1842.

37   91 High Street, where Burton was lodging, is next door but one to University College. Furthermore, Dr Greenhill was a close friend of A.P. Stanley, one of its fellows.

38   Information from the College Register. The change formed part of a radical overhaul of the College scholarships which took place on 16 Oct 1837, under University's new Master, Frederick Charles Plumptre.

39   As the records show, this did not mean that the college was awarding two open scholarships annually, but that there were two places to be filled at any one time. Examinations could only be held, therefore, when a vacancy occurred. Unusually, as happened in 1841, both scholarships fell vacant at the same time.

40   See G. Faber, *Jowett*, p.76.

41   Dr Robin Darwell-Smith who kindly checked the 1839-42 examination results for me, found that Balliol entered 39 undergraduates for honours, as against 20 entered by University College. 'If we were to concoct "Norrington Tables" for this period,' he wrote in reply, 'I think that Balliol would come out on or very near the top, and University probably somewhere in the middle.'

42   Henry Clarence Pigou was only awarded a Fourth in Classics Finals in Easter 1844, MA in 1848. Rector of Wyke Regis, Dorset from 1855-83. Edward Hayes Plumptre (1821-91) after graduating with a double first, became a Fellow of Brasenose, 1844-48, relinquishing it on his marriage to Harriet Theodosia, sister of Frederick Denison Maurice. He spent twenty-one years on the staff of King's College, London, where he introduced evening classes. He also took a leading part in promoting the higher education of women as a professor at Queen's College, Harley Street, acting as its principal, 1875-77. In 1881 he became dean of Wells, the duties of which he combined with an enormous amount of literary work.

43   Ancient Greek had, what is known as, tonic or pitch accent. This was based on the distribution throughout the sentence of long and short syllables. During the period of the Byzantine Empire, which came to an end with the fall of Constantinople in 1453, the language of administration and most writing was couched in this archaic style. The spoken language, however, changed radically, so that modern Greek, as with English, came to have dynamic stress. Burton refers again to Greek pronunciation in *The Book of a Thousand Nights and a Night*, Vol. 5, p.22n.

44   This is the reason for the unorthodox use of the vowel symbols in our spelling, which no longer correspond to the sounds which they used to represent in English. See A.C. Baugh, *A History of the English Language,* 2nd edn (London, 1962), pp.287-289.

45   Burton's comments on the history of Latin pronunciation were, undoubtedly, sparked by the controversy that broke out in 1870 concerning the pronunciation of Latin. This was only six years before he began his autobiography. A move for reform began, following the Vatican Council of that year, which revealed the diversity of pronunciations. English Catholics of the Oxford Movement too, were abandoning the traditional pronunciation for the Italianate. A full discussion of this, and the eventual standardization agreed by the Philological Society in 1885, can be read in L.P. Wilkinson, *Golden Latin Artistry* (Cambridge, 1963).

46   E.C. Mack and W.H.G. Armytage, *Thomas Hughes. The Life of the Author of Tom Brown's Schooldays* (London, 1952), pp.27-8. 'Oriel reached its highest eminence under Provosts Eveleigh and Coplestone; its decline began with Hawkins.' See W.Tuckwell, *Reminiscences*, pp.186-7. Also V.H.H. Green, *A History of Oxford*, p.136.

47   The Latin name of the 9th-10th century Persian physician and philosopher, Abu Bakr Muhammad Ibn Zakariya. Greenhill's translation was not published until 1847. Rhazes's two most significant medical works are the *Kitab al-Mansuri*, and *Kitab al-Hawi*, in which he surveyed Greek, Syrian, and early Arabic medicine, as well as some Indian medical knowledge. Burton's acknowledgement that Dr Greenhill was responsible for introducing him to Arabic is made in 'The Biography of the Book Reviewed,' *The Supplemental Nights*, 1886-8, Vol.6, p.416. He does not receive any recognition for this in *The Life*.

48   Thomas van Erpe, more commonly known as Erpenius (1584-1624) was a Dutch orientalist who published the first European manuals of Arabic (in Latin). His *Grammatica Arabica* (1613) remained, virtually, the only available tool for European students until the latter half of the nineteenth century.

49   There is a copy of Erpenius's first edition in the British Library, bound in with *Proverbia Arabica* (1614), which he co-edited with Joseph Scaliger. The text of the *Grammatica Arabica*, although in Latin, was printed in the style of an Arabic book, ie starting from the top page at, what we in the West regard as, the back of the volume, and moving inwards to the centre from right to left. It comprises 192 pages, and is divided into six chapters.

50   See L. Marchand, *The Athenaeum – A Mirror of Victorian Culture* (Chapel Hill, 1941), p.218, and G. Ticknor, *Life of William Hickling Prescott* (London, 1864), p.120, and pp.305-6, for his account of the enormous amount of time and effort which Gayangos devoted to furthering the researches of the American historian on the reign of Philip of Spain. Gayangos was also a famous bibliographer, who published a catalogue of the Arabic manuscripts in history and geography for the library of the Royal Historical Society of Madrid. He also spent much time in London compiling the catalogue of Spanish manuscripts in the British Museum, 1875-93.

51   I have to thank Ms Doris Nicholson and the Library's archivist for undertaking this research on my behalf. Such is

the Bodleian's meticulous record-keeping, that we also know precisely what Gayangos read on each of these days!

52 *The Life*, p.81. This is repeated in R.F. Burton, *The Book of the Thousand Nights and a Night*, (Benares, 1885-88), Vol.10, p.96n.

53 Among the books in the Burton Library at the Huntington (BL 624), is H.G. Ollendorf, *a New Method of Learning to Read, Write, and Speak a Language in Six Months; adapted to the Spanish* (London, 1858). Burton was clearly not averse, therefore, to looking at the systems of other linguists for the rapid learning of a foreign language.

54 See C.E. Mallett, *A History of the University of Oxford*, pp.131-2.

55 See S.N. Mukherjee, *Sir William Jones. A Study in 18th Century British Attitudes to India* (Cambridge, 1968), pp.18, 22, & 23.

56 *The Life.*, p.77.

57 See H. Hall, 'The Origin of the Lord Almoner's Professorship of Arabic,' *The Athenaeum*, No.3238, 16 Nov 1889, pp.673-4.

58 Edward Bouverie Pusey (1800-82), turned to the study of oriental languages in order to equip himself to fight against the encroaching tide of rationalism, and German biblical criticism. In June, 1825, he left for Germany, settling in Göttingen, where he attended the lectures of the distinguished biblical critic, John Gottfried Eichhorn. From there, he moved on to Berlin where he met the liberal theologian Schleiermacher, and the philosopher, Hegel. On a second visit to Germany in 1826, he studied so hard under Freytag, professor of oriental languages at Bonn, that his health was seriously undermined. See H.P. Liddon, *The Life of Edward Bouverie Pusey* (London, 1893), Vol.1, Chap IV, pp.70-80, and Chap V, pp.94-104. Burton writes somewhat ambiguously in his Terminal Essay, 'Section II, The Nights in Europe,' *The Book of a Thousand Nights and a Night*, Vol.10, p.102n. 'Dr. Pusey studied Arabic to familiarise himself with Hebrew, and was very different from his predecessor at Oxford in my day who, when applied to for instruction in Arabic refused to lecture except to a class.' Precisely what Burton meant by '*in my day*' is unclear, since Pusey took over the professorship of Hebrew from Dr Richard Lawrence in 1828.

59 W. Tuckwell, *Reminiscences.*, p.130.

60 I owe this information to the late A.F.L. Beeston, Laudian Professor of Arabic. He added that he was 'not sure when this stipulation disappeared from the statutes, but it is quite possible that it remained technically in force from the foundation of the Laudian chair in 1636 down to at least the first university reform scheme in 1850.'

61 For a comparison see *The Life*, p.77, and *The Times*, 23 March 1877, p.10. This was only a year or so after Burton began writing his autobiography. When Lady Burton's *Life* appeared in 1893, a keen-eyed reader pointed out in a letter to *The Saint James's Gazette*, 3 September 1893, that Burton's description of Newman's style of preaching was couched in the very language used of Newman by Gladstone. 'We have not at the moment, the date of Mr. Gladstone's little description,' he wrote, 'but it will be found quoted, we believe, in Mr. Hutton's little book on Newman in a series of "Leaders of Religion," published a year or two ago.' Cutting in Burton papers, WSRO. R.H. Hutton, *Cardinal Newman*, Methuen & Co, 1891, does indeed quote Gladstone's observations on Newman in their entirety on pp.97-98. However, the speech at the City Temple is incorrectly dated to 1887.

62 *The Life*, p.77. Dr Greenhill wrote to the editor of the *Spectator*, 19 August 1893, shortly after the appearance of *The Life*, denying that Burton had ever met with Newman and Arnold at his house. He stated that he had already done so, following the publication of Hitchman's biography. He was, therefore, surprised at having to do so again. 'I may add,' he went on, 'that the only time in latter years when Arnold and Newman met was at Oriel, Feb. 2nd, 1842, a full account of which meeting is given in "Newman's Letters," vol. ii, p.440- .' In a fatuous letter published in the journal a week later, Lady Burton implied that Greenhill was suffering from senility, declaring that her 'husband's memory and his accuracy were so remarkable that I am inclined to think that this statement written at the age of fifty-five must be correct.....the only mistake that could have occurred would be that, as Richard Burton spent most of his time at Oriel...that it was *there* that he met them, instead of at Dr. Greenhill's....' Cutting in the Burton papers, WSRO.

63 A full account of their meeting can be found in M. Trevor, *Newman: The Pillar of the Cloud* (London1962), pp.263-5.

64 Burton's version in his 'Little Autobiography,' p.153, reads as follows: 'After begging the paternal authority in vain for the Austrian service, the Swiss Guards at Naples, and even the *Legion étrangère*, I determined to leave Oxford,

coûte qui coûte.'[*sic.* 'qui' should read 'que.'] No mention here of his wishing to emigrate or enter the service of the East India Company.

65 Trinity College Archive: Burton's University dues for the First Quarter, ending Dec 16 1841, amounted to 10s 3d., and comprised the following charges: Arts Culets, 3d; Convocation tax, 1s; University charter, 3d; St Mary's Gallery, 6d; Divinity clerk, 1d; University lectures, 6d; Police tax, 1s 3d.; Paving tax, 6s 5d. Accounts, III/G/1841-2, Buttery Book; First Quarter, show Burton charged daily for food, fuel, etc. Accounts, III/G/1841-2, Buttery Book, Second Quarter, ending 10 March 1842, shows Burton charged daily up to, and including, the final day.

66 *The Life*, p.90.

67 See M. Ayres and G. Newbon, *Over the Sticks* (Newton Abbot, 1971), p.18. Oliver, who lived in Cheltenham, where a Grand Annual Steeplechase was inaugurated in 1834, won three Grand Nationals – on Gaylad (1842), Vanguard (1843), and Peter Simple (1853). He also came in second three times, and third once. When his favourite horse, Vanguard, died, Oliver had it skinned, using the skin to cover his sofa.

68 H.E.D. Blakiston, *Trinity*, p.218.

69 *The Life*, p.153.

70 Responsions, part of the exercises for the degree of BA, was introduced in 1808. According to the Oxford Calendar for 1840, candidates were publicly examined by Masters of the Schools 'in the Greek and Latin language (chiefly with a view to their grammatical construction), in the rudiments of logic, or in Euclid's Geometry.'

71 C. Bede, *The Adventures of Verdant Green*, pp.176-7. I have been unable to locate in any history books or reminiscences about the University, any reference to steeple-chasing taking place at Oxford, or elsewhere in the region. In a letter from the Central Library, Oxford, I was informed that, 'The Chipping Norton Steeplechases seem to have attracted little attention from historians, and are not mentioned in the *Victoria County History of Oxfordshire*, vol. 2, 1907, where county horse-racing, including an earlier Chipping Norton meeting (ca. 1734-57) is recorded.'

72 *The Life*, p.153.

73 *Ibid.*, pp.90-1. Trinity College Archive. Accounts, III/H/1841-42, Broad Book. Account for the Second Quarter ending 11 March.

74 Oriel College Archive: Details from the Tutorial Register, which records academic activity term by term. John Thomas Anderson was admitted to the Inner Temple on 21 January 1845, and called to the Bar on 28 January 1848. After practising in this country, he left for Canada, where he was appointed a QC. He died at Yowlands, Felsham, 2 April 1894.

75 Trinity College Archive. Accounts, III/H/1841-42, Broad Book. Account for the Second Quarter ending 11 March. Accounts, III/G/142. Buttery Book, Third Quarter, 11 March 1842, Burton's name is no longer on the list.

Notes to Chapter 5

1 Letters would have taken at least a week, and much more likely round about a fortnight. Storms in the Channel or snow blocking the Mt Cenis Pass would, of course, have added to the time of the journey. The route was across the Channel to Calais, from there to Paris and Lyon, then on to the frontier town of Pont de Beauvoisin, through the Mount Cenis Pass to Turin and Lucca.

2 See D. Balsdon, *Oxford Now and Then* (London, 1970), p.29. Burton's caution money was returned to him on 13 April 1842.

3 *The True Life*, p.27.

4 Col J. Davis, *History of the Queen's (Second) Royal Regt of Foot* (London, 1902), Vol.V, pp.21-23.

5 At the close of 1841, in spite of his age, poor health, and lack of recent battle experience, the unfortunate Elphinstone was given command of the British army at Kabul. Elphinstone, who had not wanted the command in the first place, was harshly criticised from every quarter. 'We have been favoured with the perusal of several Jellalabad letters of the same date,' reported *The Times* of 7 April 1842, 'and all agree in breathing the same fine spirit, when speaking of the defence of that place; the same indignation when the writers dwell on the atrocious

conduct of Akhbar Khan, and the same settled disgust when they speak of General Elphinstone….As it was our very soul sickens to think of the degradation – the force – a force of more than 5,000 British troops – actually marched out under the protection (as the old dotard deemed it) of the Envoy's assassin, and submitted to his conqueror's orders.'

6   *Ibid.*, Tuesday, 5 April 1842.

7   *Ibid.*, Friday, 11 March 1842.

8   *The Times*, 5 April 1842, reported that 'Orders were published on the 5th of February for the purpose of having a 10th Company added to every regiment in India which, with other measures adopted, will cause an increase of about 26,000 men.'

9   *The Life*, i, pp.104-105. No Company officer, for example, could appear at Court in uniform, and British Army officers took precedence over those of equal rank in the Indian service. See T.A. Heathcote, *The Indian Army – The Garrison of British Imperial India, 1822-1922* (Newton Abbot, 1974), p.121.

10   A.T. Embree, *Charles Grant and British India* (New York, 1952), pp.126, 178-184: "Report from the Committee Appointed to Inquire into the Existence of any Abuses in the Disposal of the Patronage of the East India Company, March 23, 1809," *Parliamentary Debates*, I Ser, Vol.XIII, Appendix IV, *passim*. Quoted in R. Callahan, *The East India Company and Army Reform, 1783-1798* (Cambridge, Mass., 1972), p.17.

11   In his cadet papers, OIOC, L/MIL/9/201, ff.46-49, and service record L/MIL/12/73 (1842-51). A. Burnes, *Travels into Bokhara* (London, 1835) dedicated his book to Loch, 'as a token of Respect and Gratitude….'

12   L/MIL/9/201, folio 49, extract from the Register Book, where she certified 'that no money or other valuable consideration has been or is to be paid, either directly or indirectly for the same, and that I will not pay or cause to be paid, either now or hereafter, by myself, by my nephew or the Hands of any other Person, any Pecuniary or Valuable Consideration whatsoever to any Person or Persons who have interested themselves in procuring the said nomination of my Nephew from the Director above mentioned.'

13   *Ibid.*, folio 46, which shows that the nomination was approved and passed on 7 June 1842.

14   L/MIL/9/201, f.46. Maitland's address was 41 Baker Street, Portman Square. Robert John Bagshaw lived not far off at 87 Wimpole Street.

15   J.H. Stocqueler, *The Handbook of India* (London, 1844), p.158.

16   See J.D. Aylward, *The House of Angelo – A Dynasty of Swordsmen* (London, 1953), p.175ff.

17   Swift, born in 1814, made his debut into the ring at the age of fifteen, winning more than eleven important fights before he was twenty. In a career spanning ten years he lost only two fights. Two victories ended fatally. His blows killed Anthony Noon in 1834, resulting in Swift's serving six months in jail, and Brighton Bill in 1838. Although he was acquitted of the latter's death, Swift gave up fighting. See N. Fleischer & S. Andre, *A Pictorial History of Boxing* (London, 1975).

18   According to Burton's 'Little Autobiography', *The Life*, i, p.154, he received 'a dozen lessons from Prof. Forbes.' Duncan Forbes (1798-1868), a remarkable character, born of humble parents, who knew no English until he was thirteen. Graduated MA at St Andrews University in 1823. He was appointed to King's College in 1837. Created an Hon LLD of St. Andrews in 1847.

19   Forbes later gave lessons in Hindustani to William Gifford Palgrave (1826-88) who, like Burton, won fame as an Arabian traveller with his *Narrative of a Year's Journey through Central and Eastern Arabia*, 2 vols (London, 1865). Unlike Burton, he enjoyed a brilliant academic career at Trinity, winning an Open Scholarship on 12 June 1842, and graduating with a first in Lit Hum and a second in Mathematics after only two and half years at the University. Deciding to take up soldiering in India, he took lessons in riding at the Albany Street barracks, fencing lessons at Maclaren's gymnasium in Oxford, and studied Hindustani every morning at eight o'clock with Duncan Forbes. See M. Allan, *Palgrave of Arabia* (London, 1972), p.84ff.

20   Charles Lamb was appointed to the Accounts Department in April 1792. His inimitable description of the older East India building, erected between 1726-29, is to be found in his essay, 'The South Sea House.' Other distinguished figures who served the East India Company for many years were: the philosopher, historian, and economist, John Mill (1772-1836) appointed an official in East India House in 1819, becoming head of the examiner's office in 1830. He was succeeded on his death in 1836 by the satirical novelist, Thomas Love Peacock. Mill's even more famous and

influential son, John Stuart Mill (1806-73) joined the examiner's office in 1823, rising to become its head following Peacock's retirement in 1858. See W. Foster, *The East India House, Its History and Associations* (London, 1924).

21   Cadets, then as now, were allowed to state a preference for the service which they wished to join, but that is quite different from the right to exercise it. They could go where they liked, provided there was a vacancy for them and the regimental colonel was willing to accept them. Under General Orders, Burton was initially appointed to the 14th Regiment, Bombay Native Infantry, 24 Sept 1842, and transferred to the 18th BNI on 25 Oct 1842. *The Life*, i, p.97n.

22   George Thomas D'Aguilar, 1783-1839, natural son of Benjamin D'Aguilar, of Foley Place, Marylebone, formerly a merchant at Benares. Brief details of his military career are set out in the card index of officers of the East India Company, Bengal, NAM.

23   See Frank C. Bowen, 'Passengers in East Indiamen,' *The P.L.A. Monthly*, March 1940, pp.90-92.

24   For the Overland Route and the introduction of steam navigation, see C.R. Low, *A History of the Indian Navy, 1613-1863* (London, 1877), i, pp.525-29, and ii, pp.54-56.

25   J.H. Stocqueler, *Handbook*, pp.167-168. Those who were not good sailors could shorten the sea-journey by travelling through France to Marseilles, where they could pick up a French steamer leaving every ten days or so for Malta, and thence to Alexandria.

26   Shipping News, *The Times*, 1 June 1842, p.1.

27   The biggest East Indiamen were of less than 2,000 tons. The ordinary merchant ship in general increased in tonnage from around 200 to 300 tons in the first quarter of the 19th century to 500 or 600 tons in the fifties and sixties. The *Endeavour* in which Captain Cook sailed to the South Pacific in 1768 was a bark of only 368 tons.

28   It was usual for passengers to embark at Gravesend for India rather than at Greenwich. Outward-bound East Indiamen often waited two or three days at Gravesend to embark passengers/Company officials/military etc., and to take on supplies. Robert Bagshaw may well have had a hand in arranging this, too, in order to spare the 'family harem' the long journey to Gravesend.

29   Isaac Spenser Baré Phipps Boileau, Ensign, 22nd Foot, 23 April 1842, Lt 29 Dec 1843; transferred to the 94th Foot, 25 April 1845. Died at Cannanore, British military headquarters on India's west coast, 7 June 1852. OIOC records. Charles Thompson (1823-95), Ensign, 18 June 1842, 2 European Light Infantry, Lt 30 Sept 1844. He went on to become Major-Gen, 1 Jan 1884, Lt Gen, 1 July 1887, Gen, 1 April 1894. See card index of officers of the East India Company, Bombay, NAM. There is also an obituary in *The Times*, 14 May 1895, p.10.

30   Burton could only remember the name of the first of these ladies, whose name he spelled as Mrs Lewis. I have taken the full passenger list from the Shipping Section of the *Bombay Almanac* for 1843.

31   Paradoxically, the purpose of the chair, endowed by Col John Boden, late of the East India Company, was 'that a more general and critical knowledge of the Sanskrit language will be a means of enabling his countrymen to proceed in the conversion of the Natives of India to the Christian religion, by disseminating a knowledge of the Sacred Scriptures amongst them.' See *The Oxford University Calendar*, 1840.
Haileybury, the Company's college in Hertfordshire, was founded in order to train the civilian members of the service. The subjects taught were divided into what were known as 'Orientals' and 'Europeans.' The former lasting two years was split into four terms. In the first term, students began studying Sanskrit, followed by Persian in the second, and Hindustani in the third. 'Europeans' studied Greek, Latin, and mathematics, together with law, general and Indian. See P.Woodruff, *The Men Who Ruled India* (London, 1971), Vol.1, 'The Founders,' p.279ff.

32   J.Mill, *The History of British India*, abridged and with an introduction by William Thomas (Chicago, 1975), p.xxxviii.

33   The parallel military seminary for Company officers was at Addiscombe, near Croydon. Boys who received a nomination went there for their education. The results of their final examination determined which arm of the service they were sent to. In descending order of achievement, this was the Engineers, the Artillery, or the Infantry. John Shakespeare (1774-1858) was appointed to an oriental professorship at the Royal Military College, Marlow in 1805. When the training college at Addiscombe opened in 1809, he was appointed professor of Hindustani there on a salary of £200 per annum, which was raised to £600 in 1822. While at Addiscombe he compiled a Hindustani dictionary. He made a great deal of money from the sale of his books, receiving £3,600 alone from the Directors for

his Hindustani grammar and dictionaries.

34   Mrs M. Postans, *Western India in 1838* (London, 1839), i, p.4.

Notes to Chapter 6

1   Mrs Postans, *Western India in 1838* (London, 1839), i, p.7.

2   Burton claimed in his 'Reminiscences written for Mr Hitchman, 1888,' (*sic*), *The Life*, i, p.130, that the Company made no provision for receiving its cadets. This does not appear in his earlier written chapter, p.100. I have relied for my information on J.H. Stocqueler, *The Handbook of India* (London, 1844), p.515.

3   Mrs Postans, *Western India*, p.34. This, apparently, is what she calls the Victoria Hotel, containing 'mosquitoes, a billiard table, and coffee and tap room.' *The Gazeteer of Bombay, City and Island* (Bombay, 1910), Vol III, p.299, states that there was no hotel worthy of the name prior to 1845. The Hope Hall family hotel opened in Mazagon in 1837, served for many years as the principal family hotel in Bombay.

4   James Ryan (1807-52), assistant garrison surgeon serving under Superintendent Surgeon A.C. Kane.He died at Putney in 1852.

5   Eighteenth century doctors were aware that those who had lived for some time in the tropics, were more resistant to disease than newcomers. They were thought to be 'acclimatised' or 'seasoned.' One school believed that the first sickness, called the 'seasoning sickness' was the necessary hurdle. See P.D. Curtin, *The Image of Africa* (Madison, 1964), pp.82-83.

6   There is a description of the burial grounds in *The Gazeteer of Bombay*, p.63.

7   Cremation is the traditional funeral method in Hinduism. Burial is reserved for those who have not been sufficiently purified by domestic rites, known as samskaras, and ascetics who have renounced all earthly concerns. Hindus believe in reincarnation, ie rebirth to a higher or lower state of life. Isabel Burton describes one such cremation in *The Romance*, ii, p.588.

8   An extract from the *Asiatic Journal* describing Bombay in 1843, quoted in J.H. Stocqueler, *The Handbook of India*, p.524.

9   *The Life*, i, p.130.

10   Panca-Tantra, or Panchatantra, meaning in Sanskrit 'Five Chapters.' The original text, now lost, was a mixture of Sanskrit prose and verse, with the stories contained within one of the five 'frame stories.' It is believed to have been written some time between 100 BC and AD 500.

11   Burton gives a detailed description of this vessel in *Goa and the Blue Mountains* (London, 1851), pp.2-3.

12   Staff appointments were eagerly sought after by officers, since they offered higher pay, greater prestige, and more interesting work than the routine duties of an ordinary military station. Although beneficial for the officers concerned, the system had a highly detrimental effect on the regiments which they left behind. See T.A. Heathcote, *The Indian Army – The Garrison of British Imperial India, 1822-1922* (Newton Abbot, 1974), pp.133-135.

13   From Burton's 'Little Autobiography' in *The Life*, i, p.154.

14   Captain (later Lt Gen) Houghton James, then in command of the 'wing' of the regiment at Baroda, was married, as was Lt Macdonald. Ensign Thompson who came out on the *John Knox* with Burton, married only three years after arriving in India. These were the exception, since few junior officers could exist on their pay, let alone support a wife. There was an old army saying, 'Subalterns may not marry, captains may marry, majors should marry, colonels must marry.'

15   *The Life*, i, p.109.

16   *Ibid.*, pp.135-36.

17   R.F. Burton, *The Book of the Thousand Nights and a Night*, Kamashastra Society (Benares, 1885), Vol.3, p.160.

18   For a discussion of Free trade versus imperialism, see A.G.L. Shaw (ed.), *Great Britain and the Colonies, 1815-1865*, (London, 1970), pp.164-83.

19   To shield the tent from the intense heat of the midday sun, a false roof was erected with bamboos and date leaves. See Mrs Postans, *Western India*, p.34.

20   Major-General Vans-Kennedy (1784-1846), born at Ayr in Scotland. He was a great student, published a Maharatti dictionary, and wrote on questions connected with languages and mythology, and on military law. See his entry in the *DNB*.

21   Gujarati was part of the Indo-Aryan family of languages. It derived from Sanskrit through Prakrit, and was 'spoken,' Burton said, 'throughout the country, and by the Parsees of Bombay and elsewhere.'

22   E. Rice, *Captain Sir Richard Burton* (New York, 1990), p.63.

23   See P.J. Marshall (ed.), *The British Discovery of Hinduism in the Eighteenth Century* (Cambridge, 1970). The editor writes, p.20: 'English writers in the second half of the 18th century were the heirs to over two hundred years of attempts by Europeans to interpret Hinduism. Interpretations had generally followed the same lines...between what they regarded as "popular" Hinduism and "philosophical" Hinduism. Popular cults were described to be condemned or ridiculed....'

24   The Royal Asiatic Society, Bombay, derived from the Literary Society, founded by Sir James Mackintosh, Recorder of Bombay in 1804. In 1827, the RAS of Great Britain and Ireland sent a proposal for the union of the two societies. In 1829 this was put into effect. Two years later it moved from the Fort, having been given the upper portion of the north wing of the Town Hall for its Library and Reading Room. Its first journal was published in 1841. See *The Gazeteer of Bombay*, p.330ff.

25   E. Moor, *The Hindu Pantheon* (c.1810). In his preface to 'A New Edition, With Additional Plates, Condensed and Annotated by the Rev W.O. Simpson' (Madras, 1864), the editor writes, p.vii: 'A few lines will suffice to tell all that is generally known of Edward Moor, the author of the Hindu Pantheon...He was with the British contingent under Captain Little, which acted with the Mahrattas against Tippoo Sahib in 1790 and 1791. During this time, he lived apparently on terms of close intimacy with various native chiefs of Western India. We are not precisely informed when he returned to England, but it appears to have been shortly before the publication of his book, that is somewhere about 1810. Twenty years familiar intercourse with native life was no mean preparation for such a work.' There is a copy of Moor's work in the Burton Library at the Huntington (BL 1283).

26   William Ward (1769-1823). In the autumn of 1798, Ward, a printer by trade, offered his services as a missionary to the baptist mission committee. He sailed in 1799. His time in India was chiefly occupied in superintending the printing press, by means of which the scriptures, translated into Bengali, Mahratta, Tamil, and twenty-three other languages, were spread throughout India. Suffering from bad health, he returned to England in 1818. He was then entrusted with the task of pleading for funds with which to endow a college at Serampore for the purpose of instructing the native population in European literature and science. On 28 May 1821 he sailed for India with £3,000 for the new college which had been founded during his absence. He died of cholera at Serampore on 7 March 1823.

27   J. Mill, *The History of British India*, abridged with an introduction by W. Thomas (Chicago, 1975), p.xxix.

28   Rajputs, Brahmins, and Banias, who are respectively war-lords, priests, and merchants, form an elite in Hindu society. They are distinguished from lowlier castes by being allowed to wear the sacred thread, and of assuming the epithet "twice-born".' See G.M. Carstairs, *The Twice Born, A Study of A Community of High-Caste Hindus* (London, 1961), pp.13-14. The sacred thread, *upavita*, is bestowed on them during their boyhood investiture, *upanayana*, and generally worn diagonally across the body over the left shoulder. However, during the water offering to saints, it is suspended around the neck, and over the right shoulder during ancestor rites.

29   See C.E.B. Russell, *General Rigby, Zanzibar and the Slave Trade* (London, 1935), p.33ff.

Notes to Chapter 7

1   See J.G. Lockhart, *The Life of Sir Walter Scott* (London, 1906), pp.11-12n. A much fuller account of Thomas Scott and his family can be found in J.H.C. Grierson (ed.), *The Letters of Sir Walter Scott* (London, 1932). Thomas later became an officer in the Manx Fencibles (1808-11), then paymaster to the 70th Regiment in Canada, where he died on 14 February 1823 'after much suffering of body and....mind.'

2   Scott's cadet papers are in OIOC, L/MIL/9/149, 1-80, 1822 (ff.306-10), and in L/MIL/9/144 (ff.104-08). His

service records are in the Bombay Army List, L/MIL/12/69.

3   See T. Wright, *An Autobiography* (London, 1936), p.112.

4   *The Life*, i, p.140. Burton, however, is wrong both as to the place and date of Scott's death. He attained the rank of general, 31 March 1875, and died 19 March 1876, at Halbendorf, near Dresden, Saxony. See J.H.C. Grierson, *The Lettters*, biographical note, Vol.VI, 229n.

5   Meanee was fought on 17 February 1843, and Dubba on 24 March 1843. Meanee is incorrectly dated 21 February by Burton in *The Life*, i, p.116.

6   Lt Gen Sir W. Napier, *The Life and Opinions of General Sir Charles James Napier* (London, 1857), ii, p.218.

7   See Lieutenant-Colonel Outram, C.B., *The Conquest of Scinde. A Commentary* (Edinburgh & London, 1846). Outram, whose share of the prize money amounted to £3,000, refused to accept it for himself. Instead, he distributed it among a number of charitable institutions in India.

8   *The Times*, 6 May 1843, p.5.

9   Quoted in P. Woodruff, *The Men Who Ruled India* (London, 1971), i, p.326.

10 Towards the latter part of the century, *Karachi* had become the official spelling, according to the *Imperial Gazeteer of India*. Even so, *Kurrachee* was the form which continued to be widely used in 'railway guides, shipping lists, in mercantile and domestic correspondence, in telegraphic messages, and even by the Director-General of the Post-Office of India.' See A. F. Bailiie, *Kurrachee (Karachi), Past: Present: And Future* (Bombay & London, 1890), p.2.

11 Lt Gen Sir W. Napier, *The Life and Opinions*, ii, p.356. Journal entry dated 5 April 1843.

12 *Ibid.*, iv, pp.8-9.

13 Lt Gen Sir W. Napier, *The Life and Opinions*, iii, p.95.

14 See Colonel K. Young, *Sind in the 40s*, ed. A.F. Scott (London, 1912), journal entry, Friday, 27 Oct 1843, p.19.

15 *Ibid.*, p.177, Keith Young writing to Sir Henry Lawrence.

16 A reproduction of the drawing appears in R.Lawrence, *Charles Napier. Friend and Fighter, 1782-1853* (London, 1952), p.134.

17 Burton's service records, OIOC, Bombay Army List, L/MIL/12/73, show his being qualified as an Interpreter in Maharatta from 22 October 1844.

18 OIOC, Bombay Army List, L/MIL/12/73, Appointed 2nd Assistant Surveyor in Scinde from 15 Nov last, Bengal GO 2 May 1845.

19 NLS, MS 3867, ff 95-96. Captain (later General) William Craig Emilius Napier (1818-1903) was first commissioned into the 25th (The King's Own Borderers) Regiment of Foot in 1835. After seeing active service in Natal, he became *aide-de-camp* to his uncle, Sir Charles Napier. Later, in the Crimean War, he acted as Assistant Director, Land Transport Corps to his brother-in-law, Colonel William M.S. McMurdo. Promoted general in 1877, he became Governor of the Royal Military College, Sandhurst (1875-82).

20 R.F. Burton, *The Lands of Cazembe* (London, 1873), p.9

21 Sir William Erskine Baker, 1808-81. Educated at Addiscombe, he went out to India in the Bengal Engineers in 1826. He was successively Superintendent of Canals and Forests in Sind, Director of the Ganges Canal, and Consulting Engineer to the Government of India in the Public Works Department. He was regarded as the greatest authority of his time on irrigation.

22 OIOC, Bengal Army List, L/MIL/10/27.

23 OIOC, Bengal Army List, L/MIL/10/36. Permitted to resign his appointment as Superintendent of canals and forests in Scinde and granted leave for three months to enable him to join his former appointment as Superintendent of Delhi Canals, GO 4 Oct '44. Appointed Superintendent of canals in the Dooab, and Director of the works on the Ganges canal from 1st Feb '45. GO 13 Dec '44. H.T. Lambrick, *Sir Charles Napier in Sind* (Oxford, 1952), p.311, appears to be mistaken in asserting that Baker had to depart on sick leave.

24   Lt Gen Sir W. Napier, *The Life and Opinions*, iii, p.286.

25 OIOC, Bombay Army List, L/MIL/12/69. Appointed Superintendent of Canals and Forests, Calcutta Gaz, 18 Sept, Bombay, 10 Oct 1844.

26 Thomas Colvin Blagrave 2nd son of Charles George Blagrave, Bengal Civil Service, and Jean Colvin, his wife. Born 25 March 1818; baptised Calcutta 16 April 1818. Educated by the Rev J. Bewsher, Richmond. Retired as Hon Lt

Col, 26 BNI, 31 Dec 1861. Died 21 Oct 1897, aged 79. Details from the card index of officers, Bengal Army, NAM.

27   Lt Gen Sir W. Napier, *The Life and Opinions*, iii, p.156.

28   R.F. Burton, *Scinde; or the Unhappy Valley* (London, 1851), ii, p.89.

29   See W.H. Wilkins (ed.), *The Jew, The Gypsy, and El Islam* (London, 1898). Burton who spoke Romany, was one of the original members of the Gypsy Lore Society. *The Life*, i, pp.250-53.

30   R.F. Burton, *Falconry in the Valley of the Indus* (London, 1852), p.x.

31   See E.B. Eastwick, *Dry Leaves from Young Egypt* (London, 1851), p.24. Writing anonymously as an 'Ex-Political,' Eastwick highlighted the hypocrisy of the British with regard to these shikargahs. After initially complaining that the forests were an obstacle to the navigation of the river, 'We built our agencies, our cantonments, with timber from them, without troubling ourselves as to payment….then we seized the whole on the plea of their being highly injurious to trade…..' In a footnote, he added: 'After abusing the Shikargahs ad libitum, we have thought it proper to let them stand!'

32   The most recent and scholarly account of this sect is by a descendant of Sardar Abul Hasan Khan, F. Daftary, *The Isma'ilis: their history and doctrines* (Cambridge, 1990).

33   See 'The Revolt of the Agha Khan Mahallati and the Transference of the Isama'ili Imamate to India,' H. Algar, *Studia Islamica* (Paris, 1969), pp.55-81. Also N.M. Dumasia, *The Agha Khan and His Ancestors* (Bombay, 1939). Burton's references to the Agha Khan are derisory and critical. See *Scinde;or the Unhappy Valley*, i, pp. 190-96, and *Sindh and the Races*, pp.248-49.

34   A. Burnes, *Travels into Bokhara, Containing the Narrative of a Voyage on the Indus* (London, 1835), i, p.x

35   *The Athenaeum*, No.1252, 25 October 1851, p.1112.

36   R.F. Burton, *Falconry*, p.99.

37   R. Kipling, 'Miss Youghal's Sais,' *Plain Tales From The Hills* (Calcutta & London, 1889), pp.28-29.

38   Both, of course, were policemen. One was the stepson of a British officer who had married the widow of an Afghan military leader some time between 1839-41; the other, named Christie, was a European born and brought up in India. See R.E. Harbord, *The Reader's Guide to Rudyard Kipling's Work*, ed. L. Green (Canterbury, 1961), i, pp.16-17. F. McLynn, *Snow Upon the Desert* (London, 1990), p.379, 36n, considers it 'highly significant that "Strickland," like Burton, served in the Punjab.' Burton, however, never saw service in that region. The nearest he got to it was in 1846. His regiment, forming part of Sir Charles Napier's army, temporarily halted at Bahawalpur, then capital of an independent princely state ruled over by nawabs originally from Sind. Within a day or so, after learning that the First Sikh War was over, the army was forced to return.

39   *The Life*, i, pp.160-61.

40   R. F. Burton, *Scinde; or the Unhappy Valley*, i, p.67.

41   Sir Charles Napier to Sir John Cam Hobhouse, President of the Board of Control, cited in *The Life and Opinions*, iv, p.16.

42   The phrase, 'Great Game,' was originally coined by Captain Arthur Connolly, and used by him in a letter to a friend. Following his execution at the hands of the emir of Bokhara in June 1842, his letters eventually passed to the military historian, Sir John Kaye. While it was he who first publicly introduced the term, it was Rudyard Kipling's *Kim*, which was responsible for giving it universal currency.

43   R.F. Burton, *The Book of the Thousand Nights and a Night* (Benares, 1885), x, p.205.

44   F.M. Brodie, *The Devil Drives* (London, 1984), p.66. For direct copying from this source see, M. Hastings, *Sir Richard Burton, a biography* (London, 1978), pp.55-58; E. Rice, *Captain Sir Richard F. Burton* (New York, 1990), p.128; F. McLynn, *Snow upon the Desert* (London, 1990), p.41. M.S. Lovell, *A Rage to Live* (London, 1998), p.56, while not copying from Brodie, is clearly influenced by her version.

45   See Lt Gen Sir W. Napier, *The Life and Opinions*, iv, p.28. Brodie correctly quotes the source, but misrepresents the author.

46   *The Life*, i, p.145.

47   Penzer goes beyond what Burton states, claiming that he 'was relieved of his duties and the report was in all probability burned.' See N.M. Penzer, *An Annotated Bibliography of Sir Richard Francis Burton, KCMG* (London, 1923), p.198.

48   OIOC, Bombay Service Army List, L/MIL/12/73.

49   *The Book of the Thousand Nights and a Night*, Vol.10, pp.233-4.

50   R.F. Burton, *Sindh and the Races* (London, 1851), p.vi.

51   R.F. Burton, *Zanzibar; City, Island, and Coast* (London, 1872), i, p.9.

52   NLS, Scott Papers, MS 3867, ff 109-10, 10 July 1845.

53   F.M. Brodie, *The Devil Drives*, p.64.

54   R.F. Burton, *Sindh and the Races*, p.237.

55   R.F. Burton, *Sindh and the Races*, p.13. Eastwick's comment, of which Burton's is a paraphrase, can be found in his *Dry Leaves from Young Egypt*, p.38.

56   R.F. Burton, *Sindh and the Races*, p.298.

57   H. Pottinger, *Travels in Belochistan*, p.377.

58   T. Postans, *Personal Observations* pp.49-50.

59   E.B. Eastwick, *Dry Leaves*, p.138.

60   R.F. Burton, *Scinde; or the Unhappy Valley*, ii, pp.241-42.

61   Indian Poetry Book in the QK Coll. I have cited verse 8 of a 12-stanza poem, detailing his 'adventures with fair females/That filled my history.'

62   QK Coll. In his rush, Napier has muddled up the Christian names of the two commanders, who were: Sir Hugh Gough, 1st viscount, 1799-1869, and Sir Henry Hardinge, 1785-1856. The latter had succeeded his brother-in-law, Lord Ellenborough, as governor-general of India, in 1844. Sir Charles Napier later replaced Gough as commander-in-chief in India, who was severely criticised for the heavy British losses sustained in fighting the Sikhs.

63   NLS, Scott Papers, ff 119-20. This long interesting letter is dated Rodewalla, 15 Feb 1846. Written in soft pencil, it is very badly faded in places as to be almost illegible. The Battle of Sobraon was the most decisive battle of the First Sikh War (1845-46). The Sikhs had secured their retreat by a bridge of boats strung across the river. Following a heavy artillery exchange, the British stormed the Sikh positions. More than 10,000 Sikhs were killed in their rush to escape across the Sutlej, when the pontoon collapsed, throwing them into the water. The British also suffered severe losses, with some 2,383 killed or wounded.

64   NLS, Scott Papers, ff 121-22.

65   Henry Nicholas Corsellis, son of Henry Corsellis, EICS. Born Bencoolen 13 January 1800, died Liverpool 22 January 1848. This latter date in the card index of officers of the Bombay Army in the NAM is incorrect. Corsellis's death certificate shows he died at 7 Upper Warwick Street, Toxteth Park on 21 February 1848. Cause of death is given as 'Influenza supervening in Paralysis and general decay from long residence in Tropical Climates.' His eldest daughter, Marion Isabel, died at Cheltenham on 14 February 1926, aged 96.

66   BL, Napier Papers, MSS 54520 (iii).

67   R.F. Burton, *Scinde; or the Unhappy Valley*, i, p.152.

68   See Lt General Sir W. Napier, *Life and Opinions*, iii, pp.432-3.

69   OIOC, Bombay Army List, L/MIL/12/73.

70   John Frederick Steinhaeuser, 1814-66. OIOC, Bombay Army List, L/MIL/12/85. He has an entry in V.G. Plarr, *Lives of the Fellows of the Royal College of Surgeons of England*, ed. Sir D'Arcy Power *et al*, 2 vols (London, 1930), and in Lt. Col. D.G. Crawford, *Roll of the Indian Medical Service, 1615-1930* (London, 1930).

71   Henry John Carter, FRS, 1813-95. His Service Records up to 1858 are in OIOC, Bombay Army List, L/MIL/12/85. A summary of his career is to be found in his obituary notice in *Proceedings of the Royal Society*, Vol.58, 1895, pp.liv-lvii. He is also noticed in Lt. Col. D.G. Crawford, *Rolls of the Indian Medical Service*.

Notes to Chapter 8

1   R.F. Burton, *Os Lusiadas* (London, 1880), i, p.xi

2   *Les six voyages de Jean Baptiste Tavernier, Baron d'Aubonne*, Part II, p.115.

3   R.F. Burton, *Goa and the Blue Mountains* (London, 1851), pp. 59 & 62.

4   R.F. Burton, *Camoens. His Life and his Lusiads. A Commentary* (London, 1881), i, p.185, 5: The Translation Now Offered To The Public.' The 'old Anglo-Indian newspaper' was *The Bombay Times*.

5   St. Francis Xavier, 1506-52. The Jesuit priest who became the greatest Roman Catholic missionary of modern times, bringing Christianity to India, the Malay Archipelago, and Japan. He was canonized in 1622.

6   A.C. Burnell (ed.), *The Voyage of John Huygen Van Linschoten to the East Indies*, from the Old English translation of 1598 (London, 1885), I, p.178 and note 4. Dr Burnell was told in 1879 by the Archbishop of Goa, 'that there was only one nun besides some lay sisters in the convent; that it had proved, on the whole, a failure, and would not be kept up...'

7   R.F. Burton, *Goa*, p.73.

8   *Ibid.*, pp.73-85.

9   See *The Three Voyages of Vasco Da Gama* from *The Lendas of India* of Gaspar Correa. Translated from the Portuguese with notes and introduction by the Hon E.J. Stanley: Printed for the Hakluyt Society (London, 1869), pp.330-31, and p.363.

10   *Ibid.*, p.170.

11   *Ibid.*, p.179.

12   *Ibid.*, p.222.

13   R.F.Burton, *Goa*, p.260.

14   See Sir J.F. Price, *Ootacamund: A History. Compiled for the Government of Madras* (Madras, 1908). A very rare publication. For a modern account, see M. Panter Downes, *Ooty Preserved. A Victorian Hill-Station* (London, 1967), and J. Cameron, *An Indian Summer* (London, 1974).

15   R.F. Burton, *Goa*, p.295. Panter Downes, p.111, states that Sir Frederick Price 'gives a cold mention or two to Burton and his derisive criticism...but it is plain that he cannot forgive him.'

16   *Akhlak I Hindi, or A Translation of the Hindustani Version of Pilpay's Fables*, by R.F. Burton, Lt. 18th Regt. Bombay NI, with explanatory notes and appendix by the Translator, 1847. The bound typescript, consisting of seventy-eight folios in quarto sheets, carries the signature of W.H. Wilkins, and his address, Walsingham House, Piccadilly. See N.M. Penzer, *An Annotated Bibliography of Sir Richard Francis Burton, KCMG* (London, 1923), pp.185-6. Facing page 186 is an illustration of the title-page and pages from the Preface and text.

17   See OIOC, Bombay Army List, L/MIL/12/73. There is no doubt that Burton consciously set out to match, if not to exceed, Lt C.P. Rigby's linguistic feats.

18   *The Life*, i, p.150.

19   *Ibid.*, p.150.

20   See R.F. Burton, *Personal Narrative of a Pilgrimage to El Medinah and Meccah* (London, 1885-6), iii, p.149, where he writes: 'The House of Allah *has been so fully described by my predecessors, that there is little inducement to attempt a new portrait.* [my italics]...I will do homage to the memory of the accurate Burckhardt, and extract from his pages a description which may be illustrated by a few notes.' Ali Bey's Plan of the Mosque is bound in between pp.60-1. Burckhardt had also, of course, fully described the activities in Mecca itself, during the pilgrimage season.

21   *Ibid.*, p.201.

22   *Ibid.*, p.202

23   An Iranian order, associated with the Hanbali theologian, 'Abd al-Qadir al-Jilani (1078-166) in Baghdad. It emerged in the 12th century and spread both eastwards and westwards into India and North Africa.

24   J.S. Trimingham, *The Sufi Orders in Islam* (Oxford, 1971), p.193, n.1. There is an illustration of the so-called Murshid's diploma in N.M. Penzer, *Ann. Bib.*, facing p.53. The original is in the Burton Collection, OHG.

25   Punjabi for "The First, or Original Book." It is also known as *Granth Sahib* (the *Granth* personified), and is treated with the reverence paid to a living guru. The book was initially compiled by the fifth Guru, Arjun, at Amritsar in AD 1604. In AD 1704 the tenth and last Guru, Gobind Singh, added the hymns of his predecessors. On 7 October 1708, shortly before his death, he passed on the succession to the holy book, thus ending the line of personal gurus.

26   Bombay Government Records (1855), No.XVII. New Series, Part II, pp.637-657. As N.M. Penzer points out, this is chronologically the earliest printed article by Burton. Although written in 1847, however, it was not published

until eight years later.

27 *Ibid.*, pp.613-636.

28 See R.F. Burton, *Scinde; or the Unhappy Valley*, i, pp.258-62.

29 *Journal of the Bombay Branch of the Royal Asiatic* Society, Vol.III, No.XII., Jan. 1849, Art V, pp.58-69. For the acknowledgement of his Afghan helper, see *The Life*, i, p.150, footnote 2. This did not appear in the paper itself.

30 Boris Andreevich Dorn (1805-81). After a period as Privat-Dozent (unpaid lecturer) at Leipzig University, he became professor of Oriental Literature at the Imperial Russian University of Kharkov. He was later appointed professor of History and Geography of the East in the Institute of Eastern languages attached to the Foreign Ministry. He was elected an academician in 1852.

31 *JRAS* (Bombay Branch), Vol.III, No.XII, Jan 1849, Art IX, pp.84-125.

32 *The Life*, i, pp.182-3.

33 Their epitaph at Multan reads: 'On this, the farthest frontier of the British Indian Empire, which their deaths extended, lie the remains of PETER VANS AGNEW of the Bengal Civil Service and WILLIAM ANDERSON Lieut. 1st Bombay Fusilier Regiment.' Quoted in J. Morris, *Heaven's Command* (London, 1979), p.277. Lt Anderson was James Outram's brother-in-law.

34 Letter to his cousin, Sarah Burton, dated 14 Nov 1848, printed in T. Wright, *The Life of Sir Richard Burton* (London, 1906), i, p.83. Burton's aunt died on 10 September 1848, and was buried in the family vault at Elstree parish church.

35 It first appeared in F. Hitchman, *Richard F. Burton. KCMG: His Early, Private and Public Life* (London, 1887)

36 *The True Life*, pp.53-4.

37 For example: B.Farwell, *Burton* (London, 1965), Avon paperback, p.68, where he writes: 'Unfortunately for Burton, his earlier report on pederasty in Karachi, although unpublished, had come to the attention of the Bombay Government......all roads to further advancement were now blocked.' F.M. Brodie, *The Devil Drives* London, 1984), Norton paperback, p.69: 'Their arrival in Bombay [ie the alleged reports on the Karachi bordellos] nearly precipitated a crisis which eventually drove Burton from India.'

38 OIOC, Bombay Army List, L/MIL/12/73. See *The Life*, where he writes, p.151: 'In the latter, official examinations were passed before Captain Stack, the only Englishman in the country who had an inkling of the subject.' He had written many years earlier, 'A few years ago that distinguished Orientalist Major-General Vans Kennedy, when applied to for an examination in the Sindhi dialect, replied that he was not aware of the existence of any such language.' R.F. Burton, *Sindh and the Races*, p.69. In the *Gazeteer of the Province of Sind,* compiled by E.H. Aitken (Karachi, 1907), pp.472-4, he remarks that 'Sindhi was the language of common life among all, from the Mirs to the Muhana, and though it was not considered a fit vehicle for learning, or polite correspondence, the Hindu traders kept their accounts and carried on all their business in it, using a Hindu character, based on the Devangari, of which there were several varieties.....In 1851 Mr. (afterwards Sir Bartle) Frere issued a circular requiring all officers in civil employ to pass an examination in colloquial Sindi....' However, it could not be used for official correspondence until an alphabet was agreed upon. 'Captain (afterwards Sir Richard) Burton strongly advocated the adoption of the Arabic alphabet...Captain Stack, his only equal in knowledge of the language and author of a dictionary of it in the Devangari character, contended for the adoption of one or other of the Hindu-Sindhi alphabets already in use among the traders......The contention raged for some time...In 1853..the Court of Directors of the East India Company decided that Arabic should have a trial.'

39 See F.M. Brodie, *The Devil Drives*, p.71.

Notes to Chapter 9

1 J. Conrad. *The Mirror of the Sea* (London, 1906)

2 The date of Burton's arrival off Plymouth is given in W.H. Wilkins (ed.), *Wanderings in Three Continents by the late Captain Sir Richard F. Burton, KCMG* (London, 1901), p.4.

3 R.F. Burton, *Scinde or the Unhappy Valley* (London, 1851), i, p.21. Burton glosses 'bihisht' as 'Paradise', and

'chob' as the 'bastinado', that is, flogging the feet. It was common practice then, and for some years later, for passengers to be brought ashore by pilot-boats standing on station at the entrance to the Sound. By doing so, they avoided the notoriously slow journey up-Channel to London.

4   *The Times*, Thursday, 6 September, 1849, p.4.

5   There is no truth in Georgiana's Stisted's assertion, *The True Life* (London, 1896), p.56, that, 'on his arrival in London, regardless of the unearthly hour, he went straight to the house of the aunt who had nursed him through the scarlet fever, and knocked her up at 2 am.' In 1849, there was a daily service of six trains running between Plymouth and London. The fastest, the 10.25 am express, nicknamed the *Flying Dutchman*, arrived in London at 5.25 pm.

6   Before his marriage, Robert had lived at 87 Wimpole Street, a short distance from the Barretts at Number 50.

7   He returned to England a widower. On 19 October 1820, only three years after arriving in India, his wife Mary and one of his daughters were tragically drowned, when the boat in which they were passengers on the Hooghly River, Calcutta, capsized. Robert would have been seventeen at the time. He was the only son. There were at least two other daughters, Mary Louisa and Lucy.

8   An account of the Bagshaw family, illustrated by the author, can be found in W. Cooper, The Bagshaws of Dovercourt, *Essex Countryside*, Vol. 22, May, 1974, pp.26-29.

9   See M. Stenton (ed.), *Who's Who of British Members of Parliament*, Vol.1, 1832-85 (Sussex, 1976).

10   In the 1851 Census Returns they are listed as: Thomas Whitehouse, widower, aged 66, butler; C.T. Alderney, unmarried, aged 20, footman; George Harcourt, married, aged 30, coachman; Mary Harcourt, wife, aged 32; George D. Harcourt, son, aged 10; Sarah, daughter, aged 5; Margaret, daughter, aged 6; George Riches, aged 22, groom; Jane Griffith, widow, aged 45, cook; Caroline Day, unmarried, aged 37, upper house-maid; Margaret Day, aged 23, house-maid; Margaret Webb, aged 30, house-maid. The Bagshaws occupied 9 York Place until around Christmas 1854, when they left, presumably, to occupy the first house in Orwell Terrace, appropriately named Banksea House, at Dovercourt New Town, Harwich.

11   Sarah Baker, died on 6 March 1846, aged 74 years. Her eldest daughter, Sarah, widow of Dr Francis Burton, died on 10 September, 1848, aged 51. She was interred with her late husband at Elstree. Under the terms of her will, dated 25 July 1846, Sarah Burton left all the property and personal estate to her executors in trust for her two daughters. She bequeathed £50 to Margaret Morgan. The rate-books show that the house remained occupied until Lady Day, circa 25 March 1852.

12   Burton, accompanied by his servant, Khudabaksh, probably took one of the General Steam Navigation Company's steam-packets, which left London Bridge wharf on Tuesdays and Sundays, for Boulogne. From there, they would have been able to catch a train, first to Paris, and then on to Bourges, capital of the Chér department, almost exactly in the centre of France. There was no railway line at this period to Avignon, so this leg of the journey would have been undertaken by diligence. At Avignon, they could travel once more by train to Marseilles. Information from *The Times*, 1 September 1849, and from B. Cima, *Histoire synchronoptique des chemins de fer français*, Périod 1828-49: "le temps des expériences," courtesy of Didier Durandal, Le rédacteur en chef, la vie du rail, Paris.

13   Captain (later Lt Gen Sir) Henry William Stisted (1817-1875), had a distinguished military career, an account of which can be read in the military histories of the regiments in which he served: Col J. Davis, *History of the Queen's (Second) Royal Regiment of Foot*, 9 vols (London, 1902); J. Macveigh, *Historical Records of the 78th Highlanders* (Edinburgh, 1887); Brig Gen. A.E. Cavendish, *The 93rd Sutherland Highlanders, 1799-1927* (Published privately, 1928). Stisted was appointed Colonel of this regiment in 1873. He also has an entry in the *DNB*.

14   Georgiana was born at Winchester in 1846, and Maria at Lucca in 1849. Portraits of the two girls can be found in T. Wright, *The Life of Sir Richard Burton* (London, 1906), i, p.97. Writing to me on 25 November, 1984, the late Brigadier Nigel Stisted stated, that he 'was left two large oval pastels of Georgiana and Maria Stisted aged about 20. When we moved we sold them, as we had not sufficient wall space to hang them.' Their whereabouts are now unknown.

15   Burton's account of Edward's university career (*The Life*, i, p.88), can be dismissed as an amusing piece of fiction, much like his own. His entry in J.A. Venn, *Alumni Cantabrigienses*, Part II, Vol.1 (Cambridge, 1940), p.467 reads: 'Burton, Edward Joseph Netterville, Adm. Pens. At Trinity, July 5, 1843 (2nd son of Joseph Netterville, Col. 36th

Regt [sic] – died 1857, at Bath – Matric. Michs. 1843. Entered the Army, Ensign, 37th Regt. 1845, Lieut. 1846, Capt. 37th Regt. Brother of Sir Richard Burton the well-known explorer.' Details about the activities of the regiment, which include brief references to Edward, are to be found in C.T. Atkinson, *Regimental History, The Royal Hampshire Regiment* (Glasgow, 1952). Edward is the subject of several inaccuracies. Thomas Wright, *The Life of Sir Richard Burton*, i, p.76, was the first biographer to state, incorrectly, that Edward practised as an army doctor. This mistake, with variations, has been copied by a succession of biographers: Byron Farwell (1963), Fawn Brodie (1967), Michael Hastings (1978), and Frank McLynn (1990). The latter, copying from Farwell, and adding a fictitious detail of his own, describes Edward as, 'a trainee surgeon in the 36th Regiment in Ceylon.' Mary S. Lovell (1998) refers to his being in 'the Bengal Army.'

16   *The Times*, Saturday, 13 October 1849, p.6.
17   R.F. Burton, *Wanderings in West Africa* (London, 1863), i, p.271 n.
18   G. Stisted, 'Reminiscences of Sir Richard Burton,' *Temple Bar*, Vol.92, May-July, 1891, p.335. She did not include this anecdote in her biography of Burton published five years later. As for the name Allahdad, applied to Burton's Muslim servant, it was first used in these 'Reminiscences,' and then repeated in Georgiana's *True Life*, pp. 54 and 56. This, in spite of Burton's clear statement in *Scinde, or the Unhappy Valley*, as already quoted, that his name was Khudabaksh. Perhaps even more remarkable is the fact that the name Allahdad has been copied by every one of Burton's biographers since. Khudabaksh, presumably, returned to India shortly after arriving back in England.
19   St Margaret's was not only the mother church of the city of Westminster, but the parish church of the House of Commons, where Lucy's father, John Bagshaw, was an MP. The wedding was noted in *The Times*, Monday, 3 June 1850.
20   Miscellaneous historical material relating to the Pryce family, is to be found in *Montgomeryshire Collections* (the publication of Powys Historical Society) in Vol.18 (1886), and Vol.23, (1889). Vol.18, p.118. E.S. Mostyn Pryce matriculated at Balliol College, Oxford, on 25 Jan 1871, aged 19; BA 1874; MA 1877; a student of the Inner Temple, 1873. There is an entry for him in A. Mee (ed.), *Who's Who in Wales* (1921), p.383. He died on 14 June 1932, aged 81, his occupation being given on his death certificate as HM Inspector of Schools (Retd). There is a portrait of him in T. Wright, *The Life of Sir Richard Burton.*,ii, p.273.
21   Bombay Calendar and General Directory (Civil, Army & Navy Lists), Bombay 1850, p.253.
22   The pay of an East India Company infantry lieutenant on maximum allowances in 1855, was 257 rupees per month, or £0 16s 10d per day. [approx. £25 14s 0d a month.] In this instance, it is based on an exchange rate of R10 = £1. See T.A. Heathcote, *The Indian Army, The Garrison of British Imperial India, 1822-1922* (Newton Abbot, 1974), Table 9, p.128.
23   *The True Life*, p.58.
24   F.M. Brodie, *The Devil Drives* (New York & London), p.72.
25   She was born on 16 July 1810 at Exeter, south Devon. The marriage is briefly referred to in Burton's chapter on his boyhood days in Italy. See *The Life*, i, p.64: 'There was a very nice fellow of the name of Wood, who had just married a Miss Stisted, one of the nieces of the "Queen of the Baths," with whom all the "baths" were in love.'
26   See L.A. Marchand, *The Athenaeum, A Mirror of Victorian Culture* (North Carolina, 1941).
27   *The Athenaeum*, 19 April 1851, No.1225, pp.423-5. I totally disagree with Farwell and Hastings who rubbish this and other of Burton's books. Farwell's criticism, in particular, I find quite bizarre. See his *Burton* (London, 1963), p.51.
28   Burton's service record, L/MIL/12/73, OIOC, reads as follows: 'Submits for Court's inspection the manuscript of a work which he is desirous of publishing on the Ethnography of Sind, UCI, No.1850. Request permission to dedicate it to the Court HC 25, 25 February 1851. Author of a Work entitled 'Goa and the Blue Mountains, or Six Months of Sick Leave,' HC 14, 14 May, 1851. Author of a work entitled, 'A Work on the Topography and Ethnology of Scinde,' of which the Court purchases 150 copies, and are willing to accept the dedication of the work, HC 23 July and 27 August, 1851. In his book, Burton expressed his gratitude to Lt Col Sykes, FRS, John Petty Muspratt, Esq, and Horace Hayman Wilson, 'for the kind assistance and friendly advice with which they forwarded his views and encouraged his labours.'

29   See R.F. Burton, *Personal Narrative of a Pilgrimage to El Medinah and Meccah* (London & Belfast, 1879), i, p.1 note, referring to Sir James Hogg's 'much disliking, if truth be told, my impolitic habit of telling political truths.' This was copied into the "Memorial" edition, edited by Lady Burton, 1893.

30   *Falconry in the Valley of the Indus* (London, 1852), pp.89-90.

31   *The Athenaeum*, Saturday, 17 July 1852, No.1290, pp.765-6.

32   Military Home Correspondence, 1851-52, L/MIL/2/423, OIOC.

33   The other was run by Mon Henry Dubois at 3 rue des Vieillards, a street no longer in existence.

34   R.F. Burton, *Goa.*, p.147.

35   R.F. Burton, *Personal Narrative of a Pilgrimage to El-Medinah and Meccah*, Memorial Edn. (London, 1893), i, p.269.

36   *The Life*, i, p.165. This account has been elaborated on by two biographers. Byron Farwell, *Burton* (London, 1963), p.55, calls it 'an official reprimand.' Michael Hastings, *Sir Richard Burton* (London, 1978), p.75, incorrectly describes Sykes as Burton's 'brigade commander.'

37   N. Penzer, *Ann. Bib.*, p.42.

38   Letter dated 22 August 1920, from Oscar Eckenstein to Norman Penzer, in the Oscar Eckenstein Collection, RAS, London. Precisely how Eckenstein, who was not an expert in this field arrived at this conclusion, must remain a mystery.

39   I owe this information to G.M. Wilson, Keeper of Edged Weapons, the Armouries, Tower of London. A very interesting lecture on the history of the bayonet was delivered at the Royal United Service Institution on Wednesday, 27 May 1863, by Capt Sir Sibbald David Scott, Bart, FSA. It is included as an appendix in F.J. Stephens, *Bayonets. An Illustrated History & Reference Guide* (London, 1968). Burton's work is noted on p.74.

40   See J.D. Aylward, *The House of Angelo – A Dynasty of Swordsmen* (London, 1953), p.193 & p.209.

41   Ashcombe house was rented by the celebrated portrait photographer, Cecil Beaton, in the 1930s. In 2001, the estate was bought by the pop singer, Madonna, and her film director husband, Guy Ritchie, for £9 million.

42   One of the five ICT suites at the school today is named the Gerard Room.

43   In 1794, under threat from the advancing French revolutionary armies, the school transferred to Maastricht for three months before moving to England. After being given temporary shelter by Lord Stourton at Holme Hall , Yorkshire, and then at Dean House, Wiltshire, it took up permanent residence at New Hall, near Chelmsford, Essex, in 1798. A short history of the school compiled by Sister Margaret Helen, appeared in *East Anglian Magazine*, No.6, Vol.30, April 1971.

44   The 8th Lord Arundell had considerably over-stretched himself in building the new Wardour Castle, and had sold off land in a vain attempt to keep the bailiffs at bay. The sale had been continued by James Everard's father. Financial affairs had deteriorated so badly by 1828 that his son closed Wardour Castle and left England with his wife. His creditors even pursued his yacht down river in order to seize it. See Ilchester, Earl (ed.), *The Journal of the Hon Edward Fox* (London, 1923), for a critical account of Lord Arundell and his wife during their stay in Rome. Admitted to the House of Lords as a result of the Catholic Emancipation Bill of 1829, James Everard was the only Catholic peer to vote against the Reform Bill.

45   No. 4 Great Cumberland Place, which would be No. 30 according to modern numbering, now forms part of the Marble Arch Synagogue. Isabel was the first of eleven children born to her parents over the next twenty years. The two following her died in quick succession: Raymond Everard in May 1833, Mary Julia two months later.

46   The Catholic Relief Act of 1778, passed by Peel's government, allowed Roman Catholics for the first time to join the armed services, without being obliged to take the oath of allegiance to the Church of England. Further statutes enacted between that date and 1793 made it possible for them to practise their religion without let or hindrance, enter the legal profession, sell property, become magistrates, and hold most civil and military appointments. Finally, the Catholic Emancipation Act of 1829, gave them the right to sit as MPs at Westminster.

47   Renfric died in 1877, Henry ten years later. The business moved to 68 Park Street in 1895 as Arundell & Co Wine Merchants, then to 37 Davies Street in 1905. From 1907-9, it was located at 148½ Fenchurch Street. It remained at this address for the next two years, trading under the name of Arundell and Van Zeller Wine Merchants from 1910-11. The business saw out the last two years of its existence, 1912-14, at 13 Waterloo Place.

48   In the Census returns for 1861, for example, while Renfric was quite happy to describe himself as a wine-merchant,

Henry gave his occupation as "house property." Ten years later, his rank/profession was listed as 'Not known.'

49   It still exists, although much changed. In September 1997, when I visited it, it was owned by John L. Bird, who was kind enough to show me around part of the grounds. He was still in residence in 2001. There is a short history of the house and its various owners in E.E. Wilde, *Ingatestone and the Great Essex Road* (Oxford, 1913), pp.282-8.

50   The register entry for her reads: 'Miss Isabella Arundell arrived at New Hall, 3 June 1841. She is 10 years of age. She is to take the common lessons and to learn Music and Dancing. She has not been to Confession. She abstains but one day a week. She has <u>not</u> [crossed through] had <u>either</u> [crossed through] or ['not' substituted] Hooping cough. She is to take wine when she abstains. She made her 1st Confession 22 June 1841. She made her 1st Communion 8th Decbr 1841. She had measles April 1843. She was confirmed 12th Oct 1843. She left New Hall July 24th/46.'

51   He entered the school in December 1839 (a very unusual time to arrive), and left on 5 July 1845. For some unexplained reason, he was known to his contemporaries at the school as 'Sap' Arundell. He receives a brief mention in Percy Fitzgerald, *Stonyhurst Memories* (London, 1895), p.85.

52   *The Romance*, i, pp.21-22.

53   J. Raymond (ed.), *The Reminiscences and Recollections of Captain Gronow* (London, 1964), p.43.

54   A slight misquotation from Othello, Act II, I, Iago's reply to Desdemona's question: "To suckle fools and chronicle small beer."

55   *The Romance*, pp.37-9.

56   J. Foster, *The Life of Charles Dickens* (London, 1966), ii, p.146.

Notes to Chapter 10

1   *Journal of the Royal Geographical Society*, Vol.22, 1852, pp.cxiv-cxv. The custom of a yearly survey by the President at the Anniversary Meeting began in 1838 (*JRGS*, Vol.8). By the second decade of the 1840s, the custom was well established of printing in full the Presidential Address at the Society's Anniversary Meeting, which reviewed events and publications of geographical interest, including Admiralty Surveys and records of the Survey of India.

2   G.A. Wallin, 'Narrative of a journey from Cairo to Medina and Mecca via Suez, Araba, Tawila, Al -Jauf, Jubbe, Hail, and Nejd in 1845,' *JRGS* 24 (1854), pp.115-207; 'Notes taken during a journey through part of Northern Arabia in 1848,' *JRGS* 20 (1850), pp.293-344. There is a useful article on Wallin by M. Trautz, 'G.A. Wallin and the Penetration of Arabia,' *JRGS* 76 (1930), pp.248-252.

3   See G.A. Wallin, 'Travels in Arabia (1845 & 1848),' with introductory material by W.R. Mead and M. Trautz, (Falcon Oleander ,Cambridge, 1979). Professor Mead's essay, 'Georg August Wallin: The English Connection,' is a rewrite of an article which originally appeared in a Finnish publication. That by M. Trautz, 'A Forgotten Explorer of Arabia,' is a reprint of an article first published in *JRCAS* 19 (1932), pp.131-50.

4   It had been part of Sweden since the 12th century. In 1809, however, following its defeat at the hands of the Russians, Sweden was forced to cede Finland together with the Åland Islands, an archipelago at the entrance to the Gulf of Bothnia. G.A. Wallin was born in 1811 in Sund, Åland islands, a Fenno-Swede, Swedish by blood and speech, but a native of Finland.

5   Early representations to the Russians suggesting joint sponsorship were entrusted to Sir Roderick Murchison,. He had been honoured by Tsar Nicholas for his important geological work in Russia, and was well-known to the Russian aristocracy and members of the scientific community. He had also played a leading role in the founding of the Imperial Geographical Society (1845), the constitution of which was closely modelled on its English counterpart. See H.R. Mill, *The Record of the RGS* (London, 1930), p.5, and A.I. Alekseyev, *Fedor Petrovich Litke* (Moscow, 1970), p.204.

6   Sir R. Murchison, *JRGS*, Vol.22, p.cxv.

7   OIOC, Military Home Correspondence, L/MIL/2/450, 1852.

8   OIOC, L/MIL/2/450, 1852, 'I do hereby certify that the above statement is correct and I certainly agree in Mr.

Barratt Lucas's opinions.' Signed, Archibald Colquhon, Surgeon EIC Service.'

9   Major-General William Monteith (1790-1864) had retired from the Madras Presidency five years earlier, where he had been chief engineer. He also had had political experience, having been attached to the embassy of Sir John Malcolm to Persia, and later acting as secretary to D.R. Morier.

10   Born at St. Croix in the Danish West Indies, the son of a general in the Danish Army. He was educated partly in New York, and partly in Copenhagen, where he qualified as a surgeon, later becoming MRCS, and MD. Appointed Assistant Secretary of the RGS in 1848, he became the chief support of Captain (later Admiral) W.H. Smyth, who took over the Presidency of the Society in 1849, during a period of severe financial difficulties. See H.R. Mill, *The Record of the RGS*, p.59, and Sir Roderick Murchison's obituary of Dr Shaw in *JRGS* 69 (1869), pp.cxlvii-iii..

11   Col William Henry Sykes (1790-1872), a former EIC soldier, who had passed Interpreter examinations in Hindustani and Maharatta, and acted for many years as a statistical reporter for the Bombay Government. He was particularly interested in natural history. In 1840 he was elected a Director of the East India Company, becoming Deputy Chairman in 1855, and Chairman the following year. Three years later he became President of the Royal Asiatic Society. He was a keen scientific observer, and contributed numerous scientific papers to various journals. Dr Wallin, who met Sykes at East India House in 1850, described him as 'a very interesting and learned man.' He was not, as Wallin mistakenly believed, "Director of the Cartographical Department." However, Sykes, elected to membership of the RGS Council in 1852, was keenly interested in seeing a new and accurate map of Arabia drawn up, and was grateful to use the results of Wallin's latest discoveries. See M.Trautz, 'A Forgotten Explorer of Arabia,' p.xxix.

12   RGS Archives,Correspondence Files. Burton's proposal is undated. It was received, however, at the Society, on 3 November 1852. Burton subsequently wrote: 'No one felt the want of this "silent friend" more than myself; for though Eastern Arabia would not have been strange to me, the Western regions were a terra incognita. Through Dr. Norton Shaw, Secretary to the RGS, I addressed a paper full of questions to Dr. Wallin, professor of Arabic at the University of Helsingfors. But that adventurous traveller and industrious Orientalist was then, as we after-wards heard with sorrow, no more; so the queries remained unanswered.' *Personal Narrative of a Pilgrimage to El-Medinah and Mecca*, 3 vols (London, 1855-56), i, 7n. Hereafter cited as *The Pilgrimage*.

13   Burton's service in India actually totalled six years five months, OIOC: L/MIL/2/450, 'Officer on Furlough: Entered the service, 28 Oct. 1842. Nature of Furlough & when it commenced: SC., 30 March, 1849.'

14   OIOC, L/P&J/1/62, Revenue and Judicial Committee no.318, 1852. Burton's letter is misdated, Friday being 5 November. He ended his letter as follows: 'That the object of my attempt is a worthy one, I am allowed to use in testimony the names of Sir Roderick I. Murchison, Major-General Monteith (Madras Army) and Lt.Col. Outram [Burton was mistaken. He was not appointed to this rank until June, 1853] of Bombay. The latter two officers have kindly offered & furnish opinion concerning my fitness for the undertaking. And, to conclude, I may mention Dr Carter the medical officer who accompanied Capt Saunders on his coastal survey of the region I propose to explore: he assures me that I shall find few obstacles to success.'

15   RGS Archives, Letter Book, Shaw to Wallin, 17 Nov 1851.

16   See J.R. Godsall, 'Fact and Fiction in Richard Burton's Personal Narrative of a Pilgrimage to El-Medinah and Meccah,' *JRAS*, Third Series, Vol.3, Part 3, Nov 1993, p.337.

17   Adolphe Baron von Wrede, "Account of an Excursion in Hadramaut," *JRGS* 14 (1844), pp.107-112. Dr Wallin met von Wrede in Cairo, and disliked his 'talkativeness and boastfulness, despising a man who had lived for 20 years among Arabs without learning more than a smattering of Arabic; but he granted Wrede's courage and promptitude and did not doubt his travels.' See M.Trautz, 'A Forgotten Explorer of Arabia,' p.xxvii. A. von Wrede's book on his journey in the Hadramaut was not published in Germany until 1870.

18   Fulgence Fresnel (1795-1855), a multi-lingual scholar, who studied Arabic and Persian under De Sacy, In 1831 he went to Cairo, where he became a friend of Edward Lane. Appointed French consul in Jedda, he travelled to South Arabia in order to study the region's Himyaritic inscriptions. During 1851-54, he was joint-leader of a French archaeological expedition to Mesopotamia. He became ill there, and died in Baghdad on 30 November 1855. See *Dictionnaire de Biographie Française* (Paris, 1979), xiv, pp.1234-5.

19   RGS Archives, Committee Minutes. Also present at the meeting were Capt W.H. Smyth, and the eminent cartog-

rapher, John Arrowsmith, who published the *London Atlas* (1834, 4 vols), followed later by a long series of elaborate and carefully executed maps, embodying the results of contemporary exploration.

20   RGS Archives, Letter Book,Murchison to J.C. Melvill, and OIOC, L/P&J/1/63.

21   *The Pilgrimage* (1855-56), p.2.

22   OIOC, L/P&J/1/62, no. 318.

23   OIOC, E/1/298, Miscellaneous (Jan.-June, 1853), nos.213-14,

24   *The Pilgrimage*, i, p.2.

25   OIOC, L/MIL/2/458, Military Home Correspondence (1-9 Feb.1853).

26   *Ibid.* Burton added in his undated note, written on Thursday afternoon from the East India United Service Club: 'Also would you kindly let me have one like to Norris of the Royal Asiatic asking him, or rather authorising him to let me take a book or two home instead of having to waste time at the Society's rooms. Norris told me that the only thing wanted was a note from you.' Sykes was a member of the RAS, and its president in 1858. Edwin Norris was then Secretary of the Society, becoming Librarian and Hon Sec in 1860, and Honorary Librarian ten years later. See S.Simmonds & S.Digby, (eds.) *The Royal Asiatic Society, Its History and Treasures* (Leiden & London, 1979), pp.73-74.

27   OIOC, L/MIL/2/458 (Feb. 1-9), 1853.

28   OIOC, E/1/298. Miscellaneous (Jan-June 1853), no.431, 4 Feb 1853. This rule, based on Statute of 33rd, Geo.3rd. Cap.52, Sec.70, stipulated that an officer would lose his commission if continuously absent from India for more than five years. The statute is quoted in the letter to Burton, and is referred to by him in *The Pilgrimage* (1855-56), ii, p.299, as one of the reasons for his not attempting to cross Arabia.

29   RGS Archives, Correspondence Files, undated and unlogged. Given Burton's destination, and later hostility towards missionaries, there is an interesting, if very odd letter, in the archives, dated 12 February 1853, addressed from the EIUS Club to the Secretary of the Church Missionary Society, which reads: 'Sir, Having obtained a year's leave to Egypt, I propose to start early in April for an exploring journey to Central and Eastern Arabia. If I can in any way forward the views of your Society and collect any knowledge which may be useful to them, I shall be most happy to do so. I would put you to the trouble of supplying me with a list of questions which you may wish to be answered.' This letter is not in the CMS archives. Possibly, therefore, it was never sent.

30   RGS Archives, Committee Minutes.

31   At this meeting, it will be noticed that Burton's, possibly misconstrued, offer of joining the 'Egyptian Caravan' has been corrected to joining the 'Damascus Caravan.' The former by-passed Medina. It is a matter of great regret for the correct evaluation of his later statements and actions, that the Minutes do not contain a transcription of what he planned at this stage to do 'in order to render his travels in Arabia successful.'

32   The RGS Council had originally obtained this sum from the Government and the EIC in 1846, each contributing £100, in order to enable the Rev Thomas Brockman, Vicar of St Clements, Sandwich, who was in southern Arabia searching for inscriptions, to penetrate the interior of the Hadramaut. He later wrote to the RGS from Shehr, stating that he had been advised that the Hadramaut was too dangerous for travel. He, therefore, felt unable to use the money. Brockman continued to explore along the coast, but later died of fever in Oman. For the grant, see RGS Archives, Ledger No.2, p.2 Letters to Lord Colchester, PRGS, from HM Treasury (ref No. 2963), 14 Feb 1846; and from EIC Directors, 7 March, 1846. For Brockman's activities and death see Lord Colchester, Anniversary Address, *JRGS* 16 (1846), p.xvii, and *JRGS* 17 (1847), pp.xxx-xxxi.

33   Although Burton wrote in *The Pilgrimage*, i, p.3, of 'being liberally supplied with the means of travel by the Royal Geographical Society,' he did not mention the actual amount involved.

34   *The Pilgrimage* (1855-56), i,184n.

35   See R.F. Burton, 'Journey to Medina, with Route from Yambu,' *JRGS* 24 (1854), p.210. These sentiments are similar to those expressed by an earlier explorer, Ulrich Jasper Seetzen, in the last letter he wrote before his death in 1810: 'If I live and keep my health, I shall, after concluding my journey in Arabia, hasten forward with the greatest eagerness to the goal of all my travels in Africa, where I hope the mask of Islam will do me equally good service.' See A. Ralli, *Christians at Mecca* (London, 1909), p.73.

36   *The True Life*, p.72. Once again, as with Burton's departure from India in 1849, Georgiana only refers to his

writing to his mother. It is odd that the rate books for the parish of Walcot, Bath, show Joseph Netterville Burton living at 20 Bennett Street from May 1853-May 1855. The name does not appear before or after these dates. Certainly, the latter is wrong, since Burton's mother and father died at this address, Martha on 10 December 1854, and Joseph on 6 Sept 1857. There are no means of knowing when they returned from Italy to live in this country.

Notes to Chapter 11

1   In the *Pilgrimage* (1855-56), i, p.5, Burton said that he travelled from London disguised as a 'Persian prince.' In his account written for the RGS, however, 'Journey to Medina, with Route from Yambu,' *JRGS* 24 (1854), p.209, he merely states that he 'left Southampton disguised in Persian dress.'

2   An iron, screw-driven steamer of 2,185 tons, built by Tod & MacGregor, Partick, at a cost of £70,000, first registered on 5 February 1853. Barque-rigged, she had 1,084 ihp geared beam engines, and a maximum speed of about 12 knots. She carried 135 first-class passengers and, presumably, some second-class. This was the ship's second voyage (her first left Southampton on 20 February), and after four return trips to get her "run-in" she was sent out to the Calcutta/Suez run.

3   The very important fact that one of the passengers was 'John Larking, a well-known Alexandrian…[who] was in my secret,' is not mentioned in *The Pilgrimage*. It appears in *Wanderings in Three Continents*, ed. W.H. Wilkins (London, 1901), p.10. That Burton was also known to the ship's captain and a Turkish embassy official seems highly feasible. This, too, is omitted from his narrative. It is to be found in *The Life*, ii, p.13, under a page captioned, 'Articles by Alfred Bates Richards.'

4   *The Koran*, translated with notes by N.J. Dawood (London, 1999), 5.90, p.89. The relevant section reads in full: 'Believers, wine and games of chance, idols and divining arrows, are abominations devised by Satan. Avoid them, so that you may prosper.'

5   RGS Archives, Burton to Shaw, Shepheard's Hotel, 16 Nov 1853.

6   The *Bengal* left Southampton at 15.00 hours on 4 April 1853, and arrived at Alexandria at 16.55 local time, on 17 April.

7   H. Martineau, *Eastern Life, Present and Past* (London, 1848), p.5.

8   See F.S. Rodkey, 'The efforts of Briggs and Company to guide British policy in the Levant, 1821-41.' *Journal of Modern History* (Chicago, 1933), Vol.V, pp.324-50. Larking's sister, Camilla, became Samuel Briggs's second wife in 1835. See M.L. Bierbrier, *Who was Who in Egyptology*, 3rd rev edn (London, 1995), p.236. Larking is incorrectly described in *The Life*, i, p.170, as John (sic) Thurburn's son-in-law, a mistake perpetuated in later biographies.

9   Robert Thurburn had served as secretary to Col Misset, the British Consul-General at Cairo, at whose house Burckhardt spent a month in 1815. After acting as a partner in the mercantile house of Briggs & Co, Thurburn later became a partner in Joyce, Thurburn & Company. See K.Sim, *The Desert Traveller. The Life of Jean Louis Burckhardt* (London, 1969), p.358; J.L. Burckhardt, *Travels in Nubia*, 2nd edn (London, 1822), p.lxxxi; R. Gray, *A History of the Southern Sudan* (Oxford, 1961), p.22, n 4.

10 Burton dedicated Vol.VII of *The Book of the Thousand Nights and a Night* (Benares, 1885-88) to his 'Old and Valued Friend John W. Larking.' An obituary of Larking appeared in the *Kentish Mercury*, 22 May 1891.

11 F. Steegmuller (trans. & ed.), *Flaubert in Egypt* (London, 1972), Gustave Flaubert to Louis Bouilhet, Cairo, 23 Feb 1850, p.117. According to E.W. Lane, *The Manners and Customs of the Modern Egyptians*, 5th edn (London, 1904), ii, p.92, there were two types of male dancers: "Khawals", 'who are mostly young men…..[who] personate women,' and whose 'general appearance….is more feminine than masculine.' The other group, 'whose performance, dress, and general appearance are almost exactly similar to those of the Khawals,' were known as "Gink." This was a Turkish term, 'and has a vulgar signification, which aptly expresses their character.'

12 *The Pilgrimage*, i, 103-104n.

13 R.F. Burton, *The Book of the Thousand Nights and a Night*, x, Terminal Essay, Section D, Pederasty, p.219.

14 F. Steegmuller, *Flaubert in Egypt*, Flaubert to Bouilhet, Cairo, 15 Jan 1850, p.84.

15 *The Pilgrimage*, ii, Appendix IV, p.413.

16   See K. Sim, *The Desert Traveller*, p.218.

17   The *Athenaeum*, No.3451, 16 Dec 1893, p.850.

18   R.F. Burton, *Sindh, and the Races that inhabit the Valley of the Indus* (London, 1851), p.413n.

19   See R. Hyam, *Empire and Sexuality* (Manchester, 1990), pp.75-78. The author cites the experience of Dr R.E. Foot, a former army doctor, who, frequently, 'had been appalled by the "filth collected" under the prepuces of the uncircumcised.'

20   The *Athenaeum*, 16 Dec 1893, as related by W.H.M. Jackson, Lt Col, 'an old friend and brother officer of Dr Herman Bicknell.'

21   'Early in April 1853 I left Southampton disguised in Persian dress, and landed at Alexandria regretting that I had not at once assumed an Afghan costume.' *JRGS* 24 (1854), p.209. This is Burton again being less than truthful, since the suggestion of his adopting an Afghan persona did not occur until he had moved to Cairo.

22   G.A. Wallin, 'Narrative of a Journey from Cairo to Medina and Mecca......in 1845,' *JRGS* 24 (1854), p.206, where he writes: 'My hazardous situation with the pilgrims....and the hated presence of the Persians....' Although the paper was not published until a year after Burton left for Arabia, it had been read to the Society by Dr Norton Shaw on 26 April 1852, and, no doubt, the manuscript given to Burton to read. In *The Pilgrimage*, i, p.9, he wrote, 'Dr George A. Wallin, of Finland, performed the Haj in 1845; but his "somewhat perilous position, and the filthy company of Persians," were effectual obstacles to his taking notes.' The MS at the RGS, in fact, has 'loathsome,' as the adjective applied to the Persians.

23   FO List, 1853. Appointed Feb 1848. The Agent and Consul-General was the Hon C.A. Murray, CB, appointed 27 May 1846.

24   Burton, in fact, had just turned thirty-two, perhaps a sore point. Note that in this context, he makes no mention of his supposed parentage as he does later when dealing with a change of persona. Parentage is very important in the East, and would have appeared on his documents.

25   *The Pilgrimage*, i, pp.33-34.

26   R.F. Burton, *Scinde; or, the Unhappy Valley* (London, 1851) i, p.228. He also contrived to bring it into a footnote to the 'History of Gharib and his Brother Ajib,' *The Book of a Thousand Nights and a Night*, Vol.7, p.43. This claim, copied by Lady Burton into her *Life*, was not only disputed by A.S. Bicknell in the *Athenaeum* letter already cited, but by Augustus Ralli, *Christians at Mecca* (London,1909), p.203, who took them to be her own views. He wrote, 'In no authority do we find corroboration of her views on the questionable position of Moslem converts.'

27   Now one of the items in the Burton Collection, OHG. It has more the appearance of thin oilskin than canvas, and is now somewhat fragile. In the first edition, it was described as 'the gift of a kind friend.'

28   Burton obtained his money, totalling £30 in all, from John (sic) Thurburn. Although this name appears in the Memorial Edition, in the first edition, i, p.184, he is merely referred to as 'a friend at Alexandria.' However, in Burton's letter to the RGS from Suez, 16 Oct 1853, he is named as 'Hugh Thurburn.'

29   *The Pilgrimage*, i, p.55n.

30   According to E.W. Lane, *Cairo Fifty Years Ago*, ed. S. Lane-Poole (London, 1896), p.66,'Cairo contains about 200 wekalas, and about 150 of these are within the precincts of the city.'

31   *The Pilgrimage*, p.65.

32   *Ibid.*, p.67.

33   Snoring is referred to by J.L. Burckhardt, *Travels in Nubia*, p.301: 'There are certain defects, which if met with in the male slave, authorize the purchaser to return him, even so long as a fortnight after he has bought him, unless in making the bargain, he has renounced the right. Of these defects, the principal are: 1. Snoring at night, which is considered as a capital defect; 2. Si mingit dormiens [urinating while asleep]; 3. Grinding and rubbing the teeth upon each other during sleep.'

34   E.W. Lane, *Cairo Fifty Years Ago*, p.66.

35   RGS Archives, Burton to Shaw, Cairo, 16 Nov 1853.

36   Abu 'Abd Allah ash-Shafi'i (767- 820), a Muslim theologian, founder of the Shafi'iyah school of law. This school predominates in eastern Africa, parts of Arabia, and Indonesia.

37   See *Wanderings in Three Continents*, p.14. Burton does not mention his place of study in *The Pilgrimage*.

38   *The Pilgrimage*, pp.109-10.

39   RGS Archives. In his letter of 16 Nov 1853, he wrote to Shaw, 'Egypt is little agitated by the rumours of war. I verily think we might march into it without opposition.' On 15 Dec he wrote, 'No news at Cairo. No war, no "popular feeling."

40   In *Wanderings in Three Continents*, p.12. Burton states, however, that he bought the shroud at Alexandria. 'This memento mori is a piece of cotton six feet long by five broad. It is useful, for instance, when a man is dangerously sick, or wounded, the caravan, of course, cannot wait, and to loiter behind is destruction. The patient, therefore, is ceremoniously washed, wrapped up in his Kafan, partly covered with sand, and left to his fate.'

41   *The Pilgrimage*, p.180.

42   Burckhardt wrote of the Hejaz: 'Everything is enormously dear at all times, and in the time of the pilgrimage the prices are still higher.' See *Travels in Nubia.*, p.lxii. However, his financial position was far different from Burton's. When Burckhardt left Egypt, he only had sixty dollars and an ass to carry him, and the letter of credit which he had brought from Cairo was not honoured. He was only able to carry on by procuring a supply of money from Yahya Effendi, the physician of Tousoun Pasha, who had known him in Cairo.

43   RGS Archives. Letter from Burton to RGS from Suez, 16 Oct 1853. The British Hotel, better known by its owner's name as 'Shepheard's,' was the most famous hotel in the Middle East down to the twentieth century, when it was burnt down by an anti-British mob in 1952. An account of its history and the life of its owner, is given in M.Bird, *Samuel Shepheard of Cairo* (London, 1957).

44   J.L. Burckhardt, *Travels in Arabia* (London, 1829), ii, pp.91-93, Appendix V: 'Stations of the Hajj or Pilgrim Caravan from Cairo to Mekka.'

45   *The Pilgrimage*, p.186. Alfred Septimus Walne, c.1803-93. After practising as a surgeon in London, Walne went out to Egypt in 1836. He was appointed British Vice-Consul in Cairo, 1836-41, and Consul from 1841 to 1868. He continued working as a surgeon from 1836-83, when he retired. See *Who was Who in Egyptology*, p.431.

46   *The Pilgrimage*, p.195. Burton would later command a contingent of these Bashi Bazouks at the Dardanelles during the Crimean War.

47   *Ibid.*, 218.

48   *Ibid.*, p.229.

49   *Wanderings in Three Continents*, p.15.

50   M. Trautz, 'A Forgotten Explorer of Arabia,' pp.xxviii-xxix.

51   According to the FO List, 1853, West, an unpaid Vice-Consul, had been appointed to this post as recently as 24 February 1853.

52   Burton names the person responsible as Augustus Bernal, without stating who he was. In spite of an exhaustive search, I have failed to identify him. His name does not appear in the FO List as holding any official post either at Alexandria, Cairo, or Suez.

53   R.F. Burton, *JRGS* 24 (1854), pp. 209-210.

54   *Ibid.*, p.211, the sambuk is said to have been 75 tons. On p.12, he writes of the ship that, 'Her rig and build, like that of all Red Sea craft, have a general resemblance to the Indian pattimar, which I believe to be the most ancient shape in the Eastern world, after catamaran and the "toni," or hollowed mango trunk.'

55   In Burton's account for the RGS, p.211, this incident is said to have taken place before the ship was half-way between Egypt and Yambu, and Burton's alleged pushing down of a water-jar upon the attackers is not mentioned. The '"second class" generally,' he wrote, ' made an energetic attempt to share with the "first" the lofty poop of the 'Golden Wire': but we received them with our quarter-staves, and after an elegant little defence of our vantage ground we forced them to retreat, their whitey-brown burnooses bearing large stains of a certain "curious juice."' This suggests that the large jar may well have contained urine and not fresh water, something hardly to be wasted at the start of a journey down the Red Sea.

Notes to Chapter 12

1   See *JRGS* 24 (1854), p.214. For whatever reason, perhaps related to his decision to avoid regular washing, Burton

did not include this in his book.

2   *The Pilgrimage*, i, p.326. In a footnote, Burton says that it was probably a prickle of the "egg-fruit," or echinus. He found it impossible to cure his foot in the Hejaz, every remedy seeming to make it worse. It cleared up in Egypt, however, without any medical treatment. In his paper to the RGS he makes no mention of this alleged incident.

3   *Ibid.*, p.343, there is a long footnote on the shugduf. 'The shugduf of El Hejaz differs to a large extent from that used in Syria and other countries. It is made up of two corded cots 5 feet long, slung horizontally and parallel with the camel's sides, about half-way down....' This mode of transport is not referred to in Burton's paper to the RGS.

4   *Ibid.*, pp.352-53, in a long footnote on writing and sketching, Burton refers without naming him to von Wrede's unfortunate experience: 'An accident of this kind happened not long ago in Hazramaut to a German traveller who shall be nameless...He had the mortification to see his sketch-book, the labour of months summarily appropriated & destroyed by the Arabs.' Von Wrede's own account of his journey into the Hadramaut is in *JRGS* 14 (1844), pp.107-12. That relating to his imprisonment at Seef, the demands for his execution, and the handing over of, at least, some of his papers is on pp.111-112.

5   H. Jones, *Contributions towards a Dictionary of English Book-Collectors* (London, 1898), p.2. The dictionary in question was W.F. Freytag, *Lexicon-Arabico-latinum* (Halle, 1830-7).

6   *The Pilgrimage*, p.352.

7   *JRGS* 24 (1854), p.218.

8   *The Pilgrimage*, ii, p.24. Burton glosses this as, 'they would use, if necessary, the dearest and noblest parts of their bodies (their eyes) to do the duty of their basest (ie their feet).'

9   *Ibid.*, p.27.

10 *Ibid.*, p.31.

11 *Ibid.*, p.38.

12 *Ibid.*, p.57. 'The Prophet's Mosque is one of the Haramain, or the "two sanctuaries" of El Islam, and is the second of the three most venerable places of worship in the world; the other two being the Masjid El Haram at Meccah (connected with Abraham), and the Majid El Aksa of Jerusalem (the peculiar place of Solomon).'

13 *Ibid.*, p.60.

14 *Ibid.*, p.83.

15 *Ibid.*, p.108.

16 *Ibid.*, p.272.

17 *Ibid.*, pp.281-282. This claim is repeated in *The Book of a Thousand Nights and a Night*, Vol.V, 279n.

18 *Ibid.*, p.295. There was a comet visible in late August, 1853, which was clearly seen in a number of places from June, 1853, until January, 1854, when it became too faint to observe. The following description appeared in the *Memoirs of the Royal Astronomical Society*, Vol.31, p.2, as seen at the Cape of Good Hope Observatory: 'On the 12th September, and for several days following, the image of the nucleus was of a brilliant orange colour, and nearly as well-defined as the image of a bright star under a high magnifying power. The tail was about six or seven degrees in length' – about ten times that of the full moon in diameter – 'the end curving towards the south like the tail of an ostrich feather – presenting an imposing and very beautiful object.'

19 *The Pilgrimage*, p.297.

20 J.L. Burckhardt, *Travels in Arabia.* (London, 1829), ii, p.15

21 *JRGS* 24 (1854), p.209.

22 *JRGS* 25 (1855), p.122.

23 'This is nothing but a sort of cage or pagoda of gilded tracery very richly decorated. In the days of the Mamelukes, the Mahmal represented the litter of the Sultan, and went empty like a royal carriage at a public funeral; but we were told that it now carried the tribute carpet sent annually by the carpet-makers of Cairo to the tomb of the Prophet.' A. Edwards, *A Thousand Miles up the Nile* (London, 1877), p.27.

24 *JRGS* 25 (1855), p.124.

25 *The Pilgrimage*, iii, pp.106-7,

26 *Ibid.*, p.113.

27 Further proof, if any were needed, that Burton never had any intention of by-passing Mecca to go to Muscat.

28   *The Pilgrimage*, p.199.

29   *Ibid.*, p.314.

30   *Ibid.*, iii, 76n.

31   J.L. Burckhardt, *Travels in Arabia*, ii, p.14.

32   *Ibid.*, Appendix 1, p.373.

33   *The Pilgrimage*, ii, p.279n.

34   C. Niebuhr, *Travels in Arabia* (London, 1811), pp.26-7.

35   L. Casson (trans.), *The Periplus Maris Erythraei* (Princeton, 1989), p.284.

36   F. Stark, *The Southern Gates of Arabia* (London, 1936), Appendix, pp.269-70 & p.157.

37   R.F. Burton, *First Footsteps in East Africa* (London, 1856), p.32.

38   R.F. Burton, *The Book of the Thousand Nights and a Night* (London, 1885-8), iv, p.118.

39   Burton's interest in this region stemmed from two factors: 1. The remains of Kafir or Infidel architecture said to cover a hill NE of Muwaylah; 2. More importantly, the alleged presence of gold. 'Near Muwaylah gold is still found. A Haji at Cairo [ie Burton] extracted with quicksilver no less than 6 drms of dust out of 52 drms of sand, collected in a fiumara.' [by Haji Wali]. See R.F. Burton, 'Journey to Medina , with Route from Yambu,' *JRGS* 24 (1854), p.213. Burton made no reference to this in his book. This alleged discovery of gold by Haji Wali, led many years later to Burton's explorations in Midian, which he described as a new California.

40   C.R. Low, *History of the Indian Navy,1613-1863* (London, 1877), i, p.303, writes, 'Mr. Cole, for many years British Consul at Jiddah had been at one time purser on board the *Ferooz* under Captain Frushard.....'

41   No dates for departure from Jeddah and arrival at Suez are given in the original edition. The former is supplied in the Memorial Edition, the latter, 3 October, only in *Wanderings In Three Continents*, p.69.

Notes to Chapter 13

1   Burton's three-months' stay in Egypt is briefly noted in *Personal Narrative of a Pilgrimage to El-Medinah and Meccah* (London, 1855-56), i, p.73. His departure in January, 1854, though again without a specific date, is also noted in his *The Gold Mines of Midian, and the Ruined Midianite Cities* (London, 1878), p.243. Surprisingly, these references have been overlooked by Burton's biographers. Instead, they have taken their cue from the vague and misleading statement by Lady Burton, *The Life* (London, 1893), i, p.125 , that 'Richard returned up the Red Sea to Egypt, and much enjoyed the rest and safety for a short time....', and by T. Wright, *The Life of Sir Richard Burton* (London, 1906), i, p.125, that 'Having spent a few weeks in Egypt, Burton returned to Bombay....'

2   *The Pilgrimage*, iii, p.366.

3   RGS Archives. Two letters from Suez, both dated 15 Oct 1853, and received 30 October. Neither carried an address, a good indication that Burton was concealing the fact that he was staying at the British Consulate. Two letters from Shepheard's Hotel, Cairo are dated 16 Nov & 15 Dec respectively.

4   Neither of these men is ever mentioned again, and I have been unable to trace who they were.

5   The misconception may well have arisen from a paper on Zanzibar, which Col Sykes had read to the Society in June of the previous year. In his conclusion, he had stated that, 'a comprehensive and accurate view of the territories of the Imaum of Muskat, whether in Arabia or the N.E. coast of Africa, is still a desideratum.' See, 'Notes on the Possessions of the Imam of Muscat, (&) on the Climate and Productions of Zanzibar,' *JRGS* 22 (1852), p.109.

6   Despite a thorough search of *The Times* and *The Athenaeum* for November 1853, I failed to find a report of Burton's arrival in Egypt.

7   The Egyptian Transit Company had been established by Muhammad Ali in 1841, its stations positioned along the route providing facilities for both Muslim pilgrims and foreigners travelling to and from India. The running of these was later effectively taken over by the P&O company. The transit vans, which charged £12 for the service, held six passengers, three sitting each side on knife-board seats under an arched canvas cover. The horses were changed every 5-6 miles. Burton was highly critical of the behaviour of the Europeans travelling this route, contrasting the kindness of his Eastern companions towards the Turkish mother and her baby aboard the 'Golden

Wire' with 'the savage scenes of civilization that take place among the "Overlands" at Cairo and Suez.' See *The Pilgrimage*, i, p.310.

8   Edwin de Leon, *Thirty Years of My Life on Three Continents* (London, 1890), i, p.158.

9   *The Pilgrimage*, iii, p.390. Fahsien (fl AD 399-414), was the Chinese Buddhist monk, whose pilgrimage to India in 402 was responsible for first promoting Sino-Indian relations.

10   Edwin de Leon, *Thirty Years of My Life*, p.185, described Frank Sankey as 'a versatile and accomplished man, who was by turns errant Englishman, Lieut. Colonel of Bashi Bazouks in the Crimean War, and finally Vice-Consul at Kustenje, in Asia Minor, where he died, after writing most interesting and valuable sketches of the Arabs of his neighbourhood, throwing much light on that unknown region, and the wild tribes that people it.'

11   Burton's 'revolutionary' was actually Emilio Visconti Venosta (1829-1914), the Italian patriot and statesman. Initially a follower of Guiseppe Mazzini, he switched his allegiance to Camillo Benso di Cavour after the unsuccessful revolution of 1853 in Milan.

12   This is the first ever mention by Burton that he was familiar with the *Arabian Nights* in its unexpurgated version.

13   *The Pilgrimage*, iii, 76n. 'The fair sex distinguishes itself by a peculiar laxity of conduct, which is looked upon by an indulgent eye. And the men drink and gamble, to say nothing of other peccadilloes with perfect impunity.'

14   R.F. Burton, *First Footsteps in East Africa* (London, 1856), p.xix.

15   Sir James Hogg was offered the Governorship of Bombay to succeed Lord Falkland, but declined.

16   This is not true, of course. The nature of Burton's knowledge of the eastern side of Arabia is clear from the Postscript in *Falconry in the Valley of the Indus* (London, 1852), p.100: 'Besides I knew the countries of the Gulf by heart from books.'

17   A. von Wrede, *Reise in Hadramaut, etc*, ed. H.F. von Maltzan (Brunswick, 1870).

18   A Ralli, *Christians at Mecca* (London, 1909), p.191.

19   Antoine Thomson d'Abbadie (1810-97) and his brother, Arnaud Michel (1815-93) were born in Dublin, of an Irish mother and a French father. Both were awarded the grand medal of the Paris Geographical Society in 1850. Antoine, the more distinguished of the two brothers, became a Knight of the Legion of Honour, and a member of the Academy of Sciences. Arnaud published a popular account of their travels, *Douze ans de sejour dans la Haute-Éthiope* (Paris, 1868). Their political activities in Ethiopia are described in T.E. Marston, *Britain's Imperial Role in the Red Sea, 1800-78* (Hamden, Conn., 1961)

20   R.F. Burton, *Zanzibar; City, Island, and Coast* (London, 1872), i, p.48.

21   See J.L. Krapf, *Travels, Researches, and Missionary Labours During an Eighteen Years' Residence in Eastern Africa* (London, 1860), pp.543-44. The account of Rebmann's initial sighting of Kiliamanjaro appeared in the first number of the *Church Missionary Intelligencer*, May, 1849, together with the first rough map of East Africa ever made. See E. Stock, *The History of the Church Missionary Society* (London, 1893), ii, p.127

22   The treatise of Marinus of Tyre is lost, and is known to posterity only through the criticisms and references of his successor, Ptolemy.

23   See W.D. Cooley, *Claudius Ptolemy and the Nile* (London, 1854), p.72 et seq.

24   Cooley did not consider the section on the Mountains of the Moon as part of the genuine text, but an interpolation made some five or six centuries after Ptolemy's time.

25   *The Pilgrimage*, i, p.252, 'At this moment (Nov.1853).....' There are 388 pages in the first volume. Furthermore, it must be remembered that Burton's MS was heavily edited. It is likely, therefore, that he had written much more than appears in the published version.

26   Lord John Elphinstone (1807-60), 13th Baron. Former Governor of Madras, 1837-42, he was a keen traveller himself, and had been one of the first Englishmen to explore Kashmir. On 12 November, he was the guest of honour at a splendid banquet given at the London Tavern by the Directors of the East India Company. See *The Times*, 14 Nov 1854. Although the *Euxine* left Southampton for Alexandria on 20 November, Lord Elphinstone, obviously not a keen sailor, travelled overland, and joined the ship at Malta, on 30 November. From there to Cairo was another two or three days, so he would have arrived around 3 December.

27   It appears, therefore, that Burton had been unable to meet Krapf, who was returning to England ostensibly because of worsening bowel problems. By this time, however, he had become estranged from his fellow missionaries,

Rebmann and Erhardt at Rabai. See J.L. Krapf, *Travels, Researches, and Missionary Labours etc*, 2nd Edition with an Introduction by R.C. Bridges (London, 1968), pp.36-37.

28   Captain Stafford Bettesworth Haines, the colony's first Political Agent, 1839-54. The Aden Treasury was examined by a Military Committee on 1 Sept 1852, and a deficiency of over Rs 2, 81, 979 (2 lakhs and over 81,000 Rs) was discovered. Haines was accused of embezzlement of the public funds, and was forced to relinquish his appointment, as was Cruttenden. Haines was put on trial at Bombay on 25 July 1854 and again on 1 August. On each occasion he was found Not Guilty. A printed report of the two trials is in OIOC: R20/A/116. However, by order of Government, he was cashiered from the service, and thrown into a debtor's prison. He died a week after his release on 16 June 1860.

29   OIOC, Bombay Army List, L/MIL/12/85. Steinhaueser was appointed Civil Surgeon on 19 March 1853, but did not actually take up his duties at Aden until July.

30   See C. Didier, *Sojourn with the Grand Sharif of Makkah* (Cambridge, 1985), p.x & p.6 et seq. Burton refers to his departure with these two travellers, but without giving a date, in *The Pilgrimage*, i, p.264. As we have seen, he also mentions them in his letter to Shaw of 16 Nov 1853. James Hamilton, one-time private secretary to Pope Gregory, was a traveller, interested in languages, ancient monuments etc., who had set out from Malta to visit the Siwa oasis (where he was imprisoned by the inhabitants for six weeks) and other places in North Africa. He published *Wanderings in North Africa* in 1856. He also published accounts of his later visits to Sinai, Hijaz, and Sudan. Burton refers to Hamilton's sending him a list of the southern Hejazi tribes after visiting the Sherif at Taif, and of Hamilton's conviction that in the Wady Lamun, 'he had discovered in one of the rock monuments, a "lithographed proof" of the presence of Sesotris-Rameses II.' See *The Pilgrimage*, iii, p.98, & p.137n. Charles Didier, who had published *Promenade au Maroc* (Paris, 1844), was later associated in the publication of a map of the African Red Sea coast with James Hamilton.

31   This is Burton's mistake for the winter of 1853. (He also misdated his official letter from Suez, 16 Oct 1854, instead of 1853.) Unaware of the error, F. McLynn, *Snow Upon the Desert* (London, 1990), p.74, concocted a scenario in which Burton travelled to Alexandria and Cairo in the winter of 1852, for a pre-Pilgrimage trial of his dervish disguise, before carrying on to Aden and spending Christmas with Steinhaeuser.

32   R.F. Burton, *The Book of the Thousand Nights and a Night* (Benares, 1885-8), i, p.ix.

33   OIOC, Bombay Army List, L/MIL/12/65. General Orders, 8 Nov 1851.

34   R.F. Burton, *First Footsteps in East Africa*, p.36.

35   OIOC, L/PS/9/33, Aden Correspondence, report by Lieut. Dansey to Brigadier Clarke, 14 March 1854. A similar description in R.L. Playfair, *A History of Arabia Felix or Yemen* (Bombay, 1859), pp.14-15, is probably based on Dansey's report.

Notes to Chapter 14

1   T. Wright, *The Life of Sir Richard Burton* (London, 1906), i, p.125.

2   Born at Britonferry, Glamorgan, on 18 May 1807, the son of Lt Col J. Lumsden, HM 55th Foot. Brief details about his life and career are in OIOC, J/1/41 f.146, and O/6/34. By the time Burton came to write *First Footsteps*, Lumsden had been appointed Chief Judge of Suddu Dewanee and Suddu Freydarry. He resigned the service on 12 August 1857. Nine years later he died at Torquay of cancer of the tongue. For whatever reason, he is inaccurately referred to as 'the Hon William Lumsden,' in Burton's paper, 'Narrative of a Trip to Harar,' *JRGS*, Vol.XXV, p.138.

3   The Council was the governing body of the Bombay Presidency. All government decisions were described as having been taken by 'the Rt Hon. the Governor in Council.' The other member at this time was John Warden.

4   The address is derived from Burton's letters to Government written from there. Bombay has, roughly, four seasons: (i) so-called cold weather from December to January; (ii) hot weather from March to May; (iii) the rainy season, brought by the south-west monsoon from June to September; (iv) the post-monsoon season with hot weather again through October and November.

5   One can only surmise about the circumstances of their first meeting, since Burton failed to provide any details. In fact, his only public reference to their friendship occurs in his dedication of *The Thousand Nights and One Night*, Vol.V (Benares, 1885), to Arbuthnot, where he refers to its having 'lasted nearly a third of a century.' Arbuthnot, born in 1833, entered Haileybury in 1851, and joined the Bombay Civil Service two years later. He was always known to Burton by the pet-name, 'Bunnie.'

6   Burton employed a clerk from the Booldana district of Hyderabad, Bapoojee Hurree Scindia, as an amanuensis, to copy parts of his *Pilgrimage*. He afterwards presented Bapoojee with a number of Mahratta and English books, which the clerk proudly retained over the years.

7   Dr Carter's name is mentioned several times in Burton's *Pilgrimage*. He wrote a long note for inclusion in *First Footsteps*, on a collection of geological specimens and fossils which Burton brought back from Berbera.

8   H. Salt, *A Voyage to Abyssinia and Travels into the Interior of that Country, Executed under the orders of the British Government in the Years 1809 and 1810* (London, 1814), Appendix 1, pp.iv-vi. Oddly, though Burton notices Salt's book in his *First Footsteps* as regards the Harari tongue, he says nothing about Salt's Somali vocabulary.

9   On 2 June 1811, the *Ternate*, Capt T. Smee, and the *Sylph*, Lt Hardy, sailed from Bombay on a mission to explore the African coast as far south as Zanzibar, and to collect information regarding its navigable rivers, its trade, and its political situation. The material remained unpublished until 1843, when the Secretary of the Bombay Geographical Society allowed Rigby to see Smee's papers. He, then, extracted 'such parts, as added to other sources, might be deemed interesting.' See, 'Observations during a Voyage of Research on the East Coast of Africa, from Cape Guardafui south to the island of Zanzibar, with HC Cruizers *Ternate*, Captain T. Smee, and *Sylph* Schooner, Lieutenant Hardy,' *Transactions of the Bombay Geographical Society*, VI (1841-44), pp.23-61. In the same journal, in his 'Remarks on the North-East Coast of Africa, *ibid.*, p.72, Rigby wrote that he had 'appended specimens of the Sowahil, Galla and Somauli languages, on the eastern coast, from a collection of words made by Lieutenant Smee [sic].....'

10   C.P.Rigby, 'An Outline of the Somauli Language, with Vocabulary,' *Transactions of the Bombay Geographical Society*, IX (1849-50), pp.129-84. R.F. Burton, *First Footsteps in East Africa*, p.xxix. Rigby had gathered his material for this pioneering attempt at delineating the language at Aden, where he was sent in March 1840 with a wing of the 16 BNI, to help relieve the garrison which had come under fierce attack from the Arabs four months earlier.

11   R.F. Burton, *First Footsteps*, pp.513-14n., where he writes in Appendix II; *Grammatical Outline and Vocabulary of the Harari Language*: 'Lieutenant Rigby (now Captain Rigby, 16th Regiment, Bom. N.I. in an excellent paper, of an *Outline of the Somauli Language, with Vocabulary*, asserts that the dialect of which he is writing, "has not the slightest similarity to Arabic in construction." A comparison of the singular persons of the pronoun will, I believe, lead to a different conclusion.' This initial friendliness was replaced within a few years by bitter hostility towards Rigby who, in 1858, was appointed HBM's Political Agent and Consul at Zanzibar.

12   Lt C.J. Cruttenden, 'Report on the Mijjertheyn Tribe of Somallies, inhabiting the district forming the North-East point of Africa, *Transactions of the Bombay Geographical Society*, VII (1844-46), pp.111-26. Like Lt Carless in 1838, Cruttenden found the Mijjertheyn a friendly people, who 'pride themselves upon being a peaceful nation....murder is uncommon, and the "Reesh" or ostrich feather in the hair, which to westward denotes the wearer has killed a man, is by the Tribe considered both unholy (haram) and unmanly.' He remarked on their eagerness to trade, and suggested how this might be effected. *Ibid.*, pp.118,122.

13   Lt C.J. Cruttenden, 'On Eastern Africa,' *JRGS*, XVIII (1848), p.137. This short, but very interesting paper, contains between pp.136-37, a 'Map of the Somauli Coast, showing the position of the Tribes,' drawn by Lt Cruttenden, and including additions from the surveys of Captain Owen, RN, Lieuts Barker, Christopher & Carless. Cruttenden's map later appeared in J.H. Speke, *What Led to the Discovery of the Source of the Nile* (Edinburgh & London, 1864), with additions by Speke.

14   Lt C.J. Cruttenden, 'Memoir on the Western or Edoor Tribes, inhabiting the Somali Coast of NE Africa, with the Southern Branches of the Family of Darrood, resident on the banks of the Webbe Shebeyli, commonly called the River Webbe,' *Transactions of the Bombay Geographical Society*, VIII (1847-1849), pp.177-210.

15   *Ibid.*, p.195.

16 OIOC, F/4/2570, Board's Collection 151731: letter from Lt R.F. Burton, dated 28 April 1854, to H.L. Anderson, Sec to Govt, Bombay.

17 In this letter, Burton stated incorrectly that, 'In May 1849 the RGS *obtained the permission* of the Hon. the Court of Directors to depute an officer into the Somali country....' [my italics]. See *JRGS*, Vol.XXV (1855), p.136, for another version, pre-dating the wording in *First Footsteps* already noticed.

18 See P. Santi & R. Hill (trans. & ed.), 'The Journal of J.A. Vayssière, 1833-4,' in *The Europeans in the Sudan, 1834-78* (Oxford, 1980), pp. 141 & 145 and notes.

19 See R. Gray, *A History of the Southern Sudan, 1838-1889* (Oxford, 1961), p.1ff, and P.M. Holt & M.W. Daly, *A History of the Sudan from the Coming of Islam to the Present Day* (London, 1988), p.67ff.

20 Early in January, 1843, Christopher was ordered to convey His Excellency Bin Nasser (Envoy Extraordinary from the Imam of Muscat to Her Britannic Majesty) back to Zanzibar in the brig-of-war, *Tigris*. On the return voyage, as requested by Capt Haines, Christopher landed along the southern coast at Brava and Merkha. He remarked on the great fertility of the region, went inland to what he christened, the 'Haines River,' and at Bander Khasim met a young man who had visited Harar. See Burton, *First Footsteps*, p.xxix. He thought so highly of Christopher's information that he applied to Government for copies of the full reports before leaving Bombay. See OIOC, Z/P/3373, Index to Political Diary of the Bombay Government, 1854.

21 Lt Edward Dansey (1824-59). Following the dismissal of Haines and Cruttenden, Brigadier A. Clarke was appointed officiating Political Agent, with Dansey as his assistant. He assumed charge of the office on 9 March 1854. He enjoyed a very friendly relationship with Burton and Speke, both of whom mention him in their books.

22 Lt Col Atkins Hamerton (1804-1857) was the British Political Agent and Consul at Zanzibar, following the transfer of the Imam of Muscat's power base to the island in 1840. As we shall see later, Burton and Speke were his guests at the British Consulate during their preparations for the East African Expedition. He was a very influential figure in East African politics. See C.S. Nicholls, *The Swahili Coast* (London, 1971), pp.165-94, and R. Coupland, *East Africa and its Invaders* (Oxford, 1938), p.323ff.

23 C.T. Beke, 'On the Nile and its Tributaries,' *JRGS*, XVII (1847), pp.1-84.

24 See R. Coupland, *East Africa and its Invaders*, pp.473-474. Burton, himself, later remarked on Dr Beke's theory and his hope of having it substantiated by Dr Bialloblotzky, in *Zanzibar; City, Island, and Coast* (London, 1872), i, pp. 57-58. Even earlier, J.R. Wellsted, *Travels in Arabia* (London, 1838), ii, p.380n wrote: 'From information which I acquired in the Red Sea, I have reason to believe there is a fair chance of a traveller's reaching the sources of the Nile and, possibly with a caravan, Interior Africa. Had I not proceeded to Arabia, it was my intention to have made the attempt.'

25 Lt George Edward Herne (1822-1902). Born in the Persian Gulf, on 22 May 1822, he lost both his parents, and was brought up by his cousin, Thomas Mardon, who acted as his guardian. Educated at Maidstone Proprietary School, Kent, and the Military Seminary, Addiscombe. Commissioned as an ensign, 11 December 1840, arrived in Bombay, 18 July 1841. Slightly wounded at the siege of Multan on 2 January 1849. Retired from the army with the rank of major, 11 September 1872. Died 16 March 1902. On 2 May 1843, Edward Dansey, 1st Bombay European Regiment [see note 21 above], was court-martialled at Poona, 'For conduct unbecoming the character of an officer and a gentleman, in having about the hour of ten o'clock on the night of 7th instant, when at the mess table of the Bombay European regiment, struck Ensign Herne of the same corps.' Dansey was sentenced 'to be suspended from rank and pay for two months, and to be severely reprimanded.' See W. Douglas, *Duelling Days in the Army* (London, 1887), p.19.

26 OIOC, F/4/2570, Board's Collection 151731, H.L. Anderson, Sec to Govt, in reply to Burton's letter dated 28 April 1854 – the observations of Govt communicated 6 May, No.2081 of 1854. Also in Bombay Political Consultations P/394/66, No.2142 (1854).

27 In 1854, 10 rupees = £1. See T.A. Heathcote, *The Indian Army – The Garrison of British Imperial India, 1822-92* (Newton Abbot, 1974), p.128.

28 According to I.M. Lewis, 'Peoples of the Horn of Africa: Somali, Afar and Saho,' in D. Forde, ed. *Ethnographic Survey of Africa: North Eastern Africa*, Parts 1-3 (London, 1955-56), p.70, 'In the north there are two breeds of pony: the *bari* reared by the eastern tribes and the *galbed* by the western.....Somali lavish as much care on their

horses as on their camels.' This was not the experience of Lt Cruttenden among the Mijjertheyn tribe of Somalis. 'The affection of the true Arab for his horse is proverbial,' he wrote, 'the cruelty of the Somal to his, may I think, be considered equally so....' C.J. Cruttenden, 'On Eastern Africa,' p.120.

29   All references to Henchy are listed in OIOC, Z/P/3373: Index to the Political Diary of the Bombay Government for the year 1854 (Aden).

30   This letter, addressed from 'Belair House, Chinchpoogly, Nr Bombay,' is dated 27 May 1854. Communications on the subject from Henchy to the Chief Sec To Govt, Fort St George, dated St Thomas Mount, 8 June, and from H.C. Montgomery, Chief Sec To Govt, Madras, dated 16 June, are to be found in OIOC, Bombay Political Consultations, P/394/69 (1854).

31   Herne's letter to the Sec to Govt, Bombay, dated Colaba, 31 May 1854, requesting permission to accompany Burton, and the Hon Board's resolution of 2 June 1854, allowing it, are to be found in OIOC, Bombay Political Consultations, P/394/68. Burton's note to Govt signalling his intention of leaving by the *Auckland* the following day is in P/394/69. Coincidentally, the same ship took members of the Mission to Shoa from Bombay to Aden in April 1841.

32   See R.L. Playfair, *A History of Arabia Felix or Yemen* (Bombay, 1859). Playfair, of course, as an officer in the service of the HEIC, did not question Britain's right to do so, in view of Arab attacks and hostility. For the real reasons behind its annexation see R.J. Gavin, *Aden Under British Rule, 1837-1967* (London, 1975). Also see T.E. Marston, *Britain's Imperial Role in the Red Sea Area* (Hamden, Conn, 1961).

33   *Ibid.*, p.39.

34   Major-General Sir F.J. Goldsmid, *James Outram* (London, 1880), ii, p.83n.

35   Unlike Haines, Outram had a very high profile, and numerous influential friends in high places in England and India. During Haines's term of office, there had been a separate civil and military administration, which had resulted in a great deal of friction and animosity. Now, for the first time, the two functions were combined in one man. See Gavin, *Aden Under British Rule*, p.91ff. Details of Outram's appointment are in OIOC, Bombay Secret Index, Z/P/3538, and Index to the Political Diary of the Bombay Government for the year 1854, Z/P/3373. Command of the military garrison at Aden, carried with it the brevet rank and pay of a brigadier.

36   Col Outram left Bombay for Aden on 7 June, but his vessel, the Hon Co's steam frigate, *Ajdaha*, was sixteen days at sea owing to the breaking of the monsoon. See F.J. Goldsmid, *James Outram*, pp.86-7. There is no mention in the *Index* as to the date of Burton and Herne's arrival.

37   Lt (later Sir) R. Lambert Playfair (1822-99), author and administrator. Entered the Madras Artillery in 1846. Transferred to the Madras Staff Corps, 1861. Appointed Political Agent & Consul at Zanzibar 1862-63, in succession to Lt Col C.P. Rigby. Retired from the Army in 1867, and became Consul-General in Algeria, where he remained until his retirement. Nominated KCMG in 1886. Lt G.E. Herne later married one of Playfair's sisters. Information from Sir Edward Playfair in a private letter to the author.

38   QK Coll, unpublished draft review of Major-General Sir F.J. Goldsmid's biography of Outram

39   OIOC, Bombay Political Consultations, P/394/69, No.2996 of 1854, from H.L. Anderson to Col Outram, CB, 30 June 1854.

40   OIOC, Bombay Political Consultations, P/394/73, from Col Outram to H.L. Anderson, 24 July 1854. Outram, who was a very kind-natured man, recommended that Henchy's return fare should be paid by Govt, OIOC, P/395/3.

41   See R.F. Burton, *Zanzibar; City, Island, and Coast* (London, 1872), ii, p.382. J. H. Speke, who had yet to appear on the scene, gave his own deliberately false, and malicious account of the affair in 1860, writing from the African interior to his friend and confidant, C.P. Rigby. Letter quoted in C.E.B. Russell, *General Rigby, Zanzibar and the Slave Trade* (London, 1935), p.236.

42   QK Coll. Burton was 'told that he landed on the Somali coast some time after my disaster and was driven back by force.'

43   OIOC, Bombay Political Consultations, P/395/3 (1854). Two hundred and twenty-eight rupees were spent over the next fortnight, entertaining Sharmarkay.

44   Burton gives a long account of Sharmarkay bin Ali Salih in *First Footsteps in East Africa*, pp.16-21. In a footnote to

p.18, he glosses his name, Shar –ma –arkay, as 'one who sees no harm.' His name is variously spelled, however, by different authors.

45 *Ibid.*, p.1. Henry Salt, in fact, made no attempt to reach Harar. Instead, he engaged a young man, Richard Stuart, who had joined his ship at the Cape, and 'who appeared to me well qualified for such an employment,' to undertake the enterprise on his behalf.

46 Burton deliberately avoided giving the full quotation, Cruttenden going on to say: 'From what I have been able to gather, the traveller would hardly be repaid the risk and fatigue that he would have to undergo, and if he travelled as a European, he would be much exposed to insult and ill-feeling from the bigoted ruler and inhabitants of the place, who, sunk in the lowest ignorance, still plume themselves upon their superior sanctity, as followers of the true faith.' See Lt C.J. Cruttenden, 'Memoir on the Western or Edoor Tribes........' *JRGS*, XIX (1849), p.51.

47 *First Footsteps*, pp.1-2.

48 *Ibid.*, p.xxiii. He muddies the waters by describing it as 'a further change of plans,' which, quite patently, it was not.

49 Burton made no such claim in his paper for the RGS. 'Assembled at Aden in the summer of 1854,' he wrote, 'we found the *public voice* [my italics] so loud against our project, that I offered as a preliminary to visit Harar in disguise.........' 'Narrative of a Trip to Harar,' *JRGS*, Vol.XXV (1855), p.137.

50 J.H. Speke, *What Led to the Discovery of the Source of the Nile* (Edinburgh & London, 1864), p.1. Burton's rejection of Speke's claim is in *Zanzibar; City, Island, and Coast*, ii, p.378.

51 Speke, *What Led*, p.5.

52 F.M. Brodie, *The Devil Drives* (New York, 1984), p.108.

53 Notified by Allen's *Indian Mail*, 19 September 1854, OIOC, L/MIL/12/87. Stocks died at his home in Cottingham, near Hull, E. Yorkshire, on 30 August, aged only 34. According to his death certificate, cause of death was 'Sanguineous Apoplexy 11 Days.' After meeting Burton in Cairo, Stock arrived in England 'bringing with him a large herbarium of Bombay plants, found when officiating as Inspector of Forests during the absence on furlough of Dr Gibson.' He brought these to Kew, staying there for a while in order to begin preparations for a work on the flora of Sind for the press. For a letter from Stocks on botanical matters, see *The Athenaeum*, No. 1058, 5 February 1848, p.142, and a short obituary in the same journal, No.1402, 9 September 1854, p.1091. G. Waterfield, *First Footsteps*, p.23, states incorrectly that Burton received news of Stocks's death in 'the early summer.' F.M. Brodie, p.107, also errs in stating that Stocks 'died of apoplexy shortly before he was to leave India....'

54 OIOC, Bombay Political Consultations, P/395/4, 1854. Burton's letter was written four days after Speke's application, dated 28 September, addressed through Colonel Outram to the Bombay Government. It was resolved by the Hon Board, 30 September 1854, to refer Speke's application to the Govt of India, with a recommendation in its favour. This was sent to Fort William, 7 November 1854.

55 OIOC, Bombay Political Consultations, P/395/4, Burton to Outram, Camp Aden, 4 October 1854. Speke had already written in his application to Govt, that 'arriving in Aden I was informed by Lt Burton that, preceding him far in the country I might materially injure the cause of discovery.' Speke's published version of this appears in *What Led to the Discovery*, p.7.

56 OIOC, Bombay Political Consultations, P/395/4. Outram to Speke, Political Resident's Office, 4 October 1854. Copies of this letter were sent to Burton and to the Sec to Govt, Bombay.

57 OIOC, E/4/1101, Bombay Political Despatch, No.24 of 23 August 1854, pp.461-472. Burton was only sent an extract, consisting of paragraphs 1 & 6, from this very long despatch.

58 Waterfield, *First Footsteps*, p.25.

59 William Jackson Hooker (1785-1865), distinguished botanist. In 1818, he accepted the chair of Regius Professor of Botany at Glasgow University. He was appointed the first Director of Kew Gardens, London, in 1841. Waterfield, *First Footsteps*, p.23, gives an inaccurate explanation of the change. Relying on Burton's statement in his Preface, p.xxi: 'No longer hoping to carry out his first project......etc,' Waterfield assumed that Burton was referring to his intention 'to strike into Central Africa from Zanzibar or Harar, to discover the source of the Nile, and perhaps cross to the Atlantic.' His first project, as the letter shows, was an authoritative botanical survey.

60 OIOC, P/395/4, Burton to H.L. Anderson, Sec to Govt, Bombay, Camp Aden, 10 October 1854.

61   R.F. Burton, *First Footsteps*, p.xix. William Stroyan was from Newtonstuart, Dumfries, south-west Scotland. He attended the Douglas Academy, and then studied for a short period in the mathematical department of Liverpool High School. He went on to study the construction of marine steam engines in the London Dock Company. Nominated to the Indian Navy by Lt Col P. Vans-Agnew, he was appointed to the service, 13 October 1841. His name appears several times in C.R. Low, *History of the Indian Navy,1613-1863* (London, 1877), ii, pp.209, 217, 395, 397.

62   Speke, *What Led*, pp.18-19.

63   Burton, 'Narrative of a Trip to Harar,' p.137. According to OIOC, Z/P/3383, Index to the Political Diary of the Bombay Government, 1854, Burton's letter applying for Stroyan was replied to on 4 November. On 17 November authority was given for Stroyan to be provided with a free passage to Aden. P/395/6 shows that on 22 November, he was submitting an indent on the Grand Arsenal there for ammunition and relevant accessories. Burton in his Preface to *First Footsteps*, p.xxiii, states, possibly incorrectly, that Stroyan did not join Herne at Berbera until 1 January 1855.

64   Speke, *What Led*, pp.20-21.

65   *Ibid.*, pp.22-23.

66   Speke's description of these articles and their cost, £390, is in *What Led*, pp.4-5. Burton's comments were made in his *Zanzibar*, ii, p.379. This, of course, was his later view, coloured by events of the intervening years. It may be supposed that, in 1854, he had no better idea than Speke of what was suitable for the 'simple-minded Negro of Africa.' In his letter to Outram of 2 October, just over a fortnight earlier, P/395/4, Burton referred to Speke's having 'provided himself with an expensive outfit.'

67   Burton's animosity towards Outram is evident in his only acknowledging the Resident's help in his paper for the RGS, *JRGS*, Vol.XXV (1855), pp.137-38. In *First Footsteps*, p.7, he mentions only 'Lieut Dansey, an officer who unfortunately was not "confirmed" in a political appointment at Aden.'

68   *Ibid.*, p.131.

69   OIOC, Bombay Political Consultations, P/395/3, 1854, G.F. Edmonstone, Sec to the Govt of India, to H.L. Anderson, Sec to the Govt of Bombay, Fort William, 5 Sept 1854, para.3. Speke dedicated his *What Led* 'To the Memory of Lt. Gen. Sir Jas. Outram Bart, GCB, Who First Gave Me A Start In Africa.' Outram died at Pau, France, on 11 March 1863, and was buried in Westminster Abbey.

70   G. Waterfield, *First Footsteps*, p.24, states incorrectly that, 'Owing to his bad health, Colonel Outram only stayed at Aden from July to December.'

71   F.M. Brodie, *The Devil Drives*, p.109, mistakenly describes it as 'a little steamer.'

Notes to Chapter 15

1   In his *Kitab al-Buldan* ("Book of the Countries"), a general geography, the larger part of which is now lost. See J.S. Trimingham, *Islam in Ethiopia* (Oxford, 1952), pp.61-62.

2   Zayla (also spelt Zeila or Zeyla) is rendered as 'Saylac' in *The Times Atlas of the World*, Comprehensive Edition (Times Books, 1997), Plate 87. It was known as Audal or Auzal by the Somali, a name which, earlier, had been applied to the Muslim sultanate which succeeded that of Ifat. "The kingdom of Adel (as they say) is a large kingdom, and extends over the Cape of Guardafuy, and there in that part another rules subject to Adel. Amongst the Moors they hold this King of Adel for a saint, because he always makes war upon the Christians....This Kingdom of Adel borders upon the kingdoms of Fatigar and Xio, which are kingdoms of the Prester John." See Fr F. Alvarez, *Narrative of the Portuguese Embassy During the Years 1520-27*, ed. & trans. Lord Stanley of Alderley (London, 1881), p.346. Burton wrote at length about the town in his *First Footsteps in East Africa* (London, 1856), Chaps II & III.

3   Cited by Burton, *First Footsteps*, p.69-70: 'Bartema, travelling in A.D. 1503, treats in his 15th chapter of "Zeila in Aethiopia and the great fruitfulness, thereof,.....In this city is a great frequentation of merchandise, as in a most famous mart. There is marvellous abundance of gold and iron, and an innumerable number of black slaves sold for

small prices; these are taken in war by the Mahomedans out of Aethiopia, of the kingdom of Prebyter Johannes, or Preciousus Johannes, which some also call the king of Jacobins or Abyssins, being a Christian; and are carried away from thence into Persia, Arabia Felix, Babylonia of Nilus or Alcair, and Meccah…..'

4   Ralph E. Drake-Brockman, *British Somaliland* (London, 1912), p.21, states that, 'A few of the great white three-storied buildings, erected previous to Burton's visit, still exist, but the hand of time has not dealt lightly with them, and owing to the gradual diminution of the town's trade, they have been allowed to crumble to decay. The upper stories of Sharmarkay Ali's house, where Burton resided during his short stay in the town have long been demolished; only the ground floor and a small portion of the first floor are still to be seen.'

5   *Ibid.*, pp.37-38. Burton shows here a tolerant attitude that was conspicuously absent during his later African expedition to the Lake Regions.

6   *First Footsteps*, p.101. They belong, in fact, to the so-called Cushitic ethnic group, which includes the Danakil, the Galla, Saho, and Beja.

7   *Ibid.*, p.115, and I.M. Lewis, *A Modern History of Somalia* (London, 1980), p.16.

8   R.L. Playfair, *A History of Arabia Felix or Yemen* (Bombay, 1859), p.14, described them as 'a good tempered, though lazy and indolent race, but easily excited to anger; on which account they cannot even be trusted to carry sticks.'

9   *First Footsteps*, p.109.

10 R.F. Burton, *The Book of the Thousand Nights and a Night* (Benares, 1885-8), Vol.2, p.98n.

11 R.E. Drake-Brockman, *British Somaliland*, p.147.

12 Burton's account, written in Latin, and headed 'A brief description of certain peculiar customs, noticed in Nubia, by Brown [*sic*] and Werne under the name of [*in*]-fibulation,' was meant to form Appendix IV of his book. The publisher, however, when he discovered the nature of its contents, had it removed. Fawn M. Brodie discovered a copy which still contained the offending material. She very generously placed it at the disposal of Gordon Waterfield, who printed it in his edition of *First Footsteps* (London, 1966), as Appendix 2, pp.285-86.

13 See *The Book of the Thousand Nights*, Vol.V, p.279n. What Burton means can be seen in Vol.2, p.62n, where he writes, 'The most terrible part of a belle passion in the East is that the beloved will not allow her lover leave of absence for an hour.'

14 R.F. Burton, 'Narrative of a Trip to Harar,' *JRGS*, Vol. XXV (1855), p.138.

15 *Ibid.*, p.139. In *First Footsteps*, pp.94-95, Burton alludes at some length to male emasculation, describing it in a footnote, 'as an ancient practice in Asia as well as Africa. The Egyptian temples show heaps of trophies placed before the monarchs as eyes or heads were presented in Persia. Thus in 1 Sam. xviii. 25., David brings the spoils of 200 Philistines, and shows them in full tale to the king, that he might be the king's son-in-law. Any work upon the subject of Abyssinia (Bruce, book 7. Chap. 8.), or the late Afghan war, will prove that the custom of mutilation, opposed as it is both to Christianity and El Islam, is still practised in the case of hated enemies and infidels…..'

16 *Ibid.*, pp.176-177.

17 Burton, *First Footsteps*, pp.291-92. On 8 January 1892, at an inaugural lecture of the Geographical Society of California in San Francisco, John Studdy Leigh, a British-born traveller, claimed that he and not Burton was the first person to visit Harar. See H.G. Marcus and M.E. Page, 'John Studdy Leigh: First Footsteps in East Africa?', *The International Journal of African Historical Studies*, Vol.3 (1972), pp.470-78. An examination of Leigh's own journal has shown his claim to be fraudulent, although he was at Berbera in 1838-39. See J. Kirkman, "John Studdy Leigh in Somalia," *The International Journal of African Historical Studies*, Vol.VIII (1975), pp.441-56.

18 With British trade interests and the future of the Somali Expedition in mind, the Political Resident, Brigadier W.M. Coghlan, informed the Bombay Government on 14 March 1855, that he had 'despatched a Sayyed, who pretends to some slight medical skill. In the event of failing to alleviate his sufferings….the Holiness of this man's descent will render it impossible that any suspicion of poisoning should operate against him.' See G. Waterfield, *First Footsteps in East Africa* (London, 1966), p.304n, who goes on to claim, without stating his source, that 'The Amir died in September or October of the following year and was succeeded by a relative.' According to Trimingham, *Islam in Ethiopia,*, p.120, he died in 1866. The Amir's medical condition, however, makes this late dating highly unlikely.

19   Burton, *First Footsteps*, pp.364-65. The source of his quotation is 'Death the Leveller' by the Renaissance dramatist and poet, James Shirley (1596-1666), beginning 'The glories of our blood and state/Are shadows not substantial things.....'

20   *Ibid.*, p.511, where Burton writes: 'The caution necessary for the stranger who would avoid exciting the suspicions of an African despot and Moslem bigots prevented my making any progress, during my short residence at the capital, in the Harari language. But once more safe among the Girhi Mountains, circumspection was no longer necessary.' See Appendix II: Grammatical Outline, pp.511-30; Vocabulary, pp.536-82.

21   Burton who wrote at length about Berbera in his report to Government, and in his book, advocated its occupation by Britain, describing it as 'the true key of the Red Sea, the centre of East African traffic, and the only safe place for shipping upon the western Erythroean shore, from Suez to Guardafui.' See Burton, *First Footsteps*, pp.xxxiii-xxxiv. It was occupied by the Egyptians in 1875, and by the British in 1884, serving as the capital of British Somaliland until 1931.

22   Dansey's service record, L/MIL/12/72, shows that he qualified as an interpreter in Hindustani, G.O. 8 Dec 1842; Maharatta, G.O. 23 Oct 1843; Persian, G.O. 21 Sept 1853. He was helped by a Somali, Farih Dibani.

23   OIOC, P/351/45, Bombay Public Proceedings (March, 1855), nos.1702-4. Also Spiro Collection, RGS Archives.

24   TNA, FO 7/1105, Burton to Iddesleigh, 8 Sept (1866).

25   OIOC, L/MIL/12/73.

26   OIOC, V/11/2151-2.

27   R.F. Burton, 'The Biography of the Book and its Reviewers Reviewed,' *The Book of the Thousand Nights and a Night*, Supplemental Six (Benares, 1888), p.416.

28   OIOC, P/351/43/1704, Folio 1704, No.1014 of 1855, W.Hart, Secretary to Government, Bombay Castle, to Brigadier W.M. Coghlan, 7 March 1855.

29   QK Coll, Rev G.P. Badger to Burton, London, 29 Feb 1872.

30   HL 40, Badger to Burton, London, 21 February 1872. Autograph letter inserted in Burton's *Zanzibar: City, Island and Coast* (London, 1872).

31   RGS Archives, Spiro Collection. J.H. Speke to Playfair, Camp of Hadafino, 20 December 1854. 'I have the honor to forward my journal kept precisely in accordance with the spirit of Lt. Burton's orders, & to state that I have been daily expecting from the first to be able [to] send my progress report in a short time to give some guide as to my future movements, but as will be seen from my diary I have never been able to make my arrangements.'

32   Spiro Coll. Burton to Brigadier W.M. Coghlan, Camp Aden, 21 February 1855.

33   See J.H. Speke, *What Led to the Discovery of the Source of the Nile* (Edinburgh & London, 1864), p.109, where he claimed to having been 'averse to punishing him, from the simple fact of having brought him over; but my commandant thought otherwise, and that he had better be punished, if for no other reason than to set a good moral example to the others.' Speke glossed this in a footnote: 'To say the least of it this was a very dangerous policy to play with people who consider might right, and revenge to death.'

34   OIOC, F/4/2600, Board's Collection 161093: 'Application for Lieut. Burton to be allowed to devote a second year to the Somali Expedition [Aug. 1854], Feb.-Apr. 1855.'

35   See Speke, *What Led*, pp.45, 52, & 105: His collections were sent by Burton to the Asiatic Society's Museum, Calcutta. The Curator, Edward Blythe, named a small lizard, *Tiloqua Burtoni*, and 'a very interesting rat.... very much resembling the little gilleri squirrel of the Indian plains,' *Pectinator Spekei*.' According to A. Desmond and J. Moore, *Darwin* (Penguin, 1992), p.419, Blythe 'sent Darwin reams on Indian domestic animals.'

36   This is confirmed by I.M. Lewis, *A Pastoral Democracy* (Oxford, 1961), p.30.

37   G. Stisted, *The True Life*, p.159, misdated his mother's death to 18 December 1854, while he lay dangerously ill at Sagharrah.' This error has been copied into every biography since. F.M. Brodie, *The Devil Drives*, p.118, used it as the basis for making a laboured and unconvincing psychological point. She also mistakenly stated that the cause of Martha's death was unknown.

38   Incorrectly written as 'Goranna' in Waterfield, *First Footsteps*, p.245.

39   RGS Archives, Corr Files, 1851-60.

40   RGS Archives, Spiro Collection. Burton to Brigadier W.M. Coghlan, Camp Aden, 25 March 1855.

41 J.H. Speke, *What Led*, p.112.

42 See Burton, *First Footsteps*, p.445n. where he writes: 'Since returning I have been informed , however, by the celebrated Abyssinian traveller M. Antoine d'Abbadie, that in no part of the wild countries which he visited was his life so much perilled as at Berberah.'

43 For whatever reason, Burton omitted any mention of these women in his accounts in *First Footsteps*, his paper for the RGS, and in *The Life*. Their presence was only revealed in J.H. Speke, *What Led*, p.129.

44 The Bombay Army List, L/MIL/12/85, shows that Steinhaueser was on 'Leave to Europe on sick certificate for 15 months – New Regulations – G.O. 25 April and 8 June 1855. Returned to duty, arrived at Aden 27 June 1856.' He must have left Aden, therefore, around the end of March, shortly before Burton sailed for Berbera.

45 According to Burton, *The Life*, i, p.222, the javelin 'destroyed my palate and four good back teeth…'

46 OIOC, L/MIL/12/78 (1855-57), Allowed a Furlo to Europe on SC (new Reg) from the date of his departure from Aden, GO 25 May 1855.

Notes to Chapter 16

1 28 March 1854. *The Times*, p.6, reported that 'The avenues of Westminster Hall and the Peers' entrance to the House of Lords were occupied by a large assemblage of persons anxious to see Her Majesty's Ministers come down to Parliament with the declaration of war against Russia.' The Lord Chancellor read the message 'amid the breathless silence of the House….'

2 *The Times*, 14 February 1854, p.7.

3 Sir William Howard Russell (1820-1907). Landed at Gallipoli on 5 April, 1854. His letters from here and from Varna were resented by the HQ staff, and when the army reached the Crimea he was treated as an outcast, unauthorised even to draw rations.

4 Francis Augustus Plunkett Burton (1826-1865), only son of Rear-Admiral James Ryder Burton and the Hon Anna Maria Plunkett, daughter of Lord Dunsany. Educated Eton (admitted pensioner Trinity College, Cambridge, 3 May 1844, but did not reside) and Christ Church College, Oxford, 1844-46. Became an ensign and lieutenant in the Coldstream Guards on 8 May 1846; lieutenant and captain on 27 June, 1851, and retired as captain and lieutenant-colonel on 25 May 1855. These double ranks are peculiar to the Guards' regiments. Married Sarah Frances Elizabeth Erle-Drax, 14 Sept 1853. Died 3 September 1865, at 45 Grosvenor Square, London, 'after a long and painful illness….from rheumatism, caught while serving with his regiment in the Crimea.' See Venn J. & J.A., *Alumni Cantabrigiensis*, Pt. II (1752-1900), Vol.1 (Cambridge, 1940); card index of officers, NAM; obituary, *The Dorset County Chronicle*, 7 September 1865.

5 *Personal Narrative of a Pilgrimage to El-Medinah and Meccah,*3 vols (London, 1855-56). In his Preface, dated June, 1855, Thomas Wolley wrote, p.ix, 'The concluding volume on Mecca is now in the hands of the publisher, and will appear in the autumn of the present year.' However, it was not published until early the following year.

6 I have been unable to discover anything about Wolley. At the end of the Preface he gives his address as Hampton Court Palace. R.D. Harman, the Superintendent of Hampton Court Palace, in a letter to the author, wrote, 'I have consulted my records of previous Grace and Favour Residents, but can find no mention of Wolley. That is not to deny, of course, that he might have lived there, but it does indicate that he was not the tenant of an apartment….'

7 This information first appeared in *The Athenaeum*, No.3431, 29 July 1893, in a review of *The Pilgrimage* at its reissue as the first of the Memorial Edition of Burton's works. The anonymous reviewer, almost certainly Lane-Poole, wrote, p.15, 'Nothing is said in the preface, however, about the considerable excisions which we believe were made in the original MS by the advice of Sir Gardner Wilkinson, whereby a good deal of what Burton called "anthropological" statistics was lost to the curious reader.' It was repeated in Lane-Poole's Introduction to The "Standard" Library Edition, 1898-1914, and The "York" Library Edition, 1906, p.xx, both published by G. Bell & Sons Ltd.

8 Wolley, *The Pilgrimage*., p.xii.

9 *JRGS* 25 (1855), p.cxix.

10 John Arthur Roebuck, MP for Sheffield, had asked the House of Commons on 23 January 1855, to set up such a

Select Committee. The evidence was published daily. The full report appeared on 18 June of that year.

11   General Sir James Simpson (1792-1868). Sent to the Crimea in February 1855 as chief of staff with the local rank of Lt General. Reported that he did not think that 'a better selection of staff officers could be made.'

12   Fox Maule Ramsay, 11th earl of Dalhousie (1811-74), became 2nd Baron Panmure in 1852 and earl of Dalhousie in 1860. On the formation of the first Palmerston government in February 1855, he was appointed to the new office of secretary (of state) for war. Shared the blame for the conduct of the last stage of the war.

13   'Narrative of a Trip to Harar,' *JRGS* 25 (1855), pp.136-50. Read 11 June 1855.

14   See *The True Life*, p.163 et seq. Burton's brother, Edward, had entered the army as an ensign in 1845. After ten years' service abroad, he was now on a 3 years' European furlough.

15   See C.Woodham-Smith, *Florence Nightingale* (London, 1950), p.148 et seq.

16   Alexander William Kinglake (1809-91), author of *Eothen or Traces of Travel Brought Home from the East* (London, 1844), one of the most famous travel books ever written. Mysseri, as Kinglake spells his name, acted as interpreter and guide during Kinglake's Eastern tour, 1834-5, and was praised by his employer, 'as in fact, the brain of our corps.'

17   *The Times*, 22 Nov 1853, p.8. It is highly likely that the reader, writing from the Travellers' Club, Pall Mall, and signing himself, *Memor*, was Kinglake himself.

18   See W.Filder, *The Commissariat in the Crimea* (London, 1856).

19   RGS Archives: Burton to Shaw, Camp Dardanelles, 18 August 1855.

20   *The Life* (London, 1893), i, p.228.

21   Sir James resigned on 10 November 1855, handing over the command to General Sir William Codrington.

22   R.F. Burton, *Zanzibar; City, Island, and Coast* (London, 1872), i, p.2.

23   Stratford Canning, 1st Viscount (1786-1880), the diplomat who represented Britain at the Ottoman court for almost twenty years, exerting a strong influence on Turkish policy. Known by the Turks as the *Great Elchi* or Ambassador.

24   RGS Archives, Camp Dardanelles, 18 Aug 1855.

25   OIOC, Bombay Army List, L/MIL/12/85. 'Served in the Crimea with the local rank of captain from August 17 – November 17, 1855.'

26   Burton possibly had in mind: (i) his claim that Indians were hostile to British rule, i, p.54n; (ii) his facetious remark that the donkey boys in Egypt were the only class in Egypt favourable to the English, since 'we hire more asses than any other nation.' p.162.

27   Letter from Burton to *The Times*, 6 Dec 1855, p.4.

28   *The Life*, i, p.238.

29   E. Money, *Twelve Months With The Bashi-Bazouks* (London, 1857), p.34.

30   *The Life*, i, p.240.

31   Camp Dardanelles, 18 Aug 1855.

32   S. Lane-Poole, *Lord Stratford de Redcliffe* (London, 1888), i, p.345, letter from the ambassador to his wife, 16 April 1854.

33   *The Life*, p.239.

34   J.H. Skene, *With Lord Stratford in the Crimean War* (London, 1883), p.48.

35   Burton writes, 'Brigadier T.G. Neil.' See *The Life*, p.239. I have accepted instead the initials and spelling in Lt Col M.E.S. Laws, 'Beatson's Bashi-Bazouks,' *Army Quarterly*, LXXI (1955), p.83.

36   'From Our Own Correspondent,' Constantinople, 10 Sept, reported in *The Times*, 22 Sept 1855, p.10.

37   Lt Col M.E.S. Laws, 'Beatson's Bashi-Bazouks,' p.84.

38   Lane-Poole in his biography, i, pp.426-28, defends Lord Stratford, perhaps with a degree of special pleading. He blames the earlier criticism by Col Williams that his letters were not answered on the ambassador's heavy work-load, and his disinclination to delegate. He then goes on, 'There has never, I believe, been any pretence that, after the correspondence which took place in November and December 1854, Lord Stratford neglected in any way the interests of General Williams and the armies at Erzerum and Kars. The *Blue Book on Military Affairs in Asiatic Turkey* with its 400 despatches and numerous enclosures, contains abundant evidence of the zeal and perseverance

with which the Elchi pressed the Turkish government to reinforce and provision its army in Asia.'

39 *The Life*, p.242.

40 *Ibid.*, p.242.

41 F. Hitchman, *Richard F. Burton, His Early, Private and Public Life With an Account of his Explorations* (London, 1887).

42 *The Athenaeum*, No.3173, 18 August 1888, pp.216-7.

43 *The Athenaeum*, No.3174, 25 August 1888, p.260.

44 *The Academy*, Vol.XXXIV, No.852, 1 Sept 1888, p.137.

45 *The Athenaeum*, No.3176, 8 Sept 1888, p.321.

46 This operation was unsuccessful. In spite of bad weather and other difficulties, the army reached Kutais about 120 miles from Kars. There, according to J.H. Skene, *With Lord Stratford*, p.293, it 'fought a desperate and not inglorious battle at the passage of the river Ingur with a Russian force, and finding it impossible to proceed farther, retired to its base of operations without having been able to accomplish anything in favour of the Turkish garrison of Kars.' Col Williams surrendered on 23 November 1855.

47 Charles Alison was then Oriental Secretary, later becoming Minister at Teheran. He was described by Lane-Poole, *Life of Lord Stratford de Redcliffe,* ii, p.15, as 'a man of subtle and penetrating mind....more at home in Turkish families than the ambassador could possibly be.' He was also highly eccentric. Next to him in rank was Percy Smythe, later 8th Lord Strangford who, according to Burton, *The Life*, i, p.231, 'fulfilled my idea of the typical linguist in the highest sense of the word; in fact I never saw his equal except, perhaps, Professor Palmer.'

48 *The Life*, p.244.

49 L. Oliphant, *The Russian Shores of the Black Sea* (London, 1853)

50 *Ibid.*, p.319.

51 *Ibid.*, p.321. Oliphant expressed similar sentiments the following year, in an unsigned review in *Blackwood's Magazine*, Vol.LXXV (Jan.-June 1854), May, No.CCCCLXIII, pp.611-28, entitled, *The Progress and Policy of Russia in Central Asia.*' In his final paragraph, Oliphant wrote, 'The conclusion then to which our consideration of the present state of the acquired provinces in Asia has brought us, seems to be, that they have been acquired only as a necessary prelude to the annexation of another and more important country....it is in the power of this country to check that progress at once, and thus nip in the bud her long-cherished designs upon Persia, and her deeply-laid schemes for the appropriation of those sources of wealth and power in the East, which have so materially contributed to raise this country to her present high position among European nations.'

52 The first mission was entrusted to Col Lloyd, an officer familiar with the country and fluent in Turkish. He died of cholera without ever making contact with Schamyl. See A. Taylor, *Laurence Oliphant* (Oxford, 1982), pp.28 & 35. The second was undertaken by John Longworth.

53 P. Henderson, *The Life of Laurence Oliphant, Traveller, Diplomat & Mystic* (London, 1956), p.52.

54 See *The Times*, 12 October 1855, p.7. 'The Press d'Orient has a letter from the Dardanelles, dated the 28th of September, and contains the following details of the recent disturbances.' I have based my narrative on this contemporary account, rather than Burton's written many years later.

55 I have taken Major-General Smith's initials from Law's *Army Quarterly* article. Burton refers to him as Richard Smith.

56 *The Life*, i, p.245.

57 *The Times*, 14 Jan 1860, p.10.

58 *Ibid.*, p.11.

Notes to Chapter 17

1 *Blackwood's Magazine*, No.CCCCXCII, Vol.LXX, Oct 1856, p.490. The reviewer was Laurence Oliphant.

2 *The Athenaeum*, No.1448, 28 July 1855, pp.865-6.

3 *Blackwood's Magazine*, No.CCCCLXXXI, Vol.LXXVIII, November 1855, p.590.

4   There were five, but the printers refused to bind in the fourth, written in Latin, dealing with female circumcision and infibulation among the Somali tribes. It is left blank, and carries the legend, 'It has been found necessary to omit this Appendix.' However, a copy of *First Footsteps*, one of a set of Burton books bought by Fawn Brodie, contained this Appendix thought to be lost.

5   R.F. Burton, *First Footsteps in East Africa* (London, 1856), Appendix 1, pp.502-3.

6   *Blackwood's Magazine*, No.CCCCXCII, p.499.

7   R.F. Burton, *Zanzibar; City, Coast, and Island* (London, 1872), ii, pp.384-5.

8   J.H. Speke to C.P. Rigby, Kinanga Ranga, 6 Oct 1860, quoted in C.E.B. Russell, *General Rigby, Zanzibar and the Slave Trade* (London, 1935), p.235.

9   David Finkelstein claimed in an article on Speke, 'Darkening the Image of Africa,' published in the *BBC History Magazine*, August 2001, Vol.2, No.8, pp.26-29, that it was 'the previously untold story of the "ghost writing" of….Speke's *Journal of the Discovery of the Source of the Nile*.' This is inaccurate. The difficulties experienced by Speke and his publishers in putting his notes and diaries into publishable form were first recounted by John Blackwood's daughter, Mrs Geraldine Porter, in *Annals of a Publishing House*, William Blackwood and Sons (Edinburgh & London, 1898), Vol.III, pp.95-97.

10 R.F. Burton, *First Footsteps*, pp.xxx-xxxi.

11 Burton ascribes this maxim to 'a modern sage.' Despite the quotation marks, I am convinced that it is Burton himself.

12 R.F. Burton, *First Footsteps*, p.xxxiii.

13 OIOC, Bombay Secret Consultations, July 11-Oct. 1855, Vol.3, No.296. G.H. Edmonton, Secretary to the Governor-General of India to H.L. Anderson (Bombay), dated Ootacamund, 29 June 1855.

14 R.F. Burton, *First Footsteps*, p.xxxvii.

15 R.F. Burton, *Zanzibar*, i, p.10. The delay in informing Burton and his companions may well have resulted from Lord Dalhousie's departure from India in 1856, crippled in health. He died on 19 December 1860.

16 R.F. Burton, *First Footsteps*, p.xxxviii.

17 *Edinburgh Review*, No.CXXIV, July 1835, Art III, pp.342-364, 'A Voyage of Discovery to Africa and Arabia Performed In His Majesty's Ships *Leven* and *Barracoute* from 1822 to 1826 under the Command of Captain F.W.W. Owen, RN. By Capt. Thomas Boteler, RN, 2 vol. 8vo. London 1835.'

18 *Ibid*., p.348. Ten years later, Cooley encapsulated everything he had found out about the lake in 'The Geography of N'yassi, or the great lake of Southern Africa investigated,' *JRGS* 15 (1845), pp.185-235.

19 In 1850, Rebmann had published a map containing three large lakes. See 'Journal to Jagga, 1849-50,' *Church Missionary Intelligencer*.

20 *The Athenaeum*, No.1457, 29 Sept 1855, p.1116. August Heinrich Petermann (1822-78), studied at the Geographical Art School in Potsdam, founded by the distinguished geographer, cartographer, and writer, Heinrich Berghaus. He then worked as a cartographer for Alexander von Humboldt, and later at the Johnston cartographic firm in Edinburgh. From there he went to London, where he compiled some extremely fine demographic maps, including those of the 1851 census. In 1854 he moved back to Germany to work for the firm of Justus Perthus in Gotha. In 1867 he was awarded the Founder's Medal by the Royal Geographical Society for his work in advancing geographical science. He is referred to sneeringly by Burton in *Zanzibar*, ii, p.60.

21 'Reports respecting Central Africa, as collected in Mambara and on the East coast, with a new Map of the Country.' By the Rev James Erhardt. *Proceedings of the Royal Geographical Society* (1855-56), pp.8-10. The memoir on the lake, together with its accompanying map, were inserted by Francis Galton, 'who had most to do with the then newly established Proceedings.' See F. Galton, *Memories of My Life* (London, 1908), p.198.

22 'Notes on the Geography of Central Africa from the Researches of Livingstone, Monteiro, Garcia, and other authorities,' *Proceedings*, 10 Dec 1855.

23 *The Athenaeum*, No.1498, 12 July 1856, p.867. Letter dated Rosalie, Mauritius, 10 April 1856.

24 *The Athenaeum*, No.1457, 29 Sept 1855, p.1116.

25 R.F. Burton, *The Lake Regions of Central Africa* (London, 1860), pp.3-4. 'In 1855, M. Erhardt, an energetic member of the hapless "Mombas Mission", had on his return to London, offered to explore a vast mass of water,

about the size of the Caspian Sea.' Speke also makes this claim in a letter to Sir George Back, Madeira, 10 May, 1860. RGS Archives.

26   RGS Archives, Letter from Erhardt to Shaw, addressed from 8 High St, Islington, the CMS seminary in London, and dated 17 March 1856.
27   RGS Archives, Committee Minute Book, Vol.1, 1841-65. Minutes of the Expedition Committee, 19 March 1856. Other members of the Committee were Count Strzelecki, Francis Galton, and Dr Hodgkin.
28   RGS Archives, Letter from the same address, dated 2 April 1856.
29   R.F. Burton, *The Lake Regions*, p.4.
30   RGS Archives, Burton to Shaw, 9 April 1856.
31   RGS Archives, Committee Minute Book, Vol.1, 1841-65. Minutes of the Expedition Committee, 12 April 1856.
32   RGS Archives, Burton to Shaw, 19 April 1856.
33   R.F. Burton, *Zanzibar*, i, p.8.
34   *Ibid.*, ii, pp.376-77.
35   RGS Archives, Captain Smyth to Shaw, Constantinople, 27 April 1856.
36   RGS Archives, Minutes of the Expedition Committee. The Society's President, Rear-Admiral F.W. Beechey, was in the chair. The other members present were Sir George Back and Francis Galton.
37   Dr Edward Vogel, a young German astronomer, was sent out by the British Foreign Office as a replacement for James Richardson, leader of an ill-fated mission to West Central Africa, 1849-54, who had died from fever in 1851. Other members were Heinrich Barth and Adolf Overweg, who also succumbed to fever in the following year. Vogel left Tripoli in 1853, accompanied by Corporal Church and Private Maguire of the Royal Sappers and Miners. Vogel and Maguire were never seen again, presumably murdered by the Wadai king. See B. Gardner, *The Quest for Timbuctoo* (London, 1968). References to Corporal James Church are on pp. 175, 176, and 178n.

Notes to Chapter 18

1   See 'D4 – The Albany,' an obituary in *The Spectator*, 4 March 1865, p.241, written by the novelist, Thomas Hughes. A number of famous residents have lived at this exclusive address, including George Canning, Lord Byron, Bulwer Lytton, Lord Macaulay and W.E. Gladstone.
2   F. Galton, *Memories of my Life* (London, 1908), p.171.
3   W.F. Moneypenny & G.E. Buckle, *The Life of Benjamin Disraeli*, 6 vols 1910-20. Vol.III (1846-55), *Tancred*, 1847, p.50.
4   See S. Chitty, *The Beast and the Monk. A Life of Charles Kingsley* (London, 1974), p.174. It is wrongly cited as Unpublished Letters to Fanny, No.147, 1854, instead of 1856. Kingsley's odd description of Burton as 'a splendid little fellow,' can only be put down to the novelist's being extremely tall.
5   *The Romance*, pp.64-65; pp.68-69.
6   There is a list of the names of the members of the club, which included Isabel's sister, Blanche, and Louisa Segrave, at the WSRO.
7   *The Romance.*, pp.80-81. Also see *The Life*, pp.251-2, for a transcription of Richard Burton's obituary in the *Gypsy Lore Society Journal*, Jan 1891.
8   It was the first part of the Bishop of London's estates to be built in the former parish of Paddington. The building, on a lavish scale, took place in the 1830s. It was rebuilt in the 1960s, after being badly damaged by bombing during World War II.
9   Now Queen Mary's Gardens, occupying the space within the Inner Circle. 18 acres were leased by the Royal Botanic Society from 1840-1932, and Decimus Burton commissioned to lay out the Gardens and design the buildings. See D. Edgar, *The Royal Parks* (London, 1986), p.120. They are incorrectly located at Kew by F. McLynn, *Snow Upon the Desert*, p.128, and in Hyde Park by M.S. Lovell, *A Rage to Live*, p.209.
10   For the Smyth Pigott pedigree, see Burke's Genealogical and Heraldic History of the Landed Gentry, 1937. Centenary (15th edn), Vol.2, pp.1809-10. In a letter to the author, Mrs Dorothy Flemming, (née Smyth Pigott)

stated that her grandfather was never faithful to Blanche, 'and ran through everything he could lay his hands on.' There is an interesting reference to him in J.B. Atkins and W.B. Boulton, *Memorials of the Royal Yacht Squadron* (London, 1903), p.190.

11   In *The Romance*, p.81, there is no mention of 'the friend' and 'the gorgeous creature of Boulogne – then married,' although Wilkins was, ostensibly,working from Lady Burton's personal papers.

12   RGS Archives, Burton to Shaw, received 15 August 1856. The letter is undated, and carries no address.

13   The British Consul at Damascus was James Brant, who had been appointed on 3 Dec 1855, but did not take up his position until September 1856. He was appointed a CB 31 Oct 1860, and retired two days later. Biographical details in the FO list of HM Consuls, 1861.

14   *The Romance*, p.84. However, in *The Life*, i, p.255, Isabel wrote, 'He left me, at my request, the task of breaking the fact of my engagement to my people, when, where, and how I pleased, as it would be impossible to marry me until he came back.'

15   OIOC, E/1/305, No.3771. P (or J) I.D.Dickinson to Shaw. Official notification was sent to Burton on 13 Sept 1856. It is reproduced in *The Lake Regions*, ii, p.420.

16   J.H. Speke, *What Led to the Discovery of the Source of the Nile* (London, 1864), p.157.

17   RGS Archives, Burton to Shaw, undated, June 1856.

18   See R.F. Burton, *Zanzibar*, i, p.10.

19   J.H. Speke, *What Led*, p.157.

20   See F. Galton, *Memories*, p.199.

21   They are reproduced in 'The Lake Regions of Central Equatorial Africa, with Notices of the Lunar Mountains and the Sources of the White Nile; being the results of an Expedition undertaken under the patronage of Her Majesty's Government and the Royal Geographical Society of London, in the years 1857-1859,' *JRGS* 29 (1859), pp.4-6.

22   *The Romance*, pp.84-5.

23   See R.F. Burton, *Abeokuta and the Camaroons Mountains* (London, 1863), i, p.201.

24   *Pizarro* was a popular patriotic melodrama (1799), adapted by Sheridan from August von Kotzebue's *Die Spanier in Peru*. Charles Keane (1811-68) was best-known for his revivals of Shakespearian plays. In 1842, he married Ellen Tree, regarded as one of the finest actresses of her day, after which they were closely associated for the rest of his life. In 1850 Keane co-leased the Princess's Theatre in London, where he and his wife carried out most of their performances, and where they reached the peak of their fame.

25   However, in her account written for the *Gypsy Lore Journal,* Isabel wrote: 'He had left London at six o'clock the previous evening, eight hours before I saw him in the night.' See *The Life*, p.255.

26   RGS Archives, A.B. Richards to Colonel Colt, 22 Nov 1856.

27   *The Athenaeum*, No.1505, 30 August 1856, p.1087. The news of Dr Vogel's death had not yet reached England. This expedition had been mentioned in Burton's instructions from the RGS, '......should you have acquired all the information within your means, you will be at liberty to return to England by descending the Nile, where it is possible you may fall in with the expedition under the Comte d'Escayrac, now proceeding up that river to reach its sources....' See *JRGS* 29 (1859).

28   Headed 'The Source of the Nile,' *The Times*, Saturday, 27 Sept 1856, p.9. Twyford had lately been an officer in the British Transport Service, and was chosen to assist in navigating the boats up the Nile. The other members were drawn from different European countries. The Count started on 3 September for Trieste, which he was to leave on the 18th. His companions were to join him in Cairo at the beginning of October, and the expedition would then begin its ascent of the Nile.

29   'Notes relative to the late proposed Expedition to discover the Sources of the White Nile.' By Mr. A.W. Twyford. *JRGS* 27 (1857), pp.503-8. In the RGS Archives, there are two journal MSS relating to this expedition: L'Escayrac de Lauture, Comte de. 'Papers concerning the preparations for his White Nile expedition'; and L'Escayrac de Lauture, Comte de, and Twyford, A.W. 'Accounts of the progress of the White Nile Expedition.' See 'The RGS Archives'. A handlist compiled by Christine Kelly, Part II. Africa. The Nile Region, *The Geographical Journal*, Vol.CXLII (1976), p.119.

30   OIOC, E/1/305, number 4715, dated East India House, 24 October 1856. It is reproduced in *The Lake Regions*, ii,

Appendix II, p.420.

31   OIOC, E/1/305, number 4716. James Melvill, Secretary, East India House, to Norton Shaw.

32   In *The Lake Regions*, i, pp.24-25, Burton wrote, 'At Cairo I had received from the East India House an order to return to London, to appear as a witness on a trial by court-martial then pending. The missive was, as usual, so ineptly worded, that I did not think it proper to throw overboard the Royal Geographical Society – to whom my services had been made over – by obeying it: at the same time I well knew what the consequences would be.'

33   Burton to the Military Secretary, East India House, Aden, 14 Nov 1856. *Lake Regions*, ii, Appendix II, p.421.

34   Burton to Shaw, Camp Aden, 14 Nov 1856. *Lake Regions*, ii, Appendix II, p.422.

35   See *The Life*, ii, Appendix F, p.561.

36   J.H. Speke, *What Led*, pp.158-59.

37   See *The Life*, ii, p.560.

38   R.F. Burton, *Zanzibar*, i, p.34.

Notes to Chapter 19

1   Atkins Hamerton (1804-57), son of Edward Hamerton, Clerk of ships' entries at the Port of Dublin, co. Dublin, and Elizabeth. b. St Thomas, Dublin, 29 April 1804. Lt. Col. 2nd NI. HM Consul at Mascat, 14 Dec 1841 till death, 5 July 1857. Details from the card index of officers, NAM. There is a short obituary in *The Gentleman's Magazine*, Vol.iii, NS (July-Dec.1857), p.566.

2   C.S. Nicholls, *The Swahili Coast, Politics, Diplomacy and Trade on the East African Littoral, 1798-1856* (London, 1971), p.174.

3   Guillain, *Documents sur l'Histoire, la Géographie et le Commerce de l'Afrique Orientale*, pp.22-24. Guillain's pen-portrait of Hamerton is quoted in R.H. Crofton, *The Old Consulate at Zanzibar* (London, 1935), pp.17-18.

4   J.H. Speke, *What Led to the Discovery of the Source of the Nile* (London, 1864), p.160.

5   RGS Archives, Back Collection. Burton to Sir George Back, British Consulate, Zanzibar, 9 April 1857.

6   *Ibid.*

7   R.F. Burton, *Zanzibar*, i, p.37.

8   J.H. Speke, *What Led*, p.161.

9   *JRGS* XXIX (1859), Preface, Section II, p.5.

10   R.F. Burton, *The Lake Regions*, i, p.6. See also J.L. Krapf, *Travels,Researches and Missionary Labours*, 2nd edn with an Introduction by R.C. Bridges (London, 1968), p.28 et seq.

11   R.F. Burton, *Zanzibar*, i, p.474.

12   *Ibid.*, p.479.

13   *Ibid.*, pp.488-9. Burton wrote through Major Eyre 'to Mr Joseph Francis of New York, whose application of iron had taken the place of the old copper article in which Lt Lynch of the United States, descended the Jordan rapids. The total length, 20 feet, was divided into seven sections, each weighing under 40 lbs.' Although this was an American article, manufactured by Messrs Marshall, Lefferts & Co, British technologists had been early in the field, using Africa as a proving ground to try out their new inventions. See R.Lewis & Y. Foy, *The British in Africa* (London, 1971), p.xviii.

14   M.S. Lovell, *A Rage to Live* (London, 1998), p.218.

15   Quoted in R. Hall, *Stanley: An Adventurer Explored* (London, 1974), pp.61-2.

16   J.L. Krapf, *Travels, Researches, etc*, p.40.

17   R.F. Burton, *The Lake Regions*, p.6. The reservations were not only on Burton's part. In his *Zanzibar*, i, pp. 57-8, Burton wrote rather more truthfully of Rebmann, that, 'His earliest impulse was evidently to assist us in carrying out the plans which had been first formed by the 'Mombas Mission,' and personally to verify the accuracy of the map. He was not in strong health; he had, perhaps, seen enough of the interior; and possibly after a few conversations he thought that we relied too much on the arms of flesh – sword and gun.'

18   R.F. Burton, *Zanzibar,*i, p.59.

19   J.H. Speke, *What Led*, p.166.

20   See J. Thomson, *Through Masai Land. A Journey of Exploration among the Snowclad Volcanic Mountains and Strange Tribes of Eastern Equatorial Africa* (London, 1885); also R. Coupland, *East Africa and its Invaders* (Oxford, 1938), pp.343 and 357.

21   *Ibid*., pp.166-7.

22   R.B. Burton, *Zanzibar*, i, pp.154-55.

23   *Ibid*., p.175.

24   *Ibid*., pp.179-80.

25   J.H. Speke, *What Led*, p.186. For an account of the native Africans who accompanied explorers such as Burton, Speke, Livingstone, Stanley and Cameron, see D. Simpson, *Dark Companions* (London, 1975) In 1864 the RGS awarded a silver medal to Bombay, and conferred a life pension on him of £15 a year, when he was paid off on 22 August 1876. He died at Zanzibar on 12 October 1885.

26   R.F. Burton, *Zanzibar*, p.214.

27   *Ibid*., p.217.

28   Quoted in R. Lewis and Y. Foy, *The British in Africa* (London, 1971), p.49.

29   See H.H. Scott, *A History of Tropical Medicine* (London, 1938), p.124 et seq, and P.D. Curtin, *The Image of Africa* (Madison, 1964), p.71 et seq.

30   R.F. Burton, *Zanzibar*, p.257.

31   *Ibid*., p.258.

Notes to Chapter 20

1   F. Galton, *Memories of my Life* (London, 1908), p.200, wrote of Burton's having offered him the full use of his original notebook written when in Zanzibar, for the purpose of a lecture to the Society for the Propagation of the Gospel. 'The notes made by Burton were written in a fine clear hand and most elaborate in detail. He told me that he often used a board with parallel wires....to write notes, unseen, in the night-time.'

2   'A Coasting Voyage from Mombasa to the Pangani River; Visit to Sultan Kimwere; and Progress of the Expedition into the Interior.' By Captain Richard F Burton....and J.H. Speke.....*JRGS* 28 (1858), Part 1, pp.188-202 [map]. Part II, pp.202-220. Part III, pp.220-6. Also Notes from the Journal of the East African Expedition, under the command of Captain Richard F Burton [*A letter from Zanzibar, dated 22 April 1857*]. *Proceedings of the RGS*, Vol.II, 1857, pp.52-6. Discussion, pp.56-8; Burton, Captain, 'Zanzibar; and two months in East Africa,' *Blackwood's Magazine*, No.DVIII, Vol.LXXXIII, Feb, 1858, pp.200-24, March, pp.276-90, May, pp.572-89. Burton had been introduced to John Blackwood by 'a good friend,' Laurence Oliphant, some time in September 1856. See NLS: MS 4115, ff 155-6, and NLS: MS 4119, f 39.

3   J.H. Speke, *What Led to the Discovery of the Source of the Nile* (London, 1864), p.189.

4   RGS Archives, Back Collection. Burton to Sir George Back, British Consulate, Zanzibar, 9 April 1857.

5   R.F. Burton, *The Lake Regions of Central Africa* (London, 1860), pp.5-6. Burton wrote in similar vein to the RGS, in his letter of 22 April 1857, adding that, 'Messrs. Krapf and Erhardt, of the Mombas Mission, spent a few hours in Kilwa, where they were civilly received by the governor and citizens, but they were sadly deceived in being led to imagine that they could make that port their starting-point. We shall probably land at Bagomoyo.'

6   R.F. Burton, *Zanzibar*, ii, pp. 265-66.

7   RGS Archives, Speke to Shaw, Zanzibar Consulate, 20 May 1857.

8   QK Coll, Speke to Mrs Georgina Speke, c. late May 1857.

9   Speke to C.P. Rigby, Kinanga Ranga, 6 Oct 1860, cited in C.E.B. Russell, *General Rigby, Zanzibar and the Slave Trade* (London, 1935), p.235.

10   *The Life*, i, p.281. There are two further versions. See *JRGS XXIX* (1859), p.8, where Burton adds that Dr Steinhaeuser found it difficult to obtain a passage from Aden to Zanzibar during the south-west monsoon. A third version, casting Steinhaeuser in an heroic light in which, despite the odds, he allegedly crossed the Straits to

Berbera with the intention of marching down country to join the expedition, appears in Burton's *Zanzibar*, i, pp.13-14, which was dedicated to Steinhaeuser's memory.

11   OIOC, Bombay Army Lists, L/MIL/12/85.

12   R.F. Burton, *The Lake Regions*, i, p.25.

13   *Ibid.*, p.3. Burton also stated in his *JRGS* account that Hamerton 'deemed it his duty' to accompany them. However, in his *Zanzibar*, ii, p.286, he claimed that the Consul came along at his suggestion.

14   *The Life*, i, p.278.

15   See D.B. Barrett (ed.), *World Christian Encyclopaedia* (OUP,1982), p.660. I have to thank Mary Matthewman, Secretary of the Catholic Missionary Union of England and Wales, for kindly directing my attention to this source, which confirmed my original doubts as to the truth of this particular quotation.

16   R.F. Burton, *Zanizibar*, ii, p.284.

17   *The Life*, ii, p.422.

18   R.F. Burton, *Zanzibar*, i, pp.5-6.

19   An account of this appears in the preface to Burton's *Zanzibar*, i, pp.ix-x.

20   *Ibid.*, p.361.

21   The disease, Nagana, is a form of tryanosomiasis, principally affecting cattle and horses, caused by several species of the protozoan Trypanosoma. The disease, which is endemic in Southern and Central Africa, is transmitted from animal to animal by tsetse flies. The symptoms of infection include fever, muscular wasting, anaemia, and swelling of tissues. There is also a discharge from the eyes and nose. The disease soon leads to paralysis of the hindlegs, and other parts of the body.

22   *The Lake Regions*, i, p.84.

23   *Ibid.*, pp.91-92.

24   *Ibid.*, pp.106-7.

25   See R. Oliver, *The African Experience*, revised edition (London, 1999), and S. Oppenheimer, *Out of Eden* (London, 2003).

26   R.F. Burton, *The Lake Regions*, i, p.166.

27   J.H. Speke, *What Led*, p.197.

28   See Henry M. Stanley, *How I Found Livingstone* (London, 1872), p.264, where he writes: 'Tabora is the principal Arab settlement in Central Africa.' In a footnote, obviously with Burton and Speke in mind, he pointed out that, 'There is no such recognised place as Kazeh.'

29   R.F. Burton, *The Lake Regions*, i, p.323.

30   This very important, but seemingly overlooked, remark, appeared first in Speke's article, 'The Upper Basin of the Nile, from Inspection and Information,' *JRGS* 33 (1863), p.322 [but not published until 1864]. It was then repeated in his *What Led*, 1864, p.198. However, it was omitted by Speke in his *Blackwood* articles of Sept and Oct, 1859, both of which included details of their stay at Kazeh on the outward and return journeys respectively.

31   RGS Archives, Speke to Shaw, Unyanyembe, 20 Nov 1857.

32   R.F. Burton, *The Lake Regions*, i, pp.388-9.

33   *Ibid.*, ii, p.41.

Notes to Chapter 21

1   J.H. Speke, *What Led*, p.231.

2   Primitive tools have been excavated from Kalamabo Gorge, dated by the radio-carbon method from 300,000 years BC.

3   The Ruzizi River, in fact, falls 2,000 feet on its way into Tanganyika from Lake Kiva.

4   This is taken from Speke's *Blackwood's* paper, No.DXVII, Vol.LXXXVI, Sept 1859, p.352. In his book, p.232, he continued, 'were it not that Dr. Livingstone has determined the level of Lake Nyassa to be very nearly the same as this lake.'

5   J.H. Speke. *What Led*, p.245.

6   *The Life*, i, p.308.

7   J.H. Speke, *What Led*, pp.250-1.

8   NLS, Grant Collection, Speke to Rigby, Duthumi, 22 Oct 1860.

9   *The Life*,i, p.308. J.N. Burton died at his home in Bath, aged 74. The death certificate gives the cause of death as 'Paralysis. 10 Weeks.' He was interred with his late wife, Martha, in Walcot Cemetery, on 10 Sept 1857.

10   RGS Archives, Burton to Shaw, Unyanyembe, Central Africa, 24 June 1858.

11   *Blackwood's Magazine*, Vol.LXXXVI, Oct, 1859, Part II, p.393.

12   Published in the *Proceedings of the Royal Geographical Society*, 24 Jan 1859.

13   RGS Archives, Letter Book. Sir Roderick Murchison to the Earl of Malmesbury, 30 June 1858. Murchison was President from 1856-59, his third time in that office.

14   The letter to Burton is from H.L. Anderson, Secretary to Government, and dated Bombay Castle, 23 July 1857. His reply, is dated Unyanyembe., 24 June 1858. Both are printed in *The Life*, ii, Appendix F, pp.565-6

15   RGS Archives, Speke to Shaw, 2 July 1858. There are two further letters of this date from Speke to Shaw, which are of a more technical nature.

16   J.H. Speke, *What Led*, pp.307-8.

17   *Blackwood's Magazine*, Part III, Oct, 1859, p.395.

18   J.H. Speke, *What Led*, p.370.

19   *The Life*, i, p.315.

20   *Ibid.*, p.322.

21   I owe this diagnosis of the probable cause of Speke's illness to A.J. Duggan, former Director of, what was then known as, the Wellcome Museum of Medical Science, London. 'The modern work of George Nelson and others,' he wrote in a letter, ' has emphasised the clinical manifestations of trichinosis in eastern Africa. These well-known symptoms explain the nightmares which are often associated with toxic delirium, the severe pain in his sides, the spasms of jaws, imitating hydrophobia, the barking note in his voice and changed appearance.'

22   *The Life*, p.322. Naturally, these disclosures made during Speke's delirium were not reproduced in *The Lake Regions*. In 1862 Speke wrote a letter to A.H. Layard, then on the Council of the RGS, accusing Burton, presumably around this time, of having tried to poison him. Bombay, who was supposed to have administered it in Speke's medicine, failed to do so because of his close attachment to the explorer. QK Coll, J. Grant to S. Baker, 26 June 1890. Grant believed that 'Burton felt so sore at Speke's discovery of the Vic. Nyanza that he tried to get rid of him by poison and claim the discovery himself....' It is strange, however, that Speke did not mention this allegation to Grant in 1862, nor to his close confidant, C.P. Rigby, to whom he wrote in every letter of Burton's supposed villainies.

23   QK Coll, draft letter in letter-book to N.I. Andrews, Esq, Sec to the Bombay Govt, Ugogi, Eastern Africa, 7 December 1858. Its untidier than usual handwriting , together with numerous crossings out and edits, suggest that it was written with some difficulty.

24   RGS Archives, Letter Book. Shaw to Mrs Speke, 18 Dec 1858. Lord Malmesbury's instructions giving them permission to draw on a further £250, arrived too late to affect what later happened at Zanzibar with respect to paying the personnel of the Expedition.

25   *The Life*, p.321.

26   R.F. Burton, *Zanzibar*, ii, pp.329-70, contains his account of the abortive visit to Kilwa.

27   See *Ibid.*, pp.332-3. The young German scientist was later murdered by two of his African followers. Their execution at Zanzibar was witnessed by Speke's companion, Captain Grant, on 23 August 1860.

28   C.E.B. Russell, *General Rigby, Zanzibar and the Slave Trade* (London, 1935), p.270. Rigby's observations about Burton are contained in a letter from the Zanzibar Consulate of 16 Nov 1860, to H.L. Anderson, Chief Secretary to Government, Bombay.

29   C.E.B. Russell, *General Rigby*, pp.229-30.

30   FO List, 1868.

31   C.E.B. Russell, *General Rigby*, p.247n.

32   See N.R. Bennett, *A History of the Arab State of Zanzibar* (London, 1978), p.60 et seq. According to K. Ingham, *A History of East Africa* (London, 1963), p.80, the French Consul admitted to Rigby that 'France was already negoti-ating with Thwain, and that his seizure of the Zanzibar Government would meet with French approval.'

33   C.E.B. Russell, p.243n. Undated letter to J. Miles.

34   In *Zanzibar,* ii, p.389, however, Burton wrote that Speke 'showed a nervous hurry to hasten home, although we found upon the Island that *our leave had been prolonged by the Bombay Government.*' [my italics]

35   R.F. Burton, *The Lake Regions,* ii, pp. 381-2.

36   RGS Archives, Burton to Shaw, Aden, 19 April 1859.

37   C.E.B. Russell, *General Rigby*, pp.266-7. Speke wrote a further letter to Rigby on the same subject, four days after arriving at Aden.

38   R.F. Burton, *Zanzibar,* ii, p.389.

Notes to Chapter 22

1   R.F. Burton, *The Lake Regions,* i, p.ix.

2   In fact, it was two days after his return. Burton copied from Speke, who made the initial mistake in *Blackwood's Magazine*, No.DXXV, Vol.LXVIII, May, 1860, p.561. It was then repeated in Speke's *Journal of the Discovery of the Nile* (London, 1863), p.1.

3   R.F. Burton & J. M'Queen, *The Nile Basin* (London, 1864), pp.7-8.

4   R.F. Burton, *Zanzibar,* ii, p. 390.

5   *The Times*, 28 Oct 1891. Grant's letter is reproduced in *The Life,* ii, pp.421-2.

6   *The Life*, pp.424-5. In a footnote to p.425, Isabel claimed that, 'Speke told me of this, and after his death I taxed Laurence Oliphant with it, who said so simply, "Forgive me –I am sorry – I did not know what I was doing." I could not say another word; but Richard and he were friends after that.'

7   J.H. Speke, *What Led*, pp.326-7. In his *Blackwood's* article, May 1860, p.561, Speke wrote, 'It is strange that on being obliged to abandon the prosecution of my discovery of the lake, I had made up my mind to return there again as soon as I could obtain permission to do so…then little suspecting that so much importance would be attached to it by the great geographers of Great Britain.'

8   J.H. Speke, *Journal*, pp.1-2. In what he must have regarded as sweet revenge, given Burton's later public disparage-ment of his surveying skills, Speke, in a footnote to p.2, quoted Burton's praise of them at the RGS medal ceremony in 1859.

9   A. Taylor, *Laurence Oliphant* (Oxford, 1982), p.67. The author quotes no source for this statement. A search by J.R. Elliott, Area Librarian, Plymouth, of the *Plymouth and Devonport Weekly Journal*, the *Plymouth, Devonport and Stonehouse Herald*, and *The Times*, failed to find mention of any such arrival. Speke's biographer, Alexander Maitland, *Speke* (London, 1971), pp.94-5, describes the *Furious* arriving at Southampton, although the Suez Canal was not opened until ten years later.

10   RGS Archives, Speke to Shaw, Hatchett's Hotel, Piccadilly, London, 8 May 1859. Presumably, Oliphant had alerted Shaw to Speke's being in London.

11   RGS Archives, Autograph MS: Sir C.R. Markham, *Fifty Years Work of the Royal Geographical Society*. Markham (1830-1916) served in the Royal Navy from 1844-51, taking part in the search for Sir John Franklin. In 1853 he entered the civil service, and from 1867-1877 was in charge of the geographical work of the India Office. He was PRGS from 1893-1905, becoming a KCB in 1896.

12   *Proceedings of the Royal Geographical Society of London*, Session 1858-59, pp.210-13.

13   Described in *The Times*, Saturday, 21 May 1859, p.10, as 'Captain Burton, the celebrated traveller, who has made some wonderful discoveries in the interior of Africa.'

14   R.F. Burton, *Zanzibar,* ii, p.391.

15   RGS Archives, Speke to Shaw, 3 Park St, Grosvenor Sq, 19 May 1859.

16   *The Romance*, p.145. In Jewish esoteric thought, the letters of the Hebrew alphabet are regarded as providing the

key to understanding the Torah. *Lamed*, the twelfth letter, stands for 'study'. According to Otiot de-Rabbi Akiva, the letter alludes to the heart, the source of wisdom in man, and the king of all his other organs. See M. Glazerson, *Letters of Fire*, trans S. Fuchs (Jerusalem & New York, 1991), pp. 14 & 49. Many years later, Isabel labelled two private books containing her last wishes with the first and second letters of the Hebrew alphabet. Whether she was conscious of their mystic significance is, of course, a moot point.

17 See 'Brave sisters who built a fine school,' *Eastern Evening News*, Norwich, 2 Oct 1989. Additional corroborative evidence was sent to me by Sister Mary, Headteacher of Notre Dame High School.

18 *The Life*, i, p.330. Burton, as we have seen, had landed two days earlier.

19 'Presentation of the Royal Awards,' *JRGS* 29 (1859), p.xcv.

20 *Ibid.*, p.xcvii.

21 *Ibid.*, p.clxxxii.

22 *The Times*, 24 May 1859.

23 RGS Archives, Report of the ad hoc Expedition Sub-Committee, 21 June 1859. Read and confirmed at a meeting of the Expedition Committee on 3 December 1859. According to Francis Galton, *Memories Of My Life* (London, 1908), p.172, 'Laurence Oliphant had a most winning manner and a marvellous facility of expression. I have served on more Council Meetings than could be easily reckoned, and am only too familiar with the often recurring difficulty of finding a phrase that shall cover just as much of the question under discussion as is generally accepted. Oliphant had the art of hitting upon the appropriate phrase on these occasions more deftly and aptly than anyone else I can remember. We worked together most pleasantly as joint secretaries under the presidency of John Crawfurd, the Ethnologist, who nicknamed us his two sons.'

24 G.Stisted, 'Reminiscences of Sir Richard Burton,' *Temple Bar*, Vol.92, May-July, 1891, pp.337-8.

25 The Lake Regions of Central Equatorial Africa, with Notices of the Lunar Mountains and the Sources of the White Nile; being the results of an Expedition undertaken under the patronage of Her Majesty's Government and the Royal Geographical Society of London, in the years 1857-1859. *JRGS* 29 (1859), pp.1- 464.

26 RGS Archives, Burton to Galton, 6 August 1859, 11 Marine Parade, Dover.

27 T.W. Reid, *The Life and Letters of Richard Monckton Milnes, First Lord Houghton* (London, 1891), p.454.

28 NLS, Grant Collection, MS 17910: Speke to Rigby, addressed as from Jordans, 3 Sept 1859.

29 See A. Warwick, *The Phoenix Suburb, A South London Social History* (London, 1972). According to Warwick, p.70, 'the grounds and buildings were sold by auction in 1858, and part of the land was built over.' It is evident, however, that whatever else happened, the Hydropathic Institute remained open, since Burton was using it in 1860.

30 NLS, Grant Collection, Speke to Rigby, Jordans, 17 Oct 1859.

31 RGS Archives, Speke to Shaw, Jordans, Sunday, undated, but arrived 28 Oct 1959.

32 R.F. Burton, *Zanzibar*, ii, p.392.

33 *The Life*,i, pp.332-337.

34 The word agnostic was 'Suggested by Professor Huxley at a party held previous to the formation of the now defunct Metaphysical Society, at Mr. James Knowles's house on Clapham Common, one evening in 1869, in my hearing. He took it from St. Paul's mention of the altar to 'the Unknown God.' R.H. Hutton in letter 13 March, 1881. Quoted in the *OED*, 2nd edn (Oxford, 1989), Vol.1, p.260. However, according to Huxley himself, the term *agnostic* "came into my head as suggestively antithetic to the 'gnostic' of Church history, who professed to know so much about the very things of which I was ignorant." Quoted in B. Lightman, *The Origins of Agnosticism* (Baltimore & London, 1987), p.12.

35 My own opinion is, that it was written by Isabel at a much later date especially for inclusion in her biography of Burton. The term *agnostic* appeared for the first time in print in R.H. Hutton, 'The Theological Statute at Oxford,' *The Spectator*, 42, 29 May 1869, p. 642. Thereafter, followed Huxley's *Lay Sermons, Addresses, and Reviews* in 1870, Leslie Stephen's *Essays on Freethinking and Plainspeaking* in 1873, and John Tyndall's highly controversial, 'Belfast Address,' in 1874. Two years later, Stephens used his essay, 'An Agnostic's Apology,' to justify the use of the term *agnostic* 'as an appropriate response to the bankruptcy of Christian orthodoxy.' B. Lightman, *The Origins of Agnosticism*, p.93. This was the year when Burton began first dictating his autobiography to Isabel on their voyage to India.

36 T. Cosmo Melvill to Captain R. Burton, India Office, E.C. 8 Nov 1859. This is the first letter in Appendix II, headed 'Second Correspondence,' of Burton's *Lake Regions* (London, 1860), ii, pp.430-1. The whole Appendix was transcribed in *The Life*, ii, Appendix F, pp.567-74, and provocatively headed 'Letters bearing on Speke and Rigby's Cabal.'

37 NLS, Grant Collection, Speke to Rigby, 3 Sept 1859; *Ibid.*, Jordans, 17 Oct 1859.

38 Capt Rigby, HM's Consul and British Agent, Zanzibar, 15 July 1859, to H.L. Anderson, Sec to Govt, Political Dept, Bombay, No.70 of 1859, *Lake Regions*, pp.431-34

39 C.E.B. Russell, *General Rigby*, p.249.

40 Capt R.F. Burton to T. Cosmo Melvill, East India United Service Club, St James's Sq, 11 Nov 1859. *Ibid.*, pp.434-9

41 RGS Archives, Burton to Shaw. Addressed from EIUSC, Friday morning, but with no specific date. Recd. Nov 1859.

42 NLS, Grant Collection, Speke to Rigby, 25 Nov 1859.

43 'J.H. Speke to Under-Secretary of State for India,' Jordans, Ilminster, 1 Dec 1859. Quoted in C.E.B. Russell, *General Rigby*, pp.249-55.

44 RGS Archives, Expedition Committee Meeting, 2 Dec 1859. Committee Minute Book. The rest of the Committee consisted of Sir Roderick Murchison, Mr Arrowsmith, L. Oliphant, and Dr Shaw.

45 RGS Archives, Committee Minute Book, 10 Jan 1860.

46 T. Cosmo Melvill to Captain R.F. Burton, India Office, 14 Jan 1860. Quoted in *Lake Regions*, ii, pp.439-440

47 *Ibid.*, pp.440-441. Unlike his letter from the EIUSC of 11 Nov 1859, this letter is reproduced in the *Lake Regions* without any date or address. In *The Life*, ii, p.574, it is dated as "January, 1860," so it must have been written in Boulogne.

48 TCC, Burton to Milnes, Boulogne, 22 Jan 1860.

49 See J.Pope-Hennessy, *Monckton Milnes, The Flight of Youth, 1851-85* (London, 1951), pp.121-22.

50 *Ibid.*, p.120.

51 TCC. The court hearing of Beatson's libel-suit was held at Nisi Prius, Westminster, on Friday and Saturday, Jan 13-14 1860, before Baron Bramwell and a special jury. The case was reported in *The Times* on Saturday and the following Monday. Burton's evidence is to be found in the Saturday issue, p.11. Speke, who obviously followed the case, remarked in a short note to Shaw just before leaving for Jordans on the Monday, 'How very elegantly both Beatson and Burton have come out in the court!!

52 There are two long letters in the QK Coll from Speke to Burton. The first is dated 17 June, the other 20 June 1859. Both are on the vexed question of the money owed to Burton, who had written that, 'the sooner this affair is settled the better.' In his turn, Speke wrote that, 'Taking this affair in an £. s. d. point of view I must say that your importunate demand has rather surprised me.'

53 QK Coll, Burton to Speke, an undated draft written on lined jotter paper.

54 TCC, Burton to Milnes, Hotel de Paris, Boulogne. 10 Feb 1860.

55 RGS Archives, Burton to Shaw, Hotel de Paris, Boulogne, 16 Feb 1860.

56 RGS Archives, Burton to Shaw, 16 March, no address given; probably EIUSC.

57 RGS Archives, Burton to Shaw, EIUSC, 21 March 1860.

58 OIOC, L/P & S/3/140, Draft Minute, Political Dept, India House.

59 See the Society's Bulletin, 'Assemblée générale du 20 Avril 1860,' pp.438-9. It is noteworthy that Burton makes no reference to this award in his correspondence with the RGS. A French résumé of *The Lake Regions of Central Africa*, appeared in 1860, and a complete reprint of the work two years later. For details, see N.M. Penzer, *An Annotated Bibliography*, p.68.

Notes to Chapter 23

1 N. Hawthorne, *Our Old Home* (London, 1863), i, p.11.

2 Known initially as the Church of Christ, its name was changed in May 1834 to Church of the Latter-day Saints,

and four years later to Church of Jesus Christ of Latter-day Saints, the official title by which it has been known ever since.

3 L. Arrington, *Brigham Young: American Moses* (New York, 1985), p.48.

4 Named from the Book of Mormon, which was first published in 1830 in Palmyra, New York. It is regarded by members of the Church of Jesus Christ of Latter-day Saints as divinely inspired, having been revealed to and translated by Joseph Smith.

5 Brigham Young, "History," *Deseret News*, 10 March 1858. The first number of *The Millenial Star*, which went on to have a circulation of 20,000, was printed at Manchester. It was issued monthly from May 1840, fortnightly from June 1845, and weekly from April 1852. It contained articles on doctrines, reports on conferences and missionary activities, instructions to emigrants, etc. Published at Liverpool were: Joseph Smith, *The Book of Mormon*, 1st European edn, 1841; *Doctrines and Covenants*, 1st European edn, 1845; *Journal of Discourses*, Reports of addresses by Brigham Young and other leaders, printed for the British Mission, 26 vols, 1854-86. See R.F. Burton, *The City of the Saints* (London, 1861), p.258ff.

6 *Ibid.*, pp.359-60.

7 In the preamble to the legislative act incorporating the Perpetual Emigrating Fund, it stated: 'Labor and industry is wealth, and all kinds of mechanics and laborers are requisite for building and attending the benefits of civilized society, subduing the soil, and otherwise developing the resources of a new country.' Cited in L. Arrington, *Great Basin Kingdom. An Economic History of the Latter-day Saints, 1830-90* (Cambridge, Mass, 1958), p.97.

8 Three sorts of companies were set up under the scheme: (i) PE Companies which provided a full subsidy for those too poor to pay their own way from Europe to the Salt Lake Valley. After arrival, they were expected to pay back some of the money to the Fund; (ii) Ten Pound Companies, for those who could afford that sum as part payment towards the full cost of their travel; (iii) Cash Emigrant Companies, comprising those able to afford the full cost of their transportation. See L. Arrington, *Great Basin Kingdom*, pp.97-99.

9 There were 32,894 Mormons in England in 1851, and 29,442 in 1854. See P.A.M. Taylor, 'Mormon Emigration to the United States,' unpub PhD thesis, University of Cambridge, 1950, pp.69-70. This was later published under the title, *Expectations Westward, The Mormons and the Emigration of their British Converts in the Nineteenth Century* (Edinburgh & London, 1965).

10 *The Times*, 3 June 1857, p.8. 'According to the calculation of Mr Carvalho,' it wrote, 'who was the companion of Colonel Fremont on his journey over the Rocky Mountains in 1835, and spent several weeks among the Mormons, nine-tenths of the population were the peasantry of Scotland, England and Wales.'

11 *The Times*, 4 Sept 1855, p.5.

12 WH Wilkins (ed.), *The Jew, the Gypsy and El Islam* (London, 1898), p.345.

13 *The Edinburgh Review*, April 1854, Vol.XCIX, No.CCII, p.382. The article is cited in R.F. Burton, *The City of the Saints*, p.253, where he remarks that it was reprinted 'in 112 pages, 121 mo., by Messrs Longmans, London, 1854.'

14 H.A. Murray, *Lands of the Slave and the Free, or Cuba, the United States and Canada* (London, 1855), i, p.201. In a footnote to p.212, Murray wrote: 'The doctrines of this community will be found in the Appendix A.' Murray probably learned of Horace Mann's Report from Conybeare's *Edinburgh Review* article, where it is cited in a footnote to p.376.

15 With regard to drink, the word, according to the *OED*, is used in two opposite senses: (i) sober. Now only Scottish; (ii) exhilarated by drink; partially intoxicated; half seas over.

16 NLS MS, 4154, f.9. Speke to Blackwood, 27 March 1860.

17 C.E.B. Russell, *General Rigby and the Slave Trade* (London, 1935), p.236; Speke to Rigby, Kinanga Ranga, 6 Oct 1860.

18 R.F. Burton, *Zanzibar; City, Island and Coast* (London, 1872), i, p.14. There is no record of service for Steinhaueser after 1860 included in the series, OIOC, L/MIL/12/88-101, Bombay Services, 1860-92. However, the Bombay Service Lists shows that he was on sick-leave to Europe from 15 Sept 1859, and throughout 1860.

19 The donor was a Mrs Evelyn Lindermann Letchford, related by marriage to Daisy Letchford, later Mrs Nicastro. Unfortunately, there is no further record of the provenance of the fragment, then classed as Brit Mus (now Brit

Lib) Add MS 49380L.

20 There is a page of an undated auction catalogue in the Quentin Keynes Collection, announcing the sale of an 'Autograph manuscript, a portion of a narrative of Burton's voyage to North America in 1860, *16 pp., 12 mo., lacking fol.22, text broken at beginning and at end*, foliated 8 to 24, with corrections and revisions, some written on blank versos........' What connection, if any, this has with the Brit Lib Add MS 49380L, is unclear.

21 According to the Bank of England's equivalent contemporary values of the pound, £300 in 1860 had the purchasing power of £13,161 as of June 2000.

22 He first appears in Chapter 27, 'Samuel Weller makes a Pilgrimage to Dorking, and beholds his Mother-in-law.'

23 F.M. Brodie, *The Devil Drives*, p.180.

24 M.S. Lovell, *A Rage to Live*, p.344. There is, of course, no evidence that he ever did so.

25 R.F. Burton, *Camoens: His Life and his Lusiads – A Commentary* (London, 1881), i, p.46.

26 R.F. Burton, *The Thousand Nights and One Night* (London, 1885), ii, p.234.

27 Quoted in R.F. Burton, *Gelele, King of Dahomey* (London, 1864), ii, p.186. His visit there is misdated as 1859.

28 For examples of the memorabilia, see A.H. Jutzi, Burton and his Library in, *In Search of Sir Richard Burton. Papers from a Huntington Library Symposium* (San Marino, California, 1993), pp.85-106.

29 *The Life* (London, 1893), i, p.26.

30 See R.F. Burton, *Two Trips to Gorilla Land and the Cataracts of the Congo* (London, 1876). i, p.243.

31 R.F. Burton, *The City of the Saints*, p.539.

32 I have accepted the distance given by Mark Twain, *Life on the Mississippi* (London, 1914), p.171. In 1860 the author, known by his real name as Samuel Clemens, was a licensed steamboat pilot. It is described as a '700 mile trip' in L.J. Arrington, *Great Basin Kingdom* (Cambridge, Mass, 1958), p.104.

33 See H. Parker and F.C. Bowen, *Mail and Passenger Steamships of the Nineteenth Century* (London, 1928), p.241.

34 The Hon Henry A. Murray, *Lands of the Slave and the Free* (London, 1855), i, p.213.

35 R.L. Stevenson, *Across the Plains with other Memories and Essays* (London, 1892), pp.40-41.

36 R.F. Burton, *The City of the Saints*, p.76.

37 See J.A. Hawgood, *The American West* (London, 1967), p.240, and R.A. Billington, *Westward Expansion. A History of the American Frontier* (New York, 1949), pp.637-8.

38 R.F. Burton, *The City of the Saints*, p.73.

39 The probable source for these signs, on pp.150-161, is Major S.H. Long, 'The Indian Language of Signs,' in *Expedition to the Rocky Mountains* (1823), i, pp.378-94, where the author gives 104 examples.

40 R.F. Burton, *Abeokuta and the Camaroons Mountains* (London, 1863), ii, p.109.

41 W. Chandless, *A Visit to Salt Lake City* (London, 1857), p.108. Chandless's description of South Pass was largely copied by Burton, who made adaptations here and there. For example, 'a field of battle large enough for all the armies of the world,' became in Burton, p.201, 'upon whose iron surface there is space enough for the armies of the globe to march over....'

42 L.J. Arrington and D. Bitton, *The Mormon Experience. A History of the Latter-Day Saints* (London, 1979), p.101.

43 R.F. Burton, *The City of the Saints*, p.240.

44 *Ibid.*, p.249.

45 See L.J. Arrington, *Great Basin Kingdom*, pp.211-12.

46 Mrs T.B.H. Stenhouse, *An Englishwoman in Utah* (London, 1880), p.73.

47 Her husband published *The Rocky Mountain Saints; A Full and Complete History of the Mormons* (New York, 1873). He died, aged fifty-seven, in 1882.

48 R.F. Burton, *The City of the Saints*, p.293.

49 *Ibid.*, p.300.

50 J. Remy and J. Brenchley, *A Journey to Great Salt-Lake City* (London, 1861), i, p.213.

51 *Ibid.*, p.201.

52 R.F. Burton, *The City of the Saints*, p.523.

53 Mrs T.B.H. Stenhouse, *An Englishwoman in Utah*, p.181.

54 Quoted in G.C. Ward, *The West. An Illustrated History* (London, 1999), p.269.

55 There is a copy of the fourth European edition, 1854, in the Burton Library at Huntington, California, Kirkpatrick Catalogue No.1237, p.81.

56 M. Twain, *Roughing It and the Innocents at Home* (London,1885), p.87.

57 J. Remy and J. Brenchley, *A Journey to Great Salt-Lake City*, i, p.463n.

58 *Ibid.*, p.494.

59 R.F. Burton, *The City of the Saints*, pp.411-413.

60 The best documented account is by the late and courageous Mormon historian, J. Brooks, *The Mountain Meadows Massacre* (Stanford, 1950).

61 W. Chandless, *A Visit to Salt Lake City*, p.238.

62 The letter, which is no longer extant in the RGS archives, appeared in the *Proceedings of the Royal Geographical Society*, Vol.V, 1860-1, 12 Nov 1860, pp. [I], 2. It was printed in *The Times*, 14 Nov 1860, and later in *The Life*, i, pp.338-9. Isabel omitted Burton's comment that the letter, 'gave rise to a great deal of laughter amongst the audience.'

63 The election of Abraham Lincoln as President on 6 November 1860, provoked the Southern states to secede from the Union, and led to four tragic years of civil war.

Notes to Chapter 24

1   There is a lavishly illustrated article on the house in *Country Life*, 26 Jan 1907, pp.126-33.

2   *The Times*, 28 Dec 1860, p.8, col.3.

3   R.F. Burton, *The City of the Saints, and Across the Rocky Mountains to California* (London, 1861), p.606.

4   M.S. Lovell, *A Rage to Live*, p.357, attempts to get round this difficulty by supposing that the paper was opened to page 7, with the further implication that this item was not covered by the sheet music, and that Isabel was close enough to read it.

5   M. Hastings, *Sir Richard Burton* (London, 1978), p.137. Farwell, Brodie and McLynn solve the problem by ignoring it. M.S. Lovell, *A Rage to Live*, p.358, suggests that Isabel 'persuaded a servant to travel to the telegraph office in Hull from where a telegram could be delivered to the house within hours.'

6   This matter was kindly investigated for me by Martin T. Craven, co-author with J.A. Fowler of *Postal History of Kingston upon Hull, Hedon and Holderness* (Yorkshire Postal History Society, 1974). In a letter to me, Mr Craven wrote, '....we have a clear reference to a telegraph office in 1872. My belief is that the facility was introduced at Hull around 1870.'

7   *The Life*, i, p.340.

8   Wiseman had moved from old premises in Golden Square to 8 York Place in 1855, a couple of months after the Bagshaws left No. 9 for Dovercourt in Essex.

9   Quoted in W.Ward, *The Life and Times of Cardinal Wiseman* (London, 1897), ii, p.189.

10 *Ibid.*, i, p.89, 'He can speak with readiness and point,' wrote Cardinal Newman,...... 'in half a dozen languages, without being detected by a foreigner in any of them, and at ten minutes' notice can address a congregation from a French pulpit or the select audience of an Italian academy.'

11 Information from Mgr Ralph Brown, Vicar-General, Archbishop's House, Westminster, London. 'Quinquennial faculties' was the term used for the authority granted by Rome to local bishops on a five year basis, allowing them to dispense various canonical permissions without having further recourse to Rome.

12 *The Romance*, p.161

13 *Ibid.*, pp.162-4.

14 Burton to Rigby, 14 St James's Sq, 16 Jan 1861. See *The Life*, ii, pp.575-6. Unfortunately, Rigby's letter to Shaw is not extant in the archives of the RGS.

15 R.L. Playfair, *A History of Arabia Felix or Yemen* (Bombay, 1859), Supplementary Chapter, Expedition to the Somali Country, pp.176-7.

16 R.F. Burton, *The Lake Regions of Central Africa* (London, 1860), i, pp.67-8. In this passage, Burton mentioned no

names, although it was clear to whom he was referring. Later, in his *Zanzibar*, i, p.9, where he brought up the matter again, he was more specific, writing of 'the apathy of the highest political authority – the Resident at Aden, Brigadier Coghlan – and the active jealousy of his assistant, Captain Playfair….', omitting, however, any mention of Sir James Outram who, by this date, was dead.

17 OIOC, Bombay Political Consultations, P/397/17, Vol.CCCXCVII. Letter dated 25 Aug 1860.

18 This claim is open to challenge.

19 OIOC, Bombay Public Consultations, P/397/17, Resolution of the Hon Board, 11 Sept 1860.

20 NLS, MS 4154, Speke to Blackwood, Bagomoyo, 1 Oct 1860.

21 Derived from the London Post Office Directory, years 1857 and 1861. Isabel did not disclose the Birds' address, writing in *The Life*, i, p.342, 'and drove to a friend's house (Dr. and Miss Bird, now of 49 Welbeck Street)…' The Birds did not move to this address until some time later in 1861. It is incorrectly given in *The Romance*, p.167n, and has been copied by every biographer since.

22 The church is now known as the Church of Our Lady of the Assumption & of St Gregory. For a short history with a brief guide for visitors, see R.C. Fuller, *Warwick Street Church* (London, 1973). There is also a board affixed to the wall of the church, giving details.

23 *The True Life* p.274.

24 The unmarked, original letter, written on wafer-thin paper and framed together with a copy, forms part of the Burton Collection, OHG. There is a letter at the WSRO, 2/XVI/1-110, to Lady Burton from George Etheridge of Chapman and Hall, dated 21 April 1893, in which he says, among other things, 'To me there appears no difficulty in taking out "Bury Street." It was, therefore, expunged by the simple expedient of dropping a blob of ink over the word 'Bury'. This is how it appears in volume 1 of *The Life*, between pp.342-3. The letter is omitted by Wilkins in *The Romance*.

25 *The True Life*, p.274. Burton, of course, at the date of his marriage, was two months short of his fortieth birthday.

26 T. Wright, *The Life of Sir Richard Burton* (London, 1906), i, p.166.

27 *The Romance*, p.177.

28 *The Life*, i, p.343.

29 G. Stisted, 'Reminiscences of Sir Richard Burton,' *Temple Bar*, Vol. 92, May-July, 1891, p.338.

30 *The True Life*, p.275.

31 *The Romance*, p.174.

32 *Ibid.*, p.275. Burton, of course, was not on half-pay, but on sick pay.

33 T.Wright, *The Life of Sir Richard Burton*, i, p.161.

34 *Ibid.*, p.194.

35 TNA, PROB 11/2258, S. 732, 1857. In the Probate Act Book of 1857 (PROB 8/250), the value of Lt Col J.N. Burton's personal estate is given as one thousand pounds. There is also a marginal note which reads, 'Residue at Stamp Office, Jan. 1861, under £1500.' This note is clarified in the Death Duty entry for J.N. Burton, reference IR 26/2088 folio 914 (1857) which shows that his estate was registered for Death Duty tax in 1857, and was valued at £1,000. However, the entry states that between December 1860 – January 1861 further assets belonging to him were discovered, which increased the value of the estate to under £1,500, thus prolonging the settlement of the estate until January 1861.

36 *The Life*, i, p.344.

37 *The Romance*, p.176.

38 *Vanity Fair*, 26 August 1882, 'III. Amateur Consuls,' pp.122-3.

39 Burton wrote only one line of the sailor's ditty. I have added the second line from another source, which gives a clearer picture of its import.

40 TCC. Pat.Row = Paternoster Row, the London address, close to St Paul's Cathedral, of Stationers' Hall, the premises of the Stationers' and Newspaper Makers' Company, founded in 1403 and incorporated in 1557. Until the passing of the Copyright Bill of 1911, every work published in Britain had to be registered at Stationers' Hall.

41 TNA, 2/40, 18 April 1861. The dress code laid down for members of the Foreign Office and Diplomatic Service, and the Consular Service, and the occasions when it applied, was minutely detailed. In general terms, the full-dress

of a Consul consisted of a single-breasted coat of blue cloth, with Prussian collar and nine gilt buttons carrying the Royal Arms without supporters; a cocked hat; sword with French hilt, gilt wire grip and helmet top; breeches of white Kerseymere, to be worn with white silk stockings, shoes and gilt buckles, white neck-cloth, and white gloves. Similar rules applied to half-dress and undress. See FO List, 1866, 'Uniforms,' p.204.

42   Thomas Joseph Hutchinson had been senior surgeon on board the *Pleiad*, on the expedition to the rivers Niger, Tehadda and Benue in 1854-55. He became Consul at Fernando Po on 22 Nov 1855, his appointment being terminated on 6 June 1861. He was the author of several books and a fellow of four learned societies, including the RGS and the Ethnological Society.

43   TNA, FO 84/1164. In spite of Hutchinson's being cleared by the FO of bribery charges, he is misrepresented by K.Onwuka Diké, *Trade and Politics in the Niger Delta* (Oxford, 1956), p.123, who writes: 'Later it was revealed that the Consul had received bribes and had a vested interest in the trade.' This is also the case in M.Crowder, *The Story of Nigeria* (London, 1978), 4th rev edn, p.129, where he writes: 'three years later with evidence of Hutchinson's corruption mounting, it [ie the FO] ordered a commission of Enquiry into his conduct, as a result of which he was transferred.'

44   TNA, 84/1164. John Beecroft was a dominating figure during his period as Consul to the Bights of Benin and Biafra, 1849-54, meriting an entry in the *DNB*. A fuller account is to be found in an article by K.O. Diké, 'John Beecroft, 1790-1854,' *Journal of the Historical Society of Nigeria*, I, 1956, pp.5-14.

45   TNA, FO 84/1164.

46   The 1861 Census returns for 32 Oxford Square show in residence: Henry Arundell, Head, Eliza Arundell, Wife, Isabella Burton, dau., Rodolphe, son, Renfric, brother [inaccurately entered as 'son'], John Pigott, son-in-law, Blanche Pigott, dau., Cecil H. Pigott, visitor. There were also six servants in the house. Burton's name does not appear in any of the returns for Bury Street, which indicates that he was still living at Dovercourt.

47   R.F. Burton, *Zanzibar*, i, p.183.

48   See *The Athenaeum. Club and Social Life in London, 1824-1974* (London, 1979), and A. Lejeune, *The Gentlemen's Clubs of London* (London, 1979), p.39 *et seq.*

49   Burton was elected under the normal procedure of Rule III, ie not so much exceptional merit, as the necessary attainments required for membership. J. Burton, *Sir Richard Burton's Wife* (London, 1942), p.70, states, incorrectly, that Burton belonged to the Garrick, the Beefsteak, and the Arundel Clubs at this time. This has since been copied into other later biographies. Burton was never a member of the first and last, and became a member of the Beefsteak only on 3 July 1882.

50   *The Life*, i, pp.345-6

51   OIOC, L/MIL/3/1935, Despatch No.1071, 1861, Adjutant-General's Office, Headquarters, Bombay, 4 March 1861.

52   OIOC, L/MIL/3/2415, Military No.175, Sir Charles Wood to His Excellency the Honourable the Governor in Council, Bombay, India Office, London, 15 Nov 1861. This directive is noted in Abstract of Proceedings of the Government of India for the month of December 1861, Military Ref. P/366/4, Index No.3712.

53   E. Gosse, *The Life of Algernon Charles Swinburne* (London, 1917), p.121.

54   *The Life*, i, pp.344-5.

55   *The Times*, 20 June 1861, p.9.

56   *The Life*, p.345. The numerous fires that took place in London were regularly reported in *The Times*. Nevertheless, in spite of making an exhaustive search through the newspaper for the period concerned, I was unable to find any reference to one at Grindlays. A roughly contemporary directory shows that Grindlay & Co, who were then East India Company Agents, had three premises in London. Two of these were in the City, one in Cornhill and the other at Bishopsgate Within; the third was at St Martin's Place, Charing Cross. However, the first two buildings were offices, and the third a reading room. Unfortunately, the published history of Grindlay's, G.Tyson, *100 Years of Banking in Asia and Africa* (National and Grindlay's Bank Ltd, 1963), deals with matter outside the period and scope of my enquiries. The archives of Grindlay's Bank plc do not extend back over many years. I have also tried the Guildhall Library with a similar lack of success.

57   P.B. du Chaillu, *Explorations and Adventures in Equatorial Africa* (London, 1861).

58   *Ibid.*, pp.1-2.

59   *The Times,* 8 July 1861. Burton's letter was written from the EIUSC on 6 July. The newspaper had printed M. du Chaillu's public apology on the previous day.

60   TNA, FO 2/40, 1861.

61   Burton expressed a diametrically opposite view when writing from the Bonny River to the FO in 1864: 'My health having suffered from the last rainy season…I would again request your Lordship's permission to absent myself from the Island of Fernando Po during the wet months when the climate is thoroughly malarious.'

62   TNA, FO 2/40, 1861. Sir Ronald Martin was the East India Company's official physician.

63   *The Life,* ii, pp.576-7. Despite his threat, Burton did not take legal proceedings against Rigby, and the matter is never heard of again.

64   TCC, 23 August 1861.

65   *The Life*, pp.348-9.

Notes to Chapter 25

1   R.F. Burton, *Wanderings in West Africa* (London, 1863), i, p.175.

2   *Ibid.*, p.211

3   *Ibid.*, p.217.

4   The island is now known as Bioko. The Bubi people, however, call it Otcho.

5   Beecroft was HBM's Consul to the Bights if Benin and Biafra, 1849-54. The career of this remarkable man, who acquired immense influence and authority in this region during the 1840s and early 1850s, can be read in K.O. Dike, John Beecroft, 1790-1854, *Journal of the Historical Society of Nigeria*, I, 1956,

6   R.F. Burton, *Wanderings*, i, p.294. Burton passed himself off as the consul's companion, hence his use of 'our' instead of 'my.'

7   Present-day Malabo.

8   M.H. Kingsley, *Travels in West Africa* (London,1897), p.50.

9   R.F. Burton, *A Mission to Gelele, King of Dahomey* (London, 1864), i, p.10.

10   TCC, 26 April 1862.

11   TNA, FO 2/40, draft dated 8 Oct 1861.

12   TNA, FO 2/42, 22 May 1862. Burton furnished this description in response to a request by the Foreign Office.

13   The total is £194 17s 4d, plus the carpenter's expenses of £150. The signature appears to be that of Isaac Williams. Items include palings, planking, scantling, bamboo mats, thatching, ropes, nails, posts, rafters, tar, paint, brushes, turps, whitewash. Whether by oversight, or for some other reason, the estimate when neatly set out by Burton (or someone else) on the opposite page, totalled £322 12s 0d, giving the impression of there being two different estimates. This was picked up at the FO, and questioned.

14   One perambulator, wheel-barrow shaped, one Swedish patent jug, two barometers, two maximum & minimum thermometers, two chronometers.

15   TNA, FO 2/40, Russell to Burton 27 Dec 1861.

16   TNA, FO 2/42, 24 Dec 1862.

17   R.F. Burton, *Abeokuta and the Camaroons Mountains* (London, 1863), i, p.1.

18   TNA FO 84/1176, SlaveTrade Reports, Burton to Russell, Lagos, 20 Nov 1861.

19   R.F. Burton, *Abeokuta*, i, p.1.

20   See T. Jeal, *Livingstone* (London, 1973), p.141 *et al.* Bedingfield and M'Coskry had conducted the treaty negotiations which led to the cession of Lagos to the British Government on 6 Aug 1861.

21   R.F. Burton, *Abeokuta*, pp.10-11, for Burton's long account of this remarkable man's background.

22   TNA, MR. 1804 (4), ex. CO 147/43. Admiralty Chart 143, African West Coast, River Ogun or Abeokuta. Sketch survey by Cdr Bedingfield, RN, and Capt Burton, Bombay Army, 1861. Lithographed, coloured. About 3.14 miles to an inch. 51 cm x 69cm. Published by the Admiralty, 24 March 1862. Burton's ascent of the Ogun River is

noticed in *Proceedings of the Royal Geographical Society*, Vol.VI (1861-2), p.49. Letter enclosing sketch of the river, pp.64-6.

23   R.F. Burton, *Abeokuta*, pp.121-2.

24   *Ibid.*, pp.175-6.

25   *Ibid.*, pp.201-2.

26   *Ibid.*, pp.202-3

27   *Ibid.*, ii, p.12. Mrs Grundy first appeared (always offstage) in Thomas Morton's *Speed the Plough*, 1798. She typified the censorship enacted in everyday life by current conventional opinion.

28   Samuel Crowther (1809-1891), the first African to be ordained by the Church Missionary Society. In 1864 he was consecrated bishop of the Niger territory. See E. Stock, *History of the Church Missionary Society* (London, 1899), i, p.450 and *passim*. Also see M. Crowder, *The Story of Nigeria* (London, 1978), Chapter 9, for the activities of the early explorers and missionaries, including the Rev Samuel Ajayi Crowther.

29   The River Niger, nearly 2,600 miles in length (4,200 km) is the principal river of West Africa, and the third longest in the continent. It rises in Guinea on the landward side of the Fouta Djallon highlands.

30   TCC, Burton to Milnes, Brass River, 1 Dec 1861.

31   TNA, FO 2/45, Burton to Russell, 1 April 1864.

32   T. Hutchinson, *Impressions of Western Africa*, p.101, quoted in K. Onwuka Dike, *Trade and Politics in the Niger Delta* (Oxford, 1956).

33   Gustav Mann, born in Hanover, 20 Jan 1836, died Munich, 22 June 1916. He began his botanical career as a Kew gardener and then became a plant collector. Collected for the Niger Expedition, 1859-62. See *J.Linn. Soc.*, v. 6, 1861, 2, 27-30. He was the first collector on Mt Cameroon. See S.Cable and M.Cheek (ed.), *The Plants of Mt Cameroon* (Royal Botanic Gardens, Kew, 1999). Attached to the Indian Forest Service, 1863-91. MS journals, letters, portrait and plants at Kew. See R. Desmond, *Dictionary of British and Irish Botanists and Horticulturalists* (London, 1994), p.465.

34   TNA, FO 2/45, Burton to Russell, 1 April 1864.

35   TNA, FO 84/1176, Slave Trade Reports.

36   TNA, FO 2/45.

37   'Letter from G. Mann, Government Botanist, describing his Expedition to the Cameroon Mountains.' Communicated by Sir W.J. Hooker, FRS, FLS &c. [Read 5 June 1862], *Journal of the Proceedings of the Linnean Society of London*, Vol.VII, 1869, pp.1-13.

38   R.F. Burton, *Abeokuta*, i, p.vii.

39   *Ibid.*, ii, p.129.

40   In *Abeokuta*, ii, p.153, Burton claimed that the judge had slightly sprained his ankle.

41   Although overstated, it is the impression one gets from Burton's report to the FO, sent with despatch, TNA, FO 84/1176, 14 Jan 1862, from which I have largely drawn. It was passed to the RGS, and appeared in *Proceedings of the Royal Geographical Society*, Vol.VI, 1861-2, pp.238-48.

42   L. Huxley, *Life and Letters of Sir Joseph Dalton Hooker, OM, GCSI* (London, 1918), i, p.406n.

43   RGS Archives, I. Burton to Shaw, 2 Dec 1862.

44   TNA, FO 84/1176, 'Slave Trade Reports,' Cameroons Mountains, 14 Jan 1862.

45   *Ibid.*, 14 Jan 1862.

46   TNA, FO 2/42, 21 May 1862.

47   W. Reade, *Savage Africa* (London, 1863), p.68.

48   Napoleon III, Charles-Louis-Napoleon Bonaparte, the nephew of Napoleon I, was emperor of the French from 1852-70. Failing to obtain the hand of a princess of equal birth, he married the Countess Eugenie de Montijo in January 1853. After defeat in the Franco-Prussian War of 1871, he was deposed and went into exile in England. He died at Chislehurst, Kent, 9 Jan 1873.

49   See *The Romance*, p.162, 'Rules for my Guidance as a Wife, No.7: 'Perpetually work up his interests with the world, whether for publishing or appointments. Let him feel, when he has to go away, that he leaves a second self in charge of his affairs at home…'

50 RGS Archives, I. Burton to Shaw, 31 Dec 1861. Recd 4 Jan 1862.

51 Presumably Burton's account of his ascent of the Cameroons Mountains. It was sent to the FO, 22 February, 1862, and received with despatch No.11, Slave Trade Reports, 84/1176, on 12 April 1862.

52 RGS Archives, Burton to Shaw, 11 Jan 1862. There is no evidence in the archives that either man wrote to Sir Charles Wood on Burton's behalf. Certainly, nothing official was sent.

53 TNA, FO 2/42, Fernando Po, 26 April 1862.

54 R.F. Burton, *Two Trips to Gorilla Land and the Cataracts of the Congo* (London, 1876), i, p.203.

55 *Ibid*., pp.210-11. However, Burton had earlier drawn attention in a footnote to p.66, to du Chaillu's ending his Chapter 1 with an "illustration of a Mpongwe Woman," copied without acknowledgement from Mr Wilson's 'Portrait of Yanawaz, a Gaboon Princess." On p.107, Burton also noted du Chaillu's abridgement of the Rev Mr Wilson's abstract of the Mpongwe language, 'without owning the authority, and in changing the examples he did all possible damage.'

56 TNA, FO 84/1176, Slave Trade Draft, No.3, 26 Feb 1862.

57 TNA, FO 84/1176, Slave Trade Reports, 18 Dec 1862.

58 *The Edinburgh Review*, Vol.CXV (Jan.-April), No.CCXXXIII, Article VII, 1862, p.185. In a letter to Sir Charles McCarthy, 20 Jan 1862, Milnes wrote, 'I wish I could have inserted all Burton's Mormon anecdotes; for example, one person saying to another, "Sir if you were Mr. Jesus Christ or Mr. Joseph Smith himself sitting there with your halo hanging above your head, I would pull your nose at any rate." But this, alas! the respectability of the Edinburgh Review would not allow.' See T.W. Reid, *The Life, Letters and Friendships of Richard Monckton Milnes, First Lord Houghton* (London, 1891), ii, p.76.

59 W. Reade, *Savage Africa*, p.212. Reade may well have discussed the matter with Burton before his book went to press.

60 The account which follows is taken from Burton's very long report to the FO, TNA, 84/1176, Slave Trade Reports, 22 May 1862.

61 TNA, FO 84/1176, 23 Aug.1862.

62 TNA, FO 2/40, 22 May 1862.

63 TNA, FO 84/1176, Draft No.7, 23 April 1862. Palmerston, during his tenure as Foreign Secretary, had been particularly insistent on this point. In January 1851, he wrote a minute to his Under-Secretary: 'These Consuls are too bad; there is hardly one of them that writes a decent hand and with readable Ink. Write to each of the offenders that if they do not write large and more legibly, and with black Ink, I shall be obliged to send all their despatches to them to be written over again...Life is not long enough to decipher their scribbling.' Quoted in J. Ridley, *Lord Palmerston* (London, 1970), pp.110-11.

64 TNA, FO 2/42, 6 May 1862.

65 TNA, FO 84/1176, Slave Trade Draft, No.10, 6 May 1862.

66 The four extant letters from Burton to the Hon Henry Anthony Murray, were formerly in the family of Mrs Elizabeth Murray of Edinburgh – Murray was her husband's great-uncle. In 1970 she deposited them with the papers belonging to her husband's grandfather, the Hon Sir Charles A. Murray, in the National Register of Archives, Scottish Record Office, Edinburgh.

67 'My Wanderings in West Africa. A Visit to the Renowned Cities of Wari and Benin. By an FRGS. Part I – The Renowned City of Wari,' *Fraser's Magazine*, Vol.LXVII, Feb 1863, pp.135-157; Part II – The renowned city of Benin, March, pp.273 – 89. Part III – [continuation], April, pp.407-22. Burton had become acquainted with Dr Henry and his wife on his outward journey to Fernando Po in 1861. See *Wanderings in West Africa*, ii, p.243.

68 TNA, FO 84/1176, Slave Trade Reports, 26 Aug 1862. The Governor of Lagos was Henry Stanhope Freeman.

69 See N.M. Penzer, *An Annotated Bibliography*, p.206, for reference to a 'Statement of the outrage committed upon an English Factory in Benin River,' by R.C. Henry Lemnos, Benin River, Liverpool, 1862. Penzer says that 'On pp. 16 and 17 of this rare and interesting pamphlet Burton witnesses oaths of men giving evidence to assaults and injuries received in above outrage.'

70 Burton wrote in his despatch, TNA, FO 84/1176, 26 Aug 1862: 'A comparison of it with the Hydrographic Office's Chart (Sheet No.XVIII, Jaboo to River Forcados) will show how much is still to be done in the Delta of

the Niger. I have sent originals not copies as professional surveyors prefer the former.'

71   *Fraser's Magazine*, Vol.LXVII, p.153.

72   *Ibid.*, p.155.

73   See N.M. Penzer (ed.), *Selected Papers on Anthropology, Travel and Exploration* (London, 1924), pp.230-233. The article on Belzoni had originally appeared in *The Cornhill Magazine*, Vol.XLII, July, 1880, pp.36-50. In the Archives of the RGS, there is a letter from Isabel Burton to Dr Norton Shaw (recd 6 Nov 1862), 'I find it was Belzoni's Benin that dear Richard wants if you will lend it. I shall call for it with his general books. PS. I shall be glad to know if you have this book as if not I must order it at Quaritch's.'

74   TNA, FO 74/1176.

75   *Fraser's Magazine,* March 1863, Part II, p.287.

76   *Ibid.*, Part II contd, April 1863, p.407.

77   TNA, FO 84/1176.

78   *Ibid*. Note that Burton put the date 26 August on his despatch, *before* he had actually sailed for Lagos.

79   TNA, FO 2/42, 22 July 1862. The normal entitlement was a month's leave per year on full pay. This included travelling time. Fares, both for himself and members of his family, had to be paid for out of the consul's own pocket. These rules were not changed until 1874. See D.C.M. Platt, *The Cinderella Service, British Consuls since 1825* (London, 1971), p.29.

80   Sir Austin Henry Layard (1817-94), the archaeologist whose excavations in Mesopotamia did much to reveal the ancient civilization of Babylon and Assyria. He later served as a Member of Parliament, 1852-7, and 1860-69, becoming Under-secretary of Foreign Affairs, 1861-6.

81   *The Romance*, pp.182-3.

82   *The Life*, i, p.376. Isabel's account does not mention any specific month.

83   See R.F. Burton, 'An account of an Exploration of the Elephant Mountain, in Western Equatorial Africa,' *JRGS*, Vol.33 (1863), pp.241-50. Stokes is correctly referred to as Lieutenant Commander on the first page of Burton's report. Thereafter, for whatever reason, he is described as 'Lieutenant.'

84   TNA, FO 84/1176, Slave Trade No.10, Fernando Po, 26 Sept 1862.

85   TNA, FO 84/1176, Slave Trade No.15, 23 July 1862.

86   TNA, FO 2/42, England, 17 Dec 1862.

87   According to *The Times*, 12 Dec 1862, p.12, 'nine or ten ladies and gentlemen' intended to disembark there.

88   RGS Archives.

Notes to Chapter 26

1   TCC. The letter carries the Burtons' address but is not dated.

2   TNA, FO 2/42, 17 Dec 1862.

3   *The Times*, 23 Dec 1862, p.4. The letter, headed "The Great Gorilla Controversy", was written from 14 Montagu Place, Montagu Square, the new, and final, home, of Isabel's parents.

4   TNA, FO/1203, Slave Trade Reports, 6 Jan 1863.

5   TNA, FO 84/1203, Slave Trade Reports, 20 Jan 1863.

6   'Hunt, in his dedication to Pierre Paul Broca of his translation of Vogt's *Lectures on Man*, cited Knox and Burton as the two men who had helped him to institute the new organization.' See R. Rainger, 'Race, Politics and Science: The Anthropological Society of London in the 1860s,' *Victorian Studies*, Vol.22, No.1, 1978, p.57, note 18.

7   See G. Stocking, 'What's in a Name? The Origins of the Royal Anthropological Institute, 1837-71. *Man*, March 1971, p.376. James Hunt (1833-69) had a practice in Hastings, where two of his patients were famous literary figures, Charles Kingsley and Lewis Carroll (Charles Lutwidge Dodgson), both of whom suffered from speech impediments. For a short account of Hunt, see A. Clark, *Lewis Carroll – A Biography* (London, 1979), p. 105.

8   G. Stocking, *What's in a Name?*, p.377.

9   P.D. Curtin, *The Image of Africa. British Ideas and Action, 1780-1850* (Madison, 1964), p.377. Dr Robert Knox's

book was: *The Races of Man: A Philosophical Enquiry into the Influence of Race over the Destinies of Nations* (London, 1862). See for further information, L. Poliakov, *The Aryan Myth, A History of Racist and Nationalist Ideas in Europe* (London, 1974), p.18.

10   *The Anthropological Review*, Vol.1, pp.43-54. Discussion on pp.185-7.

11   *Ibid.*, pp.145-9. There is an excellent short review of the numerous publications of the various anthropological societies in N.M. Penzer, *An Annotated Bibliography of Sir Richard Francis Burton* (London, 1923), pp.203-4.

12   *The Life*, i, p.377.

13   A photograph of the Burtons at Madeira in 1863 taken by Lord Brownlow, is in the WSRO. Lady Marianne [not Marion] Margaret Alford (1817-88), artist, art patron and author, was the elder daughter of Spenser Compton, second Marquis of Northampton. She lived at Alford House, Prince's Gate, London. In 1841 she married John Hume Cust, viscount Alford, elder son of John Cust, 1st Earl of Brownlow. He died in 1851, leaving his widow with two sons.

14   TCC, Burton to Milnes, Hollway's, Madeira, 17 Feb 1863.

15   TNA, Parliamentary Select Committee. Report from Committee, 8 vols. 'I. Africa (Western Coast), Session, 7th Feb. – 6th July, 1863. Vol.5, 412. Report from the Select Committee Appointed to Consider the State of British Establishments on the Western Coast.' Ironically, Commodore Edmonstone was one of the witnesses called to give evidence. The background to the setting up of this Select Committee can be read in K.O. Dike, *Trade and Politics in the Niger Delta* (London, 1959), pp.166-81.

16   TNA, FO 84/1203, 9 Feb 1863. (Hollway's), Madeira.

17   In his letter to Milnes, Burton wrote, 'I am off to Teneriffe and Madam insists upon going though yellow fever is still there.'

18   *The Romance*, i, p.206.

19   *Ibid.*, p.210.

20   Isabel had written to Milnes on Burton's behalf almost a year earlier, asking for his advice on the intended motto. See TCC, Isabel, Lady Burton, Letters to Lord Houghton, 1862-80, 13 [?] March 1862. The full poem, consisting of eighteen lines of Latin verse translated by J.W. Postgate, can be read in 'Catullus, Tibullus, Pervigilium Veneris,' *Loeb Classical Library* (London, 1976), No.XIX, p.336. It is headed in this edition, 'Incerti Auctoris'. Burton's extract is of lines 9-12.

21   Isabel's copy is in the Huntington Library, California.

22   *The Life*, i, p.381.

23   W. Tinsley, *Recollections of an Old Publisher* (London, 1900), i, pp.145-46.

24   *Month*, Vol.6, 1867: No.31. I. Santa Cruz to Oratava, pp.63-70; No.33. II. A Climb up the Peak, pp.237-45; No.34. III. On the Peak and Down Again, pp.339-45; No.36. IV. Some Account of the Guanches. pp.554-60. A brief account of the Burtons' ascent of the Peak of Teneriffe is in *The Life*, i, p.380. A longer version can be read in *The Romance*, pp.210-23.

25   *Ibid.*, i, p.225.

26   *The Life*, i, p.381.

27   TNA, FO 84/1203, Burton to Wylde, Lagos, 6 May 1863. William H. Wylde was for many years Senior Clerk and Superintendent of Consular and Commercial Departments at the Foreign Office.

28   TNA, FO 84/1203, Slave Trade, No.4, 27 Jan 1863.

29   See M. Crowder, *The Story of Nigeria* (London, 1978), pp 136-7, who states that it was done 'in the interests of free trade….where the ruler Posu had established himself with the rest of Kosoko's followers who had opposed the cession of Palma and Lekki to the British.'

30   TNA, FO 84/1203, Lagos, 6 May 1863.

31   It is also related in Sir R.F. Burton, "A Mission to Dahome," *Wanderings in Three Continents*, ed. W.H. Wilkins (London, 1901), p.202 *et seq.*

32   R.F. Burton, *Two Trips to Gorilla Land and the Cataracts of the Congo* (London, 1876), pp.1-2.

33   TNA, FO 84/1203, HMSS *Antelope*, 30 Nov 1863.

34   TNA, FO 84/1203, Loanda, 15 Aug. 1863. Edward Laughlan was described by Burton in his November despatch

as 'Postmaster.'

35   TNA, FO 84/1203, Slave Trade No.9, 23 June 1863. Commodore Wilmot's Reports addressed to Rear-Admiral Sir
      B. Walker, are to be found printed in extract in R.F. Burton, *A Mission to Gelele, King of Dahome* (London, 1864),
      ii, pp.335-73.

36   R.F. Burton, *Two Trips to Gorilla Land*, ii, p.33.

37   TNA, FO 84/1203, HMSS *Antelope*, 30 Nov 1863.

38   R.F. Burton, *Two Trips to Gorilla Land*, p.65. This was the first memorial column planted in 1485 by the explorer
      Diogo Cam.

39   See *Ibid.*, ii, Appendix II, pp.345-50, where Burton gives a list of 'Plants collected in the Congo, at Dahome, and
      the Island of Ammabom...' They were received at the Herbarium, Royal Gardens, Kew, London, in Sept 1864.

40   TNA, FO 84/1203, Slave Trade No.11, 23 July 1863.

41   TNA FO 84/1203, Slave Trade No.12, 20 August 1863.

42   TNA, FO 84/1203, Slave Trade No.13, 20 August 1863.

43   TNA, FO 84/1203, 27 Oct 1863.

44   This, 'The Case of Capt. R.F. Burton, Her Britannic Majesty's Consul at Fernando Po, and the brig "Harriet",' is
      contained in a bulky volume of correspondence at TNA, ref FO 97/438. It comprises 165 folios, covering events
      from May 1863 to July 1867.

45   TNA, FO 97/438. Isabel's letter, dated Santos, 16 May 1866, was sent to the then Foreign Secretary, Lord
      Clarendon.

46   It would be another year, 22 Nov 1864, before the Foreign Office would send Burton a letter instructing him 'to
      place yourself in immediate communication with the parties and furnish them with an explanation of your
      proceedings in the matter.'

47   R.F. Burton, *A Mission to Gelele*, i, p.201.

48   *Ibid.*, p.322.

49   *Ibid.*, p.325.

50   *Ibid.*, ii, p.73.

51   TNA, FO 84/1203, Agbome, 30 Dec 1863.

52   M.J. Herskovits, *Dahomey*, (New York, 1938), i, p.6.

53   Burton carried with him an illuminated letter written in Latin from Cardinal Wiseman and dated May, 1863, which
      he had obviously asked Isabel to obtain for him. It was addressed to all bishops and priests working as missionaries
      in Africa, and ran: 'We entrust to you, my true friend, R. Burton , British Consul at Fernando Po. Please ensure
      that you provide it readily, wherever and how often he needs your help and support. To do this will be a most
      welcome service to myself. In return for this kindness may God always watch over you.'

54   R.F. Burton, 'Notes on the Dahoman,' in *Selected Papers on Anthropology, Travel and Exploration* , ed. N.M.
      Penzer (London, 1924), p.116.

55   N.M. Penzer, *Selected Papers*, p.124.

56   *Ibid.*, p.121. See R.F. Burton, *The Book of The Thousand Nights and One Night* (Benares, 1885), Vol.10, p.247,
      where he writes: 'In the Empire of Dahomey I noticed a corps of prostitutes for the use of the Amazon soldier-
      esses.'

57   F.Werne, *Reise durch Sennaar nach Mandera, Nasub, Cheli, in Lande zwischen dem Blauen Nil und den Atbara*
      (Berlin, 1852), pp.25-7.

58   N.M. Penzer, *Selected Paper*, p.123. Writing to Milnes from Fernando Po, 25 Oct 1863, Burton said that he already
      had, 'some 300 pages ready for some magazine which does not legally object to an anonymous. The greater part
      will not interest you....I could not, however, insert a description of how the nymphae are artificially elongated by
      way of affording pleasant amusement in the way of pulling at them.'

59   TNA, FO 2/45, Fernando Po, 15 April 1864.

60   According to J.A. Skertchley, *Dahomey As It Is* (London, 1874), pp.49-50, 'The Wesleyans established themselves
      at Whydah in 1843, the Rev T.B. Freeman, Bishop of the Gold Coast, and Mr Dawson being pioneers.' In 1863,
      Bernasko was in sole charge. 'His reverence, however, was fond of spiritual things in more than one sense; for he

took to imbibing rum and other unholy liquids.' Skertchley, at the time of writing, described Bernasko's son as 'worthless as his father,' and claimed that the eldest girls of his large family were 'encouraged *by their father* to prostitute themselves to every white man in the place.'

61 TNA, 84/1221, Bonny River, HMSS "Jaseur", 23 March 1864.

62 Methodist Missionary Society Archives: Gold Coast, 1859-67. Extract letter from Bernasko, 4 March 1864, probably addressed to T.B. Freeman, Head of the Gold Coast Methodist Mission. Quoted in *A Mission to Gelele, King of Dahomey*, ed. with an Introduction and Notes by C.W. Newbury (London, 1966), p.23.

63 TNA, FO 2/45, Bonny River, 23 March 1864.

64 TCC, Burton to Milnes, Bonny River, 24 March 1864. At the end of his letter to *The Athenaeum*, No.1892, 30 Jan 1864, p.156, headed 'The Sources of the Nile,' Dr Charles Beke wrote, 'This is, however a point which Captain Burton himself will, no doubt, be able to explain on his arrival in England, *which I am told is shortly expected.*[my italics].

65 R.F. Burton, *A Mission to Gelele*, p.16. Burton went on: 'At certain hours the bugle-call from Santa Cecilia intimates that all about me is not savagery. And below where the smoke rises...from the dense plantation of palms, lies rich study for an ethnologist – Basile the Bube village.' It was a study, however, on which Burton, never once embarked during his stay on the island.

66 J. Hunt, 'On the Negro's Place in Nature,' *Memoirs Read Before the Anthropological Society of London*, 17 Nov 1863, pp.1-63.

67 The article on negroes in the *Encyclopedia* of Diderot and d'Alembert in France was written in the same vein.

68 R.F. Burton, *A Mission to Gelele*, ii, p.178.

69 R.F. Burton, *Wit and Wisdom from West Africa* (London, 1865), p.xvi. The Preface is dated 20 July 1863.

70 TNA, FO 2/45, 24 March 1864. The minute was dated 18 May.

71 TNA, FO 2/45, Burton to Russell, Teneriffe, 3 June 1864.

72 TNA, FO 2/45, Burton to FO, Teneriffe, 11 June 1864.

73 In his *Wanderings in West Africa*, i, p.107, Burton diplomatically tempered his admiration by writing, 'For those who admire black anywhere except in the skin, there is nothing more enchanting than the women of Teneriffe. But I will confess that one soon wearies of black eyes and black hair, and after a course of such charms, one falls back with pleasure upon brown, yellow, or what is better than all, red auburn locks and eyes of soft limpid blue.'

74 TNA, FO 2/45, FO to Burton, 30 June 1864.

75 *The Life*, i, p.388.

Notes to Chapter 27

1   TCC, Burton to Milnes, 34 Upper Montagu Street, Montagu Square, 12 Aug 1864.

2   Vambery wrote a paper for the RGS, 'Journeys through Central Asia to Khiva, Bokhara and Samarcand,' which was revised and read for him by Laurence Oliphant. It was published in *Proceedings of the Royal Geographical Society*, 1st Series, Vol.8 (1864), pp.267-69.

3   See L. Alder and R. Dalby, *The Dervish of Windsor Castle* (London, 1979), p.229. This badly printed book is also littered with inaccuracies. The authors, following Isabel Burton, wrongly date Vambery's visit to August 1861.

4   *The Life*, i, pp.347-8.

5   TNA, FO 2/45, Burton to Russell, 2 Sept 1864. Same London address.

6   TNA, FO 2/45, Burton to FO, 3 Sept 1864. Same London address.

7   TNA, FO 84/1221, Slave Trade, Russell to Burton, 10 Sept 1864.

8   RGS Archives: Speke to Murchison, 6 July 1862.

9   *The Times*, 29 April 1863, p.12.

10 *The Times*, 18 May 1863, p.12.

11 *The Illustrated London News*, Supplement (Vol.XLIII, July – December), 4 July 1863, p.17. The first page of this special issue carries full-page engravings of the two explorers, with the caption: 'The Reception of Captains Speke

and Grant at the Royal Geographical Society.' The rest of the issue is full of engraved reproductions of Grant's drawings.

12   *The Times*, 24 June 1863, p.7.

13   See G. Porter, *Annals of a Publishing House, John Blackwood* (Edinburgh and London, 1898), iii, pp.95-6. The first two volumes, *Annals of a Publishing House. William Blackwood and his Sons* (Edinburgh and London, 1897) were written by Mrs Oliphant, who died in the year of their publication. Speke's biographer, Alexander Maitland, appears not to have been aware of the problems that Speke's notes and diaries posed Blackwood's. John Hill Burton (1809-81), was educated at Marischal College, Aberdeen, and called to the Scottish bar in 1831. He contributed extensively on a wide range of subjects to *Blackwood's Magazine* from 1842 until his death. See F. Boase, *Modern English Biography* (Truro, 1892), i, pp.494-5.

14   See *The Taunton Courier*, Wednesday, 11 Nov 1863, p.4.

15   *The Athenaeum*, No.1886, 19 December 1863, pp.829-32.

16   *The Taunton Courier*, 23 December 1863, p.5.

17   A. Maitland, *Speke* (London, 1971), p.196.

18   Hume Greenfield temporarily filled the post of Asst Sec, following the resignation of Dr Norton Shaw at the end of the 1863 session. See H.R.Mill, *The Record of the Royal Geographical Society* (London, 1930), pp. 74-75, for the reasons behind this. Some time afterwards, the then Foreign Secretary, Lord Stanley, appointed Shaw to the post of British consul on the Danish island of Ste Croix. He died there in the summer of 1868. There is an obituary in *JRGS* Vol.39 (1869), pp.cxlvii-iii.

19   RGS Archives, Letter Book (Clerk's Correspondence). H.W. Farley to Capt J.H. Speke, 16 April 1864.

20   RGS Archives, Letter Book (Official Correspondence). W. Spottiswode to Capt J.H. Speke,14 May 1864.

21   'The Upper Basin of the Nile, from Inspection and Information,' by Captain J.H. Speke, FRGS,' *JRGS* Vol.33 (1863), p.322. Although the Journal is dated 1863, the problems caused by Speke's paper delayed its publication until the following year.

22   J.H. Speke, *What Led to the Discovery of the Source of the* Nile (Edinburgh & London, 1864). The three articles were entitled 'Captain Speke's Adventures in Somali Land,' and appeared in Blackwood's *Magazine*, Vol.LXXXVII (Jan. – June, 1860); May, pp.561-80; (ii) June, pp.674-93; (iii) Vol.LXXXVIII (July – Dec. 1860), July, pp.23-36.

23   NLS, MS 4185: Speke to Blackwood, 25 July 1864.

24   NLS, MS 4185: Speke to Blackwood, 6 Aug 1864.

25   *The Life*, i, p.389

26   *The Athenaeum*, No.1925, 17 Sept 1864, p.369.

27   R.F. Burton, *Zanzibar; City, Island, and Coast* (London, 1872), ii, p.397.

28   According to William Speke, the explorer's elder brother: 'It was… a marvellous dispensation of Providence that a letter was written that day, perhaps that hour, from the Chairman of the Geographers at Bath stating that the Committee of Section E has recommended that Govt.: be moved to grant honorary distinctions to Captain Speke and Captain Grant, a knighthood and civil CB to my brother, the latter distinction to Grant, with a pecuniary reward to them…' NLS, MS 4185, W. Speke to J. Blackwood, Jordans, 29 Sept 1864. Sir H. Johnston, *The Nile Quest* (London, 1903), pp.169-70, pointed out that the British government did *nothing* for Speke, 'unless there can be attributed to its influence the paltry satisfaction of granting to him through the Herald's College supporters and an additional motto to the family's coat of arms. By this grant his family is now entitled to add a hippopotamus and a crocodile as supporters to their shield, a crocodile to their crest, the flowing Nile to their coat of arms, and the additional motto, 'Honor est a Nilo.'

29   See F. Galton, *Memories of My Life* (London, 1908), pp.173-4. Galton was general secretary of the British Association from 1863-67, serving four times as sectional president, and twice declining the presidency.

30   *The Times*, 17 Sept 1864, p.6.

31   R.F. Burton, 'On the present state of Dahome,' *Report of the British Association…..*(Bath). *Transaction of the Sections*, pp. 137-9.

32   *The Athenaeum*, No.1927, 1 Oct 1864, p.435.

33 Samuel Baker (1821-93), accompanied by his second wife, Florence von Sass, set out for Lake Luta N'zige, shortly after Speke and Grant had gone north to Khartoum. They reached the lake, which Baker called Albert Nyanza, on 14 March 1864. He was knighted in August 1866, a year after his return from Africa.

34 R.F. Burton, 'Lake Tanganyika, Ptolemy's Western Lake-Reservoir of the Nile,' *Proceedings of the Royal Geographical Society*, Vol.IX, 1864-5, pp.6-8. (Précis only).

35 *The Athenaeum*, No.1927, p.435. John (later Sir John) Kirk, 1832-1922, naturalist and British administrator in Zanzibar. He accompanied Livingstone's expeditions into Central Africa, 1858-1863. Three years later he was appointed acting surgeon to the Zanzibari political agency, becoming consul-general and agent there in 1873.

36 *The Times*, 17 Sept 1864, p.12. A squat obelisk surrounded by railings, was later erected on the spot where Speke died, and inscribed with the words: 'Here the distinguished and enterprising African traveller, Captain John Hanning Speke, lost his life in an accidental explosion of his gun, Sept. 15, 1864.' During a visit in April 1981, no one in the locality I talked to appeared to know anything about it or its whereabouts. I eventually found it in a corner of a field, about 100 yards in from the road, to the side of a public footpath sign-posted Lent's Green 1/4.

37 Quotation from the original letter provided by the late Frank Wilson's son, and printed in 'An Explorer's Centenary. Richard Burton 1821-90,' *The Times*, 19 March 1921.

38 R.F. Burton, *Zanzibar*, p.398.

39 *The Times*, 19 Sept 1864, p.6.

40 *The Times*, 23 Sept 1864, p.8.

41 James A. Grant Papers, NLS 17910, Rigby to Grant, Oriental Club, Hanover Square, 12 Feb 1866.

42 *Ibid.*, 17 June 1866.

43 In a letter to Sir Roderick Murchison, merely dated Friday, 1865, Grant wrote: 'I have written to a member of Speke's family saying that fifty pounds are still required to complete the monument and if they gave it anonymously it would be very desirable.' An appreciation of Speke, 'Restoring Honour to an Explorer,' written to commemorate the centenary of his death by Donald Simpson, Librarian of the Royal Commonwealth Society, appeared in *The Times*, 12 Sept 1964, p.9.

44 Thomas Wright (1810-77), was one of the founders of the British Archaeological Association, and a pioneer in the study of Anglo-Saxon and medieval literature.

45 TNA, FO 84/1221, Slave Trade, Russell to Burton, 3 Oct 1864.

46 TNA, FO 2/45, Russell to Burton, 6 Oct 1864.

47 *The Romance*, i, p.227. It is dated, presumably by Wilkins, "Minto, Oct. 6, 1863." However, Russell's reference to Burton's mission to Dahomey, which occupied the months of December 1863 to February 1864, shows that it is mis-dated and, therefore, misplaced.

48 Captain Sir Henry Vere Huntley (1795-1864). Captain in the navy, colonial governor and author. He had served on the West Africa station in the anti-slavery squadron. In 1839 he was appointed Lieut. Governor of the settlements on the river Gambia, in 1841 Lieut. Governor of Prince Edward's Island (being knighted before going out), and afterwards arbitrator of the mixed courts of Loanda. He was then appointed to Santos, where he died on 7 May 1864.

49 TNA, FO 13/425, Russell to Burton, 28 Oct 1864.

50 See J.A. Casada, 'James A Grant and the Royal Geographical Society,' *The Geographical Journal*, Vol.140, Part 2, June 1974, p.247.

51 K.Onwuka Dike, *Trade and Politics in the Niger Delta, 1830-85* (Oxford, 1959), p.182n.

52 James M'Queen (1778-1870), was for some years manager of a large sugar plantation in Grenada, West Indies. He was the first to suggest in a treatise of 1818, that the Niger flowed out into the Bights of Benin and Biafra, an assumption which Richard Lander subsequently proved to be true. In 1821 he became editor and part owner of *The Glasgow Courier*, using the paper to support the West Indian planters' interests. He communicated a number of very interesting memoirs to the RGS, many of which were printed in the *JRGS* and the *Proceedings*. Although he wrote a *Geographical Survey of Africa*, like W.D. Cooley, he was an 'armchair geographer,' who never set foot on the African continent during the whole of his long lifetime.

53 'Dishonor Est A Nilo,' *The Saturday Review*, 2 July 1864, p.13. The title is Strangford's adaptation of the inscrip-

tion, 'Honor Est A Nilo,' on the medal struck by the King of Sardinia to commemorate Speke's achievement. Strangford at the time was a member of the Council of the RGS.

54   Sir H. Johnston, *The Nile Quest* (London, 1903), p.167.

55   *Blackwood's Magazine*, 'Nile Basins and Nile Explorers,'Vol.XCVII, No.DXCI, pp.101-11.

56   TNA, FO 97/438, Russell to Burton, 22 Nov 1864.

57   TNA, FO 97/438, Burton to Russell, Howlett's Hotel, Manchester St, Manchester Sq, 10 Dec 1864.

58   See N. Mitford (ed.), *The Stanleys of Alderley* (London, 1939), repr. 1968.

59   *The Life*, i, pp.450-1.

60   B. & P. Russell, *The Amberley Papers*, pp.349-50.

61   TNA, FO 97/438, Russell to Burton, 16 Feb 1865.

62   TNA, FO 97/438, Burton to Russell, 14 St James's Sq, 5 March 1865.

63   TNA, FO 97/438, Burton to Russell, 36 Manchester St, Manchester Sq, 11 March 1865.

64   *The Life*, pp.392-3.

65   It is inaccurately described as being in 'blank verse' by N.M. Penzer, *Ann. Bib.*, p.77.

66   *A Sketch of the Career of Richard F. Burton,* by A.B. Richards, A. Wilson, St. Clair Baddeley (London, 1886), Appendix B, pp.53-65.

67   David Livingstone to London Missionary Society, 25.5.65, LMS Archives, cited in T.Jeal, *Livingstone* (London, 1973), p.285.

68   The Parliamentary Select Committee's Report on British Establishments in West Africa. Report from Committee, 8 vols. Vol.1. Africa (Western Coast), Session 7 Feb. – 6 July, 1865, Vol.5.

69   The Mails etc – Southampton. Passenger list, *The Times*, Wednesday, 10 May 1865, p.5. The Burtons left by the Royal Mail Company's steamship, *La Plata*.

70   TNA, FO 97/438, Burton to Russell, Braganza Hotel, Lisbon, 16 May 1865.

71   TNA, FO 97/438, Burton to Russell, 14 Montagu Place, Bryanston Sq, 8 May 1865.

72   TNA, FO 97/438, internal memo, 8 May 1865.

73   TNA, FO 97/438, Russell to Burton, 23 May 1865.

74   *The Life*, p.417. The period of two months is also repeated by Wilkins in *The Romance*, i, p.233. However, it is clear from Letter IV, Jan 1866, p.85, of Burton's, 'London to Rio de Janeiro. Letters to a Friend,' *Fraser's Magazine*, Vol.LXII, No.72, Oct 1865, and LXIII, No.73, Jan 1866, that he left on 13 June, the feast of St Antonio of Lisbon, exactly a month after arriving.

75   TNA, FO 97/438, I. Burton to Earl Clarendon, Santos, 16 May 1866.

76   See T. Hall, *The Spiritualists: The Story of Florence Cook and William Crookes* (London, 1972).

77   E.E. Fournier D'Albe, *Life of Sir William Crookes* (London, 1923), p.120.

78   TCC, I. Burton to Lord Houghton, No address, 15 Aug 1865.

79   *The Romance*, pp.242-3.

Notes to Chapter 28

1   *The Life*, i, p.420.

2   TCC, Burton to Milnes, Rio de Janeiro, 23 Oct 1865.

3   *The Life*, p.422.

4   TNA, FO 97/438, I. Burton to Earl Clarendon, Santos, 16 May 1866.

5   The second part of the pamphlet was called *An Enquiry Into An Ordinance Suggested in Captain Burton's Book, and Carried out by Major Blackall, Governor of Sierra Leone,* etc, etc.

6   W. Rainy, *The Censor Censured,* (London, 1865) p.11.

7   *Ibid.*, p.14.

8   NLS, MS 17910, Rigby to Grant, Oriental Club, Hanover Sq, 13 Feb 1866.

9   *Ibid.*, 17 June 1866. There is a copy of Rainy's pamphlet in the Library of the Foreign and Commonwealth Office,

London. There are no means of knowing how many pamphlets were printed, or how widely they were circulated. Rainy, obviously, was intent on inflicting as much damage as he could to Burton's reputation in official quarters.

10   TNA, FO 97/438, Earl Clarendon to Burton, 28 May 1866.

11   They were the first two of a course of four lectures delivered before the Emperor and his court in 1866: I. 'The Visitation of El Medinah'; II. The Pilgrimage to Meccah.' The others were, 'A Ride to Harar,' and 'A Mission to Dahome.' These, and other essays, were collected by W.H. Wilkins (ed.), in *Wanderings in Three Continents by the late Captain Sir Richard F. Burton, KCMG* (London, 1901).

12   TNA, FO 128/83, Burton to Thornton, Santos, 18 May 1866.

13   See R.F. Burton, *Letters from the Battlefields of Paraguay* (London, 1870), Letter VIII, Buenos Airies, 20 Oct 1868, p.208. All the letters are addressed to: 'My Dear Z[ookins]' – one of Isabel's pet names.

14   The tales first appeared in *Fraser's Magazine*, Vol.LXXVII, April-June, Vol.LXXVIII, August-December, 1868. They were published in book form by Longmans in 1870, with illustrations by Ernest Griset. Burton dedicated the tales to his uncle, Robert Bagshaw, 'That Will Remind Him Of A Land He knows So Well.'

15   According to G. Stisted, *The True Life*, p.310, 'Burton depended much upon his writings for bringing in welcome pecuniary additions to his moderate income, and Isabel spent many an hour copying the MS, even acquiring the knack of imitating his handwriting so accurately that only his sister or myself could tell the difference.'

16   *The Romance*, p.265.

17   Edward Henry Stanley (1826-93), was the eldest son of the 14th Earl of Derby. From Rugby, he went on to Trinity College, Cambridge, taking a first in the classical tripos, and a third in the mathematical. According to his entry in the *DNB* , 'In character he was singularly cool, fair, and critical, but was too diffident of his powers and, perhaps, too undecided to become a great man of action.'

18   A well-known Latin tag meaning: 'The rigour of the law is the height of oppression.'

19   TNA, FO 97/438, Memo to draft of despatch sent by Lord Stanley to Burton, 5 Sept 1866, acknowledging his of 10 August, and stating that it had been forwarded to the Commodore of the West African squadron.

20   TNA, FO 128/83, Thornton to Burton, Rio de Janeiro, 27 Nov 1866.

21   *The Romance*, p.266.

22   *The Life*, p.424, and *The Romance*, p.266.

23   *The Life*, p.425.

24   TNA, F0 128/86, Thornton to Burton, Rio de Janeiro, 25 Jan 1867.

25   C.Y. Lang, *The Swinburne Letters* (Yale, 1959), Vol.1, No.78, p. 124. Swinburne to Milnes, 22A Dorset Street, 11 July (?) 1865. Quoted in F.M. Brodie, *The Devil Drives*, p. 198. Rodin, the name here used of Burton, was the surgeon in the Marquis de Sade's novel, *Justine, or the Misfortunes of Virtue.*

26   *The Saturday Review*, Vol.XXII, 4 Aug 1866, p.145.

27   Sir A. Quiller Couch (Q), *Studies in Literature*, First Series (Cambridge, 1923), p.234.

28   Holmwood, Henley on Thames, 11 Jan 1867, in C. Y. Lang (ed.), *The Swinburne Letters*, No.174, p.224.

29   TNA, FO 97/438, internal memo, James Murray, 22 Jan 1867.

30   TNA, FO 128/86, Burton to Thornton, Santos, ? Feb 1867.

31   *The Romance,* pp.268-9.

32   Henry Walter Bates (1825-92), naturalist and explorer whose demonstration of the operation of natural selection in animal mimicry, provided further strong evidence to support Darwin's theory of evolution. In 1848, Bates travelled with Alfred Russel Wallace to the Amazon River. Wallace returned four years later. Bates, however, remained for eleven years, amassing a vast collection of species, mostly of insects. On his return to England he wrote a famous paper, 'Contributions to an Insect Fauna of the Amazon Valley.' His only book, *The Naturalist on the River Amazon* (London, 1863), has become a classic of scientific and travel information for this area.

33   OHG. H.W. Bates to Burton, 15 Whitehall Place, 5 April 1867. Bates added a P.S. 'The first part of your Report on Brazil has been received & favourably considered by our Council, but we cannot print any of it till we get the remainder. Where is it?' There are two short references to Burton's travels in Brazil: *Proceedings of the RGS*, Vol.XII, 1867-8, p.261, Vol.XIII, 1868-9, p.311. Since the Report was never published by the Society, it has to be assumed that it remained uncompleted.

34 TNA, FO 128/86, Thornton to Burton, Petropolis, 10 May 1867.

35 TNA, FO 97/438, Burton to Lord Stanley, Rio de Janeiro, 5 June 1867.

36 TNA, FO 97/438, Lord Stanley to Burton, 23 July 1867.

37 R.F. Burton, *The Highlands of the Brazil* (London,1869), i, p.252.

38 QK Coll, Burton to Rupert Dixon, Rio de Janeiro, 12 June 1867.

39 R.F. Burton, *The Highlands of the Brazil*, ii, p.70.

40 W.S. Blunt, *My Diaries* (London, 1932), p.542.

41 TCC, I. Burton to Lord Houghton, 18 April 1868.

42 TNA, FO 128/89, Burton to Matthew, Santos, 15 June 1868.

43 *The Romance*, p.345. In *The Life*, i, p.450, the turning point in Burton's recovery is traced to the administering of ether pills and the application of mustard to his calves and thighs.

44 TNA, FO 128/89, Santos, 15 June 1868.

45 *The Romance*, p.349.

46 In *The Life*, p.453, Isabel mistakenly gives the date of embarkation from Santos as 24 July. The correct datings of her departure are given in *The Romance*, p.348, in her letter to her mother of 16 June: 'I leave São Paulo on the 31st, Santos on the 1st, Rio on the 9th, and will reach home early in September.'

47 The Paraguayan War, perhaps better known as the War of the Triple Alliance (1864-70), the bloodiest conflict in Latin American history, fought between Paraguay and the allied countries of Argentina, Brazil and Uruguay.

48 *The Life*, p.454. In this same letter, Isabel said that 'All my wealth depends on my editing a book and a poem of Richard's and two things of my own for the October press....' The book was Burton's *The Highlands of the Brazil*, and his poem '*Who Last Wins*,' an elegy on Speke's death. What she calls the two things of her own, were: *Iraçéma, The Honey Lips, a Legend of Brazil* by J. De Alencar, Translated with the Author's Permission by Isabel Burton (London, 1886), and *Manuel de Moraes, A Chronicle of the Seventeenth Century*, by J.M. Pereira Da Silva, Translated by Richard F. and Isabel Burton (London, 1886). The original manuscript of the *Iraçéma* is in the WSRO.

49 Francisco Solano Lopez (1827-70), the dictator of Paraguay, responsible for the War of the Triple Alliance. Following the capture of the capital, Asuncion, in 1869, Lopez fled northwards to wage a guerilla war. He was captured on 1 March 1870, and shot by Brazilian troops.

50 R.F. Burton, *Letters from the Battlefields of Paraguay*, Letter V, pp.166-7.

51 *Ibid.*, Letter XII, p.287.

52 W.S. Blunt, *The Diaries*, p.545.

53 R.F. Burton, *Letters from the Battlefields of Paraguay*, Letter XXIII, 10 April 1869, p.413.

Notes to Chapter 29

1   There were three boys and three girls of the marriage. The eldest son, Raymond Robert, then aged twelve, died at the early age of thirty. Edgar Clifford (1859-1921) and Gerald Arthur (1861-1939) later went on to inherit the Wardour title, as the 14th and 15th Lord Arundell, respectively.

2   Burton's translation of the *Uruguay* was not published until 1982 by the University of California Press. *Iracema* and *Manuel de Moraes* were privately printed by Isabel in 1886.

3   TCC, 14 Montagu Place, 14 Sept 1868.

4   TCC, 14 Montagu Place, 28 Oct 1868.

5   TCC, 14 Montagu Place, Sunday, u/d, but must be 8 November.

6   Quoted in *The Romance*, i, pp.350-1.

7   Maggs Catalogue, 289/1997, I. Burton to William Tinsley, u/d, c. Sept/Oct 1869.

8   Maggs Catalogue, 283/1011.

9   TCC, I. Burton to Lord Houghton, 20 Jan 1868, post-script.

10 *The Athenaeum*, 16 Jan 1869, No.2151, pp.83-4.

11   TNA, FO 881/2148, No.1, Stanley to Burton, 3 Dec 1868.

12   *The Romance*, i, p.352. The post carried a salary of £700, together with an annual allowance of £300 for office expenses. In terms of current money values, this roughly amounted to an annual salary of £40,000. To this was added £160 for outfit.

13   TNA, FO 881/2148, No.2, Burton to Hammond, Buenos Ayres, 30 March 1869.

14   TNA, FO 881/2148, No. 3, No.45 Commercial, Elliot to Clarendon, Constantinople, 3 May 1869.

15   NLS, MSS 13069, f.66. Private letter-book of Sir Henry Elliot, Therapia, 9 June 1871. Earl Granville was then Colonial Secretary in Gladstone's first cabinet.

16   TNA, FO 881/2148, No.5, Burton to Murray, Howlett's Hotel, 14 June 1869.

17   TNA, FO 881/2148, No.6, Murray to Burton, 19 June 1869.

18   TNA, FO 881/2148, No.8, Burton to Murray, Howlett's Hotel, 21 June 1869.

19   QK Coll, Grant to Murchison, Simla, 16 Oct 1866. In his letter of 12 June 1868 to Rupert Dixon (QK), Burton wrote: 'Herewith is a paper about the Nile, my case is coming. Baker knighted – I wonder that he ever accepted it. Grant offered Star of the Sudan. Speke family quarters Nile – field vert on sable. I opened up the way to the whole work of opening up Africa and have never even had a word of thanks.'

20   NLS, Grant Papers, MSS 17909, f.27, Murchison to Mackenzie, 8 Nov 1866.

21   *The Life*, ii, p.45, I. Burton to R. Murchison, Howlett's Hotel, 24 June 1869.

22   G. Lafourcade, *Swinburne: a literary biography* (London, 1932), pp.200-1.

23   E. Gosse, *The Life of Algernon Charles Swinburne* (London, 1917), p.140.

24   HL, EMC, Howlett's, Manchester Street, Manchester Square, London, 9 July 1869.

25   C. Y. Lang, *The Swinburne Letters*, Vol.2, No. 302, p.18, Hotel de France, Vichy, 29 juillet 1869.

26   E. Gosse, *Portraits and Sketches* (London, 1912), p.32. See Swinburne's elegy, 'Reminiscences: Leighton, Burton, and Mrs Sartoris, Vichy, September 1869,' *The Pall Mall Gazette*, 26 February 1896, pp.1-2, collected as 'An Evening at Vichy, September 1869. Written on the News of the Death of Lord Leighton' in CROP, 1904. There is also a rather inaccurate anecdote relating to this period in J.C. Hare, *The Story of My Life* (London, 1896), 4, pp.357-8.

27   C.Y. Lang, No. 303, pp.23-4, Swinburne to Alice Swinburne, Vichy, 10 Aug 1869. Quoted in F.M. Brodie, *The Devil Drives*, p. 247.

28   *Ibid.*, No.304, p. 24, Swinburne to Lady Henrietta Swinburne, 13 Aug 1869. Quoted in A. Symons, *Dramatis Personae* (London, 1925), p.258.

29   Stratford is now part of the London Borough of Newham. According to Jenni Munro-Collins, Local Studies Officer: 'The Chapman and André Map of 1777, clearly shows wells marked. On the Ordnance Survey map, surveyed in 1867, there are at least six wells marked within the area of Stratford. Additionally there is a pump in West Ham Lane, between 1600-1800, which served a lead pipe, which filled an underground tiled cistern serving factories.'

30   See *The Life*, pp.461-66.

31   *The Inner Life of Syria, Palestine and the Holy Land* (London, 1876), i, p.6.

32   This is taken from her account in *The Inner Life of Syria*. Jago, who later took over the Damascus consulate following Burton's recall, receives no mention in either *The Romance* or *The Life*.

33   According to the FO List, 1890, George Jackson Eldridge was attached to the HQ of the British Army in the Crimea from August 1855. Held Consulships at Kertch, appointed to Erzeroom, but did not proceed. Consul-General in Syria to reside in Beyrout, appointed 29 April 1863.

34   Burton arrived at Damascus on 3 Oct 1869. See FO 881/2148, No.11, Wood to Clarendon. Charles Wood was Acting-Consul at Damascus from 1 Jan – 28 Oct 1869.

35   See R.F. Burton and C.F. Tyrwhitt Drake, *Unexplored Syria* (London, 1872), i, pp.373 & 153.

Notes to Chapter 30

1   FO List 1884: Edward Rogers appointed Consul at Damascus, 20 Jan 1861. Was Acting Consul-General in Syria

from 10 April – 28 May 1861. Transferred to Cairo, 30 Nov 1868. Later known as Rogers Bey, he became a noted Egyptologist and Arabic scholar and the discoverer of the tombs of the Caliphs.

2   I. Burton, *The Inner Life of Syria, Palestine and the Holy Land* (London, 1876), i, p.54 *et seq.*Taken from an account which Isabel sent to *The Times* but which, for whatever reason, never reached its destination.

3   *The Life*, i, p.481.

4   After surrendering to the French in 1847, his captors reneged on their promise of safe conduct to Egypt or Palestine, and he was imprisoned in France. In 1852 he was released by Louis Napoleon, and given a pension of 150,000 francs. Three years later, he moved from the Byrsa, the citadel area of Carthage, to Damascus. During the horrendous massacre that took place there in 1860, he intervened to save the lives of some 12,000 Christians, including the French consul and his staff. His green and white standard was adopted by the Algerian liberation movement during the War of Independence, and became the national flag of independent Algeria. The government brought his remains back to Algeria, and he was interred with great ceremony on 5 July 1966, the fourth anniversary of independence. A mosque bearing his name was built as a national shrine in Constantine.

5   *The Romance*, pp.394-5.

6   Every Wednesday, according to *The Romance*, ii, p.389, which is more likely. In *The Life*, i, p.485, it is given as Friday.

7   *The Romance*, p.392.

8   R.F. Burton, *The Book of the Thousand Nights and a Night* (Benares, 1885), Vol.4, p.202.

9   The best account of his stewardship in Syria is in M.L. Gross, *Ottoman Rule in the Province of Damascus, 1869-1909*, PhD thesis, Georgetown University, 1979.

10   These series of reforms were initiated during the reigns of Abdulmecid I (1839-61) and Abdulaziz (1861-76). The most significant affected the army, the administration, and society, through changes in the educational and legal system. For an excellent study of the Tanzimat period, see R.H. Davison, *Reform in the Ottoman Empire, 1856-1876* (Princeton, 1963).

11   For Rashid's successful expeditions which resulted in the extension of direct Ottoman rule over the, then, frontier region of Transjordan, see E.L. Rogan, *Frontiers of the State in the Late Ottoman Empire, Transjordan, 1850-1921* (CUP, 1999), pp.48-52. The Druzes, known for their belligerence, are a heterodox Islamic sect professing pure monotheism and believing in the divinity of al-Hakim Bi-Amr Allah, the sixth caliph (r. 996-1021) of the Fatimid dynasty in Egypt. They keep their religious doctrines shrouded in mystery.

12   *The Life*, pp.484-5.

13   R.F. Burton & C.F. Tyrwhitt Drake, *Unexplored Syria* (London, 1872), i, Chap.1. Damascus, 7 May 1870, a section written by Isabel.

14   Dressed as a Bedouin, she rode into Palmyra in some style, astride her white stallion with its red and gold saddle. Bringing up the rear were twenty-five heavily armed horsemen, seventy Bedouin, and numerous camels loaded with provisions and presents. Hailed as "Queen of the Desert," she was feted with drums, horseback displays and women scattering petals at her feet.

15   I. Burton, *The Inner Life of Syria*, p.204.

16   *The Romance*, p.418.

17   It was not published by the Hakluyt Society until 1874.

18   HL, EMC, Burton to Tootal, Damascus, 16 May 1870.

19   At Dar Djoun, Mt Lebanon, 8 miles north-east of Sidon, where she died on 23 June 1839. She was buried in the olive grove that was once her garden.

20   Both men have entries in the *DNB*. Drake's short life- he died aged only twenty-eight in June 1874 – is also commemorated in W. Besant, *The Literary Remains of the Late Charles F. Tyrwhitt Drake. Edited with a Memoir* (London, 1877).

21   Properly, the Society for the Systematic and Scientific Exploration of Palestine. Founded in 1865, its aim was, 'the accurate and systematic exploration of the topography, geology, natural history, and ethnology of the Holy Land, particularly with a view to the interpretation of the Bible.' It published Quarterly Statements, sent free to subscribers. The Society initially sent out two members of the Royal Engineers, Major Wilson and Captain

Anderson, to report on the best method of carrying out the work. They made a reconnaissance in Galilee and along the watershed to Nablus, taking a large number of photographs and discovering several of the Galilean synagogues. The Fund then turned its attention to the archaeology of Jerusalem. In 1867, Captain Warren, RE, was sent out, his work continuing until 1870. See *Autobiography of Sir Walter Besant* (London, 1902), p.153ff, and K. Baedeker, *Palestine and Syria. Handbook for Travellers* (1876), p.125.

22 A popular account of these expeditions was published by Palmer in *The Desert of the Exodus*, 2 vols, 1871; *The Secret Sects of Syria*, British Quarterly Review, 1873.

23 *The Romance*, p.435.

24 QK Coll, Bludan, 29 August 1870.

25 I. Burton, *The Inner Life of Syria*, p.307.

26 Burton sent a despatch on the 'affair' to Sir Henry Elliot, TNA: FO 881/2148, Enclosure in No.16, Damascus, 28 Aug 1870. In this, he additionally reported that, 'Christians had been threatened in the streets and bazaars, many families left the city, and in some instances the newly-arrived troops showed a hostile animus. The Ottoman authorities, however, have been alive to their sense of danger, and as long as they do their duty there never will be a massacre at Damascus.....The Moslem population has been excited against the Christians, unjustly attributing to the latter the mustering of the Redif [militia] which has never yet been called out at Damascus.'

27 Mt Hermon, on the Lebanon-Syrian border west of Damascus. It rises to 9, 232 feet (2,814m) the highest point on the east coast of the Mediterranean Sea. There are a number of temples on its slopes, with Greek inscriptions on them dating from c. AD 200.

28 R. F. Burton & C.F.T. Drake, *Unexplored Syria*, p.137.

29 Commenting on the matter in a letter to Edmund Hammond, NLS, MS 13609, f.66, Therapia, 6 Sept 1870, Sir Henry Elliot wrote: 'The quarrel between him and Mr Mott is of such trifling importance that Eldridge is quite right in saying it need never have been reported at all; but what makes me anxious is the evidence which it seems to give that Burton is trying to be in favour with the more intolerant section at Damascus, and this may sooner or later lead to very serious trouble.'

30 These sorts of abuses practised, it has to be said, by Christian as well as Jewish money-lenders, were of long-standing concern to the authorities. See FO, 78/622, Wood to Aberdeen, No.44, 29 Dec 1845. A firman issued in 1851, fixed a rate of interest of 8 percent interest on loans in order to protect the peasants from extortion by the moneylenders, FO 78/910, Wood to Canning, No.3, incl. in Wood to Palmerston, No.2, Damascus, 28 Jan 1852. It failed through lack of enforcement, and led to a worse situation. See M. Ma'oz, *Ottoman Reform in Syria and Palestine, 1840-61* (OUP, 1968), p.158ff.

31 Under a system known as the Capitulations. These were extra-territorial rights originally granted to Europeans in the hey-day of the Ottoman Empire, allowing them to trade and be tried under Western forms of justice. Over time, what began as a concession turned into widespread abuse, embassies affording protection to all manner of people in order to enhance their prestige. See D.C.M. Platt, *The Cinderella Service. British Consuls since 1825* (London, 1971), p.136ff.

32 TNA, FO 881/2148, Encl. in No.46, Burton to Elliot, Damascus, 21 Nov 1870. This despatch was used by Isabel for her account in *The Inner Life of Syria*, p.332. She suppressed the names of the Jewish moneylenders, describing them instead as 'a triumvirate of Shylocks.'

33 Sir Francis Henry Goldsmid (1808-78), the first Jewish barrister in England. As leader of the Anglo-Jewish Association, 1871-8, he publicised the oppression of Jews in Poland, Serbia, and Rumania. Sir Moses Montefiore, 1784-1885. An outstanding philanthropist and supporter of rights for oppressed Jews all over the world.

34 HBM's Consulate, 29 Nov 1870. Wilkins who prints this letter in *The Romance*, p.456, is coy for some reason of using Goldsmid's name at the head of the letter, printing two dashes instead.

35 See his Report, *Diplomatic and Consular Services*. Ordered by the House of Commons to be printed, 16 July 1872, pp.204. Commenting on the problem of the Jewish money-lenders, Kennedy suggested retaining British protection, believing that the debtors could end up in a worse position if the moneylenders looked for protection from another consulate. See TNA, FO/1132, Beirut, 11 Jan 1871.

36 TNA, FO 881/2148, No.25, Confidential. Elliot to Granville, Constantinople, 15 Jan. 1871.

37   TNA, FO 881/2148, No.8, Kennedy to Granville, Cairo, 15 Jan 1871. In the meantime, it is clear that Sir Henry Elliot had been having second thoughts. While agreeing in principle with Kennedy's conclusions, he thought it would not be desirable for the Damascus Consulate to hold a lower rank than that of France and Russia. Only if they reduced theirs, would Britain be justified in doing the same. See FO 881/2148, No 11, Commercial, Elliot to Granville, Constantinople, 14 Feb 1871.

38   Unless Isabel was lying, it is noticeable here that Rashid Pasha makes no mention of his offering her an apology, and giving orders for the burning and sacking of the family's home, and their confinement in jail.

39   TNA, FO 881/2148, Rashid Pasha to Aali Pasha, Damascus, 11 Jan 1871.

40   TNA, FO 881/2148, No.25 Confidential, Elliot to Granville, 15 Jan 1871.

41   R.F. Burton & C.F.T. Drake, *Unexplored Syria*, i, Appendix IV, p.33, 'Notes on the Hamah Stones, with Reduced Transcripts.'

42   J.L. Burckhardt, *Travels in Syria and the Holy Land* (London, 1822) p.145.

43   The Hamah Stones and Burton's papers are discussed in N.M. Penzer, *An Annotated Bibliography*, pp.220-22. It has since been discovered that this system of pictographic writing was used in the Syrian Hittite states for writing an eastern dialect of the Luwian language chiefly from the 10th–6th century BC. Hieroglyphic Luwian was largely deciphered between 1930 to 1935. Additional information was obtained after the discovery in 1947 of the Karatepe bilingual inscriptions, written in both Hieroglyphic Luwian and Phoenician.

44   I. Burton, *The Inner Life of Syria*, ii, p.257.

45   Lord Redesdale, *Memories* (London, 1915) ii, p.572. A highly dubious claim at best. There is not the slightest evidence that Burton had any thoughts about translating the *Arabian Nights* at this period.

46   *Ibid.*, pp.563-4.

47   R.F. Burton & C.F.T. Drake, *Unexplored Syria*, i, p.142.

48   *The Life*, p.543 & pp.570-1.

49   *The Romance*, ii, p.487 *et seq.*

50   A similar incident of stone-throwing, this time by a Muslim mob, occurred at Safed four years later, involving Lt Conder, RE, and his party, working under the auspices of the Palestine Exploration Fund. See P. Magnus, *Kitchener, Portrait of an Imperialist* (London, 1958), p.14 *et seq.*

51   I. Burton, *The Inner Life of Syria*, ii, p.224.

52   *Ibid.*, p.224.

53   *The Romance*, ii, p.491.

54   TNA, FO 881/2148, Encl. 1 in No.25, Pisani to Elliot, Pera, 20 May 1871.

55   TNA, FO 881/2148, No.41 Commercial, Elliot to Granville, Constantinople, 22 April 1871.

56   TNA, FO 881/2148, No.52 Commercial, Granville to Elliot, Foreign Office, 25 May 1871.

57   *The Inner Life of Syria*, p.257.

58   QK Coll, General Government of the Vilayet of Syria, Rashid to Burton, Damascus, 6 June 1871.

59   QK Coll, H.M Consulate, Damascus, Burton to Rashid, 8 June 1871. Burton later claimed that Rashid deliberately sent out a plundering party to kill them. See *Unexplored Syria*, p.252. 'I duly appreciated the compliment,' Burton wrote, 'of sending 300 men to dispose of three…the felon act, however, failed, and their fifteen days of wandering ended without incident.' According to Isabel, *The Inner Life of Syria,*, p.262, she sent a messenger to warn them of the alleged plot, 'and by God's blessing it was in time.'

60   TNA, FO 881/2148, No.65 Commercial, Elliot to Granville, Therapia, 5 June 1871.

61   TNA, FO 881/2148, No.7, Burton to Elliot, Damascus, 7 June 1871.

62   TNA, FO 881/2148, No.8, Burton to Elliot, Damascus, 9 June 1871.

63   TNA, FO 881/2148, No.9, Burton to Elliot, Damascus, 11 June 1871.

64   TNA, FO 881/2148, Burton to Elliot, Damascus, 18 June 1871.

65   TNA, FO 881/2148, No.1, Odo Russell to Burton, FO, 14 June 1871.

66   This letter does not appear in the correspondence of the Blue Book.

67   TNA, FO 881/2148, No.79, Elliot to Granville, Therapia, 26 June 1871.

68   TNA, FO 881/2148, No.15, Burton to Elliot, Damascus, 1 July 1871.

69   The Shadhiliyah, or Shaziliyah, are a brotherhood of Islamic Sufis, founded on the teachings of the Muslim theologian Abu al-Hasan ash-Shadhili, born 1196/97, died 1258. The order, founded in Egypt, became one of the most popular of the mystical brotherhoods of the Middle East and North Africa. There is an account of the order, obviously written by Burton, which Isabel first incorporated in her chapter headed, "The Christian Revival in Syria," *The Inner Life of Syria*, pp.182-3. She then used the whole of this material, with certain additions, in *The Life*, i, p.550-51, under the same title. There is a pamphlet in the OHG, *The Review of Christianity in Syria. Its Miracles and Martyrdoms.* Related by 'P.' The author is undoubtedly Isabel, adopting the first letter of her nickname P[uss].

70   TNA, FO 881/2148, No.16, Burton Elliot, Damascus, 3 July 1871. In the opinion of one British Consular judge, missionaries were, 'next to habitual criminals, the most troublesome people in the world to deal with.' Quoted in R.H. Davison, *Reform in the Ottoman Empire,* p.74.

71   *The Life*, i, p.548.

72   R.F. Burton, *First Footsteps in East Africa* (London, 1856), pp.77-79n.

73   *The Life*, p.549.

74   *Ibid.*, p.548.

75   TNA, FO 881/2148, No.24, Burton to Elliot, Damascus, 15 July 1871. A 'rayah' is defined by the *OED* as, 'A non-Muslim subject of the Sultan of Turkey, subject to payment of the poll-tax.' Presumably Burton is using the word here in its root meaning of subjects or peasants. Later that year, *after* his recall, he wrote to his friend, Rathborne: 'If you can get a peep at last Tablet do, and you will find Tyrwhitt Drake's account of the revivalist movement in Syria. He says it may amount to 20,000 – 25,000. *Do you advise me to draw Ld Granville's attention to it?* [my italics] Mind, the affair is serious. If anything like a massacre takes place, Russia certainly and France probably will interfere and occupy Syria in force. Prussia and Austria will object and then there is a row.' EMG, Howletts, Monday, 4 Dec 1871. Rathborne's reply is not extant. There is no evidence, however, that Burton followed up the matter with the FO.

76   TNA, FO 881/2148, Telegraphic, Encl. 1, Mrs Burton to Elliot, Beyrout, 10 July 1871; Telegraphic, Encl. 2, Elliot to Mrs Burton, Constantinople, 20 July 1871. Writing between these two dates, Sir Henry complained to Edmund Hammond of Burton's 'inconvenient way of making his wife write to me on public matters and it is difficult to snub a lady beyond certain limits.....They carry the system so far that last night I got a telegram from her asking leave for him to some place four hours distance from Damascus on account of the heat....' See NLS MSS13609: f. 183. Therapia, 14 July 1871.

77   TNA, FO 881/2148, No.100, Commercial, Elliot to Granville, Therapia, 6 Aug 1871.

78   R.F. Burton & C.F.T. Drake, *Unexplored Syria*, p.4.

79   TNA, FO 881/2148, No.l3, Granville to Burton, Foreign Office, 22 July 1871.

80   TNA, 881/2148, Nos. 31 &.32, Burton to Elliot, Damascus, 9 Aug 1871. Both these complaints were followed up by the FO, the second one particularly forcefully, Lord Granville instructing Sir Henry Elliot to state, 'that HM's Government must insist on the displacement of the officers who have so grossly failed in the performance of the investigation intrusted to them, as well as on the punishment of the offenders. Your Excellency will speak very seriously to the new Grand Vizier on this point, and say that HM's Government expect a searching inquiry to be instituted without delay.' See FO 881/2148, No.16 Commercial, Granville to Elliot, FO, 12 Sept 1871.

81   *The Inner Life of Syria*, p.276; *The Romance*, p.499; *The Life*, p.569.

82   TNA, FO 881/2148, Separate, Burton to Granville, Damascus, 17 Aug 1871.

83   *The Life*, p.568.

84   These excerpts are from a copy of Jane Digby's diary in the personal collection of Mary S. Lovell.

85   *The Inner Life of Syria*, p.299.

86   *Ibid.*, p.299.

Notes to Chapter 31

1   TCC, Burton to Houghton, 20 Sept 1871.

2   *Ibid.*, Burton to Houghton, 26 Sept 1871.

3   *The True Life*, p.363.

4   TCC, I. Burton to Lady Houghton, Ashridge, 14 Nov 1871.

5   *The Life*, i, p.570. This claim is repeated in almost identical words on p.584.

6   As is clear from a letter to Burton from James Orr Scott of the Irish Presbyterian Mission, Damascus, it was widely believed there that Burton was the author of a number of critical letters which had been printed in *The Levant Herald*, an English language newspaper published in Constantinople. According to Scott, he was told by Mrs Mentor Mott, that her husband had been 'offended and injured by a severe criticism of his conduct which had appeared in the "Levant Herald," and which was supposed to be the product of Captain Burton.' She had assured Scott, 'That Mrs Burton had herself told her "Captain Burton writes the letters and I put in the spice."' See James Orr Scott to Burton, Damascus, 17 March 1871, WSRO. There is no reference to these letters either in *The Life* or *The Romance*.

7   BL, Add MSS 46, 698ff, 230-1, Rashid Pasha to Aali Pasha, 30 July 1871. Isabel, obviously unaware of Rashid Pasha's request to be allowed to return to Constantinople, claimed that, following news of his own recall, he 'fought hard to stay.' See *The Life*, p.586, and *The Romance*, ii, p.505.

8   TNA, 881/2148, Jago to Elliot, Damascus, 28 Sept 1871. Jago stated that the Wali's successor was to be Achmet Tawfik Pasha. 'He is said to belong to the old Turkish school, and a recurrence to the policy of that party, as opposed to that of progress, with which Rashid is identified, is looked forward to with impatience by some and with anxiety by others.'

9   Accounts of this incident can be found in R.H. Davison, *Reform in the Ottoman Empire, 1856-76* (Princeton, 1963), p.346, and in Sir Henry G. Elliot (ed. G. Elliot), *Some Revolutions and Other Diplomatic Experiences* (London, 1922), pp.244-45. Hasan was hanged the next day, 'helping to adjust the rope round his own neck....'

10 See M.L. Gross, *Ottoman Rule in the Province of Damascus, 1869-1909*, PhD thesis, Georgetown University (1979), p.122.

11 TCC, I. Burton to Lady Houghton, 14 Nov 1871.

12 See D.C.M. Platt. *The Cinderella Service. British Consuls Since 1825* (London, 1971), p.134, where he describes Consul-General Eldridge's reporting from Beirut in 1870, that he had frequently to interrupt his consular duties to deal with pressing political and religious problems, in order 'to save the country from the return of the disasters it had so often suffered in the past.'

13 TNA, FO 881/2148, (Separate), Burton to Granville, 14 Montagu Place, Montagu Sq, London, 16 Oct 1871. Penzer notes that a zincograph copy of this letter is on folio paper, and the actual letter occupies seven full pages and a few lines. With it are thirty-four letters of appreciation, also zincographed, occupying twenty-nine foolscap pages. See N.M. Penzer, *An Annotated Bibliography*, p.215.

14 R.H. Davison, *Reform in the Ottoman Empire*, pp.71-2, states that foreign diplomats were often disliked 'because of their frequent high-handed interference in Ottoman affairs.' In fact, London was asked three times to recall Sir Stratford de Redcliffe who 'would not allow the sultan to reign as coequal with himself.' There was an even greater dislike of foreign consuls, who 'tended 'to drag national honour into their personal arguments with the Turks, and often to conduct themselves like little lords.'

15 TNA, FO 881/2148. I have drawn on observations made by Elliot in two despatches: No.109 Commercial, Elliot to Granville, Therapia, 24 Aug 1871, and No.117 Commercial, Therapia, 9 Sept 1871.

16 *The Life*, i, p.589; *The Romance*, ii, pp.527-28. According to Wilkins, Isabel, knowing how difficult it was to get Burton to discuss verbally matters of this kind, is supposed to have put a note between the leaves of a book he was reading, 'to arouse him to a sense of the position.'

17 TNA, FO 881/2148, Granville to Burton, FO, 25 Oct 1871. Damascus was made up to a full consulate only a short time later, a fact noticed, surprisingly, without pejorative comment by Burton in a note written to his friend, Rathborne, in December.

18 TNA, FO 881/2148, (Separate), Burton to Granville, 14 Montagu Place, Montagu Sq, London, 12 Nov 1871. This is the last letter in the 'Correspondence Respecting Consul Burton's Proceedings at Damascus, 1868-71,' marked 'Confidential.' It was printed for the use of the Foreign Office in February 1872. The originals of Burton's despatches forming part of this 'Correspondence' are in the WSRO.

19   *The Life*, p.591.

20   TCC, I. Burton to Lady Houghton, Ashridge, Berkhampsted, 14 Nov 1871.

21   *The Life*, p.593. She omits to say whether or not Burton accepted the invitation.

22   See A. Geikie, *Life of Sir Roderick I. Murchison* (London, 1875), p.331.

23   *The Times*, 28 October 1871, p.6. Winwood Reade died four years later.

24   Edward Tichborne (1782-1853) = Katherine, dau. of James Arundell, 9th Lord Arundell of Wardour (1795-1853); Alfred Joseph Tichborne, 11th Baronet = Teresa Mary, eldest dau. of Benedict, 11th Lord Arundell of Wardour; Francis Catherine Tichborne (1809-36) = Henry Benedict, 11th Arundell of Wardour.

25   Extracted from Burton's evidence as reported in *The Times*, Thursday, 14 Dec 1871.

26   *The True Life*, pp.364-5.

27   Knowsley was the home of the Stanley family, Earls of Derby. Burton planted a Cedar of Lebanon there, one of several he had brought back with him. Others were planted at Garswood.

28   TCC, Burton to Houghton, Garswood, Newton le Willows, 1 Jan 1872.

29   RGS Archives, Burton to Bates, 34 Queen St., Edinburgh, 26 Jan 1872. Dr John Kirk was then Consul at Zanzibar. The Rev T. Wakefield was employed by the CMS at Mombasa.

30   R.F. Burton, *Zanzibar; City, Island and Coast* (London, 1872), i, p.xii.

31   *Ibid.*, ii, p.371.

32   NLS, Grant Papers, MS 17922, f. 107. This bitter commentary on the book is written on two foolscap sheets,

33   The extract from *The Examiner* review of 3 February 1872, to which Burton took exception, is quoted by him in *Unexplored Syria*, p.xv.

34   *The Athenaeum*, No.2309, 27 Jan 1872, pp.105-6.

35   *Ibid*, p.596.

36   Edgcumbe Staley, 1906, pp.106-7. Quoted in Richard Ormond's catalogue of the *Victorian High Renaissance* exhibition at Minneapolis, Brooklyn and Manchester, 1978-9, p.113.

37   *The Life*, p.596. This is slightly misquoted: 'shop' should read 'spirit shop.'

38   Minutes of Evidence, Select Committee on Diplomatic and Consular Services, PP 1872, 314, VII, QQ 2047-8, quoted in D.C.M. Platt, *The Cinderella Service*, p.40. The 1872 Committee recommended the division of the consular service into two classes: a salaried class restricted from trading and accounting for all fees to the Exchequer, and an unsalaried class rendering services gratuitously, but retaining such fees as it collected to cover office expenses.

39   Sir Henry Stisted was appointed Colonel of the Regiment on 25 September 1873, following the death of Lt Gen G.C. Hay. See Brig Gen A.E. Cavendish, CMG, *The 93rd Sutherland Highlanders Now 2nd Bn. The Argyll and Sutherland Highlanders, 1799-1927* (published privately, 1928), p.208. The late Brigadier J.N. Stisted, OBE, presented a photograph of Sir Henry to the Regiment in the early 1980s.

40   *The True Life*, p.366.

41   *The Life*, p.597. Charles James Lever (1808-72), Anglo-Irish writer, born in Dublin, where he trained in medicine at Trinity College. His early novels in particular, set in the post-Napoleonic Wars period in Ireland and Europe, featuring lively picaresque heroes, were immensely popular.

42   T.Wright, *The Life of Sir Richard Burton*, i, p.231.

43   *The Life*, p.597.

44   TCC, Burton to Houghton, 23 Sept 1872.

45   RGS Archives, Burton to Bates, Newton le Willows, 16 Jan 1872.

46   Quoted in R. Hall, *Stanley. An Adventurer Explored* (London, 1974), p.210.

47   *Ibid.*, pp.220-1.

48   Quoted in E. Longford, *Victoria R.I.* (London, 2000), p.458.

49   V.L. Cameron, 'Burton As I Knew Him,' *The Fortnightly Review*, Vol.LIV (XLVIII NS), Dec 1890, p.882. He was mistaken in dating it to November, since Burton left for Trieste on 24 Oct. Cameron was given the command of a new 'Livingstone Search Expedition,' which sailed from Zanzibar for Bagamoyo on 2 Feb 1873. After discovering that Livingstone was dead, he continued his march across Africa, eventually arriving at Benguella on the West

coast, the first European to traverse the African continent from east to west. For the explorer's own account, see V.L. Cameron, *Across Africa* (London, 1877). There is a biography of Cameron by W.R. Foran, *African Odyssey* (London, 1937). For a scholarly assessment see, J.A. Casada, 'Verney Lovett Cameron: A Centenary Appreciation,' *Geographical Journal*, Vol.141, Part 2, July 1975, pp.203-15.

50   The words 'Mwata ya Nvo' occur in Burton's translation of *The Lands of Cazembe*, p.12, where he writes: 'Without mentioning the information given by Godinho and De Jarric, or the well-known journey of the Pombeiros, we find that in 1845-47 the lands of "Mwata ya Nvo" on the highroad across the continent, were visited by Joaquin Rodriguez Graça, and shortly afterwards by the late Ladislaus Magyar, if what he reports was a fact.'

51   See *The Life*, p.598. His name in the Arundell genealogy is given as Henry Adolphus, 1841-72, though Isabel calls him Jack, 'our youngest and favourite brother.' According to her account, he was administered 'a very slight dose of opiate,' to which he was allergic, for rheumatic fever. It is quite possible that he took an overdose, unable any longer to bear the pain and the lack of sleep, the truth being withheld from members of the family to spare their feelings and religious sensibilities. There are photographs of him in the WSRO.

52   TNA, FO 7/803, Burton to Granville, 20 Manchester St, Manchester Sq, London, 2 Oct 1872. The Treasury register for 1872, T2/299, indicates that the FO never referred Burton's request to the Treasury.

53   See R.B. Burton, *Sindh and the Races* (London, 1851), Chap.VII, p.158ff, where he quotes highly selective extracts on the subject of matrimony from a work, 'composed by one Sayyid Hasan Ali in the Sindhi dialect, and called the Lizzat El Nisa Sharai, or the "Lawful Enjoyment of Women."' In note 1, p.401, he writes, 'As opposed to the other Lizzat El Niza.'

54   *Kama Shastra, or The Hindoo Art of Love (Ars Amoris Indica)*, Translated from the Sanskrit and Annotated by A.F.F. and B.F.R., Preface, p.xi. Note the printing of their initials in reverse. In his *One Thousand Nights and a Night*, iii, pp.92-93, Burton wrote: 'A literal translation of the Ananga-Ranga appeared in 1873 under the name of Kama-Shastra; or the Hindoo Art of Love (Ars Amoris Indica); but of this only six copies were printed. It was reissued (printed but not published) in 1885.' There is a comprehensive account of the different reprints of this work in N.M. Penzer, *An Annotated Bibliography*, pp.171-73.

55   *The Life*, ii, pp 2-3.

56   TNA, FO 7/803, Burton to Granville, Trieste, 8 Dec 1872.

57   QK Coll, I. Burton to Franks, 20 Manchester Street, 1 Nov 1872.

58   HL, EMC, Burton to Tootal, Trieste, 9 March 1873.

59   *The Life*, ii, p.3. The anecdote about the game-cock and bull-terrier was, of course, apocryphal.

Notes to Chapter 32

1   Quoted in D.C.M. Platt, *The Cinderella Service,* p.27.

2   TCC, Burton to Houghton, Trieste, 14 Feb 1873. Badakhshan is a province of north-eastern Afghanistan. In 1584 it was conquered by the Uzbeks, remaining under the control of local Uzbek mirs until 1822, when the province was overrun by Morad Beg of Qonduz. In 1859 it became tributary to Kabul, finally losing its autonomy in 1881.

3   QK Coll. There is a short entry for Lt General Wylde (1788-1877) in F. Boase, *Modern English Biography* (Truro, 1892-1921), Vol.6, p.1533. The writer of the Catalogue details for the letter's sale at one of the leading auction houses, claimed, without citing any source, that Wylde became Queen Victoria's secret envoy (whatever that meant) early on in her reign. He/she then went on: 'None of Burton's biographers have ever made a connection between Queen Victoria and Burton. However, Burton's relationship to Wylde and his special relationship with the Queen, clearly show, albeit at second hand, her interest in his career.' This is quite an unwarranted assumption, in my opinion, and reads like a sales pitch designed to increase the potential value of the letter at auction. Wylde was appointed equerry to Prince Albert on 25 Feb 1840, acting as groom of the bedchamber from 1846-61. He was never, as this writer asserts, 'Aide-de Camp to Queen Victoria.'

4   Unable to find the letter in question, a search was made on my behalf at TNA in the General Correspondence

relating to Austria, TNA, FO 7/914, without success.

5   Walburga Lady Paget, *Further Recollections* (London, 1923), i, p.282.

6   *The Life*, ii, p.22. 'Teddy' Howard was a cousin of the Duke of Norfolk, and the second cardinal in the Norfolk family since the seventeenth century. Isabel's aunt, Lady Gerard (née Harriet Clifton), wife of Sir Robert Tolver Gerard (created Lord Gerard, 1876), was a cousin of the Duchess of Norfolk. See M. Bence-Jones, *The Catholic Families* (London, 1992), pp. 224 & 226. Walburga, Lady Paget, described him as 'a jolly priest, who could never forget that he had been a lifeguardsman. There was a Tommy Atkins swagger about his walk when he strode up to St. Peter's, of which he was vicar, and the gorgeous silks and precious laces in which he clothed his stately presence, swung round him in a right militant way.' See *Further Recollections*, p.279.

7   Notes on Rome: *Macmillan's Magazine*, Vol.XXXI. I. The Seven Hills of Rome. Nov 1874, pp.57-63. II. The Actualities of Rome Dec 1874. III. The Hygienic Treatment of the Tiber. Dec 1874, pp.126-34.

8   In *The Romance*, ii, p.544, it is said that Isabel suffered from blood-poisoning as well as fever.

9   E. Lee, *Ouida, A Memoir* (London, 1914), p.49. See also Walburga Lady Paget, *Further Recollections*, pp.282-3.

10 TNA, FO 7/819, Burton to Granville, Trieste, 25 April 1873.

11 *The Athenaeum*, No.2376, 10 May 1873, pp.598-9.

12 *The Life*, ii, p.24.

13 *Ibid.*, p.25.

14 In a letter to Georgiana written from Wardour Castle, 5 July 1872, Isabel reported to her niece that 'Arundell has done an awfully kind thing.......he has desired me to assume all the family honours on arriving, and given me copies of the Patent, with all the old signatures.... He has desired my cards to be presented Mrs Richard Burton, the Countess Arundell of Wardour of the most sacred Roman Empire.' Quoted in T. Wright, *The Life of Sir Richard Burton*, p.231-2.

15 *The Athenaeum*, No.2377, 17 May 1873, p.631. Burton wrote at the end of his report, 'You will probably hear from me again when the Exhibition really opens. Meanwhile, remember that the cream of the cream will be in June and July. Earlier the works will not be completed; later on Vienna becomes a Jehannum of a climate, deserted withal. The prizes will be distributed upon the Imperial birthday, August 18th.'

16 This is the amount given later in *The Life*, ii, p.25. In a letter to her cousins, John and Lucy Arundell, Trieste, June 30 1873 (QK Coll), which I have already cited, she stated that she 'ran through £140 in 24 days without being aware of it and am paying for it now, and that with the greatest economy.'

17 'Celebrity at Home, Captain Richard F. Burton at Trieste,' *The World*, 27 Nov 1878. This account first appeared in *A Short Sketch of the Career of Captain Richard F. Burton*, by an Old Oxonian (London & Belfast, 1880), and then in the 1886 reprint, pp.30-47. It was reproduced in *The Life*, ii, pp.4-10. In spite of the fact that the author of the article is stated to be 'a passer-by on the Staff of the lively World,' *A Short Sketch*, p.24, it is incorrectly attributed to Alfred Bates (sic) Richards in the Index to *The Life*.

18 'Testimony of Captain Burton on Spiritualism,' *The Spiritualist*, No.59 (Vol.III, No.20), 1 Sept 1873, pp.309-10.

19 R.F. Burton, *The Lands of Cazembe* (London, 1873). Burton's main contribution to the book ends on p.164. Two other translations of Portuguese accounts were included. The second narrative, according to the Preface, 'the route journal of the Pombeiros, P.J. Baptista & Amaro José, who traversed Africa from Angola to Tette and crossed therefore the recent line of march of Dr. Livingstone between Cazembe and Lake Bagweolo, was translated by Mr. B.A. Beadle, Chancellor of the Portuguese Consulate in London, Captain Burton revising and editing this portion of the volume. Of the third narrative, that of Messrs Monteiro and Gamitto, whose journey to Cazembe was undertaken in 1831, it has been thought sufficient to reprint a résumé that had previously appeared from the able pen of Dr. Charles Beke.'

20 A.H. Sayce, *Reminiscences* (London, 1923), p.52.

21 See W.D. Cooley, 'The Geography of Nyassi, or the great lake of southern Africa investigated,' *JRGS* 15 (1845), pp.185-235; 'Further explanations in reference to the geography of Nyassi,' *JRGS* 16 (1846), pp.138-43; 'The journey of Joachim Rodriguez Graça to the Muata Yamvo,' *Proceedings of the RGS*, OS I, 1856, pp.92-3, and 'On the travels of the Portuguese and others in inner Africa,' *Proceedings of the RGS*, OS 8, 1864, pp.255-63.

22 The Lands of Cazembe: Lacerda's journey to Cazembe in 1798. Supplementary Papers by the Same. *The Academy*, Vol.V, 3 Jan 1874, pp.2-4.

23   'Notes on the Castellieri or Prehistoric Ruins of the Istrian Peninsula,' dated Tizu, 18 February 1874.' Published in *Anthropologia*, No.III, Oct 1874, pp.375-415. They are reproduced in *The Life*, ii, pp.27-30. The meeting later that year of the London Anthropological Society at which Burton's paper was read by Dr Carter Blake, was described as 'certainly the most interested and crowded meeting which has taken place since the palmy days of Dr. Hunt and the great negro question.' Burton's paper was fulsomely praised as 'one of the most important contributions to prehistoric literature which has ever been published.'

24   HL, EMC, Burton to Tootal, 2 March 1874.

25   TNA, FO 7/839, Derby to Burton, 21 May 1874. This was in reply to Burton's despatch No.20 of 9 May.

26   The Wiener Schneeberg, 2,076 metres high, is about 80 km south-west of Vienna. Along with the limestone massif of the Rax, it is considered as the Viener Hausberg, the 'home mountain' for the people of the Vienna region.

27   TCC, I. Burton to Houghton, 12 Aug 1874. Most of the account is reproduced in *The Life*, ii, pp.34-5. For whatever reason, connected perhaps with interference by Isabel's sister, Dilly, there is no mention of Burton's grave illness in *The Romance*.

28   *The Life*, ii, p.35.

29   *Ibid.*, p.35. In his contribution to W.Besant (ed.), *The Literary Remains of the Late Charles F. Tyrwhitt Drake, FRGS* (London, 1877), p.21, Burton wrote, 'During the spring of 1874 he caught as before mentioned the Jericho fever whilst he was camped in the rainy swamps that bound the lower Jordan. When a little better he was removed to Jerusalem where he relapsed, and where his horror of the climate was justified, as if it had been a presentiment, by the fatal result of his illness.' His successor in the work for the Palestine Exploration Fund was Lt (later Field Marshal Lord) Kitchener. He joined his friend, Lt Claude Conder in Camp at El Dhoheriyeh in the plain of Philistia on 2 November 1874. See P.Magnus, *Kitchener:Portrait of an Imperialist* (London, 1958), p.12.

30   *The Life*, ii, pp.40-41.

31   The others; *a New System of Sword Exercise for Infantry*; *Etruscan Bologna*, and *Two Trips to Gorilla Land and the Cataracts of the Congo*, were not published until 1876. His *The Lowlands of the Brazil*, completed early in 1874, which he told his friend, Albert Tootal, in a letter dated 2 March of that year, 'will be published when my wife goes to London, say June next,' failed to find a publisher, and disappeared from sight.

32   QK Coll. Letter from Isabel dated 23 Jan 1875, responding to an offer of the previous day from an unnamed correspondent, probably the publisher, William P. Nimmo.

33   WSRO. Letter to I. Burton from Alfred G. Lock, Roselands, Millbrook, Southampton, 29 Jan 1875. It appears from the letter that Burton's brothers-in-law, W. Fitzgerald, and Sir Henry Stisted had also been drawn into the enterprise, if only peripherally. The former is quoted as stating that, 'as a business man he should be sorry to depend on Capt. Burton's opinion of a mineral property and would very much rather have an Engineer's report.'

34   RGS Archives. Council of the RGS to Earl Derby, 22 March 1875.

35   A reference to the *Ananga Ranga*, which Burton and Arbuthnot had issued the previous year under the name of "*Kama Shastra*" or the "*Hindoo Art of Love.*" Burton, in fact, has mis-remembered the order of the initials, which were printed as A.F.F. and B.F.R. As we have seen, only four or six copies were printed, one, possibly, going to Lord Houghton.

36   This is the *Kama Sutra* of Vatsyayana, the first edition of which did not appear until 1883. It appeared under the imprint of the so-called Kama Shastra Society, founded by Burton and Arbuthnot in that year, mainly for the printing of Eastern erotica.

37   TCC, Burton to Houghton, Trieste, 2 March 1875.

38   TNA, FO 7/860, Burton to Derby, Trieste, 15 April 1875.

39   TNA, FO 7/860, Burton to Derby, Trieste, 26 April 1875.

40   HL, EMC. Burton to Tootal, 24 May 1875. Burton, in fact, had taken 15 days travelling from Trieste.

41   The legal agreement drawn up between Isabel and the publisher, Henry S. King & Co in 1875, forms part of The Burton Collection, George Arents Research Library, Syracuse University, Syracuse, New York.

42   *The Athenaeum*, No.2488, 3 July 1875, pp.18-19.

43   I. Burton, *The Inner Life*, ii, pp.113-14.

44   *Ibid.*, p.163.

45 Oddly, and coincidentally, he had met a Captain Burton earlier that day, but as the footnote by the editor indicates, 'Captain Henry Burton of N. Audley Street, London.' See H.C.G. Matthew (ed.), *The Gladstone Diaries* (Oxford, 1986), Vol.IX, Jan 1875 – Dec 1880, p.43.

46 TNA, FO 7/860, Burton to Derby, Howlett's Hotel, Manchester Street, Manchester Square, 14 June 1875.

47 Tiflis, present-day Tbilisi, capital of Georgia. The city, standing on the Kura River, has a strategic position commanding the route between western and eastern Transcaucasia. It was captured by the Russians in 1810.

48 TNA, FO 7/860, Burton to Derby, Howlett's Hotel, 15 June 1875.

49 R.F. Burton, *A New System of Sword Exercise for Infantry* (London, 1876). Isabel wrote in *The Life*, ii, p.42: 'This last, when he arrived, he took himself to his Royal Highness the Duke of Cambridge, who desired him to show him several of the positions of defence he most liked, and a system of *manchette*, with which he appeared particularly pleased, and Richard returned enchanted with his interview.....With this pamphlet he had done for broadsword exercise, what a score of years ago he did for bayonet exercise, and he was confident that the Horse Guards will eventually adopt it.'

50 This was Burton's carbine pistol, described with an illustration in *The Life*, i, pp.455-57, adapted by Burton from the central-fire Albini rifle, to avoid using the shoulder when on horseback.

51 TCC, Burton to Houghton, 14 June 1875.

52 *The Life*, ii, p.50.

53 It should have been held on Thursday, 1 July, but was postponed because of rain. See Court Circular: Windsor Castle, 1 July, *The Times*, 2 July 1875, p.9. The Royal Garden Party was reported in *The Times*, 6 July 1875, p.7. The huge guest list, printed in strict order of precedence, extends across 3$\frac{1}{2}$ columns of broad-sheet, 'Captain and Mrs Burton' appearing in the lower part of column three, among the lesser fry. Among the guests were Sir Robert Tolver and Lady Gerard through whom, it is likely, that Isabel obtained tickets for the event.

54 'Notes of Travel,' *The Academy*, 10 July 1875, p.38.

55 *Ibid.*, 31 July 1875, p.116. The expedition members were organised by Burton as follows: 'Captain Burton, Director General; Commissioner and Treasurer, Mr. Kent; Jäger, or Hunter, Mr. W.C. Baldwin; Master of the Horse, Mr. Tennant; Commissary General, Mr. Johnstone; Land Transport Quartermaster and Secretary, Mr. Lock; Surveyor-General or Assistant, Mr. G.F. Cole and Mr. W. Hope; Geologist-General, Mr.Germon Green; Manager and Inspector-General.'

56 Paray-le-Monial is in the Saône-et-Loire department of east central France, not far from Vichy. In the 17th century, Margaret Mary Alacoque founded the cult of the Sacred Heart of Jesus there. With the growth of the cult from the 1870s, it became second only to Lourdes as a pilgrimage site in France. The most venerated spot is the Chapel of the Visitation, where most of the apparitions said to have appeared to Margaret, took place. She was canonized by Benedict XV in 1920.

57 TNA, FO 7/860, Burton to Derby, 36 Manchester St, 22 Aug 1875.

58 TNA, FO 7/860, Burton to Derby, Hotel d'Espagne, 6 Rue Thibaut, Paris, 25 Sept 1875. Ritterbandt's address is given as 54 Manchester Sq W.

59 *The Life*, ii, p.51.

60 TNA: FO 7/860, Burton to Derby, Hotel d'Espagne, 6 Rue Thibaut, Paris, 12 Dec 1875.

61 *The Romance*, ii, pp.552-3.

Notes to Chapter 33

1 HL, EMC, Burton to Cave, Hotel d'Espagne, Paris, 15 Dec 1875. Cave, who was MP for Shoreham, Sussex, came from a rich West Indian family. Educated at Harrow, he became a lawyer, a director of the Bank of England and the London Dock Company.

2 Quoted in G. Tindall, *City of Gold. The Biography of Bombay* (London, 1982), p.29. Named after its first owner, John Watson, it was fabricated in England and erected on site between1867 and 1869. The five-storey building had 130 guest-rooms, a lobby, restaurant, bar and a large atrium lit by a glass skylight, which was used as a ballroom.

After the hotel closed in the 1960s, the owner allowed the building to deteriorate to such an extent that it was threatened with demolition. As a result of efforts by an Italian architect, the building was listed in June 2005 on the "100 World Endangered Monuments" by the World Monuments Fund based in New York.

3   *The Life*, ii, p.61.

4   TNA, FO 7/885, Burton to Derby, Watson's Hotel, Bombay, 16 Feb 1876.

5   TNA, FO 7/885, Derby to Burton, 23 March 1876.

6   The five autograph letters from Bapoojee Hurree dated 9, 15, 29 Feb, March and 14 March, are inserted in J.C.D.G. Duff, *History of the Marathas*, trans from the English original of Captain Grant Duff by Captain David Capon [Marathi text], Bombay, 1830. See B.J. Kirkpatrick (ed.), *A Catalogue of the Library of Sir Richard Burton, KCMG*, RAI, London, 1978 [BL, 1958]. A short account, with brief extracts from two of the letters, can be found in Alan H. Jutzi, 'Burton and His Library,' *In Search of Sir Richard Burton*. Papers from a Huntington Library Symposium, San Marino, Calif, 1993, pp.98-99.

7   QK Coll, Camp Dholtoa (?), 18 February 1876.

8   In 1724 Nizam–ul-Mulk Asif Jah I, founded the Asif Jahi dynasty, and seven generations of the family ruled the Deccan for 224 years up to 1948. The Nizam at the period of the Burton's visit was Mahboob Ali Pasha, then a minor aged ten. He was installed on the masnad by the British Resident and Sir Salar Jung, who also acted as the co-regent. His long rule extended from 1869-1911.

9   A watercolour of Sir Salar Jung (1829-83) by Leslie Ward, the noted caricaturist who adopted the pseudonym, 'Spy,' appeared in *Vanity Fair*, 14 Oct 1876.

10   The Salar Jung Museum, located on the southern bank of the Musi river in Hyderabad, opened to the public on 16 Dec 1951. It houses the magnificent collection of the Salar Jung family, mainly comprising Islamic art from all over Asia, including numerous illuminated Qu'rans, astrolabes, jewelled swords and daggers, and Persian carpets. It also contains examples of European art and sculpture, as well as Japanese and Chinese prints.

11   R.F. Burton, *Sind Revisited* (London, 1877), p.47.

12   *Ibid.*, pp.62-63.

13   *Ibid*, pp.256-7.

14   *The Life*, p.104.

15   *Ibid.*, p.117.

Notes to Chapter 34

1   Badly advised by his ambassador at the Porte, Sir Henry Elliot, Disraeli initially dismissed the allegations as 'coffee-house babble.' He was furious when it later emerged that the accounts were only too true. In September, Gladstone published an eloquent pamphlet, *The Bulgarian Horrors and the Question of the East* containing the famous demand that Turkey should clear out 'bag and baggage.' It became a best-seller, some 40,000 copies of the pamphlet being sold within three or four days.

2   HL, EMC, Burton to Geary, 20 June 1876. The collection consists of seventeen autograph letters from Burton to Grattan Geary dating from 1876-79. Excerpts from thirteen of them first appeared in H.J. Schonfield, *Richard Burton, Explorer* (London, 1936), Appendix to Chapter XIV, pp.271-74. He failed, however, to give any provenance for them. In 1878, Geary published a travelogue, *Through Asiatic Turkey, Narrative of a Journey from Bombay to the Bosphorus*.

3   HL, EMC, 7 Sept 1876. In writing these letters, Burton adopted the pseudonym, 'Pantellaria.' from an island of that name in the Mediterranean off the north African coast. This is confirmed by an article in *The Times of India* under the heading, 'Notes from the Mediterranean,' written under 'the Library, Pantellaria Island,' dated 4 Nov 1876, and signed F.B. Baker, Burton's favourite alias. The first of his letters to *The Times of India* was sent on 2 Nov 1876. In the second, Burton wrote: 'Please put in a deceptive date, and see that the signature is the same as the last one….The next if you want it will be on the standpoint of Austria. Then Russia-cum-Turkey and lastly the Jews. Are you prepared for strong truths about the latter?

4   The paper, intended to compete with such established prints as *The Times* and *The Morning Herald*, had been launched in 1846 by the publishers, Bradbury and Evans, with the financial backing of Joseph Paxton and the 'Railway King,' George Hudson. Charles Dickens became its first editor, but resigned after only seventeen issues. Despite teething problems, it prospered as a radical newspaper, especially under the editorship of Archibald Forbes. In his 1 Sept letter to Geary, Burton wrote: 'Dare not go to Belgrade, or F.O. would pay me out for letters in the *Daily News* (August 15th and 24th)....'

5   These are previously unstated reasons for his hatred of the former Wali. They suggest that it was motivated more by personal rancour for his wishes being thwarted while at Damascus, than any high-minded disapproval of Rashid's alleged shameless plundering of Syria.

6   HL, EMC, 10 envelopes of letters to and from Sir Richard and Isabel Burton, 4/10. Richard Burton to Dr Edward J. Burton, Trieste, 24 June 1876. Part of this letter is quoted in Thomas Wright, *Sir Richard Burton*, i, p.270. Wright incorrectly dates Sir Henry Stisted's death to 1876. In fact, he died from tuberculosis on 10 Dec 1875. Furthermore, both the *DNB* and F. Boase, *Modern English Biography*, err in stating that he died at Wood House, Upper Norwood, Surrey. His death certificate shows that he died at Wrotham Villa, Sydenham Hill, Sydenham, Kent. It now lies almost wholly within the London borough of Lewisham.

7   For whatever reason, there was a delay, and his book, *Across Africa*, published in two volumes by Daldy, Isbiter & Co, London, did not appear until early in 1877. Despite this, it became a best-seller.

8   QK Coll, Cameron to Burton, 23 July 1876.

9   RGS Archives, Correspondence Files, 22 Nov 1875. Quoted in James A. Casada, 'Verney Lovett Cameron: A Centenary Appreciation,' *Geographical Journal*, Vol.1, Part 2, July 1975, p.210.

10   V.L. Cameron, *Across Africa* (London, 1885), p.544.

11   Matteo Maria Boiardo (1441? – 1494), began his poem about 1476. It was intended to consist of three parts, but only the first two, and part of the third, were completed at his death. The first edition of Ariosto's *Orlando furioso* was published at Venice in 1516, the second at Ferrara in 1521. A third edition, Ferrara, 1532, contained 46 cantos.

12   It is the last in a list of Burton's unpublished works made by Lady Burton's secretary, Miss Plowman. After Lady Burton's death, almost everything on this list was burned under instructions from her sister, Mrs Fitzgerald. See N.M. Penzer, *Ann. Bib.*, p.183.

13   *The Bookman's Journal and Print Collector*, 21 Jan 1921, p.211. Herbert Jones was the chief Librarian at the Central Library, Kensington, where Burton's books were first housed. The author of the article, using the pseudonym, *Sermones*, may well have been Penzer himself. There is a reproduction of p.19, 'Canto Secondo,' stanzas 60-8, of this valuable Milan edition of the *Orlando furioso* in Penzer's *Annotated Bibliography*, facing p.184. Almost every part of the page is covered with Burton's miniscule handwriting. Unfortunately, this is the only place where it can be seen, since the Ariosto has, apparently, disappeared. It is not listed in B.J. Kirkpatrick (ed.), *A Catalogue of the Library of Sir Richard Burton, KCMG* (London, 1978).

14   'Journals of Major-General C.G. Gordon, C.B. at Khartoum.' Reviewed by R.F. Burton, *The Academy*, 11 July 1885, p.19.

15   Gordon to Burton, Bedden, South of Gondokoro 23 miles, 17 July 1875. *The Romance*, ii, pp.646-50. W.H. Wilkins devotes the whole of Chap.XXV, pp.645-76, to printing a selection of the numerous letters from General Gordon to Burton written between 1875 and 1885.

16   Gordon to Burton, Oomchanga, Darfur, 21 June 1877, *The Romance*, p.655.

17   Burton's reply is undated both in *The Romance*, p.656, and *The Life*, ii, p.43. Here, it is represented as a response to a letter, also undated, from Gordon (who always dated his letters): 'You and I are the only two men fit to govern the Soudan; if the one dies, the other will be left. I will keep the Soudan, you take Darfur; and I will give you £5,000 a year if you will throw up Trieste.' The only letter mentioning £5,000 is one from Gordon to Burton, dated Khartoum, 8 August 1878: 'Why cannot you get two years' leave from F.O. then write (saying it is my suggestion) to H.H., and offer it? I could give, say, £5,000 a year from London to your Government.' *The Romance*, p.663.

18   There is no trace in TNA of Burton's February 1877 letter to the FO.

19   *The Life*, ii, p.122.

20   Infection occurred usually by inhaling the virus on airborne droplets, so Rodolphe might well have picked it up in

the close confines of a hansom cab. In the past it was known that if the sores did not touch (discrete smallpox), mortality was less than ten per cent. If they merged to form huge pustules (confluent smallpox), mortality was fifty per cent. If bleeding took place beneath the skin and from the nose and mouth (haemorrhagic or black smallpox) death was inevitable.

21   TCC, I. Burton to Lord Houghton, Trieste, 20 April 1877.

22   This is clear from a letter written by Burton to Grattan Geary on 8 February, in which he asks Geary to remain 'mum' about it. Burton refers to Zagreb as Agram, the German name by which the city was known during the Austro-Hungarian era. At this period, it was the centre of the pan-Yugoslav movement and of a Croatian independence movement, in which Burton was no doubt interested as part of the Eastern Question.

23   The review of Cameron's book, across two columns, appeared in *The Times of India*, 27 March 1877.

24   Burton had written a highly critical review of The Marquis de Compiègne's two-volume account of his African travels: *L'Afrique Equatoriale: Gabonais, Pahouins, Gallois*, and *L'Afrique Equatoriale: Okanda – Bangouens – Osyeba* (Paris, 1875). Of volume 1, he wrote, 'The English public will be sorely disappointed by a book which promises so much, by a map which ignores many of the names in the narrative, by eight illustrations which are utterly deficient in originality or character, and by 354 pages which manage to say as little as could, within that compass, have possibly been said.' *The Academy*, Vol.8, 30 Oct 1875, p.444. He was equally scathing of the second volume. See *The Academy*, Vol.9, 3 June 1876, p.531.

25   R.F. Burton, *The Gold Mines of Midian*, p.63 and footnote. The latter reads: 'The only allusion to it ever published was the following statement in the Tauchnitz Ed. of my Pilgrimage (1874), Vol.2, p.218. 'The country may have contained gold, but the superficial formation has long been exhausted. At Cairo I washed some sand brought back from the eastern shore of the Red Sea, north of Wijh (El Uijh) and found it worth my while.' As pointed out earlier, Burton made an oblique reference to this in his paper, 'Journey to Medina, with Route from Yambu,' *JRGS* 24 (1854), p.213.

26   R.F. Burton, *The Gold Mines of Midian,*, p.29.

27   'The Khedive's Last Dodge,' *Punch*, 9 Feb 1878, p.57.

28   'Senior's Conversations and Journals in Egypt,' Vol.1, p.181, quoted in Earl of Cromer, *Modern Egypt* (London, 1908), i, p.21. Evelyn Baring, 1st Earl Cromer (1841- 1917), army officer, administrator, and British diplomat. In 1872 he acted as secretary to his cousin, Lord Northbrook, Viceroy of India. Seven years later, he was appointed British controller of the debt office in Egypt. After serving on the Viceroy's council in India from 1880-83, he returned to Egypt as British Agent and consul-general with plenipotentiary powers, becoming virtual ruler of the country.

29   Earl of Cromer, *Modern Egypt*, p.11.

30   R.F. Burton, *The Gold Mines of Midian*, p.63. The *OED* defines a "placer" as, 'A deposit of sand, gravel or earth, in the bed of a stream, or any alluvial or diluvial detritus, containing gold or other valuable minerals in particles.

31   Burton must have been a poor judge of age in 1853, or Haji Wali looked considerably younger than he really was. Burton reckoned his age then to be 45, or thereabouts, which would have made him 69 in 1877, not 82.

32   R.F. Burton, *The Gold Mines of Midian*, pp.356-7.

33   TNA, FO 7/914, Burton to Derby, off Port Suez, 21 April 1877.

34   TNA, FO 7/914, Derby to Burton, 7 May 1877.

35   In *The Book of the Thousand Nights and a Night* (Benares, 1885), i, p.vii, Burton said that Arabia was the land of his predilection. In 1877, his choice of the Nile Valley was an opportunistic piece of flattery.

36   R.F. Burton, *The Gold Mines of Midian*, p.372.

37   *Ibid.*, p.380.

38   'The Ogham Character,'*The Athenaeum*, No.2580, 7 April 1877, p.447. The article contains numerous examples of the characters, e.g., 'El-Mushajjar applied to Arabic,' El-Mushakkar applied to old Persian (Pehlevi).' Ogham writing, dating from the 4th century AD, was an alphabetic script used for writing the Irish and Pictish languages on stone monuments. There is no agreement among scholars as to its origin. Some connect it to the runic and, ultimately, Etruscan alphabets; others claim that it is merely a transformation of the Latin alphabet.

Notes to Chapter 35

1   R.F. Burton, *The Land of Midian (Revisited)* (London, 1879), i, p.3.

2   The Khedive's letter, written in French, offering Burton the governorship with the mission of civilising the country and suppressing the slave trade, is dated Cairo, 16 Sept 1877. Burton's draft reply, also in French, is dated 28 Sept. 'I hope that I shall continue to enjoy your Majesty's exalted permission,' he wrote in the final paragraph, 'and your powerful aid for carrying on with my investigations during this winter in the gold regions already discovered. I have spent the summer studying the geological question and in discussions with the most learned historians of Europe, and my ambition is to lead a Khedive sponsored expedition, which will successfully open up for Egypt an untapped California.' (QK Coll).

3   R.F. Burton, *The Land of Midian,*, p.6.

4   QK Coll, I. Burton to L. Ionides, Trieste, 17 Sept 1877. Lucas Alexander Ionides (1837-1924), better known as 'Luke', was the second son of Alexander Constantine Ionides (1810-90), a shipping owner and collector of Greek/Turkish origin , originally from Istanbul. On 29 August 1869, Luke married Elfrida [Elfie] Elizabeth, daughter of Dr George Bird. There were seven children of the marriage. The couple separated in 1895 after Luke lost his fortune. A collector and patron of many well-known artists of the day, particularly the pre-Raphaelites, Luke, by all accounts was a friendly, gregarious man. As is evident from Isabel's light-hearted banter, she and Luke hit it off.

5   N.M. Penzer, *An Annotated Bibliography*, p.49.

6   These details are taken from a document headed: 'Statement of the Objects and Advantages of the Syndicate' in the Burton Collection, OHG. The bankers for this enterprise were Messrs Barclay, Bevan, Tritton, Twells & Co, 54 Lombard St, London, EC. The conduct of the Pilgrimage was entrusted by the Syndicate to Messrs Fairman & Co, merchants of Jedda and London. A document dated 14 Sept 1877, shows the office of the Syndicate to have been at 60 Gracechurch St, EC.

7   In 1849 over 100,000 people had arrived in California prospecting for gold. During the next few years the output of the precious metal rose from $5 million in 1848 to $40 million in 1849, and $55 million in 1851. These amounts, large as they were, still fell far short of the debt owed by Egypt.

8   TNA, FO 7/914, Burton to Derby, Trieste, 20 Sept 1877. Isabel falsely claimed that the Khedive applied to the FO for the loan of Burton throughout the winter. See *The Life*, ii, p.122.

9   R.F. Burton, *The Land of Midian*, p.9.

10   Now known as Karlovy Vary and located in the present-day Czech Republic. The alkaline sulphur springs were patronised from medieval times by royalty, members of the aristocracy and ecclesiastics. The spa's greatest popularity dates from the 19th century when the main baths, hotels, and sanatoria were built.

11   A napoleon was a gold coin issued by Napoleon I, of the value of twenty francs. Assuming an exchange rate of roughly £1 = 10 francs, this totalled £5,000 or so.

12   TNA, FO 7/914, Burton to Derby, Fort El Molilah, Land of Midian, via Suez and Trieste, 17 Dec 1877; FO 7/942, Derby to Burton, 14 Jan 1878.

13   R.F. Burton, *The Land of Midian*, p.40.

14   HL, EMC, I. Burton to L. Ionides, Trieste, 12 Nov 1877. 'Fitz' refers to her brother-in-law, Edward Gerald Fitzgerald. What is widely regarded today as indefensible sharp practice, involving unlawful exploitation of inside or privileged information for profit in market transactions, was then perfectly legitimate. In fact, 'insider dealing' was not made illegal in Europe until the adoption of an EC Directive on Insider Trading on 13 November 1989.

15   *The Life*, ii, p.130.

16   Burton gave the reference, "My Pilgrimage, Vol.1, Chap.XI," where it is called 'Sharm Damgah.'

17   *The Life*, ii, p.131.

18   *Ibid.*, pp.131-2.

19   R.F. Burton, *The Land of Midian*, p.xvii.

20   TNA, FO 7/942, Burton to Salisbury, Cairo, 27 April 1878.

21   Earl of Cromer, *Modern Egypt*, p.44.

22   TNA, FO 7/942, Burton to Salisbury, Trieste, 15 June 1878.

Notes to Chapter 36

1   TNA, FO 7/942, Burton to Salisbury, 14 Montagu Place, Montagu Sq, London, 11 Aug 1878.

2   B.Stoker, *Personal Reminiscences of Henry Irving* (London, 1906), i, p.350. Bram Stoker (1847-1912), author of the Gothic horror romance, *Dracula* (1897). In 1878, when he met the Burtons, he had recently become Henry Irving's manager, a post which he held for twenty-seven years.

3   'The Land of Midian,' *Report of the British Association* (Dublin), Transactions of Section E, pp.630-1.

4   Sir Samuel Ferguson (1810-86), Deputy Keeper of public records of Ireland since 1867, and knighted in 1878. He became President of the Royal Irish Academy in 1882. He later wrote, 'Ogham inscriptions in Ireland, Wales and Scotland,' edited by Lady Ferguson, 1887. See F. Boase, *Modern English Biography* (Truro, 1892), Vol.1.

5   'The Ogham Runes and El-Mushajjar.' A Study. *Transactions of the Royal Society of Literature*, Vol.XII, Part 1, 1879, 46 pp.

6   *The Athenaeum*, 11 May 1878, No.2637, p.601.

7   *Vanity Fair*, 7 May 1878.

8   *The Globe*, 7 May 1878.

9   TCC, 14 Montagu Place, 15 Sept 1878.

10   Lord Salisbury succeeded Lord Derby (who resigned) in April 1878, in Disraeli's second cabinet.

11   TNA, FO 7/942, Burton to Salisbury, Athenaeum Club, Pall Mall, SW, 17 Nov 1878.

12   HL, EMC, I. Burton to A.Tootal, 18 Oct 1878. Begun at Lord Derby's residence, Knowsley, and completed at Lord Houghton's ten days later.

13   Proved in London, with a Codicil, on 9 Sept 1878. Bagshaw asked to be buried in the same grave as his first wife, Burton's favourite aunt, Georgiana.

14   *The Daily News*, 22 June 1878.

15   On the opposite side is an enclosure detailing Burton's absences: 'April 27th/75......June 18th/76; March 4th.....May 12th, 1877; Oct. 20th 1877....May 17th 1878; July 7th 1878 (still away).'

16   Quoted without date or address in T. Wright, *The Life of Sir Richard Burton*, i, pp.283-4. Isabel was at Brighton 'for the purpose of helping at a bazaar in behalf of humanity to animals.' *The Life*, ii, p.135.

17   An allusion to the remark made by Disraeli at a meeting of the Oxford Diocesan Society held at the Sheldonian Theatre, Oxford, on 25 Nov 1864: 'The question is this – Is man an ape or an angel? My Lord [to Bishop Wilberforce], I am on the side of the Angels.' Quoted in G.E. Buckle, *The Life of Benjamin Disraeli, Earl of Beaconsfield*, iv, 1855-1868 (London, 1916), p.374.

18   Huxley to F. Dyster, 9 Sept. 1860, Thomas Huxley Papers 15.115. Quoted in A. Desmond and J.Moore, *Darwin* (London, 1992), p.497.

19   *The Life*, ii, p.152. A claim, in my opinion, that needs taking with a large pinch of salt.

20   *Ibid.*, pp.154-5. Burton's paper was published in *The Spiritualist*, No.328 (Vol.XIII, No.23), 6 Dec 1878, pp.270-5. It is dated 13 December by Isabel, *The Life*, ii, p.137.

21   R.F. Burton, *The Land of Midian (Revisited)*, p.xviii.

22   Dr Percy's report, only a small part of which is summarised by Burton, is addressed from the Metallurgical Laboratory, Royal School of Mines, Jermyn Street, London, 13 Dec 1878.

23   R.F. Burton, *The Land of Midian (Revisited)*, p.xxiv.

24   HL, EMC.

25   TNA, FO 7/977, Burton to Salisbury, 14 Montagu Place, Montagu Sq W, London, 27 Jan 1879. The request was granted in FO 7/977, 1 Feb 1879.

26   B. Stoker, *Reminiscences of Henry Irving*, pp.351-55.

27   'Mrs. Burton in India,' *The Saturday Review*, 29 March 1879, p.402.

28   *The Athenaeum*, No.2681, 15 March 1879, p.337.

29   *JRGS* 49 (1879), pp. [*i*] – 150. Penzer. p.234, states that offprints of this article were made.

30   D. Hogarth, *The Penetration of Arabia* (London, 1904), pp.182-3.

31   *The Life*, p.166.
32   Heinrich Karl Brugsch (1827-94), an Egyptologist who did pioneering work in deciphering demotic, the Egyptian hieroglyphic cursive writing used in handwritten texts from the early 7th century B.C. until the 5th century A.D. He was first sent to Egypt by the Prussian government in 1853, when Burton was there following his 'pilgrimage' to Mecca. He returned in 1864 as Prussian consul, and was director of the school of Egyptology from 1870-9. His huge hieroglyphic-demotic dictionary appeared between 1867-82.
33   Addressed from Chalet Cecil, Puys, Dieppe, 22 Sept 1879. See *The Romance*, ii, p.618.
34   Earl of Cromer, *Modern Egypt*, i, p.141.
35   Some years later, Ismail was allowed by the sultan to retire to his palace of Emirghian on the Bosphorus. He remained there until his death on 2 March 1895.
36   Gordon to Burton, 'En Route to Massawah, Red Sea, 31 Aug 1879,' *The Romance*, p. 666.
37   TNA, FO 7/977, No.23, Burton to Salisbury, Trieste, 15 Oct 1879. Salisbury to Burton, 27 Oct 1879, agreeing to '3 months' leave of absence from the 15th Nov. next...'
38   TCC, I. Burton to Lord Houghton, 31 Dec 1879.
39   Journals of Major-General C.G. Gordon, C.B. at Khartoum. Review by Burton, *The Academy*, 1 July 1885, p.20.
40   TNA, FO 7/1006, Burton to Salisbury, Shepheard's, Cairo, 9 Feb 1880.
41   Gordon to I. Burton, U.S. Club, Pall Mall, 4.2.80. *The Romance*, pp.667-8.
42   *Ibid.*, pp.671-2.
43   Lady Salisbury to I. Burton, Hatfield House, Hatfield, Herts, 18 April 1880. *The Romance*, p.622.
44   *The Life*, p.123.

Notes to Chapter 37

1   'On Slavery. Captain Burton's Reports to Lord Granville on Anti-Slavery. Letter No.1, Cairo, April 27th, 1880; Letter No.2, Cairo, May 3rd, 1880.' *The Life*, ii, pp.192-94.
2   Letter No.3, Consulate, Trieste, May 11th, 1880. *Ibid*, p.194.
3   *Ibid.*, p.195. Isabel also printed a very long article, 'How to Deal with the Slave Scandal in Egypt,' *The Life*, pp.195-210. Although its source is not noted there, it was contributed by Burton to *The Manchester Examiner and Times*, 21, 23, and 24 March 1881. Isabel later had it printed in the form of a pamphlet at Trieste. For whatever reason, it is signed A.E.I., (Isabel Burton). See N.M. Penzer, *Ann.Bib.*, pp.238-9.
4   R.F. Burton, *Os Lusiadas* (London, 1880), p.xi.
5   *Ibid.*, Editor's Preface, Trieste, 19 July 1880. Burton's Preface which follows, is dated Cairo, 1 May 1880.
6   Undated letter quoted in T. Wright, *The Life of Sir Richard Burton.*, ii, p. 19. Isabel mentioned their visit in *The Life*, ii, pp.189-90, transcribing a letter which she wrote to the Editor of *The Medical Times and Gazette*, describing the baths and recommending them to English visitors. Burton also wrote an article, 'Thermae of Montfalcone (aqua dei et vitae), which was reprinted from the "Field " newspaper. The original article appeared on 12 Nov, 17 Dec and 24 Dec 1881, when it was entitled "Curious Cures."
7   T. Wright, *The Life of Sir Richard Burton*, ii, p.19.
8   R.F. Burton, *A Glance at the "Passion Play"* (London, 1881), p.13.
9   The Passion Play at Oberammagau is, and always has been from its inception in the 17th century, performed by the ordinary people of the village. Why Burton thought it was performed by 'hereditary and professional players' is not clear.
10   R.F. Burton, *A Glance at the "Passion Play,"* pp.160-1.
11   N.M. Penzer, *Ann. Bib.*, pp.97-98. Despite its poor sales, *The Kasidah* has remained in print up to the present day.
12   *The Kasidah* (London, 1974), Note 1. pp.74-6.
13   The poem is reprinted in *The Life*, i, pp.185-95. The Notes to it are in vol.ii, Appendix B, pp.456-76.
14   Chapter 49. 'In Which Mrs Harris assisted by a teapot is the cause of a Division among friends.' The scene occurs at Mrs. Gamp's rather cramped and overcrowded residence in Kingsgate Street, High Holborn: "Bother Mrs. Harris!" said Betsy Prig. Mrs. Gamp looked at her with amazement, incredulity, and indignation; when Mrs. Prig,

shutting her eye still closer, and folding her arms still tighter, uttered these memorable and tremendous words: "I don't believe there's no sich a person!"

15   F. M. Brodie, *The Devil Drives* (New York & London, 1984), p.277.

16   *The Edinburgh Review*, Vol. 178, July-Oct, Art VII, pp.439-468, 1893.

17   Letter to Miss Bishop from Opicina, 17 January 1881. Quoted in *The Romance*, ii, pp. 626-7.

18   Norman Penzer provides an illustration of the front cover of the pamphlet, which carries no date or publisher. He said that he could only trace four copies – one each at Kensington and Camberwell, one in the British Museum, and the last was sold by Quaritch in 1911. *Ann.Bib.* facing p.239. There is, however, a copy in the Oscar Eckenstein Collection of Burton's works housed at the Royal Asiatic Society. It is bound in stiff black and green marbled covers, with leather strengthening at the edges and corners. Written on the flyleaf are the words: 'Given to me by Mr. Francis Hitchman, the biographer of Lord Beaconsfield. Only 25 copies printed. R. Garnett.' Penzer writes, p.239: 'Francis Hitchman was apparently connected with its production, for not only did he write a "Life" of Beaconsfield, but the British Museum and the Quaritch copies were both presented by him.' Dr Richard Garnett (1835-1906), was Keeper of the Printed Books at the British Museum, and then Chief Keeper of the Museum.

19   R.F. Burton, *Lord Beaconsfield. A Sketch*, p.3.

20   *Ibid.*, p.4.

21   *Ibid.*, pp.5-6.

22   *Ibid.*, pp.9-10. For an excellent scholarly assessment of Burton's anti-Semitic views in this pamphlet and *The Jew, the Gypsy and El Islam*, see C. Holmes, *Anti-Semitism in British Society, 1876-1939* (London, 1979), pp.49-62.

23   Rilke was a guest of his friend, Princess Maria von Thurn und Taxis-Hohenlohe, at the castle in 1910 . He began writing the Duino Elegies there in 1912. They were completed in Switzerland ten years later. At the end of World War II, the castle served as British headquarters, during the period when it was unclear whether Trieste would be handed over to Italy or Jugoslavia.

24   Letter to Miss Bishop, Trieste, 5 Dec 1881, *The Romance*, ii, p.632.

25   R.F. Burton, *His Life and His Lusiads* (London, 1881), Vol.2. A Commentary. The Reviewer Reviewed by Isabel Burton. A Postscript, p.710.

26   *Ibid.*, pp.715-7. A forecast not fulfilled either then or now. Burton had earlier written to Gerald Massey, the poet, Shakespearian scholar and Egyptologist, 'You see my attempt is novel: no translator as yet has flown so high. Of course I must expect to "catch it" for a vicious flight over vulgar heads.' QK Coll, Trieste, 28 May 1881.

27   In a despatch, TNA, FO 7/1026, Burton to Granville, 7 April 1881, he informed the Foreign Secretary that an English sailor, the previous day, had attacked the Vice-Consul in his office. As a result of his injuries, Mr E. Brock was given leave to England, and on 27 July, Burton was given permission to appoint Mr P. Proby Cautley as Acting Vice-Consul in his place. Precisely what financial arrangement was arrived at here is not clear, since Burton's absence was not officially sanctioned. In FO 7/1026, Granville to Burton, 19 Feb 1881, when leave was official, Burton was authorised 'to pay Mr. E.W. Brock at a charge in your quarterly account with this Office the sum of £6 10s. 5d. less 3/3 [3s. 3d.] for his services as Acting Consul at Trieste, from the 17th August to the 1st Sept. 1880.' In the present case, Burton would be away for six weeks.

28   Burton's report, 'The Geographical Congress at Venice,' appeared in The Academy, Vol.XX, 1881, pp.258-60.

29   *The Life*, ii, p.224.

30   TNA, FO 7/1026, Burton to Granville, Trieste, 8 Oct 1881. Burton reported that Mr. Vice-Consul Brock had returned to his duties on 14 Sept. 'He can obtain help when required at my expense from Mr. Philip Proby Cautley who has lately been acting for him, and whose activity and excellent management of the office together with his knowledge of languages leaves nothing to be desired.'

31   *The Academy*, Vol.XV, 26 April 1879, pp.369-70.

32   *The Athenaeum*, No.2822, 26 Nov 1881, p.703.

Notes to Chapter 38

1   T. Wright, *The Life of Sir Richard Burton* (London, 1906), ii, p.34. The letter is undated, but must have been

written shortly after Burton arrived at Lisbon on 17 Dec 1881. Wright was incorrect, of course, in supposing that Cameron travelled with Burton at this stage.

2   James Irvine informed Isabel in January that Burton had 'waited at Madeira in the first place a week because I telegraphed to him to do so, and in the second place another week to await the arrival of Captain Cameron, and my last information from him was a telegram a fortnight ago requesting me to forward some photographic appliances which I am doing today.' James Irvine to I. Burton, Exchange Court, Liverpool, 19 Jan 1882, WSRO, 2667/26/2 (xviii) 1.

3   R.F. Burton, *To the Gold Coast for Gold* (London, 1883), ii, p.1.

4   *Ibid*, ii, p.92.

5   *Ibid*., p.93.

6   *Ibid*., p.172.

7   *Ibid*., p.173.

8   *Ibid*., p.190.

9   T. Wright, *The Life of Sir Richard Burton*, ii, p.35.

10   There is a journal MS in the archives of the RGS (1882), 'Cameron. V.L. 'On a sketch survey of the Ancobra and Prince's Rivers and of the Takwa range, Gold Coast.' See a handlist compiled by Christine Kelly, 'The RGS Archives, Part II: Africa,' *The Geographical Journal*, Vol.CXLII (1976), p.123.

11   R.F. Burton, *To the Gold Coast for Gold*, i, p.x.

12   Although I have been unable to locate Burton's despatch, he must have applied to the FO while in West Africa for an extension to his existing leave, 15 Nov 1881 to 16 Feb 1882, and been granted it.

13   See WSRO, letters from James Irvine to Burton: Exchange Court, Liverpool, 21 April 1882; 25 April; 27 April. Burton to Irvine, Reid's English Rooms, Funchal, 3 May 1882. In this letter expressing his disagreement with Irvine's suggestions, Burton wrote: '1.The sooner we begin perorating the better: even days are of importance; 2. A dinner is much more naturally given to a man, or held, just on arrival or when departing; 3. If the dinner is kept for London, it will look like a puff. I have no objection to the latter proceeding, but wish to do it my way.' Lord Derby declined the invitation. In a letter to Irvine of June 1882 from Knowsley, he wrote: 'I have so sincere a respect for Capt. Burton's energy, enterprise, and varied ability that I regret to be unable to join in any plan for doing him honor, but I rarely attend public dinners and during the next few weeks my engagements are so many that I fear I must decline to add to the number. No compliment can be better deserved than that which you propose to pay.'

14   TNA, FO 7/1043 (11), Burton to Granville, 31 May 1882.

15   TNA, FO 7/1043 (13), I. Burton to Mr Lister, 10 June 1882, 14 Montagu Place, Bryanston Square.

16   In his *The Life of John Payne* (London, 1919), p.249, Wright said that he called on Payne's sister, Mrs. Pritchard, as soon as he could after Payne's death. 'In a letter to her written in February 1916, I had expressed the hope that Burton's letters to Payne would be carefully preserved, as they substantiated all the principal statements made in my *Life of Sir Richard Burton* respecting the rival translations. She replied on 28 February, stating that she had given orders that all the Burton letters should be tied together and sent to her.' Despite these assurances, the originals appear to be lost. A small number of them, transcribed by Payne, are to be found in the HL, EMC, Box 11, containing 10 envelopes of letters to and from Burton and his wife.

17   QK Coll. The reason for this misdating is unclear. *To the Gold Coast for Gold* was published in 1883, *The Book of the Sword* and Camoens's *The Lyricks* in 1884.

18   T. Wright, *The Life of Sir Richard Burton*, ii, p.38. Presumably the dashes were inserted by Wright.

19   *The Academy*, Vol.XX , 17 Dec 1881, p.457.

20   TNA, FO 7/1043, R. Burton to Lord Granville, 14 July 1882.

21   TNA, FO 7/1043, 29 July 1882.

22   No reason was given for this arrangement. Cameron had offended Irvine by stating publicly that Ingotroio was unhealthy, thereby possibly putting off potential investors. Writing to Isabel (25 May 1882) , Irvine said that Cameron had 'spoilt himself – <u>this most confidential</u> – his failing is well known.' It appears that Cameron had a drink problem, and had let himself down, as well as those associated with the scheme, by being arrested for drunkenness. He later became a teetotaller.

23   Blanche Mary was the eldest daughter of Isabel's younger sister, Blanche, and John Hugh Wadham Smyth-Pigott,

of Brockley Hall, Brockley Court, and the Grove, Somerset. Like her youngest sister, Sybil Constance Mary, she remained unmarried. Of the two others daughters, Maud Isabel Mary, *m.* 1st, 1884, Baron Joseph Piers de Raveschoot, of Olsène, Belgium, and had issue. She *m.* 2ndly, Vicomte Réné de Ghellinck d'Elséghem, of Swynaerde, Belgium. Edith Florence Mary, *m.*29 Nov 1888, Lieut-Col. Walter Raleigh Chichester-Constable, of Burton Constable, Hull, and had issue. See H. Pine-Gordon (ed.), *Burke's Genealogical and Heraldic History of the Landed Gentry*, 1937. Centenary (15th edn.) Vol. 2, Smyth-Pigott of Brockley, p.1810.

24   TNA, FO 7/1043 (15), Burton to Granville, Trieste Consulate,1 Aug 1882. Recd 8 August. This was annotated by the Chief Clerk: 'I know that it is perfectly useless laying down any rule or regulation with regard to leave so far as Burton is concerned, but in common fairness to V. Consul Brock – who during some past has been carrying on the Consulate in a feeble state of health – Burton's vagaries shd. be checked.' Another hand, possibly Wylde, added: 'Capt Burton fixes three days as requisite for a journey to Trieste – allow him four and he will be liberally treated. The difference between four and fifteen should be added to his leave.'

25   The Orsini bomb was named after its inventor, the Italian revolutionary Felice Orsini (1819-58), who was executed after a failed attempt to assassinate Napoleon III in 1858. He had tested the device in England in the previous year with a fellow-conspirator, using abandoned quarries in Devonshire and Sheffield. The bomb, six of which were made for him by the gunsmith, Joseph Taylor, was fitted with horns containing the highly sensitive fulminate of mercury, which exploded on impact.

26   TNA, FO 7/1042, Burton to Granville, Trieste Consulate, 3 Aug 1882.

27   T. Wright, *The Life of Sir Richard Burton*, p.38.

28   Her Majesty's Consular Service, III. 'Amateur Consuls,' *Vanity Fair*, August 26th, 1882, p.123. I attempted, unsuccessfully, to discover the identity of the author of this very interesting series of articles. Sir Edward Playfair suggested to me, that it was possibly written by someone either working in the FO, or having close connections with one or more of its officials.

29   Letter addressed from Hotel Klinger, Marienbad, Bohemia, 1 Sept 1882, cited in *The Life*, ii, pp.238-9.

30   WSRO, 2667/26/2 (xviii). 58. Irvine to Burton, Exchange Court, Liverpool, 5 Sept 1882.

31   *The Life*, ii, p.227. Burton, himself, wrote later, 'During the autumn of 1882, after my return home from the Gold Coast (with less than no share of the noble metal which my companion Cameron and I went to find *and found a failure*)......' [my italics]. See *The Supplemental Nights to the Book of the Thousand Nights and a Night* (Benares, 1886-8), Vol. 6, p.390.

32   TNA, FO 7/1041, Burton to Granville, Trieste Consulate, 6 Sept 1882.

33   T. Wright, *The Life of Sir Richard Burton*, ii, p.39.

34   *Ibid.*, p.39. Wright avoided mentioning R.S. Poole and others by name, writing in a footnote: 'The author wishes to say that the names of several persons are hidden by the dashes in these chapters, and he has taken every care to render it impossible for the public to know who in any particular instance is intended.'

35   *Ibid.*, p.39.

36   *Ibid.*, p.40.

37   Wright plausibly suggested Antoine Galland's adaptation of *The Nights*. It was a popular version from Syrian manuscripts, freely translated, and appeared between 1704-17.

38   *Ibid.*, pp.40-1.

39   Both telegrams are quoted in *The Life*, p.242.

＊

Notes to Chapter 39

1   Prince Tewfiq had called on the sultan to put down the revolt, but the Sublime Porte was reluctant to employ Turkish troops against Muslims who were rebelling against foreign Christian interference.

2   Extract from Palmer's Journal to his wife, quoted in the *DNB* account of his mission.

3   Lt Harold Charrington, aged twenty-six, of HMS *Euryalus*,was Flag-Lt to Rear Admiral Sir William Hewitt, VC, KCB, C-in-C in the East Indies. Capt W.J. Gill, RE, was author of *The River of Golden Sand*, the narrative of a

journey through China and Eastern Tibet to Burmah, 2 vols, John Murray, London, 1880. His travel diaries and numerous other documents are in the archives of the RGS.

4   TNA, FO 7/1041, Burton to Granville, Trieste, 28 Oct 1882.

5   The telegram is undated, but obviously has to be 2 Nov 1882.

6   The letter is not to be found among the file, FO 7/914, containing the General Correspondence relating to Austria.

7   Arabi's army was defeated on 13 Sept 1882. He was captured and sentenced to death. Through Lord Dufferin's influence, his sentence was commuted, and he was exiled to Ceylon. He returned to Egypt in 1901, where he died ten years later.

8   TNA, FO 7/1041, Burton to Granville, Hotel Suez, 16 Nov 1882..

9   TNA, FO 7/1041, Burton to Granville, Consulate, Trieste, 11 Dec 1882. Col Warren, in fact, did an excellent job in reconstructing the events leading to the death of Palmer and his companions, during a minute and intricate inquiry, which resulted in the conviction of the murderers. The fragmentary remains of Palmer, Gill, and Charrington, were brought back to England, and interred in the crypt of St Paul's Cathedral. This is correctly cited in *The Life*, ii, p.247, where Isabel quotes from Burton's journal for 31 March 1883. However, in Appendix H, 'Report After Going To Search for Palmer,' *The Life*, ii, p. 613, Burton mistakenly states that the remains were buried in Westminster Abbey.

10   QK Coll. Written across the top of the first page is a note: 'We have taken Egypt and we shall have to keep it whether we like it or not. Any report of the English army leaving will drive away all Europeans....' Lord Dufferin's recommendations formed the basis of subsequent reforms. In 1884 he was appointed viceroy of India to succeed Lord Ripon. Burton's article appears not to have been accepted by *The Cornhill*. Instead, extracts were published in *The Academy*: The Late E.H. Palmer. I. Personal Reminiscences, May 5 1883, p.311; II. The Story of his Death, May 12 1883, pp.329-30; England's Duty to Egypt, May 26 1883, p.366. See N.M. Penzer, *Ann. Bib.*, pp.267-8.

11   T. Wright, *The Life of John Payne*, p.78.

12   *Ibid.*, pp.78-9. Burton used the rather restrictive word, pederasty, for such practices which, properly, referred to unnatural connection with a boy, sodomy. The word homosexuality was first used in 1892, in Krafft-Ebing, *Psychopathia Sexualis*, C.G. Chaddock (tr.), III, p.185. It was also used in the same year by John Addington Symonds in Letter 21, Oct, cited in P.Grosskurth, *J.A. Symonds* (London, 1964), p.293. Burton published an account of what he called a 'Sotadic Zone,' in his *The Book of the Thousand Nights and a Night* (Benares, 1885), Vol.10, Terminal Essay, pp.206-7.

13   T.Wright, *The Life of Sir Richard Burton*, ii, p.43.

14   T. Wright, *The Life of John Payne*, p.79.

15   *The Life*, ii, p.271 & p.272.

Notes to Chapter 40

1   T. Wright, *The Life of Sir Richard Burton*, ii, p.71.

2   Letter to the Editor, *Evening Standard*, "The True Life of Sir Richard Burton," 31 Dec 1896. Faber's letter was written in support of the claim made by Georgiana Stisted and many others at the time who knew Burton well, that his alleged conversion to Roman Catholicism on his death-bed was a sham.

3   R.F. Burton, *The Book of the Sword* (London, 1884), p.xxii. Burton dedicated his book 'To the Memory of My Old and Dear College Friend, Alfred Bate Richards, Who in Years Gone By Accepted the Dedication of These Pages.'

4   *Ibid.*, pp.xvii-xx. Only the first volume appeared, and that fell still-born from the press. Norman Penzer has given an extended account of the mass of material left behind after Burton's death, which would have been drawn on for volumes 2 and 3. Lady Burton passed it on to Mr Forbes Sieveking to edit and see through the press. However, it proved to be in such a chaotic state, that nothing could be done with it. See N.M. Penzer, *Ann. Bib.*, pp.108-12. There is an illustration of 'The MS. Notes, Cuttings, Illustrations, etc., Intended for the Continuation of the "Book

of the Sword"' facing p.112. It is now housed in the Burton Collection, Huntington Library, California.

5   *The Academy*, 10 May 1884, p.323.

6   T. Wright, *The Life of Sir Richard Burton*, p.71.

7   R.F. Burton, *First Footsteps in East Africa* (London, 1856), p.36.

8   R.F. Burton, *The Book of the Thousand Nights and a Night* (Benares,1885), i, p.ix.

9   T. Wright, *The Life of Sir Richard Burton*, ii, p.53.

10   The earliest printed texts of the *Nights* were: 1. The Shirwanee text of 1814-18 (better known as Calcutta I); 2. the Breslau text of 1824-43; 3. the Bulaq text, printed in the Bulaq suburb of Cairo in 1835; 4. the Macnaghten text of 1839-42 (generally known as Calcutta II).

11   R.F. Burton, *The Supplemental Nights* (Benares, 1886-8), The Biography of the Books and its Reviewers Reviewed, 'The Engineering of the Work,' Vol.6, p.390.

12   R.F. Burton, *The Book of the Thousand Nights and a Night*, p.xvii.

13   *Ibid.*, p.xviii.

14   *Ibid.*, p.xix. Lane's notes were highly regarded by his contemporaries, whose view of the *Nights* was radically altered by reading them. 'Undoubtedly the most important part of this new edition,' commented *The Athenaeum*, 'is the notes.' See *The Athenaeum*, No.572, Oct 1838, p.739. Lane's notes on Muslim customs and beliefs derived from his deep personal knowledge of Arabic culture, were edited by S. Lane-Poole, and appeared under the title *Arabian Society in the Middle Ages*, 1883. For a scholarly assessment of Lane's contribution to *AN* and Arabic studies generally, see L. Ahmed, *Edward W. Lane, A Study of his life and work, and of British Ideas in the Middle East in the Nineteenth Century* (London, 1978).

15   *The Arabian Nights Entertainments, carefully revised....to which is added a selection of new tales, now first translated from the Arabic originals. Also an Introduction and notes....by* Jonathan Scott, LL.D...with engravings from paintings by Smirke in six volumes. Published by Longman, Hurst, Rees, Orme and Brown, London, 1811.

16   *The Thousand and One Nights, commonly called in England The Arabian Nights' Entertainments.* A new translation from the Arabic, with copious notes. By Edward William Lane. The first edition of this highly popular translation was brought out in monthly parts between 1838-40 by Charles Knight, a pioneer in the publication of cheap literature. Each instalment, illustrated by woodcuts, after drawings by William Harvey, cost 2s 6d. Once the serialization was complete, it was bound in book form in 3 volumes selling at £4 4s. A second edition edited by E.S. Poole appeared in 1859. Frequent reprints followed. A new edition, edited by Lane's nephew, Edward Stanley Poole was published by Chatto & Windus in 1883.

17   R.F. Burton, *The Book of the Thousand Nights and a Night*, p.xii.

18   *Ibid.*, p.xiii.

19   T. Wright, *The Life of Sir Richard Burton*, ii, p.53.

20   *Ibid.*, i, p.xii. N.M. Penzer thought that it was a futile exercise trying to prove that a translator was guilty of flagrant and intentional plagiarism. He described having carefully examined the copy of Payne's "Nights" that Burton used. He found it 'very little marked, although signs of considerable use are manifest.' See *Ann.Bib.*, pp.316-7. Fawn Brodie on the other hand, thought it likely that Burton had two copies of Payne's *Nights*, one of which he cut up, and heavily annotated. There is no evidence for this, and I doubt it to be the case. Even Burton, no bibliophile as we have already seen would, in my opinion, have drawn a line at cutting up a second set of Payne's 9 volumes at a guinea a time.

21   TNA, FO/1071, British Consulate, Trieste, 3 May 1884. Dr Castiglioni was chief doctor of the Austro-Hungarian Lloyd's Steam Navigation Society at Trieste. Isabel made no mention in *The Life*, of Syria being the destination of Burton's sick-leave, since it was never his intention to go there.

22   T. Wright, *The Life of Sir Richard Burton*, ii, p.72.

23   I do not have a copy of Burton's despatch for this extension, but the FO reply to it is: FO 7/1071, 12 July 1884.

24   T. Wright, *The Life of Sir Richard Burton*, pp.72-3.

25   *Ibid.*, p.73.

26   R.F. Burton, *The Supplemental Nights*, Vol.6, The Biography of the Book and Its Reviewers Reviewed, pp.390-93.

27   T. Wright, *The Life of Sir Richard Burton*, p.74. Burton also had help from Payne with the pricing of his edition.

On 17 April 1884, he had written from Trieste (HL, EMC): 'For my guidance with that ticklish animal the publisher, it would be a great kindness to me to know what arrangements you made. I understand you printed 9 vols at £1. 1. 0 each, 500 =£4,500. What concerns me most is the cost of each volume before it was delivered to the subscribers. Whatever you tell me will be kept secret, no one shall know it but ourselves.'

28   T. Wright, *The Life of Sir Richard Burton*, p.75. Payne's dedication to Burton in Vol.9 of his translation runs: 'To Captain Richard Francis Burton In Token of Admiration and Friendship For Much Kindness.'

29   Letter from A.C. Swinburne, The Pines, Putney, 27 Nov 1884. Burton Collection, HL. There are other letters on the same subject from Alice (Lallah) Bird, St. Clair Baddeley, Oswald Crawfurd, and A.H. Sayce, all of whom were sent copies. There is also a list of names and addresses for free copies, and the printing expenses for the two volumes.

30   Cutting, dated New York, 15 Jan 1885, Burton Collection, HL.

31   *The Athenaeum*, No.3000, 25 April 1885, p.533.

32   TNA, FO 7/1086, Burton to Granville, Trieste, 25 March 1885.

Notes to Chapter 41

1   HL, EMC, I. Burton to Mr Notcutt, 23 Dorset St, Portman Square, 13 June 1885.

2   *Ibid.*, 27 June 1885.

3   QK Coll, ? July 1885. Sir George Lewis (1833-1911) a colourful lawyer of whom it was said that 'he cared for rules only so far as not to be caught breaking them,' and that 'he was a dangerous man to best.' Quoted in the *Oxford Dictionary of National Biography*, 'The Lives of the Law,' by the Rt Hon Lord Bingham of Cornhill. The Burtons had been introduced to Mrs Linton by the poet, Swinburne. The Society for the Suppression of Vice and the Encouragement of Religion and Virtue had been founded in 1801. However, as a result of financial problems it had gone out of business during the 1870s. It was succeeded in March 1886 by the National Vigilance Association, which later trumpeted its helping Lady Burton destroy many of her husband's works after his death. See D. Thomas, *A Long Time Burning. The History of Literary Censorship in England* (London, 1869).

4   TNA, FO 7/1086, Burton to Salisbury, 23 Dorset Street, Portman Sq, 3 July 1885.

5   HL, EMC, HL, late July 1885. Mrs Friswell was now a widow, her husband, Hain Friswell, having died from consumption at Bexleyheath, Kent, on 12 March 1878. Walter Herries Pollock was a well-known author, and editor of *The Saturday Review* from 1883 to 1894.

6   A short obituary by Burton appeared in *The Academy*, 22 August 1885, p.118. According to Isabel, 'his sorrow for this good old friend occupies a whole page of his journal.'

7   R.F. Burton, *Supplemental Nights*, Vol.6, p.394.

8   *Whitehall Review*, 17 Sept 1885, quoted in I. Burton, *The Life*, ii, p.619.

9   *Nottingham Journal*, 19 Sept 1885, quoted in *The Life*, p.619.

10   This sentence is quoted in *The Life*, Appendix 1, 'Opinions of the Press and of Scholars of the "Arabian Nights," p.619. However, Isabel bowdlerised Symonds's, "can under any shadow of pretence *be classed with the garbage of the brothels*," substituting her own words, "*be ignored.*" [my italics]

11   *The Academy*, Vol.XXVIII, 3 Oct 1885, p.223. The letter was written from Am Hof, Davos Platz, Switzerland, 27 Sept 1885, where Symonds had settled for the benefit of his health.

12   *The Edinburgh Review*, Vol.164, July 1886, pp.166-99.

13   R.F. Burton, *Supplemental Nights*, Vol.6, p.431. The use of the word 'deprave' recalled the wording of the judgement by the Lord Chief Justice, Sir Alexander Cockburn in the Court of Queen's Bench in Regina v Hicklin (1868). It was as a result of this case that the definition of pornography was enshrined in law: 'The test of obscenity is whether the tendency of the material charged as obscenity is to deprave and corrupt those whose minds are open to such immoral influences and into whose hands a publication of this sort might fall.' Law Reports, 3QBD, 1867-8, p.371.

14   On 6 July 1885, W.T. Stead, the flamboyant editor of *The Pall Mall Gazette* published the first of three instalments

of 'The Maiden Tribute of Modern Babylon,' a lurid exposé of child prostitution, abduction and procurement in London. Running to six pages, it carried such prurient sub-headings as, 'The Violation of Virgins,' 'The Confessions of a Brothel-Keeper,' 'How Girls Were Bought and Ruined.' The last section headed, 'A Child of Thirteen bought for £5,' recounted the case of Eliza Armstrong, which became a major scandal. When the true details of the story were later unearthed by rival newspapers, Stead was brought to trial and sentenced to three months' imprisonment.

15 R.F. Burton, *Supplemental Nights*, pp.436-7. Criticism of some of the contents of the Old Testament and Shakespeare was of long standing. Donna Elvira in M.G. Lewis's novel *The Monk*, published in 1796, refused to allow her daughter, Antonia, aged fifteen, to read the Bible, except in an expurgated version. 'That prudent mother,' wrote Lewis, 'while she admired the beauty of the sacred writings, was convinced that, unrestricted, no reading more improper could be permitted to a young woman.....' An expurgated version of Shakespeare, considered suitable for family reading, was published by Thomas Bowdler in 1818. Cited in D. Thomas, *A Long Time Burning* (London, 1969), pp.182 & 186. Gaius Petronius Arbiter was the reputed author of the *Satyricon*, which paints a vivid picture of the life, decadence, and social manners of Rome in the time of Nero. The first English translation appeared in 1694. François Rabelais' comic novels *Gargantua and Pantagruel* were first published together in English in 1567.

16 R.F. Burton, *Supplemental Nights*, pp.437-8.

17 TNA, FO 7/1086, Burton to Salisbury, 23 Dorset St, Portman Sq, London, 2 Oct 1885. The leave mentioned was, of course, official. It would have exceeded two years, had the FO been aware of Burton's unofficial absences.

18 T. Wright, *The Life of Sir Richard Burton*, ii, p.134.

19 R.F. Burton, *The Thousand Nights and One Night*, Vol.10, p.163. N.M. Penzer, *Ann. Bib.*, p.321, described his own personal experience in January 1922, of listening to the story-teller in the Great Suk at Tangier, and 'being struck with the similarity of the scene so often described by Burton.'

20 *The Life*, p.311.

21 The Most Distinguished Order of St Michael and St George is an order of chivalry founded on 28 April 1818 by the Prince of Wales, later George IV, while acting as Prince Regent for his father, George III. The Order, which ranks sixth in the British honours system, is divided into three classes. These, in ascending order, are: Companion (CMG); Knight Commander (KCMG); GCMG (Knight Grand Cross). It has been humorously suggested in more recent times, that the abbreviations actually stand for 'Call Me God' (CMG), 'Kindly (or Kings) Call Me God,' (KCMG) and 'God Calls Me God' (GCMG).

22 Henry Raymond Arundell died at 14 Montagu Place on 14 March 1886, in his eighty-seventh year.

23 QK Coll, Burton to Ouida, Trieste, Austria, 2 April 1886.

24 TNA, FO 7/1105, Rosebery to Burton, 22 May 1886.

Notes to Chapter 42

1 *The Life*, ii, p.322.

2 The entry for Henry Raymond Arundell in the Death Duty Register, IR 26/3709, f. 1888, is very complex, and it was only possible to make some sense of the figures by collating it with the original will. This was carried out for me by Edward Higgs, Search Dept, TNA, to whom I am extremely grateful.

3 WSRO, Trowbridge, Box II, 2667/26/2 (vii) (1) – (13), (9). Robson & Kerslake, English and Foreign Booksellers, 23 Coventry Street, Haymarket, 12 May 1886. For further information about this firm, see P. Mendes, *Clandestine Erotic Fiction in English, 1800-1930. A bibliographical study.* (Aldershot, 1993), pp.15-16.

4 Almost nothing is known of Shaykh Nafzawi, who appears to have come from an area to the south of what is now Tunisia. The patron for whom he wrote *The Perfumed Garden* is believed to have been Muhammad ibn 'Awana az-Zuwawi, a minister of Abu Faris, who reigned from 1394-1434. See R. Brunschvig, *La Berbérie sous les Hafsides* II (Paris, 1947), 372f.

5 This is the number from the Neville Spearman (1963) edition, p.12. However, under 'Note' at the head of the

Burton's translation (1886), see Note 7 below, the number of copies is given as twenty-five.

6   WSRO.

7   Report from the Joint Select Committee on Lotteries and Indecent Advertisements, 1908, p.40. Cited in D. Thomas, *Swinburne. The Poet in his World* (London, 1979), pp.215-16. Avery was responsible for issuing Swinburne's early two-part 94 stanza poem, 'Reginald's Flogging' in *The Whippingham Papers* (1888). Information about Avery (1851-1913) can be found in P. Mendes, *Clandestine Erotic Fiction*, pp.12-13.

8   *The Book of the Thousand Nights and a Night* (Benares, 1885), x, p.133, note 3. Penzer, *Ann. Bib.*, p.174 describes this "rival" version as resembling 'the Kama Shastra Society edition in every respect as far as the text is concerned, except for the addition of a few head and tail-pieces and other decorations and the fact that the ink is violet instead of black. The binding is very similar, but has more gold decoration on the front of the cover.' There is a copy of this pirated version in the Oscar Eckenstein Collection, RAS, London.

9   *The Perfumed Garden of the Sheikh Nefzaoui* (Cosmopoli, 1886), p.xii.

10   *Ibid.*, p.xiii. However, as one commentator has pointed out, 'Arabic MSS of the Garden do, of course, contain a section devoted to homosexuality......'See *The Perfumed Garden of the Shaykh Nefzawi*, by Sir Richard Burton. Introduction by Alan Hull Walton (London, 1963), p.68. An anonymous modern translation by H.E.J., *The Glory of the Perfumed Garden. The Missing Flowers. An English Translation from the Arabic of the Second and Hitherto Unpublished Part of Shaykh Nafzawi's Perfumed Garden* (London, 1978), treats of the subject in Chap.II: On Sodomy and the Tricks of the Sodomites, their Love for Boys and their Preference for Boys over Good-looking Girls.

11   Chapter 21 in the Burton translation is headed: 'Forming the Conclusion of this work, and Treating of the Good Effects of the Deglutition of Eggs as Favourable to the Coitus.' Precisely how a section on pederasty could naturally follow on from this is unclear.

12   Sotades was a Greek satirist of the 3rd century BC noted for the coarseness and scurrility of his writings. The *OED* notes that the adjective 'Sotadic', was first used by Milton in 1645. Sotades was also fond of writing palindromes, i.e. verses and sentences capable of being read in the reverse order. Both meanings may have been in Burton's mind in choosing this word, the latter probably predominating.

13   *The Thousand Nights and a Night,*, x, pp.206-7.

14   *Ibid.*, Vol.2, p.234. According to Karl Heinrich Ulrichs (1825-95) who began writing under the pseudonym, Numa Numantius, love between men was natural and biological. In a series of pamphlets, collected under the title of *Forschungen über das Rathsel der mannmännlichen Liebe* (Researches on the Riddle of Male-Male Love) he summed up the phenomenon as, 'a female psyche confined in a male body.' Persecuted throughout his life for his outspoken views on homosexuality, he now enjoys cult status as a pioneer of the modern gay rights movement. It appears that Burton intended to incorporate extracts from Ulrich's writings in his later edition of *The Perfumed Garden*, which he never lived to finish, and which was burned by Lady Burton after his death.

15   H. Ellis, *Studies in the Psychology of Sex* (London, 1942), Third Edn, Vol.1, Part Four, Sexual Inversion, p.58. This major seven-volume work appeared between 1897-1928. The term 'contrary sexual feeling' was a diagnostic term invented in 1869 by Dr Karl Westphal, an eminent professor of psychiatry at Berlin. It was translated from the German as 'sexual inversion.' The word 'homosexual,' was coined in the same year by the Austrian-born Hungarian journalist and human rights campaigner, Karl-Maria Kerbeny (1824-82). Given widespread currency in Richard von Krafft-Ebing's *Psychopathia Sexualis* (1886), it eventually became the standard term.

16   *The Supplemental Nights*, Vol.6, p.450. Copyright, secured by registration with the Stationers' Company in London, lasted from 1554 to 1924. The number of copies which an author was obliged to hand over to the Stationers' Company was, in fact, five, not seven, these being the number of copyright libraries at the time entitled by law to a copy of every published book. They were: the British Museum Library (now the British Library), the Bodleian Library, Oxford, the Cambridge University Library, the present National Library of Scotland, and Trinity College, Dublin. The National Library of Wales was added by an Act of 1911. The term of copyright was fixed by an Act of 1842 at forty-two years after publication, or the life of the author plus seven years, whichever proved the longer.

17   Volumes III, IV, and V came out in 1887, Vol.VI in 1888.

18   *Lady Burton's Edition of her Husband's Arabian Nights*, Translated literally from the Arabic, prepared for

Household Reading by Justin Huntly McCarthy, M.P. (London, 1886), p.vi. 23 Dorset Street, Portman Sq, W London, Oct 1886.

19   *The Supplemental Nights*, Vol. VI, p.452.

20   SWRO, Box II, 2667/26/2 (vii) (1) – (13), (9)

21   See F. Brodie, *The Devil Drives* (London, 1984), pp.310-11.

22   *The Life*, ii, p.324.

23   TNA, FO 7/1105, Burton to Rosebery, 23 Dorset St, Portman Sq, 31 July 1886. Lord Iddesleigh took over as Foreign Secretary in Lord Salisbury's second cabinet formed in August 1886. Dr Donald Baines, MD, had a practice at 44 Brook St, Grosvenor Sq. His certificate is dated 28 July 1886.

24   I have dealt with Burton's claims regarding his Arabic examination in my article, 'Fact and Fiction in Richard Burton's Personal Narrative of a Pilgrimage to El-Medinah and Meccah (1855-56),' *JRAS*, Third Series, Vol.3, Part 3, Nov 1993, Section V, pp.348-51.

25   TNA, FO 7/1105, Burton to Iddesleigh, 23 Dorset St, Portman Sq, 8 Sept 1886. The statement of, what Isabel calls, 'the modest list' of Burton's "Services" is copied into *The Life*, ii, p.325, under the heading 'The Last Appeal.' It is also transcribed in Penzer's *Ann.Bib.*, pp.13-14.

26   TNA, FO 7/1105, Burton to Iddesleigh, 23 Dorset St, Portman Sq, 14 Sept 1886.

27   B. Stoker, *Personal Reminiscences of Henry Irving* (London, 1906), i, pp.360-1.

28   MSS Bodl. Or. 550-556 has an entry under AD 1803, in W.D. Macray, *Annals of the Bodleian Library Oxford* (Oxford, 1890), 2nd edn, p.281.

29   J. Scott, *The Arabian Nights Entertainments* (London, 1811), i, p.xv. See F. Moussa-Mahmoud, 'A Manuscript Translation of the Arabian Nights in the Beckford Papers,' *Journal of Arabic Literature*, Vol.7 (Leiden, 1976), pp.8-9.

30   Burton's introductory letter, and the relevant correspondence on the subject appeared in *The Academy*, Vol. XXX, 13 Nov 1886, p.327.

31   Information provided in a letter to the author from A.D.S. Roberts, the Keeper of Oriental Books, Bodleian Library, Oxford, 29 Jan 1979.

32   Application of the kind sought by Burton, had to be approved by the Curators in full session. The Librarian was not empowered to act alone.

33   Letter from A.D.S. Roberts already cited. Burton was sent a letter informing him of the Curators' decision on Monday, 1 Nov. He sent a letter of complaint to the University Vice-Chancellor on 3 Nov. See *The Academy*, letter IV, p.327.

34   *The Life*, p.323. A highly dubious claim, I think, possibly manufactured by Isabel. Chandler was a classical scholar who devoted his life to the study of Aristotle. He could not possibly have known anything about the MSS in question, nor the capabilities of the university's professors of Arabic.

35   According to Chandler's entry in the *DNB*, however, the suggestion of photographing texts as an alternative to lending them was Chandler's own. Burton dedicated Vol.IV of his *Supplemental Nights* to Chandler on 10 March 1888, mistakenly writing his Christian names as William H. instead of Henry W. On 16 May of the following year, Chandler, who had suffered all his life from chronic insomnia, committed suicide at Pembroke College, where he was a fellow.

36   A.H. Sayce, *Reminiscences* (London, 1923), p.243.

37   *Ibid.*, p.243.

38   *The Life*, p.331.

Notes to Chapter 43

1   The hotel was used during World War II as the headquarters of the German commander of Greater Paris, Dietrich von Choltitz, who disobeyed Hitler's order to burn the city. Choltitz was captured there on 25 August 1944.

2   *The Academy*, Vol.XXXI, 22 Jan 1887, pp.60-61. Burton also gave an extended account of his find in *The Supplemental Nights* (1886-8), Vol.III, Foreword, pp. viii-ix.

3   TNA, FO 7/1125, Burton to Salisbury, Trieste, 7 April 1887. Burton had sent a further despatch on similar lines on 12 April..

4   *The Romance*, ii, p.689.

5   TNA, FO 7/1125, Burton to Salisbury, Trieste, 14 July 1887. Leave authorised by the FO on 22 July.

6   Bodleian Western MSS, J.J. Fahie Papers, Trieste, 11 Oct 1887.

7   In the above letter to Fahie, however, Isabel stated their reason for changing doctors was that, 'we have sucked this one's brain dry and I am getting another to keep till next spring who will take us home to England when I hope he [Burton] will be quite out of danger.'

8   T. Wright, *The Life of Sir Richard Burton*, ii, p.165.

9   F. Hitchman, *Richard F. Burton, K.C.M.G.: His Early, Private and Public Life* (London, 1887), i, pp.v-vi.

10 HL, Correspondence of Sir Richard F. Burton (Box 2), I. Burton to Smithers, Hotel Stephanie, Abbazia, Sudbahn, Austria, 18 Feb 1888.

11 WSRO, 26667/26. Box 4: press cuttings book.

12 *Western Daily Mercury*, 3 Dec 1887. It appears that Hitchman had connections with another Plymouth newspaper, the *Western Morning News*. The *Mercury* was incorporated with the *Western Morning News* on 1 Feb 1921.

13 WSRO, 2667/26, Box 4: press cuttings book. Isabel Burton to the Editor of *The Western Daily Mercury*, Abazzia, 12 Dec 1887. Written across the top of the letter in Isabel's handwriting are the words: 'I wanted to send this but Richard would not let me – send it back with the others.'

14 WSRO, 2667/26, Box 4: press cuttings book. I. Burton to Mr Russell, Hotel Stephanie, Abbazia, Austria, 12 Dec 1887.

15 *A Sketch of the Career of Richard F. Burton*, Collected from "Men of Eminence"; from Sir Richard and Lady Burton's Own Works; from the Press; from Personal Knowledge, and Various Other Reliable Sources.' By Alfred Bates [sic] Richards, (late Editor of the "Morning Advertiser") up to 1876: By Andrew Wilson (Author of the Abode of Snow) up to 1879: By St. Clair Baddeley, up to the present date, 1886. As Penzer pointed out, *Ann. Bib.*, p.306, 'Practically every word of these pamphlets was reproduced in Lady Burton's "Life" of 1893.'

16 *The Saturday Review*, 10 Sept 1887, pp.367-8.

17 *The Saturday Review*, 28 Jan 1888, pp.110-11.

18 HL, Correspondence of Sir Richard F. Burton, I. Burton to L.Smithers.

19 TNA, FO 7/1140, Burton to Salisbury, Trieste, 2 May 1888.

20 The coup took place on 15 November 1889, but it was not until the following day that the news was broken to Pedro II. He was then informed that he and his family would have to leave the country within twenty-four hours. See R.M. Schneider, *"Order and Progress." A Political History of Brazil* (Oxford, 1991), p.64. Pedro II died on 5 December 1891 in Paris, more than a year after Burton's death. His and his wife's remains were brought back to Brazil in 1922 and reburied in Petropolis.

21 A review by Burton of "Aladdin" in the original Arabic. *Histoire d'Ala Al-Din ou La Lampe Merveilleuse*. Text Arabe....Par H. Zotenberg, 1888, had appeared in *The Academy*, 4 February 1888, p.79.

Notes to Chapter 44

1   Wilde to Reggie Turner, 10 Aug 1897, *The Letters of Oscar Wilde* (ed.) Rupert Hart-Davis (London, 1962).

2   Wesley College had opened in 1838 as the Wesleyan Proprietary Grammar School taking day pupils and boarders from the age of nine. Six years later, it became a university college of the University of London, changing its name to reflect its new status. A prospectus published some time before 1853 shows that its curriculum included the study of Greek, Latin and Hebrew, hence Smithers' excellent knowledge of the classics. In 1903 Wesley College was sold to the City Council and was amalgamated with the Sheffield Royal Grammar School in 1905 to form King Edward VII School.

3   *Priapeia, or the Sportive Epigrams of divers Poets on Priapus* (Cosmopoli, MDCCCXC), Introduction, p.ix.

4   The French novelist, Emile Zola, stayed at the Queen's Hotel in Norwood from October 1898 to June 1899, after

fleeing to England following his famous open letter to the President of the Republic in 1898, "J'Accuse," in which he denounced the unjust conviction of the Jewish army officer, Alfred Dreyfus.

5   *The Life*, ii, p.364.

6   G. Stisted, *Temple Bar*, Vol.92, May-July 1891, pp.341-2.

7   TNA, FO 7/1140, Burton to Salisbury, 1 Nov Post Restante, Geneva, No.1, 188. However, Burton did not arrive at Geneva until the morning of 3 Nov, according to a postcard he wrote to W.F. Kirby. He was granted leave on 23 Nov 1888.

8   *The Life*, p.365. A résumé of the proceedings is in 'Séance familière du 26 Novembre en l'honneur de Sir Richard Francis Burton.' *La Globe, Journal Géographique. Organe de la Société de Géographie de Genève.* Tome Vingt-Huitième. Quatrième Série – Tome VIII. Bulletin No.1. Nov 1888 – Jan 1889, pp.15-18. See N.M. Penzer, *Ann. Bib.*, pp.241-2.

9   This was an annotated translation made by Smithers, and illustrated with etchings of the French erotic work, *Les Tableaux Vivants* first published in Brussels in 1870. Dated 1888 and issued in a limited edition of 250 copies, it was the second in the list of works printed by the Erotika Biblion Society. It formed the first in what Smithers and Nichols later named the *Bibliothèque Français* series. See J.G. Nelson, *Publisher to the Decadents: Leonard Smithers in the Careers of Beardsley, Wilde, Dowson* (Pennsylvania, 2000), p.28 and note 5, p.359.

10 HL, Burton to Smithers, 30 September 1888.

11 HL, Burton to Smithers, Geneva, 2 December 1888.

12 HL, Burton to Smithers, Tunis, 24 December 1888.

13 Penzer provides a short 'Note' on Letchford's life in *Ann. Bib.*, Appendix C, pp.325-6.

14 T. Wright, *The Life of Sir Richard Burton*, ii, p.209.

15 HL, Burton to Smithers, Trieste, 1 May and 22 May 1889.

16 These, and other similar remarks, were reprinted in the National Vigilance Association's *Pernicious Literature* (1888), p.24.

17 Somewhat on the lines of Burton's 'Black Book,' Vizetelly, before the trial, had sent to the Treasury Solicitor '*Extracts Principally from English Classics: Showing that the Legal Suppression of M. Zola's Novels would Logically Involve the Bowdlerising of some of the Great Works in English Literature..........*' Cited in D. Thomas, *A Long Time Burning* (London, 1969), p.268.

18 HL, Burton to Smithers, Trieste, 2 June 1889.

19 HL, Burton to Smithers, Trieste, 26 June 1889. Although dated 1888, the Smithers/Nichols *Priapeia* did not appear until, possibly, the middle of July 1889. It was bound in grey boards with white paper back, and limited to 250 copies. According to the prospectus among Burton MSS at the British Library, it was priced at £2 12 0 a volume, with a discount of 10 shillings if payment was received before December 1888.

20 *The Life*, p.380.

21 TNA, FO 7/1153, Salisbury to Burton, 10 August 1889.

22 TNA, FO 7/1153, Burton to Salisbury, Südbahn Hotel, Semmering, Austria, 19 Aug 1889.

23 HL, Burton to Smithers, Vienna, 29 Aug 1889.

24 HL, Burton to Smithers, Trieste, 13 Sept 1889.

25 QK Coll, Smithers to Burton, 109 Queen St, Sheffield, 17 Sept 1889. This was the address of Smithers' solicitors' chambers in the city.

26 T. Wright, *The Life of Sir Richard Burton*, pp.209-10. The FO had granted Burton four months' leave on the grounds of ill-health, from 15 Nov 1889 to 15 March 1890. He informed the FO of his imminent departure for Brindisi in TNA: FO 7/1153, Burton to Salisbury, Trieste, 15 Nov 1889.

27 The Lambert Playfair papers, University Muniments, University Library, St Andrews, Scotland. I. Burton to Lambert Playfair, Tunis, 9 Jan 1890.

28 T.Wright, *The Life of Sir Richard Burton*, pp.210-15.

29 HL, Burton Smithers, February 1890.

30 T. Wright, pp.216-7.

31 HL, Burton to Smithers, Trieste, 10 May 1890.

32   HL, Burton to Smithers Trieste, 11 May 1890.
33   HL, Burton to Smithers, 15 May 1890, deliberately omitting his address and signature.
34   HL, I. Burton to Smithers, Trieste, 16 May 1890.
35   HL, Burton to Smithers, 19 May 1890.
36   HL, Isabel Burton to Smithers, Trieste, 27 May 1890.
37   HL, Burton to Smithers, Trieste, 28 and 31 May 1890.
38   HL, I. Burton to Smithers, Trieste, 18 June 1890.
39   HL, Burton to Smithers, Trieste, 21 June 1890.

Notes to Chapter 45

1   Bertram Joseph Arundell Smyth-Pigott (*Pipestone, Manitoba*) born 26 March 1874. Smyth-Pigott of Brockley, Burke's Genealogical and Heraldic History of the Landed Gentry 1937 Centenary (15th edn.), ed. H. Pine-Gordon, ii, 1810. The young Arthur Conan Doyle was a pupil at the college from 1875-6, after passing his London matriculation examination at Stonyhurst.
2   HL, I. Burton to Smithers, 27 May 1890.
3   *Priapeia*, p.xi. Penzer, pp.151-2 quotes the passages containing the original and altered wording. Apparently, a mistake was made in binding in old pages in front of the preface in 'probably not more than a half dozen copies' which were sent out before the error was discovered. Penzer, himself, owned a copy containing a set of five plates by the French painter, Jean-Honoré Fragonard (1732-1806), chiefly known for his erotic canvases. These appear to have been 'originally bound into the book and not subsequently inserted.'
4   HL, Burton to Smithers, Hotel Baur au Lac, Zurich, 15 July 1890. Outidanos (= Good for Nothing) and Neaniskos (= A Young Man) were the pseudonyms adopted respectively by Burton and Smithers for the *Priapeia*. They had been coined by Burton, Smithers admitting in a letter to him of 17 Sept 1889 (QK Coll), of being unable to think of one.
5   QK Coll, I. Burton to Lady White-Cooper, Hotel Baur au Lac, Zurich, Suisse, 24 July 1890.
6   Quoted in 'The Burton Collection at the Royal Asiatic Society,' by C.E. Whitting, *The Royal Asiatic Society, Its History and Treasures* (ed.) S. Simmonds and S. Digby (Leiden & London, 1979), p.152.
7   Quoted in W.G. Lockett, *Robert Louis Stevenson at Davos* (London, 1934), p.33.
8   The forty-nine year old Stanley had married Dorothy Tennant, an accomplished neoclassicist painter fourteen years his junior, in Westminster Abbey on 12 July of that year. A week before the wedding, the first edition of *In Darkest Africa* appeared, containing Stanley's graphic account of the Emin Pasha Relief Expedition to 'rescue' Emin Pasha, the governor of Equatoria in the southern Sudan.
9   Letter from I. Burton to *The Morning Post*, dated Maloja, 28 August, and printed in the newspaper on 8 Sept 1890.
10   D. Stanley (ed.) *Henry M. Stanley, Autobiography* (London, 1912), pp.423-4.
11   *The Life*, ii, p.405.
12   HL, Burton to Smithers, Trieste, 8 September 1890.
13   HL, Burton to Smithers, 24 Sept 1890. Two days later, Burton wrote a postcard to Smithers confirming that he had received his copy the previous day. 'I like the book very much, but the binding must be altered…..'
14   *The Life*, p.405.
15   According to Wright who does not cite his source, the visit to Greece was to be made in the company of Dr Schliemann. He died at Naples, two months after Burton, on 26 Dec 1890. See T. Wright, *The Life of Sir Richard Burton*, p.237. There is nothing in the FO Correspondence files, which indicate that Burton had made any request for leave at this date.
16   In Assher's Collection of English authors. It now forms part of the Burton Collection at the OHG.
17   The German physician, Franz Anton Mesmer (1734-1815), had postulated a theory that the planets influenced the human body in sickness and in health, by what was thought to be a mysterious, invisible fluid. He later called this healing influence, 'animal magnetism.' It is possible that Isabel thought she could act as a conduit for this supposed

magnetism, by placing her hands on the sick person.

18   It is not clear from this description precisely how the battery was being used in an attempt to revive the action of the heart. John A. MacWilliam, (1857-1937), appointed professor of physiology at Aberdeen University at the age of 29 in 1886, was a pioneer of Cardiac Electrophysiology. 'In certain forms of cardiac arrest [he wrote] there appears to be a possibility of restoring by artificial means the rhythmic beat and tiding over a sudden and temporary danger...In order to do this in man one electrode should be applied in front over the area of cardiac impulse, and the other over the region of the fourth dorsal vertebra behind, so the induction shocks may traverse the organ...The shocks employed should be strong, sufficient to excite powerful contraction in the voluntary muscles.......' See J.A. MacWilliam: Electrical stimulation of the heart in man. *British Medical Journal*, 1889; 1: 348-350. Whether Dr Baker kept abreast of current medical thinking in this field is, of course, a moot point.

19   *The Life*, pp.413-4.

20   *The True Life*, p.414.

21   *Ibid.*, p.415n.

22   *The Romance*, ii, p.709. A letter on the subject from the Baroness had already appeared in *The Catholic Times* on 24 December 1890.

23   There is no mention in *The Life* of the short document, written in Isabel's hand and dated Gorizia, 15 February 1877, nor of 'a paper of considerable length, all of it in Sir Richard Burton's handwriting and signed by himself, in which he declared that he had lived and would die a Catholic, adhering to all the rites and usages of the Church.' See T. Wright, *The Life of Sir Richard Burton*, ii, pp.217-8, quoting from a letter to him from Mr T.D. Murray of 24 September 1904, who claimed that Lady Burton showed him the paper about a year before her death.

24   *The Romance*, pp. 706-8. 'Declaration,' (translated from the Italian) Trieste, January 12, 1897, signed by Pietro Martelani, "Formerly Parish Priest of the B.V. del Soccorso, now Prebendary and Priest of the Cathedral of Trieste."

25   *Ibid*, p.708. This was the charge laid at the door of Dr Baker by Isabel, as will be seen later.

26   *Ibid.*, p.710. In a letter to J.J. Fahie five years earlier, she had written: 'I am also as you know a Papist – an old one too – your dream is like my daily hopes and struggles from the year '56 till now, to make him a Catholic though I never speak of it to him.' Trieste, 12 May 1885, Bodleian Western MSS, J.J. Fahie Papers, MSS Eng. Mis. d 187 (1919).

27   *The Life*, p.268.

28   *The Kasidah*, Canto VI, stanzas 11 & 12.

29   See T. Wright, *The Life of Sir Richard Burton*, p.244, Major St George Burton to T. Wright, March 1905. According to Catholic doctrine, if a man is unconscious when the priest arrives, as was claimed in Burton's case, Extreme Unction may be given *conditionally*, the Latin phrase, *Si capax es*, meaning 'If you have the requirements for a valid reception,' the assumption being made that, before losing consciousness, the dying man made an act of contrition.

30   They form part of the Burton Collection at the OHG.

31   In 1868, the German chemist, August Wilhelm von Hofmann, discovered formaldehyde. It was probably this chemical which was used in Burton's embalming. The blood would have been drained from his veins and replaced by a fluid consisting of a solution of formaldehyde in water, injected into one of the main arteries.

32   Isabel was well aware that calling Burton a Catholic, and holding a Catholic service in Trieste for him, had caused Lady Stisted great offence.

33   T. Wright, *The Life of Sir Richard Burton*, 246-7. Undated. Lent to Wright by Mostyn Pryce, who inherited the Stisteds' effects when Georgiana died.

34   *The Life*, p.420.

35   *The Romance*, p.742. Letter to Madame Gutmansthal de Benvenuti, London, 1 March 1891.

36   WSRO, 2667/26/2 (xv) i, two copies, 9 pages, undated. It contains three sections headed: No.1. Stanley Picture, No.2. The Picture After Death, No.3. The Great Picture; 2667/26/2 (xii) (A) (2), 10 pages, 6 Aug 1893.

37   WSRO, 2667/26/2 (XV) [3]

38   *The Life*, pp.420-1.

39   N.M. Penzer, *Ann. Bib.*, p.181. Daisy Letchford sent one of the notebooks she managed to preserve to Penzer, and it became 'the gem' of his Burton collection. He hoped that it would eventually be housed in an appropriate museum or library. Ironically, having escaped the flames at Trieste, it perished when Penzer's house was destroyed by incendiary bombs in World War II.

40   QK Coll, I. Burton to Dr Baker, 5 Baker St, 21 July 1891.

41   Further details about Canon George Webb Waterton (1842-1911) can be found in his obituary in *The Carlisle Journal*, 7 Feb 1911, col.1&2. Among the mourners at his funeral was Mr Joseph van Zeller, Lady Burton's nephew.

42   Elaborate steps were taken to guard against any possibility of infection. The remains had to be placed in a leaden shell with a glass cover over the face. This was again closed in a coffin of steel and gilt. It was then put into a stoutly-made plain white deal case, secured with iron clamps and screws. The case was filled with sawdust in which, according to Austrian law, a bottle of carbolic acid was poured. Painted in black on the outside of the case were the words: 'To the Rev Canon Wenham, Catholic Church, Mortlake, SW, Surrey.'

43   WSRO, 2667/26/2 (xv), [8]. There are two copies on file of this letter.

44   WSRO, 2667/26/2 (xv) [14]: F. Grenfell Baker to Lady Burton, Hotel [?], Sunday Oct 25, 10.15 am.

45   In the document on the Letchford pictures, Isabel dates this last get-together with her friends to 25 January 1891, 'two evenings before I left…' In *The Life*, ii, p.428, she describes it as being the last evening, ie 26 January.

46   WSRO, 2667/26/2 (xv) [2], I. Burton to Prince Hohenlohe, undated, 67 Baker Street, Portman Square, London W. A typed letter, because she was 'too weak to write,' headed 'Private and Confidential,' probably written towards the latter part of June 1891. After describing her problems with Letchford over the paintings, she warned the Prince to 'have all your contracts in writing, taking warning of what has happened to me and not leave anything to friendship, as I did.' Isabel's order of 6 April 1892 for 500 fl was paid to Letchford on 13 April by I. & R. Priv. Austrian Society of Credit for Commerce and Industry, Trieste Branch.

Notes to Chapter 46

1   See D.C.M. Platt, *The Cinderella Service. British Consuls since 1825* (London, 1971), pp.46-7, where he points out that it was not until 1949 that widows and other dependants of civil servants received any pension rights. Furthermore, no financial help was given to families of consuls dying abroad to transport their bodies back to England.

2   The last entry in the Trieste consular files for Burton, TNA: FO 7/1165, was a despatch addressed to P.P. Cautley, 14 Nov 1890, which read: 'I am directed by the Marquess of Salisbury to transmit the accounts bill on the Chief Clerk for £31 15s 11d, representing the amount of salary due to the late Sir Richard Burton in respect of the period Oct 7 to Oct 20 less income tax.' This amounted to 16s 3d. Isabel was granted probate of Burton's will on 23 March 1891.

3   According to Lady Burton's will, £375 was invested in Great Indian Peninsular Railway five per cent guaranteed stock, and £1,197 in London and North Western Railway consolidated four pounds per cent guaranteed stock upon trust. However, this differs from her account in her journal 'Beth,' where she writes: 'My income consists of £150 Queen's pension, £204 joint annuity on Richard's and my life, and about £7,900 chiefly in railways, which produce about £261 yearly, making my income £600 without income tax.'

4   See F. Galton, FRS, *Memories of My Life* (London, 1908), p.202. Galton, aged eighty-six when his memoirs were published, claimed incorrectly that he was 'instrumental in procuring a Government Pension of £300 for Lady Burton.' It was a matter of some irony, of course, that Galton, of whom Burton had spoken in the harshest terms, was most active in procuring a Civil List pension for Burton's widow.

5   See RGS Archives, Eric Harrington Correspondence, 12 Jan 1891. The memorial was dated 6 January, and noted Burton's contribution to Literature as well as Science. The result of Galton's enquiries was 'that it was better to rest his [Burton's] claims on his wide discursiveness rather than any one specified performance.' The reply from 10 Downing Street, Whitehall, was sent to the PRGS on 22 January.

6   RGS Archives, Letter Book. I. Burton to H.W. Bates, Venice, 29 Jan 1891.

7   *The Times*, 24 Jan. 1891, p.11. Sir Polydore de Keyser (1832-98), enjoyed the distinction of being the first Roman Catholic to be elected Lord Mayor of London (1887) since the Reformation.

8   HL, I. Burton to L. Smithers, Trieste, 26 Dec 1890. Bills from the Cunard Steam Ship Company, alone, amounted to £5 0 3 for 25 packages and effects, and £25 for Burton's corpse, a total of just over £30, equivalent in modern money of more than £1,600.

9   HL, I. Burton to L. Smithers, Liverpool, 12 Feb 1891, written on Langham Hotel notepaper.

10 *The Life*, ii, p.430.

11 HL, EMC, L. Smithers to I. Burton, 26 Feb 1891.

12 *The Times*, 2 March, p.4. The letter was written on 26 Feb.

13 *The Times*, 1 April 1891. Writing to J.J. Fahie on 11 April 1891, thanking him for his generous contribution, she said that the donations then amounted to £581 13 6.

14 HL, I. Burton to L. Smithers, Langham, 22 March 1891.

15 *The True Life*, p.415.

16 F. Galton, *Memories of My Life*, p.202.

17 *The Life*, p.444. Dr Grenfell Baker, claiming to have regularly heard and discussed its contents with Burton, described it as being merely a greatly annotated edition of that issued in 1886. However, according to Thomas Wright, *The Life of Sir Richard Burton*, ii, pp.197-8, Burton had told Payne that he had compensated for his failure to locate the missing 21st chapter on pederasty 'by collecting all manner of tales and of learned material of Arab origin bearing on my special study, and I have been so successful that I have trebled the original manuscript.' Whom do we believe?

18 WSRO, 2667/26/2 (xii) (A) (2), 6 August 1893.

19 *A Problem in Modern Ethics*, *Being an Inquiry Into The Phenomenon Of Sexual Inversion*. Addressed Especially To Medical Psychologists and Jurists (London, 1896), Chap.VII. Literature: Polemical: Karl Heinrich Ulrichs, pp. 82-111. Symonds described *Memnon*, p.82, as 'the most important' of the pamphlets, 'polemical, analytical, theoretical, and apologetical,' which appeared between 1864 and 1870. At the same time, he also thought it 'necessary to study earlier and later treatises – Inclusa, Formatrix, Vindex, Ara Spei, Gladius Furens, Incubus, Argonauticus, Prometheus, Araxes, Kritische Pfeile – in order to obtain a complete knowledge of his opinions, and to master the whole mass of information he has brought together.'

20 J.A. Symonds to E. Carpenter, 7 Feb 1893, quoted in H. Kennedy, 'Karl Heinrich Ulrichs: 1825-1895,' *The European Gay Review*, Vol.1 (1986), p.74.

21 WSRO, 2267/26, Box 2 (iv) 28, L. Smithers to I. Burton, 109 Queen St, Sheffield, 16 July 1891.

22 HL, I. Burton to Smithers, letters dated 16 and 18 July 1891.

23 HL, EMC, L. Smithers to I. Burton, 109 Queen St, Sheffield, 10 Jul 1891. The shop in London Smithers referred to was, in fact, H.S. Nichols's new shop at 174 Wardour Street, sited very close to Oxford Street.

24 HL Corr [Box 2] I. Burton to L. Smithers, 5 Baker St, 21 July 1891.

25 HL, EMC, L. Smithers to I. Burton, 22 July 1891.

26 HL, EMC, Smithers to I. Burton, 13 Aug 1891.

27 HL, I. Burton to L. Smithers, 13 Aug 1891. In his autobiography, *The Early Life & Vicissitudes of Jack Smithers* (London, 1939), Smithers wrote, p.23: 'I was born into this world on the day that my sister Lena, aged two, passed out of it, on August 13 1891, at Dalkieth Terrace, Ranmoor, Sheffield.'

28 HL, EMC, L. Smithers to I. Burton, 31 Aug 1891.

29 Blanche Mary Smyth-Pigott died aged 56, on 21 Sept 1891 at 3 Royal Terrace, Weston-super-Mare. She had been separated for some time from her wastrel husband, and had been staying with her daughter of the same name, at 52 Seymour Street, Portman Sq, London. Her personal estate at the time of her death amounted to £1,561 3s. 5d. Her husband, John Hugh Wadham Smyth-Pigott, who had dissipated his fortune and lost his huge estates, died four months later on 19 January 1892, at St Helier, Jersey. He left effects valued at only £217 10s. See Calendar of the Grants of Probate and Letters of Administration made in the Probate Register of the High Court of Justice in England etc, London.

30 HL, EMC, L. Smithers to I. Burton, 16 Nov 1891.

31   *The Romance*, ii, p.751. I. Burton to E. Bishop, 27 Dec 1891.

32   E.L. Linton, 'The Partisans of Wild Women,' *The Nineteenth Century*, March 1892, p.461.

33   C.A. Swinburne, *The Fortnightly Review*, No.CCCVII, New Series, July 1 1892.

34   Isabel eventually wrote a characteristically spirited reply in 'Sir Richard Burton: An Explanation and a Defence,' *New Review*, VII, 562-76, November 1892.

35   Bodleian Western MSS, J.J. Fahie Papers, MSS Eng. Mis, d.187 (1919), I. Burton to J.J. Fahie, 67 Baker St, Portman Sq, W, 24 March 1892.

36   HL, I. Burton to L. Smithers, 17 July 1892.

37   WSRO, Trowbridge, 26677/26/2 (iv) 25 nd

38   WSRO, Trowbridge, 2667/26/2 (iv) 25.

39   WSRO, Trowbridge, 2667/26/2/ (xvii). Of the 110 letters to Isabel from George Etheridge, 1892-93, in this collection, only two belong to the former year. (i) 18 Oct 1892 in which he speaks of sending her 'per today's post some specimens of illustrations very suitable in book work,' specimens of type, and in a few days, 'some good specimens of line blocks & half-tone blocks.' He also offered help with choosing paper, and suggested someone who, he felt, would 'gladly undertake the "Index" for a reasonable remuneration.'(ii) 31 Dec 1892. This shows, that an interview with Mr Chapman had already been set up for the previous Thursday, which Isabel, possibly for reasons of ill-health, had been unable to attend.

40   Isabel's copy of The "Memorandum of Agreement made....between Chapman Hall Publishers....and Lady Isabel Burton..." for her Life of Captain Sir Richard Burton, dated 3 March 1893, is signed by Edward Chapman and Lady Burton. It forms part of the Edwards H. Metcalf Collection at the Huntington Library, call number RFB 1004. An agreement for US and Canadian rights was signed on 10 May 1893.

41   See his obituary in the *Sheffield Daily Telegraph*, 9 June 1920. The reference to Caroline Frith's fortune was made by Smithers in a letter to Isabel of 4 June 1893 in the Metcalf Coll.

42   *The Pilgrimage*, *A Mission to Gelele*, and *Vikram and the Vampire*, appeared in 1893. *First Footsteps* came out in 1894. All were published by Tylston and Edwards, possibly a cover-name for Smithers & H.S. Nichols, since none carries an identifiable publisher's address.

43   Quoted by Lady Walburga Paget, *In My Tower* (London, 1924), p.19. The MS was sold to Henry & Co, who wrote in a Publisher's Note: 'In issuing "Il Pentamerone" to the subscribers, the Publishers desire to say that the Ms was placed in their possession by Lady Burton in pursuance of agreement. In no respect has the text been abbreviated; it represents a faithful and unexpurgated rendering of these Neapolitan tales.'

44   HL, EMC, L. Smithers to I. Burton, 2 May 1893. There is a rather odd, undated typed note to Smithers from Isabel, signing herself 'Hermaphrodite', in which she writes: 'You promised me the remainder of Priapeia in exchange for Catullus.'

45   SWRO, Trowbridge, 2667/26/2 (xvii). There are letters on the subject from G. Etheridge to I. Burton from 23 June – 5 July 1893. Isabel, incensed by Chapman's action, but without any reasonable justification, wrote a strongly worded note to the publishers, but was dissuaded from sending it by Smithers, who thought it would offend George Etheridge.

46   *The Romance*, p.755, letter dated 10 Jan 1894.

47   HL, EMC, L. Smithers to I. Burton, 28 August 1893.

48   QK Coll. Mortlake, 16 September 1893.

49   Smithers and Nichols brought out a second edition of *The Kasidah* early in 1894, limited to 100 copies, and carrying a preface by Isabel, dated 15 February 1894.

50   Cited in J.G. Nelson, *Publisher to the Decadents* (Pennsylvania, 2000), p.22.

51   *The Carmina of Caius Valerius Catullus* (London, MDCCCXCIIII), Introductory letter written by Isabel, 11 July 1894, p.v.

52   *Ibid.*, Smithers's Introduction of same date, pp. xvii & xv.

53   WSRO, 2667/26/2 (ix), I. Burton to members of the Writers' Club, 67 Baker St, Portman Square, 15 Jan 1895, mistakenly dated 1894. Her long letter of explanation accompanied a set of the Library Edition, which she sent to them as a New Year's gift. The twelve volumes, which appeared in November 1894, were sold for £6 6s the set. Of

the Terminal Essay, only the article on pederasty, was omitted. See N.M. Penzer, *Ann. Bib.*, pp. 117-24, for a detailed account of the Nichols-Smithers editions.

54   See an excellent critical account in J.L. Campbell and T.H. Hall, *Strange Things. The Story of Fr. Allan McDonald, Ada Goodrich Freer, and the Society for Psychical Research* (London, 1968).

55   *Borderland*, Vol.III, 1896, p.162.

56   *Ibid.*, p.38.

57   *Borderland*, Vol.III, 1896, p.168.

58   T. Wright, *The Life of Sir Richard Burton*, p.281.

59   *Borderland*, Vol.III, p.168.

60   *The Romance*, pp.767-8. As we have seen, Ada Goodrich Freer published two accounts of the affair in *Borderland* in April 1896, and January 1897. She also read a paper on the Burton case, 'Some Recent Experiences Apparently Supernormal,' to the 83rd General Meeting of the Society for Psychical Research at the Westminster Town Hall, 4 Dec 1896. The audience 'is said to have been the largest present at any meeting of their society since its foundation.' *Borderland*, Vol.IV, 1897, p.5.

61   R.F. Burton, *The Highlands of the Brazil* (London, 1869), ii, p.101.

62   Holywell Lodge, Eastbourne, 12 March 1896. Quoted in *The Romance*, p.769.

SELECT BIBLIOGRAPHY

Note: All books were published in London unless otherwise stated

A Collection of Warrants and Regulations Issued to the Army on Matters of Finance (F. Pinkney, Military Library, Whitehall, 1837).

A Reminiscence of Sir Richard Burton, Anonymous, *Chambers's Journal*, Vol.VII, 6th Series, Dec 1903 – Nov 1904, pp. 538-40.

Abbott, J., *Sind: A Re-interpretation of the Unhappy Valley* (Humphrey Milford OUP, 1924).

Abir, Mordecai, *Ethiopia and the Red Sea* (Frank Cass, 1980).

Ahmed, Leila, *Edward W. Lane. A Study of his life and work, and of British ideas in the Middle East in the nineteenth century* (Longman Group Ltd, 1978).

Aitken, E.H., *Gazeteer of the Province of Sind* (Karachi, 1907).

Ajayi, J.F.A. and Crowder, Michael, (eds.), *History of West Africa*, 2 vols. (Longman Group Ltd, 1974).

Aldington, Richard, *Lawrence of Arabia, A Biographical Inquiry* (Collins, 1955).

Aldridge, James, *Cairo. Biography of a City* (Macmillan, 1969).

Allan, Mea, *Palgrave of Arabia* (Macmillan, 1972).

Allen, Bernard M., *Gordon and the Sudan* (Macmillan and Co Ltd, 1931).

Allgemeine Deutsche Biographie (Duncker & Humblot, Berlin, 1968).

Allgrove, George, *Love in the East* (Anthony Gibbs & Phillips, 1962).

Alvarez, Fr. Francisco, *Narrative of the Portuguese Embassy to Abyssinia, During the Years 1520-27,* Translated from the Portuguese and edited with Notes and an Introduction by Lord Stanley of Alderley (Hakluyt Society, 1881).

Anderson, Nancy Fix, *Woman Against Women In Victorian England. A Life of Eliza Lynn Linton* (Indiana University Press, 1987).

Annual Review 1991-1992, The Arundell of Wardour papers, *The Royal Commission on Historical Manuscripts* (HMSO).

Antonius, George, *The Arab Awakening. The Story of the Arab National Movement* (Hamish Hamilton, 1938).

Arberry, A.J., *British Orientalists* (Collins, 1943).

Armstrong, J.R., *The History of Sussex* (Phillimore & Co. Ltd, 1978).

Arrington, Leonard J & Bitton, Davis, *The Mormon Experience. A History of the Latter-Day Saints* (George Allen & Unwin, 1979).

Arrington, Leonard J., *Brigham Young: American Moses* (Alfred A. Knopf, New York, 1985).

——————*Great Basin Kingdom. An Economic History of the Latter-day Saints, 1830-90* (Harvard University Press, Cambridge, Mass, 1958).

Assad, Thomas, *Three Victorian Travellers* (Routledge & Kegan Paul, 1964).

Aylward, J.D., *The House of Angelo – A Dynasty of Swordsmen* (The Batchworth Press, 1953).

Badawi, M.M. (ed.), *Journal of Arabic Literature*, Vol.VII (E.J. Brill, Leiden, 1976).

Baedeker, K. (ed.), *Palestine and Syria. Handbook for Travellers* (Dulau and Co, 1876).

Bagley, J.J., *The Earls of Derby, 1485-1985* (Sidgwick & Jackson, 1985).

Baillie, Alexander F., *Kurrachee: (Karachi). Past: Present: And Future* (Thacker & Co Ltd, Bombay, 1890).

Baker, F. Grenfell, Sir Richard Burton As I Knew Him, *The Cornhill Magazine*, NS LI, Oct 1921, pp. 411-23.

Baker, Sir Samuel, *Albert N'Yanza. Great Basin of the Nile,* 2 vols (Macmillan, 1866).

Balsdon, Dacre, *Oxford Then and Now* (Duckworth & Co Ltd, 1970).

Barrett, David B., (ed.), *World Christian Encyclopaedia* (OUP, 1982).

Bartlett, Richard A., *The New Country. A Social History of the American Frontier, 1776-1890* (OUP Inc, 1974).

Bearce, George D., *British Attitudes Towards India, 1784-1858* (OUP, 1961).

Bédarida, François, *A Social History of England, 1851-1990* (Routledge, 1991).

Bede, Cuthbert, *The Adventures of Verdant Green* (James Blackwood & Co, undated).

Beer, Gavin de (ed.), *Charles Darwin. Thomas Henry Huxley. Autobiographies* (OUP, 1974).

Belany, James Cockburn, *A Treatise Upon Falconry In Two Parts* (Berwick-upon-Tweed, 1841).

Bell, Gertrude Lowthian, *The Desert and the Sown* (William Heinemann, 1907).

Bence-Jones, Mark, *The Catholic Families* (Constable & Co Ltd, 1992).

Bennett, Norman R., *A History of the Arab State of Zanzibar* (Methuen & Co Ltd, 1978)

Besant, Walter (ed.), *The Literary Remains of Charles F. Tyrwhitt Drake* (Richard Bentley & Son, 1877).

—————————*Autobiography* (Hutchinson & Co, 1902).

Best, Geoffrey, *Mid-Victorian Britain, 1851-75* (Fontana Press, 1971).

Billington, Ray Allen, *Westward Expansion. A History of the American Frontier* (The Macmillan Company, New York, 1949).

Bird, Michael, *Samuel Shepheard of Cairo. A Portrait* (Michael Joseph, 1957).

Bishop, Jonathan, The Identities of Richard Burton: The Explorer as Actor. *Victorian Studies, 1957-58,* Vol.1, No.1, Sept 1957.

Blackmansbury, Vol.1, No.3, August 1964.

Blakiston, Herbert E.D., *Trinity*. Oxford University College Histories (F.E. Robinson, 1898).

Blewett, Octavian, *The Panorama of Torquay,* 2nd edn (Simpkin & Marshall, London, and Cockrem, Torquay, 1832).

Blunt, Wilfrid Scawen, *My Diaries. Being a Personal Narrative of Events, 1888-1914.* Single volume edn (Martin Secker, 1932).

Bolt, Christine, *Victorian Attitudes to Race* (Routledge & Kegan Paul, 1971).

Bombay Calendar and General Directory (Civil, Army & Navy Lists), Bombay, 1850.

Borer, Mary Cathcart, *Mayfair. The Years of Grandeur* (W.H. Allen, 1975).

—————————An Illustrated Guide to London (Robert Hale, 1988).

Bouch & Jones, C.M.L. & G.P., The Lake Counties (1500-1830). A Social and Economic History (Manchester University Press, 1961), reprinted 1968.

Bowen, Frank C., Passengers in East Indiamen, *The P.L.A. Monthly*, March 1940.

Boxer, C.R., *The Portuguese Seaborne Empire* (Hutchinson & Co Ltd, 1969).

Bradford, Sarah, *Disraeli* (Weidenfeld and Nicolson, 1982).

Brander, Michael, *The Georgian Gentleman* (D.C. Heath Ltd, Farnborough, Hants, 1973).

Bridges, Roy (ed.), The Visit of Frederick Forbes to the Somali Coast in 1833, *International Journal of African Historical Studies* 19, 4 (1986).

Briggs, Asa, *Victorian People. A reassessment of persons and themes, 1851-67*, rev edn (University of Chicago Press, 1972).

Brooks, Juanita, *The Mountain Meadows Massacre* (University of Oklahoma Press, Norman and London, 1962).

Brown, Dee, *Wondrous Times on the Frontier* (Arrow Books Ltd, 1994).

Brown, John P., *The Dervishes; or Oriental Spiritualism* (Trübner and Co, 1868).

Bruce, James, *Travels to Discover the Source of the Nile in the Years 1768-1773*, 5 vols (G.G. J. & J. Robinson, 1790).

Bryant, Arthur, *The Years of Endurance, 1793-1802* (William Collins Sons & Co Ltd, 1975).

Bryant, Sir Arthur, *The Age of Elegance, 1812-1822* (Collins, 1975).

Bulmer's History and Directory of Westmorland, 1905.

Bunbury, E.H., *A History of Ancient Geography. Among the Greeks and Romans from the Earliest Ages till the Fall of the Roman Empire*, 2 vols (John Murray, 1879).

Burchaell and Sadleir, George Dames and Thomas Ulick (ed.), *Alumni Dublinenses* (Dublin, 1935).

Burckhardt, John Lewis, *Travels in Nubia,* 2nd edn (John Murray, 1822).

—————*Travels in Arabia,* 2 vols (Henry Colburn, 1829).

Burke, John & John Bernard, *A Genealogical and Heraldic History of the Extinct and Dormant Baronetcies of* England (London, 1838), 2nd edn 1845.

Burke, Sir Bernard, *A Genealogical History of the Dormant, Abeyant, Forfeited and Extinct Peerages of the British Empire* (Harrison, 1883).

—————*Dormant & Extinct Peerages,* 1883.

Burke's Landed Gentry, 18th edn, Vol.III, 1972.

—————*Peerage & Baronetage,* 105th edn, 1975.

—————*Irish Family Records,* 1976.

Burnand, Sir Francis C., *Records and Reminiscences, Personal and General* (Methuen & Co Ltd, 1904).

Burnell, Arthur Coke (ed.), *The Voyage of John Huyghen Van Linschoten to the East Indies* Vol.1 (Hakluyt Society, 1885).

Burnes, Alexander, *Travels into Bokhara* (John Murray, 1835).

Burnes, James, *A Narrative of a Visit to the Court of Sinde* (Robert Cadell, Edinburgh: and Whittaker, Treacher, and Arnot, London, 1831).

Burton, Elizabeth, *The Early Victorians At Home, 1837-61* (Longmans, 1972).

C. Hibbert, *George IV. Regent and King, 1811-30* (Allen Lane, 1973).

Cable, Boyd, *A Hundred Year History of the P&O, 1837-1937* (Ivor Nicholson and Watson Ltd, 1937).

Cadell, Sir Patrick, *History of the Bombay Army* (Longmans, Green & Co, 1938).

Caillié, Réné, *Travels Through Central Africa to Timbuctoo; And Across the Great Desert to Morocco. Performed In The Years 1824-1828*, 2 vols (Henry Colburn and Richard Bentley, 1830).

Cairns, H. Alan C, *Prelude to Imperialism, 1840-1890* (Routledge & Kegan Paul, 1965).

Calder, Jenni, *The Victorian Home* (T. Batsford, 1977).

Callahan, Raymond, *The East India Company and Army Reform, 1783-1798* (Harvard University Press, Cambridge, Mass, 1972).

Cameron, V.L., Burton As I Knew Him, *The Fortnightly Review,* Vol.LIV (XLVIII NS), Dec 1890, pp. 878 – 884.

Cameron, Verney Lovett, *Across Africa,* New Edition (George Philip, 1885).

Campbell, John L. and Hall, Trevor H., *The Story of Fr. Allan McDonald, Ada Goodrich Freer and the Society for Psychical Research's Inquiry into Highland Second Sight* (Routledge & Kegan Paul, 1968).

Cantlie, Lt Gen Sir Neil, *A History of the Army Medical Department* (Churchill Livingstone, Edinburgh, 1974).

Carew, Tim, *How The Regiments Got Their Nicknames* (Leo Cooper, 1974).

Carrington, Charles Edmund, *Rudyard Kipling. His Life and Work* (Macmillan & Co Ltd, 1955).

Carstairs, G. Morris, *The Twice-Born. A Study of A Community of High-Caste Hindus* (The Hogarth Press, 1961).

Cartwright, Frederick, & Biddis, Michael, *Disease and History* (Rupert Hart-Davis, 1972).

Casson, Lionel, *The Periplus Maris Erythraei.* Text with Introduction, Translation and Commentary (Princeton University Press, 1989).

Castagno, Margaret, *Historical Dictionary of Somalia.* African Historical Dictionaries No.6 (The Scarecrow Press Inc, Metuchen, New Jersey, 1975).

Catlin, George, *Letters and Notes on the Manners, Customs, and Condition of the North American Indians*, 3rd edn, Vol.1 (Tilt and Bogue, 1842).

Chaillé-Long, Charles, *My Life in Four Continents*, 2 vols (Hutchinson and Co, 1912).

Chaillu, Paul B. Du, *Explorations and Adventures in Equatorial Africa* (John Murray, 1861).

Chandless, William, *A Visit to Salt Lake, Being A Journey Across The Plains And A Residence In The Mormon Settlement At Utah* (Smith, Elder and Co, 1857).

Chew, Samuel C., The Nineteenth Century and After, 1789-1939, *A Literary History of England* (ed.) Albert C. Baugh (Appleton-Century-Crofts, Inc, New York, 1948).

Clark, Anne, *Lewis Carroll* (J.M. Dent & Sons Ltd, 1979).

Colville, Jim (tr.), *The Perfumed Garden of Sensual Delight by Muhammad ibn Muhammad al-Nafzawi* (Kegan Paul International, 1999).

Cook, H.C.B., *The Sikh Wars, 1845-6; 1848-9* (Leo Cooper, 1975).

Cooley, William Desborough, *The Negroland of the Arabs Examined and Explained* (J. Arrowsmith, 1841).

——————*Claudius Ptolemy and the Nile* (John Parker & Son, 1854).

——————*Dr Livingstone and the Royal Geographical Society* (Dulau & Co, 1874).

Cooper, Winifred, The Bagshaws of Dovercourt, *Essex Countryside*, Vol.22, May 1974, pp. 26 – 29.

Correspondence Respecting Consul Burton's Proceedings at Damascus, 1868-71. FO 881/2148, Printed for the use of the Foreign Office, February 1872.

Coupland, R., *East Africa and Its Invaders. From the Earliest Times to the Death of Seyyid Said in 1856* (OUP, 1938).

——————*The Exploitation of East Africa, 1856-90* (Faber & Faber Ltd, 1939).

——————*Livingstone's Last Journey* (Collins, 1945).

Cox, G.V., *Recollections of Oxford* (Macmillan & Co, 1868).

Crawford, Dirom Grey, *Roll of the Indian Medical Service, 1615-1930* (Thacker, 1930).

Crofton, R.H., *The Old Consulate at Zanzibar* (OUP, 1935).

Cromer, Earl of, *Modern Egypt*, 2 vols (Macmillan & Co Ltd, 1908).

Crooke, William (ed.), *Hobson-Jobson. A Glossary of Colloquial Anglo-Indian Words and Phrases* (John Murray, 1903).

Crowder, Michael, *The Story of Nigeria.* 4th revised edn (Faber and Faber, 1978).

Cruse, Amy, *The Victorians and their Books* (George Allen & Unwin Ltd, 1935).

Cullen, L.M., *Life in Ireland* (B.T. Batsford, 1968).

Curle, A.T., The Ruined Towns of Somaliland, *Antiquity*, O.G.S. Crawford & Roland Austin (eds.), Vol.XI, 1937, No.43, September.

Curling, Jonathan, *The Man in the Iron Wig. Edward Wortley Montagu, 1713-1776* (Andrew Melrose, 1954).

Curtin, Philip D., *The Image of Africa. British Ideas and Action, 1780-1850* (University of Wisconsin Press, Madison, 1964).

D'Albe, E.E. Fournier, *Life of Sir William Crookes* (T. Fisher Unwin Ltd, 1923).

Daftary, Farhad, *The Isma'ilis: their history and doctrines* (CUP, 1990).

Daniel, Norman, *Islam, Europe and Empire* (Edinburgh University Press, 1963).

Davis, H.W. Carless, *A History of Balliol College.* Revised by R.H.C. Davis & R. Hunt (Basil Blackwell, Oxford, 1963).

Davison, Roderick H., *Reform in the Ottoman Empire, 1856-1876* (Princeton University Press, 1963).

Dawood, N.J. (tr.), *The Koran.* 5th revised edn reprint (Penguin Books, 1999).

Dawson, Warren R. and Uphill, Eric P., *Who Was Who in Egyptology.* 3rd rev edn by M.L. Bierbrier (The Egyptian Exploration Society, 1995).

Dennis, Armand, *Taboo* (W.H. Allen, 1966).

Dickens, Charles, *American Notes* (Chapman and Hall, 1842).

Didier, Charles, *Sojourn with the Grand Sharif of Makkah* (The Oleander Press, 1985).

Dike, K. Onwuka, *Trade and Politics in the Niger Delta, 1830-85* (OUP, 1956).

Doe, Donald Brian, *Southern Arabia* (Thames & Hudson, 1971).

Doughty, Charles M., *Travels in Arabia Deserta* (Jonathan Cape Ltd, 1926).

Douglas, William, *Duelling Days in the Army* (Ward and Downey, 1887).

Downes, Molly Panter, *Ooty Preserved. A Victorian Hill-Station* (Hamish Hamilton, 1967).

Drake-Brockman, Ralph E., *British Somaliland* (Hurst & Blackett Ltd, 1912).

Drew, Sir William Robert Macfarlane, *Medical Officers in the British Army, 1660-1960*. Vol.1: 1660-1898 (A. Peterkin & W. Johnston, 1968).

Dumasia, Naoroji M., *The Agha Khan and his Ancestors* (The Times of India Press, Bombay, 1939).

Dunraven, Windham Quinn, Fourth Earl of, *Past Times and Pastimes* (Hodder & Stoughton, 1922).

E.R. Crawford, *The Sikh Wars, 1845-49* (Hutchinson, 1967).

Eastwick, Edward Backhouse, *Dry Leaves from Young Egypt* (John Madden, 1851). Published anonymously under pseudonym, 'An Ex-Political.'

Edwardes, F.M., *The Rise of Bombay – A Retrospect* (The Times of India Press, 1902).

Edwardes, Michael, *The Sahib and the Lotus. The British in India* (Constable & Co Ltd, 1988).

Edwards, Amelia, *A Thousand Miles Up The Nile* (Century Publishing, 1982)

Elliot, Gertrude (ed.), *Some Revolutions and Other Diplomatic Experiences by the Late Right Hon. Sir Henry G. Elliot, G.C.B.* (John Murray, 1922).

Ellis, Havelock, *Studies in the Psychology of Sex* (William Heinemann, 1942)

Erpe, Thomas van, *Grammatica Arabica* (Leiden, 1614).

Evans, Joan, *John Ruskin* (Jonathan Cape, 1954).

F. McLynn, *From the Sierras to the Pampas. Richard Burton's Travels in the Americas, 1860-69* (Century, 1991).

Faber, Geoffrey, *Jowett. A Portrait with Background* (Faber and Faber Ltd, 1957).

Fairley, *The Lion River. The Indus* (Allen Lane, Penguin Books 1975).

Falkiner, C. Litton, *Studies in Irish History and Biography, Mainly of the Eighteenth Century* (Longmans, Green, and Co., 1902).

Fleischer, Nat, and Andre, Sam, *A Pictorial History of Boxing*. revised edn (Hamlyn, 1975).

Flint, John E. (ed.), *The Cambridge History of Africa*, Vol.V, c. 1790- c. 1870 (CUP, 1976).

Fonseca, José Nicolau da, *An Historical and Archaeological Sketch of the City of Goa* (Thacker & Co Ltd, Bombay, 1878).

Foran, W. Robert, *African Odyssey. The Life of Verney Lovett Cameron* (Hutchinson & Co Ltd, 1937).

Forster, John, *The Life of Charles Dickens* (J.M. Dent & Sons Ltd, 1966).

Foster, J, *Alumni Oxonienses*, Vol.II, 1715-1886 (London, 1888).

Foster, William, *The East India House. Its History and Associations* (John Lane, 1924).

Freeth, Zara, and Winstone, Victor, *Explorers of Arabia. From the Renaissance to the Victorian Era* (George Allen & Unwin, 1978).

French, Patrick, *Younghusband. The Last Great Imperial Adventurer* (Flamingo, 1995).

Friswell, James Hain, *The Gentle Life* (Sampson Low, Son, & Marston, 1864).

Friswell, Laura Hain, *James Hain Friswell. A Memoir* (George Redway, 1898).

—————*In the Sixties and Seventies. Impressions of Literary People and Others* (Hutchinson & Co, 1905).

—————*The Sixties and Seventies. Impressions of Literary People* (Hutchinson & Co, 1905).

Froude, James Anthony, *Thomas Carlyle. A History of the First Forty Years of his Life, 1795-1835,* Vol.1 (Longmans, Green, and Co, 1882).

Fulford, Roger, *The Trial of Queen Caroline* (T. Batsford Ltd, 1967).

Fuller, R.C., *A Short History of Warwick Street Church Formerly The Royal Bavarian Chapel* (Church Of Our Lady Of The Assumption And St Gregory, 1973).

Fyfe, Christopher, *A History of Sierra Leone* (OUP, 1962).

Galton, Francis, *Memories of My Life* (Methuen & Co, 1908).

Gavin, R.J., *Aden Under British Rule, 1839-67*, (C. Hurst & Co Ltd, 1975).

Gay, Peter, *The Bourgeois Experience. Victoria to Freud. The Tender Passion* (OUP Inc, New York, 1986).

Geikie, Archibald, *Life of Sir Roderick I. Murchison – Based on His Journals and Letters* (John Murray, 1875).

Girouard, Mark, *Life in the English Country House* (Yale University Press, 1978).

——————*The Return to Camelot. Chivalry and the English Gentleman* (Yale University Press, 1981).

Glover, Michael, *Wellington's Army* (David and Charles, Newton Abbot, 1977).

Goldsmid, Sir F.J., *James Outram*, 2 vols (Smith, Elder & Co, 1880).

Gordon, Anthony, *A Treatise on the Science of Defence for the Sword, Bayonet and Pike in Close Action* (London, 1805).

Gosden, Walter (ed.), *The Langham Hotel. Guide to London.* 9th edn (The Langham Hotel Company Ltd, 1895).

Gosse, Edmund, *Portraits and Sketches* (William Heinemann, 1912).

——————*The Life of Algernon Charles Swinburne* (Macmillan and Co Ltd, 1917).

Gournay, Jean-François, *L'Appel Du Proche-Orient. Richard Francis Burton et son Temps 1821-90.* (Université de Lille, 1983).

Graham, Gerald S., *Great Britain in the Indian Ocean. A Study of Maritime Enterprise, 1810-1850* (Clarendon Press, Oxford, 1967).

Gray, Richard, *A History of the Southern Sudan, 1838-1889* (OUP, 1961).

Green, Lancelyn (ed.), *The Reader's Guide to Rudyard Kipling's Work* (R.E. Harbord, Hertfordshire, 1961).

Green, Martin, *Dreams of Adventure, Deeds of Empire* (Routledge & Kegan Paul, 1980).

Greenhill, William Alexander, *A Treatise on the Small-Pox and Measles by Abu Becr Ibn Zacariya Ar-Razi.* Translated from the Original Arabic (Sydenham Society, 1848).

Grey, Elizabeth, *The Noise of Drums and Trumpets* (Longman, 1971).

Grierson, H.J.C. (ed.), *The Letters of Sir Walter Scott*, Centenary Edition (Constable & Co, 1932).

Gross, Max L., *Ottoman Rule in the province of Damascus, 1869-1909.* PhD Thesis, 2 vols (Georgetown University, 1979).

Grosskurth, Phyllis, *John Adddington Symonds* (Longmans, Green and Co, Ltd, 1964).

Guinness, Jonathan. *The House of Mitford* (Hutchinson & Co Ltd, 1984).

Gwynn, Denis, *Cardinal Wiseman* (Brown & Nolan Ltd, Dublin, 1950).

H.C.G. Matthew (ed.), *The Gladstone Diaries, 1825-1896*, 14 vols (Clarendon Press, Oxford, 1994).

Haddon, Alfred C., *History of Anthropology* (Watts & Co, 1934).

Halévy, Elie, England in 1815, *History of the English People*, Vol.1 (Ernest Benn Ltd, 1970).

Hall, Richard, *Stanley, An Adventurer Explored* (Collins, 1974).

Hall, Trevor, *The Spiritualists. The Story of Florence Cook & William Crookes* (Gerald Duckworth, 1962).

Hallett, *Africa. A Two-Volume History* (Heinemann Educational Books Ltd, 1974).

Halsband, Robert, *The Life of Lady Mary Wortley Montagu* (Clarendon Press, Oxford, 1956).

Hamilton, Ian, *Keepers of the Flame. Literary Estates and the Rise of Biography* (Hutchinson, 1992).

Hammand, J.W. (ed.) Lake District, Ward Lock Red Guide (1973).

Hare, Augustus, J.C., The Story of My Life, 6 vols (George Allen, 1896).

Harris, Frank, *Contemporary Portraits*, First Series (Methuen & Co Ltd, 1915).

Harris, W. Cornwallis, The Highlands of Aethiopia, 3 vols (Longman, Brown, Green, and Longmans, 1844).

Hawgood, John A., *The American West* (Eyre and Spottiswoode, 1967).

Hawthorne, Nathaniel, Our Old Home, Vol.1 (Smith, Elder and Co, 1863).

——————*Passages from the English Note-Books,* Vol.1 (Strahan & Co, 1870).

Hayward, Pat (ed.), *Surgeon Henry's Trifles – Events of a Military Life* (Chatto & Windus, 1970).

Head, F.B., *The Life of Bruce. The African Traveller* (John Murray, 1830).

Heathcote, T.A., *The Indian Army – The Garrison of British Imperial India, 1822-1922* (David & Charles, Newton Abbot, 1974).

——————*The Afghan Wars, 1839-1919* (Osprey, 1980).

Henderson, Philip, *The Life of Laurence Oliphant. Traveller, Diplomat & Mystic* (Robert Hale, 1956).

Herskovits, Melville Jean, *Dahomey. An Ancient West African Kingdom* (J.J. Augustin, New York, 1938).

Hibbert, Christopher, *The Destruction of Lord Raglan* (Viking, 1984).

Hill, R., *Biographical Dictionary of the Anglo-Egyptian Sudan* (OUP, 1951).

Hindley, Geoffrey, *Tourists, Travellers and Pilgrims* (Hutchinson, 1983).

Hird, Frank, *H.M. Stanley. The Authorised Life* (Stanley Paul & Co Ltd, 1935).

Hodgkin, Thomas (ed.), *Nigerian Perspectives. An Historical Anthology* (OUP, 1960).

Hogarth, David George, *The Penetration of Arabia* (Lawrence & Bullen Ltd, 1904).

Holliday, J.S., *The World Rushed In. The California Gold Rush Experience* (Victor Gollancz, 1983).

Holmes, Colin, *Anti-Semitism in British Society, 1876-1939* (Edward Arnold, 1979).

Holt, P.M. & Daly, M.W., *A History of the Sudan from the Coming of Islam to the Present Day*, 4th edn (Longman Group, UK Ltd, 1988).

Holt, P.M., *Studies in the History of the Near East* (Frank Cass, 1973).

Honan, Park, *Matthew Arnold. A Life* (Weidenfeld and Nicolson, 1981).

Hopkirk, *The Great Game. On Secret Service in High Asia* (John Murray, 1990).

Hopwood, Derek, *Syria, 1945-1986. Politics and Society* (Unwin Hyman Ltd, 1989).

Hoskins, Halford Lancaster, *British Routes to India* (Longmans, Green and Co, 1928).

Hoskins, W.G., *Devon and Its People* (David and Charles, Newton Abbot, 1968).

Huggett, Frank, *Carriages at Eight* (Lutterworth Press, 1979).

Hughes, Thomas, *Tom Brown At Oxford* (Macmillan & Co, 1895).

Hunter, Sir William Wilson, *A History of British India* (Longmans, Green & Co, 1899).

Hutchins, Francis G., *The Illusion of Permanence* (Princeton University Press, 1967).

Hyam, Ronald, *Britain's Imperial Century, 1815-1914* (B.T. Batsford, 1976).

——————*Empire and Sexuality* (Manchester University Press, 1992).

Hyde, Francis E., *Cunard and the North Atlantic, 1840-1973* (The Macmillan Press Ltd, 1975).

Hyde, H. Montgomery, *The Other Love. An Historical and Contemporary Survey of Homosexuality in Britain* (Heinemann, 1970).

I.M. Lewis, Peoples of the Horn of Africa. Somali, Afar and Saho in Daryll Forde (ed.), *Ethnographic Survey of North Eastern Africa, Parts 1-3* (International African Institute, 1955-56).

Ingram, James, *Memorials of Oxford* (John Henry Parker, H. Slatter, and W. Graham, and Charles Tilt, 1837).

Ionides, Luke, Memories of Richard Burton, *Transatlantic Review*, March 1924.

Irwin, Robert, *Night and Horses and the Desert* (Allen Lane, The Penguin Press, 1999).

——————*The Arabian Nights: A Companion* (Allen Lane, The Penguin Press, 1994).

Jeal, Tim, *Livingstone* (Heinemann Ltd, 1973).

Jeanson, Denis, *Sites et monuments du Grand Tours* (Imprimerie Mame, 1973).

Johnston, Sir Harry H., *The Nile Quest* (Lawrence & Bullen Ltd, 1903).

——————*The Story of My Life* (Chatto & Windus, 1923).

Jones, Horace Leonard (tr.), *The Geography of Strabo.* Vol.VII (William Heinemann, 1930).

Joyce, Michael, Genes and Genealogy, *Genealogists' Magazine*, December 1999, pp.301-303.

Jutzi, Alan H. (ed.), *In Search of Richard Burton. Papers from a Huntington Library Symposium* (Henry Huntington Library and Art Gallery, San Marino, California, 1993).

Kabbani, Rana, *Europe's Myths of Orient.* (The Macmillan Press Ltd, 1986).

Kaplan, Fred, *Thomas Carlyle* (Cornell University Press, 1983).

Kaye, John William, *History of the War in Afghanistan*, 2 vols (Richard Bentley, 1851).

Ker, Ian (ed.), *The Letters and Diaries of John Henry Newman*, 10 vols (Clarendon Press, Oxford, 1978).

Khoury, Philip S., *Urban Notables and Arab Nationalism. The Politics of Damascus, 1860-1920* (CUP, 1983).

Kiernan, V.G., *The Lords of Human Kind. European Attitudes to the Outside World in the Imperial World* (Weidenfeld & Nicolson, 1969).

Kinglake, Alexander, *Eothen* (OUP, 1982).

Kingsley, Mary, *Travels in West Africa* (Macmillan & Co Ltd, 1897).

——————*West African Studies* (Macmillan & Co Ltd, 1899).

Kipling, Rudyard, *Kim* (Penguin Books, 1989).

Krafft-Ebing, Dr R., *The Psychopathia Sexualis. Abberrations of Sexual Life* (Panther Books Ltd, 1965).

Krapf, The Rev Dr J. Lewis, *Researches and Missionary Labours During An Eighteen Years' Residence in Eastern Africa* (Trübner & Co, 1860).

Laffin, John, *Surgeons In The Field* (Dent, 1970).

Lafourcade, George, *Swinburne. A Literary Biography* (G. Bell and Sons, 1932).

Lambrick, Hugh Trevor, *Sir Charles Napier and Sind* (Clarendon Press, Oxford, 1952).

Lane, Edward William, *Cairo Fifty Years Ago*, ed. Stanley Lane-Poole (John Murray, 1896).

Lane, Edward William, *The Manners and Customs of the Modern Egyptians.* 5th edn, Edward Stanley Poole (ed.), 2 vols (John Murray, 1904).

Lane-Poole, Stanley, *The Life of the Right Honourable Stratford Canning, Viscount Stratford de Redcliffe*, 2 vols (Longmans, Green, and Co, 1888).

Lang, Cecil Y. (ed.), *The Swinburne Letters*, 6 vols 1959-62 (Yale University Press, 1959).

Langley, Michael, *The East Surrey Regiment* (31st & 70th Foot) (Leo Cooper, 1972).

Lawrence, Rosamond, *Charles Napier. Friend and Fighter, 1782-1853* (John Murray, 1952).

Laws, M.E.S., Beatson's Bashi-Bazouks, *Army Quarterly*, LXXI, 1955.

Leach, F. *Longner Hall, County Seats of Shropshire* (Shrewsbury, 1891).

Lee, Albert., *History of the 33rd Foot* (Jarrold & Sons, Norwich, 1922).

Lee, Elizabeth, *Ouida: A Memoir* (T. Fisher Unwin, 1914).

Legman, G., *The Horn Book. Studies in Erotic Folklore and Bibliography* (University Books Inc, New York, 1964).

Lejeune, Anthony, *The Gentlemen's Clubs of London* (Macdonald and Jane's, 1979).

Lennox, J.T., *Sevenoaks School and its Founder, 1432-1932* (Caxton and Holmesdale Press, Sevenoaks, 1932).

Leon, Edwin de, *Thirty Years of My Life On Three Continents* (Ward and Downey, 1890).

Lewis, Bernard & Holt, P.M., (eds.), *Historians of the Middle East*, (OUP, 1962)

Lewis, Bernard, *Islam and the West* (OUP, 1993).

Lewis, I.M., *A Modern History of Somalia. Nation and State in the Horn of Africa* (Longman, 1980).

Lewis, Roy, and Foy, Yvonne, *The British in Africa* (Weidenfeld and Nicolson, 1971).

Liddon, Henry Parry, *Life of Edward Bouverie Pusey.* Rev J.O. Johnston and Rev Robert J. Wilson (eds.), 4 vols. (Longmans, Green and Co, 1893).

Lloyd, Thomas, Sir Richard Burton, *The Bookman*, May 1906, pp. 51-55.

Lockett, W.G., *Robert Louis Stevenson at Davos* (Hurst & Blackett Ltd, 1934).

Longford, Elizabeth, *A Pilgrimage of Passion – The Life of Wilfrid Scawen Blunt* (Weidenfeld & Nicolson, 1979).

Lovell, Mary S., *A Scandalous Life. The Biography of Jane Digby el Mezrab* (Richard Cohen Books, 1995).

Low, Charles Rathbone, *History of the Indian Navy (1613-1863)*, 2 vols (Richard Bentley and Son, 1877).

Ma'oz, Moshe, *Ottoman Reform in Syria and Palestine, 1840-1861* (Clarendon Press, Oxford, 1968).

Macfarlane, D.A. & Thomas, L.P., (ed.), *Textbook of Surgery*, 3rd edn (Churchill Livingstone, 1972).

Mack, Edward C. and Armytage, W.H.G., *Thomas Hughes. The Life of the Author of Tom Brown's Schooldays* (Ernest Benn Ltd, 1952).

Macray, Rev William Dunn, *Annals of the Bodleian Library Oxford*, 2nd edn (Clarendon Press, Oxford, 1890).

Magnus, P., *Kitchener, Portrait of an Imperialist* (John Murray, 1958).

Mallett, *A History of the University of Oxford*, 3 vols (First pub 1927, reprinted, Methuen & Co Ltd, 1968).

Mallock, W.H., *Memoirs of Life and Literature* (Chapman & Hall, 1920).

Marchand, Leslie A., *The 'Athenaeum' – A Mirror of Victorian Culture* (University of North Carolina Press, Chapel Hill, 1941).

Marcus, Harold G. and Page, Melvin E., John Studdy Leigh: First Footsteps in East Africa? *The International Journal of African Historical Studies*, Vol.3 (1972).

Marcus, Steven, *The Other Victorians. A Study of Sexuality & Pornography in Mid-Nineteenth Century England* (Weidenfeld and Nicolson, 1967).

Marcy, Capt. R.B., *The Prairie And Overland Traveller* (Sampson, Low, Son, and Co, 1860).

Margetson, Stella, *Leisure and Pleasure in the Nineteenth Century* (Cassell & Co Ltd, 1969).

Markham, Felix, Oxford (Weidenfeld and Nicolson, 1967).

Marriott, Sir J.A.R., *England Since Waterloo*, 14th edn (Methuen & Co Ltd, 1950).

Marshall, Dorothy, *English People in the 18th Century* (Longmans, Green & Co, 1956).

Marshall, P.J. (ed.), *The British Discovery of Hinduism in the Eighteenth Century* (CUP, 1970).

Marston, Thomas E., *Britain's Imperial Role in the Red Sea Area* (Shoestring Press Inc, Hamden, Conn, 1961).

Martineau, Harriet, *Eastern Life. Present and Past* (Edward Moxon, 1848).

Mason, Philip, *A Matter of Honour. An Account of the Indian Army, its officers and men* (Jonathan Cape, 1974).

Masters, John, *Bugles and a Tiger* (Michael Joseph, 1956).

McCarthy, Justin, *Portraits of the Sixties* (T. Fisher Unwin, 1903).

McCrindle, J.W. (tr. & ed.), *The Christian Topography of Cosmas, An Egyptian Monk* (Hakluyt Society, 1897).

Mee, Arthur, The Lake Counties – Cumberland and Westmorland, *The King's England*, (ed.) Gordon Wood (Hodder and Stoughton, 1969).

Mendes, Peter, *Clandestine Erotic Fiction in English, 1800-1930. A bibliographical study* (Scolar Press, 1993).

Meyer, Karl & Brysac, Shareen, *Tournament of Shadows* (Little, Brown and Company, 2001).

Mill, James, *The History of British India*. Abridged by William Thomas (University of Chicago Press, 1975).

Miller, James Innes, *The Spice Trade of the Roman Empire, 29 BC to AD 641* Clarendon Press, Oxford, 1969).

Mitford, Nancy (ed.), *The Stanleys of Alderley* (Hamish Hamilton, 1968).

Money, Edward, *Twelve Months with the Bashi-Bazouks* (Chapman & Hall, 1857).

Monroe, *Philby of Arabia* (Faber and Faber, 1973).

Moorhead, Alan, *The White Nile* (Hamish Hamilton, 1960).

More about the Burton messages. By Miss "X." *Borderland*, Vol.IV, 1897, pp. 37-42.

Morell, Jack & Thackeray, Arnold, *Gentlemen of Science. Early Years of the British Association for the Advancement of Science* (Clarendon Press, Oxford, 1981).

Morris, Jan (ed.), *The Oxford Book of Oxford* (OUP, 1978).

————*Oxford* (OUP, 1978).

————*Trieste And The Meaning Of Nowhere* (Faber and Faber, 2001).

Mukherjee, S.N., *Sir William Jones. A Study in 18th Century British Attitudes to India* (CUP, 1968).

Murphy, Sophia, *The Mitford Family Album* (Sidgwick & Jackson, 1985).

Murray, Hon Henry A., *Lands of the Slave and the Free or Cuba, The United States, and Canada* (John W. Parker and Son, 1855).

Musgrave, Clifford, *Life in Brighton – from the earliest times to the present* (Rochester Press, 1981).

Napier, Lt Gen Sir William, *The Life and Opinions of General Sir Charles James Napier*, 4 vols (John Murray, 1857).

Nelson, James G., *Publisher to the Decadents. Leonard Smithers in the Careers of Beardsley, Wilde, Dowson* (Rivendale Press, High Wycombe, Bucks, 2000).

Newbury, C.W., *The Western Slave Coast And Its Rulers* (OUP, 1973).

Nicholls, C.S., *The Swahili Coast. Politics, Diplomacy and Trade on the East African Littoral, 1798-1856* (George Allen & Unwin Ltd, 1971).

Noble, Mary E., (ed. & copyist), *The Registers of The Parish of Shap in the County of Westmoreland from 1559-1830* (Titus Wilson, 1912).

Norton, Lucy, *The Sun King* (Hamish Hamilton, 1983).

Notes and Queries, Third Series, Vol.XI, Jan – June 1867.

O'Byrne, William R., *A Naval Biographical Dictionary* (John Murray, 1849).

Oliphant, Laurence, *The Russian Shores of the Black Sea in the Autumn of 1852* (William Blackwood & Sons, 1853).

Oliphant, Margaret, *Annals of a Publishing House. William Blackwood and his Sons, Their Magazine and Friends* (William Blackwood and Sons, Edinburgh and London, 1897)

Oman, C.W.C, *Wellington's Army, 1809-1814* (Edward Arnold, 1912).

Oman, Carola, *Sir John Moore* (Hodder and Stoughton, 1953).

Oppenheim, Janet, *The Other World. Spiritual and psychical research in England, 1850-1914* (CUP, 1985).

Ormond, Leonée and Richard, *Lord Leighton* (Yale University Press, 1975).

Ouida, (Madame Ramée), Richard Burton, *The Fortnightly Review*, Vol.85 (LXXIX NS), Jan – June 1906, pp. 1039 – 45.

Outram, Lt Col James, *The Conquest of Scinde. A Commentary* (William Blackwood and Sons, 1846).

Page, William (ed.), Hertfordshire, Vol.II, *The Victoria History of the Counties of England* (Archibald Constable & Co Ltd, 1908).

Paget, Lady Walburga, *Scenes And Memories* (Smith Elder & Co, 1912).

——————*Further Recollections*, 2 vols (Hutchinson & Co, 1923).

——————*In My Tower* (Hutchinson & Co, 1924).

Pakenham, Thomas, *The Scramble for Africa* (Weidenfeld and Nicolson, 1991).

——————*The Year of Liberty. The story of the great Irish Rebellion of 1798* (Hodder and Stoughton, 1969).

Pankhurst, Richard, The Trade of the Gulf of Aden Ports in the Nineteenth and Early Twentieth Centuries, *Journal of Ethiopian Studies*, Vol.III, No.1 (Haile Sellasie University, Addis Ababa, 1965).

Parker and Bowen, Capt H. & Frank C., *Mail and Passenger Steamships of the Nineteenth Century* (Sampson, Low, Marston & Co Ltd).

Parkes, Samuel, *The Chemical Catechism*, 12th edn (Baldwin, Cradock and Joy, 1826).

Pearsall, Ronald, *Night's Black Angels, The Forms and Faces of Victorian Cruelty* Hodder & Stoughton, 1975).

——————*The Worm in the Bud. The World of Victorian Sexuality* (Weidenfeld and Nicolson, 1969).

Pearse, Col H.W., *History of the 31st and 70th Foot*, Vol.1, 1702-1914 (Spottiswoode, Ballantyne & Co Ltd, 1916).

Pemberton, W. Baring, *Battles of the Crimean War* (B.T. Batsford, 1962).

Penniman, T.K., *A Hundred Years of Anthropology* (Gerald Duckworth, 1935).

Perkin, Joan, *Victorian Women* (John Murray, 1993).

Peterson, Mildred Jeanne, *The Medical Profession in Mid-Victorian London* (University of California Press, Berkeley, 1978).

Petherick, Mr & Mrs John, *Travels in Central Africa and Explorations of the Western Nile Tributaries*, 2 vols (Tinsley Brothers, 1869).

Piercy, Frederick, *Route from Liverpool to Great Salt Lake Valley*, ed. James Linforth (Franklin D. Richards, 1855).

Pine-Gordon, H. (ed.), *Burke's Genealogical and Heraldic History of the Landed Gentry, 1937*, Centenary (15th edn.), Vol. 2.

Plarr, Victor Gustave, *Lives of the Fellows of the Royal College of Surgeons of England.* Revised by Sir D'Arcy Power; with the assistance of W.G. Spenser and G.E. Gask (Simpkin, Marshall Ltd, 1930).

Platt, D.C.M., *The Cinderella Service. British Consuls Since 1825* (Longman Group Ltd, 1971).

Playfair, Robert Lambert, *A History of Arabia Felix or Yemen* (Bombay, 1859)

Pocket Guide to Swiss Spas (Swiss National Tourist Office and the Association of Swiss Spas).

Poliakov, Léon, *The Aryan Myth. A History of Racist and Nationalist Ideas in Europe* (Chatto, Heinemann, for Sussex University Press, 1974).

Polk, William R., *The Arab World Today* (Harvard University Press, 1991).

Pope-Hennessy, James, *Monckton Milnes. The Years of Promise: 1809-1851* (Constable, 1949).

——————*Monckton Milnes. The Flight of Youth, 1851-1885* (Constable, 1951).

Porter, Geraldine, *Annals of a Publishing House. John Blackwood by his Daughter*, Vol.III (William Blackwood and Sons, 1898).

Porter, Rev J.L., *A Handbook for Travellers in Syria and Palestine*, 2 vols (John Murray, 1858).

——————*Two Years in Damascus*, 2 vols (John Murray, 1855).

Porter, Roy & Rousseau, G.S., *Gout. The Patrician Malady* (Yale University Press, 1998).

Postans, Mrs Marianne, *Cutch, or Random Sketches of Western India* (Smith, Elder & Co, 1838).

——————*Western India in 1838* (Saunders & Otley, 1839).

Postans, T, *Personal Observations on Sindh* (Longman, Brown, Green, and Longman, 1843).

Pottinger, Henry, *Travels in Belochistan and Sinde* (Longman, Hurst, Reed, Orme, and Brown, 1816).

Prevost, Sir G. (ed.), *The Autobiography of Isaac Williams, B.D.* Third Edition (Longmans, Green & Co, 1893).

Price, Sir John Frederick, *Ootacamund: A History. Compiled by the Government of Madras* (The superintendent, Government Press, 1908).

Prichard, James Cowles, *The Natural History of Man* (Hippolyte Bailliere, 1845).

Prothero, Rowland E., *The Life and Correspondence of Arthur Penrhyn Stanley, D.D.* 2 vols (John Murray, 1893).

Prouty, Chris and Rosenfeld, Eugene, *Historical Dictionary of Ethiopia.* African Historical Dictionaries No.32 (The Scarecrow Press Inc, Metuchen, New Jersey).

Pusey, William Allen, *The History & Epidemiology of Syphilis* (Springfield, Illinois, 1933).

Rainger, Ronald, Race, Politics and Science. The Anthropological Society of London in the 1860s, *Victorian Studies*, Vol.2, No.1, Autumn 1978.

Rainy, William, *The Censor Censured, or The Calumnies of Captain Burton on the Africans of Sierra Leone* (George Chalfont, 1865).

Ralli, Augustus, *Christians At Mecca* (William Heinemann, 1909).

Ramsey, Sherwood, *Historic Battersea* (G. Rangecroft & Co, Battersea, 1913).

Reade, W. Winwood, *Savage Africa* (Smith, Elder & Co, 1863).

Redesdale, Lord, *Memories.* 9th edn (Hutchinson & Co, 1916).

Rees, Barbara, *The Victorian Lady* (Gordon & Cremonesi, 1977).

Reid, T. Wemyss, *The Life, Letters and Friendships of Richard Monckton Milnes, First Lord Houghton*, 3rd edn (Cassell & Co, 1891).

Remy, Jules and Brenchley, Julius, *A Journey to Great Salt-Lake City* (W. Jeffs, 1861).

Rhys, Ernest, A Friend of Leigh Hunt's. Dr George Bird, *Hampstead Annual*, 1903, pp. 16- 24.

Richards, Alfred Bate, *Oxford Unmasked*. Published pseudonymously as By A Graduate (Effingham Wilson, 1842).

Richards, T. Addison, Appleton's Ilustrated Hand-book of American Travel (Trübner & Co, 1857).

Richardson, Joanna, Louis XIV (Weidenfeld and Nicolson, 1973).

Richardson, Sir Benjamin Ward, The "Asclepiad," Second Series, Vol.XI (Longmans, Green & Co, 1895).

Ridley, Jasper, *Palmerston* (Constable, 1970).

——————*The Freemasons* (Constable and Co Ltd ,1999).

Rihani, Ameen, The Coming of the Arabian Nights, *The Bookman*, Vol.XXXV (Dodd, Mead & Co, New York, 1912).

Robinson Ronald, and Gallagher John, with Alice Denny, *Africa and the Victorians – The Official Mind of Imperialism* (Macmillan & Co Ltd, 1961).

Rogan, Eugene, *Frontiers of the State in the Late Ottoman Empire* (Cambridge, 1999).

——————*Frontiers of the State. Transjordan, 1850-1921* (CUP, 1999).

Rogers, Col Hugh Cuthbert Bassett, *Wellington's Army* (J. Allan, 1979).

Royal Warrant and Regulations Regarding Army Services (W. Clowes & Sons & J.W. Parker & Son, 1855).

Russell, Bertrand and Russell, Patricia, *The Amberley Papers* (George Allen & Unwin, 1966).

Russell, Mrs Charles E.B., *General Rigby, Zanzibar & the Slave Trade* (George Allen & Unwin Ltd, 1935).

Said, Edward W., *Orientalism* (Routledge & Kegan Paul, 1978).

Salt, Henry, *A Voyage to Abyssinia and Travels Into The Interior Of That Country Executed Under The Orders Of The British Government In The Years 1809 and 1810* (F.C. and J. Rivington, 1814).

Santi, Paul & Hill, Richard (trs. & eds.), *The Europeans in the Sudan, 1834-1878* Clarendon Press, Oxford, 1980).

Schmidt, Margaret Fox, *Passion's Child. The Extraordinary Life of Jane Digby* (Hamish Hamilton, 1977).

Scholem, Gershom, *Origins of the Kabbalah (*Princeton University Press, 1987).

Schoolcraft, Henry R., *Information Respecting the History, Condition and Prospects of the Indian Tribes of the United States* (Lipincott Grambo & Co, Philadelphia, 1853).

Schweinfurth, George, *The Heart of Africa. Three Years' Travel and Adventures in the Unexplored Regions of Central Africa from 1868-71*, 2 vols (Sampson Low, Marston, Low, and Searle, 1874).

Scott, Arthur F. (ed.), *Scinde in the Forties, Being the Journal & Letters of Col Keith Young, CB* (Constable & Co Ltd, 1912).

Scott, H. Harold, *A History of Tropical Medicine*, Vol.1 (Edward Arnold & Co, 1938).

Scott, R.F., (ed.), *Admissions to the College of St John the Evangelist*, Part III (Cambridge, 1903).

Seton, Ernest Thompson, *Universal Signal Code Without Apparatus for Use in Army, Navy, Camping, Hunting and Daily Life* (Doubleday, Page & Company, Garden City, New York, 1918).

Shaw, A.G.L. (ed.), *Great Britain and the Colonies, 1815-1865* (Methuen & Co Ltd, 1970).

Short, Martin, *Inside the Brotherhood. Further Secrets of the Freemasons* (Grafton Books, 1989).

Sidebottom, John K., *The Overland Mail. A Postal Historical Study of the Mail Route to India* (George Allen & Unwin, 1948).

Sim, Katherine, *The Desert Traveller. The Life of Jean Louis Burckhardt* (Victor Gollancz, 1969).

Simmonds, Stuart, and Digby, Simon, (eds.), *The Royal Asiatic Society. Its History and Treasures* (E.J. Brill, Leiden & London, 1979).

Simpson, Donald, *Dark Companions. The African Contribution to the European Exploration of East Africa* (Paul Elek, 1975).

Simpson, Rev W.O (ed.), *The Hindu Pantheon by Edward Moor, F.R.S.* (J. Higginbotham, Madras, 1864).

Skertchley, J.A., *Dahomey As It Is* (Chapman & Hall, 1874).

Smithers, Jack, *The Early Life & Vicissitudes of Jack Smithers. An Autobiography* (Martin Secker, 1939).

Some Recent Experiences Apparently Supernatural. By Miss "X." *Journal of the Society for Psychical Research*, Vol.VIII (1897-98), pp. 3–7.

Some Thoughts on Automatism With the Story of the Burton Messages, etc. By Miss "X." (Miss Goodrich Freer), *Borderland*, Vol.III, 1896, pp. 157-72.

Spain, James W., *The Way of the Pathans* (OUP, 1962).

Speke, John Hanning, *What Led to the Discovery of the Source of the Nile* (William Blackwood & Sons, Edinburgh & London, 1864).

Sprenger, A. von, *Das Leben Und Die Lehre Des Mohammad* (Nicolaische Verlagsbuchhandlung, 1869).

Stanley, Arthur Penrhyn, *Life and Correspondence of Dr Arnold*, Teachers' Edition (John Murray, 1901).

Stanley, Dorothy (ed.), *The Autobiography of Sir Henry Morton Stanley* (Sampson Low, Marston & Co Ltd, 1909).

Stanley, Henry Morton, *How I Found Livingstone* (Sampson Low, Marston, Low, and Searle, 1872).

—————*Through the Dark Continent*, 2 vols (Sampson Low, Marston, Searle and Rivington, 1878).

Stanley, Hon Henry E.J., *The Three Voyages of Vasco da Gama and his Viceroyalty from the Lendas da India of Gaspar Correa* (Hakluyt Society, 1869).

Stedman, A.M.M. (ed.), Cardinal Newman, by Richard H. Hutton. *English Leaders of Religion* (Methuen and Co, 1891).

Steegmuller, Francis (tr. & ed.), *Flaubert in Egypt* (The Bodley Head, 1972).

Stenhouse, Mrs T.B.H., *An Englishwoman In Utah. The Story of a Life's Experience in Mormonism* (London, 1880).

Stephens, Frederick J., *Bayonets. An Illustrated History and a Reference Guide* (Arms & Armour Press, 1968).

Stevas, Norman St John, *Obscenity and the Law* (Martin Secker & Warburg, 1956).

Stevenson, Robert Louis, *Across the Plains with Other Memories and Essays* (Chatto & Windus, 1892).

Stisted, Georgiana M., Reminiscences of Sir Richard Burton, *The Temple Bar*, Vol.92, July, pp. 335- 42.

Stock, Bishop Joseph, *A Narrative of What Passed at Killala in the County of Mayo And the Parts Adjacent During the French Invasion In The Summer of 1798* (R.E. Mercier & Co, 1800).

Stock, Eugene, *The History of the Church Missionary Society*, 3 vols (CMS, 1899).

Stocking, George. What's In A Name? The Origins of the Royal Anthropological Institute, 1837-71, *Man* (RAI, March 1971).

Stocqueler, J.H., *The Hand-Book of India* (W.H. Allen & Co, 1844).

Stoker, Bram, *Personal Reminiscences of Henry Irving*, 2 vols (Heinemann, 1906).

Studia Islamica, Vol.XXIX (G.P. Maisonneuve-Larose, Paris, 1969).

Symonds, John Addington, *A Problem in Modern Ethics* (Privately printed, London, 1896).

—————*A Problem in Greek Ethics. Being An Inquiry Into the Phenomenon of Sexual Inversion* (Privately printed, London, 1901).

Symons, Arthur, *Dramatis Personae* (Faber & Gwyer Ltd, 1925).

Symons, Richard, *Oxford and Empire. The Last Lost Cause?* (The Macmillan Press Ltd, 1986).

Taylor, Anne, *Laurence Oliphant* (OUP, 1982).

Taylor, Colin F., *Native American Life. The Family, The Hunt, Pastimes and Ceremonies* (Salamander Books Ltd, 1996).

Taylor, P.A.M., *Expectations Westward. The Mormons and the Emigration of their British Converts in the Nineteenth Century* (Oliver & Boyd, Edinburgh and London, 1965).

The Annual Register, Or a View of the History and Politics of the Year 1844, Vol.86 (F. & J. Rivington, 1845).

The Arnoldian, Vol.X, No.1 (Winter, 1982).

The Athenaeum Club and Social Life in London, 1824-1974 (Heinemann, 1975).

The Cambridge Encyclopaedia of the Middle East and North Africa (CUP, 1988).

The Cambridge History of Islam, Vol.2 (CUP, 1970).

The Gazeteer of Bombay City and Island (Times Press, Bombay, 1910).

The Glory Of The Perfumed Garden, The Missing Flowers. An English Translation from the Arabic of the Second and

Hitherto Unpublished Part of Shaykh Nafzawi's Perfumed Garden (Panther, Granada Publishing Ltd, 1978).

The Hand-Book for English Visitors in Tours and Touraine (Smith, Elder and Co, 1841).

The Journal of Modern History, Vol.V, March-December 1933 (The University of Chicago Press, Chicago, Illinois).

The Quarterly Review (Aug & Nov), Vol.II, 2nd edn (1811).

Thomas Wright of Olney. An Autobiography (Herbert Jenkins Ltd, 1936).

Thomas, Bertram, *Arabia Felix. Across the Empty Quarter of Arabia* (Jonathan Cape, 1932).

Thomas, Donald, *A Long Time Burning. A History of Literary Censorship in England* (Routledge & Kegan Paul, 1969).

————*Swinburne. The Poet in his World* (Weidenfeld and Nicolson, 1979).

Thomson, J. Oliver, *History of Ancient Geography* (CUP, 1948).

Thomson, Joseph, *Through Masai Land* (Sampson Low, Marston, Searle & Rivington, 1885).

Thomson, William R.A., *Spas That Heal* (A & C Black, 1978).

Ticknor, George, *Life of William Hickling Prescott* (Routledge, Warne, & Routledge, 1864).

Tidrick, Kathryn, *Heart-Beguiling Araby* (CUP, 1981).

Tindall, Gillian Elizabeth, *City of Gold. The Biography of Bombay* (Temple Smith, 1982).

Tinsley, William, *Random Recollections of an Old Publisher*, Vol.1 (Simpkin, Marshall, Hamilton, Kent & Co Ltd, 1900).

Tomkins, W., *Universal Indian Sign Language* (San Diego, California 1926).

Transactions of the Ars Quatuor Coronatorum Lodge, Vol.xlix, London, 1939.

Trench, Richard, *Arabian Travellers. The European Discovery of Arabia* (Macmillan, 1986).

Trevor, Meriol, *Newman: The Pillar of the Cloud* (Macmillan, 1962).

Trimingham, J. Spenser, *Islam in Ethiopia* (OUP, 1952).

————*The Sufi Orders in Islam* (OUP, 1971).

Tristram, W. Outram. *Coaching Days & Coaching Ways* (EP Publishing Ltd, 1973).

Tuckwell, Rev W., *Reminiscences of Oxford* (Smith, Elder & Co, 1907).

Tussaud, John Theodore, *The Romance of Madame Tussaud's* (Odhams Press, 1919).

Twain, Mark, *The Innocents Abroad or the New Pilgrims' Progress* (American Publishing Company, Hartford, 1875).

————*Life on the Mississippi* (Chatto and Windus, 1914).

————*Roughing It and the Innocents Abroad* (Chatto & Windus, 1885).

Ullendorf, Edward, *The Ethiopians: An Introduction to Country and People*, 3rd edn (OUP, 1973).

V.H.H. Green, *A History of Oxford* (B.T. Batsford, 1974).

Valentia, George Viscount, *Voyages and Travels to India, Ceylon, the Red Sea, Abyssinia and Egypt In the years 1802, 1803, 1804, 1805, and 1806*, 3 vols (William Miller, 1809).

Vanity Fair, Her Majesty's Consular Service, August 12th, 19th, 26th, 1882.

Venn, J. & J.A., *Alumni Cantabrigienses*, Part I to 1751, Vol.1 (Cambridge,1922).

Venn, J.A., *Alumni Cantabrigieneses*, Part II, Vol.II (Cambridge, 1944)

W. Ward, Rev W, *A View of the History, Literature, and Religion of the Hindoos* (Black, Parbury, and Allen, London, 1817).

Walkowitz, Judith R., *City of Dreadful Delight. Narratives of Sexual Danger in Late-Victorian London* (Virago Press Ltd, 1992).

Wallin, George Augustus, *Travels in Arabia, 1845 & 1848* (Falcon-Oleander, 1979).

Walpole, Spenser, *Life of Lord J. Russell*, 2 vols (Longmans, Green & Co, 1889).

Ward, Geoffrey C., *The West. An Illustrated History* (The West Book Project, Inc, 1996).

Ward, Wilfrid, *The Life and Times of Cardinal Wiseman* (Longmans, Green & Co, 1897).

Warwick, Alan R., *The Phoenix Suburb* (Blue Boar Press, 1972).

Waterfield, Gordon, *Sultans of Aden* (John Murray, 1968).

Watney, John, *Travels in Arabia – Lady Hester Stanhope* (Gordon Cremonesi, 1975).

Wellsted, J.R., *Travels in Arabia*, 2 vols (John Murray, 1838).

Westminster & Foreign Quarterly Review, Vol.XXXV, April, (Trübner & Co, 1864).

Whalen, William J., *The Latter Day Saints in the Modern World* (University of Notre Dame Press, Indiana, 1967).

Wilbur, Marguerite Eyer, *The East India Company and the British Empire in the Far East* (Stanford University Press, 1945).

Wilde, Sir William R., *Loch Coirib. Its Shores and Islands With Notices of Loch Measaga*, 4th edn abridged and edited by Colm O Lochlainn (Dublin, 1955).

Wilkinson, L.P., *Golden Latin Artistry* (CUP, 1963).

Williams, Guy, *The Age of Agony* (Constable, 1975).

Williams, N.H. Garnon, *A History of Berkhamsted School, 1541-1972* (Berkhamsted School, 1980).

Wilson, W.J., *History of the Madras Army From 1746 to 1826* (R. Hill, Government Press, Madras, 1888).

Winstanley, D.A., *Unreformed Cambridge. A Study of Certain Aspects of the University in the 18th Century* (CUP, 1935).

Woodham-Smith, Cecil, *Florence Nightingale, 1820-1910* (Constable & Co Ltd, 1950).

——————*The Reason Why* (Constable, 1953).

Woodruff, Douglas, *The Tichborne Claimant. A Victorian Mystery* (Hollis & Carter, 1957).

Woodruff, Philip, *The Men Who Ruled India* (Jonathan Cape, 1953).

Wright, Alan, *Tom Sayers. The Last Great Bare-Knuckle Champion* (The Book Guild Ltd, Sussex, 1994).

Wyngaarden, James B. & Smith, Lloyd H., (eds.), *Cecil Textbook of Medicine*, 16th edn (W.B. Saunders Company, 1982).

Wynn, Antony, *Persia in the Great Game. Sir Percy Sykes, Explorer, Consul, Soldier, Spy* (John Murray, 2003).

Burton as Author, Translator, and Editor

A Chronological Listing of His Books

Goa, and the Blue Mountains; or Six Months of Sick Leave (Richard Bentley, 1851).

Scinde; or the Unhappy Valley, 2 vols (Richard Bentley, 1851).

Sindh, and the Races that inhabit the Valley of the Indus; with Notices of the Topography and History of the Province (W.H. Allen, 1851).

Falconry in the Valley of the Indus (Jan Van Voorst, 1852).

A Complete System of Bayonet Exercise (William Clowes and Sons, 1853).

Personal Narrative of a Pilgrimage to El-Medinah and Meccah, 3 vols (Longman, Brown, Green, and Longmans, 1855-56).

First Footsteps in East Africa; or, An Exploration of Harar (Longman, Brown, Green and Longmans, 1856).

The Lake Regions of Central Africa. A Picture of Exploration, 2 vols (Longman, Green, Longman, and Roberts, 1860).

The City of the Saints, and Across the Rocky Mountains to California (Longman, Green, Longman, and Roberts, 1861).

The Prairie Traveller, a Handbook for Overland Expeditions. With Illustrations, and the Itineraries of the Principal Routes between the Mississippi and the Pacific, and a Map, by Randolph B. Marcy. Edited (with notes) by Richard F. Burton (Trübner & Co, 1863).

Abeokuta and the Camaroons Mountains. An Exploration, 2 vols (Tinsley Brothers, 1863).

Wanderings in West Africa. From Liverpool to Fernando Po. By a F.R.G.S., 2 vols (Tinsley Brothers, 1863).

A Mission to Gelele, King of Dahome, With Notices of the so-called "Amazons," the Grand Customs, the Yearly Customs, the Human Sacrifices, the Present State of the Slave Trade, and the Negro's Place in Nature, 2 vols (Tinsley Brothers, 1864).

The Nile Basin. Part I. Showing Tanganyika to be Ptolemy's Western Lake Reservoir. A Memoir read before the Royal Geographical Society, November 14, 1864. With Prefatory Remarks. By Richard Burton. Part II. Captain Speke's Discovery of the Source of the Nile. A Review. By James M'Queen (Tinsley Brothers, 1864).

Wit and Wisdom from West Africa; or, A Book of Proverbial Philosophy, Idioms, Enigmas, and Laconisms. Compiled by Richard F. Burton (Tinsley Brothers, 1865).

The Guide-book. A Pictorial Pilgrimage to Mecca and Medina. Including Some of the More Remarkable Incidents in the Life of Mohammed, the Arab Lawgiver. (William Clowes & Sons, 1865).

Stone Talk. Being Some of the Marvellous Sayings of a Petral Portion of Fleet Street, London, to One Doctor Polyglott, Ph.D., by Frank Baker, D.O.N. (Robert Hardwicke, 1865).

The Highlands of the Brazil, 2 vols (Tinsley Brothers, 1869).

Vikram and the Vampire or Tales of Hindu Devilry (Longmans, Green, and Co, 1870).

Letters from the Battlefield of Paraguay (Tinsley Brothers, 1870).

Unexplored Syria. Visits to the Libanus, The Tulul el Safa, The Anti-Libanus, The Northern Libanus, and the 'Alah. By Richard F. Burton and Charles F. Tyrwhitt-Drake, 2 vols (Tinsley Brothers, 1872).

Zanzibar; City, Island, and Coast, 2 vols (Tinsley Brothers, 1872).

The Lands of Cazembe. Lacerda's Journey to Cazembe in 1798. Translated and Annotated by Captain R.F. Burton…(Royal Geographical Society, 1873).

The Captivity of Hans Stade of Hesse, in A.D. 1547-1555. Translated by Albert Tootal….and Annotated by Richard F. Burton (Hakluyt Society, 1874).

Ultima Thule; or; A Summer in Iceland. 2 vols (William P. Nimmo).

Etruscan Bologna: A Study. (Smith, Elder & Co, 1876).

A New System of Sword Exercise for Infantry (William Clowes and Sons, 1876).

Two Trips to Gorilla Land and the Cataracts of the Congo, 2 vols (Sampson Low, Marston, Low & Searle).

Scind Revisited: With Notices of the Anglo-Indian Army; Railroads; Past, Present, and Future, 2 vols (Richard Bentley and Son, 1877).

The Gold Mines of Midian and the Ruined Midianite Cities. A Fortnight's Tour in North-western Arabia (C. Kegan Paul & Co, 1878).

The Land of Midian (revisited), 2 vols (C. Kegan Paul & Co, 1879).

The Kasidah of Haji Abdu El-Yezdi, a Lay of the Higher Law. Translated and Annotated by His Friend and Pupil F.B. (Poem and notes are by Burton. Privately printed).

Os Lusiadas (The Lusiads): Englished by Richard Francis Burton: (Edited by His Wife, Isabel Burton), 2 vols (Bernard Quaritch, 1880).

Camoens: His Life and His Lusiads. A Commentary by Richard F. Burton, 2 vols (Bernard Quaritch, 1881).

A Glance at The "Passion-Play" by Richard F. Burton (W.H. Harrison, 1881).

Lord Beaconsfield. A Sketch (1882?).

To the Gold Coast for Gold. A Personal Narrative by Richard F. Burton and Verney Lovett Cameron, 2 vols (Chatto & Windus, 1883).

The Kama Sutra of Vatsyayana. ….With a Preface and Introduction. Printed for the Hindoo Kama Shastra Society,1883. [Translated by Burton and his friend, F.F. Arbuthnot].

Camoens. The Lyricks. Part I, Part II (Sonnets, Canzons, Odes, and Sextines). Englished by Richard F. Burton (Bernard Quaritch, 1884).

The Book of the Sword, (Chatto & Windus, 1884).

*Ananga Ranga; (Stage of the Bodiless One) or, The Hindu Art of Love (Ars Amoris Indica). Translated from the Sanskrit, and annotated by A.F.F. & B.F.R.….*Cosmopoli, for the Kama Shastra Society of London and Benares, and for private circulation only. (1885). [The initials, of course, are those of Arbuthnot and Burton inverted].

A Plain and Literal Translation of the Arabian Nights' Entertainments, Now Entituled The Book of the Thousand Nights and a Night. With Introduction, Explanatory Notes on the Manners and Customs of Moslem Men and a Terminal upon the History of the Nights. By Richard F. Burton. Printed by the Kamashastra Society For Private Subscribers Only. 10 vols (1885).

Supplemental Nights to the Book of The Thousand Nights and a Night. With Notes Anthropological and Explanatory By Richard F. Burton. Printed by the Kamashastra Society for Private Subscribers Only. 6 vols (1886-8).

Iracema, The Honey-lips. A Legend of Brazil. By J. De Alencar. Translated, with the Author's Permission, by Isabel Burton, and *Manuel de Moraes. A Chronicle of the Seventeenth Century*, by J.M. Pereira Da Silva. Translated by Richard F. and Isabel Burton, (Bickers & Son, 1886).

The Perfumed Garden of the Cheikh Nefzaoui. A Manual of Arabian Erotology (xvi Century). Revised and Corrected Translation. (Cosmopoli: 1886: for the Kama Shastra Society of London and Benares, and for Private Circulation only).

The Beharistan (Abode of Spring). By Jami. A Literal Translation from the Persian. (Printed by the Kama Shastra Society for Private Subscribers only, 1887). [The translator was Edward Rehatsek, with some editorial imput by Burton].

The Gulistan or Rose Garden of Sa'di, Faithfully Translated into English. (Printed by the Kama Shastra Society for Private Subscribers only, Benares, 1888). [Again, translated by Rehatsek with editorial imput by Burton].

Priapeia, or the Sportive Epigrams of divers Poets on Priapus: the Latin Text now for the first time Englished in Verse and Prose (the Metrical Version by "Outidanos") with Introduction, Notes Explanatory and Illustrative, and Excursus, by "Neaniskos." (Cosmopoli: 1890. Printed by the Translators in One Volume…For Private Subscribers Only)

Burton's Posthumously Published Works

Marocco and the Moors: Being An Account of the Travels, with a General Description of the Country and its People, by Arthur Leared. Second edition, Revised and edited by Sir Richard Burton (Sampson Low, Marston, Searle, & Rivington, Ltd, 1891).

Il Pentamerone; or the Tale of Tales. Being a Translation by the Late Sir Richard Burton of Il Pentamerone; Overo Lo Cunto de li Cunte, Trattenemiento de li Peccerille, of Giovanni Battista Basile, 2 vols (Henry and Co, 1893).

The Carmina of Caius Valerius Catullus, Now first completely Englished into Verse and Prose, the Metrical Part by Capt. Sir Richard F. Burton....and the Prose Portion, Introduction, and Notes Explanatory and Illustrative by Leonard C. Smithers, (London: 1894. Printed for the Translators: in One Volume: for Private Subscribers Only).

*The Jew, the Gypsy, and El Islam, By the Late Captain Sir Richard F. Burton...*Edited with a Preface and Brief Notes by W.H. Wilkins (Hutchinson & Co, 1898).

*Wanderings in Three Continents, By the Late Captain Sir Richard F. Burton...*Edited with a Preface, by W.H. Wilkins (Hutchinson, 1901).

The Sentiment of the Sword: A Country-house Dialogue. Edited with notes by A. Forbes Sieveking and a Preface by Theodore Cook. (London: The Field, 1911).

Selected Papers on Anthropology, Travel, and Exploration. ed. Norman M. Penzer (A.M. Philpott Ltd, 1924).

The Uruguay (A Historical Romance of South America). Edited with an Introduction, Notes and Bibliography by Frederick C.H. Garcia and Edward F. Stanton (Berkeley, California: University of California Press, 1982).

Bibliographies

Penzer, N.M., *An Annotated Bibliography of Sir Richard Francis Burton, K.C.M.G.,* (A.M. Philpott Ltd, 1923).

Kirkpatrick, B.J. (ed.), *A Catalogue of the Library of Sir Richard Burton, K.C.M.G.* (Royal Anthropological Institute, 1978).

Casada, James A., *Sir Richard F. Burton: A Biobibliographical Study* (Mansell, 1990).

Lives of Burton

Richards, Alfred Bate, Andrew Wilson, and St Clair Baddeley, A Sketch of the Career of Richard F. Burton..... (London: Waterlow & Sons Ltd, 1886).

Hitchman, Francis, Richard F. Burton, K.C.M.G., *His Early, Private and Public Life, With an Account of His Travels and Explorations,* 2 vols (Sampson Low, Marston, Searle, and Rivington, 1887).

Burton, Isabel, *The Life of Captain Sir Richd. F. Burton, K.C.M.G., F.R.G.S.,* 2 vols (Chapman & Hall, 1893).

Stisted, Georgiana M., *The True Life of Capt. Sir Richard F. Burton, K.C.M.G., F.R.G.S.,* (H.S. Nichols, 1896).

Wright, Thomas, *The Life of Sir Richard Burton,* 2 vols (Everett & Co, 1906).

Dodge, Walter Phelps, *The Real Sir Richard Burton* (T. Fisher Unwin, 1907).

Downey, Fairfax, *Burton: Arabian Nights Adventurer* (Charles Scribner's Sons, 1931).

Dearden, Seton, *The Arabian Knight: A Study of Sir Richard Burton* (Arthur Barker Ltd, 1936).

Schonfield, Hugh J., *Richard Burton, Explorer* (Herbert Joseph Ltd, 1936).

Bercovici, Alfred, *That Blackguard Burton!* (Bobbs-Merrill, 1962).

Edwardes, Allen, *Death Rides a Camel: A Biography of Richard Francis Burton* (Julian Press, 1963).

Farwell, Byron, *A Biography of Richard Francis Burton* (Longmans, 1963).

Brodie, Fawn M., *The Devil Drives: A Life of Sir Richard Burton* (Eyre & Spottiswoode, 1967).

Hastings, Michael, *Sir Richard Burton: A Biography* (Hodder & Stoughton, 1978).

McLynn, Frank, *Burton: Snow upon the Desert* (John Murray, 1990).

Rice, Edward, *Captain Sir Richard Francis Burton* (Charles Scribner's Sons, 1990).

Lovell, Mary S., *A Rage to Live* (Little, Brown and Company, 1998).

Kennedy, Dane, *The Highly Civilized Man. Richard Burton and the Victorian World* (Harvard University Press, 2005).

INDEX